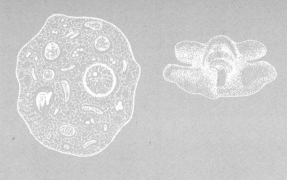

THOMAS C. CHENG, Ph.D.

Parasitologist, Northeast Shellfish Sanitation Research Center,
Public Health Service, U.S. Department of Health, Education and
Welfare, Narragansett, Rhode Island
and
Adjunct Professor of Zoology, University of Rhode Island,
Kingston, Rhode Island.

THE BIOLOGY OF
ANIMAL PARASITES

W. B. SAUNDERS COMPANY
PHILADELPHIA AND LONDON   1964

The Biology of Animal Parasites

*This book is dedicated to three outstanding
biologists to whom I am greatly indebted:*

To PROFESSOR DOMINIC L. DeGIUSTI,
Wayne State University,

> who initiated me to the excitement of studying parasitic
> animals.

To the late PROFESSOR BRUCE D. REYNOLDS,
University of Virginia,

> who encouraged and guided my first attempts at original
> investigation.

To DOCTOR HORTON H. HOBBS, Jr.,
U. S. National Museum,

> whose enthusiasm for the invertebrates has served as a beacon
> by which my humble efforts have been guided.

"Nature keeps much on her shelf, but more in her closet."

RALPH WALDO EMERSON

PREFACE

Along the course of evolution, many organisms found suitable habitats on land, in streams, ponds, estuaries, and oceans. Still other organisms accidentally entered the bodies or became attached to the exterior of dissimilar organisms and adapted to these environments. The term *free-living* has been used to describe the first group and *symbiotic,* the second group. Many biologists have taken up the study of the free-living species; others, fewer in number, have specialized in the symbiotic or parasitic species. Thus parasitology has come into being. The study of parasites and parasitism, in the broad sense of these terms, seems to have been neglected in many ways, especially when one considers that there are many more parasites than free-living animals. As the following pages indicate, the field is multifold, ranging from the chemical to the organismal to the ecological levels. No student can be well grounded in the principles of biology without being exposed to parasitology—the study of the biology of parasites. The teaching of parasitology belongs in every institution of higher learning devoted to the pursuit of scientific truths.

Although the term *parasitism* is commonly thought by the layman, and even some biologists, to be synonymous with disease, this is not the case. It is true that many parasitic animals do cause disease; however, parasitism in the majority of cases does not lead to disease. Parasitism is a natural way of life among a large number of organisms, and its study remains as one of the most challenging aspects of biology. It is true that in the past those phases of parasitology that deal with human and animal diseases have dominated the scene. Parasitologists have served humanity well, sometimes to the point of self-effacement, and it has been only in the last two or more decades that biologists have aggressively sought to understand through experimentation the basis for the evolution of parasites and the mechanisms involved in parasitism. Our knowledge at present indicates that this aspect of biology represents one of the most fascinating and rewarding avenues of investigation. As the number of biologists interested in the fundamental aspects of parasitology increases, more and more colleges and universities are offering courses in parasitology apart from those applied courses offered in schools of human and veterinary medicine. These developments have demanded teaching aids that do not place their primary emphasis on medical and veterinary parasitology.

The need for a general introductory parasitology textbook directed at courses taught in liberal arts colleges was indicated while I was teaching at the University of Virginia and at Lafayette College. Furthermore, this need has been repeatedly expressed to me by many friends and former associates who are presently teaching courses in parasitology in colleges and universities of this nature.

Because it is felt that students being introduced to parasitology should be well grounded in the basic concepts of this discipline and divorced from the medical, veterinary, and agricultural implications, lengthy discussions concerning clinical symptoms, epidemiology, chemotherapy, and field eradication programs have been omitted. Pathogenesis and pathology, as correlated with host-parasite relationships, have been discussed only briefly. Some may feel that in so doing I have overlooked some important aspects of the field. However, I believe that if parasitology is to continue to contribute to the academic world as a branch of biology, it must be presented as a basic science in the liberal arts colleges and universities, from which future specialists arise. The place for training chemotherapy experts, medical and veterinary diagnosticians, and public health officers does not lie in the liberal arts colleges but in the professional and specialized graduate schools.

The Biology of Animal Parasites is not intended to be a definitive reference book. It is an introductory textbook and guide. However, it is my hope that students and investigators will find the sections devoted to basic taxonomy, morphology, and physiology of assistance while tackling laboratory work. Some may feel that too much detail has been included in certain sections and not enough in others. The choice of material has been deliberate to emphasize the basic biology of parasites. This text emphasizes such fundamentals as taxonomy, chemical composition, morphology, development, life cycles, physiology, and ecology. It is felt that such information serves as the foundation on which more highly specialized questions can later be asked and answered.

From past experience, I know that students enrolled in an introductory course in parasitology have generally had experience with general biology or zoology, vertebrate anatomy, introductory invertebrate zoology, and perhaps some introductory phases of physiology. Hence, this book has been oriented at this level.

I have chosen to consider the parasitic animals from the phylogenetic standpoint—that is, each group of animals is considered in a separate chapter or section. My teaching experience has indicated that this is the most effective method of introducing the material. It is the most efficient from the students' standpoint, and with a book so organized, the teacher can select the particular taxa he wishes to emphasize or assign the reading of chapters on certain groups he intends to omit from his formal lectures.

Much space has been given to the morphology, both gross and microscopic, of the various animals considered. This has been done because I have found such material to be of great assistance to the beginning student in basic laboratory work. Furthermore, this volume can serve as a quick reference for advanced students being introduced to research, since morphology is the basis for almost all phases of investigation at the organismal level.

In considering the physiology of parasites, only certain aspects are included—for example, oxygen requirements, growth requirements, metabolism, effects of parasite on host, and effects of host on parasite. The excellent monographs by von Brand (1952: *The Chemical Physiology of Endoparasitic Animals*) and Rogers (1962: *The Nature of Parasitism*) should be read by those seeking greater depth in the area of chemical parasitology. For those desiring more information on immunity to parasites, the Monograph of Sprent (1963: *Parasitism*) should be consulted.

Finally, a short list of suggested readings is included at the end of each chapter. These recommended selections have been limited to the more readily available books and journals.

I am deeply indebted to several friends and authorities who have very kindly read and criticized sections of this volume during the preparative stages. Their constructive criticisms are greatly appreciated and many changes were made as the result of their advice. Errors that may still remain are totally the responsibility of the author and do not in any way reflect on these individuals.

Appreciation is due Dr. Jesse C. Thompson, Jr., Hampden-Sydney College; Dr. William J. Hargis, Jr., Virginia Institute of Marine Science; Dr. Martin J. Ulmer, Iowa State University; Dr. Arthur W. Jones, University of Tennessee; Dr. Helen Ward, Oak Ridge Institute for Nuclear Studies; Dr. John J. McDermott, Franklin and Marshall College; Dr. Harry L. Halloway, Jr., Roanoke College; Dr. Howard G. Sengbusch, University College at Buffalo, The State University of New York at Buffalo; Dr. Frank J. Etges, University of Cincinnati; Dr. Leslie A. Stauber, Rutgers University; Dr. Dominic L. DeGiusti, Wayne State University; Dr. David Causey, University of Arkansas; Dr. Robert Short, Florida State University; Dr. William D. Lindquist, Michigan State University; Dr. Marvin Meyer, University of Maine; and Dr. Edwin J. Robinson, Macalester College.

Acknowledgments are also due the following individuals who contributed invaluable assistance in checking the generic names included in this volume and for suggesting certain inclusions: Dr. Allen McIntosh and Mrs. M. B. Chitwood, both of the Beltsville Parasitological Laboratory, U. S. Department of Agriculture; Dr. Joseph P. E. Morrison, U. S. National Museum; Dr. J. C. Becquaert, Harvard University; Dr. Robert P. Higgins, Wake Forest College; and Dr. David Erasmus, University of Wales, Great Britain. A special thanks is due Dr. George W. Chu, University of Hawaii, for placing his personal library at my disposal during my stay in Hawaii.

I am also grateful to my wife Barbara Ann and to my colleagues in the Department of Biology, Lafayette College, for their patience and encouragement during the years this book was in preparation. In addition, I wish to acknowledge the hospitality offered me by the Mountain Lake Biological Station, University of Virginia, during the summer of 1963, and the Pacific Biomedical Research Center, University of Hawaii, during the academic year 1963–64, while I was completing the manuscript, and to acknowledge the receipt of an award from the National Science Foundation administered by the University of Virginia. I also wish to acknowledge the invaluable editorial assistance provided by the staff of the W. B. Saunders Company.

It is the hope of the author that teachers of parasitology will find this volume to be of assistance in initiating the student to the complexities of parasites and parasitism. Suggestions, constructive criticisms, and notices of errors will be greatly appreciated and will be given careful scrutiny.

The views expressed in this book are solely those of the author. They do not represent the official views of the U. S. Public Health Service.

Narragansett, Rhode Island   THOMAS C. CHENG

CONTENTS

**PART
ONE**

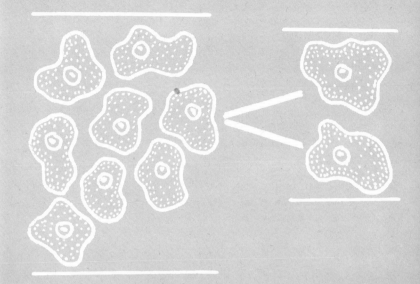

INTRODUCTION

1

PARASITES AND PARASITISM

Parasitology, the study of parasites and their relationship to their hosts, is one of the most fascinating and rewarding phases of biology. This discipline actually includes several approaches to the study of parasitic organisms. Through the years the field has enjoyed contributions from those who have studied parasites and parasitism from the phylogenetic standpoint, those who have investigated from the ecological aspect, from the morphological, physiological, chemotherapeutic, serological, immunological, and nutritional standpoints, and with advances in our understanding of biochemistry, even from the chemical standpoint.

TERMINOLOGY

The concept of parasitism is often misunderstood because of the complexity of the relationship between the parasite and its host. Any animal or plant that spends a portion or all of its life cycle intimately associated with a different and larger species of animal or plant, during which there is a physiological exchange, is considered a symbiont. The relationship is known as symbiosis. Although three subordinate categories of symbiotic relationships—parasitism, commensalism, and mutualism—are commonly distinguished to facilitate understanding, the lines of demarcation between these categories are often tenuous and almost impossible to define.

Strictly defined, the term *parasitism* is that condition of life normal and necessary for an organism that lives on or in its host (which is of a different and usually larger species) and that nourishes itself at the expense of the host without rapidly destroying it as a predator does its prey, but often inflicting some degree of injury affecting its welfare.

An organism that lives at the expense of its host but does not inflict any harm is known as a *commensal,* and the relationship is known as *commensalism.* A classic example of commensalism is the unique relationship between the pilot fish *Naucrates ductor* and the shark. The pilot fish accompanies the shark in a free-swimming manner, eating the fragments of food that become available as the shark tears apart its prey. Much as a piece of iron is attracted by a magnet, the pilot fish follows the shark, responding instantly to the incessant and irregular directional changes of the larger fish. A similar commensal relationship is that between the remora, *Echeneis remora,* and the shark, but the remora actually attaches itself to the shark by its dorsal fin, which is modified as a sucker.

3

Like the pilot fish, the remora feeds on "left-overs" and does no harm to the shark.

Another interesting commensal relationship involves a fish of the genus *Trachichthys*, which always remains among the tentacles of the large sea anemone, *Crambactis arabica*, found in the Red Sea area. When another fish comes within reach, it is immediately captured and swallowed by the sea anemone. At that instant, the *Trachichthys* follows the prey into the mouth of the "host" and takes its share of the victim. In this case, it would appear that *Trachichthys* must possess an immunity against the paralyzing poisons of the sea anemone.

Sometimes the commensal has a closer association with the host. The crab *Eumedon convictor* of the Gambier Islands, for example, lives in a large cavity formed by the fold on the back of the apical region of the sea urchin, *Echinothrix turca*. Resting in this nest, the commensal does not have to exert any energy in continuously swimming around the host, yet it is on hand to share the food of the sea urchin and enjoy its protection. A similar relationship exists between *Pocillopora* and another crab, *Hapalocarcinus marsupialis*.

The interesting associations between certain intestinal flagellates and wood-eating termites and roaches have often been cited as typical of the third type of relationship, *mutualism*. Several species of these flagellates, living in the gut of termites, are able to produce cellulases—the enzymes responsible for the digestion of cellulose, which constitutes the major bulk of the termite host's food. The host itself is unable to produce the enzymes and is dependent on the protozoa to digest its food; in return, the host provides the cellulose, which the protozoa also utilize as food. Removal of the flagellates from the host (a process known as defaunation) usually results in the death or severe starvation of the latter. This mutually beneficial relationship is cited as a classic example of mutualism.

Many rumen-dwelling ciliates of herbivores may be said to be engaged in mutualism, because several species of these protozoa produce cellulases and evidence indicates that the protozoa also utilize the cellulose ingested by their hosts. The degree of dependency of the host on these protozoa differs, however, since defaunation of lambs harboring such ciliates does not result in any appreciable change in their metabolism. In fact, the lambs continue to grow normally; thus the presence of the ciliates in their stomachs cannot be considered essential, as is the case of the flagellates found in termites and woodroaches. The ciliates of ruminants, however, do perform the service of cellulose digestion for their hosts and do derive some benefit, and so they are, by definition, engaged in mutualism.

Several types of parasitism are recognized. An organism that does not absolutely depend on the parasitic way of life, but is capable of adapting to it if placed in such a relationship, is known as a *facultative* parasite. If an organism is completely dependent on the host during a segment or all of its life cycle, the relationship becomes markedly physiological, and in such instances the parasite is known as an *obligatory parasite*. If an organism accidentally acquires an unnatural host and survives, it is known as an *incidental parasite*.

An *erratic parasite* is one that wanders into an organ in which it is not usually found; a *periodic* or *sporadic parasite* is one that visits its host intermittently to obtain some benefit; a *pathogenic parasite* is one that is the causative agent of an almost immediate disease in the host.

Parasites that live within the body of their host in such locations as the alimentary tract, liver, lungs, gallbladder, and urinary bladder are known as *endoparasites*. Those attached to the outer surface of their host, or situated subcutaneously, are known as *ectoparasites*.

The *host* is the larger of the two species in the symbiotic relationship. It may be classified as: (1) a *definitive* or *final host*, if the parasite attains sexual maturity in it; (2) an *intermediate host*, if it serves as a temporary environment but is necessary for the completion of the parasite's life cycle (for example, molluscs and arthropods commonly serve as first and second intermediate hosts in which digenetic trematodes complete a part of their development); and (3) a *transfer host*, if it is not necessary for the completion of the parasite's life cycle but is utilized as a temporary refuge until the appropriate definitive host can be reached. Arthropods and other invertebrates that serve as intermediate hosts, as well as carriers for protozoan and other smaller parasites, are referred to as *vectors;* for example, various species of mosquitoes serve as vectors for the protozoan malarial parasites, *Plasmodium* spp. From the evolutionary standpoint, some intermediate hosts may have been definitive hosts at one time. On the other hand, other intermediate hosts may have been transfer hosts.

Animals that become infected and serve as a source from which other animals can be infected are known as *reservoir hosts*.

PARASITISM IN THE ANIMAL KINGDOM

A quick survey of the Animal Kingdom shows that there are parasitic members in practically every major phylum. Among the Protozoa, many species of amoebae, flagellates, ciliates, and all of the Sporozoa are parasitic. It is of interest to note that despite their small sizes, certain protozoa, such as *Stentor* and *Spirostomum,* can serve as hosts for the flagellate *Astasia* sp. Small amoebae are known to parasitize opalinid ciliates and *Trichodina*.

The Mesozoa, which are minute, wormlike, acoelomate organisms, include forms that are common parasites in cephalopods and other marine invertebrates. *Dicyema,* for example, is a common parasite in the nephridia of squids and octopuses. *Rhopalura* is a less common mesozoan parasite encountered in various tissues and body cavities of marine turbellarians, nemerteans, brittle stars, oligochaetes, and clams.

Although parasitic coelenterates are not common, some are known (p. 622).

One of the most popular subdivisions of parasitology is *helminthology,* which deals specifically with the parasitic representatives of the Platyhelminthes, the Nematoda, and the Acanthocephala.* All platyhelminths, except the turbellarians, are parasitic, and even a few cases of parasitism have been reported among turbellarians. Numerous species of nematodes are parasitic, many as parasites of animals and others as parasites of plants. The Acanthocephala are all parasitic.

In addition to these major groups of helminths, the less commonly encountered Nematomorpha, or horsehair worms, are of interest to helminthologists, because the larvae of most species are parasitic in insects although the adults are free-living in aquatic situations.

Some species of the phylum Mollusca, in addition to serving as definitive or as inter-mediate hosts for protozoan and helminth parasites, may also be ectoparasitic continuously or during some phase of their life cycle (p. 677).

Among the Annelida, the leeches are common ectoparasites on various vertebrates.* It is estimated that 25 per cent of the leech species are parasites, but few of them are totally parasitic. Some are known to serve as vectors for protozoan parasites. The medicinal leech, *Hirudo medicinalis,* which is usually 2 inches long and less than an inch in diameter, will engorge itself with blood until its length increases to 9 inches and its diameter to approximately 2 inches. In China, North Africa, and Israel, horses and men may suffer, even fatally, from loss of blood caused by the ectoparasitic habits of the horse leeches, *Limnatis* or *Haemopis,* which enter the nasal passages and pharynx while the hosts are drinking from pools and streams. Some leeches are known to enter the urinary bladder, where they attach themselves and hang on for days, literally draining the host of its blood. Aquatic leeches are known to serve as vectors for certain species of blood flagellates that belong to the genus *Trypanosoma* and that infect fishes and amphibians.

Among the Polychaeta, *Ichthyotomus sanguinarius* and other related species are ectoparasites attached to the fins of eels and fishes. Parasitic forms are few among the Arachiannelida and Oligochaeta, but these annelids represent an important group of intermediate hosts.

The arthropods are represented by many parasitic species. Even more species serve efficiently as definitive hosts for various protozoa and helminth parasites and as intermediate and transfer hosts for both protozoa and helminths. Among members of the class Arachnoidea, the Acarina (ticks and mites), especially the mange mites (Sarcoptidae), soft ticks (Argasidae), hard ticks (Ixodidae), and members of the Dermanyssidae, are of medical and veterinary importance. They act both as ectoparasites and as vectors. The insects are represented by a large number of ectoparasites and intermediate hosts. The mosquitoes and flies (Diptera) are well known as vectors and ectoparasites. The chewing lice (Mallophaga) and sucking lice (Anoplura) are important ectoparasitic pests. Another important group is the fleas, which are both ectoparasites and transmitters of microorganisms.

---

* *Helminthological Abstracts* includes the literature pertaining to the Hirudinea, reflecting the consensus of those who consider leeches to be helminths.

The importance of the Vertebrata in parasitology needs little elaboration. Vertebrates serve as intermediate, reservoir, transfer, and definitive hosts for practically all forms of parasites. Man and domestic animals harbor numerous species of parasites, many of which are of considerable medical and veterinary importance.

This brief sampling shows that parasitic forms are well represented in the Animal Kingdom, and that many nonparasitic animals are directly or indirectly involved in the "parasitological world" as definitive hosts, vectors, intermediate hosts, and as hosts of accidental infestations.

THE PHYSIOLOGY OF PARASITISM

Of great importance in parasitology is the study of the relationship between the host and the parasite. This intimate relationship invariably involves physiological adaptations, hence investigations of parasite and host physiology have become an integral aspect of the discipline. Questions such as "How do parasites affect their hosts?" and "How do hosts affect their parasites?" are basic in parasitology. It is imperative that those interested in parasitism and parasites should become familiar with the physiology of these animals. Knowledge of the enzymatic activities, the synthesis of food, protective mechanisms, secretions and excretions, composition, respiration, and metabolism of parasites in general is of great importance to our understanding of the parasitic way of life.

Although biologists have been interested in the physiology and chemical composition of parasites since the 1800's, most of our knowledge in this area has come to light during the 1900's, especially in recent years with the advent of new techniques.

Research in such indispensable areas as morphology, taxonomy, development, phylogenetic relationships, chemotherapy, and pathology is still progressing, but in recent years the trend has been to advance our understanding of the physiology of parasites. In 1952 von Brand published a volume on the chemical physiology of endoparasites, and in 1957 he reviewed some of our knowledge of parasite physiology. More recently, Rogers (1962) contributed a stimulating treatise on the physiology of parasites and parasitism. These books,

along with the establishment of the journal *Experimental Parasitology,* reflect the upsurge of interest in this area of parasitology.

The reader will find a specific section at the end of each chapter devoted to certain aspects of the physiology and host-parasite relationships as these apply to each phylum.

As Cameron (1956) has pointed out, "No organism is an entity unto itself." All animals live in some form of relationship with surrounding organisms. One might state that all animals are directly or indirectly "parasitic" on plants, and in turn plants are "parasitic" in many ways on animals. This being the case, the traditional separation between free-living and parasitic organisms becomes less justifiable.

The study of the relationship between the host and parasite may be considered an ecological subject. Investigations of ecological relationships reveal that free-living and parasitic organisms do not represent two distinct groups. A gradient occurs between the two extremes. For example, among the platyhelminths, the free-living planarians are capable of synthesizing their own digestive enzymes, and the chemical constituents of their bodies are derived from materials ingested or absorbed from the physical environment. On the other hand, the ectoparasitic monogeneids, also capable of synthesizing their own digestive enzymes, depend mainly on the blood of their hosts (primarily fishes and amphibians) for nutrients. Although most of these chemical building blocks used in their bodies are derived from the blood of the host, this is not the only source, for oxygen and possibly other chemicals can be derived from the aquatic environment. The endoparasitic digenetic trematodes can synthesize their own enzymes, but all the constituents of their body tissues are synthesized from those obtained within their hosts, some even from the hosts' tissues. Finally, the tapeworms are largely dependent on their hosts for the digestion of food, for present information indicates that tapeworms cannot synthesize many of the essential digestive enzymes. Food already digested by the host is absorbed through ultramicroscopic microtriches on the body surfaces of the tapeworm and utilized within their bodies. Thus it is apparent that there is a gradation between free-living planarians and obligatory endoparasitic tapeworms. Quantitative studies of enzymatic activities, source of body chemicals, etc. could lead to quantitative analyses of the dependency of parasites on their hosts. Such information may in time become available and should prove to be exceedingly interesting.

EFFECTS OF PARASITES ON THEIR HOSTS

Since true parasites bring about some change within their hosts that may be interpreted as affecting the hosts' welfare, it is necessary to give some consideration to the types and degrees of changes caused by parasitic animals. With our advancing knowledge of host-parasite relationships, it is increasingly apparent that in many instances it is extremely difficult, if not impossible, to distinguish between a true parasite and a commensal, because the effect of the parasite in some cases may be so minute that it can hardly be considered injurious. However, some classic types of parasite-inflicted effects on hosts can be cited. In classifying the various types of effects, one should remember that in a number of cases multiple effects may be present, and it is often not possible to state that a given parasite causes only one specific type of effect. Furthermore, the types of effects often merge into each other so that sharp lines of demarcation between types cannot always be recognized.

Utilization of Host's Food

Utilization of the host's nutrient to a detrimental point by parasites is probably the first type of damage that comes to one's mind. Although in the past some biologists have doubted the importance of parasites in this regard, since the amount of food a microscopic parasite can utilize seems negligible, more recent physiological studies of nutritional requirements of parasites, especially endoparasitic forms, have indicated that depletion of host's nutrients by parasites may have serious consequences. *Dibothriocephalus latus* in man has been known to cause an anemia similar to pernicious anemia because of the affinity this tapeworm has for vitamin B_{12}. This tapeworm can absorb 10 to 50 times as much B_{12} as other tapeworms. Since B_{12} plays an important role in blood formation, its uptake by *D. latus* causes anemia.

Studies of cestode nutritional requirements show that tapeworms absorb not only simple sugars from their hosts but also nitrogen-containing amino acids, some constituent of yeast in the host's diet, and other nutrient essentials presumably from secretions of the host. It is not only possible but probable in cases of heavy infections that an appreciable amount of such materials is drained from the host, and in instances of undernourished hosts—poor sanitary conditions conducive to parasitic infections often go hand in hand with undernourishment —that this drainage has considerable effect.

Utilization of the Host's Non-nutritional Materials

In some cases parasites also feed on host substances other than nutrients. The endo- and ectoparasites that feed on the host's blood are examples. It is extremely difficult to estimate the amount of blood any organism can rob from its host. Table 1-1 lists some estimated amounts taken in by a few bloodfeeding species. From the data presented, it should be obvious that the blood lost through parasitic infestations can become an appreciable amount over periods of time. Lepage (1958) estimated that 500 human hookworms can remove 250 cc. of blood, or one twenty-fourth of the total volume of blood, each day. This estimate may be too high, for others have estimated that no more than 50 cc. of blood are removed. Nevertheless, the loss of even 50 cc. of blood per day constitutes a serious drainage of blood cells, haemoglobin, and serum.

Destruction of Host's Tissue

Not all parasites are capable of destroying the host's tissues, and even among those that do, the gradation in the degree of damage is large. Some parasites injure the host's tissues when they enter the host, while others inflict tissue damage after they have successfully entered. A combination of these two types of injury may occur. The hookworms, *Necator americanus* and *Ancylostoma duodenale,* exemplify the first instance, for the infective larvae of these nematodes do extensive damage to cells and underlying connective tissue during penetration of the host's skin. The cercariae of certain schistosomes that cause "swimmer's itch" while penetrating the host's skin, cause inflammation and damage the surrounding tissues. Although cercariae-caused dermatitis is extremely irritating, fortunately, as the result of host incompatibility, these worms do not become established in the host's blood. Penetration of the host's skin by schistosome cercariae not only involves slight tissue damage but, more important, involves an allergic reaction.

Various armed (with attachment hooks) helminths, such as the Acanthocephala, certain

Table 1-1. Blood Intake of Certain Bloodfeeding Parasites*

Species of Parasite	Host	Number of Parasites	Amount of Blood Ingested
TICKS			
Ixodes ricinus (larvae)	Sheep	1000	5 cc.
Ixodes ricinus (adult female)	Sheep	1	1 cc.†
LEECHES			
Haemadipsa zeylanica	Man and animals	—	Sufficient in heavy infections to cause anemia.
Limnatus nüotica	Man and animals	—	Sufficient in heavy infections to cause anemia.
NEMATODES			
Ancylostoma caninum	Dogs and man	1	0.5 cc. each day
Ancylostoma duodenale	Man	500	250 cc. each day
Necator americanus	Man	500	250 cc. each day
Haemonchus contortus	Sheep	4000	60 cc. each day

*Tabulated from data collected and presented by G. Lapage (1958) in *Parasitic Animals.*

†Heavily infected sheep may lose 250 cc. of blood per week.

flukes, and tapeworms, often irritate the cells lining the lumen of their host's intestine while they are holding on. In most cases the damage is minute, but repeated irritations over long periods can result in appreciable damage. Furthermore, microscopic lesions resulting from such irritation can become sites for secondary infections by bacteria. The amoebic dysentery-causing protozoan, *Entamoeba histolytica,* actively ingests the epithelial cells lining the host's large intestine, causing large ulcerations that are not only damaging in themselves but that also serve as sites for secondary bacterial infections (Plate 1–1). This same amoeba is known also to cause large ulcers in the host's liver. Partial or total destruction of the hepatopancreatic cells of molluscan intermediate hosts harboring larvae (rediae and sporocysts) of digenetic trematodes is also known (Plate 1–2). Cheng and James (1960) reported one such case, in which the liver of the fresh-water bivalve *Sphaerium striatinum* was completely destroyed through ingestion by the rediae of *Crepidostomum cornutum,* a fluke that as an adult is parasitic in the intestine of various species of bass. In some cases, the molluscan hosts were killed by the severe

damage. In addition to direct ingestion, disruption of hepatopancreatic cells caused by the parasites' movements, and cytolysis caused by the parasites' excreta, both contributed to the destruction.

During migration of larvae of the large nematode *Ascaris lumbricoides* within its host, these larvae pass through the lungs of the host. As the result of the migration of a large number of worms, damage sometimes is done to the lung tissue (Plate 1–3).

Ancylostoma duodenale, one of the hookworms, is a good example of a parasite that causes both internal and external tissue damage. The external damage phase has been discussed. Once established within the host's intestine, this roundworm causes considerable damage to the gut wall. It may actually engulf small pieces of tissue, thus producing small lesions.

Histopathological studies of parasite-damaged tissues reveal that cell damage other than removal by ingestion or from mechanical disruption is of three major types: (1) Parenchymatous or albuminous degeneration occurs when the cells become swollen and packed with albuminous or fatty granules, the nuclei become

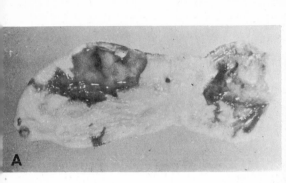

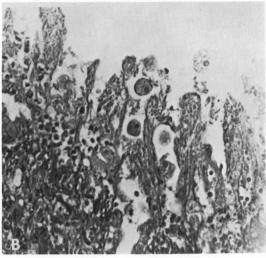

Plate 1-1   Host tissue damage caused by animal parasites. A. Section of colon of kitten experimentally infected with *Entamoeba histolytica* showing lesions of acute amoebiasis. **B.** *E. histolytica* invading gland crypts and interglandular stroma of the superficial mucosa of large intestine of kitten. (A and B after Sister Josephine, M. A., 1958. Am. Jour. Trop. Med. Hyg., *7:* 158–164.)

indistinct, and the cytoplasm appears pale. This type of damage is characteristic of liver, cardiac muscle, and kidney cells. (2) Fatty degeneration describes the condition in which the cells become filled with an abnormal amount of fat deposits that give them a yellowish appearance. Hepatic cells display this type of degeneration when in contact with parasites. (3) Necrosis occurs when any type of cell degeneration persists. The cells finally die, giving the tissue an opaque appearance. In the encystment of *Trichinella spiralis* in striated muscle,

necrosis of the surrounding tissues is followed by calcification.

Abnormal Growth

In certain parasitic infections abnormal growth of host tissues, known as hyperplasia (increase in the rate of cell division), results. The presence of the trematode *Fasciola hepatica* in bile ducts is known to effect rapid division of the lining epithelial cells. The presence of the protozoan *Eimeria stiedae* is known to cause hyperplasia of the hepatic cells of the rabbit.

Plate 1-2   Destruction of hepatopancreas of mollusc by larval trematodes. Photomicrograph showing the mechanical invasion by trematode sporocysts of the space normally occupied by the hepatopancreatic tubules of the fresh-water snail *Nitocris dilatatus.*

(H, hepatopancreatic tubules; S, sporocysts.)

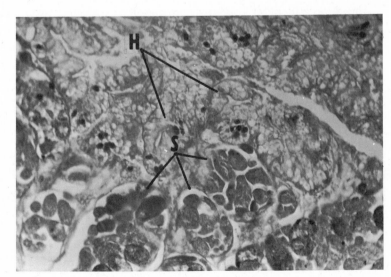

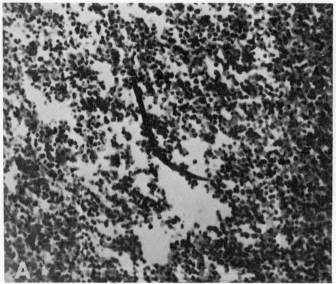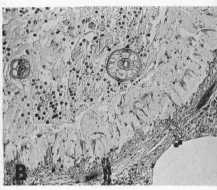

Plate 1-3   **A.** Larva of *Ascaris lumbricoides* during migration through lung of human host. Notice displacement of host cells. (Courtesy of Armed Forces Institute of Pathology, negative No. 80930.) **B.** Photomicrograph of human lung showing bronchiole entirely filled with mucopurulent material containing a larva of *A. lumbricoides* cut transversely through the esophagus and midintestine. (After Beaver and Danaraj, 1958. Photograph loaned by Dr. P. C. Beaver, Tulane University.)

The eggs of *Schistosoma haematobium* with their spinous projections are known to irritate the transitional epithelium of human urinary bladders, causing hyperplasia.

When the lung fluke *Paragonimus westermani* parasitizes man and carnivores, the normal cuboidal cells lining the bronchioles commonly undergo both hyperplasia and metaplasia (the change of one type of cell into another) and are transformed into stratified epithelium.

Hyperplasia resulting from parasitic infections may result in neoplastic reactions—that is, the development of tumors from existing tissues. Bullock and Curtis (1920) demonstrated that cysticerci of *Taenia taeniaeformis* in the livers of rats, mice, and other rodents can cause the formation of tumors. Other known instances of neoplasm development include adenoma (gland cells surrounded by connective tissue) formation from *Eimeria stiedae* infections in the epithelial lining of bile ducts of rabbits; papilloma (a core of vascularized connective tissue surrounded by epithelial cells) formation as the result of the presence of *Schistosoma mansoni* eggs in the colon of man; and growths in the stomachs of cats and dogs resulting from infections with the roundworm *Gnathostoma spinigerum*. True cancerous neoplasms have been reported associated with helminth parasites. The liver flukes *Opisthorchis sinensis* and *O. felin-*

eus have been suspected of initiating cancer in the liver of man; the lung fluke *Paragonimus westermani* has been suspected of contributing to cancer in the lungs of tigers. Siedlecki (1902, 1907) reported that the coccidian parasite *Caryotropha mesnili,* parasitizing the spermatogonial cells of the annelid *Polymnia nebulosa,* brings about hypertrophy of the parasitized cells, involving both the nucleus and the cytoplasm (Plate 1-4). Some of the surrounding cells undergo similar changes and eventually fuse with the infected cell to form a giant multinucleated cell.

Effects of Toxins, Poisons, and Secretions

Specific poisons or toxins, egested, secreted, or excreted by parasites, have been cited in many cases as the cause of irritation and damage to hosts. This phase of parasitology is in need of a great deal of research since toxins are often cited as the causative factors when no definite proof is at hand. Isolation or localization of toxic substances is the only reliable means of verifying their existence, and this involves extremely painstaking procedures.

A good example of an irritating parasite secretion that elicits an allergic reaction in the host is that which causes schistosome cercarial dermatitis. The severe inflammatory reaction of the host's tissue strongly suggests that the

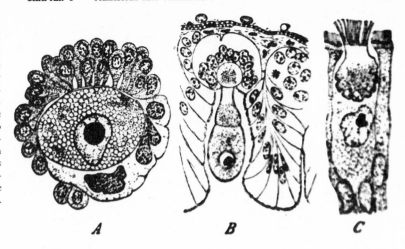

Plate 1-4   A. Hypertrophy of spermatogonial cell of the annelid *Polymnia nebulosa* infected with the coccidian *Caryotropha mesnili.* (After Siedlecki, 1902.) **B.** Invasion of intestinal epithelial cells of *Gryllomorpha* by the gregarine *Clepsidrina davini* causing host cells to fuse into a syncytium. (After Léger and Duboscq, 1902.) **C.** Hypertrophy of an intestinal epithelial cell of *Blaps* parasitized by the gregarine *Stylorhynchus longicollis.* Only epimerite of gregarine is visible in this picture. (After Léger and Duboscq, 1902.)

A   B   C

fluke secretes some substance that causes the inflammation, and indeed such a secretion is now known to exist. In the case of bloodsucking insects, such as mosquitoes, the swellings resulting from the bites represent the host's response to the irritating salivary secretions of the insect.

A known parasite toxin is the peri-intestinal or coelomic fluid of the nematode *Parascaris equorum.* The irritability of this fluid to the cornea and to the mucous membranes of the nasopharyngeal cavity is well known. Weinberg and Julian (1911, 1913) collected a quantity of this fluid under aseptic conditions and injected it into guinea pigs. Not surprisingly, they found that 0.5 cu. mm. of this highly toxic fluid kills a guinea pig. Weinberg also placed drops of this fluid in the eyes of horses and found that it generally caused a violent reaction. Some horses, however, were not affected. Further investigation revealed that the unaffected horses were heavily infected with *P. equorum,* thus suggesting that these hosts had developed an immunity against the toxin.

Mechanical Interference

Less is known about injuries to the host resulting from mechanical interferences by parasites. However, the author suspects that they are more common than is generally supposed. Probably the best known case of this type of damage is elephantiasis. In humans infected with the filarial nematode *Wuchereria bancrofti,* the adult worms become lodged in the lymphatic ducts. The continuous increase of the number of worms, coupled with the aggregation of connective tissue in the area of interference, eventually results in complete blockage of the lymph flow, and the excess fluid behind the

blockage seeps through the walls of the lymph ducts into the surrounding tissues, causing edema. The frequency of extremes of this condition, known as elephantiasis (Plate 1-5, Fig. 2), is often exaggerated in medical textbooks, which carry photographs of humans with extremely edemic legs and scrotums. Such extreme instances are of many years standing.

Mechanical damage by a nematode is also demonstrated by *Ascaris lumbricoides* in the intestine and bile ducts of their hosts. This intestinal parasite, which measures up to 14 inches in length, when present in large numbers, can easily block the normal flow of bile down the bile duct and the passage of chyme into the intestine.

The sheer occupancy of a large portion of the liver and other organs of man and dogs by hydatid cysts of the tapeworm *Echinococcus granulosus* constitutes another type of mechanical interference (Plate 1-5, Fig. 1). These fluid-filled cysts can attain a diameter of several inches, and one cyst removed from a human in Australia contained 50 quarts of fluid. *Coenurus cerebralis,* the cysticercus larva of the dog tapeworm, *Multiceps multiceps,* is known to exert extreme pressure on the brain and spinal cord of sheep, which serve as intermediate hosts. Infected sheep are said to suffer from *staggers* or *gid* because of the staggering movement resulting from pressure on the brain.

It is known that erythrocytes of chickens infected with the avian malaria organism *Plasmodium gallinaceum* have a tendency to stick together, thus clogging the fine capillaries. Blood vessels dammed up by the infected blood cells often rupture. Those rupturing in the area of the brain permit blood to leak into the brain

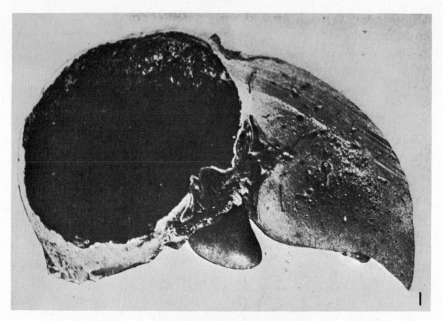

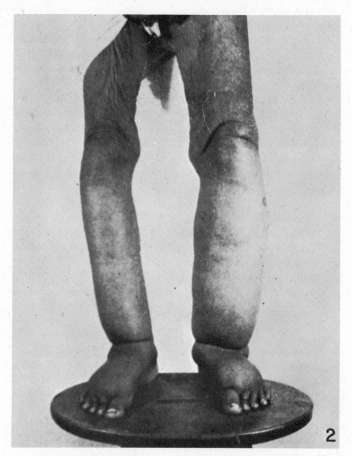

Plate 1-5   Manifestations of some human parasitic diseases. 1. Extremely large cavity in human liver caused by hydatid cyst of *Echinococcus granulosus*. (After Faust, in Brennemann, J., (ed.). 1937. *Practice of Pediatrics*. W. F. Prior Co., Hagerstown, Md.) **2.** Elephantiasis of human legs. (Courtesy of Armed Forces Institute of Pathology, negative No. A-4430-1.)

tissue, thus often causing the death of the host. Similar instances have been reported among human victims of malaria.

Strangulation of fish whose gills are parasitized by monogenetic trematodes is another good example of mechanical damage to hosts.

Biological Effects in the Host

Other interesting and challenging aspects of host-parasite relationships are the biological effects on the host. Among the most interesting of these are the secondary manifestations resulting from damage to some specific organ. Giard (1911–1913) and Smith (1910, 1911) have shown that in crabs parasitized by *Sacculina* the host's gonadal tissue is invaded by this crustacean causing drastic changes in males but not females. Seventy per cent of the parasitized male crabs acquired secondary female characteristics—abdomen broadens, appendages are modified to grasp eggs, and chelae become smaller (Plate 1–6). Histological examinations of the testes revealed that the testicular cells were at various stages of degeneration. This was found to be true also of ovarian tissue in parasitized females. However, if the parasites are removed from the male, the remaining testicular cells regenerate to form a hermaphroditic gonad that is responsible for the changes in secondary sex characteristics. Since ovarian cells cannot regenerate, the removal of the parasites from the females is not followed by changes in secondary sex characteristics. Similarly, another parasitic crustacean, *Peltogaster carvatus,* has the same effect on the male and female crabs *Eupagurus excavatus* var. *meticulosa.* Other cases of males acquiring female characteristics are known. The parasitic isopod *Entoniscus* begins as an ectoparasite, but it soon enters the body cavity of its host and eventually causes castration without ever touching the host's gonads. In the case of the nematode *Heterotylenchus aberrans,* which parasitizes the river-fly *Hylemyia,* the ovaries of female hosts fail to develop while in males the testes are functional. The destruction of gonadal tissues by a parasite is known as parasitic castration and has been reviewed by Reinhard (1956).

Another interesting aspect of parasite-caused biological change has to do with metabolic alterations in the host. Wheeler (1910) pointed out that workers of the ant *Pheidole commutata,* when parasitized by the roundworm *Mermis,* become hypertrophied, and the entire body becomes much larger than that of the normal ant. The abdomen sometimes enlarges to eight

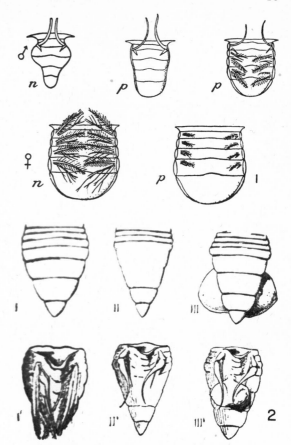

Plate 1-6   Modifications of external sex characteristics as a result of parasitism. 1. Abdomen of *Inachus mauritanicus,* showing modifications due to parasitism by *Sacculina. n,* normal individuals; *p,* parasitized individuals. Males in the first row, females in the second. (After Smith, 1910–11.) **2.** Modification of abdomen of *Carcinus maenas* due to parasitism by *Sacculina,* dorsal and ventral views. I, I′, abdomen of normal female; II, II′, abdomen of normal male; III, III′, abdomen of parasitized male. (After Giard, 1911–13.)

times the normal size. Such parasite-caused giants are known as macroergates. The explanation given for this unusual condition is that the parasitized larvae engorge themselves and undergo extensive growth.

There have been many studies of *Sacculina* because this unique crustacean parasite is known to affect the metabolism and sex life of its hosts. In one crab host, *Carcinus maenas,* the females and males are metabolically different. The difference is manifested in the chemical composition of the blood. In males the blood is generally colorless except just prior to molting when, because of the presence of tetronerythrin, it becomes pink. In sexually mature females the blood is yellowish due to the presence of lutein. The fat content varies, being 0.198 per cent in mature females, 0.086 per cent in "pink-blooded" males, and 0.059 per cent in "white-blooded" males. Smith (1910, 1911) showed that in *Sacculina*-infected males the fat content in the blood is increased considerably, approaching the level found in females. In short, *Sacculina* has caused males to alter their metabolism to that characteristic of females.

Snails infected with trematode larvae are known to be larger than uninfected ones. The reason for this phenomenon, known as gigantism, is not yet known.

For other examples of secondary biological effects on hosts caused by parasites the reader should consult two excellent essays: Geoffrey Lapage's *Parasitic Animals* and Maurice Caullery's *Parasitism and Symbiosis*.

Host Tissue Reactions

In instances of host tissue reactions, certain host cells and cell products (e.g., connective tissue fibers) aggregate around the invading parasite forming what is commonly called a cyst, although not all cysts are of host origin. For example, when the metacercaria of the yellow grub, *Clinostomum marginatum*, encysts in the skin of fish, two cyst walls are formed around the parasite. The inner one is secreted by the parasite; the outer one is laid down by the host in response to the parasitic invasion. Although the double wall of trematode metacercarial cysts is a common occurrence (Plate 1–7, Fig. 1), single-walled cysts also occur.

Another example of host tissue reaction is demonstrated by *Trichinella spiralis* encystment in mammalian muscle. Once the nematode larva reaches the musculature, it is surrounded by connective tissue cells and eosinophils. These host cells soon form a capsule around the coiled worm; hence the cyst is completely of host origin. In time, the capsule becomes calcified, the calcium coming primarily from the host, although there is some evidence that the parasite also contributes some (Plate 1–7, Fig. 2).

Immunity to Parasites

Parasites enter their hosts either actively or passively. If the infective form of the parasite penetrates into or aggressively attacks its host, admittance is said to be *active*. If the infective form has to be ingested, inhaled, or injected into the host, admittance is said to be *passive*. Active and passive admittance resulting in successful establishment can only be possible if the host is susceptible to the parasite; even

then, in many instances, the host responds to the presence of the parasite by becoming totally or partially immune. Prior to a discussion of immunity, it is appropriate to discuss two other terms—susceptibility and resistance.

A host is said to be susceptible if it is theoretically capable of being infected by a specific parasite. This implies that the physiological state of the host is such that it will not eliminate the parasite before the parasite has an opportunity to become established in the host. A host is said to be resistant if its physiological state prevents the establishment and survival of a parasite, be it during the initial or a subsequent contact.

If a parasite is established within a susceptible host so as to be able to inject some metabolic product—usually a protein or protein complex—or the body of the parasite comes in contact with the host's blood or nonprotective tissues (visceral organs, muscles, brain, etc.), these parasite products act as antigens. These antigens in turn elicit the synthesis of antibodies. Antibodies produced in response to ectoparasites either are elicited by antigenic substances introduced as the parasite feeds on the host, or the somatic proteins of the parasite have in some way challenged the host. It is not possible to discuss in detail here the various hypotheses of antigen-antibody reaction. These are given in any immunology textbook, such as that by Cushing and Campbell (1957). In short, a specific antibody combines with the antigen that elicited its production. This indicates that the molecular structure of the antibody is in some way related to its corresponding antigen.

When a host produces specific antibodies against an invading parasite, the host is said to have developed an immunity to the parasite. This immunity may be partial or complete. If it is complete, the host will readily eliminate the parasite and all similar parasites that subsequently attempt to enter, at least for the period during which the antibodies remain functional.

The host's immunological response to bacterial, viral, protozoan, and metazoan parasites is essentially the same. Response to these various antigenic agents depends on factors affecting the host's immunological competence and reactivity—for example, age, diet, stress, and the quality and quantity of the antigens and their availability to the host. The quality, quantity, and availability of the antigens are primarily responsible for the differences, both

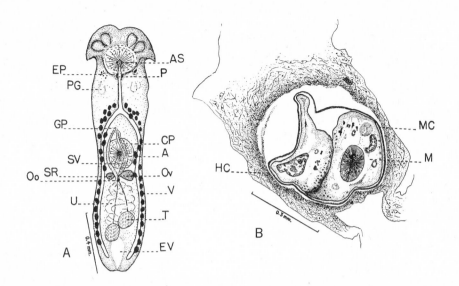

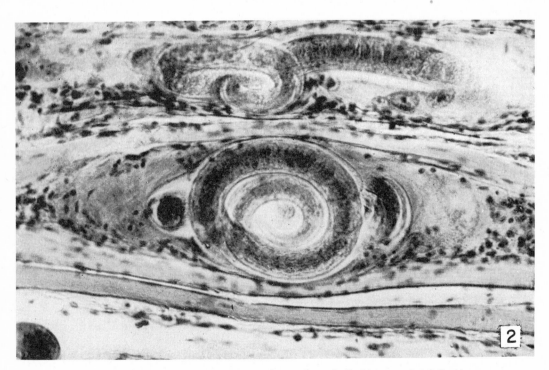

Plate 1-7   **Examples of encystment of parasites. 1. A.** Metacercaria of *Crepidostomum cornutum* removed from its cyst. **B.** Histological section of metacercaria of *C. cornutum* in body of crayfish host. Notice presence of two cyst walls. (*A*, acetabulum; AS, anterior sucker; CP, cirrus pouch; EP, eyespot pigment; EV, excretory vesicle; GP, genital pore; HC, host cyst wall; M, metacercaria; MC, metacercarial cyst wall; Oo, ootype; Ov, ovary; P, pharynx; PG, penetration gland; SR, seminal receptacle; SV, seminal vesicle; T, testis; U, uterus; V, vitelline follicle.) (After Cheng, 1957.) **2.** Larva of *Trichinella spiralis* encysted in striated muscles of rat host. (Courtesy of General Biological Supply House, Inc., Chicago.)

qualitative and quantitative, in antigenic stimulation exhibited by bacterial and viral parasites and by metazoan parasites.

Bacterial and viral parasites undergo rapid multiplication within their hosts and in so doing expose susceptible animals to relatively large quantities of homogenous antigens. In most instances the microbial antigen (or toxin) is released directly into the host's tissues. On the other hand, adult helminths do not multiply within their hosts. During the parasitic phase of helminth life cycles, it is primarily the elaboration of transitory rather than somatic antigens that elicits the immune resistance response by the host (Thorson, 1953; and later studies by others). In order to effect an antibody response to these transitory antigens, the host must ingest or be exposed to a sufficient number of infective larvae in a single dose, and the infective larvae must undergo development that results in production of the minimum threshold quantity of antigen for antibody production to be stimulated. Even if a sufficient amount of antigens is produced, production of antibodies will not occur unless the antigens are absorbed in unaltered form and reach the antibody-producing sites. Thus, the antigens of intestinal helminths must pass through the intestinal mucosal barrier of the host. Cases in which immunological responses in hosts cannot be detected are probably due to either insufficient quantities of antigens and/or failure of the antigens to reach the antibody-producing sites.

Because of the differences between microbial and metazoan antigens, the selective pressure resulting from metazoan parasites is not as noticeable as the selective pressure resulting from bacteria and viruses. In other words, metazoan infections do not result in as dramatic a disease nor cause as many deaths as bacterial and viral infections. A good example of this is myxomatosis in European and Australian rabbits. The introduction of the myxoma virus has reduced these rabbit populations by 85 to 90 per cent.

In summary, relative to immunity to metazoan parasites, (1) infection with living larvae is not a very efficient way of inducing antibody response and host resistance, for the important antigen-producing stages of these worms are transitory; (2) the antibody titers in animals naturally infected with metazoan parasites tend to be low or even lacking, and the development of resistance tends to be irregular; (3) only slight selective pressure appears to be exerted on hosts to encourage their development of antibody-producing mechanisms sensitive to the low levels characteristic of the antigens of metazoans; and (4) by employing in vitro culture techniques that allow collection of elaborated antigens in greater quantities, it is possible to induce resistance by artificial immunization, even when there is no evidence of natural immunization.

While many protozoan and most helminthic infections do not confer dramatic and long-lasting immunity to reinfection, in some cases these infections do stimulate resistance during the time the parasites are still in the host. This resistance to hyperinfection is known as premunition.

Determination of Antibodies

Antibodies in immunized hosts have been primarily associated with the gamma globulin fraction of the host's sera, but it is becoming evident that these antibodies may also be associated with the $alpha_1$, $alpha_2$, and beta globulin fractions. For this reason, the presence of antibodies in hosts can generally be detected by determining whether there are any increases in the serum globulin fractions by means of electrophoretic separations. In addition, various other methods can be employed. Some of these are briefly described here.

PRECIPITATION.   When a soluble antigen in suitable concentration is placed in the presence of a suitable concentration of the reciprocal antibody and observed under suitable conditions, the solution becomes turbid and an insoluble antigen-antibody complex precipitates.

AGGLUTINATION.   The basic mechanism of agglutination is essentially the same as that of precipitation except that the antigen in this case is larger, being particulate or cellular. Thus whole protozoan or bacterial cells, when placed in host serum that includes antibodies specific to them (antisera), clump together, or agglutinate.

LYSIS.   Although lysis is not a very common type of antigen-antibody reaction, under certain conditions the antibody may lyse the antigenic cells or organisms. Certain protozoan trophozoites and trematode cercariae are sometimes lysed if placed in antisera.

As a rule, antibodies produced against parasites can be categorized as being humoral or cellular. Humoral antibodies circulate in the blood and hence are evenly distributed throughout the host, while cellular antibodies are found only within the cells. Thus it is necessary to rupture the cells, releasing the antibodies, before any type of antigen-antibody reaction can be detected.

In recent years much attention has been focused on the utilization of immunological techniques in the diagnosis of helminthic infections. Such techniques as immunoelectrophoresis, tanned sheep erythrocyte agglutination, agar-gel diffusion, precipitation, agglutination, and various other methods have all been tested with varying degrees of success (Silverman, 1963; Kabat and Mayer, 1961). Investigations and findings of this sort are numerous and are not discussed in this book other than to state that helminths demonstrate multiple antigenicity. As the result, cross reactions, which are often observed, create a confusing picture. Sometimes even unrelated parasites cross react possibly because of common similarities in their antigenic structures. The precise characterization of helminth antigens thus must necessarily be undertaken (Kent, 1963). Interested readers are referred to the monograph edited by Jachowski (1963). Of fundamental importance, however, is the fact that in parasitic immunodiagnostic studies, two categories of antigens are used—somatic and metabolic.

Somatic antigens include suspensions of homogenized whole worms; saline or aqueous extracts of homogenized worms, extractions of specific tissues, such as, muscle, intestine, cuticle, or body fluid; and chemical fractions of homogenized worms.

Metabolic antigens, preferably known as ES (excretions and secretions) antigens, are in the form of excretions and secretions of whole worms at some stage of their life cycles, which excretions and secretions become suspended in a liquid medium in which the worms had been maintained for a period of time. The importance of ES antigens in vivo is becoming increasingly more apparent.

THE ECOLOGY OF PARASITES

EFFECT OF STRESS ON PARASITISM

From the biological standpoint, manifestations of stress by the host, caused by such conditions as crowding, lack of adequate shade and water, filth, poor ventilation, rough treatment, insufficient food, and abnormal temperatures, is basically a physiological response and not a pathological condition. The host under stress attempts to maintain its normal life processes and re-establish functional activities. It has been demonstrated that a host in stress responds differently, sometimes only in degree, to infection by parasites. Louis Pasteur was the first to discover that the susceptibility of a host is increased as the result of stress caused by effects of low environmental temperature. He found that although chickens are normally resistant to the anthrax organism *Bacillus anthracis*, reduction of their body temperature by chilling makes them susceptible. Subsequent studies revealed, however, that other factors in addition to body temperature are involved in the decreased resistance, for Pasteur later was able to culture *B. anthracis* at a temperature comparable to the body temperature of fowls.

In mice infected with the normally non-pathogenic haemoflagellate *Trypanosoma duttoni*, if the hosts are subjected to stress brought about by partial starvation and low environmental temperatures, they die much earlier than control hosts maintained at room temperature. Thus stress apparently lowers the resistance of hosts (Sheppe and Adams, 1957).

Other reports of the effects of stress on parasitism exist. For example, Josephine (1958) has shown that stress increases the invasiveness of *Entamoeba histolytica* in kittens. Robinson (1961) has found that the survival of *Trichinella spiralis* is enhanced in mice subjected to psychological stress resulting from mild electric stimulation, bright lights, and loud noise. Welter (1960) has found that there are more liver and proventriculus lesions in chickens infected with the flagellate *Histomonas* when the birds are subjected to starvation. Noble (1962) has reported that the number of coccidial oocysts and trichomonads in the feces of ground squirrels subjected to stress resulting from periodic fighting is higher than in the feces of hosts caught in the field and those maintained in the laboratory without stress. He has suggested that changes in the number of parasites may indicate altered resistance mechanisms.

The introduction of chemicals to bring about stress is also known to alter the resistance pattern in hosts. For example, Weinmann and Rothman (1961) have shown that the injection of cortisone acetate, into mice infected with the tapeworm *Hymenolepis nana*, even in quantities as small as 0.05 mg. per day for a week, enhances host reinfection. If treatment with cortisone is stopped, mice recover their ability to resist reinfection within 4 to 6 days. Nelson (1962) has shown that in lambs that had previously developed resistance to the sheep ked *Melophagus ovinus,* this resistance can be broken down within 2 weeks after injecting long-acting adrenocorticotropic hormone (ACTH) daily for a month, by oral treatment twice daily with acetylsalicylic acid (ASA), or by daily injections of cortisone for 4 weeks. It was suggested that the pituitary-adrenal system is involved in modifying the resistance in lambs to keds and that the basic annual ked population cycle can be affected by physiological or environmental stress such as pregnancy or undernourishment. The results obtained from the introduction of hormones, together with what is known concerning the effects of physically and nutritionally induced stresses on endocrine glands, suggest that the influence of stress on parasitism most probably involves the endocrines.

The zoogeography, ecology, and population densities of parasites provide intriguing problems for study. The ecology of parasites can be divided into two categories—that concerned with the relationship between parasite and exterior environment, directly or indirectly, can be considered *macroecology,* while that concerned with the relationship between parasite and the environment provided by its host can be considered *microecology.* Hence, parasitology, aside from its medical and veterinary implications, can be considered an area of ecology. Some of the more important principles of the macroecology of parasites are considered here; microecology is considered later.

The far-flung distribution of the definitive host need not mean that its parasites are also widely distributed, especially if specific intermediate hosts and vectors are involved. If the intermediate host(s) is absent in a given geographical area, even if the definitive host is parasitized, the infection will soon die out since the completion of the parasite's life cycle becomes impossible. Therefore, maintenance of a specific species of parasite depends on the availability of all its hosts. Because of this relationship, factors governing the survival of the hosts indirectly govern the presence of dependent parasites.

By means of normal evolutionary processes— that is, random mutations acted on by forces of natural selection—species of parasites have become acclimated to certain types of hosts.

For example, the trematode *Calicotyle kroyeri* is specific for a limited number of marine skates and rays, and the liver lancet fluke *Dicrocoelium dendriticum* (Plate 1–8, Fig. 1) is only found in pastoral areas where the small land snail *Cionella lubrica* and the ant *Formica fusca*—the first and second intermediate hosts—are found. One of the human malarial parasites, *Plasmodium vivax,* is only endemic to areas where suitable mosquito vectors can survive. Thus the geographical limits of the definitive host do not necessarily represent the same limits for the parasite. This is most obviously exemplified in the case of human parasites. Human population is widely distributed, but certain species of human parasites are not as widely distributed, particularly if intermediate hosts are involved. Thus, human trypanosomiasis, filariasis, and opisthorchiasis are not endemic to the United States. If an intermediate host is not involved, as in the case of the commensal *Entamoeba coli,* the geographic distribution of the parasite usually coincides with that of man.

The geographic distribution of certain well known species, especially those parasitizing man and domestic animals, has been fairly well determined. Thus, the haemoflagellate *Trypanosoma rhodesiense*—the causative agent of

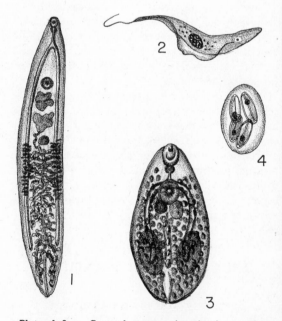

Plate 1-8   Several types of animal parasites.
1. *Dicrocoelium dendriticum* adult. **2.** *Trypanosoma rhodesiense,* a blood parasite of man. **3.** *Nanophyetus salmincola,* the salmon-poisoning trematode, adult. **4.** Oocyst of *Eimeria ellipsoidealis* recovered in feces of cattle. (Redrawn after Becker and Frye.)

one type of African sleeping sickness—is limited to Rhodesia, Kenya, Nyasaland, Portuguese East Africa, Tanganyika, and areas of eastern Uganda (Plate 1–8, Fig. 2). The "salmon poisoning" fluke, *Nanophyetus salmincola,* is limited to North America and eastern Siberia (Plate 1–8, Fig. 3). The distribution of some parasites of nondomesticated animals is known; for instance, the common intestinal fluke of wild rabbits, *Hasstilesia tricolor,* is limited to North America. In the majority of cases, however, the geographic distribution of parasites remains hazy. Part of this uncertainty is the result of difficulties in the recognition of species, especially in genera with morphologically similar species. In such instances, reports of new species have often been neglected. In due time, with the accumulation of information resulting from the continued reporting of new locales for known species, reliable geographic distribution charts may be constructed.

FACTORS THAT INFLUENCE
PARASITE DENSITY AND DISTRIBUTION

The presence or absence of a number of biological and physical factors in the environment directly or indirectly affects the densities and distributions of parasites.

Flora

Vegetation that serves as food and shelter for hosts, both intermediate and definitive, greatly influences the parasite population. This is particularly evident in the case of helminth parasites. For example, various aquatic molluscan hosts of digenetic trematodes survive only where there is an abundance of plants in the water and deciduous trees on the banks. The aquatic plants not only provide food but also oxygen for the molluscs. Leaves dropping from the trees very often serve as food for aquatic snails. If such flora are sparse or absent, the molluscan population declines, and the likelihood that the trematodes will complete their life cycles is proportionally diminished.

Although the metacercariae of the liver fluke *Fasciola hepatica* can encyst in water, these larvae usually encyst on vegetation and are later taken into their definitive host when sheep, or some other host, ingest plants on which the encysted metacercariae are found. If plants are absent or sparse, the chances of metacercarial encystment and eventual ingestion by the definitive host are greatly reduced, resulting in a much lower adult parasite population in the area.

Fauna

Since parasitism can only occur if two different species of organisms enter the symbiotic relationship, the presence and abundance of the host species are of critical importance. Furthermore, among animals the food chain is an essential factor. In nature, the presence of prey is absolutely necessary to carnivores and indirectly influences parasite density. The importance of the faunistic population forming the food chain, therefore, is obvious. For example, the larvae of the tapeworm *Taenia pisiformis* are found in the liver and mesenteries of rabbits and will only develop into adults when the viscera of infected rabbits are ingested by a carnivorous mammal—commonly the wild cat. Thus the presence and abundance of wild rabbits and wild cats are vital to maintenance of this tapeworm.

Water

Water plays a major role in the maintenance of parasitic fauna. Many sporadic parasites, such as the mosquitoes, can complete their development only when bodies of water are present. Furthermore, the absence of water would impede the development of a large number of helminths that utilize aquatic invertebrates as intermediate hosts. Moreover, the infective form of many parasites, particularly flatworms, is free-swimming and requires water to migrate and reach its host. Such is the case with the cercariae of certain digenetic trematodes and the ciliated larvae of certain monogeneids.

Not only is water of prime importance in the maintenance of certain parasites, but its physical state may also be influential. There is evidence that the velocity of flow influences the parasite population. For example, Rowan and Gram (1959) demonstrated that when the number of *Schistosoma mansoni* cercariae per unit volume of water is constant, experimentally exposed mice acquire heavier worm infections in fast-flowing water than in slow-flowing water. The explanation is that during a given period, more cercariae come in contact with each mouse in fast water than in slow water.

Not only do such physical factors as temperature, pH, salinity, and mineral content, influence the number and survival rates of intermediate hosts, but these factors also influence longevity of free-swimming stages in the life cycle of certain helminths such as the coracidia of certain tapeworms and the miracidia and cercariae of certain trematodes.

Host Population Density and Behavior

Population densities of transport, intermediate, and definitive hosts affect the parasite population density, for the latter is directly dependent on the former. In addition to population densities, the feeding, migratory, and other behavior patterns of hosts affect the parasite density. For example, the predatory feeding habits of many definitive hosts make possible the active intake of larval parasites that can only complete their development after being ingested by the host.

Although experimental evidence is slim, there is reason to believe that the parasite population, particularly the metazoan population, is an indicator of the biotic productivity of the environment. Thus, if the fish population in a lake harbors a large number of individuals and varieties of species of parasites, a concerted survey in most instances reveals a rich assortment and a large population of free-living fauna, primarily invertebrates. When one considers the fact that metazoan parasites generally require intermediate hosts—commonly invertebrates—the use of the number and variety of parasites as an indicator of biotic wealth in an area becomes reasonable.

From the foregoing it should be clear that a multitude of factors, such as the flora, fauna, presence of water and its temperature, pH, salinity, and mineral content, as well as the terrain and host population density and behavior, are all important in governing the population and distribution of the parasitic fauna.

HOST SPECIFICITY AMONG PARASITES

Host specificity is defined as the natural adaptability of a species of parasite to a certain species or group of hosts. The mechanisms responsible for host specificity are not completely known and are undoubtedly complex and varied, for the degree of specificity differs from species to species.

Wenrich (1935) postulated that host specificity among parasites evolved along two main lines:

(1) Some parasites have adapted themselves to many varieties of hosts. This is particularly true among protozoan parasites, such as mem-

bers of the genus *Trypanosoma,* which parasitize hundreds of vertebrate hosts of all major classes. Species of the sporozoan parasite *Eimeria* are again good examples of parasites having a wide range of hosts (Plate 1–8, Fig. 4). *Eimeria* spp. are known to parasitize annelids, insects, and mammals. Although the genus is well represented by species parasitizing a variety of hosts, oftentimes the individual species are quite host specific.

(2) The second group of parasites has been limited to a small category of hosts. This type of limited host specificity is convincingly demonstrated by the monogenetic trematodes (Hargis, 1957). For example, monogeneids of the family Hexabothriidae have been reported only as ectoparasites of the Elasmobranchii and are further restricted to members of the class Chondrichthyes. In addition, trematodes of the family Gyrodactylidae, of the monotypic but common genus *Gyrodactylus,* appear to be restricted to teleostomid fishes.

Obviously there are intermediates between these two main streams of host-specific adaptations. The digenetic flukes in their adult stages are generally limited to one or two groups of vertebrate hosts and hence display some degree of host specificity, although, as striking exceptions, flukes of the family Lecithodendriidae parasitize fishes, amphibians, reptiles, birds, and mammals. On the other hand, flukes of the family Bucephalidae are found only in fishes. This indicates that there are varying degrees of host specificity even among digenetic trematodes. The same may be said of tapeworms.

As a rule, a parasite that can only survive in one or a few species of hosts is more likely to require a more specific site within its host, while a parasite that is less host specific can live in a wide variety of environments. For example, the tapeworm *Taeniarhynchus saginatus,* which is specific for man, can only live in the small intestine, while the larvae of *Trichinella spiralis,* which can infect a variety of warm-blooded animals, is much less particular about which area of the host's body it encysts in.

The testing of host specificity, especially among the parasite Protozoa, is a form of experimentation popular among parasitologists. As the result of such investigations, the malarial parasites of man have been found to be quite host specific, as are the Coccidia of man. The human-infecting *Iodamoeba bütschlii,* although morphologically indistinguishable from the pig-infecting *Iodamoeba suis,* must be distinct from it, because attempts at cross infection have proven futile. Thus species differences, in such cases, need not be morphological, but may be essentially physiological. Among the less host-specific protozoan parasites, *Toxoplasma* of man is infective for a number of mammals as is the ciliate *Balantidium coli,* which occurs naturally in pigs, monkeys, apes, and man.

As our knowledge of host specificity increases, it is conjectured that the number of currently recognized species will be reduced because species reported from different hosts and established on that basis may be found to be infective to various hosts and thus shown to be identical, and because morphological variations that presently constitute the criteria for the definition of new species may well prove to be simply the result of the influence of the particular host and hence merely intraspecific variations. As Stunkard (1957) pointed out, often the specific host in which a parasitic flatworm is harbored governs the morphology of the species to some degree. It is possible, therefore, that many species of worms described from various hosts are variants of a single species.

Another interesting problem in the study of host specificity is that of geographically linked specificities. In several known cases, parasites of the same species utilize different intermediate hosts in different areas. For example, the blood fluke *Schistosoma mansoni* uses *Biomphalaria* snails as intermediate hosts in Africa, while in the West Indies and South America, *Tropicorbis centimetralis* and *Australorbis glabratus* are intermediate hosts. Interestingly enough, the Puerto Rican strain of *S. mansoni,* when tested, does not infect *Biomphalaria alexandrina,* the natural snail host in Egypt.

The compatibility of the parasite to its host, manifested by a minimal amount of host response to the invasion in the form of cellular response (encapsulation, phagocytosis, etc.) and/or production of humoral or cellular antibodies, is an important mechanism governing host specificity. The lack of strong reactions by the host's internal defense mechanisms presupposes that the parasite's body proteins are less antagonistic.

Smyth and Haslewood (1963) proposed that the biochemical composition of a mammalian host's bile could act as one possible selective biochemical agent in determining host specificity. The composition of bile varies greatly, relative to bile salts, conjugation of bile salts, fatty acids, pigments, and rate of secretion. If a helminth parasite, such as the hydatid tape-worm *Echinococcus granulosus,* enters an unfavorable host, the host's bile can rapidly destroy the invader by lysing its body cuticle, or in some way proving toxic to the parasite, or interfering with its metabolism. If the helminth enters a favorable host, the host's bile can provide the stimulus necessary for the inauguration of the next growth phase in the parasite's life cycle— hatching if an egg is introduced, scolex evagination if a larval tapeworm is introduced, or excystment if an encysted metacercarial trematode is introduced. Furthermore, the host's bile may provide a surface-activating agent that may be essential for the parasite's metabolic activities at a microsomal or mitochondrial level.

Bile is not the only biochemical agent that can serve as the stimulant for further development once the parasite enters a compatible host. Physical factors, such as pH, temperature, and salt concentration, and biochemical factors, such as enzymes and essential amino acids, can govern compatibility. Cheng (1963) demonstrated that in the trematode *Gorgodera amplicava* the normally quiescent cercariae (a larval stage) become activated and escape from their cyst-like tails when they come in contact with some component in the blood of the snail that serves as the second intermediate host. The cercariae, once activated, can develop into the next stage in its life cycle by encysting. In this case some substance in the host's blood serves as the stimulant.

BIOTIC POTENTIAL AMONG PARASITES

As a general rule, animals that have adopted the parasitic way of life possess greater biotic potentials—that is, hyperreproductivity.

In the case of parasitic Protozoa, very little work has been done in actually measuring their rates of reproduction. We do know that one mature eight-nucleate cyst of *Entamoeba coli,* when taken into the alimentary tract of the host, gives rise to eight metacystic trophozoites; a four-nucleate cyst of *E. histolytica* gives rise to four metacystic trophozoites. The free-living forms under normal conditions have little or no occasion to encyst and undergo intracystic nuclear division, which is followed by cyto-plasmic division (cytokinesis) upon excystment, thus increasing the number of individuals. In addition to this mode of reproduction, free-living and parasitic forms both are capable of asexual division (fission) in the trophozoite form, thus increasing the number of daughter amoebae. Therefore, it is apparent that parasitic entamoebae can produce more individuals in a given period, because they encyst more often (Plate 1–9).

Among parasitic helminths, the biotic potential is indeed great. A single human pinworm, *Enterobius vermicularis,* is capable of producing 4672 to 16,888 (mean 11,105) eggs during its life span. A single female *Ascaris lumbricoides,* the common intestinal roundworm, is capable of producing 200,000 eggs daily and has a total capacity of 27,000,000 eggs in her uterus. The author was able to count 2500 eggs in the uterus of *Acanthatrium oligacanthum,* a minute trematode found in the small intestine of bats. *Raillietina demerariensis,* the Celebes tapeworm of man, is estimated to possess 200 to 250 eggs per gravid proglottid and possesses approximately 5000 such proglottids. These tremendously large numbers of eggs probably represent the highest reproduction rates among living animals. Because of such great biotic

potentials, parasitic worms are able to maintain themselves despite the tremendous odds against them because of the hit-or-miss processes necessary during the completion of their life cycles. Indirectly, the fecundity of parasites is manifested by the magnitude of parasitic infections that exist despite the mortality rate. Stoll (1947) announced the astounding figure that in the world today there are 2,200,000,000 cases of human helminthic infections! This is a challenging medical problem, not to mention the millions of infections in domestic and wild animals as well as those in lower vertebrates and invertebrates.

The reproductive rate of insects is extremely great. It has been stated that, excluding the Protozoa and nematodes, there are more insects on the face of the earth than any other group of animals. Certainly the biotic potential of parasitic insects ranks among the highest in the Animal Kingdom.

The striking exception to the rule of greater biotic potential among parasites is the parasitic molluscs, which give rise to fewer progeny

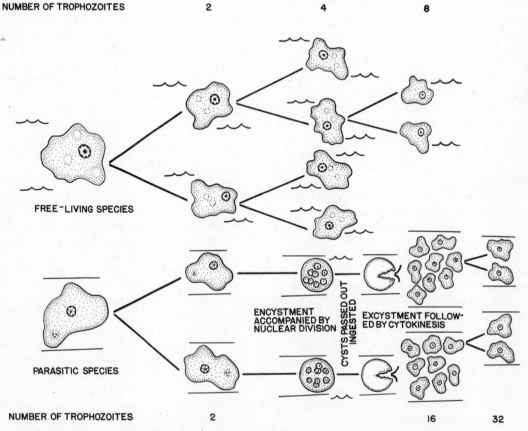

Plate 1–9   Comparison between the reproductive rates of a free-living and a parasitic amoeba.

than free-living species. This undoubtedly is due to evolutionary changes associated with the more efficient means these animals have for spreading infection (p. 677).

It is not surprising that the biotic potential is so high among parasites if one considers the tremendous odds parasites must surmount to perpetuate their species. Protozoan parasites that require an arthropod vector to carry them from one vertebrate host to another must await the right vector, and civilization with all its modern insecticides is not making life any easier for them. Digenetic trematodes exhibit what is considered one of the most complex types of life histories among animals. Most of them require one, two, three, or even four intermediate hosts to complete their life cycles. Think of the difficulties confronting these minute animals. Often the metacercaria (the last larval stage in most species of trematodes) remains encysted in an arthropod intermediate host and must be ingested by the definitive host before it can complete its development. The parasite itself is helpless. The same obstacles in varying degrees confront the cestodes, the spiny-headed worms, and other groups. Little wonder the sexually mature individuals lay so many eggs; it's nature's way of improving the odds in preserving the species. Only after more efficient methods of completing the life cycle have evolved, as among the parasitic molluscs, does the number of eggs produced decrease.

THE EVOLUTION OF PARASITES

Where and when did parasites arise? There is no clear-cut answer. As in study of the evolution of free-living plants and animals, evidence is primarily circumstantial. In postulating the origin of parasitism, most authorities agree that parasites arose from free-living progenitors. It follows that endoparasites have resulted from free-living forms that were accidentally introduced into the host. In this new environment, spontaneous genic mutations occurred, and the more proficient mutants thrived, exemplifying the concept of "survival of the fittest." Among the tapeworms, the continuous appearance of mutant forms has resulted in the appearance of modern species that lack an alimentary tract. Such mutants have obviously become highly successful, for the environment consists of a matrix of di-

gested and partially digested nutrients that can be absorbed. Thus the lack of an alimentary tract, though seemingly "degenerate," is actually a more advanced and efficient condition. Furthermore, tapeworm enzymatic systems, modes of locomotion, digestion, and sensation have also become more efficiently adapted to parasitism. Similar modifications have taken place among other parasite groups.

Where more than one host is involved in completion of the parasite's life cycle, the multi-host species usually may be considered to be more advanced, because presumably the parasite has become adapted, in time, to several species of hosts. The modern intermediate hosts may well have been definitive hosts at one time. This concept is quite popular, but in studying the evolution of parasites within the same phylum and in light of biotic potentials and life cycle patterns, perhaps the advancement in parasitism is best represented by a bell-shaped curve (Table 1–2). That is, the increasing number of intermediate hosts signifies evolutionary advancement only up to a certain point, whereafter the elimination of certain intermediate hosts should be considered a more advanced condition because the parasite enhances its chances of reaching the definitive host by eliminating one or more intermediate hosts.

This concept is borne out in the case of the *Schistosoma* blood flukes. Here the parasite requires only one intermediate host; the cercariae emerging from the snail host actively seek out and penetrate the definitive host. Both the presence of male and female schistosomes and the more highly developed type of cercarial tail suggest the advanced state of these worms as compared to that of other digenetic trematodes, in which two, three, or more intermediate hosts are required (Plate 1–10, Figs. 1 and 2).

Parasitism, commensalism, and mutualism are often examined from the evolutionary standpoint. Which is the most recent form of relationship? The concept that parasitism is most primitive was quite popular at one time, because in some cases an organism introduced into a new host results in severe pathogenicity, causing metabolic alterations that affect the welfare of the host. According to this concept, parasitism, through adaptation, is reduced to the nonharmful commensalism and still later becomes the mutually beneficial mutualism. With the advance of experimental parasitology, this concept has come into question as the result of work by several investigators. It has been shown that one species of *Plasmodium,*

Table 1-2.   The Hypothetical Evolution of Parasitic Animals As Correlated with the Number of Intermediate and Definitive Hosts

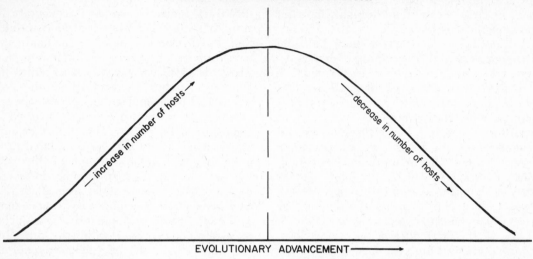

EVOLUTIONARY ADVANCEMENT⟶

when inoculated into a variety of hosts, causes death, in one species of host, modest malaria in another, and fails to produce any symptoms in a third. Packchanian (1934) reported similar results with *Trypanosoma brucei* when it was introduced into an array of hosts. Since these were all "new" hosts, the concept previously mentioned appears dubious, at least in the instances cited. It appears to be more appropriate to say that parasitism, commensalism, and mutualism are independent forms of relationships, each having arisen divorced from the other and dependent on the particular pair entering into the relationship. On the other hand, the subtle gradient between these three categories of symbiotic relationships suggests that, at least in certain instances, one type of symbiosis may have evolved from another; hence both concepts may hold true, depending

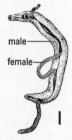
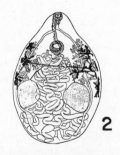

Plate 1-10   Comparison between a schistosome and a monoecious distomate trematode. 1. *Schistosoma haematobium*. (After Ward.) 2. *Prosthogonimus macrorchis*. (After Macy.)

on the species involved.   Because evolution is a continuous process—animals are forever evolving—one species may give rise to others and these in turn to still more. This brings us to the consideration of what a species is.

THE SPECIES PROBLEM AMONG PARASITES

When one considers a species, it must be understood if this is from the viewpoint of a systematist or that of a student of evolution. To the systematist, the species serves as a practical device designed as the basis for the arrangement of all living organisms into a comprehensive system. In his discussion of a species, the systematist emphasizes the methods and criteria by which the various species, or any other taxon, can be distinguished from one another. Thus the species is considered a fixed state. To the student of evolution or speciation, the species is a passing stage in the stream of evolution. As Dobzhansky (1937) puts it: "[a species is] that stage of the evolutionary process at which the once actually or potentially interbreeding array of forms becomes segregated into two or more separate arrays which are physiologically incapable of interbreeding." Thus the species is a temporary state in the stream of evolution. So the reader will not be left with the impression that the species concepts of systematists and evolutionists are mutually exclusive, it should be pointed out that the modern systematist, in attempting to arrange organisms into a comprehensive system, believes that he is employing criteria that permit his arrangement to be representative of a natural phylogenetic pattern rather than mere pigeon-holing in an artificial system.

A completely satisfactory definition of a taxonomic species, be it for free-living or parasitic organisms, but particularly the latter, remains to be contributed. Simpson (1961) stated: "The modern biological or, more strictly, genetical concept of a species among biparental, contemporaneous organisms is a group of interbreeding organisms genetically isolated from other such groups." This broad conceptual definition appears to satisfy most biologists. It should be noted, however, that the concept of the *genetic species* has changed since the days of Lotsy and other geneticists at the turn of the century, who considered a species as a group of genetically identical individuals. We now know that genetic differences, although slight in most instances, do exist among individuals of the same species and even among individuals of infraspecific groupings. In fact, as Mayr (1942) pointed out, except for identical twins, every individual in bisexually-producing species is a different biotype. The modern concept of the genetic species considers genetic identicality to mean the sharing of a common gene pool and takes into consideration the phenomenon of isolation as given in Simpson's definition. To the practicing systematist, the genetic species concept serves more as a viewpoint by which to guide his work than as a tool.

Another species concept—that based on the fertility of offsprings—has often been employed. Thus, if two organisms mate and produce fertile offspring, the parents usually belong to the same species. There is severe objection to relying too heavily on this hypothesis, however, because numerous cases are known in which members of two generally recognized distinct species mate and produce fertile offspring. Furthermore, instances are also known in which geographic races of a single species exhibit reduced fertility or are completely sterile. Thus the concept of the *fertility-linked species* is not a completely satisfactory one.

When the fertility-linked species concept is applied to experiments in parasite cross fertilization, technical difficulties arise because parasites can rarely be removed from their hosts and cultured in vitro. Certain species of protozoa and helminths have been cultured, but there is no assurance that the organisms grown outside the host are physiologically identical to or

behave in the same manner as those found in vivo. Arthropod parasites are more useful from this standpoint since they are primarily ecto- and periodic parasites and cross fertilization experiments are feasible. Furthermore, many parasites are asexual or monoecious; hence attempts at cross fertilization are technically impossible.

Because of these obstacles, the *morphological species* is the most commonly used in reference to parasites. Such a species is defined as one that is consistently different morphologically from another. This again is an idealistic definition since very often in nature, especially among the helminths, only one, two, or three specimens can be found in a given population of hosts. In such cases, how can the systematist determine whether his specimens constitute a consistently different type? Again, if many parasites are found in the same host and several of the specimens reveal slight variations, can these differences be considered specific differences or intraspecific variations? These are difficult questions to answer and so in practice "a species is a systematic unit which is considered a species by a competent systematist (preferably a specialist of the group)" (Mayr, 1942).

In determining taxonomic differences and similarities among parasites, unlike the systematist working with free-living organisms, particularly vertebrates, the parasitologist commonly takes into consideration not only the morphology but also the biology of the various stages in the life cycles of animals. This, in many ways, makes systematic studies on parasites more fascinating and challenging.

Undoubtedly many species of parasites described so far are reliable; however, dubious ones that are in need of clarification exist.

In recent years, new techniques have brought about new ways to differentiate between species. As the result, new criteria are being established in defining a species. Some biologists believe that new taxonomic tools, such as comparative serology and biochemistry, serve only to confirm what is already known. Nevertheless, these essentially biochemical approaches may well lead to the synthesis (if it is not already established) of a new species concept—the *biochemical species*. Biochemical investigations have been applied to helminth parasites by Wilhelmi (1940), who not only found serologic differences among individuals of different species, but achieved some degree of accuracy in identifying stages in the life cycles of the same species (*Cryptocotyle lingua, Zygocotyle lunata,* and *Paror-*

chis acanthus). As a result of his studies, Wilhelmi wrote: " 'Species' of helminths may be defined tentatively as a group of organisms the lipid free antigen of which, when diluted to 1:4000 or more, yields a positive precipitin test within one hour with a rabbit antiserum produced by injecting 40 mg. of dry-weight, lipid-free antigenic material and withdrawn ten to twelve days after the last of four intravenous injections administered every third day." This technique for differentiating between species of trematodes may have been effective in the case of the three species studied by Wilhelmi, but more recent investigations have revealed that different species of helminths commonly possess common antigens so that cross reactions occur. For this reason, Wilhelmi's technique is not always useful.

Although serologic techniques hold promise in systematic studies, their practical application is often limited, because in homogenizing parasites to use as antigens in forming specific antisera, the specimens are necessarily destroyed. In cases of rare infections and hypo-infections (a small number of parasites per host), such techniques are problematic.

In addition to recognizing species serologically, the identification of specific amino acids and peptides constituting specific species, the determination of specific electrophoretic patterns of homogenates or sera (the latter in the case of arthropods), and the testing of host specificities all hold promise as ways by which the differentiation of taxa may be accomplished.

The never-ending species problem among parasites, especially metazoan parasites (among all plants and animals, for that matter), is acute and will provide careers for many future parasitologists. Professor Horace W. Stunkard (1957) wrote: "In the meantime, specific determination remains exceedingly difficult. Host varieties may be recognized, but in my opinion, subspecies of trematodes and cestodes have no meaning. The problems of intraspecific variation in parasitic flatworms are formidable but not insuperable."

PARASITOLOGY AS AN ACADEMIC AND APPLIED SCIENCE

At times the question is raised as to whether parasitology should be considered as a basic academic branch of biology or as an applied science related to human and veterinary medicine, agriculture, and public health. The answer is that it should be considered both. As in many other branches of biology, such as serology, genetics, immunology, bacteriology, ecology, and marine biology, there are workers who prefer to devote their time to fundamental problems and others who prefer the application of basic information to immediate practical situations.

Academically, parasitism may be thought of as a way of life. All animals may be divided into free-living and parasitic forms, although a series of gradients do exist. The dividing line is sometimes hazy. In adopting this outlook, those interested in parasitism may be considered to be engaged in ecological studies. Those interested in the anatomy or physiology of parasites are closely akin to biologists who are interested in the anatomy and physiology of fishes, birds, reptiles, or any other group of animals. Those interested in the embryology and morphogenesis of trematodes, cestodes, or acanthocephalans are uniformly as "fundamental" in outlook as traditional embryologists working with amphibians and echinoderms.

Because parasitic forms are represented among a large number of invertebrate phyla, there are many parasitologists interested in these representatives purely from the taxonomic standpoint. The comparison of species and the grouping of species into postulated natural schemes represent a branch of invertebrate zoology.

As applied sciences, medical, veterinary, and wildlife parasitology are as prominent and as practical as pharmacy, radiology, agronomy, pathology, and economic entomology. With the rapidity and frequency of world travel today, physicians are becoming increasingly conscious of the importance of tropical medicine, which involves medical parasitology. The threats imposed by amoebiasis, filariasis, typanosomiasis, schistosomiasis, opisthorchiasis, and other parasitic diseases in many areas of the world demand the attention of farsighted and cosmopolitan physicians and public health personnel.

In veterinary medicine the situation is more acute. Capillariasis, ascariasis, dirofilariasis, and opisthorchiasis in household pets, and spiruriasis, capillariasis, ascariasis, heterakiasis, and histomoniasis (blackhead disease) in domestic fowls are but a few common parasitic diseases confronting the veterinarian. Hogs, cattle, horses, sheep, dogs, cats, and all other types of domestic animals are known to suffer from parasitic diseases, some rather commonly and with severe economic repercussions. Chemotherapy, pathology, and control work are but a few examples of secondary aspects of economic parasitology. The role of parasitology as a practical science is an essential one.

LITERATURE CITED

Bullock, F. D., and M. R. Curtis. 1920. The experimental production of sarcoma in the liver of rats. Proc. N. Y. Path. Soc., *20:* 149–175.

Cameron, T. W. M. 1956. Parasites and Parasitism. John Wiley, New York.

Caullery, M. 1952. Parasitism and Symbiosis. Sidgwick and Jackson, London, England.

Cheng, T. C. 1963. Activation of *Gorgodera amplicava* cercariae by molluscan sera. Exptl. Parasit., *13:* 342–347.

Cushing, D. H., and J. E. Campbell. 1957. Principles of Immunology. McGraw-Hill, New York.

Dobzhansky, T. 1937. What is a species? Scientia, *61:* 280–286.

Giard, A. 1911–1913. Oeuvres Diverses. Paris.

Hargis, W. J., Jr. 1957. The host specificity of monogenetic trematodes. Exptl. Parasit., *6:* 610–625.

Jachowski, L. A., Jr. (ed.). 1963. Immunodiagnosis of Helminthic Infections. American Journal of Hygiene Monograph Series, No. 22. D. Bodian, Baltimore.

Josephine, M. A. 1958. Experimental studies on *Entamoeba histolytica* in kittens. Am. Jour. Trop. Med. Hyg., *7:* 158–164.

Kabat, E. A., and M. M. Mayer. 1961. Experimental Immunochemistry. 2nd Ed., Charles C Thomas, Springfield, Ill.

Kent, N. H. 1963. Fractionation, isolation and definition of antigens from parasitic helminths. *In* Immunodiagnosis of Helminthic Infections (L. A. Jachowski, Jr., ed.). American Journal of Hygiene Monograph Series No. 22., pp. 30–46. D. Bodian, Baltimore.

Lapage, G. 1958. Parasitic Animals. W. Heffer, Cambridge, England, 2nd Ed.

Mayr, E. 1942. Systematics and the Origin of Species. Columbia University Press, New York.

Nelson, W. A. 1962. Development in sheep of resistance to the ked *Melophagus ovinus* (L.). II. Effects of adrenocorticotrophic hormone and cortisone. Exptl. Parasit., *12:* 45–51.

Noble, G. A. 1962. Stress and parasitism. II. Effect of crowding and fighting among ground squirrels on their coccidia and trichomonads. Exptl. Parasit., *12:* 368–371.

Packchanian, A. A. 1934. Experimental *Trypanosoma brucei* infection and immunity in various species of *Peromyscus* (American deer mice). Am. J. Hyg., *20:* 135–147.

Reinhard, E. G. 1956. Parasitic castration of Crustacea. Exptl. Parasit., *5:* 79–107.

Robinson, E. J. 1961. Survival of Trichinella in stressed hosts. Jour. Parasitol., *47:* 16–17.

Rowan, W. B., and A. L. Gram. 1959. Relation of water velocity of *Schistosoma mansoni* infection in mice. Am. J. Trop. Med. *8:* 630–634.

Sheppe, W. A., and J. R. Adams. 1957. The pathogenic effect of *Trypanosoma duttoni* on hosts under stress conditions. Jour. Parasitol., *43:* 55–59.

Siedlecki, M. 1902. Cycle évolutif de la *Caryotropha mesnilii,* coccidie nouvelle des polymnies; note préliminaire. Bull. Internat. Acad. Sc. Cracovie, Cl. Sc. Math. Nat., *8:* 561–568.

Siedlecki, M. 1907. O budowie i rozwoju *Caryotropha mesnilii.* Bull. Internat. Acad. Sc. Cracovie, Cl. Sc. Math. Nat., *5:* 453–497.

Silverman, P. H. 1963. In vitro cultivation and serological techniques in parasitology. *In* Techniques in Parasitology (A. E. R. Taylor, ed.). Blackwell Scientific Publications, Oxford, pp. 45–67.

Simpson, G. G. 1961. Principles of Animal Taxonomy. Columbia University Press, New York.

Smith, G. W. 1910. Studies in the experimental analysis of sex. Quart. J. Micro. Sci., *55:* 225–240.

Smith, G. W. 1911. Studies in the experimental analysis of sex. Part 7. Sexual changes in the blood and liver of *Carinus maenas.* Quart. J. Micro. Sci., *57:* 251–265.

Smyth, J. D., and G. A. D. Haslewood. 1963. The biochemistry of bile as a factor in determining host specificity in intestinal parasites, with particular reference to *Echinococcus granulosus.* Ann. N. Y. Acad. Sci., *113:* 234–260.

Stoll, N. R. 1947. This wormy world. J. Parasit., *33:* 1–18.

Stunkard, H. W. 1957. Intraspecific variation in parasitic flatworms. System. Zool., *6:* 7–18.

Thorson, R. E. 1953. Studies on the mechanism of immunity in the rat to the nematode, *Nippostrongylus muris.* Am. J. Hyg., *58:* 1.

von Brand, T. 1957. Recent trends in parasite physiology. Exptl. Parasit., *6:* 233–244.

Weinberg, M., and A. Julian. 1911. Substances toxiques de l'*Ascaris megalocephala* (Recherches expérimentales sur le cheval). Compt. Rend. Soc. Biol. Paris, *70:* 337–339.

Weinberg, M., and A. Julian. 1913. Accidents mortels observés chez le cheval a la suite de l'instillation de toxine ascaridienne. Compt. Rend. Soc. Biol. Paris, *74:* 1162–1163.

Weinmann, C. J., and A. H. Rothman. 1961. Effects of natural stressors and of cortisone upon acquired resistance to *Hymenolepis nana* in mice. Jour. Parasitol., *47:* 55.

Welter, C. J. 1960. The effect of various stresses upon histomoniasis in chickens and turkeys. Poultry Sci., *39:* 361–366.

Wenrich, D. H. 1935. Host-parasite relations between parasitic Protozoa and their hosts. Proc. Amer. Philo. Soc., *75:* 605–650.

Wheeler, W. M. 1910. The effects of parasitic and other kinds of castration in insects. J. Exper. Zool., *8:* 337–438.

Wilhelmi, R. W. 1940. Serological reactions and species specificity of some helminths. Biol. Bull., *79:* 64–90.

SUGGESTED READING DEALING WITH PARASITISM IN GENERAL

Baer, J. G. 1951. Ecology of Animal Parasites. University of Illinois Press, Urbana, Ill. (This interesting monograph is based on a series of lectures given at the University of Illinois. The monograph approaches the morphology and biology of selected parasitic animals from an ecological standpoint.)

Ball, G. H. 1943. Parasitism and evolution. Amer. Nat., *77:* 345–364. (In a presidential address, Ball considered parasitism, primarily among Protozoa, from an evolutionary standpoint.)

Cameron, T. W. M. 1956. Parasites and Parasitism. John Wiley, New York. (This is a small textbook in which the author considers and speculates on some of the major principles of parasitism. The book is arranged in phylogenetic order, with examples.)

Caullery, M. 1952. Parasitism and Symbiosis. Sidgwick and Jackson, London. (This monograph, translated from French, is an excellent discourse on the various types of symbiotic relationships with consideration of morphology and biology. The classic examples cited make reading it a necessity for serious students.)

Chandler, A. C., and C. P. Read. 1961. Introduction to Parasitology. 10th Edition, John Wiley, New York. (Parasites of humans are dealt with primarily in this introductory textbook, although much basic taxonomy, morphology, and biology are included.)

Lapage, G. 1957. Animals Parasitic in Man. Penguin Books, Baltimore. (This short monograph emphasizes the medical importance of parasitology and the diagnosis of human parasites.)

Lapage, G. 1958. Parasitic Animals. 2nd Ed., W. Heffer, Cambridge, England. (This is a short volume written for the scientifically inclined layman, with emphasis on parasites of medical and veterinary importance and dramatic examples of the harm they cause.)

Noble, E. R., and G. A. Noble. 1961. Parasitology: The Biology of Animal Parasites. Lea & Febiger, Philadelphia. (The approach to parasitology in this introductory textbook is essentially biological. The authors consider the various groups of parasitic animals phylogenetically.)

Rogers, W. P. 1962. The Nature of Parasitism. Academic Press, New York. (One of a series on theoretical biology, this excellent monograph is primarily concerned with the physiology and biochemistry of metazoan endoparasites and parasitism. The nematodes are emphasized. The references provided are most useful. This should be required reading for serious students and workers in the field.)

Stunkard, H. W. 1929. Parasitism as a biological phenomenon. Sci. Month., *28:* 349–362. (A recognized authority on zoological parasitology has written this fine article on the study of parasites from the viewpoint of a zoologist.)

von Brand, T. 1952. Chemical Physiology of Endoparasitic Animals. Academic Press, New York. (This is a classic, invaluable because of the principles and concepts established, although some details of the material are outdated. It should be read by all serious students.)

Ward, H. B. 1909. The influence of hibernation and migration on animal parasites. Proc. 7th Internat. Zool. Congr. (This comparatively old paper is still of considerable interest, for it points out the importance of the host's behavior patterns on parasites.)

HISTORY OF
PARASITOLOGY

The history of parasitology, like that of any field of human endeavor, represents an area of study with which every prospective student of the field should become familiar. Individual research soon teaches the student that besides accumulating experimental data he must become familiar with the related knowledge that has already been attained. The familiarization process, which is commonly referred to as "literature searching," is actually a study of history. This type of historical study is of the most detailed type, involving hours of concentrated mental digestion of minute details. In this brief chapter the author is not attempting to give a detailed account of the advent of modern parasitology. Rather, he is presenting an abbreviated account of the advancement of man's knowledge of animal parasites since ancient times. Professor R. Hoeppli (1959) has published a scholarly volume on the history of parasitology in its earlier days. References to almost all the existing literature concerned with the history of the field, both eastern and western, can be found in this treatise.

Accounts by various investigators have revealed that the existence of parasitic animals, especially those that infect humans, was known as long ago as 1250 to 1000 B.C. Ruffer (1910, 1921), while examining the remains of XXth

Dynasty Egyptian mummies, found eggs of the blood fluke *Schistosoma haematobium* in the kidneys. This finding confirmed the suspicion that schistosomiasis was then in existence. Furthermore, Sigerist (1951) reported that hematuria, a symptom of *haematobium*-schistosomiasis, is recorded fifty times in medical papyri of that era. In addition to blood flukes, the *Papyrus Ebers* refers to other worms, probably the tapeworm *Taeniarhynchus saginatus,* the roundworm *Ascaris lumbricoides,* and the guinea worm, *Dracunculus medinensis.* Ectoparasites—specifically fleas, flies, and mosquitoes—were also known, since this same Egyptian scroll lists prescriptions for expelling such insects.

Mosaic Law (Leviticus 11:4–7; Deuteronomy 14:7, 8) forbids eating the meat of the camel, shaphan (probably rabbit, according to Hoeppli), hare, and swine. These ancient public health laws are often cited as indicating knowledge of the presence of tapeworm larvae (cysticerci, p. 311) and the trichina worm (p. 407). Again, the fiery serpents mentioned in Numbers 21:6 are often thought to be guinea worms (p. 445), which are endemic to the area. The ectoparasitic flea is mentioned in I Samuel 24:14.

Parasites are believed to have been known even before the era of biblical Palestine and

29

the peak of Egyptian civilization. Hoeppli (1954), after studying the primitive tribes on the islands of southeastern Asia, concluded that "knowledge of parasites and the medical views held by the primitive races of today in all probability more or less represent the knowledge of their remote ancestors and of the ancestors of those races which subsequently became highly civilized." He found that these primitive peoples knew of large and small roundworms, probably *Ascaris lumbricoides,* and the pinworm *Enterobius vermicularis.*

Many writers have indicated that parasites of humans were known by the ancient Greeks and Romans. Pliny the Elder (A.D. 23–79), who completed his 37 volume *Natural History* in A.D. 77, mentioned two types of worms in man—roundworms and flatworms. Aristotle (384–322 B.C.), who wrote the *Historia Animalium,* had stated earlier: ". . . there are three kinds of helminths: those which one calls large and flat (tapeworms), those which are cylindrical [*Ascaris lumbricoides*], and thin ones, the ascarides [*Enterobius vermicularis*]." Galen (A.D. 130–200), a Greek physician who later lived in Rome, often called the last of the great biologists of antiquity, also recognized three types of worms in humans.

Although these ancient naturalists were concerned primarily with parasites of humans, some evidence suggests that they were also aware of the more conspicuous parasites of other animals. Pagenstecher (1879–1893) stated that Galen implied in his writings that the Greek physician Hippocrates (460?–357 B.C.), the Father of Medicine, knew about pinworms of horses (*Oxyuris equi*) and that Aristotle knew about helminths infecting dogs. Infected dogs were said to show an affinity for eating standing corn. Galen himself knew about "worms of fishes"—interpreted to be encysted nematodes —and roundworms from horses. Columella (middle of first century A.D.), Vegetius (second half of fourth century A.D.), and Demetrius Pegagomenus (eighteenth century) respectively wrote about helminths from calves, roundworms from horses, and worms living under the nictitating membranes of falcons.

In Asia, *Ascaris lumbricoides, Enterobius vermicularis,* tapeworms, leeches, myiasis-causing maggots, bedbugs, and probably mosquitoes were known to ancient Indians.

The voluminous writings of ancient (B.C.) Chinese physicians and natural historians indicate that *Ascaris, Enterobius,* and *Taenia* were known. The presence of *A. lumbricoides* was recorded in *Nei Ching,* written either at the end of the Chou or at the beginning of the Chin Dynasty, about 300–200 B.C. Animal parasites, described as "eye-clouding worm from the horse" and "bow-thread worm from the eye of camel"—both probably *Thelazia* spp. (p. 440)— were known. In addition to these endoparasites, leeches were known, and their properties were described in the fifth century B.C. Common ectoparasitic arthropods, such as lice, fleas, bedbugs, and itch mites, were also known.

In the Americas, parasites are known to have existed during pre-Columbian times. Lastres (1951) stated that hookworms were present in pre-Columbian Peru. *Ascaris lumbricoides* and other common human intestinal helminths, in addition to the arthropods *Scarcopsylla penetrans* and *Pediculus humanus* (body louse), were present in pre-Columbian Mexico (Ocaranza, 1934). In addition, malaria and *Leishmania brasiliensis* were present in South America and Mexico. The scars of American leishmaniasis were said to have made quite an impression on the early Spanish conquerors.

Although the Europeans led in the development and advancement of the modern biological sciences, little progress was made in parasitology between 1200 and 1650. Most investigators during that era merely redescribed and reported what had been known, including some errors. Periodically a new parasite was discovered: for example, Dunus' finding in 1592 of the tapeworm now known as *Dibothriocephalus latus;* de Brie's finding in 1379 of *Fasciola hepatica,* the first known trematode, in sheep in France; Severinus' description of the giant acanthocephalan now known as *Macracanthorhynchus hirudinaceus,* in 1645, in a pig; and Hauptmann's illustration in 1657 of *Sarcoptes scabei,* the itch mite, which was already known to the ancient Greeks, Romans, and Chinese.

During the first part of the seventeenth century, natural historians and physicians still thought that the few known parasites were formed from the excretions and bodies of man and other animals (spontaneous generation). For example, Moufet (1634) wrote: "Some putrefied, superfluous and fecal matter in us is evidently collected, the hand of benevolent nature turns it into worms and in this way purifies the body." It was not until the second half of the seventeenth century—when Francesco Redi (1626–1697) demonstrated that maggots developed from the eggs of flies, and Louis Pasteur, in 1865, convinced the scientific world that spontaneous generation did not

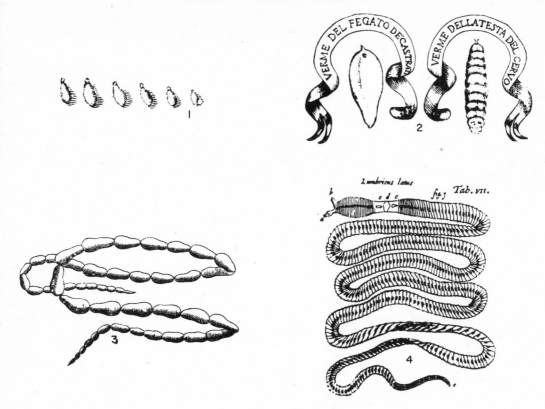

Plate 2-1   Early illustrations of animal parasites. 1. *Cysticercus pisiformis* (larva of *Taenia pisiformis*). (By Francesco Redi in *Osservazioni Intorno Agli Animali Viventi, Che Si Trovano Negli Animali Viventi,* Firenze, 1684.) **2.** *Fasciola hepatica* and an *Oestrus* larva. (By F. Redi in *Esperienze Intorno Alla Generazione Degl' Insetti,* Firenze, 1688.) **3.** First illustration of a tapeworm. (By C. Gemma in *De Naturae Divinis Characterismis Seu Raris Et Admirandis Spectaculis, Causis, Indiciis, Proprietatibus Rerum In Partibus Singulis Universi,* Antverpiae, 1575.) **4.** Early illustration of *Bothriocephalus latus* showing two small imaginary heads. (From *Nicolai Tulpii Amstelreda Mensis Observationes Medicae,* 1652.)

exist—that men sought elsewhere for the origin of parasites. Francesco Redi is considered the founder of parasitology because he was the first to actually search for parasites, and to find them, not only in the intestine and other organs of humans and other mammals, but also in the air sacs of birds and in the swim bladders of fishes.

With the perfection of Leeuwenhoek's first microscopes in the latter half of the 1600's, parasitology entered a new era, even though such prominent early helminthologists as Rudolphi and Bremser carried the idea that worms came from body excretions into the nineteenth century.

Although great advancements were made in various allied fields of biology during the Renaissance and the 1600's, the study of parasites was still clouded by misconceptions and myths. This slow growth is especially amazing

when one considers some of the great advancements in allied fields. Leonardo da Vinci (1452–1519, Italian) and Andreas Vesalius (1514–1564, Flemish) had established mammalian anatomy and physiology; William Harvey (1578–1657, English) had introduced the experimental method and explained blood circulation in addition to contributing to the field of embryology; Marcello Malpighi (1628–1694, Italian) had introduced plant and animal microscopic anatomy; and Swammerdam (1637–1680, Dutch) had explored the morphology of invertebrates, especially insects. Swammerdam also contributed to our understanding of the anatomy of the body louse. John Ray (1627–1705, English) had begun the classifying of plants; and Robert Hooke, in 1665, had seen cells in cork.

Many parasitologists of the era, if they could be so designated, believed that parasitic animals

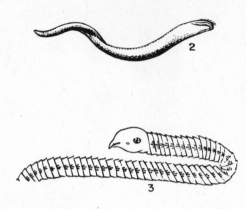

Plate 2-2   Early illustrations of animal parasites. 1. *Pediculus humanus*. (By Moufet in *Insectorum Sive Minimorum Animalium Theatrum*, London, 1634.) 2. *Enterobius* sp. (By Contoli, who reported the pinworm as a minute fish in *Historia Naturalis Et Medica Latorum Lumoricorum*, etc., Geneva, 1715.) 3. *Dibothriocephalus* scolex. (In *Nicolai Tulpii Amstelredamensis Mensis Observationes Medicae*, Amsterdam, 1652.)

were beneficial. The quotation given above from the writings of Moufet indicates this. Linnaeus believed that children were protected by lice from various diseases (Zinsser, 1935). Even toward the end of the eighteenth century and during the first half of the nineteenth, many prominent men advocated the usefulness of human parasites. Goeze (1782) and Joerdens (1801) believed that endoparasitic helminths were beneficial because they consumed the host's excess foods and intestinal mucus, which otherwise would putrefy and bring on diseases. These men also believed that intestinal worms stimulated peristalsis and hence were desirable.

Knowledge of the pathologic effects of various parasites was also highly speculative during the seventeenth and eighteenth centuries, not to mention earlier centuries. Linnaeus (1769) thought that leprosy was caused by nematodes that were normally parasitic in fish. Jenner (1749–1823), who won eternal fame for his work on smallpox vaccination, believed that the hydatid cysts of certain tapeworms (particularly *Echinococcus granulosus*) could be transformed into tuberculous tissue. Boerhaave (1728) believed that rabies resulted from a kidney infection caused by the "poisonous snake" that we know today as the nematode *Dioctophyma renale*. Numerous interesting misconceptions of this nature are described in Hoeppli's book.

Parasitic animals, by virtue of their mysterious nature, played an important role in early medicine. Many species were thought to possess therapeutic and cosmetic values. This idea was held by both Oriental and Occidental civilizations. For example, dried *Ascaris* was universally believed to be an effective anthelmintic. In Chinese medicine, various eye diseases, malig-

nant pustula, and other disorders were treated with dried ascarid powder. The medicinal leech was commonly used, and is still being used, in both eastern and western medicine as a means of bloodletting to cure fevers, high blood pressure, headaches, internal hemorrhages, and diseases of the eye, ear, and other organs. Living body lice were used in Europe as a cure for conjunctivitis, malaria, and toothache, while in China they were used to treat headaches, fevers, and even to remove corns from toes. Fly maggots were used in Europe as a remedy for sterility and epilepsy, and in Asia for dysentery, vomiting, and conjunctivitis. It is well known that even in the twentieth century maggots have been used in modern medicine to ingest decayed tissues of wounds.

The use of dried helminths in medicine has all but disappeared today except in some remote areas such as certain interior provinces of China. It is of interest to note, however, that the administration of powdered *Dibothriocephalus latus* along with gastric juices is known to be just as effective in treating pernicious anemia as the administration of vitamin B_{12}, because the tissues of this tapeworm contain a high concentration of this vitamin (p. 347).

Progress in parasitology was slow up to 1800. The greatest contributions were made by Rudolphi in the late 1700's and early 1800's and by Zeder in the 1800's. By this time Carolus Linnaeus (1707–1778, Swedish) had published his *Systema Naturae*, which had passed through 12 editions, the last in 1768. Rudolphi, in an attempt to classify worms, recognized five classes: Nematoidea, Acanthocephala, Nematoda, Cestoda, and Cystica. The last class was abandoned half a century later when cysticerci were shown to be tapeworm larvae by Leuckart, von Siebold, Küchenmeister, and others. In 1773, O. F. Müller discovered cercariae, one of the larval forms of digenetic trematodes. The occurrence of a life cycle in trematodes was finally postulated in 1842, but it was not until Thomas' (1883) detailed and complete study of the development of *Fasciola hepatica* that modern trematode life history studies began. Sharing the honors with Thomas was Leuckart, who concurrently and independently established the life cycle pattern of *F. hepatica*.

CHRONOLOGY OF THE DEVELOPMENT OF PARASITOLOGY

The most outstanding contributions in parasitology from 1550 to 1800 are listed below in chronological order. Protozoological, helminthological, and entomological discoveries are intermingled here because discoveries in one subfield often lead to discoveries in another, especially in protozoological and entomological investigations.

1570   Jean de Clamorgan rediscovered *Dioctophyma renale,** which Caessalpinus (1519–1603) mistook for a snake.

1577   Mercurialis postulated that flies carried the plague organism (virus) from the ill or dead to the food of the well.

1587   G. S. de Souza stated that flies suck poisons from sores and infect healthy persons by leaving such poisons in skin abrasions. (This represents the first recorded observation that *Spirochaeta pertenuis,* the yaws-causing organism, can be transmitted by flies.)

1665   Ruysch observed the nematode *Strongylus equinus* in the arteries of a horse.

1666   F. Baldner of Strassburg, France, first mentioned parasitic crustaceans, the argulids.

1674   Leeuwenhoek described the oocysts of *Eimeria,* which were later named by Dobell (1922).

1675   Wepfer stated that gid of sheep and cattle was caused by a bladder (bladder worm or cysticerci of *Multiceps multiceps*) in their brains.

1681   (Published in 1682) Leeuwenhoek described *Giardia intestinalis* seen in his own feces.

1683   Tyson performed the first scientific and anatomical study of *Ascaris lumbricoides.* This work was later verified by Redi (1684) and Vallisnieri (1733).

1684   Redi reported the examination of numerous domestic and wild animals for helminth parasites and recorded

*The scientific nomenclature of these parasites has been added, since it is obvious they were not correctly known at the time of these reports.

many new ones. (This report represents one of the first, if not the first, parasitological surveys conducted.)

Redi described *Cysticercus fasciolaris* (*Taenia taeniaeformis*) from a hare, and stated that this bladder worm is distinct from the liver flukes of hares.

1688   Hartmann indicated that *Cysticercus tenuicollis* of goats is a living parasite since it moves when placed in warm water. He further postulated that all *Cysticercus* spp. were larvae of *Diphyllobothrium* in fishes, thus establishing the principle that tapeworms possess larval forms.

1691   Tyson studied the anatomy of *Cysticercus tenuicollis* taken from the omentum of an antelope.

1694   Hartmann observed the first *Echinococcus* known, taken from a dog.

1699–1700   Hartsoeker, Baglivi, and Andry postulated that infections with helminths were due to their eggs, which in some way reached the host, thus establishing the principle that helminthic infections may be acquired through ingestion of microscopic eggs.

1700   Andry, in Paris, published the first treatise on human-infecting helminths.

1717   G. M. Lancisi postulated that malaria was caused by "animalic elements" transmitted by mosquitoes and that the periodicity of the fever was correlated with the copulation and multiplication of these "elements" in the human body. This report established the principle that malaria is caused by an invading parasite and correlated the clinical symptoms of chills and fever with the biology of the parasite.

1734–1743   Réaumur published an account of his observations of parasitism among certain insects, thus establishing the concept that animal parasites include insects as well as protozoa, helminths, and crustaceans.

1737–1738   Swammerdam found *Ascaris nigrovenosa* in the frog and noted that it was viviparous.

Swammerdam found rediae of trematodes in a snail but did not grasp their significance.

1752–1778   De Geer published accounts of parasitism among certain insects.

1762   Roederer and Wagler described *Trichuris trichiura,* the human whipworm, which had been known since the thirteenth century.

1770   Mongin described the first known case of *Loa loa* infection, thus establishing the concept of filarial diseases.

1782   Goez initiated the taxonomy of helminths.†

1793   Abilgaard infected ducks and other birds with *Diphyllobothrium* sp. by feeding them the larval stage from a fish.

†Goez's (1782) attempt to classify helminths was undoubtedly prompted by the increasing number of forms known at that time. To give some idea of the rapidity with which new species were being described, Linnaeus, in the 12th edition of *Systema Naturae* (1767) listed 11 helminths; Gmelin (1790) in the 13th edition listed 199; Rudolphi, in his classic *Enterozoorum Sive Vermium Intestinalium Historia Naturalis,* 2 vols. (1808–1810) and in his *Synopsis* (1819), listed 1100 forms from 756 different hosts.

Although perhaps unknown at the time, the discoveries prior to and during the eighteenth century initiated certain parasitological concepts and principles. Mercurialis' postulation in 1577 that flies can carry the plague organism initiated the principle that arthropods can serve as mechanical carriers and even as vectors of microorganisms. Ruysch's discovery in 1665 of *S. equinus* in the arteries of horses established the concept that blood parasites do exist. Redi's discovery of parasites in animals other than man further revealed that parasitism is widespread. Finally, Abilgaard's experimental infection of birds initiated the beginning of life cycle studies.

The nineteenth century might be thought of as the genesis of modern parasitology. As the student advances in this field, the names of many nineteenth century parasitologists will undoubtedly become familiar because of their repeated appearances in the literature. Men such as Zeder, Rudolphi, Frölich, Bütschli, Doflein, Dujardin, von Siebold, Schaudinn, Ross, and Looss ushered in the modern era.

Not only was the nineteenth century a progressive one in parasitology, it was also one of tremendous impact on all of biology. The concepts of organic evolution, the cell theory, metagenesis, homeostasis, and heredity; the death of the spontaneous generation myth; development of the microscope; and refinement of the experimental method have all greatly influenced the development of parasitology.

It would be an encyclopedic task to list all publications of the 1800's that referred to parasitic animals. However, many outstanding discoveries deserve mention, and these are listed below in chronologic order.

1801   **First general theory of organic evolution was put forth by Lamarck in *Philosophia Zoologique*.** Lamarck gave the first clear-cut expression of a theory to account for organic evolution. In this treatise he assumed that acquired characteristics could be inherited, a theory which has since been refuted. Nevertheless, the concept of organic evolution was made public, and its implications relative to parasitic animals was most useful to later workers.

1835   Owen described *Trichinella spiralis* in human muscle.

Von Siebold observed that *Taenia* eggs contained embryos with small hooks (hexacanth larvae).

1836   Von Siebold discovered that *Taenia* possesses spermatozoa.

1837   Creplin determined experimentally that ciliated larvae escape from the operculated eggs of *Diphyllobothrium* sp. when these are placed in water. He noted that the eggs of *Taenia* do not hatch, thus establishing the

principle that helminth eggs may be physiologically different.

Donné described *Trichomonas vaginalis,* the only human-infecting flagellate that does not live in the intestinal tract.

1838–1839   **Schleiden and Schwann formulated the cell theory.** The cell doctrine, with its basic concept that all metazoa and metaphyta are made up of similar units, represents one of the truly great landmarks in biological progress. The theory opened up a new understanding of the life process, for it gave biologists a starting point for studying the structure and function of organisms.

1839   Hake rediscovered and described *Eimeria stiedae.*

1841   Valentin discovered the first known trypanosome, found in the fish *Salmo fario,* thus establishing the existence of haemoflagellates.

1843   Gruby described trypanosomes from frogs.

Steenstrup formulated the concept of alternation of generations, which had great bearing on helmintho-logical research, especially that of trematodes.

Dubini described the hookworm *Ancylostoma duodenale* from man. This worm was first known in 1838.

1845   Dujardin showed the relationship between cysticerci and *Taenia* adults.

1846   Leidy described *Trichinella spiralis* in hog muscle.

1848   Josiah Nott of New Orleans postulated that mosquitoes give rise to both malaria and yellow fever, thus advancing the vector concept.

1849   Gros discovered the first parasitic amoeba of man, *Entamoeba gingivalis.*

1850's   **The concept of spontaneous generation of animals had been discarded by most scientists.** This move was greatly stimulated by Eschericht's publication of 1841.

1850   Van Beneden added many new cestodes from his study of the parasites of marine fishes.

1851   Bilharz discovered *Schistosoma haematobium, Hymenolepis nana,* and *Hetrophyes heterophyes,* which were later described by von Siebold and Bilharz.

Küchenmeister differentiated between *Taenia solium* and *Taeniarhynchus saginatus,* thus advancing the concept of speciation and the science of taxonomy.

1851–1852   Küchenmeister was successful in obtaining cysticerci by feeding suitable intermediate hosts with *Taenia* eggs, and recovering adult worms when the cysticerci were fed to definitive hosts. (*Taenia solium* was recovered from man fed *Cysticercus cellulosae* from infected pork in 1855.) Thus the life cycle pattern of a cyclophyllidean cestode was established.

1853   Von Siebold recovered adult *Echinococcus granulosus* from dogs that had been fed hydatid cysts.

1854   Beauperthy formulated the scientific theory that mosquitoes carried yellow fever.

1857   Malmsten described the first parasitic ciliate of man, *Balantidium coli.*

1857–1859   Leuckart and Virchow independently discovered the life history of *Trichinella spiralis.* (Read the exciting account by Reinhard, 1958.)

1859   W. D. Lambl described *Giardia intestinalis* from man.

Charles Darwin put forth the theory of organic evolution based on natural selection in *The Origin of the Species*. (Although Darwin did not originate the concept of organic evolution, his interpretation, based on natural selection, represents the greatest single landmark in biological history.)

1860   **Claude Bernard proposed the concept of homeostasis.** (This important concept of the consistency of the internal environment has greatly influenced physiological thinking. Its implication in parasitology relative to adaptation to endoparasitism and the sensitivity of endoparasites to environmental changes is most evident.)

1865–1866   **Gregor Mendel formulated the basic laws of genetics.** (Formulation of the laws of heredity established a basis for organic evolution. In parasitology, parasite speciation, host specificity, and strain differences can all be adequately explained in terms of genetic differences.)

1869   Raimbert demonstrated that the anthrax organism *Bacillus anthracis* can be disseminated by flies. (Montfils postulated this in 1776).

Melnikoff showed that the dog louse *Trichodectes canis* is the intermediate host for the tapeworm *Dipylidium caninum*.

Krabbe, a Danish physician, discovered that each order of birds possesses its particular tapeworms, thus suggesting host specificity.

1870   T. R. Lewis discovered human intestinal amoebae in Calcutta, India.

1875   Lösch discovered *Entamoeba histolytica* in St. Petersburg, Russia.

1878   Patrick Manson observed the development of *Wuchereria bancrofti* in the body of the mosquito *Culex quinquefasciatus*. (He pointed out the importance of understanding the development of parasites, not only in their definitive hosts, but in their intermediate hosts as well. Our understanding of the physiology of parasites in their intermediate hosts does contribute to our understanding of their behavior in their definitive hosts and vice versa.)

1880   Laveran discovered the malaria organism *Plasmodium malariae* (or possibly *P. falciparum*) in red blood cells of man, and first saw *P. vivax*, which Grassi and Felletti (1890) named *Haemamoeba vivax*.

1883   Thomas and Leuckart independently worked out the first complete trematode life history, that of *Fasciola hepatica* (see Reinhard, 1957). These studies served as progenitors of all modern life cycle studies.

T. Smith and Kilbourne discovered the causative agent of Texas cattle fever, *Babesia bigemina,* in the red blood cell of the host (actually found by Smith in 1889).

Leuckart discovered the heterogonic cycle of *Strongyloides stercoralis*.

1884   Wes Delage described the life cycle of *Sacculina*, a rhizocephalan parasite, and established its affinity for the Cirripeda.

1886   Alfred Giard introduced the concept of parasitic

castration and its implications in the area of parasite-caused biological effects.

1892   Johannes Müller of Berlin discovered and named *Entoconcha,* the first known parasitic snail, thus establishing that parasitism does occur among molluscs.

1893   T. Smith and Kilbourne discovered that the cattle tick *Boöphilus annulatus* is the vector of *Babesia bigemina*. (This discovery had tremendous implication for medical entomology for the concept of arthropod vectors of microorganisms had positively been proven.)

1895   Bruce discovered that the tsetse fly *Glossina morsitans* served as the vector of *Trypanosoma brucei,* the causative agent of nagana in Africa.

1897   Ronald Ross found the zygotes of the malaria parasite in anopheline mosquitoes (verified and elaborated on by Manson, 1898; MacCullum, 1898; Bastianelli, Bignami, and Grassi, 1898; and Sambon and Low, 1900).

1898   Simond succeeded in transmitting plague from rat to rat via a flea vector (verified by Verjbitski, 1908, and Liston, 1905).

This chronological presentation points out the development of several parasitological concepts. Owen's finding of *Trichinella spiralis* in human muscle emphasized that parasites are found in areas of the host's body other than the alimentary tract and the circulatory system. The finding of trypanosomes by Valentin in trout blood initiated the search for haemoflagellates, which remain not only an important group of parasites but also a favored group of experimental animals. Dujardin's keen observation in 1845 that cysticerci are the larvae of *Taenia* further advanced the popular field of life cycle studies. Nott's postulation in 1848 that mosquitoes play a role in the transmission of malaria and yellow fever advanced the vector concept. His report represents one of the first major American contributions to parasitology.

Krabbe's studies on avian cestodes in 1869 helped develop the concept of host specificity, which remains an important one in parasitology.

In the area of medical parasitology, Laveran's discovery of the human malaria organism in 1880 is a landmark. This was followed by extensive studies on malaria and 17 years later Ross, who won the Nobel prize for his studies, finally demonstrated that this dreaded protozoan parasite is carried by mosquitoes.

The year 1883 can be considered another landmark, since the solving of the first trematode life history, that of *Fasciola hepatica,* was accomplished. Life history studies among platyhelminths still remain a popular and valuable

Johannes J. Steenstrup
1813–1897

Rudolf Leuckart
1822–1898

Sir Algernon Phillips Withiel Thomas
1857–1937

Rudolf Virchow
1821–1902

Joseph Leidy
1823–1891

Louis Pasteur
1822–1895

Plate 2-3   Outstanding parasitologists of the Nineteenth Century. (All photographs except that of Pasteur from *Experimental Parasitology*, Academic Press, Inc., New York.)

form of parasitological research. Knowledge of life histories is not only of practical importance (see p. 251), but also provides insights into the phylogenetic relationships between these metazoan parasites.

By the beginning of the twentieth century, parasitology was well established as a science. In the United States, Joseph Leidy pioneered in helminthology along with E. Linton and George H. F. Nuttall, who studied in Germany

Henry Baldwin Ward
1865–1945
The University of Illinois

Charles Wardell Stiles
1867–1941
The National Institutes of Health
U. S. Public Health Service

Edwin Linton
1855–1939
Washington and Jefferson College

Harold Kirby
1900–1952
The University of California,
Berkeley

Asa C. Chandler
1891–1958
The Rice University

Charles Atwood Kofoid
1865–1947
The University of California,
Berkeley

Plate 2-4   American pioneers in parasitology. (Courtesy of the *Journal of Parasitology.*)

and later resided in England. Charles F. Craig, an army medical officer, pioneered in tropical medicine and became an authority on the parasitic protozoa of humans. G. N. Calkins was outstanding for his contributions to our understanding of the basic biology of parasitic protozoa. Henry Baldwin Ward, a young Harvard graduate who had gained his zeal for parasitology under the tutelage of Rudolph Leuckart at Leipzig, taught at the Universities of Michigan and Nebraska. Ward established a strong program in parasitology at the University of Illinois, to which site many of our present-day parasitologists can trace their academic origin. Along with the University of Illinois, Harvard University, Johns Hopkins University, and the University of California were among the first to develop strong programs in parasitology. Today most teachers and directors of programs in parasitology can trace their academic genealogy back to one of these four institutions.

The 1900's witnessed outstanding contributions in parasitology from all over the world. Norman Stoll's report of "self-cure" in sheep infected with the nematode *Haemonchus contortus* (p. 435) in 1928 marked the beginning of immunologic studies on helminth parasites. The work of William Taliaferro on the immunology of protozoan parasite infections caused a new surge of interest in this important aspect of parasitology. His monograph of 1929, *Immunology of Parasitic Infections,* deserves the attention of all serious students of parasitology.

The following is a list of some of the pioneering contributions made during the early decades of the 20th century.

1900   Reed (Carrol, Lazear, and Agramonte), while in Cuba, demonstrated that the mosquito *Aëdes aegypti* is the vector for yellow fever. Carlos Finlay also deserves credit for this finding.

1901   Forde discovered *Trypanosoma gambiense* (named by Dutton in 1902), the causative agent of Gambian sleeping sickness.

1902   Graham described dengue fever in Syria and found that *Aëdes aegypti* is the vector.

1903   Marchoux and Salimbeni proved that *Spirochaeta gallinarum,* the fowl spirochaetosis organism, is carried by the fowl tick *Argas persicus.*

Bruce and Nabarro demonstrated that *Glossina palpalis* is the vector for *Trypanosoma gambiense.*

1904   Ross and Milne demonstrated that the tick *Ornithodoros moubata* carries *Borrelia recurrentis,* the African relapsing fever organism.

Looss accidentally infected himself with the larvae of *Ancylostoma duodenale* while in Cairo, thus establishing the mode of infection of hookworms.

1906   Ricketts showed that the tick *Dermacenter andersoni* is the vector for *Dermacentroxenus rickettsi,* the causative agent for Rocky Mountain spotted fever.

1907   Castellani demonstrated that flies transmit the yaws organism, *Treponema pertenue.*

1909   Chagas proved that the cone-nosed bug *Triatoma megista* is the vector for *Trypanosoma cruzi,* the Chagas' disease organism.

1909–1910   Nicolle, Comte, and Conseil in Tunis, and Ricketts and Wilder in Mexico proved that the louse

Pediculus humanus is the vector for *Rickettsia prowazeki,* the typhus organism.

1910   Fantham described *Trypanosoma rhodesiense,* the causative agent of Rhodesian sleeping sickness, and Kinghorn and Yorke (1912) proved that *Glossina morsitans* is the vector.

1911   Kleine and Taute in Germany completed the life cycle of *Trypanosoma gambiense.*

1913   Miyairi and Suzuki in Japan worked out the life cycle of a schistosome.

1918   Rosen and von Janicki at Neuchâtel discovered that the life cycle of *Dibothriocephalus latus* requires two intermediate hosts.

1923–1925   Cleveland commenced his work on mutualistic relationships between termites and woodroaches and their intestinal flagellates, which has led to outstanding work on the physiology of mutualism and protozoan cytology.

1924   (1932)   Taliaferro demonstrated the presence of ablastin and the trypanocidal antibodies in *Trypanosoma lewisi* infections in rats, and created great interest in parasite immunology.

1926   Blacklock reported that the dipteran *Simulium damnosum* is the vector for the filarial nematode *Onchocerca volvulus.*

1927   Stokes, Bauer, and Hudson provided experimental animals for yellow fever investigations when they showed that monkeys can be infected.

1928   Stoll reported "self-cure" in sheep infected with the nematode *Haemonchus contortus.* This finding initiated subsequent studies on immunity to metazoan parasites.

1932   Hackett, Martini, and Missiroli discovered race differences among vectors of malaria, thus opening a new subfield concerned with the genetics of parasites.

1933   Kalser demonstrated that the virus for equine encephalomyelitis is transmitted by the mosquito *Aëdes aegypti.*

1934   O'Roke demonstrated that the dipteran *Simulium venustum* transmits the duck protozoan *Leucocytozoön anatis.*

The finding in 1900 that *Aëdes aegypti* is the major vector for yellow fever must be considered a landmark in parasitology as well as in medicine. For the first time a scientific approach could be taken to eradicate this disease, which had plagued mankind for centuries. Completion of the Panama Canal, with all its economic implications, was made possible because of this discovery.

Marchoux and Salimbeni's discovery in 1903 that a tick can serve as a vector for pathogenic microorganisms can be regarded as the basis for the discipline of acarology, at least the economic aspects of the field.

The beginning of Cleveland's work on mutualism during 1923 and 1925 is significant, since it revealed the intriguing phenomenon of host-parasite relationships and introduced others to studies on the basic mechanisms of symbiosis.

Although still a relatively unexplored field, the importance of genetics of parasitic organisms, as introduced by Hackett and his colleagues in 1932, was vividly demonstrated. This area of research holds much promise for future investigators.

The two world wars, especially World War II, brought about an accelerated interest in parasitology, especially the medical aspects. Scrub typhus (tsutsugamushi fever) in the South Pacific, amoebiasis in the Far East and elsewhere, malaria in various parts of the world, opisthorchiasis in China, and many other parasite-caused diseases became of immediate importance. American servicemen became afflicted with diseases that were at one time thought to be exotic and merely medical curiosities. This critical situation called for acceleration of training in medical parasitology.

While medical parasitology was being emphasized, basic research in the field continued at a steady pace, and veterinary parasitology was rapidly climbing to a position of importance. Since World War II, with the improvement of laboratory instruments and techniques, another phase of parasitology is gaining impetus— parasite physiology and biochemistry. Although such investigations date back to the last century, most of the more significant discoveries have been made during the last three decades. Increasingly more researchers are discovering that, physiologically speaking, parasites are quite similar to their free-living relatives. On the molecular level, these differences become practically nil. Hence it appears justified to state that on a broader plane the history of biology has been, in part, the history of parasitology.

The archaic practice of isolating the various fields of biology is rapidly being eliminated. As a result of the need to understand the anatomy, morphology, and physiology of hosts; the environmental conditions in which the hosts live; the migration patterns of definitive and intermediate hosts; the pathology and symptomology of parasitic infections; immunity to parasites, enzymatic actions in host and parasite, and numerous other related aspects, parasitology became one of the first disciplines to cross traditional lines. To quote from the late Professor Asa C. Chandler's (1946) address: "Parasitology touches upon or overlaps so many other sciences that a parasitologist probably has to stick his nose into more different fields of knowledge than any other kind of biologist."

The coming of age of parasitology as a discipline of the biological sciences is manifested by the number of liberal arts colleges now offering courses in parasitology. Parasitology is no longer considered only an applied science restricted to professional schools. Biologists from every discipline have finally realized that the study of symbiotic relationships is a fundamental and intriguing one. Indeed, modern parasitology might well be designated as symbiology—one of the first truly interdisciplinary biological sciences.

Both the applied and basic phases of parasitology are rapidly advancing. The large volume of original research being contributed from all over the world indicates the healthy state of this area of biology. Some of the more prominent publications which include original papers dealing with the biology of animal parasites are listed below. A more complete list is available in the *Index-Catalogue of Medical and Veterinary Zoology,* published by the United States Department of Agriculture.

Acta Tropica (Switzerland)

American Journal of Hygiene (U. S.)

American Journal of Tropical Medicine and Hygiene (U.S.)

American Midland Naturalist (U. S.)

Anais do Instituto de Medicina Tropical (Spain)

Anales del Instituto de Biologia (Mexico)

Annales de l'Institut Pasteur (France)

Annales de Parasitologie Humaine et Comparée (France)

Annals of Tropical Medicine and Parasitology (England)

Archives de l'Institut Pasteur d'Algerie (Algeria)

Archiv für Schiffs- und Tropenhygiene (Germany)

Biological Bulletin (U. S.)

Boletin Chieno de Parasitologica (Chile)

Bulletin de la Société de Pathologie Exotique (France)

Bulletin de l'Institut Pasteur (France)

Bulletin of Marine Science of the Gulf and Caribbean (U. S.)

The Canadian Journal of Zoology (Canada)

Comptes Rendus de la Société de Biologie (France)

Ecology (U. S.)

Ecological Monographs (U. S.)

Experimental Parasitology (U. S.)

Japanese Journal of Medical Science and Biology (Japan)

Journal of Economic Entomology (U. S.)

Journal of Experimental Biology (England)

The Journal of Helminthology (England)

Journal of Infectious Diseases (U. S.)

Journal of the Marine Biological Association of the United Kingdom

Journal of Morphology (U. S.)

The Journal of Parasitology (U. S.)

The Journal of Protozoology (U. S.)

Journal of Tropical Medicine and Hygiene (England)

Malacologia (U. S.)

Memorias do Instituto Oswaldo Cruz (Brazil)

Nature (England)

Parasitology (England)

Philippine Journal of Science (Philippines)

Proceedings of the Helminthological Society of Washington (U. S.)

Proceedings of the Society for Experimental Biology and Medicine (U. S.)

Quarterly Journal of Microscopical Science (England)

Revista Brasileira de Malariologia e Doenças Tropocais (Argentina)

Revista de Medicina Tropical y Parasitologia, Clinica y Laboratorio (Cuba)

Revista de Medicina Veterinaria y Parasitologia (Venezuela)

Revista di Parassitologia (Italy)

Revista Iberica de Parasitologia (Spain)

Revista Kuba de Medicina Tropical y Parasitologia (Cuba)

Science (U. S.)

Transactions of the American Microscopical Society (U. S.)

Transactions of the Royal Society of Tropical Medicine and Hygiene (England)

Veterinary Medicine (U. S.)

Wildlife Disease (U. S.)

Zeitschrift für Parasitenkunde (Germany)

Zeitschrift für Tropenmedizin und Parasitologie (Germany)

Zentralblatt für Bakteriologie, Parasitenkunde und Infektionskrankheiten (Germany)

Zentralblatt für Bakteriologie und Parasitologie (Germany)

Zoologischer Anzeiger (Germany)

Several major abstracting services abstract and/or list current papers dealing with the biology of animal parasites. The most important of these are:

Biological Abstracts (U. S.)

Helminthological Abstracts (British Commonwealth)

Index-Catalogue of Medical and Veterinary Zoology (U. S.)

Tropical Diseases Bulletin (Great Britain)

Zoological Record (Great Britain)

From the foregoing, it is apparent that parasitology is a relatively young science. Although animal parasites have been known since the beginning of history, the study of parasites as a science began with Francesco Redi in 1684 but did not gain prominence and concentration until the nineteenth century. Judging from the number of Ph.D. degrees being conferred in parasitology and by the number of liberal arts colleges and universities that are now offering courses in parasitology and that have added courses in recent years, it is quite apparent that parasitology has yet to reach its zenith.

LITERATURE CITED

Bastianelli, G., A. E. Bignami, and B. Grassi. 1898. Coltivazione delle semilune malariche dell' uomo nell' *Anopheles claviger* Fabr. (sinonimo *Anopheles maculipennis* Meig.). Nota preliminare. Atti R. Accad. Lincei, Roma, *7:* 313–314.

Boerhaave, H. 1728. Aphorism. der cur. etc. Aphorism 1134, p. 270. Lugd. Batav.

Chandler, A. C. 1946. The making of a parasitologist. J. Parasit., *32:* 213–221.

Dobell, C. C. 1922. The discovery of the Coccidia. Parasitology, *14:* 342–348.

Eschericht, D. F. 1841. Anatomisch-physiologische Untersuchungen über die Bothryocephalen. Nova Acta Acad. Lep. Carol., *19:* 1–152.

Goeze, J. A. E. 1782. Versuch einer Naturgeschichte der Eingeweidewuermer thierischer Körper. Blankenburg.

Grassi, G. B., and R. Feletti. 1890. Parassiti malarici negli uccelli. Nota preliminarie. Bull. Mens. Accad. Gioenia Sc. Nat. Catania, n. s., *13:* 3–6.

Hoeppli, R. 1954. Some early views on parasites and parasitic infections shared by the people of Borneo, Malaya and China. Proc. Alumni Assoc., Malaya, *7:* 3–17.

Hoeppli, R. 1959. Parasites and Parasitic Infections in Early Medicine and Science. University of Malaya Press, Singapore.

Joerdens, J. H. 1801. Entomologie und Helminthologie des Menschlichen Körpers. Hof. Gottfried Adolph Grau.

Küchenmeister, F. 1855. Die in und an dem Körper des lebenden Menschen vorkommenden Parasiten. Erste Abtheilung, Leipzig.

Lastres, J. B. 1951. Historia de la Medicina Peruana. Vol. I, La Medicina Incaica. Lima.

Linnaeus, C. 1769. Amoenitates academicae. VII. Holmiae.

Liston, W. G. 1905. Plague rats and fleas. J. Bombay Nat. Hist. Soc., *16:* 253–273.

MacCullum, W. C. 1898. On the haematozoan infections of birds. J. Exper. Med., *3:* 117–136.

Manson, P. 1898. Surgeon-Major Ronald Ross: Recent investigations on mosquito-malaria theory. British Med. J., *1:* 1575–1577.

Moufet, T. 1634. Insectorum Sive Minimorum Animalium Theatrum. London.

Ocaranza, F. 1934. Historia de la Medicina en Mexico. Mexico.

Pagenstecher, H. 1879–1893. Abthlg. I. a. *in* Bronn's *Klassen und Ordnungen des Thier-Reichs.* Vol. 4, C. F. Winter, Leipzig.

Redi, F. 1684. Osservazioni intorno agli animali viventi, che se trovano negli animali viventi. Florence.

Reinhard, E. G. 1957. Landmarks of parasitology. I. The discovery of the life cycle of the liver fluke. Exptl. Parasit., *6:* 208–232.

Reinhard, E. G. 1958. Landmarks of parasitology. II. Demonstration of the life cycle and pathogenicity of the spiral threadworm. Exptl. Parasit., *7:* 108–123.

Ruffer, M. A. 1910. Note on the presence of "Bilharzia haematobia" in Egyptian mummies of the twentieth dynasty (1250–1000 B.C.). Brit. Med. J., *1:* 16.

Ruffer, M. A. 1921. Studies in the paleopathology of Egypt. Chicago, 18–19.

Sambon, L. W., and G. Low. 1900. The malaria experiments in the Campagna. Brit. Med. J., *2:* 1679–1682.

Sigerist, H. E. 1951. A History of Medicine. Vol. I. Primitive and Archaic Medicine. Oxford University Press, New York.

Singer, C. 1912. Notes on some early references to tropical diseases. Ann. Trop. Med. Parasitol., *6:* 87–101, 379–402.

Taliaferro, W. H. 1929. Immunology of Parasitic Infections. Century, New York.

Thomas, A. P. 1883. The life history of the liver fluke (*Fasciola hepatica*). Quart. J. Micro. Sci., n. s., *23:* 99–133.

Vallisnieri, A. 1733. Opera fisicho-mediche raccolte da Antonio suo figliuolo. Venice.

Verjbitski, D. T. 1908. The part played by insects in the epidemiology of plague. J. Hyg., *8:* 162–208.

Zinsser, H. 1935. Rats, Lice and History. Atlantic Monthly Press, Boston.

SUGGESTED READING

Chandler, A. C. 1946. The making of a parasitologist. J. Parasit., *32:* 213–221. (In this presidential address before the American Society of Parasitologists, the author points out the complexity of the discipline and the training of a parasitologist. It should be read by all prospective students of parasitology.)

Cram, E. B. 1956. Stepping stones in the history of the American Society of Parasitologists. J. Parasit., *42:* 461–473. (This is another presidential address before the ASP. The author records the contributions of several outstanding parasitologists in their struggle to establish the Society, and in so doing helping to establish parasitology in the United States. The article should be read by all American students.)

Hoeppli, R. 1956. The knowledge of parasites and parasitic infections from ancient times to the seventeenth century. Exptl. Parasit., *5:* 398–419. (This is a short version of the author's treatise on the early history of parasitology. It should be read by all students.)

Hoeppli, R. 1959. Parasites and Parasitic Infections in Early Medicine and Science. University of Malaya Press, Singapore. (This is a complete work on the early history of parasitology. The detailed information included in this volume not only is scientifically interesting but also represents a definitive scholary work, including translations of ancient writings that refer to parasites.)

Meleney, H. E. 1942. Tropical medicine in United States military history. Bull. N. Y. Acad. Med., *18:* 329–337.

Meleney, H. E. 1943. The role of the parasitologist in World War II. J. Parasit., *29:* 1–7. (For those interested in medical parasitology, these two articles by Dr. Meleney will prove to be most enjoyable. The author recalls from firsthand experience the contributions of medical parasitology to the achievements by the U. S. armed forces.)

Reinhard, E. G. 1957. Landmarks of parasitology. I. The discovery of the life cycle of the liver fluke. Exptl. Parasit., *6:* 208–232.

Reinhard, E. G. 1958. Landmarks of parasitology. II. Demonstration of the life cycle and pathogenicity of the spiral threadworm. Exptl. Parasit., *7:* 108–123. (These two historical accounts by Dr. Reinhard should be read by all biologists. The author has presented enlightening and enthusiastic accounts of the establishment of two major landmarks in parasitology. Unfortunately, because of the death of the author, this valuable series was not completed.)

Rothschild, M., and T. Clay. 1957. Fleas, Flukes and Cuckoos. 2nd Ed., Collins, London.

Zinsser, H. 1935. Rats, Lice and History. Atlantic Monthly Press, Boston. (For the beginning student and educated layman who do not wish to be confronted with technical terminology, the preceding two volumes are excellent. Both give fascinating accounts of parasitism, the latter emphasizing medical aspects and how the flea, as vector for the plague organism, played an important role in history.)

PART TWO

PROTOZOA

3

INTRODUCTION TO THE PARASITIC PROTOZOA THE MASTIGOPHORA—
The Flagellates

Protozoa are commonly referred to as unicellular organisms because their bodies consist of a single cell that possesses all the basic characteristics of the cells of metazoans. By far the majority of protozoans are free-living, found in various aquatic and moist environments. However, some protozoans are mutualists, some commensals, and some true parasites. Some of the parasitic forms, such as *Trypanosoma gambiense* and *Entamoeba histolytica,* are actually pathogenic to their vertebrate hosts, and hence are of concern to human and veterinary medicine.

The parasitic protozoa have been the center of a great deal of attention, and as the result of concerted interest, the greatest success at in vitro culture of animal parasites has been with these unicellular forms. The nutritional requirements, the growth patterns and secretion of toxic substances, and other physiological properties of parasites can be critically studied in the majority of cases only in the laboratory on forms maintained in vitro.

The sizes of protozoa vary greatly. If the individual masses of all known species are compared with the masses of other types of cells, most protozoa would fall within the lower half of the range scale. Table 3–1 gives some idea of the comparative masses of various types of cells.

GENERAL MORPHOLOGY OF PROTOZOA

Following the systematic interpretation of Jahn and Jahn (1949), the phylum Protozoa is divided into four subphyla—Mastigophora (flagellates), Sarcodina (amoebae), Sporozoa (sporozoans), and Ciliophora (ciliates and suctorians).

Cytoplasmic Zones
Structurally all protozoa are unicellular. The cytoplasm of the trophozoite (vegetative form) is surrounded by some form of cell mem-

Table 3-1.   Comparative Masses of Various Types of Cells.*

Cell or Organism	Mass in Grams
Dinosaur egg, ostrich egg, cycad ovule	10^2 to 10^3
Valonia macrophysa (mature)	10^1
Valonia ventricola (màture)	10^0
Nitella (large internode)	10^{-1}
Frog egg	10^{-2} to 10^{-3}
Striated muscle of man	10^{-4}
Human ovum	10^{-5}
Large *Paramecium*	10^{-6}
Large sensory neuron of dog	10^{-6}
Average *Vorticella*	10^{-7}
Human smooth muscle fiber	10^{-7}
Human liver cell	10^{-7}
Entamoeba histolytica	10^{-8}
Frog erythrocyte	10^{-9}
Plasmodium spp.	10^{-9}
Human sperm	10^{-9}
Small protozoa *(Monas)*	10^{-9}
Anthrax bacillus	10^{-11}
Tubercle and pus bacteria	10^{-12}
Smallest bacteria	10^{-14}

LIMIT OF MICROSCOPIC VISION

Filterable virus	10^{-15}

*Partially after Maldane and Huxley (1927): *Animal Biology.* Oxford University Press; in Giese (1962): *Cell Physiology,* W. B. Saunders.

brane or a specialized rigid or semirigid covering. The cytoplasm is commonly divided into two areas—the peripheral ectoplasm and the medullary endoplasm. The consistency and appearance of the ecto- and endoplasms differ among species, and the delineation between the two areas may also vary markedly. In certain species the separation between the two cytoplasmic zones appears hypothetical.

Nuclei

All protozoans possess nuclei. Some have one, others have two or more essentially identical nuclei, and still others have two types of nuclei—a macronucleus and a micronucleus. In members of the subphyla Mastigophora, Sarcodina, and Sporozoa, there are one or more nuclei of the same type, while in the Ciliophora there are generally two types of nuclei.

The macronucleus (when present) is typically larger and is associated with trophic activities. The micronucleus is concerned with reproductive activities.

In addition to characterizing nuclei as either macro- or micronuclei, two morphologically distinct types of nuclei have been described—the vesicular nucleus and the compact nucleus. These two types are often referred to in the diagnosis of species.

THE VESICULAR NUCLEUS.   The vesicular nucleus is one in which the nuclear membrane, although delicate, is visible (Plate 3–1, Fig. 1). Throughout the nucleolymph, the chromatin material may be lightly diffused, but one or more prominent bodies—the endosomes—are apparent. The staining affinities of endosomes strongly suggest that they are, at least in part, clumps of DNA (deoxyribonucleic acid). The vesicular nucleus is usually found in species of Sarcodina and Mastigophora.

THE COMPACT NUCLEUS.   The compact nucleus contains a seemingly larger amount of chromatin material scattered as minute granules throughout the nucleus, and the nuclear membrane is less conspicuous (Plate 3–1, Fig. 2). Nuclei of this type are generally larger and assume varying shapes, ranging from rounded to ovate. They may be club shaped, rod shaped, filamentous, or dendritic. Kudo (1936) described the compact nucleus of the common parasite of cockroaches, *Nyctotherus ovalis*, to be 20 μ or more in diameter. Compact nuclei are usually found among the Ciliophora.

Vacuoles

The cytoplasm of most protozoa contains one or more vacuoles. These appear as light, rounded bubbles floating among the cytoplasmic granules. Vacuoles are differentiated physiologically into contractile vacuoles and food vacuoles. Contractile vacuoles function as osmoregulatory organelles, and food vacuoles—conspicuous in holozoic and parasitic species—as sites of digestion of food inclusions. Other types of vacuoles are known—for example, concrement vacuoles are characteristic of ciliates belonging to the family Bütschiidae, which inhabit the alimentary canal of mammals, and to the family Paraisotrichidae, which are endoparasitic in the caecum and colon of horses (Plate 3–1, Fig. 3). These highly specialized vacuoles, which are situated singly in the anterior third of the organism's body, are composed of a pellicular cap, a permanent vacuolar wall, concrement granules, and two fibrillar systems. During division by transverse fission, the anterior daughter retains the vacuole, while a new one is formed in the posterior daughter from the pellicle into which concrement granules flow. There are no surface pores present, and the vacuoles are believed to be sensory in function.

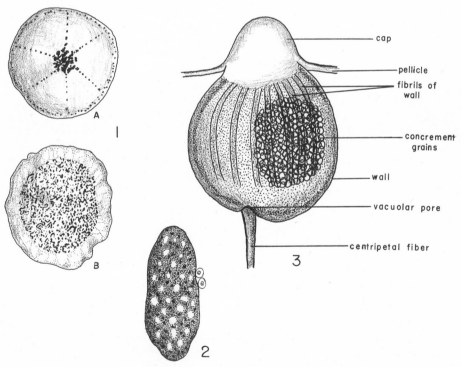

Plate 3-1   **Protozoan structures. 1. A.** Vesicular nucleus of *Entamoeba invadens*. **B.** Vesicular nucleus of *Amoeba proteus* subjected to Feulgen's reaction. (Redrawn after Kudo, R. R., 1954. *Protozoology*, Charles C Thomas, Springfield, Ill.) **2.** Compact nucleus of *Paramecium aurelia* and two vesicular micronuclei seen with phase-contrast microscope. (Redrawn after Kudo, R. R., 1954. *Protozoology*, Charles C Thomas, Springfield, Ill.) **3.** Concrement vacuole of *Blepharoprosthium* sp. (Redrawn after Dogiel.)

Cytoplasmic Inclusions

RIBOSOMES. Ribosomes (or microsomes) are believed to be the sites of protein synthesis and have regularly been recognized in the cytoplasm of metazoan cells. When examined with the electron microscope, they are found to be located on the endoplasmic reticulum and are possibly derived from it. These microorganelles generally appear as minute, RNA-rich (ribonucleic acid) bodies.

MITOCHONDRIA. Another type of cytoplasmic inclusion found in protozoan and metazoan cells is the mitochondrion.* Mitochondria are the sites of intracellular aerobic metabolism (respiration). Lindberg and Ernster (1954) arrived at this conclusion when it was discovered that the principal enzymes involved in the Krebs, or citric acid, cycle are present in mitochondria. The ultrastructure of mitochondria has been successfully defined by electron microscopy (Plate 3–2). The body is double-walled, and the inner lamella forms an undulating surface, the folds of which are known as cristae mitochondriales if they are membranous, and as tubuli mitochondriales if they are tubular. The individual cristae or tubuli serve to increase the surface on which the respiratory enzymatic reactions take place. Chemically, mitochondria are made up of proteins, phospholipids, glycerides, cholesterols, and a small quantity of RNA. More than half the solids present are proteins, mostly in the form of enzymes.

These minute bodies can be demonstrated in protozoa by supravital staining with Janus green B, Janus red, and osmium tetroxide. They may be spherical, ovoid, rod shaped, or filamentous. They are arranged in definite patterns, as in the free-living ciliate *Tillina condifera,* or are randomly scattered as in *Opalina,* the large ciliate found in the large intestine of amphibians.

In the parasite *Monocystis,* found in the coelom and seminal vesicles of oligochaetes, mitochondria can be demonstrated in the form of minute rods throughout the asexual phase of the parasite's life cycle, but with the commencement of sporulation, the mitochondria decrease both in size and number and finally are no longer visible in the definitive spore.

GOLGI BODIES. Golgi bodies represent another type of cytoplasmic inclusion, the specific function of which remains unclear. They are suspected of being associated with cell secretion and possibly with lipid storage. Golgi bodies were initially described by Hirschler (1914) in the parasitic protozoan *Monocystis ascidiae.* Since that time, these structures have been demonstrated in other protozoa as minute bodies in the cytoplasm. The arrangement and number of these structures appear to be inconsistent, even in a given species. Furthermore, the number of Golgi bodies varies at various stages in the life cycle. For example, in the ciliate ectoparasite of fishes *Ichthyophthirius* and in *Protoopalina,* an intestinal parasite of amphibians, the Golgi bodies disappear when the protozoa are encysted, but they arise de novo on excystment. Hirschler (1927) demonstrated that even the distribution of these organelles varies at different stages in the life cycle of gregarine parasites. A similar variation undoubtedly also occurs in other groups of protozoa.

Within the cytoplasm, Golgi bodies appear as osmiophilic and argentophilic granules. Chemically, they are composed of phospholipids, lipoproteins, and proteins. Their forms and sizes vary.

CYTOPLASMIC FOOD RESERVES. These inclusions have been described from various species of parasitic protozoa. The nature and amount of such stored nutrients vary with the environment. Glycogen or paraglycogen has been reported in the cysts of *Ichthyophthirius,* in the cysts of certain intestinal amoebae of mammals, and in other parasitic protozoa. This stored food material is deposited shortly before encystment and is completely utilized prior to excystment. In certain gregarines, paraglycogen is formed within a mitochondrial sphere, which disappears after the paraglycogen mass reaches a certain size. The same has been reported in *Ichthyophthirius.* In addition to the polysaccharide glycogen or paraglycogen, lipid droplets may also be present.

OTHER CYTOPLASMIC INCLUSIONS. Other types of cytoplasmic inclusions, such as the endoplasmic reticulum and lysosomes, are present in protozoa. The reader is referred to any recent text on cytology for discussions of these. The monograph by Pitelka (1963) is especially recommended.

Other Structures

Such structures as pigment granules, pyrenoids, and chromatophores—all found among the plantlike Phytomastigophorea—and photo-

---

*The term *chondriosomes* of the Protozoa, as used in the older literature, undoubtedly refers to the mitochondria since the descriptions of each correspond.

receptors—found among euglenae and dino-flagellates—are beyond the realm of this text, because these structures are found primarily in free-living species. Certain specialized organelles are present in some specific groups of protozoa; these are discussed in the following sections devoted to each taxon.

CHEMICAL COMPOSITION OF PROTOZOA

Proteins

Joyet-Lavergne, working with coccidian and gregarine parasites, reported that proteins are stored in the cytoplasm of these protozoa. Reichenow (1929) reported that volutin, composed of free nucleic acids, is stored as a reserve substance for the nucleus and is accumulated in forms such as coccidia and trypanosomes, which undergo rapid nuclear divisions. Volutin and stored proteins are not known to exist in metazoans.

Lipids

Various investigators have attempted to determine the presence and amount of lipids in parasitic protozoa. It is now known, for example, that in *Trypanosoma lewisi, T. equiperdum,* and *T. evansi,* three flagellate blood parasites, 3.3 per cent, 18.6 per cent, and 60 per cent respectively of their dry weight consists of lipids. In one malarial parasite, *Plasmodium knowlesi,* it is known that lipids form 28.8 per cent of the dry weight.

Carbohydrates

Carbohydrates stored in the bodies of parasitic protozoa are generally in the form of glycogen and/or paraglycogen. Paraglycogen is a type of animal starch similar to glycogen but can only be dissolved in water with difficulty. Glycogen is not water-soluble. Paraglycogen was first discovered in gregarines and later found in coccidia and endoparasitic ciliates. It is not known in metazoans. Within the bodies of parasitic protozoa, depending on the species, glycogen and paraglycogen are distributed either in definite locations, randomly, or in, but not restricted to, definite organelles. To exemplify the first instance, the large glycogen mass in the cysts of *Iodamoeba* is generally found at the pole opposite the nucleus. In young binucleated cysts of *Entamoeba* the large glycogen vacuole is always located between the two nuclei. The paraglycogen found in gregarines is located primarily in the deutomerite (p. 113); that found in trophozoites of *Nyctotherus* lies between the anterior end of the body and the macronucleus. Randomly scattered glycogen droplets are known to exist in *Tritrichomonas foetus* and in the trophozoites of various intestinal amoebae. The polysaccharides found in various stomach-dwelling ciliates of ruminants are commonly found in specific organelles but are not limited to these. In these ciliates, glycogen is stored primarily in the complex skeletal plates.

The amount of polysaccharides per animal varies, but none has been demonstrated in the malaria-causing sporozoans or in trypanosomes. Seasonal fluctuation of the amount of stored glycogen occurs in the flagellate *Cryptobia helicis,* a parasite in the reproductive organs of various pulmonate snails, and also occurs in other protozoa. Such fluctuations do not occur in endoparasitic helminths. In *C. helicis,* glycogen is not present during the summer but is present during the winter. This occurs because the snails are poikilothermic hosts, whose metabolism fluctuates greatly with the temperature. Seasonal variations in the amount of glycogen in the host are known to occur, hence it is not surprising that the metabolism of the parasite, which is totally dependent on the host, should fluctuate accordingly. Information available about glycogen in endoparasitic helminths has been derived from the study of only a few species occurring in warm-blooded hosts. In these cases the internal environment in which the parasites are found is maintained at a constant state (homeostasis).

Inorganic Substances

In addition to proteins, lipids, and carbohydrates, several inorganic substances have been demonstrated that are important in the metabolism of protozoan parasites. From micro-incineration of *Opalina,* a ciliate parasite in the large intestine of frogs and toads, Scott and Horning (1932) demonstrated ash deposits that indicated inorganic substances. These inorganic substances were found to be present in the myonemes, cilia, and basal granules. Analyses of the ash revealed that calcium oxide is deposited in the cytoplasm. Similar ash deposits are found in the same sites and also in the nucleus of *Nyctotherus,* a parasitic protozoan

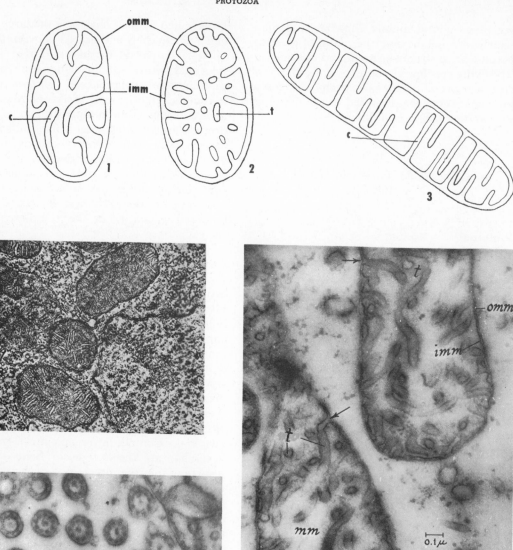

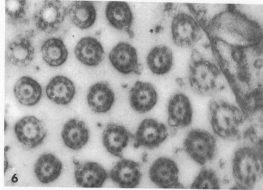

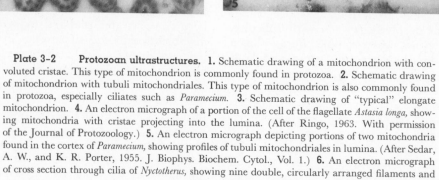

Plate 3-2 Protozoan ultrastructures. 1. Schematic drawing of a mitochondrion with convoluted cristae. This type of mitochondrion is commonly found in protozoa. **2.** Schematic drawing of mitochondrion with tubuli mitochondriales. This type of mitochondrion is also commonly found in protozoa, especially ciliates such as *Paramecium*. **3.** Schematic drawing of "typical" elongate mitochondrion. **4.** An electron micrograph of a portion of the cell of the flagellate *Astasia longa*, showing mitochondria with cristae projecting into the lumina. (After Ringo, 1963. With permission of the Journal of Protozoology.) **5.** An electron micrograph depicting portions of two mitochondria found in the cortex of *Paramecium*, showing profiles of tubuli mitochondriales in lumina. (After Sedar, A. W., and K. R. Porter, 1955. J. Biophys. Biochem. Cytol., Vol. 1.) **6.** An electron micrograph of cross section through cilia of *Nyctotherus*, showing nine double, circularly arranged filaments and

(Legend continued on opposite page.)

from the colon of amphibians. Analyses revealed that the cytoplasm is rich in sodium, while silica is present in the cytopharynx. Both calcium and iron are found lining the wall of food vacuoles in the cytoplasm. In the woodroach mutualist *Trichonympha,* most of the inorganic materials are present in the neuromotor system, the cytoplasm, and the nucleus, and the body surface is rich in calcium compounds.

Because phosphorus plays an important role in several metabolic processes (phosphorylations), it is not surprising that this element has been demonstrated in various parasitic protozoa, such as the trypanosomes. The synthesis of volutin, for example, is apparently correlated to the occurrence of phosphorus, since it has been demonstrated that when the free-living flagellate *Haematococcus pluvialis* is cultured in a phosphorus-rich medium, volutin is accumulated in large quantities and disappears when the culture is changed to a phosphorus-free one. This is of interest to parasitologists, for some parasitic flagellates accumulate volutin.

Other specific aspects of the composition and physiology of parasitic protozoa are included at the end of each chapter devoted to the specific groups.

PROTOZOAN ENCYSTMENT

Many parasitic protozoa are capable of encystment. A typical protozoan cyst is composed of a rounded mass of protoplasm enveloped within a rigid or semirigid cyst wall that is secreted by the trophozoite during the process of encystment.

Cysts of parasitic protozoa serve four primary functions: (1) They protect against unfavorable environmental conditions; (2) they function as sites for reorganization and nuclear division, followed by multiplication upon excystment; (3) they function in attachment; and (4) they serve as means of transmission from one host to another. The first function is exemplified by the cysts of the human pathogen *Entamoeba histolytica,* which are formed when the environment becomes unfavorable to the trophozoites. Such cysts can be maintained viable for many

weeks under normal conditions and for days at higher and lower temperatures and during periods of desiccation.

The cysts of *E. histolytica* also exemplify cysts that serve as sites for reorganization and nuclear division. Shortly after the trophozoite encysts, cytoplasmic reorganization occurs followed by nuclear divisions, so that the mature cyst encloses four vesicular nuclei. Similarly, cytoplasmic reorganization and nuclear divisions occur in the cysts of *E. coli,* but with eight nuclei present in the mature cyst. If mature cysts are reintroduced into a suitable host, excystment occurs, and the escaping trophozoite divides rapidly so that four metacystic trophozoites are produced from the protoplasm in each *E. histolytica* cyst and eight from that in each *E. coli* cyst.

Cysts, such as those of the fish epithelium-infecting ciliate *Icthyophthirius,* serve an additional function—that of attachment. When the encysted ciliate falls to the substratum, the cyst wall becomes attached, thus holding the parasite in place until excystment occurs.

Finally, it is well established that intestinal protozoa, such as *Entamoeba histolytica, Iodamoeba bütschlii,* and *Giardia intestinalis,* are transmitted to new hosts or become reëstablished in the same host through the swallowing of the encysted forms by the host. Thus the cysts serve as mechanisms for transmission.

Protozoan cysts vary in chemical composition. Cysts of *Entamoeba histolytica* and *Endolimax nana,* both parasitic amoebae, and those of the intestinal flagellate *Giardia intestinalis* contain proteins of keratin- or elastin-like albuminoids that on acid hydrolysis are found to be composed of lysine, histidine, arginine, tyrosine, glutamic acid, and glycine. The cysts of many ciliates also are known to be proteinaceous. Other materials, such as silicon, are present in the cysts of free-living protozoa.

CONDITIONS FAVORING ENCYSTMENT

Encysted protozoa can withstand adverse environmental conditions that would kill the vegetative or trophozoite form. The resistance

---

(Legend continued.)

a double, central filament. Flagella are identical with cilia when cross sections are studied with an electron microscope. (Courtesy of Dr. H. W. Beams, State University of Iowa).

(c, cristae mitochondriales; imm, inner mitochondrial membrane; mm, mitochondrial membrane; omm, outer mitochondrial membrane; t, tubuli mitochondriales.)

of cysts of *E. histolytica,* for example, is well known. They can withstand various extremes in physical conditions, such as heat and drying, in addition to chemical irritants (p. 101). The actual longevity of protozoan cysts varies greatly, depending on the species and other factors. Laboratory experiments suggest, however, that the conditions prevailing at the time of encystment determine longevity to a great extent. For example, cysts formed in cultures that have not dried do not live as long as cysts formed after the culture has dried.

All factors that favor encystment are not yet known. In many species the process appears to be a response to food deficiency. In addition, desiccation, increased concentration of dissolved salts in the medium, changes in temperature, low pH, decreased oxygen supply, accumulation of waste products in the medium, and crowding all appear to contribute to encystment. Among intestinal protozoa, absorption of water from the host's intestine, with resulting increase in the concentration of certain substances in the intestine, favors encystment. This may be why encysted amoebae are seldom found in diarrheic stools where trophozoites abound. What the relative importance of these factors may be in encystment in vivo is uncertain. Again, the various influencing factors appear to have different effects on different species.

CLASSIFICATION OF PROTOZOA

The taxonomy of the Protozoa is continuously being revised in light of recent findings.* Hall (1953) has given an excellent account of the various systems employed in the classification of these organisms. The author has chosen to follow the systematic pattern of Jahn and Jahn (1949). For finer details of differences and similarities between various taxa, the student is referred to either of these two volumes.

The phylum Protozoa is divided into four subphyla—Mastigophora, Sarcodina, Sporozoa, and Ciliophora. All members of the first three subphyla possess either pseudopodia or flagella as locomotor organelles during some stage in their life cycles. The Sporozoa possess no flagella or pseudopodia in their definitive stage; however, such organelles have been demonstrated in the alternating forms of certain species. The number of nuclei within the

*For a new suggested classification, see Honigsberg et al. (1964), *Journal of Protozoology, 11:* 7–20.

members of the first three subphyla vary from one to many, but the nuclei are all vesicular. Among the Ciliophora, the nuclei are usually of the compact type, and both macro- and micronuclei are usually present.

SUBPHYLUM MASTIGOPHORA

The Mastigophora, commonly known as flagellates, includes all the protozoans that possess one or more flagella in their trophozoite form. The majority of the flagellates are free-living, found in various ecological situations, but a large number are parasitic in or on both invertebrates and vertebrates. Most endoparasitic species inhabit their host's digestive tract, their host's circulatory system, and their host's tissues. That flagellates are capable of swimming aids them in adapting to different environments within their hosts. Unlike amoebae, which require a surface on which to glide, flagellates can survive in a liquid medium and thus are well adapted for living in their host's blood, lymph, and cerebrospinal fluid. The flagellate trypanosomes exhibit a further adaptation for life in a liquid medium that is evident in their body forms. They are elongate torpedo shaped and thus can swim in their host's body fluids with little resistance.

The relationships between flagellates and their hosts need not result in disease. Some flagellates apparently do little damage and are maintained in their hosts for long periods. For this reason, it is often extremely difficult to distinguish between a true parasite, a mutualist, and a commensal. Other flagellates are known to be highly pathogenic. Such is the case among the human-infecting species of *Trypanosoma* and *Leishmania*. A list of medical and veterinary significant flagellate species is given in Table 3–2.

The Mastigophora includes a large number of heterogeneous forms undoubtedly divergent in their immediate lines of descent, which although they all bear flagella, are in other respects quite different.

MORPHOLOGY

The Flagellum

The specific organelle common to all mastigophorans is the flagellum. This locomotor structure is also found on intermediate forms of certain amoebae and sporozoans but is characteristic of the definitive form of all flagellates, the number of flagella ranging from one to many, depending on the species.

The single flagellum is a filamentous cytoplasmic projection. When seen with the light microscope, the cytoplasm is observed to actually form a sheath around the axial filament, the axoneme (Plate 3–3, Fig. 1). The axoneme arises from a basal granule situated within the body proper. The cytoplasmic sheath is contractile and tapers toward the free end. In some cases, the axial filament is believed to be naked at the distal end. When studied with the electron microscope, the axial filament appears to be composed of two central and nine peripheral fibrils (Plate 3–2, Fig. 6).

The kinetic complex, associated with nuclear division and flagellar motion, is highly complex in certain species, simple in others, and not visible in still others. The constituents of the complex are: the basal granule (also known as the blepharoplast or kinetosome), which appears as a minute granule in the cytoplasm commonly situated immediately beneath the body surface and from which the flagellum arises (Recent electron microscopic studies indicate that the basal granule is morphologically identical to the flagellum.); the kinetoplast, which is a larger body closely associated with the basal granule and often appears to be combined with it; and the parabasal body, the morphology of which varies greatly among the various genera. The parabasal body is usually closely associated with the nucleus and connected with the basal granule.

In some flagellates, a delicate fibril, the rhizoblast, has been reported to connect the basal granule or blepharoplast to the nucleus. However, recent electron microscopic studies indicate that the rhizoblast does not connect with the nucleus (Pitelka, 1963). The exact functions of these organelles and the justification for considering them as separate entities are dubious, for it has suggested that the blepharoplast and rhizoblast together might be considered an enlongated centriole, because in certain species the blepharoplast has been seen to divide at the initiation of nuclear division and act much in the same way as a centriole. For this reason, the term *centroblepharoplast* has been suggested.

The parabasal body contains acid phosphatase and a polysaccharide. The currently popular hypothesis is that this structure, which can be pyriform, rodlike, or collar-like, is a part of the Golgi complex (Pitelka, 1963). More than one parabasal body may be present in each flagellate, and their sizes fluctuate with the availability of nourishment to the organism (Grimstone, 1959). During certain periods, such as when the flagellate divides, the parabasal body may become invisible under the light microscope.

The author has chosen to recognize these terms even if they may be artificial, because they are important taxonomic tools frequently used in the description of species. Variations of the kinetic complex are depicted in Plate 3–3.

MOTILITY OF FLAGELLA. The functions of flagellar movement appear to be to aid in the propelling and directing of the organism's movement, to assist in procuring food in some instances, and perhaps even to aid in tactility. The mechanics of flagellar operation has long been a problem and still is not completely resolved. Lowndes has pointed out, as the result of cinematographic studies, that flagellar undulations always originate at the base and move toward the free end. Although various types of flagellar movements are known, the source of the required energy and the mechanism(s) that controls the movements remain unknown. Probably the best hypothesis is that the basic mechanism is essentially that of muscle contraction—that is, there exists a special arrangement of protein chains whose interactions cause contraction and extension by telescoping. The energy is supplied by ATP (adenosin triphosphate). The monograph by Sleigh (1962), devoted to discussions of the morphology and function of flagella and cilia, should be consulted for further details.

Other Organelles

Certain parasitic flagellates are known to possess various specialized organelles that serve specific functions. These organelles are utilized also as diagnostic tools.

THE AXOSTYLE. The axostyle is a supporting structure embedded along the longitudinal axis in the cytoplasm (Plate 3–4, Fig. 1). It may appear as a fine filament in some species and as a broad hyaline rod in others. It may extend partially along, totally along, or beyond the length of the body, and may possess a broad, rounded anterior end known as the capitulum. In stained specimens, the axostyle varies in appearance. It may appear homogeneous, granular, naked, or sheathed. When stained with iron haematoxylin, only some axostyles are

(Text continued on page 58.)

Table 3-2. Some Important Parasitic Flagellates of Man and Domestic Animals.

Flagellate	Principal Hosts	Habitat	Main Characteristics	Disease
Leishmania donovani	Man, dogs, cats, horses, sheep, cattle	Spleen, bone marrow, liver, monocytes	$2\text{-}4\,\mu$ in diameter, eccentric rounded nucleus	Kala-azar
L. tropica	Man, dogs	Dermal sores	Indistinguishable from *L. donovani*	Oriental sore
L. braziliensis	Man, dogs, monkeys	Dermal sores, especially mucous membranes	Indistinguishable from *L. donovani*	Mucocutaneous leishmaniasis
Trypanosoma equiperdum	Horses, cattle, donkeys	Genitalia and internal reproductive organs	$25\text{-}28\,\mu$ long, $1\text{-}2\,\mu$ wide	Dourine
T. theileri	Cattle	Blood	$60\text{-}70\,\mu$ long, $4\text{-}5\,\mu$ wide, myonemes	Nonpathogenic
T. melophagium	Sheep	Blood	$50\text{-}60\,\mu$ long	Nonpathogenic
T. evansi	Horses, mules, donkeys, cattle, dogs, camels, elephants	Blood	$25\,\mu$ long	Surra
T. equinum	Horses (S. Amer.)	Blood	$20\text{-}25\,\mu$ long, no blepharoplast	Mal de Caderas
T. hippicum	Horses (Panama), mules	Blood	$16\text{-}18\,\mu$ long	Murrina
T. brucei	Horses, donkeys, mules, camels, cattle, swine, dogs	Blood	Pleomorphic, $15\text{-}30\,\mu$ long	Fatal nagana
T. simiae	Pigs, monkeys, sheep, goats	Blood	Seldom with free flagellum	Virulent
T. congolense	Cows, other domestic animals	Blood	Monomorphic, $8\text{-}19\,\mu$ long, $3\,\mu$ wide, no free flagella	Bovine trypanosomiasis
T. vivax	Ruminants, equines	Blood	$15.5\text{-}30.5\,\mu$ long, free flagellum	Virulent
T. gambiense	Man, monkeys, antelopes, dogs	Blood, lymph	$15\text{-}30\,\mu$ long, $1\text{-}3\,\mu$ wide, spiral undulating membrane	Gambian trypanosomiasis (sleeping sickness)

Species	Host	Location	Description	Pathogenicity
T. rhodesiense	Man, wild game, domestic animals	Blood, lymph	Usually indistinguishable from *T. gambiense*	Rhodesian trypanosomiasis
T. cruzi	Man, cats, dogs, monkeys, squirrels	Blood	**C** or **U** shaped, 20 μ long	Chaga's disease
T. americanum	Cattle	Blood	17-25 μ long or longer	Nonpathogenic ?
T. lewisi	Rats	Blood	Approximately 30 μ long	Nonpathogenic ?
Trichomonas canistomae	Dogs	Mouth	Four anterior flagella, one trailing; 9 μ long; 3.4 μ wide	Nonpathogenic
T. felistomae	Cats	Mouth	8.3 μ long, 3.3 μ wide	Nonpathogenic
T. gallinae	Turkeys, chickens, pigeons	Upper digestive tract, liver	6.2-18.9 μ long, 2.3-8.5 μ wide	Avian trichomoniasis
T. gallinarum	Turkeys, chickens, pigeons	Caecum	Pear shaped, 9-12 μ long, 6-8 μ wide	Nonpathogenic ?
T. anseri	Geese	Caecum	Oval body, 7.9 μ long, 4.7 μ wide, large cytostome	Nonpathogenic
T. vaginalis	Women	Vagina	10-30 μ long, 10-20 μ wide, cytostome inconspicuous	Vaginitis
T. hominis	Man	Intestine	5-20 μ long	Nonpathogenic
T. tenax	Man	Mouth	10-30 μ long	Nonpathogenic
Tritrichomonas equi	Horses	Colon, caecum	Three anterior flagella, undulating membrane, slender axostyle, 4-6.5 μ long	Nonpathogenic
T. foetus	Cattle	Genital tract	Pear shaped, three anterior flagella, undulating membrane, axostyle, 10-25 μ long, 3-15 μ wide	Tritrichomonas abortion
T. suis	Pigs	Intestine	Three anterior flagella, undulating membrane, axostyle, 8-10 μ long	Nonpathogenic
T. eberthi	Chickens	Caecum	9 μ long, 4-6 μ wide	Nonpathogenic
Retortamonas ovis	Sheep	Intestine	Pear shaped, two flagella of length of body, 5.2 μ long, 3-3.7 μ wide	Nonpathogenic
R. cuniculi	Rabbits	Caecum	Posterior flagellum thick, one-half as long as body; 7.5-13 μ long; 5.5-9.5 μ wide	Nonpathogenic
R. intestinalis	Man	Intestine	Pleomorphic, 4-9 μ long, 3-4 μ wide, cytostome one-third length of body	Diarrhea ?

(Table 3-2 Continued)

Flagellate	Principal Hosts	Habitat	Main Characteristics	Disease
Pleuromonas jaculans	Chickens	Caecum	One short anterior flagellum, one long trailing flagellum, 5-12μ long, 5μ wide	Nonpathogenic
Pentatrichomonas hominis	Man, other primates, dogs, cats	Intestine	Three to five anterior flagella	Nonpathogenic
P. gallinarum	Turkeys, chickens, guinea-fowls	Caecum	Pear shaped, five anterior flagella, one trailing flagellum, 6-8μ long	Caecal lesions
Histomonas meleagridis	Chickens, turkeys, ducks, geese	Caecum, liver, other tissues	Pleomorphic, four flagella	Blackhead histomoniasis
Monocercomonas ruminantium	Sheep, cattle	Rumen, prepuce	Three anterior flagella, 12-14μ long, 8-10μ wide	Nonpathogenic
M. cuniculi	Rabbits	Caecum	Nucleus ellipsoidal, axostyle protrudes from posterior end, 5-14μ long	Nonpathogenic
M. gallinarum	Chickens	Caecum	5-8μ long, 3-4μ wide, pear shaped, three anterior flagella, one longer trailing flagellum	Nonpathogenic
Chilomastix mesnili	Man	Large intestine	Pear shaped, three free anterior flagella, one flagellum in cytostome	Nonpathogenic
Embadomonas intestinalis	Man	Large intestine	Slipper shaped, two unequal anteriorly directed flagella, large cytostome	Nonpathogenic
Tricercomonas intestinalis	Man	Large intestine	Pear shaped, three anterior flagella, one trailing flagellum	Nonpathogenic
Giardia intestinalis	Man	Intestine	Pear shaped, bilaterally symmetrical, two nuclei, two axostyles, four pairs of flagella	Diarrhea
Hexamita spp.	Turkeys, pigeons, chickens	Small intestine	Elongate, two anterior nuclei, two pairs anterior flagella, two trailing flagella	Severe enteritis
Callimastix equi	Horses	Colon, caecum	Kidney shaped, 12-15 flagella at hilus, 12-18μ long, 7-10μ wide	Nonpathogenic
C. frontalis	Cows	Rumen	Anterior end disc shaped, 12 flagella, 30μ long	Nonpathogenic

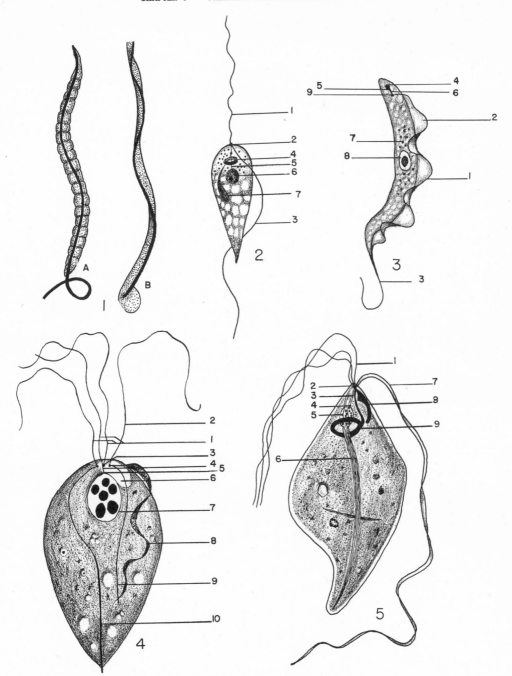

Plate 3-3   The flagellum and associated structures. 1. A. Flagellum of *Euglena,* showing centrally located axoneme, which is naked terminally. (Redrawn after Bütschli.) **B.** Flagellum of *Trachelomonas,* showing axoneme off to one side. (Redrawn after Plenge.) **2.** *Proteromonas lacertae* from the rectum of a lizard, showing (1) locomotor flagellum, (2) blepharoplast, (3) trailing flagellum, (4) cytostome, (5) rhizoplast, (6) nucleus, and (7) parabasal body. (Redrawn after Grassé.) **3.** *Trypanosoma gambiense,* showing (1) flagellum, (2) undulating membrane, (3) free terminal of flagellum, (4) kinetoplast, (5) rhizoplast, (6) axoneme, (7) metachromatic granules, (8) nucleus, and (9) basal granule. (Original.) **4.** *Trichomonas buccalis,* showing (1) locomotor flagella, (2) trailing flagellum, (3) blepharoplast, (4) rhizoplast, (5) centriole, (6) cytostome, (7) nucleus, (8) undulating membrane, (9) basal rod, and (10) axostyle. (Redrawn after Hinshaw.) **5.** *Devescovina* from the intestine of a termite, showing (1) anterior flagella, (2) blepharoplast, (3) rhizoplast, (4) centriole, (5) nucleus, (6) axostyle, (7) trailing band flagellum, (8) chromatic basal rod, and (9) parabasal body coiled around nucleus. (Redrawn after Kirby.)

deeply stained, thus suggesting differences in chemical composition. In certain species of woodroach gut-inhabiting flagellates, there are numerous axostyles, known as axial filaments.

THE PELTA. The pelta is a crescent shaped membrane that can be demonstrated in certain species of flagellates by staining with Bodian's silver or some comparable stain (Plate 3–4, Fig. 2). Kirby (1947) postulated that the pelta is homologous with the membranous extension of the axostylar capitulum.

THE COSTA. The costa is a thin, firm, rod like structure running along the base of the undulating membrane of certain flagellates, such as *Trypanosoma* spp. and *Tritrichomonas* spp. (Plate 3–4, Fig. 3). It is probably a supporting structure.

THE ACICULUM. The aciculum, a bent, fin-like organelle, has been demonstrated in *Cryptobia helicis,* a flagellate parasitic in the reproductive organ of pulmonate snails (Plate 3–4,

Fig. 4). The function of this structure is not clear. It may serve as a supportive organelle.

MYONEMES. In several parasitic flagellates, myonemes have been demonstrated. These fine fibrils are contractile and may be thought of as a primitive type of muscle fibrils that enable the protozoans to contract and extend their bodies. More commonly, myonemes are found in various free-living ciliates such as *Stentor* and *Zoothamnium,* and in free-living flagellates such as *Leptodiscus* and *Craspedotella.*

Other organelles and structures found in parasitic flagellates are common to all protozoans and have been discussed previously.

SYSTEMATICS AND BIOLOGY

There are two classes of Mastigophora— the Phytomastigophorea and the Zoomastigophorea.

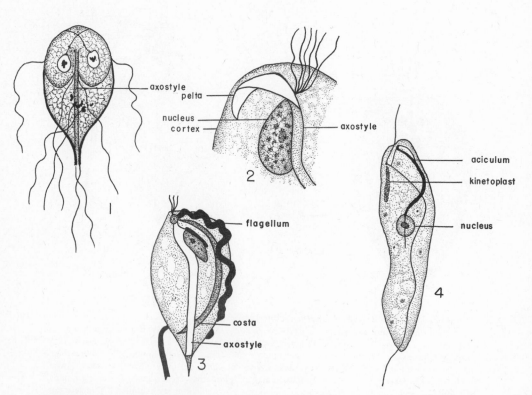

Plate 3–4   Flagellates and their specialized organelles. 1. *Giardia intestinalis,* an intestinal parasite of humans, showing axostyle. (Redrawn after Kudo, R. R., 1954. *Protozoology,* Charles C Thomas, Springfield, Ill.) **2.** *Hexamastix citelli,* showing pelta and axostyle. (Redrawn and modified after Kirby and Honigberg.) **3.** *Tritrichomonas muris,* an intestinal parasite of mice, showing costa and axostyle. (Modified after Kirby and Honigberg.) **4.** *Cryptobia helicis* from the gonads of various pulmonate snails, showing aciculum. (Modified after Kozloff.)

CLASS PHYTOMASTIGOPHOREA

The phytomastigophoreans are characterized by chromatophores (pigment-bearing organelles), and most of the species are colored. Most of these plantlike flagellates are free-living, being capable of holophytic, mixotrophic, holozoic, or saprozoic existences in various aquatic situations.

All the symbiotic members of the Phytomastigophorea belong to the order Dinoflagellida with a few exotic exceptions. For example, a species of *Astasia* of the order Euglenida has been reported in two larger protozoa, *Spirostomum* and *Stentor;* and *Chrysidella* of the order Cryptomonadida has been found in foraminiferans and radiolarians.

ORDER DINOFLAGELLIDA

The parasitic dinoflagellates all belong to the family Blastodidiidae and are ecto- and endoparasitic on both plants and animals. Representative parasitic genera include *Oodinium, Chytriodinium, Duboscquella, Haplozoon, Apodinium,* and *Blastodinium.* Discussion of the biology of a few representative species follows.

Oodinium ocellatum. This parasite is an ectoparasite attached to the gill filaments of marine fishes (Plate 3–5, Fig. 1). This small (average 60 μ by 50 μ), ovoid organism is encased within a shell that completely surrounds the body cytoplasm except for a terminal aperture through which a broad flagellum and cytoplasmic processes protrude. It is by these processes that the organism is attached to its host. Within the cytoplasm is a large spherical nucleus along with many chromatophores, starch granules, and a stigma. The smaller organisms remain attached to the fish while they are growing and finally drop off. They ultimately grow as large as 150 μ in diameter. The unattached organism withdraws its flagellum and processes, and the aperture is closed

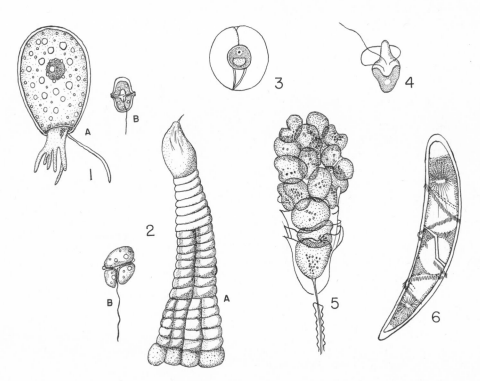

Plate 3–5   Parasitic dinoflagellates. 1. A. *Oodinium ocellatum,* recently detached from host's gill. **B.** Free-living flagellate form of *O. ocellatum.* (Redrawn after Nigrelli, 1936.) **2. A.** *Haplozoon clymenellae,* mature colony. **B.** Free-living swarmer form. (Redrawn after Shumway, 1924.) **3.** *Chytriodinium parasiticum,* found in the egg of a copepod. (Redrawn after Dogiel.) **4.** *Duboscquella tintinnicola* swarm cell. (Redrawn after Duboscq and Collin.) **5.** *Apodinium mycetoides,* swarmer formation. (Redrawn after Chatton, 1952.) **6.** *Blastodinium spinulosum.* (Redrawn after Chatton, 1952.)

off by a cellulose secretion. Within the now completely closed test, the organism undergoes division and eventually gives rise to as many as 128 cells. Each one of these daughter cells becomes flagellated and divides once more. These flagellated swarm cells (also known as swarmers) rupture out of the test and actively seek the gills of their piscine host, to which they become attached. Once situated, each swarm cell develops a test, extends cytoplasmic processes and a flagellum, and begins to increase in size. The closely related *O. poucheti* and *O. limneticum* have similar life cycles. *Oodinium poucheti* is an ectoparasite of tunicates, and *O. limneticum* is parasitic on fresh-water fishes. This last species bears green chromatophores but no flagellum or stigma. The nature of the relationship between the various species of *Oodinium* and their hosts remains uncertain; however, it appears to be an obligatory one. In some cases, as the author has noticed in Hawaii, *O. ocellatum,* when present in large numbers, can cause the death of the fish host. Death of the host appears to result from suffocation, for the parasites are commonly attached in large numbers to the surface of the gills.

Haplozoon clymenellae. Haplozoon clymenellae is an intestinal parasite of the polychaete *Clymenella torquata.* The mature forms are gathered in colonies of 250 or more individuals arranged in a pyramidal or linear fashion (Plate 3–5, Fig. 2). The swarm cells are unicellular with two pronounced flagella.

Chytriodinium parasiticum. This parasite was originally reported from the eggs of copepods (Plate 3–5, Fig. 3). The young grow at the expense of the eggs' contents, and on reaching maximal size, they divide into many daughter cells. Each daughter cell gives rise to swarmers, each of which bears four flagella. These swarmers escape from the egg to seek new copepod eggs.

Duboscquella tintinnicola. This species is an intracellular parasite of certain spirotrichous ciliates. Within the larger protozoan, the parasite appears as a large (100μ) oval body with a large nucleus. The free-swimming swarmers, which result from the division of the daughter cells which in turn originated from the parent, are biflagellate (Plate 3–5, Fig. 4).

Apodinium spp. These dinoflagellates are ectoparasitic on tunicate gill slits, and are binucleate and colorless (Plate 3–5, Fig. 5).

Blastodinium. An endoparasite of copepods, *Blastodinium* adults are spindle shaped, arched, and the noncellulose envelope often bears two spiral rows of bristles (Plate 3–5, Fig. 6).

Although the parasitic dinoflagellates are of little economic importance, they are of great interest biologically, because only a few are parasitic while their close relatives are free-living. Further study of the closely allied free-living and parasitic forms may well reveal insights into the origin of parasitism. Some additional parasitic dinoflagellates are depicted in Plate 3–6.

CLASS ZOOMASTIGOPHOREA

The zoomastigophoreans are animal-like flagellates, a large number of which are parasitic. Members of this class all lack chromatophores and are generally mononucleate. The nucleus is usually of the vesicular type. Reproduction is accomplished by longitudinal fission. The class is divided into four orders.

A KEY TO THE ORDERS OF ZOOMASTIGOPHOREA.*

1. With pseudopodia in addition to flagella . . . .
   Rhizomastigida.

1'. Without pseudopodia but with flagella . . . . 2.

2. With 1–2 flagella . . . . **Protomastigida.**

2'. With more than 2 flagella . . . . 3.

3. With 3–8 flagella . . . . **Polymastigida.**

3'. With more than 8 flagella . . . . **Hypermastigida.**

ORDER RHIZOMASTIGIDA

This order includes all the flagellates that, in addition to bearing flagella, are capable of producing pseudopodia. The number of flagella, like the number of pseudopodia, varies from one to many. Undoubtedly these unique organisms represent the borderline cases between the amoebae and the flagellates.

All the parasitic members of the Rhizomastigida are members of the family Mastigamoebidae. The individuals usually possess one to three flagella and the pseudopodia are of the lobopodial (blunt) and axopodial (filamentous) types (p. 94). The parasites belong to three genera—*Histomonas* found in fowls, *Mastigamoeba* in amphibians, and *Rhizomastix* in insects.

---

*Essentially after Kudo (1954).

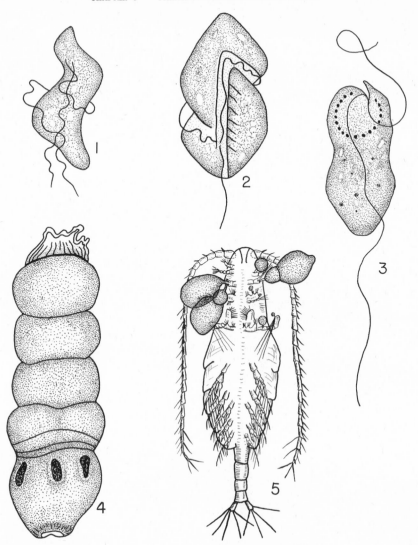

Plate 3-6   Parasitic dinoflagellates of the family Blastodiniidae. 1. *Trypanodinium ovicola* from eggs of copepods. (Redrawn after Chatton, 1920.) **2.** *Syndinium turbo* from the gut and coelom of marine copepods. (Redrawn after Chatton, 1920.) **3.** *Paradinium poucheti* from coelom of copepods. (Redrawn after Chatton, 1920.) **4.** *Paraellobiopsis coutieri* attached to appendages of Malacostraca. (Redrawn after Collin.) **5.** *Ellobiopsis chattoni* attached to *Calanus finmarchicus*. (Redrawn after Caullery.)

Histomonas. *Histomonas meleagridis* is undoubtedly the best known of the parasitic mastigamoebae (Plate 3–7, Fig. 1). Not only is this species interesting in itself, but it is also of great economic importance, because it is the etiologic agent of "blackhead" enterohepatitis, which is lethal to turkeys and other fowl. This animal is extremely interesting, because it has both amoeboid and flagellated stages. The organism in the amoeboid stage is relatively small, measuring from 8 μ to 15 μ in diameter. In this stage it occurs in caecal and hepatic tissues of the avian host, where it is found be-

tween rather than within cells. It is apparently capable of actual migration from one position to another. The flagellate form is generally larger than the amoeboid form, measuring from 8 μ to 21 μ in diameter, although smaller specimens are known. Although the presence of one flagellum is the usual condition, several flagella, up to four, are known to occur. The flagellate forms are also capable of active amoeboid movement. They ingest the host's erythrocytes, bacteria, and starch granules, all of which can be seen in their cytoplasmic food vacuoles.

Nuclear activity in *H. meleagridis* is strikingly similar to that found in *Trichomonas* (p. 174), suggesting a common ancestry. Often, nuclear division occurs without cytoplasmic division, resulting in binucleate or even tetranucleate individuals. During binary fission, the flagellum, or flagella, is lost and each daughter cell develops a new one.

Living in the intestine of the host, *H. meleagridis* actively invades and destroys the mucosa. Its habitat often extends posteriorly to the caeca. Trophozoites are commonly found invading and destroying liver cells, to which site they have undoubtedly been transported by the blood.

In turkeys, infections are acquired either through the ingestion of the parasite from the fecal droppings of infected birds or through the ingestion of eggs of the co-parasite *Heterakis gallinae,* a nematode. These eggs are very resistant and may survive for several months in soil. Hence, an infected poultry range may remain dangerous to turkeys for many months. Exactly how *H. meleagridis* enters the eggs of *H. gallinae* is uncertain. No cystic form is known for this flagellate.

Young birds are more often infected than older ones. Turkeys, especially young ones, are readily killed by this parasite, although infected chickens, especially older birds, usually survive and become carriers. Therefore, it is unadvisable to raise turkeys on a range where chickens have been kept.

Mastigamoeba. *Mastigamoeba hylae* is an elongate parasite, 80 to 135 μ by 21 to 31 μ, found in the hindgut of tadpoles of various species of frogs and toads (Plate 3–7, Fig. 2). When not in motion, the body tends to round up, and the single flagellum is not readily visible. The body elongates when in motion. The flagellum appears to be connected to the nucleus. Fine lobopodia are produced. The single large nucleus, with a prominent endosome, is located near the surface from which the flagellum protrudes.

Little is known about the biology of this organism. Infection of amphibians is probably acquired through the ingestion of flagellates

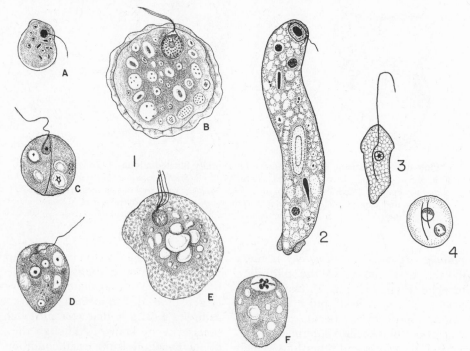

Plate 3-7   Parasitic rhizomastigids. 1. *Histomonas meleagridis.* **A.** From caecum of chicken. **B.** Large specimen from pheasant. **C.** Rounded form. **D.** Amoeboid form. **E.** Specimen from caecum of chicken, showing food vacuoles. **F.** Stage with nucleus undergoing division. (Redrawn after Wenrich, 1943; and Bishop, 1938.) **2.** Trophozoite of *Mastigamoeba hylae.* (Redrawn after Becker, 1925.) **3.** Trophozoite of *Rhizomastix gracilis.* (Redrawn after Mackinnon.) **4.** Cyst of *R. gracilis* showing two nuclei and two rhizostyles. (Redrawn after Mackinnon.)

voided from other hosts. The presence of *M. hylae* in amphibians does not appear to be injurious.

It is of interest to note that most members of the genus *Mastigamoeba* are free-living, found in damp soil and fresh water. Again, a more thorough understanding of the physiological differences between *M. hylae* and the free-living members of the genus would contribute to our understanding of the mechanisms involved during adaptation to symbiosis.

Rhizomastix. *Rhizomastix gracilis* is found in the intestine of axolotls and crane fly larvae (Plate 3–7, Fig. 3). The small (8 to 14 μ) amoeboid body gives rise to a single flagellum (20 μ long), which is joined to a blepharoplast located between the centrally situated nucleus and the posterior end of the body. A distinct fibril, probably the proximal portion of the flagellum, connects the blepharoplast with the flagellum. No vacuoles are present in the cytoplasm. Multiplication occurs within a spherical cyst, in which nuclear division is accompanied by cytoplasmic division resulting in two daughter cells (Plate 3–7, Fig. 4). The original fibril remains in one daughter, while in the second another is formed from the blepharoplast. This is a good example of how protozoan cysts can serve as sites for nuclear division and cytoplasmic reorganization.

Infection of hosts by *R. gracilis* is accomplished when cysts passed out of one host are ingested by another.

ORDER PROTOMASTIGIDA

This order includes many free-living species in addition to species parasitic in plants, invertebrates, and vertebrates. The protomastigids are generally small flagellates with one or two flagella. The body is plastic but not amoeboid as in the Rhizomastigida. Reproduction is generally by longitudinal fission, and during the life cycle, individuals usually take on more than one form (the condition is known as polymorphism). This is especially true among members of the family Trypanosomatidae.

Parasitic members of this order are included in three families—the monoflagellar Trypanosomatidae; the biflagellar Cryptobiidae, members of which possess an undulating membrane; and the biflagellar Bodonidae, members of which do not possess an undulating membrane.

Family Trypanosomatidae

Members of the family Trypanosomatidae are all parasitic and are found in the host's blood and tissues. Their bodies are typically elongate and more or less flattened and a single flagellum arises from a blepharoplast near which is located a kinetoplast. The blepharoplast varies in location from anterior, to the middle, to the posterior end of the body. When the blepharoplast is located posteriorly, the basal portion of the flagellum forms the outer margin of the undulating membrane (Plate 3–3, Fig. 3).

DEVELOPMENTAL AND DEFINITIVE FORMS. Life cycles of members of the Trypanosomatidae include more than one stage. The leishmanial, the leptomonad, crithidial, and trypanosomal stages are found during the development of various members of this family. During the development of members of each genus, at least two of these morphologic phases occur.

Designations for these life cycle stages are also used as generic names of members of this family. For example, "trypanosome" is not only a morphologic type but also a generic name—*Trypanosoma*. "Crithidia" not only indicates a type but also the genus *Crithidia*. Plate 3–8 depicts the stages the various genera undergo during their developmental cycles.

Since at least some of the stages found during the life cycles of the various genera are morphologically similar, positive identification, especially among the little known genera, depends on complete knowledge of the parasites' life cycles. For example, it is obvious that not all crithidial forms belong to the genus *Crithidia* since some may represent an intermediate stage during development of members of the *Trypanosoma*. Thus, complete life cycle information on the crithidial form should be known before a definite identification is attempted.

Leishmania. The leishmanial form is rounded or oval with a nucleus, blepharoplast, and kinetoplast. The flagellum is reduced to a tiny fibril that is totally embedded in the cytoplasm. All the members of the Trypanosomatidae exhibit this form during their life cycles. Members of the genus *Leishmania* exhibit both the leptomonad (in insect hosts) and the leishmanial forms (as an intracellular parasite of the reticuloendothelial system of vertebrates).

GENUS *Leishmania*.   *Leishmania donovani*, *L.*

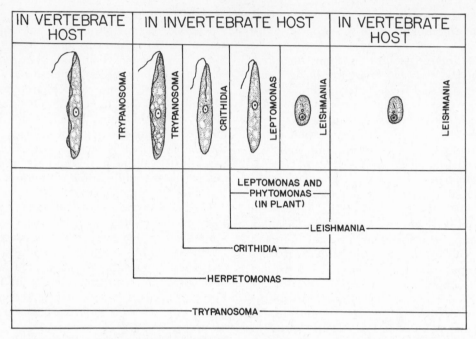

Plate 3-8   Morphological differences between members of the family Trypanosomatidae and forms attained by members of various genera during their developmental stages.

tropica, and *L. brasiliensis* are the three human-infecting species. These are indistinguishable morphologically. In the vertebrate host (man, dogs, etc.), the parasites are ovoid, 1.5 μ in diameter, and possess a distinct nucleus, blepharoplast, kinetoplast, flagellar fibril, and cytoplasmic vacuoles. All are tissue parasites of the reticuloendothelial system.

Leishmania donovani (Plate 3–9, Fig. 1) is the causative agent of visceral leishmaniasis, or kala-azar, an often fatal disease of man endemic in Greece, Malta, Italy, Spain, Sudan, North Kenya, Nigeria, China, India, a few Near Eastern countries, and in various areas of South America. In the body, the parasite is found in macrophages, certain leukocytes, spleen, liver, bone marrow, lymph glands, intestinal mucosa, and certain other cells. Typically the spleen and liver are enlarged because of an increase in the fibrous elements and the number of macrophages. Dogs in endemic areas are naturally infected and serve as reservoir hosts. The vector for *Leishmania donovani* is the sand fly *Phlebotomus argentipes* and a few related species.

During feeding on an infected vertebrate, the fly ingests the leishmanial parasites. Large numbers of small leptomonads develop within the sand fly's gut in about 3 days. These result from the longitudinal division of the original

leptomonads that develop from the leishmanial forms once the latter reach the sand fly's gut. The leptomonads migrate anteriorly to the fly's pharynx and mouth cavity, where most of them are found by the fifth day. From these anterior regions the leptomonads can easily migrate to the proboscis, ready to be introduced into the new human or canine host. On reaching such a host, they actively establish themselves via the circulatory system as intracellular leishmanial forms.

THE EFFECT OF DIETS ON TRANSMISSION OF *Leishmania.*   A fascinating aspect of the transmission of *Leishmania* spp. by *Phlebotomus* flies has to do with the diet of the vector. It was known that kala-azar and *P. argentipes* in India have a similar geographic distribution. Furthermore, it was not difficult to demonstrate that the insects do become heavily infected with the flagellated forms of *Leishmania* when fed on leishmaniasis victims. However, experimental trials at infecting humans through the bite of the insect were mostly unsuccessful until it was discovered that the substitution of a diet of raisin juice or glucose solution for blood, after the initial blood meal, made the vectors highly infective. Apparently *Leishmania* does not survive in *Phlebotomus* in nature, or at least in sufficient numbers to produce infections, unless the fly follows a blood meal with the ingestion of some fruit juice rich in glucose. It still remains undetermined what the preferred fruit juice is in nature.

Leishmania tropica causes cutaneous leishmaniasis, a relatively mild skin disease commonly known as the Oriental sore (Plate 3–9, Fig. 2). This species is endemic to countries of Europe and North Africa bordering the Mediterranean Sea. In Asia it is endemic to Syria, Armenia, Israel, Southern Russia, China, Indochina and India. *L. tropica* has also been reported from Peru, Bolivia, Brazil, the Guianas, and Mexico. Unlike *L. donovani*, *L. tropica* is primarily an intracellular parasite in endothelial cells around cutaneous sores. Beginning as a papule, the sore erupts and spreads. Such cutaneous eruptions are commonly located on the hands, feet, legs, and face. The vectors for this parasite are *Phlebotomus sergenti, P. major, P. papatasii, P.*

caucasicus, and a few less known species of sand flies. The life history of *L. tropica* parallels that of *L. donovani*. In addition to utilizing humans as the mammalian host, this species also infects dogs and cats in China, India, and a few Near Eastern nations. The monkey, bullock, and brown bear are known to be naturally infected in the Near East, as are horses and gerbils (*Rhombomys opimus, Meriones erytheurus,* and *M. meridianus*).

The third human-infecting species, *Leishmania brasiliensis* (Plate 3–9, Fig. 3), is primarily endemic to South and Central America, being found in Brazil, Paraguay, Peru, Argentina, Bolivia, Uruguay, Venezuela, Ecuador, Colombia, Panama, Costa Rica, and Mexico. Human infections have also been reported from Sudan, Somali Republic, Kenya, Italy, India, and China. It is commonly referred to

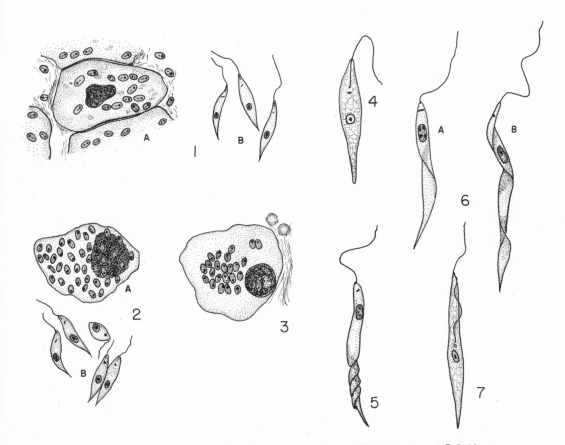

Plate 3-9   Representatives of the Trypanosomatidae. 1. *Leishmania donovani.* **A.** Leishman bodies in endothelial cell of spleen. **B.** Flagellated leptomonad forms in culture. **2.** *Leishmania tropica.* **A.** Mononuclear host cell filled with leishman bodies; from smear preparation. **B.** Flagellated leptomonad forms from culture. **3.** Leishman bodies of *L. brasiliensis* within host's macrophage. **4.** *Leptomonas ctenocephali.* (Redrawn after Wenyon.) **5.** *Phytomonas davidi.* **6.** *Phytomonas elmassiani.* **A.** As seen in the milkweed plant host. **B.** As seen in the gut of the insect transmitter, *Oncopeltus fasciatus.* (Redrawn after Holmes, 1925.) **7.** *Crithidia fasciculata.*

as the American species since it is by far more common in South and Central America. The parasite appears to prefer the mucous membranes of the nose, tongue, and mouth. The life history of *L. brasiliensis* again parallels that of the two other human-infecting species; however, in this case *Phlebotomus intermedius, P. squamipes, P. panamensis* are the primary insect vectors. It has been shown that direct infections, from sore to sore, are possible. In an attempt to determine the fate of this mucous–membrane–infecting species in nonmucous tissue, Rey (1943) inoculated *Leishmania brasiliensis* into the superficial subcutaneous connective tissue of Syrian hamsters, *Cricetus auratus,* and found that local inflammatory reactions occurred. He attributed these reactions to natural immunity. All the parasites were destroyed before 36 hours by two means: (1) substances in the connective tissue, and (2) polyblasts formed from macrophages, wandering lymphoid cells, undifferentiated perivascular mesenchymal cells, and monocytes and lymphocytes of haematogenous origin, and heterophils from the blood (rarely fibroblasts and eosinophils). These agencies of parasite destruction are complementary. This experiment, however, does not conclusively indicate that *L. brasiliensis* cannot survive in nonmucous tissue. Evidence suggests that various strains of this species exist and that some do affect dermal tissues and are not readily destroyed.

Leishmania caninum of dogs and children from the Mediterranean basin, *L. infantum* of children in China, and *L. mysxi* in the dormouse are related species the biology of which is not understood. These species are all morphologically similar to the better known species. *Leishmania chamaeleonis* was described by Wenyon from the cloaca of the lizard, *Chamaeleon vulgaris.* It is doubtful whether *L. chamaeleonis* is similar to the mammal-infecting species, because leptomonads appear to be the only form occurring in its life cycle. Furthermore, this species lives in its host's intestine. Other species of saurian leishmanias may occasionally leave the intestine and migrate into the blood. Still other species apparently have found the blood to be an ideal environment for these parasites are only found there. It may be postulated that the intestine- and blood-dwelling species are comparatively primitive and have not adapted to an intracellular existence. Little is known about the transmission of these presumably primitive leishmanias, although it is difficult to perceive how an invertebrate could serve as a vector for parasites that live in their host's intestine.

Stauber (1953 and later) has been successful in experimentally infecting chinchillas and hamsters with *Leishmania donovani* (see Stauber et al., 1954). Stauber has shown that infected hamsters exposed to high environmental temperatures of 34 to 35° C. are cured on some occasions. As in the case of numerous other pathogens, prolonged cultivation tends to reduce virulence.

The hamster is a favored experimental animal among investigators, because it usually does not develop age resistance to leishmanial infections. Furthermore, it does not show much natural immunity, although inoculations are not always successful. In the laboratory, the intraperitoneal or intracardial injection of a suspension or homogenate of infected spleen or liver in a physiologic saline solution is the usual technique for establishing experimental infections. The course of the infection, however, is dependent on the virulence of the strain of *Leishmania,* the susceptibility of the host, and the number of parasites introduced. If a virulent strain is introduced, the infected hamster generally becomes gravely ill in less than 1 month. On the other hand, if a less virulent strain is used, it may take 6 months before death occurs.

Since in nature the most common method of transmission of the human-infecting species of *Leishmania* is by way of sand-fly vectors, there is a certain degree of seasonal fluctuation in the number of new infections, correlated with the abundance and activity of the *Phlebotomus* flies.

IMMUNITY TO LEISHMANIASIS. Immunity to *Leishmania* has been studied by various investigators, primarily Stauber, who has reviewed the topic (Stauber, 1963). Leishmanias, especially *L. donovani,* are unusual in that they are entirely intracellular parasites in their host's reticuloendothelial system. Proteolytic enzymes that attack other invaders of the blood do not appear to destroy leishmanias. Within the macrophages, the parasites multiply by binary fission at an estimated rate of once in every 24 hours. Stauber has shown that in experimentally infected hamsters, the parasites accumulate rapidly in the spleen and liver, especially the liver. This rapid reproduction rate decreases sharply in the liver after 7 to 8 days. It has been suggested that cessation of reproductive activity is most probably due to the destruction of the originally infected cells. Thus, the parasites are released into the blood, where they are confronted with destructive forces (antibodies, etc.) for the first time. Similarly, the mouse and gerbil, if experimentally infected via intracardial injection with the leishmanial form of *L. donovani,* demonstrate significant acquired resistance.

If rats or rabbits are similarly infected, they are resistant. On the other hand, the golden hamster and cotton rat are highly susceptible. These findings suggest that different species of hosts possess variations in their abilities to produce immunity against the parasite. Hence, immunity, at least in part, may be responsible for host specificity. Then again, strain differences among both host and parasite also contribute to host specificity. Humans occasionally recover spontaneously from visceral leishmaniasis, while hamsters almost always die. Thus man appears to be more resistant than hamsters.

A certain degree of acquired resistance to reinfection does occur. Thus, successful vaccination of humans has been achieved by immunizing the host with living avirulent leptomonads of *Leishmania* of a rodent-infecting strain against subsequent infection by leptomonads of a human-infecting strain.

Although *L. donovani* often causes visceral leishmaniasis, *L. tropica* causes cutaneous leishmaniasis, and *L. brasiliensis* causes mucocutaneous leishmaniasis, the pathologies are not completely species specific because the extent of the infection does influence which tissues are infected.

Leptomonads.   The leptomonad form is elongate with a comparatively large nucleus. A short free-flowing flagellum arises from a blepharoplast and kinetoplast that are located near the anterior end of the body.

Genus *Leptomonas.*   Of the different genera belonging to the Trypanosomatidae, *Leptomonas* is probably the most primitive. During the life cycle of the members of this genus, these flagellates lose their free-flowing flagella, round up as leishmanial forms, and become cysts that are the infective forms. When cysts are ingested by a prospective host, excystment occurs. Each escaping organism develops a new flagellum and the typical elongate shape of the adult is attained. Under certain conditions, the flagellum of the adult may be lost and the body becomes attached to the epithelial cells lining the host's gut.

Leptomonas ctenocephali (Plate 3–9, Fig. 4) is a parasite found in the hindgut of the dog flea, *Ctenocephalides canis.* The leptomonad form

usually is found in the foregut. When the parasite reaches the hindgut, it takes on the leishmanial form. The leishmanial form is passed out in the feces of the host and later infects a new host when it is ingested, in the encysted form, by another larval flea. Other species of *Leptomonas* include *L. bütschlii,* the first known, in the gut of the nematode *Trilobus gracilis; L. patellae* in insects; and *L. pyraustae* in corn borers. Most *Leptomonas* species appear to be commensals; however, Paillot (1927) reported a pathologic condition in the European corn borer, *Pyrausta nubilalis,* caused by *Leptomonas pyraustae.* The gut apparently is the primary site of infection, but cases are known in which the flagellate has invaded the surrounding tissues.

The question of the validity of the genus *Leptomonas* has been raised, because some protozoologists suspect that these forms are actually immature representatives of *Herpetomonas,* a genus in which the organisms actually reach the trypanosomal form.

Genus *Phytomonas.*   Members of the genus *Phytomonas* are morphologically similar to members of *Leptomonas.* The distribution of the various species is worldwide. They are found both in insect vectors, usually a hemipteran, and in the ductlike vacuoles within the latex cells of plants with milky juices (families Euphorbiaceae, Asclepiadaceae, Urticaceae, Moraceae, Compositae, and Apocynaceae). The infection is transmitted from plant to plant via the insect vector. Within the vacuoles of the plant latex cells, these organisms, in the leptomonad form, feed on the milky substance and multiply by longitudinal fission. They die within the cell if not rescued by an insect vector. If ingested by a vector, they take on the leishmanial form and may aggregate as "somatella" or form chains.

Phytomonas also undergoes longitudinal fission within the gut of the insect vector and leptomonad forms appear in the salivary glands, ready to be introduced into another plant host. The transfer of leishmanial forms from insect to insect has been reported.

Phytomonas davidi and *P. elmassiani* are two rather typical members of this genus. *P. davidi* measures 15 to 20 μ by approximately 1.5 μ (Plate 3–9, Fig. 5). The posterior end of its elongate body (leptomonad form) is often twisted three or four times. *Stenocephalus agilis, Dieuches humilis,* and *Nysius euprorbiae* are the insect transmitters. *P. elmassiani* (Plate 3–9, Fig. 6) is 9 to 20 μ long and possibly is transmitted by *Oncopelus fasciatus.*

Some degree of vector specificity and plant-host specificity is recognized among *Phytomonas* spp. Holmes (1925) recorded that *P. elmassiani*, when ingested by an abnormal host, undergoes abnormal division resulting in small budlike nonflagellated cells clustered around a free-flowing flagellum. Such buds, when stained, reveal a nucleus and blepharoplast, but no flagellum.

Crithidia. The crithidial form is elongate and similar to the leptomonad form except that the blepharoplast is more posteriorly located, being immediately anterior to the nucleus. Also, the presence of an inconspicuous undulating membrane has been reported.

GENUS *Crithidia*. The genus *Crithidia* includes those species parasitic in arthropods and various other invertebrates. In the adult stage, members of this genus differ from leptomonads in the position of the blepharoplast and the point of flagellar origin. As with leptomonads, there is a leishmanial stage during the life cycle, which eventually becomes situated within a spherical cyst that is passed out in the feces of its host. Ingestion of cysts by another susceptible host is the mechanism of infection. Upon entering the new host, excystment occurs and the emerging parasite develops a new free-flowing flagellum, passing through a temporary leptomonad stage during the process. The parasite finally develops into a typical crithidia. Instances are known in which attached forms occur, as in the genus *Leptomonas*.

Crithidia fasciculata (Plate 3–9, Fig. 7) is found in the intestine of the mosquito *Anopheles maculipennis*. The leishmanial form is found in the host's hindgut. A cyst wall is formed prior to its passage out of the host. *C. gerridis* is a parasite of the common water bug *Gerris fossarum*.

Trypanosomes. The trypanosomal form is elongate. The blepharoplast and kinetoplast are located at or near the posterior end of the body. The flagellum arising from the blepharoplast is directed anteriorly, running underneath the body surface and thus forming the outer margin of the undulating membrane. The flagellum protrudes anteriorly as a free-flowing structure.

GENUS *Trypanosoma*. The genus *Trypanosoma* includes literally hundreds of species, all blood and lymph parasites of vertebrates and invertebrates. Determination of the various species is one of the most frustrating and difficult operations, because morphologically many different "species" are identical but are found naturally in different hosts and hence are generally considered host-specific species (p. 20). In addition to species similarities, trypanosomes tend to be pleomorphic (possessing many forms). This is particularly true among the species that infect amphibians. Lehmann (1959) described such a case in *Trypanosma granulosae*, a haemoflagellate of a newt (Plate 3–10). He described the narrow, medium, broad, and "tadpole" forms, all of which are quite different in appearance. Often the appearance of the nucleus, its distance from the anterior end of the body, and the shape and position of the blepharoplast are used as morphological diagnostic characteristics, because these criteria are somewhat consistent. More often, host specificity and serologic differences are used in the determination of species.

During the life cycle of *Trypanosoma* spp., the organisms attain the leishmanial, leptomonad, crithidial, and trypanosomal forms. The first three forms are found in the vector, if one exists, and the trypanosomal form in the definitive host.

The biology of *T. lewisi*, a widely distributed parasite of rats, is elucidated here because we know more about this species, which has been studied critically by a number of investigators (Plate 3–11, Fig. 1).

LIFE CYCLE OF *Trypanosoma lewisi*. The rat becomes infected while licking its fur. During this process freshly deposited rat flea feces

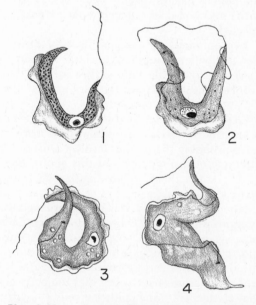

Plate 3–10   **Pleomorphism in *Trypanosoma granulosae*. 1.** The narrow form of *T. granulosae*. **2.** The medium form of *T. granulosae*. **3.** The broad form of *T. granulosae*. **4.** The "tadpole" form of *T. granulosae*. (All Figs. redrawn after Lehmann, 1959. J. Protozool., *6*: 167.)

including parasites are ingested. After several hours of incubation, the trypanosomes appear in the circulating blood as extracellular parasites. These multiply rapidly by longitudinal and multiple fission for a week or more, often resulting in rosette formation (Plate 3–11, Fig. 2). When the specific flea, *Ceratophyllus fasciatus,* feeds on the rat's blood, it also takes in the circulating trypanosomes. Approximately 25 per cent of the ingested trypanosomes persist in the flea, and each one penetrates an epithelial cell lining the host's stomach. Within the cell, the flagellate curls up and eventually becomes rounded. Sporulation (asexual reproduction) occurs within its enlarged and rounded body, resulting in many small trypanosomal forms. These enlarge and rupture out of the cell and become active within the flea's gut, seeking another cell to penetrate and thus repeat the sporogonic cycle. Eventually those free in the intestinal lumen metamorphose into the crithidial form and migrate posteriorly to the rectal region, some simultaneously undergoing longitudinal fission. In the rectum the crithidia attach themselves to the lining and become pleomorphic while undergoing longitudinal fission. Finally, some take on the trypanosomal form and are passed out in the host's feces. Infection of another rat is initiated when contaminated feces of an infected flea is ingested by that rat or introduced into the wound caused by a flea bite. The second type of transmission is known as mechanical transmission. A rat, once infected, becomes immune to reinfections even long after the parasite has disappeared from its blood.

The development of *Trypanosoma lewisi* in the posterior portion of the gut of the insect host is characteristic of a group of trypanosomes, including *T. melophagium* of sheep in sheep ticks, *T. theileri* of cattle in tabanids, and *T. cruzi* of man and other animals in triatomid bugs. This "posterior station" type of development is believed to be the more primitive as compared with the "anterior station" type of development of African sleeping sickness trypanosomes. The anterior station type of development is discussed on p. 71.

In the laboratory, experimental infection of rats can be readily achieved through intraperitoneal injection of two or three drops of blood from an infected rat suspended in citrated physiological saline to prevent clotting. This technique for the transfer of infection, which does not involve development in an insect host, has its counterpart in nature. Vectors with con-

Plate 3-11   *Trypanosoma lewisi* from rat blood. **1.** *T. lewisi,* single specimen. **2.** Rosette formation of *T. lewisi* in blood of rat host. (Drawn from slides prepared by R. F. Gartner.)

taminated mouthparts can transmit trypanosomes from one host to another without the flagellates passing through the gut-developmental stages in the vector.

The relative ease with which *T. lewisi* can be maintained in the laboratory in albino rats, although periodic transfers to new hosts are necessary, has provided the researcher with an ideal experimental situation. As a result, much has been learned about the physiology of these trypanosomes.

ANTIBODIES IN INFECTED RATS.   Multiplication of trypanosomes in the blood of a rat decreases in approximately 6 days after the infection because of the appearance of a reproduction-inhibiting antibody, ablastin (Taliaferro, 1924, 1932). The existing flagellates soon begin to decrease in number because a trypanocidal antibody, produced primarily by the host's spleen, destroys them. Generally none of the trypanosomes can be found after 3 weeks, although a few cases of longer periods of infection are known (Table 3-3). The production of ablastin represents the host's reaction to the metabolic products of the trypanosomes rather than the host's reaction to the parasites themselves, for ablastin production can be induced by immunization with the metabolic products entirely free of trypanosomes. Ablastin inhibits reproduction by interfering with nutritional and respiratory processes in that it blocks the synthesis of proteins and nucleic acids.

Ablastin has been demonstrated to be transmissible from mother rat to her offspring through the milk.

PATHOGENICITY.   *Trypanosoma lewisi* has no visible effect on the rat host and as a result of the appearance of ablastin and the trypano-

Table 3-3. Number of *Trypanosoma lewisi* in Blood of Rat Host After Experimental Infection

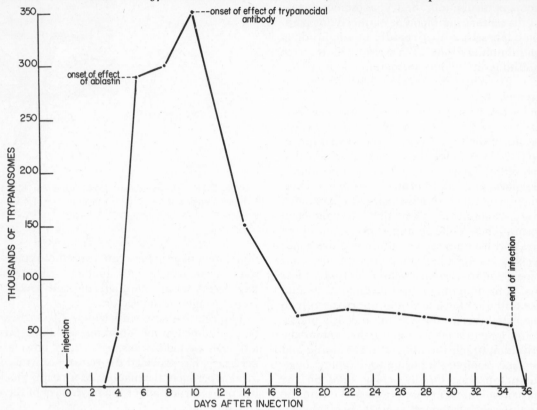

(After Taliaferro, 1932.)

cidal antibody, the infection soon dies out. However, if *T. equiperdum,* a haemoflagellate of horses, is introduced into the rat, it is able to reproduce without being inhibited and generally kills the host within a week. The cause for this striking difference in the pathogenicity of the two species remains uncertain, although it is at least in part due to genetic differences that are manifested as metabolic differences. One such difference has to do with carbohydrate metabolism. Pathogenic trypanosomes are generally greater consumers of carbohydrates than non-pathogenic species, but they fail to oxidize the carbohydrates completely. A heavy burden is thus placed on the carbohydrate reserves of the host, and possibly because of toxic by-products, the host's carbohydrate metabolism is interfered with. In horses, *T. equiperdum* produces a chronic disease with eventual involvement of the nervous system and subsequent death.

Vitamin deficiencies in the host may increase the pathogenicity of trypanosomes. For example, Becker and co-workers in 1947 demonstrated that *T. lewisi* can become pathogenic in rats deficient in pantothenic acid.

TRYPANOSOMES IN HOMOLOGOUS AND HETEROL-OGOUS HOSTS. An animal in which a parasite is normally or naturally found is referred to as a *homologous host.* An animal that is artificially or experimentally infected is known as a *heterologous host.* For instance, the rat is the homologous host for *Trypanosoma lewisi,* while mice and other animals are heterologous hosts. Certain heterologous hosts, such as mice for *T. lewisi,* can sustain the parasite, although less efficiently. Other heterologous hosts are completely refractive—that is, they do not sustain the parasite. Determination of conditions necessary to infect normally refractive heterologous hosts with trypanosomes can give valuable insight into the nature of trypanosome-host adaptations. The infection of normally refractive rats with *T. vivax,* and partially refractive mice with *T. lewisi,* has been facilitated by inoculation of normal-host serum. Desowitz (1963) has summarized such experiments and concluded that the component of normal-host serum that enhances the growth of the parasite in the case of *T. vivax,* and most probably in the case of *T. lewisi,* is a protein. It is believed that this protein present in normal-host serum (bovine, goat, and sheep in the case of *T. vivax*) protects the flagellate against the antibody elaborated by the rat. Thus it appears that host-parasite adaptation, at least in this instance, may depend upon the specific absorption of a layer of the host's serum protein that protects, in part, against an antibody.

In addition to providing protection against the antibody of a heterologous host, the specific nutritional or enzymatic contributions of normal-host serum may also be operative.

Once trypanosomes become adapted to an initially refractive or semirefractive heterologous host, drastic changes in the parasite's biology often result. There may be an alteration of virulence for the normal host as well as loss of the parasite's capability to undergo cyclical transmission in the arthropod vector. Changes in the trypanosome's antigenic constitution, metabolism, drug sensitivity, and even morphology may also result from the parasite's adaptation to the abnormal host.

AFRICAN HUMAN TRYPANOSOMIASIS. The manifestation of African human trypanosome infection is the sleeping sickness. Although trypanosomes were first discovered in 1841, human and animal trypanosomiasis are ancient diseases that have scourged mankind in Africa for centuries. To see Africans lying prostrate, drooling from the mouth, insensitive to pain, and later dying must have been a common occurrence to early slave traders. Without doubt trypanosomes have been introduced into North America and other parts of the world by infected slaves. Fortunately, the absence of compatible vectors has prevented the spread of this disease.

Although on the decline, primarily because of the introduction of modern insecticides and control techniques that have removed insect vectors, trypanosomiasis is by no means eradicated. Not only does human trypanosomiasis hinder human endeavors, but animal trypanosomiasis tends to deplete the land of both domesticated animals and game, which indirectly affects civilizations dependent on such animals for food and as beasts of burden. One can justifiably claim that trypanosomiasis is one of the primary reasons for the lack of advancement in endemic areas of Africa.

On the other hand, ironically, these parasitic flagellates have played important roles in advancing science. Observations on trypanosomes gave Ehrlich the idea that specific drugs could be found that would attack specific pathogens. His pursuance of this concept led to his discovery of "606" to combat syphilis. It was also through the study of trypanosomes that the concept of drug resistance by microorganisms became known.

The two human-infecting species of African trypanosomes are *T. rhodesiense* and *T. gambiense*. *Trypanosoma rhodesiense,* the causative agent of the virulent East African or Rhodesian sleeping sickness, is endemic to southeastern coastal Africa (Plate 3–12, Fig. 3). It is a typical trypanosome, tapering at both ends, measuring 15 to 30 μ by 1 to 3 μ. The blepharoplast is situated near the posterior end of the body. The common insect vector is the tsetse fly, *Glossina morsitans*. In addition to parasitizing man, this species is found in wild game and domestic animals in endemic areas. The reservoir hosts serve as sources of new infections. Some investigators believe that *T. rhodesiense* is a virulent strain of *T. gambiense* because morphologically the two species cannot be distinguished. Most parasitologists, however, consider the two species distinct, because when *T. rhodesiense* is experimentally inoculated into rats, the nucleus shifts to a posterior position, near or behind the blepharoplast, and the body is shortened. This does not happen when *T. gambiense* is introduced into rats.

Trypanosoma gambiense causes Gambian or Central African sleeping sickness (Plate 3–12, Fig. 4). The disease is confined to central Africa, on each side of the equator. Domestic and wild animals, such as pigs, antelopes, buffaloes, and reed bucks, serve as reservoir hosts. Experimentally, *T. gambiense* has been introduced into rats, and amazingly enough, organisms have been found in the placental blood of infected rats as well as in the livers of embryos. Transplacental infections, however, are not common, although such cases are known even in humans. The introduction of *T. gambiense* into the circulation of the vertebrate host is usually through the bite of *Glossina palpalis* and *G. tachinoides*. The mechanism of transmission differs from that of *T. lewisi* but is identical to that of *T. rhodesiense* in that the flagellate is introduced through the bite, for the infective form is in the salivary glands and not in the feces, although infection through the feces has also been reported. In addition to being a blood parasite, *T. gambiense* also invades the lymphatic glands and the central nervous system.

ANTERIOR STATION DEVELOPMENT. Development of the *lewisi* group of trypanosomes in the posterior portion of the insect vector's gut (p. 69) is referred to as *posterior station development,* characteristic of the more primitive species. African human trypanosomes, on the other hand, possess *anterior station development* within tsetse flies. Actually, three groups of anterior station trypanosomes can be recognized as forming an evolutionary series: (1) The *vivax* group consists of *T. vivax* of cattle, sheep, goats, and horses, from tsetse flies, and *T. uniforme* of cattle, sheep, and goats, from tsetse flies. This group develops only in the proboscis of the vector. (2) The *congolense* group consists of *T. congolense* of horses, cattle, and sheep, from tsetse flies; *T. dimorphon* of horses, from tsetse flies; and *T. simiae* of monkeys, from tsetse flies. Trypanosomes of this group first enter the stomach of the vector upon ingestion. Later they migrate anteriorly to the pharynx. (3) The *brucei* group includes *T. brucei* of horses, mules, etc., from tsetse flies; the two African human-infecting species, *T. rhodesiense* and *T. gambiense,* from tsetses; *T. suis* of pigs from tsetses; and *T. evansi* of horses, mules, donkeys, cattle, camels, and elephants, from tabanids and other bloodsucking flies. Trypanosomes of this group first enter the vector's stomach, where some development occurs. They then move forward and invade the salivary glands, where the infective metacyclic forms develop.

"Anterior station" trypanosomes infect the vertebrate host via the vector's bites.

AMERICAN HUMAN TRYPANOSOMIASIS. In 1909, Chagas found that the thatched roof huts in the villages of the state of Minas Gerais, Brazil, were infested with large blood-sucking bugs, *Panstrongylus megistus,* which were infected with flagellates. When he inoculated the flagellates into guinea pigs and monkeys, an acute infection developed. Later surveys revealed that among infants and young children inhabiting the infested huts, an acute disease characterized by fever, swollen glands, anemia, and nervous disturbances prevailed. Today we know this disease is the American form of trypanosomiasis caused by *Trypanosoma cruzi.*

Trypanosoma cruzi* is a smaller species, being

---

* *Trypanosoma cruzi* is also referred to as *Schizotrypanum cruzi,* because many investigators believe it to be different from members of genus *Trypanosoma. T. cruzi* multiplies intracellularly in the leishmanial form and takes on the trypanosomal form before being liberated from the cell. In genus *Trypanosoma,* free trypanosomes in the lymph or blood undergo multiplication.

C or U shaped and averaging 20 μ in length (Plate 3–12, Fig. 5). Unlike other trypanosomes, *T. cruzi* is never found dividing in the blood of its mammalian host. Furthermore, it can become established as an intracellular parasite in greatly swollen cells in various tissues of man, especially in heart cells, striated muscles, the central nervous system, and in glands. As an intracellular parasite, *T. cruzi* assumes the leishmanial form and undergoes rapid division resulting in numerous individuals. These individuals later change to the trypanosomal form and escape into the blood when the cells of the host rupture. In chronic cases of *T. cruzi* infections, the trypanosomal form is not seen in the blood, because the haemal antibodies readily kill these parasites. However, large numbers of these trypanosomes can be demonstrated in tissue cells, where they are apparently protected from the serum antibodies. In order to survive, trypanosomes rupturing out of cells must invade another cell almost immediately, before they are affected by the antibodies.

The insect vector is usually the cone-nosed or kissing bug, *Panstrongylus megistus,* or a few closely related species. However, *T. cruzi* is not very host specific as far as the insect vector is concerned. The parasite can develop not only in almost all species of reduviid bugs, but also in bedbugs, ticks, and even in the body cavity of caterpillars.

The disease caused by *T. cruzi* is known as South American trypanosomiasis or Chagas' disease. It is mainly a disease of infants and children and is widely distributed in Central and South America. In nature, cats, dogs, bats, armadillos, rodents, and other mammals have been found to be reservoir hosts. Animal infections are known to exist in southern and western United States and have recently been reported in raccoons in Maryland. This flagellate can be introduced into a large variety of mammals under experimental conditions.

Within the invertebrate host, which becomes infected by ingesting infected blood, the trypanosomes undergo longitudinal fission in the stomach and intestine and assume the crithidial form while continuing to multiply. After 8 to 10 days, the infective forms (known as metacyclic forms) appear in the vector's rectal area and are therefore of the "posterior station" type. The metacyclic forms are passed out in feces. Infection of the vertebrate host is accomplished in the same fashion as in *Trypanosoma*

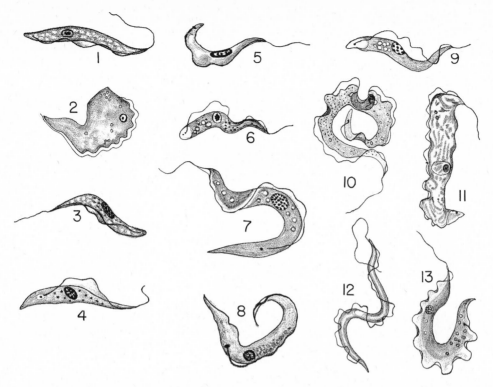

Plate 3-12   Representative species of *Trypanosoma*. 1. *T. duttoni* from mice. **2.** *T. rotatorium* from frogs. **3.** *T. rhodesiense* from experimentally infected rat. **4.** *T. gambiense* from experimentally infected rat. **5.** *T. cruzi* from experimentally infected rat. **6.** *T. brucei* from mule. **7.** *T. theileri* from cattle. **8.** *T. melophagium* from sheep. **9.** *T. evansi* from horse. **10.** *T. granulosum* from the eel, *Anguilla vulgaris*. **11.** *T. percae* from *Perca fluviatilis*. **12.** *T. diemyctyli* from the newt, *Triturus*. **13.** *T. giganteum* from *Raja oxyrhynchus*.

(All Figs. redrawn from original preparations and from others including Kudo, Minchin, Hegner, and Neuman.)

lewisi—that is, the feces are rubbed into the wound caused by the bite, or into the eyes or mucous membranes in human infections, or by ingesting the feces or infected vectors in animal infections.

TRYPANOSOMES OF OTHER ANIMALS. *Trypanosoma brucei* is extremely pleomorphic (Plate 3–12, Fig. 6). This parasite averages 20 μ in length and is transmitted to donkeys, horses, mules, camels, cattle, and dogs, by various species of tsetse flies, primarily *Glossina morsitans*. This trypanosome is extremely virulent to domestic animals, especially horses and camels, and the disease, known as "nagana", is generally lethal. Various wild animals are infected in nature, particularly antelopes, in which the parasite produces a benign infection. Most mammals can be infected except for baboons and man. *T. brucei* is endemic to areas of Africa where *Glossina* spp. thrive.

Some parasitologists are of the opinion that because of the morphological and life cycle similarities, *T. rhodesiense* is a highly modified form that has developed from *T. brucei*.

Trypanosoma theileri (= *T. americanum*) is a North American parasite of cattle (Plate 3–12, Fig. 7). Its body measures 17 to 25 μ in length, and in vitro cultures show it to take on only the crithidial form. Myonemes have been demonstrated within the cytoplasm. It is apparently nonpathogenic and is transmitted by the biting tabanid flies. *T. melophagium* is a parasite of sheep (Plate 3–12, Fig. 8). The body is 50 to 60 μ long with delicate drawn out ends. Infection is established when sheep ingest the sheep ked, *Melophagus ovinus*, or its feces. The infective trypanosome is not transmitted by the bite of the insect. The organism generally disappears in sheep 1 to 3 months after the keds have been eradicated. *T. evansi*, the causative agent of the fatal disease "surra" in camels in North Africa, is known also to parasitize horses, dogs, cattle, donkeys, and mules (Plate 3–12, Fig. 9). The disease is transient in cattle.

Other important species of *Trypanosoma* include *T. equinum,* the causative agent of acute "mal de caderas" among horses in South America; and *T. equiperdum,* the causative agent of the chronic disease dourine in various parts of the world including the United States. Unlike the other species of *Trypanosoma, T. equiperdum* does not require a vector but is transmitted directly during coitus. Infections can be transmitted in the laboratory through injection of infected blood. Furthermore, it has been demonstrated that it can be mechanically transmitted by stable- and horseflies.

Two other species, *T. duttoni* and *T. rotatorium* are commonly encountered in the laboratory (Plate 3–12, Figs. 1 and 2). The first is a blood parasite of mice and is often used in experimental work. As in *T. lewisi* infections, the reproduction-inhibiting ablastin and the trypanocidal antibody have both been shown to be present in mice infected with *T. duttoni* (Taliaferro, 1938). *T. rotatorium* is found in the blood of tadpoles and frogs. The leech, *Placobdella marginata,* has been shown to be the vector in some areas.

Trypanosomes sometimes injure their invertebrate hosts. Grewal (1957) reported that *T. rangeli,* when introduced into the bug *Rhodnius prolixus,* causes severe damage. During the first nymphal instars of this bug, the trypanosomes inhibit molting. When this species is introduced into bedbugs, the pathogenicity is even greater, causing significant numbers of these invertebrate hosts to die.

FAMILY CRYPTOBIIDAE. The family Cryptobiidae, which includes the genus *Cryptobia* (Plate 3–13, Fig. 1), is characterized by two flagella, one free and the other forming an undulating membrane. Most species of this family are parasites of the reproductive organs of invertebrates, primarily molluscs, although *Cryptobia borreli* and *C. cyprini* are found in the blood of fish.

FAMILY BODONIDAE. The family Bodonidae is characterized by two flagella, originating at the anterior end of the body, one directed anteriorly and the other trailing. There is no undulating membrane present. The parasitic members of this family include *Proteromonas,* found in the digestive tract of various lizards, and *Embadomonas* found primarily in the gut of arthropods (Plate 3–13, Figs. 2 and 3). *Embadomonas intestinalis* has been described from a human alimentary tract, probably from the colon. This species is a harmless commensal. Its cyst resembles that of *Chilomastix* but is only half as large and usually appears to have a simpler internal structure. Chandler suggested that *E. intestinalis* may be an insect symbiont that has been accidentally introduced into the human through ingestion of an infected insect. The type species of the genus is a parasite of crane flies. Those interested in the taxonomy of the Bodonidae should consult the paper by Hollande (1952).

ORDER POLYMASTIGIDA

Members of order Polymastigida consist of all the Zoomatigophorea that bear 3 to 8 or more flagella. Axostyles, costa, and crista are found in various species.

Although this order has been of considerable interest to parasitologists, the so-called parasitic members should actually be considered commensals rather than true parasites. Reproduction is asexual—through binary and multiple fission—and sexual in a few species.

The gut-dwelling genera include *Mixotricha* in termites of Australia (Plate 3–13, Fig. 4). It is suspected that this flagellate practices mutualism, digesting cellulose for its host, for wood chips have been reported in its body cytoplasm. *Enteromonas,* a four-flagellated form (three directed anteriorly, one trailing), is parasitic in mammals and is transmitted from one host to another in the encysted form. *Enteromonas hominis* is a widely distributed species commonly found in diarrheic stools of humans (Plate 3–13, Fig. 5). *Chilomastix* (Plate 3–13, Fig. 6) with various pyriform species (*C. mesnili* in humans, *C. intestinalis* in guinea pigs, *C. cuniculi* in rabbits, and *C. gallinarum* in chickens) is characterized by three anteriorly directed flagella and a fourth within a cytostomal cleft. Transmission of the various species is via the encysted form. The pear shaped *C. mesnili,* 5 to 20 μ long, is widely distributed, being found in diarrheic feces of man and pigs. The nonpathogenic *C. gallinarum,* 10 to 13 μ long, is commonly encountered in poultry. The genus *Callimastix* includes species that possess 12 to 15 long flagella, which vibrate in unison (Plate 3–14, Fig. 1). The better known species include *C. frontalis,* found in the intestine of ruminants, and *C. equi,* found in horses. Neither species is pathogenic. One species, *C. cyclopis,* is known from the body cavity of *Cyclops.*

GENUS Trichomonas. The genus *Trichomonas* includes an interesting group of flagellates.

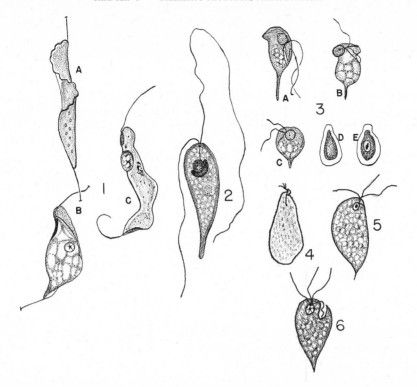

Plate 3-13   Parasitic flagellates. 1. A. *Cryptobia borreli* from the blood of various fishes. (Redrawn after Mavor, 1915.) **B.** *Cryptobia helicis* from reproductive organ of pulmonate snails. (Redrawn after Kozloff, 1948.) **C.** *Cryptobia borreli;* fixed and stained specimen. (Redrawn after Mavor, 1915.) **2.** *Proteromonas lacertae* from the gut of lizards. (Redrawn after Kühn.) **3. A.** *Embadomonas gryllotalpae* from intestine of the mole cricket *Gryllotalpa gryllotalpa.* (Redrawn after Wenrich, 1932.) **B.** *E. blattae* from colon of cockroaches. (Redrawn after Wenrich, 1932.) **C.** *E. intestinalis* from intestine of humans. (Redrawn after Wenyon, 1926.) **D.** Unstained cyst of *E. intestinalis.* **E.** Stained cyst of *E. intestinalis.* **4.** *Mixotricha paradoxa* from gut of termites. (Redrawn after Sutherland, 1933.) **5.** *Enteromonas hominis* from human intestine. **6.** *Chilomastix mesnili* from human intestine.

Grassé (1952) has listed all the known species, along with those of related genera. Students interested in identification should consult this volume. The species possess four anteriorly directed flagella and a fifth that is posteriorly directed and that forms the outer margin of an undulating membrane. Costae and axostyles are present.

Three species of *Trichomonas* are known to parasitize man although only one, *T. vaginalis,* appears to be pathogenic. The other two human-infecting species are *T. tenax* from the mouth and *T. hominis* from the colon. A rather high proportion of the world's population harbors one or more of these three species. Although no exact figures are available, various conservative samplings suggest that 25 per cent of women and 10 per cent of men are infected with *T. vaginalis;* 10 per cent of the population harbor *T. tenax;* and 2 per cent harbor *T.*

hominis. In addition to man, various simians are infected with these three species of *Trichomonas,* with *T. hominis* being the most common and *T. vaginalis* being relatively rare. It would appear very likely that both human and simian hosts have inherited these parasites, so to speak, from their common ancestral stock.

The three human-infecting species of *Trichomonas* are quite similar morphologically, although Wenrich, who has studied these organism rather extensively, suggests that certain obscure size differences are somewhat reliable in separating them. Furthermore, there appear to be physiological differences. For example, *T. vaginalis* seems to require a higher pH, ranging from 4 to 5, for optimum growth. It has been suggested that *T. tenax* was the first of the three to infect homonoids and that invasion of the colon by *T. hominis* was established when some of the more adaptable specimens of *T. tenax* were swallowed. The modern *T. vaginalis* may well have originated as a wanderer from the colon.

Trichomonas tenax (= *T. buccalis*) is a fairly common species found in the tartar and gum of the mouth (Plate 3–14, Fig. 3). It measures 5 to 12 μ long by 7 to 10 μ wide with four anteriorly situated flagella and an undulating membrane. *T. vaginalis,* measuring 7 to 23 μ long and 3 to 10 μ wide, also with four anterior flagella and an undulating membrane, is found in the vaginal tract of women, where it commonly causes inflammation and secretion (Plate 3–14, Fig. 4). This parasite is capable of secreting a toxic substance that injures cells grown in tissue culture. Although generally thought of as a parasite of women, *T. vaginalis* is fairly commonly found as an inhabitant of the male urinogenital tract and in the prostate. Infections in males are most probably acquired during intercourse.

Trichomonas hominis is a highly motile and flexible species that measures 5 to 14 μ long and 7 to 10 μ wide, with a cytostome near the anterior end and with three to five flagella (Plate 3–14, Fig. 2). As is the case with other *Trichomonas* species, no encysted form is known.

Transmission from the intestinal tract of one man to another is thought to be directly via the flagellated form. To validate this hypothesis, the eminent protozoologist Dobell swallowed a culture of a strain of *T. hominis* from a monkey, and he became infected. The apparent lack of cysts does not appear to be a handicap, because the trophozoites can endure considerable changes in environmental conditions although they cannot survive very well in highly diluted sewage. Hegner found that specimens could survive for at least 24 hours in feces-contaminated milk and suggested that transmission may well be through contaminated milk and other types of food and drink. In addition to being a parasite of man and simians, *T. hominis* can infect dogs, cats, mice, and other rodents. Such hosts serve as natural reservoirs in nature.

Experimental Morphology. Honigberg and Lee (1959), in a carefully conducted study on *Trichomonas tenax,* demonstrated that the sizes of this species can be modified in genetic strains by environmental factors, thus pointing out that size alone is not a good criterion for recognizing species. In the same study, these authors pointed out that during division, the

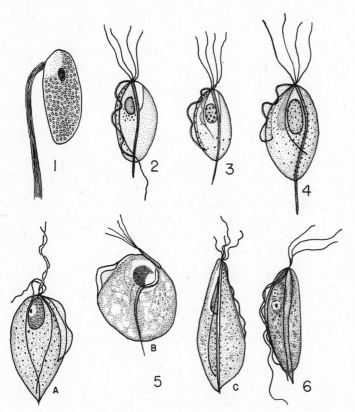

Plate 3-14   Representatives of the Polymastigida. 1. *Callimastix frontalis* from sheep. (Redrawn after Braune.) **2.** *Trichomonas hominis.* (Redrawn after Wenrich, 1944.) **3.** *Trichomonas tenax.* (Redrawn after Wenrich, 1944.) **4.** *Trichomonas vaginalis.* (Redrawn after Wenrich, 1944.) **5.** *Trichomonas gallinae* from various hosts. **A.** From a red-tailed hawk. **B.** From a turkey. **C.** From a domestic pigeon. (Redrawn after Stabler, 1941.) **6.** *Tritrichomonas foetus.* (Redrawn after Wenrich and Emmerson, 1933.)

four anterior parental flagella are equally distributed between the daughter mastigonts, two per daughter, and the full number is restored prior to complete division of the two bodies. Part of the original parental parabasal body is discarded early in the division; then two bodies are seen, one newly formed. Each daughter mastigont receives one such body and one daughter retains the undulating membrane and costa. The other daughter develops a new set of these organelles. The parental axostyle and pelta are not passed on; rather, each mastigont develops a new set of these supporting organelles. Supposedly the same mechanisms of division occurs in other flagellates.

Avian Trichomoniasis. In fowls, such as pigeons, turkeys, and chickens, *Trichomonas gallinae* is a fairly common parasite found in the upper digestive tract. This pear shaped flagellate, which measures 6.2 to 8.9 μ long, is the causative agent of avian trichomoniasis (Plate 3–14, Fig. 5). This disease is not fatal in some cases and yet extremely lethal in others, thus leading some parasitologists to believe that two strains exist. On the other hand, some suspect that this parasite has different effects on different hosts (Levine and Brandly, 1940), for new hosts (canaries, hawks, quails, and bobwhites) experimentally infected become ill. Stabler and Engley (1946), through a series of experiments, using bacteria-free cultures and bacteria-present cultures of *T. gallinae,* demonstrated that some of the squabs infected with the bacteria-free cultures died. The other type of culture had no drastic effect. These experiments strongly suggest that *T. gallinae* is only pathogenic in the absence of bacteria.

Various other species of *Trichomonas* are known in an array of hosts, including amphibians, rodents, and termites.

GENUS *Tritrichomonas.* In veterinary protozoology, *Tritrichomonas foetus* is an important pathogen, because infections in cows result in abortions by destruction of the placental attachments and the removal of the aborted fetus intact, and by the destruction of the fetal

---

*The number of anterior flagella among members of the genus *Trichomonas,* ranging from three to five, has caused some to consider the existence of three genera—*Tritrichomonas, Tetratrichomonas,* and *Pentatrichomonas. Tritrichomonas foetus* possessses three such flagella. This differentiation is essentially a taxonomic problem that is not considered here. Nevertheless, this bovine parasite is designated *Tritrichomonas foetus,* since the more recent veterinary journals and texts refer to it by this name.

membranes that are retained within the uterus (Plate 3–14, Fig. 6). In the first type of abortion, the cow may reconceive after the loss of the fetus; however, in the second type, the cow becomes permanently sterile as the result of chronic endometritis. Transmission of *T. foetus* infections occurs during copulation, and bulls are known to be susceptible. In males, the preputial cavity is the preferred site of infection. Once a bull becomes infected, the infection becomes permanent and can be transmitted to other cows during mating. Sheep, deer, and hampsters can also become infected with this flagellate.

GENUS *Giardia.* The genus *Giardia* of the Polymastigida is characterized by a blunt anterior terminal and a tapering posterior one (Plate 3–15, Fig. 1). The dorsal surface of the body is convex, and the ventral surface is flat or concave. There are two nuclei, two axostyles, and four pairs of flagella present. Cysts are known and transmission is via these. Numerous species of *Giardia* have been described from many vertebrates and even from one nematode. The hosts include tadpoles, frogs, many species of rodents, rabbits, man, and other primates, and other vertebrates. Unfortunately, the descriptions of most of the species have been based on the concept that a different host species must involve a different parasite species. Filice, in 1952, pointed out that the morphology of *Giardia* varies considerably with such factors as host diet. He considered many of the described species as "races."

Giardia intestinalis. Of the numerous species of *Giardia, G. intestinalis* (= *G. lamblia*) of man holds a prominent place. This flagellate, measuring 8 to 16 μ in length by 5 to 12 μ in width, is found in the small intestine, particularly in the duodenum and occasionally invading the bile ducts. In life, each individual holds on to the host's intestinal lining by employing its concave ventral body surface as a suction cup. Its distribution is cosmopolitan. Chandler has suggested that children are more apt to harbor this parasite than adults; however, infection among adults is fairly common. Rendtorff, for example, was able to infect 100 per cent of a group of adult men in the United States when 100 or more cysts were fed. He noted, however, that such experimentally introduced infections usually died out within 1 to 6 weeks. It has been suggested that this parasite may stimulate the production of some degree of resistance. This resistance is mani-

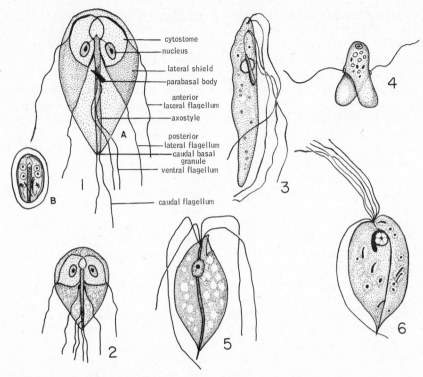

cytostome
nucleus
lateral shield
parabasal body
anterior
lateral flagellum
axostyle
posterior
lateral flagellum
caudal basal
granule
ventral flagellum
caudal flagellum

Plate 3-15   Parasitic polymastigids. 1. *Giardia intestinalis,* a human parasite. **A.** Trophozoite.
B. Cyst. (A and B redrawn after Simon, 1921.) **2.** *Giardia muris* trophozoite. **3.** *Karotomorpha bufonis*
from intestine of frogs and toads. (Redrawn after Grassé, 1952.) **4.** *Trepomonas agilis* from intestine
of amphibians. (Redrawn after Klebs.) **5.** *Eutrichomastix serpentis* from intestine of snakes. (Redrawn
after Kofoid and Swezy, 1915.) **6.** *Hexamastix termopsidis* from intestine of *Zootermopsis* spp. (Redrawn
after Kirby.)

fested in that even when there is constant exposure, only infrequent infections occur. If the
resistance declines, more frequent reinfections
ensue until the resistance is restimulated.

Although not an invader of tissue, *G. intestinalis* is considered a pathogen, because gastrointestinal symptoms and associated diarrhea
are common when these flagellates are present.
Véghelyi in 1939 found evidence of mechanical
interference with absorption, particularly of
interference with absorption through the intestinal wall, particularly of fats, as the result
of *Giardia* layered against the wall. Thus, there
is the potentiality of vitamin deficiencies
especially fat-soluble vitamins. Moreover,
heavy concentrations of this flagellate may
cause local irritation.

Encystment.   Although all the factors favoring the encystment of *Giardia* remain uncertain,
the lowering of the intestinal pH to about 6.7
in rats causes encystment to occur. On the
other hand, dilution of the feces and a short
exposure to normal body temperature apparently are sufficient to induce encystment.

Other Species of *Giardia*.   *Giardia muris,*
measuring 7 to 13 μ long, is a fairly common
parasite of rodents (Plate 3–15, Fig. 2). The
author recalls seeing thousands of these flagellates lining the intestinal wall of a white-footed
deer mouse in Virginia. *G. canis* and *G. cati* are
both fairly common species in dogs and cats
respectively and are commonly associated with
diarrhea.

Numerous other genera of the Polymastigida are known to be parasitic in various
vertebrates. A few representative forms are
depicted in Plate 3–15.

GENUS *Hexamita*.   Members of *Hexamita*
are closely related to those of *Giardia*. Their
bodies are pyriform and include two vesicular
nuclei located near the anterior end, one on
each side of the midsagittal plane. There are
eight flagella present; six originating anteriorly,
and two trailing. Two axostyles, which may be
tubular rather than rodlike, are present. *Hexamita* includes free-living as well as parasitic
species.

***Hexamita meleagridis*.**   Parasitic *Hexamita*

species include *H. meleagridis* (Plate 3–16, Fig. 1), found in the small intestine and sometimes in the caecum and bursa of Fabricius, of turkeys, various quails, pheasants, and partridges, which causes an infectious catarrhal enteritis known as hexamitosis in young birds. This parasite, measuring 6 to 12 μ in length by 2 to 5 μ in width, multiples by longitudinal fission. Transmission from one avian host to another is via feed and water contaminated with the fecal droppings of infected birds. Cysts of *H. meleagridis* have been reported but not confirmed, although certain other species of *Hexamita*—for example, *H. salmonis* (Plate 3–16, Fig. 2) in the intestine of various species of trout and salmon—are known to encyst.

Other Parasitic *Hexamita* species.   Other *Hexamita* species that are obligatory parasites include *H. columbae*, measuring 5 to 9 μ in length by 2.5 to 7 μ in width, found in the intestine of pigeons; *H. muris*, measuring 7 to 9 μ by 2 to 3 μ, found in the intestine of rats, mice, hamsters, and various wild rodents; and *H. intestinalis*, 10 to 16 μ long, found in the intestine of frogs (Plate 3–16, Fig. 3). A few species are parasites of invertebrates. For example, *H. cryptocerci*, measuring 8 to 13 μ by 4 to 5.5 μ, is found in the intestine of the woodroach *Cryptocercus punctulatus* (Plate 3–16, Fig. 4), and *H. periplanetae*, 5 to 8 μ long, is found in cockroaches.

Hexamita inflata.   Among the free-living species, which are generally found in stagnant water, *H. inflata* is of considerable interest to those interested in marine parasitology (Plate 3–16, Fig. 5). This flagellate is broadly oval with a truncate posterior end, and measures 13 to 25 μ by 9 to 15 μ. It is fairly commonly a saprobic member of the community of microorganisms found at the mud-water interface in coastal areas. It can become a facultative endoparasite of oysters, primarily found in the stomach, especially when anaerobic conditions and other environmental factors in oyster bed sediments reach such a level that the oysters are placed under stress.

Laird (1961) has suggested that hexamitiasis in oysters may be a major cause of mass oyster mortalities, especially if conditions continue to render the environment of oysters physiologically unfavorable, thus causing them to become progressively less resistant to facultative parasites. There is some disagreement as to whether *H. inflata* is the major organism lethal to oysters, for the so-called "MSX," which has

been tentatively identified as a haplosporidian sporozoa, may be more important than *H. inflata* as the lethal agent in Delaware and Chesapeake Bays (Shuster and Hillman, 1963). Nevertheless, an important ecological-parasitological principle has been established—that is, free-living organisms that can become facultative parasites can be of acute importance under certain conditions unfavorable to the host that render it increasingly less resistant to parasitism. Furthermore, the degree of harm inflicted by a parasite is influenced by the physiological state of the host, with those under certain types of stress usually being more vulnerable (p. 17).

Seasonal fluctuations in the number of *H. inflata* individuals parasitizing the American oyster *Crassostrea virginica* have been studied by Scheltema (1962). *Hexamita inflata* is most abundant in oysters (54.5 per cent) in the Delaware Bay during winter and early spring. By culturing *H. inflata* in the laboratory at different temperatures, Scheltema found that this flagellate multiplies at low temperatures, but its rate of reproduction increases with increasing water temperature up to a temperature of approximately 20° C. Temperatures above 25° C. are lethal. Because the metabolic rate of oysters is decreased at low temperatures, Scheltema postulated that during the winter and early spring when the temperature of water in Delaware Bay is low, the metabolism of the host is very low, and *H. inflata* is apparently capable of reproducing rapidly enough to be found in large numbers. During later spring and summer, however, when the host's metabolism is increased, its internal defense mechanisms (leukocytosis, phagocytosis) remove the parasite at a greater rate than the reproduction rate of the parasite. Thus, fewer parasites are present during warmer periods. If the metabolic rate of the oyster is reduced during the warm months, resulting from stress for example, large numbers of *Hexamita* are present because its reproductive rate is enhanced by the higher temperature, and at the same time the host is not as efficient at removing it. These physiological findings appear to corroborate Laird's hypothesis.

Many genera of intestinal polymastigid flagellates are mutualistic in the gut of various termites and woodroaches. These have been reported primarily by Kirby (1929, 1939, 1949), Dogiel (1916), Grassi (1917), Cleveland et al. (1934), Powell (1928), Sutherland (1933),

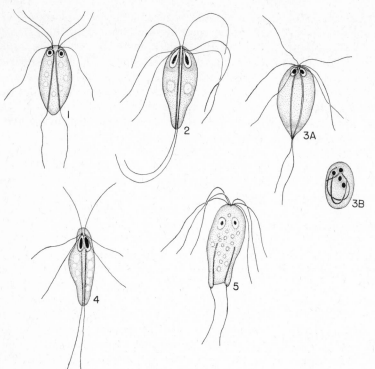

Plate 3-16   Representatives of the genus *Hexamita*. **1.** *H. mele-agridis* from a turkey. **2.** *H. salmonis* from intestine of trout. (Redrawn after Davis, 1925.) **3. A.** Trophozoite of *H. intestinalis* from intestine of frog. **B.** Cyst of *H. intestinalis*. (Redrawn after Alexeieff, 1912.) **4.** *H. cryptocerci* from intestine of *Cryptocercus punctulatus*. (Redrawn after Cleveland.) **5.** *H. inflata* from stomach of *Crassostrea virginica*.

and others. Limitation of space does not permit extensive discussion of these forms.

ORDER HYPERMASTIGIDA

The members of this order include all the multiflagellated species found in the alimentary tract of termites, woodroaches, and cockroaches. Each protozoan possesses one nucleus, and the many flagella are individually attached to numerous blepharoplasts located at the anterior region of the body. Reproduction is either asexual by binary and multiple fission, or sexual by the fusion of gametes. Asexual reproduction is by far the more common.

Generally the number of hypermastigotes per insect host is large. Various workers have estimated the fraction of the total weight of the host that these flagellates represent. Hungate (1939) estimated it to be one-seventh to one-fourth of the total weight of termite workers, and Cleveland (1925a) stated that it may be high as one-half. Katzin and Kirby (1939) estimated it to be one-third the total body weight. In any case, the number of flagellates is large and in the instances of the cellulose-digesting species found in termites of the families Kalotermitidae, Mastotermitidae, and Rhinotermitidae, the mutualistic relationship is essential to both host and flagellate.

Rigid host specificity occurs among the Hypermastigida. Flagellates of a specific host, when transferred to another (a process known as *transfaunation*), do not survive or survive only for a short period. The relationship between the host and the mutualist has become so firmly entrenched that definite correlations of the metabolic processes of both organisms exist. For example, at the time of ecdysis (molting) of the insect host, the protozoan fauna disappears and the postmolting host gains a new colony of flagellates through proctodeal feeding on other termites.

For those interested in the taxonomy of the Hypermastigida, a key to the eight families of the order and a listing of representative species are given by Kudo (1954). The order includes *Holomastigotes* characterized by a few spiral rows of flagella, *Spirotrichonympha* with 12 to 40 spiral rows of flagella, *Microspirotrichonympha* with spiral rows of flagella in the anterior half of the body only, *Joenia* with the anterior end capable of producing pseudopodia and with its body covered with immobile processes, *Staurojoenina* with four distinct tufts of flagella at the anterior end, *Kofoidia* with 8 to 16 permanently fused bundles of flagella known as loriculae, and *Teratonympha* with transverse ridges that give the appearance of metamerism (Plate

3-17, Figs. 1 to 7). All these genera are found in the intestine of termites.

The number of axostyles and flagella varies greatly among the Hypermastigida. For example, *Macrospironympha* possesses 36 to 50 axostyles; *Leptospironympha* possesses a single axostyle and two bands of spirally arranged flagella; *Barbulanympha,* members of which are acorn shaped, possesses 1500 to 13,000 flagella and 80 to 350 axostylar filaments; and *Rhynchonympha* has approximately 30 axostyles. All these genera are found in the woodroach *Cryptocercus punctulatus. Lophomonas,* among others, is found in the colon of cockroaches. Representatives of these genera are depicted in Plate 3-17.

PHYSIOLOGY OF PARASITIC FLAGELLATES

OXYGEN REQUIREMENTS

All parasitic protozoa can be grouped into two categories according to their oxygen requirements—aerobic types require some amount of molecular oxygen, and anaerobic types require none. Some anaerobic species are obligatory anaerobes—that is, they cannot utilize oxygen, and furthermore the presence of the slightest amount of oxygen is toxic. Other anaerobic species are facultative anaerobes—they can survive without molecular oxygen if it is not available. Krogh (1941) postulated that true anaerobic flagellates do not exist, because they require some amount of oxygen. This hypothesis is probably true, although many flagellates, such as those inhabiting the gut of termites, are extremely sensitive to molecular oxygen tensions and are readily killed when exposed to varying amounts of oxygen. Many such flagellates have been considered anaerobes. Very little oxygen exists in the gut of termites, for the molecular oxygen tension under the chitinous exoskeleton of insects is only 2 to 18 per cent of that found in air. In addition, these subskeletal areas have much more contact with the external environment than the gut. Nevertheless, even the slightest amount of oxygen could be sufficient for these microorganisms. Whether true obligatory anaerobes exist among the parasitic flagellates remains in doubt, although Hinshaw (1927) reported that *Trichomonas tenax* is one. At first this report may appear to be questionable, since *T. tenax* is known to live in the human buccal cavity, where oxygen abounds. However, von Brand (1946) successfully demonstrated that what little oxygen is present in the gingival crevices surrounding teeth is used up by the accompanying bacterial flora.

Various investigators have shown that some of the trichomonads can be cultured in vitro in serum with little or no oxygen. Willems et al. (1942) demonstrated that in cultures of *Trichomonas hepatica*, optimum respiration occurs when oxygen forms 5 to 10 per cent of the atmosphere. Forty per cent of the organisms died when cultured in the presence of air, and 75 per cent died when maintained in pure oxygen. These results indicate that this species should be considered a microaerobe—that is, requiring only trace quantities of oxygen. In the light of experiments such as this, Krogh's hypothesis may be correct, since many flagellates considered to be anaerobes may well be microaerobes or facultative anaerobes at best. Such is the case among certain trypanosomes that thrive best at low molecular oxygen tensions (Moulder, 1948).

Although oxygen consumption occurs among haemoflagellates, the rate of consumption varies between those found in the blood and those in tissue or culture forms. For example, 10^8 organisms of the blood forms of *Trypanosoma gambiense* consume 170 mm^3/hour of oxygen, while 10^8 organisms of the culture forms only consume 14 mm^3/hour. Tissue forms consume even less. In addition, various physical and chemical factors influence oxygen consumption. Although oxygen tension and ionic concentrations appear to have little effect, temperature and the availability of sugar have pronounced effects on oxygen consumption. Elevated temperatures are accompanied by greater consumption, up to a point. The abundance of glucose in the medium is correlated with a high rate of oxygen consumption. With the depletion of glucose in the medium, the respiratory rate declines and eventually becoming negligible.

The age of trypanosomes appears to influence the respiratory rate. For example, young dividing *Trypanosoma lewisi* show a lower oxygen consumption than older nondividing individuals. This phenomenon may be related to the presence of ablastin, which may interfere with the oxidative glucose metabolism of young individuals, since this antibody is produced early in the infection.

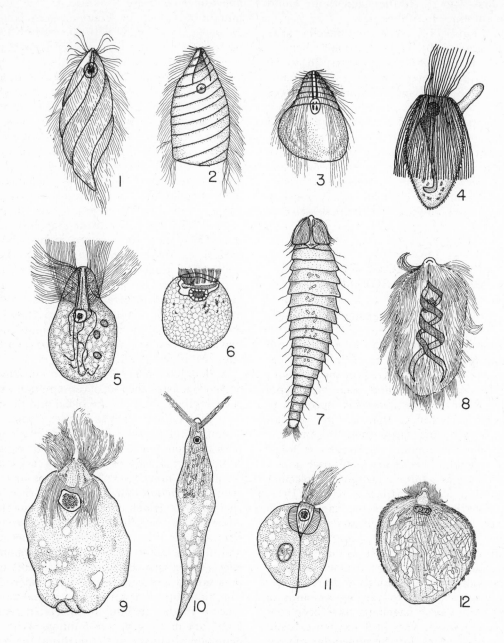

Plate 3-17   Parasitic hypermastigids. 1. *Holomastigotes elongatum* from gut of termites. (Redrawn after Koidzumi, 1921.) **2.** *Spirotrichonympha leidyi* from gut of termites. (Redrawn after Koidzumi, 1921.) **3.** *Microspirotrichonympha porteri* from gut of termites. (Redrawn after Koidzumi, 1921.) **4.** *Joenia annectens* from gut of termites. (Redrawn after Grassi and Foà, 1911.) **5.** *Staurojoenina assimilis* from gut of termites. (Redrawn after Kirby.) **6.** *Kofoidia loriculata* from gut of termites. (Redrawn after Light.) **7.** *Teratonympha mirabilis* from gut of termites. (Redrawn after Dogiel, 1916.) **8.** *Leptospironympha eupora* from gut of the woodroach, *Cryptocercus punctulatus*. (Redrawn after Cleveland et al., 1934.) **9.** *Barbulanympha ufalula* from gut of *Cryptocercus*. (Redrawn after Cleveland et al., 1934.) **10.** *Urinympha talea* from gut of *Cryptocercus*. (Redrawn after Cleveland et al., 1934.) **11.** *Lophomonas blattarum* from colon of the cockroach, *Blatta orientalis*. (Redrawn after Kudo.) **12.** *Eucomonympha imla* from gut of *Cryptocercus*. (Redrawn after Cleveland et al., 1934.)

Undoubtedly, ectoparasitic flagellates, such as *Oodinium ocellatum,* and the swarm cells of parasitic Phytomastigophorea are true aerobes, for they are continuously bathed in oxygenated water in their ecological habitats. The species of *Leishmania* can also be considered true aerobes, because in vitro cultures require the presence of molecular oxygen.

The sensitivities of various flagellates to molecular oxygen tension are not only interesting areas of study but have provided parasitologists with an ideal experimental tool. Cleveland (1925a, 1925b) demonstrated that when various hosts, such as termites, cockroaches, earthworms, frogs, goldfish, and salamanders, are placed in more than a normal abundance of oxygen, their endosymbionts are killed without the hosts themselves suffering any injury. This technique has provided workers with parasite-free hosts for experimental work. Cleveland also pointed out that the symbionts of different hosts vary in their response to various oxygen tensions. For example, the flagellates of *Leucotermes* are eliminated by an oxygen tension of 1 atmosphere within 24 hours, but those of *Reticulitermes* and *Cryptotermes* are still alive after 10 days when subjected to the same tension. The flagellates *Leptomonas* and *Polymastix* of cockroaches succumbed within 40 minutes. On the average, flagellate parasites are 67.5 times more susceptible than their hosts.

GROWTH REQUIREMENTS

Because of the relative ease with which flagellates can be cultured in vitro, more is known concerning the nutritional requirements of these protozoa. For many, a simple 1.5 per cent nutrient agar slant covered with sterile Ringer solution containing 1 to 20 parts horse serum is an effective culture medium. Unlike amoebae, many flagellates can be cultured in the absence of bacteria, thus eliminating the problem of determining what is actually being utilized by the protozoa and what by the bacteria. Recently, Lesser (1961) demonstrated that *Histomonas meleagridis* can be cultured in a bacteria-free medium. Prior to this, association with bacteria was thought to be necessary. In addition, Delappe (1953) reported that the addition of biotin (0.002 μg/ml of medium) results in better growth of this organism.

The addition of other materials to basic culture media is beneficial in the culture of a number of flagellates. Cailleau (1938 and earlier papers) demonstrated that *Tritrichomonas foetus* can be grown in human serum and *T. columbae* in pigeon serum only when cholesterol and ascorbic acid are added. The same investigator showed that in culturing *T. batrachorum,* cholesterol and linoleic acid are needed. Guthrie (1946), knowing that ascorbic acid is beneficial when added to *T. foetus* cultures, replaced this acid with thioglycolate and found that the growth was just as rich, thus suggesting that ascorbic acid per se is not the immediate requirement but its reducing ability is the beneficial property.

The common animal sterol, cholesterol, is not needed by free-living flagellates or by the more primitive parasitic flagellates, for example *Leptomonas* and *Strigomonas* (Lwoff, 1942), but is required by the more advanced forms, for example *Trichomonas* and *Eutrichomastix* (Cailleau, 1937). This sterol is not synthesized by the parasite but is derived from the host, which if a vertebrate or advanced invertebrate (molluscs and insects), can synthesize the substance. In fact, the particular type of sterol found in metazoans has been used to demonstrate phylogenetic relationships, and cholesterol utilization has been used with some degree of accuracy to determine phylogenetic relationships between parasitic flagellates.

Many other substances have been found to benefit the growth of flagellates. For example, Kupferberg et al. (1948) found that *Trichomonas vaginalis* requires pantothenic acid and shows a definite need for phosphates. Weiss and Ball (1947) found that *Tritrichomonas foetus* requires various amino acids, comparable to those required by higher animals except that the flagellate requires them in the amino acid form and cannot utilize complex proteins. If complex proteins are added to cultures, the growth rate declines.

Flagellates can incorporate amino acids from the host environment. Johnson (1962) demonstrated by paper chromatography that *Tritrichomonas foetus* includes 19 free amino acids in its protoplasm. Similar analyses of the ingredients in the medium on which the tritrichomonads were cultured revealed that identical amino acids are present except for one, β-alanine. These results suggest that the flagellate had absorbed these free amino acids from the medium. These amino acids could not have resulted from protein degradation, because proteolytic enzymes are absent in this parasite. It is possible, however, that these could have been synthesized since the presence of β-alanine, which was not present in the medium, suggests that it was synthesized.

Although the exact amino acid requirements of flagellates have been little studied, it is known that during the in vitro maintenance of *T. foetus,* the following amino acids are essential: arginine, glycine, histidine, isoleucine, leucine, lysine, methionine, phenylalanine, proline, serine, threonine, and valine.

Carbohydrate diets are generally more favorable to flagellates grown in vitro than proteins diets. This is borne out by the work of Westphal (1939), who demonstrated that growth of *Chilomastix* and *Enteromonas* is abundant when carbohydrates in digestible and readily absorbed forms are added to the media. As to exactly what sugars and related carbohydrates flagellates require appears to depend on the species. The findings of several investigators are listed in Table 3–4.

It is apparent that parasitic flagellates can utilize the simpler forms of fats, carbohydrates, and amino acids as energy sources but that carbohydrates in the form of the simpler sugars are favored. This is particularly true of trypanosomes. In their host's blood, glucose is the simple sugar normally available, and trypanosomes readily metabolize it. *T. cruzi,* however, appears to be the exception, because glucose consumption by the bloodstream form has never been demonstrated. *T. cruzi* maintained in culture, on the other hand, use glucose. There is no evidence that trypanosomes can derive energy from triglycerides of fatty acids or from lipoids in general. Lipases have not been demonstrated in these haemoflagellates.

Available information on the intermediary carbohydrate metabolism in trypanosomes is very incomplete. Although the presence of the Embden-Meyerhof glycolytic sequence (Table 3–5) is suggested in certain species, deviations do occur. The ability of trypanosomes to oxidize substrates other than carbohydrates suggests the existence of a nonglycolytic pathway.

Nonpathogenic trypanosome species, such as *T. lewisi,* are readily and simply cultured in bacteria-free media, while pathogenic species, such as *T. gambiense* and *T. rhodesiense,* are more difficult to culture and require blood or at least some haemoglobin in the media. In most instances, with members of the genus *Trypanosoma* and other Trypanosomatidae that require two hosts (invertebrate and vertebrate) only those forms found in the invertebrate host are present in in vitro cultures. Steinert (1958) demonstrated that *Trypanosoma mega* maintains the crithidial form in culture unless serum is added. When serum is added, the organism assumes the trypanosomal form. This investigator attributes the change in form to the presence of an exogenous factor, a transforming agent, that is found in the sera of various vertebrates; and an endogenous factor within the flagellate that determines the sensitivity of the crithidial form to the transforming agent.

Almost all trypanosomes and leishmanias of vertebrates cannot be satisfactorily maintained in culture in the complete absence of haemoglobin, either free or within erythrocytes. Furthermore, haematin, an iron salt of protoporphyrin found in blood, is indispensable. Although not conclusively demonstrated, it is suspected that haematin is essential to an iron-catalyzing enzyme system within the parasite. Ascorbic acid, normally present in erythrocytes, is also required, however, its definite role is not completely understood. It possibly serves to reduce the oxidation-reduction potential in the medium.

HOST–PARASITE RELATIONSHIPS

What does a parasite derive from and inflict on its host and vice versa? Besides mechanical damage and morphological change, the host-parasite relationship is often a physiological one. The diseases that such flagellates as *Trypanosoma gambiense* and *Leishmania donovani* cause have been discussed. Quite often, however, the effect of a parasite on its host is subclinical and nondamaging.

Lincicome (1963) has advanced the concept that a reciprocal exchange of chemical substances occurs between parasite and host. In *Trypanosoma lewisi* and its rat host, the enhanced growth of the host can be interpreted as evidence for a substance supplied by the parasite. Similarly, the enhanced growth of mice infected with *T. duttoni* serves as evidence. The environment provided by the host, in addition to providing growth requirements, represents evidence for the reciprocal arrangement.

Table 3-4. Carbohydrates and Related Compounds Utilized by Parasitic Flagellates*

Species	Pentoses			Hexoses				Disaccharides			Trisaccharide	Polysaccharides			Alcohols			Glucoside	Authorities
	Arabinose	Rhamnose	Xylose	Fructose	Galactose	Glucose	Mannose	Lactose	Maltose	Saccharose	Raffinose	Dextrin	Inulin	Soluble starch	Glycerol	Mannite	Sorbite	Amygdalin	
Trypanosoma equiperdum			△	▲	▲	▲	▲		▲										Plunkett (1946)
T. brucei					△	▲	▲		▲						▲		△		Kudicke and Evers (1924)
T. lewisi				▲		▲	▲		▲										Mercado (1947)
T. cruzi				▲		▲	▲		▲										Chang (1948)
Leishmania donovani				▲	▲	▲	▲		▲	▲	▲								Noguchi (1926), Chang (1948), Fulton and Joyner (1949)
L. brasiliensis				▲		▲	▲		▲	▲	▲								Kigler (1926), Noguchi (1926), Chang (1948)
L. tropica				▲		▲	▲		▲	▲	▲								Colas-Belcour and Lwoff (1925), Kigler (1926), Chang (1948)
Leptomonas ctenocephali				▲		▲													Noguchi (1926)
Herpetomonas culicidarum	▲		▲	▲	▲	▲	▲		▲	▲	▲	▲	▲			▲		▲	Noguchi (1926)
H. muscidarum	▲		▲	▲	▲	▲	▲	▲	▲	▲	▲	▲	▲			▲			Noguchi (1926)
H. parva				▲	▲	▲	▲		▲	▲	▲								Noguchi (1926)
H. media				▲	▲	▲	▲		▲	▲	▲		▲						Noguchi (1926)
Tritrichomonas foetus				▲	▲	▲	▲		▲	▲	▲	▲	▲	▲					Cailleau (1937), Plastridge (1943), Cole (1950)
Trichomonas vaginalis				▲	▲	▲			▲			▲		▲					Trussell and Johnson (1941)

*Reorganized after von Brand: *Chemical Physiology of Endoparasitic Animals*, Academic Press, N.Y.; courtesy of Academic Press.
▲ = used by flagellate
△ = very slightly used

Table 3-5.   Glycolysis and the Citric Acid Cycle (Krebs or Tricarboxylic Acid Cycle)*

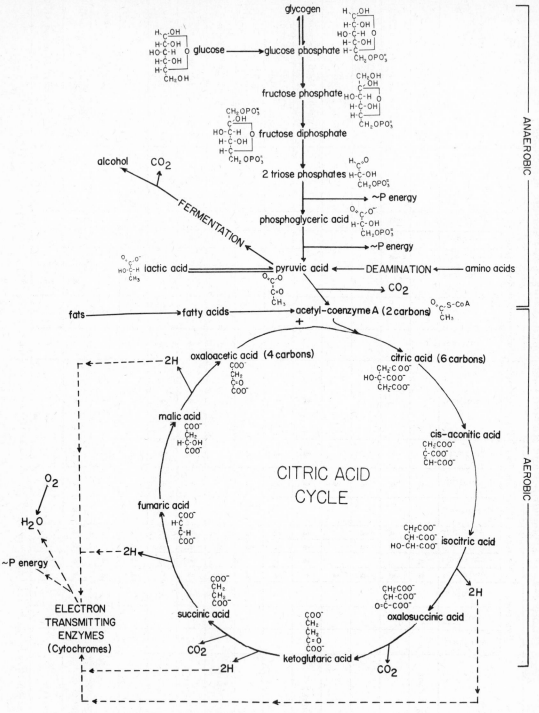

*Every step, as indicated by arrow, involves specific enzymatic action.

PHYSICAL AND CHEMICAL FACTORS WITHIN THE HOST

Various physical and chemical factors, such as the hydrogen ion concentration, the oxida-tion-reduction potential, and temperature, play important roles in the survival and normal metabolism of endoparasitic flagellates. From in vitro observations, the trichomonads appear to favor specific pH ranges. *Tritrichomonas foetus* thrives best in a pH range from 7.0 to 7.6, *Trichomonas vaginalis* from 5.4 to 6.0, and *Trichomonas gallinae* from 6.5 to 7.5. Most trichomonads multiply best at 37° C.; however, strain differences may affect optimum growth temperatures. Nevertheless, almost all species multiply in a temperature range of 32 to 40° C. When maintained at 35 to 39° C., the minimal time required for one division is 5 to 7 hours.

Host Sex and Age

Sex and age play important roles in parasitic infections. For example, male mice are more susceptible to *Trypanosoma cruzi* than females, and adult man becomes hypoglycemic when infected with *Leishmania donovani,* while children become hyperglycemic.

Metabolic Changes

In some instances, hosts are noticeably robbed of their stored food supply by parasites. Hypoglycemia in adult humans infected with *Leishmania donovani* indicates that some blood sugar is being lost. Animals infected with pathogenic trypanosomes—for example, *T. evansi, T. brucei,* and *T. congolense*—are sometimes depleted of their liver glycogen and the amount of muscle glycogen is diminished. On the other hand, there is no change in the blood sugar level in dogs and rats infected with *T. donovani* and *T. lewisi* respectively. These data have led some to believe that the relationship is one of long duration and the parasite has adjusted itself to a near-commensal relationship.

In humans infected with *T. gambiense,* Wormall (1932) has shown that liver and muscle glycogen is not depleted.

Parasite Toxicity

How does the parasite injure its host? Toxicity is often suspected. Concerning *Trypanosoma brucei* and *T. gambiense,* Laveran (1913) reported that if 0.12 to 0.15 gm. of dried trypanosomes are injected into mice, they are killed. Schilling and Rondoni (1913) amplified this experiment and showed that the trypanosomes become toxic 1 hour after death and the toxic effect is lost after 18 hours of storage, thus indicating that the autolytic decomposition processes produce the toxic effect. Coudert and Juttin (1950) indicated that some material must be secreted by *T. cruzi,* because when extracts of this flagellate are injected into tumors in experimental animals, there is regression of the growths. The tumorlytic properties of *T. cruzi* remain to be verified.

Host Diets

How does the host influence the parasite? Numerous investigations have indicated that the host's diet influences the degree of parasitemia (the presence of parasites in the host's blood) in the case of flagellates. Becker et al. (1943) showed that if vitamin B_1 and B_6 are added in large dosages to the diet of rats infected with *Trypanosoma lewisi,* the number of parasites increases and the infection persists longer. These workers attributed the results to the inhibition of the production of ablastin. Caldwell and Byörgy (1943, 1947) got similar results when their rats were fed a diet deficient in biotin.

Not only do dietary changes influence the degree of parasitemia, they can actually influence resistance. For example, hosts maintained on vitamin B complex deficient diets are more resistant to *Trypanosoma equiperdum,* and pigeons, which are normally resistant to *T. brucei,* when deprived of vitamin B complex can be infected. In mice, if vitamin E is given in the diet, the multiplication of *T. congolense* is accelerated; if cod liver oil is given, the rate of multiplication is slowed down. The same is true in rats infected with *T. vivax* (Godfrey, 1958).

Ritterson and Stauber (1949) reported that the host's protein intake influences the course of leishmaniasis in the hamster. Deficient protein diets lead to earlier emaciation and death, while excess dietary protein appears to favor host survival.

Mutualism

The voluminous work of Professor L. R. Cleveland on mutualism deserves mention in a discussion of host-parasite relationships. It is well known that the flagellates in woodroaches digest cellulose for their host. This is a remarkable mutually beneficial relationship. Other processes of the protozoa are controlled by the host. Cleveland (1947) showed that the molting hormone produced by the prothoracic glands of *Cryptocercus punctulatus* induces the sexual cycle of the intestinal polymastigote and hypermastigote flagellates. In a series of papers, Cleveland (1947, 1949, 1951) showed that in *Trichonympha, Oxymonas, Eucomonympha, Nutila,* and *Saccinobacculus,* if the roaches are treated in any way so as to slow down or stop their molting, the intestinal flagellates are slowed down or halted in their sexual cycle. The reverse also holds true. These critically synchronized relationships deserve much attention. Much of

Cleveland's work with the Hypermastigida has been summarized (Cleveland, 1959).

PHYSICAL FACTORS IN THE ENVIRONMENT

Certain physical factors in the environment are of importance in host-parasite relationships. This was well demonstrated by Wood (1954), who reported that environmental temperatures of 22 to 23° C. retard the appearance of the metacyclic form of *Trypanosoma cruzi* in the feces of *Triatoma protracta,* but temperatures from 28 to 34.5° C. increase the number of metacyclic forms.

It should be obvious that a multitude of factors, some yet unknown, may singularly or jointly influence the host-parasite relationship. As Huff (1956) and Otto (1958) brought out in their presidential addresses before the American Society of Parasitologists, the future will undoubtedly witness more investigations along the lines of host-parasite relationships and the ecology of parasites.

LITERATURE CITED

Becker, E. R., M. Manresa, and E. M. Johnson. 1943. Reduction in the efficiency of ablastic action in *Trypanosoma lewisi* infection by withholding pantothenic acid from the host's diet. Iowa State Coll. J. Sci., *17:* 431–441.

Caldwell, F. E., and P. György. 1943. Effect of biotin deficiency on duration of infection with *Trypanosoma lewisi* in the rat. Proc. Soc. Exper. Biol. Med., *53:* 116–119.

Caldwell, F. E., and P. György. 1947. The influence of biotin deficiency on the course of infection with *Trypanosoma lewisi* in the albino rat. J. Infect. Dis., *81:* 197–208.

Cailleau, R. 1937. La nutrition des flagellés tetramitidés, les stérols, facteurs de croissance pour les trichomonades (Première et seconde parties). Ann. Inst. Pasteur, *59:* 137–172; 293–328.

Cailleau, R. 1938. Le cholésterol et l'acide ascorbique, facteurs de croissance pour le flagelle tétramitidé *Trichomonas foetus* Riedmüller. Compt. Rend. Soc. Biol., *127:* 861–863.

Cleveland, L. R. 1925a. The effects of oxygenation and starvation on the symbiosis between the termite *Termopsis,* and its intestinal flagellates. Biol. Bull., *48:* 309–326.

Cleveland, L. R. 1925b. Toxicity of oxygen for protozoa in vivo and in vitro; animals defaunated without injury. Biol. Bull., *48:* 455–468.

Cleveland, L. R. 1947. Sex produced in the protozoa of *Cryptocercus* by molting. Science, *105:* 16–17.

Cleveland, L. R. 1949. Hormone-induced sexual cycles for flagellates. I. Gametogenesis, fertilization, and meiosis in *Trichonympha.* J. Morph. *85:* 197–295.

Cleveland, L. R. 1951. Hormone-induced sexual cycles for flagellates. VI. Gametogenesis, fertilization, meiosis, oöcysts, and gametogenesis in *Leptospironympha.* J. Morph. *88:* 199–243.

Cleveland, L. R. 1959. Effects of insect hormones on the protozoa of *Cryptocercus* and termites. *In* Host Influences on Parasite Physiology (edited by L. A. Stauber), Rutgers University Press, New Brunswick, N. J.

Cleveland, L. R., S. R. Hall, E. P. Sanders, and J. Collier. 1934. The wood-feeding roach, *Cryptocercus,* its Protozoa, etc. Mem. Amer. Acad. Arts Sci., *17:* 185–322.

Coudert, J., and P. Juttin. 1950. Note sur l'action d'un lysat de *Trypanosoma cruzi* vis-à-via d'un cancer greffé du vat. Compt. Rend. Soc. Biol., *144:* 847–849.

Delappe, I. P. 1953. Studies in *Histomonas meagridis.* III. The influence of anaerobic versus aerobic environments on the growth of the organism *in vitro.* Exptl. Parasit., *2:* 209–222.

Desowitz, R. S., 1963. Adaptation of trypanosomes to abnormal hosts. Ann. N. Y. Acad. Sci., *113:* 74–87.

Dogiel, V. A. 1916. Researches on the parasitic Protozoa from the intestine of termites. I. Tetramitidae (Russian text). Zool. Vestnik., *1:* 1–54 (English summary, pp. 36–54).

Godfrey, D. G. 1958. Influence of dietary cod liver oil upon *Trypanosoma congolense; T. cruzi, T. vivax* and *T. brucei.* Exptl. Parasit., *7:* 255–268.

Grassé, P. P. 1952. Traité de Zoologie. I. Fasc. I. Paris.

Grassi, G. B. 1917. Flagellati viventi nei termiti. Atti R. Accad. Lincei, Roma. Mem. Cl. Sci., Fis., Mat., Nat., *12:* 331–394.

Grewal, M. S. 1957. Pathogenicity of *Trypanosoma rangeli* Tejero, 1920 in the invertebrate host. Exptl. Parasit., *6:* 123–130.

Grimstone, A. V. 1959. Cytoplasmic membranes and the nuclear membrane in the flagellate *Trichonympha.* J. Biophys. Biochem. Cytol., *6:* 369–378.

Guthrie, R. 1946. Studies of the growth requirements of *Trichomonas foetus* Riedmüller. Doctorate dissertation, University of Minnesota, Minneapolis.

Hall, R. P. 1953. Protozoology. Prentice-Hall, New York.

Hinshaw, H. C. 1927. Cultivation of *Trichomonas buccalis,* a protozoan of the human mouth. Univ. Cal. Publ. Zool., *31:* 31–49.

Hirschler, J. 1914. Über Plasmastrukturen (Golgi'scher Apparat, Mitochondrien n.a.) in den Tunicaten—, Spangein und Protozonzellen. Anat. Anz., *47:* 289–311.

Hirschler, J. 1927. Studien über die sich mit osmium schwärzenden. Plasmakonpomenten (Golgi-Apparat, Mitochondrien) einiger Protozoenarten, nebst Bemerkungen über die Morphologie der ersten von ihnen im Tierreiche. Ztschr. Zellforsch. Mikr. Anat., *5:* 704–786.

Hollande, A. 1952. Ordre des Bodonides. *In* Grassé (1952), p. 669.

Holmes, F. O. 1925. The relation of *Herpetomonas elmassiani* to its plant and insect hosts. Biol. Bull., *49:* 323.

Honigberg, B. M., and J. J. Lee. 1959. Structure and division of *Trichomonas tenax* (O. F. Müller). Am. J. Hyg., *69:* 177–201.

Huff, C. G. 1956. Parasitism and parasitology. J. Parasit., *42:* 1–10.

Hungate, R. E. 1939. Experiments on the nutrition of *Zootermopsis.* II. The anaerobic carbohydrate dissimilation by the intestinal protozoa. Ecology, *20:* 230–245.

Jahn, T. L., and F. F. Jahn. 1949. How to Know the Protozoa. Wm. C. Brown, Dubuque, Iowa.

Johnson, A. E. 1962. The free amino acids in *Trichomonas foetus.* Exptl. Parasit., *12:* 169–175.

Katzin, L. I., and H. Kirby. 1939. The relative weights of termites and their protozoa. J. Parasit., *25:* 444–445.

Kirby, H. 1929. *Snyderella* and *Coronympha,* two new genera of multinucleate flagellates from termites. Univ. Cal. Publ. Zool., *31:* 417–432.

Kirby, H. 1939. Two new flagellates from termites in the genera *Coronympha* Kirby, and *Metacoronympha* Kirby, new genus. Proc. Cal. Acad. Sci., *22:* 207–220.

Kirby, H. 1947. Displacement of structures in trichomonad flagellates. Trans. Amer. Micro. Soc., *66:* 274–278.

Kirby, H. 1949. Systematic differentiation and evolution of flagellates in termites. Rev. Soc. Mexicana Hist. Nat., *10:* 57–79.

Krogh, A. 1941. The Comparative Physiology of Respiratory Mechanisms. University of Pennsylvania Press, Philadelphia.

Kudo, R. R. 1936. Studies on *Nyctotherus ovalis* Leidy, with special reference to its nuclear structure. Arch. Protistenk., *87:* 10–42.

Kudo, R. R. 1954. Protozoology. 4th Ed., Charles C Thomas, Springfield, Ill.

Kupferberg, A. B., J. G. Johnson, and H. Sprince. 1948. Nutritional requirements of *Trichomonas vaginalis.* Proc. Soc. Exp. Biol. Med., *67:* 304–308.

Laird, M. 1961. Microecological factors in oyster epizootics. Canad. J. Zool., *39:* 449–485.

Laveran, C. L. A. 1913. Trypanotoxines. Essais d'immunisation coutre les trypanosomes. Bull. Soc. Path. Exot., *6:* 693–698.

Lehmann, D. L. 1959. *Trypanosoma granulosae* n. sp. from the newt, *Taricha granulosa twittyi.* J. Protozool., *6:* 167–169.

Lesser, E. 1961. *In vitro* cultivation of *Histomonas meleagridis* free of demonstrable bacteria. J. Protozool., *8:* 228–230.

Levine, D., and C. A. Bradley. 1940. Further studies on the pathogenicity of *Trichomonas gallinae* for baby chicks. Poultry Sci., *19:* 205–209.

Lincicome, D. L. 1963. Chemical basis for parasitism. Ann. N. Y. Acad. Sci., *113:* 360–380.

Lindberg, O., and L. Ernster. 1954. Chemistry and Physiology of Mitochondria and Microsomes. Protoplasmatologia. Springer Verlag, Vienna.

Lwoff, A. 1942. L'Évolution Physiologique: Étude des Pertes de Fonctions chez les Microorganismes. Hermann, Paris.

Moulder, J. W. 1948. The metabolism of malarial parasites. Ann. Rev. Microbiol., *2:* 101–120.

Otto, G. F. 1958. Some reflections on the ecology of parasitism. J. Parasit., *44:* 1–27.

Paillot, A. 1927. Sur deux protozoaires nouveaux parasites des chenilles de *Pyrausta nubilalis* Hb. Compt. Rend. Acad. Sci., *185:* 673–675.

Pitelka, D. R. 1963. Electron-Microscopic Structure of Protozoa. Macmillan, New York.

Powell, W. N. 1928. On the morphology of *Pyrsonympha* with a description of three new species from *Reticulitermes hesperus* Banks. Univ. Cal. Publ. Zool., *31:* 179–200.

Reichenow, E. 1929. Lehrbuch der Protozoenkunde. 5th Ed., Jena.

Rey, H. 1943. Cellular reactions in the dermal connective tissue of the hamster to *Leishmania brasiliensis*. J. Inf. Dis., *72:* 177–124.

Ritterson, A. L., and L. A. Stauber. 1949. Protein intake and leishmaniasis in the hamster. Proc. Soc. Exp. Biol. Med., *70:* 47–50.

Scheltema, R. S. 1962. The relationship between the flagellate protozoon *Hexamita* and the oyster *Crassostrea virginica*. J. Parasit., *48:* 137–141.

Schilling, C., and P. Rondoni. 1913. Tossine tripanosomiche e immunita di fronte ai tripanosomi. Sperimentale, Arch. Biol. Norm. Patol., *67:* 595–613.

Scott, G. H., and E. S. Horning. 1932. The structure of opalinids, as revealed by the technique of micro-incineration. J. Morph., *53:* 381–388.

Shuster, C. N., Jr., and R. E. Hillman. 1963. Comments on "Microecological factors in oyster epizootics" by Marshall Laird. Chesapeake Sci., *4:* 101–103.

Sleigh, M. A. 1962. The Biology of Cilia and Flagella. Macmillan, New York.

Stabler, R. M., and F. B. Engley, 1946. Studies on *Trichomonas gallinae* infections in pigeon squabs. J. Parasit., *32:* 225–232.

Stauber, L. A. 1953. Some effects of host environment on the course of leishmaniasis in the hamster. Ann. N. Y., Acad. Sci., *56:* 1064–1069.

Stauber, L. A. 1963. Immunity to *Leishmania*. Ann. N. Y. Acad. Sci., *113:* 409–417.

Stauber, L. A., J. Q. Ochs, and N. H. Coy. 1954. Electrophoretic patterns of the serum proteins of chinchillas and hamsters infected with *Leishmania donovani*. Exptl. Parasit., *3:* 325–335.

Steinert, M. 1958. Étude sur le determinisme de la morphogénèse d'un trypanosome. Exptl. Cell Res., *15:* 560–569.

Sutherland, J. L. 1933. Protozoa from Australian termites. Quart. J. Micro. Sci., *76:* 145–173.

Taliaferro, W. H. 1924. A reaction product in infections with *Trypanosoma lewisi* which inhibits the reproduction of the trypanosomes. J. Exper. Med., *39:* 171–190.

Taliaferro, W. H. 1932. Trypanocidal and reproduction-inhibiting antibodies to *Trypanosoma lewisi* in rats and rabbits. Am. J. Hyg., *16:* 32–84.

Taliaferro, W. H. 1938. Ablastic and trypanocidal antibodies against *Trypanosoma duttoni*. J. Immunol., *35:* 303–328.

Trussell, R. E., and G. Johnson. 1941. Physiology of pure culture of *Trichomonas vaginalis:* III. Fermentation of carbohydrates and related compounds. Proc. Soc. Exp. Biol. Med., *47:* 176–178.

von Brand, T. 1946. Anaerobiosis in Invertebrates. Biodynamica Monographs. Normandy, Missouri.

Walravens, P. 1931. Influence de la trypanosomiase humaine sur la glycemie: notes cliniques. Ann. Soc. Belge Méd. Trop., *11:* 213–218.

Weiss, E. D., and G. H. Gall. 1947. Nutritional requirements of *Tritrichomonas foetus* with special reference to partially digested proteins. Proc. Soc. Exp. Biol. Med., *65:* 278–283.

Westphal, A. 1939. Beziehungen zwischen Infektionsstärke und Krankheitsbild bei Infektionen mit *Chilomastix mesnili* und anderen Dickdarmflagellaten. Ztschr. Hyg. Infektionskr., *122:* 146–158.

Willems, R., L. Massart, and G. Peeters, 1942. Über den Kohlehydratstoffwechsel von *Trichomonas hepatica*. Naturwissensch., *30:* 159–170.

Wood, F. W. 1954. Environmental temperature as a factor in development of *Trypanosoma cruzi* in *Triatoma protracta*. Exptl. Parasit., *3:* 227–233.

Wormall, A. 1932. Carbohydrate metabolism in human trypanosomiasis. Biochem. Jour., *26:* 1777–1787.

SUGGESTED READING

Cleveland, L. R. 1948. An ideal partnership. Sci. Month., *67:* 173–177. (This is a popular article that discusses the mutualist relationship between woodroaches and their intestinal flagellates.)

Fulton, J. D. 1959. Some aspects of research on trypanosomes. *In* Host Influence on Parasite Physiology (Edited by L. A. Stauber). Rutgers University Press, New Brunswick, N. J. (This article reviews the history of the pathogenic trypanosomes, the relationship between these organisms, their morphology, cytoplasmic inclusions, sex, and aspects of genetics.)

Hall, R. P. 1953. Protozoology. Prentice-Hall, New York, pp. 166–200, 527–596. (Sections of this textbook consider the morphology and taxonomy of flagellates and host-parasite relationships between protozoan parasites and their hosts.)

Hegner, R., and J. Andrews. (eds.) 1930. Problems and Methods of Research in Protozoology. MacMillan, New York.

Reynolds, B. D. Ectoparasitic protozoa. pp. 11–26.

Kirby, H., Jr. The protozoa of termites. pp. 32–48.

Hegner, R. Intestinal flagellates in general. pp. 119–123.

Wenrich, D. H. Intestinal flagellates of rats. pp. 124–142.

Hegner, R. Host-parasite specificity in the genus *Giardia*. pp. 143–153.

Kessel, J. F. Host-parasite relations among trichomonads. pp. 154–161.

Andrews, J. Blood-inhabiting flagellates in general. pp. 244–247.

Becker, E. R. The intestinal flagellates of insects. pp. 248–256.

Holmes, F. O. Protozoa of latex plants. pp. 257–275.

Taliaferro, W. H. Serological methods in the study of the Protozoa. pp. 411–438.

(Although somewhat outdated, the information in these chapters is still provocative and should provide the beginning investigator with ideas for research.)

Kudo, R. R. 1954. Protozoology. 4th Ed., Charles C Thomas, Springfield, Ill., pp. 254–434. (This section in Kudo's classic textbook is concerned with the flagellates. Although somewhat outdated, the beginning student will find a wealth of information on the biology of flagellates, both free-living and parasitic.)

Levine, N. D. 1961. Protozoan Parasites of Domestic Animals and of Man. Burgess, Minneapolis, pp. 40–128. (This section in Levine's textbook deals with the flagellate parasites of domestic animals and man. Although primarily intended for students and investigators in the field of veterinary medicine, all biologists will find the information concisely presented and the bibliography useful.)

Pitelka, D. R. 1963. Electron-Microscopic Structure of Protozoa. Macmillan, New York. (In this volume, the author deals with the ultrastructure of protozoa. The cytoplasmic and nuclear structures common to all protozoa are discussed. Structures common to protozoa and the cells of metazoans are stressed. The morphology of protozoan structures is interpreted in correlation with what is known about their biochemistry and physiology.)

Stabler, R. M. *Trichomonas gallinae:* A review. Exptl. Parasit., *3:* 368–402. (This comprehensive review of the biology of *T. gallinae* is recommended to the student. This article indicates how isolated pieces of research, in this case on a single species of flagellate, can contribute to the whole picture of our understanding.)

4

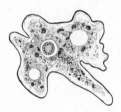

THE SARCODINA—
The Amoebae

The Sarcodina includes all the amoebae. These protozoa, unlike the flagellates, generally do not possess a form-retaining pellicle; rather, the body surface is covered by an extremely flexible plasmalemma, which permits the body cytoplasm to flow in all directions, resulting in a constant alteration of the body outline. Certain free-living amoebae, such as the freshwater *Arcella* sp., do possess rigid tests; however, none of the parasitic forms maintain such surface shells. Because of the flexibility of the body, the amoebae must be considered asymmetrical; furthermore, there is no differentiation between an anterior and a posterior end.

All amoebae are capable of producing pseudopodia, which are the locomotor and food-acquiring organelles. These body extensions result from the outward flow of cytoplasm pushing the cell or plasma membrane ahead of the direction of flow. The presence of pseudopodia in the trophozoite stage usually is considered the main distinguishing characteristic of the Sarcodina. It should be pointed out that some flagellates are capable of pseudopodial movement at some stage during their life cycles, and some amoebae possess flagella during their developmental stages; as a general rule, however, flagellates utilize flagella as their main mechanisms of locomotion, and amoebae utilize pseudopodia.

Generally the ecto- and endoplasms of parasitic amoebae are much more readily recognizable than those of free-living protozoa. In the formation of certain types of pseudopodia, both areas of the cytoplasm are involved, while in other types only the ectoplasm contributes. The type of pseudopodium formed by amoebae is quite specific and often is used in the identification of species.

Amoebae cannot swim; motility by pseudopodia is dependent on the presence of some type of substratum on which they can glide. The endoparasitic species are almost always found in the alimentary tract of their host, where they are intimately associated with the intestinal lining. The ectoparasitic species adhere to the body surface of their host.

Several amoebae are known to be pathogenic to man and domestic animals. Others live in close association with these true pathogens and hence are of importance in medical and veterinary protozoology from a diagnostic standpoint.

A list of the more commonly encountered amoebae is given in Table 4–1 to illustrate how these can be distinguished from one another. Reproduction among parasitic amoebae is

Table 4-1. Some Parasitic Amoebae of Man and Domestic Animals

Parasitic Amoeba	Principal Hosts	Habitat	Main Characteristics	Disease
Entamoeba histolytica	Man, other mammals	Large intestine	15-60 μ in diameter, distinct ecto- and endoplasms, vacuoles enclose host cells, centric endosome	Amoebiasis
E. coli	Man, monkeys, pigs	Large intestine	15-50 μ in diameter, sluggish, vacuoles do not enclose host cells, eccentric endosome	Nonpathogenic
E. gingivalis	Man, dogs, cats, monkeys	Mouth	5-35 μ in diameter, distinct ecto- and endoplasms, vacuoles rarely enclose erythrocytes	Periodontitis ?
E. bovis	Cattle	Rumen	Approximately 20 μ in diameter	Nonpathogenic
E. gallinarum	Chickens, turkeys	Caecum	9-25 μ in diameter, centric endosome	Nonpathogenic
E. anatis	Ducks	Intestine	Similar to *E. histolytica*	Enteritis ?
E. cuniculi	Rabbits	Intestine	Similar to *E. coli*, 10-20 μ in diameter	Nonpathogenic
E. polecki	Pigs	Intestine	5-15 μ in diameter, resembles precystic stage of *E. histolytica*	Nonpathogenic
Endolimax nana	Man, monkeys	Large intestine	6-15 μ in diameter, granular and vacuolated cytoplasm, sluggish, vacuoles do not enclose host cells	Nonpathogenic
Iodamoeba bütschlii	Man, pigs	Intestine	8-20 μ in diameter, broad pseudopodia, sluggish, large glycogen mass	Usually nonpathogenic
Dientamoeba fragilis	Man	Large intestine	5-12 μ in diameter, two nuclei, active	Usually nonpathogenic

essentially by mitotic cell division. This mechanism, known as binary fission, results in the production of daughter cells asexually.

CYSTS

Cyst formation is a common phenomenon among most parasitic amoebae, and it enables these animals to resist unfavorable external environments outside their hosts and to eventually be transmitted to other hosts; hence, cysts are the infective forms of most amoebae. It should be mentioned that some species do not encyst (or cysts have not been found), and transmission from host to host is via the trophozoite form. The morphology of amoebic cysts is quite consistent and commonly is used as a laboratory diagnostic tool. Some of the cysts commonly encountered in the diagnostic laboratory are depicted in Plate 4–1.

MORPHOLOGY OF PSEUDOPODIA

Pseudopodia are of four types: filopodia, lobopodia, rhizopodia, and axopodia.

Filopodia are filamentous pseudopods composed completely of ectoplasm (Plate 4–2, Fig. 2). This type of amoeboid projection is found exclusively among free-living species, such as *Amoeba radiosa* and various testaceans. Lobopodia are the common form found among parasitic amoebae (Plate 4–2, Fig. 1). This type of pseudopodium is blunt and is composed of both ecto- and endoplasm, or of ectoplasm alone. In most species, the formation of lobopodia is gradual. Watching living specimens, one can see the slow flow of granular cytoplasm into the broad projection. In *Entamoeba histolytica* and *Endamoeba blattae*, the latter a parasite of cockroaches, the lobopodia are shot out suddenly. Rhizopodia are filamentous but are even finer than filopodia (Plate 4–2, Fig. 3). This type of pseudopodium is branched and anastomosed and is found among free-living species, primarily the Foraminiferida and Testacida. Axopodia differ from the other three types of pseudopodia in that they are more or less permanent, and within each is an axial rod composed of a bundle of fibrils that are inserted near the center of the body (Plate 4–2, Fig. 4). This type of semipermanent pseudopod is generally long and needle-like and is found among the free-living Heliozoida.

The other body organelles of the Sarcodina are common to all protozoa and have been considered in Chapter 3.

SYSTEMATICS AND BIOLOGY

CLASSIFICATION

Following the taxonomic interpretation of Jahn and Jahn (1949), the subphylum Sarcodina is divided into seven orders: Proteomyxida, Mycetozoida (Myxomycetes), Amoebida, Testacida, Foraminiferida, Heliozoida, and Radiolarida. The majority of parasitic species belong to the Amoebida, but the Proteomyxida and the Mycetozoida include a few species that are parasitic in plants and animals. Since only parasitic forms are under consideration only three orders are discussed.

Order 1. Proteomyxida. Possesses numerous filopodia that are often branched and

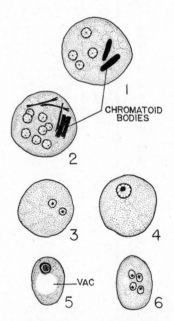

Plate 4–1   Cysts of some amoebae parasitic in man and domestic animals. 1. Mature cyst of *Entamoeba histolytica,* showing four characteristic nuclei and chromatoid bodies. **2.** Mature cyst of *E. coli,* showing eight characteristic nuclei and jagged chromatoid bodies. **3.** Cyst of *Entamoeba bovis* from cattle, showing two nuclei. **4.** Cyst of *E. polecki* from pigs, showing one characteristic nucleus. **5.** Cyst of *Iodamoeba bütschlii* from man, showing typical vacuole. **6.** Cyst of *Endolimax nana* from man, showing four characteristic nuclei.

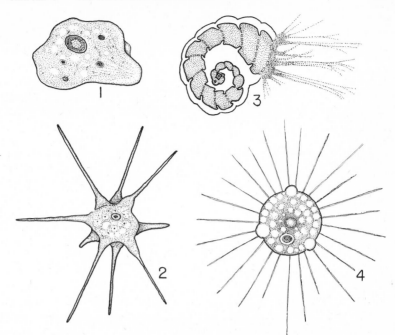

Plate 4-2   Types of pseudopodia found among the Sarcodina. 1. Lobopodia of *Endamoeba blattae* from cockroaches. 2. Filopodia of *Amoeba radiosa,* a free-living amoeba. 3. Rhizopodia of *Peneroplis pertusus,* a free-living foriminiferan amoeba. 4. Axopodia of *Actinophrys sol,* a free-living heliozoan amoeba. (All figures redrawn after Kudo, R. R., 1954. *Protozoology,* Charles C Thomas, Springfield, Ill.)

anastomosed; flagellated swarm cells common in life cycles; without external covering (tests or shells); few species parasitic in protozoa and plants.

Order 2. Mycetozoida.   Possesses rhizopodia; forms plasmodium (a multinucleate body resulting from fusion of many myxamoebae) during one phase of life cycle; without tests or shells; mostly free-living on dead vegetation but with few species parasitic in plants.

Order 3. Amoebida.   Possesses lobopodia; ecto- and endoplasm clearly differentiated; encystment common; without tests or shells; free-living and parasitic species, the latter primarily in animals.

THE ORDER PROTEOMYXIDA

The parasitic Proteomyxida are seldom considered in traditional parasitology, since these protozoa are parasites of other protozoa, algae, and higher plants and are of little economic importance. Nevertheless they are of interest from the standpoint of their morphology, life history, and physiology. The genera *Labyrinthomyxa, Pseudospora, Leptomyxa, Labyrinthula,* and *Vampyrella* are known to include ecto- and endoparasitic species.

Labyrinthomyxa sauvageaui is a commensal of the marine kelp (brown alga, *Laminaria lejolissi*). The flagellated swarm cells, measuring 7 to

18μ long, penetrate the cells of the algae, become attached head to end, and transform into the elongate amoeboid stage known as a myxamoeba, which is 7.5 to 14.0μ in length (Plate 4–3, Figs. 1, 2). The plasmodium, formed from the fusion of the myxamoebae, is known as a pseudoplasmodium, since the cytoplasms of the myxamoebae do not fuse completely but are connected by permanent filopodia (Plate 4–3, Fig. 3). Parasitized kelps are apparently not injured.

Pseudospora parasitica and *P. eudorini* are parasitic in *Spirogyra, Eudorina,* and related green algae, while *P. volvocis* is a parasite in the free-living colonial flagellate, *Volvox.* In all three species the swarm cells penetrate the host and later develop into myxamoebae that in time fuse to become plasmodia. The flagellated swarm cells develop when the plasmodia fragment.

Members of genus *Leptomyxa* are free-living soil amoebae widely found in England; however, *L. reticulata* was reported by McLennan (1930) in the root of diseased hops in Tasmania. *Labyrinthula** is another genus usually found free-living in marine waters; however, one species, *L. macrocystis,* causes a spotted disease in the leaves of the eelgrass (*Zostera marina*)

---

*Members of the genus *Labyrinthula* and related genera are considered by some to be fungi of uncertain affinity (Alexopoulos, 1962).

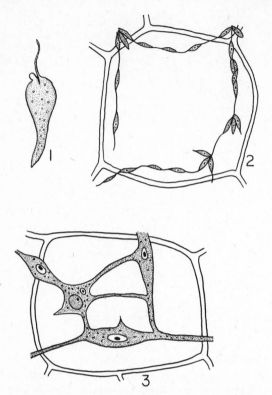

Plate 4-3   *Labyrinthomyxa sauvageaui, a parasite of plants.* **1.** Free-living flagellate form of *L. sauvageaui.* **2.** Beginning of the lining up of flagellate cells, leading to the formation of the amoeboid form within the host cell. **3.** Amoeboid form (pseudoplasmodium) of *L. sauvageaui* within a host cell. Pseudopodia are connected. (Redrawn after Duboscq, 1921.)

found along the Atlantic Coast of the United States. It also has been reported in various other algae.

The parasitism of eelgrass by *Labyrinthula macrocystis* along the Atlantic Coast of the United States has resulted in an extremely interesting and important ecologic change. As Hopkins (1957) has pointed out, prior to the early 1930's the eelgrass *Zostera marina* occupied many of the high-salinity areas along the Atlantic Coast and was a dominant member of the ecological community. Within such communities, an assemblage of organisms thrived in such numbers as found nowhere else.

During the early 1930's, the eelgrass growing in high-salinity areas became parasitized by *L. macrocystis* and eventually died out. Only those plants which grew along the low-salinity fringe of their original range survived, because apparently the protozoan parasite cannot tolerate low salinity. Occasionally, as in wet years,

Z. marina spreads from the low-salinity areas down the estuaries, only to be killed by the parasite when the salinity again is increased.

As a result of this parasite-caused shift in eelgrass distribution, many organisms that originally abounded in high-salinity eelgrass communities perished. Only those organisms that were able to adapt to low salinity are found in the new ranges. Probably the most economically important victim of this ecological shift was the bay scallop. In Virginia, for example, counties that formerly supported a sizable scallop fishing industry now have none.

The important principle revealed by the *Labyrinthula-Zostera* relationship is that the biotic nature of a community can be drastically altered by a parasite alone without the assistance of physical conditions acting directly upon the members, which in this case are the eelgrass and scallop. Hopkins has postulated that there must be many other cases, as yet undiscovered, in which the nature of a marine community is determined by parasites.

The unique *Vampyrella lateritia* is an ectoparasite on freshwater algae. This orange-red amoeba glides along the exterior of algae and occasionally breaks through the cellulose wall of the host and extracts chlorophyll bodies by means of filopodia. This species is known to encyst. The multinucleate cyst, measuring 30 to 40 μ in diameter, serves as the site of cytoplasmic reorganization, since each nucleus upon eruption of the cyst wall has gathered around it some cytoplasm and becomes a separate amoeba.

THE ORDER MYCETOZOIDA

It has long been disputed whether the slime molds, or Mycetozoida, are plants or animals. Every student who has studied general biology knows that among the lower plants and animals the borderline between the two kingdoms is extremely difficult to define. A critical review of our knowledge of these organisms, as well as a taxonomic listing, is given by MacBride and Martin (1934).

Although almost all of the Mycetozoida are free-living—found on the bark of trees and on decaying vegetation—a few species are known to be intracellular parasites in higher plants. The presence of these slime mold parasites is usually accompanied by hypertrophy of the host's tissue and the formation of galls. For those interested, Karling (1942) gives a list of plants known to be parasitized by specific mycetozoans.

GENUS *Plasmodiophora*.   The genus *Plasmodiophora* includes several species parasitic in the root cells of cabbage and related plants. The presence of these amoebae produces galls known as "root hernia." The life cycle of *Plasmodiophora* is depicted in Plate 4–4. The mature form found within parasitized cells is the multinucleate plasmodium. Plasmodia generally give rise to sporangia resulting from the condensation of cytoplasm around a number of nuclei. Within each sporangium is found a number of uninucleate spores (also known as cysts), each of which, upon being released from the sporangium and host cell, falls to the soil, excysts, and gives rise to a flagellated swarm cell known as a myxoflagellate. Myxoflagellates may be considered the "infective form," since they actively penetrate new host cells, transform into amoeboid bodies known as myxamoebae, and multiply in number. The resulting colony of myxamoebae fuses, giving rise to a plasmodium. Under certain unfavorable conditions, such as

desiccation, the large plasmodium may fragment (the process being known as plasmotomy) and give rise to smaller plasmodia. Plasmotomy is probably comparable to sclerotia formation as found among the free-living species; however, the smaller plasmodia of *Plasmodiophora* do not possess highly resistant walls.

Various investigators have described sexual reproduction in *Plasmodiophora,* in which the myxoflagellates released from the sporangia are believed to be haploid. Two of these myxoflagellates fuse, giving rise to a diploid myxamoeba. Meiosis within the sporangia prior to the formation of spores has been reported, thus confirming the concept of sexual reproduction via flagellated gametes—the haploid myxoflagellates. However, Hall (1953) is of the opinion that more cytological data are needed before it can be stated conclusively that sexual reproduction occurs.

OTHER GENERA.   Other genera of Mycetozoida known to parasitize plant cells include *Membranosorus* in the mud plantain (*Heteranthera dubia*); *Sorosphaera* in the speed-well (*Veronica*); *Spongospora,* which causes the "pow-

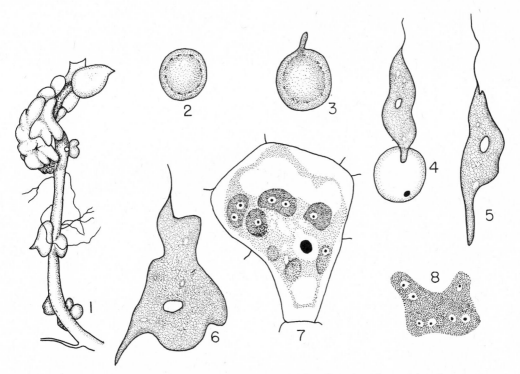

Plate 4–4   **Stages in the life history of *Plasmodiophora brassicae*, the root-hernia-causing mycetozoan.** 1. Cabbage root hernias caused by *P. brassicae*. 2. A spore of *P. brassicae*. 3. Beginning of spore germination. 4. Flagellate form escaping from spore. 5. Flagellate form of *P. brassicae*. 6. A myxamoeba of *P. brassicae*. 7. Host cell enclosing several young parasites. 8. An isolated older parasite. (All Figs. redrawn after Woronin and Nawaschin in Kudo. R. R. (ed.), 1954, *Protozoology,* Charles C Thomas, Springfield, Ill.)

dery" or "corky scab" condition in potatoes; and *Polymyxa* in wheat (*Triticum*) and other cereals. The main distinguishing characteristic among the genera is the manner of formation and arrangement of spores. For those interested in identification, the taxonomy of the parasitic Mycetozoida is given by Karling (1942).

THE ORDER AMOEBIDA

The Amoebida includes almost all the species of amoebae symbiotic in animals, including man. Although the symbiotic Amoebida generally are all classified as parasites, most of these are commensals that do little or no damage to their hosts.

As a result of the adaptation of enteric amoebae to the host's colon, their physiology has undergone certain exacting alterations. Such changes are manifested in experiments designed to cultivate them in vitro. When maintained in artificial media, enteric amoebae reveal rather precise likes and dislikes. Unless their requirements are met by the medium, these amoebae cannot survive outside their hosts.

Morphologically, the parasitic Amoebida possess one or more of the vesicular type of nucleus located in the endoplasm (in the families Amoebidae and Endamoebidae); or they possess two types of nuclei (in the family Paramoebidae). None of these amoebae possess a flagellated stage during any part of their various life cycles, and their pseudopodia are of the lobopodial type. The host's large intestine is the main habitat. This is not surprising since probably the first amoebae to enter their hosts were accidentally ingested, and as the result of their dependence on some sort of solid medium (in the form of the intestinal wall) on which to migrate, they have not been as adaptive to other environments within their hosts as have the flagellates, for example. Furthermore, the abundance of bacteria and other food materials associated with the intestinal wall has enhanced growth of amoebae.

Amoebidae
The family Amoebidae consists mostly of free-living species, including the familiar laboratory animal *Amoeba proteus*. However, at least three genera of this family include species that can live in the intestine of animals. The genus *Sappinia*, characterized by two closely associated nuclei, includes *S. diploidea*, which has been found in the feces of various animals. Neither a true parasite nor a commensal, *S. diploidea* is a coprozoic accidental parasite—that is, it feeds on rich organic materials such as feces. Some authorities contend that the cysts of this amoeba are ingested by the hosts and passed unharmed through the alimentary canal to the colon, where excystation occurs in feces, giving rise to the trophozoite form. *S. diploidea*, characterized by few short pseudopodia and highly vacuolated endoplasm with two nuclei, is mentioned here because it may be encountered during fecal analyses. The relative frequency of coprozoic amoebae, or free-living amoebae that find animal excreta a favorable environment, suggests that such an affinity may represent the initiation of the evolution of parasitism.

Vahlkampfia patuxent, found in the alimentary canal of oysters, may reach 140 μ in diameter. This species is undoubtedly an intestine-dwelling holozoic form—that is, it takes in parts of or entire organisms as food—and it feeds on bacteria causing no injury to the mollusc. It is characterized by a broad, fan shaped pseudopodium. *Acanthamoeba hyalina*, measuring 9 to 17 μ in the trophozoite form and 1 to 15 μ in the double-walled cystic form, is primarily a soil and fresh-water form but has been reported from cultures of human and animal feces. It is undoubtedly a coprozoic species. Some authorities believe that *Acanthamoeba* may be pathogenic (Culbertson et al., 1958). It has been found to cause encephalitis and death in monkeys when inoculated intracerebrally or intraspinally. Furthermore, it causes ulcers in the nasal mucous membrane of mice if introduced intranasally. If the amoeba migrates to the brain, death ensues.

Endamoebidae
The family Endamoebidae is exclusively parasitic.

GENUS *Endamoeba*. The genus *Endamoeba** includes numerous species found in the intestines of invertebrates. The members are distinguished from the closely related species of *Entamoeba* by their nuclei. A single nucleus is found in each specimen, and a conspicuous nuclear membrane is present (Plate 4–5, Fig. 1). The nucleoplasm is divided into a peripheral granular

---

*The generic names *Endamoeba* and *Entamoeba* are commonly, but erroneously, used interchangeably in parasitological literature. As indicated in the text, these are distinct genera and should be considered as such.

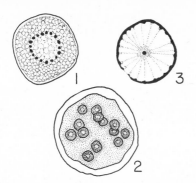

Plate 4-5   Differences between Entamoeba and Endamoeba. 1. Nucleus of a member of the genus *Endamoeba,* showing inner ring of endosomal granules and finer peripheral nucleoplasmic granules. **2.** A multinucleate cyst of *Endamoeba blattae.* **3.** Nucleus of a member of the genus *Entamoeba,* showing centrally located endosome and spokelike nucleoplasmic striations.

zone and a central hyaline zone. The two zones are separated by a ring of endosomes. *Endamoeba blattae* is a common species often encountered in the colon of cockroaches. It measures 10 to 15 μ in diameter and possesses broad lobopodia. *E. simulans,* measuring 50 to 150 μ in diameter, is found in the gut of termites.

The various species of *Endamoeba* possess multinucleate cysts, which are ingested by the host to establish the infection (Plate 4–5, Fig. 2). In the gut, according to some earlier investigators, each nucleus becomes the center of a gamete; when the cyst wall ruptures, these gametes fuse in pairs to form zygotes that in turn develop into trophozoites. This observation is in need of verification, since it does not correspond with the life cycles of other members of the family.

Genus *Entamoeba.* The genus *Entamoeba* includes numerous species parasitic in vertebrates and invertebrates. These forms possess a vesicular nucleus with a centrically or eccentrically placed endosome and with chromatin granules along the inner surface of the nuclear membrane (Plate 4–5, Fig. 3). Undoubtedly the best known species is the human parasite *Entamoeba histolytica,* which is the causative agent of amoebic dysentery, or amoebiasis, first discovered in Russia by Lösch in 1875. *E. histolytica* is universally distributed, but its prevalence varies in different areas; for example, Santos Zetina (1940) reported as high as 85 per cent infection in Merida, Yucatan. It is known that incidences of infection are high in Mexico, China, India, and sections of South America. It is important to remember that amoebiasis is not a tropical or subtropical disease, since it is found in temperate and even in arctic and antarctic zones. In the United States, the incidence of infection has varied from 1.4 per cent in Tacoma, Washington (Cresswell and Wallace, 1934), to 36.4 per cent in rural Tennessee (Milam and Meleney, 1931). The manner of infection—through the ingestion of cysts—causes the incidence to be considerably higher in densely populated institutions. For example, Faust (1931) found a 35.5 per cent infection in the clinics of New Orleans, and Reardon (1941) found 40 per cent among the patients in a mental hospital in Georgia. On the average, 8.1 per cent of Americans serve as hosts for *E. histolytica.*

Life Cycle of *Entamoeba histolytica.* The life cycle of *E. histolytica* is well known. The uninucleate trophozoite inhabits both the lower portions of the small intestine and the entire large intestine of man and other primates. Other mammals, such as dogs and cats, can be experimentally infected. This motile trophic or trophozoite form measures 15 to 60 μ in diameter (average, 18 to 25 μ) and is typically monopodial—that is, it produces one large pseudopodium at a time while moving in a given direction—and the lobopodium is formed eruptively. The cytoplasm, which is clearly differentiated into ecto- and endoplasms, contains food vacuoles that enclose the host's erythrocytes, leukocytes, fragments of epithelial cells, and bacteria. Within the host's gut, the trophozoites multiply by mitotic division (binary fission).

Not all the trophozoites are tissue invaders, but in certain instances they do invade the lining of the victim's large intestine by actually ingesting the epithelial lining by elaborating a proteolytic enzyme. Within the gut wall, some of the trophozoites are carried away by the blood circulation to various areas of the body. The liver, lung, brain, and testes are known to be sites in which these amoebae become lodged; the liver is without question the most frequently infected organ. Within the hepatic tissue, the trophozoites actively feed on liver cells, causing severe lesions that generally lead to secondary complications.

From time to time certain intestine-dwelling trophozoites assume the precystic form (Plate 4–6, Fig. 1); the cytoplasm becomes spherical and smaller, food inclusions are extruded, pseudopods are less frequently and sluggishly extruded, and chromatoidal bars begin to appear.

Amoebae at this stage are preparing to encyst. Cysts of *E. histolytica* are spherical and surrounded by a refractile cyst wall (Plate 4-1). The size varies between 3.5 and 20 μ in diameter (depending on whether the cysts are of the large or small strain). When seen in lugol iodine preparations, the cysts contain four prominent vesicular nuclei. Also characteristic of mature cysts is the presence of elongate chromatoidal bars that, unlike those in the cysts of *Entamoeba coli,* possess rounded rather than jagged ends. Such cysts, which are the infective forms, are passed out of the host in the feces.

Cysts of *Entamoeba histolytica* are highly resistant to desiccation and certain chemicals. Numerous experiments have been conducted to determine their resistance. Cysts of *E. histolytica* in water can survive up to 1 month, while those in feces on dry land survive for more than 12 days. They can survive temperatures up to 50° C., which is their thermal death point. Table 4-2 gives some idea of the effects of various common chemicals on these cysts.

When food or water contaminated with *E. histolytica* cysts is ingested by the host, the cysts pass along the alimentary tract to the ileum, where excystation occurs. In vitro studies suggest that excystment does not occur immediately. Cysts placed in fresh culture medium at body temperature excyst in 5 or 6 hours. Upon rupture of the cyst wall, a single four-nucleate organism emerges and immediately proceeds to divide until a number of small uninucleate metacystic trophozoites result. Some of the nuclei of a newly emerged trophozoite may even divide, while others merely become part of a metacystic amoeba. In instances where the nuclei divide, the daughter nuclei become lodged in metacystic amoebae that are pinched off the multinucleate parent. According to Cleveland and Sanders (1930a), metacystic forms that enclose one of the original four

nuclei can be distinguished from those that enclose a daughter of the originals since the latter are smaller. The metacystic forms pass into the large intestine and mature (Plate 4-6, Fig. 2).

Multiplication of this species thus occurs at two stages during the life cycle—by binary fission in the intestine-dwelling trophozoite stage, and by nuclear division followed by cytokinesis in the cystic and metacystic stages.

Pathogenicity and Nonpathogenicity. A curious aspect of *E. histolytica* infections in man is the apparent nonpathogenicity in some individuals. Nonaffected hosts (carriers) serve as spreaders of infective cysts and hence are of great significance from the standpoint of public health. This accounts for the almost universally required laboratory examination of fecal specimens from food handlers in the United States and other progressive nations. In addition, flies have been incriminated in the spread of this and other amoebae, because cysts can survive for some time in the gut of flies, later to be regurgitated or passed out in feces onto human food.

Several postulations have been offered to explain the nonpathogenicity of *Entamoeba histolytica* in certain individuals:

(1) A supposedly nonpathogenic race, *minuta,* measuring 12 to 15 μ in diameter, is believed to be a strict commensal, ingesting intestinal bacteria and not host tissue. However, Frye and Meleney (1938) demonstrated that these small amoebae do cause amoebiasis (tissue invasion) in experimentally infected kittens, and Neal (1957) reported pathological results when this *minuta* race was introduced into rats. It is now known that probably several races exist; one of these appears to be a harmless commensal, at least in the majority of cases.

(2) Craig and Faust (1951) proposed that hosts may acquire an immunity to *E. histolytica* infections, possibly accounting for the nonpathological conditions. This hypothesis has some merit, because it is known that when serum from infected individuals is brought into contact with antigen prepared from extracts of cultured amoebae, complement fixation does occur. However, the effectiveness of the immunity is questionable, since infected individuals definitely are not immune to reinfections.

(3) Supposedly both large and small strains of *E. histolytica* pass through a nonpathogenic phase in their development and "carriers" harbor these. This hypothesis is upheld by the

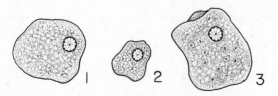

Plate 4-6   Trophozoites of *Entamoeba histolytica*. 1. Precystic stage. 2. Metacystic stage. 3. Mature trophozoite.

Table 4-2.   Effects of Various Chemical Agents and Common
Bacteriacides on the Cysts of *Entamoeba histolytica**

Chemical Agent	Time Required to Kill Cysts
50% alcohol	Immediate
1% formaldehyde	Within 4 hours
0.5% formaldehyde	30 minutes at 20-25°C. and 37°C.
Cresol (1:20)	Immediate
Cresol (1:30)	1 minute
Cresol (1:100)	30 minutes
Phenol (1:40)	15 minutes
Phenol (1:100)	7 hours
Phenol (1% solution)	30 minutes at 20-25°C. and 37°C.
0.1% $HgCl_2$	Immediate to 4 hours
2.5% NaOH	30 minutes at 20-25°C. and 37°C.
7.5% HCl	30 minutes at 20-25°C.
5% HCl	30 minutes at 37°C.
Chlorine (1:10,000)	No effect after several hours
0.2% chlorine	7 days
0.5% chlorine	36-72 hours
2% $KMnO_4$	3 days
$KMnO_4$ (1:500)	24-48 hours
Antibiotics	The majority of antibiotics kill the accompanying bacteria in *E. histolytica* cultures, and since the amoeba is dependent on associated bacteria, they are killed.

*From data compiled from various sources by R. Kudo in *Protozoology*, Charles C
Thomas, Springfield, Ill. (with the permission of publisher).

findings of Hunninen and Boone (1957), who found that in experimentally infected rabbits both large and small strain amoebae colonize in the lumen of the colon and do not invade the tissue, possibly because they were in the nonpathogenic phase. On the other hand, many "carriers" live for years without showing symptoms of amoebiasis, and it appears unlikely that the nonpathogenic phase lasts that long. (4) It has also been postulated that certain strains that produce smaller cysts are less virulent and produce only subclinical symptoms; however, Meleney and Zuckerman (1948) reported a small-cyst strain that, when maintained in culture for 5 years, produced large

cysts accompanied by a change in the chemical composition of the culture medium. This finding suggests that cyst size is not totally genetically controlled and associated with pathogenicity but is at least in part a matter of environmental influence.

(5) It has been suggested that hosts which are normally nonsusceptible to infections become susceptible when maintained on certain diets. By feeding amoebae cysts to rabbits and guinea pigs—two experimental animals that are normally not highly susceptible—maintaining them on a grain-bread diet and dry ration, and omitting greens, Westphal (1941), Tobie (1949), and others demonstrated that these

animals became heavily infected and developed amoebic ulcers. Greenberg and Taylor (1950) demonstrated that the type of dietary carbohydrate is an important factor in the susceptibility of rats to *E. histolytica*, since high concentrations of galactose and lactose favor infection. This hypothesis may hold true in the laboratory but does not explain why, in a given human population of similar dietary habits, some show clinical symptoms of amoebiasis and others do not.

It is apparent that at present there is no completely satisfactory answer to why *E. histolytica* does not cause damage in some individuals. Otto (1958) reviewed this problem and suggested that in addition to the partial answers listed, there may be a matter of proper identification of *E. histolytica* in commensal situations. Perhaps Craig (1944), following earlier workers like Dobell, was correct in saying that *E. histolytica* is an obligate tissue parasite in every case of infection and that there is no true "carrier."

Bacteria and *Entamoeba histolytica*. Another line of investigation on amoebiasis holds great promise. It has been suggested that nonpathogenic enteric bacteria may cooperate with *E. histolytica* in producing pathogenicity through tissue invasion. Phillips and co-workers demonstrated that in germ-free guinea pigs no invasion of the intestinal wall occurred when *E. histolytica* was introduced, but amoebic ulcers were produced in hosts harboring a single bacterial symbiont. The assistance provided by the bacteria is not a direct one. Rather, it is indirect, having to do with the consumption of oxygen. It is known that *E. histolytica* does not thrive very well in the presence of oxygen. In all probability, the accompanying bacteria reduce the oxygen tension in the area of amoebic infection, thus permitting the amoeba to perform normally and invade tissues. This hypothesis is borne out by experiments in which reducing chemicals, such as cysteine or thioglycollate, are introduced with amoebae. In such instances, despite the lack of bacteria, ulcers were formed.

Other *Entamoeba* Species. *Entamoeba hartmanni* is the specific name often attributed to the small race of *E. histolytica* by those who believe the two to be more than separate races. This amoeba, measuring less than 10 μ in diameter in the trophozoite form and less than 9 μ in the cyst form, is considered to be nonpathogenic. Recent observations have strongly suggested that *E. hartmanni* should be considered a distinct species. Goldman (1959) demonstrated that *E. hartmanni* is quite different from *E. histolytica* when their fluorescence is measured with a microfluorimeter after both species have been exposed to fluorescent anti-*histolytica* and normal globulins. Furthermore, Sarkisyan (1957) has shown that at least 93 to 94 per cent of cysts in *E. hartmanni* include visible glycogen stored in the form of chromatoidal bars. In *E. histolytica* the percentage is never this high. These evidences strongly suggest the *E. hartmanni* should be considered a distinct species.

Entamoeba coli, a widely distributed intestinal commensal of man and other animals, measures between 15 and 40 μ in diameter (average, 20 to 35 μ) in the trophozoite form, and 10 to 30 μ in diameter in the rounded cystic form. The incidence of infection, like that of *E. histolytica*, varies in different areas. For example, Meleney (1930) found that 31.7 per cent of a sampling of Tennesseans harbored *E. coli*; Faust (1930) found that 26.1 per cent of individuals examined in Wise County, Virginia, harbored this amoeba; and Boeck (1923), in an extensive survey of 8029 individuals from all sections of the United States, found that 19.6 per cent were infected.

Entamoeba coli does not ingest or invade host tissues. The food vacuoles present in its much granulated cytoplasm enclose bacteria, yeast cells, and other fragments of intestinal debris. *Entamoeba coli* infections are generally detected by finding the cystic form in fecal examinations. The mature cyst characteristically includes eight vesicular nuclei with eccentrically placed endosomes. Younger cysts may contain one, two, or four nuclei. The chromatoidal bodies present in cysts are irregular, with distinctly jagged ends (Plate 4–1). Although erythrocytes are occasionally found in food vacuoles of *Entamoeba coli*, and the cysts of this amoeba are commonly found in diarrheic feces, there is no other evidence to indicate that this species is in any way pathogenic.

The life history of *Entamoeba coli* parallels that of *E. histolytica*—that is, it undergoes the precystic, cyst, metacystic, and trophozoite stages; infection of the host is initiated through the ingestion of cysts.

Entamoeba polecki, measuring between 8.3 and 14.9 μ (average, 11.62 μ) in the trophozoite form and 10 to 16 μ in the cyst form, is another dubious species commonly found in intestines of pigs, goats, monkeys, dogs and has been occasionally reported from man. This species appears to be an intermediate form of *E. histolytica* and *E. coli* and is often considered to be the same as the latter; however, from time to time certain investigators have championed its recognition as a distinct species (Burrows, 1959). Like *E. coli*, this species is nonpathogenic.

Entamoeba gingivalis, the first parasitic amoeba known from man (reported by Gros in 1849), is a widely distributed species found in the tartar and debris surrounding teeth. Although food vacuoles within this species enclose host cells, leukocytes, bacteria, and in culture, erythrocytes, there is little indication that it is pathogenic. Its presence, however, is commonly associated with periodontitis. Cysts are not known for *E. gingivalis*, and transmission is believed to be either direct or indirect via the trophozoite form. Temperature resistance of the trophozoite grown in vitro has been studied by Koch (1927), who reported that the amoeba can live indefinitely at 40° C.; however, it is killed in 18 hours at 0° C., in 24 hours at 5° C., in 48 hours at 10° C., in 20 minutes at 45° C., and in 15 minutes at 50° C. Since cysts are not known, it is assumed that *E. gingivalis* multiplies strictly by mitotic division in the trophozoite form.

Another species of *Entamoeba*, *E. invadens*, is of considerable interest because it is the causative agent of reptilian amoebiasis. It measures 9 to 38 μ in diameter in the trophozoite form (average 16 μ) and 11 to 20 μ in the fournucleate cystic form. It is known to produce lesions in the stomach, large and small intestines, and liver of snakes and lizards but appears to be harmless in turtles and possibly other reptiles. It is suspected that infections can be transmitted from turtle to snake with the former serving as the carrier. The life cycle of *E. invadens* parallels that of *E. histolytica*. Lamy's (1948) report that *E. invadens* can be cultured healthily in the presence of host liver tissue, but without bacteria, represents the first successful attempt at cultivating *Entamoeba* in a bacteria-free (axenic) medium. Such cultures grow best at low temperatures, from 24 to 30° C.

Various other species of *Entamoeba* are known to parasitize domestic and wild animals. *E. bovis* is known from the rumen of cattle; *E. gallinarum* is a nonpathogenic species found in the cecal excrement of chickens and turkeys; *E. gedoelsti* and *E. equi* in horses; *E. cuniculi* in rabbits; *E. muris* in rats and mice, *E. testudinis, E. terrapinae, E. barreti* in turtles; and *E. invadens* in various reptiles. Some of these species are depicted in Plate 4–7. All species other than *E. histolytica* and *E. invadens* are nonpathogenic.

Other species of *Entamoeba* are known to parasitize insects and probably other arthropods. None of these are pathogenic.

GENUS *Endolimax*. The genus *Endolimax* of the Endamoebidae includes species found in the colon of man, other mammals, birds, amphibians, and even cockroaches. The individual species are apparently host-specific. *Endolimax nana* is a commensal in the colon of man, although from time to time it has been suspected of being pathogenic because it is commonly found in diarrheic stools, some surveys showing an incidence of nearly 30 per cent. The trophozoite is monopodial and the lobopodium is broad. The single vesicular nucleus contains an irregular endosome. This species is definitely not a tissue invader, since in all known cases the food vacuoles enclose bacteria. The life cycle of *E. nana* is typical of cyst-forming endoparasitic amoebae. The characteristic cysts, measuring 5 to 14 μ in greatest diameter, are ovoid with one or two nuclei in immature specimens and four in mature ones (Plate 4–1, Fig. 6). Very often a large glycogen body is seen in the cytoplasm. Small and large races (strains) of *E. nana* have been reported, the only difference being in their sizes.

An interesting aspect of the excystment process of *Endolimax nana* is that the tetranucleate encysted form escapes through an extremely minute pore in the cyst wall. Upon escaping from the cyst wall, the multinucleate amoeba undergoes a series of mitotic divisions during which a portion of the cytoplasm is pinched off with each nucleus so that uninucleate metacystic trophozoites are produced. The trophozoites are active feeders and multiply quite rapidly by mitotic division.

Endolimax gregariniformis, measuring 4 to 12 μ in diameter, is a commensal occasionally encountered in chickens and turkeys. The cyst is typically uninucleate. *Endolimax ranarum* is commonly found in the colon of frogs (Plate 4–7, Fig. 7). The cyst of this species is octonucleate and measures 10 to 25 μ in diameter. *Endolimax blattae* is found in cockroaches (Plate 4–7, Fig. 8). The trophozoites are 4 to

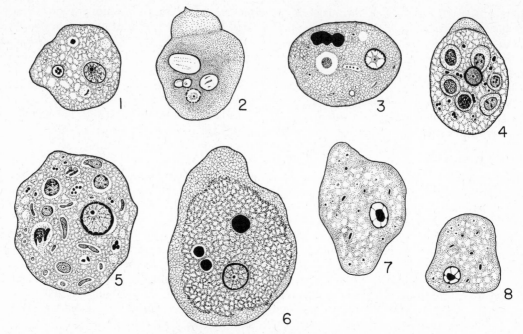

Plate 4-7   **Trophozoites of some parasitic amoebae.** 1. *Entamoeba citelli* from the caecum and colon of the striped ground squirrel. (Redrawn after Becker, 1926.) 2. *Entamoeba terrapinae* from the colon of turtles. (Redrawn after Sanders and Cleveland, 1930.) 3. *Entamoeba invadens* from the colon of various reptiles, especially snakes. (Redrawn after Geiman and Ratcliffe, 1936.) 4. *Entamoeba gingivalis* from human gingival tissue. 5. *Entamoeba coli* from human intestine. 6. *Entamoeba histolytica* from human intestine. 7. *Endolimax ranarum* from intestine of frogs. 8. *Endolimax blattae* from intestine of cockroaches.

16 μ in diameter, and the octonucleate cysts measure between 6 and 11 μ in their greatest diameter. Similar amoebae have been reported from a variety of mammals, reptiles, birds, and amphibians.

GENUS *Iodamoeba*.   The genus *Iodamoeba* includes two well recognized species, *I. bütschlii* in man and *I. suis* in pigs. These are host-specific species since morphologically they are indistinguishable. The trophozoite found in the host's intestine is 6 to 25 μ in diameter, with food vacuoles containing bacteria and yeast cells. The most characteristic feature of this genus is the large vesicular nucleus, which includes a large endosome surrounded by rounded granules (spherules). The cyst, measuring 6 to 16 μ in greatest diameter, varies from rounded to triangular and contains a large nucleus with a large endosome (Plate 4–1). Within the cytoplasm of the cyst is a large glycogen body, which is often partially wrapped around the nucleus. Because the cysts are uninucleate, the escaping form does not undergo a series of cytoplasmic divisions resulting in metacystic trophozoites. The escaping amoeba leaves through a minute pore in the cyst wall and moves with unusual rapidity. Moisture and warmth are apparently all that is required to induce excystation. Neither *I. bütschlii* nor *I. suis* are generally considered pathogenic, although Derrick, in 1948, reported a case of a Japanese prisoner-of-war who apparently died from a heavy infection of *I. bütschlii*. It is possible that occasional pathogenic strains may occur, or the commensal may become pathogenic under certain conditions such as extreme malnutrition of the host.

Because *Iodamoeba bütschlii* and *I. suis* are so similar morphologically, yet different physiologically, it is of interest to speculate whether human infections have been inherited from simian ancestors or acquired from pigs, and whether pig infections may have been acquired from man.

GENUS *Dientamoeba*.   *Dientamoeba fragilis,* a fairly common endocommensal of man, has been reported from the intestine of macaque monkeys in the Philippines. The geographic range is probably worldwide. The trophozoite, which is 4 to 18 μ in diameter, is actively amoeboid. Both one and two nuclei have been reported. As in *Iodamoeba*, the nuclei contain a prominent endosome surrounded by four or five minute chromatin granules. The cystic form is unknown, and transmission from one host to another is presumably via the trophozoite, which is extremely viable and capable of motility up to 48 hours after leaving the host in feces. Dobell (1940) suggested that transmission may be brought about with trophozoites becoming lodged in the eggs of nematode coparasites that are ingested by the host. Indeed, the pin worm (*Enterobius vermicularis*) has been suspected. This hypothesis is reasonable since this is the case in the life history of *Histomonas meleagridis* in fowls (p. 61), and Kudo (1954) suggested that *D. fragilis* may be an aberrant flagellate closely related to *Histomonas*.

Although generally considered a commensal, *Dientamoeba fragilis* may well be mildly pathogenic. Intestinal lesions due to this amoeba have never been demonstrated, but patients with gastrointestinal symptoms have been relieved of their discomforts when this amoeba is removed. Furthermore, Swerdlow and Burrows stated in 1955: "The frequency with which *Dientamoeba fragilis* is found in the appendix, its preference for red blood cells when they are available, and the concomitant occurrence of fibrosis in the appendiceal wall in all cases of *D. fragilis* infections of the appendix incriminate it as a pathogen."

Contrary to earlier beliefs, *D. fragilis* will live for several hours after being passed out of the host. Observations on the manner of division of this amoeba have revealed that cytoplasmic fission occurs first, resulting in two uninucleate daughter cells. The nucleus of each daughter then divides, restoring the binucleate condition so commonly found.

GENUS *Hydramoeba.* The genus *Hydramoeba* is represented here by *H. hydroxena*, an ecto- and endoparasite of hydra and freshwater medusae (Plate 4–8, Fig. 1). Its distribution is uncertain, although it has been reported from North Carolina, Virginia, and as far distant as Russia and Japan. The trophozoite, which measures from 25 to 200 μ in diameter, commences as an ectoparasite, primarily on the tentacles of hydra, but gradually migrates inwards, ingests the host's epidermal cells, and becomes established in the gastrovascular cavity, where it actively feeds on the gastrodermal cells (Plate 4–8, Fig. 2). Reynolds and Looper (1928) demonstrated that infected hydras die in 6 days, and the author has maintained infected hydra for as many as 10 days. Rice (1960) reported that this amoeba can destroy the medusa *Craspedocusta sowerbyi* in 6 days but apparently does not attack polyps. The host-parasite relationship appears to be an obligatory one, because once removed from its host, the amoeba disintegrates in 4 to 10 days. When the host is killed, the amoeba encysts. The cyst is spherical, measures approximately 28 μ in diameter, and contains a large nucleus, nematocysts from the deceased host, and a conspicuous vacuole. The nucleus of *H. hydroxena* is interesting in that it possesses refractile granules along the inner margin of the nuclear membrane, and as in *Entamoeba histolytica* and *E. coli,* there are spokelike radiations from the large endosome.

It is interesting to note that during the relationship between *Hydramoeba hydroxena* and hydra, the amoeba could be interpreted to be a predator that is gradually devouring its prey. This indicates that at one level a parasite may be difficult to distinguish from a predator, just as at another level a true parasite may be difficult to distinguish from a commensal.

Some other parasitic members of the Endamoebidae are depicted on Plate 4–8.

PHYSIOLOGY OF PARASITIC AMOEBAE

OXYGEN REQUIREMENTS

From knowledge obtained by observing *Entamoeba histolytica* in culture, it is apparent that this amoeba is a microaerobe capable of facultative anaerobism. Various investigators have demonstrated that *E. histolytica* grows best in a complete absence of oxygen or with only a trace present. The elevation of oxygen tension, to levels not toxic to free-living amoebae, is toxic to this parasite. *E. coli* and *E. hartmanni* behave in much the same fashion as *E. histolytica* in their sensitivity to oxygen.

GROWTH REQUIREMENTS

The actual nutritional requirements of the parasitic amoebae are not well known. *Entamoeba histolytica,* in its natural habitat, survives on the host's erythrocytes, bacteria, and dissolved substances derived from the host's tissues. In vitro culture studies have revealed some of the required nutrients. Cholesterol, vitamins (especially those of the B complex), and amino acids seem to be necessary. The most commonly used culture media for *E. histolytica* all include rice starch, because starch granules are readily engulfed and probably serve as the main energy source, thus suggesting a well developed glycolytic mechanism (Table 3–5) and fermentative activity.

Although Diamond (1961) has reported success at culturing *Entamoeba histolytica* in the absence of bacteria, it is still believed that one of the prerequisites for in vitro culture of this amoeba is the presence of accompanying bacteria or *Trypanosoma cruzi*. The latter must be present in large numbers (10^7 to 10^8 flagellates per milliter of culture medium). Although not all bacteria are compatible (Cleveland and Sanders, 1930b; Jacobs, 1950), many are excellent companions. Among the several hypotheses offered to explain the requisite of *E. histolytica* for bacteria, two are most favored:

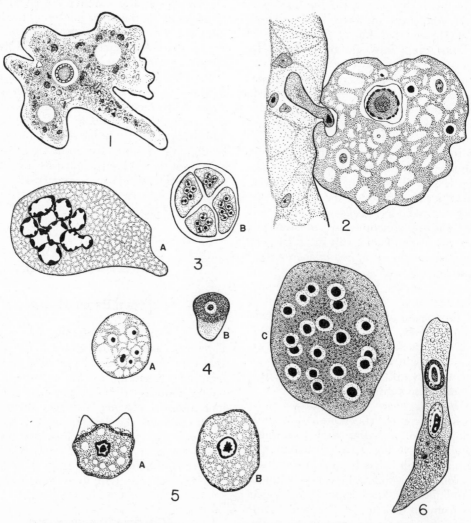

Plate 4-8   Parasitic amoebae. 1. *Hydramoeba hydroxena* trophozoite, a parasite of hydra. (Redrawn after Entz, 1912.) **2.** Section of infected hydra showing epithelial cell being ingested by *H. hydroxena.* (Redrawn after Hegner and Taliaferro. 1924. *Human Protozoology*, Macmillan, New York.) **3. A.** Stained trophozoite of *Schizamoeba salmonis* in stomach of salmonid fish. **B.** Stained cyst of *S. salmonis.* (A and B redrawn after Davis, 1926.) **4. A.** Stained cyst of *Dobellina mesnili* found between the peritrophic membrane and the epithelium in the gut of the larvae of *Trichocerca hiemalis* and other gnats. **B.** Stained uninucleate trophozoite of *D. mesnili.* **C.** Stained multinucleate trophozoite of *D. mesnili.* (A, B, and C redrawn after Bishop and Tate, 1939.) **5. A** and **B.** Stained trophozoites of *Martinezia baezi*, a parasite in intestine of iguanas. **6.** Trophozoite of *Paramoeba pigmentifera*, parasitic in coelom of chaetognaths. (Redrawn after Janicki, 1928.)

(1) A mutualistic relationship exists between the amoebae and the bacteria. The protozoa maintained in culture are suspected of having lost the ability to synthesize the essential respiratory enzymes and/or cofactors and these are provided by the bacteria. (2) Sustaining substances are acquired under in vitro and probably in vivo conditions through the ingestion of bacteria by the amoeba. This is suggested by the work of Karlsson, James, and Anderson (1952), who demonstrated that substances derived from autoclaved bacteria normally associated with E. histolytica sustained survival of the amoeba for some time. Although some maintain that the two concepts are not incompatible since the "sustaining substances" may well be the essential respiratory enzymes that the culture grown amoebae fail to synthesize, it is difficult to conceive that such enzymes can withstand the autoclaving process. It is possible, however, that some heat-resistant cofactors are involved. As stated earlier, it is believed that in life the synergistic relationship between E. histolytica and bacteria is a prerequisite to the development of amoebiasis (Phillips et al., 1958).

In the laboratory, Entamoeba histolytica can also be maintained in a medium devoid of all nutrients except the flagellate Trypanosoma cruzi, which the amoebae readily engulf. Of all the species of trypanosomes, only this species supports growth. Of course, under natural conditions T. cruzi seldom if ever comes in contact with E. histolytica since the former is a blood parasite.

In the case of Entamoeba gingivalis, accompanying bacteria are usually also necessary. Clayton and Ball (1954) reported that if the bacteria are rendered static—that is, reproduction is inhibited by the addition of antibiotics)—the amoebae die. Furthermore, observations suggest that a bacteria-feeding phase does exist, because after a period of time the existing flora is exhausted. However, if too many bacteria are present, the amoebae become static (Reeves and Frye, 1960). In culturing E. gingivalis, some factor present in saliva favors growth, since the addition of saliva enhances the culture significantly (Wysocka and Wegner, 1953).

So far as they are known, the nutrient requirements of parasitic amoebae are for the most part similar. Carbohydrates in the form of starch, especially rice starch, enhance growth. The exception is Endamoeba blattae, which thrives better if the cockroach host is maintained on a high protein diet. When Endamoeba blattae is maintained in hosts kept on a high fat diet, small quantities of fats become microscopically visible, indicating that fat utilization does occur.

As far as nitrogen requirements are concerned, it is suspected that Entamoeba histolytica and possibly other closely related enteric amoebae require only amino acids and other nitrogenous compounds of low molecular weight. This has been effectively demonstrated by Rees et al. (1945), who were able to culture E. histolytica in cellophane bags suspended in whole egg slants thus only permitting small molecules to reach the amoebae. It should be pointed out, however, that it is uncertain whether the low molecular weight nitrogenous molecules are directly beneficial to the amoebae, or are only indirectly beneficial via their bacterial associates.

PHYSICAL FACTORS

Intestinal amoebae readily adjust to changes in certain physical factors in their environment such as pH and temperature. Most amoebae grow rather satisfactorily at pH 5.4 to 8.3, although growth is definitely reduced at the two extremes. From what is known about temperature effects, it appears that individual species grow best within specific temperature ranges. For example, E. histolytica will not grow at 30° C. but will grow if placed at 32° C. and will thrive best at 37 to 38° C. On the other hand, E. invadens will grow at temperatures between 16 and 35° C., the optimum being between 24 and 30° C. A third species, E. moshkovskii, will grow between 17 and 37° C., with the optimum at 24° C.

HOST-PARASITE RELATIONSHIPS

How does the parasite affect the host? The diseases caused by pathogenic amoebae are the most readily appreciated effects. The ability of Entamoeba histolytica to invade tissues has been attributed to a combination of mechanical ingestion and the secretion of a histolytic substance (cytolysin). Bradin (1951) demonstrated that the enzyme hyaluronidase, which hydrolyzes the ground substance (specifically hyaluronic acid), is present in one strain of this amoeba that is infective for the hamster. It is conceivable that the so-called histolytic enzyme may be, at least in part, hyaluronidase. Although the presence of cytolysin appears to be universal in all *E. histolytica,* the presence of hyaluronidase cannot always be demonstrated. On the other hand, Teokharov (1956) has advanced the theory that much of the pathogenicity of *E. histolytica* results from endotoxins produced during necrosis of dying amoebae in the later stages of amoebiasis. The pathogenicity of *E. histolytica* may well be associated with host adaptation, since it is known that when amoebae are introduced into an experimental host after having been maintained in another species of host, the degree of pathogenicity is increased markedly. Again, temperature is known to affect pathogenicity, for strains adapted to growth at low temperatures (19° C.) are more virulent when introduced into hamsters (Cabrera and Porter, 1958).

EFFECTS OF HOST ON AMOEBAE

Various conditions that influence the host are known to have their effects on the parasitic amoebae. For example, if cockroaches infected with *Endolimax blattae* are starved for 8 weeks, the parasites disappear. Maintenance of hosts at high or low temperatures results in less pathogenicity of the pathogenic amoeba species; furthermore, maintenance of hosts at high or low temperatures retards the normal rate of trophic multiplication in all species.

The host's diet has a great influence on enteric amoebae. High protein diets are generally unfavorable for the parasites. Individuals suffering from amoebiasis sometimes lose their symptoms rapidly when maintained on a diet rich in proteins and vitamins. The lack of vitamins also inflicts profound effects. For example, the lack of vitamin C in guinea pigs, and of niacin in dogs, lowers resistance to amoebiasis.

The physiology of parasitic amoebae is by no means completely understood. The problems of encystment and amoeboid movement are ones that have challenged biologists for decades. A discussion of the various theories concerning these problems can be obtained from most textbooks in general physiology.

LITERATURE CITED

Alexopoulos, C. J. 1962. Introductory Mycology. 2nd Ed. John Wiley & Sons, New York.

Boeck, W. C. 1923. Survey of 8,029 persons, in the United States, for intestinal parasites, with special reference for amoebic dysentery among returned soldiers. Bull. Hyg. Lab., U. S. Publ. Health Serv., pp. 1–61.

Bradin, J. L. 1951. Hyaluronidase production by *Endamoeba histolytica.* J. Parasit., *37:* 10–11.

Burrows, R. B. 1959. Morphological differentiation of *Entamoeba hartmanni* and *E. polecki* from *E. histolytica.* Amer. J. Trop. Med. Hyg., *8:* 583–589.

Cabrera, H. A., and R. J. Porter. 1958. Survival time and critical temperatures of various strains of *Entamoeba histolytica.* Exptl. Parasit., *7:* 285–291.

Clayton, J. P., Jr., and G. H. Ball. 1954. Effects of penicillin on *Endamoeba gingivalis* in cultures with bacteria from the human mouth. J. Parasit., *40:* 347–352.

Cleveland, L. R., and E. P. Sanders. 1930a. Encystation, multiple fission without encystment, excystation, metacystic development, and variation in a pure line and nine strains of *Entamoeba histolytica.* Arch. Protistenk., *70:* 223–266.

Cleveland, L. R., and E. P. Sanders. 1930b. The virulence of a pure line and several strains of *Endamoeba histolytica* from the liver of cats and the relation of bacteria, cultivation, and liver passage to virulence. Am. J. Hyg., *12:* 569–605.

Craig, C. F. 1944. The Etiology, Diagnosis, and Treatment of Amoebiasis. Williams & Wilkins, Baltimore.

Craig, C. F., and E. C. Faust. 1951. Clinical Parasitology. Lea & Febiger, Philadelphia.

Cresswell, S. M., and C. E. Wallace. 1934. Amebiasis: survey of 1,032 stool examinations. Northwest Med., *33:* 165–168.

Culbertson, C. G., J. W. Smith, and J. R. Minner. 1958. *Acanthamoeba:* observations on animal pathogenicity. Science, *127:* 1506.

Diamond, L. S. 1961. Axenic cultivation of *Entamoeba histolytica.* Science, *134:* 336–337.

Dobell, C. C. 1940. Researches on the intestinal protozoa of monkeys and man. X. The life-history of *Dientamoeba fragilis:* observations, experiments, and speculations. Parasitol., *32:* 417–461.

Faust, E. C. 1930. The *Endamoeba coli* index of *E. histolytica* in a community. Am. J. Trop. Med., *10:* 137–144.

Faust, E. C. 1931. The incidence and significance of infestation with *Endamoeba histolytica* in New Orleans and the American tropics. Am. J. Trop. Med., *11:* 231–237.

Frye, W. W., and H. E. Meleney. 1938. The pathogenicity of a strain of small race *Endamoeba histolytica.* Am. J. Hyg., *27:* 580–589.

Goldman, M. 1959. Microfluorimetric evidence of antigenic difference between *Entamoeba histolytica* and *Entamoeba hartmanni.* Proc. Soc. Exp. Biol. Med., *102:* 189–191.

Greenberg, J., and D. J. Taylor. 1950. The effect of dietary carbohydrate on *Endamoeba histolytica* infections in the rat. J. Parasit., *36:* 21.

Hall, R. P. 1953. Protozoology. Prentice-Hall, New York.

Hopkins, S. H. 1957. Parasitism. Geol. Soc. Amer. Mem. 67, *1:* 413–428.

Hunninen, A. V., and H. A. Boone. 1957. Studies on the pathogenicity of various strains of *Endamoeba histolytica* in the rabbit. Am. J. Trop. Med. Hyg., *6:* 32–49.

Jacobs, L. 1950. The substitution of bacteria in cultures of *Endamoeba histolytica.* J. Parasit., *36:* 128–130.

Jahn, T. L., and F. F. Jahn. 1949. How To Know the Protozoa. Wm. C. Brown, Dubuque, Ia.

Karling, J. S. 1942. The Plasmodiophorales. Published by author, New York.

Karlsson, J. L., M. B. James, and H. H. Anderson. 1952. Studies on nutritional principles for *Endamoeba histolytica* in autoclaved bacterial cells. Exptl. Parasit., *1:* 347–352.

Koch, D. A. 1927. Relation of moisture and temperature to the viability of *Endamoeba gingivalis* (Gros) in vitro. Univ. Cal. Publ. Zool., *31:* 17–29.

Kudo, R. R. 1954. *Protozoology.* 4th Ed., Charles C Thomas, Springfield, Ill.

Lamy, L. 1948. Obtention d'une culture bactériologiquement pure d'amibes parasites pathogènes (*Entamoeba invadens* Rodhain), ne comportant aucune addition de germes bactériens morts, ai d'aucun extrait microbien. Compt. Rend. Acad. Sci., *226:* 1021–1022. (Also see *226:* 1400–1402.)

MacBride, T. H., and G. H. Martin. 1934. The Myxomycetes. Macmillan, New York.

McLennan, E. I. 1930. A disease of hops in Tasmania and an account of a proteomyxan organism, etc. Austral. J. Exp. Biol., *7:* 9.

Meleney, H. E. 1930. Community surveys for *Endamoeba histolytica* and other intestinal protozoa in Tennessee; first report. J. Parasit., *16:* 146–153.

Meleney, H. E., and L. K. Zuckerman. 1948. Note on a strain of small race *Endamoeba histolytica* which became large in culture. Am. J. Hyg., *47:* 187–188.

Milam, D. F., and H. E. Meleney. 1931. Investigations of *Endamoeba histolytica* and other intestinal protozoa in Tennessee: II. An epidemiological study of amoebiasis in a rural community. Am. J. Hyg., *14:* 325–336.

Neal, R. A. 1957. Virulence in *Entamoeba histolytica.* Tr. Roy. Soc. Trop. Med. Hyg., *51:* 327–331.

Otto, G. F. 1958. Some reflections on the ecology of parasitism. J. Parasit., *44:* 1–27.

Phillips, B. P., P. A. Wolfe, and I. L. Bartgis. 1958. Studies on the ameba-bacteria relationship in amebiasis. II. Some concepts on the etiology of the disease. Am. J. Trop. Med. Hyg., *7:* 392–399.

Reardon, L. V. 1941. Incidence of *Endamoeba histolytica* and intestinal nematodes in a Georgia state institution. J. Parasit., *27:* 89–90.

Rees, C. W., J. Bozicevich, L. V. Reardon, and F. S. Daft. 1944. The influence of cholesterol and certain vitamins on the growth of *Endamoeba histolytica* with a single species of bacteria. Am. J. Trop. Med., *24:* 189–193.

Reeves, R. E., and W. W. Frye. 1960. Cultivation of *Entamoeba histolytica* with penicillin-inhibited *Bacteroides symbiosus.* III. The effects of streptomycin. J. Parasit., *46:* 187–194.

Reynolds, B. D., and J. B. Looper. 1928. Infection experiments with *Hydramoeba hydroxena* nov. gen. J. Parasit., *15:* 23–30.

Rice, N. E. 1960. *Hydramoeba hydroxena* (Entz), a parasite on the fresh-water medusa, *Crapedacusta sowerbii* Lankester, and its pathogenicity for *Hydra cauliculata* Hyman. J. Protozool., *7:* 151–156.

Santos Zetina, F. 1940. Contribucion al estudio del parasitismo intestinal en Yucatan. Rev. Med. Yucatan, *20:* 271–277.

Sarkisyan, M. A. 1957. Observations on *Entamoeba hartmanni* Prowazek, 1912. Med. Parozitol. I. Parazitarn Bolezni, *26:* 618–623.

Teokharov, B. 1956. Concerning peculiarities of a pathological anatomical picture of the early stages of intestinal amoebiasis. Arkh. Patol., *18:* 106–109.

Tobie, J. E. 1949. Experimental infection of the rabbit with *Endamoeba histolytica*. Am. J. Trop. Med., *29:* 859–870.

Westphal, A. 1941. Ein Kulturverfahren für *Entamoeba gingivalis* und dessen Anwendung für die Differentialdiagnose von *E. gingivalis* und *E. histolytica*. Deutsche Tropenmed. Ztschr., *45:* 685–690.

Wysocka, F., and Z. Wegner. 1953. Spostrzezenia nad hodwola *Entamoeba gingivalis*. Biul Inst. Med. Morskie W. Gdansku, *5:* 193–207.

SUGGESTED READING

Balamuth, W., and P. E. Thompson, 1955. Comparative studies on amebae and amebicides. *In* Biochemistry and Physiology of Protozoa, Vol. II. Academic Press, New York. (This is a good review of aspects of the physiology of amoebae.)

Hall, R. P. 1953. Protozoology. Prentice-Hall, New York, pp. 544–546, 551–563. (These sections in Hall's textbook are devoted to the parasitic amoebae.)

Hegner, R., and J. Andrews. 1930. Problems and Methods of Research in Protozoology. Macmillan, New York.

Ratcliffe, H. The role of bacteria in the cultivation of intestinal protozoa. pp. 112–118.

Hegner, R. Intestinal Sarcodina in general. pp. 162–181.

Craig, C. E. Serological studies on *Endamoeba histolytica*. pp. 182–193.

Rees, C. Experimental amoebiasis in kittens. pp. 194–200.

Reynolds, B. D. Ectoparasitic protozoa. pp. 11–26.

Andrews, J. Coprozoic protozoa. pp. 59–65.

(Each of these chapters is concerned with some aspect of the biology of parasitic amoebae. Although somewhat outdated, these sections should prove to be of interest to the beginning student and may provide ideas for research.)

Hoare, C. A. 1951. The commensal phase of *Entamoeba histolytica*. Exptl. Parasit., *1:* 411–427. (This review article discusses some of the author's thoughts about the nonpathogenicity of *E. histolytica* in certain individuals.)

Hoare, C. A. 1958. The enigma of host-parasite relations in amebiasis. The Rice Institute Pamphlet, *XLV:* 23–35. (This review article discusses the host-parasite relationship between *E. histolytica* and its host. Pathogenesis, invasion, and host response to strains are discussed.)

Levine, N. D. 1961. Protozoan Parasites of Domestic Animals And of Man. Burgess, Minneapolis, pp. 129–157. (Although this section from Levine's textbook is primarily concerned with parasitic amoebae of medical and veterinary importance, the student will find these to-the-point discussions of interest and the bibliography useful.)

Lwoff, M. 1951. Nutrition of parasitic amoebae. *In* Biochemistry And Physiology of Protozoa. Vol. I. Academic Press, New York. (This is a good review of the nutritional physiology of amoebae.)

5

THE SPOROZOA

The subphylum Sporozoa includes parasitic forms exclusively. These are either intra- or intercellular parasites of hosts belonging to practically every animal phylum. In vertebrates, the sporozoans occur mainly in the blood, the redituloendothelial system, and in the epithelial lining of the intestine; in invertebrates, they are found primarily in the gut and in the digestive and excretory systems. All sporozoans theoretically share one basic characteristic—the capability to produce spores, although this ability has become lost in some. As adults, sporozoans are not capable of rapid locomotion because they possess no specialized organelles of locomotion. However, during the immature stages of certain species, pseudopodia are produced, and in the gametic stage many species exhibit flagella-like structures.

Neither the morphology nor the life cycle patterns of sporozoans give much indication of their relationship with the other protozoa. The complexities of their life cycles, which are intimately associated with the physiology of their hosts, suggest that the sporozoans have long been parasitic. Cleveland (1949) has suggested that the modern Mastigophora and Sporozoa probably arose from a common group. This hypothesis is based on the discovery that some intestinal flagellates of woodroaches and some sporozoans possess complex sexual cycles that have too much in common to have been produced by parallel evolution. He postulated that both groups were well evolved by the beginning of the Tertiary, if not earlier, hence 70,000,000 years ago.

Since the life cycle patterns, as found among the members of the various taxa subordinate to the Sporozoa, are both numerous and diverse, it is not possible to give a generalized pattern other than to state that in sporozoan life cycles there are usually two or three distinct phases. The three-phase life cycle is by far the more comon. The infective form of all sporozoans is the sporozoite. This commonly elongate form is either enveloped or not enveloped within a spore wall. Once introduced into a host, sporozoites, after undergoing certain preparative stages, reproduce asexually by multiple fission or schizogony. This is the *schizogonic phase*.

The organisms resulting from schizogony are commonly known as merozoites. Some of these differentiate into male gametes, while others become female gametes. This period of development is referred to as gamogony. When a female gamete and a male gamete fuse, the zygote is formed. Thus gamogony and subsequent fertilization may be considered the *sexual reproductive phase*. The appearance of the zygote marks the end of the reproductive stage and the beginning of the third phase, the *sporogonic phase*. During this phase, the zygote develops into one or several haploid spores, each containing a distinctive number of sporozoites. When sporozoites become established within a host, the schizogonic phase recurs.

111

Among a few sporozoans, asexual reproduction (the schizogonic phase) does not occur, hence in their life cycles only the sexual and sporogonic phases are present. This is the case among most gregarines.

Among species that require two hosts, sexual reproduction commonly occurs in one host, and asexual reproduction in the other. The host in which sexual reproduction takes place is referred to as the definitive or primary host; the host in which schizogony occurs is known as the intermediate or secondary host.

Spores constitute the transmissive form of the parasite. Spores of species confined to one host usually have a resistant membranous encasement—the spore membrane—which enables them to withstand unfavorable conditions while outside the host's body. Among sporozoan blood parasites such as the malarial *Plasmodium* spp., the infective forms (sporozoites) are naked—that is, without an encasement. These sporozoans require two hosts—an insect vector and a vertebrate host.

Unlike amoebae, sporozoans are unable to ingest particulate food or bacteria. They are dependent on soluble cellular constituents.

Many sporozoans are of medical and veterinary importance because they are responsible for some of our most widespread diseases, such as malaria.

SYSTEMATICS AND BIOLOGY

CLASSIFICATION

The systematic scheme proposed by Kudo (1954) is modified and adopted as follows*;

Subphylum Sporozoa
    Class 1. Telosporidea
        Order 1. Gregarinidia
        Order 2. Coccidia
        Order 3. Haemosporidia
    Class 2. Acnidosporidea
        Order 1. Haplosporidia
        Order 2. Sarcosporidia
    Class 3. Cnidosporidea
        Order 1. Myxosporidia
        Order 2. Actinomyxidia
        Order 3. Microsporidia
        Order 4. Helicosporidia

---

*Since the Sporozoa is undoubtedly a heterogeneous collection of divergent forms, many interpretations of the taxonomy have been proposed. The most comprehensive have been those of Grassé (1953) and Grell (1956). Students interested in phylogeny and taxonomy should consult these monographs.

Members of the class Telosporidea form simple spores that do not include a polar filament or a polar capsule. A polar filament is a long, spirally coiled, delicate thread located within a specialized chamber known as the polar capsule, which is found at one end of the spore. The polar filament is considered to be a temporary organelle that anchors the spore after it germinates and has gained entry to a suitable host's alimentary tract. There is usually more than one sporozoite within the spore of a telosporidean. Sporozoans belonging to this class are intracellular parasites during a part of their life cycle.

The members of the class Acnidosporidea form simple spores like those of telosporideans, but acnidosporidean spores include only one sporozoite. Members of this class are parasitic in cells, tissues, and coelomic cavities of invertebrates and lower vertebrates or in the muscles of mammals, birds, and reptiles.

Members of the class Cnidosporidea form spores that possess one to four polar filaments typically coiled within a polar capsule. There are one to many sporoplasms (amoeboid organisms) within each spore. Cnidosporideans are exclusively parasitic in lower vertebrates and invertebrates, in which they are found in cells and the coelom.

THE CLASS TELOSPORIDEA

The Telosporidea includes the gregarines and coccidians. Most of these probably arose from primitive flagellates but some may have arisen from primitive amoebae.

ORDER GREGARINIDIA

The gregarines are primarily parasites of invertebrates, especially arthropods, molluscs, and annelids. A few have been reported from ascidians. Since the discovery that molluscs have arisen from a segmented ancestral form, it is now reasonable to postulate that parasitism by gregarines could have been initiated in some common ancestral stock from which segmented animals were derived (Manwell, 1961). Gregarines are most commonly found in the cells lining the coelom of the host, in the cells lining the digestive tract, and in reproductive organs. These parasites obtain their nutrition by osmosis through the body surface, and the majority multiply by sexual reproduction. Among members of a small group, both sexual and schizogonic reproduction occur. Gregarines that undergo sexual reproduction only belong to the suborder Eugregarinina. Those gregarines that multiply sexually and by schizogony belong to the suborder Schizogregarinina.

SUBORDER EUGREGARININA

This suborder includes the "true gregarines," which are commonly encountered in insects and other invertebrates. The life cycles of the various species follows essentially a similar pattern.

Generalized Life Cycle

Infection of a new host is established with the ingestion of spores (oocysts) enclosing sporozoites. Typically each spore includes eight rod or sickle shaped sporozoites. Once within the gut of the host, the sporozoites escape from the spore walls and actively penetrate epithelial cells, one sporozoite to each cell. The intracellular sporozoites increase in size and eventually leave the host cell. These large organisms, now known as trophozoites, are then found in the lumen of the host's gut. After a period of wandering about, each individual, now known as a gametocyte, becomes more round and pairs up with a mate. The two then become encysted in a protective envelope known as the gametocyst.

Although the members of each pair of gametocytes are undistinguishable, it is believed that one represents a male and the other represents a female. Once enveloped within a gametocyst, each gametocyte undergoes repeated nuclear divisions, culminating finally in cytoplasmic divisions, with a portion of the parental cytoplasm surrounding each daughter nucleus. The resulting uninucleate bodies are known as gametes. The progeny of a male gametocyte are all males, while the progeny of a female gametocyte are all females. Because the male and female gametes are morphologically similar, they are known as isogametes.

The fusion of a male and a female gamete (known in this case as *isogamy*) results in a zygote. Numerous zygotes are formed within a single gametocyst. As soon as the zygotes are formed, a secondary cyst, known as an *oocyst* or sometimes as a *sporocyst*, is secreted by each zygote around itself. Three rapid divisions occur within the oocyst resulting in eight sporozoites. At this point, the gametocyst, which contains numerous sporozoite-enclosing oocysts, is discharged from the host's gut in feces. It may remain intact and be ingested by another host, or it may rupture, releasing oocysts, each enclosing eight sporozoites. If this occurs, oocysts are ingested by another host.

In the life cycle pattern elucidated above, only the sexual type of reproduction is present. Schizogonic, or asexual, reproduction does not occur. As a result, the host is not overwhelmed with parasites, especially tissue-invading parasites. Thus, injury is limited to those host cells actually attacked by the sporozoites.

Tribes of Eugregarinina

The Eugregarinina includes two tribes—the Acephalina and the Cephalina. Members of the Acephalina possess rather simple bodies that are not compartmentalized, although the trophozoite usually possesses an organ of attachment at the anterior end. Members of the Cephalina possess bodies that are divided into chambers. In those forms of Cephalina in which the trophozoite possesses two chambers, the anterior chamber is known as the *protomerite* and the larger posterior one is known as the *deutomerite*. In Cephalina with three-chambered trophozoites the chambers are designated as epi-, proto-, and deutomerites.

TRIBE ACEPHALINA. The Acephalina includes *Monocystis,* the members of which are commonly found in the coelom and in the seminal vesicles of earthworms (Plate 5–1). In addition, the members of the genera *Enterocystis, Rhabdocystis, Apolocystis,* and *Nematocystis* are all fairly common, and in each case the organism follows the life cycle pattern that does not involve schizogony. Selected members of these genera are depicted in Plate 5–2.

Enterocystis ensis is parasitic in the alimentary tract of the larvae of the ephimerid, *Caenis* sp. (Plate 5–2, Fig. 1). The spores (or oocysts) are elongate ovoid, enclosing eight sporozoites. *Rhabdocystis claviformis* is found in the seminal vesicles of *Octolasium complanatum* (Plate 5–2, Fig. 2). The trophozoites of this species measure up to 30 μ by 300 μ, and the spores are oval with a slight indentation in the middle. *Nematocystis* includes *N. vermicularis,* a parasite in the seminal vesicles of various species of earthworms (Plate 5–2, Fig. 4). The trophozoites are 1000 μ by 100 μ in size and bear tufts of cilia-like projections from each end. *Apolocystis* includes parasites of the seminal vesicles and coelom of various oligochaetes; the trophozoites are spherical and the spores are biconical (Plate 5–2, Fig. 3).

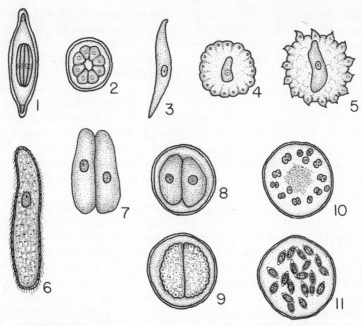

Plate 5-1   **Stages in the life cycle of** *Monocystis lumbrici,* **a gregarine parasite in the seminal vesicles of earthworms.** **1.** Spore, or oocyst, containing eight sporosoites. **2.** Cross-sectional view of a spore enclosing eight sporozoites. **3.** Single, liberated sporozoite. **4.** Sporozoite that has entered the multicellular sperm sphere of host (sperm mother cells). **5.** Growth and transformation of a sporozoite into the trophozoite form within the host's sperm sphere. **6.** A mature trophozoite surrounded by a thin layer of degenerating sperm-sphere cells, to which the tails of the spermatozoa are attached. **7.** Two trophozoites that are now free of the degenerated sperm-sphere cells and that have united as gametocytes. **8.** Gametocytes encysted within a double-walled gametocyst. **9.** Gametocytes undergoing sporulation to form isogametes. **10.** Sexual reproduction, during which isogametes unite to form zygotes. **11.** Cyst containing many young spores. The spores have arisen from the division of the zygotes to form sporozoites that secrete the spore capsules around themselves. (Some figures original; others from various authors.)

The genus *Rhynchocystis* differs from the previously mentioned genera in that the anterior end of the trophozoite is conical (Plate 5-2, Fig. 5). All the many species of *Rhynchocystis* are found in the seminal vesicles of various oligochaetes.

Other representative genera of the Acephalina are depicted in Plates 5-2 and 5-3.

TRIBE CEPHALINA. The members of this tribe are primarily parasites in the alimentary canal of arthropods. Some of the better known genera are described below. The genus *Gregarina* includes many species parasitic in insects (Plate 5-4, Fig. 1). For example, *G. blattarum* is found in the oriental cockroach, *G. oviceps* is found in various species of crickets, and *G. polymorpha* in the mealworm, *Tenebrio molitor.* The genus *Stylocephalus* is characterized by a nipple shaped epimerite and papillae-covered spores (Plate 5-4, Fig. 2). Several species of this genus have been reported from insects and molluscs.

Members of the genus *Actinocephalus* can be recognized by a sessile epimerite that has eight to ten finger-like processes at its apex and by their biconical spores (Plate 5-4, Fig. 3). This genus includes *A. parvus* in the gut of the dog flea *Ctenocephalus canis,* and *A. acutispora* in the gut of the beetle *Silpha laevigata.*

Among one group of Cephalina, members of *Porospora* and *Nematopsis,* two hosts are involved —a crustacean and a mollusc. When naked or well protected sporozoites enter the stomach or midgut of a specific crustacean host, they develop into typical cephaline trophozoites with compartmentalized bodies. One, two, or more of these trophozoites, which are also known as sporadins, become associated and encyst. Their nuclei undergo repeated division, accompanied by cytoplasmic division, so that a large number of daughter cells, known as gymnospores, are formed. The gymnospores are located in the host's hindgut and are eventually voided in feces.

When gymnospores come in contact with the molluscan host, they enter or are engulfed by amoeboid phagocytes in the mollusc's gills, mantle, or digestive tract. Gymnospores are

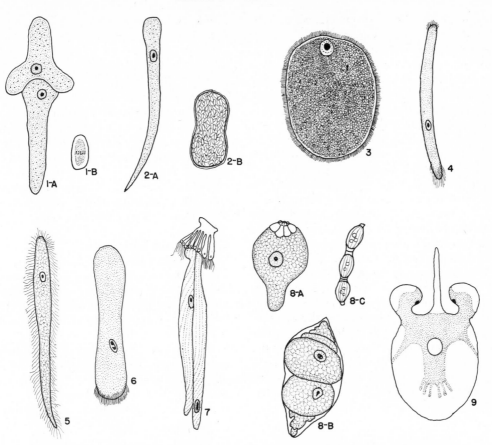

Plate 5-2   Some gregarine parasites (Acephalina). 1. A. Two trophozoites, or sporadins, of *Enterocystis ensis* in the characteristic end-to-end association known as syzygy. **B.** A single spore of *E. ensis,* found in the gut of the larvae of the ephemerid *Caenis* sp. (A and B redrawn after Zwetkow, 1926.) **2. A.** Single trophozoite, or sporadin, of *Rhabdocystis claviformis,* a parasite in the seminal vesicles of the oligochaete, *Octolasium complanatum.* **B.** Cyst of *R. claviformis.* (A and B modified after Boldt.) **3.** *Apolocystis gigantea* trophozoite, found in the seminal vesicles of the oligochaetes *Helodrilus foetidus* and *Lumbricus rubellus.* (Modified after Troisi, 1933.) **4.** Trophozoite of *Nematocystis vermicularis,* found in the seminal vesicles of various oligochaetes. (Original.) **5.** Trophozoite of *Rhynchocystis pilosa,* found in the seminal vesicles of various oligochaetes. (Redrawn after Hesse, 1909.) **6.** Trophozoite of *Zygocystis wenrichi* in the seminal vesicles of *Lumbricus rubellus* and *Helodrilus foetidus.* (Redrawn after Troisi, 1933.) **7.** Trophozoites of *Pleurocystis cuenoli* in the ciliated seminal horn of *Helodrilus longus* and *H. caliginosus.* (Redrawn after Hesse, 1909.) **8. A.** Trophozoite of *Stomatophora coronata* with sucker-like anterior epimeritic organelle; found in seminal vesicles of oligochaetes of the genus *Pheretima.* **B.** Cyst of *S. coronata.* **C.** Spores of *S. coronata* typically arranged in a chain. (A–C redrawn after Hesse, 1909.) **9.** Trophozoite of *Choanocystella tentaculata,* showing typical anterior mobile sucker and a tentacle; found in seminal vesicles of the oligochaete *Pheretima beaufortii* in New Guinea. (Redrawn after Martiis, 1911.)

commonly found in large numbers in their host's gill lacunae. Eventually the gymnospores pair off and fuse, forming zygotes that develop into sporozoites. These sporozoites are either enclosed within membranes or are naked, depending on the species.

When sporozoites that are enclosed by phagocytes are ingested by the crustacean host —normally this occurs when young infected molluscs are ingested—the portion of the life cycle that occurs within the crustacean is repeated. Some protozoologists consider the rapid

division of trophozoites, or sporadins, resulting in the formation of gymnospores to be a form of schizogony, and they thus consider these sporozoans to be members of the suborder Schizogregarinina.

As mentioned, this type of life cycle is characteristic of members of the genera *Porospora* and *Nematopsis.* Members of *Porospora* are characterized by their sporozoites, which have no protective envelope and are found in molluscan phagocytes (Plate 5–4, Fig. 4). Sporozoites of *Nematopsis,* which are also found in molluscan phagocytes, are enveloped by two membranes (Plate 5-4, Fig. 5).

Species of *Porospora* and *Nematopsis* are commonly encountered by marine parasitologists, for several are found in economically important salt-water invertebrates. For example, *Porospora gigantea* alternates between lobsters and mussels as hosts, with sexual reproduction occurring in the lobster hosts. *Nematopsis legeri*, with gymnospores measuring 7 μ in diameter; *N. ostrearum*, with gymnospores measuring 4 μ in diameter; and *N. prytherchi*, with gymnospores measuring 6 μ in diameter, all utilize crabs, and oysters or mussels as hosts. Although there are high levels of infection of oysters by *N. ostrearum* along the Atlantic and Gulf Coasts of the United States because the gregarious habit of the mud crab provides for recurring contacts (Shuster, 1960), there is little evidence that this gregarine is destructive to the oyster under normal conditions. This is probably because of the achievement of a dynamic equilibrium in the oyster between elimination of and reinfection by the parasite (Feng, 1958). Elimination of the parasite is achieved primarily by migration of the sporozoite-laden phagocytes from the oyster. This mechanism has been shown by Stauber (1950) to be more effective than intracellular digestion of the invading parasite.

SUBORDER SCHIZOGREGARININA

Members of this small suborder are intestinal parasites of arthropods, annelids, and tunicates. Some species, such as members of the genus *Lipotropha*, are extremely small, being found as intracellular parasites of fat bodies of certain dipteran larvae.

Unlike the eugregarinines, the schizogregarines undergo both sexual reproduction and schizogony during their life cycles.

Generalized Life Cycle

Infection of hosts by schizogregarines is accomplished when cysts (or oocysts) enclosing sporozoites are ingested. Once in the host's gut, the elongate sporozoites escape from the cyst wall. They may invade the host's epithelial cells or remain free in the lumen. In either case, they increase in size to become trophozoites.

The trophozoites undergo schizogony—the asexual reproductive process during which a series of nuclear divisions occur resulting in a

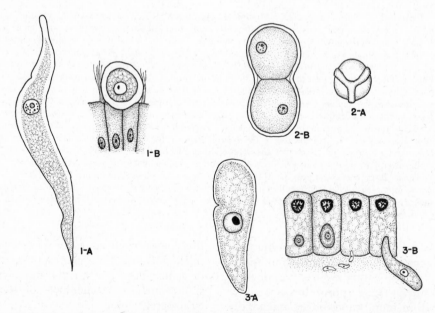

Plate 5-3   Some gregarine parasites (Acephalina). 1. A. Trophozoite of *Schaudinnella henleae*, an intestinal parasite of *Henlea leptodera*. **B.** Trophozoite of *S. henleae* within a clear wartlike epimerite attached to gut epithelium of host. (A and B redrawn after Nusbaum.) **2. A.** Cyst of *Diplocystis schneideri*, a parasite in the coelom of *Periplanata americana*. **B.** Two spherical trophozoites of *D. schneideri*, typically paired. (Modified after Kunstler.) **3. A.** Mature trophozoite of *Lankesteria culicis*, found in lumen of gut of mosquitoes of the genus *Aedes*. **B.** Entrance of sporozoites of *L. culicis* into midgut epithelium of *Aedes*; growth of trophozoites; a large trophozoite escaping. (A and B modified after Wenyon.)

large multinucleate individual. Cytoplasmic divisions occur after the nuclei have ceased to divide, resulting in a large number of uninucleate individuals. These are known as gametocytes. At this point schizogony terminates and gamogony occurs. The gametocytes pair up, presumably one of each sex, and encyst within a gametocyst. As is the case among eugregarines, each gametocyte gives rise to numerous gametes.

When two gametes of opposite sexes unite, the zygote is formed. Since gametes of schizogregarines are morphologically identical, this type of mating is isogamy. As soon as the zygotes are formed, a secondary cyst (oocyst) is secreted by each zygote around itself. Division of the zygote may or may not occur within the oocyst. If division takes place within the oocyst, several sporozoites, commonly eight, are formed. If division does not occur, the zygote becomes a single sporozoite. At this point, the gametocyst, enclosing numerous oocysts, is discharged in the host's feces. As is the case among eugregarines, the gametocyst may be ingested intact by another host, or it may rupture and the oocysts ingested singly.

The Schizogregarina includes relatively few species. Members of the genus *Ophryocystis* are found in the Malpighian tubules of coleopterans. These can be recognized both by their conical trophozoites, which are attached to host cells by pseudopods, and by their oocysts, which include eight sporozoites. Members of the genus *Schizocystis* are found in flies, annelids, and sipunculids. Trophozoites of members of this genus are known to engage in syzygy—the temporary end-to-end union of a varying number of individuals to form a long chain; they may also be connected laterally. The gametocysts of *Schizocystis* spp. include up to 30 oocysts, each containing eight sporozoites.

ORDER COCCIDIA

Coccidians are generally parasites of the epithelia that line the alimentary tracts of vertebrates and invertebrates, but they are also found in the cells of associated glands. An alternation between sexual and asexual reproduction is the general rule. Except in a few genera, such as *Aggregata* and *Lankesterella*, these parasites are associated with one host only. In the case of the exceptions mentioned, a second invertebrate host is required for the completion of the life cycles. The spores produced by coccidians are highly resistant.

The Coccidia is divided into two suborders—the Eimerida, which includes those species with similar male and female gametocytes, and the Adeleida, which includes species in which the gametocytes are quite different in size.

SUBORDER EIMERIDA

Coccidians belonging to this suborder are generally intracellular parasites of the epithelial lining of the host's alimentary canal. Both the sexual and schizogonic phases of their life cycles generally occur in one host, although some species exhibit an alternation of hosts. The infective oocysts generally include eight sporozoites.

The Eimerida includes twenty-three genera, of which only three of the better known are discussed here.

Genus *Eimeria*

Eimeria is a multi-species genus that includes several economically important parasites. The life cycle of *E. tenella*, a species found in the caeca of chickens, is representative of the group (Plate 5–5).

LIFE CYCLE OF *Eimeria tenella*—(A ONE-HOST CYCLE.)   Infection of the fowl occurs when mature oocysts are ingested. Sporozoites escape from the oocyst through a micropyle (a minute pore) in the oocyst wall and penetrate the epithelial cells lining the caeca. As an intracellular parasite, the sporozoite increases in size and schizogony begins. Rapid nuclear division takes place, resulting in a multinucleate schizont. Cytoplasmic divisions follow until a layer of cytoplasm envelops each nucleus. Thus, within a single host cell as many as 900 pyriform daughter cells, known as *merozoites,* can be found. A single merozoite measures 2 to 4 μ by 1 to 1.5 μ.

The merozoites escape from the host cell and usually invade another cell in which they increase in size (up to 4 to 5 μ in diameter) to become trophozoites. These trophozoites repeat the schizogonic cycle. The merozoites resulting from the second schizogonic cycle are larger and more elongate, measuring 15 μ by 2 μ. The merozoites may penetrate other cells and repeat the schizogonic cycle, but most of them, upon entering cells, initiate gamogony by becoming male or female gametocytes.

The female, or macrogametocyte, which is slightly larger, develops into a single macro-

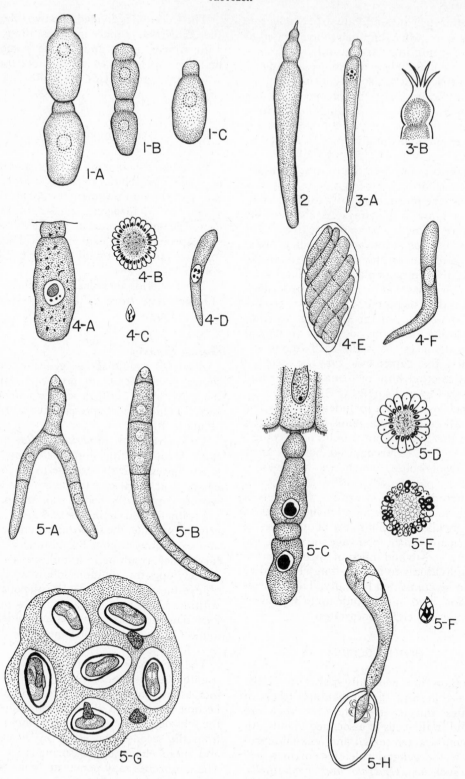

Plate 5-4   See legend on opposite page.

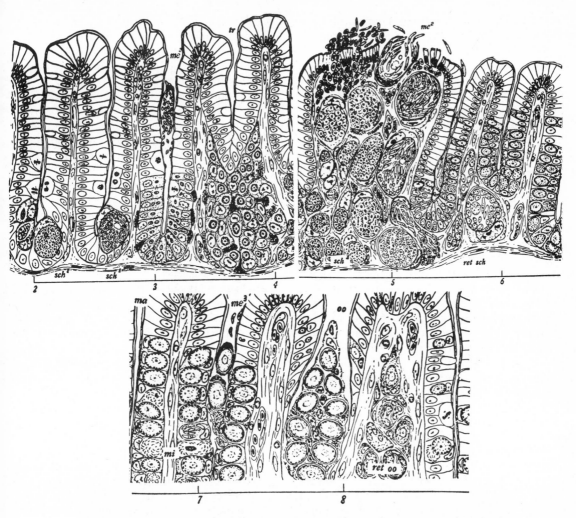

Plate 5-5   Diagram illustrating the development of *Eimeria tenella* in caecal glands of chick. Numbers below line indicate the days of infection. (ma, macrogamete; me, merozoite [me^1, me^2, me^3, generation 1,2,3 merozoites respectively]; mi, microgametocyte; oo, oocyst; ret oo and ret sch, oocysts and schizonts that failed to escape; sch^1 and sch^2, schizonts of generation 1 and 2; tr, young growing trophozoites. (After Tyzzer, 1929.)

Plate 5-4   Some representative members of the Cephalina, Gregarinida. 1. A. *Gregarina blattarum* trophozoites, or sporadins, in midgut of cockroaches. (Redrawn after Kudo, R. R., 1954. *Protozoology*. Charles C Thomas, Springfield, Ill.) **B.** *Gregarina oviceps* trophozoites, or sporadins, in grasshoppers. **C.** *Gregarina locustae* sporadin in the locust *Dissosteria carolina*. (Redrawn after Leidy, 1853.) **2.** *Stylocephalus giganteus* trophozoite, or sporadin, in various Coleoptera. (Modified after Ellis, 1912.) **3. A.** *Actinocephalus acustispora* trophozoite, or sporadin, in gut of the coleopteran *Silpha laevigata.* **B.** Anterior end of *A. acustispora,* showing some of the apical processes. (Modified after Léger, 1892.) **4. A.** Trophozoite of *Porospora gigantea,* attached to gut of *Homarus gammarus.* **B.** Gymnospores of *P. gigantea* in molluscan hosts *Mytilus minimus* and *Trochocochlea mutabilis.* **C** and **D.** Developing sporozoites of *P. gigantea* in molluscan host. **E.** Sporozoites of *P. gigantea* enveloped by host's phagocyte. **F.** Mature sporozoite of *P. gigantea.* (Modified after Hatt, 1931.) **5. A** and **B.** Trophozoites, or sporadins, of *Nematopsis legeri* in the crustacean *Eriphia spinifrons.* **C.** Trophozoites, or sporadins, of *N. legeri,* attached to gut epithelium of crustacean host. **D.** Gymnospores of *N. legeri.* **E.** Gymnospores after entering body of molluscan host. **F.** Young sporozoite of *N. legeri.* **G.** Cyst of *N. legeri* in molluscan host, enclosing six spores. **H.** Germination of spore in gut of the crustacean host. (Modified after Hatt, 1931.)

gamete. The male, or microgametocyte, gives rise to numerous biflagellated microgametes. The microgametes escape from the host cell and invade a cell in the vicinity that already harbors a macrogamete. Fertilization takes place within the host cell. The resulting zygote then lays down a cyst wall around itself formed from eosinophilic plastic granules of mucoprotein present in the cytoplasm of the macrogamete. These granules pass to the periphery, flatten out, and coalesce, forming the cyst wall after fertilization.

According to Monné and Hönig (1954), the outer layer of the oocyst wall is a quinone-tanned protein, while the inner layer is a lipid lamella closely associated with the protein layer. Completion of the cyst wall marks the transition of the zygote into an oocyst.

The oocysts eventually rupture out of their host cells and enter the intestinal lumen, from which they are expelled to the exterior in feces. The prepatent period (from the time of infection to the appearance of the first oocysts in the feces) is 7 days. Continuous daily discharge of oocysts in feces is the common occurrence, because the sporozoites initially freed in the host do not all enter host cells simultaneously. Hence, their subsequent development is staggered.

Maturation of oocysts, or sporogony, continues after the oocysts are discharged to the exterior. A single sporont is present within each newly passed oocyst. If the required aerobic condition prevails, this sporont undergoes meiotic division giving rise to four sporoblasts, each of which then develops into a sporocyst. Two sporozoites develop within each sporocyst. Thus, the mature oocyst, which is the infective form, includes eight sporozoites.

Although oxygen is required for oocysts to mature, the young oocyst that has recently passed out of a host can survive under anaerobic conditions for some time. *Eimeria tenella* infections in chickens are very commonly lethal, because hemorrhage and sloughing of the affected tissues are extremely severe. Coccidiosis accounts for one of the major causes of death on chicken farms.

OTHER SPECIES OF *Eimeria*. Many other species of *Eimeria* are known. Some of the more common, although not necessarily the most economically important, are *E. stiedae, E. magna,* and *E. sciurorum* in rabbits; *E. augusta* and *E. bonasae* in grouse; *E. debliecki* in pigs; *E. mephitidis* in skunks; *E. arloingi* in sheep and goats;

E. felina in cats; *E. canis* in dogs; *E. smithi, E. canadensis,* and *E. bovis* in cattle; *E. cavia* in guinea pigs; *E. soricis* in shrews; *E. ranarum* in frogs; *E. pigra* and *E. truttae* in trout; and *E. schubergi* in centipedes.

The pathogenicity of the various species of *Eimeria* differs. *E. zurnii* and *E. bovis,* for example, are extremely pathogenic to their bovine hosts. Diarrhea, often accompanied by blood, tenesmus, and even death, often occurs. In one experiment, the feeding of 250,000 to 1,000,000 oocysts of *E. bovis* to calves caused death within 24 to 27 days. On the other hand, other species such as *E. schubergi* have little or no effect on their hosts.

FACTORS GOVERNING PATHOGENICITY. Not all factors governing pathogenicity in *Eimeria* infections are known. Among the more important factors known are (1) the number of oocysts ingested; (2) the number of merozoite generations that occur and the number of merozoites produced during each schizogonic cycle, for these determine the number of host cells destroyed by each infecting oocyst; (3) the location of the parasites in the host tissues and within host cells; (4) the degree of reinfectivity; and (5) the degree of natural or acquired immunity.

Genus *Isospora*

Oocysts of members of this genus contain two sporocysts, which in turn each contain four sporozoites (Plate 5-6). Several species of *Isospora* parasitize birds; others parasitize amphibians, reptiles, and various mammals including man (*I. hominis*). The effect of infection by *I. hominis* is not clearly understood. The symptoms include diarrhea and fever, but the infection is apparently nonlethal.

LIFE CYCLE OF *Isospora felis*—A ONE-HOST CYCLE. Hitchcock (1955) reported the life cycle of *I. felis.* Infection of kittens is established with the ingestion of mature oocysts. Within the small intestine, the sporozoites escape from the oocyst and establish themselves as intracellular parasites of the epithelial lining. These intracellular sporozoites, known as first generation schizonts, are oval or rounded. In the less mature schizonts, the chromatin material appears in large irregular clumps that become smaller, although still irregular in outline, as the schizonts mature.

The schizonts undergo schizogonic division and give rise to merozoites that escape from the host cells, invade other cells, and having

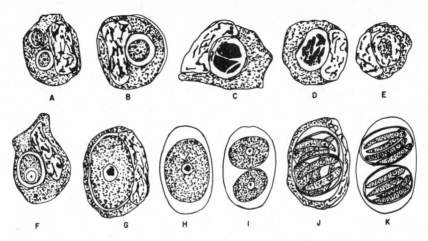

Plate 5-6   Stages in life cycle of *Isospora bigemina*. A-D. Schizogony. **E.** Possible microgametocyte with microgametes. **F** and **G.** Growth of macrogametocyte. **H-K.** Development of oocyst in tissues of villi. (After Wenyon, 1926.)

become second generation schizonts, repeat the schizogonic cycle. The greatest number of merozoites found from a single second generation schizont is 24. The second generation merozoites initiate the gamogonic phase by developing into macro- and microgametocytes while still within the host's intestinal epithelium.

A single microgametocyte gives rise to numerous microgametes, the macrogametocyte develops into a single macrogamete. When a microgamete fuses with a macrogamete within the same host cell, the resulting zygote secretes a membrane around itself and becomes an oocyst. Oocysts are expelled from the epithelial cells, and they are immature when passed out in feces. Upon completion of sporogony, which occurs outside the host, the resulting oocysts are infective.

Other Coccidian Genera

Other coccidia that possess life cycles similar to those of *Eimeria* and *Isospora* are *Dobellia* in the gut of *Petalostoma minutum*, *Wenyonella* in the intestine of birds and snakes, *Caryospora* in the lumen and cells of the peptic glands of mice, *Schellackia* in the intestine of birds and lizards, and *Pfeifferinella* in the hepatic cells of the snail *Planorbis corneus* and the slug *Limax marginatus* (Plate 5-7, Figs. 1 to 6).

Members of the genera *Aggregata* and *Lankesterella* require two hosts, both invertebrates in the former, and one vertebrate and one invertebrate in the latter. The life cycle of *Aggregata eberthi*, depicted in Plate 5-8, is given here as an example of the two-host cycle.

LIFE CYCLE OF *Aggregata eberthi*—A TWO-HOST CYCLE. Infection of the crab *Portunus depurator* is established when spores are ingested. These spores germinate in the gut, liberating three haploid sporozoites. These elongate and flexible sporozoites invade the peri-intestinal connective tissue cells and increase in size to become trophozoites. In this site, the trophozoites greatly increase in size, become rounded, and initiate the asexual reproductive, or schizogonic, phase. The haploid nucleus undergoes mitotic division resulting in the formation of many haploid nuclei. Cytoplasmic divisions ensue, resulting in the formation of individual uninuclear merozoites.

If a crab harboring merozoites is eaten by the cuttlefish *Sepia officianalis,* the merozoites escape and penetrate into the epithelial cells lining the gut of this cephalopod host. Within these cells, sexual reproduction is initiated with some merozoites developing into macrogametocytes and others into microgametocytes. Each macrogametocyte develops into an intracellular macrogamete, while each microgametocyte gives rise to numerous microgametes.

The zygote resulting from the fusion of two opposite haploid gametes is diploid. The zygotic nucleus divides first by meiosis, followed by mitosis, resulting in many haploid nuclei. Ensuing cytoplasmic divisions result in individual haploid sporoblasts that mature into haploid spores, each with three haploid sporozoites. These spores are the infective forms, which pass out with the feces and await ingestion by the decapod host.

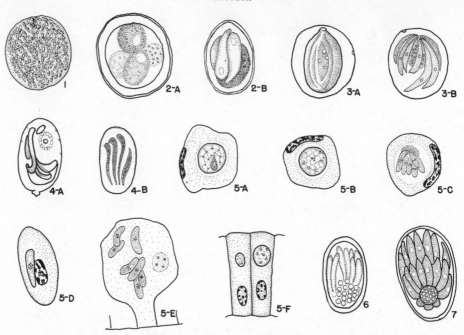

Plate 5-7   Some coccidian parasites. 1. Mature oocyst of *Dobellia ninucleata*, 20–25 μ in diameter, enclosing over 100 sporozoites, parasitic in the gut of *Petalostoma minutum*. (Original.) 2. A. Oocyst of *Wenyonella africana*, 18.5–19.2 μ × 16–17.6 μ, in small intestine of the brown snake *Boaedon lineatus*. B. Spore of *W. africana*, 9.6 × 8 μ. (A and B redrawn after Hoare.) 3. A. Oocyst of *Caryospora simplex* in the gut epithelium of the snake *Vipera aspis;* 10–15 μ in diameter. B. Spore of *C. simplex*, enclosing sporozoites. (A and B redrawn after Léger, 1911.) 4. A. Oocysts of *Cryptosporid-ium muris* in peptic glands of mouse. B. Oocyst of *C. muris*, 7 × 5 μ, enclosing four sporozoites. (Redrawn after Tyzzer, 1910.) 5. A. Zygote of *Schellackia bolivari* in midgut of lizards of the genera *Psammodromus* and *Acanthodactylus;* within epithelial cell. B and C. Development of sporozoites of *S. bolivari* from zygote. D. Sporozoite of *S. bolivari* with host's erythrocyte. E. Sporozoites of *S. bolivari* within cells of intestinal epithelium of mite vector. F. Young trophozoite and schizont of *S. bolivari* in intestinal epithelial cell of lizard after ingestion of infected mite. (A–F redrawn after Reichenow, 1919.) 6. Oocyst of *Pfeifferinella ellipsoides*, 13–15 μ long, in liver of *Planorbis corneus*, a snail. (Redrawn after Wasielewski.) 7. Spore, or oocyst, of *Lankesterella minima*, 33 × 23 μ, in endothelial cell of frog host. Parasite is transmitted by a leech. (Redrawn after Nöller, 1923.)

LIFE CYCLE OF *Lankesterella*—A TWO-HOST CYCLE. The vertebrate host of *Lankesterella* (Plate 5-7, Fig. 7) is usually an amphibian or reptile and the invertebrate host is a bloodsuck-ing form. The invertebrate introduces the para-site, in the sporozoite rather than the spore form, into the vertebrate host during feeding. The sporozoites are carried by the blood to en-dothelial cells of the body where, by schizogony, merozoites are formed that invade various cells. Macro- and microgametocytes develop from merozoites, and these later develop into ga-metes. The fusion of two opposite gametes results in a zygote that develops into a spore. Within the spore, sporogony takes place. When the spore ruptures, the sporozoites escape and invade erythrocytes. When infected blood cells are ingested by the invertebrate, the sporozoite is in position to be transferred to another vertebrate.

By comparing the life cycle of *Aggregata eberthi* with that of *Lankesterella*, it should be apparent that although both of these coccidians require two hosts to complete their life cycles, a significant difference exists. In *A. eberthi*, asexual reproduction takes place in one host, *Portunus depurator*, while sexual reproduction occurs in the other, *Sepia officianalis*. In *Lankes-terella*, both the asexual and sexual phases of reproduction occur in one host, the vertebrate host. The invertebrate host merely transports sporozoites from one vertebrate to another.

SUBORDER ADELEIDA

Members of the suborder Adeleida are characterized by the presence of macro- and microgametocytes that differ significantly in size and that are paired prior to developing into mature gametes. Unlike those of members

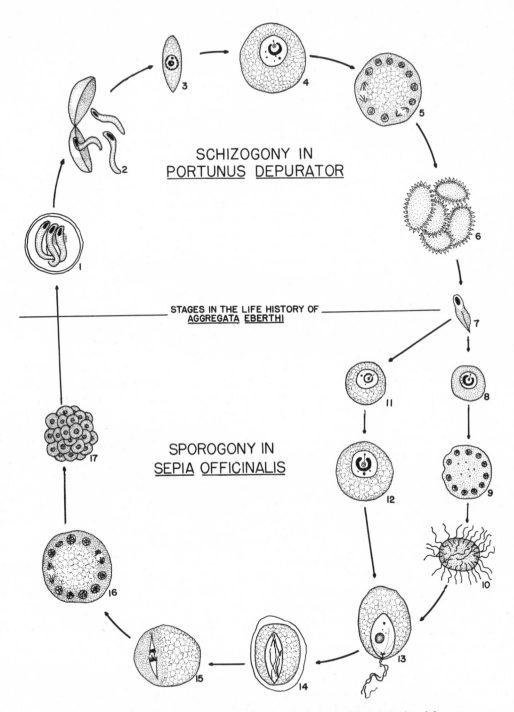

SCHIZOGONY IN
PORTUNUS DEPURATOR

STAGES IN THE LIFE HISTORY OF
AGGREGATA EBERTHI

SPOROGONY IN
SEPIA OFFICINALIS

Plate 5-8   Stages in the life cycle of *Aggregata eberthi*, a coccidian parasite of the crustacean *Portunus depurator*, and the cephalopod *Sepia officinalis*. **1.** A mature spore. **2.** The
escape of three sporozoites upon germination of spore. **3-6.** Stages of schizogony. **7.** A merozoite
swallowed by *S. officinalis*. **8-10.** Development of microgametes. **11** and **12.** Development of macrogamete. **13.** Fertilization. **14** and **15.** First zygotic division; chromosome number is reduced from
12 to 6. **16** and **17.** Development of sporoblasts. Each sporoblast eventually develops into a spore
enclosing three sporozoites. (Figs. 16 and 17 redrawn and modified after Dobell, 1925.)

of Eimerida, the adeleidan microgametocyte gives rise to only a few microgametes, and the oocysts usually contain two or four sporozoites.

The genera subordinate to the Adeleida belong to two families. Those genera that parasitize the epithelial lining and associated glands of the gut of invertebrates and occasionally in internal organs of vertebrates belong to the family Adeleidae, while those that parasitize the blood cells of vertebrates belong to the family Haemogregarinidae.

FAMILY ADELEIDAE

Members of this family possess sporocysts that are formed in oocysts. From what is known, probably only one host is involved in the life cycles of these sporozoans.

LIFE CYCLE OF *Adelina deronis.* *Adelina deronis* (Plate 5–9, Fig. 1) is selected as a representative of the family Adeleidae. Hauschka (1943) reported the life cycle of this species, which is parasitic in the mesodermal cells lining the coelom of the fresh-water oligochaete *Dero limosa.* Infection of the worm occurs with the ingestion of oocysts.

Each oocyst contains 10 to 14 spherical sporocysts ranging from 6 to 9 μ in diameter. Each sporocyst includes two elongate sporozoites. In the midgut and upper hindgut of the worm, the sporozoites escape by rupturing the sporocyst and oocyst walls. They then penetrate the gut wall and actively reach and penetrate the peritoneal cells lining the coelom. The sporozoites that fail to penetrate perish. As an intracellular parasite, the sporozoite increases in size and rounds up, often causing a marked vacuolization of the host cell's cytoplasm. No nuclei are visible in the sporozoites until they become schizonts. Merozoites resulting from the division of schizonts also possess visible nuclei. First and second generation schizonts are known. Second generation merozoites, escaping from the host cells, develop into macro- and microgametocytes in the coelomic cavity.

One gametocyte of each sex enters a new cell in the "pairing process." Instances are known, however, in which a single cell may include one macrogametocyte and two to five microgametocytes. The microgametocyte and macrogametocyte are closely associated while both are undergoing further development. The mature gametes fuse to form the zygote, which secretes a thin oocyst wall. The oocysts mature

in the coelom and enclose ten to fourteen sporocysts. It is presumed that oocysts become free and can be ingested by another host only if the host dies and its tissues disintegrate. The life cycle of *A. deronis* is completed in 18 days.

Several genera closely related to *Adelina* are depicted in Plate 5–9.

FAMILY HAEMOGREGARINIDAE

Members of the family Haemogregarinidae require two hosts to complete their life cycles. They inhabit the circulatory system in the vertebrate host and the digestive tract in the invertebrate vector. The genera *Haemogregarina* and *Hepatozoon* are presented here as representatives of this family.

Genus *Haemogregarina*

The genus *Haemogregarina* includes numerous species that utilize various amphibians, reptiles, birds, and a few mammals as the vertebrate host. During their development, the microgametocyte develops into only two or four microgametes, and the sporozoites are not enclosed within any outer walls. Lack of any type of encasement around sporozoites is a common evolutionary feature characteristic of many sporozoan species that are introduced into the vertebrate host through the bite of a vector.

LIFE CYCLE OF *Haemogregarina stepanowi.* The life cycle of *H. stepanowi,* a parasite of the turtle *Emys orbicularis,* serves as the pattern to which all haemogregarine life cycles conform (Plate 5–10).

Infection of the turtle host is established with the introduction of sporozoites into the blood during the feeding process of the leech *Placobdella catenigera.* The elongate sporozoites enter erythrocytes in the blood and grow. The infected blood cells are carried by the circulation to the bone marrow, where schizogony takes place. Each schizont produces twelve to twenty-four merozoites.

Certain merozoites may infect other red blood cells and repeat the schizogonic cycle. Some of these may produce only six merozoites. These merozoites develop into macro- and microgametocytes that escape from the host cells and individually invade new cells. These new cells are circulated in the host's blood, whence they are taken into the gut of the leech during feeding. Gamogony (the process of forming mature gametes) takes place in the leech. Four microgametes develop from a single

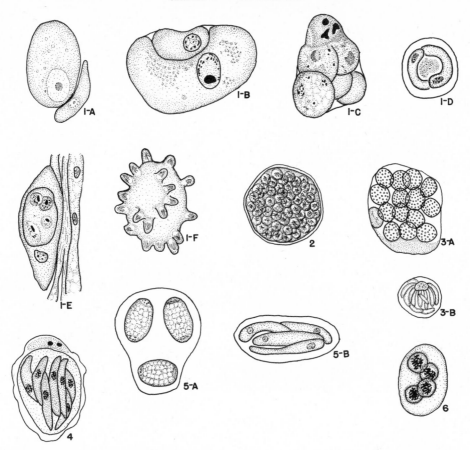

Plate 5-9   Some coccidian parasites. 1. A. Early pairing of macro- and microgametocyte of *Adelina deronis,* found in the peritoneum of the oligochaete *Dero limosa.* **B.** Later stage of pairing, with thin oocyst wall. **C.** Sporoblasts (young sporocysts) of *A. deronis* within oocyst. Remains of microgametocyte are still attached. **D.** Mature sporocyst of *A. deronis.* **E.** Young schizont of *A. deronis* in host peritoneal cell. **F.** Schizogony in *A. deronis.* (A–F redrawn after Hauschka, 1943.) **2.** Oocyst of *Klossia helicina,* found in kidneys of various terrestrial snails. Notice typical double envelope and numerous spherical sporocysts. (Original.) **3. A.** Renal cell of the mouse *Mus musculus,* enclosing 14 sporoblasts (young sporocysts) of *Klossiella muris.* **B.** A typical sporocyst of *K. muris,* enclosing sporozoites. (A and B redrawn after Smith and Johnson, 1902.) **4.** An oocyst of *Legerella hydropori,* found in the epithelium of the Malpighian tubules of the arthropod *Hydroporus palustris.* (Redrawn after Vincent, 1927.) **5. A.** An oocyst of *Chagasella hartmanni* enclosing three developing sporocysts. **B.** A single sporocyst of *C. hartmanni* enclosing four sporozoites; found in the gut of the hemipteran, *Dysdereus ruficollis.* (Redrawn after Chagas.) **6.** An oocyst of *Ithania wenrichi,* a parasite in the epithelial cells of the gastric caeca and midgut of the larvae of the crane fly *Tipula abdominalis.* (Original.)

microgametocyte; each becomes associated with a macrogamete. Fertilization occurs, and the resulting zygote undergoes three divisions, giving rise to eight sporozoites without forming oocysts and sporocysts.

Various invertebrates serve as vectors for haemogregarines. In the case of *Haemogregarina leptodactyli,* a blood parasite of the frog *Leptodactylus ocillatus,* the mite *Acarus* sp. is the vector. In the case of *Hepatozoon muris,* a blood parasite of various species of rats, another mite, *Laelaps*

echidninus, is the vector. *Hepatozoon pettiti,* a parasite of crocodiles, utilizes the tsetse fly, *Glossina palpalis,* as the vector.

ORDER HAEMOSPORIDIA

Members of this order are similar to the haemogregarines of the order Coccidia, for the schizogonic phase of their life cycles is carried out in the blood of a vertebrate host (except in the case of *Haemoproteus*) and both sexual repro-

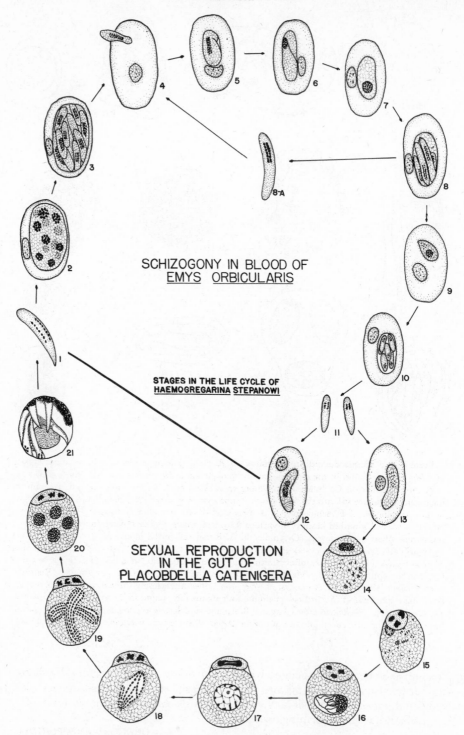

SCHIZOGONY IN BLOOD OF
EMYS ORBICULARIS

STAGES IN THE LIFE CYCLE OF
HAEMOGREGARINA STEPANOWI

SEXUAL REPRODUCTION
IN THE GUT OF
PLACOBDELLA CATENIGERA

Plate 5-10   Stages in the life cycle of *Haemogregarina stepanowi*, a coccidian parasite of the turtle *Emys orbicularis* and the leech *Placobdella catenigera*. **1.** A single sporozoite. **2-8.** Schizogonic stages. **8. A.** A single merozoite reinfecting an erythrocyte of vertebrate host, thus repeating the schizogonic phase of the cycle. **9 and 10.** Stages in gametocyte formation. **11.** Young macro- and microgametocytes. **12.** Mature microgametocyte. **13.** Mature macrogametocyte. **14 and 15.** Association of gametocytes. **16.** Fertilization taking place in gut of leech host. **17-21.** Division of the zygotic nucleus to form eight sporozoites. (All figures redrawn and modified after Reichenow, 1919.)

duction and sporogony occur in the alimentary canal of an invertebrate. It is thus apparent that the sporozoites of haemosporidians are never directly exposed to the environment and hence are not encased with any protective envelope.

The order is divided into three families.

Family 1. Plasmodiidae.   Cytoplasm includes pigment granules when present in erythrocytes. Presexual phase (schizogony) occurs in blood cells circulating in vertebrate host's peripheral blood.

Family 2. Haemoproteidae.   Cytoplasm includes pigment granules when present in erythrocytes. Schizogony does not occur in blood cells of peripheral blood. Gametocytes are found as intracellular parasites in peripheral circulation.

Family 3. Babesiidae.   Cytoplasm is without pigment granules. Are intracellular parasites of erythrocytes of vertebrate host.

FAMILY PLASMODIIDAE

The Plasmodiidae includes the multi-species genus *Plasmodium,* which is the malarial parasite of various vertebrates. Among the species that parasitize vertebrates other than man are *P. sternoceri* and *P. cnemidophori* in lizards; *P. culesbiana* in frogs; *P. bufonis* in the toad *Bufo americanus; P. gallinaceum, P. durae, P. vaughni, P. lophurae, P. rouxi,* and *P. struthionus* in various birds; *P. kochi, P. brasilianum, P. knowlesi,* and *P. cynomolgi* in various species of monkeys; and *P. berghei* in various rodents. Four species—*P. vivax, P. falciparum, P. malariae,* and *P. ovale* (and various strains)—are known to infect man, causing specific types of malaria.

Although monkey malarias were considered to be nontransmittable to humans under natural conditions in the past, it is now known from the work of Eyles et al. (1960) that at least one species, *Plasmodium cynomolgi bastianelli,* originally found in the monkey *Macara irus* in Malaya, is transmittable to man through the bite of the mosquito vector, *Anopheles freeborni.*

Malarias

One of the most vicious diseases of man is malaria. It has played a major role in shaping history, including the decline of civilizations. Human malaria is known to have contributed to the fall of the ancient Greek and Roman empires. Troops in both the Civil War and the Spanish-American War were severely incapacitated by this disease. More than one quarter of all hospital admissions in these wars were malaria patients. During World War II, epidemics of malaria severely threatened both the Japanese and allied forces in the Far East. In fact, the final success of the United States in Asia may be credited to a large degree to the parasitologists, both civilian and military, who fought and conquered a ruthless enemy, malaria.

Although this disease is finally on the decline, largely as the result of the World Health Organization (WHO) and the U. S. Public Health Service, as recently as 1937 there were at least 1 million cases of malaria each year in the United States. Malaria is still a widespread disease in many parts of the world. In 1957, it was estimated that there were 250 million cases of malaria annually, with a resulting mortality of at least 2.5 million. The disease has crippling effects on those of its victims who do not die and causes great economic loss.

GENUS *Plasmodium.* Over fifty species of *Plasmodium* are known. Human malaria is generally caused by four species of the genus *Plasmodium,* to which the genera *Leucocytozoon, Haemoproteus,* and *Hepatocystis* are closely related. The other species of *Plasmodium* are found as parasites of various other vertebrates. The species that cause malaria in birds and *P. berghei* are also interesting in their own right. *Plasmodium berghei* was first discovered in African tree rats and has since been found to be readily transmittable to other rodents, including laboratory rats, mice, and hamsters. Both the avian malaria organisms and *P. berghei* have become extremely important experimental organisms in research on human malaria. In fact, Sir Ronald Ross, the English Nobel Prize winner, discovered the transmission of malaria by mosquitoes while studying bird malaria.

It should be mentioned briefly that, although *Leucocytozoon* and *Haemoproteus* are found with relative frequency in the erythrocytes of birds, and some species of *Haemoproteus* are encountered in reptiles, these parasites are generally nonpathogenic. However, a few species are pathogenic to birds, including some economically important ones. For example, *Leucocytozoon simondi* is extremely pathogenic to ducks.

Life Cycle of *Plasmodium vivax.* *Plasmodium vivax,* the most common of the human-infecting species, is the causative agent of the type known as tertian, benign tertian, or vivax malaria (Plate 5–11). This type of malaria is characterized by a 48 hour cycle between erythrocytic merozoite production, which is manifested in the host by chills and fever at these intervals.

Infection in man is established when sporozoites are injected into the blood through the bite of the mosquito vectors *Anopheles quadrimaculatus* and others (Table 22–1). It should be noted that only female mosquitoes serve as vectors for malaria, for males feed primarily on plant juices. Once within the victim, the sporozoites almost immediately disappear from the peripheral circulation and are carried by the blood, in the plasma, to the liver, where they enter hepatic cells.*

Within hepatic cells, exoerythrocytic schizogony occurs, resulting in the formation of numerous cryptozoites (a term applied to first generation exoerythrocytic merozoites of *Plasmodium*), which escape and reinvade hepatic cells. A second schizogonic phase may occur, giving rise to metacryptozoites (second generation exoerythrocytic merozoites of *Plasmodium*).† These escape from liver cells and invade erythrocytes, thus initiating the erythrocytic phase.

Metacryptozoites invade the host's erythrocytes approximately 6 days after the initial infection in *P. vivax,* approximately 8 days in *P. falciparum,* and 75 hours in the avian *P. gallinaceum.* Thus, the initiation of the erythrocytic stage varies from species to species.

Within the red blood cell occurs the process known as erythrocytic schizogony. Morphologically, the progressive stages of this process are distinguished by the following sequence (Plate 5–11):

(1) Appearance of the ring stage, which resembles a signet ring, caused by a vacuolated area in the middle of the parasite. The surrounding cytoplasm is connected to a peripherally located nucleus, which is the "gem" of the ring. When blood smears are stained with Giemsa's or Wright's stain, the cytoplasm appears blue and the nucleus is red.

(2) An increase in size readily recognizable by the increase of blue cytoplasm.

(3) The appearance of minute red granules in the corpuscular cytoplasm—known as Shüffner's dots—which is characteristic of *P. vivax.* No such granules appear in *P. malariae* infections, while in *P. ovale* infections similar granules are present but the infected cells are not enlarged and are oval. In *P. falciparum* infections, the parasitized erythrocytes are generally found in the blood in visceral organs. The granules, known as Maurer's dots, are fewer and deeper stained with a tinge of red.

(4) The beginning of nuclear division. The single nucleus divides; each one of the daughter nuclei divides again, resulting in four; and further divisions ensue.

(5) The occurrence of segmentation, in which the nuclei are arranged peripherally with clumps of cytoplasm surrounding each nucleus.

(6) Merozoite formation, in which each unit comprised of one nucleus and surrounding cytoplasm becomes a merozoite.

These merozoites escape from the erythrocyte and invade fresh cells to repeat the erythrocyte schizogonic cycle. The "ghost cell" left behind after the merozoites escape is destroyed in the spleen. Adrenal dysfunction usually accompanies malaria and brings on the yellowish coloration of victims of the disease.

It is at the time of the escape of the merozoites specifically that chills and fever beset the host (the condition is known as paroxysm). Generations of erythrocytic schizonts occur. In time, some of the merozoites, after invading cells, do not segment but retain a single nucleus and increase in size to become rounded gametocytes (in *P. falciparum* the gametocytes are crescent shaped). The gametocytes are of two types—male and female. The female gametocytes stain a slightly lighter color, but unless viewed by the trained eye, differentiation is difficult. The gametocytes remain as intracellular parasites without further development.

When a mosquito ingests red blood cells containing gametocytes, the sexual cycle is initiated. The male gametocyte (microgametocyte) in the mosquito's gut undergoes the

---

*The discovery that sporozoites do not invade erythrocytes, as erroneously reported by Schaudinn, but are carried by the blood to the reticuloendothelial system (the liver in the case of the human and several species of avian and simian malarial parasites, but the reticuloendothelial cells of the brain, heart, lungs, and kidney in the case of *P. berghei,* a rodent form) has led to the development of a complex nomenclature. *Exoerythrocytic* is a general term used to describe stages not found within erythrocytes. *Pre-erythrocytic* is used to designate cryptozoites and metacryptozoites collectively. In certain species, especially avian species, exoerythrocytic schizogony appears to occur indefinitely. Hence, exoerythrocytic forms occur concurrently with subsequent erythrocytic forms. Such exoerythrocytic forms are commonly referred to as *phanerozoites* and their schizogonic division is known as *phanerozoic schizogony.* Exoerythrocytic forms in blood-induced infections in which the sporozoites do not take part may also be referred to as phanerozoites. (The review by Huff et al., 1948, is recommended.)

†It is still uncertain whether metacryptozoites occur in all species of *Plasmodium.* It was described for *P. gallinaceum.*

process known as exflagellation. The nucleus divides and a number of "tails" protrude from the cytoplasm, to break away as mature microgametes. The macrogametocyte matures into a single macrogamete (the cresent shaped macrogametocyte of *P. falciparum* becomes rounded). The fusion of gametes results in a zygote that increases in size and elongates to become vermiform and is then known as an *ookinete*.

The ookinete penetrates the stomach lining of the mosquito and in this location increases in size within a cyst wall that it lays down. This is known as the oocyst stage. Within the oocyst, nuclear divisions occur, resulting in a multinucleate condition. Around each nucleus a cytoplasmic aggregation appears. Each of these units is now known as a sporoblast.

Within each sporoblast, sporozoites are formed from nuclear and cytoplasmic divisions. The sporoblasts rupture and the sporozoites, over 10,000 in number, fill the cavity of the oocyst. (However, some authorities do not believe that sporoblast formation takes place in malaria.)

Within 10 to 24 days after ingestion of the gametocytes by the mosquito, the oocysts burst, releasing the sporozoites into the body cavity. These sporozoites actively migrate to and invade the salivary gland cells of the host. From their intracellular positions, sporozoites enter the lumen of the gland ducts and are thus injected into man when the mosquito partakes of its human blood meal.

EFFECT OF TEMPERATURE ON DEVELOPMENT IN MOSQUITO HOST. Environmental and climatic temperatures are known to influence the developmental time of various species of *Plasmodium* in their mosquito hosts. The optimum temperature for development varies with the species. Table 5–1 summarizes the maximum, minimum, and optimum temperatures required by three species of *Plasmodium* for development.

PERIODICITY AMONG SPECIES. Specific variations occur among the human-infecting species. For example, the time required for completion of the erythrocytic schizogonic cycle within the vertebrate host varies. In *P. malariae*, the causative agent of quartan malaria in both tropical and temperate climes, the period is 72 hours (Plate 5–11). In *P. ovale*, which causes ovale, or mild, tertian malaria, there is a 48 hour cycle (Plate 5–12). There is also a 48 hour cycle in *P. falciparum*, the causative agent of subtertian,

estivo-autumnal, or malignant tertian malaria (Plate 5–11). Diagnostic differences between the four species of human malaria organisms are given in Table 5–2.

GROUPING BY LIFE CYCLE PATTERNS. Although the life cycles of the various species of *Plasmodium* are essentially the same, variations in the duration of their exoerythrocytic and erythrocytic existences cause them to be categorized into three types.

(1) In the *malariae* group, the exoerythrocytic stage is continuous and the periodic erythrocytic forms can reinvade fixed cells to become phanerozoic. For example, in the life cycle of *Plasmodium gallinaceum* of birds the erythrocytic forms revert to the exoerythrocytic phase. Thus that segment of the cycle in the avian host can last for long periods. The invertebrate hosts in this case are *Aëdes* mosquitoes (and others). (2) In the *vivax* group, the exoerythrocytic stage is also continuous, accompanied by periodic erythrocytic activity, but it differs from the *malariae* pattern since the erythrocytic forms do not reinvade fixed cells. (3) In the *falciparum* group, the exoerythrocytic phase is short and is followed by the erythrocytic phase. Hence there are no phanerozoic forms.

If it is correctly assumed that the exoerythrocytic habitat was that of the prototype, then these three categories suggest a form of evolutionary progression with the *malariae* group (including *P. gallinaceum* and *P. elongatum* in birds, *P. berghei* in rodents, and *P. mexicanum* in reptiles) being the most primitive. Members of the *falciparum* group then should be considered the most recently evolved.

Although certain morphological differences facilitate the identification of the various species of *Plasmodium*, knowledge of which vertebrate host the organisms parasitize is extremely important in identification.

FAMILY HAEMOPROTEIDAE

The family Haemoproteidae includes two genera—*Haemoproteus* and *Leucocytozoon*. Members of *Haemoproteus* are parasitic in erythrocytes and visceral endothelial cells; members of *Leucocytozoon* are parasitic in leukocytes, liver cells, and other organs of their vertebrate hosts. Both an invertebrate and a vertebrate host are necessary for the completion of haemoproteid life cycles. The U shaped gametocytes of *Haemoproteus* spp. found within the host's red

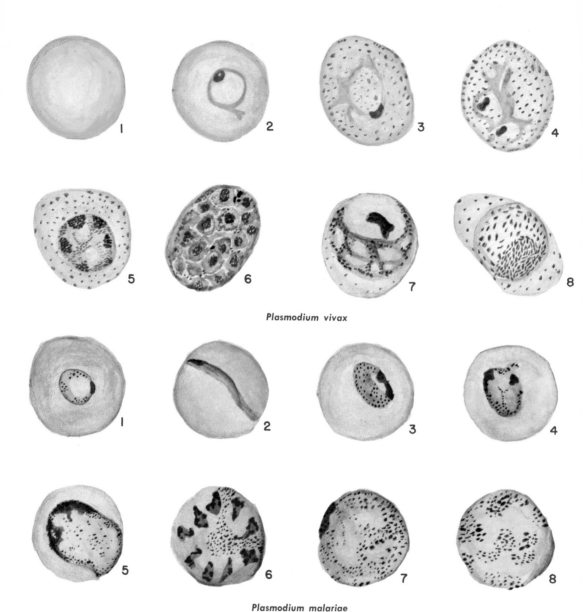

Plasmodium vivax

Plasmodium malariae

Plate 5-11   Some human malarial parasites

Plasmodium vivax. 1. Normal human erythrocyte. 2. Young signet-ring form trophozoite.
3. Older ring form trophozoite; Schüffner's dots in host cell cytoplasm. 4. Two amoeboid trophozoites with fused cytoplasm. 5. Beginning of schizont division. 6. Mature schizont. 7. Mature
macrogametocyte. 8. Mature microgametocyte. (All figures original.)

Plasmodium malariae. 1. Trophozoite in ring form, with pigment granules. 2. Band form trophozoite with elongated cytoplasm. 3. Maturing trophozoite. 4. Mature trophozoite. 5. Phase in
development of schizont. 6. Mature schizont. 7. Mature macrogametocyte. 8. Mature microgametocyte. (All figures original.)

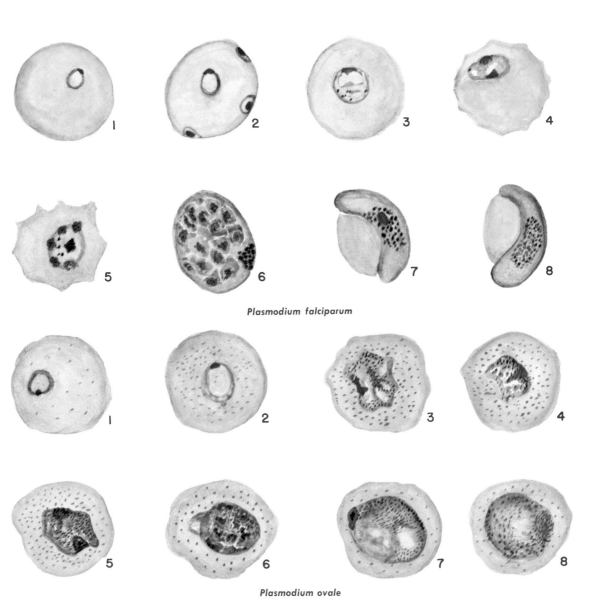

Plasmodium falciparum

Plasmodium ovale

Plate 5-12   Some human malarial parasites

Plasmodium falciparum. **1.** Ring form trophozoite. **2.** Several ring form trophozoites. **3.** Nearly mature trophozoite with pigment in cytoplasm. **4.** Mature trophozoite. **5.** Phase in development of schizont. **6.** Mature schizont. **7.** Mature macrogametocyte. **8.** Mature microgametocyte. (All figures original.)

Plasmodium ovale. **1.** Young ring form trophozoite. **2.** Older ring form trophozoite; Schüffner's dots beginning to appear in host cell cytoplasm. **3.** Maturing trophozoite. **4.** Mature trophozoite. **5.** Phase in development of schizont. **6.** Mature schizont. **7.** Mature macrogametocyte. **8.** Mature microgametocyte. (All figures original.)

Table 5-1. The Influence of Various Temperatures on the Time Required for Development of Four Species of Human-infecting *Plasmodium* in Their Mosquito Hosts.**

Species	16°C	17°C	18°C	20°C†	24°C	30°C	35°C
Plasmodium vivax	–	halted	–	16 days	9 days	7 days	None develop
Plasmodium falciparum	–	–	halted	20 days	11 days	9 days	Generally none develop*
Plasmodium malariae	halted	–	–	30 days	21 days	15 days	None develop
Plasmodium ovale			15 days at 26°C				

In addition to a suitable temperature, a mean relative humidity of over 65 per cent is required for the normal development of the human-infecting plasmodia.

*Wenyon (1926) reported that the sporogony of *Plasmodium falciparum* is even further accelerated above 30°C, with sporozoites reaching the salivary glands in less than 5 days.

**Data is based on laboratory observations but approximates what occurs in nature.

†Although sporogony takes longer at 20°C, it is commonly considered the optimum temperature since more viable sporozoites are produced.

(Adapted from Garnham, P.C.C., 1964. Factors influencing the development of Protozoa in their arthropodan hosts. *In* Host Parasite Relationships in Invertebrate Hosts, Blackwell Scientific Publications, Oxford.)

blood cells produce pigment granules. It was while working on the life cycle of *Haemoproteus* that MacCallum, in 1898, discovered microgametocytes and fertilization, which later led to our understanding of exflagellation (see p. 129).

Genus *Haemoproteus*

Many species of *Haemoproteus* have been described. Coatney (1936) composed a check list that included 45 species; other species have been added since that time. The vertebrate hosts are usually reptiles and birds. Distribution of the various species is world wide. Probably the most common and most extensively known species is *H. columbae*, a parasite of the pigeon, *Columba livia* (Plate 5–13, Fig. 1). The life cycle of this species is representative of the group.

Life Cycle of *Haemoproteus columbae*. When the infected fly vector (*Lynchia* spp., *Pseudolynchia maura,* or *Microlynchia fusilla*) bites

a pigeon, the sporozoites are discharged into the bird's blood. These infective forms are carried in the blood by the plasma to the lungs and other organs, where they invade endothelial cells. Within the endothelial cells, the uninucleate sporozoites, now known as schizonts, undergo rapid nuclear division resulting in a multinucleate form that fractures into many uninucleate bodies, known as cytomeres.

Each cytomere increases in size and its nucleus divides repeatedly. Infected host cells become hypertrophied and eventually rupture. At the time this happens, the multinucleated cytomeres also fragment, giving rise to numerous uninucleate merozoites. Thus, numerous merozoites are expelled when the host cells rupture. The merozoites may re-enter endothelial cells and repeat the schizogonic cycle, or enter red blood cells and mature into macro- or microgametocytes. These immature gametes mature within the gut of a fly that ingests infected pigeon blood cells.

Table 5-2. Diagnostic Differences Between the Four Species of Human-infecting Malaria*

	Plasmodium vivax	*Plasmodium malariae*	*Plasmodium ovale*	*Plasmodium falciparum*
Duration of schizogony	48 hours	72 hours	48 hours	36–48 hours
Motility	active amoeboid until about half grown	trophozoite slightly amoeboid	trophozoite slightly amoeboid	trophozoite active amoeboid
Pigment (hematin)	yellowish-brown, fine granules and minute rods	dark brown to black, coarse granules	dark brown, coarse granules	dark brown, coarse granules
Stages found in peripheral blood	trophozoites, schizonts, gametocytes	trophozoites, schizonts, gametocytes	trophozoites, schizonts, gametocytes	trophozoites, gametocytes
Multiple infection in erythrocyte	very common	very rare	rare	very common
Appearance of infected erythrocyte	greatly enlarged, pale with red Schüffner's dots	not enlarged, normal appearance	slightly enlarged, outline oval to irregular, with Schüffner's dots	normal size, greenish, basophilic Maurer's clefts and dots
Trophozoites (ring forms)	amoeboid, small and large rings with vacuole and usually one chromatin dot	small and large rings with vacuole and usually one chromatin dot, also young band forms	amoeboid, small and large rings with vacuole	very small and large rings with vacuole, commonly with two chromatin dots, amoeboid
Segmented schizonts	fills enlarged RBC, 12-24 merozoites irregularly arranged around mass of pigment	almost fills normal-sized RBC, 6-12 merozoites regularly arranged around central pigment mass	fills approx. 3/4 of RBC, 6-12 merozoites around centric or eccentric pigment mass	not usually seen in peripheral blood
Gametocytes	round, fills RBC, chromatin undistributed in cytoplasm	round, fills RBC, chromatin undistributed in cytoplasm	round, fills 3/4 of RBC, chromatin undistributed in cytoplasm	crescentic or kidney shaped, usually free in blood, chromatin undistributed in cytoplasm

*Wright's stain is used.

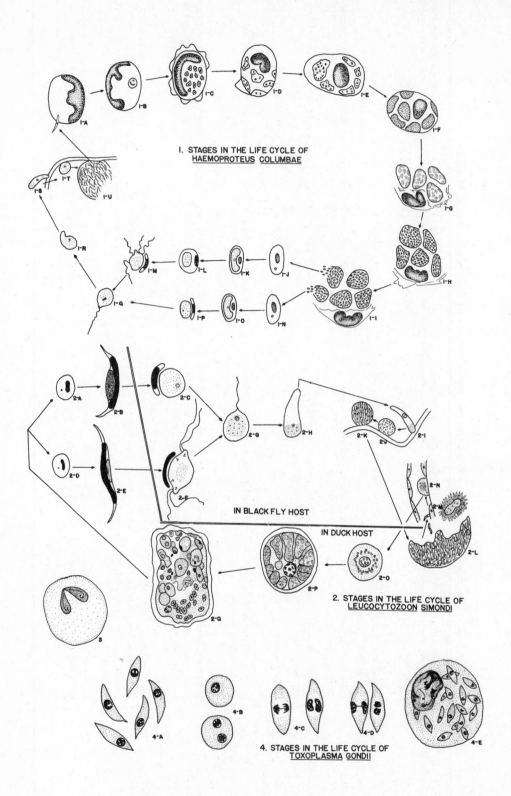

1. STAGES IN THE LIFE CYCLE OF
HAEMOPROTEUS COLUMBAE

IN BLACK FLY HOST

IN DUCK HOST

2. STAGES IN THE LIFE CYCLE OF
LEUCOCYTOZOON SIMONDI

4. STAGES IN THE LIFE CYCLE OF
TOXOPLASMA GONDII

Plate 5-13   See legend on opposite page.

The zygote formed when a micro- and a macrogamete unite enters the gut endothelium of the fly and forms the oocyst, within which sporozoites are formed. When the mature oocyst ruptures, the sporozoites are released. These find their way into the body cavity and eventually into the salivary gland, whence they can be inoculated into another avian host.

Practically nothing is known about the vectors of most species of *Haemoproteus*. Although most species were thought to be transmitted by hippoboscid flies, a species of *Haemoproteus* parasitic in ducks utilizes biting midges as vectors (Fallis and Wood, 1957).

Genus *Leucocytozoon*

Members of *Leucocytozoon* undergo schizogony in cells of visceral organs, often the liver and kidneys, and endothelium of vertebrates. These vertebrates are primarily birds and are rarely other forms (*L. salvelini* occurs in the speckled trout *Salvelinus fontinalis*). Sexual reproduction of *Leucocytozoon* takes place in bloodsucking insects. The gametocytes are found in leukocytes, or in some species, also in erythrocytes of the vertebrate host.

Life Cycle of *Leucocytozoon simondi*. O'Roke (1934) determined the life cycle of *L. simondi*, a pathogenic parasite of ducks which utilizes the blackfly *Simulium venustum* as the vector (Plate 5–13, Fig. 2). The developmental pattern is essentially the same as that given for *Haemoproteus columbae*. The schizogonic phase in the duck takes 10 days, while the sexual and sporogonic phases in the fly take 2 to 5 days. Many species of *Leucocytozoon* have been reported, including *L. smithi* in domesticated turkeys in southeastern United States and Pennsylvania, *L. bonasae* in the ruffled and spruce grouse, *L. andrewsi* in chickens, and *L. marchouxi* in the mourning dove.

FAMILY BABESIIDAE

The family Babesiidae includes those non–pigment-producing intraerythrocytic parasites of various vertebrates—mostly mammals, amphibians, and reptiles. Generally, various ticks serve as the vectors. Included in this family are several genera of considerable biological and economic interest, such as *Babesia* and *Theileria*.

Life Cycle of *Babesia bigemina*. *Babesia begemina* is found in cattle, causing the commonly lethal haemoglobinuric fever, red-water fever, or Texas fever (Plate 5–13, Fig. 3). It was during studies on the life cycle of this species that the importance of arthropods as vectors for protozoan diseases was demonstrated (see Chapter 2).

Infection of cattle is initiated with the introduction of sporozoites into the blood through the bite of the tick *Boophilus annulatus*. Within the erythrocytes the parasites increase in size and usually multiply by binary fission, which may look like budding in the early stages. Delpy (1946) recorded that there is a schizogonic phase in this species, in which several nuclei are seen within the cytoplasm, and free forms are found in the plasma that he considered to be merozoites. However, Dalpy further stated that schizogony is rare and probably only occurs under abnormal conditions.

Generally multiplication by binary fission represents the asexual reproductive phase in this species. After dividing, the daughter cells

---

Plate 5-13   Stages in the life history of some Haemosporidian and *Toxoplasma*. 1. Stages in the life cycle of *Haemoproteus columbae*, a parasite of the pigeon *Columba livia* and flies. **A.** Sporozoite entering endothelial cell of pigeon. **B.** Growth of a schizont within host cell. **C.** Segmentation of multinucleate schizont into uninucleate cytomeres. **D-I.** Development of cytomeres to produce merozoites. **J-M.** Development of microgametes. **N-P.** Development of macrogametes. **Q.** Joining of a micro- and a macrogamete in fertilization. **R** and **S.** Ookinetes. **T.** Young oocyst embedded in stomach wall of the fly host. **U.** A mature oocyst rupturing, releasing sporozoites. (Redrawn and modified after Kudo, R. R., 1954. *Protozoology*, Charles C Thomas, Springfield, Ill.) 2. Stages in the life cycle of *Leucocytozoon simondi*, a parasite of ducks and the black fly *Simulium venustum*. **A-C.** Development of macrogamete. **D-F.** Development of microgametes. **G.** Fertilization. **H.** Ookinete. **I.** Ookinete penetrating stomach wall of blackfly host. **J.** Young oocyst embedded in stomach wall of blackfly host. **K** and **L.** Development of sporozoites within mature oocyst. **M.** Sporozoites entering endothelial cell of blackfly host. **N-Q.** Schizogony. (Redrawn and modified after Brumpt in Kudo, R. R., 1954. *Protozoology*, Charles C Thomas, Springfield, Ill.) 3. *Babesia bigemina* in an erythrocyte of cattle. (Original.) 4. Stages in the life cycle of *Toxoplasma gondii*. **A.** Organisms isolated from infected cell. **B.** Trophozoites. **C.** Organisms dividing by binary fission. **D.** Host cell enclosing numerous organisms that have arisen by repeated binary fission. (Redrawn after Chatton and Blanc, 1917.)

may escape from the blood cells and reinvade others. After the tick has taken a blood meal from the cow, the intracellular parasites are released within the gut of the tick. Certain of these individuals transform into motile, vermiform isogametes. The zygotes (or ookinetes) resulting from fertilization later round up and transform into sporonts. These sporonts secrete individual cyst walls within which each sporont divides to form naked sporoblasts.

The sporoblasts give rise to multinucleate sporokinetes as the result of rapid nuclear division. These migrate and are carried by cell proliferation throughout the tissues of the tick, including developing eggs. Because much of the anterior cell mass of developing ticks is destined to develop into salivary glands, it is almost inevitable that some of the sporokinetes should come to reside in these glands. Here the sporokinetes fragment to form minute infective uninuclear sporozoites.

LIFE CYCLE OF *Babesia canis*. Regendanz and Reichenow (1933) reported that in the life cycle of *Babesia canis*, the canine-infecting species, no sexual reproduction takes place. Rather, the intracellular sporozoites, once inside the gut of the tick (*Rhipicephalus sanguineus, Dermacentor reticularis,* or *Haemaphysalis leachi*), become free and transform into vermiform bodies that invade the cells of the midgut and multiply asexually. The daughter cells enter the body cavity and some reach developing eggs of the tick.

OTHER *Babesia* SPECIES. Other species of *Babesia* are known to infect horses (*B. equi*), rodents (*B. rodhani*), ground squirrels (*B. wrighti*), cats (*B. felis*), hogs (*B. suis* and *B. trautmanni*), goats (*B. motasi*), and other mammals. Very often these infections are acute, leading to death in 7 to 10 days. In chronic infections, jaundice, anemia, and other symptoms are exhibited.

CLASS ACNIDOSPORIDEA

Members of the class Acnidosporidea, including several common forms, are little understood, and the phylogenetic affinities between the forms are still uncertain. However, all of them produce simple spores—that is, with sporoplasm (the cytoplasm within the spore) surrounded by a membrane.

Members of Acnidosporidea are either parasitic in the cells, tissues, and coelomic cavities of invertebrates and lower vertebrates or in the muscles of amphibians, birds, and mammals. The life cycle patterns of the acnidosporideans are not completely known. Based on what is known, apparently only one host is involved.

The class is divided into two orders:

Order 1. Haplosporidia. Intra- and extracellular (coelomic) parasites of invertebrates and lower vertebrates. Possesses simple spherical or ellipsoidal spores that do not possess any polar filament. Resistant spore membrane may be ridged or may possess a filamentous caudal projection. Few species have sporal operculum.

Order 2. Sarcosporidia. Parasites of muscles of reptiles, birds, and mammals. Infected muscles contain opaque white bodies (Miescher's tubes). Mature parasites are filled with banana shaped uninucleate spores (Rainey's corpuscles) that are filled with cytoplasmic granules.

ORDER HAPLOSPORIDIA

This order includes members of the genera *Bertramia,* which are coelomic parasites of aquatic invertebrates; *Anurosporidium,* which are parasitic in the sporocysts (a larval generation, p. 231) of digenetic trematodes, a fellow parasite; *Urosporidium,* which are only rarely found in the coelom of polychaetes; *Ichthyosporidium,* which are found in the musculature, connective tissue, and gills of fishes; *Coelosporidium,* found in the coelom and Malpighian tubules of cockroaches; and *Haplosporidium* found in aquatic annelids and molluscs (Plate 5–14, Figs. 1 to 5).

LIFE CYCLE OF *Haplosporidium*. The genus *Haplosporidium* includes several species found in the gut epithelium and connective tissue of annelids and in the hepatic gland of molluscs.

Although details of the life cycles of the various species remain vague, the pattern consists of a spore, which when ingested by the host, releases a small amoeboid form, the amoebula. The uninucleate or binucleate amoebula may invade a cell or penetrate through the gut wall and continue its development in the host's body cavity. Growth in size is accompanied by nuclear divisions without cytoplasmic divisions, and a multinucleate plasmodium is formed. Uninucleate sporoblasts appear within the mature plasmodium.

The plasmodium eventually fragments, and each sporoblast later matures into a spore, which may or may not bear a minute operculum at one end. How mature spores escape from one host and become ingested by another still is undetermined. In some species, the single

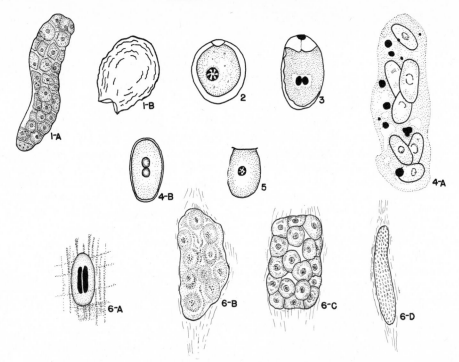

Plate 5-14   Some acnidosporidian parasites. 1. A. Cyst of *Bertramia asperospora* enclosing spores; found in the body cavity of rotifers. **B.** An empty cyst of *B. asperospora*. (A and B redrawn after Minchin.) **2.** Spore of *Anurosporidium pelseneeri*, a parasite in the sporocysts of trematodes. **3.** Stained spore of *Ichthyosporidium giganteum*, found in various organs of fishes of the genus *Crenilabrus*. **4. A.** Trophozoite of *Coelosporidium periplanetae* enclosing spores and chromatoid bodies; parasitic in lumina of Malpighian tubules of cockroaches. **B.** Spore of *C. periplanetae*, 5.5 × 3 μ or slightly larger. (A and B redrawn after Sprague, 1940.) **5.** Spore of *Haplosporidium limnodrili*, parasitic in the gut epithelium of *Limnodrilus* sp. (Redrawn after Granata, 1925.) **6. A.** Longitudinal section through *Sarcocystis muris*; initial stage of development. **B** and **C.** Successive stages in the development of *S. muris* in muscle of rat. **D.** Mature sarcocyst of *S. muris*. (A–D redrawn after Badudieri, 1932.)

nucleus within the spore is said to divide, and the daughter nuclei supposedly recombine as the spore approaches maturity (a process known as autogamy). The existence of true gametes has been claimed in some species, but this is questionable.

Life Cycle of *Icthyosporidium giganteum*. During the life cycle of *I. giganteum*, a parasite of fishes, the ingested spores germinate in the alimentary canal of the host, and the emerging amoebulae burrow through the gut wall and invade the connective tissue of various organs. As each amoebula increases in size, its nucleus undergoes repeated divisions resulting in a multinucleate plasmodium. The plasmodium divides into smaller bodies, known as *cytomeres*, which are still enclosed within the plasmodial membrane. The nuclei enclosed within each cytomere divide simultaneously. The preceding steps constitute schizogony.

Sexual reproduction is initiated when the nuclei within each cytomere pair off and the nuclear membranes become less distinct. When the plasmodial membrane ruptures, the cytomeres from within escape and eventually fracture into units known as sporonts, each with a pair of nuclei. The sporont undergoes further differentiation and division to give rise to two thick-walled, operculated spores. It is not known how the spores escape from the host.

Although the developmental patterns in *Haplosporidium* spp. and *Ichthyosporidium* spp. are similar, there are minor differences. For example, apparently the more complex forms of schizogony and sexual reproduction as found in *Ichthyosporidium* do not occur in *Haplosporidium*. Hosts harboring various Haplosporidia are not noticeably harmed.

MSX and Oyster Mortality

One of the major segments of the fishing industry along the Atlantic Coast of the United States, ranging from New England to the Gulf Coast, is the oyster industry. During 1957, and to some degree since then, heavy mortalities of oysters occurred in the Delaware and Chesapeake Bays and have threatened the entire industry in these areas. It was suspected that a parasite was responsible for these mortalities, for estuarine oyster beds provide ideal habitats for an array of microorganisms and invertebrates that either serve as convenient hosts for parasites or that can become facultative parasites if environmental conditions render the oysters physiologically vulnerable to parasitization (p. 79). Extensive investigations, conducted primarily by Haskin and Barrow, revealed that an organism, named MSX and tentatively identified as a haplosporidian, may be responsible for the oyster mortalities, although thus far it has not been demonstrated under laboratory conditions that MSX can be transmitted from infected to uninfected oysters or that this parasite is directly responsible for the death of an oyster. Since haplosporidians are known to be members of estuarine communities as hyperparasites (that is, parasites of another parasite) in gregarines that infect polychaetes and in the sporocysts and cercariae (larval stages) of the trematode *Bucephalus,* which infects oysters, Shuster and Hillman (1963) have speculated that perhaps, as the result of changing environmental conditions that render oysters increasingly more susceptible to parasites, one of these, or some other, haplosporidan could infect and kill the oysters. Since such changes in the microenvironment of oyster beds are not completely known, it is not surprising that laboratory studies on MSX infections in oysters have not been successful up to this time.

In connection with the possible role of MSX in oyster mortalities, Cort et al. (1960b) were able to infect the larval stages of strigeoid trematodes in fresh-water snail hosts with a hyperparasitic microsporidian of the genus *Nosema* by feeding spores to the snails. These workers reported that although *Nosema* became established as hyperparasites in the larval trematodes, none developed in the tissues of the snails. It thus appears probable that the haplosporidian in *Bucephalus* in oysters, like the microsporidian in strigeoids in fresh-water gastropods, normally does not invade the molluscan host's tissues. Rather, in the light of Shuster and Hillman's speculation, it may be possible that the sporozoans can invade molluscan tissues if environmental changes render the molluscs physiologically vulnerable. Investigations along these lines may prove to be extremely important.

ORDER SARCOSPORIDIA

The order Sarcosporidia includes the interesting form *Sarcocystis*. Little is known about this unusual parasite, which shows a definite affinity for striated and cardiac muscles of vertebrate hosts. Some authorities do not consider *Sarcocystis* to be a sporozoan, and some do not even consider it a protozoan. Thus, this parasite is often considered to be one of uncertain taxonomic status.

LIFE CYCLE OF *Sarcocystis muris*.[*] The life cycle of *Sarcocystis muris* is not completely known. Infection of mice and rats is initiated with the ingestion of spores that liberate amoeboid sporoblasts. These penetrate muscle fiber and become surrounded by host tissues that form an enveloping wall. This complex is known as a sarcocyst.

A single sarcocyst includes many sporoblasts which divide continuously by binary fission and eventually form numerous spores. How these spores escape remains undetermined, although the mechanism employed by *Sarcocystis* of sheep, given below, probably is found in this species also. When sarcocysts are found in muscle, they appear as elongate and more or less cylindrical bodies with pointed ends (Miescher's tubes). The spores present within mature sarcocysts are banana shaped (Rainey's corpuscles).

In *Sarcocystis* of sheep, Scott (1943) reported that secondary walls are produced by the sporoblasts within the primary sarcocyst wall. When the cyst wall ruptures, large numbers of spores are liberated. Many of these eventually reach the circulation and are carried to the intestinal lumen, from which they pass to the exterior in feces. Motility of spores by spiral rotation along the longitudinal axis accompanied by "twisting and boring" has been reported.

Sarcocystis of rodents and sheep have been

---

[*]Some protozoologists are of the opinion that only one species of *Sarcocystis, S. miescheriana,* exists, while others are merely forms found in various hosts. This viewpoint is strengthened because *Sarcocystis* shows a conspicuous lack of host specificity.

successfully transmitted by experimental oral infections.

Despite the occasional presence of incredibly large numbers of parasites (Scott reported an old ewe in which there were approximately 35,000 sarcocysts per cubic centimeter of heart muscle), sarcosporidiosis ordinarily results in no great harm to the host, although infected hosts, especially sheep, are commonly weak and lean.

Spindler and Zimmerman (1945) reported that spores of *Sarcocystis* from pigs, when cultured in dextrose solution, develop mycelia and hyphae, which are typical fungoid structures. Also they reportedly produced typical sarcosporidiosis in young pigs if such cultured spores were fed or injected. If these findings are confirmed, it is evident that *Sarcocystis* is not a protozoan, let alone a sporozoan, but is a mold.

Sarcosporidians have been reported to secrete toxic substances known as *sarcocystin;* however, this remains to be proven.

Moulé in 1888 demonstrated the extreme of scientific curiosity by personally ingesting raw beef contaminated with *Sarcocystis* to study the effects, which "fortunately" were not noticeable.

CLASS CNIDOSPORIDEA

Members of the Cnidosporidea all produce unique resistant spores that contain one to four coiled polar filaments within polar capsules. This is again a somewhat heterogeneous group that has been little studied. Although none of the cnidosporideans parasitize man, a number of species do cause serious diseases in economically important animals such as bees and fish. It was while working on *Nosema bombycis,* a cnidosporidian parasite of silkworms, that Pasteur laid the foundation for his later research on the biology of infectious diseases.

During the life cycle of cnidosporideans, they undergo schizogony and sporogony. Whether sexual reproduction occurs is uncertain, although it probably does not. During schizogony, division takes place by fission, budding, or plasmotomy. The entire life span of the parasite is spent in one host, which depending on the species, may be an insect, a fish, or some other animal.

The class is divided into four orders:

Order 1. Myxosporidia. Parasites of lower vertebrates, especially fishes, but including a few amphibians and reptiles. Spores are of varying shapes and sizes. Spore membrane bipartite (two valves) with sutural plane either twisted or straight. Membrane may be smooth or marked. Polar capsules numbering from one to four, all at one end (except in Myxidiidae). Possesses single large sporoplasm.

Order 2. Actinomyxidia. Parasites in the body cavity or gut-epithelium of fresh-water and marine annelids. Spores are of varying shapes and sizes. Spore membrane is tripartite (three valves) and may form processes. Consistently possesses polar capsules. Each spore has one to several sporoplasms.

Order 3. Microsporidia. Parasites of cells of arthropods and fishes. Spore is small (majority from 3 to 6 μ in diameter), and has single unseparated membrane. Possesses single polar filament and sporoplasm.

Order 4. Heliocosporidia. Parasites of tissues or cavities of arthropods. Spores possess single unseparated membrane with thick filament wrapped around. Possesses three uninucleate sporoplasms.

ORDER MYXOSPORIDIA

The Myxosporidia includes *Ceratomyxa,* found in the viscera of the rainbow trout and in the gallbladder of marine fishes; *Trilospora, Leptotheca,* and *Myxoproteus,* all found in the gallbladder of various fishes; *Mitraspora,* in the kidneys of fresh-water fishes; *Wardia,* in various tissues of fresh-water fishes; *Unicapsula, Myxidium,* and *Unicauda,* all tissue parasites of fishes, amphibians, and reptiles (Plate 5–15, Figs. 1 to 7).

Life Cycle of Myxosporidians

Life cycles of members of the various genera of Myxosporidia are all essentially of the same pattern. When spores are ingested by the host, the sporoplasms leave the spores as amoebulae that burrow through the epithelial lining of the host's gut and migrate to certain visceral organs where they transform into the multinucleate plasmodia. This is accomplished by an increase in size accomplished by repeated nuclear divisions.

Within a single plasmodium, groups of nuclei become surrounded by cytoplasm. Each one of these smaller multinucleate units is known as a sporont. The sporonts increase in size while their nuclei divide rapidly, resulting in six to eighteen daughter nuclei within each sporont. If the sporont, depending on the species, develops into a single spore, it is termed a monosporoblastic sporont; if it is destined to form two spores, it is known as a pansporoblastic or disporoblastic sporont.

The development of sporonts into spores is initiated in the center of a plasmodium. The

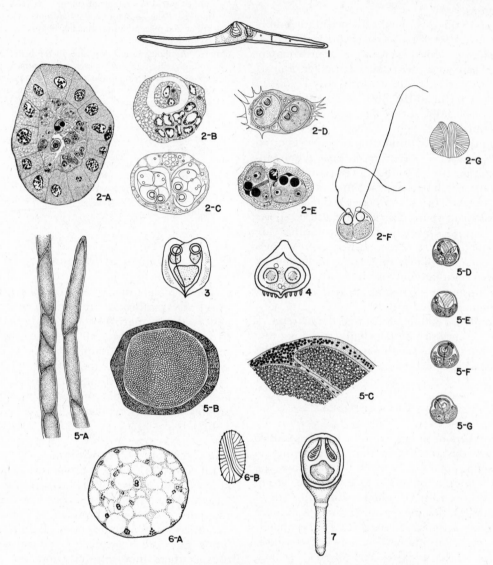

Plate 5-15   Some cnidosporidian parasites. 1. *Ceratomyxa mesospora*, found in the gall-bladder of the marine fish *Cestracion zygaena*. (Redrawn after Davis, 1917.) **2.** Stages in the life cycle of *Leptotheca ohlmacheri*, parasitic in the uriniferous tubules of the kidney of frogs and toads. **A.** Section of a uriniferous tubule of *Rana pipiens* showing trophozoites and spores. **B.** A trophozoite with a bud. **C-E.** Disporous trophozoites. **F.** A spore with extended polar filaments. **G.** Surface view of spore. (After Kudo, 1922.) **3.** A spore of *Myxoproteus cordiformis*, a parasite in the urinary bladder of the marine fish *Chaetodipterus faber*. (Redrawn after Davis, 1917.) **4.** A spore of *Wardia ovinocua*, a parasite in the ovary of the fresh-water bass *Lepomis humilis;* 10–12 μ wide. (Redrawn after Kudo, 1921.) **5.** Stages in the life cycle of *Unicapsula muscularis,* found in the muscle of marine fishes. **A.** Infected muscle fibers of host. **B.** Cross section of an infected muscle fiber. **C.** A part of a section of an infected muscle. **D** and **E.** Spores of *U. muscularis,* the causative agent of "wormy" halibut. (A–E after Davis, 1924.) **6. A.** Stained young trophozoite of *Myxidium serotinum*, 6.5 × 1.8 mm., with highly vacuolated cytoplasm, found in gallbladder of frogs and toads. **B.** An unstained spore of *M. serotinum* showing characteristic ridges on the membrane; 16–18 μ × 9 μ. (A and B redrawn after Kudo, 1943.) **7.** An unstained spore of *Unicauda clavicauda*, parasitic in the subdermal connective tissue of the minnow *Notropis blennius;* 10.5–11.5 μ × 8.5–9.5 μ × 6 μ. (Redrawn after Kudo, 1934.)

surrounding host tissue becomes hypertrophied, degenerates, and forms a cyst wall around the parasite. Such cysts are readily visible to the naked eye. If such cysts are located on the host's body surface, they rupture, thus permitting the mature spores to escape into water. If the cyst is located internally, escape of the spores must await the death and disintegration of the host.

Some myxosporidians parasitize their host's tissues, living in organs such as the kidneys, muscles, gills, or integument. Other myxosporidians prefer various body cavities such as the urinary bladder and gallbladder. Most injury caused by myxosporidians results from those species that parasitize tissues. Fishes whose integument are infected often develop tumor-like masses. If the intestinal tissues, especially muscles, are infected, the parasites are so intimately intermingled with the host's tissues that the food value of the fishes is destroyed.

ORDER ACTINOMYXIDIA

The Actinomyxida includes, among others, the genera *Triactinomyxon* and *Synactinomyxon,* both found in the gut-epithelium of oligochaetes (Plate 5–16, Figs. 1 to 3). Members of *Sphaeractinomyxon* are found in the coelom of oligochaetes (Plate 5–16, Fig. 4).

ORDER MICROSPORIDIA

The Microsporidia includes comparatively small organisms (3 to 6 μ) that are typically parasites of arthropods and fishes. However, representatives have been reported from other hosts and are generally pathogenic. Included in this order are several species of some economic importance because they parasitize such useful insects as silkworms and honeybees.

Life Cycle of Microsporidians

Microsporidians undergo both schizogony and sporogony as intracellular parasites. Very often, infected cells demonstrate marked hypertrophy.

The infective form of microsporidians is the spore, which is typically covered by a keratinous membrane. Within this membrane are found the sporoplasm and a long polar filament coiled within the polar capsule. When a spore is ingested by a compatible host, the polar

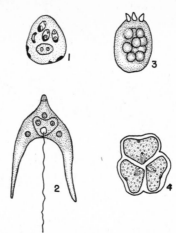

Plate 5–16   Some cnidosporidian parasites. 1. A spore of *Tetractinomyxon intermedium,* 20–25 μ in diameter, in coelom of the sipunculid *Petalostoma minutum.* (Redrawn after Ikeda, 1912.) 2. A spore of *Synactinomyxon tubificis,* parasitic in gut epithelium of *Tubifex tubifex.* (Redrawn after Stole.) 3. A spore of *Synactinomyxon globosum,* parasitic in the gut epithelium of *Limnodrilus udekemianus.* (Redrawn after Granata, 1925.) 4. A spore of *Sphaeractinomyxon stolci* in *Clitellis* and *Hemitubifex.* (Redrawn after Caullery and Mesnil, 1905.)

filament is released and anchors the escaping sporoplasm to the host's gut epithelium. The escaped sporoplasm is amoeboid and is known as an amoebula.

The amoebula usually remains in the lumen of the gut for a short period, during which it is known as a *planont.* Some planonts invade and remain in the cells lining the host's gut, while others are carried by the blood to another site of infection where they become established as intracellular forms. Within the appropriate cell, the planont becomes a trophozoite, which undergoes binary fission or schizogony giving rise to multinucleate sporonts.

Each sporont gives rise internally to a number of uninucleate spores. The number of spores produced within a sporont is often used as a generic characteristic. In certain species, the spores are capable of germinating and infecting nearby cells, thus establishing extremely heavy infections. Such instances very often lead to the death of the host.

Nosema bombycis (Plate 5–17, Fig. 1) is parasitic in silkworms and causes the fatal pébrine disease, which was initially studied by Louis Pasteur in 1870. *Nosema bryozoides* parasitizes germ cells of bryozoans, while *N. apis* (Plate 5–17, Fig. 2) affects the digestive tract and indirectly affects the ovary of worker bees and

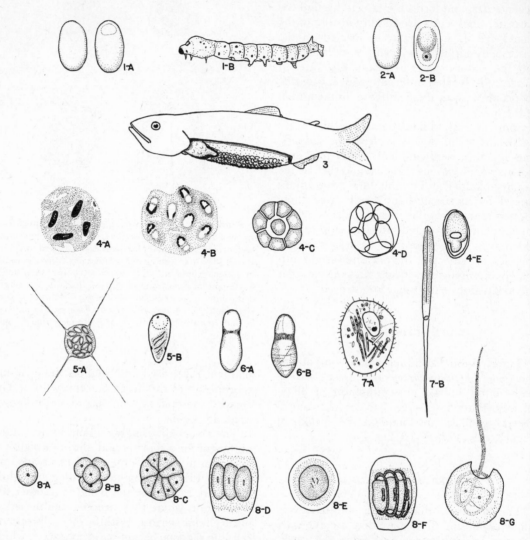

Plate 5-17   Some microsporidian and helicosporidian parasites. 1. A. Fresh spores of
Nosema bombycis, 3–4 μ × 1.5–2 μ, a tissue parasite of silkworms. **B.** A heavily infected silkworm larva,
showing characteristic pigments. (A and B redrawn after Kudo, 1913.) **2. A.** A fresh spore of
Nosema apis, 4–6 μ × 2–4 μ, a parasite in the gut of honeybees. **B.** A stained spore of *N. apis.* (A and B
redrawn after Kudo, 1921.) **3.** A smelt infected with *Glugea hertwigi.* (Redrawn after Schrader, 1921.)
4. A and **B.** Stained sporogonic stages of *Thelohania legeri,* found in fat bodies of larvae of several
species of *Anopheles.* **C** and **D.** Mature sporonts of *T. legeri.* **E.** A fresh spore of *T. legeri,* 4–6 μ × 3–4 μ.
(A–E redrawn after Kudo, 1921.) **5. A.** Mature sporont of *Trichoduboscqia epeori,* found in fat bodies
of nymphs of mayflies, 9–10 μ in diameter. **B.** A fresh spore of *T. epeori,* 3.5–4 μ long. (A and B redrawn after Léger, 1926.) **6. A** and **B.** Stained spores of *Plistophora longifilis* in testis of *Barbus
fluviatilis,* 3–12 μ × 2–6 μ. (Redrawn after Schuberg, 1910.) **7. A.** An infected lymphocyte of *Tubifex tubifex,* enclosing *Mrazekia caudata.* **B.** A spore of *M. caudata,* 16–18 μ × 1.3–1.4 μ. (A and B redrawn after Mrazek.) **8.** Stages in the life cycle of *Helicosporidium parasiticum,* parasitic in the body
cavity, fat bodies, and nervous tissue of certain Diptera and Acarina. **A.** Young growth stage.
B. Four-cell growth stage. **C.** Eight-cell growth stage. **D.** Lateral view of a developing spore showing three central cells; spiral filament not yet differentiated. **E.** End view of developing spore.
F. Mature spore showing peripheral spiral filament and three central cells. **G.** Spore membrane
ruptured and spiral filament protruding. (A–G redrawn after Keilin, 1921.)

he queen bee. It causes the so-called *Nosema* disease of bees.

Glugea hertwigi (Plate 5–17, Fig. 3) and *G. mülleri* are parasites of fishes. In *G. hertwigi,* the so-called "cysts," which are actually units of host cells surrounding sporonts, are quite conspicuous on the host's body surface.

Other species of Microsporidia are depicted in Plate 5–17.

Hyperparasitism by Microsporidians

The role of an undetermined species of *Nosema* as a hyperparasite (that is, a parasite of a parasite) in the sporocysts and developing cercariae of strigeoid trematodes in fresh-water gastropods has been mentioned in connection with MSX and oyster mortality (p. 137). The literature pertaining to hyperparasitism by microsporidians in helminths has been reviewed by Dollfus (1946) and Cort et al. (1960a). Various species of *Nosema* and *Glugea* are capable of hyperparasitism in larval and adult helminths. For example, both *Nosema légeri* and *N. spelotremae* have been found as hyperparasites in trematode larvae, specifically metacercariae, in marine bivalves; *N. distomi* was described from adult trematodes in *Bufo marinus* in Brazil; *Glugea danilewskyi* and *G. encyclometrae* are hyperparasitic in adult trematodes in snakes; and *Nosema echinostomi* is a hyperparasite in the rediae, cercariae, and metacercariae of echinostomate trematodes in the snail *Limnaea limnosa* in France. One species of *Nosema*, *N. helminthorum,* is hyperparasitic in tapeworms of the genus *Moniezia* in England and Pakistan.

Practically nothing is known about the physiological aspects and relatively little about the morphological manifestations of the host-parasite relationship between these hyperparasitic microsporidians and their helminth hosts. However, Dollfus (1946) has reported that *Nosema echinostomi* develops slowly in the rediae and cercariae in the snail host. If cercariae are not heavily parasitized, they can develop into metacercariae, but in heavy infections the cercariae are killed. Parasitized rediae lose their characteristic yellowish color and become white. Furthermore, only lightly infected rediae produce cercariae that become parasitized.

Cort et al. (1960a) have reported that the development of strigeoid cercariae is distorted if parasitized by *Nosema* (Plate 5–18), although a small proportion of the microsporidians would produce spores. Cercariae emerging from snails do not include microsporidians because infected embryonic cercariae are so injured and distorted that they cannot escape from the snail. Strigeoid larvae infected through experimental feeding of large numbers of *Nosema* spores to snail hosts become heavily infected and their microsporidians develop rapidly, producing spores in about 2 weeks, while in nature the number of microsporidians is small and their development is extremely slow, with only a few ultimately producing spores. Cort et al. (1960b) have suggested that these differences are due to some type of resistance that develops in the natural infections, most of which are probably produced by ingestion of only a few spores. In experimental infections with large number of spores, it has been suggested that the resistance may have been prevented from developing.

ORDER HELICOSPORIDIA

The Helicosporidia is a small order, presently including only one species, *Helicosporidium parasiticum,* a parasite in the fat bodies, body cavity, and nervous tissue of Diptera and Acarina (Plate 5–17, Fig. 8).

SPOROZOANS OF UNCERTAIN STATUS

Toxoplasma

Toxoplasma is a parasite that continues to elude the systematic protozoologist, for its relationship to other sporozoans remains undetermined (Plate 5–13). At one time there was even some doubt as to whether it is a true sporozoan. Its position in the Sporozoa now appears to be substantiated, since Gaven et al. (1962) reported the finding of schizogonic division in this parasite.

Although various species of *Toxoplasma* have been reported (Chatton and Blanc, 1917), it is suspected that only one, *T. gondii,* is valid, although strains, as determined by serological techniques, do exist. *Toxoplasma gondii* is usually seen as a crescent shaped organism about 6 to 12 μ long and half as wide. One end is usually more pointed than the other, and a prominent nucleus is present. When studied with the electron microscope, it was reported by Gustaf-

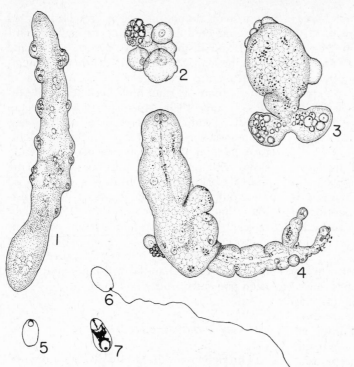

Plate 5-18 Hyperparasitic *Nosema* in intramolluscan larvae of strigeoid trematodes. **1.** Young daughter sporocyst of *Posthodiplostomum minimum,* showing effects of infection. **2.** Mass of embryonic cells from within daughter sporocyst of *Apatemon* sp. with one hyperinfected cell. **3.** Young cercarial embryo of *Apatemon* sp. showing small vesicles and protuberances characteristic of hyperparasitized individuals. **4.** Infected cercarial embryo of *Diplostomum flexicaudum,* showing some vesicles and surface protuberances. **5.** Fresh spore of *Nosema* sp., 3.9–6 μ $\times$ 2.2–3.8 μ. **6.** Fresh spore with extruded filament. **7.** Spore of *Nosema* from section stained with iron haematoxylin. (All figures redrawn from photomicrographs of Cort, Hussey, and Ameel, 1960.)

son et al. (1954) to have a system of some fifteen longitudinal fibrils (toxonemes) extending from the median portion of the cytoplasm to the anterior pointed terminal. These toxonemes supposedly account for the active motility of the organism and its ability to penetrate cells. A tiny knob (the conoid) projects from the anterior tip, which is believed to be either a "cell mouth" or a holdfast organelle.

Toxoplasma is able to parasitize an array of hosts, in which it is usually found within leukocytes and cells of the reticuloendothelial system. Animals known to be compatible hosts include humans, other mammals, and some birds. It has been successfully introduced experimentally into a variety of warm-blooded animals, including all laboratory rodents, and has been reported occasionally in poikilothermic animals.

Within its hosts, *Toxoplasma* multiplies intracellularly by longitudinal fission and schizogony, and upon rupturing out of a cell, can be carried by the blood in leukocytes to various areas of the body. It appears to possess a special affinity for nervous tissue and to some degree for the eyes. When cells are infected, pseudocysts are formed within the cells by the parasites themselves. Each pseudocyst encloses up to fifty organisms. Such cysts are commonly found in the brain, which appears to have less ability to resist infection.

It is only after the pseudocyst ruptures that the parasites can be circulated to infect other cells. How infections are acquired is still uncertain, although young mice can be parasitized through milk during maternal nursing and experimental animals can be infected by feeding with infected feces or flesh. It is suspected that human infections are acquired through the ingestion of infected meat, especially pork, although there are evidences to the contrary. In infants, infections are suspected to be acquired congenitally, being transmitted in utero or at birth from the mother.

Since *Toxoplasma* can survive for hours or even days in various blood-ingesting arthropods, it was suspected that an insect or tick intermediate host might be involved in transmission of the parasite, but there is little evidence to substantiate this hypothesis. Lack of complete knowledge of the life cycle is an important problem because *Toxoplasma* causes subclinical infections in humans (determined by the presence of antibodies), the incidence being as high as 40 per cent in some areas.

Fortunately, toxoplasmosis is usually subclinical. In acute cases where nonimmune individuals are exposed to large doses of *Toxoplasma* leath can result. Even if the victim recovers, permanent injury to the brain and eyes often occurs. Just how *Toxoplasma* injures the host remains uncertain. Although the secretion of a toxic proteinaceous substance has been suspected, no definite proof has been found. *Toxoplasma* and toxoplasmosis remain a challenge to parasitologists.

Atoxoplasma

Atoxoplasma was formerly thought to be a species of *Toxoplasma* parasitic in birds, for it is a crescent shaped intracellular parasite seen most often in leukocytes. Reproduction appears to be by binary fission and possibly by another process as well. However, it differs from *Toxoplasma* in being nontransmissible, either to other birds or to mammals. *Atoxoplasma* is considered a sporozoan because of its similarity to *Toxoplasma*. Nothing is known about its life history, transmission, or effects, although the parasite population may increase to rather high levels among English sparrows kept in captivity.

PHYSIOLOGY OF SPOROZOANS

OXYGEN REQUIREMENTS

All intraerythrocytic sporozoans, such as *Haemoproteus* spp. and *Plasmodium* spp., are true aerobes. This is not surprising because blood, especially arterial blood, is rich in oxygen, which is incorporated in oxyhaemoglobin within erythrocytes. Oxygen tension in the arterial blood of dogs, rabbits, men, and fishes is between 70 and 100 mm. Hg, while that in the venous blood of men, horses, and ducks ranges between 37 and 40 mm. Hg (von Buddenbrock, 1939). The oxygen tension in the blood of these representative vertebrates indicates that in their normal habitats, the blood-dwelling sporozoans are in continuous contact with appreciable amounts of oxygen.

Although the intraerythrocytic sporozoans are aerobic, high concentrations of oxygen are not suitable for their growth. For example, Anfinsen et al. (1946) demonstrated that if the environment contains 95 per cent O_2, *Plasmodium knowlesi* cannot be cultured. However, amounts of oxygen ranging from 0.37 to 20 per cent are equally satisfactory for the maintenance of *P. knowlesi* in vitro.

The great amount of oxygen utilized by parasitized cells can be used as an indication of oxygen consumption by the intracellular parasite. For example, the oxygen consumption of normal monkey erythrocytes rises from 0.73 mM. per hour, when 5×10^{12} cells are present, to 51.0 mM. per hour when *Plasmodium knowlesi* is present in the cells.

It should be noted, however, that among the intraerythrocytic species, some do not require oxygen during certain phases of their development. For example, during the formation of micro- and macrogametes in *Haemoproteus columbae*, no oxygen is necessary.

Studies on the respiratory rates of *Plasmodium lophurae* and *P. knowlesi* have revealed that respiration is almost completely inhibited by 0.001 M of cyanide, and approximately 64 per cent of respiration is inhibited by carbon dioxide. Thus, as in other blood-dwelling protozoans such as the trypanosomes, the presence of iron-porphyrin respiratory enzymes is indicated. Furthermore, there is some evidence to indicate the presence of flavoprotein systems.

Among the intestine-dwelling sporozoans, little oxygen is required. Again this is not surprising, for there is a minimal amount of oxygen in the lumen-gut of vertebrates. It is known that in the small intestine of such large mammals as horses, cows, and dogs, there is 0 to 6 mm. Hg of oxygen tension.

Nothing is known about the oxygen requirements of sporozoans that parasitize the lower vertebrates and invertebrates. Undoubtedly the intracellular parasites can utilize what oxygen is available within their host's cells.

Hydrogen ion concentration (pH) of the medium in which sporulated oocysts of *Eimeria* are found to some degree affects the oxygen uptake. For example, Smith and Herrick (1944) demonstrated that in *E. tenella* (p. 117), the oocysts of which are exposed to greatly variable conditions, the oxygen consumption of the oocysts remains unaltered within the remarkably wide pH range of 4.7 to 8.8. However, if the pH goes beyond this range, the rate of oxygen consumption changes.

GROWTH REQUIREMENTS

In order to obtain information concerning the growth requirements of a parasitic organism, very often it is necessary to culture the organism in vitro. Only after this has been successful can the nutritional requirements be studied. This is true for the Sporozoa. Attempts at culturing certain sporozoans in vitro, especially haemosporidians, have met with some success. Until the early 1940's most culture work on haemosporidians, primarily *Plasmodium* spp., was performed on the erythrocytic stages because the exoerythrocytic stages were not known until 1940. In discussing culture techniques for maintaining malarial organisms in vitro, it is necessary to treat exoerythrocytic and erythrocytic stages separately.

Culture of Exoerythrocytic Stages

The extensive literature pertaining to the culture of exoerythrocytic stages of *Plasmodium* spp. has been reviewed by Pipkin and Jensen (1958). Two basic types of techniques can be used to culture these stages: by placing infected cells or tissues in tissue culture flasks and culturing them by use of standard tissue culture techniques, and by maintaining suitable uninfected tissues in tissue culture and attempting to infect these with sporozoites. Of the two methods, considerable success has been attained with the first, but very little success with the second, mainly because of contamination or the failure of sporozoites to penetrate cells.

Various investigators have reported success in varying degrees in the culturing of infected host tissues. Lewert (1950) was able to maintain *Plasmodium gallinaceum* for as long as a year. He utilized a culture medium consisting of a clot of chicken plasma and Tyrode's solution (1:1), with just enough chick embryo extract to permit clotting of the plasma. The infected tissue was placed in the center of the clot, and the entire complex was covered with a supernatant consisting of 5 parts chick serum, 1 part Tyrode's solution, and 1 part chick embryo extract. The supernatant had to be changed twice weekly and fresh tissue supplied every 10 to 14 days. The conventional procedure of using roller tubes was followed.

Culture of Erythrocytic Stages

Although the erythrocytic stages of *Plasmodium* can be cultured either within their host cells or after they are removed from the cells, the first procedure is the more commonly employed. In either case it is of critical importance to provide the following conditions: a physical environment with pH, oxygen tension, CO_2 tension, osmotic pressure, and other factors that are comparable to that of blood; suitable nutrients for growth and development; and provision for the removal of metabolic by-products.

By providing these conditions, Geiman et al (1946) were able to culture *Plasmodium*, using composite medium that included inorganic salts, amino acids, vitamins (water soluble forms), purines, and pyrimidines.

Because erythrocytic stages derive most of their nutrient requirements from host cells, most in vitro cultures of these stages require the addition of whole erythrocytes. Trager (1950), however, successfully maintained *Plasmodium lophurae* for 2 to 3 days in media to which were added not whole blood cells, but extracts of duck erythrocytes.

In culture experiments with *Plasmodium knowlesi*, Anfinsen et al. (1946) showed that addition of glucose and *p*-aminobenzoic acid is necessary for success, thus suggesting the definite need for these nutrients in this and undoubtedly other species. Other sugars, such as mannose and fructose and even glycerol, can be oxidized by *Plasmodium*. However, only glucose can sustain long-term growth and reproduction. Parasitized cells utilize 25 to 100 times more glucose than normal ones. There is little evidence to indicate that sporozoans are capable of utilizing complex sugars or even disaccharides.

McKee and Geiman (1948) reported that addition of methionine enhances growth. In cultures of *Plasmodium lophurae*, calcium pantothenate also enhances growth. More recent work by Trager has demonstrated that this organism requires coenzyme A for optimum growth. From these and similar experiments, it is now known that the addition of methionine (an amino acid), *p*-aminobenzoic acid, glucose, and coenzyme A is important for cultivation of the erythrocytic stages of *Plasmodium* spp. Withdrawal of ascorbic acid from the host's diet affects malarial parasites, but parasites cultured in media that lack ascorbic acid are not appreciably affected, indicating that this acid acts through the host.

Carbohydrate Metabolism

Although *Plasmodium* can oxidize various carbohydrates, including fructose, mannose, and glucose, only glucose can satisfy the long-term requirements of growth and reproduction. In *Plasmodium gallinaceum*, glucose is quantitatively converted to lactic acid under anaerobic conditions. Enzymes of the typical Embden-Meyerhof glycolytic pathway (Table 3–5) are present, thus indicating the presence of the phosphorylative glycolytic pathway. The oxidative process during carbohydrate metabolism undoubtedly involves the Krebs tricarboxylic acid cycle (Table 3–5).

The malarial organism is extremely wasteful in its energy-producing mechanisms (Smyth, 1962), because it glycolyzes much more carbohydrate than it oxidizes, resulting is an accumulation of lactic acid, which if not removed or neutralized in culture media, impairs the respiratory activity. It has been estimated that only about 10 per cent of the total required energy is supplied by the anaerobic glycolytic process, while the remaining 90 per cent comes from the enzymatic transfer to oxygen of the electrons liberated during the tricarboxylic acid cycle.

Protein Metabolism

Although a great deal is yet to be learned about utilization of haemoglobin by malarial parasites, knowledge in this area of sporozoan physiology is advancing by great strides. Moulder and Evans (1946), for example, observed a high rate of amino nitrogen produced by erythrocytes parasitized by *P. gallinaceum*, thus suggesting that haemoglobin was utilized.

More recently, Rudzinska and Trager (1959) demonstrated that *P. berghei* ingests its food, mainly haemoglobin, from the cytoplasm of host erythrocytes by pseudopodial engulfment, although the ingested particles were either molecules or groups of molecules. Malarial organisms contain enzymes that can split haemoglobin into a nonprotein fraction and globin.

It has been estimated that approximately 76 per cent of the haemoglobin in an infected erythrocyte is destroyed during the life of the parasite. The nonprotein fraction of the split haemoglobin molecule is haematin, which is not utilized by the parasite but is released as the characteristic malarial pigment, haemozoin, when the parasite ruptures out of the host cell.

Although most of the in vivo protein and amino acid requirements of *Plasmodium* are satisfied from host cell proteins, the methionine requirement cannot be totally acquired from this source because very little of this amino acid is present. As the result, the parasite derives its methionine requirement from the surrounding plasma, thus indicating that although the protozoan appears to be an intracellular parasite of individual erythrocytes, it is physiologically parasitic on the host cell, the plasma, and other cells as well.

Once taken into the body of the parasite, the bulk of the polypeptides and amino acids are utilized for synthesis and only very small amounts are utilized in oxidative energy-producing processes.

Lipid Metabolism

Practically nothing is known about sporozoan lipid metabolism. It is known that the total lipid content in red blood cells infected with *Plasmodium knowlesi* is increased more than 400 per cent over normal. Some 25 per cent of the lipid, mainly cholesterol, is nonsaponifiable. The fatty acid content of infected cells is approximately four to five times that of uninfected cells. Among the fatty acids present in infected cells, there is an unsaturated 18-carbon monocarboxylic fatty acid that possesses lytic properties. It has been suggested that this fatty acid may be in some way associated with the rupturing of the red blood cell wall when merozoites escape.

HOST–PARASITE RELATIONSHIPS

EFFECTS OF PARASITE ON HOST

Aside from the obvious clinical symptoms of malaria and other sporozoan-caused diseases, an array of other parasite-induced effects are known.

Anemias

In infections with *Babesia* spp. and *Plasmodium* spp., anemias are known to result. Numerous hypotheses have been postulated to explain the origin of these anemias, especially those resulting from *Plasmodium* infections. (1) It has been suggested that loss of erythrocytes at the periods when merozoites escape is greater than the rate of replacement, hence the anemic condition sets in. (2) Parasitized erythrocytes in some cases are more fragile and therefore are easily ruptured and destroyed. (3) Since the spleen of a malaria victim becomes enlarged, it has been postulated that a lytic substance, lysolecithin, which destroys erythrocytes, is released by the spleen. (4) Parasitized erythrocytes are believed to serve as autoantigenic bodies that bring on production of a specific antibody, haemolysin, in the spleen. Once in the blood, haemolysin destroys red blood cells.

Possibly a combination of these major hypotheses, all of which are based on experimental evidences, is the cause of anemia. In humans infected with *Plasmodium falciparum* the erythrocyte count may drop from 4,600,000–6,200,000 per cu. mm. to 440,000 per cu. mm., and in humans infected with *P. vivax* the count may drop to 560,000 per cu. mm.

Altered Protein and Carbohydrate Composition of Host

The carbohydrate and protein composition of hosts infected with various Sporozoa are affected. For example, numerous investigators have shown that in humans infected with *Plasmodium malariae, P. vivax,* and *P. falciparum* the total serum protein is decreased. An analysis of the protein fractions has revealed that the albumin component is decreased but the globulin is increased. This is not surprising because the globulin fraction, especially gamma globulin, includes the antibodies that would be expected to increase on the introduction of the parasite into the host's blood and tissues.

Kehar (1936) reported a parallel condition in monkeys infected with *P. knowlesi*. Ghosh and Sinton (1935) reported that the blood protein remains normal in monkeys infected with *P. inui*. This sporozoan is not pathogenic and has little or no demonstrable effect on its host. That the serum protein is unaltered suggests that the virulence of the parasite is directly correlated with the degree of change in the protein composition of the host's serum.

Waxler (1941) and Pratt (1940, 1941) reported that in chickens infected with *Eimeria tenella,* hyperglycemia develops, and there is a decrease in the amount of stored glycogen. This instance serves to demonstrate disruptions in carbohydrate metabolism resulting from sporozoan infections. Furthermore, von Brand and Mercado (1956) reported that in chickens infected with *Plasmodium gallinaceum* the liver reveals less glycogenesis. Histological studies revealed that this is due to the apparent nonfunction of certain liver cells.

Effect on Endocrine Glands

The presence of malarial organisms can affect certain endocrine glands. For example, Nadel et al. (1949) reported that in chickens infected with *P. gallinaceum,* an increase in the number of adrenal cells is found. This condition reaches a maximum level at approximately one day after the number of parasites reaches its highest level.

Effect of Parasite Secretions

As in all instances of parasitic infections, parasite secretions may affect the host. This aspect of host-parasite relationship in sporozoan infections remains to be completely explored. In one instance, that of *Toxoplasma* infections, the secretion of a toxin is suspected. Weinman and Klatchko (1950) reported that when secretions of *Toxoplasma* in the peritoneal fluid of infected mice are injected into the veins of parasitized and nonparasitized mice, these animals died immediately. This toxic material is reported to be totally or partially composed of proteins. Confirmation of the existence of this toxin should be made.

Weakening Effects

Hosts of certain sporozoans demonstrate a general weakened condition. For example, sheep heavily infected with *Sarcocystis* are lean and weak. In addition to being frequently lethal to chickens, *Eimeria tenella,* when present in small numbers, is known to weaken birds. The gastrocnemius muscle, for example, of infected birds can only perform 58 per cent of the work done by those of uninfected animals, and muscle fatigue among infected birds sets in before it does in healthy ones (Levine and Herrick, 1954).

Castration

Sporozoan parasites have been incriminated in several instances for the castration of their hosts. One such case was reported by Smith (1905), who found destruction of the testes of the crustacean, *Inachus dorsettensis,* by *Aggregata eberthi* and feminization of the host's external characteristics.

EFFECTS OF HOST ON PARASITE

Sex Hormones and Susceptibility

There exists considerable evidence that the sex hormones of the host play an important role in governing its susceptibility to sporozoans, especially the haemosporidians. Chernin (1950) reported that the degree of parasitemia in ducks infected with *Leucocytozoon simondi* diminishes when female birds commence egg laying. This phenomenon is undoubtedly correlated with female sex hormones. Also young female chickens (not sexually mature) are more susceptible to *Plasmodium gallinaceum* than males and mature females. In sexually mature, egg-laying ducks, there appears to be a higher degree of resistance to *P. lophurae* than in males. Trager and McGhee (1950) indicated that some substance present in the blood is at least partially responsible for this immunity.

Age Resistance

What has commonly been termed "age resistance" to malaria, especially among avian hosts, may well be partly due to hormonal influences.

Effect of Host Diet

There is some indication that deficient host diets may result in more severe primary attacks by *Plasmodium* spp. In addition, there is a greater tendency on the part of the host to relapse and become more susceptible to super-infections.

Vitamins are known to play a role in sporozoan infections. Becker and Dilworth (1941) reported that in *Eimeria nieschulzi* infections in rats, when vitamin B_1 is present in the host's diet, there is a depressing effect on the development of the parasite, as measured by the production of oocysts. On the other hand, vitamin B_6 has a stimulating effect. If both vitamins are given together, there is a strong inhibiting effect.

PERIODICITY

The synchronized time intervals at which merozoites of specific species of *Plasmodium* escape from host cells represent an interesting phase of host-parasite relationship. Stauber (1939) has shown that the synchronous periodicity of reproduction of three strains of *Plasmodium cathemerium* and one strain of *P. relictum* in birds is affected by high and low temperatures and the amount of light to which the hosts are exposed. Environmental and climatic temperatures are also known to play important roles.

LITERATURE CITED

Anfinsen, C. B., et al. 1946. Studies on malarial parasites. VIII. Factors affecting the growth of *Plasmodium knowlesi* in vitro. J. Exper. Med., *84:* 607–621.

Becker, E. R., and R. I. Dilworth. 1941. Nature of *Eimeria nieschulzi* growth-promoting potency of feeding stuffs. II. Vitamins B_1 and B_6. J. Inf. Dis., *68:* 285–290.

Chatton, E. P. L., and G. R. Blanc. 1917. Notes et réflexions sur le toxoplasme et la toxoplasmose di gondi (*Toxoplasma gondii* Ch. Nicolle et Marceaux. 1909). Arch. Inst. Pasteur Tunis, *10:* 1–15.

Chernin, E. 1950. The relapse phenomenon in *Leucocytozoon simondi* infections in domestic ducks. J. Parasit., *36:* 22–23.

Cleveland, L. R. 1949. Hormone-induced sexual cycles of flagellates. I. Gametogenesis, fertilization, and meiosis in *Trichonympha*. J. Morph., *85:* 197–296.

Coatney, G. R. 1936. A check-list and host-index of the genus *Haemoproteus*. J. Parasit., *22:* 88–105.

Cort, W. W., K. L. Hussey, and D. J. Ameel. 1960a. Studies on a microsporidian hyperparasite of strigeoid trematodes. I. Prevalence and effect on the parasitized larval trematodes. J. Parasit., *46:* 317–325.

Cort, W. W., K. L. Hussey, and D. J. Ameel. 1960b. Studies on a microsporidian hyperparasite of strigeoid trematodes. II. Experimental transmission. J. Parasit., *46:* 327–336.

Delpy, L. P. J. 1946. Description de formes schizogonique de *Babesia bigemina*. Comparaison avec des formes identiques, descrites par E. Dschunkowsky, 1937, sous le nom *Luhsia bovis* n. sp. Arch. Inst. Hessarek., *2:* 43–53.

Dollfus, R. P. 1946. Parasites (animaux et végétaux) des helminthes. Hyperparasites, ennemis et prédateurs des helminthes parasites et des helminthes libres. Encyclopédie Biologique, Vol. 37, Lechevalier, Paris.

Eyles, D. E., G. R. Coatney, and M. E. Getz. 1960. Vivax-type malaria parasite of macaques transmissible to man. Science, *131:* 1812–1813.

Fallis, A. M., and D. M. Wood. 1957. Biting midges (Diptera: Ceratopogonidae) as intermediate hosts for *Haemoproteus* of ducks. Can. J. Zool., *35:* 425–435.

Feng, S. Y. 1958. Observations on distribution and elimination of spores of *Nematopsis ostrearum* in oysters. Proc. Nat. Shellfish. Assoc., *48:* 162–173.

Gavin, M. A., W. Theodor, and L. Jacobs. 1962. Electron microscopic studies of reproducing and interkinetic *Toxoplasma*. J. Protozool., *9:* 222–234.

Geiman, Q. M. 1948. Cultivation and metabolism of malarial parasites. Proc. 4th Internat. Cong. Trop. Med. Malaria, *1:* 618–628.

Geiman, Q. M., et al. 1946. Studies on malarial parasites. VII. Methods and techniques for cultivation. J. Exper. Med., *84:* 538–606.

Grassé, P. P. 1953. Traité de Zoologie, Masson et Cie., Paris.

Grell, K. 1956. Protozoologie. Springer, Berlin.

Gustafson, P. V., H. D. Agar, and D. I. Cramer. 1954. An electron microscope study of *Toxoplasma*. J. Trop. Med. Hyg., *3:* 1008–1021.

Hauschka, T. S. 1943. Life history and chromosome cycle of the coccidian *Adelina deronis*. J. Morph., *73:* 529–481.

Hitchcock, D. J. 1955. The life cycle of *Isospora felis* in the kitten. J. Parasit., *41:* 383–397.

Huff, C. G., et al. 1948. Symposium on exoerythrocytic forms of malarial parasites. J. Parasit., *34:* 261–320.

Kehar, N. D. 1936. Some physico-chemical factors and their relationship to protein fractions, blood cells and parasite counts, in the blood sera of monkeys infected with *Plasmodium knowlesi*. Rec. Malaria Surv. India, *6:* 499–509.

Kudo, R. R. 1954. Protozoology. 4th Ed., Charles C Thomas, Springfield, Ill.

Levine, L., and C. A. Herrick. 1954. The effects of the protozoan parasite *Eimeria tenella* on the ability of the chicken to do muscular work when its muscles are stimulated directly and indirectly. J. Parasit., *40:* 525–531.

Lewert, R. M. 1950. Alternations in the cycle of *Plasmodium gallinaceum* following passage through tissue culture. I. Tissue-culture studies. Am. J. Hyg., *51:* 155–177.

Manwell, R. D. 1961. Introduction to Protozoology. St. Martin's Press, New York.

McKee, R. W., and Q. M. Geiman. 1948. Methionine in the growth of the malarial parasite, *Plasmodium knowlesi*. Fed. Proc., *7:* 172.

Monne, L., and G. Hönig. 1954. On the properties of the shells of the coccidean oocyst. Ark. Zool., *7:* 251–256.

Moulder, J. W., and E. A. Evans. 1946. The biochemistry of the malaria parasite. VI. Studies on the nitrogen metabolism of the malaria parasite. J. Biol. Chem., *164:* 145–157.

Nadel, E. M., D. J. Taylor, J. Greenberg, and E. S. Josephson. 1949. Adrenal hypertrophy in chicks infected with *Plasmodium gallinaceum*. J. Nat. Malaria Soc., *8:* 70–79.

O'Roke, E. C. 1934. A malaria-like disease of ducks caused by *Leucocytozoon anatis* Wickware. Bull. Univ. Mich. Schl. Forest. Conserv.

Pipkin, A. C., and D. V. Jensen. 1958. Avian embryos and tissue culture in the study of parasitic protozoa. Exptl. Parasitol., *7:* 491–530.

Pratt, I. 1940. The effect of *Eimeria tenella* (Coccidia) upon the blood sugar of the chicken. Trans. Amer. Micro. Soc., *59:* 31–37.

Pratt, I. 1941. The effect of *Eimeria tenella* (Coccidia) upon the glycogen stores of the chicken. Am. J. Hyg., *34:* 54–61.

Regendanz, P., and E. Reichenow. 1933. Die Entwicklung von *Babesia canis* in *Dermacenter reticulatus*. Arch. Protistenk., *79:* 50–71.

Rudzinska, M. A., and W. Trager. 1959. Phagotrophy and two new structures in the malaria parasite *Plasmodium berghei*. J. Biophys. Biochem. Cyt., *6:* 103–112.

Shuster, C. N., Jr. 1960. On the ecology of estuarine zooparasites. Trans. N.Y. Acad. Sci., *23:* 133–137.

Shuster, C. N., Jr., and R. E. Hillman. 1963. Comments on Laird, M.: "microecological factors in oyster epizootics." Chesapeake Sci., *4:* 101–103.

Scott, J. W. 1943. Life history of the Sarcosporidia, with particular reference to *Sarcocystis tenella*. Univ. Wyoming Agr. Exp. Sta. Bull., *259:* 1–63.

Smith, B. F., and C. A. Herrick. 1944. The respiration of the protozoan parasite, *Eimeria tenella*. J. Parasit., *30:* 295–302.

Smith, G. W. 1905. Note on the gregarine (*Aggregata inachi*, n. sp.) which may cause the parasitic castration of its host (*Inachus dorsettensis*). Mitth. Zool. Sta. Neapel, *17:* 406–410.

Smyth, J. D. 1962. Introduction to Animal Parasitology. Charles C Thomas, Springfield, Ill.

Spindler, L. A., and H. E. Zimmerman, Jr. 1945. The biological status of *Sarcocystis*. J. Parasit., *31* (Suppl.): 13.

Stauber, L. A. 1939. Factors influencing the asexual periodicity of avian malarias. J. Parasit., *25:* 95–116.

Stauber, L. A. 1950. The fate of india ink injected intracardially into the oyster, *Ostrea virginica* Gmelin. Biol. Bull., *98:* 227–241.

Trager, W. 1950. Studies on the extracellular cultivation of an intracellular parasite (avian malaria). I. Development of the organisms in erythrocyte extracts, and the favoring effect of adenosine triphosphate. J. Exper. Med., *92:* 349–365.

Trager, W., and R. B. McGhee. 1950. Factors in plasma concerned in natural resistance to an avian malaria parasite (*Plasmodium lophurae*). J. Exper. Med., *91:* 365–379.

von Brand, T., and T. I. Mercado. 1956. Quantitative and histochemical studies on glycogenesis in the liver of rats infected with *Plasmodium berghei.* Exptl. Parasit., *5:* 34–47.

von Buddenbrock, W. 1939. Grundriss der vergleichenden Physiologie. 2nd Ed., Vol. 2. Borntraeger, Berlin.

Waxler, S. H. 1941. Changes occurring in the blood and tissue of chickens during coccidiosis and artificial hemorrhage. A. M. Physiol., *134:* 19–26.

Weinman, D., and H. J. Klatchko. 1950. Description of toxin in toxoplasmosis. Yale J. Biol. Med., *22:* 323–326.

SUGGESTED READING

Ball, G. H. 1960. Some considerations regarding the Sporozoa. J. Protozool., *7:* 1–6. (A presidential address before the Society of Protozoologists. Classification, morphology, and biology of the sporozoa are discussed. Need for further research is pointed out.)

Boyd, M. F. 1940. Malariology (2 volumes). W. B. Saunders, Philadelphia. (This definitive treatise on all aspects of malarial parasites, although somewhat outdated in certain sections, is an invaluable reference.)

Hall, R. P. 1953. Protozoology. Prentice-Hall, New York., pp. 597–626. (This chapter in Hall's textbook deals with the human malarias.)

Hegner, R., and J. Andrews. 1930. Problems and Methods of Research in Protozoology. The Macmillan Co., New York.
    Read:
        Hegner, R. Sporozoa in general. pp. 276–280.
        Andrews, J. Coccidiosis in birds and mammals. pp. 281–302.
        Kudo, R. R. Myxosporidia. pp. 303–347.
        Hegner, R. Malaria in general. pp. 348–353.
        Manwell, R. D. Experiments on bird malaria. pp. 381–397.
        Taliaferro, L. G. Periodicity in malaria. pp. 398–405.
        MacDougall, M. S., and G. H. Boyd. Experimental modification of bird malaria infections. pp. 406–410.
    (Although somewhat outdated, these chapters in the volume edited by Hegner and Andrews should be read by the beginning student. The various contributors have suggested experiments which may be attempted.)

Horton–Smith, C., and P. L. Long. 1963. Coccidia and coccidiosis in the domestic fowl and turkey. *In* Advances in Parasitology (B. Dawes, ed.). Academic Press, New York, Vol. I, pp. 67–108. (In this review article, the authors have considered in detail the life cycles and the pathological changes caused by species of *Eimeria* that are parasitic in fowls. These species include *E. acervulina, E. brunetti, E. maxima, E. mitis, E. necatrix,* and *E. tenella* of chickens and *E. adenoeides, E. meleagridis,* and *E. meleagrimitis* of turkeys. In addition, the cytochemical composition of the various stages in the life cycles of these parasites and immunity to coccidiosis are considered.)

Huff, C. G. 1963. Experimental research on avian malaria. *In* Advances in Parasitology (B. Dawes, ed.). Academic Press, New York, Vol. I, pp. 1–65. (In this review article, Dr. Huff has brought up to date the information on avian malaria, *Haemoproteus,* and *Leucocytozoon* since Hewitt's review paper that appeared in 1940. In this article are considered such topics as cultivation, physiology and cytochemistry, fine structure, immunity, cytology, and pathology.)

Hyman, L. H. 1940. The Invertebrates. Protozoa through Ctenophora. McGraw-Hill, New York. pp. 143–164. (Hyman has given a general discussion of the Sporozoa in these pages. The references, especially those to the older literature, are most useful.)

Levine, N. D. 1961. Protozoan Parasites of Domestic Animals and of Man. Burgess, Minneapolis. pp. 158–346. (This is a concise and up-to-date account of the different species of Sporozoa that are of economic importance or that are related to economically important species. The student will find the bibliography of great value.)

Moulder, J. W. 1955. The protein metabolism of intracellular parasites. *In* Some Physiological Aspects and Consequences of Parasitism. (Edited by W. H. Cole). Rutgers Univ. Press New Brunswick, N. J. (The author has summarized our scanty knowledge concerning protein metabolism in intracellular parasites, including viruses, malarial parasites, and typhus rickettsiae.)

Pipkin, A. C., and D. V. Jensen. 1958. Avian embryos and tissue culture in the study of parasitic protozoa. I. Malarial parasites. Exptl. Parasit., *5:* 491–530. (The techniques, usefulness and successes at in vitro culturing of malarial parasites in tissue culture are discussed.)

Trager, W. 1955. Studies on the cultivation of malaria parasites. *In* Some Physiological Aspects and Consequences of Parasitism. (Edited by W. H. Cole). Rutgers Univ. Press. New Brunswick, N. J. (The author has summarized the biochemical requirements and techniques employed in the cultivation of *Plasmodium*. This chapter should be read by all students who intend to work on the physiology of malarial parasites.)

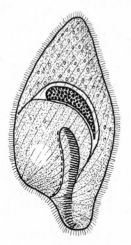

6

THE CILIOPHORA—
The Ciliates and
Suctorians

The subphylum Ciliophora, which includes two major groups of protozoa—the ciliates and the suctorians—differs from the Mastigophora, Sarcodina, and Sporozoa in that the members bear cilia during some stage in their development. Except for the Protociliatia, which is a primitive group of ciliates, ciliophorans also possess two types of nuclei—the macronucleus and the micronucleus. Among the Protociliatia there may be more than one nucleus present but all the nuclei are of the same type.

Most ciliophorans are free-living, being found in fresh, brackish, and marine waters, but there are several genera of parasitic forms. Some of these, such as the pathogen *Balantidium coli* in humans, are true parasites, but by far the majority are epizoic and commensalistic species.

Reynolds (1930) has listed 55 species of ciliates known to attach to the body surface of various vertebrates and invertebrates. These unique species are often categorically classified as parasites, although they are more properly considered epizoic, since their relationship with their hosts is generally devoid of any type of physiological interactions (nutritional, sensory, etc.). The relationship is purely one of mechanical attachment. In a few instances, however, some physiological bond does exist, for if removed from their hosts the ciliates cannot survive. Such is the case between *Trichodina scorpenae* and its fish host.

At the other extreme, *Ichthyophthirius multifiliis* is a true ectoparasite that inflicts severe damage to its piscine host. Another true ectoparasite, *Enchelys parasitica*, causes a fatal skin disease of the rainbow trout. Economically important species of ciliates are listed in Table 6–1.

Although there is a lack of fossil evidence, most biologists agree that the ciliates represent a very ancient group, although not as ancient as the flagellates and the amoebae. Perhaps for this reason there are fewer parasitic ciliates than flagellates or amoebae. It is also possible that the greater specialization of structure of the ciliates through evolution implies refinements in their physiological requirements that make adaptation to the parasitic way of life more difficult.

Morphologically, the class Ciliatea can be distinguished from the class Suctorea by the

Table 6-1. Some Important Parasitic Ciliates of Man and Economically Important Animals

Organism	Principal Hosts	Habitat	Main Characteristics	Disease
Balantidium coli	Pigs, monkeys, man	Large intestine	50-100μ long, large ovoid body, anterior end more pointed, peristome leading into distinct cleft, two contractile vacuoles, kidney shaped nucleus	Balantidiasis (in man)
Balantidium sp.	Sheep	Intestine	45μ long, 33μ wide	Nonpathogenic
Ichthyophthirius multifiliis	Fish	Integument	100-1000μ long, ovoid, with large cytostome measuring 30-40μ in diameter	Ichthyophthiriasis
Enchelys parasitica	Trout	Integument	Flask shaped, cytostome slitlike, about 120μ long	Enchelysiasis

presence of cilia throughout life. Among the suctorians, cilia are present only during the young developmental stages (swarm cells). Once suctorians become mature, they develop characteristic tentacles that serve as locomotor and food-acquiring mechanisms.

CLASS CILIATEA

MORPHOLOGY

The body shapes and sizes among the various species of Ciliatea vary greatly, but they all have cilia, which may be uniformly distributed over the entire body surface or grouped in heavier concentrations in certain areas. Microscopically, cilia appear as extremely fine, short, hairlike projections which are usually arranged in definite rows (Plate 6-1, Figs. 1 to 4). Each cilium is attached at the basal granule (also known as the basal body), situated immediately below the pellicle, which is a definite membrane surrounding the cytoplasm (Plate 6-1, Fig. 5).

Structurally, the single cilium is similar to a flagellum (p. 52). There is an axoneme surrounded by an elastic cytoplasmic sheath (Plate 6-1, Fig. 6). When studied with the electron microscope, the axoneme is seen to be composed of eleven fibrils, nine peripherally arranged, and two centrally situated.

Cosgrove (1948) reported that in *Opalina obtrigonoidea,* found in the colon of frogs and toads, there are extremely fine fibrils that originate at the basal granules, traverse the body cytoplasm dorsoventrally, and are connected individually with a basal granule on the opposing body surface (Plate 6-1, Fig. 7). Similarly, ciliary rootlets have been reported in other species. However, these rootlets, which also arise from the basal granules, do not traverse the body cytoplasm but end therein (Plate 6-1, Fig. 8).

In addition to these fibrils, longitudinal, and in some species transverse, fibrils connect the basal granules, forming a network that is readily demonstrable when stained with various modifications of the silver impregnation technique (Plate 6-2, Fig. 1).

Other types of networks are known to exist independent of that connecting the basal granules (Plate 6-2). These networks have been termed the silverline, the infraciliature, or the neuromotor (neuroneme) system (Hall, 1953,

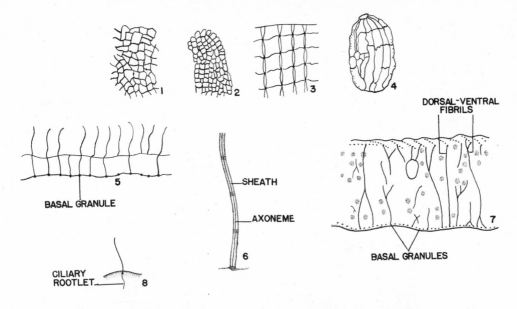

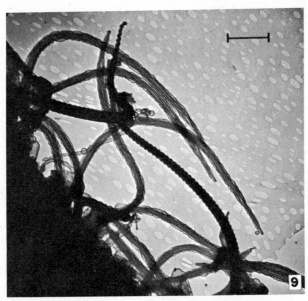

Plate 6-1   **Some ciliary patterns.** 1. Silverline system of *Prordon teres,* an aquatic ciliate, showing the narrow-mesh type of organization with some orientation of fibrils. (Redrawn after Klein, 1932.) 2. Silverline system of a ciliate, showing the primitive narrow-mesh type of arrangement. (Redrawn after Klein, 1932.) 3. Silverline system of *Cinetochilum margaritaceum,* showing the double striation pattern of arrangement. (Redrawn after Klein, 1932.) 4. Silverline system of *Cyclidium glaucoma,* showing the striation system of arrangement. (Redrawn after Klein, 1932.) 5. Longitudinal section of *Entorhipidium echini* through cortex, showing cilia attached to individual basal granules and a longitudinal fibril joining the basal granules. (Redrawn after Lynch, 1929.) 6. Enlarged drawing of the basal portion of a single cilium, showing the elastic sheath and axoneme. (Original.) 7. Section of *Opalina obtrigopoidea,* showing dorsal-ventral fibrils joining basal granules. (Redrawn after Cosgrove, 1947.) 8. Ciliary rootlet, projecting inwardly from basal granule. (Original.) 9. Electronmicrograph of cilia (and one trichocyst) of *Paramecium,* showing fibrils within sheath. Bar indicates 1 μ. (Courtesy of Dr. T. F. Anderson, Institute for Cancer Research, Philadelphia.)

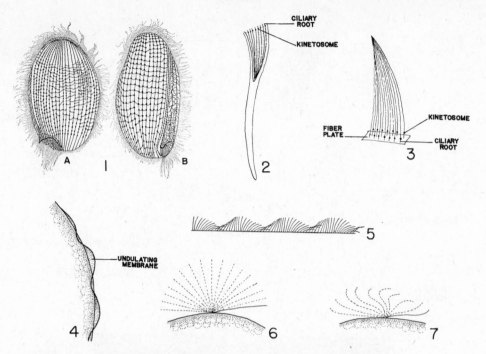

Plate 6-2   Some ciliary and flagellar arrangements. 1. Silverline system of *Ancistruma mytili*, a commensal in the mantle cavity of various marine mussels. **A.** Ventral view. **B.** Dorsal view. (After Kidder, 1933.) **2.** Anal cirrus of *Euplotes eurystomus*, a free-living spirotrichous ciliate from fresh and brackish waters. (Redrawn after Taylor, 1920.) **3.** A membranelle of *E. eurystomus*. (Redrawn after Taylor, 1920.) **4.** Portion of a flagellate, showing the undulating membrane. (Original.) **5.** Metachronous movement of cilia in a longitudinal row. (After Kudo, R. R., 1954. *Protozoology,* 4th Ed. Charles C Thomas, Springfield, Ill.) **6.** Diagrammatic drawing showing pendular movement of a single cilium: (Original.) **7.** Diagrammatic drawing showing flexural movement of a single cilium. (Original.)

pp. 21 to 25). The neuromotor system is thought to represent a primitive type of nervous system that coordinates ciliary motion. This is postulated because it is well known that the movement of cilia, unlike the random beating of flagella, is well coordinated in a rhythmic sway. Recently, Pitelka (1961) has contributed a thorough study of the silverline and fibrillar systems of three tetrahymenid ciliates. The monographs by Pitelka (1963) and Sleigh (1962), in which are considered the ultrastructure and function of cilia, should be consulted by those interested in these aspects.

Specialized Ciliary Organelles

The fusion of adjacent cilia in definite patterns gives rise to various types of specialized organelles. Those commonly found on parasitic species include the cirrus, composed of a tuft of cilia from two or three adjacent rows that have fused together to give the appearance of long flexible spines; the membranelle, composed of two fused layers of cilia (lamellae) forming a triangular platelike structure; and the undulating membrane (oral membrane)*, composed of one or more lamellae forming a flap that is generally associated with the oral groove or peristome (Plate 6–2, Figs. 2 to 4).

These specialized ciliary organelles are not only of functional but also of diagnostic importance. For example, cirri are commonly found among the Hypotrichida, membranelles are found among the more advanced ciliates except certain Holotrichida, and undulating membranes are most commonly, although not exclusively, found among the Holotrichida.

Functionally, cilia not only serve as mech-

---

*The undulating membrane of ciliates is not to be confused with that of flagellates, which is formed by the undulating distentions of a flagellum underneath the body surface.

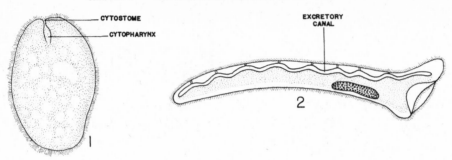

Plate 6-3 **Some specialized structures of ciliates.** **1.** Hypothetical ciliate, showing cytostome and cytopharynx. (Original.) **2.** Specimen of *Haptophrya michiganensis*, showing longitudinally oriented excretory canal. (Redrawn after MacLannan, 1944.)

anisms of locomotion but also serve in the acquisition of food particles and as sensory organelles. Cirri are associated with specialized movement and are used as stalks or paddles. Undulating membranes and membranelles are generally associated with food acquisition.

It is known that cilia beat in a uniform wave-like fashion (known as metachronism), but the mechanisms of movement and coordination have not been determined definitely (Plate 6–2, Fig. 5). Probably the most logical hypothesis offered thus far to explain ciliary motion is the alternating contraction of one side then the other of the elastic sheath.

Ciliary motion has been classified into two types: (1) Pendular movement, in which the single cilium sways from one side to the other, flexing only at the base (Plate 6–2, Fig. 6). This type of motion is characteristic of cirri of hypotrichs. (2) The common flexural movement (Plate 6–2, Fig. 7), in which the cilium first bends at the free end and the bending passes towards the base. During recovery, the cilium straightens out from the base upwards.

Sharp (1914) reported that the so-called neuromotor network, which lies beneath the body surface in the ectoplasm, is connected with a "coordinating center"—the motorium. This organelle presumably governs the pattern and rhythm of motion. The coordinating function of the motorium has been suggested in *Chlamydodon* by MacDougall (1928), who reported that if this organelle is destroyed, the coordinated movement of the membranelle is disrupted.

MacLennan (1935b) demonstrated that if the neurofibrillar system of *Ichthyophthirius* is injured, the ciliary movement becomes disorganized. Similar phenomena have been demonstrated in other parasitic species. Ciliary motion

and a coordination center should be investigated further before this concept is fully accepted.

Other Specialized Structures

In addition to cilia and specialized ciliary organelles, several other types of structures are found among the ciliates. The ingestion of food particles is made possible by a minute "mouth" —the cytostome—which leads into the cytopharynx (Plate 6–3, Fig. 1). This structure is rarely visible in most ciliates because of the membranelles and/or undulating membranes in the peristomal zone surrounding the cytostome. It is of some interest to note that cytostomes have been demonstrated in certain parasitic amoebae—for example, trophozoites of *Dientamoeba fragilis* and *Entamoeba muris*.

The remaining organelles and cell inclusions in the Ciliatea correspond with those found in other protozoa and have been discussed in Chapter 3. In the large symbiotic ciliate *Haptophrya michiganensis*, found in the gut and gallbladder of salamanders, a specialized contractile canal is oriented along the dorsal aspect of the longitudinal axis of the sausage shaped body. Located along the wall of this canal are accessory vacuoles that gradually unite with one another and later with the main canal (Plate 6–3, Fig. 2). The contents of the expanded canal empty to the exterior through several short excretory ducts.

This unique excretory system rids the body of waste materials—carbon dioxide, water, and nitrogenous materials. Because endoparasitic sporozoans, amoebae, and flagellates live in near isotonic environments, contractile vacuoles are usually not seen in their bodies. However, vacuoles do exist in ciliates and suctorians, but the reason for their visibility has not been determined.

SYSTEMATICS AND BIOLOGY

CLASSIFICATION

The class Ciliatea is divided into two subclasses: the Protociliatia,* which includes a small number of more primitive species that are characterized by two or more nuclei of the same type, cilia, of uniform length, and the absence of a cytostome; and the Euciliatia, which includes far more numerous advanced species. The euciliates are characterized by macro- and micronuclei, a cytostome, and various specialized ciliary organelles (cirri, membranelles, etc.).

SUBCLASS PROTOCILIATIA

The protociliates are all parasitic, being found in the colons of amphibians, reptiles, and fishes. The taxonomy of this group is not given here but may be found in Metcalf (1923, 1940). Reproduction is generally asexual by transverse fission. However, the sexual fusion of gametes has been reported in *Protoopalina intestinalis,* an intestinal parasite of amphibians, and in other species.

There is some doubt as to exactly what the relationship between the protociliates and the other ciliates is. Metcalf, who studied protociliates extensively, considered them to be primitive ciliates. However, more recently, Grassé, Corliss, and others have suggested that the protociliates are more truly associated with the Zoomastigophorea. The protociliates are considered here in their more traditional position in the Ciliatea. Indeed, Corliss himself remarks: ". . . their organization seems to show a very high degree of differentiation and specialization indicating a long evolutionary history of their own far removed from the main line of development of any other protozoan group." Although the protociliates are considered with the Ciliatea, the author does so with reservations.

The best known genera of the Protociliatia are *Opalina, Protoopalina,* and *Zelleriella.*

GENUS *Opalina*. The genus *Opalina* includes over 150 species found in the colons of frogs and toads (Plate 6–4, Fig. 1). *Opalina* bodies are dorsoventrally flattened, include many nuclei, and are enveloped by a relatively tough pellicle. *Opalina obtriganoidea,* measuring 400 to 840 μ long by 175 to 180 μ wide, is found in most common frogs and toads. It is quite representative of the genus, both in size and morphology. Another species, *O. ranarum,* measuring from 500 to 700 μ long, is also relatively common.

Life Cycle of *Opalina ranarum*. In *Opalina ranarum,* the large multinucleate trophozoites inhabit the frog host's large intestine. During the nonbreeding terrestrial phase of the host *Rana temporaria,* El Mofty (1959) reported that only the large trophozoites are found. These divide occasionally by binary fission.

In the spring, just before commencement of egg-laying by the host, the multinucleate trophozoite undergoes division (plasmotomy) and gives rise to a number of smaller ciliates with fewer nuclei, each measuring 30 to 90 μ long. These smaller forms soon encyst and are passed out of the host. Thus cysts, which are the infective forms and measure 30 to 70 μ in diameter and with two to twelve nuclei, are plentiful at the bottom of ponds when young tadpoles develop. When cysts are ingested by tadpoles, excystment occurs.

The liberated form undergoes a series of divisions culminating in production of gametes. Such gametes are of two sizes, the larger female macrogametes, and the smaller male microgametes. The fusion of a male and a female gamete results in the formation of a diploid zygote. The zygote increases in size and undergoes a period of active division, presumably ending only when the opalinid population has reached the limit of available food supply. Zygotes are also known to undergo encystment, and such cysts are passed to the exterior. When zygote-bearing cysts are ingested by a second tadpole, the escaping form develops into a multinucleate adult.

The synchronization between plasmotomy of the multinucleate trophozoites and their subsequent encystment and the commencement of egg laying by the host suggests adaptation of the parasite to the hormonal mechanism of the host. Indeed, El Mofty and Smyth (1960) have shown that the injection of urine from pregnant females or gonadotrophin into immature frogs induces cyst formation in *Opalina* within 9 to 13 days.

Sexual maturation of the host is under endocrinal control by gonadotrophic hormones secreted by the anterior pituitary, and injection of male and female hormones into prebreeding frogs, even castrated or hypophysectomized frogs, produces similar results. Injection of testosterone propionate induces sexual maturity

---

*Some taxonomists consider the Protociliatia, not as members of the Ciliatea, but as being more closely related to the flagellates.

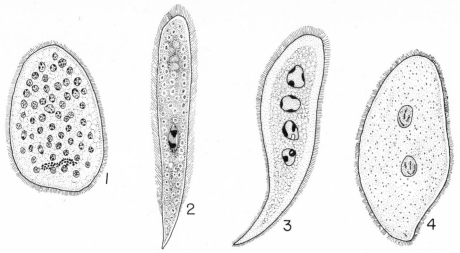

Plate 6-4   **Some parasitic protociliates.** 1. *Opalina ranarum* from large intestine of frogs. (Original.) **2.** *Protoopalina saturnalis* from large intestine of the marine fish *Box boops*. (Redrawn after Léger and Duboscq.) **3.** *Cepedea lanceolata* from colon of amphibians. (Redrawn after Bezzenberger.) **4.** *Zelleriella elliptica* from colon of *Bufo valliceps*. (Redrawn after Chen, 1948.)

in the host during any time of the year, and this in turn induces encystment of the parasite.

On the other hand, injection of estrone is only effective prior to the breeding season. The results with testosterone propionate suggest that the encystment of *O. ranarum* is induced by sex hormones, their breakdown products, or some factor in the host elicited by the presence of these substances. Some of the results of El Mofty and Smyth are given in Table 6–2.

When cultured in vitro in a saline–serum-albumin medium, *Opalina* is less sensitive to hormones than it is in vivo. When cultured in the presence of pregnancy urine, smaller ciliates and eventually cysts appear. This is interpreted as being due to the presence in the urine of catabolic products of estrone. Ciliates cultured in the presence of gonadotrophin fail to encyst.

Genus *Protoopalina*.   Members of the genus *Protoopalina* possess two nuclei and are cylindrical or spindle shaped (Plate 6–4, Fig. 2). All *Protoopalina* species are endocommensals in amphibians except for *P. saturnalis*, which is found in the intestine of the marine fish *Box boops*.

Other Protociliatia Species.   The Protociliatia also includes *Cepedea*, a cylindrical or spindle shaped multinucleate form found in amphibians, and *Zelleriella*, a binucleate flattened form found in amphibians (Plate 6–4, Figs. 3 and 4).

Although the protociliates are categorized as parasites, they are best described as commensals because in no instance are they known to cause any disturbance to the host.

SUBCLASS EUCILIATIA

The euciliates are mostly free-living, but many representatives are endosymbionts and others are epizoic. Reproduction is both sexual by conjugation and asexual by fission. As a rule, all the euciliates possess two types of nuclei—macronuclei and micronuclei—although some are amicronucleate. This large group of protozoa is subdivided into four orders on the basis of the distribution and types of ciliary organelles.*

Order 1. Holotrichida.   Body cilia are of equal length; cytostome, if present, is not surrounded by adoral zone with special ciliary organelles. Encystment is common. Asexual reproduction is usually by transverse fission; sexual reproduction by conjugation. Are mostly free-living; some epizoic. Are commensalistic or endoparasitic.

Order 2. Spirotrichida.   Possesses adoral membranelle arranged clockwise. Body cilia are present. Peristome does not protrude beyond surface of body. Sexual and asexual reproduction is known. Are mostly free-living; few species are parasitic.

Order 3. Chonotrichida.   Possesses adoral specialized cilia arranged clockwise; body cilia are present. Body is generally flask shaped with protruding apical cytostome. Cytostome and cytopharynx are sunk below body sur-

---

*For different interpretations of the classification of the Euciliatia, the reader is referred to Hall (1953), Kudo (1954), Jahn and Jahn (1949), and Corliss (1961).

Table 6-2. Cyst Formation in *Opalina*

Material Injected	Pre Breeding Season Condition of Frog Host			Post Breeding Season Condition of Frog Host		
	Normal	Hypophysectomized	Gonadectomized	Normal	Hypophysectomized	Gonadectomized
Pregnancy urine	+	+	-	-	0	0
Chorionic gonadotrophin	+	+	-	-	0	0
Serum gonadotrophin	+	+	-	-	0	0
Progesterone	-	-	0	-	0	0
Estrone	+	+	-	-	0	0
Testosterone propionate	+	+	+	+	0	0
Adrenalin	+	+	-	+	0	0

* The encystation of *Opalina* signals the beginning of its "sexual" reproductive cycle. Results of experiments performed just prior to the host's breeding season must be interpreted with caution, because during this period the endocrine balance is easily disrupted and the control experiment, in which saline was injected, often gives positive results also. (Data from El Mofty, 1959; El Mofty and Smyth, 1960.)

0 = no experiments performed

- = cysts absent

+ = cysts present

face. Macronucleus generally is located in middle of body. Asexual reproduction is by lateral budding; sexual reproduction by conjugation. Many are epizoic on aquatic animals.

Order 4. Peritrichida.   Possesses adoral cilia arranged counterclockwise. Body cilia are more or less limited. Possesses disc-like anterior region around cytostome. Asexual reproduction is by fission; sexual reproduction by conjugation. Majority are free-living; few species are parasitic.

ORDER HOLOTRICHIDA

The holotrichs include many free-living species, among which is the well known laboratory ciliate, *Paramecium*. Most of the so-called parasitic species are either epizoites or commensals. Although none are known to cause any pathological disturbances in their hosts, their biology warrants some discussion.

Several of the genera that parasitize higher animals are depicted in Plate 6–5.

Genus *Ichthyophthirius*.   One of the most genus *Tetrahymena* are normally free-living but are commonly found as facultative commensals in various vertebrate and invertebrate animals (Plate 6–5, Fig. 17). Certain species can be induced to parasitize various hosts by experimentally injecting them into those hosts (Thompson, 1958). Corliss (1960) has contributed a monograph on the facultative commensalism of *Tetrahymena* spp. and has listed the various animals known to serve as hosts.

Genus *Ichthyophthirius*.   One of the most important parasitic holotrichous ciliates is *Ichthyophthirius multifiliis,* an ectoparasite of fish (Plate 6–6). This ovoid parasite, which measures 100 to 1000 μ long, possesses a large cytostome that is 30 to 40 μ in diameter and is located at the anterior extremity. The ciliation is uniform. The large macronucleus is horseshoe shaped with the micronucleus usually situated adjacent to it. The cytoplasm is exceptionally granular and includes numerous fat-like globules and contractile vacuoles. Living in the skin of both fresh and salt water fishes, it causes a skin disease—icthyophthiriasis— which is characterized by the formation of pustules and which often results in the death of the host. The distribution of *I. multifiliis* is cosmopolitan, being known in fresh-water ponds, hatcheries, and marine waters.

Life Cycle of *Ichthyophthirius multifiliis*. The life history of this important ciliate has been studied by MacLennan (1935a, b; 1937; 1942). The stages in its life cycle are depicted in Plate 6–6. The trophozoites, which are found

in thin-walled cysts underneath the host's epidermis, rotate continuously. They increase in size and divide to form two to four individuals. When the trophozoites reach a certain size, they escape from their hosts and drop to the bottom of the aquarium, where the cysts are attached to the substratum by a specialized surface organelle.

Within the cyst wall, the cytostome is absorbed and the body cytoplasm fragments into 100 to 1000 minute spherical ciliated cells known as tomites. Each tomite measures from 18 to 22 μ in diameter. These rounded cells soon elongate, becoming 40 to 100 μ in length. They eventually rupture out of the cyst wall and are then known as theronts. The free-swimming theronts seek out new piscine hosts and penetrate the epithelium.

Theronts can attack fish during the first 96 hours after excystment but are most effective during the initial 48 hours. The free-swimming forms possess only incompletely developed cytostomes, which become completely formed only when the ciliates are firmly established under the host's epidermis. At this site, the trophonts, or trophozoites, actively ingest cell components.

Some of the holotrichous ciliates found in mammals are depicted in Plate 6–7. For a comprehensive listing of ciliates (including holotrichs) found in the rumen and reticulum of American cattle, the reader is referred to Becker and Talbott (1927), and to Chavarria (1933) for those found in Mexican cattle.

ORDER SPIROTRICHIDA

The spirotrichous ciliates include an array of symbiotic species. Among these is *Balantidium coli,* which is a true pathogen of man and which also parasitizes pigs. Several genera of large spirotrichs found in the alimentary tract of mammals are odd-looking ciliates that have been considered by many to be mutualists (p. 4) because a few are known to digest their host's food. However, Becker et al. (1930) and Mowry and Becker (1930) prefer to consider these as commensals, thus again pointing out that commensals are sometimes difficult to distinguish from mutualists. The question as to whether the spirotrichs of ruminants, at least certain species, should be considered mutualists or commensals is by no means completely resolved (p. 172).

In some spirotrichs, cirrus-like projections, in

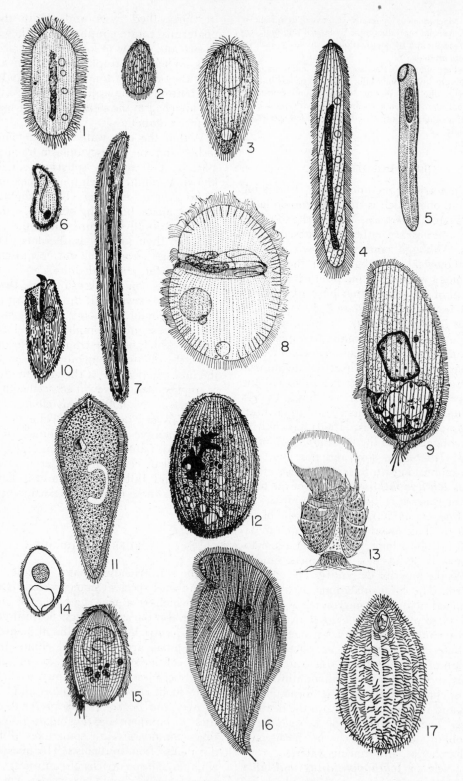

Plate 6-5   See legend on opposite page.

addition to individual cilia, are present on the body. The cilia, may not all be of equal length. The macronucleus is generally large and the micronucleus small. Both sexual (conjugation) and asexual (fission) reproductive mechanisms exist.

Genus *Balantidium*. The genus *Balantidium* includes numerous species found in the intestine of vertebrates and invertebrates. Although some biologists still prefer to recognize *B. coli* in man and *B. suis* in pigs as two distinct species, Levine (1940), after finding that the morphology of the organism could be altered in various culture media, suggested that the two are synonymous. Furthermore, Lamy and Roux (1950) successfully obtained forms similar to

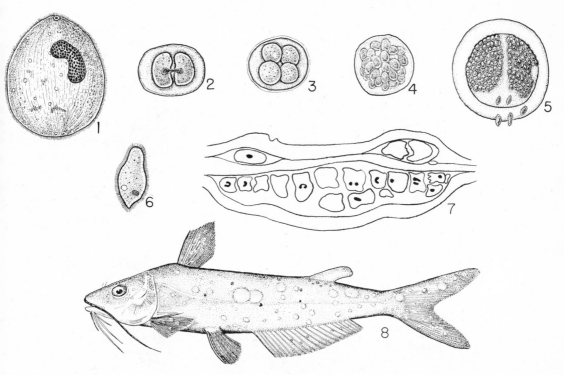

Plate 6-6   *Ichthyophthirius multifiliis,* a parasite in the skin of fish. 1. A mature trophont, or trophozoite. 2. An encysted individual undergoing first division. 3. Four daughter individuals within cyst wall. 4. Numerous daughter tomites within cyst wall. 5. Fully mature cyst enclosing numerous tomites. 6. Young theront that has escaped from cyst. 7. Section through fin of infected carp, showing numerous parasites. 8. A catfish, *Ameiurus albidus,* heavily infected by the ciliate. (Figs. 1 and 5 redrawn and modified after Bütschli; 2 through 4 and 6 redrawn and modified after Fouquet; 7 redrawn after Kudo; and 8 redrawn after Stiles.)

Plate 6-5   **Some symbiotic holotrichous ciliates.** 1. *Anoplophrya marylandensis* in the gut of *Lumbricus terrestris* and *Helodrilus caliginosus*. (After Conklin, 1930.) 2. *Perezella palagica* in the coelom of copepods. (After Cépède, 1910.) 3. *Dogielella sphaerii* in the fresh-water bivalve, *Sphaerium corneum*. (After Poljansky, 1925.) 4. *Bütschliella opheliae* in *Ophelia limacina*. (After Cépède.) 5. *Haptophrya michiganensis* in gut and gallbladder of salamanders. (After Woodhead, 1928.) 6. *Lachmannella recurva* in intestine of *Planaria limacina*. (After Cépède.) 7. *Monodontophyra kijenskiji* in anterior portion of gut of *Tubifex inflatus*. (After Cheissin, 1930.) 8. *Lechriopyla mystax* in gut of sea urchins of the genus *Strongylocentrotus*. (After Lynch, 1929.) 9. *Biggaria bermudense* in intestine of sea urchins. (After Powers, 1935.) 10. *Espejoia musicola* in gelatinous envelope of eggs of insects and molluscs. (After Penard.) 11. *Ophryoglena intestinalis* in gastrovascular cavity of *Dicotylus* sp. (After Rossolimo, 1926.) 12. *Conchophthirus caryoclada* in mantle cavity of the clam *Siliqua patula*. (After Kidder, 1933.) 13. *Hemispeira asteriasi,* an ectocommensal on the starfish *Asterias glacialis*. (After Wallengren, 1895.) 14. *Protophrya ovicola* in uterus and brood chamber of marine molluscs of the genus *Littorina*. (After Kidder, 1933.) 15. *Ancistruma mytili* in mantle cavity of marine molluscs, *Mytilus* spp. (After Kidder, 1933.) 16. *Entorhipidium echini* in intestine of the starfish, *Strongylocentrotus purpuratus*. (After Lynch, 1929.) 17. *Tetrahymena pyriformis,* a facultative parasite of various animals. (After Furgason, 1940.)

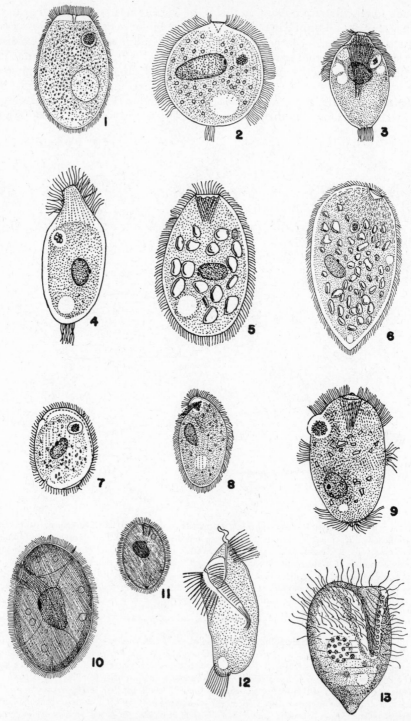

Plate 6-7   **Some symbiotic holotrichous ciliates.** 1. *Bütschlia parva* from stomach of cattle.
2. *Blepharosphaera intestinalis* from caecum and colon of horses. 3. *Blepharoconus cervicalis* from colon
of horses. 4. *Polymorpha ampulla* from caecum and colon of horses. 5. *Holophryoides ovalis* from colon
and caecum of horses. 6. *Blepharozoum zonatum* from caecum of horses. 7. *Paraisotrichopsis composita*
from caecum of horses. 8. *Paraisotricha colpoidea* from colon of horses. 9. *Alloiozona trizona* from colon
or caecum of horses. 10. *Isotricha prostoma* from stomach of cattle. 11. *Dasytricha ruminantium* from
stomach of cattle. 12. *Blepharocorys uncinata* from caecum and colon of horses. 13. *Cyathodinium piri-
forme* from caecum of guinea pigs. (Figs. 1–4 and 7–9, after Hsiung, 1930; 5 and 6, after Gassovsky;
10 and 11, after Becker and Talbott, 1927; 12 after Reichenow; and 13 after Lucas, 1932.)

both "species" in a culture originating from a single ciliate, thus indicating that the two species should be considered one.

Different strains of *B. coli* may exist, for morphologically identical forms have been found in guinea pigs and rats. At any rate, humans most probably acquired the first *Balantidium* infections from pigs when the latter became domesticated and very often lived under the same roof.

Balantidium coli. *Balantidium coli*, measuring 30 to 200 μ (average 50 to 80 μ) by 20 to 70 μ, is a relatively large ovoid ciliate commonly found in the caecum or colon of pigs, sometimes in humans, and even in other primates (Plate 6–8, Fig. 1). The cytostome and cytopharynx are located at the anterior end. There is a distinct peristomal zone lined with coarser cilia. The macronucleus is typically elongate and kidney shaped, and the vesicular micronucleus is rounded.

Most specimens possess two prominent contractile vacuoles, one in the middle of the body and the other near the posterior end. Food vacuoles in the cytoplasm enclose debris, bacteria, starch granules, erythrocytes, and fragments of host epithelium. The usual reproductive method is asexual by transverse fission, with the posterior daughter cell forming a new cytostome after division. Conjugation is also known to occur in this species.

In man, *B. coli* inhabits the large intestine, in which it is a true parasite invading and ingesting tissue. In a few cases, this ciliate has been transported by the blood into the spinal fluid. As in *Entamoeba histolytica* infections, diarrhea and secondary complications accompany balantidiasis. Mild cases in man are known in which clinical symptoms cannot be recognized.

Transfer of *Balantidium coli* from host to host is via the cystic form. Cysts of *B. coli*, measuring 40 to 60 μ in diameter, are round and the wall consists of two membranes (Plate 6–8, Fig. 2). The large macronucleus and contractile vacuoles can be seen within the cyst wall. Cysts can be found in the feces of hosts and are generally not considered as sites of reproduction, although cysts containing two individuals have been reported.

Other *Balantidium* Species. Balantidial infections are common in numerous species of vertebrates, including frogs, toads, fish, tortoises, birds, and cattle. In each of these cases, a different species of *Balantidium* is generally believed to be involved. For example, *B. duodeni* is the common parasite of frogs, and the incidence of infection is rather high. Balantidial infections of invertebrates are also common. *B. praenucleatum* is the species found in cockroaches.

GENUS *Nyctotherus*. Members of the genus *Nyctotherus* are commonly encountered in the large intestine of amphibians, fishes, and invertebrates (Plate 6–9, Fig. 1). The many species have been catalogued by Wichterman (1938).

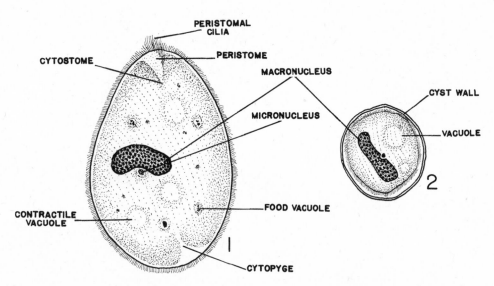

Plate 6-8   Trophozoite and cyst of *Balantidium coli*, an intestinal parasite of pigs and man. **1.** Trophozoite. **2.** Encysted form. (Original.)

Ciliates belonging to this genus may be recognized by the deep, laterally situated peristome that ends in a cytostome and gullet. The peristome begins at the anterior end and is lined with a row of long cilia. Lying in the cytoplasm is a large reniform macronucleus with a small micronucleus lying in its concavity.

Nyctotherus ovalis in cockroaches and millepedes, measuring 90 to 185 μ long, and *N.*

cordiformis, measuring 60 to 200 μ long, in frogs are the two most commonly encountered species. These ciliates are commensals. It is of interest to note that a ciliated cytoproct (primitive "anus") has been reported in *Nyctotherus* (Plate 6-9, Fig. 2).

Life Cycle of *Nyctotherus*. The trophozoites of *Nyctotherus* are found in the rectum of frogs and toads, where they occasionally divide

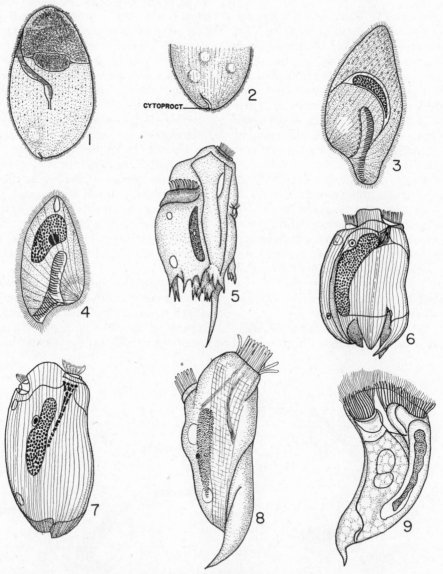

Plate 6-9 **Some symbiotic spirotrichous ciliates.** 1. *Nyctotherus ovalis* from colon of frogs. (Redrawn after Kudo.) 2. Posterior end of *Nyctotherus,* showing cytoproct. 3. *Clevelandella panesthiae* from colon of woodroaches *Panesthia javanica* and *P. spadica.* (Redrawn after Kidder, 1938.) 4. *Paraclevelandia brevis* from colon of same woodroaches. (Redrawn after Kidder, 1938.) 5. *Ophryoscolex caudatus* from stomach of sheep, goats, and cattle. (Redrawn after Dogiel, 1927.) 6. *Diplodinium dentatum* from stomach of cattle. (Redrawn after Kofoid and MacLennan, 1932.) 7. *Eremoplastron bovis* from stomach of cattle and sheep. (Redrawn after Kofoid and MacLennan, 1932.) 8. *Epidinium caudatum* from stomach of cattle, camels, and reindeer. (Redrawn after Becker and Talbott, 1927.) 9. *Cunhaia curvata* from caecum of guinea pig *Cavia aperea.* (Redrawn after Hasselmann.)

by binary fission. In the spring, when the host's breeding season commences, a change from asexual to sexual reproduction occurs. This is first noticeable when the trophozoites divide more frequently, finally forming mononuclear precystic forms. Once encystment occurs, the cysts pass out into the water with the host's feces. Such cysts are ingested by tadpoles and the preconjugants excyst. These conjugate and undergo a series of nuclear changes like that which occurs in *Paramecium*. After conjugation, the postconjugants separate. These are found almost exclusively in recently metamorphosed frogs, in which the postconjugants undergo a series of binary fission.

As in *Opalina,* the injection of pregnancy urine or male and female hormones into hosts under certain conditions induces the encystment of *Nyctotherus,* thus suggesting that the process is correlated with the level of sex hormones in the host.

Genus *Euplotaspis*.   Members of the family Cycloposthiidae, which are characterized by the presence of a rigid pellicle and endoskeleton, are endocommensals of horses and primates (Plate 6–10).

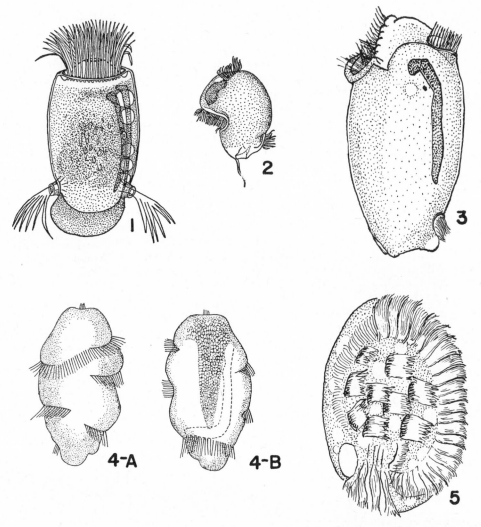

Plate 6-10   **Some symbiotic spirotrichous ciliates.** 1. *Cycloposthium bipalmatum,* found in caecum and colon of horses. (After Bundle.) **2.** *Triadinium caudatum,* found in caecum and colon of horses. (After Hsiung, 1935.) **3.** *Ditoxum funinucleum,* found in colon of horses. (Redrawn after Hsiung, 1930.) **4. A.** Ventral view of *Troglodytella abrassarti,* found in colon of chimpanzees. **B.** Dorsal view of *T. abrassarti.* (A and B, after Brumpt and Joyeux, 1912.) **5.** Ventral view of *Euplotaspis cionaecola,* found in branchial cavity of the ascidian Ciona intestinalis. (Redrawn after Chatton and Seguela, 1936.)

The genus *Euplotaspis* of the Cycloposthiidae is closely related to the common fresh-water ciliate *Euplotes* (Plate 6–10, Fig. 5). *Euplotaspis* includes an unusual species, *E. cionaecola,* which is an endocommensal in the branchial cavity of the acidian *Ciona intestinalis.*

OTHER SPIROTRICHS. Other symbiotic spirotrichs include members of the genera *Clevelandella* and *Paraclevelandia,* all of which are commensals found in the gut of wood-eating roaches, *Panesthia javanica* and *P. spadica* (Plate 6–9, Figs. 3 and 4). Members of *Metopus,* including *M. circumlabens,* are found in the alimentary tract of sea urchins.

Several genera of Spirotrichida are known from the digestive tract of domestic animals. Those species found in the stomach pouches of American cattle are listed and described by Becker and Talbott (1927). These elongate ovoid ciliates of the family Ophryoscolecidae all possess one or two membranellar zones. Representative genera are depicted in Plate 6–9.

ORDER CHONOTRICHIDA

The chonotrichs include a small group of ciliates that are free-living, but because of their epizoic habitats they are briefly mentioned here. The various genera and species that are members of this order have been monographed by Kahl (1935). These ciliates are typically vase shaped with an apical peristome that is surrounded by a cytoplasmic collar bearing cilia.

Reproduction is generally asexual by transverse fission, although conjugation is known to occur. Several genera are normally attached to the body surface of crustaceans and other aquatic invertebrates. For example, *Spirochona* is attached to fresh-water *Gammarus, Stylochona* is found on marine *Gammarus,* and *Trichochona* is attached to the marine crustacean *Amphithoë* (Plate 6–11, Figs. 1 to 3). The distribution of the many species is universal and has been recorded by Mohr (1948).

ORDER PERITRICHIDA

The peritrichs are primarily free-living ciliates with some species, like the well known *Vorticella,* attached to aquatic plants and animals. The body of peritrichs is typically cone shaped with an enlarged disc shaped peristome (sometimes termed an epistome) lined with conspicuous cilia. These adoral cilia are arranged in a counterclockwise pattern when viewed from the front. Reproduction is by transverse fission or by conjugation.

A few unique species of the Peritrichida have been reported in or on various invertebrates. For example, *Paravorticella clymellae* (Plate 6–11, Fig. 4) is found in the large intestine of the annelid *Clymenella torquata* in the Woods Hole, Massachusetts, area. *Trichodina* (Plate 6–11, Fig. 5), a genus characterized by a ring of hooked teeth on the posteriorly located attaching disc, includes *T. pediculus* found attached on fish, hydra, and on the gills of *Necturus* and *Triturus.*

The biology of members of this genus, like that of most of the parasitic peritrichs, is not well understood. However, *Trichodina scorpenae* appears to be more than a mere epizoic form. It is a true ectocommensal and cannot be separated from its host. *Trichodina ranae* and *T. urinicola* (Plate 6–11, Figs. 6 and 7) are fairly commonly found in the urinary bladder of frogs and toads.

Among members of the epizoic genus *Epistylis, E. niagarae* is found attached to the antennae and body of crayfish (Plate 6–11, Fig. 8). This is a colonial peritrich and a colony generally consists of from 40 to 50 telotrochs (individuals). Members of the genus *Glossatella* are commonly found attached to fish and amphibian larvae (Plate 6–11, Fig. 9). Members of *Ellobiophrya* are unique in possessing two armlike processes at the posterior end of their bodies by which they are attached to the gill bars of mussels (Plate 6–11, Fig. 10).

None of the symbiotic peritrichous ciliates can be considered true parasites, because in no instance are they known to cause any unfavorable changes in their hosts. These ciliates are either epizoic or commensals.

CLASS SUCTOREA

The Suctorea includes an unusual group of protozoa that are considered to be closely related to the ciliates, because they possess both macro- and micronuclei and bear cilia during their free-swimming larval stage. As adults, these protozoa lose their cilia and develop specialized tentacles that distinguish them from all other protozoa.

The commonly spherical body surface of

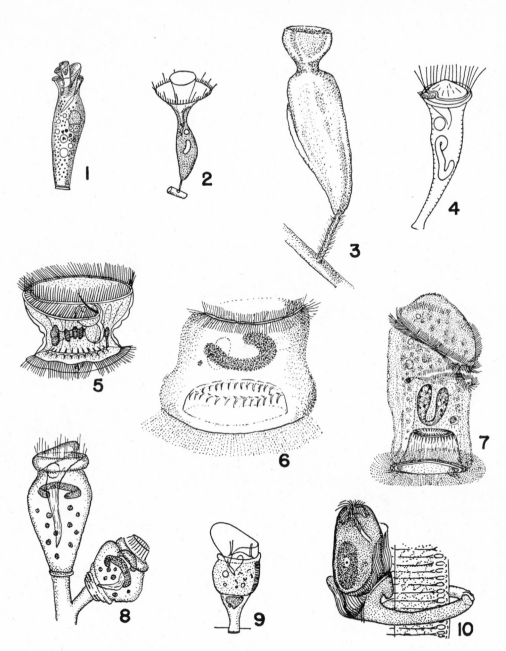

Plate 6-11   Some parasitic and epizoic ciliates. 1. *Spirochona gemmipara,* a chonotrichous ciliate found attached to gill plates of *Gammarus pulex.* (After Hertwig.) **2.** *Stylochona coronata,* a chonotrichous ciliate attached to marine *Gammarus* spp. (After Kent.) **3.** *Trichochona lecythoides,* a chonotrichous ciliate attached to appendages of the marine crustacean *Amphithoë* sp. (Redrawn after Mohr, 1948.) **4.** *Paravorticella clymenellae,* a peritrichous ciliate found in colon of the annelid *Clymenella torquata.* (After Shumway.) **5.** *Trichodina pediculus,* a peritrichous ciliate found on *Hydra* and on the gills of *Necturus* and salamanders. (After James–Clark.) **6.** *Trichodina* sp. from the skin and gills of frog and toad tadpoles. (Redrawn after Diller, 1928.) **7.** *Trichodina urinicola,* a peritrichous ciliate from the urinary bladder of *Bufo* sp. and in frogs. (After Fulton, 1923.) **8.** *Epistylis niagarae,* a peritrichous ciliate found attached to crayfishes and turtles. (Redrawn after Bishop and Jahn, 1941.) **9.** *Glossatella tintinnabulum,* a peritrichous ciliate found attached to the epidermis and gills of newts. **10.** *Ellobiophrya donacis,* a peritrichous ciliate found holding fast to the gill bars of the mussel *Donax vittatus* by means of two armlike processes. (After Chatton and Lwoff.)

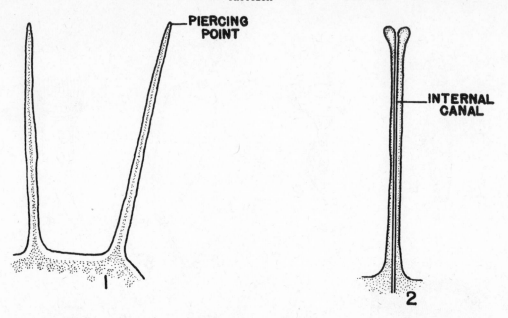

Plate 6-12   **Types of suctorian tentacles.** 1. Piercing type. 2. Suctorial type. (Original.)

adult suctorians is covered with a pellicle and in some species with a more rigid lorica. Because there is no cytostome, ingestion of food particles occurs through the tentacles. The tentacles of suctorians are of two types: the piercing type, which possesses a sharp, pointed terminal and is used to pierce the body wall of its prey; and the suctorial type, which possesses a rounded or flattened knob at the terminal and is used for attachment and the absorption of nutrients (Plate 6–12, Figs. 1 and 2). Suctorians commonly prey on ciliates, paralyzing their victims and drawing in their cytoplasm and inclusions through the tentacles. This food becomes enclosed in food vacuoles, which are formed at the proximal end of the tentacles.

Most suctorians are free-living, either attached or unattached, and prey on ciliates. A few species, however, have been reported by Reynolds (1930) as epizoites on various invertebrates (Plate 6–13), while others have been reported in other protozoa and in mammals. A few representative endosymbiotic species are considered here.

Suctorian Genera

Allantosoma, a genus with several species found in the intestine of horses, possesses an elongate ovoid body with one or more tentacles at each end (Plate 6–14, Fig. 1). The development, life cycles, and general biology of these

unique suctorians remain to be resolved. They are probably commensals.

The genus *Sphaerophrya* includes mostly free-living species found in fresh water, but one species, *S. stentoris,* is an endoparasite of the ciliate *Stentor* (Plate 6–14, Fig. 2). During the life cycle of *S. stentoris,* two forms are evident—the larval swarmer cells that invade the host's cytoplasm and that bear cilia at the posterior end and tentacles at the anterior end, and the adult form in the cytoplasm of *Stentor.* The adults are spherical and bear tentacles on their entire body surface.

Endosphaera includes several species parasitic in fresh-water and marine ciliates (Plate 6–14, Fig. 3).

The various species symbiotic in ciliates and other protozoa could be considered endopredators because, while feeding on the cytoplasm, they rapidly destroy their hosts.

PHYSIOLOGY OF SYMBIOTIC CILIATES

Oxygen Requirements

The oxygen requirement of endoparasitic ciliates varies among the species and with the location of the organisms within their hosts. It

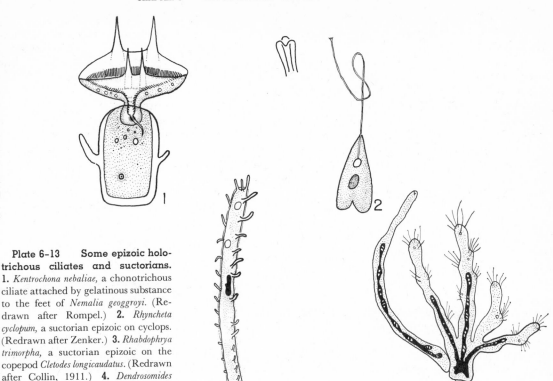

Plate 6-13   Some epizoic holo-trichous ciliates and suctorians.
1. *Kentrochona nebaliae*, a chonotrichous ciliate attached by gelatinous substance to the feet of *Nemalia geoggroyi*. (Redrawn after Rompel.) 2. *Rhyncheta cyclopum*, a suctorian epizoic on cyclops. (Redrawn after Zenker.) 3. *Rhabdophrya trimorpha*, a suctorian epizoic on the copepod *Cletodes longicaudatus*. (Redrawn after Collin, 1911.) 4. *Dendrosomides paguri*, a suctorian epizoic on the marine crabs *Eupagurus* spp. (Redrawn after Collin, 1911.)

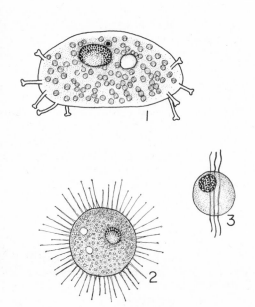

Plate 6-14   Some parasitic suctorians. 1. *Allantosoma intestinalis* attached to various ciliates that live in the colon and caecum of horses, (Redrawn after Hsiung, 1928.) 2. *Sphaerophrya stentoris*, parasitic in *Stentor*. (Original.) 3. *Endosphaera engelmanni*, embedded in the cytoplasm of *Opisthonecta henneguyi* and other peritrichous ciliates. (Redrawn after Lynch and Noble.)

is apparent that both aerobic and anaerobic (perhaps microaerobic) species exist. Daniel (1931) reported that *Balantidium coli* does consume oxygen and is thus aerobic. Unlike microaerobes, *B. coli* can be maintained for hours even under high O_2 tensions. On the other hand, Pütter (1905), Lwoff and Valentini (1948), and others have repeatedly cultured *Nyctotherus* in the absence of O_2, indicating that this endoparasitic species is capable of anaerobic respiration, perhaps as a facultative anaerobe.

Osmoregulation

Unlike the parasitic Mastigophora, Sarcodina, and Sporozoa, the parasitic ciliates contain visible contractile vacuoles in the cytoplasm. No completely satisfactory explanation has yet been advanced to explain why these vacuoles should be present in intestinal ciliates and not in intestinal flagellates and amoebae. Contractile vacuoles in ciliates perform a definite function—that of osmoregulation, and the associated function of excretion of waste materials.

MacLennan (1933) demonstrated that in the rumen-dwelling ciliates *Epidinium* and *Ophryo-*

scolex of cattle, the intervals between contractions of the vacuoles vary from 1 minute to more than 1 hour for the former and from 2 to 4 minutes for the latter. This investigator pointed out that there is very little absorption or diffusion of water through the cell membrane of these species, for the body walls are relatively impermeable.

Wertheim (1934a, b) verified MacLennan's results by finding that the intervals between contractions of vacuoles in rumen-dwelling ciliates are lengthy when compared to those of free-living species. He recorded that in *Entodinium, Isotricha, Ostrachodinium,* and *Ophryoscolex* the intervals ranged from 1 to 12 minutes. On the other hand, Strelkow (1931a, b) reported that the intervals are rapid in *Cycloposthium* (25 to 30 seconds) and *Tripalmaria* (30 to 45 seconds), two species found in the caecum of horses.

Specific, and probably even more important, habitat differences are responsible for the discrepancies in the results. Nevertheless, these observations all indicate that the contractile vacuoles of endoparasitic ciliates are present and functional.

Growth Requirements

Little is known definitely about the nutrient requirements of symbiotic ciliates. It is known that many of the rumen ciliates can utilize highly complex carbohydrates and cellulose as energy sources and that *Balantidium coli* possesses a starch-splitting enzyme. These species differ from the parasitic flagellates at least in this respect, for the flagellates can utilize only simple sugar in most instances and are dependent on their hosts to break down the more complex molecules of food.

Balantidium coli has been successfully maintained in vitro in human serum diluted with saline and kept at 30 to 37° C. when accompanying bacteria are present. It is suspected that as in *Entamoeba histolytica* cultures, the bacteria aid in the synthesis of necessary enzymes and coenzymes for the protozoa. Nevertheless, because serum is protein in composition, it is apparent that *B. coli* can utilize proteins as food. This is borne out by the tissue-ingesting habits of the parasite.

Observations on *B. coli* grown in culture have revealed that addition of starch granules is highly favorable. Ciliates can be seen to enclose numerous starch granules. In addition, erythrocytes and yeast cells are also avidly devoured. However, if given the choice, *B. coli* prefers starch granules.

Gutierrez and Davis (1959) have shown that at least two genera of rumen ciliates—*Entodinium* and *Diplodinium*—can utilize bacteria, which are mostly protein, as food. The utilization of fats has been shown in some instances.

Effects of Temperature

When *Balantidium coli* is maintained at 37° C. in a diphasic medium consisting of a coagulated horse serum slant covered with diluted serum to which starch is added, the ciliates conjugate regularly. If the temperature is lowered to 25° C., conjugation ceases after about a month, thus indicating the importance of temperature as an environmental factor in the biology of this species.

HOST-PARASITE RELATIONSHIPS

Considerable discussion can be found in the literature as to whether rumen- and reticulum-dwelling ciliates should be considered commensals or mutualists. Oxford (1955) and Hungate (1955) have reviewed the arguments relative to this question. It appears that certain species, such as *Diplodinium*, should be considered mutualists because they possess the enzyme cellulase and harbor cellulytic bacteria. Thus they aid their hosts in cellulose digestion. Furthermore, the holotrichs occurring in both artiodactyles and perissodactyles aid the accompanying bacteria in breaking down carbohydrates and starch ingested by their hosts. Since these species do perform such services for their hosts, they might be considered mutualists. However, Oxford (1955) cautioned against sweeping generalities because some of the so-called mutualists are also injurious to their hosts, causing destruction of B vitamins and production of lactic acid, waste bacterial proteins, etc. Hence, these organisms are truly parasitic.

The stomach-dwelling ciliates represent an interesting group for study, for few general statements can be made that apply to all of them. For example, *Diplodinium maggii* possesses cellulase, but coexisting species of *Isotricha, Oütschlia,* and *Entodinium* do not. Thus it appears wise to consider each species as a separate physiological organism in spite of their common habitat.

Several interesting observations have been made about the physiology of the host-parasite relationship between *Balantidium coli* and its hosts. The clinical symptoms and tissue pathology of *B. coli* infections have been mentioned. Since host cells and cell fragments are known to occur in the food vacuoles of this ciliate, it has been generally assumed that *B. coli* brings about ulceration through mechanical ingestion. However, Tempelis and Lysenko (1957) have demonstrated that hyaluronidase—the enzyme that hydrolyses hyaluronic acid, a component of the ground substance that binds tissues—is present in *B. coli* and is suspected of contributing to the tissue-invading process.

Although *Balantidium coli* of pigs and man cannot be conclusively differentiated by their morphology, attempts at infecting man with specimens from pigs have mostly been futile. This then suggests the occurrence of two physiologically distinct strains, but many authorities are of the opinion that *B. coli* is normally a parasite of pigs and only in rare and ideal situations does it become established in man. They believe the so-called "failures" at infecting man result from nonideal conditions. This concept appears logical, because natural *B. coli* infections in man are relatively rare.

LITERATURE CITED

Becker, E. R., and M. Talbott. 1927. The protozoan fauna of the rumen and reticulum of American cattle. Iowa State Coll. J. Sci., *1:* 345–371.

Becker, E. R., J. A. Schulz, and M. A. Emmerson. 1930. Experiments on the physiological relationships between the stomach infusoria of ruminants and their hosts, with a bibliography. Iowa State Coll. J. Sci., *4:* 215–251.

Chavarria, C. M. 1933. Estudios protistologicos I. Fauna del tubo digestivo del toro (*Bos laurus* Linn.) de Mexico. A. Inst. Biol. Univ. Nac. Mexico, *4:* 109–142.

Corliss, J. O. 1960. *Tetrahymena chironomi* sp. nov., a ciliate from midge larvae, and the current status of facultative parasitism in the genus *Tetrahymena*. Parasitology, *50:* 111–153.

Corliss, J. O. 1961. The Ciliated Protozoa. Pergamon Press, New York.

Cosgrove, W. B. 1948. Fibrillar structures in *Opalina obtrigonoidea* Metcalf. J. Parasit., *33:* 351–357.

Daniel, G. E. 1931. The respiratory quotient of *Balantidium coli*. Am. J. Hyg., *14:* 411–420.

El Mofty, M. M., and J. D. Smyth. 1959. Endocrine control of sexual reproduction in *Opalina rananum* parasitic in *Rana temporaria*. Nature, *186:* 559.

Gutierrez, J., and R. E. Davis. 1959. Bacterial ingestion by the rumen ciliates *Entodinium* and *Diplodinium*. J. Protozool., *6:* 222–226.

Hall, R. P. 1953. Protozoology. Prentice-Hall, New York.

Hungate, R. E. 1955. The ciliates of the rumen. *In* Hutner, S. H., and A. Lwoff. Biochemistry and Physiology of Protozoa. Vol. II, pp. 159–179. Academic Press, New York.

Jahn, T. L., and F. F. Jahn. 1949. How to Know the Protozoa. William C. Brown, Dubuque, Iowa.

Kahl, A. 1935. Urtiere oder Protozoa, etc. *In* Dahl's Die Tierwelt Deutschlands, Part 30. G. Fischer, Jena.

Kudo, R. R. 1954. Protozoology. 4th Ed. Charles C Thomas, Springfield, Ill.

Lwoff, A., and S. Valentini. 1948. Culture du flagelle opalinide *Cepedea dimidiata*. Ann. Inst. Pasteur, *75:* 1–7.

Lamy, L., and H. Roux. 1950. Remarques morphologiques, biologiques et spécifiques sur les *Balantidium* de culture. Bull. Soc. Path. Exot., *43:* 422–427.

Levine, N. D. 1940. Changes in the dimensions of *Balàntidium* from swine upon cultivation. Am. J. Hyg., *32:* 1–7.

MacDougall, M. S. 1928. Neuromotor system of *Chlamydodon*. Biol. Bull., *54:* 471–484.

MacLennan, R. F. 1933. The pulsatory cycle of the contractile vacuoles in the Ophryoscolecidae. Ciliates from the stomach of cattle. Univ. Cal. Publ. Zool., *39:* 205–250.

MacLennan, R. F. 1935a. Observations on the life history of *Ichthyophthirius*, a ciliate parasitic on fish. Northwest Sci., *9:* 12–14.

MacLennan, R. F. 1935b. Dedifferentiation and redifferentiation in *Ichthyophthirius*. I. Neuromotor system. Arch. Protistenk., *86:* 191–210.

MacLennan, R. F. 1937. Growth in the ciliate *Ichthyophthirius*. I. Maturity and encystment. J. Exper. Zool., *76:* 423–440.

MacLennan, R. F. 1942. Growth in the ciliate *Ichthyophthirius*. II. Volume. J. Exper. Zool., *91:* 1–13.

Metcalf, M. M. 1923. The opalinid ciliate infusorians. Bull. U. S. Nat. Mus. No. 120.

Metcalf, M. M. 1940. Further studies on the opalinid ciliate infusorians and their hosts. Proc. U. S. Nat. Mus., *87:* 465–634.

Mohr, J. L. 1948. *Trichochona lecythroides*, a new genus and species, etc. Allan Hancock Foundation Publ., Occasional Papers, No. 5. (From Kudo).

Mowry, H. A., and E. R. Becker. 1930. Experiments on the biology of infusoria inhabiting the rumen of goats. Iowa State Coll. J. Sci., *5:* 35–60.

Oxford, A. E. 1955. The rumen ciliate protozoa: their chemical composition, metabolism, requirements for maintenance and culture, and physiological significance for the host. Exptl. Parasit., *6:* 569–605.

Pitelka, D. R. 1961. Fine structure of the silverline and fibrillar systems of three tetrahymenid ciliates. J. Protozool., *8:* 75–89.

Pitelka, D. R. 1963. Electron-microscopic Structure of Protozoa. Macmillan, New York.

Pütter, A. 1905. Die Atmung der Protozoan. Ztschr. Allg. Physiol., *5:* 566–612.

Reynolds, B. D. 1930. Ectoparasitic protozoa. *In* Hegner, R., and J. Andrews: Problems and Methods of Research in Protozoology. Macmillan, New York.

Sharp, R. G. 1914. *Diplodinium ecaudatum*, with an account of its neuromotor apparatus. Univ. Cal. Publ. Zool., *13:* 43–122.

Sleigh, M. A. 1962. The Biology of Cilia and Flagella. Macmillan, New York.

Strelkow, A. A. 1931a. Morphologische Studien über oligotriche Infusorien aus dem Darme des Pferdes. II. Cytologische Untersuchungen der Gattung Cycloposthium Bundle. Arch. Protistenk., *75:* 191–220.

Strelkow, A. A. 1931b. Morphologische Studien über oligotriche Infusorien aus dem Darme des Pferdes. III. Körperbau von *Tripalmaria dogieli* Gassovsky Arch. Protistenk., *76:* 221–254.

Tempelis, C. H., and M. G. Lysenko. 1957. The production of hyaluronidase by *Balantidium coli*. Exptl. Parasit., *6:* 31–36.

Thompson, J. C., Jr. 1958. Experimental infections of various animals with strains of the genus *Tetrahymena*. J. Protozool., *5:* 203–205.

Wertheim, P. 1934a. Über die Pulsation der kontracktilen Vakuolen bie den Wiederkäuermageninfusorien. Zool. Anz., *106:* 20–24.

Wertheim, P. 1934b. Zweiter Beitrag zur Kenntnis der Vakuolenpulsation bei Wiederkäuerinfusorien nebst einigen biologischen Beobachtungen. Zool. Anz., *107:* 77–84.

Wichterman, R. 1938. The present state of knowledge concerning the existence of species of *Nyctotherus* (Ciliata) living in man. Am. J. Trop. Med., *18:* 67–75.

SUGGESTED READING

Corliss, J. O. 1960. *Tetrahymena chironomi* sp. nov., a ciliate from midge larvae, and the current status of facultative parasitism in the genus *Tetrahymena*. Parasitology, *50:* 111–153. (This is a comprehensive review of facultative parasitism in various species of *Tetrahymena*. The student will find the lists of host and parasites useful.)

Hegner, R., and J. Andrews. 1930. Problems and Methods of Research in Protozoology. Macmillan, New York. Read:

    Hegner, R. Parasitic infusoria in general. pp. 222–224.

    Hegner, R. The genus *Balantidium*. pp. 225–233.

    Metcalf, M. M. Research problems in the Opalinidae. pp. 234–243.

(Although the book is outdated, the beginning student will find these articles interesting and may obtain ideas of relatively simple experiments to try.)

Levine, N. D. 1961. Protozoan Parasites of Domestic Animals and of Man. Burgess, Minneapolis, pp. 347–376. (The ciliates found in man and domestic animals are listed and briefly discussed. The reader will find the bibliography useful.)

Oxford, A. E. 1955. The rumen ciliate protozoa: their chemical composition, metabolism, requirements for maintenance and culture, and physiological significance for the host. Exptl. Parasit., *6:* 569–605. (This review summarizes and analyzes the literature pertaining to an interesting group of ciliates—those symbiotic in the rumen of domestic animals.)

PART
THREE

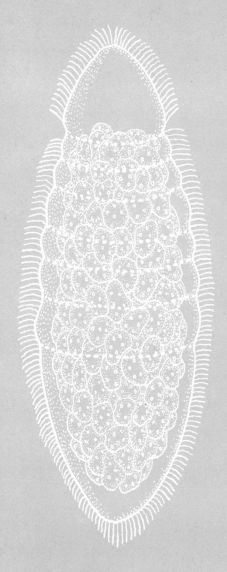

MESOZOA

7

THE MESOZOA

The Mesozoa is a small group of interesting but little understood multicellular endoparasites found in the nephridia of squids and octopuses, and in the body spaces and tissues of various other marine invertebrates. Although the morphology of both larval and adult forms of the known species has been studied by several workers, the complete life histories of a whole group, the Dicyemida, continues to elude biologists.

The relationship between the Mesozoa and the other multicellular invertebrates is uncertain, although some consider the Mesozoa to be degenerate forms of one of the lower invertebrate groups, specifically the digenetic trematodes.

Members of this phylum lack digestive, excretory, circulatory, and nervous systems. Their bodies consist of two layers of cells that are not comparable to the epidermis (ectoderm) and endodermis (endoderm) of diploblastic animals (Plate 7–1, Fig. 1).

SYSTEMATICS AND BIOLOGY

CLASSIFICATION

The few known species of the Mesozoa are divided into two orders—the Dicyemida and the Orthonectida.

Order 1. Dicyemida. Are parasitic in the nephridia of cephalopods. Uninucleate agametes are found in uninucleate axial cells. Somatoderm is not grooved. Parasitic infusorigen the only known sexual stage. Complete life cycle pattern not known.

Order 2. Orthonectida. Are parasitic in internal spaces and tissues of turbellarians, nemerteans, brittle stars, annelids, gastropods, and bivalve molluscs. Agametes are formed from multinucleate plasmodia of one or two sexes. Somatoderm of sexual individuals bears transverse grooves. Complete life cycle pattern, including parasitic asexual and free-living sexual stages, are known.

ORDER DICYEMIDA

The order Dicyemida includes such genera as *Dicyema, Pseudicyema,* and *Dicyemennea* (Plate 7–1, Figs. 2 to 4). Members of these genera are distinguished from one another by the number and arrangement of the cells that constitute the anterior end, known as the polar cap.

In *Dicyema* there are two tiers of oppositely arranged polar cells (the anterior tier is known as propolar and posterior as metapolar), four cells in each tier. In *Pseudicyema* there are also two tiers of four cells each, but the cells composing the tiers are alternately arranged. In *Dicyemennea* there are four cells in the first tier and five in the second. These tiers are alternately arranged. McConnaughey (1949) has presented a classification of these animals and has given a key to the species known up until that time.

Life Cycle of *Pseudicyema truncatum*

Lameere (1916) and Nouvel (1933) investigated the life cycle and developmental pattern of *Pseudicyema truncatum,* a species commonly found in the nephridia of the European cuttlefish squid, *Sepia officinalis.* The developmental stages are depicted in Plate 7–2 and diagrammatically represented in Plate 7–3. The youngest form, found free-swimming in the kidneys of young hosts, is a ciliated larva known as the larval stem nematogen. Its body and the body of the adult stem nematogen into which it matures are essentially the same as that of the primary nematogen, differing in that there are three axial cells present and there is a larger number of somatic cells. There are two layers of cells. The outer cilia-bearing layer, known as the somatoderm (somatic cells), envelops the inner axial cells.

The somatic cells can be divided into five types. Those making up the head region or polar cap are termed propolar and metapolar cells, those immediately posterior to the polar cap in the neck region are known as parapolar cells, those making up the trunk proper are referred to as diapolars, and those comprising the posterior terminal are known as uropolars. In the larval stem nematogen of *P. truncatum* there are four propolars, four metapolars, three parapolars, seventeen diapolars and uropolars combined, and three axial cells. The axial cells are the generative (or reproductive) cells of the animal. In the ciliated larval stem nematogen, each axial cell includes two nuclei, one vegetative, and one generative. The generative nucleus soon is surrounded by cytoplasm and becomes an agamete.

The ciliated larval stem nematogen develops into a second form, the adult stem nematogen, which is made up of the same number of somatoderm cells as the ciliated larva, but during the differentiation from larval stem nematogen to adult stem nematogen, each agamete has divided and is seen as an aggregate of cells. Division of the agametes is strikingly similar to the early cleavage stages in the asexual stages of digenetic trematodes. This similarity plus the presence of the ciliated larva has influenced some to consider the Mesozoa to be closely related to the Platyhelminthes, specifically the Digenea (Stunkard, 1954).

The agametes in adult stem nematogens develop into the common form of the animal—the primary nematogen—which is attached to the host's kidney tissue by its polar cap. The body of the primary nematogen of *P. truncatum* consists of four propolars, four metapolars, two parapolars, ten to fifteen diapolars and uropolars combined, and a single axial cell. The development of primary nematogens from agametes within adult stem nematogens, is a rather complex process. Each agamete undergoes several divisions, resulting in two types of cells—the smaller somatic cells and a larger axial cell. The somatic cells divide again repeatedly, and the resulting group of somatic cells envelop the axial cell, thus forming a primary nematogen.

Fully developed primary nematogens escape from the parent into the host's kidney fluid. Subsequent generations of identical primary nematogens arise from these, and the number of individuals increases until the renal organ of the cephalopod becomes heavily infected.

A primary nematogen gives rise to others in the following manner. During the formation of each member of the first primary nematogen generation, the single nucleus within the single

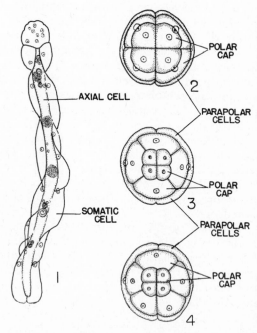

Plate 7-1　　Morphology of some Dicyemida. 1. Entire rhombogen of *Dicyema briarei,* a parasite of *Octopus briareus,* showing centrally located axial cell and peripheral somatic cells. (Redrawn after Short, 1961.) 2. Head-on view of *Dicyema,* showing geometric arrangement of polar cap and parapolar cells. 3. Head-on view of *Pseudicyema,* showing geometric arrangement of polar cap and parapolar cells. 4. Head-on view of *Dicyemennea* showing geometric arrangement of polar cap and parapolar cells. (Figs. 2–4 redrawn after Nouvel, 1933.)

axial cell divides forming two nuclei, one of which remains as the axial cell nucleus. The other nucleus is surrounded by cytoplasm and becomes an agamete. This agamete divides rapidly so that by the time the primary nematogen is fully developed, its axial cell includes a large number of agametes. From these agametes, other primary nematogens develop in the same manner as from the agametes in adult stem nematogens.

The production of primary nematogens continues while the host is growing but generally ceases when it attains sexual maturity. When this condition is reached, the existing primary nematogens either give rise to another generation—the primary rhombogens, which develop from agametes within the last generation of primary nematogens—or metamorphose into secondary rhombogens. Rhombogens are essentially identical to nematogens except that their somatic cells become filled with lipoproteins (yolk-like material) and glycogen and protrude from the body surface of the parasite as verruciform cells.

The agametes found in primary rhombogens represent products of the germ cell lineage from agametes in primary nematogens or from agametes carried over from primary nematogens that have metamorphosed into secondary rhombogens. Some of the agametes in rhombogens degenerate, while others divide to form infusorigens (Plate 7–2, Fig. 10). Infusorigen formation from agametes is comparable to formation of primary nematogens from agametes, except that the cells surrounding the axial cell are not ciliated.

Most authorities on the Mesozoa now agree that infusorigens are hermaphrodites, for they produce male and female gametes that fuse during sexual reproduction. The female gametes, or ova, result from the rounding up and differentiation of some of the surface cells of the infusorigen, while the agametes in the axial cell undergo meiosis and form sperms that fertilize the ova (McConnaughey, 1951). The resultant eggs are given off from the surface of the infusorigens. These eggs undergo cleavage to form balls of cells that eventually differentiate into ciliated free-swimming infusoriform larvae (Plate 7–2, Fig. 11).

The infusoriform larvae escape from the parent rhombogen and leave the host. It is suspected that in sea water these larvae seek and enter another host in which they undergo further development. The manner in which young cephalopods become infected remains uncertain.

According to some experts (McConnaughey, 1951), certain rhombogens may cease producing infusorigens and start producing nematogens, known as secondary nematogens, which in turn produce primary rhombogens (Plate 7–3).

Rhombogens that remain in the host's nephridia disintegrate in time. Within the cephalopod, these parasites apparently do little damage. They acquire their nutrition through their body surfaces and also engulf and digest the host's spermatozoa present in the kidney. Stored glycogen exists in young nematogens and is gradually used up, but quantities reappear in the rhombogens.

ORDER ORTHONECTIDA

The two most common genera included in the order Orthonectida are *Rhopalura*, the members of which are found in brittle stars and other marine invertebrates, and *Stoecharthrum*, a hermaphroditic species parasitic in marine annelids (Plate 7–4, Figs. 1 and 2). A taxonomic revision of the order is given by Caullery and Mesnil (1901).

The life cycle pattern of the Orthonectida is better understood than that of the Dicyemida (Plate 7–5). Through the work of Caullery, Mesnil, and Lavallée (Caullery and Lavallée, 1912), it is known that although hermaphroditic species exist, the majority of these parasites are dioecious. All the known species, which are seldom more than 300 μ in length, have been reported from Europe and England except for Meinkoth's report (1956) of *Rhopalura linei* from the nemertean *Amphiporus ochraceus* off the Massachusetts coast.

Life Cycle of *Rhopalura ophiocomae*

In *R. ophiocomae*, a parasite of the brittle star, the largest forms are the multinucleate plasmodia found in the host's gonads (Plate 7–6, Fig. 1). Some of these plasmodia are males while others are females. Within the individual plasmodium, a certain amount of cytoplasm surrounds each nucleus and through subsequent fragmentation, individual uninucleate agametes are formed. These undergo cleavage to form individual solid masses of embryonic cells— each mass known as a morula (Plate 7–6, Fig. 2).

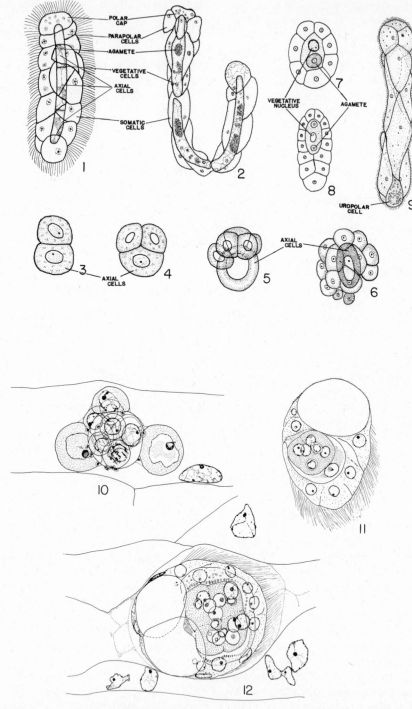

Plate 7-2   Stages in the life cycle of *Pseudicyema truncatum*, a parasite of *Sepia* and of *Dicyema briarei*, a parasite of *Octopus*. 1. Larval stem nematogen of *Pseudicyema truncatum* with three axial cells. (Redrawn after Lameere, 1916.) **2.** Adult stem nematogen of *P. truncatum*, developed directly from larva. Surface cilia are omitted. (Redrawn after Lameere, 1916.) **3.** Two-cell stage during development of a primary nematogen of *P. truncatum* from an agamete. **4.** Three-cell stage during development of a primary nematogen of *P. truncatum* from an agamete. **5.** Six-cell stage during development of a primary nematogen of *P. truncatum* from an agamete. The axial cell is gradually being enveloped by the dividing somatic cells. **6.** Further division of somatic cells during

(Legend continued on opposite page.)

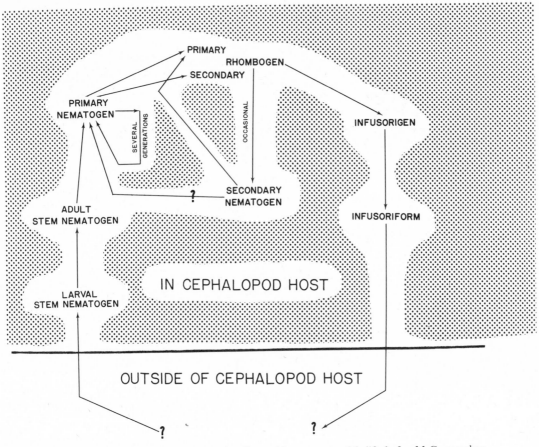

Plate 7-3   Life cycle pattern of a dicyemid mesozoan. (Modified after McConnaughey, 1951.)

Differentiation occurs in each morula. The outer surface cells become the somatoderm and bear cilia, while the inner cells, 200 to 300 in number, become sex cells. The body increases in size and becomes elongate (rather long and slender in certain species), with the females becoming two to three or four times larger than the males. Concentric rings appear on the body surface of these sexual forms in areas where rows of somatic cells form grooves. Generally the males possess fewer rings (Plate 7-6, Fig. 4).

The number, width, and position of these rings are important characteristics in the identification of species (Plate 7-6, Fig. 3). Three distinct regions are recognizable on the body

---

(Legend continued.)

formation of primary nematogen of *P. truncatum*. **7.** Optical section of a developing primary nematogen of *P. truncatum* showing axial cell completely enveloped by smaller somatic cells. The original axial cell nucleus has given rise to an agamete and a vegetative nucleus. **8.** Later stage showing presence of two agametes within the axial cell. **9.** Primary nematogen of *P. truncatum* showing uropolar cell. **10.** Infusorigen and paranucleus of *Dicyema briarei* in axial cell. **11.** Parasagittal optical section of infusoriform larva of *D. briarei* within axial cell, which is not shown. **12.** Dorsal view of infusoriform larva within axial cell. Note also nuclei of uropolar cells of rhombogen. (Figs. 3–9 redrawn after Whitman, 1882. Figs. 10–12 after Short, 1961; drawings loaned by Dr. R. B. Short, Florida State University.)

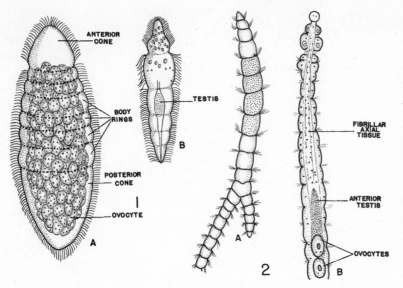

Plate 7-4   Some Orthonec-
tida. 1. A. Mature female of *Rho-palura granosa,* a parasite of the clam *Heteranomia.* B. Mature male of *R. granosa.* (Redrawn after Atkins, 1933.) 2. A. Anterior portion of *Stoecharthrum giardi,* a parasite in the body cavity of the marine annelid *Scoloplos mülleri.* Drawn from living specimen. B. Anterior portion of *S. giardi.* Drawn from stained specimen. (Redrawn after Caullery and Mesnil, 1901.)

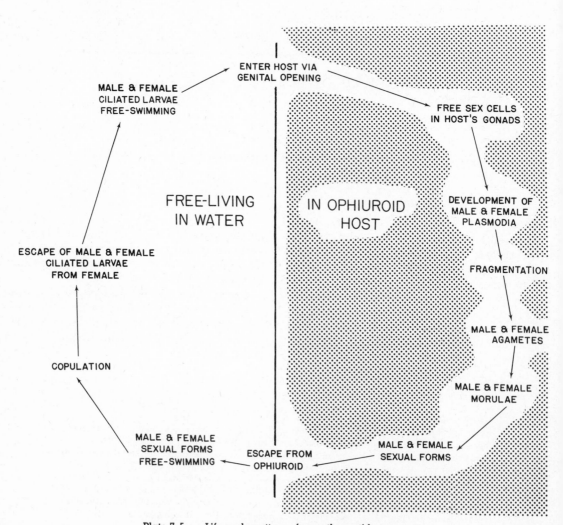

Plate 7-5   Life cycle pattern of an orthonectid mesozoan.

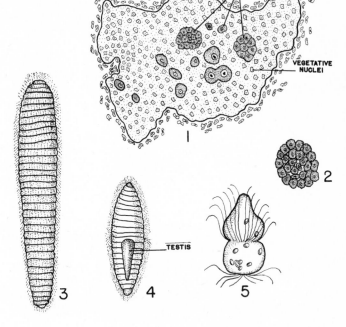

Plate 7-6   **Stages in the life cycle of Orthonectida. 1.** Male plasmodium of *Rhopalura ophiocomae,* a parasite of the brittle star. (Redrawn after Caullery and Mesnil, 1901.) **2.** Morula of *R. ophiocomae.* **3.** Free-living female of *R. ophiocomae.* (Redrawn after Caullery and Mesnil, 1901.) **4.** Free-living male of *R. julini,* a parasite of an annelid. (Redrawn after Caullery and Mesnil, 1901.) **5.** Ciliated larva of *R. granosa,* a parasite of the clam *Heteranomia.* (Redrawn after Atkins, 1933.)

surface—an anterior cone made up of somatic cells on which the cilia are pointed anteriorly, a body region on which the cilia are directed posteriorly, and a posterior cone that is marked off from the body. Some of the cells include birefringent bodies that presumably represent stored nutrients.

Male and female ciliated sexual forms escape from the host and are free-swimming in sea water. When a male and a female make contact, the spermatozoa, which are formed by the sex cells in the male, are introduced into the sex cell mass of the female via the slender posterior end of the male. The fertilized ovum undergoes maturation division, during which polar bodies are extruded on long conical projections. Unequal cleavage follows the fusion of the pronuclei, resulting in another morula-like stage with central cells enveloped by smaller peripheral cells. During this phase of development, chromatin material is eliminated from some of the cells. Ciliated larvae thus formed mature in about 24 hours after fertilization, escape from the genital pore of the female, seek out another host, invade it via the genital openings, and in the process lose their outer somatic layer. The inner sex cells scatter within the host's gonads, primarily in the gonaducts, and

through repeated nuclear division, male and female plasmodia are formed.

In the hermaphroditic species, both male and female morulae are formed from the same plasmodium.

The Orthonectida that parasitize gonadal tissues destroy cells—a case of host castration by a parasite.

It is difficult and speculative to compare the stages in the life cycle of dicyemid and orthonectid mesozoans. However, the sexual forms of orthonectids resemble the nematogens of dicyemids in that both are ciliated. On the other hand, they differ in that there are from several to many more cells in the center of the sexual forms of orthonectids than there are axial cells in dicyemids. Furthermore, all the cells comprising the inner cell mass of the sexual forms of orthonectids are true reproductive cells, being either ovocytes or spermatogonia, depending upon the sex of the individual. In dicyemids, only the agametes enclosed within the axial cells are true reproductive cells.

The plasmodia of orthonectids probably correspond to the axial cells of dicyemid nematogens, because these plasmodia represent the central mass of reproductive cells of ciliated larvae. Again, there is a difference in that the nuclei of each orthonectid plasmodium eventually all become the nuclei of agametes, while only some of the nuclei in dicyemid nematogen axial cells become the nuclei of agametes, the other nuclei becoming the nuclei of somatic cells.

PHYSIOLOGY OF MESOZOA AND HOST-PARASITE RELATIONSHIPS

Practically nothing is known about the physiology of the Mesozoa. What little is known concerning the life history pattern and effects of the parasites on their hosts has already been mentioned.

In dicyemids, Nouvel (1933) reported that the required nutrition is presumed to be absorbed from the surrounding medium, in addition to phagocytosis of particulate material, including the host's spermatozoa, by somatodermal cells. It has also been reported that the infusoriform larvae that escape from the host require oxygen, but the other stages are apparently anaerobic.

To students who have access to laboratory facilities in marine waters, the field of parasitology relative to the Mesozoa presents a challenging and practically virgin field of research.

LITERATURE CITED

Caullery, M., and A. Lavallée. 1912. Recherches sur le cycle évolutif des orthonectides. Les phases initiales dans l'infection expérimentale de l'ophiure, *Amphiura squamata,* par *Rhopalura ophiocomae* Giard. Bull. Scient. France Belgique, *46:* 139–171.

Caullery, M., and F. Mesnil. 1901. Recherches sur les orthonectides. Arch. Anat. Micr., *4:* 381–463, 464–470.

Lameere, A. 1916. Contributions à la conaissance des dicyémides. Première partie. Bull. Scient. France Belgique, *50:* 1–35. (Also see Deuxième partie. *Ibid, 51:* 347–390.)

McConnaughey, B. H. 1949. Mesozoa of the family Dicyemidae from California. Univ. Cal. Publ. Zool., *55:* 295–336.

McConnaughey, B. H. 1951. The life cycle of the dicyemid Mesozoa. Univ. Cal. Publ. Zool., *55:* 295–335.

Meinkoth, N. A. 1956. A North American record of *Rhopalura* sp. (Orthonectida: Mesozoa), a parasite of the nemertean *Amphiporus ochraceus* (Verrill). Biol. Bull., *111:* 308.

Nouvel, H. 1933. Recherches sur la cytologie, la physiologie et la biologie des dicyémides. Ann. Inst. Oceanogr. Monaco, *13:* 163–255.

Stunkard, H. W. 1954. The life history and systematic relations of the Mesozoa. Quart Rev. Biol., *29:* 23–224.

SUGGESTED READING

Hyman, L. H. 1940. Phylum Mesozoa. pp. 233–247. In The Invertebrates: Protozoa Through Ctenophora. McGraw-Hill, New York. (This is a good summary of the Mesozoa).

McConnaughey, B. H., and E. McConnaughey. 1954. Strange life of the dicyemid mesozoans. Sci. Monthly, *79:* 277–284. (This article is written in a popular style, describing the complex life cycle pattern of dicyemids.)

Stunkard, H. W. 1954. The life history and systematic relations of the Mesozoa. Quart. Rev. Biol. *29:* 230–244. (Life history patterns of the Mesozoa are reviewed. The author has used this information to speculate on the phylogenetic relationship of mesozoans with other invertebrates.)

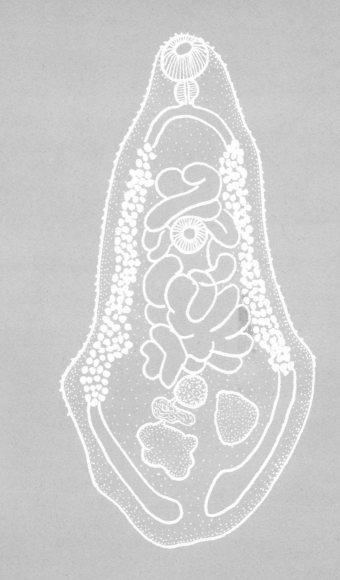

PART FOUR

PLATYHELMINTHES

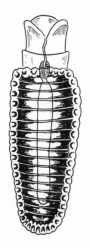

INTRODUCTION TO THE PARASITIC FLATWORMS THE SYMBIOTIC TURBELLARIA THE ASPIDOBOTHREA—
The Aspidobothrid Trematodes

The parasitic platyhelminths are among the oldest parasites known (see Chapter 2). The liver fluke *Fasciola hepatica* was reportedly first found by Jehan de Brie in 1379 in the liver of sheep in France. The importance of these worms from medical and veterinary standpoints cannot be over emphasized. From the zoological standpoint, these animals are extremely interesting, for they represent an important group of invertebrates in which both their physiology and anatomy have been altered to meet the parasitic way of life.

GENERAL MORPHOLOGY

The phylum Platyhelminthes includes the various acoelomate, dorsoventrally flattened animals that are commonly known as the flatworms. All members are typically bilaterally symmetrical and possess the flame cell or protonephritic type of excretory (osmoregulatory) system. They usually lack a definitive anus, and also lack skeletal, circulatory, and respiratory systems. The spaces between the body wall and the internal organs are filled with free-flowing and fixed cells of various types (Cheng and Provenza, 1960); the intercellular spaces in living specimens are filled with body fluids. The cells and the spaces between them are referred to collectively as the parenchyma (mesenchyme).

The platyhelminth body shape varies from that of a broad, dorsoventrally flattened, leaf like, monozoic animal, such as the liver fluke *Fasciola hepatica,* to that of a long chain of proglottids (polyzoic) as in the true tapeworms. Among the cestodes, or tapeworms, the body segments near the anterior or holdfast end of the chain are generally immature and smaller than those near the opposing end. Various intermediate forms exist among both the monozoic and polyzoic flatworms.

All platyhelminths possess a nervous system, which may be in the form of a primitive epidermal net, as in a few free-living forms. However, most parasitic species possess a relatively well developed nervous system comprising a "brain," or cephalic ganglion made up of ganglionic cells and fibers that may either form a definite mass or be arranged in the parenchyma as a ring looped around the anterior end of the alimentary tract.

From the brain, numerous nerve fibers are directed anteriorly, laterally, and posteriorly to innervate the various tissues of the body. Generally, the number of nerve cords directed posteriorly is consistent in a given group. Transverse commissures generally connect the longitudinally oriented cords (Plate 8–1, Figs. 1 and 2). The specific arrangement patterns of the nervous system in each major taxonomic group of the Platyhelminthes are given in following sections.

Except in a few cases, the parasitic flatworms are monoecious—that is, both male and female reproductive systems are found in the same individual. In sexually mature worms, both the testes and the ovaries often function simultaneously. Internal fertilization is the rule and may be accomplished by self-fertilization, which is extremely rare; by fertilization between proglottids, as in some tapeworms; or by cross fertilization between two individuals.

Not all platyhelminths are parasitic, for a large number of flatworms, members of the class Turbellaria, are free-living. A few parasitic turbellarians are known, such as the rhabdocoel *Collastoma pacifica,* found in the gut of the sipunculid worm *Dendrostoma pyrodes* (Kozloff, 1953). In addition, members of the family Fecampidae and members of the suborder Temnocephalida, both of the order Rhabdocoela, are symbiotic.

The more commonly encountered parasitic flatworms belong to the classes Trematoda (the flukes) and Cestoidea (the tapeworms). The adult trematodes and cestodes differ from the turbellarians in lacking a cellular or syncytial epithelial covering on their body surface. Instead, the bodies of trematodes and cestodes are covered by a noncellular cuticular layer. The cuticle consists of proteins, an acid mucopolysaccharide, lipids, mucoids, alkaline and acid phosphatases, and RNA.

Recent evidence indicates that the cuticle is secreted by certain specialized cuticle-secreting cells in the subcuticular zone, embedded in the parenchyma. This protective cuticle appears to be resistant to digestion by the host, especially in the gut-dwelling species. Pratt (1909) suggested that the resistance of flatworm parasites to being digested is not totally due to the body cuticle. In addition, certain subcuticular cells secrete a substance that neutralizes the host's

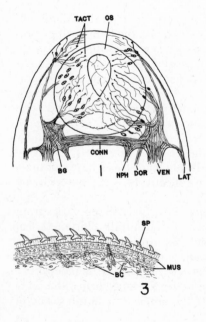

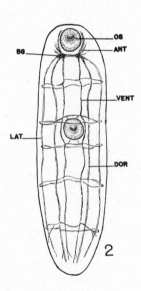

Plate 8–1   Trematode morphology. 1. Innervation of the anterior end and oral sucker of a digenetic trematode. (BG, brain ganglion; CONN, connective between two lateral brain ganglia; DOR, dorsal nerve cord; LAT, lateral nerve cord; NPH, nerve to muscular pharynx; OS, oral sucker; VEN, ventral nerve cord.) (Redrawn after Bettendorf, 1897.) 2. Nervous system of a distome. (ANT, anterior nerves; BG, brain ganglion; DOR, dorsal nerve cord; LAT, lateral nerve cord; OS, oral sucker; VENT, ventral nerve cord.) (Redrawn after Looss, 1894.) 3. Longitudinal section through portion of the cuticle and subcuticular zone of *Hasstilesia tricolor,* an intestinal trematode of rabbits, showing cuticular spines embedded in the cuticle. (BC, parenchymal beta cells; MUS, subcuticular muscles; SP, cuticular spines.) (Original.)

digestive enzymes. This hypothesis is in need of further verification.

Odlaug (1949), while studying the body cuticle of three frog-parasitizing flukes from different internal environments—a bladder-dwelling trematode, *Gorgoderina attenuata,* a lung-dwelling species, *Haematoloechus medioplexus,* and *Loxogenes arcanum,* an encysted form found in the pyloric end of the stomach and in the duodenum—found no significant differences in the thicknesses or constitution of the cuticle. This suggested that either the resistance of the cuticle cannot be appreciated through the measurement of thicknesses, or that Pratt's contention may be correct.

Very often, especially among digenetic trematodes, the body cuticle bears spines that are anchored in the cuticular layer (Plate 8–1, Fig. 3).

Attachment Mechanisms

The mechanisms of attachment of helminth parasites on or within their hosts are definitely the result of adaptation to the parasitic way of life. The most common type of attachment organ is the sucker,* which may be modified into various forms. Most digenetic trematodes have two suckers—the anterior sucker and the ventral sucker, or acetabulum.

Monogenetic trematodes are characterized by a single large sucker, a number of circularly arranged suckers, or a muscular wedge shaped or spatulate enlargement known as an opisthaptor, at the posterior terminals of their bodies. The tapeworms generally possess true cup shaped suckers on their scoleces, or modified flaplike suckers known as bothria. The taxonomic significance of these sucker shapes is discussed in Chapter 12.

The suckers of helminths are highly muscular protrusible cups that not only adhere to the surface of the host's tissue, but actually embrace the tissue (Plate 8–2).

In addition to suckers, the monogenetic flukes often possess an array of hooks, clamps, and sucker-clamps, all of which are located on the posterior sucker and which aid in attachment by digging into or embracing the host's tissue. Some tapeworms, commonly referred to as armed tapeworms, have a spinous rostellum.

In these tapeworms, one or more circular rows of hooks are located at the end of the scolex, and these also become embedded in the host's tissue. These attachment organs are of great importance to flatworms, for in their natural habitats within or on their hosts, the parasites must remain permanently and strongly attached so they cannot be sloughed off with the chyme in the case of intestinal forms, or be washed away by water in the case of aquatic forms.

Alimentary Tracts

Trematodes have incomplete alimentary canals that vary from one extremely short, blind-sac caecum or two extremely short caeca (in *Brachycoelium,* a parasite of salamanders) to two long caeca with side branches (in the liver fluke *Fasciola hepatica*). A few obscure cases of complete alimentary tracts are known (Stunkard, 1931).

Partially or completely digested nutrients, in which the worms are bathed, are taken into the caeca, primarily via the mouth and esophagus, and are distributed to the body tissues by diffusion through the caecal wall. Some nutrients, such as certain amino acids, are absorbed through the body wall. The extreme of parasitic adaptation is exemplified among the cestodes, in which an alimentary tract is completely wanting. In cestodes, nutrients are totally absorbed into the body through the body wall.

Chemical Composition

The chemical composition of endoparasitic platyhelminths has been studied by various investigators.

PROTEINS. Weinland and von Brand (1926) reported that in *Fasciola hepatica,* 58 per cent of the dry substance is protein. The proportion of protein to total dry weight of certain tapeworms was reported as follows: 60 per cent in *Dibothriocephalus* (= *Diphyllobothrium*) *latus* (Smorodintsev and Bebesin, 1936), 36 per cent in *Railletina cesticillus* (Reid, 1942), 33 per cent in *Taeniarhynchus saginatus* (Smorodintsev et al., 1933), and 30 to 36 per cent in *Moniezia expansa* (Wardle, 1937a; von Brand, 1933).

In larval forms, Hopkins (1950) demonstrated that 36 per cent of the dry substance of plerocercoids of *Schistocephalus solidus* is protein, and Salisbury and Anderson (1939) reported that in *Cysticerus fasciolaris* (larva of *Taenia taeniaeformis*) 31 per cent of the dry weight is protein.

The various protein fractions isolated from

---

*The term *sucker,* although frequently used, is not completely descriptive. The term *acetabulum* in its broad sense is probably a better one, because these holdfast structures grasp by pinching as well as by sucking.

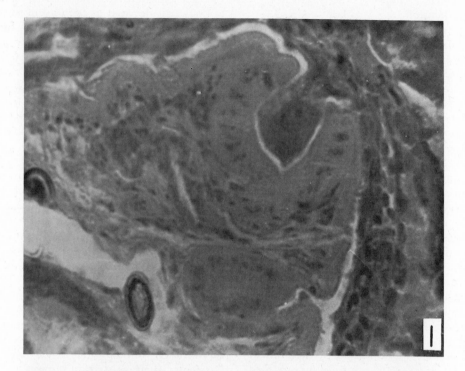

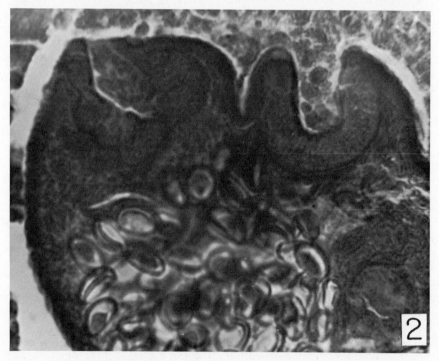

Plate 8-2   Function of trematode suckers. 1. Photomicrograph showing oral sucker of *Hasstilesia tricolor* holding on to intestinal wall of rabbit host. (Original.) **2.** Photomicrograph showing both oral sucker and acetabulum of *H. tricolor* holding on to intestinal lining of rabbit host. (Original.)

platyhelminths include albumins, globulins, albumoses, neucleoproteins, keratin, elastin, collagen, and reticulin. Kent (1947), in breaking these fractions down further into their component amino acids in the tapeworm *Moniezia expansa*, found alanine, valine, leucine, isoleucine, aspartic acid, glutamic acid, arginine, and histidine. The number of amino acids is comparatively few when compared to those of protozoa. However, Kent employed histochemical methods that may have left out some other of the constituent amino acids.

More recently Robinson (1961) employed paper chromatography in the identification of acid hydrolysates of *Schistosoma mansoni* adults and found eighteen amino acids present. Cheng (1963), by employing similar techniques, identified fifteen and nineteen bound, and eight and fourteen, free amino acids in the sporocysts of the trematodes *Gorgodera amplicava* and *Glypthelmins quieta* respectively, and fifteen and eighteen bound, and seven and fourteen free amino acids in the free-swimming cercariae of these species. In addition, he identified seventeen bound and thirteen free amino acids in the rediae of another trematode, *Echinoparyphium* sp., and seventeen bound and twelve free amino acids in the cercariae of this fluke. In the same paper, Cheng reviewed what is known about the chemical composition and utilization of amino acids in larval trematodes.

The proteins found in platyhelminths are not a part of the stored food, since metazoans do not store proteins per se. Hence these proteins must be considered a part of the makeup of the animal's tissues. However, free amino acids do exist in platyhelminths, making up the amino acid pool, but these are continuously being utilized in the synthesis of proteins and for energy production.

CARBOHYDRATES. Glycogen is stored within the body of flatworms. Numerous studies have indicated that glycogen is not found in the cuticle but in the subcuticular areas, which are important as storage sites. The parenchyma and the muscular suckers are also sites for glycogen storage. In the liver fluke *Fasciola* and related genera, glycogen has been reported in the vitelline glands and in eggs located in the uterus. Similarly, glycogen is present in the vitellaria of the tapeworm *Hymenolepis diminuta* and also in its sperm. On the other hand no glycogen is present in the vitellaria and in the eggs of the blood fluke *Schistosoma*. Furthermore, Bueding and Koletsky (1950) reported

that in the dioecious *Schistosoma*, less glycogen is present in females than in males.

It is apparent from this information that in the Platyhelminthes glycogen is primarily stored in the subcuticular areas, the sucker musculature, and in the parenchyma, but in certain species it may be found in the sperms, eggs, and vitelline glands; and there may be a difference in the quantity of glycogen in males and females in dioecious species.

The amount of glycogen in the bodies of platyhelminths does not fluctuate with the season. Known percentages of fresh and dry weight glycogen in platyhelminths is given in Table 8-1.

LIPIDS. Tötterman and Kirk (1939) reported that 1.6 per cent of the fresh substance of *Dibothriocephalus latus* is lipid, and von Brand (1933) and Smorodintsev and Bebesin (1936) demonstrated that lipids form 3.4 per cent, 1.3 per cent, and 1.4 per cent of the fresh substance of the tapeworms *Moniezia expansa*, *M. denticulata*, and *Taenia solium*, respectively; and 30.1 per cent and 16.2 per cent of the dry substance of *M. expansa* and *M. denticulata*.

Flury and Leeb (1926) and Weinland and von Brand (1926) reported that 1.9 to 2.4 per cent of the fresh substance and 12.2 to 13.3 per cent of the dry substance of the liver fluke *Fasciola hepatica* consists of lipids.

Fractionation of these lipids has yielded phosphatids, unsaponifiable matter, saturated fatty acids, unsaturated fatty acids, hydroxy fatty acids, and glycerol.

INORGANIC SUBSTANCES. In addition to proteins, carbohydrates, and lipids, certain inorganic substances are present in flatworms. Weinland and von Brand (1926) showed that inorganic substances form 1.14 per cent of the fresh weight of *Fasciola hepatica* and 4.9 per cent of its dry weight. Similarly 0.43 per cent of fresh weight and 4.8 per cent of dry weight of the tapeworm *Dibothriocephalus latus* are composed of inorganic materials (Smorodintsev and Bebesin, 1936). Again, 1.85 per cent and 5.8 per cent of the fresh and dry weights of *Raillietina cesticillus*, 1.11 to 1.4 per cent and 9.3 to 10.5 per cent of the fresh and dry weights of *Moniezia expansa*, 1.85 per cent and 5.8 per cent of the fresh and dry weights of the plerocercoids of *Schistocephalus solidus* are inorganic. The last three flatworms mentioned are tapeworms.

From what is known, it is apparent that cestodes possess higher quantities of inorganic

Table 8-1. Amounts of glycogen in some platyhelminths expressed as percentages of the fresh and dry weights of whole worms

	Glycogen in Percent of		Habitat	Availability of Significant Amount of O_2	Authority
	Fresh Weight	Dry Weight			
TREMATODES					
Schistosoma mansoni	–	14-29 ♂ 3-5 ♀	Bloodstream	Yes	Bueding and Koletsky (1950)
Fasciola hepatica	3.1; 3.7	15; 21	Bile ducts	No	Flury and Leeb (1926) Weinland and Von Brand (1926)
CESTODES					
Dibothriocephalus latus	1.9	20	Intestine	No	Smorodintsev and Bebesin (1936)
Railletina nodulosus	–	14	Intestine	No	Reid (1942)
Moniezia expansa	2.7; 3.2	24; 32	Intestine	No	Weinland (1901) Von Brand (1933) Wardle (1937)
Taenia solium	2.2	25	Intestine	No	Smorodintsev and Bebesin (1936)
Taeniarhynchus saginatus	7.4	60	Intestine	No	Smorodintsev and Bebesin (1936)
Cysticercus fasciolaris	–	28	Liver	?	Salisbury and Anderson (1939)

*Selected from von Brand, *Chemical Physiology of Endoparasitic Animals*, Academic Press, N.Y., 1952; with permission of Academic Press.

substances than trematodes. This can be explained by the accumulation of calcareous corpuscles in the parenchyma of cestodes. These corpuscles are composed of an organic base together with inorganic substances.

These inorganic materials have been determined to be potassium, sodium, magnesium, calcium phosphate, and sulfate in the body tissues of the larva of the cestode *Taenia taeniaeformis* (= *Cysticercus fasciolaris*) (Salisbury and Anderson, 1939); and CaO, MgO, P_2O_5, and CO_2 in the calcareous corpuscles of the cestode *Taenia marginata* (von Brand, 1933). Iron, in extremely small quantities, has been located in the intestinal epithelia of male *Schistosoma japonicum* and in *Paragonimus ringeri,* both trematodes. It is believed that these traces of iron represent the breakdown product of the host's haemoglobin.

Potassium, sodium, magnesium, calcium, chlorine, sulfur, iron, phosphorus, and silicon have been reported from the body fluids of helminths, especially the cystic fluids of the tapeworms *Cysticercus tenuicollis* and *Echinococcus granulosus.*

HOSTS OF PLATYHELMINTHS

The number of hosts required by flatworm parasites to complete their life cycles varies. Among the Digenea, there are always one or more intermediate hosts. Among the Monogenea, no intermediate hosts are required. Among the Cestoidea, the number again varies from one to many. The number of hosts required by parasites may be utilized as an auxiliary tool in the determination of the phylogenetic relationship between these animals (p. 23).

All parasitologists agree that the parasitic platyhelminths arose from some free-living ancestral form, probably a primitive turbellarian. Based on this assumption, it appears that some of the free-living flatworm ancestors became adapted to ectoparasitism, and like the modern Monogenea, did not require an intermediate host. The endoparasites, especially those living in their host's intestine must have arrived therein through accidental ingestion. Some of these parasites apparently survived and entered various tissues and organs associated with the alimentary tract. Those that found such sites satisfactory, survived.

Utilization of intermediate hosts, necessary for transport and later for a phase of the parasite's development, is considered a later development. On the other hand, the intermediate hosts may have been the original definitive hosts. The problem, however, is not easy to solve. It is also conceivable that parasites with more than one intermediate host may gradually lose their dependency on the several hosts, thus reducing the number if not relinquishing all intermediate hosts. The two seemingly opposing concepts are discussed on page 23.

The life history patterns of platyhelminths are discussed in following chapters. However, at this point it should be mentioned that although flukes and tapeworms parasitize vertebrates in their adult stages, larval forms generally are found in invertebrates. The exceptions to this rule are found among some of the aspidobothrid trematodes and parasitic turbellarians that are known to parasitize various invertebrates.

CLASSIFICATION

The phylum Platyhelminthes includes three classes—the essentially free-living Turbellaria, the parasitic Trematoda, and the parasitic Cestoidea.

The subdivisions of these classes are as follows:

Class Turbellaria
    Order 1. Acoela (free-living, marine)
    Order 2. Rhabdocoela (all free-living except for members of suborder Temnocephalida and a few members of suborder Lecithophora).
    Order 3. Alloeocoela (free-living, few ectosymbiotic, mostly marine, few fresh-water).
    Order 4. Tricladida (free-living, few symbiotic, marine, fresh-water, terrestrial).
    Order 5. Polycladida (almost all free-living, few symbiotic, almost exclusively marine).

Class Trematoda
    Order 1. Aspidobothrea*
    Order 2. Monogenea
    Order 3. Digenea
Class Cestoidea
    Subclass Eucestoda
        Order 1. Protecocephala
        Order 2. Tetraphyllidea
        Order 3. Disculicepitidea
        Order 4. Lecanicephala
        Order 5. Trypanorhyncha
        Order 6. Cyclophyllidea
        Order 7. Aporidea
        Order 8. Nippotaeniidea
        Order 9. Caryophyllidea
        Order 10. Spathebothridea
        Order 11. Pseudophyllidea
    Subclass: Cestodaria
        Order 1. Amphilinidea
        Order 2. Gyrocotylidea
        Order 3. Biporophyllidea

Considerations of the various taxa are given in the respective sections.

SYMBIOTIC TURBELLARIANS

The turbellarians are primarily free-living. Most species are found in salt and fresh water, but some inhabit moist terrestrial niches. The class is divided into five orders—Acoela, Rhabdocoela, Alloeocoela, Tricladida, and Polycladida.

A group belonging to the Rhabdocoela, members of the small suborder Temnocephalida, are all symbiotic. These turbellarians are characterized by the absence of cilia or reduced ciliation, tentacles, a single genital pore, and one or two adhesive discs at the posterior end of the body.

In addition to the temnocephalid rhabdocoels, a few members of another suborder of the Rhabdocoela—the Lecithophora—are symbiotic. The lecithophorans are distinguished by their bulbous pharynx, paired protonephridia, and ventral genital pores.

---

*It should be pointed out that Stunkard (1962), in following the systematic interpretation of Burmeister in 1856, considers the order Aspidobothrea along with the order Digenea to be subordinate to the subclass Malacobothridia, and the so-called monogeneids he assigns to a separate subclass—the Pectobothridia. Both Malacobothridia and Pectobothridia are assigned to the class Trematoda.

Almost all alloeocoels are marine; only a few are found in fresh water. Among the marine species, a few are symbiotic. These small turbellarians can be distinguished by their small, bulbous or plicate pharynx, numerous testes, a digestive tract that may include short diverticula, paired protonephridia that often include more than one main branch and excretory pore, and the usual penial papilla.

A few symbiotic species are known among the marine triclads. These are large, elongate turbellarians possessing a plicate pharynx that is generally directed posteriorly. The intestinal tract is characteristically divided into three highly diverticulated branches—one directed anteriorly and the remaining two directed posteriorly. There is one pair of ovaries and from two to many testes. A penial papilla is present and there is only one genital pore.

A few marine polyclads are also permanently or temporarily associated with other animals. These turbellarians are large and conspicuously flattened, possessing digestive tracts that include many irregularly branched diverticula that radiate to the periphery of the body. Numerous eyespots are also present.

Order Rhabdocoela

SUBORDER TEMNOCEPHALIDA

Members of the suborder Temnocephalida of the order Rhabdocoela are all ectocommensals on fresh-water animals, primarily crayfishes, prawns, isopods, and other crustaceans. They are less frequently found on turtles and snails, on which are attached to the external surface or in the branchial chamber. The relationship between the host and the symbiont appears to be commensalistic, for rather than deriving nutrient from the host, these helminths feed on small animals and diatoms available in the habitat. Only one species, *Scutariella didactyla,* found on prawns in Montenegro, apparently feeds on its host's body fluids and hence may be considered a parasite.

Although temnocephalids do not normally leave their hosts, attempts to remove them have revealed that some species can live for some time away from the host, while others die in a short time. Thus, some physiological dependence, especially in the latter cases, must exist.

Geographically, these ectosymbionts are limited to tropical, subtropical, and certain temperate areas. They are commonly found in South America, Australia, and New Zealand. Species have been reported from the Balkan Peninsula, India, Central America, and the islands of the South Pacific.

MORPHOLOGY

Temnocephalid rhabdocoels are small, flattened organisms that measure between 0.3 and 2 mm. in length. They are generally colorless and somewhat transparent. Their body surface includes structures that represent adaptations to symbiosis. Body projections are present on all known species. For example, in *Temnocephala* there are six prominent anteriorly directed tentacles; in *Actinodactylella* there are twelve tentacles distributed along the body; and in *Caridinicola, Monodiscus,* and other genera there are only two short stumpy tentacles (Plate 8–3, Figs. 1 to 3). Only in members of *Didymorchis* are tentacles lacking. In others, such as *Craspedella* (Plate 8–3, Fig. 4), papillae are present on the dorsal posterior region in addition to tentacles.

In addition to the conspicuous tentacles, almost all temnocephalids possess a posteriorly situated adhesive disc. In members of *Caridinicola,* the adhesive disc is absent but in its place exists a pair of adhesive pits (Plate 8–3, Fig. 3). In some genera an anterior adhesive organ is also present. The adhesive disc of temnocephalids are not as specialized as the suckers of trematodes. By alternately attaching themselves by their tentacles and adhesive discs, the temnocephalids are able to move about on their hosts.

In addition to their locomotor function, the tentacles are also tactile. Furthermore, the tentacles apparently also serve as defense mechanisms, for internally a pair of gland cells furnish rhabdites similar to those of free-living planarians to the anterior tips of the tentacles.

The syncytial body surface of temnocephalids is different from that of other turbellarians in that there is usually a noncellular border that is cuticular. Although thinner than the cuticle of trematodes and cestodes, this border resembles their cuticle.

Internal Structures

REPRODUCTIVE SYSTEM. The temnocephalid rhabdocoels are monoecious. There is usually

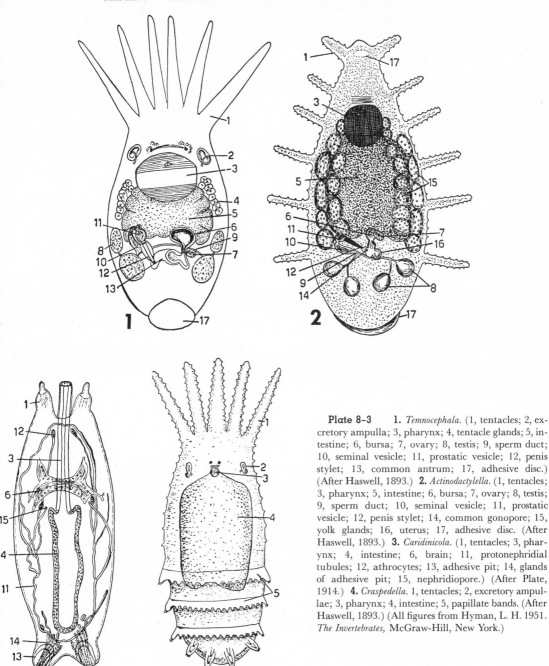

Plate 8-3   **1.** *Temnocephala.* (1, tentacles; 2, excretory ampulla; 3, pharynx; 4, tentacle glands; 5, intestine; 6, bursa; 7, ovary; 8, testis; 9, sperm duct; 10, seminal vesicle; 11, prostatic vesicle; 12, penis stylet; 13, common antrum; 17, adhesive disc.) (After Haswell, 1893.) **2.** *Actinodactylella.* (1, tentacles; 3, pharynx; 5, intestine; 6, bursa; 7, ovary; 8, testis; 9, sperm duct; 10, seminal vesicle; 11, prostatic vesicle; 12, penis stylet; 14, common gonopore; 15, yolk glands; 16, uterus; 17, adhesive disc. (After Haswell, 1893.) **3.** *Caridinicola.* (1, tentacles; 3, pharynx; 4, intestine; 6, brain; 11, protonephridial tubules; 12, athrocytes; 13, adhesive pit; 14, glands of adhesive pit; 15, nephridiopore.) (After Plate, 1914.) **4.** *Craspedella.* 1, tentacles; 2, excretory ampullae; 3, pharynx; 4, intestine; 5, papillate bands. (After Haswell, 1893.) (All figures from Hyman, L. H. 1951. *The Invertebrates,* McGraw-Hill, New York.)

a pair of testes present. Each member of the pair may be divided into two to six parts. Leading from each testis is the vas efferens, which unites with its counterpart to form the common vas deferens, or sperm duct. Sperm within the sperm duct are deposited in the seminal vesicle, from which they are conducted to the cirrus—an eversible and protrusible structure—or the cuticular penial apparatus. A group of unicellular glands (prostate glands) either empty into the base of the penis or into the prostatic vesicle, which in turn empties into the terminal end of the male reproductive tract.

The female reproductive system consists of a single ovary, from which the oviduct arises.

Material from the paired yolk glands empties into the female tract. These glands are subdivided in some species, and branched to form an anastomosing network in others. Beyond the point where the ducts from the yolk glands enter, the female tract generally becomes enlarged to form the seminal bursa, which is extremely active in digesting and absorbing excess yolk.

In some species, one or more small seminal receptacles are present. The uterus, which conducts the zygotes away from the seminal bursa, possesses thickened walls of secretory cells that produce the materials to surround the zygote and yolk, thus forming the capsule. The uterus opens into the atrium, into which the terminal end of the male reproductive system also opens. Thus it is a common genital atrium. The opening through which the atrium communicates with the exterior is the gonopore, or genital pore.

ALIMENTARY TRACT. The alimentary tract is incomplete. The mouth is situated at the anterior end of the body and leads into a bulbous or elongate pharynx, depending on the species. The pharynx in turn leads into a blind-sac intestinal caecum.

NERVOUS SYSTEM. The nervous system consists of a cephalic ganglion, or "brain," situated near the pharynx (Plate 8–4). From this nerve center, a series of nerve cords arise that form both subepidermal and submuscular nets. The submuscular net contains many sensory nerves, which lead from the tentacles to the brain. Also included in the submuscular net are three pairs of longitudinal nerve cords with transverse connectives.

Many species possess a pair of eyes. Each eye is double, with a retinal cell at each end and a pigment cell in between.

SUBORDER LECITHOPHORA

FAMILY FECAMPIIDAE

Another group of symbiotic rhabdocoels, members of the family Fecampiidae of the suborder Lecithophora, are endoparasitic in various marine crustaceans. *Fecampia* (Plate 8–5) is found as adults in the body cavity (haemocoel) of various marine crustaceans. For example, *F. xanthocephala* is found in the marine isopod *Idotea neglecta. Fecampia* is the only known parasitic turbellarian that includes a free-living

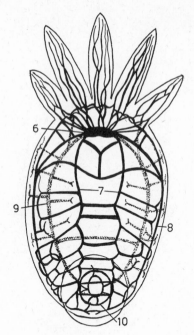

Plate 8–4   **Brain of** *Temnocephala.* (6, brain; 8, lateral cords; 9, ventral cords; 10, nerve ring in adhesive disc.) (After Merton, 1913.) (From Hyman, L. H. 1951. *The Invertebrates.* McGraw-Hill, New York.)

larval stage that is morphologically distinct from the adult.

Life Cycle of *Fecampia*

The larvae of *Fecampia* possess eyes, a mouth, a long buccal tube, a pharynx, and intestine. In the posterior end of the body are found the so-called embryonic germinal cells. These larvae are free-living. By some means yet unknown, they enter their host's haemocoel and grow to sexual maturity. Each larva loses its mouth and pharynx, while the intestinal caecum remains as a longitudinal slit closed at both ends. The eyes gradually disappear. Upon completion of this series of regressive metamorphoses, the reproductive structures develop and the body becomes increasingly more opaque because of an increase in size of the numerous subepidermal cells. The adult bears cilia as does the larva.

Adults escape from the host, presumably by penetrating through the less heavily chitinized areas of the exoskeleton, and drop to the bottom of the sea. Secretions from their subepithelial gland cells form a pear shaped cocoon, within which they lay their eggs. The eggs are surrounded by capsules, each enveloping two eggs and many yolk globules (Plate 8–5, Fig. 2).

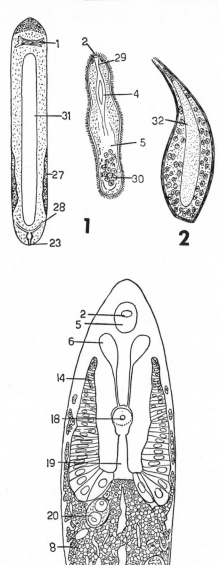

Upon completion of oviposition, the adult gradually disintegrates.

Several species of *Fecampia* are known. *F. erythrocephala* occurs in hermit crabs, and *F. spiralis* in an Antarctic isopod. Aside from *F. spiralis,* the various species are found only in European coastal waters.

OTHER RHABDOCOEL SYMBIONTS

A few other rhabdocoels have been reported to be symbiotic in marine animals. In all instances, however, little morphological difference exists between symbiotic and free-living relatives. The most striking difference rests in the fact that rhabdites are absent or only present in restricted parts of the body of the endoparasitic species. This can be interpreted as an adaptation to endosymbiosis because free-living turbellarians utilize rhabdites as defensive or offensive mechanisms. The endo-symbiotic species, being in constant and continuous contact with nourishment and free from predators, have completely or partially lost their rhabdites.

Parasitic rhabdocoels are known to occur in echinoderms, marine molluscs, and the shipworm *Teredo. Paravortex gemellipara* lives in the clam *Modiolus* off the New England coast (Plate 8–5, Fig. 3). *Paravortex cardii* is found in the ovary of *Cardium edule; Oekiocolax plagiostomorum* in the mesenchyme of the marine turbellarian *Plagiostomum,* causing parasitic castration; and *Graffilla* in the viscera of marine gastropods and shipworms.

OTHER SYMBIOTIC TURBELLARIANS

Among the alloeocoelan turbellarians, a few are ectocommensalistic or ectoparasitic on marine invertebrates. For example, certain species of *Hypotrichina* are found on the crustacean *Hebalia* in the Mediterranean. Among the Tricladida, again a few species are either ectocommensals or ectoparasites. Certain species of *Bdelloura* and *Syncoelidium pellucidum,* for example, are found on the horseshoe crab, *Limulus.*

Micropharynx, which is attached to the body surface of rays in northern waters, participates in a true parasitic relationship. This triclad feeds on the host's epithelial cells. Adaptations to parasitism occur in this species—its pharynx is much smaller than that of closely related free-living species, probably reflecting its type

Plate 8–5   1. *Fecampia* adult and juvenile stage. Adult lacks mouth or pharynx. Juvenile stage has digestive system and eyes. (1, brain; 2, mouth; 4, pharynx; 5, intestine; 23, common gonopore; 27, hermaphroditic gonad; 28, gonoduct; 29, buccal tube; 30, yolk in intestine; 31, space.) (After Caullery and Mesnil, 1903.) 2. *Fecampia* secreting capsule containing many egg clusters and yolk cells. (32, worm inside capsule.) (After Caullery and Mesnil, 1903.) 3. *Paravortex gemellipara* from the clam *Modiolus.* (2, mouth; 5, pharynx; 6, testes; 14, ovary; 18, common gonopore; 19, female antrum; 20, capsule containing two embryos. (After Ball, 1916.) (From Hyman, L. H. 1951. *The Invertebrates.* McGraw-Hill, New York.)

of nutrition, and a subventral attachment organ allows the worm to attach itself to the host.

Many polyclads are found associated with other organisms in a more or less permanent fashion. The nature of such associations has not been studied in any detail. Although polyclads are found in the shells of marine molluscs, feeding on mucus, detritus, and small organisms, the same species also occur free. Thus, their presence in molluscs is probably accidental and not obligatory. In some cases a true commensalistic relationship may exist.

Stylochus inimicus, S. ellipticus, and *S. frontalis,* the so-called oyster "leeches," penetrate through the shells of oysters and feed on their soft parts. These polyclads are considered predators and are of economic importance to the oyster industry. Pearse and Wharton reported that oysters attempt to defend themselves against *Stylochus* by walling it off with a layer of conchiolin secreted by the mantle.

The related *Stylochus zebra* is found in shells inhabited by hermit crabs. Its relationship with the hermit crab remains undetermined.

Certain other species of polyclads are associated with marine invertebrates. These appear to be on the borderline of parasitism. *Euplana takewakii,* for example, is found in the genital bursae of ophiuroids, and *Hoploplana inquilina* is found in the mantle chamber of marine snails.

It is of evolutionary interest to emphasize that certain modern turbellarians do engage in symbiotic relationships. Because present day trematodes and cestodes are believed to have arisen from some ancient turbellarians that are also the progenitors of modern turbellarians, it is significant to know that the ability to engage in ecto- and endosymbiosis is still present in the turbellarian stock.

CLASS TREMATODA

All trematodes are parasitic monozoic flatworms. The class is divided into three orders—Aspidobothrea, Monogenea, and Digenea. The endoparasitic aspidobothrid trematodes lack an oral sucker but possess an enormous ventral holdfast organ—the opisthaptor—that occupies the entire ventral body surface and is usually subdivided into compartments. No paired anterior adhesive structures or hooks are present. The single nephridiopore, or excretory pore, is located posteriorly.

The ecto- or endoparasitic monogenetic trematodes may or may not possess an oral sucker. If one is present, it is weakly developed. A large attachment organ—also known as an opisthaptor—armed with hooks is present at the posterior end of the body of monogenetic trematodes. Generally, a pair of adhesive structures are located at the anterior end. The anterodorsal excretory pores are paired.

The endoparasitic digenetic trematodes all possess a well developed oral sucker. In addition, a second sucker is present on most species. The suckers are not armed with hooks. Generally, a single posterior excretory pore is present. Unlike the monogenetic trematodes, which only contain a few large eggs in their uteri, the uterus of digenetic trematodes is long and contains numerous eggs.

All trematodes are obligatory parasites as adults. If a free-living phase occurs during their larval development, it lasts for an extremely short period. For example, the onchomiracidia of monogenetic trematodes and the miracidia and cercariae of certain digenetic trematodes are free-swimming for relatively short periods, but these larvae must reach a suitable host before further development can occur.

ORDER ASPIDOBOTHREA

The Aspidobothrea, sometimes referred to as the Aspidogastrea or the Aspidocotylea, includes relatively few species of flatworms, which have been considered by various authorities as members of either the Digenea or the Monogenea. However, Faust and Tang (1936) and Williams (1942) have advocated recognition of the aspidobothrids as a trematode group distinct from both the Digenea and the Monogenea. This interpretation has become widely accepted, for although the aspidobothrids undoubtedly resemble members of each of the other orders, they are sufficiently different so as to be readily identified.*

Aspidobothrids are primarily endoparasites of poikilothermic vertebrates and invertebrates, both fresh-water and marine, but they are most commonly encountered in molluscs, specifically pelecypods and gastropods. The common species, *Aspidogaster conchicola,* is often seen in fresh-water clams of the genera *Unio* and *Anodonta.* Sometimes as many as 15 to 20 specimens can be seen surrounding the heart

---

*The opinion of Stunkard (1962) is expressed in the footnote on p. 193.

through the transparent pericardium. Ecto-parasitic species of aspidobothrids are also known.

MORPHOLOGY

All aspidobothrids are readily recognized by the large, oval, ventral sucker—the opisthaptor—that covers the entire ventral surface of the body. The opisthaptor is an extremely strong holdfast organ by which the animal is attached to its host. This sucker is generally subdivided by septa into one to several longitudinal rows of depressions known as alveoli. The number and arrangement of the alveoli are important as taxonomic tools.

The anterior end of the body tapers to a somewhat blunted terminal, where the mouth is located. The mouth is funnel shaped, with the wide end opening externally. Although an oral sucker is said to be absent, such species as *Aspidogaster conchicola* and *A. limacoides* possess a band of muscles that surrounds the mouth, giving the appearance of a rudimentary oral sucker.

The mouth opens into a prepharynx (mouth tube), which in turn leads into a muscular pharynx. The pharynx opens into a long, blind-sac intestinal caecum that in most species terminates near the posterior end of the body. The caecum is lined with a layer of columnar epithelium that is surrounded externally by two thin layers of muscles—an inner longitudinal and an outer circular layer.

Reproductive Systems

The aspidobothrids are monoecious. The reproductive organs resemble those of digenetic trematodes, but the male system generally includes one testis, although two are found in some species. The posteriorly located testis leads into the seminal vesicle via the vas deferens. Spermatozoa are expelled from the system through the copulatory organ—the cirrus. The cirrus may protrude through the cuticularized genital atrium to the outside by the ventral genital pore at the anterior margin of the opisthaptor. In some genera, such as *Cotylaspis* and *Aspidogaster,* a cirrus sac surrounds the seminal vesicle and the cirrus; in other genera, such as *Lissemysia,* such a sac is absent.

The female system consists of a single ovary located anterior to the testis(es), near the mid-length of the body. The ovary, like that of monogenetic trematodes, is commonly folded. Leading from the ovary is the oviduct, which enters the ootype—an enlargement in the oviduct where the definitive egg is formed.

Three ducts are connected to the ootype or to a portion of the oviduct near the ootype: (1) The vitelline duct, which leads into the ootype, originates from the union of the left and right vitelline ducts coming from the vitelline glands. (2) The Laurer's canal, which originates at the ootype, is a long tube that runs posteriorly and ends blindly in the parenchyma or empties into the excretory vesicle, as in *Aspidogaster limacoides.* (3) The uterus leads from the ootype to the common genital atrium.

The aspidobothrid oviduct is unique in that it is lined with ciliated epithelium. Presumably, ciliary motion facilitates passage of ova into the ootype. It has been postulated by Dawes (1946) that the Laurer's canal is a reservoir for excess shell material, thus preventing the blockage of the oviduct, vitelline duct, and uterus by such matter. Another interpretation is that this canal is a vestigial vagina. The vitelline glands are distributed as two lateral groups and function identically to those found in the other trematodes and cestodes (p. 236).

Both self-fertilization and cross fertilization between two individuals are possible among the Aspidobothrea. During copulation, the worm inserts the cirrus either to its own uterus or into the uterus of its mate. The spermatozoa are introduced down the uterus to the ootype, where fertilization takes place. In living specimens, motile sperm can sometimes be seen along the length of the uterus, and for this reason the uterus is considered a uterine seminal receptacle.

Osmoregulatory System

The osmoregulatory (excretory) system of these worms is composed of flame cells and collecting tubes. However, the protonephridia have separate excretory vesicles that empty to the outside through either separate pores or through a common pore located on the dorsal surface of the body near the posterior extremity.

Body Tissues

The body surface of the Aspidobothrea, as in all parasitic trematodes and cestodes, is covered with a thin layer of cuticle. Immediately underlying the cuticle are four strata of mus-

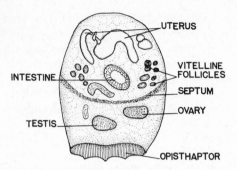

Plate 8-6   Aspidobothrea morphology. Transverse section through region of testis of *Aspidogaster conchicola,* showing muscular septum. (Modified after Stafford, 1895.)

cles. (1) The outermost layer is of circularly arranged muscles. (2) The underlying layer of longitudinal muscles is unique inasmuch as the striated cytoplasm is limited to the periphery of each fiber. Hence, they are sometimes described as shallow longitudinal muscles. (3) Next comes a layer of diagonal muscles. (4) The last layer is of circularly arranged myofibers. All these muscles have their origin and insertion in the cuticle. The spaces between the body wall and the internal organs are packed with parenchyma. In the anterior and posterior regions, dorsoventral muscles extend through the parenchyma.

Unique among some aspidobothrids, such as *Taeniocotyle,* is a deep bowl shaped muscular septum that divides the animal into upper and lower regions (Plate 8-6). This septum is composed of an upper layer of transverse muscles and a lower layer of longitudinal muscles. The partition is situated so that the upper cavity contains the intestinal caecum, the extremities of the reproductive ducts, and the vitelline glands, while the lower cavity contains the gonads. The function of this septum is unclear, although it has been suggested that the contraction and extension of the myofibers create a current in the parenchyma that causes the body fluids to circulate.

ASPIDOBOTHREAN SYSTEMATICS AND BIOLOGY

All known aspidobothrids have been systematically catalogued by Yamaguti (1963).

Some authorities recognize two families in the order Aspidobothrea. However, the author follows Dawes (1946) and recognizes only the Aspidogastridae. By far the most common

genus in North America is *Aspidogaster,* which is recognized by its four rows of alveoli (Plate 8-7, Fig. 1). Other genera include *Cotylogaster,* which possesses two testes and three rows of alveoli and is found in the intestine of fishes; the ectoparasitic *Cotylaspis,* also with three rows of alveoli but with only a single testis (Plate 8-7, Figs. 2 and 3). Some species of *Cotylaspis* have been reported from the intestine of turtles and the branchial chamber of bivalves. *Multicotyle* was reported from the river turtle *Siebenrochiella crassicollis,* in England (Plate 8-7, Fig. 4). This unusual species possesses 2 testes and 144 alveoli. The genus *Lophotaspis* is different inasmuch as the septa of the opisthaptor bear numerous sensory papillae (Plate 8-7, Fig. 5). In most aspidobothrids, such flasklike sensory bodies are present along the outer edges of the alveoli (Plate 8-7, Fig. 6). The genus *Stichocotyle* includes elongate forms that parasitize the bile ducts or spiral valves of skates (Plate 8-7, Fig. 7).

Life History of *Aspidogaster conchicola*— a One-host Cycle

Only a few life cycles are known among the Aspidobothrea. Williams (1942) reported that the larva of *Aspidogaster conchicola* develops in utero. The larva escapes from the shell (capsule) when laid. It lacks swimming organs and is sluggish. During development, two suckers are formed on the body—one anteriorly and the other posteroventrally. The anterior sucker is larger than the posterior sucker. Larvae at this stage of development are taken into another clam through its incurrent siphon. These eventually enter the renal pore and migrate through the kidney to the pericardial cavity, where they continue their development.

As development progresses, the posteroventral sucker increases in size, eventually covers the entire ventral surface of the worm's body, becomes partitioned by septa, and takes on the form of the definitive opisthaptor. The anterior sucker remains inconspicuous, forming the muscular ring around the mouth of the adult— hence the contention that there is a true oral sucker among these aspidobothrids. The life cycle is direct, without an intermediate host. However, Williams noted that if parasitized clams are ingested by fish, frogs, or turtles, the parasites are liberated in the intestine of these poikilothermic hosts, and these thus become potential hosts. Stages in the life cycle of *A. conchicola* are depicted in Plate 8-8.

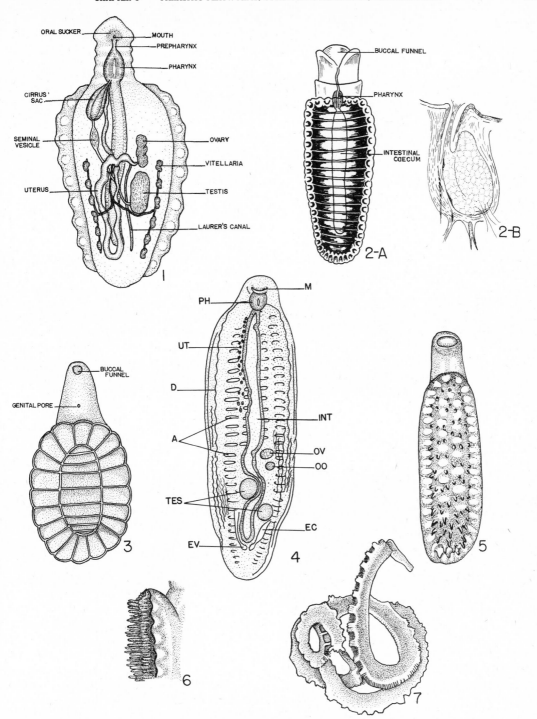

Plate 8-7   Some aspidobothrid trematodes. 1. *Aspidogaster conchicola.* (Original.) **2. A.** *Cotylogaster* sp. (Redrawn and modified after Hyman, 1949. *The Invertebrates,* McGraw-Hill, New York.) **B.** Longitudinal section of sense organ of sucker margin of *Cotylogaster.* (Redrawn after Nickerson, 1902.) **3.** *Cotylaspis* sp. (Redrawn after Osborn, 1903.) **4.** *Multicotyle purvisi,* dorsal view. (A, alveoli of outer rows; D, disc of adhesive apparatus; EC, excretory canal; EV, excretory vesicle; INT, intestine; OO, ootype; OV, ovary; PH, pharynx; UT, uterus.) (Redrawn after Dawes.) **5.** *Lophotaspis* sp., ventral view. (Redrawn from photograph by Ward and Hopkins, 1931.) **6.** Sensory papillae on margin of opisthaptor of *Lophotaspis.* (Original.) **7.** *Stichocotyle cristata.* (Redrawn from photograph by Faust and Tang, 1936.)

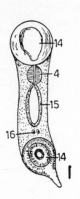
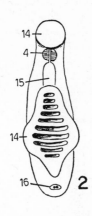
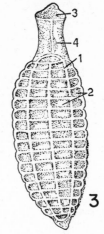

Plate 8-8   Developmental stages of *Aspidogaster*. 1 and 2. Larval stages of *Aspidogaster*. (After Veeltzow, 1888.) 3. Adult of *Aspidogaster conchicola*. (After Monticelli, 1892.)

(1, sucker; 2, alveoli; 3, mouth funnel; 4, pharynx; 14, larval suckers; 15, intestine; 16, nephridiopore.)

An alternative life cycle pattern for *A. conchicola* is possible. Eggs passing out of adults in the pericardium of clams may hatch immediately. The escaping larvae begin developing within the pericardium and reach the sexually mature stage therein, thus never leaving the host.

Van Cleave and Williams (1943), in an attempt to determine whether turtles can serve as hosts, introduced *A. conchicola* into the stomach of a turtle and found that the parasites clung to the host's stomach wall and lived for 14 days. The results of Van Cleave and Williams are not particularly surprising since adults of certain other species of *Aspidogaster*—*A. limacoides*, for example—have been found to naturally infect poikilothermic vertebrates in the form of fresh-water and marine fishes in addition to molluscs. This suggests that these aspidobothrids may have originally been parasites of molluscs but have more recently become adapted to poikilothermic vertebrates, resulting from ingestion of infected molluscs. *Aspidogaster limacoides* is found in the intestine of various fishes in the Caspian Sea and the Volga delta.

Life Histories of *Lophotaspis* and *Stichocotyle*—Two-host Cycles

Wharton (1939) demonstrated that *Lophotaspis* requires an intermediate host. The larva lives in a marine snail that is ingested by a turtle in which the parasite develops into the adult form. Cunningham (1887), Nickerson (1895), and Odhner (1910) all concluded that in *Stichocotyle nephropsis*, a parasite of skates, the larva dwells in the intestine of lobsters and develops into the adult only when the intermediate host is ingested by the skate.

It is obvious from the few life cycles presented why some authorities have considered the Aspidobothrea to be akin to the Monogenea and why others considered them closely related to the Digenea. Morphologically, these worms are quite distinct from the members of either order, but their life cycles are either direct—without an intermediate host—as in *Aspidogaster conchicola*, or indirect—with an intermediate host—as in *Lophotaspis* and *Stichocotyle*.

Although certain aspidobothrids require intermediate hosts, the parasite does not undergo asexual multiplication within intermediate hosts as is the case in digenetic trematodes. The similarities between the aspidobothrids and digenetic and monogenetic trematodes suggest their proximity in phylogenetic relationship to one or the other. All this only serves to strengthen the argument that the use of a single characteristic is often insufficient in determining the taxonomic position of animals. Often both morphology and physiological evidences must be utilized.

ASPIDOBOTHREAN PHYSIOLOGY AND HOST-PARASITE RELATIONSHIP

Practically nothing is known concerning the physiology of the Aspidobothrea. In an attempt to understand the nutritional needs of *Aspidogaster conchicola*, Van Cleave and Williams (1945) maintained specimens in mussel blood at 2 to 9° C. and found that they could be maintained for 75 days. This was a startling discovery because endoparasites such as the digenetic trematodes could hardly be maintained in this fashion. This comparatively successful maintenance of *A. conchicola* in vitro strongly suggests that the aspidobothrids are not "entrenched" endoparasites—hence another argument for their affinity to the ectoparasitic Monogenea.

Several investigators, including the author, have noticed that *Aspidogaster*-infected clams display a less healthy appearance. As to exactly how this parasite affects the host remains to be determined.

Osborn (1905) reported that the excretory vesicle of the ectoparasitic species *Cotylaspis insignis* pulsates rapidly, excreting water, thus indicating that the protonephritic system probably serves primarily as an osmoregulatory system. However, most investigators believe that the protonephritic system serves as dual function—that of osmoregulation as well as excretion.

LITERATURE CITED

Bueding, E., and S. Koletsky. 1950. Content and distribution of glycogen in *Schistosoma mansoni*. Proc. Soc. Exp. Biol. Med., *73:* 594–596.

Cheng, T. C. 1963. Biochemical requirements of larval trematodes. Ann. N.Y. Acad. Sci., *113:* 289–320.

Cheng, T. C., and D. V. Provenza. 1960. Studies of cellular elements of the mesenchyma and of tissues of *Haematoloechus confusus* Ingles, 1932 (Trematoda). Trans Amer. Micro. Soc., *79:* 170–179.

Cunningham, J. T. 1887. On *Stichocotyle nephropsis,* a new trematode. Trans. Roy. Soc. Edinburgh, *32:* 273–280.

Dawes, B. 1946. The Trematoda. Cambridge Univ. Press.

Faust, E. C., and C. C. Tang. 1936. Notes on new aspidogastrid species with a consideration of the phylogeny of the group. Parasitology, *28:* 487–501.

Flury, F., and F. Leeb. 1926. Zur Chemie und Toxikologie der Distomen (Leberegel). Klin. Wchnschr., *5:* 2054–2055.

Kent, F-H. N. 1947. Études biochimiques sur les proteines des *Moniezia* parasites intestinaux du mouton. Bul. Soc. Neuchâtel Sc. Nat., *70:* 85–108.

Kozloff, E. N. 1953. *Collastoma pacifica* sp. nov., a rhabdocoel turbellarian from the gut of *Dendrostoma pyroides* Chamberlin. J. Parasit., *39:* 336–340.

Nickerson, W. S. 1895. On *Stichocotyle nephropsis* Cunningham, a parasite of the American lobster. Zool. Jahrb., *8:* 447–480.

Odhner, T. 1910. *Stichocotyle nephropsis* J. T. Cunningham ein aberranter Trematode der Digenenfamilie Aspidogastridae. K. Svenska Vetensk. Acad. Handl., *45:* 3–16.

Odlaug, T. O. 1949. The finer structure of the body wall and parenchyma of three species of digenetic trematodes. Trans. Amer. Micro. Soc., *67:* 236–253.

Osborn, H. L. 1905. On the habits and structure of *Cotylaspis insignis* Leidy, from Lake Chautauqua, New York, U. S. A. Zool. Jahrb., *21:* 201–242.

Pratt, H. S. 1909. The cuticula and subcuticula of trematodes and cestodes. Am. Nat., *43:* 705–729.

Reid, W. M. 1942. Certain nutritional requirements of the fowl cestode *Raillietina cesticillus* (Molin) as demonstrated by short periods of starvation of the host. J. Parasit., *28:* 319–340.

Salisbury, L. F., and R. J. Anderson. 1939. Concerning the chemical composition of *Cysticercus fasciolaris.* J. Biol. Chem., *129:* 505–517.

Smorodintsev, I. A., and K. V. Bebesin. 1936. Beiträge zur Chemie der *Helminthen.* Mitt. IV. Die chemische Zusammensetzung des *Diphyllobothrium latum.* J. Biochem., *23:* 21–22.

Smorodintsev, I. A., K. V. Bebesin, and P. I. Pavlova. 1933. Beiträge zur Chemie der Helminthen. I. Mitteilung: Die chemische Zusammensetzung von *Taenia saginata.* Biochem. Ztschr., *261:* 176–178.

Stunkard, H. W. 1931. Further observations on the occurrence of anal openings in digenetic trematodes. Ztschr. Parasit., *3:* 713–725.

Stunkard, H. W. 1962. *Taeniocotyle* nom. nov. for *Macraspis* Olsson, 1869, preoccupied, and systematic position of the Aspidobothrea. Biol. Bull., *122:* 137–148.

Tötterman, G., and E. Kirk. 1939. Om innehallet av lipoider i *Bothriocephalus latus.* Nord. med., *3:* 2715–2716.

Van Cleave, H. J., and C. O. Williams. 1943. Maintenance of a trematode, *Aspidogaster conchicola,* outside the body of its natural host. J. Parasit., *29:* 127–130.

von Brand, T. 1933. Untersuchungen über den Stoffbestand einiger Cestoden und den Stoffwechsel von *Moniezia expansa.* Ztschr. Vergleich Physiol., *18:* 562–596.

von Brand, T. 1952. Chemical Physiology of Endoparasitic Animals. Academic Press, New York.

Weinland, E. 1901. Ueber den Glykogengehalt einiger parasitischer Würmer. Ztschr. Biol. *41:* 69–74.

Weinland, E., and T. von Brand. 1926. Beobachtungen an *Fasciola hepatica*. (Stoffwechsel und Lebensweise). Ztschr. Vergleich Physiol., *4:* 212–285.

Wharton, G. W. 1939. Studies on *Lophotaspis vallei* (Stossich, 1899) (Trematoda: Aspidogas tridae). J. Parasit., *25:* 83–86.

Williams, C. O. 1942. Observations on the life history and taxonomic relationships of the trematode *Aspidogaster conchicola*. J. Parasit., *28:* 467–475.

Yamaguti, S. 1963. Systema Helminthum. Vol. 4. Monogenea and Aspidocotylea. John Wiley New York.

SUGGESTED READING

Baer, J. G. 1952. Ecology of Animal Parasites. University of Illinois Press, Urbana, Ill., pp 34–35. (This is a general discussion of parasitic turbellarians. The literature cited can indicate to the student where to look for further detailed information.)

Dawes, B. 1946. The Trematoda. Cambridge University Press, London, pp. 37–44. (This is an excellent review of the taxonomy and biology of the Aspidobothrea.)

Hyman, L. H. 1951. The Invertebrates: Platyhelminthes and Rhynchocoela. The Acoelomat Bilateria. McGraw-Hill, New York, pp. 248–250. (This is also a review of the Aspidoboth rea. The material devoted to the morphology and basic biology of this group other than taxonomy is emphasized.)

Stunkard, H. W. 1962. *Taeniocotyle* nom. nov. for *Macraspis* Olsson, 1869, preoccupied, an systematic position of the Aspidobothrea. Biol. Bull., *122:* 137–148. (Aside from the discus sion concerning the substitution of a generic name, this article should prove to be e interest to the student from the standpoint of the classification of aspidobothrids.)

THE MONOGENEA—
The Monogenetic Trematodes

The monogenetic trematodes, or mono-geneids, are a group of flukes that as a rule are ectoparasitic in nature, infesting poikilothermic vertebrates. A few species, however, have been reported to be attached to mammals, crusta-ceans, and cephalopods. At least three species are known to be true endoparasites—*Dictyocotyle* sp. in the coelom of the ray *Raja lintea, Acolpen-teron ureterocetes* in the ureters of fresh-water fish, and *Polystoma integerrimum* in the bladder of amphibians. The affinity of *P. integerrimum* for the bladder represents one of the unsolved problems of parasitism—that of host and tissue specificity. Other species are known to be present in bladders, buccal cavities, and other body spaces that open directly to the exterior.

As ectoparasites, the monogeneids are usually attached to the gills, scales, and fins of fish hosts. In many cases the parasites show a marked preference for a particular gill or gills. For example, *Diclidophora merlangi* attaches most frequently on the first gill of the whiting, *D. luscae* favors the second and third gill of the pout. All species attached to gills take up the same general position while attached. Llewellyn

(1956) reported that the posterior terminal of the parasite is located closer to the host's gill arch, and the anterior end of the parasite is closer to the distal end of the host's primary lamellae. The mouth of the parasite in all instances faces downwards.

Serious students of the Monogenea should consult the extensive monograph of Bychowsky (1957).

MORPHOLOGY

Members of the order Monogenea possess the characteristics of the phylum Platyhel-minthes and the class Trematoda, both given in Chapter 8. In addition to these distinguish-ing features, monogeneids possess characteristic holdfast suckers, paired excretory pores that are located anteriorly on the dorsal surface of the body, and comparatively short uteri con-taining few eggs. Above all, they have direct life cycles that do not include intermediate hosts.

Generally the monogeneids are medium-sized animals when compared with the other monozoic platyhelminths. These worms seldom exceed 3 cm. in length.

Body Suckers

The monogeneids superficially are not unlike the digenetic trematodes, except for the presence of a posteriorly situated adhesive structure—the opisthaptor—by which the parasite is attached to its host. The opisthaptor is undoubtedly the most specialized of the various types of attachment organs found among platyhelminths. This large, circular, muscular disc generally is separated, completely or partially, into smaller suckers by septa (Plate 9–1, Fig. 1).

In the family Gyrodactylidae no secondary divisions are present, but the opisthaptor does bear two to four large hooks known as anchors, which are accompanied by auxiliary smaller haptoral hooks. A single anchor is subdivided into the root, which is the proximal portion, normally forked, and embedded in the body tissue; the shaft, which is the more or less straight portion protruding from the embedded zone; and the base, which is the shorter portion that forms the junction between the root and the shaft (Plate 9–1, Fig. 2). In addition to the anchors and haptoral hooks, some species have transversely situated sclerotized bars. These bars may or may not articulate with the anchors (Plate 9–1, Fig. 3).

Anchors, haptoral hooks, and bars are not limited to the Gyrodactylidae, for all monogeneids possess anchors and hooks at some stage during their development. Many species possess various numbers of small suckers divided by septa, ranging from 6 to 240 depending on the species. These small suckers are armed with anchors and hooks. In some monogeneids, such as the Polyopisthocotylea, there is a single cotylophore, which bears multiple suckers or clamps. Plate 9–2 depicts several types of opisthaptors found on monogenetic trematodes.

Llewellyn (1958) made comparative studies on nine species of the genus *Diclidophora* (Polyopisthocotylea). He reported that in these species there are both a pair of hinged jaws in each sucker operated by intrinsic muscles, and a more powerful extrinsic muscle that acts on a diaphragm, producing suction that is converted into a clamping action.

In addition to the opisthaptor, monogeneids usually possess two anteriorly located auxiliary

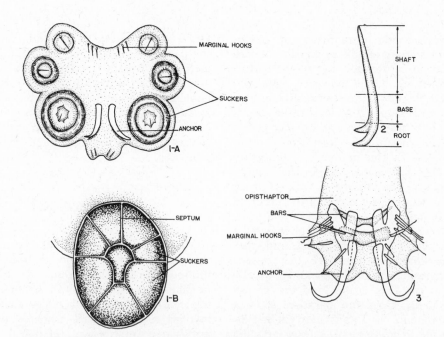

Plate 9–1   Some morphological features of monogeneids. 1. A. Opisthaptor of *Polystoma* showing various structures. (Redrawn after Zeder, 1872.) **B.** Opisthaptor of *Tristoma* showing various structures. (Redrawn after Goto, 1894.) **2.** A single anchor showing the three regions. (Original.) **3.** Posterior end of *Dactylogyrus* showing various structures; notice the bars. (Redrawn after Mueller and Van Cleave, 1932.)

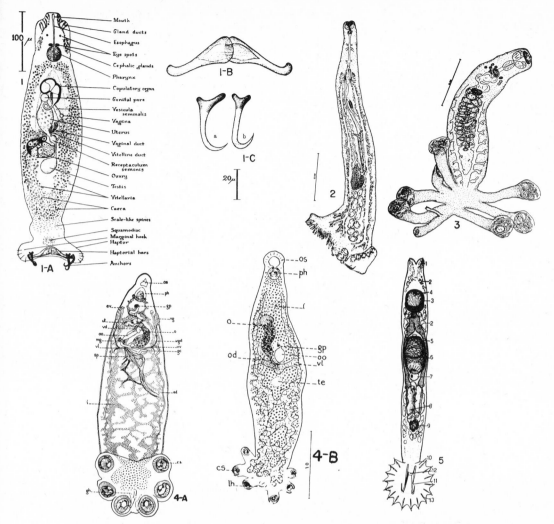

Plate 9-2   Several species of monogeneids showing various types of opisthaptors.
1. A. *Diplectanum melanesiensis* from the serranid fish *Epinephelus merra.* **B.** Scalelike spines of posterior
part of body. **C.** Dorsal (a) and ventral (b) anchors. (After Laird.) **2.** *Axinoides raphidoma* from Gulf
of Mexico fishes. (After Hargis.) **3.** *Choricotyle louisianensis* from gills of the Southern whiting. (After
Hargis.) **4.** *Polystoma integerrimum nearcticum* from the urinary bladder of the tree-frog *Hyla versicolor.*
A. Bladder generation. **B.** Gill generation. (A and B after Paul.) **5.** *Gyrodactylus* sp. (1, anterior adhesive organ; 2, adhesive glands; 3, pharynx; 4, mouth; 5, intestine; 6, embryo; 7, uncleaved egg;
8, ovary; 9, testis; 10, opisthaptor; 11, anchors; 12, bar; 13, marginal hooks.) (After Mueller and
Van Cleave, 1932.)

suckers—the prohaptors—situated one on each
side of the mouth. The prohaptors may appear
as pits, suckers, or discs.

Alimentary Tract

The internal anatomy of a monogenetic
trematode is depicted in Plate 9–3, Fig. 2. The
mouth is located at the anterior end of the
body, flanked on each side by a prohaptor. In
some species, such as *Discocotyle sagittata,* a
parasite of trout and salmon, the prohaptors

are modified as buccal suckers and are located
in the buccal funnel, which is that tube leading from the mouth (Plate 9–3, Fig. 3). In
some species the buccal funnel is protrusible,
and if such is the case, the true mouth lies as
the base of the funnel when it is withdrawn.
The mouth is seldom surrounded by an oral
sucker as in digenetic trematodes (Plate 9–3,
Fig. 1).

Head glands and head organs are commonly
present. The secretions of the glands and the

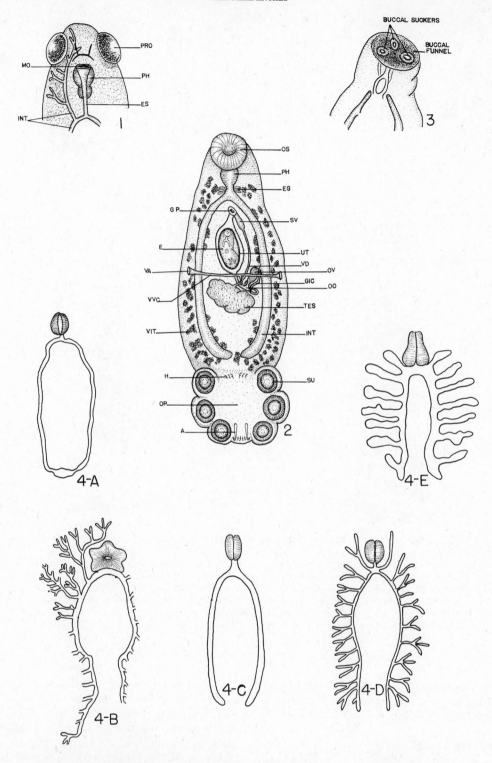

Plate 9-3   **Anatomical features of monogenetic trematodes. 1.** Anterior end of *Tristoma,*
parasitic on the gills of swordfish. (ES, esophagus; INT, intestinal caeca; MO, mouth; PH, pharynx;
PRO, prohaptors.) (Redrawn and modified after Goto, 1894.) **2.** *Polystomoidella oblongum,* parasitic
in the urinary bladder of turtles. (A, anchors; E, egg enclosing embryo; EG, esophageal glands;
GIC, genitointestinal canal; GP, genital pore; H, hooks; INT, intestinal caeca; OO, ootype; OV,

(*Legend continued on opposite page.*)

adhesive nature of the organs suggest that these function primarily as auxiliary attachment organs. Near the suckers, certain gland cells are frequently present in the body wall, and these cells secrete into the prohaptors and opisthaptors.

The buccal funnel leads into the muscular pharynx, which in turn leads into the esophagus. The intestinal tract most frequently is in the form of an inverted Y, with the caeca bifurcating from the posterior extremity of the esophagus which represents the stem of the Y. Modifications of this pattern are known.

In *Dactylogyrus amphibothrium* and related species, the two caeca are not only united posteriorly, but possess side branches (diverticula). In *Udonella*,* the gut is unbranched and resembles a single blind tube with fenestrations in the region of the gonads. In *Polystoma* and *Diclidophora*, the caeca not only give rise to numerous diverticula, but some of these actually extend into the disc shaped opisthaptor. Plate 9–3 depicts some of the intestinal tract variations found among the Monogenea.

The intestinal caeca are lined with epithelial cells that are either closely packed or sparsely arranged. As Dawes (1946) pointed out, much more can be done concerning histological studies of the intestinal lining of these worms.

Monogeneids feed primarily on blood, sloughed epithelial cells, and mucus, but they can undoubtedly also derive oxygen, and probably other chemicals, from the aquatic environment in which they are bathed. Hence, the body wall is important as an absorptive layer.

Although nothing is known about the digestive enzymes present, a black pigment is often produced that is a breakdown product of ingested haemoglobin.

---

*Bychowsky (1957) doubts that *Udonella* is a true monogenetic trematode.

Tissues of the Body Wall

The body surface of monogenetic trematodes is covered by a thin layer of noncellular cuticle (Plate 9–4, Fig. 1). The cells responsible for the secretion of the cuticle are not readily visible in the Monogenea. It is suspected that these cuticle-secreting cells (comparable to the secreting beta cells of the Digenea) have sunk into the parenchyma. Immediately beneath the protective cuticle is a thin layer of circular muscles, which may be absent in certain species.

Underneath the circularly arranged muscles is found a thin stratum of diagonally arranged muscles (the diagonal muscles), and beneath this second layer is a thick layer of well developed longitudinal muscles. The region between the body wall and the internal organs is packed with a loose parenchyma consisting of cells, fibrils, and spaces. The cellular elements are generally independent and not syncytially arranged. In certain species, however, the cellular elements situated toward the center are discrete, while those located in the periphery are syncytially arranged.

If the inner and outer parenchyma are separated, the medial zone is termed the medullary parenchyma and the outer zone the cortical parenchyma. Little is known concerning the finer structure of the parenchyma of monogenetic trematodes. The parenchyma serves as a site of glycogen storage.

Nervous System

The nervous system in the Monogenea generally consists of two large clusters of nerve ganglia and cells, both of which are situated at the anterior end of the body. These two nerve masses are connected by a transverse commissure (Plate 9–4, Fig. 2). From this primitive "brain," nerve fibers arise and extend anteriorly, laterally, and posteriorly. These nerve trunks are scattered throughout the parenchyma but

---

(*Legend continued.*)
ovary; OS, oral sucker; PH, pharynx; SU, suckers; SV, seminal vesicle; TES, testis; UT, uterus; VD, vas deferens; VIT, vitellaria; VVC, vitellovaginal canal.) (Modified after Cable, 1958.) **3.** Anterior end of *Discocotyle sagittata,* parasitic on the gills of sea trout and salmon, showing buccal suckers located within buccal funnel. (Redrawn and modified after Dawes, 1947.) **4. A.** Arrangement of intestinal caeca of *Sphyranura,* parasitic on the gills of *Necturus.* (Original.) **B.** Pattern of intestinal caeca of *Benedenia melleni.* (Modified after Jahn and Kuhn, 1932.) **C.** Pattern of intestinal caeca of *Thaumatocotyle concinna,* attached to the nasal fossae of the stingray. (Modified after Price, 1938.) **D.** Pattern of intestinal caeca of *Microbothrium apiculatum,* attached to the skin of the piked dogfish. (Modified after Price, 1938.) **E.** Pattern of intestinal caeca of *Leptobothrium pristiuri,* attached to the skin of the black-mouthed dogfish. (Modified after Gallien, 1937.)

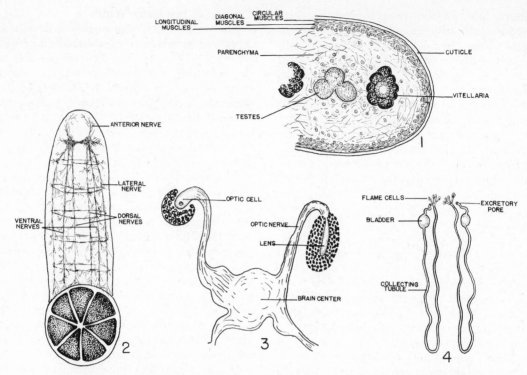

Plate 9-4   Morphology of trematodes (Monogenea). 1. Cross section of *Sphyranura* sp., showing the histology of the body wall. (Original.) **2.** Generalized drawing of a monogenetic trematode, showing arrangement of the body nerves. (Original.) **3.** Section through a young *Cercaria pellucida* (Digenea), showing relation of pigment cup to nerve ending in the paired lateral eyespots. (Redrawn after Faust, 1918.) **4.** Arrangement of the excretory system found in most monogenetic trematodes. (Original.)

especially in the ventral, lateral, and dorsal regions.

In some species, such as certain members of the Polystomatidae and Capsalidae, the "brain" is arranged in a well formed circumesophageal ring. Nerve fibers extend from this ring anteriorly, laterally, and posteriorly, one pair being dorsal, one pair ventrolateral, and one pair ventral. The ventral nerves, which are the most highly developed, are often connected by a series of transverse commissures. Branches of the nerve fibers innervate the various sucker muscles and other portions of the body.

In the Monogenea, one or two pairs of eye spots are commonly present and in most cases are comparable to those found in certain digenetic trematode cercariae. Each eye is composed of a rounded retinal cell surrounded by rods made up of pigment granules (Plate 9-4, Fig. 3). In a few complex forms, a simple lens is present.

Nervous systems among the monogeneids reach an extremely complex condition in members of the genus *Tristoma*, in which a rudimentary type of taste organ is present.

Osmoregulatory System

The osmoregulatory (excretory) system among the monogenetic trematodes, like that found in the other platyhelminths, is of the protonephritic type—with flame cells at the end of collecting tubules. Although a mesh like network of tubules has been reported, the general rule is the presence of two main lateral tubes that begin anteriorly and extend posteriorly. Each tube makes a U curve prior to reaching the posterior end of the body and then extends anteriorly (Plate 9-4, Fig. 4).

Toward the end of each ascending tube, there is a swelling known as the contractile bladder. The tubes leaving the bladders empty to the outside through two separate excretory pores (nephridiopores) situated dorsolateral to the mouth. The flame cells are located at the free ends of branches of these main collecting tubes.

Because of the usual opaqueness and thickness of the bodies of these worms, detailed studies of the osmoregulatory system, resulting in flame cell patterns as known among the Digenea (p. 237), are not so easily achieved.

Reproductive System

THE MALE SYSTEM. The male system contains either one testis, as in *Thaumatocotyle, Heterocotyle,* and *Leptocotyle,* or two or three testes, as in *Entobdella* and *Monocotyle* (Plate 9–5, Figs. 1 to 5). Some genera are multitesticular—members of *Tritestis* possess three testes, and members of *Rajonchocotyle* possess 200 testes.

The primitive number was probably two, as in the Digenea.

A single vas efferens arises from each testis. These unite to form the common vas deferens, which proceeds to either a cirrus (a protrusible and eversible copulatory structure) or a penis (only protrusible). Prior to entering the cirrus or penis, the vas deferens is enlarged in certain species to form the seminal vesicle.

Generally, the cirrus opens to the outside through a genital atrium located on the ventral surface of the body behind the caecal bifurcation. In some species, the female reproductive system also leads into this chamber, hence

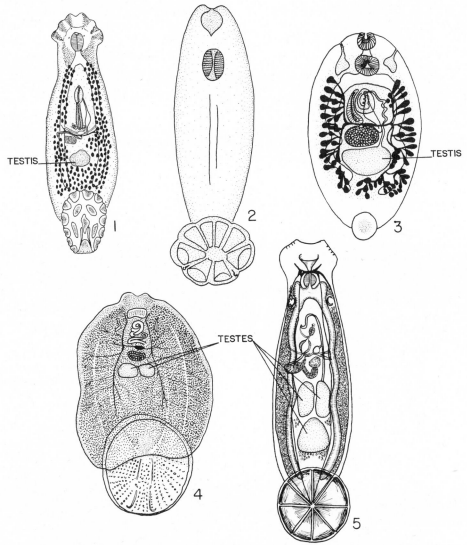

Plate 9–5   Some monogenetic trematodes. 1. *Thaumatocotyle dasybatis* (Monopisthocotylea), showing single testis. (Redrawn after Price, 1938.) 2. *Heterocotyle pastinacae* (Monopisthocotylea) with single testis that is not shown. (Redrawn after Scott, 1904.) 3. *Leptocotyle minor* (Monopisthocotylea), showing single testis. (Redrawn after Johnstone, 1911.) 4. *Entobdella hippoglossi* (Monopisthocotylea) with two testes. (Redrawn and modified after Dawes, 1947.) 5. *Monocotyle* sp. (Monopisthocotylea), showing three testes. (Redrawn after Goto, 1894.)

a common atrium. The aperture of the atrium is the genital pore (gonopore).

The degree of development of the copulatory structure varies. In *Merizocotyle,* prostate glands empty into the cirrus. In *Udonella,* a definite cirrus or penis is lacking, self-fertilization being the rule. In *Microcotyle* and *Hexabothrium,* the end of the vas deferens is modified to form a pointed protruberance. In *Diclidophora* and others, the cirrus is armed with hooklets that aid in maintaining it in the atrium of the copulatory mate.

The reproductive systems of monogenetic trematodes are depicted in Plate 9–6.

THE FEMALE SYSTEM.   The female reproductive system contains a single ovary, the shape of which may range from globular to elongate and which is usually folded (Plate 9–6). In some species the ovary may even be lobed. The oviduct arises from the surface of the ovary. The exact positions of the junctions between the oviduct and the seminal receptacle, the common vitelline duct, the genitointestinal canal, and the vagina vary among the species. Generally these various ducts, which may not all be present, connect with the oviduct before it enlarges to form the ootype.

Unicellular glands, collectively known as the Mehlis' gland, surround and secrete into the ootype. The secretions of these glands apparently serve as a lubricant that facilitates the passage of completely formed eggs from the ootype up the uterus. The short uterus may possess a muscular terminal in some species. Such a muscular area is known as the metraterm. The terminal of the uterus opens into the genital atrium.

Functionally, the common vitelline duct is the tube through which the vitellarial materials (primarily shell-forming materials and some yolk) are carried into the oviduct. The seminal receptacle serves as a storage for spermatozoa received by the female system during copulation.

The genitointestinal canal, which is found only in members of the suborder Polyopisthocotylea, is a unique tube, connecting the oviduct with the right intestinal caecum. Its presence, although quite common, has not been satisfactorily explained. It is known, however, that a similar structure is present in many turbellarians, especially among the Polycladida. It has been postulated that the presence of this canal indicates that originally the eggs were discharged through the alimentary canal.

The vagina of the Monogenea is either single or double—that is, there may be one or a pair of copulation canals, which open to the outside through one or two pores located on the ventral, lateral, or dorsal surfaces of the body. The vaginal pore is independent of the uterine pore, or genital pore, if the uterus enters the common atrium.

In certain species there is an enlarged portion along the length of the vagina known as the seminal receptacle. This type of seminal receptacle represents a modification of the distinct blind-sac type which is independent of the vagina. If two vaginae are present, these may unite somewhere along their course.

The male cirrus is inserted in the vagina of the female during copulation and the spermatozoa are introduced down this tubular canal. Some monogeneids do not possess a separate vagina, in which case the uterine pore serves as the site of entrance for spermatozoa. The vitelline glands in monogeneids are generally

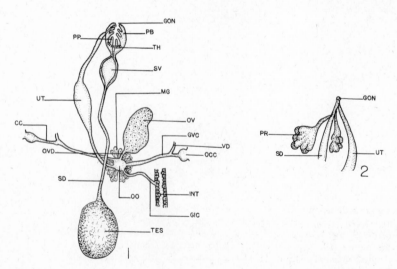

Plate 9-6   Male and female reproductive systems in monogeneids. 1. Reproductive systems of a monogenetic trematode. (CC, copulatory canal; GIC, genitointestinal canal; GON, gonopore; GVC, common genitovitelline canal; INT, intestine; MG, Mehlis' gland; OCC, opening of copulatory canal; OO, ootype; OV, ovary; OVD, oviduct; PB; penis bulb; PP, penis papilla; SD, sperm duct; SV, seminal vesicle; TES, testis; TH, thorns; UT, uterus; VD, vitelline duct.) (Original.) **2.** Terminal of another type of reproductive system as found among monogenetic trematodes. (GON, gonopore; PR, prostate glands; SD, sperm duct; UT, uterus.) (Original.)

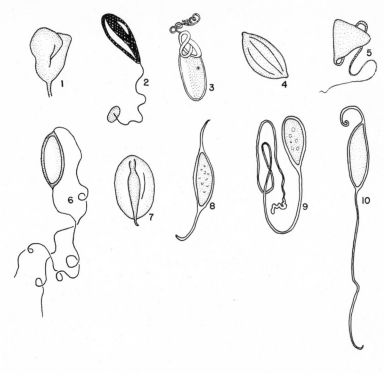

Plate 9-7   Types of eggs of monogenetic trematodes. 1. Egg of *Thaumatocotyle dasybatis,* parasitic in olfactory organs and gills of the stingray. (Redrawn after Price, 1938.) 2. Egg of *Udonella caligorum,* parasitic on various fishes. (Redrawn after Price, 1938.) 3. Egg of *Diplozoon paradoxum,* parasitic on gills of various fishes. (Redrawn after Dawes, 1946.) 4. Egg of *Rajonchocotyle alba,* parasitic on gills of the Burton skate. (Redrawn after Fuhrmann, 1928.) 5. Egg of *Nitzschia monticellii,* parasitic on gills of sturgeons. (Redrawn after Fuhrmann, 1928.) 6. Egg of *Squalonchocotyle apiculatum,* parasitic on fishes. (Redrawn after Fuhrmann, 1928.) 7. Egg of *Microbothrium apiculatum,* parasitic on piked dogfish and orkneys. (Redrawn after Price, 1938.) 8. Egg of *Erpocotyle laevis,* parasitic on gills of fish. (Redrawn after Guberlet, 1933.) 9. Egg of *Hexabothrium canicula,* parasitic on gills of fishes. (Redrawn after Guberlet, 1933.) 10. Egg of *Diclidophora denticulata,* parasitic on gills of fishes. (Redrawn after Dawes, 1947.)

follicular, lying in the two lateral zones. In *Gyrodactylus,* vitelline glands are absent. Instead, the ovary contains cells capable of performing the same function and hence is a germovitallarium.

Ova leaving the ovary are immediately fertilized and then pass on to the ootype, where the yolk material is laid down around it (except in *Gyrodactylus*), as is the shell or capsule. The typical shell of a monogeneid egg bears a lid-like cap (the operculum) at one end (Plate 9–10, Fig. 2). Fairly commonly, the eggs bear a filament at one or both ends by which they can become attached to the host or to each other in large masses after being laid (Plate 9–7). The smaller number of comparatively large eggs, generally one to twelve in the uterus of an individual worm, is quite characteristic of monogenetic trematodes. The shells are commonly yellow or brown and probably consist of a quinone-tanned protein as do those of digenetic trematodes.

GENERAL DEVELOPMENT AND LIFE CYCLE

Eggs lodged in the uterus are soon discharged through the genital pore. These eggs become attached to the host by means of the polar fila-

ment or filaments and hatch into ciliated larvae (onchomiracidia). The onchomiracidia become free-swimming and seek out a new host to which they become attached and gradually develop into adults.

In certain cases, such as *Polystoma integerrium,* the life cycle is slightly more complex, involving migration of the larvae through the host's alimentary tract. These larvae finally become lodged in the bladder, where they eventually reach maturity.

In *Diplozoon,* parasitic on various fishes, the larva hatching from the attached egg is known as the diporpa larva and becomes attached to the host's gills. Two such larvae become attached to each other in a cross fashion and remain in this position throughout life, even after reaching sexual maturity. The reproductive systems actually become interconnected.

In another curious group—the species of *Gyrodactylus,* commonly found on fresh-water fishes and amphibians—a form of polyembryony is found (Kathariner, 1904). Eggs laid by the members of this genus do not contain visible yolk and are fused within the uterus of the parent. During the unusual development, a second embryo is formed within the first, a third within the second, and a fourth within the third. When the first larva completes its development, it passes out of the parent and immediately becomes attached to the host. This larva soon develops into an adult, but the enclosed larval generations are maintained within.

Details of life cycles representative of the Monogenea are given in following pages. The important fact to keep in mind is that, despite several variations in the development patterns, an intermediate host is never required, and in this respect monogeneids differ from the digenetic trematodes.

A summary of monogeneid life histories is given by Bychowsky (1957).

SYSTEMATICS AND BIOLOGY

CLASSIFICATION

The taxonomy of the Monogenea has been monographed by Price (1937, 1938, 1939a,b, 1942, 1943a,b) and Sproston (1946), which list the species known up to 1943. Various new North American species have been reported since that time, primarily by Mizelle and his co-workers and by Hargis. The British and European forms have been adequately treated by Dawes (1946).

More recently, Yamaguti (1963) has contributed a comprehensive catalogue of all the known monogeneids.

According to Price, following the systematic interpretation of Odhner (1912), the order Monogenea is divided into two suborders—the Monopisthocotylea and the Polyopisthocotylea.

Suborder 1. Monopisthocotylea. Oral sucker is poorly developed or absent. Has prohaptors that take the form of small lateral pits or suckers, or has head organs. Opisthaptor is in the form of a disc or sucker, with or without radial septa, usually provided with one to three pairs of large hooks (anchors) and twelve to sixteen marginal hooks (hooklets). Genitointestinal canal is absent; eye spots are generally present.

Suborder 2. Polyopisthocotylea. Prohaptor either as oral sucker or as two distinct suckers opening into the oral cavity or as two lateral pits; opisthaptor, armed or unarmed, with a number of suckerlets or with clamps borne on a disc or on the ventral body surface; genitointestinal canal present; eye spots generally absent.

SUBORDER MONOPISTHOCOTYLEA

The absence of a genitointestinal canal and the absence of suckerlets or clamps on the single opisthaptor are considered the main distinguishing characteristics of the members of this suborder. However, other correlated characteristics, as listed above, are present.

Generally, a few adhesive glands are closely associated with the prohaptors. In fact in certain genera, such as *Dactylogyrus,* prohaptors are lacking, and the adhesive glands empty to the outside through ducts ending in bulbous terminals known as head organs.

The sizes and arrangements of the anchors and hooklets on the opisthaptor are important taxonomic characteristics.

Representative genera of the order Monopisthocotylea are depicted in Plate 9–8.

Several complete life cycles are known among the Monopisthocotylea—those of *Gyrodactylus, Dactylogyrus, Benedenia, Ancyrocephalus, Acolpenteron,* and others.

Life Cycle of *Gyrodactylus elegans*

Kathariner (1904) reported the developmental pattern in *G. elegans,* a common ectoparasite of fresh-water and marine fishes. The eggs within the parent lack visible indications of yolk. Two such eggs fuse and development occurs within the parental uterus.

A form of polyembryony takes place in *G. elegans,* although some differential factor is present because not all embryos develop at the same rate. On completion of its development, the first embryo passes to the outside, attaches to the piscine host, and develops into an adult. Only then does the second embryo, within the first, mature. Up to four generations may develop within the first larva, like a series of Chinese boxes.

This particular parasite is occasionally suspected of being detrimental to its host. Yin and Sproston (1948) reported a case in which a number of fantail goldfish were killed by gyrodactyliasis. Death of these fish was attributed to the hypersecretion of mucus on the host's gill surfaces due to the irritation caused by the large number of parasites present. In addition, Van Cleave (1921) reported the death of bullheads, *Ameiurus melas,* from gyrodactyliasis.

Life Cycle of *Benedenia melleni*

Jahn and Kuhn (1932) reported the life history of *B.* (= *Epibdella*) *melleni,* a parasite on the Pacific puffer *Speroides annulatus,* the spadefish *Chaetodipterus faber,* various species of angel fishes *Angelicthys* spp., and *Pomacanthus* spp. (Plate 9–9).

In *B. melleni,* the egg is tetrahedral and has a single long filament at one end and two shorter filaments at the opposing end that are recurved giving the appearance of hooks. Unlike *Gyrodactylus elegans,* the parent lays the egg unhatched. On the fourth to sixth day after the egg is laid, the larva is visible within the shell.

The fusiform onchomiracidium, which later actively escapes from the egg shell, is approximately 225 μ long and 60 μ wide and bears two bands of cilia at its anterior end, two bands mediolaterally, and two posterolaterally. The onchomiracidium possesses a folded opisthaptor bearing the definitive anchors that are characteristic of the adult. In addition, a number of marginally situated larval hooks are present.

This larva soon loses its ciliated epithelial layer, and concomitantly the opisthaptor unfolds and the larva becomes attached to the fish host. Only after the larva reaches its host does further development take place (namely, the appearance of prohaptors, the bifurcation of intestinal caeca, the development of the reproductive organs, etc.) and the adult form is attained.

Benedenia melleni inflicts injuries on its host. Because this trematode can attach to the host's epidermis and conjunctiva, the body scales of the fish fall off in untreated cases, revealing large areas of connective and muscle tissue, or the fish becomes blind. Such injuries generally lead to the death of the host.

Life Cycle of *Acolpenteron catostomi*

Another example of the direct life cycle of the Monopisthocotylea, and all monogenids for that matter, is that of *A. catostomi*, a species found in the ureters of the hosts—the common white sucker *Catostomus commersonii* and the hog molly *Hypentelium nigricans*. Fischthal and Allison (1942) reported that single, operculated eggs are found in the parental uterus and also are found free in the host's ureters. When passed out of the host along with urine, the eggs contain an uncleaved zygote, which undergoes development in water and hatches after 6 to 9 days, giving rise to an onchomiracidium. This free-swimming larva bears four groups of ciliated epithelia, four pigmented eyes, and fourteen larval hooklets on a cup shaped opisthaptor.

The larvae of *A. catostomi* do not require a transfer host, for Fischthal and Allison demonstrated that infected fish kept in an isolated tank free from other organisms were infected by second generation worms in 6½ months. The stages in the life cycle of this species are depicted in Plate 9–10.

Eggs of *Dactylogyrus*

Groben (1940) reported that *Dactylogyrus vastator,* a gill parasite of carp, possesses two kinds of eggs, the production of which is apparently related to the environmental temperature. One type, laid during the warmer periods of the year, develops quite rapidly, while the other type, produced in the autumn, develops slowly. Furthermore, the adult worm usually dies after having produced the second type of eggs. The second type of egg remains over winter in mud, hatching the following spring. This phenomenon explains why mortality in carp hatcheries due to these parasites increases at the end of a cold spell, for this coincides with the mass hatching of the "winter eggs." It is possible that similar slow-developing eggs may exist in other species.

SUBORDER POLYOPISTHOCOTYLEA

The monogeneids belonging to the suborder Polyopisthocotylea are readily recognized by the presence of multiple posteriorly situated suckers (known as suckerlets) or clamps. These suckerlets are borne on a single main disclike "trunk" —the cotylophore. A double vagina usually is present along with a genitointestinal canal.

Life Cycle of *Polystoma integerrimum*

Probably the best known North American species of the Polyopisthocotylea is *Polystoma integerrimum,* a parasite found in the urinary bladder of various frogs and toads. This unique species has been the subject of numerous investigations and is an interesting but not typical monogeneid. Its life cycle, reported by Halkin (1901), is quite well known. Stages in the life cycle are depicted in Plate 9–11.

The monoecious adult inhabits the bladder of amphibians. During the winter months the gonads are nonfunctional, but activity commences with the coming of spring. The worms copulate in the spring, producing large eggs. The number of eggs produced ranges from 4 to 122 per day for 1 week. These eggs are expelled to the exterior.

Embryonic development within the capsule (shell) is affected by temperature. At suitable temperatures above 50° F., development of the onchomiracidium normally takes less than 3 weeks. If, however, the temperature drops below 50° F., development may take 6 to 13 weeks.

The correlation between the hatching of *P. integerrimum* eggs and the development and metamorphosis of the frog is one of astounding natural synchronization and suggests a hormo-

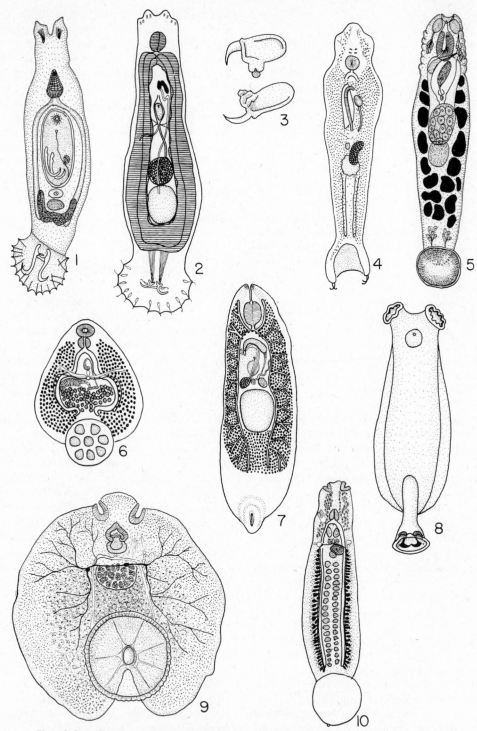

Plate 9-8   Some monopisthocotyleid monogenetic trematodes. 1. *Gyrodactylus* sp. on gills of fishes; possesses two head organs. (Redrawn after Bychowsky, 1933.) **2.** *Dactylogyrus* sp. on gills of fishes; possesses two pairs of head organs. (Redrawn after Bychowsky, 1933.) **3.** Hooks of *Ancyrocephalus paradoxus,* parasitic on gills of perch. (Redrawn after Lühe, 1909.) **4.** *Diplectanum aequans* on gills of bass and other fishes. (Redrawn after Maclaren, 1904.) **5.** *Udonella caligorum* on various fishes; prohaptor has a pair of small sucker-like organs. (Redrawn after Price, 1938.) **6.** *Calicotyle kröyeri* in cloaca of various species of rays. (Redrawn after Lebour, 1908.) **7.** *Microbothrium apiculatum,* on skin of the piked dogfish; has pair of sucker-like organs in wall of prepharynx. (Redrawn after
(*Legend continued on opposite page.*)

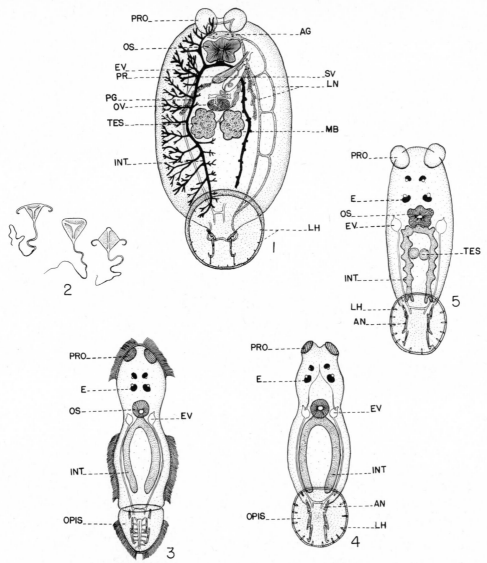

Plate 9-9   Stages in the life cycle of *Benedenia melleni*. 1. Adult showing fully developed reproductive organs and accessories, intestinal caeca with secondary diverticula, oral sucker with irregular outline, well developed longitudinal nerves, opisthaptor bearing anchors, and disappearing larval hooks. **2.** Typical eggs, which are discharged from the parent and later hatch in water. **3.** Free-swimming larva, drawn from living specimen shortly after hatching, showing six distinct patches of ciliated epidermis, rounded oral sucker, bifurcate intestinal caeca without secondary diverticula, eyes, and folded opisthaptor. **4.** Free-swimming larva that has shed its ciliated epidermis and has unfolded its opisthaptor. **5.** Young adult from fish host, showing beginning of secondary branching of intestinal caeca, beginning of irregular outline of oral sucker, developing testes, and fully expanded opisthaptor.

(AG, anterior nerve ganglion; AN, anchor; E, eye; EV, excretory vesicle; INT, intestinal caeca; LN, longitudinal nerve trunk; LH, larval hook; MB, muscular band through testis; OS, oral sucker; OV, ovary; OPIS, opisthaptor; PG, prostate gland; PR, prostatic reservoir; PRO, prohaptor; SV, seminal vesicle; TES, testis.) (All figures redrawn after Jahn and Kuhn, 1932.)

(*Legend continued.*)
Price, 1938.) **8.** *Encotyllabe nordmanni*, attached to pharynx of the black sea bream; body has thin lateral margins that are turned ventrally. (Redrawn after Fuhrmann, 1928.) **9.** *Capsala martinieri*, on gills of sunfish. (Redrawn and modified after Dawes, 1947.) **10.** *Acanthocotyle* sp. on various fishes. (Redrawn after Dawes, 1946.) (All figures from Dawes, 1946. *The Trematoda*. Cambridge University Press, and Dawes, 1947. *The Trematoda of British Fishes*. The Ray Society.)

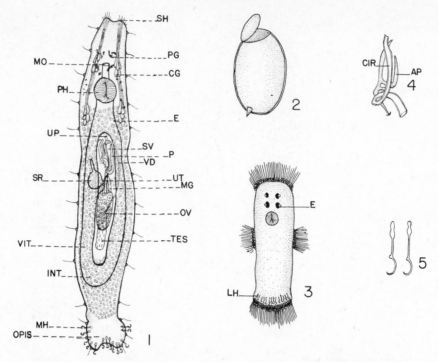

Plate 9-10   **Stages in the life history of** *Acolenteron catostomi.* **1.** Adult, ventral view.
2. Egg, showing operculum and posterior process. **3.** Ciliated larva, showing four zones of ciliated
epidermis, four eyes, and larval hooklets. (E, eyes; LH, larval hooklets.) **4.** Enlarged ventral view
of cirrus and accessory piece. (AP, accessory piece; CIR, cirrus.) **5.** Enlarged drawing of marginal
hooks found on opisthaptor of adult. (Redrawn after Fischthal and Allison, 1942.) (Legend to letters
used in figure 1. CG, cephalic glands; E, esophagus; INT, intestinal caeca; MG, Mehlis' gland;
MH, marginal hooklets; MO, mouth; OPIS, opisthaptor; OV, ovary; P, prostate gland; PG, pigment granules of disintegrated eyes; PH, pharynx; SH, sensory hair; SR, seminal receptacle; SV,
seminal vesicle; TES, testis; UP, uterine pore; UT, uterus; VD, vas deferens; VIT, vitelline glands.)

nal influence. The barrel shaped onchomiracidium, which bears 16 arrow shaped hooklets
on its opisthaptor, emerges from the egg and
becomes free-swimming at the time that the
tadpoles lose their external gills and acquire
internal ones. The larva actively seeks out such
a tadpole and enters the gill chamber, in which
it becomes attached to the gill filaments by its
armed opisthaptor. In this attached position,
development continues for about 8 weeks while
the larva subsists on mucus and sloughed host
cells.

When the frog undergoes further metamorphosis by losing its gills and developing into
a young adult, the worm passes out of the
branchial chamber, migrates down the host's
alimentary canal, and eventually becomes established in the host's bladder, which by this time
has developed. During its migration, the larva
loses its ciliated epidermis through atrophy,
develops six suckerlets on the cotylophore,
loses its larval hooks, and develops adult-type
anchors—in other words the larva matures. In

the bladder of the frog, sexual maturity of the
parasite is attained within 3 years.

In exceptional situations in which a larva of
P. integerrimum becomes attached to the external
gills of a younger tadpole, an unnatural acceleration in larval development takes place.
Shortly before the tadpole metamorphoses
into an adult, the trematode larva develops
into a neotenic form—that is, it becomes sexually mature and produces viable eggs. The
other anatomical characteristics of the neotenic
worm are not like those of the bladder form.

The correlation between the maturation
process of the host and the developmental
pattern of the parasite again strongly suggests
that the parasite is controlled by the hormonal
influence of the host. Hyman (1951) suggested
that the neotenic form may be an alternating
one with the bladder form, whereby the larvae
produced from eggs laid by the branchial form
directly invade the bladder of the frog through
the anus. Gallien (1935), however, proposed
that the larvae of branchial forms leave the

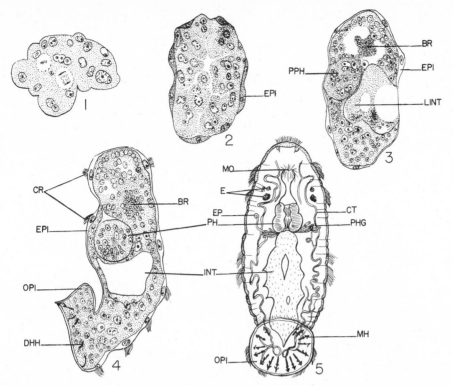

Plate 9-11   Stages during development of *Polystoma integerrimum*. 1. Early stage showing epiboly. **2.** Later stage, epidermis separating from cell mass. **3.** Formation of organs from cell
masses, cavity differentiating into digestive lumen. **4.** Later stage. **5.** Larva with areas of ciliated
epidermis.
   (BR, brain ganglion; CR, ciliary ridge; CT, collecting tubule (nephridium); DHH, developing
haptorial hook; E, eyespots; EP, excretory pore; EPI, epidermis; INT, intestine; LINT, lumen of
intestine; MH, marginal hooks; MO, mouth; OPI, opisthaptor; PH, pharynx; PHG, pharyngeal
glands.) (Redrawn after Halkin, 1901.)

host and seek out other tadpoles at the internal
gill stage and follow the normal pattern after
that.

Recent experiments by Miretski (1951) have
revealed that maturation of *Polystoma* is controlled directly or indirectly by the hormonal
activity of the frog. This investigator reported
that when hypophysis extract is injected into
an infected immature frog, the polystomes
within the frog mature within 4 to 8 days and
produce a small number of eggs for approximately one week. This period of time corresponds approximately to the time frogs spend
in spawning. This synchronized mechanism
results in the release of the parasite's eggs only
when the frogs enter water to breed. In addition, it also assures that by the time the onchomiracidia hatch, there are abundant tadpoles
available for reinfection.

How the hypophysis extract affects the
maturation of monogeneids is still uncertain.
It is possible that either the increased level

of gonadotrophins or sex hormones, brought
about by the hypophysis extract, could be responsible, as is in the ciliates *Opalina* and
Nyctotherus (pp. 158, 167).

Other representative genera of the Polyopisthocotylea are depicted in Plate 9–12.

In addition to the life cycle of *Polystoma
integerrimum,* the life cycles of several other poly-
opisthocotyleans are known. Those of *Sphyranura*
and *Diplozoon* are of particular interest, because
in each case unique variations of the "typical"
monogeneid life cycle (as that of *Benedenia
melleni*) are exhibited. In *Sphyranura,* the free-
swimming larval stage is absent, while in
Diplozoon the precocious condition of permanent
copula is unmatched even in the more complex
digenetic trematodes.

Life Cycle of *Sphyranura oligorchis*

Alvey (1936) gave an account of the life
cycle of *S. oligorchis,* a parasite on the gills of

Necturus maculosus. In this species, the adult releases eggs that enclose undeveloped zygotes. During the first 4 weeks after the eggs are released into water, embryonic development takes place. However, the developing larvae do not show any motility. On approximately the 27th or 29th day, motility is initiated and an active nonciliated larva escapes from each egg. This unique larva appears as a juvenile fluke resembling the adult.

The larva soon sinks to the bottom of the water bed and creeps along the bottom seeking a new host. If another host is not found, the larva soon dies. If it is successful in finding a host, it becomes attached and within a few days it develops into a sexually mature adult. This unique nonciliated larva possesses a well developed opisthaptor armed with hooks and hooklets and can be thought of as a precocious larva or a juvenile. If the latter interpretation

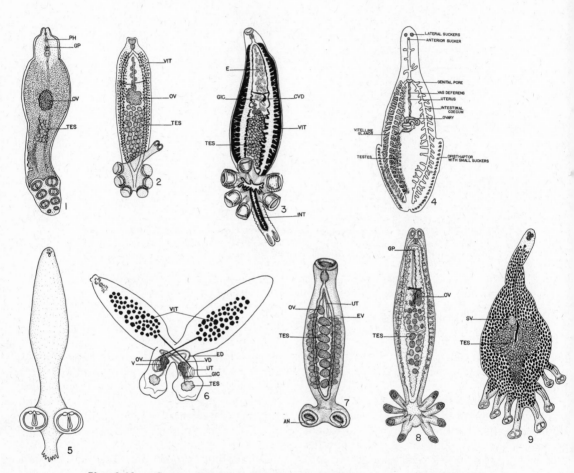

Plate 9-12   Some polyopisthocotyleid monogenetic trematodes. 1. *Hexastoma extensicaudum,* on the gills of the tunny *Thunnus thynnus.* (GP, genital pore; OV, ovary; PH, pharynx; TES, testis.) (Redrawn after Dawes, 1940.) **2.** *Erpocotyle* sp., on various marine fishes including sharks. (OV, ovary; TES, testis; VIT, vitellaria.) (Redrawn after Dawes, 1946. *The Trematoda.* Cambridge University Press.) **3.** *Rajonchocotyloides emarginata,* on gills of the thornback ray, *Raja clavata.* (TES, testis; VIT, vitellaria.) (Redrawn after Price, 1940.) **4.** *Microcotyle* sp., on various marine fishes. (Redrawn after Hyman, 1951. *The Invertebrates.* McGraw-Hill, New York.) **5.** *Anthocotyle merlucii,* on gills of the hake *Merluccius merluccius,* and the coalfish *Gadus virens.* (Redrawn after Cerfontaine, 1896.) **6.** *Diplozoon paradoxum,* on gills of numerous fishes. (ED, ejaculatory duct; GIC, genitointestinal canal; OV, ovary; TES, testis; UT, uterus; V, vagina; VD, vitelline duct; VIT, vitellaria.) (Redrawn after Dawes, 1946. *The Trematoda.* Cambridge University Press.) **7.** *Sphyranura* sp., on gills of *Necturus.* (AN, anchor; EV, excretory vesicle; OV, ovary; TES, testis; UT, uterus.) (Original.) **8.** *Octodactylus minor,* on gills of the poutassou *Gadus poutassou,* and the whiting *Gadus merlangus.* (GP, genital pore; OV, ovary; TES, testis.) (Redrawn after Gallien, 1937.) **9.** *Diclidophora merlangi,* on gills of the whiting *Gadus merlangus.* (SV, seminal vesicle; TES, testis.) (Redrawn after Dawes, 1947. *The Trematoda of British Fishes.* The Ray Society, London.)

is adopted, then one must surmise that *Sphyranura oligorchis* lacks a larval stage and develops directly from the egg.

Life Cycle of *Diplozoon paradoxum*

The development of *D. paradoxum* is unique. The various stages are depicted in Plate 9–13. The larva hatching from the egg in water is completely covered by a layer of ciliated epithelium. In addition, the larva possesses two pigmented eye spots, a well developed pharynx, and a blind-sac intestinal caecum. The opisthaptor is well developed, bearing a pair of clamps. This ciliated larva is free-swimming and after it searches out a host, becomes attached.

The natural hosts include minnows and other suitable cyprinid fishes. While attached to the gills of the fish host, the larvae metamorphose, losing the eyespots and developing branched intestinal caeca. The posterior end of the body becomes elongate and wider. A small sucker appears on the midventral surface and a small conical projection appears at about the same point on the dorsal surface. This larva type has been designated a diporpa.

After development, two diporpae become intimately associated, so that the ventral sucker of one embraces the conical protuberance of the other. By a twist of the two bodies, the free sucker of the one also embraces the conical protuberance of its mate. Not only do the two worms become fused at these points of contact but also at the external openings of their genital ducts. The male pore of the one becomes in apposition with the vaginal pore of the other and vice versa. Thus the two mates remain in permanent copula. It is usually after the two worms are thus united that the two additional pairs of clamps take form. The first pair is formed prior to the union. The three pairs of clamps are characteristic of the sexually mature adult.

PHYSIOLOGY OF MONOGENEIDS

Osmoregulation

Little is known concerning the physiology of the monogenetic trematodes. Relative to osmoregulation, Wright and Macallum (1887) observed that the excretory bladder of *Sphyranura osleri* pulsates fairly rapidly during the excretion of its contents. The intervals between pulsations vary from 0.5 to 1.5 minutes. These observations suggest that the Monogeneids, as ectoparasites and hence primarily surrounded by an aquatic environment, must possess relatively efficient osmoregulatory systems in order to maintain an ionic equilibrium between the body and its surrounding environment to resist shrinkage and bloating. Since the protonephritic excretory system is known to remove metabolic wastes from the body as well as perform the osmoregulatory function, it seems logical to conclude that the rapid pulsations of the excre-

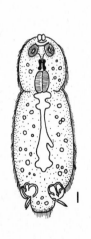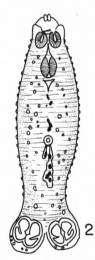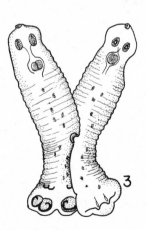

Plate 9-13   Stages in the life cycle of *Diplozoon paradoxum*. The adult of *D. paradoxum* is depicted on Plate 9–12, Figure 6, and the egg is depicted on Plate 9–7, Figure 3. **1.** Free-living ciliated larva. (Redrawn after Baer, 1952. *Ecology of Animal Parasites*. University of Illinois Press, Urbana, Ill.) **2.** Single diporpa larva. (Redrawn after Baer, 1952. ibid.) **3.** Two diporpa larvae in permanent copula. (Redrawn after Zeller, 1892.)

tory vesicle suggest a rather efficient excretory system.

Oxygen Requirement

Because of the ectoparasitic nature of the monogeneids, it is generally assumed that they carry on true aerobic respiration, utilizing the oxygen in the surrounding water.

HOST-PARASITE RELATIONSHIPS

From what little is known concerning the effect of monogeneids on their hosts, it is apparent that in some cases the host is injured in an indirect fashion. Several workers have reported the blinding of fishes as the result of *Benedenia melleni* becoming attached to their eyes. Mellen (1928) listed *Gyrodactylus, Microcotyle,* and *Ancyrocephalus* as genera that cause diseases in fishes. Gyrodactyliasis is of special concern in fish hatcheries. These parasites can ingest the host's blood from superficial capillaries. Hypersecretion of mucus by hosts infested with monogeneids is a well established fact, and this condition is known to clog the gills, thus suffocating the host. *Microcotyle* infestations have caused 90 per cent mortality among angelfish and butterfly fish in the New York Aquarium, brought about through mucus suffocation.

The fact that fishes infested with *Benedenia melleni* demonstrate varying degrees of susceptibility and resistance suggests that they may possess a natural immunity or are able to acquire immunity in varying degrees. The black angelfish, for example, is susceptible to *B. melleni* infestations for 1 to 2 weeks as young adults but soon acquire an immunity that lasts until old age, when it once again becomes susceptible.

To further test the idea that immunity occurs, Nigrelli (1937) tried to produce immunity by injecting extracts prepared from living *B. melleni;* from ground, dried worms; and serum from infected fishes. His results suggested that the secreted mucus of immunized fishes does afford some protection, for worms placed in the mucus died in less than 8 hours, while worms placed in the mucus of susceptible fishes and sea water survived for 3 days.

It is also known that the minute tears made by monogeneids on the gills and skin of fishes are ideal sites for the invasion of fungus infections.

Host Specificity

Associated with the phenomenon of host-parasite compatibility is that of host specificity. Host specificity has been repeatedly demonstrated among the Monogenea (Jahn and Kuhn, 1932; Bychowsky, 1933; Mizelle et al., 1943; Koratha, 1955; Hargis, 1953, 1957). These workers have pointed out that the monogeneids are highly host specific. Hargis (1957) suggested that this specificity "may be either physiological and genetic and/or ecological in basis. . . ."* The same author concluded that host specificity among the Monogenea may well be used as a tool in determining the phylogenetic relationships of the hosts parasitized by related parasites and vice versa.

---

*For a detailed review of host specificity among monogenetic trematodes and a discussion of infra- and supra-specificity, see Hargis (1957).

LITERATURE CITED

Alvey, C. H. 1936. The morphology and development of the monogenetic trematode *Sphyranura oligorchis* (Alvey, 1933) and the description of *Sphyranura polyorchis* n. sp. Parasitology, *28:* 229–253.

Bychowsky, B. E. 1933. Die Bedeutung der monogenetischen Trematoden für die Erforschung der systematischen Beziehungen der Karpfenfische. Erste Mittellung. Zool. Anz., *102:* 243–251. (Also see *Ibid, 105:* 17–38.)

Bychowsky, B. E. 1957. Monogenetic Trematodes, Their Systematics and Phylogeny. (Edited by W. H. Hargis, Jr.). AIBS Publ. 1961.

Dawes, B. 1946. The Trematoda. Cambridge University Press, London.

Fischthal, J. H., and L. H. Allison. 1942. *Acolpenteron catostomi* n. sp. (Gyrodactyloidea: Calceostomatidae), a monogenetic trematode from the ureters of suckers, with observations on its life history and that of *A. ureteroecetes.* Trans. Amer. Micro. Soc., *61:* 53–56.

Gallien, L. 1935. Recherches expérimentales sur le dimorphisme évolutif et la biologie de *Polystomum integerrimum* Fröl. Trav. Sta. Zool. Wimereux, *12:* 1–181.

Groben, G. 1940. Beobachtungen über die Entwicklung verschiedener Arten von Fischschmarotzern aus der Gattung *Dactylogyrus.* Ztschr. Parasit., *11:* 611–636.

Halkin, H. 1901. Recherches sur la maturation, la fécondation et le dévelopment du *Polystomum integerrimum.* Arch. Biol., *18:* 291–363.

Hargis, W. J., Jr. 1953. Monogenetic trematodes of Westhampton Lake fishes. III. Part 2. A discussion of host specificity. Proc. Helminth. Soc. Wash., *20:* 98–104.

Hargis, W. J., Jr. 1957. The host specificity of monogenetic trematodes. Exptl. Parasit., *6:* 610–625.

Hyman, L. H. 1951. The Invertebrates: Platyhelminthes and Rhynchocoela. The Acoelomate Bilateria, Vol. II. McGraw-Hill, New York.

Jahn, T. L., and L. R. Kuhn. 1932. The life history of *Epibdella melleni* MacCallum, 1927, a monogenetic trematode parasitic on marine fishes. Biol. Bull., *62:* 89–111.

Kathariner, L. 1904. Ueber die Entwicklung von *Gyrodactylus elegans* v. Nrdm. Zool. Jahrb., *70:* 519–550.

Koratha, K. J. 1955. Studies on the monogenetic trematodes of the Texas coast. I. Results of a survey of marine fishes of Port Arkansas, with a review of Monogenea reported from the Gulf of Mexico and notes on euryhalinity, host specificity, and relationships of the ramora and cobia. Inst. Mar. Sci., *4:* 234–239.

Llewellyn, J. 1956. The host specificity, microecology, adhesive attitudes and comparative morphology of some gill trematodes. J. Mar. Biol. Assoc. U. K., *35:* 113–127.

Llewellyn, J. 1958. The adhesive mechanisms of monogenetic trematodes: the attachment of species of the Diclidophoridae to the gills of gadoid fishes. J. Mar. Biol. Assoc. U. K., *37:* 67–79.

Mellen, I. 1928. The treatment of fish diseases. Zoopathologica, *2:* 1–31.

Miretski, O. Y. 1951. Experiment on controlling the processes of vital activity of the helminth by influencing the condition of the host. Dok. Ob. Sob. Akad. Nauk USSR, *78:* 613–615.

Mizelle, J. D., D. R. LaGrave, and R. P. O'Shaughnessy. 1943. Studies on monogenetic trematodes. IX. Host specificity of *Pomoxis tetraonchinae.* Am. Midl. Nat., *29:* 730–731.

Nigrelli, R. F. 1937. Further studies on the susceptibility and acquired immunity of marine fishes to *Epibdella melleni,* a monogenetic trematode. Zoologica, *22:* 185–191.

Odhner, T. 1912. Die Homologien der weiblichen Genitalwege bei den Trematoden und Cestoden. Nebst Bemerkungen zum natürlichen System der monogenen Trematoden. Zool. Anz., *39:* 337–351.

Price, E. W. 1937. North American monogenetic trematodes. I. The superfamily Gyrodactyloidea. J. Wash. Acad. Sci., *27:* 146–164.

Price, E. W. 1938. North American monogenetic trematodes. II. The families Monocotylidae, Microbothriidae, Acanthocotylidae and Unonellidae (Capsaloidea). J. Wash. Acad. Sci., *28:* 183–198.

Price, E. W. 1939a. North American monogenetic trematodes. III. The family Capsalidae (Capsaloidea). J. Wash. Acad. Sci., *29:* 63–92.

Price, E. W. 1939b. North American monogenetic trematodes. IV. The family Polystomatidae (Polystomatoidea). Proc. Helminth. Soc. Wash., *6:* 80–92.

Price, E. W. 1942. North American monogenetic trematodes. V. The family Hexabothriidae. n.n. (Polystomatoidea). Proc. Helminth. Soc. Wash., *9:* 39–56.

Price, E. W. 1943a. North American monogenetic trematodes. VI. The family Diclidophoridae (Diclidophoroidea). J. Wash. Acad. Sci., *33:* 44–54.

Price, E. W. 1943b. North American monogenetic trematodes. VII. The family Discocotylidae (Diclidophoroidea). Proc. Helminth Soc. Wash., *10:* 10–15.

Sproston, N. G. 1946. A synopsis of monogenetic trematodes. Trans. Zool. Soc. London, *25:* 185–600.

Van Cleave, H. J. 1921. Notes on two genera of ectoparasitic trematodes from fresh-water fishes. J. Parasit., *3:* 33–39.

Wright, R. R., and A. B. Macallum. 1887. *Sphyranura osleri;* a contribution to American helminthology. J. Morph., *1:* 1–48.

Yamaguti, S. 1963. Systema Helminthum. Vol. 4. Monogenea and Aspidocotylea. John Wiley, New York.

Yin, W. Y., and N. G. Sproston. 1949. Studies on the monogenetic trematodes of China; Parts 1–5. Sinensia, *19:* 57–85.

SUGGESTED READING

Baer, J. G. 1951. Ecology of Animal Parasites. University of Illinois Press, Urbana. (This is an interesting summary of the biology, especially life cycles and ecology, of monogeneids.)

Bychowsky, B. E. 1957. Monogenetic Trematodes, Their Systematics and Phylogeny (edited by W. J. Hargis, Jr.). AIBS Translation Series, 1961. (This definitive treatise on the taxonomy and biology of the monogenea, originally in Russian, has been translated into English. It is recommended to those planning to work on the monogeneids.)

Dawes, B. 1946. (Reprint 1956.) The Trematoda. Cambridge University Press, Cambridge. (This is a well written account of the taxonomy and biology of monogeneids. The biological aspects are somewhat outdated).

Hargis, W. J., Jr. 1957. The host specificity of monogenetic trematodes. Exptl. Parasit., 6: 620–625. (This comprehensive review article deals with an interesting phase of monogeneid ecology—that of host specificity.)

Hyman, L. H. 1951. The Invertebrates: Platyhelminthes and Rhynchocoela. The Acoelomate Bilateria. Vol. II. McGraw-Hill, New York. (This section in Hyman's classical monograph on the invertebrates deals with the monogenetic trematodes. The information on morphology, along with the references, is most useful.)

Llewellyn, J. 1963. Larvae and larval development of monogeneans. In Advances in Parasitology (edited by B. Dawes). Academic Press, New York, Vol. I, pp. 287–326. (This review article should be read by all students interested in helminthology. This recognized authority of the monogenetic trematodes has presented a detailed account of the development, including organogenesis, of the larvae of monogenetic trematodes. From such embryological data, the author has drawn some extremely interesting evolutionary hypotheses.)

Sproston, N. G. 1946. A synopsis of the monogenetic trematodes. Trans. Zool. Soc. London, 25: 185–600. (Sproston's monograph of the monogenetic trematodes is an indispensable reference, especially for those interested in the systematics of these helminths.)

10

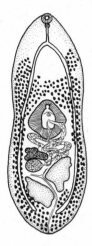

THE DIGENEA—The
Digenetic Trematodes

The digenetic trematodes comprise the largest group of monozoic platyhelminths. Within their hosts, these parasites are found in the intestine, gallbladder, urinary bladder, blood, esophagus, mouth, and practically every major organ. Although biologists have been finding new trematodes since the days of Francesco Redi in the 17th Century, the wealth of unknown trematode fauna is by no means exhausted. Even today parasitologists are continuously discovering new species of digenetic trematodes in various hosts. The number of known species is well over 40,000 and each one is a potential experimental animal.

Morphologically, the Digenea have the characteristics of the Platyhelminthes as given in Chapter 8. Unlike the aspidobothrid and monogenetic trematodes, however, the adult digenetic trematodes generally possess two prominent suckers on their body surface—the anteriorly located anterior sucker, often referred to as the oral sucker when it surrounds the mouth, and a ventrally located holdfast sucker called the acetabulum. Among certain species, such as the monostomes, only the anterior sucker is present.

From the standpoint of development and life history, the Digenea not only possess by far the most complex developmental cycles among the Platyhelminthes, but also among all members of the Animal Kingdom. During the "typical" life cycle of a digenetic trematode, the worm utilizes two, three, four, or more hosts—one being the definitive host and the remainder being intermediate hosts. In each host the parasite takes on one or more different forms. In the intermediate hosts, the parasite assumes various larval forms, each of which developed asexually from the preceding generation. It is only in the adult that sexual reproduction occurs.

All digenetic trematodes, except the schistosome blood flukes, are monoecious. Sexual reproduction may be brought about by either self-fertilization or cross fertilization between two individuals. Among the schistosomes, the individuals are either males or females. The blood flukes are of great medical importance because the species that cause schistosomiasis are widespread and are menacing hazards to human health. Numerous other species of trematodes are of medical and veterinary importance because, as true parasites, they are the causative agents of various human and animal diseases. A list of the more important digenetic trematodes is given in Table 10–1.

(*Text continued on page 231.*)

Table 10-1. Some Trematodes Found in Man and Domestic Animals

Trematode	Principal Hosts	Habitat	Main Characteristics	Disease Caused
Schistosomatoidea				
Schistosoma mansoni	Man	Blood	Male and female paired, male 6.4-9.9 mm. long, female 7.2-14 mm. long, conspicuous tuberculations on male, 6-9 testes, eggs 114-175μ by 45-68μ	Schistosomiasis mansoni
S. japonicum	Man, dogs, cats, rats, mice, cattle, pigs, horses	Blood	Male and female paired, male 12-20 mm. long, female 26 mm. long, cuticle spinous on males, seven testes, eggs 70-100μ by 50-65μ	Schistosomiasis japonicum
S. haematobium	Man, monkeys	Blood	Male and female paired, male 10-15 mm. long, female 20 mm. long, cuticular tuberculations on males, four to five testes, eggs 122-170μ by 40-70μ	Schistosomiasis haematobium
Schistosomatium douthitti	Muskrats, (skin of man)	Blood	Anterior 2/5 of male body is flattened, 14-18 testes	Schistosome dermatitis in man and dogs
Fascioloidea				
Fasciola hepatica	Man, sheep, cattle	Bile ducts	20-30 mm. long, 13 mm. wide, cone shaped process at anterior end, eggs 130-150μ by 63-90μ	Fascioliasis (liver rot)
F. gigantica	Horses, cattle	Bile ducts	Similar to *F. hepatica* only larger	Fascioliasis gigantica
Fascioloides magna	Cattle, horses, sheep	Liver	Larger than *F. hepatica*, often over 200-300 mm. long, eggs 109-168μ by 75-100μ	Fascioloidiasis
Fasciolopsis buski	Man, pigs	Duodenum, jejunum	Broadly ovate, 30-75 mm. long, 8-20 mm. wide, highly dendritic testes, eggs 130-140μ by 80-85μ	Fasciolopsiasis
Plagiorchioidea				
Dicrocoelium dendriticum	Sheep, cattle, goats, horses, pigs, rabbits, dogs, man	Liver, bile ducts	Slender, lancet shaped, 5-12 mm. long, 1 mm. wide, extremities pointed, eggs 38-45μ by 22-30μ	Dicrocoeliasis
Opisthorchioidea				
Opisthorchis felineus	Cats, rarely man	Biliary and pancreatic ducts	Lancet shaped, rounded posteriorly, 7-12 mm. long, 2-3 mm. wide, intestinal caeca along entire length of body, eggs 30μ by 11μ	Opisthorchiasis

Opisthorchioidea—Cont'd				
Opisthorchis (=Clonorchis) sinensis	Man, dogs, cats	Bile ducts	10-25 mm. long, 3-5 mm. wide, deeply lobed testes, eggs 27.3-35 μ by 11.7-19.5 μ	Clonorchiasis
Metorchis conjunctus	Dogs, cats, foxes, man	Gallbladder, bile ducts	1-6.6 mm. long, 590 μ to 2.6 mm. wide, linguiform, testes slightly lobed, cirrus absent, eggs 22-32 μ by 11-18 μ	Experimental hosts killed in heavy infections
Parametorchis complexus	Cats	Bile ducts	3-10 mm. long, 1.5-2 mm. wide, uterus rosette shaped and located in anterior half of body	Cirrhosis of liver ?
Amphimerus pseudofelineus	Cats, coyotes	Bile ducts	12-22 mm. long, 1-2.5 mm. wide, uterus with only ascending limb, eggs 25-35 μ by 12-15 μ	Cirrhosis of liver ?
Paramonostomum parvum	Ducks	Intestine	Ovoid, 250-500 μ long, 200-350 μ wide	Nonpathogenic
Notocotylus imbricatus	Water fowls	Caecum	2-4 mm. long, no acetabulum	Nonpathogenic
Heterophyoidea				
Heterophyes heterophyes	Man, cats, dogs, foxes	Small intestine	Elongate, pyriform, 1-1.7 mm. long, 0.3-0.4 mm. wide, small oral sucker	Heterophyiasis
Metagonimus yokogawai	Man, dogs	Small intestine	Similar to H. heterophyes but with acetabulum deflected to right of midline	Metagonimiasis
Apophallus venustus	Cats, dogs, raccoons	Small intestine	950 μ to 1.4 mm. long; 250-550 μ wide; no cirrus or cirrus sac; few eggs, 26-32 μ by 18-22 μ	Nonpathogenic
Cryptocotyle lingua	Usually in fish-eating birds, also found in dogs and cats	Small intestine	902 μ to 1.6 mm. long, 430-470 μ wide, conspicuous genital pore at anterior margin of acetabulum, anterior portion of body often attenuated, eggs 32-48 μ by 18-22 μ	Nonpathogenic
Phagicola longa	Dogs, cats, foxes, wolves	Small intestine	500 μ to 1 mm. long, 300-400 μ wide; oral sucker surrounded by double row of 16 spines, eggs 18 μ by 9 μ	Nonpathogenic ?
Euryhelmis monorchis	Minks	Small intestine	410 μ long, 610 μ wide, only one testis, eggs 29 μ by 14 μ	Nonpathogenic
Strigeata				
Alaria americana	Dogs	Small intestine	4-5 mm. long, posterior portion of body cylindrical, crescentric projection on each side of oral sucker, testes bilobed, eggs 106-134 μ by 64-80 μ	Nonpathogenic

(Table 10-1 continued)

Trematode	Principal Hosts	Habitat	Main Characteristics	Disease Caused
Strigeata—Cont'd				
A. arisaemoides	Dogs, foxes	Small intestine	7-10 mm. long, small projections on each side of oral sucker, body constricted, eggs 140μ by 90μ	Nonpathogenic
A. michiganensis	Dogs	Small intestine	1.8-1.91 mm. long, right testis bilobed, genital atrium more than twice the size of suckers, eggs $80\text{-}140\mu$ by $76\text{-}80\mu$	Nonpathogenic
A. canis	Dogs	Small intestine	2.8-4.2 mm. long, small projections on each side of oral sucker, anterior testis lobed, posterior testis horseshoe shaped, eggs $107\text{-}133\mu$ by $70\text{-}99\mu$	Nonpathogenic
Strigea falconis	Turkeys	Intestine	Body divided, vitellaria extend into both portions, eggs $110\text{-}125\mu$ by $75\text{-}80\mu$	Nonpathogenic
Cotylurus flabelliformis	Ducks, chickens	Small intestine	Body divided, $560\text{-}850\mu$ long, 200μ wide, eggs $100\text{-}112\mu$ by $68\text{-}76\mu$	Nonpathogenic ?
Postharmostomum gallinum	Chickens	Caecum	Elongate body, 3.5-7.5 mm. long, 1-2 mm. wide, vitellaria well developed along lateral margins of body	Irritation in heavy infections
Sphaeridiotrema globulus	Ducks, swans	Small intestine	Body subspherical; $500\text{-}850\mu$ long; uterus short, in front of acetabulum, containing four to five eggs; eggs $90\text{-}105\mu$ by $60\text{-}75\mu$	Ulcerative enteritis
Ribeiroia ondatrae	Chickens, fish-eating birds, muskrats	Proventriculus	1.6-3 mm. long, testes at posterior end of body, ovary anterior to testes, eggs $82\text{-}90\mu$ by $45\text{-}48\mu$	Proventriculitis
Echinostomatoidea				
Clinostomum attenuatum	Chickens	Trachea	5.7 mm. long, 1.6 mm. wide, dorsal body surface convex, ventral surface concave, oral sucker surrounded by collar	Nonpathogenic
Euparyphium melis	Mink	Stomach, small intestine	Lancet shaped; 3.86-10.5 mm. long; 650μ to 2.1 mm. wide; collar of 27 spines; eggs large, $117\text{-}130\mu$ by $72\text{-}84\mu$	Nonpathogenic ?
Echinoparyphium recurvatum	Chickens, turkeys, usually in water birds	Small intestine	700-4.5μ long, $500\text{-}600\mu$ wide, collar of 45 spines around oral sucker, four larger corner spines, others arranged in two rows	Severe inflammation of small intestine

Echinostomatoidea—Cont'd

Echinostoma ilocanum	Man, rats, dogs	Small intestine	2.5-6.5 mm. long, 1-1.35 mm. wide, circumoral disc with 49-51 spines, eggs 83-116 μ by 58-69 μ	Colic, diarrhea
E. revolutum	Chickens, usually in water birds	Caecum, rectum	10-22 mm. long, 2-3 mm. wide, collar of 37 spines, five grouped together as corner spines, eggs 90-126 μ by 59-71 μ	Hemorrhagic diarrhea in heavy infections
Himasthla muehlensi	Man	Intestine	11-17.7 mm. long, 0.41-0.67 mm. wide, body thin, elongate, collar of 32 spines, two on each side, remaining 28 arranged in horseshoe pattern, eggs 114-149 μ by 62-85 μ	Unknown
Hypoderaeum conoideum	Ducks, chickens, pigeons	Small intestine	6-12 mm. long, 1.3-2 mm. wide, collar of 47-53 spines in two rows, eggs 95-108 μ by 61-68 μ	Nonpathogenic
Troglotrematoidea				
Paragonimus westermani	Man, cats	Encapsulated in lungs	Plump, ovoid, 7.5-12 mm. long, 4-6 mm. wide, scalelike spines, deeply lobed testes, no cirrus pouch or cirrus, ovary lobed, eggs 80-118 μ by 48-60 μ	Paragonimiasis
P. kellicotti	Man, dogs, cats, sheep, goats, rats, lions	Encapsulated in lungs	Plump, ovoid, 9-16 mm. long, 4-8 mm. wide, similar to *P. westermani*, eggs 78-96 μ by 48-60 μ	Kellicotti paragonimiasis
Nanophyetus (= *Troglotrema*) *salmincola*	Dogs, foxes, bobcats, coyotes, cats, raccoons, man	Intestine	Pyriform, 0.8-1.1 mm. long, 0.3-0.5 mm. wide, uterus simple with few eggs, vitellaria profuse, eggs 60-80 μ by 34-50 μ	Salmon poisoning
Sellacotyle mustelae	Mink, foxes	Intestine	335 μ long, 190 μ wide, pyriform, eggs 60 μ by 54 μ	Slight enteritis
Collyriclum faba	Chickens, turkeys	Encysted in skin	Each cyst with two worms unequal in size 4-5 mm. long, 3.5-4.5 mm. wide, eggs 19-21 μ by 9-11 μ	Emaciation and anemia resulting in death

(Table 10-1 continued)

Trematode	Principal Hosts	Habitat	Main Characteristics	Disease Caused
Paramphistomatoidea				
Watsonius watsoni	Man	Intestine	Pear shaped, 8-10 mm. long, 4-5 mm. wide, thick body, acetabulum near posterior end, eggs 122-130μ by 75-80μ	Severe diarrhea
Gastrodiscoides hominis	Man	Caecum	Pyriform, 5-10 mm. long, 4-6 mm. wide, prominent genital cone, large acetabulum covering posterior half of body, eggs 150-152μ by 60-72μ	Mucous diarrhea
Paramphistomum microbothrioides (*Cotylophoron cotylophorum*)	Cattle	Rumen	3-11 mm. long, 1-3 mm. wide, conical, convex dorsally, concave ventrally, acetabulum at posterior end, testes large and lobate, eggs 132μ by 68μ	Paramphistomiasis
P. cervi	Cattle, moose, deer	Rumen	Similar to *P. microbothrioides*	Nonpathogenic ?
Zygocotyle lunata	Chickens, usually in water birds	Caecum, small intestine	3-9 mm. long, 1.5-3 mm. wide, testes lobed, acetabulum at posterior end, ovary behind posterior testis, eggs 130-150μ by 72-90μ	Nonpathogenic
Cyathocotylioidea				
Mesostephanus appendiculatum	Dogs, cats	Small intestine	900μ to 1.75 mm. long, 400-600μ wide, large adhesive organ behind acetabulum, genital pore posterior, uterus short with four to five eggs, eggs 117μ by 63-68μ	Nonpathogenic ?
Cyclocoelioidea				
Typhlocoelum cymbium	Ducks, geese	Trachea, bronchi and air sacs	6-12 mm. long, 3-6 mm. wide, caeca form complete ring, eggs 122-154μ by 63-81μ	Suffocation in heavy infections

GENERAL MORPHOLOGY

Since the digenetic trematodes pass through various stages during their life cycles, it is advisable to consider the morphology of each generation separately and to cite the variations commonly encountered. In order to consider the various stages more intelligently, a generalized hypothetical life cycle pattern is given below.

Generalized Life Cycle Pattern

The zygote, resulting from the fusion of the male and female gametes, is encased within an egg shell. The eggs, which are quite numerous, become lodged in the long uterus. From their in utero position the eggs are released into the host's intestinal lumen through the genital pore and are later passed to the outside in the host's feces. The eggs are deposited in water and eventually hatch, and from each egg a free-swimming miracidium emerges.

The miracidium penetrates the integument of a molluscan host (the first intermediate host) and sheds its ciliated epidermis in the process. The naked miracidium penetrates to the host's alimentary tract, migrates through it, up the blood vessels that supply the hepatopancreas (liver), and eventually becomes lodged in that organ. In some species, the eggs enter the molluscan host passively—that is, the eggs are ingested by the host, and the miracidia hatch out within the host's digestive tract and then migrate to the hepatopancreas.

Although the hepatopancreas is a common site for further development of the miracidia, it is not the only one, for instances are known in which the mantle, the lymph spaces surrounding the intestine, the gill chambers, and other areas have served as sites for further development. Once established in a suitable position, the now nonciliated body continues to transform and eventually gives rise to the second larval generation, called the sporocyst.

Within the sporocyst, which is commonly elongate and hollow, germinal cells are present. These cells increase in number by mitotic division and eventually differentiate into germ balls. Each germ ball further increases in size and differentiates into the next larval generation, called the redia.

As in the sporocyst, certain germinal cells in the broad chamber of the redia eventually give rise to tail-bearing cercariae, which constitute the fourth larval generation. Cercariae escape from their molluscan host and become free-swimming. In some species, the cercariae never leave the molluscan host and enter the next host only if the infected mollusc is ingested.

When free-swimming cercariae come in contact with a compatible second intermediate host—usually an arthropod, but it could be some other invertebrate or even a vertebrate—they actively penetrate the host's body and encyst. The encysted larva is known as a metacercaria. When the second intermediate host is ingested by the vertebrate definitive host, the encysted metacercaria excysts in the host's intestine and gradually matures into the adult.

During the life cycle of various digenetic trematodes, it is not uncommon to find mother and daughter generations of sporocysts and rediae. The number of generations of these different larval forms is usually consistent in the members of a specific taxon. Variations of this generalized life history pattern are known. From the foregoing, it is evident that stages in the life cycle of this hypothetical trematode include the adult, egg, miracidium, sporocyst, redia, cercaria, and metacercaria.

The Adult

Sexually mature adult digenetic trematodes can be separated into morphological types.

(1) The most frequently encountered morphological type is the distome (Plate 10-1, Fig. 1). In this type, the body is commonly elongate oval. The size, depending on the species, varies from 30 μ to approximately 30 mm. in length, as in the liver fluke, *Fasciola hepatica*. In some unusual species, such as those that parasitize scombriid fishes, the length may be several inches. Both the anteriorly situated oral sucker and the acetabulum are present. The mouth is located in the center of the oral sucker, and the intestinal caeca usually are forked although the caeca of members of the family Cyclocoeliidae are joined posteriorly forming a ring.

(2) The amphistome type (Plate 10-1, Fig. 2) is characterized by the position of the acetabulum, which is located at the posterior terminal of the body and is often referred to as the posterior sucker. The ovary is located posterior to the testes. Although this arrangement is also found among other types of trematodes, it appears to be always the case among the amphistomes.

(3) The monostome morphological type is characterized by the presence of only one sucker—the anteriorly located oral sucker (Plate 10-1, Fig. 3).

(4) The gasterostome type, which is limited

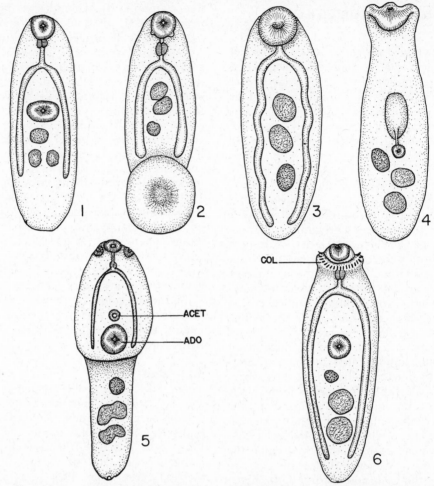

Plate 10-1   Some morphological types of adult digenetic trematodes. 1. Distome.
2. Amphistome. 3. Monostome. 4. Gasterostome. 5. Holostome. (ACET, acetabulum; ADO,
additional adhesive organ or tribocytic organ.) 6. Echinostome. (COL, collar of spines.) (All
figures original.)

exclusively to certain species parasitic in fishes, is characterized by the mouth being located not in the center of the anterior sucker but in the middle of the ventral sucker (Plate 10–1, Fig. 4). Thus, in this case the ventral sucker is the oral sucker.

(5) The holostome morphological type, found primarily in the intestine of birds and less frequently in mammals and other vertebrates, is characterized by its peculiar body shape (Plate 10–1, Fig. 5). The elongate body is divided into the forebody and the hindbody. The mildly ventrally concave forebody bears the anterior sucker and the acetabulum. Quite commonly the anterior sucker is provided with auxiliary suckers flanking it. A special glandular adhesive organ—the tribocytic organ—is present on holostomes located immediately posterior to the acetabulum.

(6) The echinostome type is actually a special-ized distome, for the positions of the suckers are comparable to those found in distome (Plate 10–1, Fig. 6). However, it may be con-sidered a distinct type, because there is a collar of large spines surrounding the oral sucker.

These six morphological types do not neces-sarily indicate six distinct phylogenetic group but are merely useful in the describing of adul trematodes.

ANATOMY OF THE ADULT. Despite super ficial differences, the anatomy of the variou: groups of digenetic trematodes is quite simila morphologically. For this reason the autho: has chosen to use the anatomy of a hypothetica distome to exemplify the various details (Plat 10–2, Fig. 1).

Alimentary Tract. The digenetic trematode possess an incomplete digestive system. The

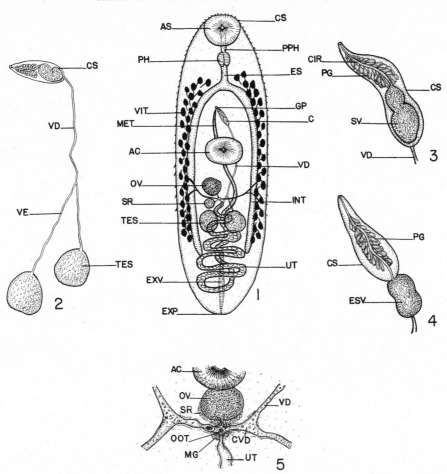

Plate 10-2   **Morphology of a hypothetical distome.** **1.** Hypothetical adult digenetic trematode. (AC, acetabulum; AS, anterior sucker; C, cirrus sac or pouch; CS, cuticular spines; ES, esophagus; EXP, excretory pore; EXV, excretory vesicle; GP, genital pore; MET, metraterm; INT, intestinal caecum; OV, ovary; PH, pharynx; PPH, prepharynx; SR, seminal receptacle; TES, testis; UT, uterus enclosing eggs; VD, vas deferens; VIT, vitellaria.) **2.** Male reproductive system of digenetic trematode. (CS, cirrus sac or pouch; TES, testis; VD, vas deferens; VE, vas efferens.) **3.** Cirrus sac, showing internal structures. (CIR, cirrus; CS, cirrus sac or pouch; PG, prostate glands; SV, internal seminal vesicle.) **4.** Cirrus sac complex with external seminal vesicle. (ESV, external seminal vesicle; PG, internal prostate glands; SC, cirrus sac.) **5.** Female reproductive system of *Glypthelmins pennsylvaniensis,* an intestinal parasite of frogs. (AC, acetabulum; CVD, common vitelline duct; MG, Mehlis' gland; OOT, ootype; OV, ovary; SR, seminal receptacle; UT, uterus; VD, vitelline ducts.) (Figs. 1–4, original; Fig. 5, after Cheng, 1961.)

mouth is located anteriorly in the center of the oral sucker (except in the gasterostomes). The mouth leads into a bulbous muscular pharynx via a short prepharynx. The prepharynx is absent in some species. The pharynx serves primarily as a masticatory organ, from which the ingested food particles pass into the esophagus.

The esophagus is lined with a single layer of epithelial cells. At the posterior terminal of the esophagus the alimentary tract bifurcates, giving rise to two blind-sac intestinal caeca that ter-

minate posteriorly in the parenchyma. The lengths of the esophagus and intestinal caeca are somewhat variable within a given species. However, these variations are within a limited range and hence, as in *Brachycoelium* and *Margeana,* both members of the same family (Brachycoeliidae) and both intestinal parasites of amphibians and reptiles, the genera are distinguished by their caecal lengths (Plate 10–3, Figs. 1,2).

Generally the cells lining the intestinal caeca are described categorically as being epithelial,

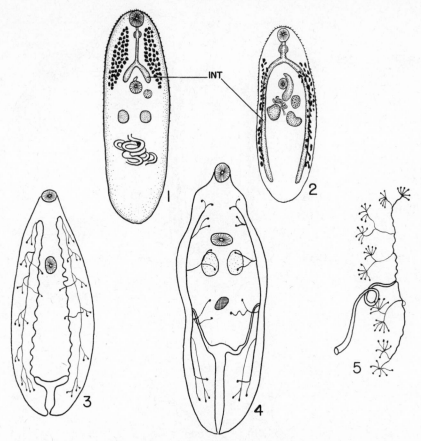

Plate 10-3   Morphology of some digenetic trematodes. 1. *Brachycoelium salamandrae,* an intestinal parasite of amphibians, showing short intestinal caeca (INT). (Redrawn after Cheng, 1958.) **2.** *Margeana linguatula,* an intestinal parasite of frogs and toads, showing long intestinal caeca (INT). (Redrawn after Cheng, 1959.) **3.** Flame cell pattern of *Opisthorchis pedicellata* (Opisthorchiidae). (Redrawn after Faust, 1932.) **4.** Flame cell pattern of *Dicrocoelium* sp. (Dicrocoeliidae). (Redrawn after Faust, 1932.) **5.** Right half of excretory system of *Otodistomum* sp. (Azygiidae). (Redrawn after Faust, 1932.)

but at least in one instance (in *Haematoloechus confusus,* a lung fluke of frogs), Cheng and Provenza (1960) have shown that specialized cells are intermingled among the smaller epithelial cells. These specialized cells are larger and presumably secrete digestive enzymes (Plate 10–4, Fig. 1). It is strongly suspected that similar cells are present in other trematodes. These cells may not be permanent, for Gresson and Threadgold (1959) have suggested that the gut epithelium in *Fasciola hepatica* passes through glandular and absorptive cycles during which changes in cell form occur. More recently, Dawes (1962) has shown that the caecal epithelium in *F. hepatica* does undergo a secretory cycle characteristic of apocrine gland cells.

Adults generally feed on sloughed cells, lymph, blood, and organic debris present in the immediate environment.

Reproductive System.   The reproductive systems, both male and female, of digenetic trematodes are somewhat similar to those found in the Monogenea and Aspidobothrea.

THE MALE SYSTEM.   The male reproductive system generally includes two testes, although multitesticular species are known. For example, members of several families (Spirorchiidae, Schistosomatidae, etc.) are multitesticular. Digenetic trematodes with a single testis also exist. The testes are located in the parenchyma in rather exact positions. In fact, the positions of these gonads are of considerable importance in the identification of species.

Leading from each testis is a vas efferens. These ducts generally unite anteriorly to form the common vas deferens, which opens into the cirrus pouch (Plate 10–2, Fig. 2). In some species the vasa efferentia enter the cirrus pouch independently. The cirrus pouch (or

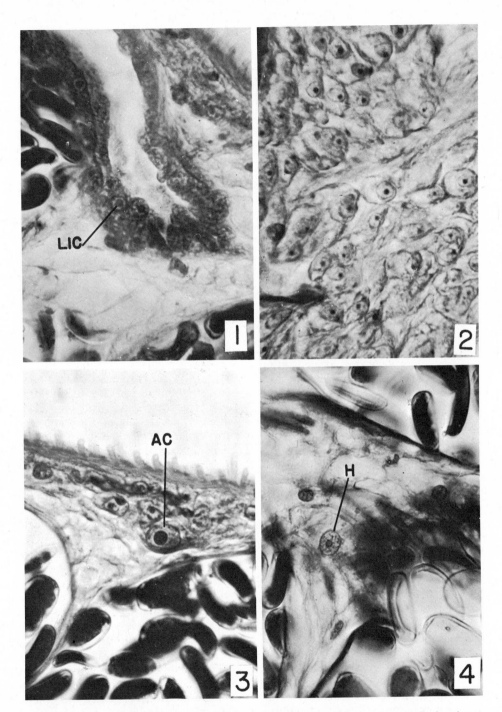

Plate 10-4   Photomicrographs of cells of digenetic trematodes. 1. Longitudinal section through intestinal caecum of *Haematoloechus confusus,* a lung fluke of frogs, showing large cells of epithelial lining of caecum (LIC). **2.** Cross section through body of *H. confusus,* showing mass of beta cells of parenchyma. **3.** Longitudinal section of *H. confusus,* showing single large alpha cell (AC) in parenchyma. **4.** Cross section of *H. confusus,* showing single haemocyte (H) in parenchyma. (All figures after Cheng and Provenza, 1960.)

cirrus sac) is saccular and is situated at the terminal of the male reproductive system, enclosing the seminal vesicle, prostate glands, and the protrusible cirrus (Plate 10–2, Fig. 3). In some trematodes a permanent penis is present. In others, the seminal vesicle is located outside the pouch and is known as an external seminal vesicle (Plate 10–2, Fig. 4). Not all digenetic trematodes possess a cirrus pouch; in some the vas deferens empties directly to the outside via the genital pore.

Spermatozoa, formed in the testes, are conducted via the vasa efferentia and vas deferens to the seminal vesicle and are stored there. During copulation, the sperms are ejected through the eversible cirrus, which is inserted in the genital atrium of the female system. The unicellular prostate glands, which surround and empty into the cirrus are believed to secrete a fluid in which spermatozoa survive.

THE FEMALE SYSTEM. The female reproductive system generally includes a single ovary located in the parenchyma, either anterior or posterior to the testes, depending on the species. Ova (actually secondary oocytes) formed within the ovary are released from that organ via a short oviduct that opens into a minute chamber —the ootype. Three auxiliary organs empty into the ootype: (1) The Mehlis' gland is a cluster of unicellular glands surrounding and independently emptying into the ootype. (2) The common vitelline duct receives the materials from the vitelline glands via the left and right ducts, and deposits these in the ootype. (3) The duct from the seminal receptacle (absent in some species) empties into the ootype.

In some species a fourth structure—the vitelline reservoir—is present in the form of an outpocket of the common vitelline duct. The function of this reservoir is for temporary storage of vitelline materials.

The function of the Mehlis' gland remains unclear. It was believed that these glands were merely responsible for the formation of the shell of the egg, but Stephenson (1947), Rennison (1953), and Johri and Smyth (1955) have shown definitely that this cannot be the case, because the shell of trematode eggs is rich in various proteins, phenols, and phenolases that are not present in these glands. Several hypotheses have been suggested to explain the function of the Mehlis' gland. (1) These glands secrete a fluid that enhances the hardening or tanning process of newly formed eggs by maintaining the desired pH, redox potential, etc. (2) The secretion of these cells causes release of the shell globules from the vitelline glands. (3) The secretion forms a thin membrane (as yet not demonstrated) around the cells forming the egg, and the shell globules then build up from within this membrane. (4) The secretion lubricates the uterus facilitating passage of the eggs. (5) The secretion activates spermatozoa, which are passed down to the ootype. All or some of these hypotheses may be valid and investigations along these lines deserve attention.

The function of the vitelline secretions is now known. In addition to contributing yolk material for incorporation within the egg, the vitelline glands also secrete large globules— known as shell globules—which envelop the developing egg and eventually coalesce and become hardened to form the shell. This hardening process involves the tanning of the protein or sclerotin present within the coalesced globules by quinone. Thus, the vitelline glands contribute both yolk and shell materials.

The uterus, which is attached to the ootype, is the long and often convoluted tube in which the formed eggs are transported to the exterior. In some trematodes, the distal segment of the uterus is muscular and by peristaltic movement expels the eggs. This muscular portion is referred to as the metraterm. The terminal portion of the uterine tract empties into the genital atrium, which in most species, is the common chamber into which the cirrus also opens. The atrium opens to the exterior through the genital spore.

During self- or cross-fertilization (the latter being the more common) the cirrus is evaginated—that is, with the inside surface becoming the outside, much in the same fashion as pulling a sock inside out—and is inserted in the female aperture. Spermatozoa introduced down the uterus become lodged in the seminal receptacle, from which they enter the ootype, where fertilization and egg formation occur.

In some species, a Laurer's canal is present. This tube originates on the surface of the ootype and is directly dorsally through the parenchyma and may not open to the exterior. If the canal opens to the exterior, it may serve as a vagina.

The vitelline glands, or vitellaria, are groups of glands (acini) commonly located along the two lateral sides of the body, but in some species these may converge along the midline. Arising from each acinus is a vitelline duct. The ducts arising from the acini located on the left side of the body unite to form the left vitelline duct and those on the right side form the right vitelline duct. The left and right ducts may either converge to form the common vitelline duct, which enters the ootype, or they may enter the ootype independently. The function of the vitelline or yolkshell glands has been discussed.

Excretory System. The excretory or osmoregulatory system of digenetic trematodes is of protonephritic type. In these worms the arrangement of the individual flame cells along the collecting tubes is so consistent in a given taxon that Faust (1919) promoted the utilization of their arrangement pattern—known as the flame cell pattern—as a taxonomic tool to indicate phylogenetic relationships. For example, two flukes that reveal similar anatomical features and also possess identical flame cell patterns could be considered members of the same genus. Faust's concept has been widely adopted despite the fact that exceptions to the rule are known. Flame cell formulae are now often used not only to indicate relationships among adult flukes but to demonstrate affinities between larval (cercariae and metacercariae) and adult forms. The arrangement of flame cells can be expressed in a formula. For example, the pattern found in *Opisthorchis pellicellata,* a species parasitic in the gallbladder of fishes (Plate 10–3, Fig. 3), can be thus expressed:*

$$2[2 + 2 + 2 + 3 + 3 + 3 + 2] = 34$$

The formula for *Dicrocoelium dendriticum,* a liver fluke of sheep (Plate 10–3, Fig. 4),* can be expressed as:

$$2[2 + 2 + 2 + 2 + 2 + 2] = 24$$

The formula for *Otodistomum veliporus,* parasitic in British skates and rays (Plate 10–3, Fig. 5),* is expressed as:

$$2[(6 + 6) + (6 + 6) + (6 + 6) + \\ (6 + 6) + (6 + 6)] = 120$$

The collecting tubules empty into a common excretory vesicle. This vesicle is singular and opens to the exterior through a pore located at or near the posterior extremity of the body. Again, the shape of the vesicle is often used as a taxonomic tool. The shape may be in the form of a V, a Y, or an I (Plate 10–5). Among the members of the family Lecithodendriidae, for example, the excretory vesicle is mostly V shaped, and in the Plagiorchiidae the vesicle is Y shaped.

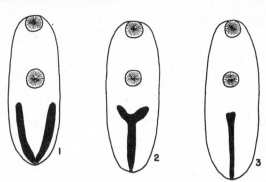

Plate 10-5   Shapes of excretory vesicles of digenetic trematodes. 1. V shaped excretory vesicle. **2.** Y shaped excretory vesicle. **3.** I shaped excretory vesicle. (All figures, original.)

Although the excretory system functions in excretion and osmoregulation, not all details associated with these functions are known. For example, alkaline phosphatase is present in the walls lining the collecting tubules and in the flame cells, but not in the lumina. The concentration of this enzyme is heaviest in that portion of each tubule in the immediate proximity of each flame cell. The exact function of this enzyme is not known except that it probably serves in the selective transfer of chemical substances.

The Egg

The ovoid eggs of digenetic trematodes are typically operculated— that is, there is a lid-like structure at one end (Plate 10–6). In some species there is a minute pointed projection at the opposite end. The eggs of schistosomes, on the other hand, do not possess an operculum. The shell is split during the hatching process. Within the shell, the fully or partially developed miracidium is surrounded by a vitelline membrane, which is formed during the development of the miracidium by the fusion of certain small surface somatic cells.

Rowen (1956, 1957) demonstrated that in the operculated egg of the liver fluke *Fasciola hepatica,* there is a viscous and granular cushion at the opercular end of the egg, situated immediately beneath the operculum. He demonstrated that the hatching process is initiated by the internal secretion (presumably by the miracidium) of a proteolytic hatching enzyme and the expansion of the granular cushion. The hatching enzyme is secreted in response to exposure to light. The enzyme dissolves the cementing material by which the operculum is attached, thus releasing the operculum. Expan-

---

*The reader must refer to Plate 10–3 in order to understand how the formula represents arrangement of the flame cells.

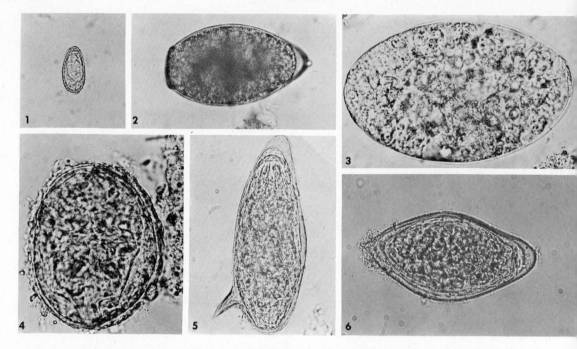

Plate 10-6   Eggs of some human-infecting digenetic trematodes. 1. Egg of *Opisthorchis sinensis,* 27 to 35 μ × 12 to 20 μ, flask shaped with operculum at narrow end. **2.** Egg of *Paragonimus westermani,* 80 to 118 μ × 48 to 60 μ, oval, with operculum at flattened end. **3.** Egg of *Fasciolopsis buski,* 130 to 140 μ × 80 to 85 μ, ellipsoidal, with inconspicuous operculum. **4.** Egg of *Schistosoma japonicum,* 70 to 100 μ × 50 to 65 μ, round to oval, with short lateral spine. **5.** Egg of *Schistosoma mansoni,* 114 to 175 μ × 45 to 68 μ, elongate oval, with long lateral spine. **6.** Egg of *Schistosoma haematobium,* 112 to 170 μ × 40 to 70 μ, spindle shaped, with posterior terminal spine. (All photomicrographs, courtesy of Ward's Natural Science Establishment, Inc., Rochester, N. Y.)

sion of the granular cushion, accompanied by exosmosis of salts and other materials from within the egg, pushes off the operculum. The cushion resembles a colloid, is at least partially composed of protein, and changes from a gel to a sol during the expanding process.

As mentioned earlier, the eggs of some species hatch in water, and the free-swimming miracidia penetrate the first intermediate host. In other species, the eggs must be ingested by the molluscan host before they are hatched. In the latter case, the miracidium hatches only after the egg comes in contact with the host's digestive juices.

The characteristics of trematode eggs, especially those of medically important species, are commonly used in diagnosis of infections. The eggs of some of these species are depicted in Plate 10–6.

The Miracidium

When the egg hatches, the escaping larva is known as a miracidium. This larva is minute, elongate, and ovoid, covered with flattened ciliated epidermal plates. The arrangement of these plates can only be appreciated when special silver-impregnation staining techniques are employed.

Arrangement of the ciliated plates is quite consistent and is of considerable value in determining phylogenetic relationships (Plate 10–7, Fig. 1). For example, members of the family Fasciolidae, which includes the liver flukes, possess six plates in the anteriormost tier, six in the next tier, and three, four, and two in each tier after that. Among the echinostomes the arrangement is six, six, four, and two; in the amphistomes it is six, eight, four, and two; and in the strigeids the pattern is six, eight, four, and three. Bennett (1936) has assembled the various patterns known at the time.

At the anterior tip of the miracidium is found a mobile apical papilla, which is armed with a stylet in some species (Plate 10–7, Fig. 2). The penetration or cephalic glands, located in the parenchyma, empty to the outside near the apical papilla. The secretion of these glands aids in dissolving the host's tissue during the

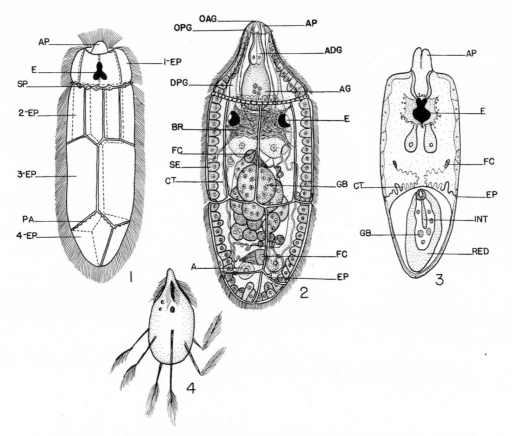

Plate 10-7   Morphology of miracidia of digenetic trematodes. 1. Miracidium of *Parorchis acanthus,* showing ciliated epidermal plates. (AP, apical papilla; E, eyespot; 1-EP, first tier of epidermal plates; SP, ring of sensory papillae; 2-EP, second tier of epidermal plates; 3-EP, third tier of epidermal plates; PA, ring of papillae between third and fourth tiers; 4-EP, fourth tier of epidermal plates. (Redrawn after Rees, 1940.) **2.** Miracidium of *Heronimus,* showing various internal organs and structures. (AG, apical gland; ADG, additional glands of uncertain nature; AP, apical papilla; BR, brain; A, anthrocyte; CT, collecting tubule; FC, flame cell; E, eyespot; EP, excretory pore; GB, germ ball; OAG, opening of apical gland; SE, subepithelium.) (Redrawn after Lynch, 1933.) **3.** Miracidium of *Parorchis acanthus* with cilia not shown. (AP, apical papilla; E, eyespot; EP, excretory pore; FC, flame cell; CT, collecting tubule; GB, germ ball within brood chamber of redia; INT, intestinal caecum of redia; RED, redia.) (Modified after Rees, 1940.) **4.** Miracidium of a bucephalid trematode, showing stalked tufts of cilia. (Redrawn after Woodhead, 1929.)

miracidium's penetration process, and the stylet serves as an "arrowhead" during penetration. In the astylet species, the papilla may become partially invaginated during penetration and thus function as a suction cup into which the glandular secretion is secreted (Dawes, 1960).

The sensory organs of the miracidium may include two, sometimes three, eyespots and lateral papillae, one on each side of the body between the first and second tiers of ciliated plates. In some species, such as *Parorchis acanthus,* a rectum-dwelling parasite in gulls and flamingos, there are additional sensory papillae that are circularly arranged in the same groove

(Plate 10–7, Fig. 1). The "brain" of the miracidium is a large cephalic ganglion lying in the parenchyma behind the apical region. From this nerve center, fibers are oriented in all directions to innervate the various body tissues.

In some miracidia a distinct multinucleate gland can be seen attached to the inner surface of the apical papilla. This unusual gland is distinct from the previously mentioned penetration glands (Plate 10–7, Fig. 2). Its function is uncertain although it probably also secretes some substance that aids in the process of penetration.

The flame cell type of excretory system is

present in the miracidium. The body fluids containing wastes are collected by the individual flame cells, which generally number two or three on each side, and are deposited to the exterior through two excretory pores, one for each side, laterally situated at some level along the length of the body (Plate 10–7, Fig. 3).

During the differentiation of the miracidium within the egg shell, certain germinal cells become trapped in the parenchyma. These develop into germ balls by increasing in size and number and becoming enveloped, eventually giving rise to the next larval generation. Such germ balls are usually located in the posterior portion of the body.

Miracidia of flukes belonging to the families Bucephalidae (gasterostomes) and Brachylaimidae are unique in that the body plates do not bear cilia, and the cilia are arranged in tufts borne on stalks (Plate 10–7, Fig. 4).

The Sporocyst

The first generation sporocysts, having differentiated from miracidia, frequently are found between the tubules in the hepatopancreas of the molluscan host. However, in plagiorchioid trematodes (members of the superfamily Plagiorchioidea), the first generation or mother sporocysts are inconspicuous budlike sacs attached to the snail's alimentary tract (Cort et al., 1954). The shape of sporocysts ranges from ovoid buds to elongate sausage shaped bodies to branched structures. The branched forms are found in members of the families Bucephalidae, Heronimidae, Brachylaimidae, and to some extent Dicrocoeliidae. In these, the branching arms ramify throughout the host's tissues (Plate 10–8, Figs. 1 to 3).

In cross section, the sporocyst wall varies in thickness depending on the age and the species. The outermost layer is generally composed of noncellular cuticle, under which is a thin layer of circularly arranged muscles followed by an inner layer of parenchymal cells (Plate 10–9, Fig. 4). In the thin-walled species, these three layers are not readily visible. The brood chamber is a hollow space in the center of the sporocyst within which are found the germ balls that eventually give rise to the next generation. Sporocysts contain no alimentary, excretory, nervous, or reproductive systems. In some, there is an inconspicuous birth pore, through which the fully formed larvae escape. The larvae within those species without a birth pore rupture the sporocyst wall to escape.

In some species, mother sporocysts give rise to daughter sporocysts and the daughter sporocysts to still further generations of sporocysts. In other species, although rare, mother sporocysts give rise immediately to the next larval generation—the redia—or directly to cercariae (Table 10–2). Although daughter sporocysts for the most part are similar to mother sporocysts, the daughter sporocysts can be distinguished by the inclusion of rediae or cercariae, whichever is the case in the particular species; by being larger and longer; and by being found in the hepatopancreas of the molluscan host as among the plagiorchioid and certain other trematodes.

The Redia

In species that include a redial stage, these larvae either develop directly from the miracidium or are found within the brood chambers of sporocysts. They eventually escape into the host's tissue, usually in the hepatopancreas. In echinostomes whose rediae are found in bivalved molluscs, the rediae are commonly found embedded between the inner and outer lamellae of the host's gills.

The redia is an elongate structure often possessing two or four budlike projections—the ambulatory buds—two located anterolaterally and two posterolaterally (Plate 10–9, Fig. 1). Unlike the sporocyst, the redia possesses a mouth located at the anterior terminal of the elongate body. The mouth leads into a muscular pharynx, which in turn leads into a blind-sac caecum. The redia is capable of motility through the movement of the ambulatory buds and body contractions, and it ingests host cells.

The rediae of certain trematodes possess a pair of cephalic ganglia on each side of the pharynx. From these ganglia nerve fibers radiate in all directions.

The protonephritic osmoregulatory (excretory) system is present in some rediae. Figure 2 of Plate 10–9 depicts the excretory system found in the redia of *Cotylophoron cotylophorum*, an amphistome fluke parasitic in the rumen of cattle. In this species, the collecting ducts on each side empty into separate excretory vesicles, which in turn empty to the exterior through two laterally located excretory pores. The flame cell pattern found in these larvae is of the same general pattern found in the adult, but the number of individual flame cells is less.

The histology of the body wall of rediae is identical to that of sporocysts. More often

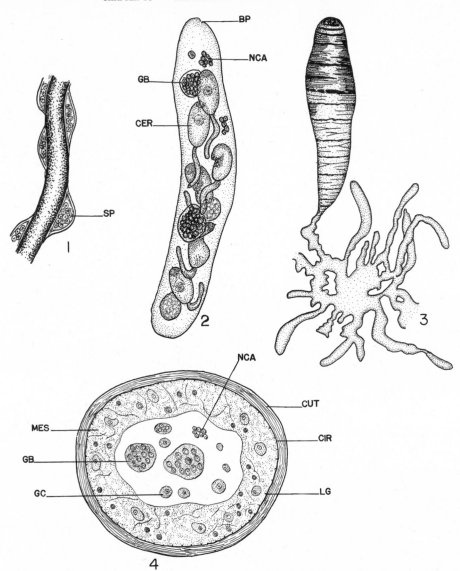

Plate 10-8   **Structure of sporocysts of digenetic trematodes. 1.** Mother sporocysts of *Glypthelmins pennsylvaniensis* attached to outer surface of intestinal tract of the molluscan host. (SP, mother sporocyst.) (Original.) **2.** A sausage shaped trematode sporocyst. (BP, birth pore; NCA, naked cell aggregates within brood chamber; GB, germ ball; CER, fully developed cercaria.) (Original.) **3.** Pigmented and branched sporocyst of *Leucochloridium macrostoma.* (Redrawn after Wesenberg-Lund, 1931.) **4.** Cross section through a sporocyst. (CIR, circular muscle layer; CUT, cuticle; GB, germ ball; GC, germinal cell; LG, longitudinal muscle layer; MES, mesenchyme; NCA, naked cell aggregate. (Redrawn after Tennent, 1906.)

than not, a birth pore is present, lateral to and in the proximity of the mouth. Within the brood chamber are found germ balls that either differentiate into another generation of rediae (daughter rediae) or into the next larval generation (the cercariae).

The Cercaria

Cercariae are differentiated from the germ balls in the brood chamber of sporocysts or rediae, whichever may be the pattern in the particular species (Table 10–2). After escaping from the brood chamber of the preceding generation, cercariae actively leave the molluscan host and either (1) become free-swimming in water, actively seeking the next host; (2) encyst on vegetation; (3) encyst in the slime trail of terrestrial snails; (4) encyst in the mantle cavity of the mollusc; or (5) develop into a tailless nonencysted metacercaria within the

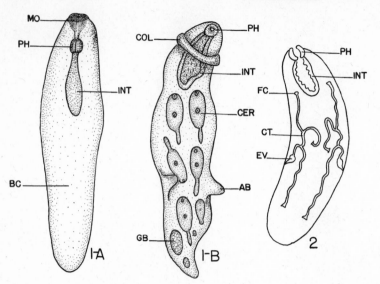

Plate 10-9   Morphology of rediae of digenetic trematodes.
1. A. Redia (mother) of *Crepidostomum cornutum,* showing various structures. (BC, brood chamber; INT, intestinal caecum; MO, mouth; PH, pharynx.) (Original.) **B.** Redia of liver fluke. (AB, ambulatory bud; CER, fully developed cercaria; COL, collar; GB, germ ball; INT, intestinal caecum; PH, pharynx.) (Redrawn after Ross and McKay, 1929.) **2.** Redia of the amphistome *Cotylophoron.* (CT, collecting tubule; EV, excretory vesicle; FC, flame cell; INT, intestinal caecum; PH, pharynx.) (Redrawn after Bennett, 1936.)

Table 10-2.   Variations in Life Cycle Patterns Among Digenetic Trematodes

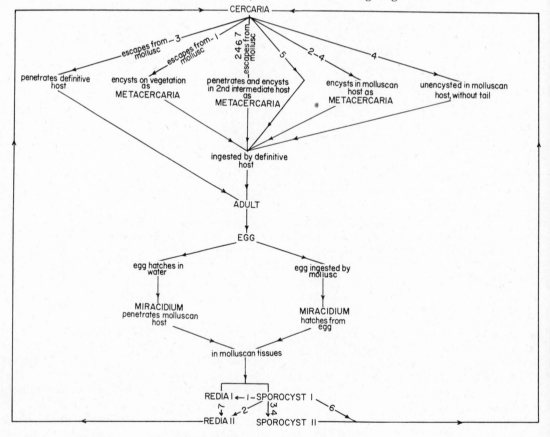

1. Fascioloidea
2. Some Opisthorchioidea
3. Schistosomatoidea
4. Some Plagiorchioidea
5. Azygiidae
6. Bucephaloidea
7. Gorgoderidae

molluscan host. Thus, except in the first instance, these larvae await ingestion by the definitive or another intermediate host.

CERCARIAL TYPES. Before describing the internal anatomy of the cercaria, it appears advisable to consider the types of cercariae, based on their external morphology. Lühe (1909) and Lebour (1912) were the first helminthologists to classify cercariae by their external features, and many of their ideas relative to designations are still in use in the description of these larval trematodes. The separation of cercariae into the following types by no means indicates that the species belonging to each type are closely related. These categories are purely descriptive, although in many cases closely related flukes do possess similar cercariae.

1. Monostome cercariae possess one sucker only—the anteriorly situated oral sucker (Plate 10–10, Fig. 1). They possess two eyespots and long simple tails, usually with pointed locomotor processes directed posteriorly from the posterior extremity of the body proper. This type of cercaria develops in rediae and gives rise to monostomate adults.
2. Amphistome cercariae possess a posterior sucker and eyespots (Plate 10–10, Fig. 2). These cercariae develop in rediae and give rise to amphistome adults (Superfamily Paramphistomoidea).
3. Gasterostome cercariae possess a mouth located on the ventral surface of the body, and they eventually develop into gasterostome adults of the family Bucephalidae (Plate 10–10, Fig. 3).
4. Distome cercariae possess two suckers—the anteriorly located oral sucker and the ventrally located acetabulum (Plate 10–10, Fig. 4). This is by far the most common type of cercaria.

The four types of cercariae listed above are classified according to the position and number of body suckers. The following descriptive types are categorized according to the shape and relative size of their tails.

1. Pleurolophocercous cercariae are characterized by a dorsoventral finlike fold along the length of the tail (Plate 10–10, Fig. 5). These cercariae commonly possess eyespots and an extremely small acetabulum that is readily overlooked. Pleurolophocercous cercariae are produced in

rediae, encyst in cold-blooded vertebrates, and when ingested by the definitive host, develop into adults belonging to the superfamily Opisthorchioidea.

2. Cystocercous cercariae are characterized by a cavity or "cyst" at the base of the tail into which the body proper can be withdrawn (Plate 10–10, Fig. 6). These are usually parasites of amphibians as adults and belong to the family Gorgoderidae.
3. Furcocercous cercariae are characterized by a forked tail (Plate 10–10, Fig. 7). Some species may possess eyespots. Those with a pharynx are the larvae of holostomes and strigeids, while those without a pharynx are schistosomes or schistosome-related forms.
4. Microcercous cercariae are characterized by a small tail that may be knoblike or conical (Plate 10–10, Fig. 8). These nonswimming larvae do not represent any specific taxonomic group.
5. Gymnophallus cercariae are characterized by the complete absence of a tail (Plate 10–10, Fig. 9).
6. Rhopalocercous cercariae are characterized by a broad tail that is as wide or wider than the body proper. (Plate 10–10, Fig. 10).
7. Leptocercous cercariae are characterized by a straight tail that is slender and narrower than the body proper (Plate 10–10, Fig. 11).
8. Trichocercous cercariae are characterized by tails armed with spines or bristles (Plate 10–10, Fig. 12). These are marine forms.
9. Cercariaea, like the gymnophallus cercariae, lack a tail but differ from the latter in that they generally do not leave the molluscan host (Plate 10–11, Fig. 1). In the few marine species that do leave their hosts, the cercariae move by inching along in a wormlike crawl.
10. Rat-king (rattenkönig) cercariae are all marine and are characterized by their colonial arrangement (Plate 10–11, Fig. 2). The tails of the individuals are joined and the bodies are arranged in a radial pattern.
11. Cotylocercous cercariae are similar to the microcercous type except that the short tail is shaped like a cup (Plate 10–10, Fig. 13), generally with large gland cells lining the concavity.

Cercariae can also be categorized morpho-

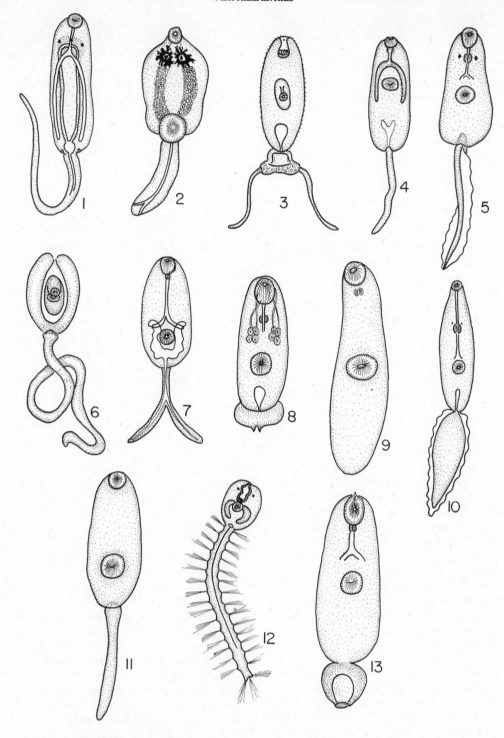

Plate 10-10   Morphological types of cercariae. 1. Monostome cercaria (*Notocotylus seineti*). (Redrawn after Faust, 1930.) **2.** Amphistome cercaria (*Cercaria frondosa*). (Redrawn after Faust, 1930.) **3.** Gasterostome cercaria (*Bucephalopsis gracilescens*). (Redrawn after Lebour, 1911.) **4.** Distome cercaria. (Original.) **5.** Pleurolophocercous cercaria (*Glypthelmins quieta*). (Original.) **6.** Cystocercous cercaria (*Gorgoderina* sp.). (Original.) **7.** Furcocercous cercaria (*Cercaria dichotoma*). (Redrawn after Lebour, 1911.) **8.** Microcercous cercaria (*Cercaria brachyura*). (Redrawn after Lebour, 1911.) **9.** Gymnophallus cercaria. (Original.) **10.** Rhopalocercous cercaria (*Cercaria isopori*). (Redrawn after Lühe, 1909.) **11.** Leptocercous cercaria. (Original.) **12.** Trichocercous cercaria (*Opechona bacillaris*). (Redrawn after Lebour, 1916.) **13.** Cotylocercous cercaria. (Original.)

logically by specialized body structures. Some of these descriptive types are listed below.

1. Echinostome cercariae are characterized by the presence of a collar of spines around the anterior sucker (Plate 10–11, Fig. 3). These larvae develop in rediae and mature into adults belonging to the superfamily Echinostomatoidea.
2. Gymnocephalus cercariae are typical distomes that, unlike the echinostome cercariae, lack a spinous collar (Plate 10–11, Fig. 4).
3. Xiphidiocercariae possess an anteriorly located stylet (Plate 10–11, Fig. 5). Penetration glands are exceptionally well developed in these. These cercariae develop in sporocysts. Certain xiphidiocercariae possess a bipartite, transparent, fluid-filled sac that overlaps the oral sucker. This sac is known as a virgulate organ and such cercariae are known as virgulate cercariae. Most, if not all, of these cercariae belong to the family Lecithodendriidae. The material secreted by the virgulate organ aids the cercariae in becoming attached to their hosts while penetrating, and it is also protective (Kruidenier, 1951).
4. Ophthalmocercariae include all the forms that possess eyespots.

Since all these types of cercariae are distinguished by one major characteristic, combinations of these can be used in describing specific cercariae that possess more than one of these characteristics. For example, the cercaria of *Crepidostomum cornutum,* an intestinal parasite of fishes (Plate 10–11, Fig. 6), can be described as a distomate, leptocercous, ophthalmoxiphidiocercaria.

INTERNAL ANATOMY. Since the internal anatomy of all cercariae, irrespective of morphological type, is essentially the same, that of *C. cornutum* is used here to illustrate the internal structures (Plate 10–11, Fig. 6M).

Alimentary Tract. Except in the gasterostomes, the mouth is situated at the anterior end of the body and is surrounded by the oral sucker. Food ingested through the mouth passes down the prepharynx and through the pharynx and esophagus to enter the bifurcate intestinal caeca.

Penetration Glands. Cephalic, or penetration, glands are arranged in two groups, one on each side of the esophagus. All these glands empty to the outside anteriorly via individual ducts.

In some species, the penetration glands are arranged into an anterior preacetabular group and a posterior postacetabular group. The functions of the two groups may differ, as in *Schistosoma mansoni* cercariae. In this case, the preacetabular glands secrete the lytic substance that aids in penetration, and the postacetabular glands secrete a mucoid film believed to be protective in nature (Stirewalt, 1963). However, in the cercariae of *Posthodiplostomum minimum,* where pre- and postacetabular glands also occur, Bogitsh (1963) has shown that the functions of both sets of glands appear to be identical. Two types of secretions are synthesized in all the gland cells—a carbohydrate-protein complex, probably a glycoprotein, and an acid mucopolysaccharide. Bogitsh interpreted this to mean that the secretions of all the glands function as the adherence medium and probably also serve as the penetration medium.

Genital Primordium. Near the acetabulum is found the genital primoridium, which is composed primarily of reproductive cells that eventually differentiate into gonads.

Excretory System. Cercariae have a protonephritic excretory system. However, unlike the protonephritic system in earlier larval stages—that is, miracidium and redia—the two lateral collecting ducts empty into a common, posteriorly situated excretory vesicle, from which a tube extends posteriorly into the tail. Various numbers and positions of excretory pores are known. For example, in the cercaria of *Cotylophoron cotylophorum* there are two pores, one on each side of the tail (Plate 10–12, Fig. 1). In the furcocercous cercaria of *Sanguinicola,* there are two pores, one at the tip of each branch of the fork (Plate 10–12, Fig. 2). The larval excretory pores become nonfunctional and are discarded with the tail when the cercaria develops into the metacercaria.

LaRue (1957) presented a revised classification of the Digenea based on the embryonic development of the excretory system. Space does not permit detailed descriptions of the known variations of the developmental patterns. However, in the fork-tailed cercariae and others—for example, amphistomes, brachylaimids, and fellodistomes—the excretory vesicle is formed through the fusion of the two collecting ducts and does not involve mesodermal cells (Plate 10–13).

In other trematodes, such as plagiorchids, opisthorchids, and allocreadids, the development pattern follows that found in the cercaria of *Cercaria dioctorenalis,* a xiphidiocotylocercous

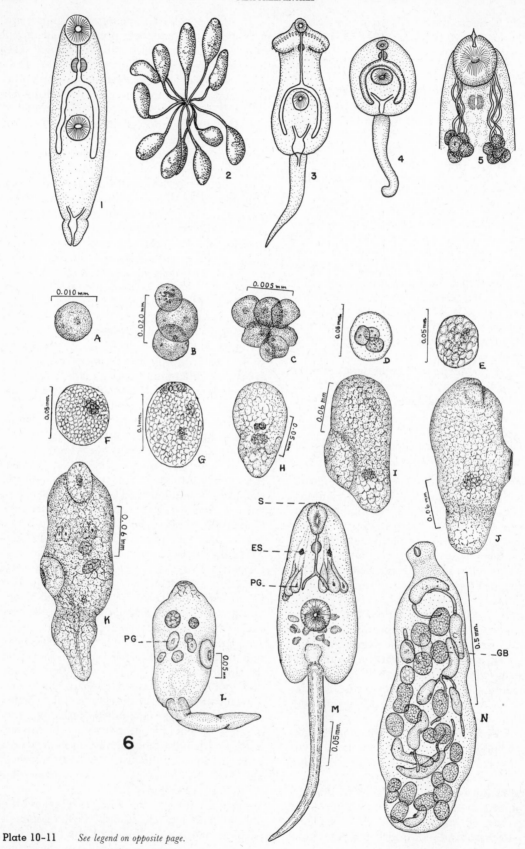

Plate 10-11 *See legend on opposite page.*

cercaria. Excretory system development of this cercaria has been studied by Dobrovolny (1939) (Plate 10–13). During development, the two ducts fuse in the center of a mesodermal mass, and the resulting excretory vesicle is lined with a layer of mesothelium. The flame cell pattern found in the cercaria usually coincides with that found in the adult. Thus, if one knows the formula of a particular cercaria, it can be used in associating the larva with the adult.

Cystogenous Glands. In most cercariae conspicuous cystogenous glands can be seen in the subcuticular zone of the body (Plate 10–14, Fig. 1). The secretion from these glands is responsible for the laying down of the cyst wall when the cercariae are ready to encyst. These glands can be distinguished from the penetration glands by their position and by their affinity for certain stains. For example, they take on a bluish color when stained with dilute thionine or toluidine blue.

Mucoid Glands. Certain glands, known as mucoid glands, have been reported along the midventral surface of various cercariae (Plate 10–14, Fig. 2). It has been demonstrated that the mucoid secretion of these cells not only protects the cercaria from harmful substances, including its own cytolytic secretions during the penetration process, but also aids movement along the substrate and serves as a lubricant during penetration.

The histology of the body wall of cercariae is identical to that of adults and is considered on page 249.

The Metacercaria

The final larval stage of digenetic trematodes is the metacercaria. When the free-swimming cercaria comes to rest on suitable vegetation or penetrates a compatible host, it loses its tail and encysts. Within the cyst wall or walls (p. 248), the body proper of the cercaria metamorphoses into the metacercaria, which is

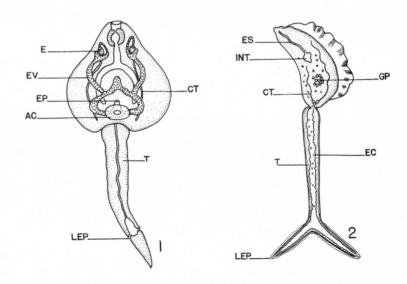

Plate 10-12 Excretory system of some larval trematodes. 1. Cercaria of *Cotylophoron*, showing excretory canal leading into tail. (AC, acetabulum; E, eyespot; EV, excretory vesicle; CT, collecting tubule; EP, excretory pore; LEP, larval excretory pore; T, tail.) (Redrawn after Bennett, 1936.) **2.** Cercaria of *Sanguinicola*, showing excretory canal leading to tips of tail. (EC, excretory canal; ES, esophagus; GP, genital primordium; INT, intestinal caecum; LEP, larval excretory pore; T, tail.) (Redrawn after Ejsmont, 1925.)

Plate 10-11 Morphology and development of cercariae. 1. Cercariaeum (*Cercaria politae nitidulae*). (Redrawn after Harper, 1929.) **2.** Rat-king cercaria. (Original.) **3.** Echinostome cercaria (*Echinoparyphium recurvatum*). (Redrawn after Harper, 1929.) **4.** Gymnocephalous cercaria (*Fasciola hepatica*). (Redrawn after Harper, 1929.) **5.** Anterior end of xiphidiocercaria, showing stylet. (Original.) **6.** Stages in the morphogenesis of the cercaria of *Crepidostomum cornutum*. **A.** Single germinal cell. **B.** Single germinal cell and two somatic cells. **C.** Single germinal cell and five somatic cells. **D.** True germ ball with membrane surrounding single germinal cell and two somatic cells. **E.** Germ ball enclosing somatic and germ cells. **F** and **G.** Older germ balls. **H.** Elongating germ ball. **I.** Differentiating cercaria. **J** and **K.** Older differentiating cercariae. **L.** Differentiating cercaria, showing primordia of penetration glands (PG). **M.** Fully developed cercaria, showing stylet (S), eyespots (ES), and penetration glands (PG). **N.** Daughter redia enclosing germ balls (GB) and cercariae in brood chamber. (All figures after Cheng and James, 1960.)

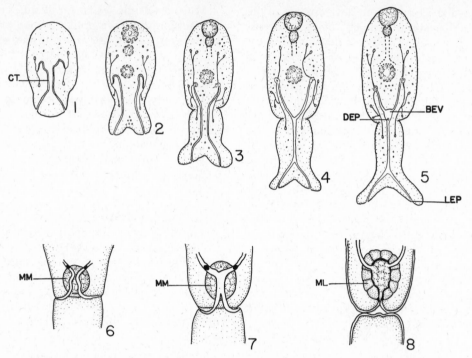

Plate 10-13   Development of the excretory system in cercariae. 1 to 5. Development of the excretory system in a furcocercous strigeid cercaria. (BEV, beginning of definitive excretory vesicle; CT, collecting tubule; DEP, definitive excretory pore; LEP, larval excretory pore.) (Redrawn after Komiya, 1938.) **6 to 8.** Development of the excretory vesicle in *Cercaria dioctorenalis*, showing the eventual lining of the bladder by mesodermal cells. (ML, mesodermal lining; MM, mesodermal mass.) (Redrawn after Dobrovolny, 1939.)

actually a juvenile replica of the adult. The cercarial characteristics, such as the stylet, penetration glands, cytogenous and mucoid glands, and eyespots, all soon disappear. The genital primordium differentiates into gonads that are usually nonfunctional. However, in certain progenetic metacercariae, sterile eggs are formed. Generally the excretory vesicles in metacercariae are greatly distended and enclose a large quantity of waste materials that appear as refractile granules.

The histology of the various structures found in metacercariae corresponds to that of the adult.

CYST WALL. The cyst wall surrounding certain metacercariae is double layered, while that enveloping others is single layered. Bogitsh (1962) reported that in the double-layered type, the outer layer is fibroblastic, apparently elaborated by the host, while the inner one is noncellular and most probably is secreted by the parasite. Chemically, metacercarial cysts are composed of carbohydrate-protein complexes similar to those found in the ground substance of vertebrate connective tissue. Lynch

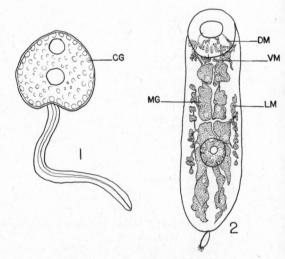

Plate 10-14   Glands of trematode cercariae. 1. Cercaria of *Fasciola hepatica* beginning to form a cyst, showing cytogenous glands in body. (Redrawn after Thomas, 1883.) **2.** Cercaria of *Paragonimus kellicotti*, showing arrangement of mucoid glands in body. (DM, dorsal mucoid reservoir; LM, lateral mucoid reservoir; MG, mucoid gland; VM, ventral mucoid reservoir.) (Redrawn after Kruidenier, 1953.)

and Bogitsh (1962) were able to identify sixteen amino acids and five sugars in acid hydrolysates of *Posthodiplostomum minimum* cysts found in the tissues of fresh-water fish.

BODY TISSUES

The histology of the body wall of adult flukes has been studied most recently by Odlaug (1948) and Cheng and Provenza (1960). The outermost layer of the wall is formed of non-cellular cuticle that in many species bears spines that appear as distinct structures embedded in the cuticle (Plate 10–15, Fig. 1).

Immediately beneath the cuticle are three layers of muscles—the outermost circular layer, the medial longitudinal layer, and the inner diagonal layer. In addition to these muscles, others make up the suckers and pharynx. Still others—the parenchymal muscles—are dorsoventrally oriented along the lateral regions of the body (Plate 10–15, Fig. 2).

Immediately beneath the body wall musculature are numerous cells, known as beta cells (Plate 10–4, Fig. 2). Some of the beta cells possess cytoplasmic tubules that penetrate through the muscular layers and reach the cuticle. These specialized beta cells are thought to secrete cuticular materials that reinforce the existing cuticle.

The body wall of trematodes is more than an inert protective layer; it is a dynamic structure of great importance in the metabolism of the organism. Although trematodes derive a great deal of their nutrients through ingestion, certain chemicals such as certain amino acids, which are necessary as energy sources and as raw materials for the synthesis of complex body chemicals, are absorbed through the body wall. It is also possible that certain metabolic wastes are discharged through the cuticle.

Within the body wall, the spaces between the internal organs are filled with parenchyma. The parenchyma includes several cellular types. In addition to beta cells (Plate 10–4, Fig. 2), alpha cells (Plate 10–4, Fig. 3), which are fewer and larger, are presumed to have differentiated from the more primitive beta cells. Alpha cells are only intermediate in their stage of differentiation, because they differentiate further into myofibers in adults and into gland cells and muscle cells in cercariae. There is also reason to believe that certain alpha cells may be nerve centers, perhaps as neuromuscular cells. There are also haemocytes, which are primitive blood cells capable of phagocytosis (Plate 10–4, Fig. 4).

Primitive blood cells are present in the so-called lymphatic canals of amphistome trematodes (Willey, 1930, and others) and few distomes (Manter, 1937), but in *Haematoloechus confusus,* a lung fluke of frogs, and *Hasstilesia tricolor,* an intestinal fluke of rabbits, this author demonstrated the presence of blood cells that are not confined to lymph canals, since such canals are not present in these two distomes. Because at least one distome, *Apocreadium maxicanum,* from the fish, *Labrisomus xanti,* does possess lymphatic canals, it appears that a series of evolutionary progression occurs here: the distomes *Haematoloechus* and *Hasstilesia* do not possess lymphatic canals but have blood cells in their parenchyma; the distome *Apocreadium* has haematocytes in lymphatic canals; and practically all amphistomes possess blood cells in lymphatic canals. The occurrence of blood cells in certain trematodes is not particularly surprising, because blood vessels (lymphatic canals) enclosing blood cells are consistently present in a closely related group of acoelomate worms—the rhynchocoelans (p. 666).

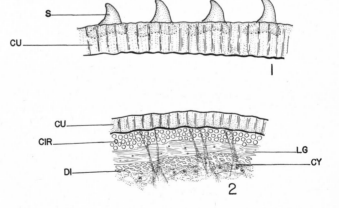

Plate 10-15   Histology of cuticle and subcuticular zone of Digenea. 1. Longitudinal section through cuticle of a digenetic trematode, showing embedded cuticular spines (S) and cuticle (CU). (Original.) **2.** Longitudinal section through surface of an aspinous trematode, showing cuticle (CU), layer of circular muscles (CIR), longitudinal muscles (LG), diagonal muscles (DI), and cytoplasmic processes of parenchymal cells leading to cuticle (CY). (Original.)

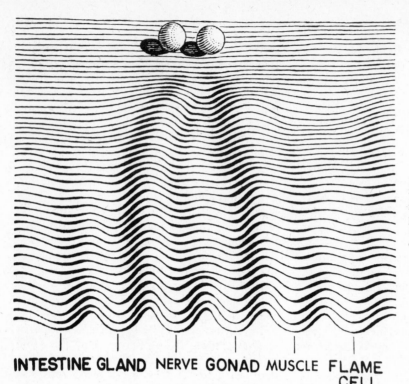

INTESTINE GLAND NERVE GONAD MUSCLE FLAME CELL

Plate 10-16   Differentiation. Epigenetic landscape depicting various possible avenues of differentiation of a primitive cell—a parenchymal beta cell of trematodes. (Modified after Waddington, 1953; courtesy of *Scientific American*.)

The primitive beta cells, which are capable of various avenues of differentiation, are of great interest to those concerned with cell and tissue differentiation. Plate 10–16 depicts a modification of the hypothetical epigenetic landscape drawing of Waddington, which illustrates how undifferentiated cells, such as the beta cells of trematodes, can follow any of the valleys of differentiation.

The beta cells are syncytially arranged with intercytoplasmic spaces scattered throughout (Plate 10–17, Fig. 1). In living worms, these spaces are filled with body fluids. Willey (1930) postulated that it is through the alignment of such intercytoplasmic spaces that the lymphatic canals of amphistomes had their origin (Plate 10–17, Fig. 2).

Other than gonadal tissues, the internal organs of trematodes are formed as the result of the differentiation of undifferentiated somatic cells. For example, the uterus of the Digenea is composed of a number of large flattened

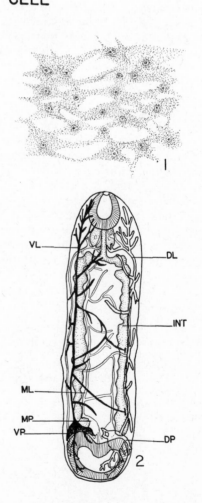

Plate 10-17   Morphology of digenetic trematodes. 1. Syncytially arranged parenchymal (beta) cells in body of digenetic trematode. (Original.) 2. The lymph system of a sexually mature specimen of *Megalodiscus temperatus* seen from ventral aspect. Reconstructed from a series of 140 frontal sections. (DL, dorsal lymph vessel; DP, dorsal posterior lymph sinus; INT, intestinal caecum; ML, medial lymph vessel; MP, medial posterior lymph sinus; VL, ventral lymph vessel; VP, ventral posterior lymph sinus. (Redrawn and slightly modified after Willey, 1930.)

250

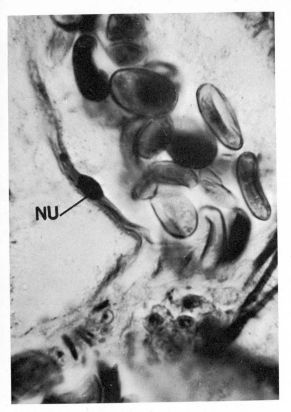

Plate 10-18   Uterine wall. Photomicrograph of longitudinal section of *Haematoloechus confusus,* showing large nucleus of cell of uterine wall. (After Cheng and Provenza, 1960.)

cells that connect with each other much in the same fashion as do endothelial cells of vertebrate blood vessels—that is, the cell walls interlock (Plate 10–18, Fig. 1). These cells have differentiated from stem somatic cells.

LIFE CYCLE STUDIES

The complex life history patterns of the Digenea have been studied extensively. Stunkard (1937, 1940) has pointed out the importance of this phase of helminthology. Investigations on life cycles are fascinating from the biological standpoint because such information can contribute to our understanding of the phylogenetic relationships between species since related trematodes almost always demonstrate similar developmental patterns. Furthermore, a complete understanding of the detailed morphology of the various stages, both larval and adult, contributes to our understanding of host-para-

site relationships, for the manner in which the parasite is specifically adapted to its host is commonly manifested in its structure. For example, ophthalmoxiphidiocercariae are always free-swimming and penetrate their host utilizing their stylets and exceptionally large penetration glands.

From the more practical standpoint, information on the life cycles of medically important species (Table 10–2) is invaluable because eradication of these species largely depends on knowledge concerning which snails serve as the intermediate hosts and how the larvae enter humans. If the answers to the questions are known, then various means can be devised to eradicate both the larvae and their intermediate hosts, thus preventing the completion of their development—that is, the entering of the final host. The human blood fluke *Schistosoma mansoni* serves as a good example. If the snail host for this important human pathogen is eliminated, for example through the application of chemicals, the cercariae die along with the snails. In addition, newly developed miracidia cannot find a suitable host and hence also perish. This type of eradication program is now in common practice.

HOST SPECIFICITY

The Digenea are as a rule not as host specific as the Monogenea. However, the degree of specificity varies with the various stages. The miracidia, sporocysts, and rediae are quite host specific and can only survive in one or a limited few closely related hosts, usually molluscs. On the other hand, adults are not as specific and in many cases can be induced to develop in an array of experimental hosts.

The factors that govern host specificity among digenetic trematodes—that is, the successful establishment of a parasite within either a single or a group of closely related species of hosts—are far from being completely understood. Natural immunity and factors of incompatible metabolism and environment are undoubtedly responsible for the failure of certain trematodes to successfully infect certain hosts. The mechanisms governing host specificity in several species of schistosome miracidia have been studied by Sudds (1960). He reported that when the miracidia of *Trichobilharzia elvae, T. physellae, Schistosoma mansoni,* and *Schistosomatium douthitti* were exposed to seven species of normal or natural snail hosts and nineteen species of abnormal hosts, these miracidia successfully penetrated, and underwent further development in all the natural hosts. The miracidia attempted to penetrate seventeen of the nineteen species of abnormal hosts but were successful in only five of the species, and these were species that are closely related to the hosts normally utilized by the parasites.

Subsequent histological studies revealed that there was severe tissue response on the part of the abnormal hosts, resulting in encapsulation that rapidly destroyed the parasites. No such host-tissue response occurred in the normal hosts. Thus, the compatibility of molluscs for these miracidia appears to be governed by factors involved in penetration and successful intramolluscan development of the parasites.

GERM CELL CYCLE

Space does not permit a detailed account of the embryonic development of each stage in the life history of digenetic trematodes but it should be apparent that reproduction in the miracidium-sporocyst-redia-cercaria phase is essentially asexual and the progeny arise through differentiation of germinal cells that are passed on from one generation to the next. This phenomenon, known as the germ cell cycle, has been reviewed by Cort et al. (1954). The metacercaria and adult are actually stages in the maturation process of the cercaria, the adult being the mature form. It is only in the adult that sexual reproduction occurs.

The life cycle pattern in a given species is almost always the same and because many researchers have contributed life cycle data for numerous representative trematodes, it is now possible to draw some conclusions relative to developmental patterns in the various taxonomic groups. Table 10–2 depicts the typical life cycles found in several taxa of the Digenea.

SYSTEMATICS AND BIOLOGY

CLASSIFICATION

The taxonomy of the Digenea is being investigated continuously. Other than a few fairly well recognized superfamilies, taxonomic groups above the familial level still are being questioned. The British and continental European trematodes have been adequately monographed by Dawes (1946), and more recently Yamaguti (1958) has contributed a taxonomic study of all known digenetic trematodes. In addition, LaRue (1957) has contributed a taxonomic scheme for the higher categories. Students interested in identification and classification of these parasitic worms should consult these publications.

Digenetic trematodes are separated into two suborders—the Gasterostomata and the Prostomata.*

Suborder 1. Gasterostomata. Mouth is situated on ventral body surface surrounded by ventral oral sucker; anterior sucker is imperforate. Intestinal caecum is a simple blind sac; genital pore is on ventral body surface near posterior end. Cercariae are furcocercous; adults are parasitic in aquatic vertebrates, primarily fishes.

Suborder 2. Prostomata. Includes most species of the Digenea, hence a great array of morphological variations exist. All members have the mouth located at the anterior (terminal) or near the anterior end (subterminal) of body. Cercariae are of all types; adults are parasitic in every group of the Vertebrata.

SUBORDER GASTEROSTOMATA

FAMILY BUCEPHALIDAE

All gasterostomes belong to the family Bucephalidae.

Life Cycle of *Bucephalus*

The common species *Bucephalus polymorphus* is found in the stomach, intestine, and rarely in the pyloric caeca of various carnivorous fishes (Plate 10–19, Fig. 1). The adult measures 1 to 6 mm. long and possesses the typical ventrally situated mouth. During the life cycle of this species, eggs laid by the adult are passed out into the water in the host's feces. A unique miracidium with stalked cilia escapes from each egg and is free-swimming (Plate 10–7, Fig. 4). When the miracidium comes in contact with fresh-water clams of the genera *Unio* and *Anodonta*, it penetrates the first intermediate host and gives rise to highly branched sporocysts that are located in the bivalve's hepatic tissue (Plate 10–19, Fig. 2).

The sporocysts give rise directly to furcocer-

*Division of the Digenea into the suborders Gasterostomata and Prostomata, although a commonly used system, is probably artificial, since the gasterostomes are believed closely related to the prostomes that possess furcocercous cercariae (see Stunkard, 1946. *Biological Reviews* Cambridge, Vol. 21).

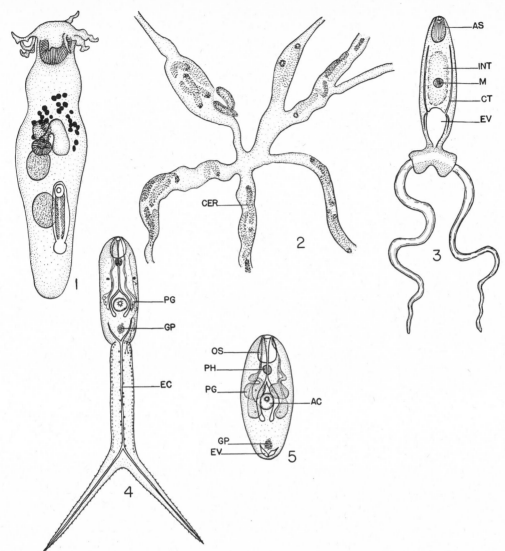

Plate 10-19   Morphology of some trematodes with furcocercous cercariae. 1. Adult of *Bucephalus polymorphus* from intestine of various fresh-water fishes, showing characteristic tentacles extending from head. (Redrawn after Nagaty, 1937.) **2.** Branching type of sporocyst of *B. polymorphus*, showing enclosed cercariae (CER). (Redrawn after Palombi, 1934.) **3.** Oxhead cercaria of *B. polymorphus*, showing anterior sucker (AS), intestinal caecum (INT), mouth (M), collecting tubules of excretory system (CT), and excretory vesicle (EV). (Redrawn after Palombi, 1934.) **4.** Furcocercous cercaria of *Alaria*. (EC, excretory canal; GP, genital primordium; PG, penetration glands.) (Redrawn after Bosma, 1934.) **5.** Mesocercaria of *Alaria* in frogs and tadpoles. (EV, excretory vesicle; AC, acetabulum; GP, genital primordium; OS, oral sucker; PG, penetration glands; PH, pharynx.) (Redrawn after Bosma, 1934.)

cous cercariae that escape from the clam and are free-swimming (Plate 10–19, Fig. 3). The long forks of the cercarial tail become entangled in the fins of small fishes, and thus the cercariae become attached to the second intermediate host and become encysted under the host's scales and on the fins. However, metacercariae are known to be encysted in the buccal cavity of some fishes. When the small fish is ingested by a larger carnivorous fish, the metacercariae excyst once they reach the alimentary tract and mature into adults. In certain other gasterostomes, snails rather than clams serve as the first intermediate host.

Other Bucephalid Species

In addition to the numerous species of *Bucephalus,* all of which bear hornlike projections on their cephalic region, the family Bucephalidae also includes *Rhipidocotyle* (Plate 10–20,

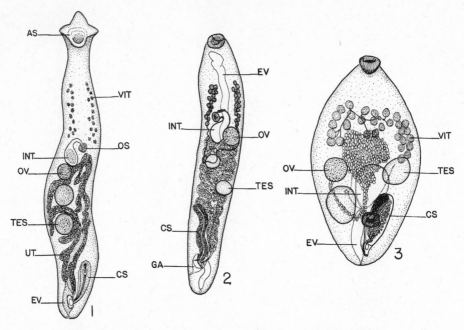

Plate 10-20 **Some gasterostome trematodes. 1.** *Rhipidocotyle pentagonum* in fishes *Scomberomorus* and *Thynnus*. (Redrawn after Ozaki, 1934.) **2.** *Bucephalopsis ovata* in intestine of fishes of the genus *Lobotes*. (Redrawn after Yamaguti, 1940.) **3.** *Prosorhynchus magniovatum* in intestine of the marine fish *Conger myriaster*. (Redrawn after Yamaguti, 1938.)

(AS, anterior sucker; CS, cirrus sac; EV, excretory vesicle; INT, intestinal caecum; OS, oral sucker; OV, ovary; TES, testis; UT, uterus; VIT, vitelline glands.)

Fig. 1), *Bucephalopsis* (Plate 10-20, Fig. 2), *Prosorhynchus,* and other genera, all found in various fishes. The life cycles of the various gasterostomes all follow the basic pattern found in *Bucephalus polymorphus.*

SUBORDER PROSTOMATA

The number of families subordinate to the Prostomata is numerous. Table 10-3 lists some of the families along with some major familial characteristics.

The nature of this text does not warrant the listing of every recognized family of the Digenea along with a discussion of representative genera. Instead, below are listed some of the major groups of trematodes along with some pertinent information concerning each.

THE STRIGEOID TREMATODES

The flukes that belong to this group are characterized by a divided body. The anterior portion or forebody is either flattened, curved, or cupped and functions as an attachment apparatus. The hindbody, which contains the gonads, is conical, ovoid, or cylindrical. There is a special holdfast or adhesive organ on the ventral body surface that is provided with histolytic glands. The genital pore is located toward the posterior end of the body. The eggs are either operculate or with polar filaments. The life cycle of strigeoids includes furcocercous cercariae and metacercariae encysted in molluscs, leeches, or even lower vertebrates. The metacercariae reach the definitive vertebrate host when the second intermediate host is ingested.

The strigeoid-type trematodes include members of the families Strigeidae and Diplostomatidae, and a few minor families. The biology of this group of flukes has been extensively reviewed and studied by Szidat (1929) and Dubois (1937, 1938). Dubois has contributed two monographs considered to be classics on the strigeoid trematodes. All strigeoids parasitize aquatic birds, reptiles, and mammals that feed on aquatic amphibians, fish, and invertebrates. The biology of strigeoid parasites of fish has been summarized by Hoffman (1960). This publication should be consulted by those interested in the parasites of fishes.

FAMILY STRIGEIDAE

The family Strigeidae includes the genera *Strigea* with numerous species parasitic in the intestine of fish-eating scavenger birds (Plate 10–21, Fig. 1), *Ophiosoma* in gulls and bitterns, *Parastrigea* in the domestic duck, and *Cotylurus* in various aquatic birds (ducks, geese, plovers, etc.) (Plate 10–21, Fig. 2). Other representative strigeids are dipicted in Plate 10–21.

Life Cycle Pattern

The miracidia of strigeids are free-swimming and possess two pairs of flame cells. These ciliated larvae actively penetrate snails, primarily lymnaeid snails, and pass through two sporocyst generations. The daughter sporocysts give rise to furcocercous cercariae that possess a conspicuous pharynx. These free-swimming cercariae penetrate various aquatic animals—

(*Text continued on page 260.*)

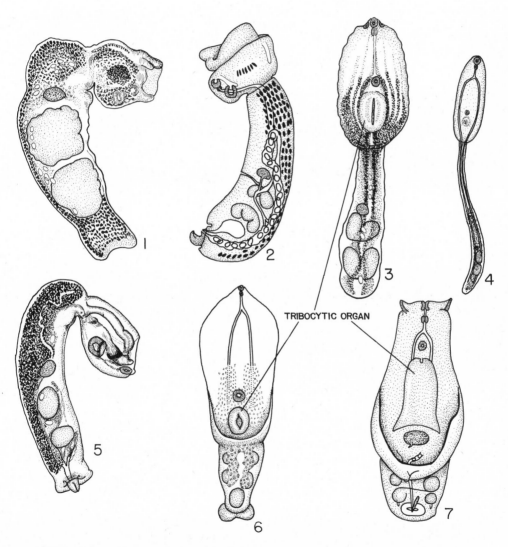

Plate 10-21   Some adult strigeoid trematodes. 1. *Strigea strigis* in intestine of various fish-eating birds. (Redrawn after Dubois, 1938.) **2.** *Cotylurus erraticus* in intestine of fish-eating birds. (Redrawn after Fuhrmann, 1928.) **3.** *Diplostomum spathaceum* in intestine of fish-eating birds. (Redrawn after Dubois, 1938.) **4.** *Uvulifer gracilis* in intestine of the bird *Ceryle lugubris*. (Redrawn after Yamaguti, 1934.) **5.** *Apatemon gracilis* in intestine of fish-eating anseriform birds. (Redrawn after Dubois, 1938.) **6.** *Neodiplostomum orchilongum* in intestine of hawks. (Redrawn after Noble.) **7.** *Alaria alata* in intestine of dogs, cats, and foxes. (Redrawn after Baylis, 1929.)

Table 10-3. General Characteristics of Common Digenetic Trematode Families†

Family	Hosts	Size	Shape	Cuticle	Suckers	Pharynx	Caeca	Genital Pore
Acanthocolpidae	F	s-m	E-VEc	S	2	+	l	Am
Acanthostomatidae	F	m	EO-Esf	S	2	+	l	Am
Allocreadiidae	F	s-m	EO-Esf	s-S	2	+	m-l	Am-l
Aporocotylidae	F	fs	E	S	0	−	m-lH	PPm-lG
Azygiidae	F	fs-fl	EO-Esf	s-w	2	+l	l	Am
Brachycoeliidae	AR	s-m	EO-sf	S-Sa	2	+	sml	Am
Brachylaemidae	(AR)BM	s-fs	EO-Esf	s-S	2	+	l	PP
Bunoderidae	F	s	EO-f*	s	2	+	l	Am
Campulidae	Mpc	fs-m	Esf	S	2	+	lHb	Am
Cathaemasiidae	B	fl	EO-E		2	+	l	Am
Cephalogonimidae	ARB	s	E-sf	S-Sa	2	+	s-m	AAm-l
Clinostomatidae	RB	m-vl	Ef	s	2	±	ld	P
Cyathocotylidae	RB	s	O	s	2	+	l	PP
Cyclocoelidae	B	fl-vl	EOf	s	1-o-o±v	+	(ld)	AAm
Dicrocoeliidae	ARBM	s-m	EO-Esf	s-S	2	+	m-l	Am
Didymozoidae	F	l	VE-c	s	1-2±v	±	l	AA
Diplostomatidae	BM	s	EOfacp*	s	1-2±v	+	l	PP
Echinostomatidae	BM	s-vl	EO-Ef	S-Sa	2p	+	l	Am
Eucotylidae	B	fs-m	Ef		1-v	+	l	A
Fasciolidae	M	l-vl	O-EOf*	s-S	2	+	lb	Am
Fellodistomatidae	F	s-fs	O-EOsf	S	2	+	m	Am-l
Gorgoderidae	FAR	s-fs	EO-Ecfp	s	2p	±	l	Am

†Modified from B. Dawes: *The Trematoda*, Cambridge University Press, 1946. With permission of publisher.

Explanation of abbreviations

HOSTS: F = fishes; A = Amphibia; R = Reptilia; B = Birds; M = Mammalia; pc = pinnipedes and cetaceans; ( ) = rarely.

SIZE: s = small; vs = very small; fs = fairly small; m = medium; l = large; fl = fairly large; vl = very large.

SHAPE: O = oval; EO = elongate oval; E = elongate; VE = very elongate; sf = slightly flat; f = flat; fa = flat anteriorly; sfa = slightly flat anteriorly; fp = flat posteriorly; c = cylindrical; cp = cylindrical posteriorly; * = shape distinctive.

CUTICLE: s = smooth; w = wrinkled; S = spinous; Sa = spinous anteriorly; S' = scaly; S'a = scaly anteriorly.

SUCKERS: 1, 2, 3 = number present; −o = oral sucker absent; −v = ventral sucker (acetabulum) absent; ± = present or absent; p = powerful.

PHARYNX: − = absent; + = present; ± = present or absent; l = large.

CAECA: s = short; m = medium length; l = long; d = with diverticula; b = with branched diverticula; ( ) = joined posteriorly; H = H-shaped; o = with anal openings either to exterior or into excretory vesicle; S = single caecum.

GENITAL PORE: A = immediately in front of acetabulum; AA = far forward, near mouth; P = posterior to acetabulum; PP = near posterior extremity; m = median; l = lateral; d = dorsal; G = with sucker or gonotyl.

Cirrus Pouch	Testes	Ovary	Uterus	Laurer's Canal	Seminal Receptacle	Vitellaria	Excretory Vesicle	Eggs	Family
+e	RT	ARm	A	·	·	W	Y	NN	Acanthocolpidae
–	RT	ARm	A	·	·	F-W	Y	Ns	Acanthostomatidae
+l	RT	AR-Ll	A	+	+	W	FT	NN	Allocreadiidae
+	N	PR	A	–	–	W	Y	NN	Aporocotylidae
+	RT	PRm	A	+	–	W	Y	NNE	Azygiidae
+s-l	R-T-O	A-P-R	DA	+	+	W	VY	NM	Brachycoeliidae
±s	RT	BRm	AD	+	–	W	Y	·	Brachylaemidae
+	RT-D	ARl	DA	+	+	W	S	N	Bunoderidae
+	R-L-BT	AR-Lm-l	A	+	+	W	T	NN	Campulidae
+	BT	ARm	A	+	–	W	S	NNl	Cathaemasiidae
+e	RT	ARl	DA	+	+	W	Y	N	Cephalogonimidae
+	LT	BRm	A	·	·	W	·	NN	Clinostomatidae
+l	RD	BRm	D	·	·	W	MB?	Fl	Cyathocotylidae
+s	R-LD	A-BRm	A	–	–	F-W	Sd	NM	Cyclocoelidae
+s	RT-O	PRm	DA	+	+s	F-W	TS	N	Dicrocoeliidae
–	R-LOe	Bme	A	–	·	Fcs	S	Ns	Didymozoidae
–	RT	ARm	A	·	·	W	MB	Fl	Diplostomatidae
+	R-LT	ARl-m	A	+	–	W	Y	NNl	Echinostomatidae
–	RO	ARl	AD	·	·	F	·	N	Eucotylidae
+	BT-D	ABl	A	+	+	W	MB	N	Fasciolidae
+s	RT-O	AR-Ll	DA	+	–	W	YV	NE	Fellodistomatidae
–	R-LO	ARm-l	DA	+	+	F	Td	Nl	Gorgoderidae

CIRRUS POUCH: – = absent; + = present; ± = present or absent; s = short or small; l = large; e = elongate.
TESTES: R = rounded or entire; L = lobed; B = branched; T = tandem; O = approximately in same transverse plane (opposite); D = diagonal; e = elongate; N = numerous; S = single.
OVARY: A = anterior to testes; P = posterior to testes; B = between or on same plane as testes; R = rounded or entire; L = lobed; B = branched; m = median; l = lateral; e = elongate.
UTERUS: A = with ascending limb only; DA or AD = with ascending and descending limbs; – = absent; ( ) = rare.
LAURER'S CANAL: – = absent; + = present.
SEMINAL RECEPTACLE: – = absent; + = present; s = small; l = large.
VITELLARIA: W = well developed; F = feebly developed; c = compact; s = single.
EXCRETORY VESICLE: F = funnel-shaped; Y = Y-shaped; V = V-shaped; T = tubular; S = sac-like; MB = much branched; d = with dorsal pore.
EGGS: N = numerous; NN = not numerous; E = each containing embryo; F = few; s = small; l = large; f_1, f_2 = with 1 or 2 terminal filaments; M = containing a miracidium.

(*Table continued on page 258.*)

(*Table 10–3 continued.*)

Family	Hosts	Size	Shape	Cuticle	Suckers	Pharynx	Caeca	Genital Pore
Halipegidae	FA	m-fl	EO-c	s	2	+	l	AAm
Haploporidae	F	vs-s	O-EOsf	S-Sa	2	+l	s	Am
Haplosplanchnidae	F	fs	O-EO		2	+	(S)	AAm
Hemiuridae	F(A)	s-m	O-EOc	s-w	2	+	l	Am
Heterophyidae	BM	vs-s	EOsf	S'-S'a	1-3	+	l	Pm-lG
Lecithodendriidae	ARBM	s	O-EOsf	s-S	2	+	m-l	Am-l-d
Mesometridae	F	s-fs	O		1-v	+	m	A(A)
Microphallidae	B	vs-s	O	S-Sa	2	+	s-m-l	
Monorchiidae	F	s	O-sf	S	2	+	l	Am-l
Notocotylidae	BM	s-fs	EOf	Sa	1-v	+	l(d)	AAm
Opisthorchiidae	RBM	s-m	EO-Ef	s-S	2	+	m-l	Am
Orchipedidae	B	s-m	E	s	2	+	l	AAm
Paramphistomatidae	FARBM	fl-l	EO-Ec	s	2p	±	m-l	Am
Philophthalmidae	B	m-l	EO-Esf	s-S	2	+l	l	Am
Plagiorchiidae	FARBM	fs-m	O-EOsf	S-S	2	+	m-l	A(A)m-l
Psilostomatidae	B	s-fs	EO-Ef	s-S	2p	+	l	Al
Ptychogonimidae	F	fs-m	O-EOsf	s-w	2p	+l	lo	Am
Sanguinicolidae	F	vs	Ec	s	0	–	l	PP
Schistosomatidae	BM	l-vl	VEc*	s-S	0-2±0±v	–	(l)	AAm-l
Stomylotrematidae	B	fs	O-EO	s	2	+l	m-l	AAl
Strigeidae	RBM	s	EOfacp*	s	1-2±v	+	l	PP
Troglotrematidae	BM	m-fl	Osfa	S	1-2±v	+	m-l	A-Pm-l
Zoogonidae	F	s	Osf	S	2	±	s	Al

†Modified from B. Dawes: *The Trematoda*, Cambridge University Press, 1946. With permission of publisher.

Explanation of abbreviations

HOSTS: F =fishes; A =Amphibia; R =Reptilia; B =Birds; M =Mammalia; pc =pinnipedes and cetaceans; ( ) =rarely.

SIZE: s =small; vs =very small; fs =fairly small; m =medium; l =large; fl =fairly large; vl =very large.

SHAPE: O =oval; EO =elongate oval; E =elongate; VE =very elongate; sf =slightly flat; f =flat; fa =flat anteriorly; sfa =slightly flat anteriorly; fp =flat posteriorly; c =cylindrical; cp =cylindrical posteriorly; * =shape distinctive.

CUTICLE: s =smooth; w =wrinkled; S =spinous; Sa =spinous anteriorly; S' =scaly; S'a =scaly anteriorly.

SUCKERS: 1, 2, 3 =number present; –o =oral sucker absent; –v =ventral sucker (acetabulum) absent; ± =present or absent; p =powerful.

PHARYNX: – =absent; + =present; ± =present or absent; l =large.

CAECA: s =short; m =medium length; l =long; d =with diverticula; b =with branched diverticula; ( ) =joined posteriorly; H =H-shaped; o =with anal openings either to exterior or into excretory vesicle; S =single caecum.

GENITAL PORE: A =immediately in front of acetabulum; AA =far forward, near mouth; P =posterior to acetabulum; PP =near posterior extremity; m =median; l =lateral; d =dorsal; G =with sucker or gonotyl.

Cirrus Pouch	Testes	Ovary	Uterus	Laurer's Canal	Seminal Receptacle	Vitellaria	Excretory Vesicle	Eggs	Family
–	RO	PRl	A	+	–	Fc	Y	Nf_1	Halipegidae
+	SR	BRl-m	DA	+	–	W	S	NNf_1M	Haploporidae
–	SR	AR	A	–	+l	F	Y	M	Haplosplanchnidae
–	RT-O	PRm	DA	+	+	Fc	Y	Ns	Hemiuridae
–	R-L-T-O	AR-Lm-l	(D)A	+	+	W	Y	NN	Heterophyidae
+	R-LO	A-Pl	DA	+	+	F-W	V	N	Lecithodendriidae
–	RO	PL	A	·	·	W	·	NNf_1	Mesometridae
±	RO	Am-l	DA	·	±	W	·	N	Microphallidae
+e	SR	ARl	DA	+	±	W	YT	Ns	Monorchiidae
+e	R-LO	BR-Lm	A	+	–	W	Yd	Nf_2	Notocotylidae
–	R-BD	ARm	A(D)	+	+	W	Y	Ns	Opisthorchiidae
–	N	AR	A	+	+	W	TY	NNl	Orchipedidae
±	R-LT-D-O	PRm	A	+	·	W	Sd	NorNN	Paramphistomatidae
+e	R-LT-D	ARm	A	+	–	F	·	NM	Philophthalmidae
+	R-LT-D-O	AR-Ll	DA	+	±	W	Y	Ns	Plagiorchiidae
+l	RT	ARm	A	+	+s	W	Y	Nl	Psilostomatidae
–	R-LT	Am	DA	+	–	W	V	NM	Ptychogonimidae
–	NRT-O	PLm	–	–	–	W	Y	Fl(one)	Sanguinicolidae
–	NR	–Rm	A	–	–	W	YV	Fl	Schistosomatidae
+	RO	ARl	AD	+	+	F	·	Ns	Stomylotrematidae
±	RT	ARm	A	+	+	W	MB	Fl	Strigeidae
±	L-BOe	ALl	A	+	+	W	TYS	Ns-l	Troglotrematidae
+e	RO	PRm	DA	+	+	Fcs	S	NNM	Zoogonidae

CIRRUS POUCH: – =absent; + =present; ± =present or absent; s =short or small; l =large; e =elongate.
TESTES: R =rounded or entire; L =lobed; B =branched; T =tandem; O =approximately in same transverse plane (opposite); D =diagonal; e =elongate; N =numerous; S =single.
OVARY: A =anterior to testes; P =posterior to testes; B =between or on same plane as testes; R =rounded or entire; L =lobed; B =branched; m =median; l =lateral; e =elongate.
UTERUS: A =with ascending limb only; DA or AD =with ascending and descending limbs; – =absent; ( ) =rare.
LAURER'S CANAL: – =absent; + =present.
SEMINAL RECEPTACLE: – =absent; + =present; s =small; l =large.
VITELLARIA: W =well developed; F =feebly developed; c =compact; s =single.
EXCRETORY VESICLE: F =funnel-shaped; Y = Y-shaped; V = V-shaped; T =tubular; S =sac-like; MB =much branched; d =with dorsal pore.
EGGS: N =numerous; NN =not numerous; E =each containing embryo; F =few; s =small; l =large; f_1, f_2 =with 1 or 2 terminal filaments; M =containing a miracidium.

for example, snails, fish, leeches, tadpoles, frogs, salamanders, and snakes—and develop into encysted or nonencysted metacercariae. When the definitive host ingests the second intermediate host, the cycle is completed.

Lautenschlager (1959) and others have reported meningeal tumors associated with the presence of the metacercariae of *Diplostomulum* sp. in the brain of salamanders. The author has observed many extremely sluggish aquatic newts, *Triturus,* that upon investigation were found to contain metacercariae of *Diplostomulum* in their brains. In addition, when large numbers of metacercariae are present in the eyes of fish, blindness ensues.

Cyathocotyle bushiensis

Erasmus and Öhman (1963) have contributed an illuminating study of one aspect of the relationship between *Cyathocotyle bushiensis,* a strigeid trematode, and its duck host. The metacercariae of this trematode are encysted in the fresh-water snail *Bithynia tentaculata.* When infected snails are ingested by ducks, the adult trematodes develop in the bird's caecum where these parasites are intimately associated with the caecal wall. This association is made possible primarily by the muscular, ventrally situated, adhesive organ of the parasite, which actually draws the host's tissue up into its cup shaped chamber. Microscopic examination of this adhesive organ has revealed that clusters of spindle shaped secretory cells are associated with it.

Histochemical examinations further revealed that these secretory cells are rich in proteins and RNA granules, thus suggesting that they are sites of active protein synthesis. Indeed, these cells are now known to secrete various enzymes, including alkaline phosphatase, esterases, and leucine aminopeptidase. Such enzymes act on the host's tissue and thus the lining epithelial cells of the duck's caecum are eroded. Furthermore, the position of the trematode's mouth suggests that the sloughed host cells are ingested. Thus the adhesive organ complex in this strigeid not only serves as an attachment organ but also as a site from which enzymes are secreted that make possible ingestion of the host's cells by the parasite. Such secretory cells are also associated with the adhesive organ of metacercariae.

Immunity in Molluscan Hosts of Strigeids

It was while studying the infection of the fresh-water snail *Lymnaea stagnalis* by the larvae of the strigeid *Cotylurus flabelliformis* that Winfield (1932) and Nolf and Cort (1933) discovered that acquired immunity may occur in molluscan intermediate hosts of larval trematodes. These investigators reported that the presence of sporocysts of *C. flabelliformis* in varieties of *L. stagnalis* prevents almost all cercariae of this strigeid from penetrating, even when the infected snails are exposed to very large numbers of cercariae. Normally, the cercariae of *C. flabelliformis* invade noninfected snails of the same or some closely related species and encyst therein as metacercariae.

Cort et al. (1945) discovered that when *Cotylurus flabelliformis* sporocysts infect another snail, *Stagnicola emarginata angulata,* the mollusc also becomes refractile to penetration by free-swimming cercariae. The few cercariae that do succeed in penetrating infected snails do not develop into metacercariae unless they enter sporocysts. This suggests that some type of antibody is present in infected snails that acts against unprotected cercariae, since only those cercariae that successfully enter sporocysts, and thus presumably are protected from the mollusc's antibodies, succeed in developing into metacercariae.

FAMILY DIPLOSTOMATIDAE

The family Diplostomatidae includes the genera *Diplostomum* (Plate 10–21, Fig. 3) and *Neodiplostomum* (Plate 10–21, Fig. 6), both found primarily in birds. The genus *Alaria* includes *A. alata,* a species parasitic in the intestine of dogs, cats, and foxes (Plate 10–21, Fig. 7). This unusual fluke differs from the other strigeoids in that it requires three intermediate hosts to complete its life cycle (Bosma, 1934; Odlaug, 1940). The furcocercous cercariae (Plate 10–19, Fig. 4) penetrate frogs and tadpoles but do not develop into metacercariae; instead, they only undergo slight metamorphosis and develop into mesocercariae (Plate 10–19, Fig. 5). When the second intermediate host is ingested by the third intermediate host—usually mice, rats, and raccoons—the mesocercariae develop into metacercariae. Finally, when the third intermediate host is ingested by the definitive host, the adults develop.

STRIGEOID METACERCARIAL TYPES

Since the metacercariae of the strigeoids are probably the most frequently encountered stage, it should be mentioned that these metacercariae can be separated into three types: (1) The tetracotyle type characterized by a

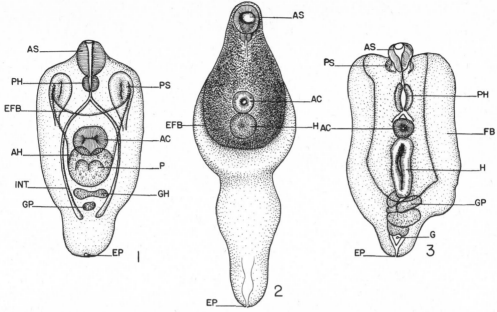

Plate 10-22   Strigeid types. 1. Tetracotyle larva from a garter snake. (Redrawn after Hughes, 1929.) **2.** Neascus larva from a bass. (Redrawn after Hughes, 1927.) **3.** Diplostomulum larva. (Redrawn after Bosma, 1934.)

(AC, acetabulum; AH, anterior lobes of holdfast organ; AS, anterior sucker; EFB, edge of cup-like forebody; EP, excretory pore; GH, glands of holdfast organ; GP, genital primordium; INT, intestine; P, posterior lobes of holdfast organ; PH, pharynx; PS, pseudosucker; H, holdfast organ; FB, forebody; G, gonopore.)

pyriform body, with or without a hindbody, but with well developed pseudosuckers, holdfast organs, acetabulum, and an auxiliary excretory vesicle (Plate 10–22, Fig. 1). (2) The neascus type is characterized by a cup shaped forebody with a well developed hindbody and auxiliary vesicle but lacking pseudosuckers (Plate 10–22, Fig. 2). (3) The diplostomulum type is characterized by a large concave forebody, a small conical hindbody, pseudosuckers, and an auxiliary tubular vesicle (Plate 10–22, Fig. 3). Diplostomula in the host are not surrounded by parasite-elaborated cyst walls.

THE SCHISTOSOMATOID TREMATODES

The schistosome and schistosome-like trematodes belong to the families Sanguinicolidae, Spirorchidae, and Schistosomatidae. The adults are either dioecious or monoecious and are found in the blood of their definitive hosts. Their elongate slender bodies are well adapted to this habitat. They lack a muscular pharynx and may or may not possess acetabula. The eggs of schistosomes typically lack an operculum. The life history pattern includes a free-swimming miracidium, two generations of sporocysts in a molluscan intermediate host, and furcocercous cercariae that penetrate the integument of the definitive host and develop into adults in the blood of the portal system.

FAMILY SCHISTOSOMATIDAE

The family Schistosomatidae includes the genus *Schistosoma,* which in turn includes several species parasitic in the blood of man and domestic animals. The three human-infecting species are *S. mansoni, S. japonicum,* and *S. haematobium**

Human Schistosomiasis

Although two major human parasitic diseases —malaria and hookworm disease—appear to be on the decline in recent years as the result of concerted efforts involving drugs, insecticides, and public health measures, another dreaded parasitic disease—schistosomiasis,†—is on the upgrade. Some 114 million cases of human schistosomiasis exist in the world. In Communist China alone, it has been estimated that 11

*The three human-infecting species of schistosomes are believed by some to be complexes of closely related species or varieties that infect man and other animals (Kuntz, 1955).

†Known as bilharziasis among European parasitologists.

million cases exist, and this disease is regarded as the most serious parasitic disease in that country. Another heavily affected nation is Egypt. In lower Egypt, an incidence of 60 per cent infection has been estimated in most areas, with an incidence as high as 90 per cent in some localities. In all, close to 10 million cases of human schistosomiasis exist in that country.

With the advent of jet airplanes, the world is rapidly shrinking. Schistosomiasis is no longer a disease of distant lands. Indeed, human cases of this parasite-caused disease exist in considerable numbers in such metropolitan areas as New York, Chicago, and Philadelphia, primarily among immigrants from endemic areas.

Schistosomiasis has even influenced world history. To cite a recent example, Kierman at-

tributed a decisive role to this disease in the prevention of an assault on Formosa by Communist China early in 1950. In that instance, between 30,000 and 50,000 acute cases of schistosomiasis among soldiers postponed the attack. During World War II, schistosomiasis among American troops in the Pacific caused great problems. For example, the infection of nearly 2000 troops during the recapturing of Leyte in 1944 caused the loss of over 300,000 man-days and $3,000,000 for medical care. The scourge of schistosomiasis on mankind is of such a magnitude that the World Health Organization has earmarked it as one of its major targets.

Schistosoma mansoni. This parasite is a dioecious species widely distributed in Africa,

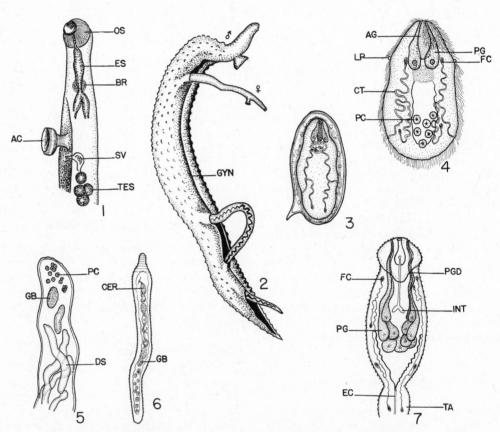

Plate 10-23   Stages in the life cycle of *Schistosoma mansoni*. 1. Anterior portion of a male specimen. (AC, acetabulum; BR, brain; ES, esophagus; OS, oral sucker; SV, seminal vesicle; TES, testes.) (Redrawn and modified after Hyman, L. H. 1951. *The Invertebrates,* McGraw-Hill, New York.) 2. Adult male and female in copula with female in gynecophoric canal (GYN) of male. (Redrawn after Gönnert.) 3. Egg enclosing miracidium. (Redrawn after Faust in Craig and Faust, 1951. *Clinical Parasitology,* Lea and Febiger, Philadelphia.) 4. Miracidium. (AG, apical gland; CT, collecting tubule of excretory system; FC, flame cell; LP, lateral papilla; PC, propagative (germinal) cell; PG, penetration gland.) (Original.) 5. Mother sporocyst enclosing propagative cells (PC), germ balls (GB), and daughter sporocysts (DS). (Original.) 6. Daughter sporocyst enclosing germ balls (GB), and cercariae (CER). (Original.) 7. Body proper of cercaria, showing internal structures. (EC, excretory canal leading into tail; INT, intestinal caeca; PG, penetration glands; PGD, ducts of penetration glands; TA, tail. (Redrawn after Faust and Hoffman, 1934.)

parts of Brazil, Venezuela, Guiana, Puerto Rico, and the Dominican Republic (Plate 10–23). Its occurrence in the New World is not as concentrated or as prevalent as it is in Africa. Its presence in the Western Hemisphere is believed to be a by-product of the African slave trade.

The females and males found in the host's portal blood, usually in the smaller branches of the inferior mesenteric vein in the region of the lower colon, are often in close association. The male, measuring 6.4 to 9.9 mm. in length, is broader than the female. The two lateral borders of its body are curved to form a groove—the gynecophoric canal—in which the female, measuring 7.2 to 14 mm. in length, is snugly held. Minute sensory papillae cover the body surface of the male, and microscopic tufts of cilia are found on these protuberances (Plate 10–23, Fig. 2). Both suckers are present and are located in the anterior portion of the body (Plate 10–23, Fig. 1). The internal anatomy of this fluke is similar to that of other trematodes except that a pharynx is wanting and the males are multitesticular.

The major molluscan hosts of *S. mansoni* are listed in Table 10–4. *S. mansoni* is readily maintained in certain laboratory mammals, such as the hamster, mouse, and cotton rat. The relative susceptibilities of some common laboratory mammals are tabulated in Table 10–5.

Life Cycle of *Schistosoma mansoni*. In *S. mansoni*, fertilization occurs when spermatozoa from the male are introduced into the female. The fully formed egg measures 114 to 175 μ by 45 to 68 μ, is nonoperculate, and bears a large posterolateral spine (Plate 10–23, Fig. 3). Such eggs are laid by the female in the smallest blood vessels of the host to which they migrate after copulation. The eggs become free in the mesenteric vessels and are carried by the blood to the proximity of the large intestine, where they gradually penetrate the intestinal wall, become included in the lumen, and are passed out in feces. Sometimes a few eggs become trapped in various tissues and cause inflammation. Andrado and Barka (1962), by employing histochemical techniques, demonstrated that eggs in the liver of experimentally infected mice contain acid phosphatase, nucleotidases, ATPase, aminopeptidase, alkaline phosphatase, and a nonspecific esterase. In addition, a complex carbohydrate, believed to be antigenic, is also present. The reticuloendothelial cells of the host's liver and spleen became sites of high acid phosphatase activity.

When the eggs of *S. mansoni* come in contact with water, the enclosed miracidia break out of the shells by cracking them. The free-swimming miracidium (Plate 10–23, Fig. 4) finds and penetrates a pulmonate snail and transforms into mother sporocysts (Plate 10–23, Fig. 5), which are located in the region of the host's foot. Daughter sporocysts (Plate 10–23, Fig. 6), differentiating from the germ balls in mother sporocysts, migrate to the host's hepatopancreas and eventually produce large numbers of furcocercous cercariae (Plate 10–23, Fig. 7). These escape from the daughter sporocysts through the birth pore, leave the snail, and become free-swimming in water. When the cercariae come in contact with the skin of man in the water, they actively penetrate it.

The penetration process of the cercariae of *Schistosoma* is understood (Stirewalt and Hackey, 1956). It involves lysis by secretions of the penetration glands coupled with muscular boring movements. In cases of heavy infections, inflammation occurs at the sites of penetration.

If successful penetration occurs, usually in several minutes, the cercariae lose their tails during the process. Such tailless cercariae can be found in the skin for approximately 18 hours after penetration. They then enter the blood circulation and are carried to the host's lungs via the heart. Young adults, known as schistosomulae, can be found in the lungs by the second or third day after penetration. Later, by about the fifteenth day, they can be found accumulated in the liver, where they feed on portal blood and undergo rapid growth.

By the twenty-third day, migration of the young adults to the mesenteric veins takes place, and sexual maturation and mating occur. Egg production generally occurs by the fortieth day. If cercariae are taken in with drinking water, these larvae will penetrate through the lining of the mouth and throat. Rodents can be experimentally infected through the ingestion of infected snails.

The sex of *S. mansoni*, like that of the other dioecious species, is genetically controlled. A male miracidium eventually gives rise to all male adults and a female miracidium results in female adults.

Schistosoma japonicum. This parasite is geographically confined to the Far East (Plate 10–24, Fig. 1). It is found primarily in Japan, China, and the Philippine Islands. The life cycle of this species parallels that of *S. mansoni*. The eggs are readily distinguished from those of *S. mansoni* because there is only a very small lateral spine on the shell (Plate 10–24, Fig. 2). The entire egg measures 70 to 100 μ by

Table 10-4. Major Molluscan Hosts of *Schistosoma mansoni**

Species of Snail	Geographic Location
Australorbis glabratus	Puerto Rico, Dominican Republic, St. Kitts, Guadeloupe, Martinique, St. Lucia, Dutch Guiana, Venezuela, Brazil
A. tenagophilus	Brazil
Tropicorbis centimetralis	Brazil
T. philippianus	Ecuador†
T. chilensis	Chile†
T. albicans	Puerto Rico†
T. riisei	Puerto Rico†
Biomphalaria pfeifferi gaudi	Gambia, Portuguese Guiana, Sierra Leone, Liberia, Guiana, Mauritania, Senegal, Sudan, Ivory Coast, Ghana, Nigeria
B. sudanica	Cameroons, Congo, Kenya, Uganda, Tanganyika, Nyasaland
B. rüppellii	Congo, Sudan, Eritrea, Ethiopia, Kenya, Uganda, Tanganyika
B. pfeifferi	Uganda, the Rhodesias, Tanganyika, South Africa, Mozambique, Madagascar
B. choanomphala	Uganda
B. smithi	Uganda
B. stanleyi	Uganda
B. alexandrina	Egypt, Saudi Arabia, Yemen
B. sudanica	Congo
B. bridouxiana	Congo

* Data from Malek, E.A. 1962. *Laboratory Guide and Notes for Medical Malacology.* Burgess Publ. Co.
† Experimental infections.

Table 10-5. Susceptibilities of Common Laboratory Mammals to *Schistosoma* Infections*

Host	Per cent Maturing	Per cent Fatality among Hosts	Presence of Eggs in Host's Feces
Hamster	31.8	71	++
Mouse	22.1	49	+
Cotton rat	17.2	12	+
Guinea pig	6.4	9	–
Cat	10-45	0	–
Albino rat	2.6	1	–
Rabbit	0-18	0	–
Dog	0	0	–

* Data from Stirewalt, Kuntz, and Evans (1951).

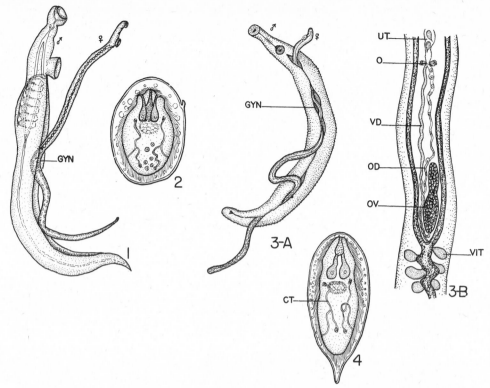

Plate 10-24   *Schistosoma japonicum* and *S. haematobium.* 1. *Schistosoma japonicum* female lying in gynecophoric canal (GYN) of male. 2. Egg of *S. japonicum* enclosing miracidium. Note small lateral spine. 3. **A.** *Schistosoma haematobium* female lying in gynecophoric canal (GYN) of male. (Redrawn after Looss.) **B.** Reproductive system of female. *S. haematobium.* (O, ootype; OD, oviduct; OV, ovary; UT, uterus; VD, vitelline duct; VIT, vitelline gland.) 4. Egg of *S. haematobium* enclosing miracidium, showing collecting tubules of excretory system (CT). Note prominent posterior terminal spine. (Figs. 1, 2, 3B, and 4 redrawn after Faust in Craig, C. and Faust, E. 1951. *Clinical Parasitology,* Lea & Febiger, Philadelphia.)

50 to 65 μ. The body cuticle of adult male *S. japonicum* does not bear cuticular projections, rather true cuticular spines are present. The snail hosts include *Oncomelania formosana* in Formosa; *O. fausti, O. tangi,* and *O. hupensis* in China; *O. nosophora* in Japan; and *O. quadrasi* in the Philippines.

Within the human host, *S. japonicum* adults inhabit the branches of the superior mesenteric vein in the proximity of the small intestine. In addition, the inferior mesenterics and caval system may also be invaded, for the worms tend to migrate away from the liver as they become older. Adult males may reach 22 mm. in length, while females may reach 26 mm. in length.

Schistosoma haematobium. This schistosome is endemic to North Africa (particularly in the valley of the Nile), central and west Africa, and the Near East (Plate 10–24, Fig. 3). Stoll (1947) estimated that 39.2 million human infections exist; the majority are limited to Africa. Again, the life cycle of *S. haematobium*

parallels that of *S. mansoni* except the eggs do not pass into the lumen of the large intestine but pass into the urinary bladder and are expelled in urine. These eggs measure 112 to 170 μ by 40 to 70 μ and are readily identified by a distinct terminal spine (Plate 10–24, Fig. 4).

After maturing in the sinusoids in the host's liver, *S. haematobium* adults, as with other human-infecting schistosomes, migrate from the liver. The majority of *S. haematobium* adults reach the vesical, prostatic, and uterine plexuses by way of the inferior haemorrhoidal veins. Adult males may become 15 mm. long, while females may reach 20 mm. in length.

The snail hosts for *S. haematobium* are listed in Table 10–6.

PATHOLOGY. The injuries inflicted by schistosomes depend on the degree of infection and the prolonged period of infection and reinfection. During migration of the eggs through tissues to reach the colon (*S. mansoni* and *S. japonicum*) or the urinary bladder (*S. haemato-*

Table 10-6. The Gastropod Hosts of *Schistosoma haematobium*[*]

Species of Snail	Geographic Location
Bulinus truncatus	Morocco, Tunisia, Algeria, Egypt, Libya, Sudan, Turkey, Syria, Israel, Saudi Arabia, Yemen, Iraq, Iran
B. *guernei*	Ghana, Cameroons, Gambia, Mauritania
B. *truncatus rohlfsi*	Ghana, Cameroons, Gambia, Mauritania
B. *senegalensis*	Senegal, Gambia
B. *globosus*	Portuguese Guiana, Gambia, Sierra Leone, Liberia, Cameroons, Ghana, Nigeria, Sudan, Angola, Uganda, Tanganyika, the Rhodesias, South Africa, Mozambique
B. *africanus*	South Africa, the Rhodesias, Mozambique
B. *jousseaumei*	Portuguese Guiana, Le Soudan, Gambia

[*] Data from Malek (1962).

bium), tissue reactions in the form of inflammation, necrosis, connective tissue encapsulation, and eventual scar formation take place. *Schistosoma mansoni* and *S. japonicum* eggs may become lodged in the intestinal mucosa, causing pseudoabscesses. Since the females force their way into small blood vessels, disruptions of the vessel walls commonly occur. During migration of the eggs through the wall of the urinary bladder in *S. haematobium*, or through the colon wall in *S. mansoni* and *S. japonicum*, hemorrhage generally occurs. This is accompanied by diarrhea in *mansoni* and *japonicum* schistosomiasis.

In endemic areas, where reinfections occur, repeated penetration of the intestinal and bladder walls results in extensive scar formation, which prevents migration of the eggs through these structures. As the result, many eggs are transported to the liver and rarely to other sites, such as the brain and spinal cord. Wherever these aberrant eggs become lodged, local inflammation, fibrosis, and necrosis ensue. Cirrhosis of the liver is not uncommon. Swelling of the liver and spleen is of common occurrence. In instances of heavy infections, mature worms may migrate to the brain, lungs, uterus, oviduct, and gonads. As expected, their presence at these sites provoke pathological changes.

Acute cases of schistosomiasis, especially schistosomiasis *japonicum*, which is highly pathogenic, often lead to death.

IMMUNITY. Immunity to human schistosomiasis is not well understood, although it is known that animals experimentally infected with the human-infecting schistosomes do develop an immunity. Vogel and co-workers have demonstrated that the exposure of monkeys to moderate numbers of infective cercariae of *S. mansoni* and *S. japonicum* monthly, so as not to elicit schistosomiasis, brought about a state of tolerance. Subsequent exposures of these monkeys to cercariae in numbers sufficiently large to kill an unexposed host did not cause symptoms of schistosomiasis, nor was the number of parasites in the body increased. This process of protecting against reinfection as a result of an existing infection is known as premunition. No doubt some degree of premunition must occur among humans in endemic areas where constant reinfections occur while earlier infections still exist.

In addition to infecting man, the three important species of schistosomes can infect various other animals. Natural infections of monkeys and rodents with *S. mansoni* are known. Similarly, monkeys can be naturally infected with *S. haematobium*, and various rodents can be experimentally infected with this parasite. *Schistosoma japonicum* can infect cattle, goats, pigs, dogs, cats, shrews, weasels, and various wild rodents. Different strains of *S. japonicum* have been recognized among those that naturally infect animals other than man, and there is reason to believe that certain strains are not as virulent as the natural human-infecting strain. Furthermore, geographic strains—

namely, Chinese, Formosan, and Japanese strains—have also been recognized. The various strains, and the three human-infecting "species" for that matter, interbreed.

OTHER SCHISTOSOMES.   Other economically important schistosomes include *S. bovis* in cattle and sheep. Also, this species can be experimentally induced to mature in guinea pigs. *Schistosoma indicum* is found in the veins of horses, cattle, goats, and buffaloes in India; *S. nasale* in the nostrils of cattle in India; and *S. suis* in the portal veins of pigs and dogs in India.

Genus *Schistosomatium*

Among members of *Schistosomatium*, found in rodents is *S. douthitti*, a parasite in the hepatic portal system of field mice, albino mice, deer mice, and muskrats. *Schistosomatium doutthitti* is commonly used in the laboratory as an experimental animal because it is not infective to man. This species is dioecious. The body of the male measures from 1.9 to 6.3 mm in length, and is divided into the anterior forebody, which is flattened and occupies two-fifths of the body length, and the hindbody, which is curved to form the gynecophoric groove. There are 14 to 16 testes present in *S. douthitti*, and the body cuticle is spinous.

The female, measuring from 1.1 to 5.4 mm.

Table 10-7. Development of *Schistosomatium douthitti* in Various Hosts

Host	Development in Host
Deer mouse	normal
Field mouse	normal
Hamster	normal
Muskrat	normal
Albino mouse	normal
Lynx	normal
Rat	abnormal
Rabbit	abnormal
Cat	abnormal
Monkey	Immunity develops in 3 weeks

in length, bears spines along the lateral edges of the dorsal and ventral surfaces. These cuticular spines extend from the anterior portion of the body posteriorly to the level of the ovary. The oral sucker also bears spines. When in copula, the female worm is held within the male's gynecophoric groove with her dorsal body surface against the ventral surface of the male and with only her anterior end protruding.

The eggs of *S. douthitti* are smaller than those of the human-infecting species. They measure from 42 to 80 μ by 50 to 58 μ and do not possess a lateral spine.

The molluscan hosts for *S. douthitti* include various subspecies of *Lymnaea stagnalis, Physa gyrina elliptica, Lymnaea palustris, Stagnicola exilis,* and *Stagnicola emarginata angulata.* Attempts to infect various mammals with this schistosome have produced varied results, as shown in Table 10-7. It is interesting to note that Short and Menzel (1959) reported that some of the eggs of *Schistosomatium douthitti* can develop parthenogenetically, giving rise to haploid females.

Swimmer's Itch

An interesting phase of schistosome biology concerns so-called cercarial dermatitis, or "swimmer's itch." Cercariae of species that normally infect birds and other vertebrates attempt to penetrate the skin of humans and in so doing sensitize the areas of attack, resulting in itchy rashes. Since humans are not suitable definitive hosts for these cercariae, the flukes do not enter the blood and mature, rather they perish in the process of attempting to penetrate the skin. In fresh-water lakes of North America, cercariae of the genera *Trichobilharzia* and *Bilharziella*, which normally infect birds, are the most common dermatitis-producing flukes. Chu (1958) has contributed an extensive review of cercarial dermatitis and has listed the various causative cercariae—both fresh-water and marine—in areas bordering the Pacific. This paper should be consulted by those interested in schistosome dermatitis.

FAMILY SANGUINICOLIDAE

The family Sanguinicolidae includes several monoecious genera primarily parasitic in the blood of fishes. These slender trematodes lack suckers and a pharynx, and possess X or H shaped intestinal caeca. They possess follicular testes and separate male and female genital pores. Three of the most important genera are *Sanguinicola, Cardiocoa,* and *Cardicola* found mainly in fishes (Plate 10–25, Figs. 7 and 8).

Life History of *Sanguinicola*

Scheuring (1920) reported that eggs of *Sanguinicola inermis* discharged into the blood of fish undergo further development and are eventually located in the capillaries of the host's gills. In this location the eggs hatch and the miracidia escape into the water. The intermediate host is the snail *Lymnaea* sp. The furcocercous cercariae that escape from the gastropod become attached to the gills of carp and actively penetrate into the blood. Some species of *Sanguinicola* do not live in the host's blood vessels but are found in the heart, liver and other highly vascularized organs.

Cardiocoa davisi

In North America, a sanguinicolid blood fluke of trout, known as *Cardiocoa davisi,* has caused severe trout mortality in hatcheries. Adults of this fluke normally reside in the main gill capillaries, lying parallel with the gill cartilages. It differs from most digenetic trematodes in that only one egg is produced at a time, and this egg is carried by the blood into the capillaries of the gill filaments, where development of the miracidium is completed and hatching occurs.

The active miracidium works its way through the epithelium to the surface of the gill filament, where a lobule forms. When the lobule ruptures, the miracidium becomes free-swimming. After penetrating the snail host *Oxytrema* (*Goniobasis*) *circumlineata,* the miracidium transforms into a mother sporocyst. Mother sporocysts give rise to daughter sporocysts that in turn give rise to rediae. The furcocercous cercariae are formed within rediae.

These cercariae, like the adults, lack suckers and a pharynx. Its caecum terminates in three short bulbous sacs. When a cercaria comes in contact with a fingerling trout, it penetrates through the surface of a fin, actively migrates through veins to the heart and from there to the gill capillaries, where it matures.

Cardicola klamathensis

Cardicola klamathensis is closely related to *Cardiocoa davisi,* but is smaller. It is found in the efferent renal veins of trout. The eggs are spherical, and the cercariae bear a longitudinal fin over the dorsal body surface. The gastropod host is *Fluminicola seminalis.*

FAMILY SPIRORCHIDAE

The family Spirorchidae includes relatively small distomate and monostomate species found in the blood of reptiles, primarily turtles. The biology of these blood flukes has been reviewed by Stunkard (1923) and Byrd (1939). These trematodes possess an oral sucker but lack a pharynx, and in some species the intestinal caeca are divided while in others there is a single unbranched caecum. The principal genus is *Spirorchis* (Plate 10–25, Fig. 9) containing several species, the validity of which are questioned. Although most commonly found in the blood of turtles, Ulmer and his co-workers have shown that *Spirorchis* can be embedded in the submucosa of the esophagus of turtles. Other representative genera are depicted in Plates 10–25 and 10–26.

Wall (1941) reported the life history of *Spirorchis.* The miracidium is free-swimming. There are two generations of sporocysts in the snail host, *Helisoma* spp., and the escaping cercariae are furcocercous. These penetrate the integument of the turtle host.

An interesting aspect of the influence of larval trematodes on their molluscan hosts was reported by Goodchild and Fried (1963) while studying the small planorbid snail *Menetus dilatatus buchanensis* infected with a species of *Spirorchis.* They reported that infected snails maintained in groups lived longer, began releasing cercariae sooner, and had a greater cercarial output per snail than snails individually maintained. As in many other species of cercariae, the shedding of *Spirorchis* cercariae by *M. dilatatus buchanensis* reflects periodicity, for the cercariae in this case are released at night. Goodchild and Fried were able to reverse the nocturnal shedding by employing a 12 hour alternation of day and night using artificial light. Thus, they have shown that the periodicity is in some way regulated by light.

There are other less well known schistosome-like families—for example, Aporocotylidae—the members of which are parasitic in the blood of fishes. The life cycle pattern is similar in all known cases. There is a free-swimming miracidium—mother sporocyst—daughter sporocyst—furcocercous free-swimming cercaria—adult type of life history pattern.

THE PLAGIORCHIOID TREMATODES

This group of flukes is included in a number of distome families, the more prominent being Plagiorchiidae, Dicrocoeliidae, Brachycoeliidae, and Lecithodendriidae. These small-to-medium worms are generally intestinal parasites, but certain species are found in the gallbladder, bile duct, lungs, and pancreatic ducts of their vertebrate hosts. There are various life history variations among the various families (Table 10–2). However, the cercariae usually possess thin, straight tails and stylets.

FAMILY PLAGIORCHIIDAE

The family Plagiorchiidae includes numerous species parasitic in fishes, amphibians, reptiles, birds, and mammals. Those found in fishes include species of *Astiotrema* (Plate 10–26, Fig. 3), and *Glossidium* (Plate 10–26, Fig. 4). The species of *Glossidium* are limited to fresh-water fish. Those found in amphibians include species of *Plagiorchis* (Plate 10–26, Fig. 5) in frogs, toads, and salamanders; *Haplometra* (Plate 10–26, Fig. 6) in the lungs of frogs; the extremely large genus *Haematoloechus* (Plate 10–26, Fig. 7) with over forty species all found in the lungs of various frogs and toads; and *Dolichosaccus* in the alimentary tract of frogs.

Plagiorchiid genera that parasitize reptiles include *Plagiorchis; Astiotrema; Opisthogonimus* (Plate 10–26, Fig. 8) in the intestine of snakes; *Stomatrema* (Plate 10–26, Fig. 9) in the mouth and esophagus of snakes; *Styphlodora* (Plate 10–26, Fig. 10) with various species in the gallbladder, kidneys, ureters, and intestines of snakes; *Dasymetra* (Plate 10–26, Fig. 11) in the intestine of water snakes; *Lechriorchis* (Plate 10–26, Fig. 12) in the lungs or oviducts of snakes; *Ochetosoma* (Plate 10–27, Fig. 1) with numerous species parasitic in the mouth, esophagus, or lungs of snakes; and *Zeugorchis* (Plate 10–27, Fig. 2) in the alimentary canal of various reptiles.

Life Cycle of *Ochetosoma*

The life cycles of the reptile-infecting species are mostly of the same general pattern. Byrd (1935) reported the life cycle of *Ochetosoma aniarum*, found in the mouth and esophagus of snakes, *Natrix* spp. The eggs laid by the monoecious adults contain fully formed miracidia. These do not hatch until the eggs are ingested by the snail *Physa helei*. It is suspected that the digestive juices of the gastropod play an important role in the hatching process, in activating the miracidia, and perhaps in some way effecting the opening of the operculum. There are two generations of sporocysts in the snail host. The daughter sporocysts give rise to thin and long-tailed xiphidiocercariae, which encyst in tadpoles. When infected tadpoles are ingested by snakes, the cycle is completed.

Life Cycle of *Plagiorchis*

The second developmental pattern, found among the plagiorchids, is typified by *Plagiorchis ramlianus,* an intestinal parasite of snakes. After the miracidium-enclosing egg is ingested by the snail *Bulinus contortus,* it hatches and the miracidium eventually gives rise to a redia instead of a sporocyst. The escaping xiphidiocercariae encyst in dragonfly larvae and hemipteran larvae, and when these are ingested by the definitive host, the cycle is completed.

***Plagiorchis* SPECIES.**   Numerous species of *Plagiorchis* have been reported from the intestine of birds; some, such as *P. arcuatus* and *P. petrovi,* are found in chickens.

Plagiorchids parasitic in mammals include *Plagiorchis javensis* and *P. philippinensis* in man, and *P. muris* in rats, dogs, and also man and birds. The genus *Neoglyphe* includes several species found in dogs, rodents, and other mammals in Japan, Russia, and Switzerland.

LIFE CYCLE OF *Plagiorchis muris.*   The life history of *Plagiorchis muris* has been studied by Tanabe (1922) and Dollfus (1925). The pattern is unusual for the xiphidiocercariae, which are formed in sporocysts, encyst in the same sporocysts. The molluscan host is *Lymnaea pervia.* When the snail is ingested by the definitive host, the cycle is completed. In this instance, the snail is the only intermediate host. Yamaguti (1943) did, however, demonstrate that if cercariae of *P. muris* are experimentally removed from the sporocysts, they will encyst in an experimental second intermediate host. This observation strongly suggests that *P. muris* originally required two intermediate hosts but has recently discarded its requirement for the second host, thus indicating that hosts can be eliminated during progressive evolution (see Chapter 1).

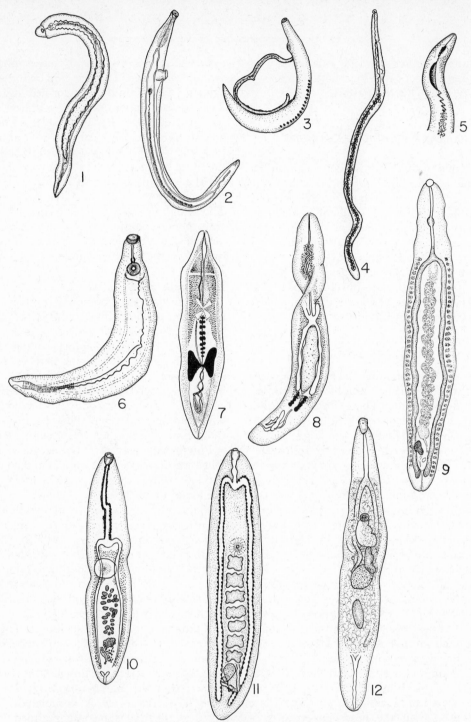

Plate 10–25   Some digenetic trematodes parasitic in the circulatory systems of their hosts.
1. Male of *Bivitellobilharzia loxodontae* (Schistosomatidae) in veins of intestinal wall of the elephant
Loxodonta africana. (Redrawn after Vogel and Minning, 1940.) **2.** Male of *Ornithobilharzia odhneri*
(Schistosomatidae) in portal vein of the bird *Numenius arquatus*. (Redrawn after Faust, 1924.) **3.**
Male and female of *Microbilharzia chapini* (Schistosomatidae) in mesenteric veins of various birds.
(Redrawn after Price, 1929.) **4.** *Trichobilharzia kowalewskii* (Schistosomatidae) in *Anas* spp. (Re-
drawn after Ejsmont, 1929.) **5.** Anterior extremity of male *Gigantobilharzia acotylea* (Schistosoma-
tidae) in intestinal veins of gulls and other birds. (Redrawn after Odhner, 1910.) **6.** Male of
Heterobilharzia americana (Schistosomatidae) in mesenteric veins of *Lynx* sp. (Redrawn after Price,
1929.) **7.** *Sanguinicola inermis* (Sanguinicolidae) in heart of the fish *Cyprinus carpio*. (Redrawn after
Plehn, 1905.) **8.** *Cardicola cardicola* (Sanguinicolidae) in circulatory system of the marine fish
Calamus bajonado. (Redrawn after Manter, 1947.) **9.** *Spirorchis innominatus* (Spirorchidae) in
blood vessels of various fresh-water turtles. (Redrawn after Ward, 1921.) **10.** *Learedius learedi* (Spirorchidae) in circulatory system of the marine turtle *Chelone mydas*. (Redrawn after Price, 1934.)

(*Legend continued on opposite page.*)

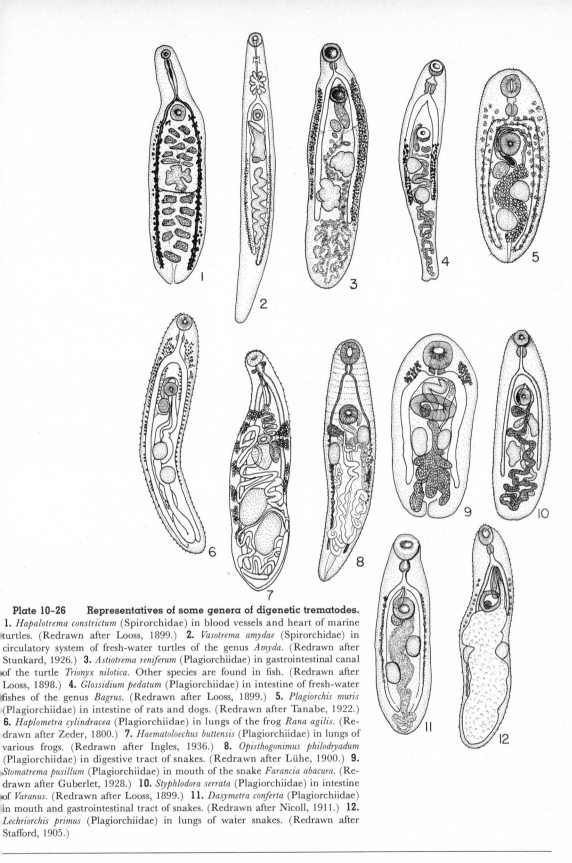

Plate 10-26   Representatives of some genera of digenetic trematodes.
1. *Hapalotrema constrictum* (Spirorchidae) in blood vessels and heart of marine
turtles. (Redrawn after Looss, 1899.) **2.** *Vasotrema amydae* (Spirorchidae) in
circulatory system of fresh-water turtles of the genus *Amyda*. (Redrawn after
Stunkard, 1926.) **3.** *Astiotrema reniferum* (Plagiorchiidae) in gastrointestinal canal
of the turtle *Trionyx nilotica*. Other species are found in fish. (Redrawn after
Looss, 1898.) **4.** *Glossidium pedatum* (Plagiorchiidae) in intestine of fresh-water
fishes of the genus *Bagrus*. (Redrawn after Looss, 1899.) **5.** *Plagiorchis muris*
(Plagiorchiidae) in intestine of rats and dogs. (Redrawn after Tanabe, 1922.)
6. *Haplometra cylindracea* (Plagiorchiidae) in lungs of the frog *Rana agilis*. (Redrawn after Zeder, 1800.) **7.** *Haematoloechus buttensis* (Plagiorchiidae) in lungs of
various frogs. (Redrawn after Ingles, 1936.) **8.** *Opisthogonimus philodryadum*
(Plagiorchiidae) in digestive tract of snakes. (Redrawn after Lühe, 1900.) **9.**
Stomatrema pusillum (Plagiorchiidae) in mouth of the snake *Farancia abacura*. (Redrawn after Guberlet, 1928.) **10.** *Styphlodora serrata* (Plagiorchiidae) in intestine
of *Varanus*. (Redrawn after Looss, 1899.) **11.** *Dasymetra conferta* (Plagiorchiidae)
in mouth and gastrointestinal tract of snakes. (Redrawn after Nicoll, 1911.) **12.**
Lechriorchis primus (Plagiorchiidae) in lungs of water snakes. (Redrawn after
Stafford, 1905.)

(Legend continued.)

11. *Plasmiorchis orientalis* (Spirorchidae) in heart of the turtle *Kachuga dhongoka*. (Redrawn after
Mehra, 1934.) **12.** *Hapalorhynchus gracile* (Spirorchidae) in artery of the turtle *Chelydra serpentina*. (Redrawn after Stunkard, 1922.)

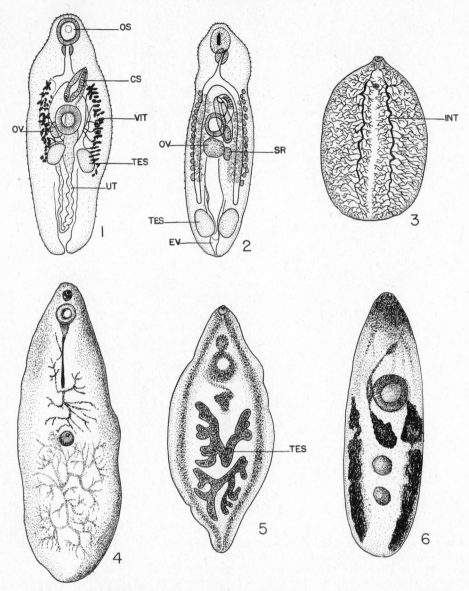

Plate 10-27   **Morphology of some adult digenetic trematodes. 1.** *Ochetosoma ellipticum* (Plagiorchiidae) in mouth, esophagus, or lungs of snakes. (CS, cirrus sac; OS, oral sucker; OV, ovary; TES, testis; UT, uterus; VIT, vitelline glands.) (Redrawn after Pratt, 1903.) **2.** *Zeugorchis aequatus* (Plagiorchiidae) in alimentary canal of the snake *Thamnophis sirtalis*. (EV, excretory vesicle; OV, ovary; SR, seminal receptacle; TES, testis.) (Redrawn after Stafford, 1905.) **3.** *Fascioloides magna* (Fasciolidae) in liver and lung of cattle. (INT, multibranched intestinal caeca.) (Redrawn after Ward and Whipple, 1917.) **4.** *Fasciolopsis buski* (Fascididae) in intestine of man. (Redrawn after Odhner, 1902.) **5.** *Parafasciolopsis fasciolaemorpha* (Fasciolidae) in biliary ducts of the ungulate *Alces alces*. (Redrawn after Ejsmont, 1932.) **6.** *Protofasciola robusta* (Fasciolidae) in intestine of the African elephant. (Redrawn after Odhner, 1926.)

FAMILY DICROCOELIIDAE

The family Dicrocoeliidae includes many genera parasitic in birds, reptiles, and mammals. Undoubtedly the best known of the members is the lancet liver fluke *Dicrocoelium dendriticum* (Plate 10–28, Fig. 1). This economically impor-

tant trematode is found in the bile ducts and gallbladder of sheep, cattle, deer, the wood-chuck, rabbits, and other mammals in upper New York State, Europe, and occasionally elsewhere. *Dicrocoelium dendriticum* possesses an unusual life cycle in that it does not require an aquatic environment at any time. The egg hat pass out from the definitive host are ingested by the land snails *Cionella lubrica.* Although *C. lubrica* is the major molluscan host in the United States and elsewhere, other snails can also serve as hosts. *Planorbis marginatus, P. complanatus, Limax* sp., *Helicella itala, H. candidula, H. ericetorum, Zebrina detrita, Theba carthusiana, Abida rumentum, Ena obscura,* and *Euomphalia stingells* all have served as hosts.

The mother and daughter sporocysts develop in the snail and the xiphidiocercariae are passed out in the "slime balls" of the snail. These are ingested by the ant *Formica fusca,* and other ants. When the ants are eaten along with grass by sheep, the adult parasites develop (Krull and Mapes, 1952; Mapes, 1952).

FAMILY BRACHYCOELIIDAE

The family Brachycoeliidae includes several multi-species genera, all parasitic in the small intestine (one exception in bile ducts) of amphibians and reptiles. In the life cycles of *Brachycoelium obesum, Glypthelmins quieta, G. pennsylvaniensis,* and *Mesocoelium lanceatum,* all members of representative genera, only one intermediate host, a gastropod, is required. In *B. obesum* and *M. lanceatum,* the cercariae develop into unencysted metacercariae, which remain in the molluscan host and mature into adults when infected snails are ingested by the amphibian host. In *Glypthelmins,* the metacercariae encyst in the skin of the definitive frog host; when sloughed epithelium is ingested, the cycle is completed.

FAMILY LECITHODENDRIIDAE

The Lecithodendriidae includes numerous species parasitic in the intestine of all classes of vertebrates. Although these parasites are of little economic importance, their biology is extremely interesting. Many of these trematodes are intestinal parasites of chiropterans. The developmental pattern of *Prosthodendrium anablocami* in bats involves two intermediate hosts —a snail and a mayfly nymph (Etges, 1960).

THE FASCIOLID TREMATODES°

These trematodes belong mostly to the family Fasciolidae. Members are all large flat distomes parasitic in mammals.

---

*The Fasciolid trematodes are considered by LaRue (1957) to be members of the Echinostomatoidea.

The intestinal caeca may be simple or with dendritic lateral branches, as in the common liver fluke *Fasciola hepatica* (Plate 10–29, Fig. 1). The genus *Fasciola* includes *F. hepatica* and *F. gigantica,* both found in the liver and bile ducts of herbivorous mammals.

Human infections with *F. hepatica* are cosmopolitan in distribution and are of increasing importance in Cuba and other Latin-American countries, as well as in France and Algeria. Ecologically, sheep- and cattle-raising areas are the primary zones in which human infections are found. Fascioliasis is characterized by the destruction of the host's liver tissues, damage to bile ducts, atrophy of the portal vessels, and secondary pathological conditions. In many cases the disease leads to the death of the host.

Life Cycle of *Fasciola hepatica*

Fasciola hepatica holds a prominent place in parasitology because its life cycle was the first digenetic trematode life cycle to be completely worked out (Thomas, 1883), which has stimulated all subsequent discoveries in life cycle investigations. The life cycle pattern of *F. hepatica* is unusual, for encystment of the metacercaria occurs on vegetation.

The typical eggs of *F. hepatica* are large, 130 to 150 μ by 63 to 90 μ, and are operculate (Plate 10–29, Fig. 2). These eggs are laid before complete formation of the miracidium and pass into the alimentary tract via the bile ducts. They eventually pass out of the host in the feces.

After being in water for 4 to 15 days at 22° C., the miracidium within the shell is completely developed and escapes. This ciliated larva bears eyespots. Within the first 8 hours after hatching, the miracidium must seek out and penetrate a snail (*Lymnaea, Succinea, Fossaria,* or *Practicolella*).

Each miracidium develops into a sporocyst, which in turn gives rise to mother rediae. The mother rediae give rise to daughter rediae (Plate 10–29, Figs. 3,4). The germ balls in the brood chamber of daughter rediae develop into cercariae, which escape from the snail and become free-swimming (Plate 10–29, Fig. 5). When these free-swimming cercariae reach aquatic vegetation, they lose their tails and encyst as metacercariae (Plate 10–29, Fig. 6). Some cercariae can encyst in water.

Metacercariae swallowed by the definitive host excyst once they reach the duodenum. They then penetrate the intestinal wall and are found in the coelomic cavity. From the body cavity, they penetrate to the liver, migrate

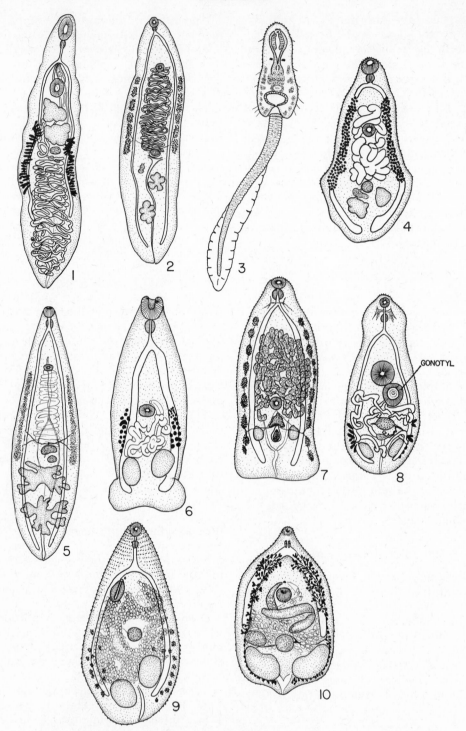

GONOTYL

Plate 10-28   Some adult digenetic trematodes. 1. *Dicrocoelium dendriticum* (= *D. lanceatum*) (Dicrocoeliidae) in gallbladder and bile ducts of cattle, sheep, deer, rabbits, man, and other mammals. (Redrawn after Dawes, B. 1946. *The Trematoda,* Cambridge University Press, New York.) 2. *Opisthorchis tenuicollis* (Opisthorchiidae) in bile ducts of cats, dogs, and man. (Original.) 3. Cercaria of *O. tenuicollis* (Opisthorchiidae). (Original.) 4. *Metorchis albidus* (Opisthorchiidae) in gallbladder of dogs, wolves, and cats. (Redrawn after Price, 1932.) 5. *Opisthorchis sinensis* (Opisthorchiidae) in bile ducts of man and other mammals. (Original.) 6. *Pseudamphistomum* sp. (Opisthorchiidae)

(*Legend continued on opposite page.*)

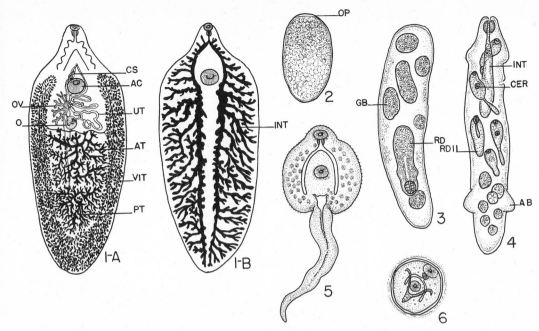

Plate 10-29   Stages in the life cycle of Fasciola hepatica. 1. A. Adult *Fasciola hepatica*, showing reproductive systems. (AC, acetabulum; AT, anterior testis; CS, cirrus sac; O, ootype; OV, ovary; PT, posterior testis; UT, uterus, VIT, vitellaria.) (Original.) **B.** Drawing showing multibranched intestinal caeca of *F. hepatica* (INT). (Original.) **2.** Egg, showing operculum (OP). (Original.) **3.** Sporocyst enclosing germ balls (GB) and redia (RD). (Original.) **4.** Redia with intestinal caecum (INT), and ambulatory buds (AB), enclosing germ balls, cercariae (CER), and daughter redia (RD II). (Original.) **5.** Cercaria. (Original.) **6.** Metacercaria encysted on grass. (Redrawn after Faust in Craig, C., and Faust, E. 1951. *Clinical Parasitology,* Lea & Febiger, Philadelphia.)

through the parenchyma, and become established in the bile ducts where they mature. During migration through the liver, the young adults actively feed on the host's liver cells.

The rate and extent of development of *F. hepatica* within the snail host is dependent upon the degree of infection and upon the availability of nutrients within the snail, primarily those stored in the hepatopancreas. Table 10–8 gives a comparison of the number of larvae in fed and starved snails.

Other Fasciolid Trematodes

Other species of *Fasciola* include *F. halli* in cattle and sheep in Louisiana and Texas, and

F. indica in Indian cattle. In Hawaii, *F. gigantica* is the predominant species that parasitizes cattle. In some areas the infection may be as high as 80 per cent. The presence of this parasite in Hawaii is not only of concern to cattlemen but is also a public health problem, for watercress is grown in large quantities in many areas where cattle are raised, and the metacercariae will encyst on this vegetable, which is commonly eaten raw or only slightly cooked.

The genus *Fascioloides* includes *F. magna* in cattle and sheep (Plate 10–27, Fig. 3). Its life history parallels that of *Fasciola hepatica* except that the intermediate snail host is *Galba, Pseu-*

(*Legend continued.*)

in bile ducts and gallbladder of mammals, including man. (Redrawn after Mönnig, 1934.) **7.** *Microtrema truncatum* (Opisthorchiidae) in liver of pigs. (Redrawn after Kobayashi, 1915.) **8.** *Heterophyes heterophyes* (Heterophyidae) in digestive tract of cats, dogs, foxes, wolves, and man. (Redrawn after Looss, 1896.) **9.** *Metagonimus yokogawai* (Heterophyidae) in intestine of dogs, cats, pigs, mice, and man. (Redrawn after Leiper, 1913.) **10.** *Centrocestus cuspidatus* (Heterophyidae) in intestine of *Milyus parasiticus.* (Redrawn after Looss, 1896.)

Table 10-8.   Rediae and Fully Formed Cercariae of *Fasciola hepatica* in Fed and Starved *Lymnaea trunculata**

Fed Snails			Starved Snails		
Shell length (cm.)	Number of rediae	Number of cercariae	Shell length (cm.)	Number of rediae	Number of cercariae
0.96	151	1,353	0.62	133	200
0.82	296	1,308	0.74	215	218
0.92	141	1,078	0.72	169	374
1.02	133	1,299	0.67	215	134
0.82	152	952	0.74	119	391
0.93	156	1,390	0.61	159	14
0.93	136	1,160	0.68	196	9
1.09	136	1,593	0.62	30	131
1.22	344	2,275	0.63	57	292
1.08	200	2,018	0.62	82	480

* Data after Kendall (1949).

dosuccinea, or *Fossaria.* Other fasciolid trematodes include *Fasciolopsis buski* (Plate 10–27, Fig. 4), which is found in the intestine of man and other mammals and which utilizes the molluscs *Planorbis coenosus* or *Segmentina largillierti* as intermediate hosts; *Fasciolopsis fuelleborni,* found in man in India and Egypt; *Parafasciolopsis fasciolaemorpha* (Plate 10–27, Fig. 5) found in the biliary ducts of ungulates in eastern Europe; and *Protofasciola robusta* (Plate 10–27, Fig. 6) found in African elephants.

THE OPISTHORCHIOID TREMATODES

These flukes belong to the families Opisthorchiidae, Heterophyidae, Acanthostomatidae, and a few other smaller families. All members are relatively small worms with testes situated posterior to the ovary. They possess small eggs, lack a cirrus pouch, and possess pleurolophocercous cercariae that develop in rediae.

FAMILY OPISTHORCHIIDAE

The Opisthorchiidae includes the well known *Opisthorchis tenuicollis* (= *O. felineus*), found in the bile ducts of fish-eating mammals, including cats, dogs, and man (Plate 10–28, Fig. 2).

Life Cycle of *Opisthorchis tenuicollis*

During development of *O. tenuicollis,* the eggs, which pass out in the host's feces, include fully developed miracidia that do not hatch until they are swallowed by snails of the genus *Bithynia.* In the gastropod, one sporocyst and one redial generation develop. The redial generation possesses neither a birth pore nor ambulatory buds. The pleurolophocercous cercariae penetrate the skin of cyprinid fishes and encyst under the body surface (Plate 10–28, Fig. 3). When infected fishes are eaten by the definitive host, the metacercariae develop into adults that live in the bile ducts.

Other Opisthorchiids

Other members of the Opisthorchiidae include *Opisthorchis sinensis* (= *Clonorchis sinensis*) (Plate 10–28, Fig. 5), an important liver parasite of man in Asia; *O. canis* in Indian dogs; *O. tonkae* in muskrats; *Metorchis* (Plate 10–28, Fig 4), with various species found in the gallbladders of mammals and birds; *Pseudamphistomum* (Plate 10–28, Fig. 6) in the bile ducts or gallbladders of mammals; and *Microtrema* (Plate 10–28, Fig. 7) in the livers of cats and pigs in China.

Human Opisthorchiasis

Although unknown in the western hemisphere, opisthorchiasis caused by *O. sinensis* is a widespread disease of humans, especially in China, Japan, Korea, Vietnam, and parts of India. Since human infections are acquired through eating poorly cooked or raw fish in which metacercariae are found, one would expect to find a high percentage of infection among the Chinese, Japanese, and Koreans, because raw fish is considered a delicacy among these people. It is estimated that 19 million human cases of opisthorchiasis exist in the Far East. Because this trematode is found in biliary ducts, thickening of duct walls and involvement of hepatic tissue take place. Severe cases usually lead to cirrhosis and ultimate death.

Nonhuman Opisthorchiasis

Cats and dogs are commonly infected by *O. sinensis* and serve as reservoir hosts from which human infections can be acquired.

Usually young adults, developing from ingested metacercariae, migrate up the bile duct of the host within a few hours after being eaten. However, even if the bile duct is tied off, certain worms still make their way to the liver. Apparently an alternate route that still is undetermined, must exist.

FAMILY HETEROPHYIDAE

The family Heterophyidae includes small distomes and monostomes that are found in the intestines of birds and mammals. The genital pore of heterophyids opens into a retractile sucker-like structure—the gonotyl—which is either incorporated in the acetabulum or lies to one side of it. This family includes the genera *Heterophyes, Metagonimus,* and *Centrocestus,* which all include human-infecting species.

Heterophyes heterophyes is an intestinal parasite of dogs, cats, man, and other mammals, and is commonly found in Asia and Egypt (Plate 10–28, Fig. 8). There is reason to believe that it has been introduced into Hawaii. Its life cycle parallels that of *Opisthorchis tenuicollis.* The molluscan host is usually a member of the family Thiaridae, although *Pirenella* is the common host in the Middle East.

Metagonimus yokogawai is an intestinal parasite of man, dogs, cats, pigs, and mice in the Far East and countries surrounding the Baltic Sea (Plate 10–28, Fig. 9). Again, infections are caused by the eating of infected raw or poorly cooked fish.

Centrocestus spp. are found in fishes as well as in cats, dogs, and man (Plate 10–28, Fig. 10). The metacercariae of these species encyst in cyprinid fishes and when these are ingested by another fish or a mammal, the cycle is completed.

Haplorchis taichui is an intestinal trematode of birds and mammals, including man. Its life cycle parallels that of *Opisthorchis tenuicollis.*

Numerous other genera of the Heterophyidae are known. Some nonhuman-infecting representative genera are depicted in Plate 10–28.

Host Specificity among Heterophyids

Experimental infection with various species of Heterophyidae indicates that these trematodes are usually not very host specific and can be induced to develop in an array of vertebrate hosts. Although these trematodes can develop in most experimental hosts, their behavior pattern in abnormal hosts suggests that such hosts are not completely satisfactory. For example, when heterophyids of night herons are experimentally introduced into mammals, these heterophyids gradually shift their position toward the posterior portion of the alimentary tract, and they are eventually expelled. When heterophyids normally not found in dogs and man are introduced into these hosts, the parasites become buried deep in the mucous lining of the intestine and their eggs, which are normally passed out in feces, do not escape in this manner. Instead, the eggs are taken up by the blood and lymph and distributed throughout the host's bodies. Furthermore, many of these worms die after a short period of development. As a rule, heterophyids introduced into abnormal hosts cause some degree of tissue pathology.

FAMILY ACANTHOSTOMATIDAE

The Acanthostomatidae is a relatively small family the members of which possess eyespots in the adult stage. Many members also possess a circumoral coronet of spines (Plate 10–30, Fig. 7). All species are parasitic in teleost marine fishes and only occasionally in reptiles.

THE ECHINOSTOMATOID TREMATODES

The majority of echinostomatoid termatodes belong to the family Echinostomatidae. They live in the intestine and less commonly in the bile ducts of various vertebrates. The main distinguishing characteristic of these flukes is a collar of spines around the oral sucker.

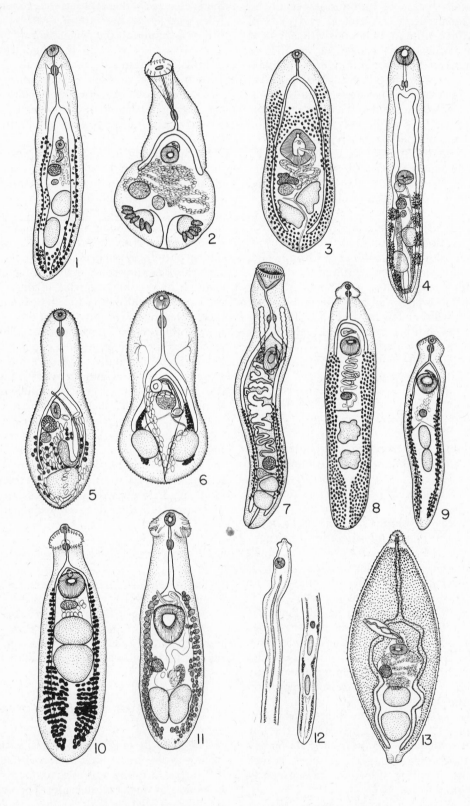

Plate 10-30   See legend on opposite page.

FAMILY ECHINOSTOMATIDAE

The family Echinostomatidae includes the genus *Echinostoma* with over 80 species parasitic in birds, reptiles, and mammals. *Echinostoma revolutum* is an intestinal parasite of birds, dogs, cats, muskrats, and man (Plate 10–30, Fig. 8). The biology of this species has been reviewed by Beaver (1937). Echinostomiasis in humans is not very serious, often causing nothing more than diarrhea.

Representatives of other larger genera of the Echinostomatidae are depicted in Plate 10–30.

Life Cycle of *Echinostoma revolutum*

The life cycle of *E. revolutum* typifies that of most echinostomes. The eggs, which pass out of the host in the feces, contain uncleaved zygotes. A miracidium is fully developed in each egg after it has been in water for about 2 to 5 weeks. The miracidium hatches from the egg while in the water and penetrates snails of the genera *Lymnaea, Physa,* and *Bithynia.* Various fresh-water pelecypods and gastropods serve as hosts for other echinostomes. A single sporocyst generation and two redial generations develop in the snail host. The free-swimming cercariae penetrate and encyst in other molluscs (other members of the family encyst in snails, clams, planaria, tadpoles, and fish), and when snails infected with encysted metacercariae are swallowed by the definitive host, the life cycle is completed.

Not all echinostome cercariae bear a coronet of spines around the oral sucker. However, a ringlike collar is usually present, and the horns of the excretory vesicle extend to near the anterior end of the body and include conspicuous globules.

*THE TROGLOTREMATOID TREMATODES**

The members of this group of flukes are all small and fleshy. They are either intestine-dwellers or are encysted in the respiratory tract and in connective tissues of birds and mammals. The cercariae are of the microcercous type. Almost all species belong to the families Troglotrematidae and Nanophyetidae. Undoubtedly the best known species are *Paragonimus westermani, P. kellicotti,* and *Nanophyetus* (= *Troglotrema*) *salmincola.*

Life Cycle of *Paragonimus westermani*

Paragonimus westermani is an encysted (encapsulated) form found in the lungs of man and crab-eating mammals (Plate 10–31, Fig. 1). This parasite is found primarily in Asia, although it exists in Africa and South and Central America. The eggs are expelled from the definitive host in sputum when the cysts encapsulating the adult worms rupture into the bronchioles and the eggs are coughed up, and the miracidia develop in 3 weeks in moist environments. In Asia, eggs and miracidia are found in rice and vegetable paddies, because infected farmers habitually spit while working. This situation is an ideal one as far as the trematode is concerned, for the snail intermediate hosts are present in the paddies within easy reach.

After penetrating the snail host (*Semisulcospira libertina, S. amurensis, Thiara granifera,* or *Brotia asperata*), each miracidium gives rise to one sporocyst generation followed by two redial

---

*The Troglotrematoid trematodes are considered by LaRue to be members of the Allocreadioidea.

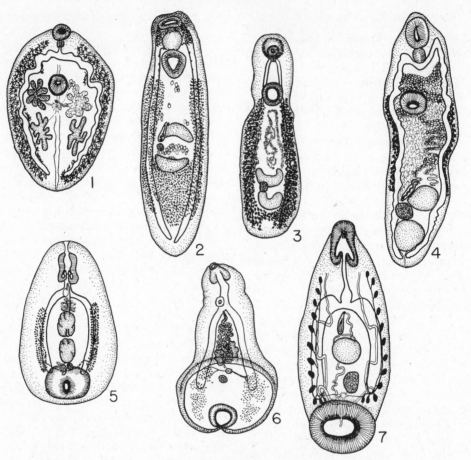

Plate 10-31   Some adult digenetic trematodes. 1. *Paragonimus westermani* (Troglotrematidae) in lungs of man and other crab-eating mammals. (Redrawn after Yamaguti, S. 1958. *Systema Helminthum,* Interscience, New York.) **2.** *Clinostomum complanatum* (Clinostomatidae) in buccal cavity and esophagus of various fish-eating birds. (Redrawn after Braun, 1900.) **3.** *Euclinostomum heterostomum* (Clinostomatidae) in buccal cavity of fish-eating birds (Ardeiformes). (Redrawn after Braun, 1901.) **4.** *Brachylaima suis* (Brachylaimidae) in small intestine of *Xerophila mendranoi.* (Redrawn after Balozet, 1937.) **5.** *Watsonius watsoni* (Paramphistomatidae) in small intestine of man and monkeys. (Redrawn after Stiles and Goldberger, 1910.) **6.** *Gastrodiscoides hominis,* in large intestine of man and other mammals. (Redrawn after Badanin, 1929.) **7.** *Diplodiscus subclavatus,* in rectum of amphibians. (Redrawn after Lühe, 1909.)

generations. Each sporocyst gives rise to approximately twelve mother rediae each of which in turn gives rise to twelve daughter rediae.

The cercariae are formed within the brood chambers of the daughter rediae. The escaping microcercous cercariae are 175 to 240 μ long and possess a spinous cuticle and fourteen penetration glands. These cercariae are emitted from the snail host approximately 78 days after the initial infection of the snail. The cercariae crawl rather than swim, and once they come in contact with the crustacean second intermediate host, they penetrate the body at various vulnerable sites and then encyst.

In China, Japan, and the Philippines, various species of fresh-water crabs serve as suitable second intermediate hosts, and in Korea, a crayfish is the intermediate host.

Although other species of *Paragonimus* tend to encyst in the second intermediate host's cardiac region, *P. westermani* tends to form metacercarial cysts in the gills and muscles of the body and legs, and sometimes in the liver. Encystment in the heart is also possible. The encysted metacercariae, measuring 0.5 mm. or less in diameter, are not doubled over ventrally as do most trematode metacercariae, but lie within the cyst wall in an extended position. When the definitive host, which includes man, ingests the flesh of infected crustaceans, excystment of the parasite occurs in the intestine. However, the fluke does not attain maturity in the intestine but instead bores through the intestinal wall into the coelom, through the diaphram, and into the lungs, where it becomes encapsulated

Sometimes wandering adults do not enter the lungs but become lodged in the spleen, liver, urinary system, intestinal wall, eye, or muscles, causing tissue reactions at these sites. Adults flukes also invade brain tissue, causing a type of eosinophilic meningitis. Encysted worms in the lungs are commonly found in pairs, although a single individual or several specimens may occur within a single cyst.

Within the cysts are found infiltrated cells and numerous eggs in a reddish semifluid mass. Infected lungs have a peppered appearance because of abscesses. Infected individuals are not seriously hampered, although the symptoms include coughing, intermittent blood-stained sputum, mild anemia, and slight fever. Discovery of eggs in the sputum is probably the most reliable diagnostic sign. Yokogawa et al. (1960) have contributed a critical review of the genus *Paragonimus* and human paragonimiasis. This excellent review should be consulted for further data.

Paragonimus kellicotti is a lung fluke of cats, dogs, and pigs. Its life cycle parallels that of *P. westermani* with crayfish serving as the second intermediate host.

Life Cycle *Nanophyetus salmincola*

Nanophyetus salmincola, the salmon-poisoning fluke, has been recently studied by Bennington and Pratt (1960) (Plate 1–5, Fig. 3). This unique trematode is commonly called the salmon-poisoning fluke because it serves as the vector for the rickettsial organism, *Neorickettsia helminthoeca*, which is extremely toxic to canine hosts that ingest raw salmon parasitized by *N. salmincola*.

The eggs of *N. salmincola* do not include fully formed miracidia when passed out of the host. In fact, development of the miracidium is extremely slow. Bennington and Pratt reported that it takes 185 to 200 days before the free-swimming miracidium hatches. The snail host is *Goniobasis plicifera silicula*. Within the gastropod, the miracidia give rise to mother rediae, which in turn simultaneously give rise to daughter rediae and cercariae. The escaping cercariae are microcercous xiphidiocercariae. These penetrate and encyst as metacercariae in the kidney and under the skin of various fishes, primarily salmon and trout. When infected fish are eaten by dogs, cats, foxes, bears, minks, hogs, or other animals, the metacercariae excyst and develop into adults in the definitive host's small intestine.

Other *Nanophyetus* and Closely Related Species

Another species of *Nanophyetus*, *N. schikhobalowi*, has been reported from man in eastern Siberia.

Closely related to *Nanophyetus* spp. is *Sellacotyle mustelae*, a minute form that occurs in the small intestine of minks. The cercariae of this species develop in rediae in the large freshwater viviparous snail *Campeloma rufum*. Metacercariae, developing from the free-swimming cercariae, are found encysted in fish, primarily the bullhead *Ameiurus melas*. These metacercariae become infective after 8 days and develop to maturity in the mink by the fifth day after ingestion.

THE CLINOSTOMATOID TREMATODES

These trematodes are members of the families Clinostomatidae, Brachylaimidae,* and other minor families. All the species are comparatively large and have the anterior sucker and acetabulum closely associated. These flukes also lack a muscular pharynx. Their excretory system is unique in that in addition to the protonephritic system, a secondary network of ramified lacunae is present.

The most common genera of clinostomatoid trematodes are *Clinostomum* (Plate 10–31, Fig. 2) in the mouth, pharynx, and esophagus of herons and herring gulls; *Euclinostomum* (Plate 10–31, Fig. 3) in the nasal passages and mouths of herons and reptiles; and *Brachylaima* (Plate 10–31, Fig. 4) in the intestine of small mammals. Ulmer (1951a, b) has reviewed the systematics of the subfamily Brachylaiminae and contributed the life history of *Postharmostomum helicis*, a parasite of the wild mice *Peromyscus maniculatus* and *P. leucopus*.

Also included in the family Brachylaimidae is the extremely interesting fluke *Leucochloridium macrostoma* (=*L. paradoxum*), the life cycle of which is given on page 282.

---

*La Rue (1957) considers the Brachylaimidae as representing the superfamily Brachylaimoidea.

Life Cycle of *Postharmostomum helicis*

Adults of *P. helicis* are found in the caecum of their rodent hosts. The trematode eggs include well developed embryos when they pass out in the host's feces. When such eggs are ingested by the land snail *Anguispira alternata*, miracidia hatch from the eggs and migrate through the intestinal wall into the surrounding connective tissue or into the hepatopancreas, where they develop into large multibranched mother sporocysts.

The mother sporocysts give rise to daughter sporocysts in 7 to 10 days. The daughter sporocysts are localized within the gastropod's hepatopancreas, where they increase in size and become branched, thus being very similar to the mother sporocysts. Short-tailed cercariae are produced within the daughter sporocysts in about 12 weeks during the summer. These cercariae escape into the host's mantle cavity through birth pores situated at the tips of the branches. The production of cercariae continues for a year or longer and possibly for the life span of the snail. Those cercariae in the mantle cavity escape to the exterior via the host's respiratory pore and become incorporated in the mollusc's slime trail.

Various species of snails (*Polygyra, Anguispira, Stenostoma, Derocercas*), crawling over slime that includes cercariae become infected when the cercariae enter the pore of their primary ureter. The larval trematodes then migrate through the ureters into the kidney and through the renal canal. They then become lodged in the pericardial chamber. The small tail of each cercariae is lost in approximately 10 days, but the metacercariae remain unencysted. Mice and chipmunks become infected when they ingest snails harboring metacercariae.

It is of interest to note that snails infected with sporocysts of *P. helicis* do not become infected with cercariae. Although not yet demonstrated, some type of immunity undoubtedly occurs as in the molluscan hosts of *Cotylurus flabelliformis* (p. 260).

Once ingested by the mammalian host, the metacercariae reach the caecum and commence feeding on blood. Sexual maturity is attained in 8 to 20 days. Ulmer has noted that metacercariae of *P. helicis* can become progenetic—that is, produce eggs before attaining the adult form.

Life Cycle of *Leucochloridium macrostoma*

Leucochloridium macrostoma, a brachylaimid trematode found in the caeca and bursa Fabricii of birds, and occasionally in mammals, is an extremely interesting organism, for certain features of its life cycle suggest that it is well adapted and probably a parasite of long standing. Eggs of *L. macrostoma*, passed out in the feces of the avian host, are dropped onto vegetation, and some are ingested by terrestrial and amphibious snails. *Succinea* is the major molluscan host, although *Planorbis, Limax,* and *Helix* are also compatible hosts.

Miracidia hatching from ingested eggs burrow through the intestinal wall into tissues and transform into mother sporocysts that in turn give rise to daughter sporocysts. The daughter sporocysts develop from germ cells within the brood chambers of mother sporocysts. As the daughter sporocysts grow, they become highly branched (Plate 10–8, Fig. 3), and they migrate toward the host's tentacles. Branches eventually extend into the tentacular cavity.

As a result of the comparatively large diameters of the sporocysts, the host's tentacles become greatly distended and their surfaces become transparent. Because the sporocysts of *Leucochloridium* bear bright green, brown, or orange rings and pulsate continuously, infected snails appear to possess colorful sausage shaped, pulsating tentacles, which are noticeable at a distance of several feet. It is believed that the sporocyst-enclosing tentacles attract birds, which peck at them and thus ingest large numbers of encysted tailless cercariaea that are located within the daughter sporocysts. Once ingested by a bird, the cercariaea excyst and migrate to the avian host's cloaca or bursa and mature.

In addition to the method of infection of birds just described, encysted cercariaea are also readily released from infected snails, for the swollen snail skin ruptures at the slightest touch. Such cercariaea may be individually deposited on vegetation on which infected snails feed or entire cercariae-enclosing sporocysts may be released and deposited. These sporocysts continue to pulsate and thus presumably attract birds. Young birds are more susceptible to *Leucochloridium* infection than adults. In nature, sporocysts picked up by parent birds are undoubtedly often fed to nestlings.

The unique appearance and behavior pattern of the intramolluscan larvae of *Leucochloridium* suggest that the relationship between this trematode and its molluscan host has resulted from evolutionary changes over a long period. These evolutionary adaptations on the part of the parasite without doubt are beneficial to the maintenance of the trematode species, for they enhance the parasite's chances of reaching a definitive host, thus to complete its life cycle, develop to maturity, and produce eggs.

Life Cycles of Other Clinostomatoids

Similar seemingly beneficial adaptations are found among certain other digenetic trematodes. For example, in the case of *Ptychogonimus megastoma* (Family Ptychogonimidae, Table 10–3), a stomach parasite of selachian fishes, cercariae developing in sporocysts do not escape from the scaphopod intermediate host but remain within the sporocyst's brood chamber. It is the sporocysts that escape and remain at the bottom of the water, where they contract and extend slowly by muscular action. Their movements attract *Carcinus* crabs, which ingest the cercariae-enclosing sporocysts. Once within the crab host, the cercariae escape from partially digested sporocysts, penetrate the body cavity of the crab, and encyst. Selachian fishes become infected by eating crabs harboring encysted metacercariae.

Although *Leucochloridium* utilizes only one intermediate host, a terrestrial mollusc, the life cycle pattern of brachylaimid members normally involves two intermediate hosts, both snails, which may or may not be of the same species. The life cycle of *Postharmostomum helicis* reflects this pattern. In addition, the life cycles of several other brachylaimids reflect this pattern. For example, the sporocysts of *Postharmostomum gallinum*, a parasite of chickens, develop in *Eulota similaris* and the metacercariae are found in *Subulina octona;* the sporocysts of *Brachylaimus virginianus* of opossums develop in *Polygyra thyroides*, while the metacercariae are found in another snail of the same species; and the sporocysts and metacercariae of *Leucochloridiomorpha constantiae* of ducks are found in different specimens of the same species of the viviparous aquatic snail *Campeloma decisum.*

In those brachylaimids in which the sporocysts and metacercariae are usually found in different specimens of the same molluscan species, it is suspected that some type of acquired immunity has developed in the sporocyst-enclosing specimens, so that the metacercariae cannot successfully develop in the same individuals. In *Leucochloridium macrostoma*, the ancester of which probably also utilized two molluscan hosts, the cercariae are able to encyst in the same snail in which the sporo-

cysts are found, probably because the encysted cercariaea are found within daughter sporocysts and thus protected against the immune mechanism of the molluscan host.

THE PARAMPHISTOMATOID TREMATODES

These flukes are characterized by fairly large fleshy bodies that possess a posteriorly situated acetabulum. The best known species include *Watsonius watsoni* and *Gastrodiscoides hominis*, which are human-infecting (Plate 10–31, Figs. 5 and 6), and *Diplodiscus subclavatus* (Plate 10–31, Fig. 7), which is found in the rectum of frogs, toads, and newts.

The paramphistomes possess a primitive type of lymphatic system embedded in the parenchyma (Plate 10–17, Fig. 2) and has been studied extensively by Willey (1930). Enclosed within the lymphatic canals are primitive blood cells (p. 249).

One of the most frequently encountered paramphistomatoid trematodes in American biological laboratories is *Megalodiscus temperatus*, which is found in the rectum of frogs. This fluke measures up to 6 mm. in length and approximately 2 to 2.25 mm. in thickness.

Life Cycle of *Megalodiscus temperatus*

Eggs laid by adult flukes in the rectum of frogs and tadpoles pass into water within the host's feces. These eggs enclose fully developed miracidia that hatch almost immediately. If young snails (*Helisoma trivolvis, H. campanulatum*, or *H. antrosum*) are present, the miracidia penetrate them and transform into sporocysts.

Three generations of rediae are found in the snail's hepatopancreas. The last redial generation gives rise to ophthalmocercariae that are positively phototropic (infected snails emit more cercariae during the afternoon and on bright days). If frogs or tadpoles are close by, the cercariae quickly become attached to their skin and encyst. The amphibians become infected when sloughed skin, including encysted metacercariae, are ingested. Excystation occurs in the host's rectum.

When cercariae become attached to the skin of adult frogs, they adhere tenaciously and appear to prefer the pigmented portions of the host's fore- and hindlimbs. Why these positively phototropic cercariae prefer pigmented areas of the host is not understood, but it may be due to some chemotactic response. When cercariae become attached to tadpoles, they adhere lightly and can be readily knocked off. Also of interest is the fact that during the metamorphosis of infected tadpoles to adults, adult trematodes that are not expelled from the rectum migrate anteriorly and are commonly found in the host's stomach. On completion of metamorphosis of the host, these adult trematodes once again migrate into the rectum. The physiological basis for this migratory pattern has not been determined.

Maturation of *M. temperatus* individuals in the frog's rectum is influenced by the number present. Although individuals may mature within 27 days, the normal maturation period is 2 to 3 months. When a large number of flukes are present, maturation is delayed and may take as long as 3 to 4 months.

Life Cycles of Other Paramphistomatoids

The known life cycles of other paramphistomatoids exhibit certain variations from the life cycles of *Megalodiscus temperatus*. For example, in *Stichorchis subtriquetrus,* a parasite in the caecum of beavers, the eggs do not include fully developed miracidia when they pass to the exterior. In fact, development of the miracidium takes approximately 3 weeks. The miracidium of *S. subtriquetrus* is unusual in that it contains a single fully developed mother redia. When such a miracidium penetrates a suitable aquatic gastropod, such as *Fossaria parva* in North America or *Bithynia tentaculata, Planorbus vortex, Succinea putris,* and others in Russia, the enclosed mother redia is discharged into the snail's

mantle cavity. From the mantle cavity, the mother rediae migrate to the hepatopancreas, where they produce daughter rediae. The miracidium disintegrates shortly after the mother redia escapes.

Megalodiscus temperatus is a member of the family Diplodiscidae, while *Stichorchis subtriquetrus* is a member of Paramphistomatidae. Morphological differences between the adults of these two species plus life cycle differences have brought about the different familial designations. However, not all members of the Paramphistomatidae possess life cycles like that of *S. subtriquetrus.* In species that parasitize ruminants, the metacercariae, like those of *Fasciola hepatica,* encyst on vegetation.

THE HEMIUROID TREMATODES

These parasites are all medium to large trematodes normally found in the intestines of fishes and sometimes of amphibians. The eggs contain fully developed miracidia when laid. The cercariae are of the cystophorous type— without stylets—and develop in rediae. The metacercariae are encysted in copepods and sometimes in insects and fishes. Most members belong to the family Hemiuridae, although one human-infecting species, *Isoparorchis hypselobagri,* belongs to the small family Isoparorchidae.

The type genus for the family Hemiuridae is *Hemiurus* (Plate 10–32, Fig. 1) with numerous

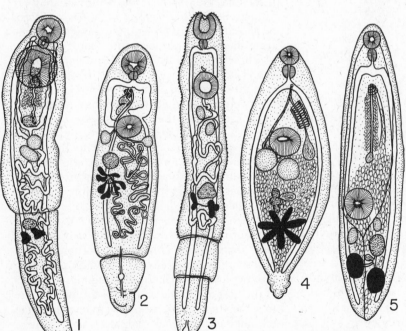

Plate 10-32   Some adult digenetic trematodes of the family Hemiuridae. 1. *Hemiurus appendiculatus* in stomach, sometimes in intestine and pyloric caeca, of various fresh-water fishes. (Redrawn after Fuhrmann, 1928.) 2. *Lecithochirium rufoviride* in stomach of anglers, congers, and eels. (Redrawn after Johnstone, 1907.) 3. *Brachyphallus crenatus* in stomach of various marine fishes. (Redrawn after Fuhrmann, 1928.) 4. *Lecithaster gibbosus* in intestine of various species of fish. (Redrawn after Lebour, 1908.) 5. *Derogenes varicus* in stomach, sometimes in intestine, of various species of fish. (Redrawn after Lebour, 1908.)

species parasitic in fishes. Other genera are depicted in Plate 10–32.

Isoparorchis hypselobagri is a common parasite found in the swim bladder of siluroid fishes in the Far East and India. Occasionally this fluke is found in man. It is suspected that human infections result from the ingestion of raw fish. No serious symptoms accompany this parasite.

PHYSIOLOGY OF DIGENETIC TREMATODES

Oxygen Requirements

Digenetic trematodes are mostly all facultative anaerobes. They can be maintained under anaerobic conditions but are capable of utilizing oxygen if kept in its presence. Table 10–9 gives the survival time of several species under both aerobic and anaerobic conditions. In their natural environments, trematodes are subjected to varying amounts of oxygen, depending on the stage of development and the particular host. It is obvious that free-swimming miracidia and cercariae are aerobic, utilizing the oxygen present in the aquatic environment. On the other hand, the intramolluscan larvae, particularly when found in the reproductive systems or in the hepatopancreas of their hosts, are essentially in anaerobic or microaerobic environments. However, rediae, at least, utilize oxygen if it is present. Thus, intramolluscan

larvae depend primarily on carbohydrate metabolism as the main energy source.

Although fatty acids are present in the bodies of developing cercariae, these acids are generally not useful as substratum for anaerobic energy production, because their carbon atoms (with the exception of the carboxyl carbon) are largely reduced. These atoms therefore do not lend themselves readily to the internal oxidation-reductions characteristic of anaerobic processes. Adult trematodes, except for those that are found in the blood or that ingest oxygen-containing erythrocytes, and those found in relatively highly aerated sites such as the lungs, are exposed to oxygen-poor surroundings. This appears to be substantiated by the fact that certain adult trematodes, such as *Fasciola hepatica,* excrete higher fatty acids.

Some authors have drawn phylogenetic correlations from the oxygen requirements of parasitic worms. Bunge (1889) assumed that helminths that can survive under anaerobic conditions are descended from ancestrial forms that inhabited oxygen-poor habitats such as mud. This hypothesis is not completely acceptable because it is quite possible that a true aerobic ancestor could have gradually inclined toward anaerobism during the process of adapting itself to the endoparasitic way of life.

Bueding (1949) discovered that although *Schistosoma* sp. lives under relatively high oxygen tensions in its adult stage in the blood of its host, it depends primarily on anaerobic metab-

Table 10-9.   Survival Time of Several Species of Digenetic Trematodes under Aerobic and Anaerobic Conditions*

Species	Medium	Temperature °C.	Survival time (in days)		Authority
			Anaerobic	Aerobic	
Fasciola hepatica	Blood	38-39	1.5	1.5	Weinland and von Brand (1926)
Fasciola hepatica	Borax-saline and glucose	38	1.5	2	Stephenson (1947)
Opisthorchis felineus	Ringer's	37	18	18	Erhardt (1939)
Schistosoma mansoni	Serum ultrafiltrate	37	5	12	Ross and Bueding (1950)
Sphaerostoma bramae	1% NaCl	Room temperature	5	4	Hausmann (1897)
Cryptocotyle lingua (metacercariae)	Modified Ringer's and glucose	Room temperature	4	12	Stunkard (1930)

* From data accumulated by von Brand in *Chemical Physiology of Endoparasitic Animals.*

olism for energy production. This signifies that the amount of oxygen present in the environment need not indicate the type of respiration used by the parasite. However, in the case of lung flukes (e.g., *Haematoloechus, Haplometra*) and esophagus-dwelling flukes (e.g., *Leptophallus, Otodistomum*) their ability to survive in the presence of oxygen for relatively long periods in vitro suggests that they are true aerobes. The frog lung fluke *Haematoloechus* spp. actually ingests the host's erythrocytes, which are rich in oxygen.

Most of the quantitative information available on oxygen consumption by digenetic trematodes has been contributed by Vernberg and Hunter using the delicate Cartesian diver respirometer. Verberg (1963) has reviewed these data. It is now known that all the different life cycle stages of trematodes utilize oxygen if it is available, although there is the tendency for the species or stages in the life cycle that are located in regions of low oxygen tension to regulate their respiratory rates. Differences in oxygen consumption by various stages in the life cycle of *Gynaecotyla adunca,* a parasite of birds, are given in Table 10-10.

Growth Requirements

Numerous attempts have been made to culture digenetic trematodes in vitro. However, no completely satisfactory medium has yet been devised. Ferguson (1940) was able to maintain metacercariae of *Posthodiplostomum minimum* in a sterile medium consisting of chicken serum, diluted Tyrode solution, and yeast extract kept at 39° C. These metacercariae actually developed into young adults within a few days, but the young adults could not be maintained for any length of time. Furthermore, these adults produced only inactive spermatozoa and sterile, abnormal eggs.

Ferguson (1943) attempted to culture *Diplostomum flexicaudum* cercariae in Tyrode solution but found that they did not grow nor was maintenance continuous. However, upon the addition of the lens of a sunfish or a rat to the medium, the cercariae developed into metacercariae that, however, were noninfective for birds. These experiments suggest that the cercariae of *D. flexicaudum* are dependent on some substance or substances in the lens of the intermediate host to trigger their development into metacercariae.

Inorganic substances play an important role in the maintenance and maturation of trematodes in vitro. Ferguson, in his experiments with *Diplostomum flexicaudum,* showed that if amphibian Ringer's solution, consisting primarily of inorganic salts, was substituted for Tyrode solution, some of the cercariae did develop into metacercariae. Furthermore, Stephenson (1947) reported that adult *Fasciola hepatica* survived best (for about 60 hours) in a medium containing 150 mM NaCl, 10 mM KCl, 1 mM $CaCl_2$ and 6 mM Na_3BO_3—all inorganic salts—and 30 mM glucose maintained at a pH of 8.6.

The best survival record thus far was reported

Table 10-10. Oxygen Consumption of Various Life Cycle Stages of *Gynaecotyla adunca**

Stage in Life Cycle	Temperature	Oxygen Consumption in microliters/hour/mm^3
Free cercariae†	30.4	5.35
3-4 days after penetrating crab†	30.4	not measurable
Immediately prior to encystment†	30.4	0.159
Encysted metacercariae	30.4	5.62×10^{-3} (per worm)
Adults 24 hours after excystment	30.4	0.153
Adults 48 hours after excystment	30.4	0.120
Adults 72 hours after excystment	30.4	0.104

* Measurements were made on individual organisms by use of the Cartesian diver respirometer. Data from Hunter and Vernberg, 1955; Vernberg and Hunter, 1956.
† Indicates stages later determined not to be those of *G. adunca* but those of *Zoogonus rubellus,* a parasite of fish.

by Hoeppli and Chu (1937) for *Opisthorchis sinensis,* which they successfully maintained for 5 months in serum plus Tyrode solution.

The ideal medium for helminth cultivation should provide more than mere maintenance. Ideally, the parasites should undergo growth and development. Development has not yet been attained, but Senft and Weller (1956) reported that growth of adults of *Schistosoma mansoni* was achieved when maintained in a medium comprised of 45 per cent bovine amniotic fluid, 45 per cent Hanks' balanced salt solution, 5 per cent inactivated horse serum, and 5 per cent beef embryo extract. Penicillin, streptomycin, and phenol red were added, and the medium was maintained at pH 7.4. Mouse erythrocytes were added later.

Eventual success in culturing trematodes will undoubtedly be attained when more thorough knowledge concerning the metabolism of these parasites in vivo is achieved.

Protein Synthesis

From observations on in vivo worms, it is well known that the degree and rate of protein synthesis among the Digenea must be considerably higher than in closely related free-living forms. The tremendous output of reproductive cells alone, especially ova, is 10,000 to 100,000 times greater than in free-living relatives, and these reproductive cells are proteinaceous. During the development of larval generations, the mutiplication of the amount of protein is manyfold. For example, it has been reported that 10,000 cercariae may be derived from a single miracidium of *Schistosoma japonicum,* and in *S. mansoni* a single miracidium may give rise to as many as 200,000 cercariae. Meyerhof and Rothschild (1940) reported that in the snail *Littorina* infected with *Cryptocotyle lingua,* 1.3 million cercariae are produced in one year.

The fecundity of larval trematodes through asexual reproduction suggests that within the body of the molluscan host, these parasites must have a substantial source of amino acids. The author has investigated this phase of trematode biochemistry. In four species of trematodes it was demonstrated that sporocysts and rediae can acquire amino acids from two sources— from the free and bound amino acids in the sera of the hosts, and from the free amino acids and those amino acids resulting from the degradation of cells in the immediate vicinity of the parasites. Although proteases have been demonstrated in the soma of only one larval

trematode, such are found widely in adults. No doubt proteases will be found in more larvae, especially cercariae.

Carbohydrate Metabolism

Adult digenetic trematodes can utilize carbohydrates, a considerably lesser amount of lipids, and some proteins. Bueding found that adult *Schistosoma mansoni* consumes 79 to 96 gm. per 100 gm. wet weight of carbohydrates at 37 to 41° C. under anaerobic conditions, and 79 to 96 gm. per 100 gm. wet weight under aerobic conditions. Weinland and von Brand reported that *Fasciola hepatica* consumes 2.6 gm. per 100 gm. wet weight of carbohydrates under anaerobic conditions at 37 to 41° C. The large quantity of carbohydrate consumed by *S. mansoni* is the highest known in any parasitic animal.

Embden-Meyerhof phosphorylative glycolysis (Table 3–5) most probably is utilized by adult trematodes, although the detailed pathways have not all been demonstrated. The rate of glucose utilization is essentially the same under aerobic and anaerobic conditions in *S. mansoni,* hence the bulk of the energy produced is by glycolysis, even under aerobic conditions. The main end-product of glucose metabolism is lactic acid. Despite the importance of glycolysis in the production of energy, oxygen may be necessary for the normal maturation of the worms, possibly to permit the synthesis of essential intermediate metabolites.

Although no quantitative studies are yet available on carbohydrate consumption among larval trematodes, the author and co-workers have shown that sporocysts and rediae fulfill their carbohydrate requirements from adjacent host cells. This is particularly true with those larvae found in the mollusc's hepatopancreas or in the musculature. In *Gorgoderina* sporocysts, which are found between the inner and outer lamellae of the gill filaments of the fresh-water bivalve *Musculium,* the required sugars are derived from the host's blood because very little glycogen is stored in gill epithelium. Since carbohydrate is stored in host cells in the form of glycogen, this polysaccharide must first be broken down to glucose, the size of which molecule enables it to permeate sporocyst walls. Developing cercariae within rediae and sporocysts also absorb much of this glucose. A portion of the glucose is resynthesized as glycogen within the bodies of the cercariae while the rest is utilized in energy production. Rediae derive some of their required carbohydrate by absorption, as do sporocysts, but mainly through ingestion of glycogen-containing host cells.

The utilization of carbohydrates by larval trematodes, however, does not appear to hold true for all species. Vernberg, by utilizing respiratory rate as an indicator of metabolic rate, reported that the metabolic rate of the rediae of the echinostome *Himasthla quissetensis* is not altered when glucose, mannose, ribose, and fucose are added to the medium in which the rediae are maintained in vitro. The addition of some of the amino acids, particularly proline, causes increased respiratory rates. Malonate, on the other hand, decreases the respiratory rate. The respiratory rate of the cercariae of *H. quissetensis* is not increased by any of these substrates. These findings suggest that the rediae and cercariae of this trematode do not utilize sugars.

The nonusage of sugars by cercariae is not surprising, for free-swimming cercariae most probably depend on lipid metabolism (see following discussion) as their source of energy. In the case of the rediae of *H. quissetensis,* Vernberg's findings suggest species differences. Nevertheless, there exists the perplexing question of whether intramolluscan larval trematodes maintained in an aerobic in vitro environment behave in the same manner as they would in their natural anaerobic in vivo environment.

Lipid Metabolism

Lipase activity has been reported in adult *Fasciola hepatica* and *Schistosoma mansoni,* thus suggesting the utilization of fats, although the levels of activity are extremely low. Since most intestinal trematodes live in microaerobic or even anaerobic environments, one would not expect to find high levels of lipid metabolism. On the other hand, the author suggested in 1963 that lipid metabolism as an energy source is undoubtedly of great importance among free-swimming cercariae. This is borne out because considerable fatty acids are stored in the bodies of developing cercariae while very little is present in the bodies of adults. This indicates that these fatty acids have been exhausted during the free-swimming, aerobic cercarial stage.

The presence of larval trematodes in the hepatopancreas of gastropods induces hyper-synthesis of neutral fats within the cells of that organ. In time, these neutral fats are broken down to fatty acids, which are readily absorbed through sporocyst walls and are stored, not as neutral fats, but as fatty acids in the bodies of enclosed cercariae.

HOST-PARASITE RELATIONSHIPS AMONG THE DIGENEA

Most of the flukes listed in Table 10–1 are detrimental to their hosts. This phase of host-parasite relationship—that is, the production of diseases—is the most obvious effect digenetic trematodes inflict on their hosts.

Effects of Parasite on Host

Although adult trematodes are not suspected of playing important roles in depriving their hosts of nutrients, it is suspected that they may play an important role in depriving their hosts of vitamins and trace elements, which can result in disrupting host metabolism.

Intramolluscan larval trematodes deplete the host's carbohydrates, lipids, and amino acids, which probably causes some harm to the host. In fact, infected molluscs generally do not survive as long as uninfected ones. However, death is not attributed completely to the loss of nutrients but to a large degree to the mechanical and lytic damage caused by the larvae.

Other forms of metabolic disruption are known. For example, in rabbits infected with *Schistosoma japonicum* or *Opisthorchis sinensis,* the blood calcium decreases and blood potassium and sodium increase. In cattle and sheep infected with *Fasciola hepatica,* there is a slight increase of blood chlorides. In rabbits infected with *O. sinensis* and in man infected with *Schistosoma mansoni,* hyper- and hypoglycemia may occur.

Lipid metabolism of the host is disrupted in *Schistosoma japonicum* and *Opisthorchis sinensis* infections. Hiromoto (1939) reported that blood cholesterol of rabbits is raised when *S. japonicum* is present. A parallel condition develops in rabbits infected with *O. sinensis*. Host protein metabolism is also disrupted. Khalil and Hassan (1932) reported that serum albumin and globulin are decreased and increased respectively in humans infected with *Schistosoma haematobium*. Faust and Meleney (1924) and Hiromoto (1939) reported that in humans and rabbits infected with *S. japonicum,* the total serum protein is decreased but the globulin and nonprotein nitrogen fractions are increased.

Toxins

Certain endoparasitic trematodes secrete toxic substances. For example, the liver lesions produced by *Fasciola hepatica* are only partially due to the traumatic destruction of liver tissue. These lesions are also due to the trematode's proteolytic, amylolytic, and lipolytic enzymes, to the toxic effect of the excreta of the flukes, and to the absorption of the dying worms' autolytic products. Injections of *F. hepatica* excreta into experimental animals produce toxic reactions, and if the material is injected locally, it produces edema, fever, inflammation, and sometimes anemia. In *S. japonicum,* an ether-soluble haemolysin is present.

Azimov (1958) reported that the polysaccharide antigens extracted from *Dicrocoelium* are toxic when injected intra-abdominally into various laboratory animals. Specifically, 90 to 150 mg. of the extract suspended in saline was toxic to mice, 350 to 400 mg. was toxic to guinea pigs, and 840 to 1000 mg. was toxic to rabbits.

Effects of Larvae on Molluscs

Several investigators have studied the effects of larval trematodes on their molluscan hosts. These have been reviewed by Cheng and Snyder (1962). The range of effects varies from none to considerable, the latter being the rule.

The effects of larval trematodes on their molluscan hosts can be categorized in three groups—the effect on the host's hepatopancreas, the effect on the host's gonads and reproductive structures, and the effect on the general physiological state of the host.

Effects on the hepatopancreas of the host by larval trematodes include (1) accumulation of fatty bodies in the cytoplasm of hepatopancreatic cells; (2) the appearance of vacuoles in the cytoplasm; (3) karyolysis; (4) sloughing of tissues due to mechanical damage; (5) formation of fibromata and granulomata; (6) decrease in the amount of glycogen; (7) rupturing of the covering epithelium, resulting in the penetration of foreign bodies; (8) histolytic effects inflicted by the excretory products of the larvae;

(9) secretion of granular substances by the host cells; (10) release of cell pigments by host cells; (11) metabolic degeneration of host cells; and (12) displacement and destruction of hepatopancreatic tubules.

Effects on the host's gonads and reproductive structures include (1) direct ingestion of the host's gonadal tissue by rediae or mechanical destruction of gonads by sporocysts, resulting in parasitic castration; (2) sex reversals; and (3) inhibition of normal gametogenesis through the disruption of normal vascularization, crowding, and toxicity. Effects on the general physiological state of the host include (1) gigantism of the host in some cases, retardation of growth in others, and no influence on growth in still others, depending on the particular host-parasite team; (2) pigmentation, thinning and "ballooning" of shells; (3) a rise in body temperature; (4) blockage and destruction of circulation, and (5) increased calcium content in the tissues.

Effects of Host on Parasite

The diet of the host is known to affect trematodes. For example, Krakower et al. (1944) reported that in *Schistosoma mansoni* infection of guinea pigs, although the worms are not affected if the host is maintained on diets deficient in vitamin C, the trematode eggs produced possess weakly formed shells. It is believed that lack of vitamin C affects the shell globule-forming ability of the vitelline glands. These same investigators reported that if the guinea pigs are maintained on diets deficient in vitamin A, more of the initially introduced parasites survive.

In other instances, Rothschild (1939) found that gulls deprived of vitamins do not affect *Cryptocotyle lingua,* but Beaver (1937) reported that if pigeons are fed diets deficient in vitamins A and D, their *Echinostoma revolutum* parasites are either retarded in their development or do not develop at all.

Finally, an interesting aspect of the growth pattern of digenetic trematodes in their definitive hosts has been studied by Willey (1941). This investigator reported that individuals of the amphistome *Zygocotyle lunata* vary in size within the same host depending on the number of individuals present. The fewer the worms, the larger the individuals. This phenomenon, known as the crowding effect, occurs in *Opisthorchis* and *Megalodiscus* infections and among some cestodes.

LITERATURE CITED

Andrado, Z. A., and T. Barka. 1962. Histochemical observations on experimental schistosomiasis of mouse. Am. J. Trop. Med. Hyg., *11:* 12–16.

Azimov, S. A. 1958. (Toxicity of antigens extracted from *Dicrocoelium* and *Thysaniezia*). Dokl. Akad. Nauk. Uzbek SSR, *10:* 61–63. (In Russian.)

Beaver, P. C. 1937. Experimental studies on *Echinostoma revolutum* (Froel.), a fluke from birds and mammals. Ill. Biol. Monogr., *15:* 1–96.

Bennett, H. J. 1936. The life history of *Cotylophoron cotylophorum,* a trematode from ruminants. Ill. Biol. Monogr., *16:* 1–119.

Bennington, E., and I. Pratt. 1960. The life history of the salmon-poisoning fluke, *Nanophyetus salmincola* (Chapin). J. Parasit., *46:* 91–100.

Bogitsh, B. J. 1962. The chemical nature of metacercarial cysts. I. Histological and histochemical observations on the cyst of *Posthodiplostomum minimum.* J. Parasit., *48:* 55–60.

Bogitsh, B. J. 1963. Histochemical observations on the cercariae of *Posthodiplostomum minimum.* Exptl. Parasit., *14:* 193–202.

Bosma, N. J. 1934. The life history of the new trematode *Alaria mustelae,* Bosma, 1931. Trans. Amer. Micro. Soc., *53:* 116–153.

Bueding, E. 1949. Metabolism of parasitic helminths. Physiol. Rev., *29:* 195–218.

Bunge, G. 1889. Weitere Untersuchungen über die Athmung der Würmer. Ztschr. Physiol. Chem., *14:* 318–324.

Byrd, E. E. 1935. Life history studies of Reniferinae parasitic in reptilia of the New Orleans area. Trans. Amer. Micro. Soc., *54:* 196–225.

Byrd, E. E. 1939. Studies on the blood flukes of the family Spirochiidae. Part II. Revision of the family and descriptions of new species. Jour. Tenn. Acad. Sci., *14:* 116–161. (Also see *ibid., 13:* 133–136.)

Cheng, T. C., and D. V. Provenza. 1960. Studies on cellular elements of the mesenchyma and of tissues of *Haematoloechus confusus* Ingles, 1932 (Trematoda). Trans. Amer. Micro. Soc., *79:* 170–179.

Cheng, T. C., and R. W. Snyder. 1962. Studies on host-parasite relationships between larval trematodes and their hosts. I. The status of our present knowledge. II. Host glycogen utilization by the sporocysts and cercariae of *Glypthelmins pennsylvaniensis* Cheng and associated phenomena. Trans. Amer. Micro. Soc., *81:* 209–228.

Chu, G. W. T. C. 1958. Pacific area distribution of fresh-water and marine cercarial dermatitis. Pacific Sci., *12:* 299–312.

Cort, W. W., D. J. Ameel, and A. Van der Woude. 1954. Germinal development in the sporocysts and rediae of the digenetic trematodes. Exptl. Parasit., *3:* 185–225.

Cort, W. W., S. Brackett, L. Olivier, and L. O. Nolf. 1945. Influence of larval trematode infections in snails on their second intermediate host relations to the strigeid trematode, *Cotylurus flabelliformis* (Faust, 1917). J. Parasit., *31:* 61–78.

Dawes, B. 1946. The Trematoda. Cambridge University Press.

Dawes, B. 1960. Penetration of *Fasciola gigantica* Cobbold, 1856 into snail hosts. Nature, *185:* 51–53.

Dawes, B. 1962. A historical study of the caecal epithelium of *Fasciola hepatica* L. Parasitology, *52:* 483–493.

Dobrovolny, C. G. 1939. Life history of *Plagioporus sinitsini* Mueller and embryology of new cotylocercous cercariae (Trematoda). Trans. Amer. Micro. Soc., *58:* 121–155.

Dollfus, R. P. 1925. Distomiens parasites de Muridae du genre *Mus.* Ann. Parasitol., *3:* 85–102.

Dubois, G. 1937. Contribution a l'étude des Diplostomes d'oiseaux (Trematoda: Diplostomatidae Poirier, 1886) du Musée de Vienne. Bull. Soc. Neuch. Sci. Nat., *62:* 99–128.

Dubois, G. 1938. Monographie des Strigeida (Trematoda). Mém. Soc. Neuch. Sci. Nat., *6:* 1–535.

Erasmus, D. A. and C. Öhman. 1963. The structure and function of the adhesive organ in certain strigeid trematodes. Ann. N. Y. Acad. Sci., *113:* 7–35.

Etges, F. J. 1960. On the life history of *Prosthodendrium* (*Acanthatrium*) *anaplocami* n. sp. (Trematoda: Lecithodendriidae). J. Parasit., *46:* 235–240.

Faust, E. C. 1919. The excretory system in Digenea. Biol. Bull., *36:* 315–344.

Faust, E. C., and H. E. Meleney. 1924. Studies on schistosomiasis japonica. Amer. J. Hyg. Monogr. Ser. No. 3.

Ferguson, M. S. 1940. Excystment and sterilization of metacercariae of the avian strigeid trematode, *Posthodiplostomum minimum,* and their development into adult worms in sterile cultures. J. Parasit., *26:* 359–372.

Ferguson, M. S. 1943. In vitro cultivation of trematode metacercariae free from microorganisms. J. Parasit., *29:* 319–323.

Goodchild, C. G., and B. Fried. 1963. Experimental infection of the planorbid snail *Menetus dilatatus buchanensis* (Lea) with *Spirorchis* sp. (Trematoda). J. Parasit., *49:* 588–592.

Gresson, R. A. R., and C. T. Threadgold. 1959. A light and electron microscope study of epithelial cells of the gut of *Fasciola hepatica* L. J. Biophys. Biochem. Cyt., *6:* 157–162.

Hiromoto, T. 1939. Chemische Untersuchungen des Blutes bei experimenteller Kaninchen-schistosomiasis japonica. (English summary). Okayama Igakkai Zasshi., *51:* 1633–1637.

Hoeppli, R. J. C., and H. J. Chu. 1937. Studies on *Clonorchis sinensis* in vitro. Festschr. Nocht., pp. 199–203.

Hoffman, G. L. 1960. Synopsis of Strigeoidea (Trematoda) of fishes and their life cycles. Fishery Bull. 175, v.S. Fish and Wildlife Serv. U. S. Gov't Printing Office, Wash., D. C. pp. 439–469.

Khalil, M., and A. Hassan. 1932. The serum globulin in human schistosomiasis. J. Egypt Med. Assoc., *15:* 211–231.

Krakower, C. A., W. A. Hoffman, and J. H. Axtmayer. 1944. Granulación en la cubierta de los huevos de *Esquistosoma mansoni.* Puerto Rico J. Pub. Health, *19:* 669–677.

Kruidenier, F. J. 1951. The formation and function of mucoids in virgulate cercariae, including a study of the virgula organ. Amer. Midl. Nat., *46:* 660–683.

Krull, W. H., and C. Mapes. 1952. Studies on the biology of *Dicrocoelium dendriticum* (Rud., 1819) (Trematoda: Dicrocoeliidae), including its relation to the intermediate host, *Cionella lubrica.* Cornell Vet., *42:* 252–285. (Also see *Ibid.,* *42:* 277–285; *42:* 339–351; *42:* 464–489; *42:* 603–605; (1953) *Ibid.,* *43:* 199–202; *43:* 389–410).

Kuntz, R. E. 1955. Biology of the schistosome complexes. Am. J. Trop. Med., *4:* 383–413.

LaRue, G. R. 1957. The classification of digenetic trematoda: a review and a new system. Exptl. Parasit., *6:* 306–349.

Lautenschlager, E. W. 1959. Meningeal tumors of the newt associated with trematode infection of the brain. Proc. Helminth. Soc. Wash., *26:* 11–14.

Lebour, M. V. 1912. A review of the British marine cercariae. Parasitology, *4:* 416–456.

Lühe, M. 1909. Parasitische Plattwürmer. I: Trematodes. Süsswasserfauna Deutschlands (Brauer), *1:* 1–217.

Lutz, A. 1921. Zur Kenntnis des Entwicklungszyklus der Holostomiden Vorläufige Mitteilung. Zbl. Bakt. I. Orig., *86:* 124–129.

Lynch, D. L., and B. J. Bogitsh. 1962. The chemical nature of metacercarial cysts. II. Biochemical investigations on the cyst of *Posthodiplostomum minimum.* J. Parasit., *48:* 241–243.

Manter, H. W. 1937. A new genus of distomes (Trematoda) with lymphatic vessels. The Hancock Pacific Expeditions, *2:* 11–23.

Mapes, C. R. 1952. *Cionella lubrica* (Muller), a new intermediate host of *Dicrocoelium dendriticum* (Rud., 1819) Looss, 1899. J. Parasit., *38:* 84.

Meyerhof, E., and M. Rothschild. 1940. A prolific trematode. Nature, *146:* 367–368.

Nolf, L. O., and W. W. Cort. 1933. On immunity reactions of snails to the penetration of the cercariae of the strigeid trematode, *Cotylurus flabelliformis* (Faust). J. Parasit., *20:* 38–48.

Odlaug, T. O. 1940. Morphology and life history of the trematode, *Alaria intermedia.* Trans. Amer. Micro. Soc., *59:* 490–510.

Odlaug, T. O. 1948. The finer structure of the body wall and parenchyma of three species of digenetic trematodes. Trans. Amer. Micro. Soc., *67:* 236–253.

Rothschild, M. 1939. A note on the life cycle of *Cryptocotyle lingua* (Creplin) 1825 (Trematoda). Novitat. Zool., *41:* 178–180.

Rowen, W. B. 1956. The mode of hatching of the egg of *Fasciola hepatica.* Exptl. Parasit., *5:* 118–137.

Rowen, W. B. 1957. The mode of hatching of the eggs of *Fasciola hepatica.* II. Colloidal nature of the viscous cushion. Exptl. Parasit., *6:* 131–142.

Scheuring, L. 1920. Die Lebensgeschichte eines Karpfenparasiten (*Sanguinicola inermis* Plehn). Allg. Fisch. Ztg., *45:* 225–230.

Senft, A. W., and T. H. Weller. 1956. Growth and regeneration of *Schistosoma mansoni in vitro.* Proc. Soc. Exptl. Biol. Med., *93:* 16–19.

Short, R. B., and M. Y. Menzel. 1959. Chromosomes in parthenogenetic miracidia and embryonic cercariae of *Schistosomatium douthitti.* Exptl. Parasit., *8:* 249–264.

Stephenson, W. 1947. Physiological and histochemical observations on the adult liver fluke *Fasciola hepatica* L. III. Egg-shell formation. Parasitology, *38:* 128–139.

Stirewalt, M. A., and J. R. Hackey. 1956. Penetration of host skin by cercariae of *Schistosoma mansoni*. I. Observed entry into skin of mouse, hamster, rat, monkey and man. J. Parasit., *42:* 565–580.

Stoll, N. R. 1947. This wormy world. J. Parasit., *33:* 1–18.

Stunkard, H. W. 1923. Studies on North American blood flukes. Bull. Amer. Mus. Nat. Hist., *48:* 165–221.

Stunkard, H. W. 1937. The physiology, life cycle and phylogeny of the parasitic flatworms. Amer. Mus. Novitat., No. 908.

Stunkard, H. W. 1940. Life history studies and the development of parasitology. J. Parasit., *26:* 1–15.

Sudds, R. H. Jr. 1960. Observations of schistosome miracidial behavior in the presence of normal and abnormal snail hosts and subsequent tissue studies of these hosts. J. Elisha Mitchell Sci. Soc., *76:* 121–133.

Szidat, L. 1929. Beitrage zur Kenntnis der Gattung *Strigea* (Abilag.) I. Allgemeiner Teil: Untersuchung über die Morphologie, Physiologie und Entwicklungsgeschichte der Holostomiden nebst Bemerkungen über die Metamorphose der Trematoden und die Phylogenie derselben. II. Spezieller Teil: Revision der Gattung *Strigea* nebst Beschreibung einer Anzahl neuer Gattungen und Arten. Zeit. Parasitenk., *1:* 612–764.

Tanabe, H. 1922. Contribution to the knowledge of the developmental cycle of digenetic trematodes. On a new species of trematode *Lepoderma muris* n. sp. Okayama Igakkai Zasshi., *385:* 47–58.

Thomas, A. P. W. 1883. The life history of the liver fluke (*Fasciola hepatica*). Quart. J. Micro. Sci., *23:* 99–133.

Ulmer, M. J. 1951a. *Postharmostomum helicis* (Leidy, 1847) Robinson, 1949, (Trematoda), its life history and a revision of the subfamily Brachylaeminae. Part I. Trans. Amer. Micro. Soc., *70:* 189–238.

Ulmer, M. J. 1951b. *Postharmostomum helicis* (Leidy, 1847) Robinson, 1949, (Trematoda), its life history and a revision of the subfamily Brachylaeminae. Part II. Trans. Amer. Micro. Soc., *70:* 319–347.

Vernberg, W. B. 1963. Respiration of digenetic trematodes. Ann. N. Y. Acad. Sci., *113:* 261–271.

von Brand, T. 1952. Chemical Physiology of Endoparasitic Animals. Academic Press, New York.

Wall, L. D. 1941. Life history of *Spirorchis elephantis* (Cort, 1917), a new blood fluke from *Chrysemys picta*. Amer. Midl. Nat., *25:* 402–412.

Willey, C. H. 1930. Studies on the lymph system of digenetic trematodes. Jour. Morph. Physiol., *50:* 1–37.

Willey, C. H. 1941. The life history and bionomics of the trematodes, *Zygocotyle lunata* (Paramphistomidae). Zoologica, *26:* 65–88.

Winfield, G. F. 1932. On immunity of snails infested with the sporocysts of the strigeid, *Cotylurus flabelliformis*, to the penetration of its cercariae. J. Parasit., *19:* 130–133.

Yamaguti, S. 1943. Cercaria of *Plagiorchis muris* (Tanabe, 1922). Annot. Zool. Japan, *22:* 1–3.

Yamaguti, S. 1958. Systema Helminthum. Vol. I (Two Parts). Interscience, New York.

Yokogawa, S., W. W. Cort, and M. Yokogawa. Paragonimus and paragonimiasis. Exptl. Parasit., *10:* 81–137, 139–205.

SUGGESTED READING

Cort, W. W., D. J. Ameel, and A. Van der Woude. 1954. Germinal development in the sporocyst and rediae of the digenetic trematodes. Exptl. Parasit., *3:* 185–225. (This classic paper reviews what is known about the modes of asexual reproduction in larval trematodes and points out how these differences may be of phylogenetic importance.)

Dawes, B. 1946. The Trematoda. Cambridge University Press. (This is a well known monograph of the Trematoda. The sections devoted to trematode taxonomy and biology are particularly useful to the student.)

Hyman, L. H. 1951. The Invertebrates: Platyhelminthes and Rhynchocoela. The Acoelomate Bilateria. McGraw-Hill, New York, pp. 250–311. (This section in Hyman's treatise of the invertebrates discusses the digenetic trematodes. The discussion of morphology is particularly useful.)

LaRue, G. R. 1957. The classification of digenetic trematoda: A review and a new system. Exptl. Parasit., *6:* 306–344. (This rather technical paper presents a new interpretation of the classification of the higher taxa of digenetic trematodes based on the embryology of the excretory system.)

Manter, H. W. 1955. The zoogeography of trematodes of marine fishes. Exptl. Parasit., *4:* 62–86. (In this review, Manter has summarized results from some of his own research and those of others relative to the distribution of digenetic trematodes of marine fishes.)

Smyth, J. D., and J. A. Clegg. 1959. Egg-shell formation in trematodes and cestodes. Exptl. Parasit., *8:* 286–323. (This research paper is rapidly becoming a classic in the area of trematode physiology. The authors discuss the biochemistry of eggshell formation in the parasitic platyhelminths. The student can derive some good research ideas from this paper.)

11

THE CESTOIDEA—
The Tapeworms
THE CESTODARIA—
The Unsegmented Tapeworms

The Cestoidea constitutes another very interesting group of parasitic flatworms. Members of this class display the characteristics of the phylum Platyhelminthes as given in Chapter 8. In addition, they lack a mouth and digestive tract, and like the other parasitic platyhelminths they possess a layer of noncellular cuticle that covers the body surface. A large number of the Cestoidea are true tapeworms of the subclass Eucestoda,* while a smaller, less known group belongs to the subclass Cestodaria. The true tapeworms generally possess segmented bodies with a specialized holdfast segment—the scolex —at the anterior end by which the adults are attached to the intestinal wall of the host. A few tapeworms, however, do not possess segmented bodies, and still others are segmented internally but lack external body divisions. De-

tailed accounts of these forms are given in Chapter 12. The cestodarians, on the other hand, do not possess segmented bodies and superficially portray a certain degree of affinity to the trematodes.

One phase of host-parasite relationship among these worms is that concerned with species that parasitize man and domestic animals, and in so doing cause varying degrees of pathologic conditions and hence are of great interest to the medical and veterinary professions. Although the effects of this type of parasitic infection tend to be regarded as disease-causing, from the biological standpoint, the resulting conditions might best be regarded as manifestations of host response to parasitism. Such is the case of the broad fish tapeworm, *Dibothriocephalus latus,* which becomes parasitic in man when larvae are ingested along with raw or poorly cooked fish. As an intestinal parasite, it may produce no symptoms or may produce severe systemic toxemia and even a

---

* The designation Cestoda is often used in place of the older Eucestoda, and the true tapeworms are often referred to as cestodes.

type of anemia (p. 347). Another example can be drawn from the dwarf tapeworm, *Hymenolepis nana*. When this worm parasitizes man, it causes eosinophilia and severe systemic toxemia, especially in children.

Not only are the morphology and life cycles of tapeworms of great interest to biologists, but also recent studies on the biochemical physiology of these parasites have greatly enhanced our understanding of parasitism.

SUBCLASS CESTODARIA

The cestodarians, which are all endoparasites in the intestine and coelomic cavities of various fishes and rarely in reptiles, show affinities to both the true tapeworms and to the trematodes. Nevertheless, since these animals lack a digestive tract and possess fairly well developed parenchymal muscles, most modern zoologists consider them to be more closely related to the Eucestoda than to the Trematoda. Their position in the class Cestoidea is suggested not only by the two previously mentioned characteristics, which they share in common with the true tapeworms, but also because their larvae are quite similar to those of the Eucestoda. The major difference is that the cestodarian larva—the lycophore—characteristically bears ten hooks while the larva of tapeworms bears six. On the other hand, the cestodarians are similar to the trematodes in that some species possess suckers similar to those found on certain digenetic flukes. Furthermore, the cestodarians are devoid of scoleces, and only one set of reproductive organs is present in each individual. The apparent lack of strobilation (proglottization) has caused the cestodarians to be described as monozoic in contrast to the polyzoic condition of the Eucestoda.

Cestodarians are believed to be rather ancient parasites that were once a flourishing group, which originated in fresh-water hosts, in which many modern members of one order —the Amphilinidea—are still found, but which later passed into the sea along with their hosts. These hosts were most probably primitive elasmobranchs, of which the chimaerids are among the only survivors today. Indeed, almost all of the known modern members of another order, the Gyrocotylidea, are intestinal parasites of marine chimaerid fishes. If this concept is valid, then these worms must

have originated during the early Mesozoic and possibly during the Paleozoic. Aside from anatomical characteristics, the fact that cestodarians parasitize primitive fishes suggests their ancient origin.

Wardle and McLeod (1952) recognize three orders subordinate to the subclass Cestodaria— Amphilinidea, Gyrocotylidea, and Biporophyllidea. The members of these orders, especially those belonging to the first two, are quite different from each other, even in certain aspects of their basic histology. These differences make it impractical to discuss a general anatomical pattern. Rather, the patterns are expounded on in the respective sections devoted to each order.

Body Tissues

Basically, the body wall of all cestodarians consists of the outermost noncellular cuticle, which is thinner in the amphilinids than in the gyrocotylids. Immediately underneath the cuticle are two layers of muscles, the outer being circularly arranged and the inner being longitudinally arranged. These subcuticular muscles are better developed in gyrocotylids. Certain large parenchymal cells are present in the subcuticular region of amphilinids. The parenchymal muscles of the gyrocotylids are generally better developed than those of the amphilinids. However, the long boring muscles, which extend from the proboscis to the so-called anchor cells in the posterior region of the body, are quite well developed in amphilinid cestodarians. Being acoelomate animals, the body spaces between the body wall and the internal organs are filled with a meshlike parenchyma, similar to that found in the flukes and tapeworms.

SYSTEMATICS AND BIOLOGY

CLASSIFICATION

The three orders comprising the Cestodaria are:

Order 1. Amphilinidea. Adults are parasitic in the coelom of sturgeons, other primitive fishes (Osteoglossidae, Haemulidae, Siluridae, Acipenseridae), and tortoises. Body is elongate and dorsoventrally flattened, with calcareous corpuscles in parenchyma. Cuticle has no armature. Protrusible proboscis is present at anterior end. Frontal glands are present; no suckers. Male and female genital pores are separate but closely situated to each other at posterior end of body. Testes are follicular, usually as two lateral bands, but scattered throughout parenchyma in certain species. Ovary is singular, located in posterior half of body. Uterus is pre-ovarian, with N shaped coil, opening in proximity of proboscis. Vitellaria are in form of two lateral bands, two lateral osmoregulatory (excretory) canals and their branches forming peripheral network, opening into excretory vesicle at posterior end of body.

Order 2. Gyrocotylidea. Adults are primarily parasitic in intestine of chimaerid fishes. Body is elongate, dorsoventrally flattened. Anterior end has eversible cup shaped proboscis (considered a sucker by some). Posterior end has rosette adapted as holdfast organ. Cuticle is spinous at anterior terminal. Male genital aperture is on ventral surface, female genital aperture on dorsal surface. Testes are follicular, scattered throughout parenchyma in anterior portion of body. Ovarian follicles are scattered in posterior portion of body. Uterus opens on ventral surface of body. Vitellaria are scattered throughout parenchyma, especially in lateral regions. Osmoregulatory system is in form of a mesh of minute canals generally opening through two excretory pores on ventral surface in anterior half of body.

Order 3. Biporophyllidea. Adults are parasitic in intestine of sharks. Body is elongate, dorsoventrally flattened, containing calcareous corpuscles in parenchyma. Cuticle is spinous. Proboscis is present at anterior end of body. Male and female genital pores open into laterally situated common atrium in anterior half of body. Testes are follicular, scattered throughout parenchyma in anterior half of body. Ovary is lobed, in posterior half of body. Sac-like uterus opens dorsomedially. Osmoregulatory system is mesh of tubules, and two longitudinal canals lead into a common excretory vesicle at posterior end of body.

ORDER AMPHILINIDEA

The major characteristics of the members of Amphilinidea are listed above. These monozoic worms are ribbon-like and measure up to 15 inches in length.

The Proboscis and Related Structures

The proboscis, which is located at the anterior end of the body, is a powerful boring apparatus. It can be retracted into the body proper. A bundle of well developed muscle fibers extends posteriorly from the interior of the proboscis to certain large cells—the anchor cells—located at the posterior end of the body. These muscles, which are twisted anteriorly, cause the proboscis to twist partially during the boring process. In addition, they lend support to the anterior end of the worm during boring, and drag the posterior end of the body through the perforation made by the proboscis. In addition to these long muscle fibers, true retractor muscles are present, which are responsible for the extension and retraction of the proboscis.

Within the proboscis in some species, clusters of frontal glands secrete to the outside through minute pores on the proboscal surface.

Osmoregulatory System

The osmoregulatory (excretory) system in members of this order has been little studied. It is known, nevertheless, that in *Amphilina* each flame cell includes a group of 18 to 30 flame bulbs (Plate 11–1, Fig. 1). The main lateral canals lead into a common excretory vesicle located at the posterior end of the body, which vesicle empties to the outside through a single excretory pore.

Nervous System

The nervous system of amphilinids is quite similar to that found in the other platyhelminths. There is a large ganglionic mass located immediately behind the proboscis. From this primitive brain, two main nerve trunks are directed anteriorly and two posteriorly. The posteriorly directed trunks are joined near the posterior end of the body by a commissure.

Reproductive Systems

The cestodarians are monoecious, with a complement of single male and female reproductive organs.

MALE SYSTEM. In amphilinid cestodarians, the male system consists of follicular testes, which are generally limited to the two lateral fields (Plate 11–1, Fig. 2). However, in *Amphilina* the testes are scattered throughout the parenchyma. An individual vas efferens arises from each follicle, and these unite to form the common vas deferens (also known as the sperm duct), which is directed posteriorly and opens to the exterior through the male genital pore situated at the posterior end of the body. Prior to opening to the exterior, the vas deferens is provided with a muscular zone, into which prostate glands secrete. In some amphilinids, a genital papilla is present at the copulatory terminal.

FEMALE SYSTEM. The female system consists of a single ovary located near the posterior end of the body (Plate 11–1, Fig. 2). An oviduct arises from the surface of the ovary and eventually enlarges to become a winding uterus, which terminates at the uterine pore located near the proboscis. Branching off the oviduct is the slender vagina, which extends posteriorly and opens to the outside in one of three ways, depending on the species. The vagina can join the vas deferens and open through a common genital pore, open through a separate female genital pore, or bifurcate and open through two separate pores. The vitelline glands are poorly developed and are

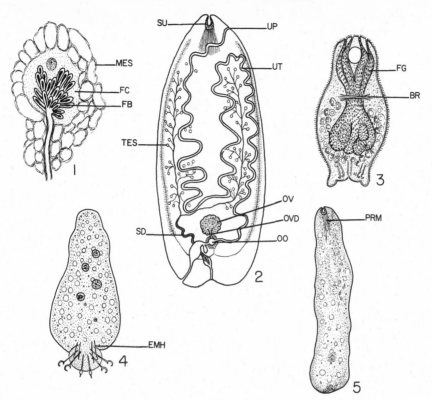

Plate 11-1   **Morphology and stages in life cycle of *Amphilina*.** 1. Flame cell of *Amphilina* with cluster of flame bulbs. (Redrawn after Hein, 1904.) 2. Adult specimen of *Amphilina foliacea*, showing male and female reproductive systems. (Redrawn after Benham, 1901.) 3. Lycophore of *Amphilina*, showing large frontal glands. (Redrawn after Janicki, 1928.) 4. Procercoid of *Amphilina*. (Redrawn after Janicki, 1928.) 5. Plerocercoid of *Amphilina*. (Original.)

(BR, brain; EMH, embryonic hooks; FB, flame bulbs; FC, flame cells; FG, frontal glands; MES, mesenchyme; OO, ootype; OV, ovary; OVD, oviduct; PRM, developing proboscis protractor muscles; SD, sperm duct; SU, sucker; TES, testis; UP, uterine pore; UT, uterus.)

arranged in two lateral bands, with the common vitelline duct entering the oviduct near the vagino-oviductal junction.

During copulation, spermatozoa are introduced into the vagina through the female or common genital pore, depending on which is present. The spermatozoa ascend the vagina and enter the oviduct, where fertilization takes place. The vitelline secretions are laid down around the fertilized ovum to form part of the egg. The eggs pass up the uterus and in some species hatch before their expulsion from the uterine pore. Such species are ovoviviparous. In other species, the eggs are oviposited, and development of the enclosed embryo continues on the outside, and hence they are oviparous.

The embryology of one species, *Gephyrolina paragonopora*, has been studied along with a portion of its life cycle (Woodland, 1923) (Plate 11–2). One other life cycle, that of *Amphilina foliacea*, has also been studied (Salensky, 1874;

Janicki, 1928). The patterns in these two species are essentially the same. The zygote is enveloped by a coat of yolk material within a thin, irregularly ovoid shell. Embryonic development occurs while the egg is in utero. The escaping larva—known as a decacanth larva, or lycophore (Plate 11–1, Fig. 3)—is approximately 100 μ long and has ten hooks embedded in the posterior end. The lycophore of *G. paragonopora* is not ciliated. The lycophore of *A. foliacea* is ciliated and there is a cluster of large frontal glands present that open to the outside at the anterior end of the body.

Woodland postulated that the lycophore of *Gephyrolina* escapes through the uterine pore of the parent only after the parent has burrowed through the body wall of the fish host, because he observed that lycophores that were hatched prematurely within the host's body cavity became surrounded with histolytic tissue and were eventually destroyed.

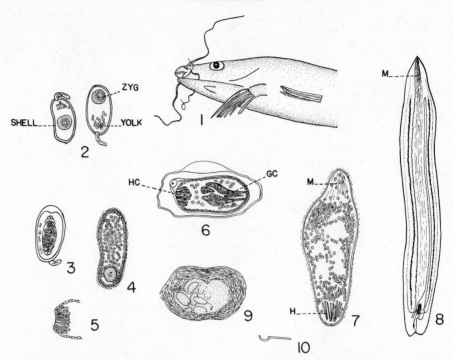

Plate 11-2   Stages in the life cycle of *Gephyrolina paragonopora.* **1.** Adult escaping from body cavity of fish host. **2.** Eggs in the proximal segment of the uterus, showing zygote (ZYG), yolk, and shell. **3.** Egg in medium segment of uterus, showing morula stage of embryo surrounded by invested membrane. **4.** Early larva in longitudinal section, showing one large blastomere. (Shell not shown.) **5.** Section through posterior end of larva, showing formation of hooklet-forming cells. **6.** Early larva in section, showing gland cells (GC) and hooklet-forming cells (HC). **7.** Late larva with fully developed hooklets (H) at posterior end. Muscle fibers (M) are visible, but gland cells are not. **8.** Sexually mature adult, dorsal view, showing reproductive organs. (M, muscle fibers.) **9.** Young cyst developing from the mesentery of fish host and enclosing degenerate larva and disintegration products. **10.** Larval hooklet in posterior end of fully developed larva. (All figures, redrawn after Woodland, 1923.)

AMPHILINID GENERA

None of the genera subordinate to the Amphilinidea are common. The type genus, *Amphilina,* is probably the most frequently encountered. *Amphilina foliacea,* a parasite in the coelom of European sturgeons, has been known since 1819, when Rudolphi originally thought it to be a trematode. Several other species of *Amphilina* have been recorded in various species of sturgeons. In North America, *A. bipunctata* has been reported from a sturgeon in Oregon. The genus *Gephyrolina* includes several species from siluroid fishes in India and Brazil (Plate 11–3, Fig. 2). *Gigantolina* includes extremely large forms, measuring up to 380 mm. in length, which are found in the fish *Diagramma crassispinum* in Ceylon. A ribbon-like amphilinid, *Austramphilina elongata,* has been found in the body cavity of the tortoise, *Chelodina longicollis,* in Australia (Plate 11–3, Fig. 3).

Life Cycle of *Amphilina foliacea*

Janicki has contributed the only completely known amphilinid life history, that of *A. foliacea.* The ciliated larva of this species, although fully developed, does not escape from the eggshell until the egg is ingested by the intermediate host—an amphipod crustacean. Within the gut of the amphipod, the lycophore hatches and sheds its ciliated epidermis. The secretions of the frontal glands aid the now naked lycophore in penetrating the gut wall of the intermediate host, and the lycophore finally inhabits the coelom of the host. In this new location, the lycophore undergoes dedifferentiation—it loses most of its body structures, including the frontal glands, and develops a rounded tail somewhat similar to the cercomer of some true tapeworms. Ten hooks of the lycophore are not enclosed within this tail. This larval form is referred to as the procercoid (Plate 11–1, Fig. 4).

The procercoid continues to develop—the body elongates, the tail is shed, the adult pro-

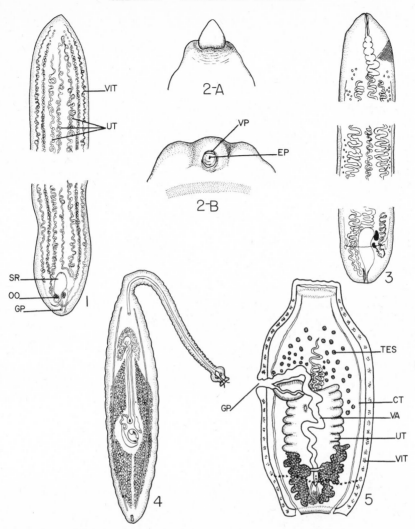

Plate 11-3   **Some cestodarians.** 1. *Gigantolina magna* from intestine of *Diagramma cras-sispinum* from Ceylonese waters. (Redrawn after Southwell, 1928.) **2. A.** Anterior terminal of *Gephyrolina paragonopora.* **B.** Posterior terminal of *Gephyrolina paragonopora.* (Redrawn after Woodland, 1923.) **3.** *Austramphilina elongata* from the body cavity of the tortoise *Chelodina longicollis* in Australia. (Redrawn after Johnston, 1931.) **4.** *Gyrocotyloides nybelini* in *Chimaera monstrosa.* (Redrawn after Fuhrmann, 1931.) **5.** *Biporophyllaeus madrassensis* in the shark *Chiloscyllium griseum* in Indian waters. (Redrawn after Subramanian, 1939.)

(CT, collecting tubule of osmoregulatory system; EP, excretory pore; GP, genital pore; OO, ootype; SR, seminal receptacle; TES, testes; UT, uterus; VIT, vitelline glands; VA, vagina.)

boscis is formed along with the frontal glands, and the body muscles begin to take form. The animal is now known as a plerocercoid (Plate 11–1, Fig. 5). When the amphipod host is ingested by a sturgeon, the plerocercoid burrows through the fish's gut wall and becomes lodged in the coelom and attains maturity. In *Amphilina* and related genera, for example *Gigantolina* (Plate 11–3, Fig. 1), the embryonic hooks are maintained throughout life in the parenchyma near the posterior end.

ORDER GYROCOTYLIDEA

The gyrocotylid cestodarians are quite different from the amphilinids. In fact, upon gross inspection, the two orders do not bear much resemblance to each other. The gyrocotylids possess a wrinkled bundle of flaps—the rosette—which resembles a minature carnation, at the posterior end of their bodies surrounding a conical depression (Plates 11–5 and 11–6).

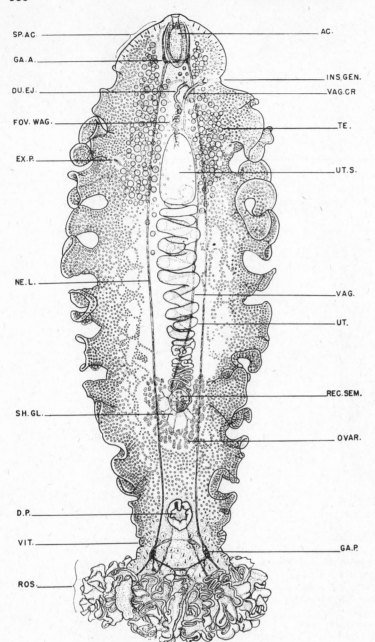

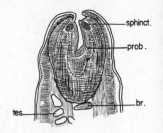

Plate 11-4   *Gyrocotyle.* Longitudinal section through proboscis of *Gyrocotyle,* showing sphincter (sphinct.), proboscis (prob.), brain (br.) and testes (tes.). (Redrawn after Watson, 1911.)

Plate 11-5   *Gyrocotyle fimbriata,* **dorsal view.** (AC., acetabulum; D.P., dorsal pore of funnel; DU.EJ, ejaculatory duct; EX.P., excretory pore; FOV.WAG., fovea Wageneri (ventral); GA.A., anterior ganglion; GA.P., posterior ganglion; INS.GEN., genital notch; NE.L., longitudinal nerve trunk; OVAR., ovary; REC.SEM., seminal receptacle; ROS., rosette; SH.GL., shell gland; SP.AC., acetabular spines; TE., testicular follicles; UT., uterus; UT.S., uterine sac; VAG., vagina; VAG.C., vagina (thickened terminal portion); VIT., posterior limit of vitelline follicles. (After Lynch, 1945.)

Within the coelom of the fish host, these parasites are attached by the rosette. A muscular cup shaped proboscis (also referred to as a sucker) is located at the anterior end (Plate 11-4). This proboscis is eversible. Quite characteristic of the gyrocotylids are the ruffled body margins and cuticular spines. The spines are generally limited to the anterior and posterior ends of the body. The spines located at the posterior end are arranged in front of the rosette. The parenchymal muscles are well developed. A sphincter is located at the posterior end of the proboscis, and the retractor muscles, which control the eversion and retraction of the proboscis, are attached to it.

Nervous System

The nervous system of gyrocotylid cestodarians is unique in that it appears to be better developed at the posterior end. Immediatel in front of the rosette are located a commissure, two ganglia, and a nerve ring (Plate 11–5). Anteriorly, a commissure is located behind the proboscis and two lateral nerve cords extend posteriorly from it. The nerve cords join the posteriorly situated ganglia. Watson (1911) described two ridges and pits at the anterior tip of the proboscis of *Gyrocotyle,* which are richly innervated and are presumed to be tactile regions.

Osmoregulatory System

The osmoregulatory system consists of a network of partially ciliated vessels that bear minute tubules bearing flame cells at their terminals. The main tubes empty to the outside of the body through two nephridiopores (excretory pores) at the anterior end of the body. There is no excretory vesicle present (Plate 11–5).

Reproductive System

The male reproductive system consists of numerous testes, which are scattered throughout the parenchyma in the anterior portion of the body (Plate 11–5). The individual vasa efferentia unite to form a common vas deferens, or sperm duct, which leads to the exterior through a minute genital papilla projecting from the body surface. This papilla is laterally located on the ventral body surface near the anterior end (Plate 11–6). Prior to entering the papilla, the vas deferens first forms a spermiducal vesicle followed by a muscular area.

The female reproductive system consists of numerous ovarian follicles located in the posterior region of the body (Plate 11–5). A single oviductule arises from each follicle. These oviductules unite to form the oviduct, which enlarges to become the uterus. The uterus is coiled and terminates at the female genital pore, situated on the mid-dorsal line in the anterior part of the body, posterior to the proboscis. The vitelline glands are scattered throughout the parenchyma, especially in the two lateral regions. The common vitelline duct enters the oviduct, as does the Mehlis' gland and the duct of the large seminal receptacle, if present. The seminal receptacle is the storage site for spermatozoa, which enter the anteroventrally located vaginal pore (female genital pore) during copulation and which swim down to the oviduct, which empties into the receptacle.

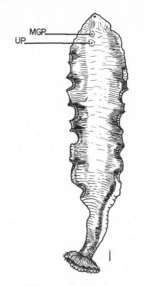
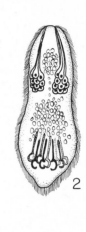

Plate 11-6   *Gyrocotyle urna.* **1.** Fully extended adult specimen of *G. urna,* ventral view. (MGP, male genital pore; UP, uterine pore.) (Redrawn after Wardle, 1932.) **2.** Lycophore larva of *G. urna,* showing two groups of glands and ten larval hooks. (Redrawn after Ruskowski, 1931.)

GYROCOTYLID GENERA

The Gyrocotylidea includes the genera *Gyrocotyle* and *Gyrocotyloides* (Plate 11–3, Fig. 4), both parasitic in primitive fishes. In *Gyrocotyloides* the body cuticle is smooth and devoid of spines; the rosette is poorly developed.

Life Cycle of *Gyrocotyle urna*

Complete life history data on gyrocotylids are wanting. Ruszkowski (1932), however, reported phases of the developmental cycle of *Gyrocotyle urna* (Plate 11–6), a parasite of the chimaeroid fishes *Chimaera* and *Hydrolagus.* In this species, the eggs secrete a gelatinous capsule a few hours after being ejected through the uterine pore. The in utero development of the lycophore is incomplete; hence, further development ensues only after the operculated egg escapes into the water. Again, the parent bores through the body wall of the fish host to lay its eggs. Subsequent development is shown in Table 11–1.

The lycophores of *Gyrocotyle urna* (Plate 11–6, Fig. 2) and *G. rugosa* possess a ciliated epidermis, although gyrocotylid lycophores generally lack a ciliated epidermis, possessing instead an embryonic membrane, presumably epidermal, between the larva and the capsule (shell).

Table 11-1. Development of *Gyrocotyle urna*

Days after leaving parent	Stage of development
5–7	Yolk cells fuse
10–15	Embryonic hooks (10) appear
12–20	First movement observed
25–30	Lycophore fully developed, leaves shell

Ruszkowski's attempts to infect various molluscs (*Cardium, Lima,* and *Mytilus*) were unsuccessful, but he reported finding larvae (procercoids) 3 to 5 mm. long in fish hosts on which the rosettes were already formed and the ten embryonic hooks grouped together where the rosettes had formed. This finding has been interpreted by some to mean that no intermediate host is necessary, but others feel that larval development in an intermediate host does exist but is as of yet unknown. Linstow's (1903) *Gyrocotyle medusarum,* found in a jellyfish, *Phyllorhiza rosacea,* in the Pacific, is thought by those who champion the second interpretation to be a gyrocotylid larva using the jellyfish as the intermediate host.

Life Cycle of *Gyrocotyle rugosa*

Manter (1951) reported that the eggs of *Gyrocotyle rugosa,* a parasite of the elephant fish *Callorhynchus milli* commonly found in New Zealand waters, hatch almost immediately in sea water. The emerging ciliated lycophores readily penetrate samples of the host's mucus and pieces of tissues cut from the spiral valve of the elephant fish. However, the lycophores demonstrate no affinity for hermit crabs and molluscs placed in their presence. Once within the tissues of the elephant fish, the larvae enter the muscular layers and a few also enter blood vessels. Manter also found numerous post larval forms in the mucus from the anterior part of the spiral valve of the host.

Dollfus (1923) and Lynch (1945) have included extensive bibliographies on *Gyrocotyle.*

ORDER BIPOROPHYLLIDEA

This obscure order of cestodarians includes only one species, *Biporophyllaeus madrassensis,* in the shark *Chiloscyllium griseum* from the Indian Ocean (Plate 11-3, Fig. 5). This species possesses a laterally located common atrium in the anterior half of the body, into which the male and female genital pores empty. The two longitudinal osmoregulatory canals lead into an excretory vesicle situated at the posterior end of the body.

PHYSIOLOGY OF CESTODARIANS AND HOST-PARASITE RELATIONSHIPS

Very little is known about the physiology of cestodarians because these unique monozoic worms are relatively rare and seldom encountered let alone maintained in the laboratory where they can be studied. It is apparent that their body forms and structures are the results of adaptive evolution correlated with their parasitic way of life. The rosette of the gyrocotylids and the powerful proboscis of the amphilinids are manifestations of such adaptations that facilitate host-parasite contact. That cestodarians lack an alimentary tract suggests that they acquire their nutrients by absorption through the body cuticle. Such is the case among the cestodes. The highly muscular proboscis of cestodarians is a necessity because the adults must bore through the body wall of their fish host in order to give birth to the young, or they must lay their eggs on the outside.

Some interest has been directed to the function of the frontal glands of the Amphilinidea. Janicki (1928) reported that these glands in the lycophore secrete a substance that aids in the larval penetration of the intestinal wall of the amphipod intermediate host. On the other hand, Woodland (1923) believed that these glands, as found in adults, are not actually glands but are fibers of the boring muscle.

It is interesting to note that adult amphilinids are parasitic in the coelomic cavity of their hosts, because this is one of the sites occupied by the larvae of certain Eucestoda. Some zoologists have interpreted this to mean that modern amphilinids are the neotenic larvae of a group of ancestral tapeworms whose definitive hosts have become extinct. These neotenic larvae have become able to attain sexual maturity and no longer require the original definitive host for the completion of the life cycle. This interpretation seems reasonable and is generally accepted.

LITERATURE CITED

Dollfus, R. P. 1923. L'orientation morphologique des *Gyrocotyle* et des cestodes en général. Bull. Soc. Zool. France, *48:* 205–242.

Janicki, C. von. 1928. Die Lebensgeschichte von *Amphilia foliacea* G. Wagener, Parasiten des Wolga-Sterlets. Nach Beobachtungen und Experimenten. Arbeiten Biologischer Wolga-Station No. 10, Saratov.

Linstow, O. F. B. von. 1903. Parasiten, meistens Helminthen, aus Siam. Arch. Mikrockop. Anat. Entwicklungsmech. *62:* 108–121.

Lynch, J. E. 1945. Redescription of the species of *Gyrocotyle* from the ratfish, *Hydrolagus colliei* (Lay and Bennet), with notes on the morphology and taxonomy of the genus. J. Parasit., *31:* 418–446.

Manter, H. W. 1951. Studies on *Gyrocotyle rugosa* Diesing, 1850, a cestodarian parasite of the elephant fish, *Callorhynchus milii.* Zool. Publ. Victoria Univ. College, New Zealand, No. 17.

Ruszkowski, J. S. 1932. Études sur le cycle évolutif et sur la structure des cestodes de mer. II. Sur les larves de *Gyrocotyle urna* (Gr. et Wagen.). Bull. Intern. Acad. Polon. Sci. Classe Sci. Math. Nat. B., pp. 629–641.

Salensky, W. 1874. Ueber den Bau und die Entwicklungsgeschichte der *Amphilina* (*Monostomum foliaceum* Rud.) Z. Wiss. Zool., *24:* 291–342.

Wardle, R. A., and J. A. McLeod. 1952. The Zoology of Tapeworms. University of Minnesota Press, Minneapolis.

Watson, E. E. 1911. The genus *Gyrocotyle* and its significance for problems of cestode structure and phylogeny. Univ. Calif. Publ. Zool., *6:* 353–468.

Woodland, W. N. F. 1923. On *Amphilina paragonopora* sp. n. and a hitherto undescribed phase in the life history of the genus. Quart. J. Micro. Sci., *67:* 47–84.

SUGGESTED READING

Baer, J. 1952. Ecology of Animal Parasites. University of Illinois Press. Urbana, Ill., pp. 136–138. (This is the short chapter in Dr. Baer's monograph devoted to cestodarians. The author emphasizes life cycle patterns and their possible significance relative to the phylogeny of these flatworms.)

Hyman, L. H. 1951. The Invertebrates: Platyhelminthes and Rhyncocoela. The Acoelomate Bilateria. Vol. II. pp. 344–350. McGraw-Hill, New York. (This section in Dr. Hyman's monographic series describes the morphology and classification of cestodarians.)

Wardle, R. A., and J. A. McLeod. 1952. The Zoology of Tapeworms. University of Minnesota Press, Minneapolis, pp. 653–665. (Although brief, this is by far the most complete and detailed review of the Cestodaria available in book form.)

12

THE EUCESTODA—
The True Tapeworms

The Eucestoda, or true tapeworms, includes a large and important group of the Platyhelminthes. These are by far the most highly specialized metazoan parasites known. All adult members of this subclass are endoparasitic in the alimentary tract and associated ducts of various vertebrate hosts. During their life cycles, one or two (or more) intermediate hosts—vertebrates and invertebrates—are required in which the tapeworms undergo a phase of their development.

The body of the adult tapeworm is dorsoventrally flattened and often white; however, some species display coloration, usually yellow or gray. These pigments are presumably due to the food materials absorbed by the parasite.

The origin and phylogeny of tapeworms have been the subject of much speculation. Most modern zoologists agree that the Eucestoda had their origin in some platyhelminth ancestor that arose from a primitive prototype—the common stock from which modern trematodes also arose. Wardle and McLeod (1952, Chapter 4) give an excellent account not only of the origin and evolution of the class but of the various subordinate orders as well.

MORPHOLOGY

The body of the typical eucestode can be divided into three regions (Plate 12–1, Fig. 1): (1) the scolex—the holdfast organ, which is generally considered the anterior end.* Its morphology and dimensions are important in the identification of these worms; (2) the neck region, which is situated immediately posterior to the scolex. This is an unsegmented, poorly differentiated area that is generally narrower than the scolex and the strobila proper, and is

---

*There are two schools of thought concerning the interpretation of the structure of tapeworms. Some consider a single scolex and connected strobila to be a single animal. Others consider each proglottid to be an individual—hence a single tapeworm is a colony of many individuals. The author considers that the entire body constitutes a single animal, and he refers to it as such. Some helminthologists argue that the scolical end of the cestode is actually the posterior end. However, the author agrees with Hyman (1951) that the evidence for considering the scolex as the posterior end is not convincing. Furthermore, the more recent literature indicates the scolical end should be considered the anterior, or cephalic, end.

the continuously differentiating zone that gives rise to immature proglottids, or body segments, of these worms; and (3) the strobila, which constitutes the main bulk of the body and is made up of a chain of proglottids. The most anteriorly situated proglottids are generally immature—that is, the reproductive organs, although visible, are nonfunctional. Proglottids posterior to the immature proglottids are sexually mature, while those towards the posterior end of the body are usually gravid, that is, filled with eggs. In some species, the gravid proglottids drop off from time to time, thus permitting the eggs to escape from the host along with fecal wastes.

Monoecious and dioecious species of the Eucestoda are known. Self-fertilization within a single proglottid and between proglottids, and copulation between two worms take place among the monoecious species, although the former is extremely rare.

Even continuous cross fertilization between different proglottids of the same tapeworm, known as "selfing," appears to be deleterious. Rogers and Ulmer (1962) have shown that when infections of *Hymenolepis nana* are established in mice, one tapeworm per mouse, thus assuring self-fertilization, the frequency of abnormalities among cysticercoids (larval forms) is increased. Also the proportion of eggs developing into cysticercoids when fed to *Tribolium confusum*, the confused flour beetle—a suitable but not an obligatory intermediate host (p. 337)—appears to decrease, and the proportion of cysticercoids developing into adults when fed to mice decreases. In addition, no "selfed" strain could be maintained beyond the fifth "selfed" generation. These observations suggest that cross fertilization between individuals, resulting in what is genetically termed hybrid vigor, is necessary for the normal perpetuation of the species.

When there are separate male and female individuals, cross fertilization is necessary. The occurrence of separate sexes in the Eucestoda is limited to the genus *Dioecocestus*, a parasite of grebes and ibises (Plate 12–1, Fig. 2); however, anomalies among members of other genera exist.

During development and maturation of reproductive organs, the tapeworms demonstrate protandrous hermaphroditism—that is, in mature proglottids the male organs become functional before the female organs. Also,

asexual and "intersexual" conditions exist, and these present another interesting avenue of investigation.

BODY TISSUES

The basic body tissues—the osmoregulatory structures, the reproductive systems, and the nervous system—of all tapeworms, except for certain morphological variations among the different taxa, are essentially the same and are discussed generally rather than separately under each taxonomic grouping.

Body Wall

The body wall of cestodes is made up of several layers (Plate 12–1, Fig. 3). The outermost layer of the body surface is called the cuticle. This layer is more or less transparent, noncellular, and without visible pores. When studied with the electron microscope, minute projections known as microtriches are present on the cuticular surface. Rothman (1963) suggests that the distal portion of each microthrix, which is solid, is concerned with two functions: (1) it may serve as a means of resisting the intestinal current, since the body surface is in intimate contact with the microvilli of the striated border of the cells lining the host's small intestine; and (2) it may serve to agitate the microhabitat in the vicinity as the worm moves, thus stirring up the intestinal fluids so that nutrient materials as well as waste products are always in a state of flux. The proximal portion of each microthrix is medullated and could very well serve as sites of absorption. In addition to these projections, ultramicroscopic pore canals that communicate with the parenchyma are present in the cuticle. These may be sites of absorption also. Rothman also reports the presence of mitochondria in the cuticle of cestodes. Thus, it is apparent that this outer body layer is a dynamic structure rather than a mere covering.

The cuticle consists of two, perhaps more, strata. Immediately beneath the cuticle is the basement membrane. This noncellular connective tissue layer contains vacuoles and granules. The protoplasmic layer, underneath the basement membrane, is comparatively thick. This layer is believed to be cellular, because occasionally disintegrating nuclei can be seen embedded in the matrix, but cell outlines are not visible. The subcuticular muscles are

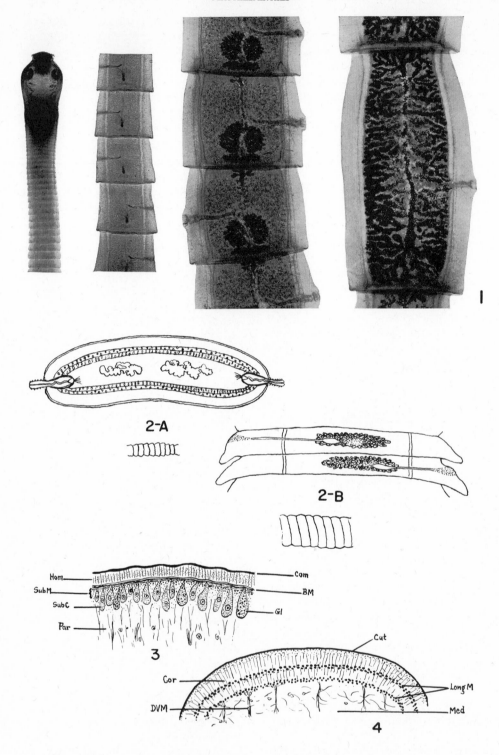

Plate 12-1   Tapeworm morphology. 1. Photomicrograph of sections along the body length
of *Taenia pisiformis*. From left to right—scolex and neck region, immature proglottids, mature
proglottids, and gravid proglottid. (Courtesy of Ward's Natural Science Establishment, Rochester,
N. Y.) 2. A. Transverse section of a proglottid of male of *Dioecocestus acotylus*. Irregularly outlined
bodies in center represent the testes. B. Ventral view of two proglottids of female specimen of
D. acotylus. Irregular dark bodies in middle of proglottids represent ovaries. (Redrawn after
(*Legend continued on opposite page.*)

located beneath the protoplasmic layer. These are arranged in two layers—the outer layer is circularly or transversely arranged, and the inner layer is longitudinally oriented.

A thin layer of neuromuscular cells is situated underneath the subcuticular muscles. These cells are in the form of multipolar bodies, which possess cytoplasmic processes, some joining similar processes from neighbouring neuromuscular cells, and still others joining the fine nerve fibers of the nervous system. Beneath the neuromuscular layer is the subcuticle, composed of bipolar, elongate, epidermal cells that are randomly situated at various depths. These are oriented at right angles to the body surface. The cytoplasmic projections of these cells are believed by some to pass through the overlying strata, penetrate the body cuticle, and appear on the surface as "pseudocilia," which are probably equivalent to microtriches.

Parenchyma

The space enclosed by the body wall, except for that occupied by the reproductive organs, osmoregulatory structures, muscle fibers, and nervous tissue, is filled with a spongy type of tissue—the parenchyma. Although the histology of this tissue is in need of further study, it is known that certain syncytially arranged cells form a network. In living animals, the spaces present between the cells are filled with fluid. The parenchymal cells, and to some extent the spaces, serve as sites for the storage of glycogen.

Body Muscles

The parenchymal musculature, as distinguished from the subcuticular musculature, is characteristic of cestodes. Parenchymal musculature does not exist in trematodes, cestodaria, and turbellarians. One type of these long, bipolar muscle cells is arranged longitudinally in a circle lying in the parenchyma approximately equidistant between the body wall and an imaginary body axis, thus dividing the parenchyma into the outer cortical and inner medullary zones (Plate 12–1, Fig. 4). The muscle cells rest between bundles of fibers that have their origin in the cells. The other type of parenchymal muscles are circularly arranged and line the inner surfaces of the longitudinal muscles, one group running from one lateral margin of the body to the other in the dorsal half of the body, and the other oriented in the same fashion but located ventrally. The two bow shaped bundles enclose the medullary parenchyma. These circularly arranged muscles are laid down by the longitudinally arranged ones and are inserted terminally in the cuticle by fine cytoplasmic processes.

The most complex set of muscles in a tapeworm's body is that which controls the actions of the holdfast structures on the scolex. Basically, these are sets of criss-crossing muscle fibers attached to the inner surfaces of the suckers, thus permitting contraction of these areas (Plate 12–2, Fig. 1). These are specialized subcuticular muscles and are not related to the parenchymal musculature.

Osmoregulatory System

The osmoregulatory system (sometimes known as the excretory system) in the Eucestoda is essentially the same as the protonephritic type found in trematodes (Plate 12–2, Fig. 2). The typical cyclophyllidean system is given here to familiarize the reader with the terminology.

Four main collecting canals traverse the entire length of the strobila. The two ventral canals are ventrolaterally located, and the two dorsal canals are dorsolateral. All these canals are situated in the peripheral zone of the medullary parenchyma. A single transverse canal connects the two ventral canals at the posterior end of each proglottid. The ventral vessels carry the water away from the scolex, the dorsal vessels toward it. Within the scolex the four longitudinal canals may be joined by a network of canals or joined by a single ring vessel or the dorsal and ventral canals on each side may be joined by a simple connection with no apparent exchange between the two sides (Plate 12–2, Figs. 3 to 5).

Along the length of the ventral canals, a series of secondary tubules arise that may in turn give rise to tertiary tubules. At the free end of the terminal tubules are flame cells, which are generally arranged in groups of

---

(*Legend continued.*)

Fuhrmann, 1932.) **3.** Cross section through body wall of a tapeworm. (Com, comidial layer of cuticle; Hom, homogeneous layer of cuticle; BM, basement membrane; SubC, subcuticular cells; Gl, gland cells; Par, parenchyma.) (Original.) **4.** Cross section through proglottid of tapeworm. (Cut, cuticle; Cor, cortical parenchyma; Med, medullary parenchyma; LongM, longitudinal muscles; DVM, dorsoventral muscles.) (Original.)

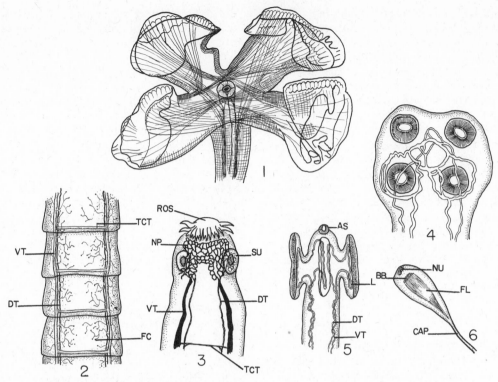

Plate 12-2   Morphologic features of Eucestoda. 1. Expanded holdfast of *Anthobothrium auriculatum,* showing muscle fibers. (Redrawn after Rees, 1943.) **2.** Osmoregulatory canals in consecutive proglottids. (Original.) **3.** Scolex of *Taenia,* showing network type of nephridial (osmoregulatory) plexus. (Redrawn after Riehm, 1881.) **4.** Scolex of *Proteocephalus torulosus,* showing single ring type of connection of the osmoregulatory canals. (Redrawn after Wagner, 1917.) **5.** Scolex of *Echeneibothrium,* showing lateral loop type of connection of the osmoregulatory canals. (Redrawn and modified after Hyman, L. B. 1951. *The Invertebrates,* McGraw-Hill, New York.) **6.** Single flame cell of a tapeworm.

(AS, anterior sucker; BB, basal bodies; CAP, capillary; DT, dorsal excretory tubules; FC, flame cell; FL, flame of cilia; L, loop of bothridium; NP, nephridial plexus; NU, nucleus; ROS, rostellum; SU, sucker; TCT, transverse collecting tubule; VT, ventral excretory (collecting) tubule.)

fours. The individual flame cell is a stellate body with granular cytoplasm and a nucleus (Plate 12–2, Fig. 6). The "flame" is actually a group of cilia that arise from a concave basal plate located near the cell nucleus. The cilia are enveloped in the funnel shaped enlargement of the free end of the tubule. Water collected through the flame cells is passed down the tubules into the main tubes.

In young worms, there is an excretory vesicle in the posteriormost proglottid, into which the ventral tubes empty. However, as the neck region produces more proglottids, the older proglottids are pushed further back, and eventually the segment containing the vesicle is broken off. Thus, in most older specimens the posterior ends of the tubes open independently to the exterior.

Nervous System

The nervous system of cestodes is relatively complex considering the lack of coordination in these animals. The most striking "coordinated" movement of tapeworms is the contraction of the body, for example, when it is placed in tap water. The "brain" lies in the scolex and is more or less rectangular (Plate 12–3, Fig. 1). Two large major nerve trunks of the body extend posteriorly along the entire length of the strobila. Two shorter nerve trunks extend anteriorly to innervate the tissues anterior to the "brain." The anterior long side of the rectangle is the anterior commissure, the posterior long side is the posterior commissure. The rectangle itself is the cephalic ganglion. Modifications of this pattern are known. In *Grillotia erinaceus,* for example, two anterior commissures (or a split commissure) exist, and the anterior and posterior nerve trunks leave the ganglionic complex at 45° angles.

Reproductive Systems

The reproductive system of cestodes is essentially the same as that of digenetic trematodes except in some (Cyclophyllidea) where the female system includes a blind-sac uterus.

THE MALE SYSTEM.   The male reproductive system consists of one or many testes situated in the medullary parenchyma except in certain subfamilies of the Proteocephala, in which the testes are arranged in the cortical parenchyma (Plate 12–3, Fig. 2). From each testis, a single vas efferens arises, and if more than one testis is present, the vasa efferentia unite to form a common vas deferens. In certain species there is an enlargement of the vas deferens—the seminal vesicle—for storage of spermatozoa. The vas deferens enters the cirrus, which is located within a cirrus pouch.

In certain species the seminal vesicle is located within the confines of the cirrus pouch and is known as an internal seminal vesicle. In other species, the vesicle is located outside the pouch and is hence an external seminal vesicle. In still others, both an internal and an external seminal vesicle are present. Within the cirrus pouch, there are generally glandular cells—the prostate glands—which open into the cirrus through cytoplasmic ducts. The cirrus is protrusible and in most cestodes empties into a common male and female external opening —the genital pore—situated at the surface opening of the cup shaped atrium.

THE FEMALE SYSTEM.   The female reproductive system consists of a single lobed or unlobed ovary, from which an oviduct arises (Plate 12–3, Fig. 3). The oviduct leads to a minute chamber—the ootype—where various components of the egg are assembled. Also leading into the ootype are (1) the Mehlis' gland, the cells of which form an amorphous complex surrounding the ootype; (2) the single common vitelline duct, which results from the union of many primary vitelline ducts arising from the vitelline glands. These glands range from a single compact body to numerous individual follicles scattered throughout the parenchyma; (3) the duct of the seminal receptacle, the latter being an enlarged portion in the vaginal tube that generally opens into the common atrium.

The tube leaving the ootype is the uterus. In certain orders of tapeworms, such as the Pseudophyllidea, the uterus opens to the outside of

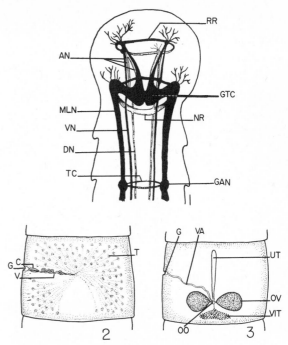

Plate 12–3   Anatomy of Eucestoda. 1. Lateral view of nervous system in anterior end of *Moniezia*. (Redrawn after Tower, 1900.) 2. Male reproductive system of *Taenia*. 3. Female reproductive system of *Taenia*. Figures 2 and 3 are separated; however, in actuality, the two systems are surmounted on each other in this monoecious worm.

(AN, anterior nerve; C, cirrus sac enclosing cirrus; DN, dorsal nerve; G, genital pore; GAN, ganglion at origin of transverse commissure; GTC, genglionated transverse commissure; MLN, main lateral nerve; NR, nerve ring; OO, ootype; OV, ovary; RR, rostellar ring; T, testis; TC, transverse commissure in proglottid; UT, uterus; V, vas deferens; VA, vagina; VIT, vitellaria; VN, ventral nerve.)

the body through the genital pore. In such cases, the proglottid continuously forms eggs, which are expelled. In other tapeworms, such as certain members of the order Cyclophyllidea, the uterus is a blind sac. The proglottids of these tapeworms become filled with eggs in distended uteri. These eventually break away from the strobila and rupture, thus permitting the individual eggs to escape, or the proglottids may remain intact and still containing the eggs when passed out of the host. In other cyclophyllideans, such as *Dipylidium caninum*, the double-pored tapeworm of dogs, the gravid uterus breaks up into egg capsules, each containing from one to approximately sixty eggs. Such eggs are either passed out of the host in sloughed proglottids or in egg capsules.

The vitelline glands secrete materials that contribute to the formation of the yolk and shell, while the function of Mehlis' gland is identical with its function in trematodes (p. 236).

During copulation, the cirrus of one proglottid may be introduced into the vagina—a tube connecting the genital atrium with the seminal receptacle—of another proglottid of the same worm or into a proglottid of another worm. Spermatozoa are stored in the seminal receptacle, from which they enter the ootype for fertilization. As indicated on p. 305, cross fertilization between two worms appears to be necessary, at least periodically to permit hybridization, thus guarding against the deleterious effects of "selfing."

It should be mentioned that although the ootype is the site of egg formation in most species, in such tapeworms as *Hymenolepis* spp., the envelopes surrounding the zygote or blastomeres (the inner membrane, the embryophore, and the capsule or shell) are laid down after the cleaving zygote enters the uterus, rather than in the ootype.

Details of cestode prelarval embryology are only known in a few pseudophyllideans (Schauinsland, 1886) and cyclophyllideans (Janicki, 1907; Spätlich, 1925). Among pseu-

dophyllideans, the cleavage is total and equal, with one early blastomere becoming separated and later flattening out to form the vitelline membrane. Among cyclophyllideans, cleavage is total but unequal.

LIFE CYCLE STUDIES

Generally, cestode life cycles are not as complicated as those of trematodes because they usually do not involve asexual reproductive phases. However, most tapeworms also require at least one or two intermediate hosts.

Life cycle patterns among the Eucestoda are of considerable phylogenetic importance, for they often indicate the membership of particular species in specific orders. Unfortunately, the complete representative developmental patterns of all tapeworm orders are as yet not known. The patterns for the Proteocephala, the Cyclophyllidea, and the Pseudophyllidea, however, are known. Some variations in the life cycle of the Eucestoda are given in Table 12-1.

Table 12-1.   Some Variations in the Life Cycle Patterns of Eucestoda

1. *Dibothriocephalus*
2. *Caryophyllaeus*
3. *Archigetes*
4. *Hymenolepis nana*
5. *Dipylidium*
6. *Echinococcus*
7. *Multiceps*
8. *Taenia*

Proteocephalan Life Cycle Pattern

In the order Proteocephala, eggs containing larvae known as onchospheres leave the host in the feces. Generally these eggs are ingested by a copepod, in which the onchospheres escape and actively penetrate the gut wall, reaching the host's haemocoel. In this position, the onchospheres develop into procercoid larvae. The procercoids often lack the characteristic cercomer—a small caudal appendage commonly associated with this type of larva. If a cercomer is present, the characteristic hooks embedded in it are often absent. When the intermediate host is ingested by a definitive host, the procercoids invade such tissues as hepatic, muscular, and intestinal epithelium, and develop into plerocercoid larvae with invaginated scoleces. These larvae migrate back into the lumen of the gut and metamorphose into adults.

Cyclophyllidean Life Cycle Pattern

In the Cyclophyllidea, the hexacanth embryo, or onchosphere, remains passive in the eggshell or the unciliated embryophore (a flexible membrane) until the embryo is ingested by a vertebrate or invertebrate intermediate host. In species that require a vertebrate intermediate host, the onchosphere either invades the villi lining the intestine and develops into a cysticercus larva, as in *Hymenolepis nana*, or the onchosphere penetrates the intestinal wall and is carried by the circulation to some other body area where it develops into a cysticercus. The penetration by onchospheres of the host's intestinal wall is made possible by secretions from glands present in each onchosphere. These glandular structures, first discovered by Reid (1946, 1948), secrete a substance that acts on the ground substance of the host's mucosa and also has a cytolytic effect. The secretion contains a polysaccharide that is not hydrolyzed by salivary amylase.

The cysticercus, known also as a bladder-worm, is a bladder-like form in which a thickened portion of the wall invaginates and develops into a scolex.

In certain species, several scoleces are formed in the same individual. Such a multiscolical form is known as a coenurus.

In *Echinococcus granulosus*, the larvae display a third variation of scolex formation. In these parasites, daughter and grand-daughter cysts are formed, the daughters having originated as invaginations on the wall of the mother, and the grand-daughters as invaginations on the walls of the daughters. The walls of the second

and third generation cysts in turn give rise to a number of scoleces, which protrude into the cystic spaces referred to as brood capsules. Thus a large cyst, known as a hydatid cyst, is formed enclosing numerous heads, each of which will develop into a worm. A hydatid cyst commonly measures about 10 mm. in diameter. Sometimes thousands of worms result from a single hydatid cyst. When the intermediate host harboring hydatid cysts, cysticerci, or coenuri is ingested by the definitive host, each scolex develops into an adult.

In species that utilize an invertebrate intermediate host—commonly an arthropod—the onchosphere develops into a solid cysticercoid larva in the host's body cavity. The cysticercoid larva lacks a bladder but possesses an inverted scolex located at one end. On reaching the definitive host, the larva develops into an adult.

The evagination of certain tapeworm larvae, once they reach the definitive host's intestine, is referred to as excystment because these larvae are enveloped within a protective cyst wall. Rothman (1959) has shown that larvae of species such as, *Hymenolepis diminuta*, *H. nana*, *H. citelli*, and *Oochoristica symmetrica*, require the host's bile salts for activation and excystment, while the larvae of *Taenia taeniaeformis* do not. Furthermore, the larvae of *T. taeniaeformis*, *Hymenolepis diminuta*, *H. nana*, and *H. citelli* require a proteolytic enzyme to dissolve their cysts. In addition, the environmental temperature may influence excystment. The influences of bile salts, pepsin, trypsin, and temperature on the excystment of certain cyclophyllidean cestodes are listed in Table 12–2.

Pseudophyllidean Life Cycle Pattern

In the Pseudophyllidea, the onchosphere is covered with a ciliated embryophore. The larva hatching from the egg is free-swimming and is known as a coracidium. Coracidia are ingested by the first intermediate host—usually a copepod—and in the intestine of this host the coracidia shed their ciliated coat while penetrating the gut wall. In the copepod's haemocoel, the larvae develop into elongate oval procercoids that bear six hooks each. The hooks are situated in a caudal protruberance, the cercomer. When the first intermediate host is ingested by a second intermediate host, procercoids develop into solid, wormlike plerocercoids, each with an invaginated scolex at one end. Finally, when the second intermediate

Table 12-2. Some Factors Contributing to Excystment of Larval Cestodes

Cestode Species	Acid Pepsin (effect on cyst digestion)	Trypsin (effect on excystment)	Bile Salts (effect on excystment)	Temperature (effect on excystment) 18-26° C.	37° C.	Authority
Hymenolepis citelli	Initiates	None*	Activation only	None	Excyst	Rothman, 1959
H. diminuta	Initiates	None*	Some excystment	None	Excyst	Rothman, 1959
H. nana	Initiates	None*	Activation only	None	Excyst	Rothman, 1959
Taenia taeniaeformis	Essential	None	Some excystment	Excyst	Excyst	Rothman, 1959
T. solium	Essential	None*	Excyst	Excyst	Excyst	Butning, 1927
T. pisiformis	Unessential		Excyst	Excyst	Excyst	DeWaele, 1934; Edgar, 1941
T. tenuicollis			Excyst	Excyst	Excyst	Malkani, 1933
Taeniarhynchus saginatus		None	Excyst	Excyst	Excyst	Malkani, 1933
Oochoristica symmetrica	Unessential	None	Excyst	Excyst	Excyst	Rothman, 1959
Raillietina kashiwariensis	Unessential	Excyst†	Some excystment	None	Excyst‡	Sawada, 1959

* Produces excystment if bile salts are present.
† Pancreatin active, lipase relatively inactive, amylase not tested.
‡ Temperature at 40 to 42° C.
(After Read and Simmons, 1963.)

Table 12-3.   Light Requirement for Hatching of Eggs of Some Pseudophyllidean Cestodes

Cestode Species	Light Requirement for Hatching	Authority
Dibothriocephalus latus	Essential	Vogel, 1930
D. ursi	Not essential	Hilliard, 1960
D. dalliae	Not essential	Hilliard, 1960
D. dendriticum	Essential	Hilliard, 1960
D. oblongatum	Essential (?)	Thomas, 1947
Schistocephalus solidus	Essential	Smyth, 1955
Spirometra mansonoides	Essential (?)	Mueller, 1959
Triaenophorus lucii	Not essential	Guttowa, 1958
Bothriocephalus clavriceps	?	Jarecha, 1959

(After Smyth, 1963.)

host is ingested by the definitive host, the adult form of the parasite is attained.

Pseudophyllidean eggs, enclosing coracidia, are similar to those of digenetic trematodes in that there is an operculum at one end. For the coracidium to escape, the operculum must be released. Because Rowen had indicated that light releases an enzyme or proteolytic substance that attacks the opercular seal of the egg of the trematode *Fasciola hepatica,* thus allowing the miracidium to escape (p. 237), it was suspected that the action of light also affects the hatching of pseudophyllidean eggs. Studies in this area have indicated that although the eggs of a number of pseudophyllideans can hatch in the dark, light is required in some other species. However, even in species of the same or closely related genera, the eggs of some require light for hatching while the eggs of others do not. For example, Hilliard (1960), in addition to confirming Vogel's finding that eggs of *Dibothriocephalus latus* require light for hatching, also found that light is not essential in two related species. At 20° C., 60 per cent of eggs of *Dibothriocephalus dalliae* and 20 per cent of eggs of *Dibothriocephalus ursi* hatched in the dark after 31 days. Since eggs of both *D. dalliae* and *D. ursi* have been found in muddy pools and in deep lakes, it appears that the ability of their eggs to hatch in darkness is of survival value. Table 12-3 lists some findings relative to the light requirement for the hatching of pseudophyllidean eggs.

SYSTEMATICS AND BIOLOGY

Classification

Several excellent taxonomic monographs are available for identifying the Eucestoda. The most outstanding recent publications of this nature are by Skrjabin (1951), Wardle and McLeod (1952), and Yamaguti (1959). Other manuals are available for the identification of medically important species of tapeworms. Species parasitic in man and domestic animals are given in Table 12–4.

The subclass Eucestoda, according to Wardle and McLeod, is divided into eleven orders.

Order 1. Proteocephala.   Adults are parasitic in freshwater fishes, amphibians, and reptiles. Small tapeworms with an extremely mobile scolex provided with four simple, cup shaped suckers set flush with its surface. Apical sucker is present in some. Common atrium is marginal; vitellaria, ovary, uterus, and testes are usually medullary, cortical in a few. Vitellaria are follicular, as lateral bands; ovary is bilobed, posterior in position. Uterus has numerous lateral diverticula and one or more medioventral apertures.

Order 2. Tetraphyllidea.   Adults are parasitic in intestine of Selachii (elasmobranch fishes). Moderate-sized tapeworms with four leaf-, trumpet-, or ear-like outgrowths on scolex; these outgrowths may or may not be supplemented by true suckers. Common atrium is marginal; testes are entirely in front of ovary. Vagina is dorsal to cirrus pouch and uterus, opening in front of male aperture. Ovary is bilobed, posterior, X shaped in cross section. Vitellaria are in two lateral fields. Uterus appears as small uterine duct dorsal to vagina, or as

(*Text continued on page 318.*)

Table 12-4.   Common Cestodes Parasitic in Man and Domestic Animals

Cestode	Principal Hosts	Habitat	Main Characteristics	Disease Caused
Pseudophyllidea				
Dibothriocephalus latus (=*Diphyllobothrium latum*)	Man, dogs, cats, minks, bears, other fish-eating mammals	Intestine	Extremely large; 3-10 meters long; consisting of 3000 or more proglottids; scolex 2.5 mm. long; 1 mm. wide; eggs 70μ by 45μ, operculate	Dibothriocephaliasis, sometimes anemia
Diplogonoporus grandis	Normally a parasite of whales, occasionally in man	Intestine	1.4-5.9 meters long; two sets of reproductive organs per proglottid; eggs 63-68μ by 50μ, operculate	Diarrhea, constipation, secondary anemia
Spirometra erinaceieuropaei	Dogs, cats, man	Intestine	85-100 cm. long; multiple testes larger than those of *D. latus*; vitellaria numerous; eggs 57-60μ by 33-37μ, operculate	Similar to *D. latus* infections
S. mansonoides	Dogs, cats, usually bobcats	Small intestine	Rarely over 1 meter long; scolex 200-500μ wide; bothria shallow; cirrus and vagina open independently on ventral surface; eggs 65μ by 37μ, operculate	Diarrhea and secondary anemia. Larvae may cause sparganosis in man.
Ligula intestinalis	Fish-eating birds, occasionally in man	Intestine	Specimens found in humans small, less than 80 cm. long	Nonpathogenic
Cyclophyllidea (Anoplocephalidae)				
Bertiella studeri	Monkeys, apes, man	Small intestine	275-300 mm. long; 10 mm. wide; scolex subglobose, set off from strobila; eggs irregular in outline, 45-46μ by 50μ, nonoperculate	No apparent symptoms
Anoplocephala magna	Horses	Intestine	350-800 mm. long; 20-50 mm. wide; 400-500 testes per mature proglottid; eggs 50-60μ in diameter, nonoperculate	Anoplocephaliasis, secondary anemia
A. perfoliata	Horses	Large and small intestine	10-80 mm. long, 10-20 mm. wide, scolex 2-3 mm. in diameter with lappet behind each sucker	Anoplocephaliasis, secondary anemia
Paranoplocephala mamillana	Horses	Small intestine	6-50 mm. long; 4-6 mm. wide; suckers slitlike; eggs 50-88μ in diameter, nonoperculate	Nonpathogenic

Cyclophyllidea (Anoplocephalidae)—Cont'd

	Host	Location	Description	Disease
Moniezia expansa	Sheep, goats, cattle	Small intestine	Up to 4-5 meters long, 1 cm. wide; two sets of reproductive organs per proglottid; proglottid much wider than long; 100-400 testes per segment; eggs 50-60μ in diameter, nonoperculate	Nonpathogenic
M. benedeni	Sheep, goats, cattle	Small intestine	Up to 4 meters long, larger scolex than *M. expansa*	Nonpathogenic
Thysanosoma actinioides	Sheep, cattle	Small intestine	150-300 mm. long; large and prominent suckers; proglottids broader than long with fringe along posterior margin; two sets of reproductive organs per proglottid; eggs expelled in capsules; each egg 19.25μ to 26.95μ in diameter, nonoperculate	Thysanosomiasis
Aporina delafondi	Pigeons	Small intestine	70-160 mm. long, no rostellum, genital pore irregularly alternate, 100 testes per proglottid	Nonpathogenic ?
Taeniidae *Taenia solium*	Pigs, man	Small intestine	Up to 2-7 meters long; scolex quadrate with diameter of 1 mm.; rostellum armed with double row of hooks; eggs 31-43μ in diameter, nonoperculate	Taeniasis solium
(*Cysticercus cellulosae*)	Various animals, including man	Various tissues	Ovoid, whitish, 6-18 mm. long	Cysticercosis cellulosae
Taenia taeniaeformis	Cats, dogs, man	Small intestine	15-60 cm. long, 5-6 cm. wide, armed rostellum, double row of usually 34 hooks	Taeniasis taeniaeformis
(*Cysticercus crassicollis*)	Rats	Various tissues	—	—
Taenia hydatigena	Dogs	Small intestine	Up to 5 meters long, 4-7 cm. wide, scolex armed with double row of 26-44 hooks, 600-700 testes per segment, gravid uterus with 5-10 lateral branches	Taeniasis hydatigena

Table 12-4 continued.

Cestode	Principal Hosts	Habitat	Main Characteristics	Disease Caused
Taeniidae—Cont'd				
Taenia ovis	Dogs	Small intestine	Approximately 1 meter long, scolex armed with two rows of 24-36 hooks, 300 testes per proglottid, gravid uterus with 20-25 lateral branches	Taeniasis ovis
T. tenuicollis	Minks	Small intestine	Up to 70 mm. long, large suckers, 237-303μ in diameter, two rows totaling 48 hooks, eggs 17-20μ in diameter	Taeniasis tenuicollis
T. pisiformis	Dogs, cats, rabbits	Small intestine	500 mm. long; 5 mm. wide; scolex with double row of 34-48 hooks; genital pores alternate irregularly; gravid uterus with 8-14 branches; eggs 36-40μ long, 31-36μ wide, nonoperculated	Taeniasis pisiformis
Taeniarhynchus saginatus	Cysticercus in cows, adults in man	Small intestine	10-12 meters long, no rostellum, unarmed, 1000-2000 proglottids, eggs similar to those of *T. solium*	Taeniasis saginatus
Multiceps multiceps	Dogs, foxes, coyotes, man	Small intestine	Up to 1 meter long, 5 mm. wide, scolex armed with double row of 22-32 hooks, approximately 200 testes per proglottid, gravid uterus with 9-26 lateral branches, eggs 31-36μ in diameter	"Gid" in cysticercus infections; like taeniasis in adult infections
M. serialis	Dogs, occasionally man	Small intestine	70 cm. long, 3-5 cm. wide, rostellum with double row of 26-32 hooks, gravid uterus with 20-25 lateral branches	Like taeniasis
Echinococcus granulosus	Hydatid cysts in sheep, horses, deers, pigs, man	Liver and other organs	Hydatid cysts with thick two-layered wall, filled with fluid (adult morphology given in text)	Hydatid disease
Hymenolepididae				
Hymenolepis nana	Rats, mice, man	Intestine	25-40 mm. long, 1 mm. wide, short rostellum with 20-30 hooks in one ring, three testes, eggs 30-47 mm. in diameter	Hymenolepiasis nana
H. diminuta	Rats, mice, man dogs	Intestine	200-600 mm. long, 1-4 mm. wide, rostellum unarmed, eggs 60-80μ by 72-86μ	Hymenolepiasis diminuta
H. carioca	Chickens, turkeys	Small intestine	300-800 mm. long, 500-700μ wide, rostellum unarmed	Hymenolepiasis carioca
H. cantaniana	Chickens, turkeys, quails	Duodenum	2-12 mm. long, rostellum shorter than that of *H. carioca*, otherwise the two species are	Hymenolepiasis cantaniana

	Host	Location	Description	Pathogenicity
Hymenolepididae—Cont'd				
Fimbriaria fasciolaris	Chickens, ducks	Small intestine	14-85 mm. long, with pseudoscolex	Nonpathogenic
Dilepididae				
Dipylidium caninum	Dogs, cats, foxes, occasionally man	Small intestine	15-70 cm. long, 3 mm. wide, conical rostellum, armed with 30-150 hooks, 200 testes per proglottid, eggs in capsules, each egg 35-60 μ in diameter	Chronic enteritis dipylidiasis
Choanotaenia infundibulum	Chickens, turkeys, pheasants	Small intestine	Up to 20 cm. long, 1-2 mm. wide, posterior proglottids much wider than anterior ones, rostellum with single row of 16-20 hooks	Nonpathogenic
Amoebotaenia sphenoides	Chickens, turkeys	Small intestine	2-4 mm. long, entire worm roughly triangular in shape, rostellum with single row of 12-14 hooks, uterus lobed	Nonpathogenic
Metroliasthes lucida	Turkeys	Small intestine	Up to 20 mm. long, 1.5 mm. wide, scolex unarmed, uterus as two simple round sacs	Nonpathogenic
Davaineidae				
Raillietina cesticillus	Chickens, pheasants	Small intestine	100-130 mm. long, 1.5-3 mm. wide, scolex broad and flat and about 100 μ in diameter, rostellum armed with double row of 400-500 hooks	Enteritis and hemorrhage
R. tetragona	Chickens, turkeys	Small intestine	Up to 250 mm. long, 1-4 mm. wide, rostellum with double row of 90-130 hooks, suckers armed with 8-12 rows of hooklets, 6-12 eggs in single capsule	Enteritis and hemorrhage
R. echinobothrida	Chickens, turkeys	Small intestine	Up to 250 mm. long, 1-4 mm. wide, rostellum with double row of 200-250 hooks, suckers with 8-15 rows of hooklets	Enteritis and hemorrhage
R. salmoni	Rabbits	Small intestine	85 mm. long, 3 mm. wide, retractile rostellum with double row of hooks	Nonpathogenic
R. retractilis	Rabbits	Small intestine	35-105 mm. long, 3 mm. wide, short neck, rostellum with two rows of hooks, genital pore unilateral	Nonpathogenic

Table 12–4 continued.

Cestode	Principal Hosts	Habitat	Main Characteristics	Disease Caused
(Davaineidae)—Cont'd				
Davainea proglottina	Chickens	Small intestine	Up to 4 mm. long, usually only 2-5 proglottids, rostellum with 66-100 small hooks, one egg per capsule	General physiological retardation
D. meleagridis	Turkeys	Small intestine	Up to 5 mm. long, composed of 17-22 proglottids, rostellum with double row of 100-150 hooks, suckers armed with 4-6 rows of hooklets	Unknown
Mesocestoididae				
Mesocestoides latus	Cats, skunks, raccoons	Small intestine	12-30 cm. long, 2 mm. wide, scolex unarmed, vitellaria bilobed in posterior region of proglottid	Nonpathogenic
M. lineatus	Dogs	Small intestine	30 cm. to 2 meters long, genital atrium midventral	Nonpathogenic

stemlike median uterine sac ventral to vagina. Gravid uterus is broad, occupying most of proglottid. Uterine pores, delayed in appearance, appear as single pore or slit, or as several tubular canals.

Order 3. Disculicepitidea. Adults are parasitic in Selachii. Comparatively large tapeworms with scolex possessing neither suckers, bothria, nor hoods, but with large cushion-like pad at anterior end followed by a collar. Proglottids are subsquare. Special cortical granulation is present. Common atrium ventral. Vaginal aperture is anterior to male aperture. Ovary is voluminous, at extreme posterior end of proglottid, occupying its full width. Testes are numerous. Vitellaria are condensed, located posteriorly. Osmoregulatory system in form of net. Uterus is lobed, greatly thickening in gravid proglottids. Uterine aperture is wanting.

Order 4. Lecanicephala. Adults are parasitic in Selachii. Scolex lacks bothria or bothridia but is subdivided by transverse groove into dome shaped anterior region that may be flattened anteroposteriorly, that may appear as a deep, cup shaped sucker or as retractile tentacles; and cushion shaped posterior region with four suckers that may be collar-like or suspended on tentacles. Vitellaria usually appear as two lateral bands.

Order 5. Pseudophyllidea. Adults are mainly parasitic in fishes. Body ranges from a few millimeters to more than 30 meters in length. Scolex typically possesses a dorsal and a ventral bothrium; sometimes these are lacking. Genital apertures are suficial or marginal. There are one (usually) or two sets of reproductive organs per proglottid. Testes are numerous, follicular, and scattered; ovary is bilobed. Vitellaria are follicular; uterine pore is ventral. Eggs are generally operculate.

Order 6. Trypanorhyncha. Adults are parasitic in Selachii. Relatively small tapeworms. Scolex provided with two or four sessile bothria and four tentacles that are armed with hooks and that can be withdrawn into scolex. Vitellaria are arranged in continuous layer in cortical parenchyma, surrounding medulla, or in medulla, alternating with bundles of longitudinal muscles. Testes extend posteriorly beyond level of ovary. Vagina is ventral to uterus and cirrus with aperture lateral to, ventral to, or behind cirrus aperture.

Order 7. Cyclophyllidea. Adults are parasitic in amphibians, reptiles, birds, and mammals. Small to extremely large (30 meters or more) tapeworms. Scolex typically is provided with four large suckers. Apical rostellum is common. Genital pores are on one or both margins. Testes located in medullary parenchyma. Ovary is slightly or multi-lobed. Vitellaria are follicular, postovarian in medulla. Gravid uterus appears as main tube with lateral diverticula; transverse tube; or tubular network that may break down into compartments (depending on the genus). Uterine aperture is lacking.

Order 8. Aporidea. Adults are parasitic in birds. Comparatively small tapeworms, up to 13 mm. long. Scolex usually lacks suckers, may possess elaborate glandular rostellum and large suckers. External segmentation of strobila is lacking. Male and female reproductive systems have no external apertures. Ootype is lacking. Vitellaria are present or absent. Ovaries form sheath around testes in cortex. Adults are protandrously hermaphroditic, some without female reproductive system.

Order 9. Nippotaeniidea. Adults are parasitic in fishes. Body is subcylindrical. Scolex possesses single, well developed sucker. Parasites have few proglottids, each with one set of reproductive organs.

Plate 12-4   Stages in the life cycle of *Ophiotaenia perspicua*. **1.** Hexacanth larva enveloped within membrane. (After Thomas, 1931.) **2.** Procercoid. (After Thomas, 1931.) **3.** Anterior end of *Ophiotaenia*. (After Nybelin, 1917.)

(AS, apical sucker; CA, calcareous bodies; H, hooks; HE, hexacanth; IM, inner membrane; OGM, outer gelatinous membrane.)

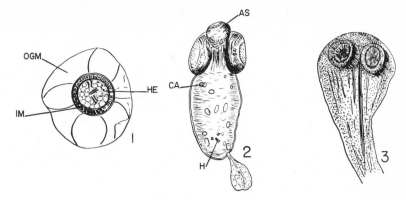

Order 10. Caryophyllidea.   Adults are parasitic in fishes. Small unsegmented tapeworms. Genital and uterine apertures appear on same flat surface of body; uterine aperture is between separate vaginal and cirrus openings. Eggs are operculated, nonembryonated when laid.

Order 11. Spathebothridea.   Adults are parasitic in ancient, probably primitive, fishes. These small tapeworms possess scolex varying in degree of differentiation but without suckers or bothria. Strobila possesses internal segmentation but without external proglottid formation. Genital pores are on ventral surface. Uterine aperture is located between vaginal and cirrus openings. Testes are medullary, appear as two lateral bands. Ovary is median, markedly lobed. Eggs are thick-shelled, operculate.

ORDER PROTEOCEPHALA

Members of the order Proteocephala have been rather comprehensively studied because they are comparatively plentiful. Generally one family—the Proteocephalidae—is recognized, and this taxon includes eight subfamilies, which are distinguished from one another by the arrangement of the reproductive organs within each proglottid.

Life Cycle of *Ophiotaenia perspicua*

The life cycle of *Ophiotaenia perspicua*, an intestinal parasite of the snake *Natrix rhombifer* (also *N. sipedon* and *Thamnophis sirtalis*), is representative of the pattern of proteocephalid cestodes (Plate 12–4).

The eggs are voided from the definitive snake host in the feces. Within each eggshell is a completely formed onchosphere. These ciliated larvae soon hatch into water and actively penetrate the body cavity of copepods, *Cyclops vulgaris, C. viridis, Mesocyclops obsoletus,* or *Microcyclops varicans*. Within these first intermediate hosts, the larvae develop into procercoids in approximately 14 days. When infected copepods are ingested by tadpoles, the procercoids invade

the mesenteries and livers of the amphibian host and develop into plerocercoids that are enclosed within cysts. The plerocercoids continue to grow, and with the metamorphosis of the tadpole into a frog, the plerocercoids may break out into the host's coelom. When an infected frog is eaten by the snake definitive host, the plerocercoids develop into adult tapeworms.

Space does not allow inclusion of the numerous genera of tapeworms belonging to the Proteocephala, but *Proteocephalus* in fresh-water fishes and rarely in amphibians and reptiles, *Corallobothrium* (Plate 12–5, Fig. 1) in siluroid fishes, and *Acanthotaenia* (Plate 12–5, Fig. 2) primarily in varanid reptiles should be mentioned because they are relatively common.

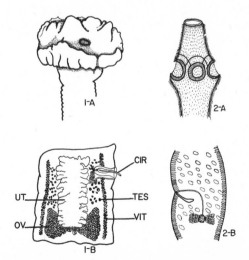

Plate 12-5   **Some proteocephalan cestodes. 1. A.** Expanded scolex of *Corallobothrium fimbriatum*. **B.** Mature proglottid of *Corallobothrium giganteum*. (CIR, cirrus; TES, testis; UT, uterus; OV, ovary; VIT, vitelline glands.) (Redrawn after Essex, 1927.) **2. A.** Scolex of *Acanthotaenia shipleyi*. **B.** Mature proglottid of *A. shipleyi*. (Redrawn after Southwell, 1930.)

ORDER TETRAPHYLLIDEA

The tetraphyllidean cestodes are readily recognizeable by four prominent outgrowths on the scolex. These flaplike holdfast organs are properly termed bothridia (Plate 12–6, Fig. 1), as opposed to the bothria of Pseudophyllidea. Often the single bothridium is subdivided into aroelae (or loculi) by septa, as in *Trilocularia*. Each proglottid contains a single set of male and female reproductive organs. These worms seldom, if ever, exceed 10 cm. in length, and no more than a few hundred proglottids form the strobila.

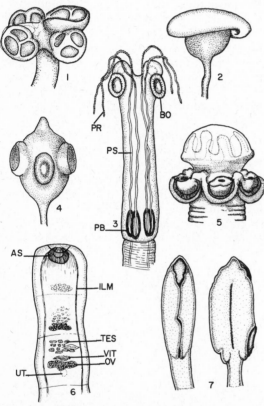

Plate 12-6   Types of eucestodan scoleces. 1. Scolex of *Trilocularia gracilis* (Tetraphyllidea), showing areolae. (Redrawn after Linton, 1924.) **2.** Scolex of *Disculiceps pileatum* (Disculicepitidea). (Redrawn after Southwell, 1925.) **3.** Scolex of *Gilquinia anteroporus* (Trypanorhyncha). (Redrawn after Hyman, L. B. 1951. *The Invertebrates*, McGraw-Hill, New York.) **4.** Cyclophyllidean scolex, showing prominent acetabula. (Original.) **5.** Scolex of *Nematoparataenia southwelli* (Aporidea). (Redrawn after Fuhrmann, 1933.) **6.** Anterior end of *Nippotaenia chaenogobii* (Nippotaeniidea). (Redrawn after Yamaguti, 1939.) **7.** Scolex of *Adenocephalus pacificus*, two views. (Redrawn after Nybelin, 1931.)

(AS, anterior sucker; BO, bothria; ILM, internal longitudinal muscles; OV, ovary; PB, proboscis bulb; PR, proboscides; PS, proboscis sheath; TES, testes; UT, uterus; VIT, vitelline glands.)

Life Cycle Pattern

The complete life cycle of the Tetraphyllidea is not known in any of the species. However, larval forms have been described from various hosts and attributed to this order. Baylis (1919), for example, reported a cysticercoid stage of *Phyllobothrium* encysted in the peritoneum of a dolphin. Similar larvae have also been found in cephalopod molluscs, marine teleostean fishes, and marine mammals. *Dinobothrium planum*, another supposedly tetraphyllidean larva, was described by Linton (1922) from *Omnastrephes illecebrosa*. The scolex of this larva includes two pairs of flattened bothridia arranged back to back. These incomplete pieces of life cycle data suggest that the Tetraphyllidea follow the two intermediate host cycle pattern —the two examples cited are in the second intermediate host. The adults are all parasitic in the intestine of elasmobranchs.

Several representative genera of the Tetraphyllidea are depicted in Plate 12–7.

ORDER DISCULICEPTIDEA

The Disculiceptidea is comprised of only one species, *Disculiceps pileatum* (Plate 12–6, Fig. 2), found in the spiral valves of the selachian fish, *Carcharias obscurus*, in the Atlantic Ocean off the Massachusetts coast. The parasite is 530 mm. or less in length and 3 to 5 mm. wide. The peculiarities of this species do not permit its inclusion in any of the other orders; hence, Wardle and McLeod (1952) established the order Disculiceptidea to include it.

The unusual shape of the scolex—without bothria, bothridia, or suckers—is unique and has caused much postulation as to its phylogenetic position among the Eucestoda. It has been suggested that the Disculiceptidea is closely related to the Tetraphyllidea but not to such a degree that it could be considered a member.

The life cycle of the single species is unknown.

ORDER LECANICEPHALA

The Lecanicephala includes, among others, *Lecanicephalum* in elasmobranchs, *Tetragonocephalum* in elasmobranchs of the genus *Trygon*, and *Polypocephalus* also in elasmobranchs (Plate 12–8, Figs. 1 to 3). All known species are intestinal parasites in their elasmobranch hosts.

The accompanying illustrations give some

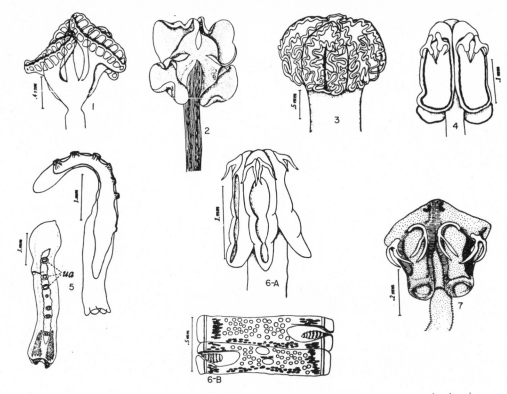

Plate 12-7   Some tetraphyllidean cestodes. 1. Scolex of *Echeneibothrium myzorhynchum,* in the elasmobranch *Raja binoculata.* (After Hart, 1936.) **2.** Scolex of *Anthobothrium cornucopia* in intestine of elasmobranchs. (After Southwell, 1925.) **3.** Scolex of *Phyllobothrium lactuca* in elasmobranchs. (After Beneden, 1850.) **4.** Scolex of *Pedibothrium brevispine* in elasmobranchs. (After Southwell, 1925.) **5.** Proglottids of *Calliobothrium verticillatum* in various elasmobranchs, showing uterine apertures. (ua, uterine aperture.) (After Woodland, 1927.) **6. A.** Scolex of *Acanthobothrium coronatum* in elasmobranchs. **B.** Mature proglottids of *A. coronatum.* (After Southwell, 1925.) **7.** Scolex of *Platybothrium hypoprioni* in the elasmobranch *Hypoprion.* (After Potter, 1937.)

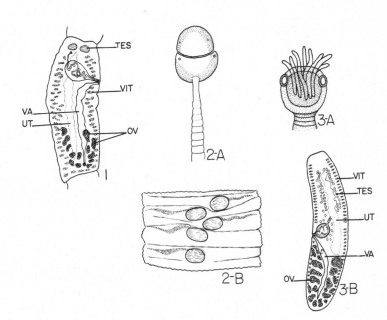

Plate 12-8   Lecanicephalan cestodes. 1. Mature proglottid of *Lecanicephalum peltatum.* (Redrawn after Southwell, 1925.) **2. A.** Scolex of *Tetragonocephalum.* **B.** Immature proglottids. (After Shipley and Hornell, 1906.) **3. A.** Scolex of *Polypocephalus medusia.* **B.** Mature proglottid. (Redrawn after Southwell, 1925.)

(OV, ovary; TES, testes; UT, uterus; VA, vagina; VIT, vitelline glands.)

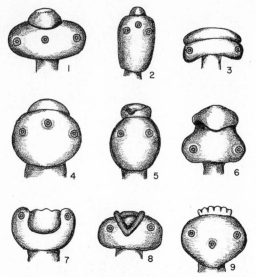

Plate 12-9   Variations in shape of the scolex of *Tylocephalum dierama.* (Redrawn after Southwell, 1925.)

idea of the variations in the scolical morphology of the various genera (Plate 12-8). Variations of the scolex of *Tylocephalum dierama* are depicted in Plate 12-9.

Life Cycle Data

Life cycle data concerning members of this order are lacking. However, Jameson (1912) reported globular larvae, which he believed to be those of *Tylocephalum,* commonly found in the digestive tract of various bivalve molluscs in the Orient. Experiments in feeding these larvae to sharks failed to verify his suspicion, for adults were not recovered.

ORDER PSEUDOPHYLLIDEA

The pseudophyllidean tapeworms are characterized by true bothria on their scoleces. These holdfast organs appear as slitlike depressions on the body surface, although various modifications do exist (Plate 12-6, Fig. 7). The scolex is not clearly demarked from the strobila in most species, and a definite neck region is lacking. These worms are comparatively small, ranging from a few millimeters to a few centimeters in length, but certain members of the family Dibothriocephalidae are as long as 30 meters.

Excluding the Cyclophyllidea, the Pseudophyllidea is the largest order of tapeworms. Numerous species have been reported from

fishes and occasionally in mammals. The order is divided into seven families. In Haplobothriidae and Dibothriocephalidae, the genital pore(s) is located on the same surface of the dorsoventrally flattened body as the uterine pore. In Bothriocephalidae and Ptychobothriidae, the genital pore(s) is on one surface, while the uterine pore opens on the other. In Echinophallidae, Triaenophoridae, and Amphicotylidae, the genital pore(s) opens on one of the lateral margins.

FAMILY HAPLOBOTHRIIDAE

The family Haplobothriidae includes the genus *Haplobothrium,* parasites in fresh-water teleost fishes (Plate 12-11, Fig. 3). This genus is unique because it appears to be an intermediate form between the Pseudophyllidea and the Trypanorhyncha. The bothria are located at the tips of four tentacle-like projections.

During the life cycle of *H. globuliforme,* the procercoid develops in about 10 days in the haemocoel of *Cyclops viridis.* When infected cyclops are ingested by the definitive host, which is a fish, development of the adult commences. It is not until the final stages of adult development that the tentacle-like proboscides develop.

FAMILY DIBOTHRIOCEPHALIDAE

The Dibothriocephalidae is comprised of numerous genera, among which is *Dibothriocephalus,* including *D. latus,* commonly called the "broad fish tapeworm." This species normally is found in various terrestrial and marine fish-eating carnivores, including canines, cats, the mongoose, the mink, foxes, bears, seals, and sea lions. In North America, the normal host is probably the brown bear, *Ursus americanus.* This tapeworm also parasitizes man. Human infections have taken place in central Europe, especially in Finland and the Baltic areas, Ireland, Israel, central Africa, Siberia, Japan, Chile, Canada, and in American states surrounding the Great Lakes.

Life Cycle of *Dibothriocephalus latus*

Stages in the life cycle of *D. latus* are illustrated in Plate 12-10. Adult worms have been reported as large as 10 to 30 feet long and 10 to 20 mm. wide and composed of 3000 to 4000 proglottids. The ovoid eggs do not include completely formed embryos when laid. Such eggs lay dormant in water after passing out of the host, and these eggs actively consume oxygen. Within the shell, the embryo becomes fully developed in 8 to 12 days. Typical of the Pseudophyllidea, the individual embryo is covered with a ciliated embryophore and is known as a coracidium.

Upon hatching, the coracidium may become free-swimming or free-crawling but must be ingested by specific copepods, such as *Diaptomus* spp., within 24 hours or else they perish. Coracidia are quite host specific. If a coracidium successfully enters the copepod host, it loses its ciliated coat and becomes a naked onchosphere. The onchosphere bores through the copepod's intestinal wall and ultimately lodges in the coelomic cavity. In 14 to 18 days, the onchosphere has metamorphosed into a solid, elongate (500 μ) larva—the procercoid. This larva possesses six hooks embedded in its cercomer, which projects from the posterior end.

When an infected copepod is ingested by a fish (such as, *Esox stizostedion* in North America and *Salmo* and *Oncorhynchus* in the Far East), the escaping procercoid in the piscine host's intestine slowly works its way through the intestinal wall and eventually becomes situated in the body musculature, where it develops into a long, solid plerocercoid. This second larval form bears an evaginated scolex at one end. The plerocercoid of *D. latus* may measure 2 to 4 cm. in length.

Unlike most pseudophyllidean plerocercoids, that of *D. latus* is coiled and can be either unencysted or encysted, although the unencysted form is more common. Encystment of the plerocercoid depends on their location in the fish host. When the plerocercoid is situated in the muscles of the body wall, encystment does not occur; however, if it should settle in or on the viscera, a cyst is formed around the plerocercoid. Although the body wall musculature appears to be a favored site for plerocercoids, they can be located elsewhere in the fish host. Infection of the definitive host is caused by the eating of plerocercoids in poorly cooked or raw fish.

Human Dibothriocephaliasis

Human infection with *Dibothriocephalus latus* is primarily, although not exclusively, limited to areas where fresh fish is a part of the everyday diet or where the fishing industry, involving handling and cleaning of fish, is carried on. Human infections are contracted when poorly cooked fish, including plerocercoids in the flesh, are ingested or when plerocercoids clinging to the hands of fish cleaners are accidentally introduced into the mouth.

In Finland, approximately 20 per cent of the population is infected, while in some communities in the Baltics nearly 100 per cent infection exists. In North America, 50 to 70 per cent of pikes and walleyes found in some small lakes in northern United States and Canada harbor plerocercoids of *D. latus*. The author has found infections in fish in the Delaware River.

Symptoms of human dibothriocephaliasis include abdominal pain, loss of weight, and rarely by a unique type of pernicious anemia (see p. 347).

Although the typical life cycle of the Pseudophyllidea includes a free-swimming coracidium, a procercoid in the first intermediate host, a plerocercoid in the second, and the sexually mature adult in the definitive host, certain species, such as *D. latus* and *Spirometra* spp., pass through more than two intermediate hosts. However, the larval stages found in the second and all subsequent intermediate hosts remain comparable, merely retaining the plerocercoid form while being transferred through the third and fourth hosts. The plerocercoid larva of such pseudophyllidean tapeworms is often referred to as a sparganum. In many instances spargana can live in human flesh causing sparganosis.

Other Dibothriocephalid Genera

Some of the other more prominent genera of the Dibothriocephalidae are *Ligula* in diving and wading birds and *Diphyllobothrium* in tooth whales (Plate 12–11, Figs. 4 and 5). Worms belonging to the genus *Diphyllobothrium* may exceed 2500 mm. in length by 15 mm. in width. Another fairly common member of the Dibothriocephalidae is *Spirometra,* which is parasitic in various fish-eating birds, dogs, and cats (Plate 12–11, Fig. 6). In these three genera, various fishes serve as the second or last intermediate host, in which the spargana (plerocercoids) are often encountered encysted in the musculature.

Experimental Sparganosis

Although loss of weight by the host is commonly associated with parasitism, especially among mammals, Mueller (1963) has found that when the spargana of *Spirometra mansonoides* are injected subcutaneously into young female mice, the infected mice show accelerated gain in weight when compared to control uninfected

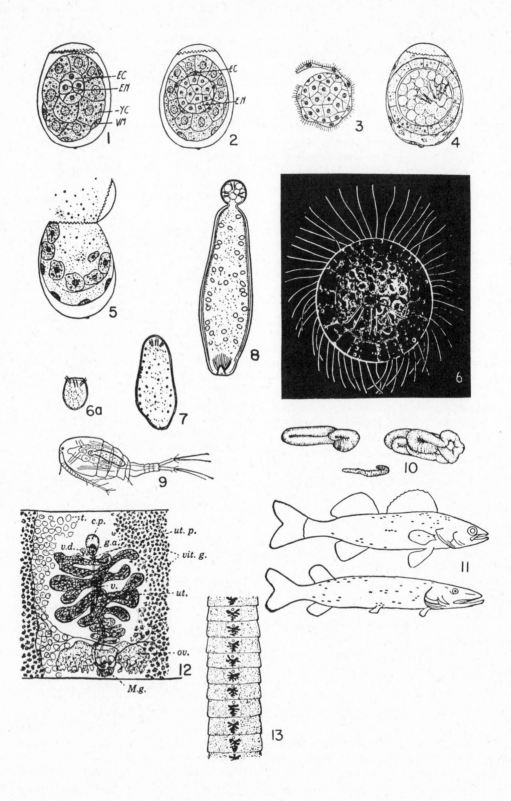

Plate 12-10   See legend on opposite page.

mice. Although the reason for the weight gain is not yet understood, the gain cannot be accounted for by the weight of the parasites or by the associated host tissue reaction, which is slight. Infected mice behave no differently from control mice, nor is their longevity affected. Within limits, the accelerated weight gain in infected mice appears to be proportional to the number of spargana introduced. Experiments in which spargana whose scoleces had been removed were injected revealed that the host's gain in weight is not dependent on growing scoleces.

Similar weight gains occur when the haemoflagellate *Trypanosoma duttoni* is introduced into mice, when *Trypanosoma lewisi* is introduced into rats, and when certain molluscs are infected by certain larval trematodes. In trypanosome infections in mice and rats, the accelerated gains in weight are only temporary, declining by the third week of infection. This aspect of host-parasite relationship—parasite-caused accelerations in growth—represents an area of study that will undoubtedly prove to be most intriguing, and the *Spirometra*-mouse relationship appears to be an ideal model for investigations.

OTHER PSEUDOPHYLLIDEAN FAMILIES

The family Bothriocephalidae includes *Bothriocephalus*, which is often encountered in fresh-water fishes in the United States. The family Ptychobothriidae includes *Ptychobothrium* in elasmobranchs, *Senga* in fresh-water labyrinthid and cyprinid fishes, *Polyonchobothrium* in African fishes, and *Clestobothrium* in fishes of the family Merluccidae (Plate 12–12, Figs. 1 to 4).

The Echinophallidae, Thriaenophoridae, and Amphicotylidae are minor families, al-though the last mentioned includes *Eubothrium*, with several species fairly common to teleost fishes (Plate 12–12, Fig. 5).

ORDER TRYPANORHYNCHA

Members of the Trypanorhyncha are small to medium tapeworms, ranging from 2 to 100 mm. in length. They are readily recognized by their four spiny proboscides, which can be everted from the scolex (Plate 12–6, Fig. 3). These proboscids are blind tubes and when retracted, their spiny surfaces face the interior of the scolex. When retracted, each proboscis rests in a proboscis sheath, which terminates posteriorly as a proboscis bulb. The shapes, sizes, and numbers of spines on the proboscides are taxonomically important.

Except in *Hepatoxylon*, in which there is a double set of reproductive organs, all the trypanorhynchid worms possess one set of reproductive organs per proglottid.

All known adult trypanorhynchans are parasitic in the stomach or spiral valves of elasmobranchs.

Life Cycle Data

Life cycle data concerning the Trypanorhyncha are lacking. Very few of the species possess operculated eggs, although one species, *Grillotia erinaceus*, is known to have them. The complete life cycle of *G. erinaceus* alone is known because of the work of Ruszkowski (1932), but most helminthologists do not consider the cycle typical of members of this order.

In *G. erinaceus*, the eggs escape from the host and hatch into ciliated coracidia, which are ingested by copepods (*Acartia longiramus, Pseudocalanus elongatus*, and others). Within the crustacean host, the coracidia develop into

---

Plate 12-10   Stages in the life cycle of *Dibothriocephalus latus*. 1 and 2. Eggs enclosing blastomeres, showing origin of ectoderm and endoderm. Tissues have shrunk away from the shell because of fixation. (Modified after Schauinsland.) 3. Immature embryo, showing development of cilia. (After Schauinsland.) 4. Egg, a few hours before hatching. 5. Eggshell immediately after liberation of coracidium. 6. Coracidium, as seen with dark field microscopy. (After Vergeer.) 6a. *Cyclops* embryo after having shed ciliated coat. 7. Procercoid growing in *Cyclops*. 8. Fully grown procercoid in *Cyclops*. 9. *Cyclops* enclosing fully grown procercoid larva. (After Brumpt.) 10. Plerocercoid larvae as they appear in the flesh of fishes. 11. Outline drawings of walleyed pike and pickerel, showing distribution of plerocercoids of *D. latus*. (After Vergeer.) 12. Mature proglottid of *D. latus*. 13. A segment of strobila of *D. latus*. (After Chandler, A. C. 1955. *Introduction to Parasitology*, John Wiley, New York.)

(c.p., cirrus pouch; EC, ectodermal cell; EN, entodermal cell; g.a., genital atrium; M.g., Mehlis' gland; ov., ovary; t., testis; ut., uterus; ut.p., uterine pore; v., vagina; v.d., vas deferens; vit.g., vitelline glands; VM, vitelline membrane; YC, yolk cell.)

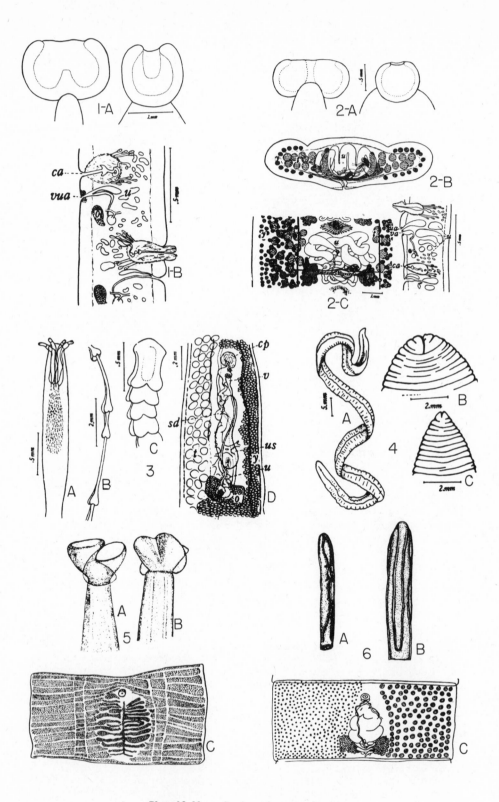

Plate 12-11   See legend on opposite page.

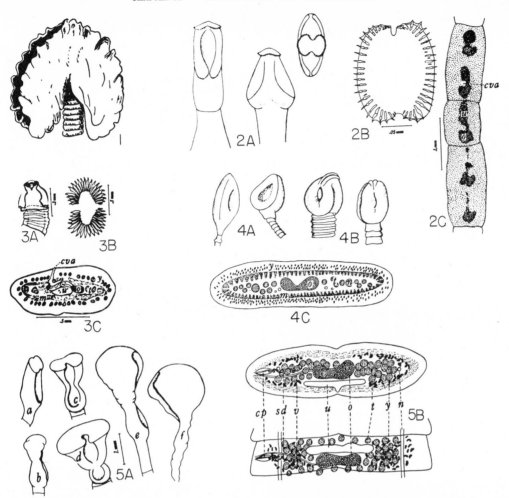

Plate 12-12   **Pseudophyllidean cestodes. 1.** Scolex of *Ptychobothrium* sp. (After Lönneberg, 1889.) **2. A.** Views of scolex of *Senga besnardi.* **B.** Hooks from scolex. **C.** Three proglottids. (After Dollfus, 1934.) **3. A.** Scolex of *Polyonchobothrium gordoni.* **B.** End-on view of crown of rostellar hooks. **C.** Cross section through cirrovaginal aperture. (After Woodland, 1937.) **4. A.** Scolex of *Clestobothrium crassiceps,* living. **B.** Scolex of *C. crassiceps,* fixed. **C.** Cross section of mature proglottid. (After Wardle, 1935.) **5. A.** Successive stages between the normal holdfast (a) and the deformed holdfast (f) of *Eubothrium rugosum.* **B.** Sectional and ventral views of mature proglottid. (After Ekbaum, 1933.)

(cp, cirrus pouch; cva, cirrovaginal atrium; m, parenchymal muscle zone; n, nerve cord; o, ovary; sd, sperm duct (vas deferens); t, testes; u, uterus; v, vagina; y, vitelline glands.)

Plate 12-11   **Some spathebothridean and pseudophyllidean cestodes. 1. A.** Scolex of *Bothrimonus fallax* from marine fish. **B.** Sagittal view of two consecutive proglottids. (After Nybelin, 1922.) **2. A.** Scolex of *Diplocotyle olrikii* in fishes. **B.** Cross section of mature proglottid. **C.** Mature proglottid, ventral view. (After Nybelin, 1922.) **3. A.** Scolex of primary segmented worm of *Haplobothrium globuliforme* in fishes. **B.** Twelfth, thirteenth, and fourteenth proglottids of *H. globuliforme.* **C.** Scolex and first three proglottids of secondary segmented worm. **D.** Mature proglottid. (After Cooper, 1914, 1918.) **4. A.** Entire worm of *Ligula intestinalis* in intestine of birds. **B.** Anterior end of larval stage. **C.** Anterior end of adult. (After Neveu Lemaire, 1936.) **5. A and B.** Scolex of *Diphyllobothrium stemmacephalum* in dolphins. **C.** Gravid proglottid. (After Cohn, 1912.) **6. A and B.** Scolex of *Spirometra mansoni,* in mammals. **C.** Mature proglottid of *S. ranarum.* (A and B after Joyeux, 1927; C after Faust *et al,* 1929.)

(ca, cirrus aperture; cp, cirrus pouch; o, ovary; sd, vas deferens; t, testes; u, uterus; ua, uterine aperture; us, uterine sac; v, vagina; vua, vaginouterine aperture; y, vitelline glands.)

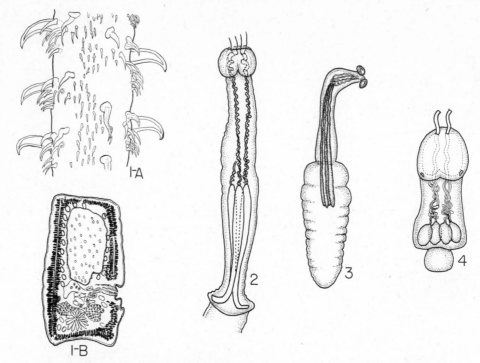

Plate 12-13   Trypanorhynchan cestodes. 1. A. External face of metabasal armature of a tentacle of *Grillotia erinaceus.* (Redrawn after Dollfus, 1942.) **B.** Mature proglottid. (Redrawn after Fuhrmann in Kükenthal, 1931.) **2.** Scolex of *Dasyrhynchus talismani.* (Redrawn after Dollfus, 1942.) **3.** *Eutetrarhynchus ruficollis* larva. (Redrawn after Eysenhardt, 1829.) **4.** Scolex of *Otobothrium.* (Redrawn after Dollfus, 1942.)

typical procercoids, which possess a cercomer. In the second intermediate host, a fish, the procercoids develop into typical plerocercoids. When the second intermediate host is ingested by the selachian host, the adults develop.

Although our knowledge of complete life cycles in the Trypanorhyncha is lacking, except for that of *G. erinaceus,* many plerocercoid larvae have been reported in marine snails, bivalves, cephalopods, crustaceans, teleost fishes, and rarely in reptiles. The plerocercoids, such as that of *Nybelinia,* possess a fully developed scolex and may or may not possess a tail. A few cysticercoid larvae have also been reported in which the scolex is enclosed in a tail. Because these larvae represent the last stage of larval development, ready to be ingested by the definitive host and hence are found in a second intermediate host, it is suspected that there is a first intermediate host in which the procercoids are to be found. Several representative genera of the Trypanorhyncha are depicted in Plate 12–13.

ORDER CYCLOPHYLLIDEA

The cyclophyllidean cestodes are undoubtedly the most common tapeworms encountered by inland helminthologists, because among these tapeworms are found most of the species that parasitize mammals, a large majority of those that parasitize birds, and some that are found in amphibians and reptiles. All members are characterized by four true suckers, or acetabula, which are symmetrically arranged on the scolex (Plate 12–6, Fig. 4). Some species possess an anteriorly projecting rostellum, which may or may not be armed with one or more rows of hooks. The number, size, shape, and arrangement of these rostellar hooks are important taxonomic tools. The rostellum can be retracted into the rostellar sac within the scolex.

Cyclophyllidean tapeworms are commonly referred to as taenoid cestodes, because the designation Taenioidea is often used. Furthermore, the order includes the genus *Taenia,* which is the most widely known of its genera. These worms range from 1 or 2 mm. up to 10 meters in length, although the majority are between 1 mm. and 3000 mm.

Fourteen families are represented in the Cyclophyllidea; some include species of medical and veterinary importance. The families Mesocestoidae, Tetrabothriidae, Nematotaeniidae, and Catenotaeniidae include those species that do not possess a rostellum, while the Taeniidae,

Davaineidae, Hymenolepidae, Dilepididae, Biuterinidae, Amabiliidae, Acoleidae, Diploposthidae, and Dioicocestidae possess a rostellum.

The families Acoleidae, Amabiliidae, and Dioicocestidae include various genera reported from avian hosts.

FAMILY MESOCESTOIDAE

The family Mesocestoidae includes the genus *Mesocestoides*, which includes numerous species commonly found in birds and mammals (Plate 12–14, Fig. 1). All the species possess ventrally

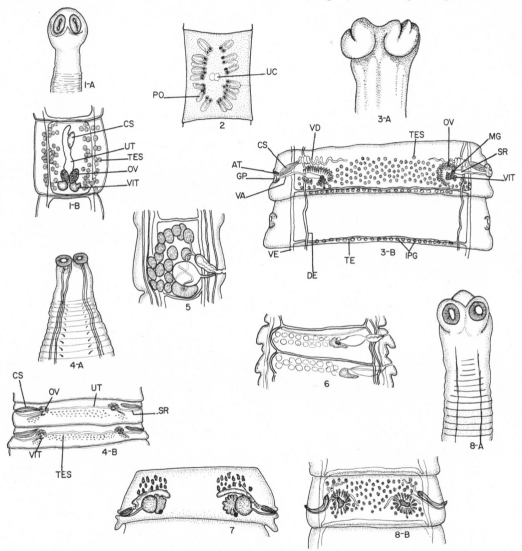

Plate 12-14   Some mesocestoid, nematotaeniid, and anoplocephalid cyclophyllideans.
1. **A.** Scolex of *Mesocestoides lineatus* (Mesocestoidae). **B.** Mature proglottid. (Redrawn after Witenberg, 1934.) **2.** Gravid proglottid of *Nematotaenia dispar* (Nematotaeniidae), showing arrangement of paruterine organs. **3. A.** Scolex of *Moniezia expansa* (Anoplocephalidae), the common tapeworm of sheep. (Redrawn after Stiles, 1898.) **B.** Mature proglottids of *M. expansa,* showing double set of reproductive organs. **4. A.** Scolex of *Cittotaenia pectinata* (Anoplocephalidae). (Redrawn after Arnold, 1938.) **B.** Mature proglottid of *Cittotaenia.* (Redrawn after Stiles, 1896.) **5.** Mature proglottid of *Andrya primordialis*) (Anoplocephalidae). (Redrawn after Douthitt, 1915.) **6.** Mature proglottid of *Paranoplocephala mamillana* (Anoplocephalidae). (Redrawn after Douthitt, 1915.) **7.** Mature proglottid of *Progamotaenia diaphana* (Anoplocephalidae). (Redrawn after Zschokke, 1907.) **8.** Mature proglottid of *Paronia pycnonoti* (Anoplocephalidae). (Redrawn after Yamaguti, 1935.)

(AT, genital atrium; CS, cirrus sac; DE, dorsal excretory tubule; GP, genital pore; IPG, interproglottidal glands; MG, Mehlis' gland; OV, ovary; PO, paruterine organs; SR, seminal receptacle; TE, transverse excretory tubule; TES, testes; UC, uterine capsules; UT, uterus; VA, vagina; VD, vas deferens; VE, ventral excretory tubule; VIT, vitelline glands.)

located genital apertures. Voge (1955) has contributed a monograph on the North American species of *Mesocestoides.*

The larva of *Mesocestoides,* known as a tetra-thyridium, is commonly found in the coelom or peritoneum of dogs, cats, mice, snakes, and other vertebrates. Such a larva resembles a cysticercus except that its body is long and slender, but not segmented. The anterior end, which includes an invaginated ,scolex, is comparatively large and bulbous. When the definitive host, including dogs, cats, raccoons, other carnivores, and even birds, ingests the carcass of an intermediate host infected with tetrathyridia, these larvae develop into adults in the host's intestine. The hexacanths of *Mesocestoides* are not infective to the hosts in which the tetrathyridia are found. Thus, a first intermediate host, yet unknown, most probably is required.

FAMILY NEMATOTAENIIDAE

The Nematotaeniid cestodes are unique in possessing cylindrical bodies instead of being dorsoventrally flattened. This family includes the genus *Nematotaenia* with the species *N. dispar,* which is found universally in various frogs and toads (Plate 12–14, Fig. 2).

FAMILY ANOPLOCEPHALIDAE

Members of the family Anoplocephalidae have unusual life cycles. Stunkard, in a series of papers published from 1937 to 1941, definitely showed that the three representative genera *Bertiella, Moniezia,* and *Cittotaenia* utilize soil-dwelling oribatid mites as the sole intermediate host. This pattern is true for *Moniezia expansa,* a parasite of lambs (Plate 12–14, Fig. 3). Although oribatid mites are now known to be the intermediate hosts of this economically important tapeworm, eradication programs have been hampered because these microscopic mites are extremely difficult to control. It is most probable that all anoplocephalids utilize oribatid mites as the intermediate host.

To students of wildlife zoology, the common tapeworms of rabbits and hares in North America, *Cittotaenia* spp. are of some interest because of their common occurrence (Plate 12–14, Fig. 4). Other common members of the Anoplocephalidae are depicted in Plates 12–14 and 12–15.

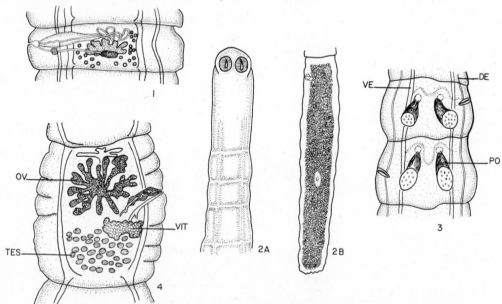

Plate 12-15   Some anoplocephalid cyclophyllidean cestodes. 1. Mature proglottid of *Linstowia semoni* (Anoplocephalidae). (Redrawn after Baer, 1927.) **2. A.** Scolex of *Oochoristica taborensis* (Anoplocephalidae). **B.** Gravid proglottid of *O. taborensis.* (A and B redrawn after Loewen, 1934.) **3.** Proglottids of *Stilesia* (Anoplocephalidae), showing two paruterine organs per proglottid. (Redrawn after Gough, 1911.) **4.** Mature proglottid of *Catenotaenia pusilla* (Anoplocephalidae) in intestine of mice. (Redrawn after Joyeux and Baer, 1945.)

(DE, dorsal excretory tubule; OV, ovary; PO, paruterine organ; TES, testes; VE, ventral excretory tubule; VIT, vitelline glands.)

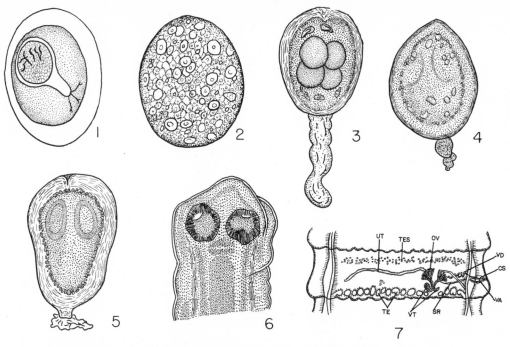

Plate 12-16   Stages in the life cycle of Bertiella studeri. 1. Egg removed from gravid proglottid. **2.** Larva from oribatid mite host that had been fed eggs of *B. studeri*. **3.** Immature cysticercoid removed from oribatid mite host. **4.** Cysticercoid from oribatid mite host. **5.** Cysticercoid from different genus of oribatid mite host (*Galumna* sp.). **6.** Scolex of mature worm. **7.** Proglottid enclosing reproductive organs that have not completely differentiated.

(CS, cirrus sac; SR, seminal receptacle; TE, transverse excretory tubule; TES, testes; UT, uterus; VA, vagina; VD, vas deferens; VT, vitelline glands.) (All figures redrawn after Stunkard, 1940.)

Life Cycle of *Bertiella studeri*

The life cycle of *Bertiella studeri*, a parasite of primates, including man, in the Eastern Hemisphere, was studied by Stunkard (1940). It is given here to demonstrate the unusual modification of the cyclophyllidean life cycle pattern as found among the anoplocephalid tapeworms (Plate 12–16).

Stunkard fed eggs removed from gravid proglottids of *B. studeri* to 24 species of mites and found that cysticercoids developed in *Schelribates laevigatus, Notaspis coleoptratus, Scutovertex minutus,* and *Galumna* spp. These cysticercoid larvae are spherical, ovoid, or pyriform, measuring 0.1 to 0.15 mm. in diameter, and they possess a small cercomer. When infected mites are accidentally eaten by primates, the tapeworm larvae develop into adults. Stunkard's experimental data do not completely explain how the cycle is completed in nature, for *Bertiella studeri* eggs are not laid and passed out in the host's feces. Instead, gravid proglottids are shed, generally 24 at a time, and these are passed out of the host. It is suspected, however, that these egg-containing body segments soon disintegrate, releasing the eggs so that they can be ingested by oribatid mites.

FAMILY TAENIIDAE

The family Taeniidae includes many medically and economically important species (Table 12–4).

Echinococcus *granulosus*

Echinococcus granulosus, or the hydatid worm, primarily parasitizes members of the canine family. In addition, human infections with the hydatid larvae have been reported from Iceland, South Australia, Tasmania, New Zealand, southern South America, northern and southern Africa, southern and eastern Europe, Siberia, Mongolia, northern China, Japan, and the Near East. In these areas, cattle, sheep, rabbits, horses, and hogs are also infected with hydatid cysts. Human cases of the hydatid disease have occurred in the Atlantic coastal states, the states surrounding the Great Lakes, Missouri, the deep South, and California.

The adult of *E. granulosus* is typically cyclophyllidean and measures from 2 to 8 mm. in length. The strobila generally consists of three or four proglottids. The rostellum is armed with a double row of from 20 to 80 hooks. In heavy infections, it is not unusual to find hundreds of worms attached to the host's intestine. Recently, Smyth (1963) has reported the presence of a group of cells lying just beneath the anterior tip of the rostellum. These cells not only contain droplets but actually secrete small viscid droplets to the exterior. The function of this secretion is still unknown but in view of the fact that the scolex of *E. granulosus* is in close contact with the canine host's intestinal mucosa, the secretion may be important from the immunological standpoint, acting as an antigenic agent.

LIFE CYCLE OF *Echinococcus granulosus.* Stages in the life cycle of *E. granulosus* are depicted in Plates 12–17 and 12–19. The life cycle and developmental pattern of *E. granulosus* is somewhat unusual because hydatid cysts are formed and asexual reproduction by budding takes place within the cysts.

Eggs resembling those of taenoids, especially the canine taenoid worms, are nonoperculate and measure approximately 30 by 38 μ. Eggs are expelled from adult worms in definitive hosts, which are primarily dogs, wolves, and foxes. These eggs gain entrance into the intermediate host either through water or in forage. Each egg contains a fully developed onchosphere. Human infection develops from too intimate an association with dogs. Infection of children is commonly established when dogs are permitted to lick their mouths. Eggs can also be ingested from contaminated fingers.

Once swallowed, the eggs pass to the duodenum, where they hatch. The escaping onchospheres penetrate the intestinal wall, enter the mesenteric venules, and become lodged in the capillary beds of various organs. Among moose, deer, and caribou, hydatid cysts usually develop in the lungs, but among other animals, including man, these larvae develop in the liver, lungs, and other tissues, with the liver being the most common site. Cysts have been known to form in the kidneys, spleen, heart, muscles, brain, and bone marrow. Development of the hydatid from the onchosphere is a slow process, with the host laying down an envelope of connective tissue around the parasite.

In a matter of months, the cyst reaches approximately 10 mm. in diameter, whereupon invaginations of its wall produces daughter cysts that project into the lumen of the mother cyst. The cavities are filled with a sterile fluid known as hydatid fluid. Within some daughter cysts, tertiary, or grand-daughter, cysts form by invagination, each one with a cavity known as the brood chamber. From the walls of these brood chambers, minute scoleces form. Scolex formation may occur from the invagination of the walls either of the daughter or grand-daughter cysts. These inverted scoleces develop and turn right-side-out, some falling into the brood chamber. In older cysts, some as large as an orange, minute daughter and grand daughter cysts and free scoleces are found a "hydatid sand" in the fluid. Such cysts, known as unilocular cysts, generally cause grea damage, if not death, to the host.

In man and certain domestic animals, the formation of hydatid cysts represents the end of the life line for the parasite. But in rabbits foxes, and other wild animals, when predator feed upon the viscera of the infected prey hydatid cysts are ingested. Upon reaching th intestine of the new host, each scolex develop into an adult worm. This cycle is interestin biologically because asexual reproduction b endogenous budding takes place during th formation of daughter and grand-daughte cysts and scoleces. Other than this deviation the cycle is typically cyclophyllidean.

Echinococcus multilocularis

In addition to the unilocular type of hydati cyst of *Echinococcus granulosus,* a second typ known as a multilocular or alveolar cyst, wa first recorded by Virchow in 1855. This typ of cyst is not a single, roughly spherical hollo body that undergoes endogenous buddin Rather, it proliferates by exogenous buddin resulting in a cluster of comparatively smalle cysts that metastasize through the surroundin host tissues.

Ever since multilocular cysts were first foun a controversy has existed as to whether the represent a modification of the unilocula hydatid cyst of *E. granulosus,* resulting fror pressure exerted by the surrounding hos tissue, or whether they represent the larvae c another species of *Echinococcus*—namely *E multilocularis.* Rausch (1952, 1953), whil investigating hydatid disease in Alaska, recog nized a species that is morphologically an ecologically different from *E. granulosus* on S Lawrence Island in the Bering Sea and tha

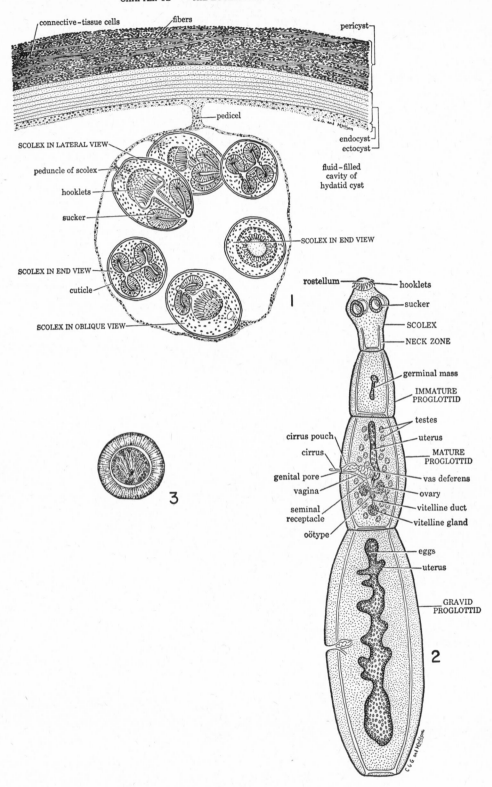

Plate 12-17   Stages in the life cycle of *Echinococcus granulosus*. 1. Section through a portion of hydatid cyst. **2.** Adult specimen of *E. granulosus*. **3.** Egg of *E. granulosus*, enclosing embryo. (All figures after Brown, F. A., Jr. 1950. *Selected Invertebrate Types,* John Wiley, New York.)

was later named *E. sibiricensis*. Because larvae of this species form multilocular cysts, it was believed to be conspecific with *E. multilocularis* in Europe and Eurasia. Since that time, Vogel (1955, 1957) has convincingly established that the Alaskan species is the same as *E. multilocularis* and is the cause of multilocular hydatid disease in man. The Alaskan form is now generally considered a subspecies of the European species.

Echinococcus multilocularis appears to be restricted in North America to the Alaskan tundra. In Eurasia, it is found on Bering and Rebun Islands. It is widely distributed in the Soviet Union, particularly in eastern, as well as western, Siberia. In Europe, human cases have been diagnosed in northern Switzerland, in the French Jura, and throughout southern Germany (see Rausch, 1958).

LIFE CYCLE OF *Echinococcus multilocularis*. The general life cycle pattern of *E. multilocularis* parallels that of *E. granulosus*. In nature, foxes, dogs, cats, and wolves serve as the definitive host, while microtine rodents, especially voles, serve as the intermediate host. Specifically, the arctic fox *Alopex lagopus* is a common definitive host in Alaska, Eurasia, and Siberia. In addition, the red fox *Vulpes vulpes*, the dog *Canis familiaris*, the wolf *Canis lupus*, and the gray fox *Urocyon cinereoargenteus* are naturally infected in Alaska. In Siberia, in addition to the arctic fox, the Azerbaidzhan fox also serves as a natural definitive host. In Germany, the red fox is the common definitive host.

The natural rodent intermediate hosts include the redback vole *Clethrionomys rutilus* and the tundra vole *Microtus oeconomus* in Alaska, Eurasia, and Siberia. In addition, the shrew *Sorex tundrensis* is a natural intermediate host in Alaska, and the muskrat *Ondatra zibethicus* is a natural intermediate host in Siberia. In Germany, the vole *Microtus arvalis* and other microtine rodents indigenous to central Europe serve as the intermediate host.

Eggs of *Echinococcus multilocularis*, passing out of the definitive host in feces, are ingested by the intermediate host. Ingestion need not occur immediately, for Schiller (1955) has shown that eggs of the Alaskan subspecies can withstand subfreezing temperatures. Some eggs are still infective after being maintained at $-26°$ C. for 54 days or at -51 °C. for 24 hours. Upon ingestion by the intermediate host, the onchospheres, escaping from the egg capsules in the small intestine, penetrate the intestinal wall and are carried by the portal circulation to the liver. Here the onchospheres penetrate the walls of the interlobular veins and enter the hepatic lobules, where growth commences. The hydatid larvae proliferate by exogenous budding. As in the case of *E. granulosus*, the definitive host becomes infected when it ingests an intermediate host or its viscera that harbor cysts with scoleces. The adult worms are found in the small intestine.

Human cases of multilocular hydatid disease may result when fruits and vegetables contaminated by the feces of infected canines are consumed (Rausch, 1958). Close association of man with dogs and cats, as is common in arctic regions, is very dangerous. In addition, water contaminated by egg-containing feces may be an important source of infection. The hydatid cysts of *E. multilocularis* most commonly develop in the liver of man; however, growth and proliferation are extremely slow. Yamashita et al. (1955) reported that the first human cases of multilocular hydatid disease on Rebun Island were diagnosed approximately 12 years after the introduction of the eggs. Furthermore, larval development in man is commonly abnormal, because as the larva increases in size, the central portion often dies and undergoes degeneration. Only the peripheral cysts survive and continue to proliferate, thus resulting in a large cavity containing purulent material. The cysts produce only few or no scoleces in human infections. This abnormal development suggests that humans are not very satisfactory intermediate hosts. If the development of the cysts reaches such a stage that they cannot be removed surgically, death commonly ensues.

Other Taeniid Genera

Also included in the Taeniidae are the genera *Fossor*, parasitic in the badger; *Taeniarhynchus*, which includes *T. saginatus*,* (Plate 12–18, Fig. 1) parasitic in humans and with cysticercus larvae in bovines; *Cladotaenia* (Plate 12–18, Fig. 2) in birds (except for *C. mirsoevi* in mammals); *Multiceps*, which includes *M. multiceps* (Plate 12–18, Fig. 4) the adults of which are common in dogs, foxes, and jackals, with coenuri being commonly found in rabbits, pigs, goats, and rarely in sheep, cattle, horses, and humans.

---

*Taeniarhynchus saginatus is often referred to as *Taenia saginata;* however, it properly belongs in the genus *Taeniarhynchus*.

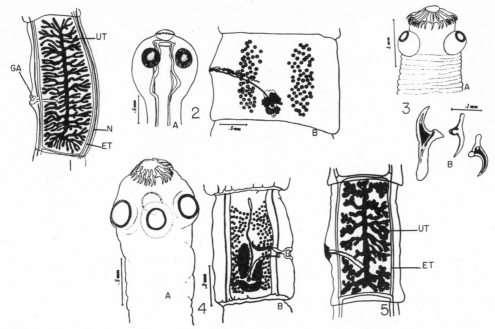

Plate 12-18   Some cyclophyllidean cestodes. 1. Gravid proglottid of *Taeniarhynchus saginatus*, showing characteristic branching uterus. (After Stiles, 1898.) 2. A. Scolex of *Cladotaenia foxi*, parasite of birds. B. Mature proglottid of *C. foxi*. (A and B after McIntosh, 1940.) 3. A. Scolex of *Taenia taeniaeformis*, parasite of the domestic cat. B. Large and small hooks of *T. taeniaeformis*. (A and B after Hall, 1919.) 4. A. Scolex of *Multiceps packi,* parasite of canines. B. Mature proglottid of *M. packi*. (A and B after Christenson, 1929.) 5. Gravid proglottid of *Taenia solium,* showing typical branching uterus. (After Blanchard, 1888.)

(ET, excretory tubule; GA, genital atrium; N, nerve cord; UT, uterus.)

Human Taeniasis

Probably the best known of the cyclophyllidean cestodes belong to the genus *Taenia,* which includes many interesting species such as *T. solium* (Plate 12–18, Fig. 5), with adults in man and cysticerci in hogs; *T. pisiformis* (Plate 12–19), with adults in dogs and cats and cysticerci in rabbits and hares; and *T. taeniaeformis* (Plate 12–18, Fig. 3), with adults commonly found in cats and strobilocercous cysticerci in rats. A strobilocercous cysticercus or strobilocercus is one in which the eversion of the scolex occurs and a short strobila is formed with the bladder attached to the posterior end while the larva is still within the intermediate host.

Taenia solium, commonly referred to as the "pork tapeworm," is a common parasite of man in areas where raw or poorly cooked pork is a part of the normal diet. The adult is usually 6 to 10 feet long, comprised of 800 to 900 proglottids (Plate 12–18, Fig. 5). The small scolex, measuring about 1 mm. in diameter, is armed with 22 to 32 rostellar hooks.

These hooks are of two sizes—the long hooks (180 μ) and short hooks (130 μ) are alternately arranged.

Segments of gravid proglottids are passed out of the host daily, each enclosing thousands of eggs. Each egg measures from 35 to 42 μ in diameter. When proglottids are eaten by pigs, dogs, monkeys, camels, and even man, the onchospheres are liberated, and these bore through the intestinal wall. They are carried in blood or lymph to muscles, where they develop into cysticerci.

The cysticerci of *T. solium,* often called *Cysticercus cellulosae,* are ovoid and have whitish bodies that measure from 6 to 18 mm. in length. The tiny, more dense white spot on one side represents the invaginated scolex. When infected pork is eaten, the scolex evaginates and becomes anchored to the wall of the host's small intestine, and the animal grows to maturity in about 2 to 3 months. Man is the only known definitive host, although some growth will occur in experimentally infected dogs.

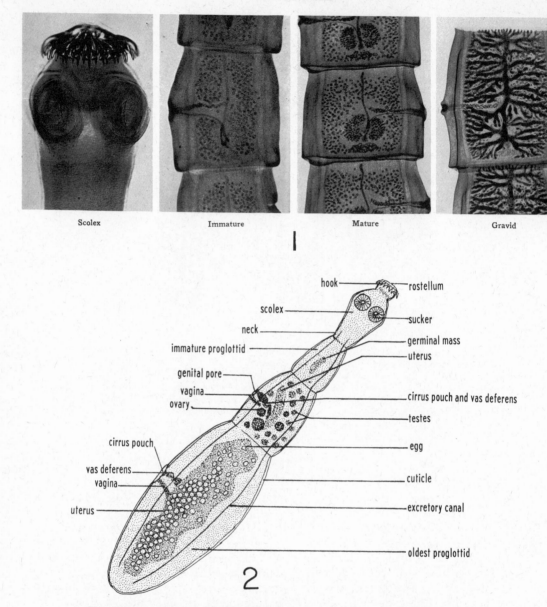

Scolex   Immature   Mature   Gravid

1

hook

rostellum

scolex

sucker

neck

germinal mass

immature proglottid

uterus

genital pore

vagina

cirrus pouch and vas deferens

ovary

testes

cirrus pouch

egg

vas deferens

vagina

cuticle

uterus

excretory canal

oldest proglottid

2

Plate 12-19   *Taenia pisiformis* and *Echinococcus granulosus.* **1.** Photomicrographs showing
regions along the body length of *Taenia pisiformis.* (Courtesy of General Biological Supply House,
Inc., Chicago.) **2.** Adult specimen of *Echinococcus granulosus.* (After D. E. Beck and L. F. Braithwaite.
1961. *Invertebrate Zoology Laboratory Workbook,* Burgess Publishing Co, Minneapolis.)

Not only do the adults of *T. solium* parasitize
the intestinal tract, but cysticerci can develop
in man, causing cysticercosis. Self-infection
with eggs can result either from contaminated
fingers or from eggs hatching in the intestine
and carried to the stomach by reverse peristalsis.
Cysticerci in man may form in the muscles or
subcutaneous tissues, where they do little
damage. However, if cysticerci are located in
the eye, heart, spinal cord, brain, or some

other important organ, the mechanical pressure
exerted by these larvae may cause secondary
complications. Violent headaches, convulsions,
local paralysis, vomiting, and optic disturbances
are common symptoms, depending on the site
of infection.

Taeniarhynchus saginatus.   This parasite is
the most common large tapeworm of man. It
is cosmopolitan in distribution. In parts of the
world where raw or rare beef forms a part of

the normal diet, as high as 75 per cent of the population may harbor this parasite. The adult is usually 15 to 20 feet long, although individuals as long as 35 to 50 feet are known. There are approximately 1000 or more proglottids comprising the strobila. Unlike *Taenia solium,* the scolex of *Taeniarhynchus saginatus* is unarmed. The life cycle of this species is similar to that of *T. solium* except that the intermediate host is the cow or some related animal. Antelopes, llamas, and giraffes are known to be naturally infected with cysticerci, while lambs and kids can be infected experimentally. Human infections are contracted through the ingestion of cysticerci in beef, particularly the head muscles and the heart. It should be mentioned that the eggs of both *T. solium* and *T. saginatus* can be carried by birds and spread in this fashion.

Saginatus taeniasis in humans may bring on such symptoms as abdominal pain, excessive appetite, weakness, and loss of weight. These symptoms generally are present in physically weak individuals.

FAMILY DAVAINEIDAE

Members of the family Davaineidae are parasites of birds and mammals. The species are relatively small, measuring between 20 and 80 mm. in length. All members possess a single set of reproductive organs per proglottid except *Cotugnia,* which is parasitic in tropical pigeons and parrots. Members of this genus possess two sets of reproductive organs per proglottid.

The more common genera of the Davaineidae are *Davainea,* with several common species in domestic fowls; *Idiogenes* in nondomesticated

birds; and *Raillietina* in birds and mammals (Plate 12–20, Figs. 1 to 3). *Raillietina* includes *R. madagascariensis, R. celebensis, R. demerarlensis, R. asiatica,* and *R. loechesalavezi,* all of which have been reported from humans.

FAMILY HYMENOLEPIDIDAE

Probably the best known family of the Cyclophyllidea from the standpoint of systematics and physiology is the Hymenolepididae. Members of this family are small to medium-sized tapeworms that characteristically possess a rostellum armed with a single row of 8 to 30 hooks. However, there are unarmed hymenolepid tapeworms, such as *H. diminuta,* an intestinal parasite of rodents and occasionally of man.

Common genera include *Hymenolepis; Diorchis* (Plate 12–23, Fig. 1) in birds; *Fimbriaria* (Plate 10–23, Fig. 2), which possesses a unique pseudoholdfast organ, in anseriform birds; and *Pseudohymenolepis* in mammals.

Life Cycle of *Hymenolepis nana*—A One-Host Cycle

The type genus of Hymenolepididae is *Hymenolepis,* which probably includes more known species than any other cestode genus. The life cycle of one of these, *H. nana,* a parasite of humans and rodents, is of special biological interest because it represents a modification of the typical cyclophyllidean life cycle pattern in that the parasite only requires one host in which to complete its development. Stages in the life history of *H. nana* are depicted in Plate 12–21.

The adult worm, which is the smallest of the

Plate 12-20 **1. A.** *Davainea proglottina* (entire worm), a parasite of fowls. (After Joyeaux and Baer, 1936.) **B.** Scolex of *D. proglottina.* (After Blanchard, 1891.) **2.** Proglottid of *Idiogenes.* (After Clausen, 1915.) **3.** Scolex of *Raillietina echinobothrida* with spiny suckers. (After Blanchard, 1891.)

(1, rostellum; 2, sucker; 3, cirrus protruded; 4, cirrus sac; 5, vas deferens; 6, vagina; 7, uterus; 8, vitelline gland; 9, testes; 10, uterine capsules; 11, seminal receptacle; 12, rostellar hook enlarged; 13, rostellar hooks; 14, paruterine organ; 15, ovary.)

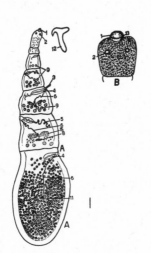
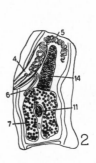

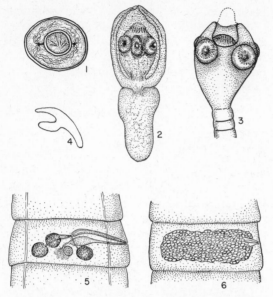

Plate 12-21   Stages in the life cycle of *Hymenol-*
epis nana. **1.** Egg enclosing hexacanth embryo. Note
typical polar filaments attached to each end of embryophore.
2. Cysticercoid larva with retracted scolex. **3.** Scolex of
adult specimen. **4.** Rostellar hook of adult. **5.** Mature
proglottid enclosing male and female reproductive organs.
6. Gravid proglottid, showing uterus distended with eggs.

several species of tapeworms that can infect
man, ranges from 7 to a little over 100 mm. in
length. The "crowding effect" is demonstrated
beautifully in cases of *H. nana* infections, for
the size of the worms is inversely proportional
to the number of worms present. Adult worms
release their onchosphere-containing eggs
through their ruptured posterior ends. These
eggs pass out, and when ingested by another
suitable rodent or human host, they hatch,
releasing the onchospheres. These larvae
burrow into the villi of the host's intestine,
where they develop into cysticercoid larvae,
completing metamorphosis usually by the
fourth day. Fully developed cysticercoids
escape into the lumen of the gut and while
attached to the gut lining, they develop into
adults.

This life cycle pattern exemplifies the elimination of an intermediate host by an advanced
parasite (p. 23), because experimentally *Hyme-*
nolepis nana can be induced to undergo cysticercoid formation of fleas and grain beetles,
thus suggesting that its immediate ancestor
utilized an invertebrate intermediate host.

Hymenolepis diminuta

Hymenolepis diminuta, the other rodent and

human-infecting species, has the typical two-
host cycle and utilizes several grain-ingesting
insects (*Tenebrio, Tribolium, Pyralis,* and *Aniso-*
lobis) and roaches as the intermediate host
The cysticercoid larvae are found in the invertebrate host. The stages in its developmental
cycle are depicted in Plate 12–22.

Human Hymenolepiasis

Three species of *Hymenolepis*—*H. nana, H*
diminuta, and *H. lanceolata*—are known to infect
man, although *H. lanceolata,* normally a parasite of ducks and geese, has been reported only
once in man. Adult *H. nana,* the smallest of the
three species, ranges from 7 to over 100 mm. in
length. Its rostellum is armed with 20 to 30
hooks and the proglottids are characteristically
broader than long. Its eggs are ovoid, measuring
about 40 by 50 μ; they include the larva, which
is enveloped within an embryophore. There is
a tiny knob at both ends of the embryophore
from which arise a number of long, wavy
filaments.

Hymenolepis diminuta, although very common
in rodents, is less frequently found in man. A
single worm may reach a length of 1 to 3 feet
with a maximum diameter of 3.4 to 4 mm.
The scolex in this species is unarmed and each
proglottid is broader than long. The eggs,
measuring 60 to 80 μ in diameter, are usually
yellowish brown and spherical. Unlike *H. nana,*
the embryophore in these eggs does not bear
conspicuous knobs and filaments at the poles.

Hymenolepis diminuta possesses a typical cyclophyllidean life cycle, including as intermediate
host one of many grain-infecting insects, both
adults and larvae. Most commonly, the adults
of the grain beetles *Tenebrio* and *Tribolium,* and
cockroaches serve as the intermediate host.
Humans become infected when cereals, dried
fruits, and other similar foods containing insects
that had become infected by ingesting rodent
feces including tapeworm eggs are eaten.

In cases of hymenolepiasis, severe symptoms
of toxicity may occur, especially in children,
including abdominal pain, diarrhea, convulsions, and insomnia.

It has been claimed that *H. nana* in humans
is physiologically different from *H. nana fraterna*
in rodents, since humans are to a certain degree
incompatible with the rodent variety. However, humans can be experimentally infected
with the rodent variety, and the relatively high
incidence of human infections with this tapeworm in communities where sanitary conditions

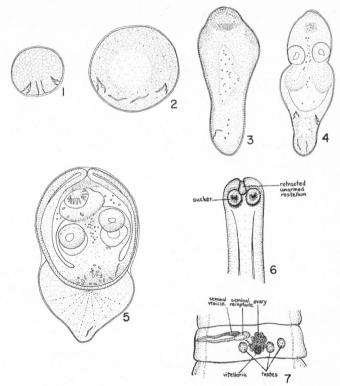

Plate 12-22   Stages in the life cycle of *Hymenolepis diminuta.* **1.** Developing embryo as solid sphere, showing paired hooks and external membrane. **2.** Appearance of cavity and dispersal of onchosphere hooks. **3.** Appearance of two body zones, elongation of the cavity, and beginning of rostellar and sucker differentiation. **4.** Process of withdrawal, showing separation of neck tissue, which will become the layer immediately enveloping scolex. **5.** Scolex withdrawn with large rostellum, partially developed hooks, and clearly defined suckers—the cysticercoid larva. **6.** Scolex of adult specimen with scolex withdrawn. **7.** Mature proglottid of adult showing male and female reproductive organs. (Figures 1 to 5 after Voge and Heyneman, 1957.)

make human contamination highly improbable strongly suggests that human infection does occur readily with the rodent variety.

Other *Hymenolepis* Species

Other species of *Hymenolepis* include parasites of ground squirrels (*H. citelli*), shrews (*H. anthocephalus* and others), muskrats (*H. evaginata* and *H. ondatrae*), various wild ducks (*H. megalops*), anseriform birds (*H. collaris* and *H. tritesticulata*), gulls (*H. ductilis* and others), poultry and game birds (*H. cantaniana, H. carioca,* and others), and passeriform birds (*H. corvi, H. microcirrosa* and *H. turdi*).

FAMILY DILEPIDIDAE

The family Dilepididae includes, among others, *Dipylidium* in mammals, *Paradilepis* (Plate 12–23, Fig. 3) in various birds, *Liga* (Plate 12–23, Fig. 4) in birds, and *Dilepis* (Plate 12–23, Fig. 5) in birds. Included also is *Ophiovalipora,* the only genus in this family found in an animal other than a bird or mammal; it is a snake parasite.

Life Cycle of *Dipylidium caninum*

The genus *Dipylidium* includes *D. caninum*

found in dogs, cats, and humans. Stages in the life cycle of this species are depicted in Plate 12–24. This species commonly attains a length of 1 foot and possesses a rostellum armed with one to eight (commonly four to six) rows of hooks. The uterus is unique in that initially it is in the form of a network, but as it becomes filled with eggs, it breaks up into individual uterine balls, each containing one to forty eggs.

Eggs are passed out of the vertebrate host in packets and are ingested by flea larvae of the genera *Pulex* and *Ctenocephalides,* or by the dog louse *Trichodectes canis.* The onchospheres hatch in the arthropod's gut and burrow through the gut wall. When the flea reaches maturity, the parasites develop into cysticercoids.

Infection of the vertebrate host is accomplished when the dog or cat ingests the flea. Infections are established in children when a dog that has just nipped a flea licks the child's mouth. Other *Dipylidium* species infect various members of the canine and feline families.

Dipylidium caninum **AND THE FLEA HOST.** Larvae of *Dipylidium caninum* are extremely destructive to the larval fleas that serve as intermediate hosts (Chen, 1934). Pathogenesis in the larval flea occurs in varying degrees. In some instances, mortality as high as 60 per cent has been observed within 24 hours after

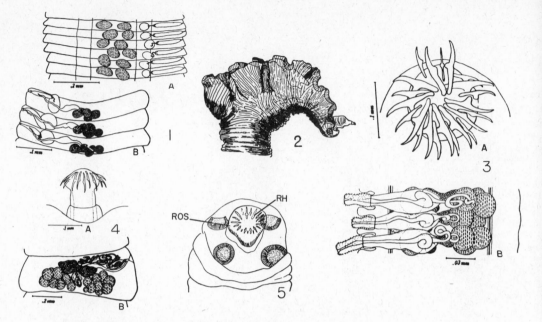

Plate 12-23   **Some cyclophyllidean cestodes. 1. A.** Successive proglottids of *Diorchis nyrocae,* showing male genitalia. **B.** Successive proglottids of *D. nyrocae,* showing female genitalia. (A and B after Long and Wiggins, 1939.) **2.** Scolex and pseudoholdfast of *Fimbriaria fasciolaris,* a parasite of domestic and wild anseriform birds. (After Wolffhügen, 1900.) **3. A.** Apex of scolex of *Paradilepis brevis* in birds. **B.** Mature proglottid. (A and B after Burt, 1940.) **4. A.** Scolex of *Liga brasiliensis,* found in birds, with rostellum extended. **B.** Mature proglottid. (A and B after Ransom, 1909.) **5.** Scolex of *Dilepis.* (RH, rostellar hooks; ROS, rostellum.) (After Burt, 1936.)

the cestode eggs are ingested. Deaths occurring during this period represent the initial mortality phase. Just prior to death, the flea larvae become lethargic and translucent white to reddish. The cause of death appears to be the mechanical damage inflicted on the larval flea's gut walls due to penetration by onchospheres migrating to the haemocoel.

A second series of developments, representing the second mortality phase, may cause the death of an additional 20 per cent of the larvae prior to pupation. Instead of spinning their cocoons at the appointed time, some mature larvae wander about or lie dormant for days and eventually die. Other larvae spin their cocoons but delay pupation. During the pupal period, a third series of reactions that represents the third mortality phase causes the death of an additional 10 per cent of the fleas.

Deaths occurring during the second and

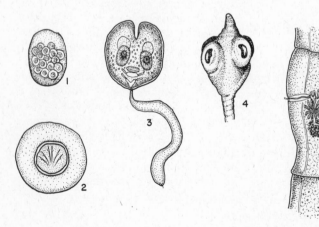

Plate 12-24   **Stages in the life cycle of *Dipylidium caninum.*** **1.** Cluster of eggs in membrane of uterine ball. **2.** Single egg, showing three pairs of hooks. **3.** Cysticercoid larva. **4.** Scolex with armed rostellum. **5.** Single mature proglottid enclosing two sets of reproductive organs. (Figs. 1 and 4 redrawn after Stiles; others, original.)

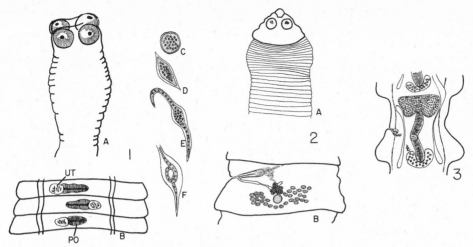

Plate 12-25   Some dilepidid cyclophyllidean cestodes of birds. 1. A. Scolex of
Anonchotaenia globata, in birds. **B.** Gravid proglottids. **C.** Young spherical embryo of *A. globata* from
uterus with investing nucleated membrane. **D.** Embryo beginning to elongate. **E.** Elongated
nematodiform embryo with middle region dilated. **F.** Coiled, fully grown, nematodiform embryo
in capsules formed by nucleated membranes; within paruterine organ. (A and B after Fuhrmann,
1908; C to F after Woodland, 1929.) **2. A.** Scolex of *Rhabdometra similis,* in galliform birds. **B.**
Mature proglottid. (A and B redrawn after Ransom, 1909.) **3.** Gravid proglottid of *Sphaeruterina
punctata* in birds. (PO, paruterine organ; UT, uterus.) (Redrawn after Fuhrmann, 1906.)

third mortality phases result from the depletion
of reserves in the flea's fat bodies, caused by
the rapidly developing cysticercoids and displacement and distortion of organs when large
numbers of cysticercoids are present.

Chen also reported that macrocytes, which
are normally found only in flea larvae, persist
through the pupal and adult stages of infected
fleas. These cells represent the defense mechanism of the host, for they form capsules about
the cysticercoids during larval life and may
kill the tapeworms. However, if the cysticercoids
survive and grow, the capsules of macrocytes
become thinner, as no new cells are added. By
the time the flea reaches maturity, the capsule
surrounding each cysticercoid is no more than
a thin web and does not appear to harm the
parasite.

Other Dilepidid Genera

Other better known genera of the Dilepididae include *Anonchotaenia, Rhabdometra,* and
Sphaeruterina, all found in birds (Plate 12–25).

Order Aporidea

The aporid cestodes are small, seldom measuring over 3.5 mm. in length. The scolex, when
compared to those of members of other orders,
is large and prominent (Plate 12–6, Fig. 5).
The strobila does not show any signs of external
segmentation. Only two genera, *Nematoparataenia*
and *Gastrotaenia,* are known (Plate 12–26, Figs.
1 and 2). Members of both genera are parasitic
in birds.

Wolffhügel (1938) suggested that the large
cushion-like rostellum is nutrition-acquiring in
function and that through pulsating movements
it attracts a stream of the host's blood and
mucus, which are absorbed by grandular cells
located within the rostellum.

Complete aporid life cycles are not known.
However, some consider *Fimbriaria fasciolaris,* a
cystocercus larva from the gizzard of a duck, to
be the larval form of an aporid tapeworm.

Order Nippotaeniidea

Yamaguti (1939) established Nippotaeniidea
to include the type genus *Nippotaenia,* which is
parasitic in fishes (Plate 12–26, Fig. 3). A
second genus, *Amurotaenia,* from the fish *Per-
cothes glehni* from Russia, has been added to the
order. These tapeworms are unique in the possession of only one true sucker or a poorly differentiated scolex (Plate 12–6, Fig. 6).

No life cycle information is yet available on
members of this order.

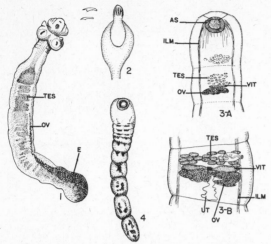

Plate 12-26   Some aporidean and nippotaeniidean cestodes. 1. Entire specimen of *Nematoparataenia southwelli* from swans. (Redrawn after Fuhrmann, 1933.) **2.** Scolex of *Gastrotaenia cygni* from birds. (Redrawn after Wolffhügel, 1938.) **3. A.** Anterior end of *Nippotaenia chaenogobii* from the fresh-water fish *Chaenogobius*. **B.** Mature proglottid. (A and B redrawn after Yamaguti, 1939.)

(AS, anterior sucker; E, eggs; ILM, internal longitudinal muscles; OV, ovary; TES, testes; UT, uterus; VIT, vitelline glands.)

ORDER CARYOPHYLLIDEA

The Caryophyllidea includes those tapeworms that are truly unsegmented (monozoic) and that possess only one set of reproductive organs. The few known species have all been found in the intestine of fishes and oligochaetes. Their unusual form strongly suggests that they possibly are neotenic procercoid larvae. Because it has been postulated that these monozoic tapeworms arose from polyzoic forms, the caryophyllideans have been considered in the past to be a specialized group of the Pseudophyllidea. However, Wardle and McLeod (1952) established the new order on the assumption that these monozoic forms are sufficiently different from the pseudophyllidean tapeworms to warrant their recognition as a separate order.

The Caryophyllidea includes such fairly well known genera as *Archigetes, Caryophyllaeides, Biacetabulum, Glaridacris,* and *Caryophyllaeus* (Plate 12–27).

The life cycle of *Archigetes cryptobothrius* was reported by Wisniewski (1928), who suggested

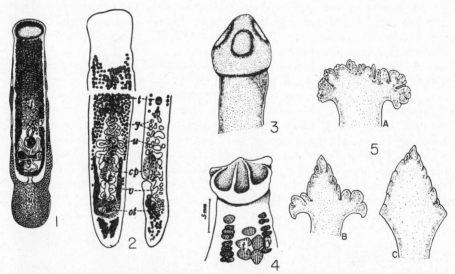

Plate 12-27   Some caryophyllidean cestodes. 1. Whole specimen of *Archigetes cryptobothrius,* parasitic in body cavity of turbificid annelids. (After Wisniewski, 1930, *In* R. A. Wardle and J. A. McLeod, 1952. *The Zoology of Tapeworms,* University Minnesota Press.) **2.** Whole specimen and sagittal section of *Caryophyllaeides fennica* in rutilid fishes. (After Nybelin, 1922, *In* R. A. Wardle and J. A. McLeod, 1952. *The Zoology of Tapeworms,* University of Minnesota Press.) **3.** Scolex of *Biacetabulum meridianum* from catostomid fishes. (After Hunter, 1927.) **4.** Scolex of *Glaridacris* sp. in catostomid fishes. (After Hunter, 1927, *In* R. A. Wardle and J. A. McLeod. 1952. *The Zoology of Tapeworms,* University of Minnesota Press.) **5. A** to **C.** Shapes of scolex of *Caryophyllaeus laticeps* in cyprinid and catostomid fishes. (After Benham, 1901.)

(cp, cirrus pouch; ot, ootype; t, testes; u, uterus; v, vagina; y, vitelline glands.)

that the worm is a neotenic procercoid, because its entire life cycle is limited to an oligochaete worm. The annelid ingests the tapeworm eggs, which then develop into procercoids, and these larvae gradually attain sexual maturity. The adults are like procercoid larvae but are filled with undeveloped operculated eggs. No free-swimming onchospheres are liberated.

ORDER SPATHEBOTHRIDEA

The spathebothrid tapeworms, like members of Aporidea, do not possess external demarcations of segmentation. However, there is a series of reproductive organs internally, hence incomplete proglottidization is present. Longitudinal parenchymal muscles are lacking. The adult worms have all been reported as parasites in the gut of various fishes.

The order includes the genera *Didymobothrium* in marine teleost fishes, *Bothrimonus* (Plate 12–11, Fig. 1) in sturgeons, and *Diplocotyle* (Plate 12–11, Fig. 2) in marine teleost fishes.

Life Cycle Pattern

In general, eggs passed out of the fish host are ingested by amphipod crustacea, in which the eggs develop into procercoids. When infected amphipods are ingested by a fish, the procercoids develop into sexually functional procercoids (progenetic larvae). When the infected fish host is eaten by the definitive fish host, these precocious procercoids develop into adults.

PHYSIOLOGY OF EUCESTODES

Oxygen Requirements

Although the natural habitats of adult tapeworms—the intestine of their hosts—contain a minimum of oxygen, many investigators have found that various tapeworms absorb oxygen in culture media provided that the in vitro environment is maintained below 38° C. Furthermore, there is an increased consumption of oxygen following anaerobiosis. This suggests that cestodes are capable of building up an oxygen debt, which in turn implies that some anaerobically formed substances are retained in the tissues and become available for oxidation during subsequent aerobic periods. This evidence has led others to investigate whether the metabolic processes within tapeworms are aerobic or anaerobic.

Investigations along these lines show that the metabolic by-products of certain species maintained in vitro are carbon dioxide, lactic acid, lighter fatty acids, and succinic acid. These metabolites are associated with glycolysis (glycogen degradation), an anaerobic process, as well as with the citric acid cycle, an aerobic process (Table 3–5). Glycolysis represents only one phase of the metabolic activity of organisms and takes place, even in definite aerobes.

Von Brand (1952) pointed out that one cannot generalize concerning the anaerobic or aerobic needs of tapeworms, and it appears pointless to categorize them one way or the other. Instead, each species must be considered separately concerning its oxygen requirements. Nevertheless, from the information available, cestodes appear to have a predominantly anaerobic metabolism, although aerobic metabolism does occur.

Aerobic metabolism in cestodes appears to be influenced by the amount of glucose in the medium. In media lacking glucose, the respiratory quotient (R.Q.) is between 0.5 and 0.9; if glucose is added, the R.Q. generally shows a marked increase. Furthermore, the metabolic rate appears to be influenced by oxygen tension. This is especially true when the tension is at a level of 2 to 5 vol. per cent.

Read (1956) has suggested that although the body surface of cestodes is exposed to oxygen from the host's mucosa, the oxygen tension in the medullary parenchyma of a large part of the strobila essentially must be zero. Thus, anaerobic fermentative metabolism most probably occurs here. The end products of such fermentative metabolism in the central regions of each proglottid would diffuse toward the body surface and become available for further oxidation in the peripheral tissues. Such a mechanism might be considered advantageous in terms of useful energy, because high energy-requiring systems, such as the muscular and nervous systems, are for the most part situated in the peripheral regions of the body.

This interpretation coincides with the earlier observations by Harnisch who in a series of papers published between 1932 and 1937 suggested that the apparent absorption of oxygen by tapeworms need not be associated with their respiratory activities per se, but is associated with the oxidation of certain oxidizable products that are produced during anaerobic metabolism and that are not removed from the body.

MAINTENANCE OF TAPEWORMS IN VITRO

For decades, helminthologists have attempted to maintain cestodes in vitro. The most outstanding studies have been those of Smyth (1955, 1956, 1958), who successfully cultured *Schistocephalus, Ligula,* and *Dibothriocephalus;* and Mueller (1958, 1959), who cultured *Spirometra mansonoides.* In these instances, not only were the plerocercoids of these pseudophyllidean tapeworms merely maintained in culture, but they actually developed to sexual maturity.

Schiller et al. (1959) reported a thirtyfold increase in *Hymenolepis diminuta* grown in vitro, and Berntzen (1961) reported success in getting cysticercoids of *H. diminuta* to develop into onchosphere-enclosing adults. The medium consisted of extracts, hormones, and various other organic materials, which were added to a base medium of whole human blood plasma and Tyrode's solution. The amount of growth observed in various cestodes maintained in vitro is shown in Table 12–5.

As in trematode cultures, the criteria for a successful artificial culture medium should include growth and development in addition to maintenance. The ideal medium obviously is one in which the egg to egg cycle can occur.

Growth Requirements

Carbohydrates, proteins, and perhaps fats are utilized by tapeworms as nutrients for the production of energy. The utilization of fats, however, is doubtful.

CARBOHYDRATE METABOLISM. Carbohydrates are by far the most commonly employed energy source. Of the carbohydrates, however, most species can utilize only certain monosaccharides (Read, 1959). In *Hymenolepis diminuta,* for example, only glucose and galactose are actively absorbed, while fructose, lactose, maltose, and trehalose are not absorbed. Upon absorption, those monosaccharides in excess of what is immediately required are converted to and stored as glycogen.

Although the lack of protein in the host's diet has little or no effect on cestodes, the lack of adequate carbohydrates results in stunting of growth, retardation of egg production, and the development of morphologically abnormal eggs. Interestingly enough, the growth of worms in hosts fed starch is better than that of worms in hosts fed disaccharides and monosaccharides. This is most probably because the simpler sugars are more readily absorbed by the host and hence less sugar is available to the parasites.

Most of the stored food in tapeworms is in the form of glycogen. Because the amount of stored glycogen along the length of the strobila of a worm differs, there is a difference in the metabolic rate along this length. For example, Daugherty and Taylor (1956) reported that in *Hymenolepis diminuta,* the glycogen content is highest in the region near the scolex, drops in the next 10 cm., rises in the succeeding 10 to 20 cm., and finally declines in the posteriormost gravid proglottids. If the rat hosts are fasted for 24 hours, there is a marked drop in stored glycogen in the first 20 to 30 cm. sections, but little effect is noticed in the more posterior segments.

If the strobila of *H. diminuta* is divided into four equal quarters, differences in the amount of stored glycogen between the portions are noticeable (Table 12–6).

The nature of the glycogen stored in cestodes has not been studied to any great extent. In vertebrate muscle, glycogen exists in two forms —that which is soluble in trichloroacetic acid and that which is insoluble in trichloroacetic acid. The soluble type is more readily available to meet the metabolic demands of the body and is the first to disappear during exercise. These two types of glycogen exist in *Hymenolepis diminuta* with the soluble type forming approximately 80 per cent of the total body glycogen. (Daugherty and Taylor, 1956).

As a rule, larval cestodes include a greater and relatively more consistent amount of glycogen than adults of the same species do. This reflects the more stable environment present in the intermediate host, usually the coelomic cavity or tissues.

PROTEIN METABOLISM. Very little information is available on the protein metabolism of cestodes. Nevertheless, it is known that unlike the protein composition of other animals, the amount of protein comprising the body of tapeworms is less than the sum of the stored glycogen and fats. Studies on the amino acid composition of cestodes have revealed nothing exceptional except that there is a close parallel between the types of amino acids and their concentrational distributions in the worms and in their host's intestinal tissue. Although this suggests that the parasite derives its required amino acids from the host tissues with which it is in close contact, recent studies by Chandler and associates (see review by Read and Simmons, 1963) indicate that at least in the case of *Hymenolepis diminuta* the parasite does not derive its nutrition from direct contact

Table 12-5. Some Recent Growth Data in Cestodes Cultured in Vitro

Cestode Species	Hosts Definitive	Hosts Intermediate	Culture Medium	Growth	Authority
Crepidobothrium lonnbergi	Snake	?	Veal broth medium	Growth of adults took place, but new proglottids were abnormal and sterile.	Stunkard, 1932
Hymenolepis nana	Mouse	-	Dilute Baker's medium	Adults maintained for 20 days, approximating their longevity in mice.	Green and Wardle, 1941
H. diminuta	Rat	Grain beetles	50% horse serum with glucose; 50% horse serum ultrafiltrate with glucose; Complex synthetic medium	Growth and strobilization of segments consisting of scolex and small portion of neck took place. Differentiation of reproductive organs was abnormal.	Schiller, Read, and Rothman, 1959
H. diminuta	Rat	Grain beetles	Complex undefined medium	Cysticercoid to adult	Berntzen, 1961
Schistocephalus solidus	Birds	Cyclops,* Gasterosteus,† Pygosteus †	Buffered horse serum-saline medium (semi-anaerobic)	Differentiation and maturation of reproductive organs in plerocercoids	Smyth, 1946, 1950, 1952, 1954
Ligula intestinalis	Birds	Cyclops,* fishes †	Buffered horse serum-saline medium (semi-anaerobic)	Differentiation and maturation of reproductive organs in plerocercoids	Smyth, 1947, 1949
Spirometra mansonoides	Cats, dogs	Cyclops,* snake,† mouse †	Calf serum-embryo extract medium containing mixture 199	Procercoids developed into plerocercoids.	Mueller, 1959

* First intermediate host.
† Second intermediate host.

Table 12-6. Glycogen Content in Linear Quarters of the Strobila of *Hymenolepis diminuta**

Worm Number	Anterior Quarter	Second Quarter	Third Quarter	Posterior Quarter
1	21.0	44.2	42.9	40.2
2	23.6	42.7	43.0	26.4
3	22.5	44.8	40.5	27.0

* Values are expressed as per cent of the dry weight (from Smyth, 1962, after data recalculated from Read, 1956).

with the host mucosa, but directly from materials passing into the host's intestine. Indeed, it has been shown that both *Hymenolepis diminuta* and *Raillietina cesticillus* actively absorb S^{35} labelled L-methionine and L-cystine. For those interested, the biophysics of amino acid absorption by *H. diminuta* has been reviewed by Read, Rothman, and Simmons (1963). Studies by these investigators indicate that competition exists between various amino acids relative to absorption by cestodes.

Not all cestodes absorb amino acids at the same rate. *R. cesticillus,* for example, absorbs amino acids four to six times as fast as *H. diminuta* does. Even within the individual worm, there exists a gradient of the absorption rate, with the anterior end absorbing at a greater rate than the posterior end. Cestodes also absorb amino acids more rapidly at their host's body temperature than at lower temperatures (Daugherty and Foster, 1958).

Proteolytic enzymes have been reported from various adult cestodes, including *Taeniarhynchus saginatus, Taenia solium, Dibothriocephalus latus, Dipylidium caninum,* and *Moniezia expansa.*

Amino acids taken into the bodies of tapeworms are not only utilized in protein synthesis but also for production of energy via protein metabolism. The end products of protein metabolism, although not extensively known, include ammonia, urea, uric acid, creatinine, and betaine. It is not surprising that ammonia is included among the end products because not only is it found in *Fasciola* and *Ascaris,* but it also occurs in many free-living invertebrates, such as polychaetes, sipunculoids, leeches, certain crustaceans, echinoderms, and cephalopod molluscs.

Kent has demonstrated that in several species of cestodes—*Taeniarhynchus saginatus, Moniezia expansa, Hymenolepis diminuta,* and *Raillietina*

cesticillus—less than 1 per cent of the proteins present are in the pure form. The remainder occur as conjugated proteins linked with glycogen, cerebrosides, and bile acids. These data suggest that the interrelationship between carbohydrate and protein metabolisms in cestodes is probably closer than the interrelationship normally found in other organisms.

Evidence indicates that protein metabolism in larval cestodes is in some way correlated with their infectivity. Hopkins and Hutchison (1958) demonstrated that the nitrogen composition in the *Taenia taeniaeformis* strobilocercus larvae, all of the same age, is of the same percentage except when heavy infections of over 100 worms exist. During the subsequent growth of these larvae, the nitrogen content drops to the constant level of 4.25 ± 0.25 per cent of the dry weight 67 days after the initial infection of the mouse host. This period corresponds almost exactly with the earliest time (63 days) at which the strobilocercus larvae become infective to the cat definitive host. The reason for the correlation between the drop in nitrogen content and infectivity has not been determined. After *T. taeniaeformis* becomes established in the cat, there is a sharp rise in the nitrogen level until it reaches 6.4 ± 0.7 per cent of the dry weight.

LIPID METABOLISM. The lipid content of cestodes varies greatly. In *Taenia hydatigena,* a parasite of carnivores, lipids form 4.9 per cent of the dry weight, while in *Moniezia expansa,* lipids form 30 per cent of the dry weight. (Results of fractionations of such lipids are discussed on page 191.) Histochemical examinations have revealed that most of the body lipids in tapeworms are stored in the parenchyma, although almost all organs include some lipids.

Practically nothing is known about lipid

metabolism in these animals, and there is no evidence at this time that suggests cestodes require fats. The fatty acids present, especially those found in the excretory system, undoubtedly represent by-products of carbohydrate metabolism. Lipases with low activity are present in *T. taeniaeformis* and *T. pisiformis*.

OTHER NUTRITIONAL REQUIREMENTS. As with practically all helminths, the nutritional requirements of cestodes vary with the life cycle stage. For example, the cysticercoid larva of *Hymenolepis diminuta*, found in the haemocoel of *Tenebrio molitor*, maintained at 25° C., would require considerably less in the way of nutrition than the egg-producing adult in the intestine of the rodent host at 38° C.

As in most metazoans, tapeworms require certain accessory growth factors. The chemical nature of most of these auxiliary factors is still unknown. For example, certain species, such as *H. diminuta*, is dependent on some factor or factors present in brewer's yeast for normal establishment and growth.

Certain vitamins are known to serve as accessory growth factors. *Hymenolepis diminuta* is not dependent on vitamin B_1 in the host's diet for normal establishment but this vitamin does influence growth (p. 348). This parasite is not dependent on vitamins A, D_1, and E for growth, but it is dependent on the fat soluble vitamins for normal establishment. Although similar information for other species is still scanty, it is strongly suspected that the vitamin requirements for various species differ in both quality and quantity.

HOST-PARASITE RELATIONSHIPS

The effect of cestodes on their hosts has been little studied aside from the clinical aspects of parasite-caused diseases. *Dibothriocephalus latus* infections in humans cause an anemia similar to pernicious anemia in a small percentage of individuals. Von Bonsdorff (1948) has written a recent review of *D. latus*-caused anemia. In Finland this anemia is present in 5 to 10 out of every 10,000 individuals infected with this tapeworm. This anemia develops because *D. latus*, unlike other tapeworms, demonstrates a special affinity for vitamin B_{12}, which plays an important role in blood formation in the host. This species absorbs 10 to 50 times more vitamin B_{12} than any other species. As the result of depriving the host of this vitamin, blood

formation is retarded and the anemia sets in.

In addition to causing this anemia, *D. latus* also disrupts the host's metabolism. For example, Becker (1926) and others reported that there may be an increase or decrease in the potassium and iron levels in infected humans.

It should be mentioned briefly that *Taenia taeniaeformis* in rats is known to cause sarcoma.

Enzymatic Activities

Relative to the enzymatic activity of tapeworms, there is a high degree of proteolytic enzyme activity in *D. latus* that is probably associated with the movement of the worm's own proteins rather than being secreted to prepare proteins for diffusion into the parasite's body. On the other hand, Erasmus (1957) demonstrated that both acid and alkaline phosphates are present in the cuticle and other regions of adult *Moniezia expansa*. When placed in a substrate and incubated, the external substrate was broken down through hydrolysis within a short period. This suggests that the cuticular enzymes might be capable of hydrolyzing some substrate or substrates present in the contents or secretions of the host's intestine. Similar phosphatase activity is most probably present in the cuticle of cysticercus larvae.

In *Echinococcus granulosus*, Lemaire and Ribère (1935) reported the presence of proteolytic enzymes in hydatid fluid. The function of these enzymes is not known. Apparently hydatid fluid does not contain toxic substances, and the known cases of deaths resulting from rupture of cysts are due to anaphylactic shock. Only when large quantities of extracted fluid are injected into an experimental animal does death occur; even then, the symptoms are those of shock and not toxicity.

In most cases, tapeworms appear to have little visible effect on their hosts; however, as mentioned earlier, heavy infections may bring about anemias, loss of weight, and various secondary conditions.

Effect of Host's Diet

The diet and starvation of hosts have considerable effect on their parasites. For example, Reid (1942) has shown that chickens starved for 24 hours expel proglottids of *Raillietina cesticillus*, and when the expelled strobilae are examined, they reveal a marked decrease in body glycogen. Since glycogen is primarily responsible for muscle energy within the worm, it is suggested that these tapeworms are expelled as the result of their loss of muscular ability to cope with the peristaltic contractions of the host's intestines.

Since tapeworms thrive primarily on carbohydrates in the form of certain simple sugars, hosts maintained on carbohydrate-rich diets consisting of starch enhance the growth of their intestinal helminths. Such is the case in rodents infected with *Hymenolepis diminuta* and in chickens infected with *Raillietina cesticillus.*

Some effects on hosts maintained on vitamin-deficient diets, have been recorded relative to the growth of their parasites. In instances where vitamins A, D, and E are withheld, there are no visible effects on the growth of *Hymenolepis diminuta,* but fewer worms become established from the initial infection (Addis and Chandler, 1944, 1946). However, if vitamin B₁ is withheld, the worms become stunted. Although thiamine is absorbed by *Hymenolepis* (Chandler et al., 1950), the withholding of this substance has no apparent effect on the tapeworm, for it apparently still can acquire the minute amount it needs from the traces present in the host. This and similar findings exemplify the principle that, just as in certain trematodes, some tapeworms are not directly dependent on the vitamins and perhaps other growth factors, for example, trace elements, found in their host's diets; rather, they can acquire what is necessary from host tissues.

Beck (1951), in experiments on rats infected with *Hymenolepis* and maintained on various deficient diets, found that effects on the parasites were particularly noticeable when immature, female, and castrated male rats were employed. The same effects were noticeable in normal adult males only if these were maintained on deficient diets over long periods.

Beck's results suggest the influence of male sex hormones. Further evidences of the influence of male hormones are available. For example, the number of *Hymenolepis diminuta* eggs eliminated from the host in 24 hours over a period of 3 months declines in castrated male rats maintained on "complete" diets. The number eliminated is comparable to that eliminated by normal males maintained on "deficient" diets. However, the number of eggs discharged by worms in castrated males maintained on "deficient" diets exhibits a more severe decline, the number being comparable to that eliminated from identically infected normal female rats maintained on "deficient" diets. Administration of testosterone and progesterone (1 mg. per day) restores to normal the level of egg output in worms in castrated males. Although pro-

gesterone has no effect on worm egg production in female hosts maintained on "deficient" diets, the administration of testosterone, on the other hand, increases the egg count. These results all suggest that the male hormone, testosterone, does influence the egg-producing ability of *Hymenolepis.*

Larsh (1947) demonstrated that if mice infected with *Hymenolepis nana* var. *fraterna* were fed alcohol, a considerably larger number of cysticercoids developed from a given number of ingested eggs. He concluded that the increased susceptibility resulted from reduced intake of food by mice that were fed alcohol, because controls maintained on scanty diets demonstrated a similar susceptibility. This and similar experiments have indicated that the success of the tapeworm depends to some degree not only on the quality but also on the quantity of the host's diet.

Effect of Host's Age

Generally, young mice are more susceptible to infections by *Hymenolepis nana.* However, Larsh (1950) showed that daily feedings of 3.3 mg. of thyroid extract to older mice eliminated their resistance to a great degree. In mice thus treated, a greater degree of susceptibility developed, even more than that found in normally raised young hosts.

Host Immunity

The immunology of tapeworm infections has interested parasitologists for some time. Through the work of H. M. Miller, Jr., it is known that rats can be immunized against new infections of *Taenia taeniaeformis* by the injection of material from adult tapeworms, and blood from infected rats. The introduced antigen (in the case of tapeworm extracts) and antibody (in the case of rat blood) brought about no effect on the growth of pre-existing worms in the rat's liver. If material from a closely related cestode, *Taenia pisiformis,* is introduced into the host, the host will also develop an immunity to new *T. taeniaeformis* infections, thus indicating that the antigen-antibody mechanism is probably a group reaction directed against all species of *Taenia.* Miller further demonstrated that this induced immunity, which usually lasts for 167 days, can be passed on to offspring, for the young of immunized mothers show some degree of resistance for a few weeks after birth.

In *Hymenolepis nana* infections, the formation of the host's antibody is usually caused by the antigenic substances elaborated by cysticercoids while within the host's villi. Heyneman (1953) found that immunity developed from an egg infection can affect other worms that are introduced later in the cysticercoid stage. In this instance, it is not the eggs that elicit antibody formation; rather, it is the parenteral cysticercoids that develop from the eggs that are antigenic. The literature pertaining to immunity to *Hymenolepis* has been reviewed by Heyneman (1963).

Essex et al. (1931) reported acquired immunity against tapeworms. These investigators found there is a marked decline in the blood pressure of uninfected dogs when dried and powdered *Taenia pisiformis* is injected intravenously, but if the same material is injected into dogs that have been previously infected, no such drop in blood pressure occurs. Finally, immune sera from hosts give the usual immune reactions (complement fixation and precipitation tests) when brought in contact with extracts of adults or larval cestodes.

It is now known that in all cases of invasion by intestinal parasites, immunity develops only if the mucosa of the host's intestinal tract is damaged or invaded and antigenic substances are introduced therein. Thus, tapeworms with a parenteral phase in their development can cause immunity. If cysticercoids of *Hymenolepis nana* raised in beetles are fed to rats, no parenteral phase follows, hence no specific immu-

Table 12-7. Mass Attained by *Hymenolepis diminuta* in Various Hosts*

Host	Host Weight (in grams)	Worm Volume (in milliliters)
Mouse	27.6	0.28
Hamster	123.0	0.57
Albino rat	377.0	1.11
Hooded rat	452.0	1.33

* Data from Read and Voge (1954).

Table 12-8. Development of *Dibothriocephalus dendriticum* in Various Hosts*

Experimental Host	Number of Feeding Experiments	Number of Successful Infections	Per cent Infections
Birds			
Anas boschas domestica	2	0	0
Ardea cinerea	3	0	0
Columba domestica	1	0	0
Larus argentatus	5	3	60
L. canus	13	10	77
L. ridibundus	59	24	40
Serinus canariensis	1	0	0
Sterna hirundo	2	1	50
Turdus merula	1	0	0
Mammals			
Canis familaris	2	1	50
Felis domestica	3	2	66
Cavia cobaya	1	0	0
Mus musculus	6	2	33
Rattus rattus	3	1	33
Homo sapiens	3	0	0

* Data after Kuhlow (1953).

nity is developed. It is not necessary that the parasite include a parenteral phase in its development, because adult trematodes and nematodes that injure their host's enteral mucosa while holding on or feeding, and in so doing inject antigens, can bring about antibody formation. On the other hand, cestodes and acanthocephalans, both of which lack an alimentary tract, do not cause antibody formation in the host if no parenteral phase exists, because no antigenic agents are inoculated into the host during their passive feeding process.

Antibodies react against parasites by interfering with their enzymatic activities in connection with nutrition acquisition and consequently with their growth and reproduction; destroy them by combining with their body chemicals; or protect the host by neutralizing toxic products.

Host Species Differences

Not all hosts are equally susceptible to certain cestode infections. Fortuyn and Feng (1940) reported that not all strains of mice are equally susceptible to *Taenia taeniaeformis*. This phenomenon—known as natural immunity—is apparently genetic in origin, because crossing a resistant male to a less resistant female produces hybrids with less resistance than the father. Natural immunity may be the reason why some hosts infected by *Dibothriocephalus latus* develop anemia and others do not.

The growth of cestodes is influenced by differences in various species of compatible hosts. Size differences among worms of *Hymenolepis diminuta* maintained in four species of hosts are given in Table 12–7.

The compatibility of certain species of cestodes for certain hosts—that is, host specificity—need not be restricted to closely related hosts. The work of Kuhlow (Table 12–8) on *Dibothriocephalus dendriticum*, normally a parasite of gulls (*Larus* spp.), indicates that this species apparently does not develop in certain other birds but does develop in certain mammals.

LITERATURE CITED

Addis, C. J., Jr., and A. C. Chandler. 1944. Studies on the vitamin requirement of tapeworms. J. Parasit., *30:* 229–236.

Addis, C. J., Jr., and A. C. Chandler. 1946. Further studies on the vitamin requirements of tapeworms. J. Parasit., *32:* 581–584.

Baylis, H. A. 1919. A collection of entozoa, chiefly from birds, from the Murman coast. Ann. Mag. Nat. Hist. (ser. 9), *3:* 501–513.

Beck, J. W. 1951. Effect of diet upon singly established *Hymenolepis diminuta*. Exptl. Parasit., *1:* 46–59.

Berntzen, A. K. 1961. The in vitro cultivation of tapeworms. I. Growth of *Hymenolepis diminuta* (Cestoda: Cyclophyllidea). J. Parasit., *47:* 351–355.

Chandler, A. C., C. P. Read, and H. O. Nicholas. 1950. Observations on certain phases of nutrition and host-parasite relations of *Hymenolepis diminuta* in white rats. J. Parasit., *36:* 523–535.

Chen, H. T. 1934. Reactions of *Ctenocephalides felis* to *Dipylidium caninum*. Zeit. Parasitenk., *6:* 603–637.

Daugherty, J. W., and D. Taylor. 1956. Regional distribution of glycogen in the rat cestode, *Hymenolepis diminuta*. Exptl. Parasit., *5:* 376–390.

Erasmus, D. A. 1957. Studies on phosphatase systems of cestodes. II. Studies on *Cysticercus tenuicollis* and *Moniezia expansa* (adult). Parasitology, *47:* 81–91.

Essex, H. E., J. Markowitz, and F. C. Mann. 1931. Physiological response and immune reactions to extracts of certain intestinal parasites. Am. J. Physiol., *98:* 18–24.

Fortuyn, A. B. D., and L. C. Feng. 1940. Inheritance in mice of resistance against infection with the eggs of *Taenia taeniaeformis*. Peking Nat. Hist. Bull., *15:* 139–145.

Heyneman, D. 1953. Auto-reinfection in white mice resulting from infection by *Hymenolepis nana*. J. Parasit. (suppl.), *39:* 28.

Heyneman, D. 1963. Host-parasite resistance patterns—some implications from experimental studies with helminths. Ann. N. Y. Acad. Sci., *113:* 114–129.

Hilliard, D. K. 1960. Studies on the helminth fauna of Alaska. XXXVIII. The taxonomic significance of eggs and coracidia of some diphyllobothriid cestodes. J. Parasit., *46:* 703–716.

Hopkins, C. A., and W. M. Hutchison. 1958. Studies on cestode metabolism. IV. The nitrogen fraction in the large cat tapeworm *Hydatigera* (*Taenia*) *taeniaeformis*. Exptl. Parasit., *7:* 349–365.

Jameson, H. L. 1912. Studies on pearl oysters and pearls. (1) The structure of the shell and pearls of the Ceylon pearl oyster (*Margaritifera vulgaris* Schumacher) with an examination of the cestode theory of pearl formation. Proc. Zool. Soc. London, pp. 260–358.

Janicki, C. von. 1907. Ueber die Embryonalentwicklung von *Taenia serrata* Goeze. Z. Wiss. Zool., *87:* 685–724.

Larsh, J. E., Jr. 1947. The role of reduced food intake in alcoholic debilitation of mice infected with *Hymenolepis*. J. Parasit., *33:* 339–344.

Larsh, J. E., Jr. 1950. The effect of thiouracil and thyroid extract on the natural resistance of mice to *Hymenolepis* infection. J. Parasit., *36:* 473–478.

LeMaire, G., and R. Ribère. 1935. Sur la composition chimique du liquide hydatique. Compt. Rend. Soc. Biol., *118:* 1578–1579.

Linton, E. 1922. A contribution to the anatomy of *Dinobothrium,* a genus of selachian tapeworms. Proc. U. S. Nat. Mus., *60:* 1–16.

Mueller, J. F. 1958. In vitro cultivation of the sparganum of *Spirometra mansonoides* to the infective stage. J. Parasit. (suppl.), *44:* 14–15.

Mueller, J. F. 1959. The laboratory propagation of *Spirometra mansonoides* (Mueller, 1935) as an experimental tool. III. In vitro cultivation of the plerocercoid larva in a cell-free medium. J. Parasit., *45:* 561–569.

Mueller, J. F. 1963. Parasite-induced weight gain in mice. Ann. N. Y. Acad. Sci., *113:* 217–233.

Rausch, R. 1952. Hydatid disease in boreal regions. Arctic, *5:* 157–174.

Rausch, R. 1953. The taxonomic value and variability of certain structures in the cestode genus *Echinococcus* (Rud., 1801) and a review of recognized species. Thapar Commemoration Vol., University of Lucknow, India.

Rausch, R. 1958. *Echinococcus multilocularis* infection. Proc. 6th Internat. Cong. Trop. Med. Malaria, *2:* 597–610.

Read, C .P. 1956. Carbohydrate metabolism in *Hymenolepis diminuta*. Exptl. Parasit., *5:* 325–344.

Read, C. P. 1959. The role of carbohydrates in the biology of cestodes. VIII. Some conclusions and hypotheses. Exptl. Parasit., *8:* 365–382.

Read, C. P., and J. E. Simmons, Jr. 1963. Biochemistry and physiology of tapeworms. Physiol. Rev., *43:* 263–305.

Read, C. P., A. H. Rothman, and J. E. Simmons, Jr. 1963. Studies on membrane transport, with special reference to parasite-host integration. Ann. N. Y. Acad. Sci., *113:* 154–205.

Reid, W. M. 1942. The removal of the fowl tapeworm, *Raillietina cesticillus,* by short periods of starvation. Poultry Sci., *21:* 220–229.

Reid, W. M. 1946. Penetration glands in tapeworm onchospheres. Biol. Bull., *91:* 232.

Reid, W. M. 1948. Penetration glands in cyclophyllidean onchospheres. Trans. Amer. Micro. Soc., *67:* 177–182.

Reid, W. M., and J. E. Ackert. 1941. Removal of chicken tapeworms by host starvation and some effects of such treatment on tapeworm metabolism. J. Parasit. (suppl.), *27:* 35.

Rogers, W. A., and M. J. Ulmer. 1962. Effects of continued selfing on *Hymenolepis nana* (Cestoda). Iowa Acad. Sci., *69:* 557–571.

Rothman, A. H. 1959. Studies on the excystment of tapeworms. Exptl. Parasit., *8:* 336–362.

Rothman, A. H. 1963. Electron microscopic studies of tapeworms: the surface structures of *Hymenolepis diminuta* (Rudolphi, 1819) Blanchard, 1891. Trans. Amer. Micro. Soc., *82:* 22–30.

Schauinsland, H. 1886. Ueber die Körperschichten und deren Entwicklung bei den Plattwürmern. Sitzb. Ges. Morph. Physiol. München, *2:* 7–10.

Schiller, E. L. 1955. Studies on the helminth fauna of Alaska. XXVI. Some observations on the cold-resistance of eggs of *Echinococcus sibiricensis*. Rausch & Schiller, 1954. J. Parasit., *41:* 578–582.

Schiller, E. L., C. P. Read, and A. H. Rothman. 1959. Preliminary experiments on the growth of a cyclophyllidean cestode in vitro. J. Parasit. (suppl.), *45:* 29.

Skrjabin, K. I. (ed.). 1951. Essentials of Cestodology. Vols. I and II. Academy of Sciences of the USSR, Moscow (English translation available from U. S. Dept. of Commerce, Washington 25, D. C.).

Smyth, J. D. 1955. Problems relating to the in vitro cultivation of pseudophyllidean cestodes from egg to adult. Iber. Parasit. Tomo Extraordinario por Prof. Lopez-Neyra, pp. 65–86.

Smyth J. D. 1956. Studies on tapeworm physiology. VIII. Occurrence of somatic mitosis in *Diphyllobothrium* spp. and its use as a criterion for assessing growth in vitro. Exptl. Parasitol., *5:* 260–270.

Smyth, J. D. 1958. Cultivation and development of larval cestode fragments in vitro. Nature, *181:* 1119–1122.

Smyth, J. D. 1963. Secretory activity by the scolex of *Echinococcus granulosus* in vitro. Nature, *199:* 402.

Spätlich, W. 1925. Die Furchung und Embryonalhüllenbildung des Eies von *Diorchis inflata* Rud. Zool. Jahrb., Abt. Anat., *47:* 101–112.

Stunkard, H. W. 1937. The life cycle of anoplocephaline cestodes. J. Parasit., *23:* 569.

Stunkard, H. W. 1939a. The role of oribatid mites as transmitting agents and intermediate hosts of ovine cestodes. Verhandl. VII. Intern. Kongr. Entomol. Berlin, 1938, *3:* 1617–1674.

Stunkard, H. W. 1939b. Observations on the development of the cestode, *Bertiella studeri.* Abstr. 3 Intern. Congr. Microbiol., New York, p. 179.

Stunkard, H. W. 1939c. The life cycle of the rabbit cestode, *Cittotaenia ctenoides.* Ztschr. Parasitenk., *10:* 753–754.

Stunkard, H. W. 1940. Observations on the development of the cestode, *Bertiella studeri.* Proc. 3 Intern. Congr. Microbiol., New York, pp. 461–462.

Stunkard, H. W. 1941. Studies on the life history of the anoplocephaline cestodes of hares and rabbits. J. Parasit., *27:* 299–325.

Voge, M. 1955. North American cestodes of the genus *Mesocestoides.* Univ. Cal. Publ. Zool., *59:* 125–156.

Vogel, H. 1955. Über die Entwicklungszyklus und die Artzugehörigkeit des europäischen Alveolarechinococcus. Dtsch. Med. Wschr., *80:* 931–932.

Vogel, H. 1957. Über den *Echinococcus multilocularis* Süddeutschlands. I. Das Bandwurmstadium von Stämmen menschlicher und tierischer Herkunft. Ztschr. Tropenmed. Parasit., *8:* 404–456.

Von Bonsdorff, B. 1956. *Diphyllobothrium latum* as a cause of pernicious anemia. Exptl. Parasit., *5:* 207–230.

Wardle, R. A., and J. A. McLeod. 1952. The Zoology of Tapeworms. University of Minnesota Press, Minneapolis.

Wisniewski, L. W. 1928. *Archigetes cryptobothrius* n. sp. nebst Angaben über die Entwicklung im Genus *Archigetes* R. Leuck. Zool. Anz., *77:* 113–124.

Yamaguti, S. 1939. Studies on the helminth fauna of Japan. Part 28. *Nippotaenia chaenogobii,* a new cestode representing a new order from freshwater fishes. Japan. J. Zool., *8:* 278–289.

Yamaguti, S. 1959. Systema Helminthum. Vol. II. The Cestodes of Vertebrates. Interscience, New York.

Yamashita, J., Z. Ono, H. Takahashi, and K. Hattori. 1955. On the occurrence of *Echinococcus granulosus* (Batsch, 1786) Rudolphi, 1805, in the dog in Rebum Island, and the discussion about the course of infection of the echinococcosis (In Japanese, with English summary). Mem. Fac. Agric. Hokkaido Univ., *2:* 147–150.

SUGGESTED READING

Hyman, L. H. 1951. The Invertebrates: Platyhelminthes and Rhyncocoela. The Acoelomate Bilateria. Vol. II. pp. 311–422. McGraw-Hill, New York. (This section in Hyman's treatise discusses the tapeworms. The parts on morphology are exceptionally informative and the references are extremely useful.)

Read, C. P. 1959. The role of carbohydrates in the biology of cestodes. VIII. Some conclusions and hypotheses. Exptl. Parasit., *8:* 365–382. (This last of a series of research papers by Read and his co-workers on the carbohydrate metabolism of cestodes summarizes and gives the author's conclusions on this phase of cestode physiology.)

Read, C. P., and J. E. Simmons, Jr. 1963. Biochemistry and physiology of tapeworms. Physiol. Rev., *43:* 263–305. (This is a general review of the current status of our knowledge of cestode physiology. Carbohydrate, lipid, and nitrogen metabolism; oxygen consumption; nutrition; growth; and osmotic relationships are discussed along with certain aspects of organismal physiology pertaining to eggshell formation, in vitro culture, and adaptations of larval cestodes.)

Smyth, J. D. 1947. The physiology of tapeworms. Biological Reviews. *22:* 214–238. (This is a comprehensive review of the physiology of cestodes by a recognized authority. Although it is somewhat outdated, the reasoning and lines of thinking in the book will benefit the student.)

Smyth, J. D. 1963. The biology of cestode life-cycles. Commonwealth Bureau of Helminthology, St. Albans, Herts, England. Publ. No. 34. (In this short review of the functional morphology and physiology of cestodes, the author emphasizes the importance of the adaptive features of the pre-adult stages. Although much of the material pertains to *Hymenolepis diminuta* and *Echinococcus granulosus,* two popular experimental animals, the presentation is concise, stimulating, and clear, and the student will undoubtedly derive ideas to stimulate his own investigation.)

Von Bonsdorff, B. 1956. *Diphyllobothrium latum* as a cause of pernicious anemia. Exptl. Parasit., *5:* 207–230. (This review article expounds an interesting and important aspect of cestodology. This article can impart to the reader the importance of biochemical physiology in understanding parasitism and its consequences.)

Wardle, R. A., and J. A. McLeod. 1952. The Zoology of Tapeworms. The University of Minnesota Press, Minneapolis, pp. 3–169. (This section in Wardle and McLeod's monograph on cestodes deals with the evolution, development, morphology, and basic biology of this group of parasites. It is by far the most comprehensive treatise available.)

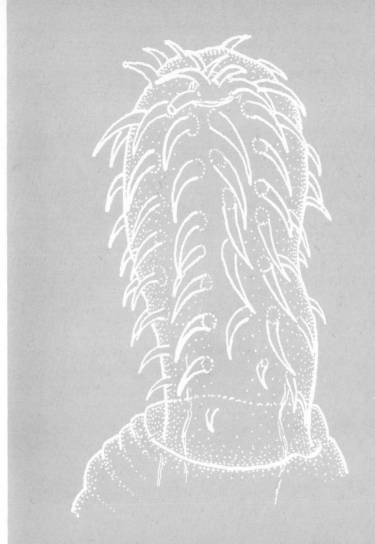

ACANTHOCEPHALA

13

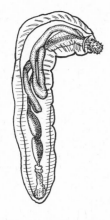

THE ACANTHOCEPHALA—
The Spiny-headed Worms

The Acanthocephala, or spiny-headed worms, represents a small but interesting and important group of helminth parasites. These worms generally measure under 35 mm. in length, although the common intestinal parasite of pigs, *Macracanthorhynchus hirudinaceus*, can measure up to 70 cm. in length. All species are endoparasitic, living as adults in the alimentary tract of various vertebrates. The number of parasites per host varies from 1 or 2 to as many as 1500.

All the acanthocephalans are elongate, most species being cylindrical and tapering at both ends. Laterally flattened forms also exist. The body resembles a tube, the body wall enclosing the pseudocoel (body cavity), in which are suspended the reproductive organs and the proboscis sheath. The main characteristic of the Acanthocephala is the protrusible, armed proboscis at the anterior terminal.

The sexes are separate (dioecious) among these worms, and there is some degree of sexual dimorphism. The female worms, as a rule, are larger than the males, and in species that possess spines on the body proper, these armatures are better developed in males. Furthermore, the copulatory apparatus of males easily distinguishes them from females.

Dorsal and ventral differentiation exists; however, in many species recognition is difficult externally. In the naturally curved forms, the convex surface is the dorsal side. In certain genera, such as *Rhadinorhynchus* and *Aspersentis*, the spines on the proboscis are larger ventrally than dorsally (Plate 13–1, Fig. 1).

A digestive tract is completely lacking in members of the Acanthocephala. Like the tapeworms, acanthocephalans, through adaptation to their parasitic way of life, take nutrients into the body by absorption through the body surface. It has been suggested that the cuticular spines may play a role in absorption.

The biotic potential is great in certain acanthocephalan species. Kates (1944) reported that gravid females of *Macracanthorhynchus hirudinaceus* may contain up to 10 million embryonated eggs at one time.

MORPHOLOGY

The body of acanthocephalans is divided into two major regions (Plate 13–1, Fig. 2). (1) The presoma, which includes the proboscis and neck, is the anterior region. The proboscis,

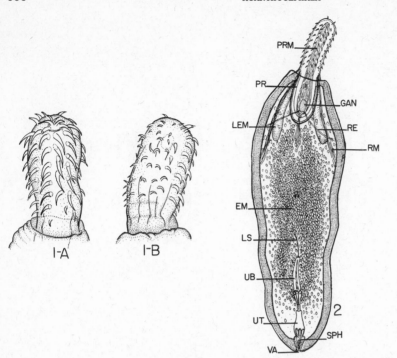

Plate 13-1   Morphology of Acanthocephala. 1. A. Ventral surface of proboscis of *Aspersentis*, showing large hooks. B. Dorsal surface of proboscis of *Aspersentis*, showing smaller hooks. (A and B redrawn after Van Cleave, 1941.) 2. Gravid female *Acanthocephalus* (Palaeacanthocephala), showing internal organs. (EM, embryos; GAN, ganglion; LEM, lemniscus; LS, ligament sac; PR, proboscis receptacle; PRM, proboscis retractor muscle; RE, retinacula; RM, retractor muscles; SPH, sphincter; UB, uterine bell; UT, uterus; VA, vagina.) (Redrawn after Yamaguti, 1935.)

which is the anteriorly situated retractile organ, is armed with rows of hooks and spines. The neck is the unarmed region situated immediately posterior to the proboscis. The neck usually equals the proboscis in diameter but various modifications exist among the species. (2) The body proper, or trunk, forms the major bulk of the animal. It is separated from the presoma by a crease in the cuticle.

Acanthocephalan proboscal hooks are defined as the larger recurved projections that are embedded by roots in the hypodermis. Spines are defined as the smaller armatures that are not rooted in the proboscis. The larger armatures may be located anteriorly, followed posteriorly by a decreasing gradation of spines, or the larger armatures may be medially situated on the proboscis, with the other spines decreasing in size anteriorly and posteriorly. These hooks and spines are generally arranged in rows. Their exact sizes and arrangements are quite consistent and are extremely useful in the identification of species.

The smaller anterior portion of the body proper, or trunk, is called the foretrunk; the posterior portion is the hindtrunk. The trunk is generally broader than the presoma, although exceptions exist.

Immediately posterior and lateral to the neck, the inner layers of the body wall invaginate to form two diverticula that protrude into the pseudocoel. These diverticula are known as lemnisci. The sac into which the retracted proboscis fits is known as the proboscis sheath, or receptacle. This structure is muscular, one cell thick in some species, two in others, and very thick in still others. In one family, the Oligacanthorhynchidae, the wall is very thick dorsally but nonmuscular and thin ventrally.

Body Tissues

The body wall is made up of several recognizable layers (Plate 13-2, Fig. 1). Covering the entire body is an extremely thin layer of noncellular cuticle. Immediately underneath the cuticle is the syncytially arranged hypodermis, which consists of three strata. (1) The outermost stratum is made up of radially arranged fibers, the entire thickness of which approximates that of the cuticle. (2) The medial layer is composed of randomly arranged fibers and is slightly thicker than the outer layer. (3) The innermost layer, like the outermost layer, consists of radially arranged fibers. The innermost layer is the thickest of the three layers and includes a series of channels known as lacunae. The lacunae are filled with a fluid that reportedly represents nutrients the animal has absorbed from the environment. Arrangement of the lacunae is of sufficient consistency to be of taxonomic importance. Although the

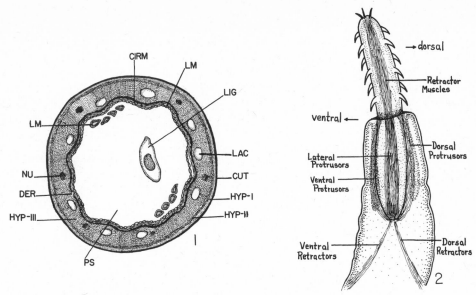

Plate 13-2   Morphology of Acanthocephala. 1. Cross section through trunk of an acantho-cephalan. (CIRM, circular muscles; CUT, cuticle; DER, dermis; HYP-I, outermost stratum of hypodermis; HYP-II, medial stratum of hypodermis; HYP-III, inner stratum of hypodermis; LAC, lacuna; LIG, ligament sac; LM, longitudinal muscles; NU, giant nucleus; PS, pseudocoel.) (Original.) **2.** Anterior end of an acanthocephalan, showing major muscles. (Original.)

channels do not penetrate either the outer layers of the hypodermis or the underlying layers, the nutrient fluid can diffuse throughout the tissues of the body. Thus, the lacunar system might be thought of as a nutrient-circulating system. The lacunae do connect with the lemnisci, which are considered storage spaces.

Giant nuclei are found embedded in the inner radial layer of the hypodermis. These nuclei are so consistent in size, number, and location in certain species that they are commonly relied on as taxonomic tools. For example, in the family Neoechinorhynchidae, six nuclei are always present; five are located dorsally along the main dorsal lacuna, and one ventrally, near the anterior end of the ventral lacuna. In other taxa, the larval stages possess consistent numbers of nuclei, but during the maturation process, these divide (fragment) and give rise to a greater number of smaller nuclei. These unique nuclei of the Acanthocephala may be round, oval, rosette, or even amoeboid in shape.

Beneath the hypodermis is a thin layer—the basement layer (dermis)—which invades the underlying muscles.

The muscles in the body wall are arranged in two layers. The outer one is circularly arranged while the inner one is longitudinally oriented. These myofibers are also syncytially arranged with scattered nuclei. Since the Acanthocephala are pseudocoelomates, no epithelial layer lines the body cavity.

In some species, the body cuticle possesses superficial circular creases suggesting segmentation. However, even in the most severe cases of cuticular folding, there are no indications of internal segmentation except perhaps for the longitudinally arranged muscles that may be attached to the areas where the body wall invaginates. Again, varying degrees of spination of the cuticula exist among the various taxa, ranging from large spines covering the entire trunk to aspinous forms.

Very often freshly obtained specimens show pronounced coloration. Meyer (1933) assumed that this is not due to native pigmentation but to the inclusion of colored nutrients. Nevertheless, in certain forms, pigmentation is suspected (von Brand, 1952).

Proboscis Musculature

The armed proboscis serves as an attachment organ. Within the host's intestine, the proboscis is embedded in the lining of the gut and the hooks anchor the parasite in place so that it is not passed posteriorly with the chyme. The mechanism behind the extension and retraction of the proboscis is extremely complex in certain species (Plate 13–2, Fig. 2). Generally, there originate a group of muscle fibers, known as retractor muscles, on the inner surface of the anterior tip of the proboscis. These muscles run posteriorly and are attached at the base of the proboscis sheath. Some, however, continue through the sheath and split; one group is directed dorsally as the dorsal retractor, attaching on that side of the trunk, and the other group is directed ventrally as the ventral retractor, attaching on the ventral surface of the trunk. The function of the retractors is to withdraw the proboscis into the receptacle. Another group of muscles, known as the protrusors, originate in a circle at the base of the neck and are situated outside the proboscis sheath, attaching along the posterior end of the sheath. These muscles are known as the dorsal, ventral, and lateral protrusors, depending on their location. The function of the protrusors is to extend the proboscis out of the receptacle.

Excretory System

The excretory system in the Acanthocephala is interesting for such a system exists only among members of the order Archiacanthocephala. In the other orders, no excretory system is present; waste materials diffuse from the body through the body surface.

In the Archiacanthocephala, the excretory system is of the protonephritic type, consisting of a pair of minute bodies lying on each side of and closely associated with the reproductive organs. Each body is made up of a group of flame bulbs that bear cilia. These are not individual cells like those found in the trematodes and cestodes for they do not possess nuclei. Waste materials in the pseudocoel are brought into the flame bulbs by the ciliary beats. From the bulbs the waste is either emptied into a common sac, as in *Nephridiorhynchus,* or is carried away in a common collecting tubule. In the first system, a common collecting tubule leads from the sac. The tubules, one from each side, join medially, and in male worms the common duct empties into the sperm duct. In females, the common duct empties into the terminal portion of the uterus and hence forms part of a urogenital system.

Nervous System

The acanthocephalan nervous system is basically uniform. However, in certain genera, secondary specialized tactile sense organs occur.

The "brain" appears as a cephalic ganglionic mass located along the ventral border within the proboscis sheath. This structure consists of a mass of nerve fibers enveloped by ganglionic cells. In *Macracanthorhynchus,* there are 86 ganglia; in *Bolbosoma,* there are 73; and in *Hamanniella,* there are 80.

Leading from the cephalic nerve center, certain fibers extend anteriorly, innervating the sensory organs at the tip of the proboscis and on each side of the neck region. Other fascicles of fibers—generally two lateral bundles —lead posteriorly, giving off branches along their length. In males, an auxiliary pair of ganglia—the genital ganglia—are located posteriorly at the base of the cirrus and are joined with each other by a ring commissure. Certain branches of the lateral nerve fibers lead into these auxiliary ganglia, and other branches lead from them to innervate the sensory organs of the copula and bursa. The two main lateral nerve bundles are wrapped within a muscular sheath known as the retinaculum (Plate 13–3).

Reproductive System

The reproductive system in the Acanthocephala is unique because the organs are suspended within a ligament sac (Plate 13–4). This hollow sac of semitransparent connective tissue is attached anteriorly to the posterior extremity of the proboscis sheath or to the body wall in the immediate area. Posteriorly,

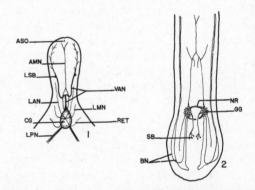

Plate 13-3   **Nervous system of Acanthocephala.**
1. Nervous system of anterior end of *Macracanthorhynchus hirudinaceus.* **2.** Posterior terminal of male of same species. (Figs. 1 and 2 redrawn after Brandes, 1899.)

(AMN, anterior median nerve; ASO, apical sensory organ; BN, bursal nerves; CG, cerebral ganglion; GG, genital ganglia; LAN, lateral anterior nerve; LMN, lateral medial nerve; LPN, lateral posterior nerve; LSB, lateral sensory bulb; NR, nerve ring in genital sheath; RET, retinacula; SB, sensory bulb of penis; VAN, ventral anterior nerve.)

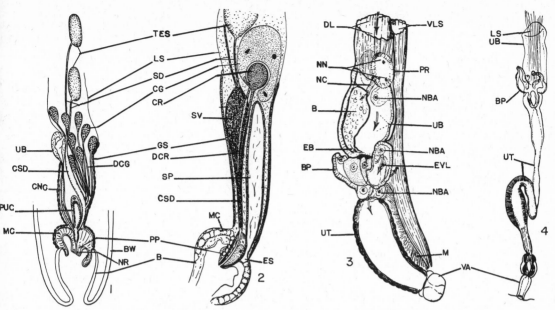

Plate 13-4   **Male and female reproductive systems in acanthocephala.** **1.** Male reproductive system of *Hamanniella* (Archiacanthocephala), lateral view. (After Hyman, L. H. 1951. *The Invertebrates,* McGraw-Hill. New York.) **2.** Male reproductive system of *Neoechinorhynchus* (Eoacanthocephala), lateral view. (After Hyman, L. H. 1951. *The Invertebrates,* McGraw-Hill, New York.) **3.** Female reproductive system of *Oligacanthorhynchus* (Archiacanthocephala), lateral view. (After Meyer, 1931.) **4.** Female reproductive system of *Bolbosoma* (Palaeacanthocephala). (After Yamaguti, 1939.)

(B, bladder (excretory vesicle); BW, body wall; BP, bell pockets; CG, cement glands; CNC, common excretory (nephridial) canal; CR, cement reservoir; CSD, common sperm duct; DCG, ducts of cement glands; DCR, ducts of cement reservoirs; DL, dorsal ligament sac; EB, exit of bladder into bell; ES, entrance of Saefftigen's pouch into bursa cap; EVL, exit into ventral ligament sac; GS, genital sheath; LS, ligament sac; MC, muscular cap of bursa; M, membrane, part of ventral ligament sac; NBA, nuclei of bell apparatus; NC, excretory (nephridial) canal; NN, excretory (nephridial) nuclei; NR, nerve ring; PP, penis papilla; PR, protonephridium; PUC, pouch of urogenital canal; SD, sperm ducts (vas deferens); SP, Saefftigen's pouch; SV, seminal vesicle; TES, testes; UB, uterine bell; UT, uterus; VA, vagina.)

t is attached to the genital sheath in males and to the uterine bell in females.

In members of the order Archiacanthocephala, the females possess two ligament sacs—one dorsal and one ventral (Plate 13-4). In these, the posterior attachment of the ventral sac is on the posterior extremity of the body. In the order Eoacanthocephala, there are also two ligament sacs in females. In these two orders, the ovaries are located in the dorsal sac, which communicates anteriorly with the ventral sac through an opening. In the order Palaeacanthocephala, there is only one sac in each sex. Furthermore, in females the sac ruptures when the worms reach sexual maturity, thus permitting the developing cells to escape into the pseudocoel.

In addition to the ligament sac(s), Haffner (1942a, b, c) pointed out that a nucleated auxiliary strand—the ligament strand—is present. In worms with two sacs, the strand is situated between them; in unisaccular forms, the strand runs along the ventral surface of the sac. The function and origin of this strand are hypothetical. Haffner considered it to be a vestigial midgut, the remnant of an ancestral alimentary tract.

In male acanthocephalans, there are two rounded or elongate testes that are tandemly arranged within the ligament sac. Arising from the posterior extremity of each testis is an individual sperm duct (vas efferens) that is directed posteriorly. Shortly after passing the level posterior to the posterior testis, one or two minute ducts empty into the sperm ducts. These ducts, known as cement gland ducts, arise from the union of many primary ducts that originate in the conspicuous unicellular cement glands lying posterior to the caudal testis. In the order Eoacanthocephala, these cement glands form a syncytium with several giant nuclei. A single cement gland duct carries the secretion to a cement reservoir from which a pair of ducts extend to join the sperm duct. The sperm ducts continue posteriorly within the narrower continuation of the ligament sac known as the genital sheath. This sheath includes myofibers from the body wall. Within the genital sheath, the two sperm ducts unite to form the single vas deferens, which may include an enlarged segment known as the seminal vesicle. The vas deferens enters the cirrus, which terminates in a muscular and eversible cup, the bursa.

The ovaries of female acanthocephalans are large bodies in the larval forms, but are fragmentary in the adults. The small ovaries of the adults are unattached in the ligament sac and are known as ovarian balls. Ova expelled from the ovarian balls become fertilized by spermatozoa introduced into the female during copulation. Developing eggs are collected by a funnel shaped uterine bell, which although thicker, is continuous with the posterior extremity of the ligament sac. The eggs pass posteriorly through the uterine tube into the long muscular uterus. A pair of large bell pouches arise as diverticula from the uterine tube and extend anteriorly. The terminal end of the genital tract is nonmuscular and is known as the vagina.

During copulation, the bursa of the male everts as the result of hydrostatic pressure due to the injection of fluid into the bursal spaces by the Saefftigen's pouch (an extension of the bursa internally into the genital sheath). The bursa is wrapped around the posterior end of the female, the cirrus is introduced into the gonopore, and spermatozoa migrate up the vagina, uterus, and uterine tube. Next "cement" is secreted from the cement glands and serves as a plug blocking the gonopore and vagina, thus preventing the escape of spermatozoa.

The acanthocephalan egg possesses three, sometimes four, membranes: (1) The ovocyte membrane surrounds the elliptical ovum when it is expelled from the ovarian ball. (2) The fertilization membrane is laid down inside the ovocyte membrane after the sperm enters. (3) The shell membrane is deposited between the ovocyte and fertilization membranes when development of the embryo is initiated.

The texture of the shell membrane varies among acanthocephalan species. In species that utilize a terrestrial intermediate host, the shell is generally hard, while in species that utilize an aquatic host, the shell is soft. The expelled eggs are highly resistant and remain viable for several months in some instances.

The in utero embryology of the giant species, *Macracanthorhynchus hirudinceus* has been studied by various investigators (Plate 13–5); however, the reports of Meyer (1928, 1936, 1937, 1938a, b) are considered the classic studies. The zygote cleavage is of the spiral determinate type, but the positions of the blastomeres are displaced because of the elliptical shape of the egg shell. Before the egg is discharged by the worm, a partially developed acanthor is already formed within the thick shell.

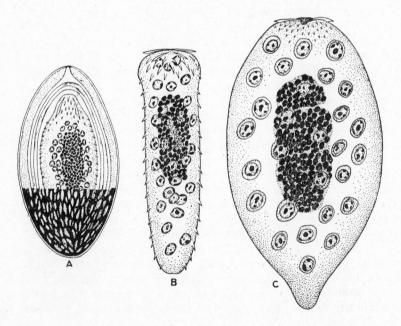

Plate 13-5   Egg and acanthor of *Macracanthorhynchus hirudinaceus*. **A.** Egg, or shelled embryo. Surface appearance shown only in lower portion. Rest of egg shown as optical section. **B.** Acanthor, stage I, from lumen of midgut of beetle larva. Note the larval rostellar hooks and spinous body. **C.** Acanthor, stage II, after penetrating wall of midgut of beetle larva. (A after Kates, 1943; B and C after Van Cleave.)

CHEMICAL COMPOSITION

The chemical composition of Acanthocephala has been studied in only the more common and larger species. Von Brand (1939) reported that 70 per cent of the dry substance of *Macracanthorhynchus hirudinaceus* is protein. Some of this undoubtedly is represented by the sclero-proteins that make up the body cuticle. In the same species, stored glycogen is found primarily in the body wall (80 per cent), in the ovaries and eggs (12 per cent), and in the body fluid within the lacunar system (8 per cent). Some glycogen is also present in the noncontractile portions of the muscle cells. Bullock (1948) stated that the subcuticulum is probably the site of glycogenesis.

Von Brand and Sauerwein (1942) reported that besides glycogen, a small amount of a type of polysaccharide (galactogen?) has been isolated from *M. hirudinaceus*. In addition, tre-halose, glucose, fructose, mannose, and maltose are the main carbohydrate reserves. These can be utilized under aerobic and anaerobic conditions, while galactose, which is also present, is only utilized under anaerobic conditions.

Lipids have been determined to form 1.0 to 2.1 per cent of the fresh substance of *M. hirudinaceus* (von Brand, 1939, 1940). These lipids have been determined, through fractionization, to be 27 per cent phosphatids, 24 per cent un-saponifiable matter, 2 per cent saturated fatty acids, 32 per cent unsaturated fatty acids, and 2 per cent glycerol. The unsaponifiable material may well be cholesterol. Body lipids in this species occur in the body wall, in the reproductive organs, and in the body fluid. Lipid droplets have also been found in the lacunar system. Bullock (1948) stated that fat synthesis and hydrolysis, under the control of lipase, also occurs in the subcuticula of the trunk and to some extent in the lemnisci.

The body musculature of various acanthocephalans contains specific differences in the amount of accumulated fats. In *Macracanthorhynchus*, there is little fat; but in *Neoechinorhynchus, Pomphorhynchus*, and *Echinorhynchus*, there are considerable accumulations. Specific types of lipids are found in specific areas. Phospholipids, for example, are found primarily in the subcuticula accumulated around the lacunae, while cholesterol and cholesterol esters are limited to the innermost margins of the subcuticula.

In addition to proteins, carbohydrates, and lipids, certain inorganic materials are found in acanthocephalans. In *M. hirudinaceus,* inorganic materials make up 0.58 per cent of the fresh body weight and 5 per cent of the dry weight (von Brand and Saurwein, 1942). Potassium, sodium, calcium, magnesium, aluminum, iron, manganese, silicon, chlorine, copper, phosphate, sulfate, and carbonate are all found in this species.

LIFE CYCLE STUDIES

An invertebrate intermediate host is required for completion of all the life cycles known among the Acanthocephala (Plate 13–6). Eggs passed out in the feces of the vertebrate host, either on land or in water, contain a partially developed acanthor. If the egg is ingested by the invertebrate host (usually an arthropod), development within the egg continues, and a fully formed elongate acanthor ruptures from the egg. The acanthor possesses pointed ends, is armed with a rostellum with hooks, and has a spinous body cuticle. In some species, a definite suture is visible on the shell and represents the line of rupture upon hatching. The active acanthor, with the aid of its rostellar hooks and body motions, penetrates the gut wall of the invertebrate host and becomes located in the haemocoel. This penetration process usually takes from 2 to 5 weeks.

In the haemocoel of the host, the acanthor rounds up and loses its rostellum, hooks, and body spines. It develops a rudimentary proboscis, proboscis sheath, cephalic ganglia, ligament sheath, primitive gonads, etc., and is then known as an acanthella. Further differentiation takes place, and all the features of the adult become readily recognizable, although the gonads are nonfunctional. When such a degree of differentiation is reached, accompanied by the elongation of the body, the animal is known as a juvenile.

The juvenile is generally enclosed within a sheath and is referred to as a cystacanth. It is inactive and its proboscis is retracted. In certain species cystacanths are found encysted in mesenteries and visceral organs in addition to the body cavity of the intermediate host.

When the invertebrate host is ingested by the appropriate vertebrate host, the cystacanth in the vertebrate's intestine loses its sheath and becomes sexually mature. Complete development within the intermediate host takes from

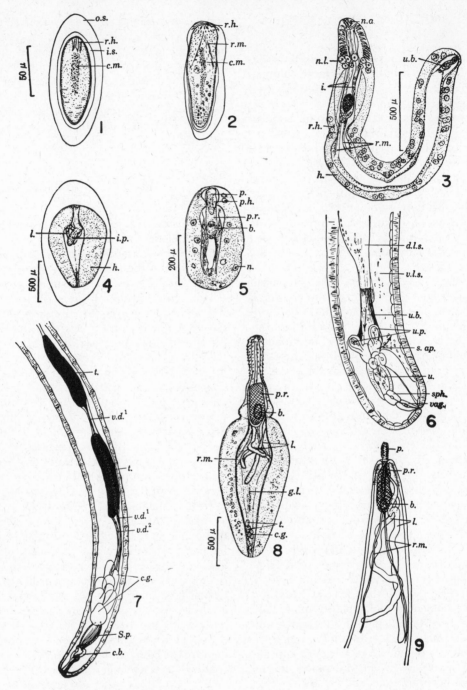

Plate 13-6 **Stages in the life cycle of** *Moniliformis dubius.* 1. Egg. 2. Acanthor in process of escaping from eggshell and membranes. 3. Acanthella dissected from enveloping sheath, about 40 days after infection. 4. Cystacanth, from body cavity of roach, with proboscis inverted, about 50 days after infection. 5. Median section of acanthor from body cavity of roach, 29 days after infection. 6. Posterior end of female adult. 7. Posterior end of male adult. 8. Cystacanth freed from cyst and with proboscis evaginated. 9. Anterior end of adult. (Figs. 1 to 5 and 8 after Moore, 1946; Figs. 6, 7, and 9 after A. C. Chandler and C. P. Read, 1961. *Introduction to Parasitology,* John Wiley, New York.)

(b., brain; c.b., copulatory bursa; c.g., cement glands; c.m., central nuclear mass; d.l.s., dorsal ligament sac; g.l., genital ligament; h., hypodermis; i., inverter muscle; i.p., inverted proboscis; i.s.,

(Legend continued on opposite page.)

6 to 12 weeks. In some cases, a second intermediate host is required.

It is generally agreed that acanthocephalans originated as parasites of fishes and the original life cycle, as is the common pattern today, included a single invertebrate intermediate host. Furthermore, many instances are known in which juvenile acanthocephalans are found encapsulated in the bodies of vertebrates and occasionally invertebrates that normally feed on invertebrates. These hosts are referred to as paratenic hosts. They undoubtedly represent hosts whose internal environment is not conductive for development of the worm to sexual maturity. For example, the normal intermediate host of *Neoechinorhynchus emydis* are ostracods. If infected ostracods are ingested by snails (*Campeloma, Pleurocera,* and *Ceriphasia*), the worm becomes encysted around the mouth and in the foot of the molluscan paratenic host. That juvenile acanthocephalans are able to re-encapsulate in paratenic hosts, particularly vertebrates that feed on arthropods, has rendered possible the adaptation of acanthocephalans to such hosts as reptiles, birds, and mammals.

Paratenic hosts are not necessary in the life cycle of acanthocephalans, although in many instances they are advantageous to the parasite, because such hosts can be considered transport hosts since, as links in the food chain, they do carry the immature worm to a suitable definitive host.

Another interesting aspect of acanthocephalan life cycles is the cohabitation of cystacanth and adult worms of the same species within the same fish host. The cystacanths are generally found within the body cavity of the host. This suggests that the same fish can serve as both the definitive and the intermediate host. Fish can become a potential intermediate host if the ingested larval acanthocephalan has not reached full development in the normal intermediate host. For example, DeGuisti (1939) has shown that when eggs of *Leptorhynchoides thecatus* are fed to amphipods, fully developed infective cystacanths are formed in 32 days. When such larvae are fed to small black bass,

they attach themselves to the fish's intestinal mucosa and develop to maturity. If, however, larvae less than 32 days old are fed to black bass, the larvae do not remain in the gut but burrow through the intestinal wall and become re-encapsulated in the body cavity. Thus the black bass can serve as both an intermediate and a definitive host, depending on the degree of maturity of the cystacanth. This unusual phenomenon may also be interpreted as advantageous to the parasite, because if small black bass harboring re-encysted cystacanths are eaten by larger fish, the cystacanths can reach sexual maturity in the larger fish.

SYSTEMATICS AND BIOLOGY

CLASSIFICATION

According to Van Cleave (1936), the phylum Acanthocephala is divided into three orders. Meyer's (1932, 1933) monograph of the Acanthocephala includes all the species of this order described up to 1933, and Ward (1951, 1952) lists species described since 1933. Yamaguti (1963) has catalogued all the known species of Acanthocephala. All of these references are useful to those interested in the identification of acanthocephalans.

Order 1. Archiacanthocephala.   Are parasites in the intestine of terrestrial hosts. Invertebrate hosts include roaches and grubs. Proboscis spines are concentrically arranged. Possess protonephridia. Main lacunar channels are median. Females possess two persistent ligament sacs. Males have eight cement glands.

Order 2. Palaeacanthocephala.   Are parasites in the intestine of fishes, aquatic birds, and mammals. Invertebrate hosts are usually Crustacea. Proboscis hooks are arranged in alternating radial rows. Protonephridia are lacking. Main lacunar channels are lateral. Possess single ligament sac, which ruptures upon sexual maturity in females. Males normally possess six cement glands.

Order 3. Eoacanthocephala.   Are parasites in intestine of fishes and reptiles. Invertebrate hosts are usually Crustacea. Proboscis hooks are radially arranged. Protonephridia are lacking. Main lacunar channels are median. Females possess two ligament sacs, which persist. Cement glands in males are syncytial, with a reservoir.

(*Legend continued.*)
inner shell; l., lemnisci; n., subcuticular nuclei; n.l., nuclei of lemnical ring; o.s., outer shell; p., proboscis; p.h., developing proboscis hooks; p.r., proboscis receptacle; r.h., rostellar hooks; r.m., retractor muscles; s.ap., sorting apparatus; S.p., Saefftigen's pouch; sph., sphincter; t., testes; u., uterus; u.b., uterine bell; u.p., uterine pouches; vag., vagina; v.d., vasa differentia; v.l.s., ventral ligament sac.)

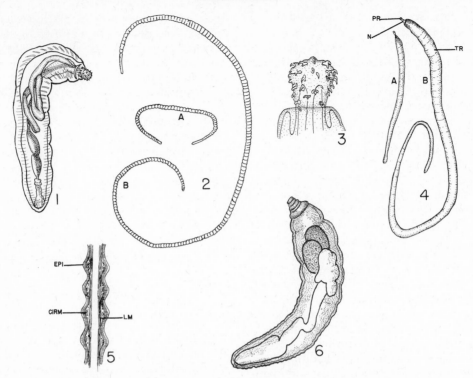

Plate 13-7   Some species of acanthocephala. 1. Male specimen of *Mediorhynchus sipoco-tensis* (Archiacanthocephala) in birds. (Redrawn after Tubangui, 1935.) 2. *Gigantorhynchus echinodiscus* (Archiacanthocephala) in mammals. **A.** male. **B.** female. (A and B redrawn after Travassos, 1917.) 3. Proboscis of *Nephridiorhynchus palawanensis* (Archiacanthocephala) in mammals. (Redrawn after Tubangui and Masiluñgan, 1938.) 4. *Macracanthorhynchus hirudinaceus* (Archiacanthocephala) in pigs. **A.** male. **B.** female. (A and B original.) 5. Part of *Moniliformis* (Archiacanthocephala) in mammals, showing relation of longitudinal muscle layer to the superficial segmentation. (Redrawn and modified after Hyman, L. H. 1951. *The Invertebrates,* McGraw-Hill, New York.) 6. Male of *Oncicola travassosi* (Archiacanthocephala) in mammals. (Redrawn and modified after Witenberg, 1938.)

(PR, proboscis; N, neck; TR, trunk; CIRM, circular muscles; EPI, epidermus (hypodermis); LM, longitudinal muscles.)

ORDER ARCHIACANTHOCEPHALA

In addition to the general characteristics described for all acanthocephalans, members of the Archiacanthocephala exhibit "unfragmented," large epidermal nuclei, and spines are absent from the body trunks. Species of this order are generally parasitic in terrestrial birds and mammals, although a few are found in fishes.

Among the genera represented in this order are: *Mediorhynchus,* parasitic in birds; *Gigantorhynchus* in mammals; *Heteracanthorhynchus* in birds; *Oligacanthorhynchus* in fishes and birds; *Nephridiorhynchus* in mammals; *Macracanthorhynchus* in mammals, including the common giant hog species *M. hirudinaceus; Moniliformis* in mammals, mostly rodents, including the two relatively common species, *M. dubius* in rats and *M. moniliformis* in other small mammals; and *Oncicola* in mammals, including *O. canis,* the species found, sometimes in large numbers, in dogs of North America (Plate 13–7).

Among members of the Archiacanthocephala, *Macracanthorhynchus hirudinaceus* has been reported in man, but rarely. Because of its large size and its easy accessibility from slaughter houses, it has been the subject of physiological and biochemical studies. Mueller (1929) reported that the cuticle of *M. hirudinaceus* is 14.78 per cent nitrogen and 0.564 per cent sulfur, thus giving some idea of the nature of the body cuticle.

ORDER PALAEACANTHOCEPHALA

Members of the Palaeacanthocephala include forms found almost exclusively in fishes, although a few are parasites of aquatic birds and mammals. Representatives of the order include *Illiosentis, Rhadinorhynchus, Tegorhynchus,* and *Pseudorhynchus* (Plate 13–8, Figs. 1 to 3).

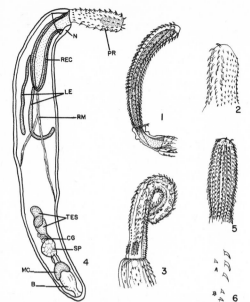

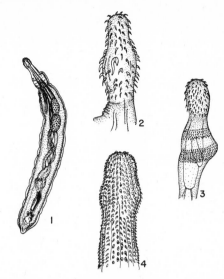

Plate 13-9   Some palaeacanthocephalan Acan-thocephala. 1. Male of *Polymorphus marilis* in birds. (Re-drawn after Van Cleave, 1939.) 2. Proboscis of *Corynosoma turbidum* in birds. (Redrawn after Van Cleave, 1937.) 3. Proboscis of *Bolbosoma thunni* in fish. (Redrawn after Harada, 1935.) 4. Proboscis of *Centrorhynchus conspectus* in birds. (Re-drawn after Van Cleave and Pratt, 1940.)

Plate 13-8   Some Acanthocephala 1. Proboscis of *Illiosentis furcatus* (Palaeacanthocephala) in fish. (Redrawn after Van Cleave and Lincicome, 1939.) **2.** Proboscis of *Rhadinorhynchus peltorhamphi* (Palaeacanthocephala) in fish. (Redrawn after Baylis, 1944.) **3.** Proboscis of *Tegorhynchus pectinarius* (Palaeacanthocephala) in fish. (Redrawn after Van Cleave, 1940.) **4.** Male of *Leptorhynchoides thecatus* (Palaeacanthocephala) in fish. (B, bursa; CG, cement glands; LE, lemnisci; MC, muscular cap of bursa; N, neck; PR, proboscis; REC, receptacle; RM, retractor muscles; SP, Saefftigen's pouch; TES, testes.) (Redrawn after Van Cleave, 1919.) **5.** Proboscis of *Gorgorhynchus lepidus* (Palaeacantho-cephala) in fish. (Redrawn after Van Cleave, 1940.) **6.** Proboscis hooks (A) and body spines (B) of *Mehrarhynchus prashadi* (Palaeacanthocephala) in fish. (Redrawn after Datta, 1940.)

Another species, *Neoechinorhynchus emydis*, is common in turtles in North America.

Other genera comprising the Eoacantho-cephala include *Pallisentis, Acanthosentis, Quad-rigyrus, Raosentis, Octospinifer, Eosentis,* and *Tenuisentis,* all common in various piscian hosts (Plate 13–10).

These genera all possess dorsoventral differences in the shapes and sizes of proboscal hooks. *Illiosentis* possesses genital spines, in addition to anterior trunk spines.

Other fish-parasitizing genera include *As-persentis* and *Leptorhynchoides.* The latter includes *L. thecatus,* a common species in the eastern United States (Plate 13–8, Fig. 4). Other representative genera of this order are depicted in Plate 13–9.

ORDER EOACANTHOCEPHALA

Included in the Eoacanthocephala is the common species *Neoechinorhynchus cylindratus,* which parasitizes fish in many fresh-water ponds and streams in North America. In the life cycle of this species, Ward (1940) demonstrated that ostracods serve as the intermediate host and smaller fish serve as transport hosts— that is, when these transport hosts are eaten by larger fishes, the worms are passed on.

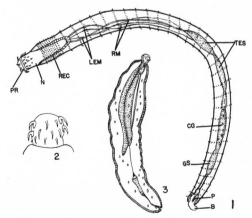

Plate 13-10   Some eoacanthocephalan Acantho-cephala 1. Male of *Pallisentis ophiocephali,* showing girdles of trunk spines. (B, bursa; CG, cement gland; GS, genital sheath; LEM, lemnisci; N, neck; P, penis (cirrus); PR, proboscis; REC, receptacle; RM, retractor muscles; TES, testes.) (Redrawn after Thaper, 1930.) **2.** Proboscis of *Octospinifer.* (Redrawn after Van Cleave, 1919.) **3.** Female of *Eosentis devdevi,* in fish. (Redrawn after Datta, 1936.)

PHYSIOLOGY

The physiology of acanthocephalans has been little studied. From what is known, the physiology of this phylum appears to resemble that of cestodes rather than nematodes.

Oxygen Requirements

Von Brand (1940) suggested that acanthocephalan metabolism is primarily anaerobic in vivo, although these worms can survive in the presence of oxygen. Laurie (1957) demonstrated that *Moniliformis dubius* is capable of anaerobic metabolism and that it ferments glucose, galactose, mannose, fructose, and maltose to acidic catabolites under anaerobic conditions. Even under aerobic conditions, this fermentative type of metabolism is carried on.

Ability to metabolize under anaerobic and aerobic conditions is exemplified by *Macracanthorhynchus hirudinaceus,* which is capable of absorbing and consuming carbohydrates. Under anaerobic conditions, these worms consume 1 gm. per 100 gm. wet weight of carbohydrate; while under aerobic conditions, they consume only 0.8 gm. These data suggest that these worms, as parasites in the intestine, where the oxygen tension is practically nil, are more adapted to anaerobism.

Metabolism

In analyses of stored nutrients in the body, von Brand (1939) reported that glycogen is found in varying quantities in *Macracanthorhynchus hirudinaceus*. His results are presented in Table 13–1.

These findings suggest that most of the body glycogen in this species is stored in the body wall. However, some glycogen is found in the body fluid, which serves as the medium for transporting nutrients. Glycogen found in the ovaries and eggs probably is utilized by the developing acanthors. In addition to glycogen, von Brand (1939) reported 70 per cent protein in dry substance analysis. Von Brand (1939, 1940) also found 1.0 to 2.1 per cent lipids in fresh substance analysis. These lipids included 27 per cent phosphatids, 2 per cent saturated fatty acids, 32 per cent unsaturated fatty acids, and 2 per cent glycerol.

The pseudocoelomic fluid of *Macracanthorhynchus* is capable of splitting starch into simpler sugars because it includes amylases. However, the fluid demonstrates no lipolytic activity but does affect proteolysis when placed in an alkaline medium.

In various histochemical studies on the Acanthocephala, Bullock (1949) reported the presence of alkaline phosphatase in *Echinorhynchus* and *Pomphorhynchus,* where it is restricted to the subcuticular hypodermis of the trunk.

An interesting aspect of parasite dependency on the host was reported by Pflugfelder (1949) on *Acanthocephalus ranae* in frogs. He found that the worm does not elaborate the fat-digesting enzyme, lipase, into the medium, but does absorb the degradation products of fat digested by lipases in the frog host. In this case, the parasite, as far as its fat requirements are concerned, is dependent on the host for predigestion.

Osmoregulation

Van Cleave and Ross (1944) demonstrated that osmoregulation and tolerance for salinity in the surrounding medium occur among acanthocephalans, specifically in *Neoechinorhynchus emydis*. Individuals of this species are normally ventrally flattened and maintain this form when placed in a solution containing 0.8 to 0.85 per cent sodium chloride. However, when the specimens are placed in a 0.7 to 0.75 per cent salt solution, they become turgid

Table 13-1. Glycogen Content in Organs and Structures of a *Macracanthorhynchus hirudinaceus* Female*

Body Wall		Ovaries and Eggs		Body Fluid	
% of Fresh Substance	% of Total Glycogen	% of Fresh Substance	% of Total Glycogen	% of Fresh Substance	% of Total Glycogen
1.5	80	0.9	12	0.2	8

* Data from von Brand (1939).

and survive less effectively. If placed in tap water, the animals become completely turgid in one hour and usually perish. The same results can be obtained by injecting salt solutions of given concentrations into the intestines of turtles.

Also experimenting with *N. emydis,* Gettier (1942) obtained slightly different results. He reported that these worms survived best in a solution of 0.5 per cent sodium chloride and 0.02 per cent calcium chloride. Potassium chloride and magnesium chloride were added without benefit. Apparently the presence of calcium chloride, even in a more dilute sodium chloride solution, is beneficial for survival. Gettier also reported that worms placed in 2 per cent sodium chloride solution died rapidly.

Resistance of Eggs

Manter (1928) reported that eggs removed from females of *Macracanthorhynchus hirudinaceus* and *Mediorhynchus* sp. can be induced to hatch by first drying them and later rewetting them. However, eggs isolated from the host's feces can not be hatched by this technique.

Eggs of acanthocephalans that utilize a terrestrial intermediate host are extremely resistant to normal environmental conditions. This has been demonstrated by Spindler and Kates (1940), who exposed eggs of *M. hirudinaceus,* in soil mixtures including and not including pig feces, to desiccation by sunlight and found that the exposed eggs remained viable and hatched readily when fed to beetle grubs. Eggs of *M. hirudinaceus* can withstand temperatures from $-10°$ to $45°$ C for as long as 140 days, and these eggs can resist desiccation at temperatures up to $39°$ C for as long as 265 days!

HOST-PARASITE RELATIONSHIPS

Acanthocephalans demonstrate host specificity, usually supraspecificity. A single species can exist in more than one species of host—in fact, the same species may occur in several different families of fish—but a parasite of fishes is not found in birds, mammals, or any other vertebrate host.

Effects of Host on Parasite

Burlingame and Chandler (1941) reported that experimentally starved rats infected with *Moniliformis dubius* lose approximately 30 per cent of the original number of parasites in 5 days; however, this loss is not due to the development of host immunity since reinfections are possible. It is now known that no true immunity to Acanthocephala is developed. There is, however, a "first come, first serve" effect, for newcomers in subsequent infections do not become attached and are sloughed through the alimentary tract because the desirable positions in the gut are occupied by worms from previous infections. Refractivity of the host to reinfections is thus a manifestation of parasite competition for nutrients and favorable locations.

Invertebrate intermediate hosts—at least certain ones—respond to the presence of larval acanthocephalans. For example DeGuisti (1949) reported that when developing *Leptorhynchoides* is present in the crustacean *Hyalella,* a mass of host epithelial cells is proliferated at the site when the acanthor penetrates the gut wall. Once the parasite enters the host's haemocoel and encysts, the coelomic side of the developing cyst is covered by motile host blood cells. When the cyst wall ruptures, host cells respond as to a foreign body, and the larval acanthocephalan is enveloped by a layer of amoeboid cells that form a syncytium. In some cases, the syncytial envelope checks the growth of the parasite and eventually causes its death. If this occurs, the dead parasite is walled off by a brown sclerous membrane.

Similarly, walled larvae of *Macracanthorhynchus hirudinaceus* have been found in the larvae of the Japanese beetle, which is a suitable intermediate host for this parasite. Temperature appears to influence the intermediate host's response to acanthocephalan larvae, for these parasites are more often walled off at low temperatures than at high temperatures.

Effects of Parasite on Host

Exactly how many ways acanthocephalans can injure their hosts remains in doubt. The main type of injury is mechanical, for the proboscal hooks and spines do pierce and rupture the lining of the host's intestine, and in the case of *Acanthocephalus anguillae* in fish, even the underlying muscularis may be perforated. In hosts harboring large numbers of worms, the amount of nutrients absorbed by the parasites may be of some consequence.

The number of worms required to kill a host

varies. Webster (1943) suggested that the presence of one or two *Plagiorhynchus formosus* in the intestine is sufficient to kill a robin, and Boyd (1951) reported that the presence of one to seven acanthocephalans of the same species causes emaciation and blackening of the visceral contents of starlings. Clark et al. (1958) reported the presence of large numbers of *Polymorphus botulus*—up to 610 worms per bird—in dead or dying eider ducks along the New England coast. In contrast to the acanthocephalan-caused pathogenicities and mortalities just described, there are numerous reports of the presence of exceedingly heavy acanthocephalan infections in fish with much vaguer pathogenicity.

Bullock (1963) has studied the histopathology of the postcaecal intestinal wall and rectum of two species of trout—*Salvelinus fontinalis* and *Salmo gairdneri*—infected with *Acanthocephalus jacksoni*. He reported that there is proliferation of the connective tissue of the lamina propria in the area where the proboscis of the worm is attached. The lamina propria is increased as the result of the development of collagenous fibrous tissue, and there is an increase in the number of host cells—primarily macrophages, fibroblasts, lymphocytes, polymorphonuclear leukocytes, and granular cells. There is also damage to the lining epithelium. The cells at the point of attachment are completely destroyed, and the cells in adjacent areas are compressed.

Although no capsule is formed around the parasite, a layer of mucus is interposed between the parasite and the host's epithelium. Bullock believed that the worm absorbs nutrients from this layer, which contains the end products of the host's digestion as well as secretions from the host's mucosa. In the case of *Polymorphus*

infections in birds, Pflugfelder (1956) reported that a capsule is formed around the acanthocephalan. Similarly, Prakash and Adams (1960) reported that a capsule is formed around *Echinorhynchus langeniformis* in flounder.

Within the fish host, the younger specimens of *Acanthocephalus jacksoni* are more anteriorly attached in the intestine than are older specimens. As the worms grow, they migrate posteriorly, and as a result, new lesions are formed each time the worms become reattached. Thus, a number of lesions can result from each worm during its migration. Although wound healing does occur, nevertheless, the lesions are injurious. This type of migration is also characteristic of *Acanthocephalus anguillae* infections in fish. Wurmbach (1937) reported that although the proboscis of *Pomphorhynchus* invariably penetrates both the mucosa and the underlying muscle layer of the fish host, it is not as destructive as *A. anguillae*, for the latter migrates and causes more lesions.

There is little evidence that acanthocephalans secrete any toxic substances under normal conditions. However, dogs infected with *Oncicola canis* do exibit symptoms of toxicity that simulate those of rabies. Again, humans infected with *Moniliformis moniliformis* may portray symptoms of toxicity in the form of diarrhea and humming of the ears. The pseudocoelomic fluid of *Macracanthorhynchus hirudinaceus* is capable of slight haemolytic activity in pigs and cattle.

Le Roux (1931) reported an interesting case of "castration" resulting from Acanthocephala infection. The worm *Polymorphus minutus* does not interfere with the normal functions of the testes of males of the intermediate host, *Gammarus pulex;* but in females, the normal functions of the ovaries are arrested and the hosts revert to certain juvenile characteristics.

LITERATURE CITED

Boyd, E. M. 1951. A survey of parasitism of the starling *Sturnus vulgaris* L. in North America. J. Parasit., *37:* 56–84.

Bullock, W. L. 1948. Histochemical studies on the Acanthocephala: A contribution to helminth metabolism. Abstract of Ph. D. thesis, University of Illinois, pp. 1–5.

Bullock, W. L. 1949. Histochemical studies on the Acanthocephala. I. The distribution of lipase and phosphatase. J. Morph., *84:* 185–200. (Also see Part II, *Ibid., 84:* 201–226.)

Bullock, W. L. 1963. Intestinal histology of some salmonid fishes with particular reference to the histopathology of acanthocephalan infections. J. Morph., *112:* 23–44.

Burlingame, P. L., and A. C. Chandler. 1941. Host-parasite relations of *Moniliformis dubius* (Acanthocephala) in albino rats, and the environmental nature of resistance to single and superimposed infections with this parasite. Am. J. Hyg., *33:* 1–21.

Clark, G. M., D. O'Meara, and J. W. Van Weelden. 1958. An epizootic among eider ducks involving an acanthocephalid worm. J. Wildl. Manag., *22:* 204–205.

DeGuisti, D. L. 1939. Further studies on the life cycle of *Leptorhynchoides thecatus.* J. Parasit., *25* (suppl.): 22.

DeGuisti, D. L. 1949. The life cycle of *Leptorhynchoides thecatus* (Linton), an acanthocephalan of fish. J. Parasit., *35:* 437–460.

Gettier, D. A. 1942. Studies on the saline requirements of *Neoechinorhynchus emydis.* Proc. Helminth. Soc. Wash., *9:* 75–78.

Haffner, K. von. 1942a. Untersuchungen über das Urogenitalsystem der Acanthocephalen. I. Teil. Das Urogenitalsystem von *Oligacanthorhynchus thunbi* forma juv. Ztschr. Morphol. Oekol. Tiere, *38:* 251–294.

Haffner, K. von. 1942b. Untersuchungen über das Urogenitalsystem der Acanthocephalen. II. Teil. Das Urogenitalsystem von *Giganthorhynchus echinodiscus* Diesing. Ztschr. Morphol. Oekol. Tiere, *38:* 295–316.

Haffner, K. von. 1942c. Untersuchungen über das Urogenitalsystem der Acanthocephalen. III. Teil. Theoretische Betrachtungen auf Grund eigener Ergebnisse. Ztschr. Morphol. Oekol. Tiere, *38:* 317–333.

Kates, K. C. 1944. Some observations on experimental infections of pigs with the thorn-headed worm, *Macracanthorhynchus hirudinaceus.* Am. J. Vet. *5:* 166–172.

Laurie, J. S. 1957. The *in vitro* fermentation of carbohydrates by two species of cestodes and one species of acanthocephala. Exptl. Parasit., *6:* 245–260.

Le Roux, M. L. 1931. Castration parasitaire et caractères sexuels secondaires chez les gammariens. Compt. Rend. Acad. Sci., *192:* 889–891.

Manter, H. W. 1928. Notes on the eggs and larvae of the thorny-headed worm of hogs. Trans. Amer. Micro. Soc., *47:* 342–347.

Meyer, A. 1928. Die Furchung nebst Einbildung, Reifung und Befruchtung des *Gigantorhynchus gigas.* Ein Beitrag zur Morphologie der Acanthocephalen. Zool. Jahrb., *50:* 117–218.

Meyer, A. 1932. Acanthocephala. Bronn's Klass u. Ordnumg. TierReichs, *4:* 1–332.

Meyer, A. 1933. Acanthocephala. Bronn's Klass u. Ordnumg. TierReichs, *4:* 333–582.

Meyer, A. 1936. Die plasmodiale Entwicklung und Formbildung der Riesenkratzers (*Macracanthorhynchus hirudinaceus* (Pallas). I. Teil. Mit Forschungsstipendium der Notgemeinschaft der Deutchen Wissenschaft 1930–1931. Zool. Jahrb., Abt. Anat., *62:* 111–172.

Meyer, A. 1937. Die plasmodiale Entwicklung und Formbildung des Riesenkratzers (*Macracanthorhynchus hirudinaceus*). II. Teil. Zool. Jahrb., Abt. Anat., *63:* 1–36.

Meyer, A. 1938a. Die plasmodiale Entwicklung und Formbildung der Riesenkratzers (*Macracanthorhynchus hirudinaceus* (Pallas) III. Teil. Zool. Jahrb., Abt. Anat., *64:* 131–197.

Meyer, A. 1938b. Die plasmodiale Entwicklung und Formbildung das Riesenkratzers (*Macracanthorhynchus hirudinaceus* (Pallas). IV. Allgemeiner Teil. Zool. Jahrb., Abt. Anat., *64:* 198–242.

Pflugfelder, O. 1949. Histologische Untersuchungen über die Fettresorption darmloser Parasiten: Die Funktion der Limnisken der Acanthocephalen. Ztschr. Parasitenk., *14:* 274–280.

Pflugfelder, O. 1956. Abwehrreaktionen der Wirtstiere von *Polymorphus boschadis* Schr. (Acanthocephala). Ztschr. Parasitenk., *17:* 371–382.

Prakash, A., and J. R. Adams. 1960. A histopathological study of the intestinal lesions induced by *Echinorhynchus lageniformis* (Acanthocephala-Echinorhynchidae) in the starry flounder. Can. J. Zool., *38:* 895–897.

Spindler, L. A., and K. C. Kates. 1940. Survival on soil of eggs of the swine thornheaded worm, *Macracanthorhynchus hirudinaceus.* J. Parasit., *26* (suppl.): 19.

Toryu, U. 1933. Contributions to the physiology of the Ascaris. I. Glycogen content of the Ascaris, *Ascaris megalocephala.* Cloq. Sci. Rep., Tohoku Imp. Univ., 4s (Biol.), *8:* 65–74.

Van Cleave, H. J. 1936. The recognition of a new order in the Acanthocephala. J. Parasit., *22:* 202–206.

Van Cleave, H. J., and E. L. Ross. 1945. Physiological responses of *Neoechinorhynchus emydis* (Acanthocephala) to various solutions. J. Parasit., *30:* 369–372.

von Brand, T. 1939. Chemical and morphological observations upon the composition of *Macracanthorhynchus hirudinaceus* (Acanthocephala). J. Parasit., *25:* 329–342.

von Brand, T. 1940. Further observations upon the composition of Acanthocephala. J. Parasit., *26:* 301–307.

von Brand, T. 1952. Chemical Physiology of Endoparasitic Animals. Academic Press, New York.

von Brand, T., and J. Saurwein. 1942. Further studies upon the chemistry of *Macracanthorhynchus hirudinaceus*. J. Parasit., *28:* 315–318.

Ward, H. L. 1940. Studies on the life history of *Neoechinorhynchus cylindratus* (Van Cleave, 1913) (Acanthocephala). Trans. Amer. Micro. Soc., *59:* 289–291.

Ward, H. L. 1951. The species of Acanthocephala described since 1933. I. Jour. Tenn. Acad. Sci., *26:* 282–311.

Ward, H. L. 1952. The species of Acanthocephala described since 1933. II. Jour. Tenn. Acad. Sci., *27:* 131–149.

Webster, J. D. 1943. Helminths from the robin, with the description of a new nematode, *Porrocaecum brevispiculum*. J. Parasit., *29:* 161–163.

Wurmbach, H. 1937. Zur krankheitserregenden Wirkung der Acanthocephalan. Die Kratzterergrankung der Barben in der Mosel. Ztschr. Fischerei, *35:* 217–232.

Yamaguti, S. 1963. Systema Helminthum. Vol. 5. Acanthocephala. John Wiley, New York.

SUGGESTED READING

Baer, J. G. 1952. Ecology of Animal Parasites. University of Illinois Press, Urbana, pp. 111–116. (This section, dealing with the Acanthocephala, emphasizes the life history and evolution of these parasites.)

Hyman, L. H. 1951. The Invertebrates: Acanthocephala, Aschelminthes, and Entoprocta. The Pseudocoelomate Bilateria. Vol. III. McGraw-Hill, New York, pp. 1–52. (This section deals with the Acanthocephala. The sections on morphology and the related references are particularly useful.)

Van Cleave, H. J. 1951. Some host-parasite relationships of the Acanthocephala, with special reference to the organs of attachment. Exptl. Parasit., *1:* 305–330. (This review article presents the author's ideas concerning the development and evolution of the proboscis of acanthocephalans.)

ASCHELMINTHES

14

INTRODUCTION TO THE SYMBIOTIC ASCHELMINTHES

THE NEMATOMORPHA—
The Horsehair Worms

THE ROTIFERA—
The Rotifers

Phylum Aschelminthes includes an array of bilaterally symmetrical pseudocoelomate animals. These unsegmented animals are mostly vermiform and are enveloped by a layer of noncellular cuticle. They possess a complete digestive, or alimentary, tract. The classes comprising Phylum Aschelminthes are: Rotifera, Gastrotricha, Kinorhyncha, Priapulida,* Nematomorpha, and Nematoda. Among these,

only certain species of the Nematoda are actually parasitic; in addition, the larvae of Nematomorpha are parasitic in various arthropods, and a few adult marine rotifers are symbiotic.

The parasitic aschelminthes, especially the nematodes (roundworms), are of great interest to biologists because not only are they plentiful and frequently encountered as endoparasites of a large array of hosts—invertebrates as well as vertebrates—but some of them are of considerable importance to human and animal health. Furthermore, certain soil-dwelling nematodes are of great interest in agriculture, for they often parasitize economically important plants and in so doing, inflict considerable injury.

---

*Although the Priapulida is usually classified as a group of pseudocoelomate aschelminths, Shapeero (1961. Science, 133 (3456): 879–860) pointed out that this small group is eucoelomate, distinct from the aschelminths.

Such is the case with the sugar beet nematode *Heterodera schachtii*. In the majority of plant-parasitizing species, the eggs are deposited either in the roots of the plant host or in the soil. When these eggs hatch, the young worms are found within plant cells or soon become established therein by actively penetrating the roots. These larvae actively ingest plant tissues, often resulting in the formation of galls or "root knots." In some instances, the destruction of plant tissues is so severe that it results in the death of the plant. Horne (1961) has contributed an introductory volume to plant nematodes.

ASCHELMINTH CHEMICAL COMPOSITION

The chemical composition of the parasitic aschelminths has only been studied among certain species of nematodes.

Proteins

In *Ascaris lumbricoides,* the common intestinal parasite of man and other mammals, Weinland (1901) reported that proteins represent 54 per cent of the dry substance of the worm, and Smorodintsev and Bebesin (1936) reported the percentage to be 48. Flury (1912) reported peptones, albumins, globulins, albumoses, and purine bases as the protein fractions isolated from bodies of *A. lumbricoides.* Similarly, Bondouy (1910) isolated albumins, albumoses, purine bases, and mucin from *Strongylus equinus,* the double-toothed strongyle nematode found in the caecum of horses. Going one step further, Yoshimura (1930) isolated and identified the bound amino acids found in *A. lumbricoides.* He reported the presence of glycine, alanine, valine, serine, leucine, isoleucine, tyrosine, phenylalanine, glutamic acid, aspartic acid, lysine, arginine, histidine, and proline. It is suspected that most intestinal nematodes have comparable amino acids comprising their protein fractions.

Relative to proteinaceous materials, Chitwood (1936) identified a mucoid substance in the cuticle of *Ascaris* and reported that glycoproteins are present in the spicules of parasitic nematodes. Chitwood (1938) also reported that the opercula of the eggs of *Dioctophyma renale*—a species found in the kidney of dogs, minks, and other fish-eating mammals—are proteinaceous.

Carbohydrates

Carbohydrates in nematodes are found both as stored nutrient in the form of glycogen, and as simple sugars in the body fluids. Fauré-Fremiet (1913) reported that glucose forms 0.15 per cent of the fresh weight of the body fluid of *Parascaris,* and Rogers (1945) reported 0.22 per cent in *Ascaris.* The glycogen content has been studied in a number of nematodes, and Table 14–1 lists the percentages of glycogen found in several representative species of roundworms.

The location of body glycogen in *Parascaris equorum* has been studied by Toryu (1933) (Table 14–2). He reported that in male worms, 4.9 per cent of the fresh weight and 96 per cent of the total body glycogen are found in the body wall; in females, 5.8 per cent of the fresh weight and 66 per cent of the total body glycogen are in the body wall. In both males and females, 0.6 per cent of the fresh weight and 9 per cent of the total glycogen are found in the intestinal wall.

The male and female reproductive organs also contain glycogen. In ovarian tissues, glycogen is found primarily in oogonia. There is little or no glycogen in oocytes and little in mature eggs. The total glycogen in the ovaries and eggs of *Parascaris equorum* represents 6.5 per cent of the fresh weight and 23 per cent of the total body glycogen. In testicular tissue, the glycogen amounts to 0.5 per cent of the fresh body weight and 2 per cent of the total glycogen.

As a rule, parasites found in oxygen-poor habitats or in habitats where periodic deficiencies of oxygen exist—for example, the stomach and small intestine—contain more glycogen.

In addition to the sugars found in body fluids and stored glycogen, other carbohydrates have been detected. The egg shell of nematodes, for example, includes polysaccharides.

Fats

Fats are found in the body of nematodes. In *Ascaris lumbricoides,* for example, lipids constitute 1.1 to 1.8 per cent of the fresh substance and 10.9 per cent of the dry substance of the body. In the larvae of *Eustrongylides ignotus,* von Brand (1938) reported that lipids constitute 1.1 per cent of the fresh substance and 4.4 per cent of the dry substance. The fat content of hookworm larvae is considered to be a good indicator of the physiological age of the specimens, for the degree of activity parallels the amount of fat content. In fact, hookworm

Table 14-1. Glycogen Content in Nematodes and Its Relation to Habitat and Oxygen Availability*

Species	Glycogen % of Fresh Weight	Glycogen % of Dry Weight	Habitat	Availability of Significant Amounts of Oxygen
Strongylus vulgaris	3.5		Intestine	?
Ancylostoma caninum	1.6		Intestine	Yes
Ascaridia galli	3.6-4.7		Intestine	?
Parascaris equorum	2.1,3.8	10,23	Intestine	No
Ascaris lumbricoides	5.3-8.7	24	Intestine	No
Dirofilaria immitis	1.9	10	Heart	Yes
Litomosoides carinii	0.8	5	Pleural cavity	Yes
Dipetalonema gracilis	0.2		Abdominal cavity	Yes
Trichinella spiralis (larvae)	2.4		Muscle	Moderate
Eustrongylides ignotus (larvae)	6.9	28	Various organs	Yes

*Data from various authors.

Table 14-2. Glycogen Content and Distribution in *Parascaris equorum**

Sex	Body Wall A	Body Wall B	Intestine A	Intestine B	Uterus A	Uterus B	Ovaries and Eggs A	Ovaries and Eggs B	Male Reproductive System A	Male Reproductive System B
Male	4.9	96	0.6	2	—	—	—	—	0.5	2
Female	5.8	66	0.6	2	1.6	9	0.5	23	—	—

*Data after Toryu (1933).

A = per cent of fresh substance.

B = per cent of total glycogen.

larvae in which the fat content has been completely exhausted are no longer infective.

The most important sites of fat deposition in nematodes are the thickened portions of the body wall musculature. In addition, the subcuticula, intestinal cells, cells of the reproductive system, and nerve ganglia are known to contain lipids. Timm (1950) reported that the vitelline membrane of nematode eggs contains myricyl palmitate, which is lipid in nature.

The lipid fractions of nematodes have been determined by Flury (1912) and Schulz and Becker (1933) to be 6.6 per cent phosphatids, 24.7 to 26 per cent unsaponifiable matter, 30.9

per cent saturated fatty acids, 34.1 per cent unsaturated fatty acids, and 2.4 to 8.8 per cent glycerol.

Inorganic Substances

In addition to proteins, carbohydrates, and lipids, certain inorganic substances are found in nematodes. Weinland (1901) and Flury (1912) reported that inorganic substances comprise 0.70 to 0.78 per cent of the fresh weight and 4 to 5.1 per cent of the dry weight of *Ascaris lumbricoides*. Rogers (1945) reported that in the body fluid of *A. lumbricoides* are found traces of potassium, magnesium, sodium, iron, copper, zinc, chlorine, and phosphorus. Among these, sodium is most abundant, followed by chlorine.

CLASS NEMATOMORPHA

The nematomorph worms, commonly called horsehair or gordiacean worms, are long, slender, cylindrical animals. The body surface is covered by a thin layer of cuticle, which is generally rough in texture. The sexes are separate and the individuals lack both lateral cords, which are longitudinal thickened portions of the body wall, and an excretory system. The adults are unique because the straight alimentary tract is degenerate at the anterior and posterior ends and hence is not functional.

MORPHOLOGY

Adult nematomorphs commonly reach 0.5 to 1 meter in length and up to 3 mm. in diameter. Sexual dimorphism exists. The males are shorter than the females, and the posterior end of the male is usually ventrally coiled as in nematode males. Living specimens vary from yellowish to dark brown.

Unlike the nematodes, the body of nematomorphs does not taper at both ends; rather, both ends are blunt and rounded. The anteriormost tip of the body—known as the calotte—is not pigmented and is set off from the rest of the body by a pigmented collar (Plate 14–1, Fig. 2). The mouth is located on the calotte, either terminally or ventrally. The posterior end of the body is often split into two or three lobes, depending on the sex and genus, and the cloacal aperture is located between the lobes or anteroventrad to these (Plate 14–1, Fig. 3).

The cuticle of many nematomorphs is rough. The roughness is due to rounded or polygonal plates—the areoles—arranged on the surface (Plate 14–1, Fig. 4). In some species, the areoles may project as conical papillae bearing bristles (Plate 14–1, Fig. 5), while in others minute pores are present. The interareolar spaces may bear bristles, minute projections, or pores, depending on the species. The function of the areoles remains undetermined, although it is suspected that they are sensory in nature. They represent thickenings of the cuticle.

Body Tissues

When seen in cross section, the body wall consists of three major layers.

(1) The outermost cuticular layer is composed of an outer thin homogeneous layer and an inner stratified fibrous layer (Plate 14–2, Fig. 1). The areoles appear as thickening of the outer homogeneous layer.

(2) Beneath the cuticle is a cellular epidermal layer composed of a single layer of cuboidal to columnar epithelial cells. In members of the order Nectonematoidea, there is a layer of pigment granules embedded between the cuticle and the epidermis. In most nematomorphs, the epidermis is thickened along the midventral body line to form the ventral cord. However, in Nectonematoidea, there are two thickened lines, the midventral ventral cord and the mid-dorsal dorsal cord.

(3) Mediad to the epidermis is the body wall musculature. These muscles, like those in nematodes, are all longitudinally oriented. Again, in all nematomorphs except members of the Nectonematoidea, these muscles are similar to those in acanthocephalans in that the striated portion of contractile fibrils envelop the cytoplasmic portion (Plate 14–2, Fig. 2). In *Nectonema*, the muscles resemble those in nematodes in that there is a slender fibrillar portion and a broadly elongate cytoplasmic portion to each fiber (Plate 14–2, Fig. 3).

Alimentary Tract

Along the middle of the body is found the alimentary tract (Plate 14–2, Fig. 4). The mouth opens on the calotte, and leading from the mouth is a slender pharynx that is not hollow but consists of a cord of cells. This nonfunctional pharynx leads into a mass of cells that presumably represents a pharyngeal bulb. Leading posteriorly from the bulb is the hollow intestine, which is lined with epithelial cells. It has been postulated that since the intestine obviously does not serve a digestive function, it probably is excretory in function.

Posteriorly, the genital ducts empty into the intestine. Immediately after these ducts join the intestine, the tube is enlarged, forming the cloaca, which is lined with cuticle.

The alimentary tract, as described here, is comparable to that found in most nematomorphs. In the Nectonematoidea, however, the tract is somewhat different. In these worms, the mouth leads into a hollow cuticularized tube—the pharynx—which in turn leads into the long intestinal tract. The intestine is composed of two to four large cells that constitute the wall (Plate 14–2, Fig. 5). These cells may be distinct or syncytially arranged. The intestine of the nectonematoids does not extend to the cloaca; rather, it soon becomes indiscrete and fades out. The cloaca in these worms functions as a portion of the reproductive system.

The space between the body wall and the alimentary tract is the pseudocoel. In most nematomorphs this space is packed with mesenchymal (parenchymal) cells so that very little true space is evident. In the Nectonematoidea, however, the pseudocoel is clear and extends from one end of the animal to the other with a septum separating a small chamber anteriorly in the area of the cerebral mass, or brain.

Nervous System

Within the pseudocoel of nematomorphs are embedded the nervous and reproductive systems. The nervous system of these worms has been studied primarily by Montgomery (1903). It consists of a large anteroventral cerebral mass lying within the calotte. Within this mass of ganglia can be found two distinct types of cells—the giant nerve cells and the small nerve cells. The main nerve of the body is the ventral nerve, which lies within the ventral epidermal cord in the nectonematoid species and dorsal to the ventral cord in the other nematomorphs. In the latter case, the main nerve is connected to the epidermal thickening by a thin nervous lamella.

Toward the anterior terminal of the ventral nerve, the single cord is split into three tracts that enter the cerebral mass. It is presumed that these terminate as giant nerve cells. The ventral nerve joins a thickened cloacal ganglion posteriorly (Plate 14–3, Fig. 1). Nerve fibers arising from this ganglion innervate the external reproductive structures.

In *Paragordius,* Montgomery (1903) reported a primitive eye located in the calotte (Plate 14–3, Fig. 2). This eye is sac-like. The cuticle and epidermis of the calotte are modified to form a thin lens. The sac is filled with a gel-like fluid in which are located a number of small fusiform cells that have been interpreted to be retinal cells. The eye is densely innervated by nerve fibers arising from the cerebral mass. Minute nerve fibers branch from the entire length of the ventral nerve, and they innervate the body surface.

A slight modification of the position of the ventral nerve cord is found in members of the Nectonematoidea. In these parasites, the nerve is neither dorsal to nor connected to the ventral cord by the nervous lamella; rather, it is permanently situated in the epidermal thickening.

Reproductive Systems

All nematomorphs are dioecious. The gonads are located in the pseudocoel surrounded by mesenchyme. In males, the two elongate cylindrical testes are situated side by side along the entire length of the body (Plate 14–3, Fig. 3). In certain species, the posteriormost segment of each testis is slightly swollen and is commonly referred to as the seminal vesicle. Each testis empties independently into the cloaca via its own sperm duct.

In females, the ovaries in young individuals are grossly indistinguishable from testes, because they are also in the form of two elongate cylindrical tubes longitudinally arranged in the body. However, in older specimens, a series of 3000 to 4000 diverticula extend laterally from each ovary into the pseudocoel (Plate 14–3, Fig. 4). It has been reported that eggs mature in these side branches before being ejected back into the main tube. The posterior segment of each ovary is known as the uterus and becomes smaller in diameter caudally to become the oviduct. The two oviducts enter the antrum independently.

The antral chamber is lined with glandular epithelium. The antrum may be considered the anterior portion of the cloaca, but it differs from the cloaca proper, because the latter is lined with cuticle. Also arising from the glandular antrum is a slender seminal receptacle, which is directed anteriorly. The cloaca, like that found in males, empties to the exterior through the cloacal aperture located in the midst of the caudal lobes. The histology of the various portions of the genital systems among the nematomorphs is in need of clarification.

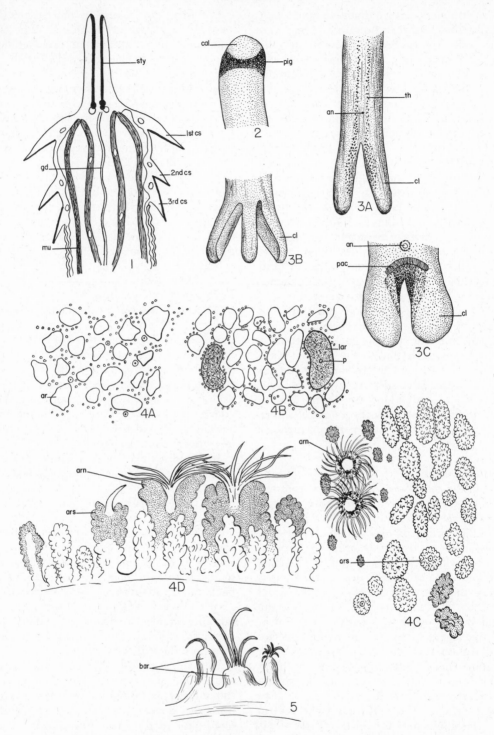

Plate 14-1   Morphology of Nematomorpha. 1. Anterior end of larva of *Paragordius* with armed proboscis protruding. (Redrawn after Montgomery, 1904.) **2.** Anterior end of *Gordius,* showing pigment ring. (Redrawn after Heinze, 1937.) **3. A.** Posterior end of male of *Paragordius.* (Redrawn after May, 1919.) **B.** Posterior end of female of *Paragordius.* (Redrawn after Montgomery, 1898.) **C.** Posterior end of male of *Gordius.* (Redrawn after Heinze, 1937.) **4. A.** Surface view of areoles of *Gordionus.* (Redrawn after Heinze, 1937.) **B.** Surface view of areoles of *Parachordodes.* (Redrawn after Heinze, 1937.) **C.** Surface view of areoles of *Chordodes.* (Redrawn after Camerano, 1897.) **D.** Side view of areoles of *Chordodes.* (Redrawn after Camerano, 1897.) **5.** Side view of
(Legend continued on opposite page.)

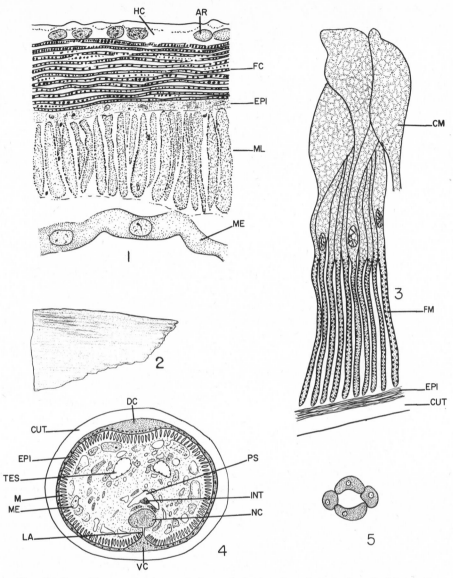

Plate 14-2   Nematomorph morphology. 1. Section through the body wall of *Paragordius.* (Redrawn after Montgomery, 1903.) **2.** Section of a muscle fiber of a nematomorph. **3.** Muscle cells of *Nectonema.* (Redrawn after Rauther, 1914.) **4.** Cross section through *Paragordius.* (Redrawn after Hyman, L. H. 1951. *The Invertebrates,* McGraw-Hill, New York.) **5.** Cross section through intestine of *Nectonema.* (Redrawn after Bürger, 1891.)

(AR, areoles; CM, cytoplasmic portion of muscle cell; CUT, cuticle; DC, dorsal cord; EPI, epidermis; FC, fibrillar layer of cuticle; FM, fibrillar portion of muscle cell; HC, homogeneous layer of cuticle; INT, intestine; LA, lamella connecting nerve cord to ventral cord; M, muscle layer; ME, mesenchyme; ML, muscle layer; NC, nerve cord; PS, pseudocoel surrounding intestine; TES, testis; VC, ventral cord.)

(*Legend continued.*)
nematomorph areoles, showing some with single and others with several bristles. (Redrawn after Müller, 1927.)

(an, anus; ar, areole; arn, areole with numerous bristles; ars, areole with single bristle; bar, bristle-bearing areoles; cal, calotte; cl, caudal lobes; 1st cs, first circlet of spines; 2nd cs, second circlet of spines; 3rd cs, third circlet of spines; gd, gland duct; lar, large areole; mu, muscle; p, pore on large areole; pac, postanal crescent; pig, pigment ring; sty, stylet; th, tracts of thorns.)

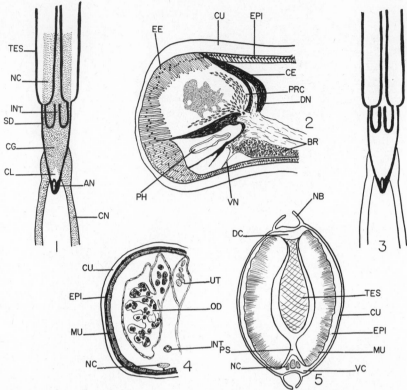

Plate 14-3　　Nematomorph structures. 1. Male reproductive system of *Paragordius*. (Redrawn after Montgomery, 1903.) 2. Section through anterior terminal of *Paragordius,* showing eye and associated structures. (Redrawn after Montgomery, 1903.) 3. Arrangement of testes in nematomorpha. (Modified after Montgomery, 1903.) 4. Section through female *Paragordius,* showing lateral diverticula of ovaries. (Redrawn after Montgomery, 1903.) 5. Section through male *Nectonema*. (Redrawn after Feyel, 1936.)

(AN, anus; BR, brain; CE, capsule of eye; CG, cloacal ganglion; CL, cloaca; CN, caudal nerves extending into caudal lobes; CU, cuticle; DC, dorsal cord; DN, dorsal nerve; EE, altered epidermis of eye; EPI, epidermis, INT, intestine; MU, muscle layer; NB, natatory bristles; NC, nerve cord; OD, ovarian diverticula; PRC, presumed retinal cells; PS, pseudocoel; PH, pharynx; NC, nerve cord; SD, sperm duct; TES, testis; UT, uterus; VC, ventral cord; VN, ventral nerve.)

The reproductive systems described here represent those found in all nematomorphs except for the nectonematoid species. Nectonematoid reproductive systems are not completely understood. Feyel (1936) reported that in male parasitic juvenile nectonematoids there is a single testis suspended from a dorsal epidermal cord (Plate 14-3, Fig. 5), which leads to the exterior dorsally through a tube. In females, no compact ovary is present; rather, there are individual ovocytes that arise through the differentiation of certain mesenchymal cells. These ovocytes originally are attached to the epidermis but soon become free in the pseudocoel. There is a short genital tube at the posterior end of the worm, through which the eggs pass to the exterior. This tube is interpreted to be the vestige of a cloaca.

LIFE CYCLE PATTERN

The Nematomorpha are of interest to parasitologists because they are closely related to the nematodes, but primarily because they spend their developmental period—that is, their larval stages—as parasites of invertebrates. The worm undergoes almost all of its development within an arthropod host. When it emerges, it is identical to the mature adult except that it is not sexually mature, but it soon attains maturity. There appears to be a seasonal preference for emergence, for most species become free-living either in late spring or summer. Sexual maturity ensues immediately and copulation occurs.

Copulation is accomplished by the male coiling its posterior end around the posterior end of the female. The spermatozoa are introduced from the cloacal aperture of the male into that of the female (Plate 14–4, Fig. 1). The spermatozoa ascend the cloaca and are stored in the seminal receptacle. Ova, passing through the glandular antrum, are fertilized, and the eggs are passed to the exterior in strips presumably formed from the secretions of the antrum (Plate 14–4, Fig. 2). Interestingly, the emergence of adults from their hosts always occurs near bodies of water—lakes, ponds, and streams—while the females are generally found along the banks. Males reportedly are capable of swimming.

Larvae enter the arthropod host by direct penetration in some species and through ingestion while in the encysted form in others. The boring ability of certain species is manifested by specialized stylets (Plate 14–1, Fig. 1). Dorier (1925, 1930) stated that the stylet is employed by *Gordius aquaticus,* the larvae of which, after hatching from the eggshell, are capable of secreting a mucous cyst wall around themselves. Certain glands located in the anterior portion of the intestine are believed to secrete the mucus. In the case of *Chordodes japonensis,* Inoue (1958, 1960) reported that the larvae emerge from eggs incubated at $23 \pm 3°$ C. in approximately 30 days. These larvae are not encysted nor do they penetrate the body wall of *Culex* and *Chironomus* larvae and *Cloeon* nymphs, but they are ingested. It is apparent that nematomorph larvae, encysted or nonencysted in water, can reach their anthropod hosts—which include grasshoppers, crickets, beetles, roaches, centipedes, millipedes, and others—only when the host migrates to a location near or is naturally found in the water.

Within the arthropod host, the larvae are situated in the body cavity, where they gradually develop into juveniles. Development does not involve drastic metamorphosis; rather, the larval structures, such as the body cuticle and muscles, gradually become strengthened. During this period of development, such larval structures as the hooks, stylets, and associated muscles degenerate and gradually disappear. In conjunction with the disappearance of these larval structures and the continued growth of other larval structures, certain additional structures, such as the cerebral mass, ventral nerve, and reproductive organs, soon appear in the juvenile and continue to develop.

In the case of *Chordodes japonensis,* Inoue reported that once the larvae are ingested by

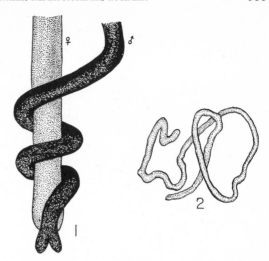

Plate 14-4   Nematomorpha. 1. Male specimen of *Gordius robustus* wrapped around posterior end of female, in copula. (Redrawn after May, 1919.) **2.** Egg string of a nematomorph worm. (Redrawn after Müller, 1927.)

the insect host, they penetrate through the intestinal wall into the coelom and encyst in 2 to 3 days. It is not known why the larvae of this nematomorph should encyst. It is possible that the three species of larval insects used as experimental hosts were unnatural ones, and the cyst walls served to protect the immature parasites from the defense mechanisms of the host. On the other hand, the cyst walls could have been of host origin and served to wall off the invading parasites.

The period of development within the host varies among species. May (1919) reported that in *Paragordius* and *Gordius* the parasitic phase lasts from several weeks to several months.

SYSTEMATICS AND BIOLOGY OF NEMATOMORPHA

CLASSIFICATION

The class Nematomorpha is divided into two orders—the Gordioidea and the Nectonematoidea, which only includes one genus.

ORDER GORDIOIDEA

The Gordioidea includes all the species that possess a ventral epidermal cord only, a ventral nerve that is distinct from the ventral cord and

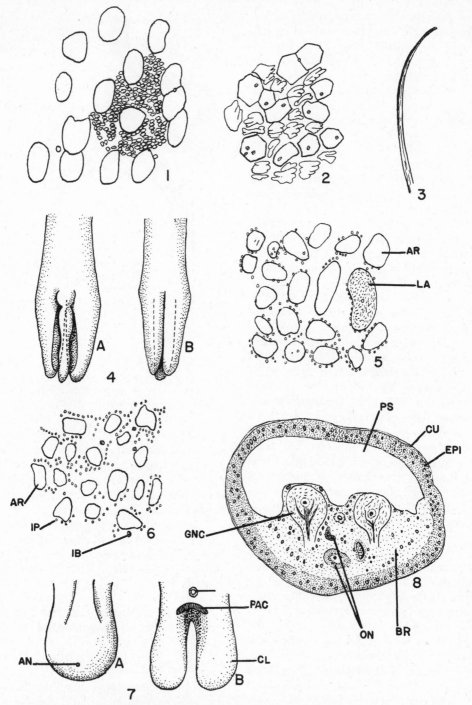

Plate 14-5   Representation genera of Nematomorpha. 1. Surface areoles of *Neochordodes talensis*. (Redrawn after Carvalho, 1942.) **2.** Surface areoles of *Pseudochordodes pardalis*. (Redrawn after Carvalho, 1942.) **3.** Anterior end of *Chordodes*. (Redrawn after Römer, 1896.) **4.** Posterior end of *Paragordius esavianus*. **A.** Female, dorsal view. **B.** Female, ventral view. (Redrawn after Carvalho, 1942.) **5.** Areoles of *Parachordodes*. (Redrawn after Heinze, 1937.) **6.** Areoles of *Gordionus*. (Redrawn after Heinze, 1937.) **7. A.** Posterior terminal of female *Gordius*. **B.** Posterior terminal of male *Gordius*. (A and B redrawn after Heinze, 1937.) **8.** Section through the brain of *Nectonema*. (Redrawn after Feyel, 1936.)

(AN, anus; AR, areole; BR, brain; CL, caudal lobes; CU, cuticle; EPI, epidermis; GNC, giant nerve cell; IB, interareolar bristle; IP, interareolar papillae; LA, large areole with central pore; ON, ordinary nerve cells; PAC, postanal crescent; PS, pseudocoel.)

connected to it by a nervous lamella, a pseudo-coel that is filled with mesenchymal (paren-chymal) cells, paired gonads, and lateral ovar-ian diverticula in sexually mature females.

The taxonomy of the order Gordioidea has been reviewed and revised by Müller (1927), Heinze (1934, 1935, 1937), and Carvalho (1942). The order is subdivided into two fami-lies—the Chordodidae and Gordiidae. A key to these is given below.

1. With conspicuous cuticular
   areoles . . . . **Chordodidae**
2. With inconspicuous cuticular areoles
   or without areoles . . . . **Gordiidae**

FAMILY CHORDODIDAE

The family Chordodidae includes, among others, the genera *Neochordodes, Pseudochordodes, Chordodes, Paragordius, Parachordodes,* and *Gordionus* (Plate 14–5, Figs. 1 to 6).* These genera are distinguished from one another primarily by their morphology, by the number of pos-terior lobes, and by the types of areoles present.

In *Neochordodes,* which is seldom found in the United States, there are no pore canals in the furrows between the areoles, the posterior end is blunt and without lobes, and only one type of areole is present. In *Pseudochordodes,* also little known in the United States, there is no postcloacal crescent shaped fold, the posterior end is bilobed in males, and there are two kinds of areoles present. In *Chordodes* the pos-terior end is not lobed in either sex, and a midventral groove extends the length of the body.

In *Paragordius* the posterior end is bilobed in males as in *Parachordodes.* However, there is only one type of areole, the posterior lobes are two and one half to three times as long as they are wide, and the lobes are not armed with hairs or papillae. Several members of *Paragordius* are known in the United States. In *Parachordo-des,* not commonly found in the United States, the posterior end of the male is also bilobed. These lobes are shorter and broader than those of *Paragordius,* and there are rows of bristles present on the lobes. In *Gordionus,* which is represented by several North American species,

there is only one type of areole. The two pos-terior lobes found on males are approximately twice as long as they are wide, and they are armed with rows of long papillae on either side of the cloacal aperture.

FAMILY GORDIIDAE

Family Gordiidae includes only one genus, *Gordius.* The females possess unlobed posterior ends; the males possess strongly bilobed pos-terior terminals that are not armed with bristles or tubercles (Plate 14–5, Fig. 7). In addition, there is a distinct crescent shaped fold in the postcloacal region.

ORDER NECTONEMATOIDEA

The Nectonematoidea includes the single genus *Nectonema* (Plate 14–5, Fig. 8). The genus, and therefore the order, is character-ized by a hollow pseudocoel that extends along the length of the body, a ventral nerve cord located within the ventral epidermal thicken-ing, a dorsal and a ventral epidermal cord, and a single gonad.

The only species known in the United States is *N. agile,* the males of which are 5 to 20 cm. long and 0.3 to 1 mm. thick; the females are 3 to 6 cm. long. This species is grayish-white, marine and pelagic, and it has been reported off the coast of Newport, Rhode Island, and Woods Hole, Massachusetts. Other known species of *Nectonema* have been listed by Feyel (1936). The juvenile of *N. agile* parasitizes small crustaceans (*Palaemonetes* sp.).

PHYSIOLOGY OF NEMATOMORPHA

Oxygen Requirements

Little is known concerning the physiology of the Nematomorpha. It is known, however, that the adults require an environment abun-dant in oxygen, while the parasitic juveniles live in environments with less oxygen.

Attraction to Water

Various investigators have reported that hosts harboring nematomorphan juveniles actively seek water when the parasites become ready to emerge. Others have postulated that juveniles preparing to leave their hosts can sense the presence of water. The coincidence of the host's nearness to water and the emergence of young

---

*For a key to the genera of Nematomorpha found in the United States, the reader is referred to p. 236 of Professor Robert W. Pennak's Fresh-water Invertebrates of the United States, Ronald Press, New York.

adults must be considered more than a matter of chance.

Male nematomorphs are more active than females, since males do move around on moist banks in a serpentine manner. Some males are active swimmers. Females, on the other hand, are generally nonmotile, or at most only slightly motile.

NEMATOMORPHAN HOST-PARASITE RELATIONSHIPS

Unlike many parasites, nematomorphs generally reveal little host specificity, for a single species can develop in an array of beetles and grasshoppers. Vertebrates have been reported to occasionally serve as hosts for juveniles. This is particularly evident in the case of fishes; however, Carvalho (1942) and others have reported that occasional human infestations do occur. Carvalho reported that in one such instance, a nematomorph was recovered from a patient's urinary passage. Undoubtedly the few known cases of human infestation have originated through drinking water containing larvae or during bathing in larvae-infested water.

Since almost all nematomorphs lack a functional alimentary tract, it is presumed that nutrition is absorbed through the body wall, as in cestodes and acanthocephalans. May (1919) reported that juveniles in hosts are situated in cavities in the host's viscera. These cavities are presumed to have resulted from the digesting of the original tissues by digestive enzymes secreted through the parasite's cuticle. Apparently the destruction of host tissues is not of a sufficient degree to cause any drastic injury.

CLASS ROTIFERA

The rotifers, or wheel animalcules, are almost all free-living, being found in abundance in fresh water, salt water, leaf axils of mosses, and various other niches where moisture is present. The bodies of these aschelminths are more or less cylindrical, and in most species a ciliated disc—the corona—is located at the anterior terminal and a forked foot is located at the posterior terminal. The body wall is comprised of a syncytium covered by a thin cuticular layer.

The digestive tract is complete in some (with a mouth and anus) and incomplete in others (with a mouth but no anus). The excretory system of rotifers is similar to that of platyhelminths, since it consists of flame cells and collecting tubules that empty into vesicles. The nervous system consists of a dorsal ganglic mass, from which nerve fibers arise to innervate the various areas of the body. Some species possess eyespots and sense organs in the form of tuftlike hairs projecting from the body.

Rotifers are dioecious and usually oviparous. Among the free-living species, parthenogenesis has been reported, in addition to sexual reproduction. Development of rotifers is direct—there are no larval stages.

SYSTEMATICS AND BIOLOGY OF THE ROTIFERA

The class Rotifera is usually divided into three orders—Seisonacea, Bdelloidea, and Monogonata. Almost all of the 1300 or more species are free-living. However, members of order Seisonacea—which actually includes only one genus, *Seison*—and a single member of the order Bdelloidea, *Zeilinkiella synaptae,* are symbiotic.

Genus *Seison*

Members of the genus *Seison,* hence of the order Seisonacea, are a small group of marine rotifers ectosymbiotic on the crustacean *Nebalia* in European waters. The unusual external appearance of the bodies of these rotifers is undoubtedly reflective of their adaptation to the symbiotic way of life.

The body, measuring up to 3 mm. in length, is covered by a segmented cuticle. It is divided into a small oval head, a slender and elongate neck, a thicker fusiform trunk, and a stalklike foot that does not bear typical rotiferan toes but terminates in an adhesive disc for attachment (Plate 14–6, Fig. 1). Typical pedal glands secrete into the disc. The corona is also modified, for instead of numerous cilia, only a few tufts of bristles exist.

Both male and female *Seison* are known. In males, which are slightly smaller and less abundant than females, there is a pair of testes, from which a common sperm duct conducts the spermatozoa to two ciliated chambers, the spermatophoral vesicles, in which the sperm are formed into spermatophores

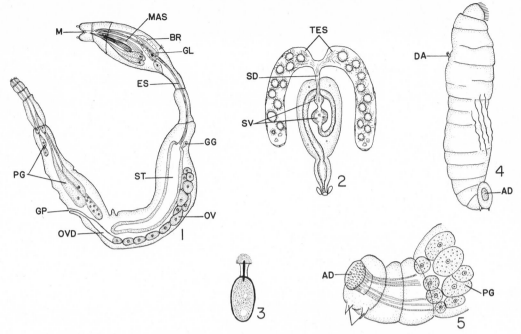

Plate 14-6   Symbiotic Rotifera. 1. Adult female *Seison*. (Redrawn after Plate, 1887.) **2.** Reproductive system in male *Seison*. (Redrawn after Remano, 1929.) **3.** Spermatophore of *Seison*. (Redrawn after Plate, 1887.) **4.** *Zelinkiella synaptae* adult with corona retracted. **5.** Foot of *Zelinkiella*, showing adhesive disc and pedal glands. (Redrawn after Zelinka, 1888.)

(AD, adhesive disc; BR, brain; DA, dorsal antenna; ES, esophagus; GG, gastric gland; GL, gland cell; GP, genital pore; M, mouth; MAS, mastax; OV, ovary; OVD, oviduct; PG, pedal glands; SD, sperm duct; SV, sphermatophoral vesicles; ST, stomach; TES, testes.)

(Plate 14–6, Figs. 2 and 3). The spermatophores are ejected from the male during copulation via the terminal portion of the intestine, which opens on the anterior part of the trunk. In females, there is a pair of ovaries connected with a common oviduct, which in some species opens to the exterior via a genital pore (Plate 14–6, Fig. 1). In others, the oviduct connects with the intestine to form a cloaca, which in turn communicates with the exterior. A female *Seison* produces only one type of egg, and parthenogenesis is not known to occur.

In life, *Seison* moves about the body surface of *Nebalia* in a leechlike manner, alternately attaching its mouth and adhesive disc. It feeds primarily on minute detritus, although it also sucks out the contents of the host's eggs. Because *Seison,* from what is known, does not acquire any nutritional requirements directly from the host, except as a predator of eggs on

occasions, and because it does not engage in any known physiological reciprocity with its host, there is some doubt that it is a true parasite. However, since it is consistently found on *Nebalia* and there are conspicuous morphological adaptations, such as the presence of an adhesive disc instead of toes, and reduced ciliature on the corona, it is suspected that the relationship is one of long standing. The term *phoresis* may be applied to this type relationship, during which the host acts as no more than a passive means of transport.

Genus *Zeilinkiella*

The order Bdelloidea includes a large number of free-living rotifers, including some of the most common species. Only the genus *Zelinkiella* —with only one species, *Z. synaptae*—is symbiotic. *Zelinkiella synaptae* is found living in pits in the skin of sea cucumbers (Plate 14–6, Figs.

4 and 5). As with *Seison*, the typical rotiferan toes are lacking on *Zelinkiella*. Instead, an adhesive disc, on which open the ducts of twelve pedal glands, is present. Nothing is known about the relationship between *Zelin-* *kiella* and its host, although the apparent specificity of this rotifer for sea cucumbers and the modification of its toes as a disc suggest that it is more than a recent or temporary relationship.

LITERATURE CITED

Bondouy, T. 1910. Étude chimique du *Sclerostomum equinum*. Arch. Parasitol., *14:* 5–39.

Carvalho, J. C. M. 1942. Studies on some Gordiacea of North and South America. J. Parasit., *28:* 213–222.

Chitwood, B. G. 1936. Observations on the chemical nature of the cuticle of *Ascaris lumbricoides* var. *suis*. Proc. Helminth. Soc. Wash., *3:* 39–49.

Chitwood, B. G. 1938. Notes on the physiology of *Ascaris lumbricoides*. Proc. Helminth. Soc. Wash., *5:* 18–19.

Dorier, A. 1925. Sur la faculté d'enkystement dans l'eau de la larve du *Gordius aquaticus* L. Compt. Rend. Acad. Sci., *181:* 1098–1099.

Dorier, A. 1930. Recherches biologiques et systématiques sur les gordiaces. Trav. Lab. Hydrobiol. Piscicult. University of Grenoble.

Fauré-Fremiet, E. 1913. Le cycle germinatif chez l'*Ascaris megalocephala*. Arch. Anat. Micro., *15:* 435–578.

Feyel, T. 1936. Recherches histologiques sur *Nectonema agile* Ver. Étude de la forme parasite. Arch. Anat. Micro., *32:* 197–234.

Flury, F. 1912. Zur Chemie und Toxikologie der Ascariden. Arch. Exp. Path. Pharmakol., *67:* 275–392.

Heinze, K. 1934. Zur Systematik der Gordiiden. Zool. Anz., *106:* 189–192.

Heinze, K. 1935. Über das Genus *Parachordodes* Camerano, 1897 nebst allgemeinen Angaben über die Familie Chordidae. Ztschr. Parasitenk., *7:* 657–678.

Heinze, K. 1937. Die Saitenwürmer, (Gordioidea) Deutschlands. Eine systematischfaunische Studie über Insectenparasiten aus der Gruppe der Nematomorpha. Ztschr. Parasitenk., *9:* 263–344.

Horne, G. 1961. Principles of Nematology. McGraw-Hill, New York.

Inoue, I. 1958. Studies on the life history of *Chordodes japonensis*, a species of Gordiacea. I. The development and structure of the larva. Jap. J. Zool., *12:* 203–218.

Inoue, I. 1960. Studies on the life history of *Chordodes japonensis*, a species of Gordiacea. II. On the manner of entry into the aquatic insect-larvae of *Chordodes* larvae. Annot. Zool. Jap., *33:* 132–141.

May, H. G. 1919. Contribution to the life histories of *Gordius robustus* Leidy and *Paragordius varius* (Leidy). Ill. Biol. Monogr., *5:* 1–118.

Montgomery, T. H. 1903. The adult organization of *Paragordius varius* (Leidy). Zool. Jahrb., Abt. Anat., *18:* 387–474.

Müller, G. W. 1927. Über Gordiaceen. Ztschr. Morphol. Oekol. Tiere *7:* 134–218.

Rogers, W. P. 1945. Studies on the nature and properties of the perienteric fluid of *Ascaris lumbricoides*. Parasitology, *36:* 211–218.

Schulz, F. N., and M. Becker. 1933. Über Ascarylalkohol. Biochem. Ztschr., *265:* 253–259.

Smorodintsev, I. A., and K. V. Bebesin. 1936. Beitrage zur Chemie der Helminthen. Mitt. V. Die chemische Zusammensetzung der *Ascaris lumbricoides*. J. Biochem., *23:* 23–25.

Timm, R. W. 1950. Chemical composition of the vitelline membrane of *Ascaris lumbroicoides* var. *suis*. Science, *112:* 167–168.

Toryu, Y. 1933. Contributions to the physiology of the Ascaris. I. Glycogen content of the Ascaris, *Ascaris megalocephala*. Cloq. Sci. Rep. Tohoku Imp. Univ. 4s. (Biol.), *8:* 65–74.

von Brand, T. 1938. Physiological observations on a larval *Eustrongylides* (Nematoda). J. Parasit., *24:* 445–451.

Weinland, E. 1901. Über Kohlenhydratzersetzung ohne Sauerstoffaufnahme bei *Ascaris*, einen tierischen Gärungsprozess. Ztschr. Biol., 42, n.F. *24:* 44–90.

Yoshimura, S. 1930. Beiträge zur Chemie der Askaris. J. Biochem., *12:* 27–34.

SUGGESTED READING

Hyman, L. H. 1951. The Invertebrates: Acanthocephala, Aschelminthes, and Entoprocta. McGraw-Hill, New York, pp. 455–472. (This section in Hyman's treatise discusses the Nematomorpha. The part on microscopic morphology is particularly valuable.)

Hyman, L. H. 1951. The Invertebrates: Acanthocephala, Aschelminthes, and Entoprocta. McGraw-Hill, New York, pp. 59–151. (This section of Hyman's treatise discusses the rotifers. Since the rotifers are almost all free-living, it is only natural that the material included is almost completely concerned with free-living species.)

Pennak, R. W. 1953. Fresh-water Invertebrates of the United States. Ronald Press, New York, pp. 232–239. (In this section of his book, Pennak discusses the Nematomorpha. The taxonomic section is very helpful to those interested in North American fauna.)

15

THE NEMATODA—
The Roundworms
THE APHASMID
NEMATODES

CLASS NEMATODA

The class Nematoda includes free-living as well as parasitic species. Many of the latter species are parasites of plants, while the remaining species parasitize animals. Most free-living nematode species are microscopic, as are parasites that live in the host's body fluids, such as the blood and lymph. Nematodes that live in the host's intestine are generally larger. Within the host, nematodes parasitize the eye, mouth, tongue, stomach, intestinal tract, lungs, liver, and practically every body cavity. Some of these parasitic nematodes are relatively harmless; others can cause some of the most severe diseases of man and beast. It is difficult to estimate how many cases of animal parasitism by nematodes exist. Stoll (1947) estimated that there are some 2 billion human infections.

MORPHOLOGY

The bodies of nematodes are generally elongate and cylindrical, tapering at both ends.

Certain species, such as *Capillaria* sp., possess an almost uniformly cylindrical and extremely thin body. A certain degree of sexual dimorphism exists, for the posterior end of males is commonly armed with special structures, for example, alae and papillae (p. 392)—and is curved ventrally. Very often males are smaller than females.

The various nematode species differ greatly in size. Some species are microscopic; others measure no more than 1 mm. in length; still others, such as the guinea worm *Dracunculus medinensis*, may measure more than a meter in length. Most species are opaque and whitish when examined in the living state, although some may have absorbed some of the coloration of the surrounding host tissues or fluids.

The cuticle of parasitic nematodes is generally smooth. However, various structures such as spines, bristles, warts, punctuations, papillae, striations, and ridges may be present. The arrangements and positions of such structures are of taxonomic importance. For example, the species of *Gnathostoma* possess minute cuticular spines that cover practically the entire body, diminishing in number toward the posterior end; the species of *Cooperia* bear longitudinally ribbed depressions and elevations along the length of the body; and the species of *Gongylonema* possess thickenings known as warts that cover the body surface (Plate 15–1, Fig. 1).

Under the layer of cuticle that covers the nematode body is a thin layer of hypodermis. Mediad to the hypodermis is a relatively thick muscular layer. In between the myofibers are found the dorsal cord at the mid-dorsal position, the ventral cord at the midventral position,

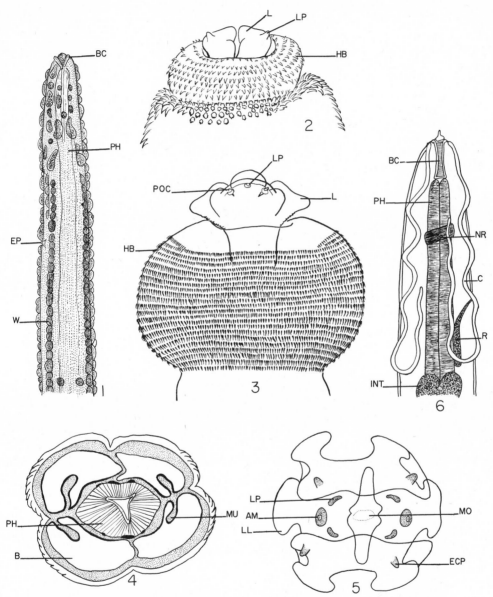

Plate 15-1   Nematode structures. 1. Anterior portion of *Gongylonema*, showing surface structures. (Redrawn after Ward, 1916.) **2.** Anterior end of *Gnathostoma*, showing head bulb. (Redrawn after Baylis and Lane, 1920.) **3.** Head of *Echinocephalus*. (Redrawn after Baylis and Lane, 1920.) **4.** Cross section through the head bulb of *Tanqua*, showing ballonets. (Redrawn after Baylis and Lane, 1920.) **5.** Head-on view of head of *Parabronema*, an intestinal parasite of elephants, showing head shields and cordons. (Redrawn after Baylis, 1921.) **6.** Anterior end of *Dispharynx*, a parasite of birds, showing recurved cordons. (Redrawn after Seurat, 1916.)

(AM, amphid; B, ballonet cavity; BC, buccal capsule; C, cordon; ECP, external circlet of papillae; EP, excretory pore; HB, head bulb; INT, intestine; L, lip; LL, lateral lips; LP, labial papilla; MO, mouth; MU, muscle; NR, nerve ring; PH, pharynx; POC, papilla of outer circlet; R, renette; W, warts.)

and two lateral cords. The pseudocoel separates the muscular layer from the internal organs.

Specialized Structures of the Body Surface

THE MOUTH AND ASSOCIATED SENSE ORGANS. The alimentary tract of nematodes is complete. The mouth is located at the anterior tip of the body.

Lips. In primitive, free-living marine species, the mouth is surrounded by six prominent lips and an array of sensory bristles and papillae. However, in parasitic species, the number of lips usually varies from one to three. It is postulated that in the tri-lipped species, the formation of three lips has resulted from fusion of the six lips found in the more primitive marine forms. If three lips are present, one is dorsal and the remaining two are ventrolateral.

Ballonets and Head Bulb. Various specialized structures and sensory organs may be found on certain species surrounding the perioral lips. For example, among the gnathostomes, there are four cuticular bulbs known as ballonets, which are located immediately posterior to the lips. These four ballonets are adjacent to one another and form a swollen ring known as the head bulb (Plate 15–1, Fig. 2). This structure is armed with spines, the number and arrangement of which are of taxonomic value. In *Gnathostoma,* the head bulb is armed with relatively few circular rows of spines; in *Echinocephalus*, there are numerous rows of minute spines (Plate 15–1, Fig. 3); and in *Tanqua,* transverse striations subdivide the head bulb (Plate 15–1, Fig. 4).

Head Shields. Another type of specialized head organ is the head shield. These shields form a cuticular collar located posterior to the lips. The dorsal and ventral portions of the lips are recurved, shielding the lips (Plate 15–1, Fig. 5). Head shields are generally found in the superfamily Spiruroidea.

The Cordon. A third type of specialized head organ is the cordon. This is a longitudinal cuticular cordlike thickening that varies in number, depending on the particular species (Plate 15–1, Fig. 6).

AMPHIDS. Although not so conspicuous in parasitic nematodes as they are in the free-living species, especially marine species, amphids are present in reduced form on many parasites. These special structures, which are thought to be chemoreceptors, appear as a pair of depressions on each side of the cephalic end, lateral or posteriolateral to the other specialized head structures. The amphids are richly innervated and are often supplied with a gland (Plate 15–2, Fig. 1).

PHASMIDS. Another type of sensory organ is the phasmid. These are minute structures, thought to be olfactory receptors, usually found in pairs, the openings of which are at the terminal minute papillae behind the anus. Again, glands are usually associated with these organs (Plate 15–2, Fig. 2). The presence or absence of phasmids determines whether a particular nematode is a member of the subclass Phasmidia or a member of the Aphasmidia.

ALAE. In addition to the specialized cuticular structures already mentioned, alae are present on certain species. These surface structures appear as compressed ridges, longitudinally oriented. Several types of alae are referred to in describing the species. Those alae situated at the anterior margin of the body are known as cervical alae (Plate 15–3, Fig. 1); those located toward the posterior terminal, normally in males, are known as caudal alae (Plate 15–3, Fig. 2); and those situated along almost the entire length of the body are known as lateral or longitudinal alae. These ridges usually number from one to four, commonly two, and are primarily cuticular extensions.

COPULATORY BURSAE. These are found at the posterior terminal of certain male nematodes—members of the superfamilies Strongyloidea and Dioctophymoidea. These specialized flaplike extensions are commonly subtended by riblike muscular rays (Plate 15–3, Fig. 3). The function of the bursa is to enable the male to grasp and envelop the female during copulation. The bursae of strongyloids are strictly cuticular extensions, while those of dioctophymoids are formed from the flattening of the entire posterior portion of the body.

Alimentary Tract

BUCCAL CAPSULE. The mouth opens into the buccal capsule, which is a strongly cuticularized chamber lined, in a number of species, with ridges, rods, and plates, all serving to maintain the shape of the chamber. Buccal capsules are not present in all nematodes. The filarioids (p. 447), for example, possess almost nonexistent cavities. In rhabditoids (p. 415), the buccal capsule is divided into three sections —the anterior vestibule, the cheilostome; the middle protostome, which is the longest; and the posterior small telostome. The buccal capsule is armed with spears, stylets, or teeth in several species. For example, in the hook-

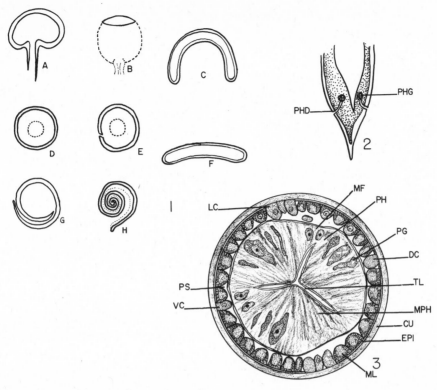

Plate 15-2   **Nematode morphology.** 1. Types of amphids. **A.** *Plectus.* **B.** Cyathiform.
C. Chromadoroidea. **D.** Circular type. **E.** Variant of circular type; **F.** Chromadoroidea.
G. Variant of spiral type. **H.** Spiral type. (A to H redrawn after Stekhoven and de Coninck, 1933.)
2. Posterior section of *Rhabditis,* showing phasmids. (PHD, duct of phasmid; PHG, gland of
phasmid.) (Redrawn after Chitwood, 1930.) **3.** Cross section through level of esophagus of a nematode, showing histology. (CU, cuticle; DC, dorsal cord; EPI, epidermis; LC, lateral cord; MF,
marginal fibers; ML, muscle layer; MPH, muscle fibers of esophagus (pharynx); PG, sections of
esophageal glands; PH, esophagus (pharynx); PS, pseudocoel; TL, triradiate lumen; VC, ventral
cord.) (Redrawn after Chitwood, 1931.)

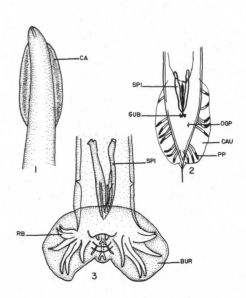

Plate 15-3   **Nematode structures.** 1.
Anterior end of nematode with cervical alae
(CA). **2.** Posterior end of *Rhabditis maupasi*
with caudal alae and pedunculated papillae.
(Redrawn after Stekhoven and Teunissen,
1938.) **3.** Posterior end of male hookworm,
showing copulatory bursa.

(BUR, copulatory bursa; CAU, caudal
alae; GUB, gubernaculum; OGP, ordinary
genital papillae; PP, pedunculated papillae;
RB, muscular rays of bursa; SPI, spicules.)

worms *Ancylostoma duodenale* and *Necator americanus,* two lateral cutting plates are present, each one armed with three teeth (also known as hooks).

THE ESOPHAGUS. The buccal capsule leads into the esophagus,* which is an elongate structure enveloped by a membranous wall. The lumen of the esophagus is characteristically triradiate when seen in cross section (Plate 15–2, Fig. 3).

Within the membranous sheath of the esophagus is a thick muscular layer surrounding the lumen. Three branched esophageal glands are embedded between the muscle fibers—one dorsal and two ventrolateral. These glands empty into the esophagus, and their secretions are emptied from there into the buccal capsule.

The esophagus commonly includes bulbs that appear as swellings. If the bulb is situated at the posterior terminal of the esophagus, it is referred to as an end bulb;† if it is located along the midlength of the esophagus, it is known as a median bulb. Distinction is made between a true bulb and a pseudobulb. The bulbous chamber of the true bulb is separated

*The esophagus of nematodes is sometimes referred to as the pharynx; however, the former term is the more commonly used among nematologists.

†The terms cardiac bulb and posterior bulb also refer to the end bulb.

from the lumen of the esophagus by sclerotized valves that regulate the aperture of the opening into the bulb. No such valves exist between a pseudobulb and the esophagus proper. In members of the superfamilies Filarioidea and Spiruroidea, the esophagus is muscular only anteriorly, being glandular posteriorly. Among certain ascaroids, such as *Porrocaecum* (Plate 15–4, Fig. 1), a diverticulum known as the esophageal caecum arises from the esophagus. In other genera more than one esophageal caecum may be present.

THE INTESTINE. The esophagus empties into the intestine. The junction of esophagus and intestine is referred to as the esophagointestinal valve. The intestine of nematodes is a straight tube lined with a single layer of cuboidal or columnar epithelium. In some genera, such as *Contracaecum* (Plate 15–4, Fig. 2), a hollow intestinal caecum arises as a diverticulum from the anterior portion of the intestine. The cell lining the intestine are unusual in that each cell possesses a brush border of parallel rod (Plate 15–4, Fig. 3). The epithelial cells are typically uninucleate; however, those found in some strongyloids are multinucleate.

THE RECTUM. The intestine empties into the rectum, which is a short, flattened tube joining the intestine and the anus. In most parasitic nematodes there are a number of unicellular rectal glands—three in females, six

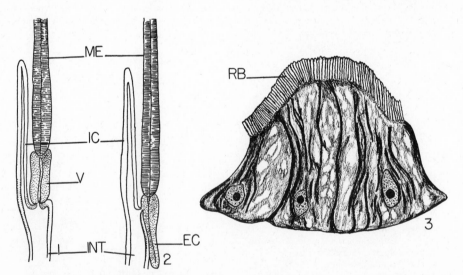

Plate 15-4   Nematode structures. 1. Alimentary tract of *Porrocaecum,* showing lateral intestinal caecum. **2.** Alimentary tract of *Contracaecum,* showing lateral intestinal caecum. (1 and 2 redrawn after Baylis, 1920.) **3.** Cross section through segment of nematode intestine. (Redrawn after Chitwood, 1931.)

(EC, esophageal caecum; IC, intestinal caecum; INT, intestine; ME, muscular portion of esophagus; RB, rod borders of intestinal epithelium; V, ventriculus.)

n males—which empty into the rectum. The rectum is lined with a thin layer of cuticle enveloped by a layer of large epithelial cells that in turn is covered by muscle cells.

The Anus. The alimentary tract opens posteriorly through the anus, located on the ventral body surface near the posterior tip. In females of the guinea worm, *Dracunculus medinensis,* the anus is lacking.

Nervous System

The nervous system consists of a circumenteric ring, composed primarily of nerve fibers, and a few ganglia, that surround the esophagus. Connected to this ring are a number of ganglia that are also connected to each other by commissures. Six nerves extend anteriorly from the circumenteric ring—two ventrolateral, two lateral, and two dorsolateral. These six fibers and their branches innervate the various structures and tissues in the anterior portion of the body. A mid-dorsal nerve, a midventral nerve, and one to three pairs of lateral nerves are directed posteriorly (Plate 15–5, Fig. 1). These nerves and their branches innervate the various structures and tissues posterior to the nerve ring. In *Ascaris* and certain other genera, a number of commissures join the ventral nerve with the lateral nerves (Plate 15–5, Fig. 2). Many of the branches of the main anteriorly and posteriorly directed nerves terminate as free endings and are sensory in nature.

Excretory System

The excretory system of nematodes, when present, is unique and not comparable to excretory systems of other aschelminths, nor is it like the protonephritic system found in platyhelminths. Each worm is provided with either a single renette or a pair of renettes. A renette is a large gland cell that empties to the outside through the excretory pore, which is generally located anteriorly at the level of the circumenteric nerve ring, or slightly anterior to or posterior to that level (Plate 15–5, Fig. 3). In some genera, such as *Ancylostoma* and *Oesophagostomum,* there is a tubular extension from the renette. In *Ancylostoma,* the tubular extension arises directly from the renette (Plate 15–5, Fig. 4); in *Oesophagostomum,* the canal is lateral to the renette and embedded in the lateral line of the body wall. In the latter case, the canal is joined to the renette by a short duct (Plate 15–5, Fig. 5). The renettes may empty independently to the exterior through the excretory pore, as in *Rhabdias* (Plate 15–5, Fig. 6), or the two renettes may join to form an H. The crossbar of the H is connected with a common contractile ampulla, which in turn expels the excreta by a pulsatory motion through the excretory pore via a common stem. This pattern is found in *Ancylostoma* (Plate 15–5, Fig. 4). The two renettes may also join anteriorly, in which case the excreta is emptied into a common stem leading into the excretory pore. This pattern is found in *Oesophagostomum* (Plate 15–5, Fig. 5).

The renette and associated tubes serve as absorptive bodies that collect wastes found in the pseudocoel. An excretory system is not present in all parasitic nematodes; for example, members of the superfamilies Trichuroidea and Dioctophymoidea lack an excretory system in their adult stage. However, a system similar to that found in *Oesophagostomum* is present in the larvae.

Reproductive System

Nematodes are, as a rule, dioecious animals. The males generally can be distinguished externally from the females by their smaller size, curved posterior ends, and the presence of bursae and other accessory reproductive structures. Although protandric hermaphroditism is found in certain free-living nematodes, true intersexual fertilization is the rule among the parasitic species. However, monoecious species are known that may be either parthenogenic or self-fertilizing hermaphrodites.

The Male System. In males, there is generally a single testis; diorchic forms, however, are not uncommon. The testis is tubular and usually convoluted and/or recurved (Plate 15–6, Fig. 1). Two types of testes are recognized among nematodes—the telogonic type, in which the proliferation of germ cells occurs only at the blind end of the elongate testis; and the hologonic type, found in members of the superfamilies Dioctophymoidea and Trichuroidea, and in which germ cell proliferation occurs along the entire length of the testis.

Ascaris lumbricoides, the common intestinal nematode of pigs and man, is a very popular animal in cytological studies, because the various stages of gametogenesis can be readily found in sequence along the telogonic testis. The slender vas deferens (sperm duct) is continuous with the proximal end of the testis. The vas deferens is directed posteriorly and

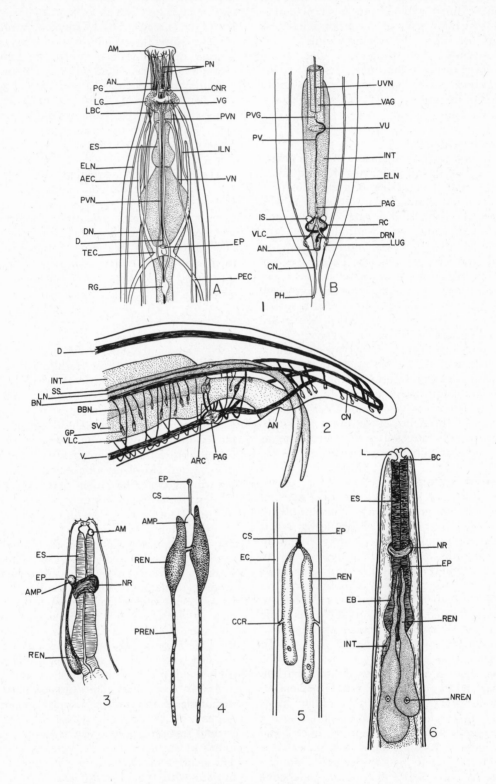

Plate 15-5   See legend on opposite page.

swells toward its terminal to form the seminal vesicle. The wall of the seminal vesicle includes muscle fibers. This vesicle leads into the rectum through a muscular ejaculatory duct (Plate 15–6, Fig. 2). In certain species, unicellular prostate glands are found along the length of the ejaculatory duct, and these glands empty into the duct.

Male nematodes are commonly armed with one or two copulatory spicules, the latter being far more common. These cuticular structures, which most commonly resemble slightly curved, pointed blades, are inserted within their respective spicule pouches located as side pockets in the rectal (commonly referred to as cloacal) wall. Each spicule is comprised of a cytoplasmic core and is secreted by the cells lining the spicule pouch.

In addition to spicules, a sclerotized gubernaculum is present in some species. This structure is located along the dorsal wall of the spicule pouch and commonly has incurved margins (Plate 15–6, Fig. 3). The gubernaculum serves as a guide along which the spicules can follow when they are extended. In some members of the superfamily Strongyloidea, another structure—the telamon—is found. It is a partially sclerotized double-bent structure. Each of its two arms subtend the lateral walls of the cloaca, and the medial section subtends the ventral wall of the cloaca (Plate 15–6, Fig. 4). The telamon also serves as a guide for the copulatory spicules when they are extended. The movement of the spicules is controlled by certain muscle bands. The shapes, sizes, and number of copulatory spicules and their auxiliary structures are of taxonomic importance. Copulatory spicules are lacking in some nematodes such as the pork worm, *Trichinella spiralis*.

THE FEMALE SYSTEM. The female reproductive system usually comprises two ovaries (didelphic), which extend in opposing directions—one anteriorly and one posteriorly (Plate 15–7, Fig. 1). In a few species, only one ovary is present (monodelphic) and extends either anteriorly or posteriorly, depending on the species. The ovaries appear as straight, convoluted, or much folded tubes.

An oviduct, lined with columnar epithelium, is continuous with the proximal terminal of each ovary. At the proximal terminal of each oviduct is a slightly swollen chamber—the seminal receptacle—which connects the oviduct to the tubular uterus. The two uteri, one associated with each ovary, join in the area of the female gonopore to form the vagina, which in turn opens to the exterior through the gonopore.

The gonopore is generally located along the midventral line in the middle one-third of the body. However, it may be more anteriorly or posteriorly located, depending on the species. In certain members of the superfamilies Strongyloidea and Spiruroidea, the vagina is highly muscular and ejects eggs through muscular contraction and distention. A vagina that functions in this manner is called an ovijector. Its histology and function are comparable to those of the metraterm found in certain flatworms.

FERTILIZATION. In parasitic nematodes, copulation between a female and a male as a rule is necessary for fertilization, except in the genus *Strongyloides* (p. 419). During copulation,

---

Plate 15-5   Nervous and excretory systems of nematodes. 1. A. Nervous system in anterior portion of *Cephalobellus*. **B.** Nervous system in posterior portion of same species. (A and B redrawn after Chitwood and Chitwood, 1933.) **2.** Nervous system present in posterior region of *Ascaris*. (Redrawn after Hesse, 1892.) **3.** Anterior end of *Linhomeus* showing excretory system. (Redrawn after Kreis, 1929.) **4.** Excretory system in larva of *Ancylostoma* with posterior canals developing from renette cells. (Redrawn after Stekhoven, 1927.) **5.** Excretory system in *Oesophagostomum* showing lateral connections of renettes to excretory canals. (Redrawn after Chitwood, 1931.) **6.** Excretory system in *Rhabdias* showing two-celled renette. (Redrawn after Stekhoven, 1927.)

(AEC, anterior excretory canal; AM, amphid; AMP, contractile ampula; AN, anus; ARC, anorectal connectives; BBN, branch of bursal nerve; BC, buccal capsule; BN, bursal nerve; CCR, connection between renette and excretory canal; CN, caudal nerve; CNR, circumcentric nerve ring; CS, common stem; D, dorsal nerve; DN, dorsal lateral nerve; DRN, dorsorectal nerve; EB, esophageal bulb; EC, excretory canal; ELN, external lateral nerve; EP, excretory pore; ES, esophagus; GP, genital papilla; ILN, internal lateral nerve; INT, intestine; IS, intestinorectal sphincter; L, lips; LBC, lateroventral brain connective; LG, lateral ganglion; LN, lateral nerve; LUG, lumbar ganglia; NR, nerve ring; NREN, nucleus of renette cell; PAG, preanal ganglion, PEC, posterior excretory canal; PG, papillary ganglion; PH, phasmid; PREN, posterior extension of renette cell; PVN, paired ventral nerves; RC, rectal commissure; REN, renette cell; RG, retrovesicular ganglion; SS, spicule sheath; SV, seminal vesicle; TEC, transverse excretory canal.)

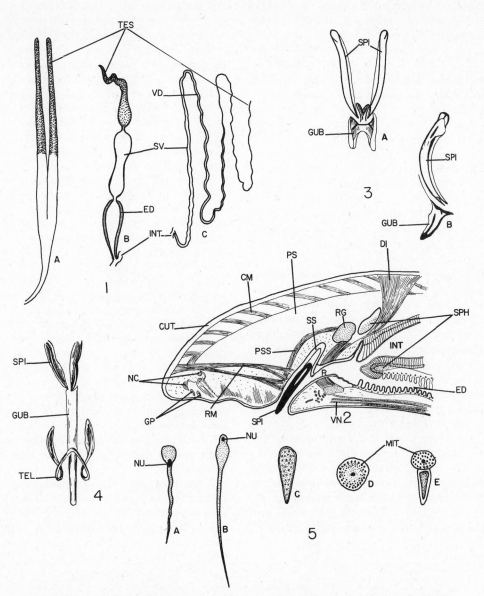

Plate 15-6   Reproductive structures of nematodes. 1. A. Male reproductive system of *Heterodera marioni* with two parallel testes (diorchic). (Redrawn after Atkinson, 1889.) **B.** Male system of *Camallanus* with one anterior testis (monorchic). (Redrawn after Törnquist, 1931.) **C.** Male system of *Ascaris* with single long coiled testis and duct. (Redrawn after Hyman, L. H. 1951. *The Invertebrates,* McGraw-Hill, New York.) **2.** Sagittal section through posterior end of *Ascaris,* showing relationship of spicules to rectum. (Redrawn after Voltzenlogel, 1902.) **3. A.** Spicules and gubernaculum of a chromadoroid nematode. **B.** Side view of same. (A and B redrawn after de Man, 1907.) **4.** Male reproductive armature of a trichostrongyloid nematode. (Redrawn after Hall, 1921.) **5. A.** Sperm of *Passalurus.* (Redrawn after Meves, 1920.) **B.** Sperm of *Trilobus.* (Redrawn after Chitwood, 1931.) **C.** Sperm of *Thoracostoma.* (Redrawn after de Man, 1888.) **D.** Sperm of *Anaplostoma.* (Redrawn after de Man, 1907.) **E.** Sperm of *Parascaris equorum.* (Redrawn after Hyman, L. H. 1951. *The Invertebrates,* McGraw-Hill, New York.)

(CM, copulatory muscles; CUT, cuticle; DI, dilator of intestine; ED, ejaculatory duct; GP, genital papillae; GUB, gubernaculum; INT, intestine; MIT, mitochondria; NC, nerve cells; NU, nucleus; PS, pseudocoel; PSS, protractor of spicule sheath; R, rectum; RG, rectal gland; RM, retractor muscle; SPH, sphincters; SPI, spicule; SS, spicule sheath; SV, seminal vesicle; TEL, telamon; TES, testis; VD, vas deferens; VN, ventral nerve.)

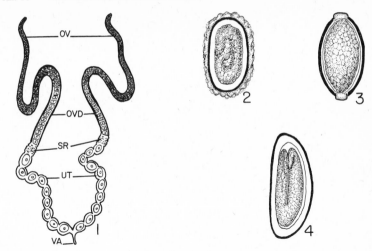

Plate 15-7   Female reproductive system and eggs of
nematodes. 1. Female system of
Heterodera. (OV, ovary; OVD,
oviduct; SR, seminal receptacle;
UT, uterus; VA, vagina.) (Redrawn after Magakura, 1930.) 2.
Fertilized egg of *Ascaris lumbricoides*
with outer albuminous coat. (Original.) 3. Egg of *Trichuris trichiura*
with two polar plugs. (Original.)
4. Egg of *Enterobius vermicularis,*
enclosing larva. (Original.)

the spicules of the male are guided by the various
auxiliary structures—for example, the gubernaculum and the telamon—and are inserted
into the gonopore of the female. The spermatozoa, which are elongate, conical, or spherical,
and without a flagellated tail, are capable of
amoeboid movement (Plate 15–6, Fig. 5). They
migrate up the vagina and uteri and are lodged
in the seminal receptacle, where fertilization
occurs.

THE EGG.   The entire sperm enters the
ovum (ovocyte), and a fertilization membrane
is secreted by the cell soon after the sperm
enters. This membrane gradually increases in
thickness to form the chitinous shell. A second
membrane, commonly referred to as the vitelline
membrane, is secreted by the zygote within the
shell. This membrane is lipoid in nature. As
the egg passes down the uterus, a third proteinaceous membrane is secreted by the uterine wall
and deposited outside the shell. This third
membrane is rough in texture (Plate 15–7,
Fig. 2) and is absent from the eggs of some
species, such as the human whipworm, *Trichuris
trichiura* (Plate 15–7, Fig. 3).

Commonly the eggs of nematodes parasitic
in animals are laid by the females and pass
from the host in feces. These eggs, depending
on the species, may still contain the uncleaved
zygote, a group of blastomeres, or even a completely formed larva, as in the human pinworm,
Enterobius vermicularis (Plate 15–7, Fig. 4). In
species parasitic to plants, the eggs are deposited
either in soil or in plant cells. They may also
be accumulated in the body of the parent;
eventually the body of the parent worm dries
up and its tissues form a cyst wall surrounding
the eggs.

Body Tissues

CUTICLE.   The body surface of nematodes is
covered by a thin layer of noncellular cuticle
(Plate 15–8, Fig. 1). This layer is divided into
three strata: (1) the dense cortical layer composed of a keratin-like material that is resistant
to digestion; (2) the middle matrix layer, which
appears as a spongy stratum that Chitwood
(1936) reported to be composed of sulfur-rich
matricin; and (3) the innermost fibrous layer
composed of two to three layers of fibrous
connective tissue in which the fibers in each
layer are oriented in a different direction. The
chemical composition of the fibers is primarily
collagen. A basement membrane is found
mediad to the cuticle.

HYPODERMIS.   Beneath the basement membrane is the hypodermis (sometimes referred
to as the epidermis). This comparatively thick
layer is either distinctly cellular or appears as
a syncytium. Four longitudinal thickenings of
the hypodermis—one mid-dorsal, one midventral, and two lateral—form the longitudinal
cords. The two lateral cords are the most
prominent and in most species can be seen on
the outside of the body as lateral lines. The
nuclei of the hypodermis are located in the
region of these hypodermal thickenings.

MUSCLES.   The muscles of the body wall are
all longitudinally oriented and lie beneath the
hypodermis. Since the four hypodermal cords
separate the body wall into four quadrants
when seen in cross section, the muscle fibers
are distinctly separated into four zones (Plate
15–8, Fig. 2). When examined in cross section,
each myofiber is composed of a heavily fibrous
zone that lies adjacent to the hypodermis, and
a less fibrous cytoplasmic zone that lies along

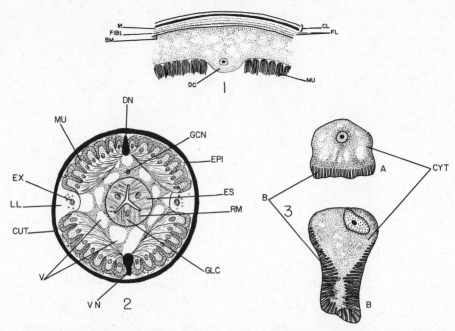

Plate 15-8   Histology of nematodes. 1. Cross section through portion of body wall of a nematode, showing various strata. (Original.) **2.** Cross section through level of esophagus of *Ascaris*. (Redrawn after Hegner, 1933.) **3. A.** Platymyarian type of muscle cell. **B.** Coelomyarian type of muscle cell. (A and B redrawn after Chitwood, 1931.)

(B, band portion of muscle cell; BM, basement membrane; CL, cortical layer; CUT, cuticle; CYT, cytoplasmic portion of muscle cell; DC, dorsal cord; DN, dorsal nerve; EPI, epidermis; ES, esophagus; EX, excretory canal; FL, fibrillar layer; FIBL, fiber layer; GCN, giant cell nucleus; GLC, gland cell; LL, lateral line; M, matrix; MU, muscles; RM, radial muscles; V, vacuoles; VN, ventral nerve.)

the medial side (Plate 15–8, Fig. 3). The pseudocoel occupies the space between the longitudinal muscles and the alimentary tract.

LIFE CYCLE STUDIES

The detailed representative life cycle patterns of various parasitic nematodes are given under the various taxa listed below. However, it appears appropriate to discuss some of the generalized life history patterns found among the parasites of plants and animals. Table 15–1 depicts some of the life cycle patterns found among superfamilies that include economically important species.

The parasitic nature of nematodes varies in degrees from accidental parasitism during the larval or adult stages to obligatory parasitism. The following categorization of the degrees of parasitism may be helpful in understanding the progression of host-parasite relationships among the Nematoda.

I. Nonparasitic Direct Cycle.
  A. Completely Free-living. Free-living nematodes usually lay their eggs in water or in soil. The developing larvae undergo several molts with little morphological change and eventually mature into adults. This pattern represents a direct life cycle without the utilization of hosts, definitive or intermediate.
  B. External Feeding. Certain free-living nematodes, while in the larval form, pierce and feed on plant juices and sap. However, the worms never enter plant tissue. This form of life might well be considered the twilight zone between the free-living and ectoparasitic states.
II. Partial Parasitic Cycle.
  A. In the Larval Form.
    1. Host Utilized for Transport. Certain free-living nematodes require a phase of parasitic existence during their life cycle. This parasitic phase occurs during the larval stages, at which time the worms penetrate and

Table 15-1.   Life History Patterns of Some Major Groups of Parasitic Nematodes

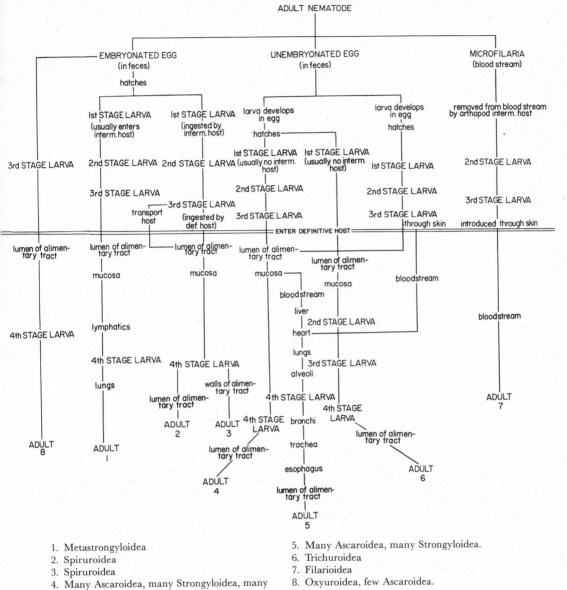

1. Metastrongyloidea
2. Spiruroidea
3. Spiruroidea
4. Many Ascaroidea, many Strongyloidea, many Trichostrongyloidea.

5. Many Ascaroidea, many Strongyloidea.
6. Trichuroidea
7. Filarioidea
8. Oxyuroidea, few Ascaroidea.

become ensheathed in insects and depend on the host to carry them to more favorable climes. An example of this type of relationship is the larva of *Agamermis decaudata,* parasitic in grasshoppers. (Plate 15–9, Fig. 1).

2. Host Utilized for Food. In another form of host-parasite relationship, the larval nematode infects an invertebrate host. The host does not serve as a transport host; rather, the nematode larva lives, ensheathed or not ensheathed, within the invertebrate and remains in a quiescent condition until the host dies. At that time, the worm actively feeds on the carcass of the host.

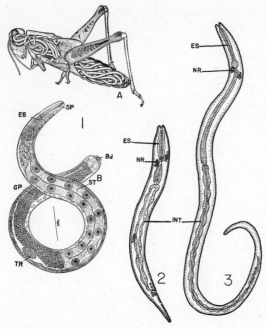

Plate 15-9   Nematoda. 1. A. Larvae of *Agamermis decaudata* in grasshopper. **B.** Larva of *Agamermis decaudata* after 6 days in host. (After Christie, 1936.) **2.** Rhabditiform larva. **3.** Filariform larva.

[BJ, breaking joint; ES, esophagus; GP, genital primordium; INT, intestine; NR, nerve ring; SP, spear; ST, stichosome; TR, trophosome (intestine).]

3. Host Utilized as Site for Partial Development. Among certain free-living nematodes, the normal cycle is of the nonparasitic direct type. Occasionally, however, larvae become parasitic in an invertebrate host when infective eggs or ensheathed larvae are ingested. Within the host, the larvae undergo development and eventually escape as adults. Such a nematode generally undergoes several generations as a nonparasite before reverting to the parasitic phase. This type of occasional parasitism is characteristic of the Mermithidae.

B. In the Adult Form. Females only. Nematodes belonging to this category are free-living in soil during their larval stages. On reaching sexual maturity, males and females copulate. The males perish after mating, while the females penetrate an invertebrate host, in which they produce a new generation of larvae that escape and become free-living.

C. In Alternately Parasitic and Free-living Adults. This type of alternating life cycle is best exemplified by *Strongyloides stercoralis,* an intestinal parasite of man and other primates. The free-living adults are smaller than the parasitic forms. The males and females copulate, and zygotes found inside the resulting eggs often develop so rapidly that they hatch prior to the laying of the eggs. Hence, these nematodes are ovoviviparous. These larvae, known as rhabditiform larvae, molt and increase in size to become infective filariform larvae. Such larvae enter the host, either through penetration or orally, and develop into parasitic males and females. After the parasitic adults copulate, the females lay eggs that hatch into rhabditiform larvae, which pass out of the host and develop into free-living males and females. Variations to this cycle are discussed on page 419.

III. Total Parasitism.

A. One Host.

1. Larvae Penetrate Host. In many nematode parasites of plants and animals, the entire life span is spent as endoparasites. In some endoparasites, the eggs are released or passed out of the host. When these hatch, the young larvae actively bore into the host and become dependent on the host throughout the remainder of their lives. Plant parasites belonging to the genus *Heterodera* are included in this category, as are certain parasites of animals.

2. Eggs Ingested by Host. *Enterobius vermicularis,* the common human pinworm, belongs in this category. The eggs are laid outside the host when gravid females expose their gonopores to the exterior to oviposit. Eggs containing larvae are ingested by the host, thus establishing the infection. The entire life span of the worm is spent as an endoparasite.

3. Continuous Existence in Host. Very few nematodes are capable of living continuously in a host without spending some phase of the life

cycle, even as eggs, outside the host. Most worms belonging to this category are parasites of invertebrates. However, *Probstmayria vivipara,* an oxyurid found in the large intestine of horses, apparently is capable of this type of cycle. *Ollulanus tricuspis,* a stomach-dwelling species in members of the cat family, is also capable of this type of cycle. In these instances, the females are ovoviviparous, giving birth to larvae instead of eggs.

B. Multiple Hosts.
   1. One Intermediate Host. Nematodes included in this category possess infective larvae that are ingested by or penetrate an invertebrate host in which they continue to develop. However, these larvae do not reach sexual maturity until they gain entrance to the definitive host, be it a plant or animal. *Angiostrongylus cantonensis,* the rat lungworm, belongs in this category. During its life cycle, first stage larvae, hatching from eggs deposited in the rodent host's lungs, migrate up the bronchioles, bronchi, and tracheae, and are swallowed. These pass to the exterior in the host's feces. These first stage larvae enter the invertebrate intermediate host, a mollusc, either by ingestion or by penetration. Within the mollusc, the larvae are found embedded primarily in the foot musculature, where they undergo two molts. When molluscs harboring third stage larvae are ingested by the rodent host, they migrate to the brain, undergo two more molts and become young adults. These adults migrate to the host's lungs, primarily in the pulmonary arteries, where they mature (p. 437).
   2. Two Intermediate Hosts. Nematodes of this category are exemplified by *Gnathostoma.* During its life history, this worm utilizes *Cyclops* as the first intermediate host. When the arthropod is ingested by a fish, frog, or snake, one of the latter serves as the second intermediate host. Finally, when the infected fish, frog, or snake is ingested by a carnivorous mammal, the nematode reaches the definitive host.

It should be apparent that the life cycles of nematodes do not involve asexual reproduction in the larval stages, as found in digenetic trematodes and some cestodes.

LARVAL FORMS

All parasitic nematodes generally undergo four molts (ecdysis) during their life cycles. All the forms prior to the final molt are commonly referred to as first, second, third, or fourth stage larvae. Various designations have been assigned to the larval forms of nematodes.

RHABDITIFORM LARVA.   The first stage larva of such parasitic species as *Strongyloides stercoralis* and *Necator americanus* is known as a rhabditiform larva. These small larvae possess an esophagus that is joined to a terminal esophageal bulb by a narrow isthmus (Plate 15–9, Fig. 2).

FILARIFORM LARVA.   After molting, rhabditiform larvae become filariform larvae. (Plate 15–9, Fig. 3). The esophagus in the filariform larva is typically elongate, cylindrical, and without a terminal bulb. This is the infective larval form.

MICROFILARIA.   The youngest larvae of nematodes belonging to the superfamily Filarioidea—for example, *Wuchereria bancrofti* and *Loa loa*—are known as microfilariae. These larvae (which are discussed in greater detail on page 447) are actually embryos, rather than fully developed larvae. The body surface is covered by a thin layer of flattened epidermal cells. Within the pseudocoel are found the primordia of various adult structures. A cord of cytoplasm containing nuclei is quite conspicuous, extending the length of the body. This represents the anlagen of the alimentary canal. In addition to this cord, there are: (1) a dash at the anterior tip of the body that is claimed by most parasitologists to represent the beginning of the mouth; (2) a developing nerve ring; (3) a V shaped invagination that represents the future excretory pore; (4) a renette cell; (5) the so-called G cells, which eventually develop into a portion of the gut; and (6) a tail spot in the posterior region that represents the developing anus. Microfilariae are generally found in circulating blood and are extremely small, usually measuring between 0.2 and 0.4 mm. in length.

Systematics and Biology

CLASSIFICATION

The taxonomy of the Nematoda is in a great degree of flux. As a result of isolated interests of soil and plant nematologists and of animal parasitologists, two divorced systems of classification were in use for many years. It is only recently, primarily through the efforts of Dr. Filipjev in Russia, and Dr. B. G. and Mrs. M. B. Chitwood in the United States, that plant nematologists have begun to compare notes with animal parasitologists, and a more natural system of classification has started to evolve.

Several volumes are available for those interested in the identification of parasitic nematodes. The parasites of vertebrates were catalogued by Yorke and Maplestone (1926). More recently, Yamaguti (1962) has published his definitive treatise on the nematode parasites of vertebrates. For those interested in the identification of species parasitic in domestic animals, the manual of Morgan and Hawkins (1949) is most helpful.

No comprehensive volume is yet available for the parasites of plants, but recently Sasser and Jenkins (1960) edited a volume on nematology that is primarily concerned with species parasitic on plants. Furthermore, Horne (1961) has contributed an introductory text to plant nematodes.

In the description of nematodes, various systems have been devised to express morphological characteristics—for example dimensions and ratios—in terms of symbols. The system advocated by de Man is currently the most widely used. According to this method, various body dimensions are given in millimeters or microns and followed by a series of ratios. The following is a list of symbols designating the various ratios.

a (α) = body length/greatest body width
b (β) = body length/distance of esophagus from anterior tip.
c (γ) = body length/distance from anus to tip of tail.
V = distance of vulva from anterior end as a per cent of total body length.

G_1 = length of anterior gonad as a per cent of body length.
G_2 = length of posterior gonad as a per cent of body length.

Taxa of the class Nematoda that include animal parasites are divided into 11 super-families.* A listing of these together with a short diagnosis of each follows.

Subclass Aphasmidia. Phasmids are absent. Excretory system is poorly developed or absent. mesenterial tissue is well developed.
  Superfamily Trichuroidea. Are parasites of vertebrates. Body is filiform anteriorly. Mouth is not surrounded by lips. Long tubular esophagus is embedded for most part in column of glandular cells (known as stichocytes). Females possess one ovary; males have one copulatory spicule or none.
  Superfamily Dioctophymoidea. Are parasites of animals, large worms. Mouth is not surrounded by lips but with six, twelve, or eighteen papillae. Esophagus is long and cylindrical. Females possess one ovary; males have one spicule and muscular bursa without supporting rays.
  Superfamily Mermithoidea. Larvae are parasitic in invertebrates, chiefly insects. Adults are usually free-living in soil and water. Smooth body is filiform. Cephalic sensory organs (usually sixteen) are reduced to papillae. Amphids are cyathiform or reduced. Esophagus is long, leading into blind intestine. Alimentary tract is modified for food storage.
Subclass Phasmidia. Phasmids are present. Possesses excretory system. Mesenterial tissue is weakly developed.
  Superfamily Rhabditoidea. Are free-living and includes parasitic members in plants and animals, primarily invertebrates. Cuticle is smooth or ringed. Cephalic papillae are arranged in two rings—an inner ring of six and an outer ring of four, six, or ten. Esophageal bulb is present; esophagus possesses long anterior cylindrical portion; esophageal swelling anterior to nerve ring usually is present. Amphids resemble small pockets. Caudal glands are absent. Females are didelphic or monodelphic. Copulatory spicules of males are equal in size, accompanied by gubernaculum.
  Superfamily Rhabdiasoidea. Parasitic stage in vertebrates is either parthenogenic or hermaphroditic. Free-living stages develop into males and females. Cuticle is smooth. Lacks definite esophageal bulb.
  Superfamily Oxyuroidea. All members are parasitic in animals—invertebrates and vertebrates. Are small pin shaped nematodes. Esophagus has bulb that is usually separated from esophagus proper by valves. Females have long, pointed tails. Males possess one or two spicules of equal length. Usually possesses caudal alae that form cuticular bursa. Terminal portion of female reproductive system is often heavily muscular.

---

*The various taxonomic groups listed here as superfamilies are considered orders by some authors.

Superfamily Ascaroidea.   All members are parasitic in vertebrates. Are mostly large nematodes. Mouth is surrounded by three prominent lips. No buccal capsule is present. Esophagus usually lacks bulb; if esophageal bulb is present, it is not separated from the esophagus proper by valves. Alimentary tract often has caeca. Tail of females is blunt; tail of males is pointed and ventrally coiled, usually without alae. Two spicules in males are of equal or unequal length.

Superfamily Strongyloidea.   Are parasites of vertebrates. Mouth is not surrounded by lips but minute crowns are present in many, considered by some as indistinct lips. Buccal capsule is well developed. Lacks esophageal bulb. Females usually possess ovijector. Males have two copulatory spicules. Well developed copulatory bursa is supported by six pairs of lateral rays and one dorsal ray.

Superfamily Spiruroidea.   Are parasitic in animals. Mouth usually has two lateral lips (pseudolips), sometimes four or six. Buccal capsule is chitinized. Lacks esophageal bulb. Esophagus is muscular anteriorly, glandular posteriorly. Males lack copulatory bursa. Spicules are unequal and dissimilar. Tail of male is spirally coiled with broad alae supported by papillae.

Superfamily Dracunculoidea.   Are parasites of vertebrates. Simple mouth lacks definite lips and cuticularized buccal capsule. Ring of papillae surrounds mouth. Lacks esophageal bulb. Esophagus is muscular anteriorly, glandular posteriorly. Alimentary canal and vulva are atrophied in adult females. Embryos escape through ruptured uterus and mouth. Males are much smaller than females. Lacks copulatory bursa. Spicules are filiform and equal in length.

Superfamily Filarioidea.   Are parasites of vertebrates. Are filiform, delicate worms. Mouth is not surrounded by lips. Buccal capsule is small or rudimentary. Lacks esophageal bulb. Esophagus as in Dracunculoidea. Vulva is far anterior. Males are small, with coiled tails, with or without alae, always with papillae. Lacks bursa. Spicules are unequal and dissimilar. Microfilariae are found in blood or skin and develop in blood-sucking insects.

SUBCLASS APHASMIDIA

SUPERFAMILY TRICHUROIDEA

Members of the superfamily Trichuroidea primarily are parasitic in the digestive tracts of birds and mammals, although species are found in amphibians. Only one species, *Oncophora neglecta,* has been reported from a marine animal, in the gallbladder of the fish *Thunnus vulgaris.* All of the other trichuroids are parasites of terrestrial and fresh-water vertebrates.

The life cycle of these nematodes is direct— that is, without an intermediate host. However, in at least one species, *Cystoopsis acipenseri,* found in the skin of the Volga sturgeon,

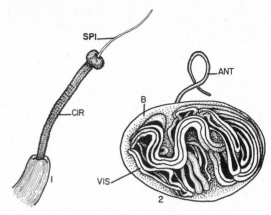

Plate 15-10   **Nematode structures. 1.** Cirrus and spicule of *Trichuris ovis,* everted. (Modified after Ransom, 1911.) **2.** Female specimen of *Cystoopsis* dissected from cyst. (Drawn from photograph after Janicki and Rasin, 1930.)
   (ANT, anterior end; B, body; CIR, cirrus; SPI, spicule; VIS, coils of viscera in body.)

amphipods do serve as the intermediate host. Most trichuroids are oviparous.

The Trichuroidea includes four families, a key to which is given below.

1. Stichosome is composed of a single longitudinal row of cells; cirrus is armed with single spicule (Plate 15–10, Fig. 1)... **Trichuridae**
2. Males lack copulatory apparatus; males are not enclosed in females..... **Trichinellidae**
3. Males are minute, lack copulatory apparatus, retain stylet and other larval structures, and are found in uterus or vagina of females ....**Trichosomoididae**
4. Males possess eversible spicule sheath armed with one spicule; posterior end of female is swollen, enclosing intestine and coiled single reproductive system (Plate 15–10, Fig. 2).................**Cystoopsidae**

Family Trichuridae

The family Trichuridae includes two prominent genera—*Trichuris* and *Capillaria.* The genus *Trichuris* includes numerous species found in various mammals—for example, *T. felis* in the caecum and colon of cats, *T. discolor* in cattle, *T. leporis* in rabbits, *T. muris* in rats, *T. suis* in pigs, *T. vulpis* in dogs, *T. ovis* in cattle and sheep, and *T. trichiura* in man.

All *Trichuris* species possess direct life cycles. For example, *Trichuris* (= *Trichocephalus*) *trichiura,* the whipworm of man, which is cosmopolitan in its distribution, is found in the area of the caecum (Plate 15–11, Fig. 1). The males are slightly smaller than the females, the latter

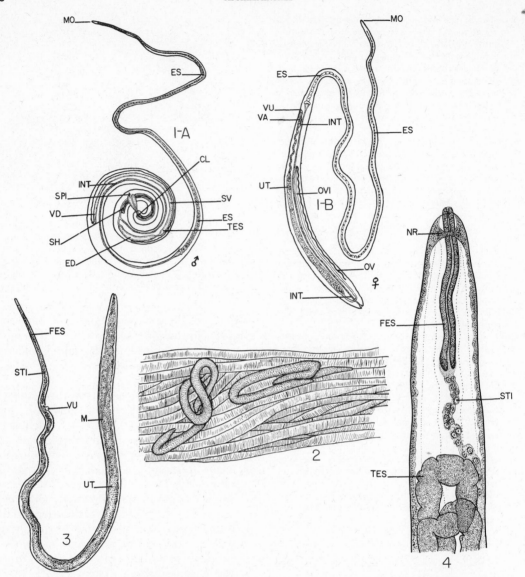

Plate 15-11   Species of nematodes. 1. A. Male of *Trichuris trichiura*. **B.** Female of *T. trichiura*. (A and B greatly modified after Gradwohl and Kouri, *Clinical Laboratory Methods and Diagnosis,* C. V. Mosby, St. Louis.) **2.** Larvae of *Trichinella spiralis* about to encyst in striated muscle of mammalian host. (Modified after Chandler, A. C., and Read, C. P. 1961. *Introduction to Parasitology,* John Wiley, New York.) **3.** Female of *Trichosomoides crassicauda* with male in uterus. (Redrawn after Hall, 1916.) **4.** Anterior portion of male of *Cystoopsis acipenseri*. (Redrawn after Janicki and Rasin, 1930.)

(ED, ejaculatory duct; ES, esophagus; FES, free portion of esophagus; INT, intestine; M, male in female; MO, mouth; NR, nerve ring; OV, ovary; OVI, oviduct; SH, sheath; SPI, spicule; STI, stichosome; SV, seminal vesicle; TES, testis; UT, uterus; VA, vagina; VD, vas deferens; VU, vulva.)

measuring 30 to 50 mm. in length. In both sexes, the long esophagus occupies two-thirds of the body length. The eggs oviposited by females are typically barrel shaped, measuring 50 by 22 μ, and containing an uncleaved zygote (Plate 15–7, Fig. 3).

It has been estimated that a single female may lay as many as 1000 to 46,000 eggs a day. These eggs pass to the exterior in feces and develop slowly in damp soil. The larva within the shell is completely formed in 3 to 6 weeks. Developing eggs are fairly resistant to unfavorable conditions. These developing eggs will die, however, in a week's time if exposed to desiccation.

Moisture is necessary for embryonic development. Within the eggshell, the larva does not molt, nor does it hatch while in the soil. Infection of man is effected when embryonated eggs are ingested—through the drinking of contaminated water, in food, or from the fingers. The eggshell is destroyed once the egg reaches the host's caecum. The escaping larva burrows into the intervillar spaces, where it remains a few days before re-entering the lumen of the caecum, there growing to maturity.

In the canine-infecting *Trichuris vulpis,* Miller (1941) reported that age resistance is probably nonexistent. Certain dogs, however, are capable of developing an immunity to this parasite. The immunity is manifested by the mass elimination of the nematodes. Nematode parasites that perforate the intestinal lining of their hosts during feeding, and thus introduce antigenic substances, generally elicit the synthesis of rather specific antibodies in their hosts.

GENUS *Capillaria.* The genus *Capillaria* includes species parasitic in the crop and esophagus of birds, in mammals, in fishes, and in amphibians, especially salamanders. Of the species found in mammals, *C. hepatica* is most frequently encountered. This nematode has been reported in a variety of animals, including man; however, it is most commonly found in rodents. The habitat of *C. hepatica* is the host's liver, surrounded by connective tissue.

Life Cycle of *Capillaria hepatica.* Although the life cycle of *C. hepatica* may be interpreted as being direct, it does include a transport host. Few eggs are released in the feces of the host, and these only occur early in the infection. Normally, eggs are released when the infected host is devoured by a predator. The infected liver tissue is digested away, and the eggs pass through the alimentary tract of the transport host and are passed out in the feces. Eggs are thus deposited in the soil. Freeman and Wright (1960) demonstrated that such eggs, enclosing fully or partially developed larvae, can survive temperatures as low as −15° C., but development usually requires warmer climates.

Infection of the host is accomplished with ingestion of embryonated eggs. Ingested eggs hatch in the caecum and the larvae penetrate through the wall, become incorporated in the portal circulation, and are carried to the liver,

where they develop to maturity. When experimentally hatched larvae are injected into hosts, these larvae eventually migrate via the blood stream to the liver.

Three additional avenues of escape for eggs of *Capillaria* spp. are displayed by *C. aerophila* parasitic in the lungs of foxes; *C. annulata,* in the esophagus and crop of turkeys, chickens, and various wild birds; and *C. plica,* found in the kidneys and urinary bladder of dogs and foxes. The eggs of *C. aerophila* are discharged in the lungs and pass up the air passages to the epiglottis. They are then coughed up and ingested and finally pass out in the host's feces. Earthworms of the genera *Lumbricus* and *Allolophora* serve as the intermediate host. The eggs of *C. annulata* are oviposited in the esophagus and crop and pass out posteriorly in feces. *Helodrilus foetidus* and *H. caliginosus,* both earthworms, serve as the intermediate host for *C. annulata.* Eggs expelled from the avian host must be ingested by an earthworm before attaining the infective form. Birds become infected when they ingest infected worms. The eggs of *C. plica* are passed out in the urine of the host. An intermediate host is required in this species also.

Many species of *Capillaria* are found in the intestine of their hosts. *Capillaria bursata* and *C. caudinflata* are parasitic in the small intestine of chickens and other birds, *C. columbae* in the small intestine of pigeons, *C. brevipes* and *C. bovis* in cattle and sheep, and *C. linearis* in the intestine of cats.

Family Trichinellidae

The family Trichinellidae contains only the species *Trichinella spiralis.* This parasite has been studied extensively. The adult males, measuring 1.4 to 1.6 mm. in length by 0.04 to 0.06 mm. in diameter, are approximately half the length of the females. The adults are found in the small intestine of the host. *Trichinella spiralis* naturally infects many mammals, including rats, mice, rabbits, cats, dogs, wolves, ferrets, muskrats, badgers, pigs, raccoons, moles, porcupines, and man. Various birds, including chickens, pigeons, crows, and owls, have been infected experimentally.

Within the small intestine, the adults are embedded in the mucosa and crypts. Soon after copulation, the males perish and the females actively penetrate the crypts of Lieberkühn. Here, the females give birth to living larvae (ovoviviparous) and then die. A single female may give birth to as many as 1500 larvae. These larvae, measuring 0.1 mm. in length, are carried by the lymphatic and blood vessels into the venous blood, which carries them to the heart.

From the heart the larvae find their way via the hepatic and pulmonary capillaries into the peripheral circulation, which in turn carries them to various tissues of the body. It is only in the striated muscles, however, that the larvae develop into the infective stage. Such larvae are found within the myofibers, first longitudinally oriented, but soon coiled and encapsulated in calcified cysts, one worm per cyst (Plate 15–11, Fig. 2). The encysted larvae generally measure 1 mm. in length and represent the fourth larval stage. Sexual differentiation has commonly begun in these forms.

Robinson and Olsen, and others have shown that in a few rare instances, larvae of *T. spiralis* are released in the lumen of the host's intestine. Thus, infections can be established via the ingestion of feces including such larvae.

When infected meat is ingested by a suitable host, the larvae escape from the encapsulating cysts, once these reach the small intestine. However, if myofibers enclosing encysted larvae are not ingested, as in human flesh, the larvae eventually die. Encysted larvae have been known to remain viable for 6 or 7 years. After gravid females have released their larvae into the submucosal zone along the intestine, the host may react severely. Muscular pains and stiffness often accompany trichinosis. Human cases of infection most commonly result from the ingestion of poorly cooked pork.

Merkushev (1955) found that the larvae of certain necrophagous beetles and other insects, which form part of the food of some carnivores, can act as temporary reservoir hosts for *T. spiralis* larvae. Such insect hosts could serve to transfer infections from infected carcasses to carnivores, insectivores, and omnivores. The insects are only temporary hosts, however, since the nematode can only survive up to 6 to 8 days in the insect larvae.

Much has been written concerning the public health aspects of trichinosis, but such data are beyond the scope of this volume. It should be mentioned that larvae encysted in meat can be rendered uninfective by lowering the temperature to less than $-15°$ C. for no less than 20 days, or less than $-35°$ C. for 24 hours. The importance of *T. spiralis* as a human parasite cannot be underestimated. Stoll (1947) estima-

ted that 27,800,000 cases of human trichinosis exist, 21,100,000 of these in North America.

IMMUNITY TO *Trichinella.* It has been demonstrated that hosts (rats, guinea pigs, pigs) infected with *T. spiralis* develop an immunity, because upon recovery from the initial infection, they resist reinfection. Although the resistance is never complete, it is transmittable in many cases from immune mothers to their offspring. *Trichinella* antigen appears within 24 hours when the worms are maintained in serum, and precipitation is known to occur within 5 days.

Antibodies produced by the host (acquired resistance) against *Trichinella* are directed against the intestinal stage of the parasite, for if infective larvae are experimentally fed to immune animals, the larvae are eliminated without development. The host's antibodies are most probably serum antibodies, although it is still uncertain how the intestinal larvae come in contact with the serum. It is possible that the larvae make contact with the host's serum when the larvae begin to penetrate the blood vessels in the intestinal wall, but then again, the antibodies may enter the lumen of the gut in some way.

Levine and Evans (1942), and Gould et al. (1955) have demonstrated that partial immunity to *T. spiralis* can be induced by feeding infective larvae irradiated with 3250 to 3750 r of x-rays or 10,000 r of gamma rays from cobalt[60]. These dosages sterilize the larvae, but growth is not inhibited. If higher dosages are used, growth of the larvae is inhibited and no immunity is induced. Although host immunity produced by feeding irradiated larvae is incomplete, the number of adults maturing in the intestine and the number of larvae that reach the muscles is greatly reduced (Table 15–2).

Not only are the body tissues of *T. spiralis* antigenic, the excretions and secretions of larvae cultured in nutrient media for 2 to 5 days are also antigenic (Chipman, 1957). When excretions and secretions are injected into mice, immunity is manifested by the significantly smaller number of larvae and adults found in the treated hosts. The effect is more readily appreciated among the larvae.

Family Trichosomoididae

The family Trichosomoididae also includes a single species, *Trichosomoides crassicauda* (Plate 15–11, Fig. 3), found in the kidney but primarily

**Table 15-2.   Effect of Reinfecting Rats with *Trichinella spiralis* Larvae
40 Days after Initial Infection to Show Presence of a Partial Immunity Induced by
Using Co⁶⁰ Irradiated Larvae***

Days after Reinfection	Group I (not irradiated)		Group II (irradiated with 10,000r from Co⁶⁰)	
	Adult Worms in Intestine	Larvae Recovered from Muscles	Adult Worms in Intestine	Larvae Recovered from Muscles
2	17	181,000	1,912	15
	165	32,200		
4	0	166,000	848	11
	8	25,800		
6	0	164,000	42	0
	4	47,240		
8	52	101,000	9	0
	0	640,000		
10	0	156,000	0	22
15	0	190,000	0	0
	0	—		
20	0	96,000	0	496

*Data after Gould et al. (1955).

in the urinary bladder of rats. The eggs pass out in urine and when ingested by another rat, hatch in the stomach. The escaping larvae penetrate the stomach wall and are carried by the blood to various parts of the body. However, only larvae that reach the urinary tract develop to maturity.

Trichosomoides crassicauda is an unusually interesting species, because the males are hyperparasitic—that is, parasitic on another parasite—in the uterus of the female. Usually three or four males occur within a single female.

Family Cystoopsidae

The family Cystoopsidae also includes a single species, *Cystoopsis acipenseri* (Plate 15-11, Fig. 4). Janiki and Rasin (1930) have studied the biology of this nematode, which is parasitic in the skin of the Volga sturgeon. The eggs are ingested by amphipods that serve as the intermediate host. In laying their eggs, the female worms rupture out of their encapsulating cysts in the host's skin. Furthermore, the uterus is ruptured in the process releasing the enclosed eggs. Within the amphipod intermediate host, the eggs hatch and the larvae each armed with a stylet penetrate the intestinal wall. After undergoing development in the haemocoel, these larvae encyst in the host's appendicular muscles. When infected amphipods are ingested by a sturgeon, the larvae burrow through the intestinal wall, become encysted in the skin, and grow into maturity.

SUPERFAMILY DIOCTOPHYMOIDEA

The major diagnostic characteristics of the superfamily Dioctophymoidea are listed on page 404. The superfamily is composed of two families—the Dioctophymidae, whose members lack an oral sucker; and the Soboliphymidae, whose members possess such a sucker.

Family Dioctophymidae

The family Dioctophymidae includes the genera *Dioctophyma, Hystrichis,* and *Eustrongylides.*

Dioctophyma renale.   A bright red species, *Dioctophyma renale* is generally found in the kidney and coelom of carnivores, such as dogs, minks, foxes, and wolves. It has also been reported from pigs, cattle, horses, and even man (Plate 15-12, Fig. 1). This nematode, which is apparently worldwide in its distribution, is highly destructive, often destroying the host's kidney, and may even bring about death.

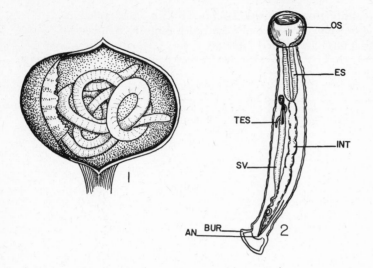

Plate   15-12   Dioctophymoid
nematodes. 1. *Dioctophyma renale* coiled
in host's kidney. (Redrawn after Hyman,
L. H. 1951. *The Invertebrates,* McGraw-Hill,
New York.) 2. Male of *Soboliphyme.* (Redrawn after Petrow, 1930.) (AN, anus;
BUR, bursa; ES, esophagus; INT, intestine; OS, oral sucker; SV, seminal vesicle;
TES, testis.)

The life span of the worm ranges from 1 to
3 years. With the death of the parasite, the
host's kidney generally shrivels and dries up.
Dioctophyma renale is one of the largest parasitic
nematodes known. The females may measure
up to 103 cm. in length and have a diameter
of 5 to 12 mm. The males are 35 cm. long by
3 to 4 mm. in diameter.

Life Cycle of *Dioctophyma renale.* The
life cycle of this nematode has puzzled parasitologists for decades. According to Woodhead
(1950), two intermediate hosts are involved.
The first intermediate host is a branchiobdellid
oligochaete, *Cambarincola chirocephala* or *C.
vitrea,* which is epizoic on or in the branchial
chamber of crayfishes.

Eggs passing out in the definitive host's
urine require approximately 6 months before
they enclose fully developed first stage larvae
(the eggs used by Woodhead were 11 months
old.) Such eggs are ingested by the oligochaete,
which periodically becomes unattached to the
crayfish. The first stage larvae hatch from the
ingested eggs and penetrate the oligochaete's
intestinal wall into the coelom, where they
undergo the first molt and become encysted.

When a crayfish on which infected oligochaetes are attached is ingested by the second
intermediate host—the bullhead *Ameiurus melas
melas*—the second stage larvae penetrate the
fish's coelom, undergo two molts, and encyst
on the mesentery. The mammalian host
becomes infected by eating infected fish. Within
the mammal, the fourth stage larvae migrate
to the kidney, less commonly to the peritoneal

cavity, and mature after undergoing the final
molt.

This spectacular life cycle pattern, reported
by Woodhead, was puzzling, for the life cycles
of closely related nematodes—for example,
Hystrichis tricolor—include only one intermediate
host. Furthermore, Woodhead reported that
the second and third stage larvae of *D. renale*
are indistinguishable from larval nematomorphs.
In fact, he called these unusual larvae "gordiid
larvae."

Recently, Karmanova (1960) restudied the
life cycle of *Dioctophyma renale* in the Kzyl-
Orda region of Kazakhstan, USSR. He confirmed Woodhead's finding that the first stage
larva develops slowly within the eggshell. However, he found that the first stage larva, hatching from the shell after ingestion by the
oligochaete *Lumbriculus variegatus,* penetrates the
annelid's blood vessels, where it passes through
the second, third, and fourth larval stages, with
the latter stages found in the abdominal blood
vessel. All of the larvae reportedly are typical
of nematodes and not of the so-called gordiid
type.

According to Karmanova, when infected
oligochaetes are eaten by the mammalian host,
the fourth stage larva molts, migrates to the
kidney, and matures. Karmanova's findings
appear to be correct, for they indicate that the
life cycle of *D. renale* conforms to the single-
intermediate-host pattern of the Dioctophymidae. Furthermore, it explains how such
mammals as pigs, horses, and cattle, which do
not as a rule feed on fish, but may accidentally

ingest infected oligochaetes while grazing or drinking water, can become infected.

Karmanova did point out, however, that in certain cases, if an infected oligochaete is swallowed by a fish, the development of *D. renale* larvae is arrested, but they are not killed. Thus, the fish becomes a transport or paratenic host. Therefore, mammals feeding on infected fish could become infected. It is now clear that the bullhead, which Woodhead believed to be the second intermediate host, is actually a paratenic host, and the gordiid larvae were probably larval nematomorphs.

Family Soboliphymidae

The family Soboliphymidae includes the genus *Soboliphyme* with the main species *S. baturini* parasitic in the intestine of cats, sables, and foxes in Kamchatka and Siberia, and in wolverines in North America (Plate 15–12, Fig. 2). This nematode is unique among the members of its class in that an oral sucker surrounds the mouth. The females are oviparous.

SUPERFAMILY MERMITHOIDEA

The Mermithoidea includes a group of unique nematodes that are generally free-living as adults. The exception to the rule is *Tetradonema plicans*, a member of the family Tetradonematidae. The entire life span of this nematode is spent as a parasite of the fly *Sciara*.

The cuticle of the mermethoid nematodes is smooth and the body is comparatively long, reaching 50 cm. in some species. The esophagus is quite distinct, for it originates at the mouth and extends posteriorly to the midlength of the body and sometimes beyond (Plate 15–13, Fig. 1). The intestine is also unusual in that it consists of two or more rows of large cells that are richly packed with food (Plate 15–13, Fig. 2). This type of intestinal tract is known as a trophosome. The trophosome does not empty to the exterior posteriorly through an anus; rather, it ends as a blind sac. The nutrients stored in the trophosome cells supply the adults, which apparently do not feed.

Sexual dimorphism is apparent among the Mermithoidea. The males are smaller than the females, and both male and female possess a pair of gonads.

The superfamily Mermithoidea includes two groups of species—those belonging to the more primitive family Tetradonematidae, and those belonging to the more advanced and larger family Mermithidae.

Family Tetradonematidae

The Tetradonematidae includes three species —*Tetradonema plicans, Mermithonema entomophilum,* and *Aproctonema entomophagum* (Plate 15–13, Figs. 3 and 4). Two variations of the mermithoid life cycle pattern are portrayed by *T. plicans* and *A. entomophagum.* In the first pattern, the entire life span is spent as a parasite, while in the second only a portion of the cycle is parasitic.

LIFE CYCLE OF *Tetradonema plicans.* Cobb (1919) and Hungerford (1919) reported that the fly *Sciara* is infected in all stages by *Tetradonema plicans,* but especially while in the soil-dwelling larval stage. A single fly may harbor from two to twenty worms of both sexes. The fly maggots become infected when they ingest eggs of the parasite. These eggs hatch in the host's intestine and the larvae burrow through the intestinal wall to become established in the fly's haemocoel. Within the haemocoel, the nematode feeds on the host's fat bodies and other tissues and grows to maturity. Female *T. plicans* measures up to 5 mm. in length, while the male measures approximately 1 mm. Copulation occurs within the fly, and the eggs are deposited in the subcuticular zone near the gonopore. When the fly host dies and disintegrates, the females are released, but soon perish, dispersing their eggs in the soil.

LIFE CYCLE OF *Aproctonema entomophagum.* Keilin and Robinson (1933) reported that *A. entomophagum* undergoes a similar life cycle. However, after copulation within the haemocoel of the host (also *Sciara*) the females escape, lay their eggs, and perish. These eggs hatch in decaying wood, giving rise to free-living larvae that molt after a period of growth. It is the second stage larva of the parasite that penetrates the larva of *Sciara,* thus establishing the parasitic phase of its life cycle.

Family Mermithidae

Species of the family Mermithidae have been listed by Polozhentsev (1952, 1954). This family includes most of the mermithoid nematodes. Some of the more common genera are *Mermis, Paramermis, Agamermis, Allomermis,* and *Hexamermis.*

Life cycles of several of these nematodes have been worked out. In each case the parasitic stage of the worm has been found to be the larva. The larvae generally parasitize insects; however, larvae of some species parasitize crustaceans, arachnids, and even molluscs.

LIFE CYCLE OF *Paramermis contorta.*   The

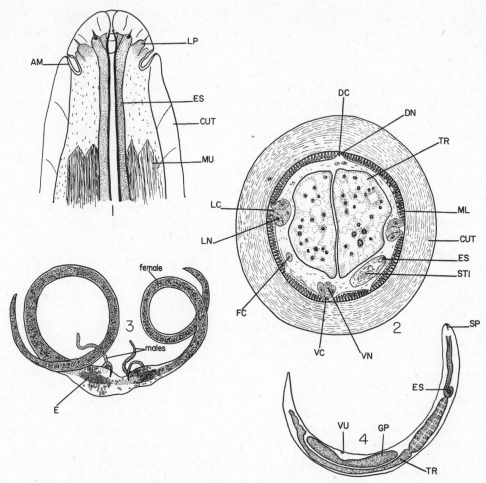

Plate 15-13   Mermithoid nematodes. 1. Anterior end of mermithoidean nematode, showing origin of esophagus in mouth. (Redrawn after Hagmeier, 1912.) **2.** Cross section through mermithoidean nematode, showing trophosome (intestine) and other structures. (Redrawn after Rauther, 1916.) **3.** Male and female of *Tetradonema plicans* in copula. (Redrawn after Hungerford, 1919.) **4.** Young female of *Aproctonema entomophagum*. (Redrawn after Keilen and Robinson, 1933.)

(AM, amphid; CUT, cuticle; DC, dorsal cord; DN, dorsal nerve; E, accumulation of eggs in region of gonopore; ES, esophagus; FC, fat cells in pseudocoel; GP, genital primordium; LC, lateral cord; LN, lateral nerve; LP, lateral papillae; ML, muscle layer; MU, body wall muscles; SP, spear; STI, stichosome; TR, trophosome; VC, ventral cord; VN, ventral nerve; VU, vulva.)

larvae of *P. contorta* parasitize the larvae of the midge *Chironomus*. When the nematode larvae attain maturity, they escape from the host and live in the mud at the bottom of a pond or stream. Adults live only 3 to 5 days, during which time copulation takes place and the female lays her eggs. The eggs hatch in 14 to 16 days and the young larvae become free-living. If such a larva comes in contact with a molting or newly molted *Chironomus* larva, it penetrates the soft cuticle and begins its parasitic life. Aquatic fly larvae of the genus *Simulium* can also serve as hosts.

LIFE CYCLE OF *Agamermis decaudata*.   In

A. decaudata, the larvae are parasitic in the haemocoel of grasshoppers. The nematode remains within the host from 1 to 3 months, after which time the nematode emerges through the intersegmental joints of the body and migrates into the soil. These worms enter the soil from August to October and remain therein until the following June, at which time they molt and become sexually mature adults. Copulation takes place, and the females lay eggs during the remaining summer months and continue to do so all through the following summer. By the end of the second summer, the stored food in the trophosomes is exhausted, and the females perish with the onset of cold weather. The sexually mature females measure up to 46.5 cm. in length.

Development of the embryo begins soon after the eggs are laid but is not completed until the following spring, when the larva undergoes one molt while still within the eggshell. The larva then hatches and becomes free-living in the soil. The soil-dwelling larva, measuring 5 to 6 mm. in length, possesses a miniature spearlike structure—the dorylaim stylet—at its anterior terminal. This stylet is characteristic of most infective larvae of the Mermithoidea. In addition to this anteriorly located stylet, there is a node at the midlength of the body of *A. decaudata*.

During rainy weather, the larvae of *A. decaudata* migrate to the surface of the soil and are often found on vegetation. Here, they are prepared to penetrate the thin exoskeleton of grasshopper nymphs. During the penetration process, the elongate body of the worm breaks at the node, leaving the posterior half outside. If the posterior portion of the body is taken into the host, it soon atrophies.

NEMATODES AND THE BIOLOGICAL CONTROL OF INSECTS

The biology of insect-parasitizing nematodes has been the subject of considerable investigation. Welch (1958) reviewed this topic and pointed out that such nematodes are being used as biological control agents in the suppression of destructive insects. Apparently a significant degree of natural control is exercised among insects by their nematode parasites. For example, because these larval nematodes usually bring about the death or impair the reproductive capacity of their hosts, infection by nematodes reduces the mosquito population in endemic locales.

PHYSIOLOGY AND HOST-PARASITE RELATIONSHIPS

The physiology and host-parasite relationships of nematodes—both aphasmids and phasmids—are discussed in Chapter 16.

LITERATURE CITED

Chipman, P. B. 1957. The antigenic role of the excretions and secretions of adult *Trichinella spiralis* in the production of immunity in mice. J. Parasit., *43:* 593–598.

Chitwood, B. G. 1936. Observations on the chemical nature of the cuticle of *Ascaris lumbricoides* var. *suis.* Proc. Helminth. Soc. Wash., *3:* 39–49.

Cobb, N. A. 1919. *Tetradonema plicans* nov. gen. et spec., representing a new family, Tetradonematidae, as now found parasitic in larvae of the midge-insect *Sciara coprophila* Lintner. J. Parasit., *5:* 176–185.

Freeman, R. S., and K. A. Wright. 1960. Factors concerned with the epizootiology of *Capillaria hepatica* (Bancroft, 1893) (Nematoda) in a population of *Peromyscus maniculatus* in Algonquin Park, Canada. J. Parasit., *46:* 373–382.

Gould, S. E., et al. 1955. Studies on *Trichinella spiralis* I-V. Am. J. Path., *31:* 933–963.

Hungerford, H. B. 1919. Biological notes on *Tetradonema plicans,* Cobb, a nematode parasite of *Sciara coprophila* Lintner. J. Parasit., *5:* 186–192.

Janicki, C., and K. Rasin. 1930. Bemerkungen über *Cystoopsis acipenseri* des Wolga-Sterlets, sowie über die Entwicklung dieses Nematoden im Zwischenwirt. Ztschr. Wissensch. Zool., *136:* 1–37.

Karmanova, E. M. 1960. The life cycle of the nematode *Dioctophyme renale* (Goeze, 1782). Dokl. Akad. Nauk SSSR, *127:* 700–702.

Keilin, D., and V. C. Robinson. 1933. On the morphology and life history of *Aproctonema entomophagum* Keilin, a nematode parasite in the larvae of *Sciara pullula* Winn. (Diptera-Nematocerca.) Parasitology, *25:* 285–295.

Levine, A. J., and T. C. Evans. 1942. Use of roentgen radiation in locating an origin of host resistance to *Trichinella spiralis* infections. J. Parasit., *28:* 477–483.

Merkushev, A. V. 1955. [Rotation of *Trichinella* infections in natural conditions and their natural foci]. Meditsinsk. Parazit. Parazitarn. Bolez. Moscow, *24:* 125–130.

Miller, M. J. 1941. Quantitative studies on *Trichocephalus vulpis* infections in dogs. Am. J. Hyg., *9:* 58–70.

Polozhentsev, P. A. [New mermithids found in rocky soil of a pine forest]. Trudy Lab. Gel'mint., Akad. Nauk SSSR, *6:* 376–382.

Polozhentsev, P. A. 1954. [Contribution to the knowledge of Nematoda of the family Mermithidae Braun, 1883] Rabot. Gel'mintol. 75-Let. Skrjabin, pp. 532–542.

Sasser, J. N., and W. R. Jenkins. 1960. Nematology. University of North Carolina Press, Chapel Hill.

Stoll, N. 1947. This wormy world. J. Parasit., *33:* 1–18.

Thorne, G. 1961. Principles of Nematology. McGraw-Hill, New York.

Toryu, Y. 1935. Contributions to the physiology of the Ascaris. III. Survival and glycogen content of the Ascaris, *Ascaris megalocephala* Cloq. in presence and absence of oxygen. Science Rep., Tohoku Imp. Univ., 4s. (Biol.), *10:* 361–375.

Villela, G. G., and J. C. Teixeira. 1937. Blood chemistry in hookworm anemia. J. Lab. Clin. Med., *22:* 567–572.

Welch, H. E. 1958. A review of recent work on nematodes associated with insects with regard to their utilization as biological control agents. Proc. Tenth Intern. Congr. Entomology, *4:* 863–868.

Woodhead, A. E. 1950. Life history cycle of the giant kidney worm, *Dioctophyma renale* (Nematoda), of man and many other mammals. Trans. Amer. Micro. Soc., *70:* 21–46.

Yamaguti, S. 1962. Systema Helminthum. Vol. III. The Nematodes of Vertebrates. 2 parts. Interscience, New York.

Yorke, W., and B. Maplestone. 1926. Nematode Parasites of Vertebrates. Blakiston, Philadelphia. (Reprinted in 1962 by Hafner Publishing Co., New York.)

SUGGESTED READING

The *Suggested Reading* list is at the end of the next chapter.

THE PHASMID
NEMATODES

The nematodes discussed in this chapter all belong to the subclass Phasmidia. Although the species portray morphological and life cycle differences, all possess one major characteristic in common. They possess phasmids—the minute, usually paired, presumably olfactory receptors found posterior to the anus. The Phasmidia (see p. 404) is divided into nine superfamilies. These are discussed below.

SYSTEMATICS AND BIOLOGY

SUPERFAMILY RHABDITOIDEA

The superfamily Rhabditoidea includes an array of species, some free-living, others symbiotic in animals, primarily invertebrates, still others symbiotic in or on plants. These species usually possess two esophageal bulbs. The more anterior one, known as the pseudobulb, is actually a swelling of the elongate esophagus, while the posterior one is a true valvulated bulb (Plate 16–1, Fig. 1). The other major diagnostic characteristics of the superfamily are listed on page 404. Most of the species parasitic to animals are found in the family Rhabditidae,

while the rhabditoid parasites of plants belong primarily to the families Tylenchidae* and Allantonematidae.

FAMILY RHABDITIDAE

Genus *Rhabditis*

A large number of the parasitic species of the Rhabditoidea belong to the genus *Rhabditis*. None of the species belonging to this genus, however, are continuously parasitic—that is, they are parasites during only certain phases of their life cycle. In fact, many of these are only facultative parasites. Many parasitic species are found in animal droppings, on which they feed, and they are dependent on some coprophagous insect to transport them to new food sites. This dependency on an insect transport host has become so intimate in some species that the continued development of the nematode is halted if it does not come in contact with the insect carrier. *Rhabditis coarctata* represents such a case. In this species, the third stage larvae (the form that has undergone two molts) do not develop into sexually mature adults until

---

*The family Tylenchidae is considered a separate superfamily by some nematologists.

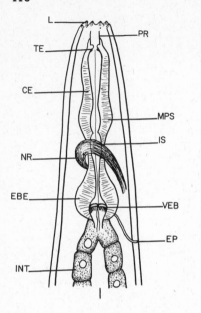

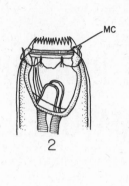

2

Plate 16-1 Anterior body structures of nematodes. 1. Anterior end of *Rhabditis maupasi*, showing rhabditoid type of arrangement of esophagus. (Redrawn after Reiter, 1928.) **2.** Anterior end of *Strongylus* sp., showing mouth collar.

(CE, corpus of esophagus; EBE, end bulb of esophagus; EP, excretory pore; INT, intestine; IS, isthmus of esophagus; L, lips; MC, mouth collar; MPS, median pseudobulb; NR, nerve ring; PR, protostom; TE, telostom; VEB, valve apparatus of end bulb.)

they are carried in the ensheathed form on a dung beetle to fresh dung (Plate 16–2, Fig. 1). If this transport occurs, the larvae escape from their sheaths and attain maturity.

An intermediate stage of dependency is exemplified by *Rhabditis dubia*. Normally this species can complete its life cycle in cow dung. However, occasionally a third stage larva develops that requires being transported by a psychodid fly to fresh dung before it can develop into a sexually mature adult. Earthworms are known to be suitable transport hosts for some species of *Rhabditis*.

A few species of *Rhabditis* can parasitize mammals. For example, *R. strongyloides* can establish itself in cutaneous ulcers on dogs. Species that reportedly parasitize man are undoubtedly accidental temporary parasites.

Other Rhabditid Genera

Other genera of Rhabditoidea parasitic in animals include *Angiostoma,* occasionally found in the intestine of the salamander *Plethedon* and in snails; and *Diplogaster* with some species (e.g., *D. bütschlii*) on bark beetles in the ensheathed form or in the intestine and haemocoel of beetles.

Members of the genus *Neoaplectana* are facultative parasites of insects. *Neoaplectana glaseri* has been introduced into North America and elsewhere as a biological control agent against the destructive Japanese beetle. The adaptability of *N. glaseri* has been utilized by Dumbleton (1945), who introduced this nematode into New Zealand to control various native melolon-

thids. As in most rhabditoids, this species is normally free-living, in this case, on insect carcasses. However, occasionally a third stage filariform larva develops that requires penetration into the larvae and adults of the beetles. Ingestion by the beetle may also be possible. Within the beetle's gut, these parasite larvae develop into sexually mature adults and they copulate. The ovoviviparous females each give birth to approximately fifteen young. During this parasitic phase, the host is killed and the parasite larvae become free-living, feeding on the host's carcass.

FAMILY TYLENCHIDAE

Genus *Heterodera*

Probably the best known plant parasites belong to the genus *Heterodera*. *Heterodera schachtii,* the sugar beet nematode; *H. rostochiensis,* the golden potato nematode; and *H. marioni,* the root-knot nematode, are among the most destructive plant parasites and are responsible for great losses to agriculture (Plate 16–2, Figs. 2 to 4).

LIFE CYCLE OF *Heterodera*. The life histories of *Heterodera* spp. all follow the same basic pattern with only minor variations. There are alternating free-living and parasitic phases in the cycle. The infective (second stage) larvae actively penetrate and enter plant cells, where they feed on the cell contents and attain sexual maturity. Both males and females continue to grow and molt, usually three times. The females then become inseminated and increase in size,

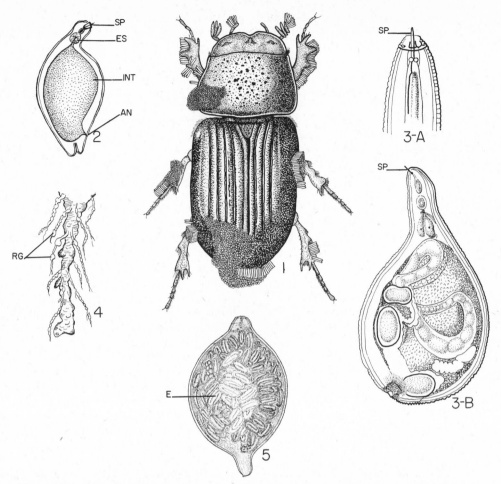

Plate 16-2   Rhabditoid nematodes. 1. Numerous ensheathed larvae of *Rhabditis coarctata* attached to the dung beetle *Aphodius*. (Redrawn after Triffitt and Oldham, 1927.) **2.** Mature female of *Heterodera schachtii*. (Redrawn after Strubbel, 1888.) **3. A.** Anterior end of male of *Heterodera rostochiensis*. **B.** Entire specimen of female of *H. rostochiensis*. (After Chitwood in Thorne, G. 1961. *Principles of Nematology,* McGraw-Hill, New York.) **4.** Root of parsnip, showing nodules caused by *Heterodera marioni*. (Modified after Atkinson, 1889.) **5.** Sugar-beet nematode cyst containing eggs. (After Maggenti and Allen.)

(AN, anus; E, eggs; ES, esophagus; INT, intestine; RG, root galls; SP, spear.)

taking on a bloated form, resembling minute gourds.

The eggs are stored within the females. The mother parasite eventually dies, but her cuticle remains intact, serving as a cyst in which the eggs are ensheathed. Upon the death and decomposition of the plant tissue, these egg-containing sacs are deposited in the soil. Within the eggshells, the larvae continue to develop until they reach the second stage, at which time they rupture out of the cyst and become free-living in the soil. This soil-dwelling form does not feed and can live for several months without additional nutrient. When the soil-dwelling larva comes in contact with a suitable

plant, it penetrates the plant host and repeats the cycle. The males escape the plant hosts after reaching sexual maturity and seek out females, which are still in plants, and impregnate them. After fertilizing a female, the male dies. Plant tissues infected with *Heterodera* spp. usually form galls.

In *Heterodera schachtii*, the sexually mature female protrudes partially from the gall and becomes impregnated by a male while she is in this position. The eggs are ensheathed, not only by the cuticle of the mother, but also by a gelatinous coat secreted from the vulva of gravid females (Plate 16–2, Fig. 5). In *H. marioni,* the body of the female does not become a cystlike enclosure for the eggs; rather, the parent secretes a gelatinous mass in which the eggs are embedded. This species is parthenogenic.

Tylenchid Host Specificity

Host specificity has been demonstrated repeatedly among the tylenchid parasites of plants. Sometimes morphologically indistinguishable forms demonstrate strict specificity; hence, these must be considered as distinct strains or races (Christie and Albin, 1944).

FAMILY ALLANTONEMATIDAE

Members of the family Allantonematidae utilize both an insect and a plant as hosts. The sexually mature worms are found in the insect host, but the young pass into plant cells when the insect host punctures the plant. Examples of such nematodes are *Heterotylenchus aberrans,* which parasitizes onion flies; and *Fergusobia curriei,* found in the larvae of the fly *Fergusonina.* When the larvae of *F. curriei* are introduced into the flowers and leaf buds of *Eucalyptus,* galls are formed.

SUPERFAMILY RHABDIASOIDEA

Genus *Rhabdias*

One of the best known of the rhabdiasoid nematodes is *Rhabdias bufonis,* a species commonly encountered in the lungs of frogs (Plate 16–3, Fig. 1).

LIFE CYCLE OF *Rhabdias bufonis.* The life cycle of this parasite deserves attention because its common occurrence in captured or commercially acquired frogs makes this parasite readily available as an experimental animal. *Rhabdias bufonis* is unique in that there are two sexual generations—a protandrous hermaphroditic stage during the parasitic phase, and a dioecious stage during the free-living phase of its life cycle. The form found in the frog's lungs is hermaphroditic. The testes develop before the ovary, and the spermatozoa produced are stored in a seminal receptacle and remain in that structure until the ovary becomes fully developed and gives rise to ova.

After fertilization, the zygotes are encapsuled within individual eggshells. These eggs containing the zygotes are coughed up into the host's bronchi and enter the buccal cavity and are swallowed. When the eggs reach the digestive tract of the frog, rhabditiform larvae hatch and migrate posteriorly. They become concentrated in the cloaca and pass out in the feces.

The rhabditiform larvae mature into soil-dwelling adult males and females, which constitute the dioecious generation. After copulation, the females give rise to ovoviviparous filariform larvae that remain within the mother and feed on her tissues. They eventually destroy the parent and are freed. The escaping larvae are ensheathed. Infection of the frog is accomplished when the ensheathed larvae penetrate the skin of the host and are carried by the lymphatic system to the various organs. However, only

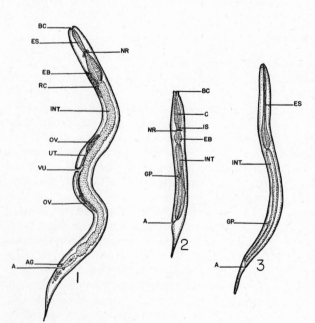

Plate 16–3   Adult and larval rhabdiasoid nematodes. 1. Parasitic female of *Rhabdias bufonis.* (Redrawn and slightly modified after Metschnikoff, 1865.) **2.** Rhabditiform larva of *Strongyloides* in soil. **3.** Filariform larva of *Strongyloides* in soil.

(A, anus; AG, anal glands; BC, buccal capsule; C, corpus of esophagus; EB, end bulb of esophagus; ES, esophagus; GP, genital primordium; INT, intestine; IS, isthmus of esophagus; NR, nerve ring; OV, ovary; RC, renette cell; UT, uterus; VU, vulva.)

larvae that reach the host's lungs survive to repeat the cycle (Fülleborn, 1928).

Certain snails may serve as transport hosts for *R. bufonis*. The cytology of *R. bufonis* has yet to be worked out and undoubtedly is of great interest, considering the uniqueness of the occurrence of both hermaphroditic and dioecious phases in the life cycle.

OTHER *Rhabdias* SPECIES. Many other species of *Rhabdias* are parasitic in the lungs of snakes. In these reptile-parasitizing species, the infective form is an ensheathed rhabditiform larva which is ingested by the host and which eventually migrates to the lungs.

Genus *Entomelas*

The superfamily Rhabdiasoidea also includes the genus *Entomelas,* the members of which are found in amphibians. *E. dujardinii* in *Anguis* (the blind worm) probably utilizes snails and earthworms as transport hosts.

Genus *Strongyloides*

Strongyloides stercoralis. The best known rhabdiasoid nematode is the medically important *S. stercoralis,* an intestinal parasite of man and other mammals. This nematode is found primarily in the tropics and subtropics; however, its occurrence has been reported in temperate climes. Relative to the frequency of its occurrence, Lopes Pontes (1946) found 24.8 per cent infection among humans in Santa Casa de Miseracordia, Rio de Janeiro; and Moraes (1948) found 58.3 per cent infection in humans in Rio Doca. Stoll (1947) estimated that 34.9 million human cases of strongyloidiasis exist— 21 million in Asia, 900,000 in Russia, 8.6 million in Africa, 4 million in tropical America, 400,000 in North America, and 100,000 in Pacific islands.

Life Cycle of *Strongyloides stercoralis.* The life cycle of *S. stercoralis* can be divided into three phases—the free-living generation, the parasitic generation, and the autoinfection phase.

THE FREE-LIVING GENERATION. Free-living *S. stercoralis* consistently can be found in moist soil in warm climes. The free-living form serves as a natural reservoir for infections. The free-living males are fusiform and smaller than the females (Plate 16–4, Fig. 1). The males, measuring 0.7 mm. in length by 0.04 to 0.05 mm. in diameter, possess a pointed and ventrally coiled tail. The females, measuring 1 mm. in length by 0.05 to 0.07 mm. in diameter, do not possess a coiled tail.

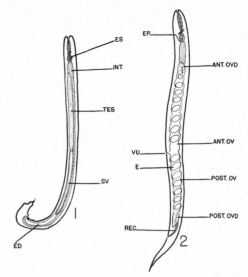

Plate 16-4   Free-living forms of *Strongyloides stercoralis.* **1.** Free-living male in soil. **2.** Free-living female in soil. (Figs. 1 and 2 redrawn after Craig, C., and Faust, E. 1951. *Clinical Parasitology,* Lea & Febiger, Philadelphia.)

(ANT. OV, anterior ovary; ANT. OVD, anterior oviduct; E, eggs in utero; ED, ejaculatory duct; EP, excretory pore; ES, esophagus; INT, intestine; POST. OV, posterior ovary; POST. OVD, posterior oviduct; REC, rectum; SV, seminal vesicle; TES, testis; VU, vulva.)

After copulation, the uterus of the female is filled with eggs, which occupy most of the body space. When these eggs are laid, they contain partially developed larvae. Development is completed in soil within a few hours, and the escaping larvae are rhabditiform (Plate 16–3, Fig. 2). These larvae feed actively on organic debris, undergo one molt, continue to feed, and gradually develop, after four molts, into sexually mature adults.

The free-living cycle may go on continuously without interruption. However, if the environment becomes unfavorable, the rhabditiform larvae molt and metamorphose into nonfeeding filariform larvae (Plate 16–3, Fig. 3). This larval type is the infective form of *S. stercoralis.* When several generations intervene between parasitic generations, the cycle is said to be indirect.

THE PARASITIC GENERATION. When filariform larvae come in contact with man or some other suitable host, they readily penetrate the skin and are carried by the fine dermal blood vessels to larger vessels. They eventually pass through the right atrium and ventricle of the heart to the lungs via the pulmonary artery. The filariform larvae can enter dogs and cats through ingestion. Once within the lungs, these larvae rupture out of the pulmonary capillaries and become lodged in the alveoli.

Faust (1933) reported that in the alveoli, the filariform larvae develop through the postfilariform and preadolescent stages, attaining the adolescent stage. Males at this stage of development are sexually mature and impregnate females. Copulation takes place while the worms are still within the alveoli or while they are migrating up the bronchi and trachea into the zone of the epiglottis, from which they are coughed up and swallowed.

Fertilization is still possible even when the adolescents migrate down to the upper section of the small intestine. However, fertilization cannot take place once the females penetrate and become established within the epithelial cells lining the small intestine, because the males are not capable of cell penetration. Instead, the males pass out of the host in feces.

Some females adolescents have been known to penetrate the lining of the bronchi and trachea and lay their eggs therein, but the majority of these larvae reach the small intestine. Sexual reproduction among adolescents of *S. stercoralis* is different from that reported in *S. ratti* in rats. In the latter species, the presence of males is not necessary, for the females give rise to their young parthenogenically. Parthenogenic development is also considered possible in *S. stercoralis*.

Larvae that hatch from eggs deposited by fertilized females in the host's epithelial cells escape from these cells and become established in the lumen. Males are typically rhabditiform and have a slightly larger buccal cavity than that found in free-living males. The females are delicate filiform worms measuring up to 2.2 mm. in length. The esophagus in the female is long, extending through the anterior third of the body length. On reaching maturity, the females, after copulation, lay their eggs in the mucous membrane in the wall of the host's small intestine. These eggs hatch into typical rhabditiform larvae, which feed in the intestine but eventually pass out of the host in feces. Larvae from the stools of infected individuals measure between 300 and 800 μ in length. Once established in moist soil, the rhabditiform larvae may develop into free-living adults (heterogonic development), or transform into filariform larvae and become infective (homogonic development). If homogonic development takes place, the cycle is referred to as

direct. Lumen-dwelling rhabditiform larvae have been known to metamorphose into filariform larvae, penetrate the intestinal wall, migrate to the lungs, and repeat the cycle. Such an instance is referred to as the hyperinfective phase.

THE AUTOINFECTION PHASE. As an alternative to the hyperinfective phase, infective filariform larvae, while en route to the exterior in feces, can reinfect the host. If these larva come in contact with perianal skin, they can penetrate and are eventually carried to the lungs by the blood. This is referred to as the autoinfective phase of the life cycle.

OTHER *Strongyloides* SPECIES. Other *Strongyloides* species of economic importance include *S. papillosus* in sheep. In this species, Ransom (1911) discovered that the males are extremely scarce in the free-living generation. The females are believed to give birth parthenogenically. *Strongyloides ransomi* is a fairly common species found in pigs. During its life cycle, unlike *S. stercoralis,* the eggs of the parasitic females do not give rise to rhabditiform larvae in the intestine; rather, the eggs pass to the exterior and then hatch.

SUPERFAMILY OXYUROIDEA

The major diagnostic characteristics of the Oxyuroidea have been discussed on page 404. The chief characteristic is the presence of an oxyuroid, or bulbous type of esophagus, which includes an end bulb. The species belonging to this superfamily are parasitic in invertebrates as well as in vertebrates.

Some common oxyuroid species that are readily available for laboratory studies are listed in Table 16–1. Several representative oxyuroid species are considered in the following discussion.

Enterobius vermicularis. Undoubtedly the best known oxyuroid nematode is the human pin- or seatworm, *E. vermicularis* (Plate 16–5). Children, especially early school-age children, are most frequently infected with this nematode. The geographic distribution of *E. vermicularis* is worldwide; however, the incidence of infection varies with each locale. For example, Hitchcock (1950) reported that at least 51 per cent of Alaska Eskimos are infected; Cates (1953) reported a 26.85 per cent infection rate among students of five elementary schools in and around Tallahassee, Florida; Leedy and Howard

Table 16-1. Some Common Oxyuroid Nematodes

Nematode Species	Host
Blatticola blattae	*Blatella germanica*
Hammerschmidtiella diesingi	*Periplanata americana*
Leidynema appendiculata	*Periplanata americana*
Thelastoma bulhoesi	*Periplanata americana*
Thelastoma icemi	*Periplanata americana*
Aspicularis tetraptera	mouse
Syphacia obvelata	rat and mouse
Enterobius vermicularis	man

(1952) reported a 58 per cent infection rate among the pupils in a preschool nursery in San Francisco, California; Cram and Reardon (1939) reported a 51 per cent infection rate among school children in Washington, D. C.; Kessel et al. (1954) reported only a 9 per cent infection rate among 5 to 9 year olds in Tahiti, French Oceania; Ricci (1952) reported a startling infection rate of 77.14 per cent among Sicilian children, but in that same population only 6.09 per cent of the adults were infected. Iwanczuk (1953) reported that 8.6 per cent of 1119 children up to 4 years of age in Warsaw, Poland, were infected; Cintra and Rugai (1955) reported only a 1.7 per cent infection rate among 2879 schoolboys from 4 to 14 years old in Baurú, São Paulo, Brazil. Cheng (1960), in surveying a group of children from a wide geographic range in the United States, found that 32.93 per cent were infected. This figure probably comes as close as any in portraying the average of infection among preschool age children in the United States.

Life Cycle of *Enterobius vermicularis*. The life cycle of *Enterobius* is direct; no intermediate host is required. Within the host's intestine, both the males and females are commonly attached to the epithelial wall. After copulation, gravid females become packed with eggs. These females demonstrate a rhythmic periodicity, since they migrate posteriorly during the night but seldom during the day. They lay their eggs, which become lodged in the perianal folds. Most females migrate back into the large intestine after ovipositing; however, some do pass to the exterior. Deposited eggs enclose a motile larva. The transparent eggshell is composed of a hyaline outer albuminous layer; a shell proper, composed of two layers of chitin; and an inner lipoid embryonic layer.

It has been estimated that a single female deposits from 4672 to 16,888 (mean, 11,105) eggs. Infections or reinfections become established when these infective eggs are ingested by the host. These eggs are usually picked up from bedclothes or fingernails that become contaminated while scratching the itchy perianal zone caused by the migrations of the females. However, the lightweight eggs can be air-borne and inhaled. Schüffner and Swellengrebel (1949) suggested that retroinfections are possible in which case larvae hatching from perianally located eggs migrate back up the intestinal tract.

Usually, ingested eggs hatch once they reach the duodenum. The escaping larvae migrate posteriorly and molt thrice in the process. These larvae become mature by the time they reach the large intestine. The life cycle of the *E. vermicularis* generally takes 2 months. Eggs are comparatively resistant and remain viable for a week or more under cool, humid conditions.

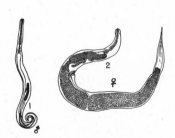

Plate 16-5 *Enterobius vermicularis*. **1.** Male specimen. **2.** Female specimen. (Figs. 1 and 2 after Beaver.)

Other Oxyuroid Genera

Other representative members of the Oxyuroidea from domestic animals are depicted in Plate 16–6.

The life cycle of *Oxyuris equi,* in horses, parallels that of *Enterobius vermicularis.* The life cycles of *Skrjabinema ovis,* the sheep pinworm, and *Passalurus ambiguus,* the rabbit pinworm, are presumably the same, although not completely known.

Numerous other oxyuroid nematodes inhabit the intestine of rabbits, hares, and rodents. These include the genera *Dermatoxys* and *Passalurus* in rabbits (Plate 16–6, Figs. 3 and 5). Members of both these genera are armed with three buccal teeth. *Aspiculuris* and *Wellcomia* are found in rodents (Plate 16–6, Fig. 6). The species of the genus *Syphacia* are parasitic in rodents but one species, *S. obvelata,* a common caecal parasite of laboratory rats, has been reported occasionally from humans. The life cycle of this species parallels that of *Enterobius vermicularis.* Another commonly encountered oxyuroid nematode is *Probstmayria vivipara,*

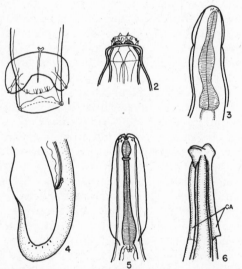

Plate 16-6   Some parasitic oxyuroid nematodes.
1. *Oxyuris equi.* Posterior end of male, ventral view. **2.** Anterior end of *Skrjabinema ovis,* the sheep pinworm. **3.** Anterior end of *Passalurus ambiguus,* the rabbit pinworm. **4.** Lateral view of posterior end of male of *Probstmayria vivipara,* the minute pinworm of horses. **5.** Anterior end of *Dermatoxys veligera,* a parasite in the caecum of rabbits. **6.** Anterior end of *Aspiculuris tetraptera,* a parasite of rats and other rodents. (CA, cervial alae.) (Redrawn after Hall, 1916.) (Figs. 1 to 5 redrawn after Schiller in Morgan, B. B. and Hawkins, P. A. 1949. *Veterinary Helminthology,* Burgess, Minneapolis.)

found in equines the world over. In *P. vivipara,* the horse pinworm, the gravid females give rise to larvae that hatch within the uteri of the parents.

Several genera of Oxyuroidea are parasitic in the intestine of reptiles. These include *Pharyngodon, Thelandros,* and *Atractis* in lizards and tortoises (Plate 16–7, Fig. 1), and *Labiduris* in turtles.

OXYUROIDS FROM INVERTEBRATES

Many species of Oxyuroidea have been reported in invertebrate hosts.

FAMILY THELASTOMATIDAE

Most species found in various insects belong to the family Thelastomatidae, members of which are characterized by eight simple papillae that make up the outer circlet surrounding the mouth, and by one or no copulatory spicules in males. Representatives found in cockroaches include members of *Leidynema, Hammerschmidtiella* (Plate 16–7, Fig. 2), and *Blatticola.*

The life cycle of *Leidynema appendiculata* is known (Plate 16–7, Fig. 3). The eggs, which pass out in the cockroach feces, include partially developed larvae that do not hatch in available culture media or outside the host. However, when the enclosed larvae complete their development, they hatch from the eggshell if the eggs are ingested by a roach host and if such eggs reach the host's midgut.

Other genera of Thelastomatidae include *Thelastoma* in cockroaches and scarabaeid beetles (Plate 16–7, Fig. 4), and *Pseudonymus* in water beetles. In *Pseudonymus,* the peculiar eggs are enveloped within two coiled filaments that uncoil when they come in contact with water and become entangled in aquatic plants (Plate 16–7, Fig. 5). Members of *Aorurus* are found in passalid beetles (Plate 16–7, Fig. 6). The female members of the three last-mentioned genera all possess spines in the cervical region.

FAMILY RHIGONEMATIDAE

The family Rhigonematidae, characterized by four double papillae that form the outer circlet and two copulatory spicules of equal length in males, includes, among others, the genera *Dudekemia* and *Rhigonema* (Plate 16–8, Fig. 2) in millipedes.

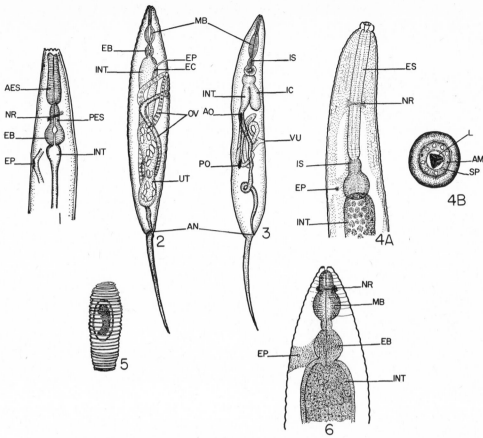

Plate 16-7   Some oxyuroid nematodes. 1. Anterior end of *Atractis* in intestine of lizards and tortoises. (Redrawn and modified after Thapar, 1925.) **2.** Female of *Hammerschmidtiella diesingi* in cockroaches. (Redrawn after Chitwood, 1932.) **3.** Female of *Leidynema appendiculata* in cockroaches. (Redrawn after Dobrovolny and Ackert, 1934.) **4. A.** Anterior end of *Thelastoma*, parasitic in cockroaches and scarabaeid beetle larvae. **B.** Face-on view of anterior end of *Thelastoma*. (A and B redrawn after Christie, 1931.) **5.** Egg of *Pseudonymus* enclosed in spiral filaments. (Redrawn after Györy, 1856.) **6.** Anterior end of *Aorurus*, in millipedes and scarabaeid beetle larvae. (Redrawn after Christie, 1931.)

(AES, anterior portion of esophagus; AM, amphid; AN, anus; AO, anterior ovary; EB, end bulb of esophagus; EC, excretory canal; EP, excretory pore; ES, esophagus; IC, intestinal canal; INT, intestine; IS, isthmus of esophagus; L, lip; MB, median bulb of esophagus; NR, nerve ring; OV, ovary; PES, posterior portion of esophagus; PO, posterior ovary; SP, sensory papilla; UT, uterus; VU, vulva.)

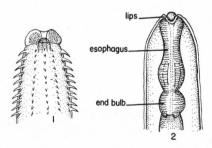

Plate 16-8   Parasitic rhigonematid nematodes. 1. Anterior end of the oxyuroid nematode *Hystrignathus*, parasitic in passalid beetles. (Redrawn after Christie, 1934.) **2.** Anterior end of the oxyuroid nematode *Rhigonema*, parasitic in millipedes. (Redrawn and modified after Artigas, 1926.)

SUPERFAMILY ASCAROIDEA

The ascaroid nematodes are comparatively large and plump worms found in the intestine of various vertebrates. The most common and best known member is *Ascaris lumbricoides*, an intestinal parasite of man and other vertebrates. Various names have been established to designate the forms found in different hosts. The validity of some of these has been challenged because the specimens recovered from certain hosts other than man are morphologically indistinguishable from *A. lumbricoides*. This is true for *A. lumbricoides* found in man and *A.*

suum in pigs. However, physiological evidence strongly suggests that these two species are distinct. For example, the pig-infecting species does not infect man, or vice versa. Hence, the two should be considered distinct physiological, or host specific species (see Chapter 1). Only recently has Sprent reported that the pig-infecting and human-infecting species of this worm can be distinguished by denticle differences.

FAMILY ASCARIDIDAE

Genus *Ascaris*

Ascaris lumbricoides. This species is cosmopolitan. Stoll (1947) estimated that there are 644 million human infections in the world, of which 3 million are found in North America, 42 million in tropical America, 59 million in Africa, 488 million in Asia, 32 million in Europe, 19.9 million in the USSR, and 500,000 in the Pacific islands. Males, measuring 15 to 31 cm. in length by 2 to 4 mm. in diameter, are smaller than the females, which measure from 20 to 40 cm. in length by 3 to 6 mm. in diameter (Plate 16–9). As in most nematodes, the posterior terminal of the males is curved ventrally. The mouth in both sexes is surrounded by a dorsal and two ventrolateral lips (Plate 16–9, Fig. 3).

Life Cycle of *Ascaris lumbricoides*. Adults of *A. lumbricoides* live in the small intestine of the host, where they feed on chyme. However, it is suspected that the adults are capable of puncturing the intestinal wall to suck blood. Copulation occurs in the host's intestine.

Egg production is extremely prolific. It has been estimated that a single female may contain as many as 27 million eggs. Eggs laid by fertilized females measure from 60 to 70 μ by 40 to 50 μ and possess a thin transparent shell covered by an irregular coat of albumin that is usually brownish in color (Plate 16–19, Fig. 4). Unfertilized eggs are often found intermingled among fertilized eggs in the host's feces. These eggs are less regularly ovoid and the albuminous coat is less prominent, or absent (Plate 16–19, Fig. 5). Also, the unfertilized egg includes amorphous globules rather than a well formed zygote.

When fertilized eggs are deposited by the female, the zygote is uncleaved. It is in this state that the eggs pass out in the host's feces. Further development of the zygotes occur only if their environment has temperatures lower than that of the host's body. The zygotes develop at temperatures between 60° and 98° F. However, development ceases at temperatures below 60° F., and the eggs disintegrate at temperatures above 100° F.

Under natural conditions, eggs develop readily in moist soil in the presence of oxygen. Active larvae are formed within each eggshell in 10 to 14 days, but ingestion of eggs enclosing such larvae does not result in the establishment of an infection. It is only after the first stage larva undergoes a molt within the eggshell and matures into the second stage larva that the egg becomes infective.

When infective eggs are swallowed, the larvae hatch in the host's small intestine. These larvae actively burrow through the intestinal lining and are carried to the liver via the mesenteric lymphatics or venules. From the liver, the larvae are transported to the right side of the heart, and are transported from there to the lungs via the pulmonary artery. The larvae generally remain in the lungs for a few days, where they increase in size before they rupture out of the pulmonary capillaries and enter the air sacs. From there they are carried up the bronchioles, bronchi, and trachea to the area of the epiglottis. Larvae lodged in the epiglottis are coughed up, swallowed, and pass down to the small intestine. During this complex migratory process, the individual worms increase from 200 to 300 μ in length to approximately ten times that size. Ecdysis occurs in the small intestine between the 25th and 29th day from the time of oral ingestion of the eggs. Only larvae that have successfully completed the fourth ecdysis can survive in the intestine and develop to maturity.

The life cycle of the majority of the other ascaroids parallels that of *A. lumbricoides*. Sprent (1952) categorizes the migratory behavior of ascarids in mice into two types—the tracheal type, in which the larvae migrate through the viscera and eventually disappear from the tissues; and the somatic type, which consists of permanent encystment of living larvae within the tissues. The migratory pattern of *A. lumbricoides* given above represents the tracheal type.

Not all ascarids possess direct life cycles—that is, without an intermediate host. For example, *Ascaris devosi* in the martin and *A. columnaris* in the skunk have rodent intermediate hosts.

Ascaris suum (= A. suilla). This nematode is morphologically indistinguishable from *A. lumbricoides* except for minor denticle differences and is considered by some to be the same; however, these two species can be considered distinct host specific species. *Ascaris suum* is a very common parasite of pigs. The fertilized eggs are extremely resistant and remain viable in damp soil for 4 to 5 years.

Various hypotheses have been advanced to explain why adult nematodes, living in their host's intestine, are not digested by their host's digestive enzymes. The mostly widely accepted theory at this time is that the parasites are capable of secreting antienzymes that inhibit the host's digestive enzymes. Indeed, Rhodes et al. (1963) have demonstrated that trypsin and chymotrypsin inhibitors are present in the body wall and perienteric (or pseudocoelomic) fluid of *Ascaris suum*.

Genus *Neoascaris*

Neoascaris vitulorum. This parasite is a relatively common large nematode found in the small intestine of cattle, particularly calves (Plate 16–10, Fig. 2). The males measure up to 25 cm. in length, while the females are from 22 to 30 cm. long. As in some *Ascaris* infections, verminous pneumonia and hemorrhages result from the migration of the larvae through the lungs. These symptoms are more frequently encountered in *N. vitulorum* infections. *Neoascaris* infections are probably always prenatally acquired.

Genus *Parascaris*

Parascaris equorum. This large intestinal

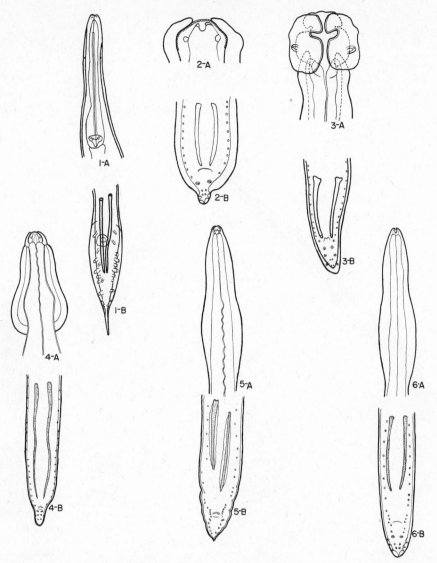

Plate 16–10   Some parasitic nematodes of veterinary importance. 1. *Heterakis gallinae*. **A.** Dorsal view of anterior end. **B.** Ventral view of posterior end of male. 2. *Neoascaris vitulorum*, large roundworm of cattle. **A.** Anterior end. **B.** Ventral view of posterior end of male. 3. *Parascaris equorum*, large roundworm of horses. **A.** Ventral view of anterior end. **B.** Ventral view of posterior end of male. 4. *Toxocara cati*, in dogs, cats, other felines, and rarely man. **A.** Ventral view of anterior end. **B.** Ventral view of posterior end of male. 5. *Toxocara canis*, in dogs. **A.** Ventral view of anterior end. **B.** Ventral view of posterior end of male. 6. *Toxascaris leonina*, in canines and felines. **A.** Ventral view of anterior end. **B.** Ventral view of posterior end of male. (All figures redrawn after Schiller in Morgan, B. B., and Hawkins, P. A. 1949. *Veterinary Helminthology*, Burgess, Minneapolis.)

roundworm of horses is generally distributed throughout North America (Plate 16–10, Fig. 3). The males measure from 150 to 280 mm. in length, while the females range from 180 to 350 mm. in length. The life cycle of *P. equorum* parallels that of *Ascaris lumbricoides*. This nematode causes severe damage to its host, especially young animals. During migration of the larvae in the lungs, hemorrhages, pneumonia, and

fever result. Intestinal obstructions and perfora- tions by the intestinal form have been reported

Genus *Toxocara*

Toxocara canis AND *T. cati*.   The genus *Toxocara* includes, among others, *T. canis* in dog and *T. cati* in cats (Plate 16–10, Figs. 4 and 5) The life cycles of both species may be similar t that of *Ascaris lumbricoides*—that is, direct, by ingesting embryonated eggs, followed by the complex migration. This is not the only life cycle pattern, however. Sprent (1956) has shown that *T. cati* eggs can hatch and develop to the second stage larvae in earthworms, cockroaches, chickens, mice, dogs, lambs, and cats. Cats can become infected by ingesting mice harboring larvae in their tissues. In this method of infection, the larvae are mostly confined to the host's digestive tract.

Prenatal infection with *T. canis* is relatively common, but it is not known to occur with *T. cati.*

Occasionally, a syndrome known as visceral larva migrans is reported in man, resulting from the ingestion of embryonated eggs of *T. canis* and *T. cati* and the subsequent migration of the larvae in viscera of the human host (p. 465).

Owen (1930) reported that, during the development of the larva in the egg of *T. canis,* the embryonic morphogenesis is completed within 35 days when the eggs are exposed to 16.5° C., but development ceases if the eggs are maintained below 12° C. and in as few as 3.5 to 5 days when exposed to 30° C. However, death occurs if the eggs are exposed to 37° C. Although eggs do not develop at temperatures below 12° C., they are not killed, for they can survive at temperatures as low as −25° C. provided there is a certain amount of oxygen present.

LIFE CYCLE OF *Toxocara canis.* As a result of research by Sprent (1958) and others, it is now known that two different avenues of development—the tissue and the intestinal phases—can occur in the case of *T. canis,* depending on the age and the species of the host. In addition, prenatal infection in dogs—that is, the passage of the parasite from mother to offspring via the uterine and umbilical circulation—is also possible. These findings emphasize that the physiology of the host can be an important factor in influencing the developmental pattern of the parasite, especially among nematodes.

Adult *T. canis* males, measuring up to 10 cm. in length, and females, measuring up to 18 cm. in length, are found in the small intestine of dogs. The eggs oviposited by females after copulation are unembryonated when passed out in the host's feces. Embryonic development occurs outside the host, and infective eggs enclosing second stage larvae develop in 5 to 6 days, or longer.

When infective eggs are ingested by the host, they hatch in the small intestine, and the larvae enter hepatic portal venules and are carried to the lungs via the liver and heart, as in the case of *Ascaris lumbricoides.* From this stage on, the migration route varies, depending on the age and the species of the host.

Tissue Phase. If the host is an older dog, a rodent, or a human (especially a child), some of the larvae that migrate to the liver and lungs remain in the parenchyma of these organs, while other larvae continue through the pulmonary veins and heart into the arterial circulation. Larvae in the arterial circulation are carried to the capillaries of the skeletal muscles and kidneys, or to the central nervous system, where they enter tissues and remain inactive.

In rodents, further development is possible if infected rodents are ingested by a dog, especially a young dog. If this occurs, larvae freed in the dog's stomach migrate into the intestine, where they burrow through the intestinal wall and enter the hepatic portal vein. The larvae are thus carried to the lungs via the liver and heart.

Within the lungs, the larvae migrate out of the blood vessels and enter bronchioles. From the bronchioles, they migrate up the bronchi and the trachea and are swallowed. Once the larvae reach the small intestine, they begin to mature.

Intestinal Phase. If the host is a young pup, almost all the larvae reach the lungs, where they escape from the blood vessels and enter alveoli. From these sites, they migrate up the bronchi and trachea and are swallowed. On reaching the small intestine, they develop to maturity. Thus, the migration pattern within the host is essentially the same as that of *Ascaris lumbricoides.*

Prenatal Infection. If *T. canis* larvae are present in the tissues of pregnant dogs, they are activated by the hormones of pregnancy and re-enter the blood stream. They are carried to the uterine circulation and reach the developing fetus via the umbilical artery. Thus, third stage larvae are found in the heart and lungs of full-term but unborn fetuses.

At the time of birth, and during the first few days after birth, larvae are found in the lungs. By the fourth day after birth, fourth stage larvae appear in the intestine; by the second week after birth, the final molt occurs and the worms mature in the host's intestine.

Genus *Toxascaris*
Toxascaris leonina. This parasite is found

in the small intestine of dogs, cats, lions, tigers, and other carnivorous animals (Plate 16–10, Fig. 6). During the life cycle of this species, the larvae hatching from the eggs do not migrate through the viscera as in *Ascaris*. Rather, once liberated in the small intestine, the larvae burrow into the crypts of Lieberkühn, the submucosa, and into the muscular layer. Within 9 to 10 days after ingestion of the eggs, the larvae return to the lumen of the small intestine and grow to maturity. This pattern is another variation in the life cycle pattern found in the Ascaroidea.

Genus *Ascaridia*

In addition to *Ascaridia galli,* a well known chicken parasite, various ascarid nematodes are known to parasitize reptiles, for example, *Polydelphis* and *Ophidascaris.*

Ascaridia galli. The biology of *Ascaridia galli,* the comparatively large intestinal nematode of chickens, has been studied extensively (Plate 16–11, Fig. 1). The males measure from 30 to 80 mm. in length, and the females are 60

to 120 mm. long. As in most parasitic nematodes, *A. galli* undergoes four molts—one while in the eggshell and three within the chicken. The life history of this species parallels that of *Toxascaris leonina.* Infection of the chicken is established when eggs containing the first stage larva are ingested. These larvae hatch; once the eggs reach the host's small intestine.

For the first 9 days, the larvae survive as lumen-dwellers or as intervillar space-dwellers in the small intestine. On approximately the 10th day, the larvae begin to burrow into the mucosa, causing severe hemorrhage and tissue damage. From the 10th to the 17th day, the larvae are partially lodged in the mucosa, but with their tails protruding into the lumen. Following the 17th day, these nematodes return as lumen-dwellers and remain permanently as such. The three molts in the host take place at intervals of approximately 6 days.

Resistance to *Ascaridia galli.* Age resistance to *Ascaridia galli* has been demonstrated repeatedly. Chickens older than 3 months and maintained on normal diets are quite resistant;

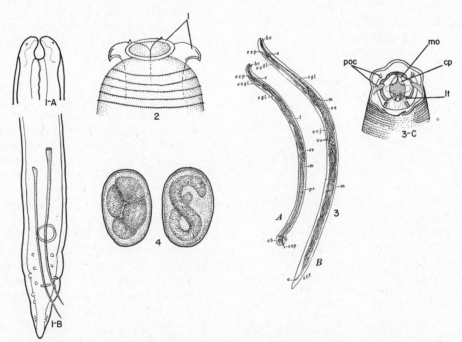

Plate 16-11   Some ascaroid and strongyloid nematodes. 1. *Ascaridia galli,* in chickens. **A.** Anterior end. **B.** Posterior end of male. (Redrawn after Schiller in Morgan, B. B., and Hawkins, P. A. 1949. *Veterinary Helminthology,* Burgess, Minneapolis.) **2.** Anterior end of *Goezia* in fishes. (Redrawn after Maplestone, 1930.) **3. A.** Male of *Necator americanus.* **B.** Female. **C.** Anterior end. (A, B and C after Craig, C., and Faust, E. 1951. *Clinical Parasitology,* Lea & Febiger, Philadelphia.) **4.** Eggs of *N. americanus*—one showing blastomeres, the other enclosing larva.

(a, anal pore; bc, buccal capsule; cb, copulatory bursa; c gl, paired cephalic gland; cp, cutting plates; c sp, copulatory spicules; e, esophagus; ex gl, excretory gland; ex p, excretory pore; l, lips; lt, lateral teeth; m, midgut; mo, mouth opening; ov, ovary; ovj, ovejector; poc, papillae of outer circlet; pr, prostate gland; sv, seminal vesicle; t, testis; vu, vulva.)

worms that are present are smaller than those in younger hosts. Ackert et al. (1939) attributed resistance in older birds to the increased number of goblet cells present in the intestinal wall, because the secretions of these cells inhibit growth and development of the worms. This phenomenon has been demonstrated by Eisenbrandt and Ackert (1941), who reported that duodenal mucous extracts of dogs and pigs hasten the death of worms maintained in vitro. The administration of the sex hormones testosterone and estradiol to male and female birds respectively also causes resistance. This resistance is thought to be an indirect rather than a direct effect.

Various workers (Ackert et al., 1935) have demonstrated that certain genetic strains of chickens are more resistant to *Ascaridia galli* than others.

FAMILY HETEROCHEILIDAE

The heterocheilid nematodes, including *Filocapsularia, Raphidascaris, Augusticaecum, Porrocaecum, Contracaecum,* and *Dujardinascaris,* can be distinguished from one another by the position and arrangement of unique digestive diverticula located in the area of the esophageal bulb (Plate 16–12). Species of *Filocapsularia* parasitize marine mammals such as seals and dolphins. Species of *Raphidascaris* are found in fishes; *Augusticaecum* spp. are found in amphibians and reptiles; *Porrocaecum* spp. in birds, fishes, and marine mammals; and *Contracaecum* spp. in fishes and certain reptiles.

Life Cycle of the Heterocheilidae

The life cycles of the various members of the Heterocheilidae involve one or more inter-

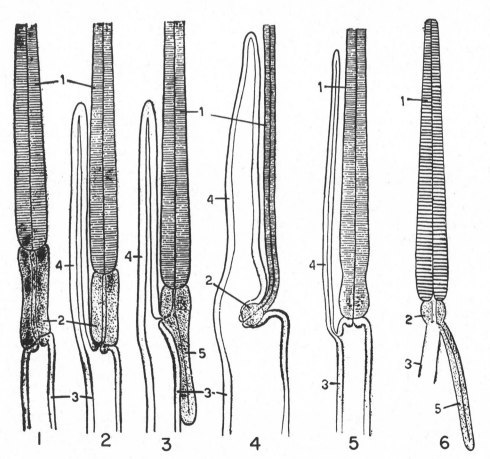

Plate 16-12   Types of digestive diverticula in heterocheilid ascaroids. 1. *Filocapsularia.* **2.** *Porrocaecum.* **3.** *Contracaecum.* **4.** *Dujardinascaris.* **5.** *Augusticaecum.* **6.** *Raphidascaris.* (Figs. 1–5 after Baylis, 1920; Fig. 6 after Yamaguti, 1935.)

(1, muscular portion of esophagus; 2, ventriculus; 3, intestine; 4, intestinal caecum; 5, esophageal caecum.)

mediate hosts. The involvement of intermediate hosts represents further variations of the developmental patterns found in the Ascaroidea. For example, in the life cycle of *Contracaecum,* eggs that pass out in the feces of the definitive host include undeveloped or poorly developed larvae. Larval differentiation continues once the eggs reach water, resulting in the formation of infective larvae armed with a cuticular stylet (also known as a boring tooth).

The infective larva either hatches or remains in the shell, but in either case it is ingested by the first intermediate host—usually a copepod, an amphipod, a jellyfish, or a fish. Within this host, the larva burrows through the intestinal wall and continues to develop within the body cavity or in the surrounding tissues. Some larvae may encyst. When such an infected host is eaten by the second intermediate host (a fish), the larva again burrows through the intestinal wall and encysts in the host's body cavity or tissues. When a fish containing encysted larvae is eaten by another fish or some other fish-eating animal, the cycle is completed. During maturation, the nematode loses its penetration stylet.

Thomas (1937) reported that in *Raphidascaris* only one intermediate host is required. In this small fish host, the nematode larvae penetrate through the intestinal wall and encyst in the liver and mesenteries. When the smaller infected fish is eaten by a pike, the cycle is completed. Similarly, a single intermediate host is necessary in the life cycle of *Porrocaecum.*

Members of the genus *Goezia,* which are characterized by rows of cuticular spines, are found in fishes (Plate 16–11, Fig. 2). Again, one intermediate host is required.

FAMILY HETERAKIDAE

Genus *Heterakis*

Heterakis gallinae. This parasite is the common caecal worm of chickens, turkeys, pheasants, and other fowls (Plate 16–10, Fig. 1). Both males and females bear cervical alae, and the males also possess caudal alae and twelve pairs of papillae. The males are 7 to 13 mm. long, while the females are 10 to 16 mm. long. As in *Ascaris lumbricoides,* the eggs passed out in the host's feces contain uncleaved zygotes. However, after embryonated eggs are ingested and hatched in the gizzard or duodenum of the bird, the larvae migrate to the caecum and usually remain in the lumen or migrate in between the crypts, rarely in the lymph glands.

These larvae do not follow the migratory pattern of *A. lumbricoides. Heterakis gallinae* also undergoes four molts—one within the eggshell while in the soil, the second 4 to 6 days after infection of the host, the third and fourth in 9 to 10 days and 14 days respectively. Not all the embryonated eggs ingested by the fowl host develop. The percentage of survival is greater when smaller numbers of eggs are ingested by a single host. For example, Clapham reported that in her experimental series of 200 eggs fed to a host, 23 per cent developed. On the other hand, when she fed 1000 eggs to a host, only 0.3 per cent developed.

Although *H. gallinae* is apparently nonpathogenic, it is the vector for *Histomonas meleagridis,* the highly pathogenic "blackhead" disease-causing flagellate (p. 61).

Heterakis spumosa. This nematode is a commonly encountered and widely distributed parasite of wild rats. The sexually mature adults inhabit the caecum and colon. The life cycle is direct.

SUPERFAMILY STRONGYLOIDEA

The superfamily Strongyloidea includes the hookworms and related bursate nematodes. The characteristics of the superfamily are listed on page 405. Many strongyloids are intestinal parasites of man and domestic animals. These parasites often result in serious diseases.

Only five of the better known families of the Strongyloidea are discussed here. A key to these follows.

1. Two ventrolateral cutting plates with or without teeth at entrance to large buccal capsule. Small teeth (lancets) at base of capsule.................**Ancylostomidae.**
2. Lips absent. Mouth surrounded by a mouth collar (corona radiata) (Plate 16–1, Fig. 2), which may or may not be lobed. **Strongylidae.**
3. Lacks cutting plates or corona radiata. Buccal capsule is poorly developed or lacking.................**Trichostrongylidae.**
4. Buccal capsule is more or less hexagonal with heavily cuticularized walls. Small teeth at base of capsule......**Syngamidae.**
5. Body laterally compressed. Buccal capsule is bivalved..........**Diaphanocephalidae.**

FAMILY ANCYLOSTOMIDAE

The family Ancylostomidae includes all the hookworms. Species of *Necator* and *Ancylostoma* infect man, while species of *Bunostomum, Globocephalus, Anclyostoma,* and *Uncinaria* parasitize various domestic animals.

Hookworm Disease

Until recent years, the human hookworm disease was numbered among the most prevalent and important of the parasitic diseases of man. Unlike malaria, amoebiasis, or schistosomiasis, hookworm disease is not spectacular. Hookworm affects populations by gradually sapping its victims of their strength, vitality and health. As exemplified in certain parts of the Middle East and the Far East, and not too many years ago in most of the southern states in the United States, the victims become lazy, shiftless, and nonproductive. The resultant economic loss is beyond computation.

LARVA MIGRANS.   As in schistosome dermatitis, hookworms of animals, for which humans are incompatible hosts, often attempt to penetrate man. These normally fail to pass through the stratum germinativum of the skin and migrate for some time at that level, causing a skin eruption known as larva migrans, or creeping eruption. This aspect of host-parasite relationship is expounded upon more fully in another section (p. 465).

Although skin penetration is the most common avenue of infection, hookworms, especially those of animals, can become established within their hosts through oral ingestion of the strongyliform larvae. Ortlepp (1925), for example, showed that *Gaigeria pachyscelis* of sheep and goats can be established through oral ingestion. Furthermore, Foster (1932) has demonstrated that intra-uterine infections are also possible.

Genus *Necator*

Necator americanus.   The New World, or American, hookworm is widely distributed in southern United States, Central and South America, and in the Caribbean area (Plate 16–11, Fig. 3). Its presence has been reported in Asia and South Africa. The males, measuring 7 to 9 mm. in length by 0.3 mm. in diameter, possess a large bursa, while the females, measuring 9 to 11 mm. in length by 0.4 mm. in diameter, are larger and lack a bursa.

Life Cycle of *Necator americanus.*   The life history of *N. americanus* is direct, with a free-living larval phase. The adults are parasitic in the small intestine of man. The worms hold on to the intestinal wall and feed on blood and tissue exudates (Plate 16–13, Fig. 1). Von Brand (1938) postulated that the erythrocytes

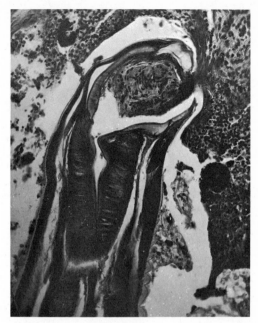

Plate 16-13   Photomicrograph of hookworm holding onto intestinal wall of host. (Courtesy of Armed Forces Institute of Pathology; Negative No. 33810.)

ingested by adult hookworms provide much of the oxygen necessary in the worm's metabolism, since these parasites live in a portion of the alimentary tract that contains very little oxygen.

The females of *N. americanus* are prolific egg producers. It has been estimated that a single female can produce 5000 to 10,000 eggs per day. When the eggs pass out of the host in feces, the embryo is at the four-blastomere stage (Plate 16–11, Fig. 4).

The embryo continues to develop in moist soil that is rich in oxygen. If such an ideal habitat exists, the egg hatches within 24 hours, and the escaping larva is of the rhabditiform type (Plate 16–14, Fig. 1). The rhabditiform larva undergoes two molts and becomes a strongyliform larva, which is characterized by a long cylindrical esophagus with a terminal bulb that is not sharply demarked from the anterior truncate portion of the esophagus (Plate 16–14, Fig. 2). The free-living larvae feed primarily on soil bacteria. A considerable amount of the nutrients, especially lipids, is stored in the body and serve as reserve food until the larva enters the host. When the rhabditiform larva undergoes the second ecdysis, usually on the fifth day, giving rise to the infective strongyliform larva, its cuticle is retained as an enclosing sheath. This sheath is usually

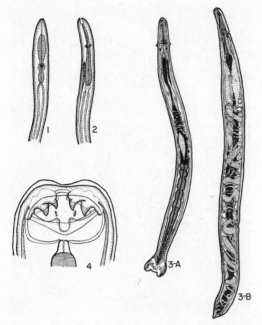

Plate 16-14   Human-infecting hookworms. 1. Rhabditiform larva of *Necator americanus.* **2.** Strongyliform larva of *N. americanus.* **3. A.** Male of *Ancylostoma duodenale.* **B.** Female of *A. duodenale.* (A and B redrawn after Looss.) **4.** Anterior end of *A. duodenale,* showing buccal capsule with two pairs of teeth. (Redrawn after Faust in Craig, C., and Faust, E. 1951. *Clinical Parasitology,* Lea & Febiger, Philadelphia.)

retained until the infective larva penetrates the skin of the host.

Infection of man is accomplished when ensheathed strongyliform larvae penetrate the skin, usually of the feet and legs. Although little damage is done during the initial burrowing, the minute perforations on the skin do serve as sites for secondary infections by bacteria and fungi. If large numbers of larvae penetrate a restricted area, dermatitis usually ensues. Once within the dermis, the larvae cause considerable damage while penetrating the minute blood vessels and lymphatics in which they are eventually carried to the right side of the heart. These larvae pass through the heart and are carried to the lungs via the pulmonary artery. Like the larvae of *Ascaris lumbricoides,* the larvae of *N. americanus* rupture out of the capillaries within the lungs and become lodged in the alveoli. From here they migrate up the bronchioles, bronchi, and trachea, and are coughed up and swallowed.

Once the larvae reach the small intestine, they actively burrow into the intervillar spaces. At this point the third molt takes place on the third to fifth day after the initial entrance

into the host. After the third ecdysis, the larvae become lumen-dwellers and increase greatly in size, reaching 3.5 mm. in length. A fourth molt follows, after which the worms develop to maturity. The entire life cycle of *N. americanus* takes approximately 6 weeks. Other species of *Necator* have been described from other mammals.

Genus *Ancylostoma*

Ancylostoma duodenale. The Old World hookworm has been reported in southern Europe, North Africa, India, China, and Japan (Plate 16–14, Fig. 3). It also has been reported in the New World among Paraguayan Indians. Stoll (1947) estimated that 72.5 million humans are infected with this hookworm, the majority, 59 million, in Asia.

A. duodenale males measure from 8 to 11 mm. by 0.5 mm., while the females measure from 20 to 13 mm. by 0.6 mm. The cutting plate is armed with two pairs of teeth (Plate 16–14, Fig. 4). This species is primarily a human parasite, but it can be induced experimentally to parasitize monkeys, dogs, and cats. Its life cycle parallels that of *Necator americanus.*

Ancylostoma braziliense. Other species of *Ancylostoma* include *A. braziliense,* a parasite of dogs and cats in the tropics and subtropics including, southeastern United States along the Atlantic and Gulf Coasts. This species has been reported from man.

Ancylostoma caninum. This relatively large species with females measuring up to 20 mm. in length, is commonly found in dogs, cats, foxes, wolves, and other carnivores in temperate as well as in tropical and subtropical areas (Plate 16–15).

A considerable amount of work has been done on the biology of *Ancylostoma caninum.* Several investigators have reported the interesting phenomenon that strains of this hookworm adapted to canine hosts produce fewer eggs when introduced into cats. However, the reverse does not hold true. An explanation has yet to be determined. Wells (1931) reported that a single hookworm may ingest as much as 0.8 cc. of blood in 24 hours, although a more conservative amount is 0.1 cc. This alone is severe enough damage, but considerable additional damage is incurred when worms hold onto the intestinal mucosa. Sites of attachment usually become necrotic.

Hookworms secrete an anticoagulant during the biting process. This secretion prevents the clotting of the host's blood during feeding and

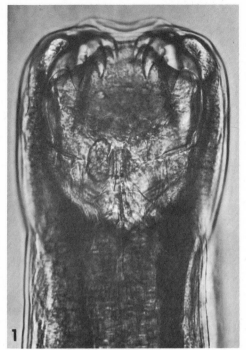

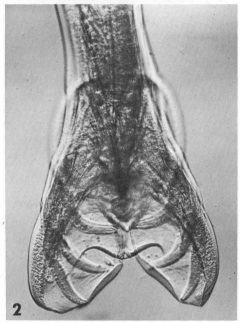

Plate 16-15   *Ancylostoma caninum,* the dog hookworm. **1.** Anterior end of adult, showing the three pairs of dorsal teeth. **2.** Copulatory bursa of male. (Photomicrographs for Figs. 1 and 2 courtesy of General Biological Supply House, Inc., Chicago.)

for a short period afterwards. Again, age resistance to *A. caninum* exists, and repeated infections result in immunity. Furthermore, Otto (1941) demonstrated that the degree of immunity is dependent on the degree of the initial infection. For example, if a dog is initially challenged with 1000 to 2000 infective larvae, an immunity to a second challenge of 50,000 larvae will result. However, if the initial challenge consists of only 500 larvae, the immunity developed is insufficient to withstand a second challenge of 50,000 larvae, and the host will be killed.

Genus *Bunostomum*

Bunostomum phlebotomum is a hookworm found in the small intestine of cattle (Plate 16–16, Fig. 1). Its life cycle is essentially the same as that of *Necator americanus.* However, infection of cows is more commonly accomplished through oral ingestion than it is by larval penetration through the skin. *Bunostomum trigonocephalum* is the hookworm of sheep.

Genus *Globocephalus*

Globocephalus urosubulatus is the hookworm of hogs (Plate 16–16, Fig. 2). The males measure 4.5 mm. by 0.38 mm., while the females measure 6.5 to 7.5 mm. by 0.52 mm. Its life cycle, although not completely understood, is presumed to be like that of the other hookworms.

Genus *Uncinaria*

The genus *Uncinaria* includes *U. stenocephala,* which is found in dogs, cats, foxes, and other carnivores. It is commonly found in colder climates such as Canada, whereas *Ancylostoma caninum* is found further south, in the United States.

FAMILY STRONGYLIDAE

The family Strongylidae includes numerous species parasitic in domestic animals. Some species are parasitic in wild animals, among which is *Oesophagostomum apiostomum* in simians of West Africa, China, and the Philippine Islands. This species is capable of infecting man.

Many of the strongylids are parasitic in the colon and caecum of horses, as are members of the genera *Strongylus, Triodontophorus, Cyathostomum,* and *Cylicocercus,* and many others (Plate 16–16, Figs. 3 to 5). Members of *Oesophagostomum,* commonly termed "nodular worms," are frequently found in pigs, ruminants, and primates. These nematodes inflict severe damage to their hosts because their larvae cause swellings or nodules in the intestinal wall of their hosts.

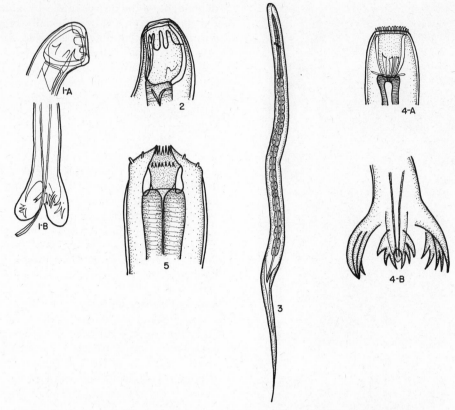

Plate 16-16   Parasitic nematodes. 1. *Bunostomum phlebotomum,* hookworm of cattle. **A.** Lateral view of anterior end. **B.** Ventral view of posterior end of male. **2.** Anterior end of *Globocephalus urosubulatus,* the swine hookworm. **3.** *Strongylus vulgaris,* the horse strongyle. **4.** *Triodontophorus tenuicollis,* in horses. **A.** Lateral view of anterior end. **B.** Ventral view of posterior end of male. **5.** Ventral view of anterior end of *Cylicocercus goldi,* parasitic in horses. (All figures after Schiller in Morgan, B. B., and Hawkins, P. A. 1949. *Veterinary Helminthology,* Burgess, Minneapolis.)

The pathogenicity of strongylid nematodes is of great importance and is of grave concern to veterinarians. The student is referred to Morgan and Hawkins (1949) for discussion of this aspect of the biology of equine-infecting and other species of strongylids.

Strongylid Life Cycles

Life cycles among the strongylids are essentially identical during the initial phases. Eggs passing out of the host contain blastomeres. Development continues in damp soil in the presence of oxygen. The escaping larvae are of the rhabditiform type. These larvae undergo two molts and metamorphose to the third stage strongyliform larvae, which are ensheathed within the cuticle of the second stage rhabditiform larvae.

The ensheathed larvae are ingested by the horse, or whatever the host may be, and once they reach the small intestine, the pattern varies, depending upon the species. Some of the known variations are as follows.

(1) The strongyliform larvae burrow into the intestinal mucosa, causing inflammation and nodule formation. The larvae dwell in the swellings until after the fourth molt, at which time they re-enter the lumen of the intestine. This pattern holds true for members of *Oesophagostomum, Basicola* in cattle, and *Cyathostomum.*

(2) The strongyliform larvae burrow through the intestinal wall and become established in the circulatory system. They are carried through an extensive migratory pathway involving the liver and lungs, and finally become lodged primarily in the anterior mesenteric artery, where they cause aneurism and thrombosis. Such is presumably the pattern in the case of *Strongylus vulgaris* in the horse.

(3) The larvae penetrate the intestinal wall,

molt, and re-enter the lumen of the intestine. This pattern is exemplified by *Strongylus equinus,* also a parasite of horses.

(4) The larvae penetrate the intestinal wall but do not migrate. Rather, they come to lie against the intestinal wall under the peritoneum and gradually shift toward the colon and caecum, where they burrow back into the intestinal wall, form nodules, molt, and eventually return to the lumen. This is the case in *Strongylus edentatus* in the horse.

FAMILY TRICHOSTRONGYLIDAE

The trichostrongylids are small and slender intestinal nematodes that lack corona radiata or cutting plates. Their buccal capsules are poorly developed and in some instances even lacking. This family includes a large number of species parasitic in all groups of vertebrates. Two well known species, *Haemonchus contortus* and *Nippostrongylus muris,* are described here as representative of the family. Other species are mentioned briefly and depicted.

Genus *Haemonchus*

Haemonchus contortus.   This parasite, called the twisted stomach worm, is a blood-sucking nematode occurring in the abomasum (the fourth stomach) of sheep and other ruminants (Plate 16–17, Fig. 2). The males measure 10 to 20 mm. in length, while the females are 18 to 30 mm. long. Freshly acquired specimens generally are reddish due to the host's blood contained within.

Haemonchus contortus is of considerable interest to veterinarians, since in heavy infections, the host dies. Even when medium infections exist, the host is weakened physically. It has been estimated that 4000 worms can suck about 60 ml. of blood a day, and it is not uncommon to find thousands of worms in a single host.

Life Cycle of *Haemonchus contortus.*   Eggs laid by the females pass to the exterior in the host's feces. They hatch under favorable climatic conditions, and the first stage larvae are free-living in soil. Two molts ensue, hence, three nonparasitic generations occur in soil. The third stage larva retains the "skin" after the second molt, so it is unable to feed. It survives at a low metabolic rate on stored nutrients. This is the infective stage of *H. contortus.* It is unable to enter its host by penetration; rather, it must be ingested while the host grazes. On reaching the sheep's abomasum, the larvae undergo two more molts and attain maturity.

Immunity to *Haemonchus.*   Stoll's report in 1928 on the so-called "self-cure" in sheep to *H. contortus* can be regarded as the beginning of studies on host immunity to helminths. Stoll experimented with two lambs. He infected one with 45 *H. contortus* larvae and left the other uninfected. Both lambs were permitted to graze in the same field. Nineteen days after the first lamb was infected, it began to pass eggs, thus contaminating the pasture. The second lamb, which was not experimentally infected, began passing eggs on the 54th day. Approximately 10 weeks after the first egg passing, both lambs reached their highest peak in egg passing; 10,600 and 13,000 eggs per gram of feces were passed by the originally infected and noninfected lambs, respectively.

Plate 16-17   Trichostrongylid nematodes. 1. Anterior end of *Trichostrongylus axei.* (Redrawn after Yorke and Maplestone, 1926.) **2.** Anterior portion of *Haemonchus contortus.* (Redrawn after Ransom, 1911.) **3.** Anterior portion of *Nematodirus filicollis.* (Redrawn after Ransom, 1911.)

(CP, cervical papillae; ES, esophagus; INT, intestine; NR, nerve ring.)

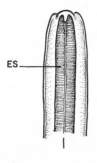

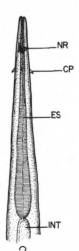

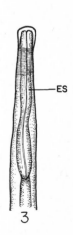

A rapid decline in the number of eggs passed followed, until none were passed at the second and third weeks after the peak. Although the lambs continued to ingest up to 14,000 infective larvae per day, no eggs were recovered thereafter. No new nematodes were established and those present were for the most part expelled. These findings caused Stoll to describe what are obviously cases of acquired immunity as "self-cure." Since that time, investigations into the development of immunity to nematodes have revealed that partial immunity to reinfection occurs in most cases.

Genus *Nippostrongylus*

Nippostrongylus muris. This nematode parasite is the hookworm of rats. It was originally a parasite of the Norway rat, *Rattus norvegicus,* but has since been experimentally transmitted to a number of laboratory animals including albino rats, cotton rats, hamsters, and rabbits. Not all these laboratory animals are completely satisfactory hosts, however, since nematodes introduced into some of these animals are stunted or abnormally developed. Within the host, *N. muris* is located in the anterior portion of the intestinal tract, either in contact with the mucosa or partially embedded in it.

In its natural host, male specimens measure 3 to 4 mm. in length, and females measure 4 to 6 mm. in length. In unnatural hosts, such as the cotton rat, males only measure 1.7 to 3.0 mm. in length, and females measure 1.7 to 3.4 mm. in length. This nematode is readily recognized by its small head, which bears a cephalic expansion of the cuticle. Furthermore, the body cuticle includes transverse striations and ten prominent longitudinal ridges. Both the mouth and buccal cavity are small, and two teeth are present, one on each side. Males can be distinguished from females by a prominent copulatory bursa and also by their smaller size.

Life Cycle of *Nippostrongylus muris.* Eggs passing out of the host in feces must fall into soil with an abundance of oxygen and moisture. Under these conditions, development of the enclosed larvae progresses until the first stage rhabditiform larvae hatch. In the laboratory, where eggs can be induced to hatch by mixing them with charcoal and spreading the mixture on moist filter paper placed in a petri dish, rhabditiform larvae hatch in 18 to 24 hours when placed at 18 to 22° C. The first stage rhabditiform larvae grow and molt to become second stage rhabditiform larvae in about 48 hours. Four or 5 days after the first molt, the second stage rhabditiform larvae undergo the second ecdysis to become third stage filariform larvae. Unlike the larvae of *Haemonchus,* the filariform larvae of *N. muris* sheds its sloughed cuticle (the process is known as exsheathing) and actively penetrates the skin of the rat host.

The infective filariform larva of *N. muris* is markedly thermotactic. It is readily stimulated and becomes quite motile if the warmth of an animal's body is made available. This larva is also negatively geotropic. If it occurs in soil, it actively migrates to the top and awaits a suitable host. Worms cultured in the laboratory on filter paper migrate to the edges of the paper and extend themselves into the air and wave back and forth.

Infection of the rat is generally accomplished by skin penetration. However, infections can be established, at least in the laboratory, by oral feeding, although this method of infection is rather ineffective. Furthermore, in the laboratory, rats can be infected by hypodermic injection. Usually the application of approximately 5000 larvae on the skin of rats results in a heavy but nonlethal infection. A much smaller dosage is required if the larvae are injected hypodermically.

Once within the host's blood, the larvae are carried to the lungs via the heart. Here they feed on whole blood and undergo rapid growth and development culminating in the third ecdysis to become fourth stage larvae. These larvae are carried up the bronchi and trachea and eventually pass down the pharynx to the intestine. The fourth stage larvae first appear in the host's intestine about 41 hours after the infection. Approximately 50 per cent of the larvae arrive between 45 and 50 hours after the infection. The fourth and final ecdysis occurs in the intestine, and adult males and females develop. Maturation is rapid and eggs appear in the host's feces by the sixth day after infection.

Adults in the rat's intestine feed mainly on blood and host cells. However, some of the intestinal contents are undoubtedly ingested because intestinal flagellates have been reported in the gut of *N. muris.* Not all third stage filariform larvae that penetrate the rat's skin develop to maturity. Only about 60 per cent do.

Genus *Trichostrongylus*

Trichostrongylus axei. This minute stomach worm of cattle, sheep, and horses, is another important trichostrongylid (Plate 16–17, Fig.

1). Its life cycle is direct. The eggs that pass out of the host include 16 to 32 blastomeres. These hatch in damp soil in 3 to 4 days, and the escaping larvae undergo two molts and are transformed into third stage infective larvae. These larvae are ensheathed within the cuticle of the second stage larvae. When ingested by horses, they exsheath and burrow into the stomach mucosa, where they undergo two more molts and attain maturity.

OTHER *Trichostrongylus* SPECIES.   Other familiar species of *Trichostrongylus* include *T. ransomi, T. affinis,* and *T. calcaratus*—all found in the small intestine of rabbits; *T. longispicularis, T. colubriformis,* and *T. capricola* in the stomach and small intestine of ruminants; *T. delicatus* in squirrels; and *T. tenuis* in domestic and wild birds.

Other Trichostrongylid Genera

The Trichostrongylidae also includes the genera *Ostertagia,* with various species parasitic in the stomach of ruminants; and *Crenosoma* in skunks, cats, and dogs. Hobmaier (1941) reported that an amphibian or reptile is utilized as a transport host in the life cycle of *Crenosoma. Cooperia* is a rather common intestinal parasite of cattle, and *Nematodirus* is found in the small intestine of rabbits and others in ruminants (Plate 16–17, Fig. 3).

FAMILY METASTRONGYLIDAE

Genus *Angiostrongylus*

Angiostrongylus cantonensis.   In recent years *Angiostrongylus* (= *Rattostrongylus*) *cantonensis,* the rat lungworm, has come into medical prominence since it has been reported as the causative agent of human meningoencephalitis in Hawaii. Furthermore, it is strongly suspected as the causative agent of a similar disease in various areas of the Pacific and in areas of Asia.

Life Cycle of *Angiostrongylus cantonensis.* In infected rats, eggs containing uncleaved zygotes are deposited in the blood stream, where they become lodged as emboli in the smaller vessels in the lungs. Embryonic development occurs here. The first stage larvae, rupturing from the thin-shelled eggs, enter the respiratory tract. They then migrate up the trachea, down the alimentary tract, and are discharged in feces. This nematode requires an intermediate host, usually snails, *Subulina octona, Bradybaena similaris,* or *Achatina fulica;* or slugs, *Veronicella*

leydigi, Agriolimax laevis, and others. Occasionally larvae of *A. cantonensis* are found in the land planarian *Geoplana septemlineata.* However, these flatworms cannot be infected with first stage larvae and presumably serve as paratenic or transport hosts, which acquire third stage larvae from feeding on naturally infected snails and slugs. The first stage larvae actively penetrate molluscs, although it is suspected that they may also gain entrance through ingestion. Within the intermediate host, the larvae undergo two molts but do not exsheath. When an infected mollusc is ingested by a rat, the larvae exsheath in the rodent's stomach and burrow through the ileum and become blood-borne. The blood-borne larvae in the hepatic portal system are carried to the right chambers of the heart via the hepatic vein and posterior vena cava. The third stage larvae are carried from the right ventricle to the pulmonary capillaries via the pulmonary artery. From the pulmonary capillaries the larvae are carried to the left chambers of the heart via the pulmonary vein. Still later, the larvae are conducted out of the left ventricle in the aortic arch, common carotid artery, and capillaries of the brain, and eventually they congregate in the central nervous system, especially in the anterior portion of the cerebrum, where they undergo the third and fourth molts. The resulting young adults emerge to the brain surface on the 12th to 14th day, remain in the subarachnoid space for approximately 2 weeks, then migrate via the venous system through the heart to the pulmonary arteries and tissues of the lungs, where they mature by the 42nd to 45th day in the rat.

In a series of experiments involving the infection of growing albino rats with known numbers of third stage larvae, the author has shown that if 150 or more infective larvae are fed to each rat, 100 or more of the worms succeed in becoming established in the brain, and the rodent host is killed between the 28th and 36th day post infection when the young adults begin to migrate from the subarachnoid space to the lungs.

Death is believed to be due to hemorrhage caused by young adult worms as they penetrate the venules on the surface of the brain, interference with the normal flow of blood through the right chambers of the heart, and blockage of the normal circulation through the pulmonary artery. If 100 or less infective third stage larvae are introduced into each rat, less than 100 worms—generally between 65 and 80—become established in the brain. In such instances, death does not occur during the period the young adults are migrating from the brain. However, if 30 or more worms are present, death generally does occur later during the course of the infection as a result of secondary pulmonary congestion and necrosis of lung tissue.

In addition, young rats infected with *A. cantonensis* do not grow as fast as uninfected ones. Histopathological examinations of the brain of infected rats have revealed that host cellular response is practically nonexistent. This is in contrast to results of similar studies of the brain of infected rabbits, rhesus monkeys, and humans. In these abnormal hosts, the host cellular response is extensive. These data exemplify the principle that parasites in tissues of abnormal hosts generally elicit much more severe cellular response than in normal hosts.

Human Meningoencephalitis. The author has spent some time in the Pacific Basin, studying *Angiostrongylus cantonensis* and experimental meningoencephalitis, and has been intimately familiar with this parasite since 1963. The importance of *A. cantonensis* as a parasite of humans was first reported by Nomura and Lin in 1944 when they recovered six adult worms in the cerebrospinal fluid of a patient in Formosa. A second discovery of *A. cantonensis* as a human parasite occurred in 1961 when Rosen et al. reported its presence in the brain of a mental patient in Hawaii who had died with an eosinophilic meningoencephalitis (the case was fully described by Rosen et al., 1962).

Aware of the presence of *A. cantonensis* in Hawaii as a result its detection in rats by Ash (1962), Alicata postulated that *A. cantonensis* might be of considerable medical importance. After observing a Japanese gardener believed to be suffering from meningoencephalitis as the result of swallowing a slug from an area where these slugs harbor third stage larvae (Horio and Alicata, 1961), Alicata (1962) further postulated that *A. cantonensis* is the causative agent of meningoencephalitis in Hawaii and Tahiti.

Although *A. cantonensis* was not positively identified in humans, Alicata and Brown (1962), as the result of field observations, reported that human infections in Tahiti could be acquired from eating raw fresh-water prawns, *Macrobrachium* sp., or native foods that included prawn juice, for they found the larvae

of *A. cantonensis* in prawns in Tahiti. Furthermore, it was suggested that human infections could be acquired from eating fresh vegetables and fruits on which small, infected slugs are found.

Continuous surveys by Alicata and others have indicated that *A. cantonensis* is regularly found on various Pacific islands where human cases suggesting eosinophilic meningoencephalitis are also found. The few actual reports of *A. cantonensis* in man coupled with the geographic overlap of the disease and the parasite, and the successful experimental production of the disease in rhesus monkeys fed *A. cantonensis* larvae, strongly suggest that this nematode is the major etiologic agent of human eosinophilic meningoencephalitis in the Pacific.

Human cases of meningoencephalitis, characterized by pleocytosis (mostly of eosinophils), headache, stiffness of the neck and back, and paresthesias of various types, need not indicate infection by *Angiostrongylus cantonensis*. In Japan, the invasion of the central nervous system, especially the brain of man, by the trematode *Paragonimus westermani* causes a similar condition.

In certain cases of larva migrans in man by *Toxocara canis,* the larvae may invade the brain and thus cause symptoms almost identical to those of eosinophilic meningoencephalitis. Production of eosinophils is characteristic of hosts infected by helminth parasites. If the numerous cases of human eosinophilic meningoencephalitis in the Pacific are due to *A. cantonensis,* as suspected, then human angiostrongyliasis, although painful, is seldom lethal.

In some cases of angiostrongyliasis in experimental animals, adult worms may migrate down the spinal cord from the brain and cause paralysis. Furthermore, young adults may migrate to the eyes and cause blindness. In one case of human angiostrongyliasis in Thailand, a young adult worm was recovered from the patient's eye.

FAMILY SYNGAMIDAE

Genus *Syngamus*

Syngamus trachea. The family Syngamidae includes the unusual worm *Syngamus trachea,* found in the trachea of chickens, turkeys, pheasants, and other birds (Plate 16–18, Fig. 1). In life, these worms are bright red. The males are 2 to 6 mm. long, while the females

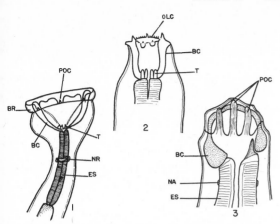

Plate 16-18   Syngamid nematodes. 1. Anterior end of *Syngamus trachea,* in the respiratory tract of domestic poultry. (Redrawn after Yorke and Maplestone, 1926.) **2.** Anterior end of *Stephanurus dentatus,* the swine kidney worm. (Redrawn after Tayler, 1899.) **3.** Anterior end of *Kalicephalus,* in intestine of reptiles; lateral view. (Redrawn after Ortlepp, 1923.)

(BC, buccal capsule; BR, buccal ring; ES, esophagus; NA, nuclei of amphidial glands; NR, nerve ring; OLC, outer leaf crown; POC, papillae of outer circlet; T, teeth.)

are 15 to 20 mm. long. These worms remain in copula so that the pair appears as a Y. Although the forms found in various birds are morphologically indistinguishable, some forms are infective to other bird species while others are not, suggesting the existance of different strains, if not species. For example, the strain found in robins, known as *S. merulae,* is highly host specific.

Life Cycle of *Syngamus trachea.*   The life cycle of *S. trachea* is extremely interesting. The eggs laid by the females are coughed up, ingested, and passed out in the feces of the bird. In 1 to 2 weeks the enclosed embryo develops, undergoes two molts, and either hatches out as an infective larva or remains within the eggshell. From this stage on, two alternatives are possible —direct infection occurs, or a transport host is utilized. If development follows the first course, the egg hatches in the intestine, and the larva burrows through the intestinal wall and is carried by the blood to the heart and lungs. Here, the larva invades the alveoli and passes up the trachea where it reaches maturity.

If the second avenue is taken, the eggs are ingested by earthworms (*Helodrilus foetidus, H. caliginosus*), slugs, snails, and arthropods. Earthworms are the most common transport hosts. Within the annelid, the larvae hatch out, burrow through the intestinal wall, and encyst

in the host's body musculature. Such encysted larvae have been reported to survive for as long as 3½ years. When the infected worm is eaten by the bird host, the nematode larvae reach the lungs and trachea, probably via the circulatory system, and the cycle is completed. Since the nematode actually hatches from the eggshell and encysts in the annelid, the latter might well be considered a true intermediate host.

OTHER *Syngamus* SPECIES.   Another species of *Syngamus* is *S. laryngeus* found in certain birds and mammals, including cattle and cats. Humans can be infected with this parasite. Other species of *Syngamus* infect a variety of birds and mammals.

Genus *Stephanurus*

Stephanurus dentatus.   This parasite is the common and extremely destructive kidney worm of hogs (Plate 16–18, Fig. 2). Its morphology and life cycle have been reported by Schwartz and Price (1932) and Alicata (1935).

FAMILY DIAPHANOCEPHALIDAE

The small family Diaphanocephalidae includes the little understood genera *Kalicephalus* (Plate 16–18, Fig. 3) and *Diaphanocephalus,* both found in the intestine of reptiles.

SUPERFAMILY SPIRUROIDEA

This group of medium-sized slender nematodes is parasitic in vertebrates, and include several species parasitic in man and domestic animals. The superfamily is composed of seven families, a key to which is given below.

1. Possesses elongate oval or hexagonal mouth surrounded by small or obscure lips. Approximately eight single or four double papillae form external circlet. . **Thelaziidae**
2. Possesses inflated bulb (head bulb) located behind lips. Four ballonets present; are continuous with individual cervical sacs, which hang free in pseudocoel. . . . **Gnathostomidae**
3. Possesses two unlobed or trilobed pseudolips (also known as pseudolabia) surrounding mouth. Head shields or interlabia often present. . . . . **Spiruridae**
4. Possesses cuticular ornamentations (cordons, etc.) on anterior half of body . . . **Acuariidae**

5. Possesses two large unlobed lips armed with one or more teeth on inner surface. Cuticular collar present behind lips. . **Physalopteridae**
6. Possesses two large lateral lips surrounding slitlike mouth. Buccal capsule is noncuticularized. Esophagus extends anteriorly to surround buccal capsule . . . . **Cucullanidae**
7. Lacks lips. Mouth is elongate, situated dorsoventrally . . . . **Camallamidae**

FAMILY THELAZIIDAE

The family Thelaziidae includes species found in various habitats in an array of hosts. Members of *Pneumonema* are found in the lungs of turtles and other reptiles; *Echinonema* in the intestine of marsupials; *Rictularia* in the small intestine of mammals; *Rictularoides* in the small intestine of rodents; *Ascarophis* in the digestive tract of cod and other fishes; and *Gongylonema* in the stomachs of ruminants (Plate 16–19, Figs. 1 to 3).

Also included in the Thelaziidae are the genera *Thelazia* (Plate 16–19, Fig. 4) and *Oxyspirura*. Members of both these genera are commonly referred to as the eye worms of domestic animals and man.

Genus *Thelazia*

Thelazia rhodesii. This parasite is found in the tear ducts between the eyes and the lids of cattle. During migration, it may leave the ducts and be found on the surface of or in the eyeball, or under the nictitating membrane.

The males are 8 to 12 mm. long, while the females are 12 to 18 mm. long. Presence of this worm may lead to ulceration of the eye and surrounding membranes and eventual loss of sight. *T. rhodesii* utilizes flies of the genus *Musca* as intermediate hosts. The first stage larva, found in the secretion of the host's eye, is picked up by the flies and carried to the eye of another host. *Thelazia rhodesii* has been found in California.

OTHER *Thelazia* SPECIES. Other species of *Thelazia* include *T. erschowi* in pigs, *T. leesei* in camels, *T. lacrymalis* in horses, and *T. callipaeda* in dogs, deer, cats, sheep, bears, and rarely man in California. Other species are known from birds.

Genus *Oxyspirura*

The genus *Oxyspirura* includes *O. mansoni*, the "eyeworm" of chickens and other birds. The life history of this species has been determined by Fielding (1926–1928) and Sanders (1928). Another species, *O. petrowi*, is found in grouse.

Life Cycle of *Oxyspirura mansoni*. The embryonated eggs oviposited by the females are passed down the tear ducts, swallowed, and passed out in feces. Such eggs may either hatch in damp soil, in which case the larvae are ingested by the intermediate host, or the eggs may be ingested without hatching. The intermediate host is the cockroach, *Pychoscellus surinamensis*. Within the roach, the larvae penetrate the intestinal wall. Some larvae are found in the coelom or even in the legs, but others become

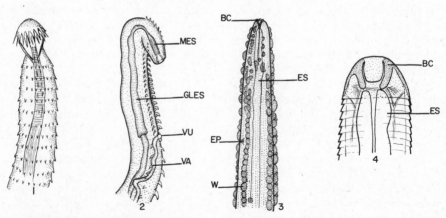

Plate 16-19 **Thelaziid nematodes. 1.** Anterior end of *Echinonema* in the small intestine of marsupials. (Redrawn after von Linstow, 1898.) **2.** Anterior end of *Rictularia* in small intestine of mammals. (Redrawn after Hall, 1916.) **3.** Anterior end of *Gongylonema* in esophagus and stomach of birds and mammals. (Redrawn after Ward, 1916.) **4.** Anterior end of *Thelazia callipaeda* parasitic in eye and associated ducts of mammals. (Redrawn after Herde, 1942.)

(BC, buccal capsule; EP, excretory pore; ES, esophagus; GLES, glandular portion of esophagus; MES, muscular portion of esophagus; VA, vagina; VU, vulva; W, warts or plaques.)

encysted along the external surface of the alimentary tract or in the adjacent adipose tissues. The time required for development from the initial entrance into the roach until the infective form is reached is 50 days.

When an infected roach is eaten by a chicken, the infective larvae become free in the crop. From here they migrate up the esophagus into the mouth, to the nasopharynx, and up the tear ducts. Worms may appear in the region of the host's eye within 15 minutes after entering the host. No explanation has yet been provided to explain why *O. mansoni* shows an affinity for the eye, because tissue and habitat affinities remain one of the mysteries of host-parasite relationships.

FAMILY GNATHOSTOMATIDAE

Genus *Gnathostoma*

The family Gnathostomatidae includes the important genus *Gnathostoma,* which includes nineteen species that have been described from all continents except Europe and Australia (Plate 16–20, Fig. 1). Miyazaki (1960) has contributed a review of the biology and distribution of members of this genus and has listed the various species. Although most of the species have been reported embedded in the stomach wall of mammals, where they are commonly associated with tumorous growths (Plate 16–20, Fig. 2), *G. gracile* was reported in the intestine of a fish, *Arapaima gigas,* from Brazil, *G. occipitri* was found subcutaneously in

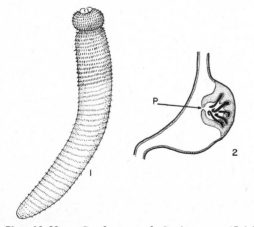

Plate 16-20   *Gnathostoma.* 1. *Gnathostoma* sp. (Original.) **2.** Cut-away view of stomach of host infected with *Gnathostoma* in cyst, showing pore (P) through which eggs of the parasites escape into lumen of host's alimentary tract. (Redrawn after Miyazaki, I. 1960. *Experimental Parasitology,* Academic Press, New York.)

an eagle in Turkestan, and *G. minutum* was found in the connective tissue of a serpent in the Congo.

Life Cycle of *Gnathostoma spinigerum.* The life cycle and migratory pattern of *G. spinigerum,* the type species, has been investigated by numerous helminthologists. The stages in the development of this species are depicted in Plate 16–21. Usually, cats and dogs serve as the definitive host, but human hosts are also known. The eggs passing out of the definitive host enclose one or two blastomeres. When such eggs fall into water of a suitable temperature (27° C. is the ideal experimental temperature), a fully developed first stage larva is visible in 5 days enveloped in a delicate sheath within the eggshell. This larva hatches in 7 days and becomes free-swimming. Development continues if the first stage larva is ingested by a suitable species of cyclops—that is, *Mesocyclops leuckarti, Eucyclops serrulatus, Cyclops strenuus,* or *C. vicinus.*

In cyclops the larva sloughs off the enveloping sheath and penetrates the gastric wall to become lodged in the host's body cavity. At this site, the larva molts within 7 to 10 days after ingestion, increases in size, reaching 0.5 mm. in length, and becomes a second stage larva.

If an infected cyclops is ingested by a second intermediate host—usually a fish, aquatic reptile, or amphibian—the larva again penetrates the host's gastric wall, migrates to the body musculature, molts, increases to a length of 4 mm., encysts within a fibrous membrane, and is then known as the third stage larva. Various crustaceans, birds, and mammals, especially rodents, can also serve as the second intermediate host. Infection of the second intermediate host is known as primary infection. Gnathostomes are unusual in that they can pass through several "second" intermediate hosts without further development. Such infections are known as secondary infections.

Finally, when hosts harboring third stage larvae are eaten by the definitive host, the larvae penetrate the gastric wall (rarely through the intestinal wall) and enter the liver. From the liver, the larvae migrate into muscles and then into connective tissue, increasing in size and molting twice during the process. When these nematodes attain their maximum size— males from 11 to 25 mm. long, females from 25 to 54 mm. long—they enter the gastric wall from the exterior and become embedded in typical nodules that possess an opening to the lumen of the stomach. It is through this aper-

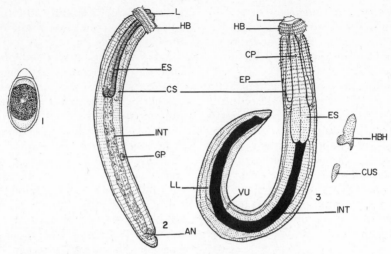

Plate 16-21   Stages in the life cycle of *Gnathostoma spinigerum*. **1.** Egg. **2.** Second stage
larva. **3.** Third stage larva.
(AN, anus; CP, cervical papilla; CS, cervical sac; CUS, cuticular spine of body in proximity of
head bulb; EP, excretory pore; ES, esophagus; GP, genital primordium; HB, head bulb; HBH,
lateral view of head bulb hook; INT, intestine; L, lip; LL, lateral line; VU, vulva.)

ture that eggs are eventually passed out. Such
nodules, as found in natural hosts, are referred
to as gnathostomiasis interna. In human infections, contracted from eating the raw flesh of
second intermediate hosts, the worms never
reach maturity and are found in peripheral tissues, usually in the subcutaneous layers. Such
a condition is known as gnathostomiasis ex-
terna. Larva migrans is known to occur in
human infections in which the worm creeps
along under the skin.

Other Genera

The family Gnathostomatidae also includes
the genera *Tanqua,* in the stomachs of lizards
and aquatic snakes; and *Echinocephalus,* in the
spiral valves of elasmobranchs (Plate 16-22,
Figs. 1 and 2). In *Echinocephalus,* larval forms
have been found encysted in pearl oysters,
suggesting that oysters serve as intermediate
hosts. The complete life cycle remains undetermined.

FAMILY SPIRURIDAE

The family Spiruridae includes several genera
all found in the esophagus and primarily in the
stomachs of their hosts. Of the various genera,
Habronema includes species found in the stomachs
of equines; *Draschia* in horses; *Spirocerca* in
nodules in the stomach and esophagus of dogs,
foxes, and other carnivorous mammals; *Tetram-*

eres, the globular stomach worm of poultry;
Physocephalus, Ascarops, and *Simondsia,* found in
the stomach of pigs and other animals; and
Seurocyrnea in the proventriculus of birds (Plate
16-22, Figs. 3 to 5 and 7 to 9).

Spirurid Life Cycle Pattern

The life cycle of most spirurids includes an
intermediate host, usually an arthropod.

Life Cycle of *Habronema muscae*. This
nematode is a stomach parasite of horses. The
eggs of the parasite pass out of the host, and
the enclosed larvae hatch in the deposited feces.
Such larvae are ingested by maggots of the
housefly, *Musca domestica.* Within the fly, the
nematodes undergo several molts and attain
the infective form by the time the fly leaves the
puparium. Horses are infected when flies deposit infective larvae on their lips or mouths or
become ingested along with food.

Life Cycle of *Spiroxys contortus*. The
commonly encountered threadworm of turtles,
Spiroxys contortus, another spirurid worm, utilizes
Cyclops as the intermediate host. However, in
this instance, transport hosts in the form of
fish, tadpoles, and dragonfly nymphs may be
utilized in addition to the intermediate host.

Genus *Gongylonema*

Another interesting spirurid genus is *Gongylonema,* members of which are parasitic in the
alimentary tract of birds and mammals, the

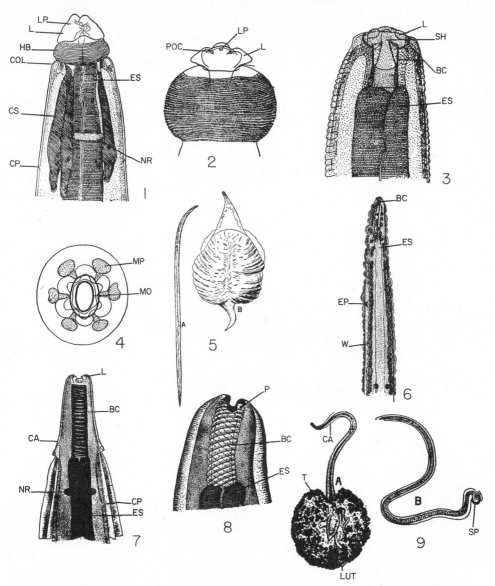

Plate 16-22   Nematodes of the families Gnathostomatidae and Spiruridae. 1. Anterior end of *Tanqua,* showing ballonets and cervical sacs. (After Baylis and Lane, 1920.) **2.** Anterior end of *Echinocephalus.* (After Baylis and Lane, 1920.) **3.** Anterior end of *Habronema muscae.* (After Ransom, 1913.) **4.** Head-on view of anterior end of *Spirocerca lupi.* (After Yorke and Maplestone, 1926.) **5.** *Tetrameres.* **A.** Male. **B.** Female. (After Cram, 1931.) **6.** Anterior end of *Gongylonema* with plaques. (After Ward, 1916.) **7.** Anterior end of *Physocephalus sexalatus.* (After Foster, 1912.) **8.** Anterior end of *Ascarops strongylina.* (After Foster, 1912.) **9.** *Simondsia.* **A.** Female. **B.** Male. (After Cobbold, 1883.)

(BC, buccal capsule; CA, cervical alae; COL, collar; CP, cervical papilla; CS, cervical sac; EP, excretory pore; ES, esophagus; HB, head bulb; L, lip; LP, labial papilla; LUT, lobes of uterus with eggs; MO, mouth; MP, masses attached to papilla; NR, nerve ring; P, papillae; POC, papillae of outer circlet; SH, shield; SP, spicule; T, tail; W, warts.)

latter primarily in subtropical and tropical countries (Plate 16–22, Fig. 6). The best known species is *G. neoplasticum,* which occurs in the tongue, esophagus, and stomach of rodents. It utilizes the American cockroach, *Periplaneta americana,* or the German cockroach, *Blatella germanica,* as the intermediate host. Within the roach, active larvae can be found encysted in the leg muscles within 2 to 3 months after feces that include eggs are ingested.

FAMILY ACUARIIDAE

The family Acuariidae includes several genera parasitic in the esophagus, stomach, and gizzard of birds. In these locations, the worms may be lumen-dwellers or be embedded in the wall. The life cycle pattern of the species parallels that of the spirurid worms in that an arthropod intermediate host is required. For example, in the life cycle of *Acuaria anthuris,* the proventricular worm of chickens, turkeys, pheasants, pigeons, and other wild birds, the pill bug *Amadillidium vulgara* and the sow bug *Porcellio scaber* are suitable intermediate hosts (Plate 16–23, Fig. 1). It takes approximately 25 days within the isopod before the infective larva is formed, and it takes 27 days for the worms to reach sexual maturity, once established within the definitive host.

Dispharynx nasuta causes nodules on the proventricular wall of grouse and pigeons in the United States. It may cause death. *Cheilospirura hamulosa* is another economically important acuariid worm found in the gizzard of chickens, turkeys, and pheasants. Grasshoppers, sand hoppers, weavils, and beetles serve as the intermediate hosts.

FAMILY PHYSALOPTERIDAE

The family Physalopteridae includes a few genera found in the stomachs of amphibians, reptiles, birds and mammals. The type genus, *Physaloptera,* includes many species found in an array of hosts, including amphibians, reptiles, birds, and mammals (Plate 16–23, Fig. 2). *Proleptus* is found in the stomach and intestine of elasmobranchi (Plate 16–23, Fig. 3). *Skrjabinoptera* is represented in the United States by *S. phyronosoma,* found in horned lizards in the Southwest. Another member of the Physalopteridae is *Abbreviata,* which is found in amphibians, reptiles, and few mammals (Plate 16–23, Fig. 4). The complete life history of the Physalopteridae has not been determined, although utilization of two intermediate hosts is suspected.

FAMILY CUCULLANIDAE

The Cucullanidae is a little understood

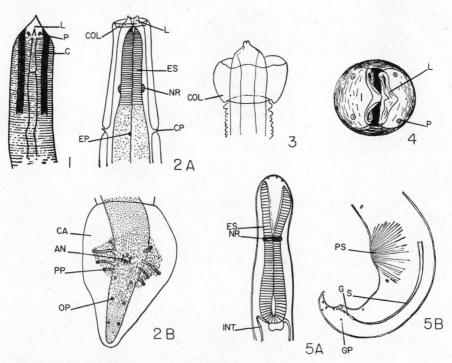

Plate 16-23   Acuariidae, Physalopteridae, and Cucullanidae. 1. Anterior end of *Acuaria.* (After Gendre, 1912.) **2.** *Physaloptera.* **A.** anterior end. **B.** Posterior end of male. (After Ortlepp, 1922.) **3.** Anterior end of *Proleptus,* showing cuticular collar. (After Lloyd, 1920.) **4.** Head-on view of *Abbreviata.* (After Chitwood and Wehr, 1934.) **5. A.** Posterior end of male of *Cucullanus.* (After Yamaguti, 1935.) **B.** Anterior end of *Cucullanus.* (After Törnquist, 1931.)

(AN, anus; C, cordon; CA, caudal ala; COL, collar; CP, cervical papilla; EP, excretory pore; ES, esophagus; G, gubernaculum; GP, genital papilla; INT, intestine; L, lips; NR, nerve ring; OP, other genital papilla; P, papilla; PP, pedunculated papilla; PS, pre-anal sucker; S, spicule.)

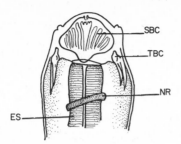

Plate 16-24   Camallanidae. Anterior end of *Camallanus*, lateral view. (ES, esophagus; NR, nerve ring; SBC, shell shaped half of buccal capsule; TBC, trident support of buccal capsule.)

family. It includes *Cucullanus,* which is found in the intestine of fishes and a few other cold-blooded vertebrates (Plate 16–23, Fig. 5).

FAMILY CAMALLANIDAE

The family Camallanidae includes the genera *Camallanus* and *Procamallanus,* both found in cold-blooded vertebrates, primarily fish (Plate 16–24). Young larvae of these nematodes escape from the host in feces and a copepod intermediate host is necessary. Transport hosts, in the form of small fishes, are customary.

SUPERFAMILY DRACUNCULOIDEA

Members of the superfamily Dracunculoidea are slender worms of moderate to large size. These nematodes are parasitic in the body cavity, its surrounding membranes, and the connective tissues of vertebrates.

Genus *Dracunculus*

Dracunculus medinensis.   Undoubtedly, the best known of the dracunculoid nematodes is *Dracunculus medinensis,* the guinea worm (Plate 16–25). This long worm is known to infect man, dogs, horses, cattle, wolves, various cats, monkeys, and baboons in the Old World, and minks, foxes, raccoons, and dogs in North America. It is widely distributed in Africa, the Near East, the East Indies, and India. Stoll (1947) estimated that there are 48 million cases of human dracunculiasis in the world.

Life Cycle of *Dracunculus medinensis.* Stages in the life cycle of *Dracunculus medinensis* are depicted in Plate 16–25. The males, measuring 12 to 40 mm. in length and 0.4 mm. in diameter, are much smaller than the females, which measure 70 to 120 cm. in length and 0.9 to 1.7 mm. in diameter. No vulva is visible in females. The worms usually develop in the body cavities and connective tissues of their hosts. On reaching the gravid state, the females migrate to the subcutaneous tissues. By this time, the ovaries are no longer functional and the uteri are filled with active larvae. This species is ovoviviparous.

In the subcutaneous tissues of the host, the females point their cephalic end toward the skin, and by secreting an irritant, cause the formation of papules in the host's dermis. Such a papule soon increases in size and resembles a blister from the exterior. The blister soon ruptures, leaving a cup shaped ulcer on the skin surface. Such eruptions usually occur on the ankles or wrists. When the open ulcer comes in contact with water, a loop of the nematode's uterus either prolapses through a ruptured anterior end or through the mouth. The uterus ruptures, enabling numerous first stage larvae to escape into the water.

The first stage rhabditiform larvae are 500 to 700 μ long and possess distinctly striated cuticula. They are free-living and their food reserves enable them to live for several days. If ingested by a suitable species of *Cyclops,* they burrow through its midgut and enter the coelom. Seldom is there more than one larva in a single *Cyclops.* The presence of more than five or six larvae results in the death of the intermediate host.

Within the coelom of *Cyclops,* the larvae continue to develop, undergo two molts, and attain the ensheathed form in approximately 20 days. If such an infected *Cyclops* is swallowed in contaminated drinking water, the larvae become freed when the intermediate host is digested and are stimulated by gastric juices and exsheath in the duodenum of the human host. They burrow through tissues, undergo two additional molts, and become lodged in the body cavity or subcutaneous tissues, where they take 8 months to 1 year to reach maturity.

During an experimental series, Moorthy fed infected *Cyclops* to dogs and found the first specimens, measuring 12 to 24 mm. in length, deep in the connective tissues in about 10 weeks. Furthermore, vaginas of females 24 mm. long already contained a mucoid plug, indicating that they had already been fertilized.

Human hosts of *D. medinensis* usually demonstrate eosinophilia, nausea, vomiting, diarrhea, asthma, and fainting. These symptoms are believed to result from the absorption of toxin secreted by the female worm while forming the blister.

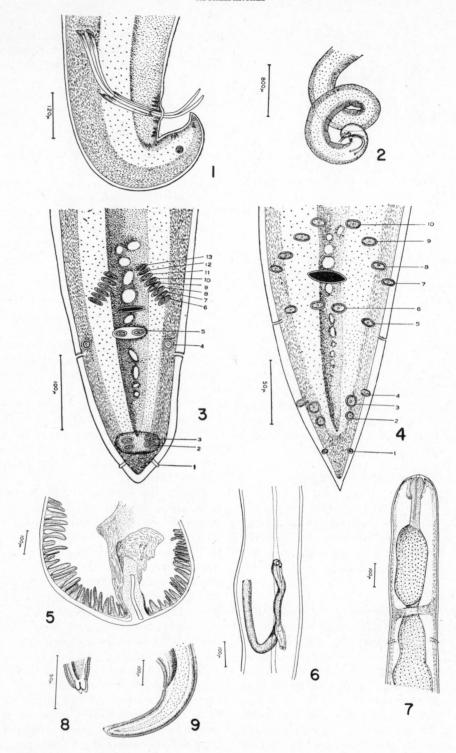

Plate 16-25   *Dracunculus.* 1. Lateral view of tail end of male. **2.** General view of posterior end of male. **3.** Ventral view of tail of male of *D. dahomensis.* (6–13, preanal papillae; 2–5, postanal papillae; 1, phasmid.) **4.** Ventral view of tail of male of *D. medinensis.* (7–10, preanal papillae; 1–6 postanal papillae.) **5.** Cross section through mature female of *D. medinensis* at level of vulva, showing mucoid plug. **6.** Portion of female of *D. medinensis,* showing vulva, vagina containing mucoid plug, and origin of uteri. **7.** Anterior end of male of *D. medinensis,* showing esophagus. **8.** Tail end of immature female of *D. medinensis,* showing four caudal mucrones. **9.** Posterior end of immature female, showing position of anus. (All figures after Moorthy, 1937.)

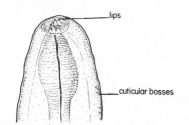

Plate 16-26   Dracunculoidea *Philometra* sp., anterior end. (Redrawn after Thomas, 1929.)

OTHER *Dracunculus* SPECIES. Other species of *Dracunculus* include *D. houdemeri* from the snake *Natrix piscator* in Vietnam and *D. ophiolensis* in garter snakes. In *D. ophiolensis,* Brackett (1938) reported that *Cyclops* also serves as the intermediate host, and tadpoles serve as the transport host.

Other Dracunculoid Genera

Other prominent genera of Dracunculoidea include *Philometra* (Plate 16–26) found in the body cavity and tissues of fishes and *Micropleura* found in the coelom and associated membranes of crocodilian reptiles. In *Philometra,* Furuyama (1934) demonstrated that gravid females escape from the fish host and rupture, thus releasing the larvae that are then ingested by *Cyclops.*

SUPERFAMILY FILARIOIDEA

The filarioid worms include some of the most important nematode parasites of man and domestic animals. The long, threadlike adult worms are found in the host's lymphatic glands, tissues, and body cavities, while the "larvae," known as microfilariae, are found in the blood (p. 403). Most of these nematodes are ovoviviparous. Some species that parasitize birds are oviparous. At the time of oviposition in the ovoviviparous species, the microfilariae uncoil and are released from the female. If the eggshell becomes elongate and forms a covering membrane over the microfilaria, the larva is termed a sheathed microfilaria; but if the shell ruptures and does not form a sheath, the larva is termed unsheathed or naked.

The isolation and identification of microfilariae very often is the only possible way to determine infections; therefore, the diagnostic characteristics of microfilariae of the most prominent species are given below and depicted in Plate 16–27.

The designations of families subordinate to the Filarioidea remain controversial. The reader is referred to Wehr (1935) and Chabaud and Choquet (1953) for detailed discussions on the systematics of the group.

Genera of filarioids known to parasitize man include *Wuchereria, Brugia, Onchocerca, Dipetalonema, Mansonella, Dirofilaria,* and *Loa.*

Genus *Wuchereria*

Wuchereria bancrofti. This parasite is the causative agent of Bancroft's filariasis and is found in eastern Europe, China, Korea, Japan, Vietnam, Malaya, the Philippine Islands, the East Indies, Australia, Burma, India, the Arabic nations of the Near East, Central and Mediterranean Africa, Madagascar, Central and South America, and formerly found in South Carolina (Plate 16–28). A Pacific strain occurs throughout the Pacific islands except Hawaii. Stoll (1947) estimated that millions of human cases of this type of filariasis are in existence.

Microfilaria bancrofti. The body is 220 to 300 μ in length. The sheath stains red with dilute Giemsa's stain. The tail is not coiled. No nuclei are in the tail. These larvae are nocturnal or are only slightly diurnal in their periodicity, depending on the strain (p. 455). They are usually found in the blood, or less often in urine.

Life Cycle of *Wuchereria bancrofti.* The stages in the life cycle of *W. bancrofti* are given in Plate 16–28. The males measure 40 mm. in length by 0.1 mm. in diameter, and the females measure 80 to 100 mm. in length by 0.24 to 0.3 mm. in diameter. These worms are found in the lymph glands and associated ducts of humans. The gravid females give rise to sheathed microfilariae that are 127 to 320 μ long. Nocturnal periodicity—that is, the microfilariae are located in the peripheral circulation at night—has been reported in most instances. However, certain strains do not demonstrate this phenomenon. For example, in the Pacific strain of *W. brancrofti,* found on various Polynesian islands in the South Pacific, the microfilariae only show slight periodicity, and it is diurnal—that is, appearing in greater numbers in the peripheral blood during the day.

Several hypotheses have been contributed to explain nocturnal periodicity: (1) There is a chemotactile force that attracts the microfilariae to the saliva of mosquito hosts (vectors), which are more plentiful at night. (2) The relaxation of the host during sleep induces the microfilariae to migrate into the peripheral circulation. (3) The migration results from a response to oxygen and carbon dioxide supply. (4) The microfilariae survive for only a short period, and it

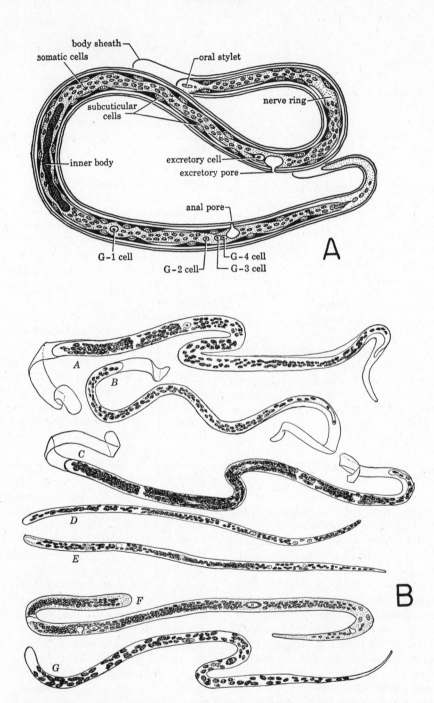

Plate 16-27   Microfilariae. A. Microfilaria of *Wuchereria bancrofti*. (After Brown, F. A., Jr. (ed.). 1950. *Selected Invertebrate Types,* John Wiley, New York.) **B.** Various species of microfilariae, drawn to scale. **A.** *Wuchereria bancrofti.* Sheathed, no nuclei in tip of tail, 270 × 8.5 μ. **B.** *Brugia malayi.* Sheathed, two nuclei in tail, 200 × 6 μ. **C.** *Loa loa.* Sheathed, nuclei to tip of tail, 275 × 7 μ. **D.** *Acanthocheilonema perstans.* No sheath, tail blunt, with nuclei to tip, 200 × 4.5 μ. **E.** *Mansonella ozzardi.* No sheath, pointed tail without nuclei at tip, 205 × 5 μ. **F.** *Onchocerca volvulus.* No sheath, no nuclei in end of tail, 320 × 7.5 μ. **G.** *Dirofilaria immitis.* No sheath, sharp tail without nuclei in end, 300 × 6 μ. (Fig. B after Chandler, A. C., and Read, C. P. 1961. *Introduction to Parasitology,* John Wiley, New York.)

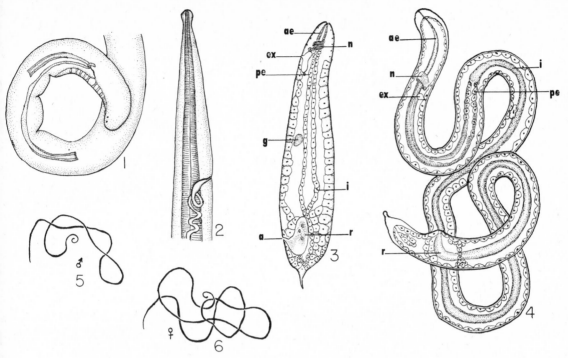

Plate 16-28   Stages in the life cycle of *Wuchereria bancrofti*. 1. Tail of adult male showing spicules and small papillae on narrow alae. **2.** Anterior end of adult, showing bulbous head and position of vulva. **3.** Sausage stage of larva. **4.** Infective larva from mosquito. **5** and **6.** Male and female shown at natural size. (All figures redrawn after Looss and Maplestone *in* Chandler, A. C., and Read, C. P. 1961. *Introduction to Parasitology,* John Wiley, New York.)

(a, anus; ae, anterior portion of esophagus; ex, excretory pore; g, genital primordium; i, intestine; n, nerve ring; pe, posterior portion of esophagus; r, rectum.)

is during the nocturnal period that they are most abundant and readily found in the peripheral circulation. None of these hypotheses has proven to be completely satisfactory. The phenomenon of microfilarial periodicity is discussed in more detail on page 455.

In strains that demonstrate nocturnal periodicity, microfilariae are most plentiful in the peripheral circulation between 10:00 P.M. and 2:00 A.M. If these microfilariae are ingested by a mosquito that has imbibed a blood meal, the mosquito phase of the life cycle commences. Unlike the malaria organisms, filarial worms show little specificity in regard to mosquito hosts. *W. bancrofti* can utilize *Culex* spp., *Aëdes* spp., *Mansonia* spp., *Anopheles* spp., and *Psorophora* spp. as vectors.

On reaching the midgut of the mosquito, the microfilariae lose their sheaths within 2 to 6 hours and penetrate the gut wall to become established in the thoracic muscles. At this new site, the organism becomes shortened by metamorphosing into a short sausage shaped body measuring between 124 and 250 μ. At this stage of development, the first true molt

occurs, after which the tail portion atrophies and the intestinal tract becomes well defined. A second molt follows and the resulting filiform third stage larva, measuring 1.4 to 2 mm. in length, migrates anteriorly into the proboscis sheath, contaminating the mouthparts of the mosquito.

When an infected mosquito bites another host, the larvae are introduced back into a vertebrate. The last two molts occur within the vertebrate. It has been determined that the infection of mosquitoes can occur only if fifteen or more microfilariae are present in every 20 cu. mm. of blood. If there are 100 or more microfilariae in every 20 cu. mm. of blood, the mosquito is killed. Under experimental conditions, development in the mosquito takes 2 weeks at 80° F., if maintained at 90 per cent humidity.

Genus *Brugia*

Up until 1960, several species of the Filaroidea with similar microfilariae were considered members of the genus *Wuchereria*. In that year, Buckley, as a result of studies of adult worms, established the genus *Brugia* to include the "malayi" group consisting of *B. malayi*, which parasitizes man, other primates, and cats; *B. pahangi*, found in the lymphatics of cats, dogs, tigers, and other wild animals in Malaya; and *B. patei* found in the lymphatics of various cats and dogs in Kenya. Recently two additional species of *Brugia*—*B. guyanensis* and *B. beaveri*—have been reported. These are the first *Brugia* species to be reported from the Western Hemisphere. *Brugia guyanensis* is found in the lymphatic system of the coatimundi *Nasua nasua vittata* in British Guiana; *B. beaveri* is found in the lymph nodes, skin, and carcass of the raccoon *Procyon lotor* in Louisiana.

Of all known species of *Brugia*, only *B. malayi* is known to parasitize man, causing what is called Malayan filariasis (Plate 16–29, Fig. 1). The range for this species extends from India to China, Japan, Formosa, Malaya, and Indonesia. A *malayi*-like form has been reported on an island off the coast of Kenya. Species of the mosquitoes *Mansonia* and *Anopheles* are the principal vectors, although in Japan *Aëdes togoi* appears to be the only vector.

Two strains of *Brugia malayi* are now recognized—the periodic and the semiperiodic strains. According to Laing (1960) and Laing et al. (1960), the periodic strain is quite host specific. It is restricted to humans. Its microfilariae portray nocturnal periodicity. On the other hand, the semiperiodic strain is less host specific, for its hosts include man, cats, the macaque monkey, and other animals, although its normal host is the leaf monkey *Presbytis*. The periodicity of its microfilariae is less pronounced.

The microfilariae of the various species of *Brugia* are quite similar and are extremely difficult to differentiate. *Brugia* can be distinguished from *Wuchereria* by the adults. *Brugia* spp. are smaller filarioids. The males measure up to 25 mm. by 100 μ, and the females measure up to 60 mm. by 190 μ. Furthermore, there are typically eleven papillae, known as anal papillae, at the posterior end of *Brugia* —four pairs situated ventrolaterally, two pairs situated postanally, and a single large preanal papilla.

In *Wuchereria*, there are about twenty-four anal papillae; nine to twelve pairs situated ventrolaterally, two pairs postanally, and also a single preanal papilla. In addition to these groups of anal papillae, there are typically two additional papillae situated between them and the tip of the tail in *Brugia* and about four such papillae in *Wuchereria*.

Both *W. bancrofti* and *B. malayi* block lymphatic canals when present in large numbers, causing enlargement of limbs and scrota, a condition known as elephantiasis (Plate 1–5, Fig. 1).

Genus *Onchocerca*

Onchocerca volvulus. This parasite causes onchocerciasis (Plate 16–29, Fig. 2). It is estimated that 19.8 million human cases of this disease exist, of which 19 million are found in tropical Africa and 800,000 in western Guatemala and northeastern Venezuela.

Microfilaria volvulus. The body is 300 to 350 μ by 5 to 8 μ. It is unsheathed and the tail is sharply pointed. There are no nuclei in the tail. The larva displays no periodicity. In the host, it is located primarily in the subcutaneous area.

Life Cycle of *Onchocerca volvulus*. The adult worms dwell in tumors in the subcutaneous connective tissue of man. In most instances there are two worms, a male and a female, in each tumorous nodule. However, numerous worms have been found coiled within a single swelling. The males, measuring 19 to 42 mm. in length, are considerably smaller than the females, which measure 33.5 to 50 cm. in length.

The eggshells rupture upon oviposition and the escaping microfilariae become unsheathed. Such microfilariae are of two sizes, suggesting sexual dimorphism. Instead of being located in the blood circulation, the microfilariae are found in lymphatics, but especially in the connective tissues of skin and rarely in the corneal conjunctiva. These larvae are phototactic. Blackflies, *Simulium* spp., serve as the insect hosts (or vectors) for *O. volvulus*. Wanson (1950) reported that development in the blackfly is essentially the same as that of *Wuchereria* in mosquitoes.

Other *Onchocerca* Species. Other species of *Onchocerca* include *O. gibsoni*, which forms hard nodules in the hide of cattle, thus destroying its value as leather, and *O. reticulata* in the neck ligaments of horses. Both of these species are found in the United States and are transmitted by *Culicoides* spp. *Onchocerca armillatus* is found in the aorta of cattle in Africa and often causes death through aneurysm. *Onchocerca gutturosa* is also found in cattle.

Genus *Dipetalonema*

Dipetalonema perstans. This filaroid nematode is primarily parasitic in man, although various primates do serve as natural reservoirs of infection. *Dipetalonema perstans* is found in Africa, South America, and the West Indies (Plate 16–29, Fig. 3). Stoll (1947) estimated that 27 million cases of human infections exist, mostly in Africa. Microfilariae of *Dipetalonema* are found in the blood of dogs in the United States.

Microfilaria perstans. The body is approximately 200 μ by 4 μ. It is unsheathed and the tail is blunted. The tail contains nuclei. No definite periodicity is evident. In the host, the larva is found in blood.

Life Cycle of *Dipetalonema perstans.* The adults are found in the host's body cavities, primarily the peritoneal cavity, although worms reportedly have also lodged in the pericardial cavity. The males, measuring 45 mm. by 60 μ, are smaller than the females, which measure from 70 to 80 mm. in length by 120 μ. The tail end of both sexes is curved and is bifurcated to form two nonmuscular flaps (Plate 16–29, Fig. 4). The microfilariae are unsheathed and are found in the blood. Although no definite periodicity is evident, more microfilariae are found during the night than during the day.

The fly *Culicoides austeni* is the principal vector. The larvae develop in the fly's thoracic muscles, and the infective form appears 8 to 9 days after the microfilariae enter the fly.

Dipetalonema streptocerca. This parasite is also primarily parasitic in man, with other primates serving as reservoirs of infection. *Dipetalonema streptocerca* is known only in its microfilarial form and has been reportedly found in the subcutaneous area of man in Africa.

Culicoides grahami has been found to be the fly vector for *D. streptocerca.* In both *D. perstans* and *D. streptocerca* infections, there appear to be little or no serious consequences. However, local inflammations are associated with the sites at which the nematodes are found in the host.

Microfilaria streptocerca. The body is approximately 220 μ by 3 μ. It is unsheathed, and the tail is blunt and hooked. The tail possesses nuclei. The body stains poorly with supravital methylene blue. This larva displays no periodicity, and is located in the subcutaneous regions of the host.

Dipetalonema reconditum. In the United States, Newton and Wright reported that there is a common species of *Dipetalonema*, probably *D. reconditum*, which is found in dogs. Dog fleas serve as the vector of this species. Undoubtedly the microfilariae of this nematode have been commonly mistaken for that of the pathogenic *Dirofilaria immitis*, discussed below.

Genus *Mansonella*

Mansonella ozzardi. This parasite is also a human-infecting species (Plate 16–29, Fig. 5). Adults are found in body cavities, usually embedded in the visceral adipose tissues, while the unsheathed microfilariae are found in the blood.

The fly *Culicoides furens* is the vector for *M. ozzardi* in northern South America. *Culicoides paraënsis* is probably another suitable vector. Other than local tissue reactions in the form of hydrocoels and lymph swellings, no drastic symptoms are connected with Ozzard's filariasis.

Microfilaria ozzardi. The body is approximately 200 μ by 5 μ and unsheathed. The tail is pointed and without nuclei. Living specimens are readily stained with methylene blue. It displays no periodicity and is found in the host's blood.

Genus *Dirofilaria*

Dirofilaria immitis. The genus *Dirofilaria* includes *D. immitis*, the fairly common heartworm of dogs, cats, foxes, and wolves (Plate 16–29, Fig. 6). Surveys have revealed that although this parasite is widely distributed in the United States, it is most frequently encountered in the southern states. The males, measuring 120 to 250 mm. in length by 1 mm. in diameter, possess tails that are blunted, armed with caudal alae, and are spirally coiled. The females, which measure 250 to 310 mm. by 1 mm., are larger, and the vulva is situated near the posterior extremity of the esophagus.

The microfilariae, measuring 218 to 330 μ by 5 to 6 μ, are unsheathed and are found in the peripheral circulation. Microfilariae can be found for several months in the blood. Hinman (1935) reported that a certain degree of periodicity exists, for the maximum number of microfilariae are present between 11 P.M. and 3 A.M., while only half of that number are present between 3 A.M. and 7 A.M.

Life Cycle of *Dirofilaria immitis.* The insect vector for *D. immitis* is a mosquito. Again, there appears to be little host specificity, for many species of mosquitoes belonging to the genera *Aëdes, Culex,* and *Anopheles* can serve as vectors. Other insects, such as lice, flies, and ticks, have been suspected as possible vectors. The wide assortment of vectors, however, may be the result of the misidentification of the parasite.

Within 24 to 36 hours after ingestion by the

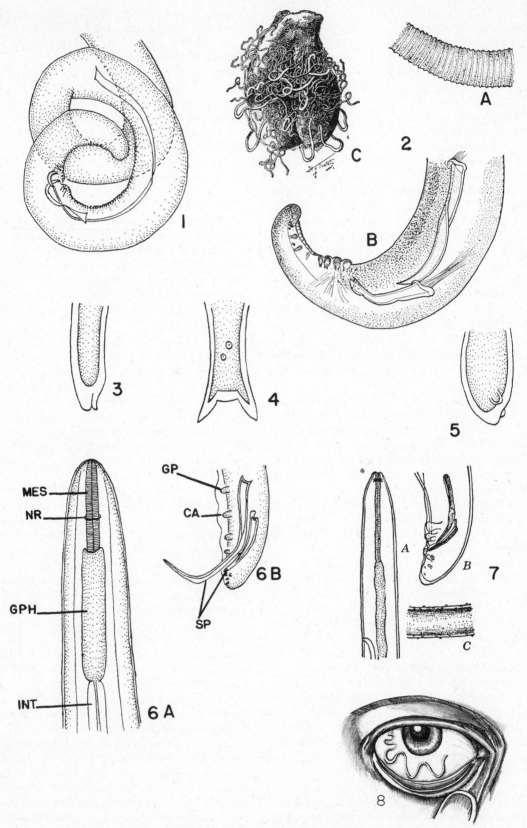

Plate 16-29   See legend on opposite page.

mosquito, the larvae are found primarily in the cells of the Malpighian tubules. The cell membranes of some of these tubules are ruptured as the result of the penetration. The larvae attain the infective stage within these cells and reach a length of approximately 900 μ.

The infective larvae escape from the Malpighian tubules and migrate to the coelom. Eleven to 12 days after their escape, most of the larvae are found in and among the fat bodies in the lower half of the thorax. From here, they migrate to the mouthparts and are in position to be introduced into another vertebrate when the mosquito partakes of another blood meal.

The adults appear in the vertebrate's heart, particularly the right ventricle and pulmonary arteries, in 8 to 9 months. In addition, *D. immitis* has been found in subcutaneous tissue, in the anterior chamber of the eye, and in pulmonary nodules of the host. Infected animals may suffer from chronic endocarditis, liver enlargement, and inflammation of the kidneys. Ascites tumors have been reported associated with this nematode. Infected dogs become extremely ill.

OTHER *Dirofilaria* SPECIES.   Other species of *Dirofilaria* include *D. magalhaesi,* reported from the left ventricle of a Brazilian child, and *D. louisianensis,* from the inferior vena cava of an elderly Negress in New Orleans.

Genus *Loa*

Loa loa.   This species, commonly known as the eye worm, dwells in the subcutaneous tissues of man and baboons in Central and West Africa (Plate 16–29, Fig. 7). Stoll (1947) estimated that 13 million cases of human infections exist. The threadlike adults are comparatively large. The males measure 30 to 34 mm. in length and 0.35 to 0.43 mm. in diameter; the females measure 50 to 70 mm. in length by 0.5 mm. The cuticle is covered with wartlike processes.

These worms are encased only rarely in connective tissue cysts. Rather, they migrate in the subcutaneous area over the entire body and are sometimes seen passing in front of the eyeballs, thus, the common name. Swellings often result from the migration of this worm and may be as large as a chicken's egg. Low (1934) postulated that such swellings result from the host's tissue reacting to toxins secreted by the worms.

Microfilaria loa.   The body is sheathed and 250 to 300 μ by 6 to 8.5 μ in size. The body stains poorly, or not at all, with Giemsa's stain. The tail is short and recurved and contains nuclei. The body will take on supravital methylene blue stain. This larva displays diurnal periodicity and is found in blood.

The sheathed microfilariae are unique among the human-infecting filarioids in that they demonstrate diurnal periodicity. The insect vector, therefore, must be a daytime biting form, and such is the case, for it has been determined that daylight feeding tabanid flies, *Chrysops dimidiata* and *C. silacea,* serve as the vectors. In the fly host, the larvae undergo three larval stages in the thoracic muscles before entering the fly's mouthparts, from which they are introduced into another vertebrate host. As with almost all filarioid worms, the last two molts occur within the vertebrate.

Genus *Litomosoides*

Litomosoides carinii.   Special attention is being paid to *Litomosoides carinii,* a parasite in the pleural cavity of the cotton rat, *Sigmodon hispidus littoralis,* since this is a filarioid worm commonly used in research laboratories as an experimental animal, especially in the United States and South America, where the rat host is commonly found in open grasslands.

Adults of *L. carinii* are long and thin. The buccal cavity is narrow. The males, which measure 24 to 26 mm. in length, lack alae or papillae at the caudal end. The females, which

---

Plate 16-29   Filarial nematodes.   1. Caudal end of male of *Brugia malayi,* showing copulatory spicules, naviculate gubernaculum, and the distribution and types of papillae. (Redrawn after Rao and Maplestone.) 2. A. Portion of body of *Onchocerca volvulus,* showing annular thickenings. B. Posterior end of male, showing spicules and papillae. C. *Onchocerca* nodule opened, showing tangled worms inside. (After Fülleborn and Brumpt.) 3. Posterior terminal of *Dipetalonema* (= *Acanthocheilonema*) *perstans* female. 4. Posterior terminal of *D. perstans* male, showing bifurcation. (Redrawn after Highby, 1943.) 5. Posterior end of *Mansonella ozzardi* female. 6. *Dirofilaria immitis.* A. Anterior end. B. Posterior end of male. (Redrawn after Canavan, 1929.) 7. *Loa loa.* A. Anterior end. B. Posterior end of male. C. Portion of body, showing warts on cuticle. 8. *Loa loa* in eye. (After various authors in Chandler, A. C., and Read, C. P. 1961. *Introduction to Parasitology,* John Wiley, New York.)

(CA, caudal ala; GP, genital papilla; GPH, glandular portion of esophagus; INT, intestine; MES, muscular portion of esophagus; NR, nerve ring; SP, spicules.)

454 ASCHELMINTHES

measure 50 to 130 mm. in length, possess both a bulbous enlargement near the vulva, and a long ovijector. Both male and female adults occur in the rat's pleural cavity; occasionally they invade the peritoneal cavity.

Life Cycle of *Litomosoides carinii*. Mature females give birth ovoviviparously to thin, sheathed microfilariae within the host's pleural cavity. These microfilariae migrate to the blood stream via various routes, the most common being via the lungs. The insect vector is the tropical rat mite *Bdellonyssus bacoti*. When mites feed on an infected rat, microfilariae are taken into the mite's intestine, where the larvae burrow through the intestinal wall to become established in the haemocoel.

Approximately 8 days after entering the mite, the larva becomes sausage shaped and undergoes the first ecdysis. The second ecdysis occurs on the 9th or 10th day and the larva increases in size until it measures 500 to 950 μ long. By the 14th or 15th day, the third stage larva is fully developed and infective. The temperature at which the mite host is maintained influences the time required for development. The periods given above are for worms in mites maintained at 23 to 25° C.

It is suspected that rats become infected when infective larvae penetrate the skin. In the laboratory, infective larvae removed from mites can be injected subcutaneously to establish the infection. Once within the rat's blood, the larva migrates to the pleural cavity and undergoes the third ecdysis in about a week. Further

growth takes place during the next 17 days, the male larva attaining a length of 6.4 ± 0.5 mm. and the female attaining a length of 8.7 ± 0.2 mm. External sex characteristics are evident by this time.

The fourth and final ecdysis occurs about 23 or 24 days after the initial infection, and growth toward the adult form commences. Sexual maturity is reached within 70 to 80 days, and microfilariae can then be found in the host's blood. No microfilarial periodicity exists. The peak of microfilarial production occurs between the 17th and 20th week after infection. The adults can live for 60 weeks or more.

Other Filarioid Genera

Other filarioid nematodes include members of *Filaria*, found in the subcutaneous tissues of rodents and some carnivores; *Setaria*, found in the abdominal cavity of domestic animals (*S. equina* in horses, *S. cervi* in cattle) and the sheathed microfilariae found in blood; *Litomosa* and *Litomosoides* found in the pleural cavities of bats and rats, respectively (Plate 16–30, Fig. 1); *Foleyella*, found in the subcutaneous tissues of amphibians and reptiles (Plate 16–30, Fig. 2); *Stephanofilaria*, with the principal American species, *S. stilesi*, found in the abdominal skin of cattle, where it causes lesions (Plate 16–30, Fig. 3); *Elaeophora*, in sheep, goats, and sometimes deer; *Aprocta*, found in the orbital and nasal cavities of birds (Plate 16–30, Fig. 4); and *Tetracheilonema*, found in the abdominal cavity and subcutaneous tissues of birds.

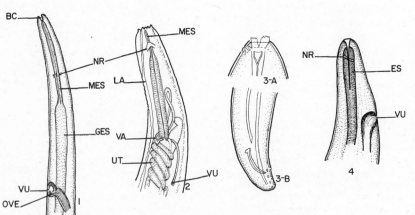

Plate 16–30   Parasitic nematodes. 1. Anterior end of *Litomosoides carinii*, in rats. (Redrawn after Chandler, 1931.) 2. Anterior end of *Foleyella* in subcutaneous tissues of amphibians and reptiles. (Redrawn after Walton, 1929.) 3. *Stephanofilaria stilesi* in skin of abdomen of cattle. A. Lateral view of anterior end. B. Lateral view of posterior end of male. (Redrawn after Schiller *in* Morgan, B. B., and Hawkins, P. A. 1949. *Veterinary Helminthology,* Burgess, Minneapolis.) 4. Anterior end of female of *Aprocta* in nasal and orbital cavities of birds. (Redrawn after Skrjabin, 1917.)

(BC, buccal capsule; ES, esophagus; GES, glandular portion of esophagus; LA, longitudinal ala; MES, muscular portion of esophagus; NR, nerve ring; OVE, ovejector; UT, uterus; VA, vagina; VU, vulva.)

PATHOGENICITY OF FILARIOIDS IN VECTORS

Filarioid nematodes cause severe damage to their insect vectors. In *Aëdes aegypti* infected with *Dirofilaria*, the pathogencity is so severe that the mortality rate is many times that for uninfected mosquitoes. The greatest injury to the mosquito occurs when the filarioids penetrate the epithelial lining of the midgut. Furthermore, worms in the Malpighian tubules cause degeneration of the cytoplasm of the cells lining the tubules, initially leaving the nuclei intact.

As the result of the destruction of the cytoplasm, cells of walls of the Malpighian tubules resemble distorted, multinucleated cells. By the time the nematodes reach the infective stage, however, the cells lining the tubules are totally disintegrated, so that the worms are enclosed in translucent bags of basement membrane. Although in need of verification, it has been reported that the pathogenicity of *Dirofilaria* is less severe in unfertilized female mosquitoes than in fertilized ones.

Species of insect vectors differ as to their ability to survive infections by filarioids. For example, *Simulium damnosum* cannot survive heavy infections of *Onchocerca volvulus*. Similarly, mortality is high when *S. callidum* and *S. ochraceum* are infected with large numbers of *O. volvulus*. On the other hand, Dalmat (1955) found that *S. metallicum* is somewhat resistant to heavy infections.

Although the histopathology of blackflies infected with *O. volvulus* has not been studied to any extent, Lavoipierre (1958) has found that thoracic muscles of *Simulium* in the vicinity of the growing larvae degenerate.

MICROFILARIAL PERIODICITY

As briefly mentioned in connection with certain microfilariae, especially *Wuchereria bancrofti* (p. 447), a definite rhythmicity occurs in the appearance of large numbers of microfilariae in the host's peripheral circulation. This phenomenon, known as microfilarial periodicity, is of fundamental interest to biologists, because it represents one form of biological rhythm—that is, the predictable recurrence of some biological phenomenon.

Microfilarial periodicity, first discovered in 1879 by Patrick Manson in human infections of *Wuchereria bancrofti* in South China, is now known to occur in a number of filarioid species (Table 16–2). In some, such as the common strain of *W. bancrofti* and the periodic strain of *Brugia malayi,* the periodicity is nocturnal,

while in others, such as *Loa loa* and *Dipetalonema reconditum,* it is diurnal. The timing and extent of these rhythms vary according to the species but are consistent for the species under natural conditions (Tables 16–3 and 16–4).

The evolution of microfilarial periodicity is of survival value, for it enhances changes in the ingestion of microfilariae by the insect vectors. For example, in the case of the common strain of *W. bancrofti* of man, the microfilariae are most abundant in the host's peripheral circulation during the night hours when the mosquito vector *Culex fatigans* (and others) are most active in their feeding. Similarly, in the case of *Loa loa,* the appearance of microfilariae in large numbers in the host's peripheral circulation during the day coincides with the active feeding period of various *Chrysops* species that serve as vectors.

Interestingly, the so-called Pacific strain of *Wuchereria bancrofti,* unlike the common strain, portrays a certain degree of diurnal periodicity. This opposite rhythmic pattern coincides with the feeding period of its mosquito vectors, *Aëdes pseudoscutellaris* and others.

In some species, for example, *Litomosoides carinii,* periodicity does not occur. Hawking (1962) has expressed the opinion that possibly these worms are not yet sufficiently evolved to be capable of periodicity, or perhaps the host's habits are not sufficiently imprinted with the 24-hour rhythm to make the evolution of parasite periodicity feasible. Hawking has also pointed out that (as suggested by the data in Table 16–2) periodicity seems to be well defined among species that parasitize birds and large mammals, especially man and simians, while it is usually absent among species that parasitize small rodents, amphibians, and reptiles.

Although numerous studies have been carried out in attempts to explain the cause of microfilarial periodicity, this aspect of helminth physiology has yet to be completely resolved. It is known, nevertheless, that periodicity is not dependent on the alternation of night and day, but on the 24-hour habits of the host. Therefore, if a host is made to reverse its routine so that it sleeps by day and moves about at night, the periodicity of the microfilariae is reversed. This reversal process takes about a week, thus indicating that the microfilariae are not affected by sleeping and waking as such but only by the entire 24-hour rhythm. In man and higher mammals, this rhythm is characterized by a decrease in body temperature and oxygen pressure, an increase in carbon

Table 16-2. The Periodicity of Some Species of Microfilariae from Various Hosts

Periodicity	Parasite	Host	Authority
Nocturnal	*Wuchereria bancrofti*	Man	
	Brugia malayi	Man	
	B. pahangi	Cat, monkey	Edeson (1959)
	B. patei	Cat	Heisch, Nelson, and Furlong (1959)
	Dirofilaria immitis	Dog	
	D. repens	Dog	
	D. corynodes	Monkey	Hawking (1962)
	D. uniformis	Rabbit	Bray and Watton (1961)
	D. tenuis	Raccoon	Pistey (1959)
	Loa loa	Monkey	Duke and Wijers (1958)
	Edesonfilaria malayensis	Monkey	Hawking (1962)
	Monnigofilaria setariosa	Mongoose	Hawking (1962)
	Splendidofilaria quiscali	Grackle	Odetoyinbo and Ulmer (1960)
	S. columbigallinae	Dove	Augustine (1937)
	S. lissum	Partridge	Raghavan and David (1955)
	Microfilaria	Crows (United States)	Boughton, Byrd, and Lund (1938), Robinson (1955)
	Microfilaria	Canaries (Algiers)	Sergent (1941)
Diurnal	*Loa loa*	Man	
	Wuchereria bancrofti var. *pacifica**	Man	
	Dipetalonema reconditum	Dog	Newton and Wright (1956)
	Ornithofilaria fallisensis	Duck	Anderson (1956)
Absent	*Mansonella ozzardi*	Man	
	Dipetalonema perstans	Man	
	D. magnilarvata	Monkey	Hawking (1959)
	D. witei	Bird	Hawking (1962)
	Litomosoides carinii	Cotton rat	
	Setaria cervi	Cattle	McFadzean (1955)
	Microfilaria fijiensis	Bat	Symes and Mataika (1959)
	Conispiculum guindiense	Lizard	Raghavan (in Hawking, 1962)
	Foleyella sp.	Frog	
	Icosiella sp.	Frog	

*Slight periodicity

(Data from Hawking, 1962. References to the authorities cited can be found in Hawking's review paper.)

Table 16-3.   Fluctuation in the Number of Microfilariae in the Peripheral Circulation of Man Infected with the Normal and Pacific Strains of *Wuchereria bancrofti**

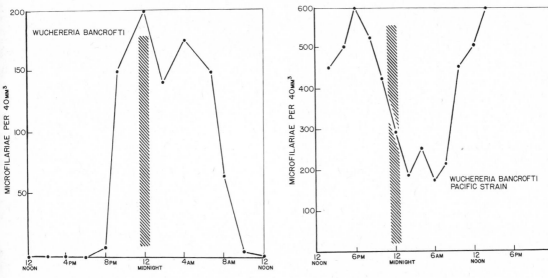

* Normal strain left; Pacific strain right.
The shaded bar represents midnight in each graph.
(After Hawking, 1962.)

Table 16-4.   Fluctuation in the Number of Microfilariae in the Circulation of Man Infected with *Loa loa* and Dog Infected with *Dirofilaria immitis**

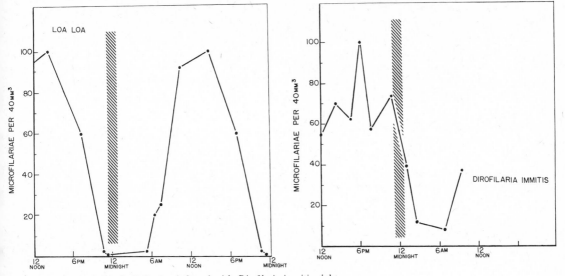

* Man infected with *Loa loa,* left; dog infected with *Dirofilaria immitis,* right.
The shaded bar represents midnight in each graph.
(After Hawking, 1962.)

dioxide pressure, increased body acidity, less excretion of water and chlorides by the kidneys, less adrenal activity, and so forth during sleep. Some or all of these physiological changes may affect the microfilariae, resulting in the rhythmic cycle.

To understand microfilarial periodicity, it is necessary to know what happens to the microfilariae during the period when they are not present or are only sparsely present in the peripheral circulation. It is now known, mainly as the result of the extensive studies of Hawking and associates, that when microfilariae are completely or almost completely absent from the peripheral circulation, they accumulate primarily in the capillaries and small blood vessels of the lungs.

Hawking (1962) has suggested that because microfilariae cannot mechanically attach to the blood vessel walls, they are maintained therein by some kind of electrostatic attraction. If the charge on the microfilariae or on the vessel wall is changed or removed by some physiological change, the parasites are swept into the general circulation. Although experimental proof of this explanation remains to be contributed, the general concept of accumulation of microfilariae in the lungs during the active phase (when they are not found in great numbers in the peripheral circulation) and the release of microfilariae by some physiological triggering mechanism into the general circulation during the passive phase (when they are found evenly distributed throughout the blood and thus appear abundantly in the peripheral circulation) has greatly enhanced our understanding of microfilarial periodicity.

The stimuli controlling alternation between the active and passive phases have been searched for extensively (see Hawking, 1956; McFadzean and Hawking, 1956). The only natural stimuli that may be of significance are increased oxygen intake and exercise.

It has been shown that if an individual parasitized by the common strain of *Wuchereria bancrofti* inhales air containing increased oxygen tension during the night, there is a marked decrease of microfilariae in the peripheral circulation following the intake of oxygen, and the number of microfilariae in the lungs is increased. Similarly, if the parasitized individual exercises during the night, a marked decrease in the number of microfilariae in the peripheral circulation follows, and their number increases in the lungs.

On the other hand, the intake of oxygen during the day by hosts of the Pacific strain of *W. bancrofti,* which normally displays diurnal periodicity, causes an increase in the number of microfilariae in the peripheral circulation. Similarly, the intake of oxygen by dogs infected with *Dirofilaria immitis* and by monkeys infected with *D. corynodes* causes a rise in the microfilarial count in the peripheral circulation. Thus, it would appear that different species of microfilariae respond differently to such stimuli.

Recently Wang et al. (1958) and Fukamachi (1960) have shown that the subcutaneous injection of acetylcholine (12 to 19 mg. per kg. of body weight) or pilocarpine (1 to 2 mg. per kg. body weight) causes a dramatic increase in the number of *Dirofilaria immitis* microfilariae in the peripherial blood of dogs. Injection of adrenalin, ethylamine, chlorpromazine, atropine, and promethazine has no effect. Furthermore, electric shock also produces a rise in the peripheral microfilarial count.

Fukamachi concluded that the periodicity is probably due to some physiological stimulus to the host's parasympathetic nervous system, which in turn stimulates the worms, for acetylcholine and pilocarpine are parasympathomimetic agents—that is, they mimic the function of the parasympathetic nervous system.

Hawking has since verified the effects of acetylcholine on microfilarial periodicity in the case of *D. immitis* infections in dogs. In addition, he reported that the intravenous injection of acetylcholine does not cause an increase in the number of microfilariae in the peripheral blood in *Wuchereria bancrofti* infections. Furthermore, there is no evidence for a relationship between the parasympathetic nervous system and the periodicity of human microfilariae. This again indicates that different species of microfilariae respond differently to similar stimuli.

IMMUNITY AND MICROFILAREMIA

Although hosts of filarioid nematodes generally maintain their parasites for long periods, it has been repeatedly recognized since Manson's report of 1899 that there is an absence of circulating microfilariae in humans with severe elephantiasis. Gordon (1955) has stated: "that it is the very persons who suffer most severely from filariasis who are least likely to show the presence of microfilariae." These observations suggest that hosts develop an immunity to filarial worms that suppresses microfilaremia, or the presence of microfilariae in the circulating blood.

Attempts made by a number of investigators to use saline suspensions of dried, powdered microfilariae in skin tests, precipitin tests, and in complement-fixation tests to detect antibodies in humans with apparent *Wuchereria bancrofti* microfilaremias have been far from satisfactory. On the other hand, conspicuous positive reactions have been observed in similar tests in patients who show clinical symptoms of filariasis without microfilaremia. These findings suggest that the host's antibodies are only present in amounts sufficient to be detected in severe cases of filariasis.

Recently Wong (1963), while studying dogs infected with *Brugia pahangi* or *Dirofilaria immitis,* has shown that such is probably the case. Wong demonstrated that uninfected dogs receiving multiple immunizing inoculations of microfilariae did not show microfilaremia after subsequent inoculations of large numbers of microfilariae. Sera taken from these dogs caused agglutination of living microfilariae of the same species, whereas no such agglutination occurred in sera from uninfected control dogs and from infected dogs with patent microfilaremia. Absorption tests indicated that these agglutinations were specific. When the sera of dogs given multiple immunizing inoculations of microfilariae were added to media used for the in vitro maintenance of adult worms, the production of microfilariae was inhibited in the adults. Furthermore, when such sera were injected intravenously into infected dogs with microfilaremia, the number of microfilariae in the circulating blood was reduced significantly.

These experiments suggest that the antibody demonstrated in vitro is also effective in vivo and that a relationship exists between the number of microfilariae present in the circulating blood and the concentration of specific antibodies produced by the host in response to the presence of microfilariae. Thus, it appears possible that the presence of a high titer of such antibodies is responsible for the absence of microfilariae in the circulating blood of hosts suffering from severe filariasis.

PHYSIOLOGY OF NEMATODES

OXYGEN REQUIREMENTS

It is now apparent that one cannot generalize as to whether adult intestinal nematodes are completely aerobic or anaerobic, nor as to whether free-living larvae are all completely aerobic. The volume of experimental data now available strongly suggests that each species must be considered individually relative to its utilization of oxygen. Some known survival rates of parasitic nematodes are listed in Table 16–5 as recorded by various investigators under aerobic and anaerobic conditions.

To illustrate the differences in oxygen requirement in several intestine-dwelling species, Rogers (1949) reported that *Nippostrongylus muris* is found in a region of the small intestine where the oxygen tension is 19 to 30 mm. Hg (average 24 mm. Hg), while *Nematodirus* sp. is located in a section of the gut where the oxygen tension is lower. These results strongly suggest that the amount of oxygen present at a particular level of the alimentary tract is at least partially responsible for the location of specific nematode species.

Wells (1931) reported that adult hookworms, which ingest their host's erythrocytes, obtain a portion of their oxygen requirement from these red blood cells. It has been estimated that approximately 0.2 mg. of oxygen is available to hookworms from this source. Hookworms and certain other adult nematodes require oxygen in their metabolism. For example, *Nippostrongylus muris* exhibits respiratory quotients (R. Q.) as high as 6.8. The R. Q. of most common ascaroids, however, is of the order of 0.4.

On the other hand, horse and pig ascarids undoubtedly lead an essentially anaerobic existence. This is confirmed in that their oxygen uptake, when such occurs, is totally unaffected by cyanide, and cytochrome oxidase has never been demonstrated in their tissues. Although these adult nematodes are essentially anaerobic, they are facultative rather than obligatory anaerobes and utilize oxygen if it is provided. Ascarids of pigs and horses utilize oxygen at a relatively high rate after a period of anaerobiosis, thus indicating the occurrence of an oxygen debt. The amount and rate of oxygen uptake is governed by the quantity of end products of anaerobic fermentation accumulated in the tissues.

There is some doubt whether the amount of oxygen required by adults is the same when maintained in vitro as it is in vivo. To illustrate this point, Rogers (1949) recorded that *Nippostrongylus muris* and *Nematodirus* spp., when in their hosts, utilize only 80 per cent and 40 per cent, respectively, of the oxygen they consume when maintained in vitro. In *Haemonchus contortus,* the amount of oxygen required in vivo is even lower than that reported for *Nippostrongylus muris* and *Nematodirus* spp. It was noticed, however, that worms maintained in vitro are considerably more active than those observed

Table 16-5.   Survival Time of Nematode Species in Vitro under Anaerobic and Aerobic Conditions*

Species	Medium	Temperature (in degrees centigrade)	Survival Time in Days	
			Anaerobic	Aerobic
Litomosoides carinii	Ox serum	37	<1	7
Parascaris equorum	Ringer's	35-38	2-5	2
Raphidascaris acus	1% NaCl	Room temperature	6	—
Ascaris lumbricoides	1% NaCl	35-38	7-9	6
Trichostrongylus colubriformis	Ringer's	37	<1	4-12
T. vitrinus	Ringer's	37	<1	4-12
Ostertagia circumcincta	Ringer's	37	<1	4-12
Cooperia oncophora	Ringer's	37	<2	4-12
C. curticei	Ringer's	37	<1	4-12
Nematodirus filicollis	Ringer's	37	<2	4-12
Trichinella spiralis (larvae)	Tyrode	37	7 or more	—
Ancylostoma caninum (larvae)	Tapwater	17	21	—
Eustrongylides ignotus (larvae)	1% NaCl	37	3	19
	0.85% NaCl	20	21	several months

*Data from various authors, mainly after von Brand (1946).

in vivo. This phenomenon is directly correlated to the amount of oxygen consumed.

The respiratory rate and sometimes the type of respiration (that is, aerobic or anaerobic) of the egg and larval stages of nematodes generally differ from those of adults (Table 16-6). Eggs of many species, for example, embryonate and hatch in the aerobic environment provided by moist soil. When investigated, the R. Q. for eggs varies between 0.6 and 0.9. The consumption of oxygen plus histochemical evidences suggests that the energy required during embryonic development within the egg is provided mainly from oxidation of fat, although protein and carbohydrate metabolisms contribute some of the energy. Passay and Fairbairn (1957) have demonstrated that a net decrease in the lipid content in developing eggs corresponds with an increase in carbohydrate. This suggests the synthesis of carbohydrates (trehelose and glycogen) from triglycerides.

The inhibition of respiration in nematode eggs by cyanide, carbon dioxide, or hydrozoic acid indicates dependency on a cytochrome system (Table 3-5).

From the standpoint of growth and development of the larva within the egg, the amount of oxygen present in the environment is of critical importance. For example, larvae in the eggs of *Ascaris lumbricoides* can survive a minimum oxygen tension of 30 mm. Hg, although even then growth is retarded by 50 per cent. In larvae in the eggs of *Parascaris,* growth is barely maintained when the oxygen tension is 5 mm. Hg, and growth is extremely slow at 10 to 80 mm. Hg, but is normal at tensions above 80 mm. Hg.

The eggs of some nematodes are able to survive for a period of time in the absence of oxygen, although oxygen is required for complete development and hatching of the larvae. In the egg of *Parascaris,* the embryo can undergo the first cleavage stages under anaerobic conditions but requires oxygen for further development. Again, in *Oxyuris equi,* the embryo can reach the gastrula stage in the absence of oxygen but requires oxygen from then on. In eggs of *Enterobius vermicularis,* the larva can reach the tadpole stage without oxygen; however, further development requires aerobic conditions.

In the species that have been studied, respiration in larval nematodes is aerobic. The R. Q. of the infective larvae of *Nippostrongylus* and

Table 16-6.   Respiratory Quotients (R. Q.) of Various Stages of Nematode Species*†

Nematode Species	Eggs	Respiratory Quotient Larvae	Adults
Haemonchus contortus	0.58-0.60	0.64	–
Ascaris lumbricoides	–	–	3-4
Ascaridia galli	–	–	0.96
Trichinella spiralis	–	1.1	–
Nippostrongylus muris	–	0.66-0.73	0.69
Litomosoides carinii	–	–	0.44
Eustrongylides ignotus	–	1.0	–
Syphacia obvelata	–	–	1.1
Neoaplectana glaseri	–	–	0.59

*Oxygen tension is about 160 mm. Hg, and sugar is absent. Unless otherwise specified, values are given for 37-38°C.

†Data from von Brand, 1952, in Smyth, 1962. *Introduction to Parasitology*, Charles C Thomas.

Haemonchus is approximately 0.7. The energy requirements in these larvae are also primarily provided through lipid metabolism. In larvae found in the host's tissues—for example, *Trichinella spiralis* in mammalian muscles and *Eustrongylides ignotus* in fish muscles—the R. Q. is higher, being 1.0 or more, because energy production is provided predominantly through metabolism of the large glycogen supply in the body of the parasites.

Although respiration in larval nematodes is primarily aerobic, certain larvae can withstand anoxic conditions for some time. Stoll (1940) reported that the first parasitic molt of *Haemonchus contortus* occurs best in cultures with limited oxygen tension. *Trichinella spiralis* can be maintained anaerobically, although oxidative metabolism brings about greater motility. In addition, certain small intestinal nematodes succumb rapidly when exposed to anaerobic conditions.

Haemoglobin in Nematodes

Haemoglobin, the oxygen-carrying pigment, has been detected in certain nematodes. For example, it is present in *Nippostrongylus muris* in amounts of approximately 6 mg. per gram of dry weight, and in *Nematodirus* and *Haemonchus contortus* approximately 0.8 mg. per gram of dry weight. Rogers demonstrated that if the environmental oxygen decreases to below 13 mm. Hg, the oxyhaemoglobin in *Nippostrongylus muris* becomes deoxygenated, and if it decreases to below 9 mm. Hg, the same occurs in *H. contortus* and *Nematodirus*.

In other nematodes, haemoglobin has been found in *Trichinella* larvae, and a haemoglobin-like substance has been reported in *Camallanus trispinosus*. Haemoglobin has also been detected in the hypodermis of *Ascaris*. It is generally presumed that haemoglobin in nematodes aids in the incorporation and conduction of oxygen from the environment to the inner tissues of the body.

GROWTH REQUIREMENTS

The maximum survival rates of some nematode species in various culture media are tabulated in Table 16–7. Some investigators have been able to maintain parasitic nematodes in culture media, others have actually found media in which the worms grew, while still others have accomplished the extremely desirable result of finding media in which the worms not only increased in size but also actually molted and developed through the various stages of their normal life cycles. To cite a few examples of each, von Brand and Simpson (1944, and earlier papers) were able to maintain *Eustrongylides ignotus* for 5 months in Bacto broth glucose solutions at 37° C. and for 4 years in Bacto proteose peptone glucose solutions at 20° C. Among the many larvae maintained in this fashion, only one specimen grew to maturity.

Hoeppli et al. (1938) were able to keep the larvae of *Ascaris lumbricoides* alive for 1 week in diluted horse serum mixed with debris of fresh liver. Fenwick (1939), using a strictly inorganic medium, was able to maintain *Ascaris* larvae

Table 16-7.   Maximum Survival Rates of Nematodes in Various Culture Media

Species	Medium	Temperature (in degrees C.)	Survival Time	Source
Ascaris lumbricoides, adults	Kronecker's solution	27-30	26 days	Hall (1917)
Spirocerca sanguinolenta, larvae	Ringer's solution	37	42 days	Hoeppli, Feng, and Chu (1938)
Camallanus americanus, adults	Witte peptone and turtle blood agar	25	2 months	Magath (1919)
Dirofilaria immitis, microfilariae	Defibrinated blood and glucose	37	15 days	Johns and Guereus (1914)
Wuchereria bancrofti, microfilariae	Saline plus haemoglobin	22-27	32 days	Couteleu (1929)
Eustrongylides ignotus	Bacto proteose peptone glucose	37	5 months	Von Brand and Simpson (1944)
E. ignotus	Bacto proteose peptone glucose	20	4 years	Von Brand and Simpson (1944)

for 5.5 days in a salt solution consisting of 0.80 per cent NaCl, 0.02 per cent KCl, 0.02 per cent $CaCl_2$, and 0.01 per cent $MgCl_2$.

In the second category, Ackert et al. (1938) were able to maintain *Ascaridia lineata* for 9 days on salt dextrose agar plates and these worms actually increased in length during the period. In the most impressive third category, Glaser (1931, 1932) was able to maintain *Neoaplectana glaseri,* a parasite of the Japanese beetle, through 32 generations on veal infusion dextrose agar with baker's yeast growing on the surface. The various stages in the life cycle of this nematode took place. The culture eventually died out when the ovaries in females failed to develop to maturity. Two other species, *Nippostrongylus muris* and *Haemonchus contortus,* have been successfully cultured through their entire life cycles, from egg to adult (Weinstein and Jones, 1956; Silverman, 1959).

Jackson (1962) has provided the first chemically defined culture medium for a parasitic nematode, *Neoaplectana glaseri,* consisting of salts, amino acids, taurine, urea, and various intermediary metabolites associated with the Kreb's cycle. It is now known that free-living larvae of *Ancylostoma caninum, A. duodenale,* and *Nippostrongylus muris* molt and metamorphose into the infective stage when maintained on homogenates of fresh chick embryos and rat liver. The sustaining substance or substances in the liver are readily destroyed by heat, for if the rat liver extracts are heated for 15 minutes at 55° C. or for 1 minute at 100° C., the growth-stimulating ability is inactivated. Dough-

erty (1951) reported that a heat-labile proteinaceous substance, or substances, is also required by *Rhabditis briggsae* for growth and reproduction when cultured under axenic conditions. This substance, known as factor Rb, can be precipitated with ammonium sulfate.

The ability of *Neoaplectana glaseri, Ancylostoma caninum, A. duodenale,* and *Nippostrongylus muris* to undergo ecdysis in vitro suggests that a molt-stimulating substance is present in the culture media, for Sommerville (1957) demonstrated that in vivo ecdysis is dependent on a dialyzable factor or factors present in the host's intestine. This factor stimulates the secretion of an "exsheathing fluid" within the nematode. The sheath of the fourth stage larva of *Nippostrongylus muris* is composed of protein, carbohydrate, and lipid. The amino acid composition of the protein fraction resembles that of collagen only in the content of tyrosine.

Our present knowledge concerning the culture of nematodes has been reviewed by Dougherty (1960) and Rogers (1962).

CARBOHYDRATE METABOLISM

As is the case among most helminth parasites, especially those that live in environments where there is little or no oxygen, nematodes depend primarily on carbohydrate metabolism as the energy source, because proteins and lipids do not lend themselves to the internal oxidation-reduction reactions characteristic of anaerobic processes. Even in certain nematodes that live in environments where oxygen abounds, carbohydrate metabolism predominates. For example, the filarial worm *Litomosoides,* which lives in the tissues or the blood stream of its host, where oxygen is available, utilizes carbohydrate metabolism as the main method of producing energy. In such cases, however, carbohydrate catabolism is of such a nature that the sugars are not oxidized completely to carbon dioxide and water, indicating that the process is of a fermentative type.

Glycogen is the main type of reserve nutrient in the bodies of nematodes. When the worms are starved, glycogen is depleted rapidly resulting in the production of fermentation acids and carbon dioxide. The metabolic end products in all species studied include for the most part volatile fatty acids, among which acetic, lactic, butyric, valeric, and caproic acids have been identified. Among these, valeric acid or its isomers comprise the major excretory product. For example, in *Trichinella spiralis,* valeric acid represents 80 per cent of the acids produced. There is some evidence that part of the usual glycolytic pathway of the Embden-Meyerhof scheme occurs (Table 3–5).

Little is known about how body glycogen is synthesized in nematodes. In *Ascaris,* however, it is known that stored glycogen is synthesized from fructose, sorbose, maltose, and sucrose, which are absorbed; but lactose and mannose are not utilized. Furthermore, larger nematodes, such as *Dracunculus* and *Litomosoides,* consume nearly forty times more carbohydrate per gram of tissue than such smaller species as *Eustrongylides.* The reason for such differences is not known, although the presence of different types of metabolism is suggested. Again, the degree of maturity of the worms studied most probably is responsible for some of these differences. For example, young worms do not require as much carbohydrate as older ones that are producing eggs.

PROTEIN METABOLISM

As with most parasitic helminths, the biotic potential of nematodes is great (p. 22). Although the exact essential amino acids of nematodes have not been determined satisfactorily, the uptake of these must be rapid and in relatively large quantities, especially in egg-producing individuals. Furthermore, the conversion of proteins and amino acids that are taken into eggs must be highly efficient.

The end products of nitrogen metabolism are known in only a few species, and in these ammonia is given off in relatively large quantities (ammoniotelic metabolism). For example, Savel (1955) reported that *Ascaris lumbricoides* excretes 39 mg. of nitrogen per 100 gm. of wet body weight per day, of which 79 per cent is ammonia, 7 per cent urea, and 21 per cent polypeptides. Similarly, Haskins and Weinstein (1957a, b) reported that *Trichinella spiralis* larvae excrete 2.8 mg. of nitrogen per 1 gm. of wet body weight, of which 33 per cent is ammonia, 7 per cent volatile amine nitrogen, 20 per cent peptide nitrogen, and 29 per cent amino acid nitrogen.

Ammoniotelic nitrogen metabolism also is found in such free-living aquatic animals as annelids, echinoderms, teleost fishes, and reptiles. Among these aquatic organisms, water is readily available from the environment in which ammonia can be diluted and kept below the toxic level. Since ammonia is also highly toxic to nematodes, it could be assumed that the intestinal nematodes are able to derive water from the host's intestinal contents to dilute the ammonia. Since the larvae of certain nematodes pass through a terrestrial phase in which water is not readily available, nitrogen metabolism in these is most probably uricotelic and hence does not involve the production of a large quantity of ammonia.

LIPID METABOLISM

Although lipases and esterases have been found in the intestine of certain intestinal nematodes, it is not known whether fatty acids can be absorbed through their intestinal wall.

In aerobic nematodes, such as the free-living larvae of human hookworms and *Nippostrongylus,* the lipids in their bodies, as determined histochemically, decrease with the age of the organism, thus suggesting that lipid metabolism occurs. Similarly, larvae of *Trichinella spiralis* maintained in vitro utilize fat as an energy source.

In essentially anaerobic adult nematodes, such as *Ascaris,* lipid catabolism is limited. Even after 5 days of starvation, the lipid content in their bodies is not decreased appreciably.

In recent years, much has been done on the biochemistry of nematode parasites. Fairbairn (1957) has reviewed the work done on *Ascaris,* and his essay deserves the attention of serious students of helminth physiology.

MOTILITY OF LARVAE

The motility of nematodes, especially that of the larvae within the host, has caused some interest. It still remains unexplained why the larvae of *Trichinella spiralis* prefer glycogen-poor muscles as sites for encystment. Relative to motility, Parker and Haley (1960) have demonstrated that the filariform larvae of the rat nematode, *Nippostrongylus muris,* is positively thermotactic. This is possibly the explanation, or one of the explanations, for the affinity these infective larvae show for their warm-blooded hosts.

HOST-PARASITE RELATIONSHIPS

The clinical symptoms of nematode-caused diseases in man and domestic animals are thoroughly discussed in volumes devoted to these aspects of helminthology. The host-parasite relationships of nematodes parasitic in plants have been authoritatively discussed by Dropkin (1955), Mountain (1960), and Christie (1960). The relationships between animal hosts and nematodes is discussed by Rogers (1962). In the following paragraphs, the author has attempted to bring out some of the less severe but nevertheless still important effects nematodes have on their hosts.

Anti-enzymes

It is known that *Ascaris* secretes anti-enzymes the primary function of which is to protect the parasite from being digested by the digestive enzymes of the host. However, the extent of the action of these anti-enzymes does not stop there. The antitryptic and antipeptic enzymes secreted by *Ascaris* and other nematodes also hinder digestion of a certain amount of the food passing through the host's alimentary tract.

Nutrient Deprivation and Metabolic Changes

Hall (1917) reported that in one instance a human harbored 11 pounds of *Ascaris.* The amount of food utilized by these worms has been estimated to comprise 8 per cent of the normal 2500 calories of the human host. In addition to robbing the host of nutrients, other effects are inflicted on the host. For example, the blood proteins of hosts are altered in certain nematode infections. Such changes most probably reflect immune responses on the part of the host (p. 16). Wright and Oliver-Gonzalez (1943) pointed out that in dogs and rabbits infected with *Trichinella spiralis,* the plasma albumin fraction decreases while the globulin fraction increases. Weir et al. (1948)

pointed out that the total protein in the blood plasma of sheep infected with *Haemonchus contortus* decreases, and Villela and Teixeira (1937) reported a decrease in both total protein and albumin in the blood of man harboring hookworms. These same authors (Villela and Teixeira, 1929) also reported that, in human hookworm infections, potassium and sodium levels in blood plasma are increased.

Sugar metabolism in the host is sometimes disrupted by nematodes. In man, *Ascaris lumbricoides* occasionally causes hypoglycemia. Numerous investigators have shown that in man, dogs, and rabbits infected with *Trichinella spiralis,* occasional hypoglycemia also occurs.

Nematode Toxins

Toxins have often been suspected as causative agents of nematode-affected metabolic disruptions (see p. 10). The toxicity of nematodes has been reviewed by Schwartz (1921), although a more recent review should be forthcoming. Although in some instances, incrimination of toxic substances has been unfounded, in other instances it is justified. It is well known that persons working with *Ascaris* and infected animals often develop an allergy. A similar phenomenon is found in some other roundworms (Sprent, 1949). In addition to developing an allergy, infected animals sometimes display other symptoms, which disappear when the worms are removed, thus strongly suggesting that some toxic substance is being secreted.

Various investigators have shown that the peudocoelomic fluids of ascarids are toxic if injected into hosts. Similarly, tissue extracts of such nematodes as *Ascaris, Parascaris, Strongylus,* and *Dirofilaria* can be lethal when injected into experimental animals.

The nature of nematode toxins has not yet been completely determined. Flury (1912) suggested that irritation of mucous membranes by ascarids is due to aldehydes formed during the metabolism of the worms. Bondouy (1908) reported that the toxic secretion of *Strongylus equinus* is alkaloid-like and is strongly haemolytic. Shimamura and Fujii (1917) reported that the toxin of *Ascaris* is an albumose-peptone fraction, Macheboeuf and Mandoul (1939) thought it to be polypeptides. Deschiens and Poirier (1949) reported that lesions produced when extracts of *Parascaris equorum* are applied to tissues resemble histamine poisoning.

In addition to producing damage to tissue in the form of lesions and symptoms of toxicity, the secretions of some nematodes actually disrupt the host's metabolism. For example,

Mönnig (1937) reported that even when the worms are removed from sheep heavily infected with *Oesophagostomum columbianum,* the hosts die. He interpreted this finding to mean that the defaunated sheep could not overcome the physiological disarrangements caused by the toxic secretions of the parasites.

Larva Migrans

In connection with nematode host-parasite relationships, the medically important and biologically interesting phenomena collectively known as larva migrans should be mentioned. The term larva migrans denotes migration of a larva of a parasitic nematode in the skin or in the internal organs of an unnatural host, or in a natural host whose immune state or some other condition renders its relationship to the parasite similar to that of an unnatural host.

Migration in the skin is commonly referred to as cutaneous larva migrans, or creeping eruption, while migration in internal organs is known as visceral larval migrans. These conditions are medically important, because they represent parasite-caused pathological conditions. They are interesting biologically, because they reflect the behavior of parasites in unnatural or abnormal hosts and the responses of such hosts to the parasites.

Although larva migrans in various animals accidentally infected with nematode larvae for which they are not the natural hosts undoubtedly occurs, most research concerning these phenomena has been centered around larva migrans in humans. The experimental or accidental inoculation of larvae of four species of nonhuman hookworms—*Ancylostoma braziliense, A. caninum, Unicinaria stenocephala,* and *Bunostomum phlebotomum*—causes creeping eruption (cutaneous larva migrans) in man.

Although *A. braziliense* is generally considered a nonhuman hookworm, adults of this species have been reported from humans on a number of occasions. Its normal hosts are dogs, cats, and related wild animals. *Ancylostoma caninum* adults, although known in humans, are normally parasites of dogs. Adults of the two other species, *U. stenocephala* and *B. phlebotomum,* are normally parasites of canines and bovines, respectively, and have not been reported from humans.

Cutaneous larva migrans is initiated when the infective larvae of any of these four nematodes penetrate the skin of man and migrate under the surface, primarily in the dermis, in a tortuous linear fashion. The paths of migration appear as tortuous elevations (Plate 16-31). These larvae seldom develop to maturity in the abnormal human host. Rarely, in the case of *Ancylostoma braziliense,* and even less frequently in the case of *A. caninum,* a few larvae may become blood-borne in man and are carried to the lungs, eventually become established in the intestine, where they develop to maturity, as is normally the case with *A. duodenale* (p. 432).

In addition to the hookworms mentioned, *Strongyloides stercoralis* larvae have been reported to cause cutaneous larva migrans. In such instances, the larvae participate in autoinfection (p. 420)—that is, they penetrate the host's skin in the anal area and produce urticarial swellings that often take on the tortuous linear patterns of creeping eruption.

Visceral larva migrans is commonly, but not exclusively, caused by the ascarid *Toxocara canis,* adults of which parasitize dogs and cats.

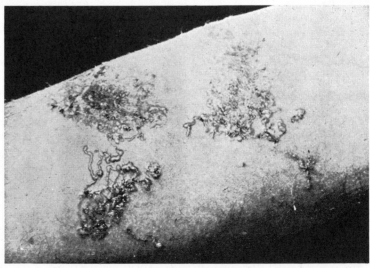

Plate 16-31   Cutaneous larva migrans, human. Note tortuous canals in skin. (After Weiner, 1960; with permission of *Veterinary Medicine.*)

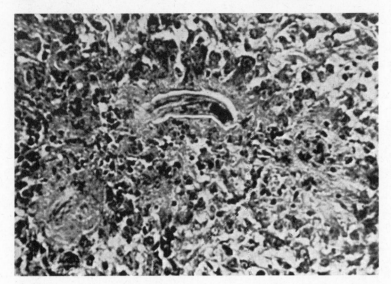

Plate 16-32   Visceral larva migrans, human. Note section of ascarid larva surrounded by host reaction cells. (After Weiner, 1960; with permission of *Veterinary Medicine.*

Human infections, which are most common in children, are contracted when soil containing embryonated *T. canis* eggs is ingested. Larvae hatching from the eggs penetrate the intestinal wall and soon reach the liver. Although the majority of these larvae remain in the liver, some pass on to the lungs and other areas. In addition, larvae have been known to invade the central nervous system and eyes. If invasion of the eyes occurs, formation of a neoplasm that may cause blindness and death can result. Hence, removal of the infected eye by surgery becomes necessary.

Although most of the larvae eventually come to rest in one location and become encapsulated by host tissues, there is a period of at least several weeks during which they actively migrate through tissues leaving long trails of inflammatory and eosinophilic granulomatous reactions (Plate 16–32). Thus, a few microscopic larvae can produce extensive lesions, especially in the liver and brain. Visceral larval migrans is manifested clinically by eosinophilia, sometimes accompanied by enlargement of the liver, hyperglobulinemia, infiltration of the lungs, and neurological symptoms. Eosinophilia —an increase in the number of leukocytes—is characteristic of almost all diseases caused by animal parasites, especially helminths.

In addition to *Toxocara canis*, *T. cati* (the feline ascarid), *Capillaria hepatica* (usually found in the liver of rodents but also known in dogs and other mammals), and *Ancylostoma caninum* may possibly be responsible for visceral larva migrans in humans (Karpinski et al., 1956; Weiner, 1960).

It should be emphasized that although nonhuman hookworms are usually associated with cutaneous larva migrans and *Toxocara canis* is associated with visceral larva migrans in humans, the locations of the lesions and even the resulting symptoms are not completely reliable in the specific identification of the etiologic agent (Beaver, 1956).

In recent years, an unusual clinical entity, characterized by acute eosinophilia and asthmalike symptoms and termed eosinophilic lung (or tropical eosinophilia), has been identified in humans. The causative agent is believed to be nonhuman filarial worms, because Buckley (1958) was able to reproduce the disease in a human volunteer by inoculating him with microfilariae obtained from mosquitoes that had fed on a monkey and a cat, respectively. This experiment suggests that eosinophilic lung is closely akin to larva migrans.

EFFECTS OF HOST ON PARASITE

The amount of food material within the host governs the maintenance of certain nematode parasites. Reid and Ackert (1941) have shown that if chickens infected with *Ascaridia galli* are starved for a period of time, the parasites are completely removed in 48 to 96 hours. Others have shown similar phenomena in other intestinal nematodes. Analysis of the expelled worms revealed that their body glycogen was decreased considerably. When host starvation does take place, it does not affect larvae, but only adults. Again, hosts maintained on complete and normal diets harbor more parasites than otherwise.

Space does not permit elaboration on the role of vitamins in parasite maintenance; however, such does exist. In *Ascaridia galli* infections of chickens, deficiency of vitamins A and B complex favors growth of the worms, which attain greater dimensions. Deficiency of vitamin D has no effect. On the other hand, deficiency of vitamin A hinders establishment of *Enterobius vermicularis* infection. These contradictory findings suggest that the influence of vitamins varies among species.

The role of host age and sex in nematode parasitosis is not completely clear. Instances are known in which age resistance or immunity do occur. Todd and Hollingsworth (1952) reported that more worms develop from a given number of *Ascaridia galli* eggs in male chicks than in females. This suggests sex differences.

Sadun (1948, 1951) tested the hypothesis that sex hormones may play a role in host-parasite relationships. He injected testosterone benzoate and α-estradiol benzoate into immature male and female chicks respectively and found that the *A. galli* in males were temporarily retarded, while those in females were temporarily accelerated in their growth. After the initial retardation and acceleration, the parasites were eliminated from the host at a rate greater than normal. Furthermore, the injection of these sex hormones into noninfected hosts increased their resistance to *Ascaridia*.

From such investigations it appears that sex hormones are of considerable importance to the host-parasite relationship. The same holds true for other endocrine secretions. To illustrate this point, Todd (1949) showed that *A. galli* in chickens suffering from experimentally induced hypothyroidism attained greater lengths.

The effect of mineral-deficient diets on the resistance of fowls to parasitism has been critically reviewed by Gaafer and Ackert (1953).

Factors Governing Infectiveness

One of the most important effects hosts have on nematode parasites is that of affecting infectiveness. The mere ingestion of eggs or larvae does not ensure infection. Activation of these infective stages must be accomplished. This is triggered by physical and chemical components in the host's gut. Of these, dissolved gaseous carbon dioxide or undissolved carbonic acid is the most important. In addition, oxidation-reduction potential, temperature, and pH all influence infectiveness by stimulating secretion of hatching fluids in eggs such as those of ascarids, or secretion of exsheathing fluids in larvae such as those of trichostrongylids. The excellent review by Rogers (1960) should be consulted for details.

Immunity

Immunity to nematode infections is known. For example, Macdonald and Scott (1953) reported that cotton rats previously infected with the filarial worm, *Litomosoides carinii*, must develop an antibody, because worms of subsequent infections are hindered in their normal growth and are smaller. Immunity to *L. carinii*, as in other helminth infections, is directed primarily against metabolic products of the worm rather than against the body proteins (p. 16).

Thorson (1954) discovered that if infective larvae of *Nippostrongylus muris* are introduced into rats along with immune serum, the infectivity decreases proportionally with the exposure time to immune serum.

The antibodies formed against nematodes are usually humoral in nature.

The nature of nematode antigens has been reviewed by Soulsby (1963). This investigator has found that after the parasite enters the host, a certain degree of development must occur before the functional antigens are produced and also before the parasite is affected by the host's immune mechanisms. In many cases, the degree of parasite development appears to include at least one ecdysis. In species such as *Nippostrongylus braziliensis* and *Haemonchus contortus*, definite substances associated with molting can be related to the immune response, but in many other species no clear evidence is available.

Although immunity to nematode infections, such as that developed against *L. carinii*, is elicited primarily by the metabolic products of the worm, Soulsby has successfully demonstrated that antigens can be prepared from both the metabolic products and the bodies of larvae grown in vitro. Hence it is now clear that nematode antigens can be both somatic and metabolic products. In either case, these functional antigens are very labile (they are most satisfactorily prepared at 4° C. and cannot be stored even after freezing at −20° C.) and may well be macromolecules.

LITERATURE CITED

Ackert, J. E., S. A. Edgar, and L. P. Frick. 1939. Goblet cells and age resistance of animals to parasitism. Trans. Amer. Micro. Soc., *58:* 81–89.

Ackert, J. E., L. Eisenbrandt, J. H. Willmonth, B. Glading, and I. Pratt. 1935. Comparative resistance of five breeds of chickens to the nematode *Ascaridia lineata.* J. Agric. Res., *50:* 607–624.

Ackert, J. E., A. C. Todd, and W. A. Tanner. 1938. Growing larval *Ascaridia lineata* (Nematoda) in vitro. Trans. Amer. Micro. Soc., *57:* 292–296.

Alicata, J. E. 1935. Early developmental stages of nematodes occurring in swine. U. S. D. A. Tech. Bull. No. 489. Washington, D. C.

Alicata, J. E. 1962. *Angiostrongylus cantonensis* (Nematoda: Metastongylidae) as a causative agent of eosinophilic meningoencephalitis of man in Hawaii and Tahiti. Can. J. Zool., *40:* 5–8.

Alicata, J. E., and R. W. Brown. 1962. Observations on the method of human infection with *Angiostrongylus cantonensis* in Tahiti. Canad. J. Zool., *40:* 755–760.

Ash, L. R. 1962. The helminth parasites of rats in Hawaii and the description of *Capillaria traverae* sp. n. J. Parasit., *48:* 66–68.

Beaver, P. C. 1956. Larva migrans, a review. Exptl. Parasit., *5:* 587–621.

Bondouy, T. 1908. Sur quelques principes constitutifs du *Sclerostomum equinum.* Présence, chez ce parasite, d'un alcaloide cristallisé éminemment hémolytique. Compt. Rend. Acad. Sci., *147:* 928–930.

Brackett, S. 1938. Description and life history of the nematode *Dracunculus ophidensis* n. sp., with a redescription of the genus. J. Parasit., *24:* 353–361.

Buckley, R. 1958. Tropical pulmonary eosinophilia in relation to filarial infections (*Wuchereria* spp.) of animals. Trans. Roy. Soc. Trop. Med. Hyg., *52:* 335–336.

Cates, S. S. 1953. The prevalence of pinworm infection among first graders of Tallahassee, Florida, and vicinity. Quart. J. Florida Acad. Sci., *16:* 239–242.

Chabaud, A. G., and M. T. Choquet. 1953. Nouvel essai de classification des filaires (super-familie des Filaroidea). Ann. Parasit., *28:* 172–192.

Cheng, T. C. 1960. A survey of *Enterobius vermicularis* infestation among pre-school age transient children; with the description of a modified Graham swab. Jour. Tenn. Acad. Sci., *35:* 49–53.

Christie, J. R. 1960. Some interrelationships between nematodes and other soil-borne pathogens. *In* Nematology (edited by J. N. Sasser and W. R. Jenkins). University of North Carolina Press, Chapel Hill.

Christie, J. R., and F. M. Albin. 1944. Host-parasite relationships of the root-knot nematode, *Heterodera marioni.* The question of races. Proc. Helminth Soc. Wash., *11:* 31–37.

Cintra, J. F., and E. Rugai. 1955. Helmintiasis entre escolares da cidade de Bauru. Rev. Inst. Adolfo Lutz, *15:* 155–157.

Cram, E. B., and L. Reardon. 1939. Studies on oxyuriasis XII. Epidemiological findings in Washington, D. C. Am. J. Hyg., *29:* 17–24.

Dalmat, H. T. 1955. The black flies (Diptera: Simuliidae) of Guatemala and their role as vectors of onchocerciasis. Smithson. Misc. Coll., *125:* 1–425.

Deschiens, R. E. A., and M. Poirier. 1949. Anatomie pathologique de l'intoxication experimentale subaigue et chronique par les substances toxiques vermineuses. Bull. Soc. Path. Exot., *42:* 70–76.

Dougherty, E. C. 1951. The axenic cultivation of *Rhabditis briggsae* Dougherty and Nigon, 1949 (Nematoda: Rhabditidae). II. Some sources and characteristics of "factor Rb." Exptl. Parasit., *1:* 34–45.

Dougherty, E. C. 1960. Cultivation of Aschelminthes, especially rhabditid nematodes. *In* Nematology (edited by J. N. Sasser and W. R. Jenkins). University of North Carolina Press, Chapel Hill.

Dropkin, V. H. 1955. The relations between nematodes and plants. Exptl. Parasit., *4:* 282–322.

Dunbleton, L. J. 1945. Bacterial and nematode parasites of soil insects. New Zealand J. Sci. Tech., Agric. Sect., *27:* 76–81.

Eisenbrandt, L. L., and J. E. Ackert. 1941. Effects of duodenal mucus of dogs and swine upon the viability of *Ascaridia lineata* in vitro. J. Parasit., *27:* 36.

Fairbairn, D. 1957. The biochemistry of *Ascaris.* Exptl. Parasit., *6:* 491–554.

Faust, E. C. 1933. Experimental studies on human and primate species of *Strongyloides.* II. The development of *Strongyloides* in the experimental host. Am. J. Hyg., *18:* 114–132.

Fenwick, D. W. 1939. Studies on the saline requirements of the larvae of *Ascaris suum.* J. Helminth., *17:* 211–228.

Fielding, J. W. 1926. Preliminary note on the transmission of the eye worm of Australian poultry. Austral. J. Exper. Biol. Med. Sci., *3:* 225–232.

Fielding, J. W. 1927. Further observations on the life history of the eye worm of poultry. Austral. J. Exper. Biol. Med. Sci., *4:* 273–281.

Fielding, J. W. 1928a. Additional observations on the development of the eye worm of poultry. Austral. J. Exper. Biol. Med. Sci., *5:* 1–8.

Fielding, J. W. 1928b. Observations on eye worms of birds. Queensland Agric. J., *30:* 37–41.

Flury, F. 1912. Zur Chemie und Toxikologie der Ascariden. Arch. Exper. Path. Pharmakol., *67:* 275–392.

Foster, A. O. 1932. Prenatal infection with the dog hookworm, *Ancylostoma caninum.* J. Parasit., *19:* 12–118.

Fukamachi, H. 1960. Experimental studies on the periodicity of microfilariae. I. Provoking effect of stress stimuli upon the migration to the peripheral circulation of microfilariae. End. Dis. Bull. Nagasaki Univ., *2:* 27–38.

Furuyama, T. 1934. On the morphology and life-history of *Philometra fujinotoi* Fururyama, 1932. Keijo J. Med., *5:* 165–177.

Gaafar, S. M., and J. E. Ackert. 1953. Studies on mineral deficient diets as factors in resistance of fowls to parasitism. Exptl. Parasit., *2:* 185–208.

Glaser, R. W. 1931. The cultivation of a nematode parasite of an insect. Science, *73:* 614–615.

Glaser, R. W. 1932. Culture of a parasitic nematode. J. Parasit., *19:* 173.

Gordon, R. M. 1955. The host parasite relationship in filariasis. Trans. Roy. Soc. Trop. Med. Hyg., *49:* 496–507.

Hall, M. C. 1917. Animal parasites. *In* Handbook of Practical Treatment, Musser and Kelly. pp. 389–419.

Haskins, W. T., and P. P. Weinstein. 1957a. Nitrogenous excretory products of *Trichinella spiralis* larvae. J. Parasit., *43:* 19–24.

Haskins, W. T., and P. P. Weinstein. 1957b. Amino acids excreted by *Trichinella spiralis* larvae. J. Parasit., *43:* 25–27.

Hawking, F. 1956. The periodicity of microfilariae. IV. Stimuli affecting the migration of the microfilariae of *Dirofilaria aethiops, D. immitis, D. repens, Dipetalonema blanci* and *Litomosoides carnii.* Trans. Roy. Soc. Trop. Med. Hyg., *50:* 397–417.

Hawking, F. 1962. Microfilaria infestation as an instance of periodic phenomena seen in host-parasite relationships. Ann. N. Y. Acad. Sci., *98:* 940–953.

Hinman, E. E. 1935. Studies on the dog heartworm, *Dirofilaria immitis,* with special reference to filarial periodicity. Am. J. Trop. Med., *15:* 371–383.

Hitchcock, D. J. 1950. Parasitological study of the eskimos in the Bethel area of Alaska. J. Parasit., *36:* 232–234.

Hobmaier, M. 1941. Description and extramammalian life of *Crenosoma mephitidis* n. sp. (Nematoda) in skunks. J. Parasit., *27:* 229–232.

Hoeppli, R. J. C., L. C. Feng, and H. J. Chu. 1938. Attempts to culture helminths of vertebrates in artificial media. Chinese Med. J. (Suppl.), *2:* 343–374.

Horio, S. R., and J. E. Alicata. 1961. Parasitic meningo-encephalitis in Hawaii. A new parasitic disease of man. Hawaii M. J., *21:* 139–140.

Iwanczuk, I. 1953. Badania nad zarzzenium pasozytami jelitowyni dzieci w zobkach Warszay (in Polish with English summary). Acta Parasitol. Polonica, *1:* 133–147.

Jackson, G. J. 1962. The parasitic nematode *Neoaplectana glaseri,* in axenic culture.II. Initial results with defined media. Exptl. Parasit., *12:* 25–32.

Karpinski, F. E., E. A. Everts-Suarex, and W. G. Sawitz. 1956. Larval granulomatosis (visceral larval migrans). Am. J. Dis. Children, *92:* 34–40.

Kessel, J. F., M. Parrish, and G. Parrish. 1954. Intestinal Protozoa, helminths and bacteria in Tahiti, French Oceania. Am. J. Trop. Med., *3:* 440–446.

Laing, A. B. G. 1960. A review of recent research on filariasis in Malaya. Indian J. Malariol., *14:* 391–408.

Laing, A. B. G., J. F. B. Edeson, and R. H. Warton. 1960. Studies on filariasis in Malaya: the vertebrate hosts of *Brugia malayi* and *B. pahangi.* Ann. Trop. Med. Parasit., *54:* 92–99.

Lavoipierre, M. M. J. 1958. Studies on the host-parasite relationships of filarial nematodes and their arthropod hosts. I. The site of development and the migration of *Loa loa* in *Chrysops silacea,* the escape of the infective forms from the head of the fly, and the effect of the worm on its insect host. Ann. Trop. Med. Parasit., *52:* 103–121.

Lopes Pontes, J. P. 1946. Incidencia das infestaçoes helminticas intestinals no Rio de Janeiro. Rev. Brasil. Med., *3:* 180–187.

Low, G. C. 1934. The skin conditions found in *Loa loa* infections. J. Trop. Med. Hyg., *37:* 359–360.

Macdonald, E. M., and J. A. Scott. 1953. Experiments on immunity in the cotton rat to the filarial worm, *Litomosoides carinii.* Exptl. Parasit., *2:* 174–184.

Macheboeuf, M., and R. Mandoul. 1939. A propos do la toxicité des extraits d'*Ascaris.* Compt. Rend. Soc. Biol., *130:* 1032–1034.

McFadzean, J. A., and F. Hawking. 1956. The periodicity of microfilariae. V. Stimuli affecting the periodic migration of the microfilariae of *Wuchereria bancrofti* and of *Loa loa* in man. Trans. Roy. Soc. Trop. Med. Hyg., *50:* 543–562.

Miyazaki, I. 1960. On the genus *Gnathostoma* and human gnathostomiasis, with special reference to Japan. Exptl. Parasit., *9:* 338–370.

Mönnig, H. O. 1937. Helminth toxins. S. African J. Sci., *33:* 845–849.

Morgan, B. B., and P. A. Hawkins. 1949. Veterinary Helminthology. Burgess, Minneapolis.

Mountain, W. B. 1960. Theoretical considerations of plant-nematode relationships. Mechanisms involved in plant-nematode relationships. *In* Nematology, (edited by J. N. Sasser and W. R. Jenkins). University of North Carolina Press, Chapel Hill.

Onorato, A. R. 1932. The effects of temperature and humidity on the ova of *Toxocara canis* and *Trichuris vulpis.* Am. J. Hyg., *16:* 266–287.

Ortlepp, R. J. 1925. Observations on the life history of *Triodontophorus tenuicollis,* a nematode parasite of the horse. J. Helminth., *3:* 1–14.

Otto, G. F. 1941. Further observations on the immunity induced in dogs by repeated infections with the hookworm, *Ancylostoma caninum.* Am. J. Hyg., *33:* 39–57. (Also see J. Parasit., *27:* 25.)

Owen, W. B. 1930. Factors that influence the development and survival of the ova of an ascarid roundworm, *Toxocara canis* (Werner, 1782) Stiles, 1905, under field conditions. Tech. Bull. (71) Minn. Agric. Exp. Sta., St. Paul., Minn.

Parker, J. C., and A. J. Haley, 1960. Phototactic and thermotactic responses of the filariform larvae of the rat nematode *Nippostrongylus muris.* Exptl. Parasit., *9:* 92–97.

Ransom, B. H. 1911. The nematodes parasitic in the alimentary tract of cattle, sheep, and other ruminants. Bull. (127) Bureau Animal Indust., Washington, D. C.

Reid, W. M., and J. E. Ackert. 1941. Removal of chicken tapeworms by host starvation and some effects of such treatment on tapeworm metabolism. J. Parasit., *27:* 35.

Rhodes, M. B., C. L. Marsh, and G. W. Kelley, Jr. 1963. Trypsin and chymotrypsin inhibitors from *Ascaris suum.* Exptl. Parasit., *13:* 266–272.

Ricci, M. 1952. Sulla diffusione delle parasitosi intestinali in un piccolo cotro siciliano. Rend. 1st. Super. Sanita, *15:* 57–63.

Rogers, W. P. 1949. Aerobic metabolism in nematode parasites of the alimentary tract. Nature, *163:* 879–880.

Rogers, W. P. 1960. The physiology of infective processes of nematode parasites; the stimulus from the animal host. Proc. Roy. Soc., B, *152:* 367–386.

Rogers, W. P. 1962. The Nature of Parasitism. Academic Press, New York.

Rosen, L., J. Laigret, and S. Bories. 1961. Observations on an outbreak of eosinophilic meningitis on Tahiti, French Polynesia. Am. J. Hyg., *74:* 26–41.

Rosen, L., R. Chappell, G. L. Wallace, and P. P. Weinstein. 1962. Eosinophilic meningoencephalitis caused by a metastrongylid lung worm of rats. J. Am. Med. Assoc., *179:* 620–624.

Sadun, E. H. 1948. Relation of the gonadal hormones to the natural resistance of chickens and to the growth of the nematode, *Ascaridia galli.* J. Parasit., *34:* 18.

Sadun, E. H. 1951. Gonadal hormones in experimental *Ascaridia galli* infection in chickens. Exptl. Parasit., *1:* 70–82.

Sanders, D. A. 1928. Manson's eyeworm of poultry. J. Am. Vet. M. A., *72:* 568–584.

Saval, J. 1955. Études sur la constitution et le métabolisme protéiques d'*Ascaris lumbricoides* Linné, 1758. I and II. Rev. Path. Comp. d'Hyg. Gen., *55:* 52–121; 213–282.

Schüffner, W., and N. H. Swellengrebel. 1949. Retroinfection in oxyuriasis. A newly discovered mode of infection with *Enterobius vermicularis.* J. Parasit., *35:* 138–146.

Schwartz, B. 1921. Hemotoxins from parasitic worms. J. Agric. Res., *22:* 379–432.

Schwartz, B., and E. W. Price. 1932. Infection of pigs and other animals with kidney worms, *Stephanurus dentatus,* following ingestion of larvae. J. Am. Vet. M. A., *81:* 325–347.

Shimamura, T., and H. Fujii. 1917. Über das Askaron, einen toxischen Bestandteil der Helminthen besonders der Askariden und seine biologische Wirkung (Mitteilung I). J. Coll. Agric. Imp. Univ. Tokyo, *3:* 189–258.

Silverman, P. H. 1959. In vitro cultivation of the histotrophic stages of *Haemonchus contortus* and *Ostertagia* spp. Nature, *183:* 197.

Sommerville, R. I. 1957. The exsheathing mechanism of nematode infective larvae. Exptl. Parasit., *6:* 18–30.

Soulsby, E. S. L. 1963. The nature and origin of the functional antigens in the immune response to nematode infections. Ann. N. Y. Acad. Sci., *113:* 492–509.

Sprent, J. F. A. 1949. On the toxic and allergic manifestations produced by the tissues and fluids of *Ascaris.* I. Effect of different tissues. J. Infect. Dis., *84:* 221–229.

Sprent, J. F. A. 1952. On the migratory behavior of the larvae of various *Ascaris* species in white mice. I. Distribution of larvae in tissues. J. Infect. Dis., *90:* 165–176. (Also see 1953. Ibid., *92:* 114–117.)

Sprent, J. F. A. 1958. Observations on the development of *Toxocara canis* (Werner, 1782) in the dog. Parasitology, *48:* 184–209.

Stoll, N. 1940. In vitro conditions favoring ecdysis at the end of the first parasitic stage of *Haemonchus contortus* (Nematoda). Growth, *4:* 383–405.

Stoll, N. 1947. This wormy world. J. Parasit., *33:* 1–18.

Thorson, R. E. 1954. Effect of immune serum from rats on infective larvae of *Nippostrongylus muris.* Exptl. Parasit., *3:* 9–15.

Todd, A. C. 1949. Thyroid condition of chickens and development of parasitic nematodes. J. Parasit., *35:* 255–260.

Todd, A. C., and K. P. Hollingsworth. 1952. Host sex as a factor in development of *Ascaridia galli.* Exptl. Parasit., *1:* 303–304.

Villela, G. G., and J. C. Teixeira. 1929. Exame do sangue no anemia helminthica. Mem. Inst. Osw. Cruz (Suppl.), *6:* 62–68.

von Brand, T. 1938. The nature of the metabolic activities of intestinal helminths in their natural habitat: Aerobiosis or anaerobiosis? Biodynamica, No. *41:* 1–13.

von Brand, T., and W. F. Simpson. 1944. Physiological observations upon a larval *Eustrongylides.* VII. Studies upon survival and metabolism in sterile surroundings. J. Parasit., *30:* 121–129.

Wang, C. F., C. L. Lin, and W. H. Chen. 1958. The mechanism of microfilarial periodicity. Chinese Med. J., *77:* 129–135.

Wanson, M. 1950. Contribution à l'étude de l'onchocercose africaine humaine (problèmes de prophylaxis a Léopoldville). Ann. Soc. Belge Med. Trop., *30:* 667–863.

Wehr, E. E. 1935. A revised classification of the nematode superfamily Filarioidea. Proc. Helminth. Soc. Wash., *2:* 84–88.

Weiner, D. 1960. Larva migrans. Vet. Med., *55:* 38–50.

Weinstein, P., and M. F. Jones. 1956. The in vitro cultivation of *Nippostrongylus muris* to the adult stage. J. Parasit., *42:* 215–236.

Weir, W. C., et al. 1948. The effect of hemopoietic dietary factors on the resistance of lambs to parasitism with the stomach worm, *Haemonchus contortus.* J. Animal Sci., *7:* 466–474.

Wells, H. S. 1931. Observations on the blood sucking activities of the hookworm, *Ancylostoma*

Wong, M. M. 1963. Studies on microfilaremia in dogs. II. Levels of microfilaremia in relation to immunologic responses of the host. Am. J. Trop. Med. Hyg., *13:* 66–77.

Wright, G. G., and J. Oliver-Gonzalez. 1943. Electrophoretic studies on antibodies to *Trichinella spiralis* in the rabbit. J. Inf. Dis., *72:* 242–245.

SUGGESTED READING

Beaver, P. C. 1956. Larva migrans. Exptl. Parasit., *5:* 587–621. (This is a review article on larva migrans by a recognized authority. Not only is the text comprehensive and informative, but the references cited should prove to be most helpful.)

Dropkin, V. H. 1955. The relations between the nematodes and plants. Exptl. Parasit., *4:* 282–322. (Although this excellent review article is concerned primarily with plant parasites, this article is recommended so the reader can appreciate how much in common there is between plant and animal parasites.)

Fairbairn, D. 1957. The biochemistry of *Ascaris.* Exptl. Parasit., *6:* 491–554. (This review article is rapidly becoming a classic in physiological parasitology. It should be required reading for all those interested in this aspect of the field.)

Gaafer, S. M., and J. E. Ackert. 1953. Studies on mineral deficient diets as factors in resistance of fowls to parasitism. Exptl. Parasit., 2: 185–208. (One of the most interesting and important aspects of host-parasite relationships is that concerned with the effects of the host's diet on parasites. This outstanding article not only gives the reader a good account of what is known but also may suggest various research problems.)

Hyman, L. H. 1951. The Invertebrates, Acanthocephala, Aschelminthes and Entoprocta. The Pseudocoelomate Bilateria. Vol. III. McGraw-Hill, New York, pp. 197–455. (This section in Hyman's treatise discusses the nematodes, both parasitic and free-living. The sections on evolution and morphology are particularly useful.)

Larsh, J. E. 1963. Experimental trichiniasis. In Advances in Parasitology (B. Dawes, ed.). Academic Press, New York, Vol. I, pp. 213–286. (This article presents the information known concerning experimental trichiniasis in hamsters, rats, and mice. Both morphological and physiological alterations in these hosts are considered. Immunity and immunological studies are also considered under physiological alterations.)

Miyazaki, I. 1960. On the genus *Gnathostoma* and human gnathostomiasis, with special reference to Japan. Exptl. Parasit., 9: 338–370. (Gnathostomiasis in humans is not a common condition in this country. This review article discusses the biology of *Gnathostoma* spp. and gnathostomiasis authoritatively. It should be read by all students of parasitology, especially those interested in nematode-caused diseases, because it points out the importance of understanding the basic biology of an organism as a prerequisite to understanding the pathology.)

Reinhard, E. G. 1958. Landmarks of parasitology. II. Demonstration of the life cycle and pathogenicity of the spiral threadworm. Exptl. Parasit., 7: 108–123. (This is the second, and unfortunately the last, of the colorful historical series on animal parasites by the late Dr. Reinhard. This article should be mandatory reading for all students of parasitology.)

Rogers, W. P., and R. I. Sommerville. 1963. The infective stage of nematode parasites and its significance in parasitism. In Advances in Parasitology. (B. Dawes, ed.). Academic Press, New York, Vol. I, pp. 109–177. (This is an extremely well written review of the biology of parasitic nematodes. The authors have considered such important physiological phenomena as hatching of eggs, molting of larvae, food reserves, oxygen requirements, metabolism, permeability and osmoregulation, and modes of infection. In addition, the behavior, survival, and the nature of infectiousness are discussed in detail. This article should be required reading by all students interested in helminth physiology.)

Sasser, J. N., and W. R. Jenkins. 1960. Nematology. University of North Carolina Press, Chapel Hill. This series of papers was given at a symposium on nematology. Although somewhat specialized, they are highly recommended to students interested in the morphology and biology of nematodes:

   Allen, M. W. Alimentary canal, excretory and nervous systems, pp. 136–139.

   Christie, J. R. The role of the nematologist, pp. 8–11.
      Some interrelationships between nematodes and other soil-borne pathogens, pp. 432–436.

   Dougherty, E. C. Cultivation of aschelminths, especially rhabditid nematodes, pp. 341–415.

   Fairbairn, D. The physiology and biochemistry of nematodes, pp. 267–296.

   Hirschmann, H. Gross morphology of nematodes, pp. 125–129.
      External characters and body wall of nematodes, pp. 130–135.
      Reproduction of nematodes, pp. 140–146.

   Mountain, W. B. Theoretical considerations of plant-nematode relationships, pp. 419–421.
      Mechanisms involved in plant-nematode relationships, pp. 426–431.

   Steiner, G. Nematology an outlook, pp. 3–7.
      The Nematoda as a taxonomic category and their relationship to other animals, pp. 12–18.

   von Brand, T. Influence of size, motility, starvation and age on metabolic rate, pp. 233–241.
      Influence of oxygen on life processes, pp. 242–248.
      Influence of pH, ions, and osmotic pressure on life processes, pp. 249–256.
      Influence of temperature on life processes, pp. 257–266.

   Winslow, R. D. Some aspects of the ecology of free-living and plant-parasitic nematodes, pp. 354–357.

PART
SEVEN

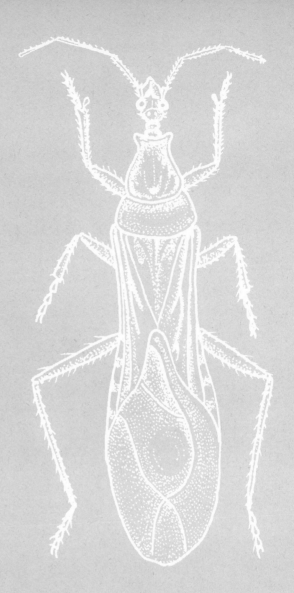

ARTHROPODA

17

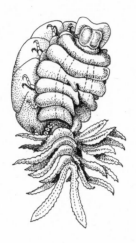

INTRODUCTION TO THE PARASITIC ARTHROPODS THE SYMBIOTIC CRUSTACEA, TARDIGRADA, AND PYCNOGONIDA

The members of the phylum Arthropoda represent the largest number of known animals. There are at least 740,000 species of arthropods in existence. The phylum is subdivided into twelve classes,* the Crustacea, the Trilobita, the Arachnoidea,† the Chilopoda, the Diplopoda, the Onychophora, the Pycnogonida, the Pentastomida, the Tardigrada, the Symphyla, the Pauropoda, and the Insecta. Most members of these classes are free-living and are found in an array of aquatic (fresh-water and marine) and terrestrial habitats. However, some members of the classes Crustacea (that is, Copepoda, Isopoda, Cirripedia, Amphipoda), Insecta, Arachnoidea, Tardigrada, and Pentastomida are parasitic. In addition, the larvae of many species of Pycnogonida are parasitic.

Although many of these arthropod parasites are of little medical and economic importance, they are of considerable interest to biologists, specifically parasitologists, from the biological standpoint. On the other hand, some of these parasitic arthropods, such as certain ticks, mites, and insects, are of considerable importance from the medical and veterinary standpoints, not only because they cause direct injury to their hosts but also because many serve as vectors for various phyto- and zooparasites, in-

---

*Some groups of arthropods listed as classes are considered phyla by certain workers.

†The designation "Arachnida" is often used in substitution for "Arachnoidea" (Bull. Entomol. Soc. Amer., *6:* 208, 1960).

cluding numerous pathogenic microorganisms. As a result of the concentrated interest of certain parasitologists on these economically important forms, a subfield of parasitology known as medical and veterinary entomology has become an established discipline of biology.

Although members of the various classes of arthropods demonstrate a wide range of characteristics, all share a few major characteristics in common. These triploblastic bilaterally symmetrical animals all possess segmented bodies bearing jointed appendages. The body surface is always covered by a rigid or semirigid chitinous exoskeleton. These animals possess complete digestive tracts (incomplete in some cirripeds, such as the Rhizocephala) with mouthparts adapted for biting, chewing, or sucking, depending on the species. There is an open circulatory system with or without a dorsally situated heart, which pumps the blood via arteries into the various organs and body tissues. The blood is returned to the heart through body spaces known as haemocoels. In addition, breathing, excretory, and nervous systems are present.

Arthropods are usually dioecious and exhibit a marked degree of sexual dimorphism. The specific anatomical characteristics of each group considered are given in subsequent sections.

Exoskeleton

The exoskeleton of arthropods is of considerable interest, not only because it serves as the protective covering for these animals but also, as Wigglesworth (1939) points out, because the physiology of arthropodan growth is greatly influenced by the integument. The mobility and growth of arthropods, as well as their reactions to the habitat, are all influenced by the integument. Morphologically, the cuticle is comprised of three (sometimes two) layers (Plate 17–1, Fig. 1).* These are: an outer thin refractile layer known as the epicuticle, which is extremely thin and is usually less than 1 μ in thickness; the middle layer, or exocuticle, which is relatively thick and pigmented in most insects, and the innermost layer, or endocuticle, which is elastic, nonpigmented, and which is the thickest of the three cuticular layers. The three cuticular layers are noncellular and are secreted by the cellular hypodermis (sometimes

---

*The cuticle of arthropods should not be confused with that of helminths, which is quite different chemically.

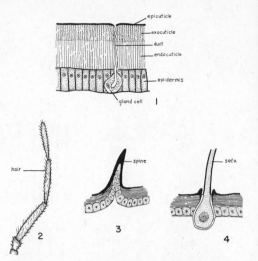

Plate 17-1   Body surface structures of Arthropoda. 1. Cross section through exoskeleton of an arthropod, showing various layers and associated cells and glands. (Original.) 2. Hairs on an antenna of the bedbug *Cimex lectularis*. (Original.) 3. Histological presentation of a spine. 4. Histological presentation of a seta.

referred to as the epidermis), which lies directly underneath the cuticle.

The cuticle may be smooth, notched, pitted, ridged, or spinous, depending on the species and the location on the body of the animal. When seen in cross section, a series of parallel perpendicular lines is found running through the exo- and endocuticles. These lines, known as pore canals, have been interpreted as cytoplasmic processes of the hypodermal cells, projecting into the cuticle. Others have suggested that although these canals are of cytoplasmic origin, in time they are transformed into cuticular material. It is possible that both types of pore canals exist. However, in most cases the canals remain as vital cytoplasmic processes.

In addition to the perpendicularly oriented pore canals, a horizontally oriented lamellar system is present in the endocuticle. These lamellae are thicker toward the basal region and originate in the shifting of the hypodermal cells as successive layers of cuticle are deposited.

The cuticle includes chitin, the chemical composition which is of a nitrogenous polysaccharidal nature. The empirical formula of chitin is $(C_8H_{13}O_5N)_x$. The following molecular configuration of chitin, which is in the form of acetylated glucosamine residues linked together, is known from the work of Bergmann and his associates.

CH=
CH · NH · Ac
CHOH
—O—CH   O
CH
CH₂OH

CH=
CH · NH · Ac
CHOH
—O—CH   O   —O—
CH
CH₂OH

Chitin is insoluble in water, dilute acids, bases, alcohol, ether, and other organic solvents. It is soluble, however, in concentrated mineral acids. In addition to chitin, the integument of arthropods includes proteins, pigments, salts (for example, $CaCO_3$), and cuticulin, which is a complex molecule containing fatty acids and cholesterol. Space does not permit an extensive review of our knowledge of arthropodan integument, which is a field of specialization in itself. Interested individuals are referred to the monographs of Richards (1951) and Wigglesworth (1954), and the volumes edited by Waterman (1960, 1961).

Chemical Composition

Von Kemnitz (1916) demonstrated that 43 per cent of the dry substance of the larva of the fly *Gasterophilus intestinalis* is composed of protein. Levenbook (1950), in analyzing the haemolymph (blood) of the same larva, found the amino acid components to be glycine, alanine, valine, serine, leucine, isoleucine, phenylalanine, tyrosone, glutamic acid, lysine, aspartic acid, arginine, histidine, and proline.

Carbohydrates, primarily glycogen, have been found in various parasitic arthropods. However, there is some doubt as to whether the glycogen found in these forms is identical to that found in vertebrates, because the optical rotation of such glycogens is somewhat different from that of mammalian glycogen. The amount of glycogen present has been determined for various larval flies and ranges between 1.1 and 9.4 per cent of the fresh weight of these animals.

Lipids are also present in parasitic arthropods. In *Gasterophilus intestinalis* larvae, von Kemnitz (1916) determined that lipids constitute 5.2 per cent of the fresh substance and 16.2 per cent of the dry substance. Similarly, Reinhard and von Brand (1944) demonstrated that lipids form 26.6 per cent of the dry substance of the rhizocephalan cirriped *Peltogaster paguri*.

Relative to inorganic materials, Levenbook (1950) demonstrated that the body fluid of *Gasterophilus intestinalis* larvae includes K, Na, Mg, Ca, Zn, Cu, Cl, S, and P. Undoubtedly, similar inorganics exist in other parasitic arthropods. For example, Dinulescu (1932) and Beaumont (1949) have found Fe in fly larvae. The exact function of the iron is not known, although it is suspected that the iron serves as an oxygen conductor, as does the iron in the haemoglobin molecule.

THE SYMBIOTIC ARTHROPODS

As mentioned previously, the parasitic arthropods are limited to the classes Crustacea, Tardigrada, Pycnogonida, Arachnoidea, Pentastomida, and Insecta. There also may be incidental parasitic species found in other classes. Most arthropodan parasites are ectoparasites, but endoparasitic species are known. Each of these groups is considered in the following sections.

CLASS CRUSTACEA

The crustaceans include an array of arthropods such as lobsters, crabs, crayfishes, barnacles, and pill bugs. Most members of this class are free-living. However, certain members of various subclasses do lead the parasitic way of life.

The class Crustacea, which includes over 26,000 known species, is subdivided into eight subclasses.* Among these subclasses, three—Copepoda, Cirripedia, and Malacostraca—include symbiotic species. Some of the other subclasses, such as the Ostracoda, include epizoic species. These epizoic species are not discussed; only the Copepoda, Cirripedia, and Malacostraca are included.

SUBCLASS COPEPODA

The Copepoda includes some 4500 known species, of which the majority are free-living aquatic animals. The symbiotic members of this subclass are found as ecto- and endosymbionts of vertebrates and invertebrates. The ectosymbiotic species commonly are found attached to the body surfaces of fishes and

---

*The subclasses subordinate to the class Crustacea are Cephalocarida, Branchiopoda, Ostracoda, Mystacocarida, Copepoda, Branchiura, Cirripeda, and Malacostraca.

Plate 17-2　　Parasitic copepods.
1. *Ive balanoglossi;* the larger is a female, the smaller is a male. (After Mayer, 1879.) 2. *Siphonobius gephyreicola,* found in *Aspidosiphon brocki.* (After Augener, 1903.) 4. Copepodid larva of *Salmincola edwardsii,* the free-swimming form. (After Wilson.)

amphibians, more commonly on the fishes. On fish hosts, copepods attach to the fins and the gills, and in the mouth. These copepods are true ectoparasites rather than epizoic, for they draw their nourishments from the host's tissues.

Numerous copepods have been reported on or in invertebrates and lower chordates. For example, *Ive balanoglosii* is found in the coelom of the hemichordate *Glossobalanus minutus* (Plate 17-2, Fig. 1). Other species have been found on the lophophore of the brachiopod *Argyrotheca* and attached to the exterior of chaetognaths. *Siphonobius gephyreicola* has been reported on the rector muscle of the sipunculid *Aspidosiphon brocki* and copepodids (a larval form) within the coelom of this host (Plate 17-2, Fig. 2).

Not only are the symbiotic copepods of interest to parasitologists because of their parasitic habits, but the whole group is of interest because many of the free-living species serve as intermediate hosts for helminth parasites, especially cestodes and nematodes.

COPEPOD MORPHOLOGY

The external form of most parasitic copepods, especially members of the orders Arguloida and Caligoida, has become so modified as the result of their adaptation to ectoparasitism that they can hardly be recognized as copepods except to the trained eye. By basing the following generalized discussion of the external anatomy of copepods on the most "typical" forms, it is felt the student can acquaint himself with the terminology and interrelationships between parts as applied to these minute crustaceans.

The Body

Basically, the body of a copepod is divided into three regions—the head, the thorax, and the abdomen. These regions are covered by a rigid or semirigid chitinous exoskeleton. The thorax is typically composed of seven segments. The first two segments are fused with the head to form the cephalothorax, which is covered dorsally by a large and somewhat flattened chitinous shield, the carapace. The seventh, or last, thoracic segment is known as the genital segment because it includes the external genitalia. The lines of division between the body segments are commonly fused among the parasitic species. In fact, in some species these sutures are not visible. If the intersegmental zones are not fused and are flexible, they are referred to as the annular zones.

The abdomen typically is composed of four segments. However, there may be one more or less in some species and quite often all of the abdominal segments are fused among the parasitic copepods. In members of the Cyclopoida and Arguloida, there is an articulation between the fifth and sixth thoracic segments. In these copepods, the portion of the body anterior to the movable joint is known as the metasome, and the portion posterior to it is known as the urosome.

The Appendages

The appendages of copepods, like those of all arthropods, are jointed. There are typically five pairs of appendages on the head. (1) The first pair is represented by the 1st antennae, which are long and comprised of up to 25 segments. These antennae serve in sensory and locomotor functions. Among members of the Cyclopoida, this pair of antennae is usually modified as auxiliary copulatory structures. (2) The second pair are the 2nd antennae, which are shorter and may be uniramous, as are the first pair, or may be biramous (forked). The function of these antennae is primarily sensory, but they also aid in locomotion. (3) The third pair of appendages are the two mandibles. (4)

The fourth pair are the two 1st maxillae. (5) The fifth pair are the two 2nd maxillae.

The last three pairs of head appendages, together with the first pair of thoracic appendages, the maxillipeds, comprise the mouthparts and are concerned primarily with the acquisition of food particles. However, on some copepods, the 2nd maxillae are modified as holdfast structures.

The thorax bears the ambulatory appendages. The first pair of thoracic appendages, the maxillipeds, are concerned with food acquisition, but thoracic segments 2 to 6 each bear a pair of biramous swimming legs (swimmerets). There may be a vestigial seventh pair of swimmerets on segment 7. In many parasitic copepods the swimmerets are absent. If swimmerets are present, each is composed of three main joints—the basal basipodite, comprised of three segments; the medial endopodite, also with three segments; and the laterally located trisegmented exopodite. The endopodite and the exopodite are both based on the distal terminal of the basipodite.

In addition to appendages, other types of smaller outgrowths from the exoskeleton are found. These include the following: (1) The aesthetasks are elongate and blunted projections on the antennae and presumably function in a sensory capacity. (2) The hairs are fine, long projections found on various zones of the body but especially on the legs (Plate 17–1, Fig. 2). These flexible structures serve in sensory, locomotor, food-capturing, and sometimes in balancing roles. (3) The spines are short and stout inflexible rods. (4) The setae are longer and flexible rods (Plate 17–1, Fig. 4).

Internal Anatomy

Below the hypodermis are thick bands of muscles that have their origin and insertion on the inner surfaces of the exoskeleton. Parasitic copepods do not have a heart. Copepod blood is a reddish noncellular fluid and is circulated through the body cavities (haemocoels) by movements of the body musculature and the alimentary tract. Some members of the order Lernaeopodoida actually possess a closed vessel system.

The digestive tract is complete, and the interesting posterior portion is capable of active pulsations made possible by extrinsic muscles. Not only do these pulsations aid in the egestion of wastes, but they also serve as auxiliary mechanisms in respiration, for oxygen enters with incoming water and carbon dioxide is discharged with each contraction. Most of the gaseous exchange, however, occurs through the body surface.

Copepods possess a rather efficient and specialized nervous system, in which most of the ganglionic cells are located toward the anterior end of the body (cephalization), and the fibers innervate the various tissues.

COPEPOD LIFE CYCLE STUDIES

Almost all knowledge of the life cycles of parasitic copepods has been obtained from observations on naturally infected hosts. Few experimental studies are available; hence, certain aspects remain as assumptions. Development and morphogenesis of copepods are extremely fascinating, for the body form alters so drastically during maturation. In fact, the adults of some parasitic species have become so modified in their appearance that they can hardly be recognized as arthropods, let alone copepods.

During development, the egg hatches into a small, active larva known as the nauplius. Among free-living copepods, such as the well known *Cyclops* spp., the nauplius molts five times, and the six nauplius stages are designated as nauplius I, nauplius II, nauplius III, etc. Some authors prefer to assign the term metanauplius to the stages beyond nauplius I.

Among the parasitic species, the number of molts is generally reduced. For example, some members of the order Cyclopoidea display only five nauplius stages. As one nauplius stage molts and metamorphoses into the subsequent stage, the body elongates and the number of appendages increases (Plate 17–3, Fig. 1). Active feeding occurs in between ecdyses.

After feeding, the last nauplius generation, which possesses the full complement of appendages (11 to 12 in free-living forms, reduced in parasitic species), undergoes another molt and is transformed into the enlarged and elongate copepodid. In certain species, such as *Caligus rapax*, commonly found on the pectoral fins of fishes, the nauplius transforms into the chalimus stage, which is characterized by a long filament secreted from a frontal head gland. The copepodids possess distinct sutures between the head, thorax, and abdomen. Copepodids feed in between molts, usually four in free-living species and fewer among parasitic members. Finally, the terminal copepodid stage (copepodid V) molts and transforms into the adult (Plate 17–3, Fig. 2).

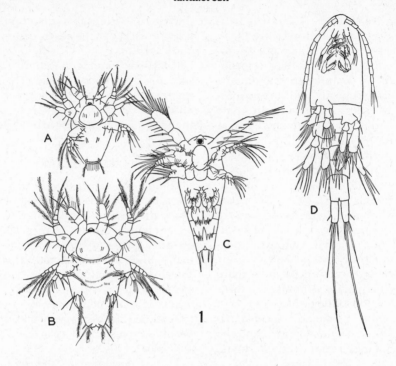

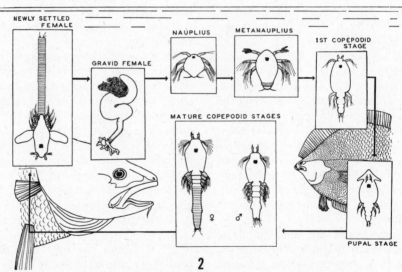

Plate 17-3   Nauplius stages of copepods. 1. Nauplius stages of free-living copepods. **A.**
Nauplius I of *Cyclops*. **B.** Nauplius IV of *Cyclops*. **C.** Nauplius VI of *Diaptomus;* **D.** Copepodid of
Cyclops. (A and B redrawn from Gurney; C modified from Gurney. From Pennak, R. W. 1953.
Freshwater Invertebrates of the United States. Ronald Press, New York.) **2.** Stages in the life cycle of
Lernaeocera branchialis, parasitic on codfish as an adult and on flatfish as a larva. (After Cameron,
T. W. M. 1956. *Parasites and Parasitism*, Methuen, London.)

COPEPOD SYSTEMATICS AND BIOLOGY

Classification

The taxonomy of the parasitic Copepoda
needs clarification. There are approximately
4500 species of copepods known, most of which
are free-living or mere accidental symbionts.
These species are divided into eight orders—
Calanoida, Harpacticoida, Cyclopoida, Noto-
delphyoida, Monstrilloida, Caligoida, Lernaeopodoida, and Arguloida. Most of the parasitic
species, however, are limited to the orders

Cyclopoida, Caligoida, Lernaeopodoida, Arguloida, Monstrilloida, and Harpacticoida. Only orders that include the more commonly encountered North American parasitic copepods are diagnosed here. Yamaguti's monograph (1963) of the copepod parasites of vertebrates should be consulted by those interested in the systematics of this group.

Order Cyclopoida.   Parasitic on fishes and in a few invertebrates. Usually only adult females are parasitic, but parasitic males are known, for example, *Bomolochus*. The body is less than 3 mm. long and only slightly flattened dorsoventrally. Abdominal segments not fused. Articulation is present between 5th and 6th thoracic segments. The fifth swimmeret and often the sixth swimmeret are present. The metasome is wider than the urosome. The first antennae have seventeen segments or less. Approximately 1000 species are known.

Order Caligoida.   Parasitic on gills and body surfaces of fishes and amphibians. Adults are elongate, wormlike. Usually more females than males are found as permanent parasites. The body measures from 7 to 15 mm. in length. The body is fused, not capable of articulation. Body segmentation is not visible in some species. Approximately 400 species are known.

Order Lernaeopodoida.   Is parasitic on gills and fins of fishes. The body is 3 to 8 mm. long, is fused, is not capable of articulation, and is not wormlike. The cephalothorax is not broad and flat. Legs are lacking in fresh-water species. Males are rarely found, are seen as minute individuals clinging to females. Approximately 300 species are known.

Order Monstrilloida.   Mostly parasitic in or on invertebrates. Parasitic during larval stages only. Free-swimming as adults. Mouthparts and second antennae are lacking in adults that are nonfeeders. Approximately 35 species are known.

Order Arguloida.*   Parasitic on body surface or in branchial chambers of fishes. Body is dorsoventrally flattened, giving ovoid appearance. Possesses movable joint between 5th and 6th thoracic segments. Abdominal segments are fused. Body is usually less than 10 mm. in length; some species are longer. Second maxillae are modified as suckers in *Argulus* found in the United States; second maxillae are not modified as suckers in other genera, for example, *Dolops*. Approximately 75 species are known.

ORDER CYCLOPOIDA

The order Cyclopoida includes a large number of free-living copepods, including the commonly encountered *Cyclops* spp. A few genera subordinate to this order reportedly are parasitic.

Genus *Ergasilus*

The genus *Ergasilus*, possessing at least twelve species in fresh-water situations, is parasitic on the gill filaments of fishes (Plate 17–4, Fig. 1). The taxonomy and distribution of members of this genus have been reviewed by

---

*The order Arguloida, which includes the parasitic genus *Argulus*, is considered by many to be subordinate to the subclass Branchiura of the class Crustacea, and independent of the Copepoda.

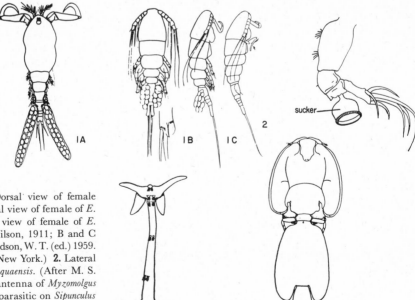

Plate 17–4   **1. A.** Dorsal view of female *Ergasilus versicolor*. **B.** Dorsal view of female of *E. chautauquaensis*. **C.** Lateral view of female of *E. chautauquaensis*. (A after Wilson, 1911; B and C after M. S. Wilson *in* Edmondson, W. T. (ed.) 1959. *Fresh-water Biology*, Wiley, New York.) **2.** Lateral view of male of *E. chautauquaensis*. (After M. S. Wilson, ibid.) **3.** Second antenna of *Myzomolgus stupendus*, showing sucker; parasitic on *Sipunculus nudus*. (After Bocquet and Stock, 1957.) **4.** Ventral view of female *Lernaea cruciata*. (After LeSeuer.) **5.** Dorsal view of female of *Lepeophtheirus salmonis*. (After Kröyer.)

Smith (1949). An identification key is furnished by Causey (1957).

After nauplii hatch from the eggs, they are free-swimming, as are the copepodids. However, when copepodids attain sexual maturity, the females become parasitic and attach to their hosts by specialized 2nd antennae, which have become adapted as two muscular claws. The sexually mature males are free-swimming in most cases, but parasitic males are known. These can be distinguished from the females by the presence of maxillipeds (Plate 17–4, Fig. 2).

All species of *Ergasilus* possess 1st antennae composed of six segments. The first four pairs of swimmerets are biramous, while the fifth pair is reduced and uniramous. During copulation, the female stores sufficient spermatozoa to fertilize all her eggs, which when formed, pass into the egg sacs attached to the genital segment.

Other Cyclopoids

In addition, *Myzomolgus stupendus* and *Catinia plana* have been reported by Bocquet and Stock (1957d) attached to sipunculid worms by stalked suckers on the third joint of the 2nd antennae (Plate 17–4, Fig. 3). Several genera of Cyclopoida have been reported on sedentary sea invertebrates, but it is strongly suspected that these are epizoites or commensals rather than true parasites.

Bocquet and Stock, in papers published between 1956 and 1958, discussed many of the copepods found on invertebrates. Their papers should be consulted by those interested in these copepods.

ORDER CALIGOIDA

The order Caligoida includes parasitic genera exclusively. The most commonly encountered genera are *Lernaea* (Plate 17–4, Fig. 4); *Lepeophtheirus,* the sea louse (Plate 17–4, Fig. 5); and *Caligus* on marine fish.

Genus *Lernaea*

In *Lernaea,* which includes thirteen or more species, it is the vermiform females, bearing hornlike processes on their cephalothorax, that are parasitic. When attached to their piscine and amphibian hosts, the entire anterior end is deeply embedded in the host's flesh and permanently anchored by these hornlike processes. Characteristically two ovisacs (egg sacs) are attached to the posterior end. These females measure between 5 and 23 mm. in length.

Haley and Winn (1959) reported finding *Lernaea cyprinacea* attached to the gills and fins of nine fish species in College Park, Maryland (Plate 17–5, Fig. 1). These parasites, like all ectoparasitic copepods, actually suck and feed on the blood and tissue fluids of their hosts and cause severe damage. Infected areas are commonly hemorrhagic, spongy, and necrotic. Heavy lernaean infections are known to kill the hosts.

LIFE CYCLE OF *Lernaea.* During the life cycle of *Lernaea,* the nauplii are free-swimming but the copepodids require a temporary host, usually a fish, to which they cling. These parasites copulate while still in the larval form, and after copulation, the males perish and the females leave the temporary host to become free-swimming. This free-swimming form (Plate 17–5, Fig. 2) is quite different from the parasitic form, to which it metamorphoses once it finds a suitable definitive host and becomes attached to it. Haley and Winn (1959) found numerous copepodids as temporary parasites on the fishes that they surveyed and suggested that perhaps these lernaeans can complete their life cycles on either one or two hosts. This hypothesis remains to be explored.

Genus *Lepeophtheirus*

The genus *Lepeophtheirus* includes several species parasitic on marine fishes (Wilson, 1944). Both male and female adults are parasitic, although males are comparatively rare. Unlike the vermiform *Lernaea,* species of *Lepeophtheirus* possess an ovoid or circular dorsoventrally flattened cephalothorax covered with a distinguishable carapace. The body segments are fused and the swimmerets are reduced. One species, *L. salmonis,* is parasitic on salmon, being attached to the body surface near the fish's anus. This species has been reported in fresh water, having been carried to that habitat by its host during its upstream migration. However, the copepod is capable of surviving for only a few days in fresh water, apparently unable to adjust to the change in the salinity of the water.

Other Caligoid Genera

Other genera of the Caligoida include *Dysgamus, Achtheinus, Teredicola, Pennella,* and *Lernaeenicus,* all found on marine fishes including sharks (Plate 17–6, Figs. 1 to 3).

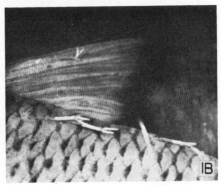

Plate 17-5   *Lernaea.* **1. A** and **B.** *Lernaea cyprinacea* on gills of fish host. (After Haley and Winn, 1959. **2. A.** Adult ovigerous female *Lernaea.* **B.** Free-swimming female with legs 2 to 4 shown on one side only. (Fig. 2 after M. S. Wilson *in* Edmondson, W. T. (ed.). 1959. *Fresh-water Biology,* Wiley, New York.)

LIFE CYCLE OF *Lernaeenicus.* The life cycle of this genus is rather intriguing, since the form of the animal changes greatly during the developing copepodid stages. The copepodid I seeks and attaches itself to the same fish on which the adult females are found. The copepodid attaches by utilizing the 2nd antennae. Soon after attachment, the larva cements itself to the host by means of strong frontal filaments.

Subsequent generations of copepodids actually exhibit dedifferentiation in that the swimmerets and mouthparts disappear and the segments of the antennae become invisible. Such copepodids are referred to as pupae. At the end of the last pupal copepodid stage, these structures reappear. The young males and females are free-swimming and copulation does not take place on the host. Soon after mating, the males die and the females seek out the same species of host and burrow in. In some instances, *Lernaeenicus* actually embeds its anterior end into the aorta of the host; in other instances, it merely burrows into the tissues of the body, whereupon a tumorous growth results.

ORDER LERNAEOPODOIDA

The order Lernaeopodoida includes the genera *Achtheres, Salmincola, Brachiella, Lernaeosolea, Krøyerina* and, *Paeonodes* (Plate 17–6, Figs. 4 to 9). Of these, only members of the first two genera are found on fresh-water fishes, and the remaining genera are found on marine fishes, primarily on the gills and spiracles of sharks. A key to the species of *Achtheres* is given by Wilson (1915) and Causey (1957). A key to *Salmincola* is also given by Wilson (1915). These should be consulted by those interested in identification.

Very little is known about the marine members of Lernaeopodoida.

Genus *Achtheres*

Species of *Achtheres* attain an extremely

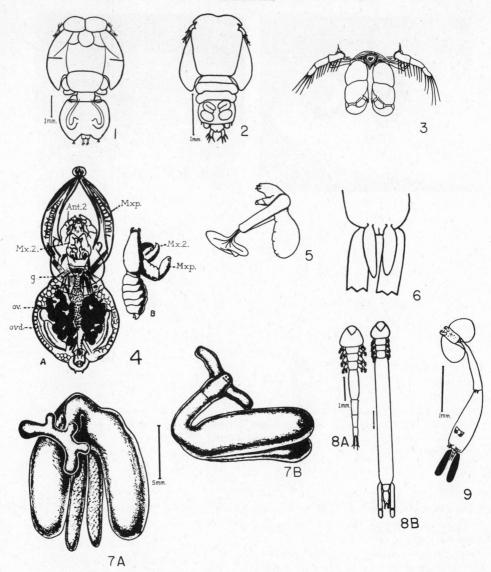

Plate 17-6   Some parasitic copepods. 1. *Dysgamus atlanticus,* dorsal view of female. **2.** *Achtheinus dentatus,* dorsal view of male. **3.** *Pennella filosa,* dorsal view of first and second antennae. **4. A.** Female of *Achtheres percarum.* **B.** Male of *Achtheres percarum.* **5.** *Salmincola beani,* side view. **6.** *Brachiella squali,* dorsal view of posterior processes and ovisacs. **7.** *Lernaeosolea lycodis.* **A.** Dorsal view of female. **B.** Lateral view of same specimen. **8.** *Krøyerina elongata.* **A.** Dorsal view of male. **B.** Dorsal view of female. **9.** *Paeonodes exiguus,* ventral view of female with ovisacs. (Figs. 1, 2, 6–9 after Wilson, 1944; Fig. 3 after Wilson, 1917; Fig. 4 after Gerstaecker; Fig. 5 after Wilson, 1915.)

modified form when found attached to their hosts. The females, usually measuring over 3 mm. in length, possess soft bellies that are more or less segmented, and they lack swimmerets. The second maxillae are greatly modified to form two long tubular armlike appendages, the ends of which are attached to a saucer-like structure, the bulla. The bulla is embedded in the flesh of the host and serves as the absorptive mechanism through which the host's blood is taken in. The males are dwarfed, and when seen, are attached to the host during their early immature stages. They soon become attached to the females before, during, and after copulation, sometimes even permanently after copulation.

LIFE CYCLE OF *Achtheres.* The life cycle of *Achtheres* is somewhat modified from the

generalized developmental plan found in copepods. The nauplius never leaves the eggshell;
rather, the hatched larva is the copepodid I
form, which is free-swimming and eventually
becomes attached to a host.

Genus *Salmincola*

Species of *Salmincola* are quite similar to those
of *Achtheres* except that the body of the females
is completely unsegmented. The maxillae of
females are also modified as arms, joining
at the bulla (Plate 17–6, Fig. 5). The size of the
females approximates that of the *Achtheres*
species. The males, measuring 1.5 mm. or less,
lack arms and are attached to the females.
Fasten (1919), in reporting the development of
Salmincola edwardsii, stated that there is only

one free-swimming copepodid stage, and this
later becomes attached to a host and undergoes modification of form (Plate 17–2, Fig. 3).

ORDER MONSTRILLOIDA

The most familiar genera of the suborder
Monstrilloida are *Haemocera* (Plate 17–7) and
Monstrilla.

Genus *Haemocerca*

Haemocerca danae.   This copepod is parasitic during its copepodid stages in the body
cavities of polychaete worms. The nauplius
hatching from the egg is free-swimming, and
upon coming in contact with the host, burrows
through its body wall and transforms into an

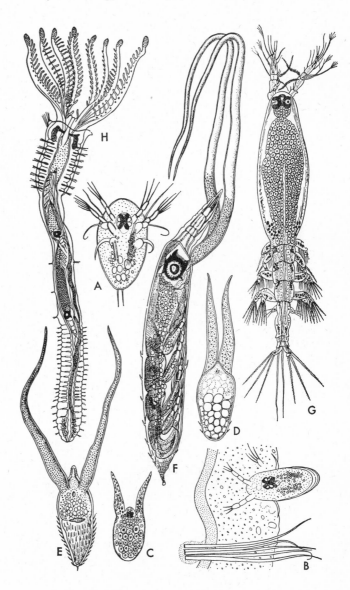

Plate 17–7   **Stages in the life cycle of**
Haemocera danae. **A.** Nauplius. **B.** Nauplius
in act of penetrating body of host. **C** to **E.**
Successive larval stages, showing the development of the appendages and also the spinous
sheath enclosing the larva. **F.** Fully developed
copepodid. **G.** Adult female copepod devoid
of mouth. **H.** Annelid host enclosing two
copepodid larvae within its coelomic cavity.
(After Baer, J. G. 1952. *Ecology of Animal Parasites,* University of Illinois Press, Urbana, Ill.)

ovoid mass of cells that migrates to the area of the host's ventral blood vessels. Once in this position, the larva secretes a wall around itself with two elongate tubular processes extending from it through which nutrients are absorbed from the host. The body elongates during this parasitic phase of its life cycle (Plate 17–7). Once the copepodid reaches the adult form within the enveloping wall, it escapes from the host by rupturing out and becomes free-swimming.

Genus *Monstrilla*

Monstrilla heligolandica.   This species is closely related to *Haemocerca danae* and is parasitic on gastropods that are in turn parasitic on lamellibranchs. The copepod, which is a parasite of a parasite, is known as a hyperparasite.

ORDER ARGULOIDA
(OR SUBCLASS BRANCHIURA)

Genus *Argulus*

The most common members of the Arguloida belong to the genus *Argulus* and are commonly referred to as fish lice. Many of the species are parasitic on marine fishes, and some fifteen are found on fresh-water fishes. At least one species has been reported on an amphibian. *Argulus* is so different morphologically from the other copepods that it is often considered to belong to a distinct subclass, the Branchiura. The body is ovoid and dorsoventrally compressed (Plate 17–8, Fig. 1). The cephalothorax is covered dorsally by the carapace, which is recurved medially onto the ventral surface of the body. Specialized respiratory areas are located on the two ventrolateral margins of the carapace. When the animal is viewed from the ventral aspect, the abdominal segments are seen to be fused. There are only four pairs of legs (swimmerets); the fifth and sixth pairs are lacking.

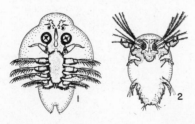

Plate 17–8   *Argulus*. 1. Female, ventral view. **2.** Newly hatched larva. (After Cameron, T. W. M. 1956. *Parasites and Parasitism,* Wiley, New York.)

The mouthparts of *Argulus* are greatly reduced, and the most striking feature is the modification of the 2nd maxillae into two suction cups by which the parasite holds onto its host. *Argulus* also possesses a preoral sting by which the animal pierces its host in order to obtain the required blood meal. When seen from the dorsal aspect, two prominent movable compound eyes are visible in the head region.

Both male and female *Argulus* are parasitic. The female, measuring 5 to 25 mm. in length, is larger than the male. Although usually attached to their hosts, these parasites leave their hosts periodically and become free-swimming. This habit is particularly true of gravid females, which lay their eggs attached to sticks and stones at the bottom of the aquatic environment.

The breeding season of *Argulus* normally occurs three times per year. The eggs are laid several hundred at a time and enveloped in a jelly-like mass. As each egg is laid, it is fertilized by a sperm stored in the female at the time of copulation. The eggs hatch in approximately 3 weeks. The escaping larva is a copepodid, quite similar to the adult except for modifications of certain appendages. For example, the 2nd antennae are plumose (in some species) and function as locomotor structures, and the 2nd maxillae are modified as clasping structures armed with hooks. In a few days, the copepodid molts; after several such molts, each of which is accompanied by structural modifications, the adult, parasitic form is attained.

ORDER HARPACTICOIDA

The order Harpacticoida includes the *Unicaltheutha*, containing a single species, *U. ovalis*. This parasite is found attached to the exoskeleton of lobsters in Placentia Bay, Newfoundland. Both the females and males of this copepod are parasitic.

COPEPOD PHYSIOLOGY

Oxygen Requirements

Very little is known about the physiology of parasitic copepods. The physiology of Crustacea in general, including information on free-living species, has been compiled in volumes edited by Waterman (1960, 1961). It is known that parasitic copepods are true aerobic animals that derive their oxygen from the surrounding aquatic media.

Haemoglobin, similar to, although not

identical with, mammalian haemoglobin, has been detected in several species. Fox (1953, 1957) reported haemoglobin in *Dolops ranarum,* a species found on siluroid fishes. The presence of haemoglobin is undoubtedly responsible for the red color of the copepod blood. Not all copepods, however, possess red blood. Van den Berghe (1933) reported red acellular blood in *Lernaeocera* and Fox (1957) reported it in *Dolops,* but *Argulus foliaceus* possesses pale blood containing no haemoglobin.

Among copepods, the types of haemoglobin differ. For example, Fox (1945) reported that the type found in *Lernaeocera branchialis* is different from that found in *Daphnia* and other free-living species. Undoubtedly haemoglobin facilitates oxygen transport throughout the body tissues, but it is not a necessity, for some species do not possess haemoglobin.

There are no special breathing mechanisms in copepods. The exchange of gases occurs through the exoskeleton and through the posterior terminal of the alimentary tract.

Osmoregulation

Panikkar and Sproston (1941) demonstrated the adaptability of *Lernaeocera branchialis,* an ectoparasite on the teleost fish *Pollachius pollachius,* relative to osmotic equilibrium. These investigators found that the salt concentration in the internal medium of the copepod is 57 to 82 per cent that of the salt concentration of the surrounding sea water as opposed to a concentration of only 43 per cent within the host itself. If these copepods are removed from their host and isolated in sea water, they become isosmotic. This suggests that while the copepod is in the attached state, the salt concentration of its internal medium is diluted by fluids (blood, etc.) obtained from the host. Not all parasitic copepods are as adaptable as this species; for example, *Lepeophtheirus salmonis* dies in a few days if brought into fresh water by its host.

Sex Determination

The fact that lernaeopodoid males are hyperparasitic, being attached to females, has influenced several workers to investigate this relationship. Amazingly enough, Reverberi and Pitotti (1942) and Reverberi (1947) found that if young males of *Ione thoracica,* a parasite of *Callianassa,* are removed from the females and transplanted directly to the host, these males alter their sex, becoming females. Furthermore, if juvenile females are purposely placed on adult females, they transform into males. From this and other similar experiments, it appears that development of copepodids into males is brought about by their affixation to females. However, some critics feel there is some unexplained genetic basis behind sex determination and that it is not totally determined by association.

COPEPOD HOST-PARASITE RELATIONSHIPS

Little is known about host-parasite relationships. The sometimes drastic body modifications of parasitic copepods while in the adult, attached state undoubtedly result from evolutionary changes caused by adaptation to the parasitic way of life. The feeding habits of parasitic copepods—that is, ingestion the host's blood and body fluids—causes injuries. In nature, the number of parasites is sufficiently sparse so that often no serious effects are noticeable. However, in small isolated areas, such as ponds and hatcheries, copepod parasites, especially lernaeans, do cause serious injuries. Furthermore, since the exoskeleton of these animals is fairly resistant to chemicals, weak acids, and alkalis, infected fishes in hatcheries must frequently be disposed of.

In addition to some copepods being true parasites and others being commensals, some copepods are also predators. Marshall and Orr (1955) reported that *Anomalocera patersoni* actually catches and ingests young anglerfish, while *Pareuchaeta norvegica* eats fish larvae. Furthermore, *Centropages hamatus* and *Femora longicornis* always have much greater than normal amounts of other crustaceans in their guts.

SUBCLASS CIRRIPEDIA

The cirriped crustaceans, including barnacles, are sessile as adults, commonly being attached by antennules located on their heads. The carapace consists of a fleshy mantle, which is armed or not armed with calcareous plates. Typically, the body is indistinctly segmented with six pairs of biramous thoracic appendages known as cirri. The abdomen is vestigial. Compound eyes and antennae are absent in the adult and a heart is lacking. The cirripeds are usually hermaphroditic. The female genital pore is located on the first thoracic segment and the male pore is located at the posterior end of the body.

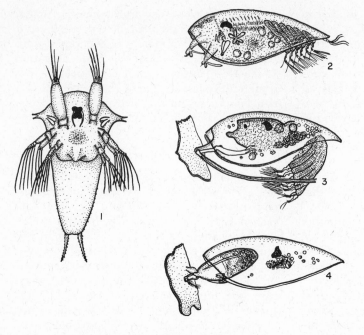

Plate 17-9   Nauplius and cypris
larvae of *Sacculina carcini*. **1.** Nauplius.
2. Cypris larva. **3.** Cypris, attached to host
by its antennae, sheds its locomotory appendages. **4.** Cypris transformed into kentrogon larva. Degenerate structures of
cypris are still visible. (Redrawn after
Delage, 1884.)

CIRRIPED LIFE CYCLE PATTERN

The life cycles of the various species of cirripeds are essentially identical.

The cirripeds are oviparous. The eggs, upon
hatching, give rise to free-swimming nauplii
that are distinguishable from nauplii of other
crustaceans by the presence of frontal horns on
the carapace (Plate 17–9, Fig. 1). The nauplius
may undergo several molts. The terminal
nauplius gives rise to the cypris (Plate 17–9,
Fig. 2). The cypris larva is readily distinguishable by its bivalvular shell; its pair of compound eyes; six pairs of two-jointed feet, which
are adapted for swimming; and the single pair
of anterior antennules, each of which is armed
with a sucking disc at its terminal and has a
cement gland at its base. Among free-living
species, such as the common barnacles, the
cypris larva becomes attached to a rock, a
plank, or some other solid surface, casts off its
shell, loses its eyes, and metamorphoses into
the adult possessing swimming legs that elongate to become typical cirri.

CIRRIPED SYSTEMATICS AND BIOLOGY

Classification

The Cirripedia, which includes some 800
known species, is divided into five orders with
the free-living barnacles belonging to the
Thoracica and other free-living forms belonging to the Acrothoracica. Members of Acrothoracica bore holes in the shells in which they
dwell. The parasitic cirripeds are subordinate
to one of the three remaining orders diagnosed
below.

Order 1. Ascothoracica.   Members are marine and are ecto-
or endoparasites of coelenterates or echinoderms. They
do not attach at the preoral region. Mantle lacks calcareous plates. Body is bivalved or saclike. Cirri, numbering six or fewer, are usually rudimentary. Abdomen
is present. Mouthparts are modified for piercing-sucking. Antennules are often modified for grasping. Cement
glands are lacking. Digestive and reproductive systems
possess diverticula extending into mantle. These parasites are usually dioecious, and males are smaller than
females. Nauplii lack frontal horns. Approximately
twelve species are known.
Order 2. Apoda.   Animals are attached by preoral region.
Mantle is lacking. Body is segmented. Abdomen is present. Cirri are lacking. Mouth is suctorial. Alimentary
canal is incomplete and lacks mid- and hindguts.
Antennules and cement glands are present. Animals are
hermaphroditic, and metamorphosis is not known. There
is only one known species.
Order 3. Rhizocephala.   Primarily parasites of other crustaceans, principally decapods (shrimps, crabs, etc.).
Adult body is greatly modified as thin-walled sac enclosing visceral mass, primarily of gonads. Members are
hermaphroditic except Seylonidae. Body segmentation
is not apparent. Lacks cirri, sense organs, or alimentary
tract. Rootlike system extends into interior of host in
all directions through which nourishment from host
body fluids are absorbed. Fertilized eggs develop in
brood chamber. Nauplii escape through aperture at
summit of sac, which also permits the entrance of oxygenated water. Parasites attach to host by short stalk at
base of saccular body. Approximately 200 species are
known.

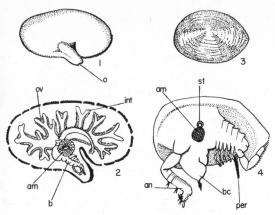

Plate 17-10 *Baccalaureus japonicus.* **1.** Female, external view. **2.** Female, right valve of carapace removed. **3.** Male, external view. **4.** Male, left valve of carapace removed. (All figures redrawn after Yosii, 1931.)

(am, adductor muscles; an, antenna; b, body of animal; bc, buccal cone; int, intestine; per, pereiopods; o, orifice of the carapace; ov, ovary; st, stomach.)

ORDER ASCOTHORACICA

The ascothoracicans are parasites of coelenterates and echinoderms. These animals somewhat resemble ostracods in that the adults do not shed the bivalved cypris larval shell. The alimentary tract and gonads send rootlike branches into the mantle cavity. Nutrition is supplied by the host's body fluids. In the endoparasites, the host's body fluids are absorbed directly into the dendritic alimentary canal. In the ectoparasites, the mouthparts are adapted for piercing the host's integument, and the body juices are drawn out.

Although the adult body is comparatively small, the shells of certain species, especially those found on coelenterates, are well developed, and both a female and a small male are found within each shell. Eggs enclosed within the branched ovaries hatch into nauplii that in turn give rise to free-swimming cypris larvae. It is the cypris larva that becomes parasitic in or on the host and develops into adults. *Baccalaureus japonicus* (Plate 17-10) is quite representative of this order.

ORDER APODA

The Apoda is a little understood group, and its complete metamorphosis is not known. The order was erected by Darwin based on a single species represented by one specimen found in a peduculate barnacle.

ORDER RHIZOCEPHALA

The rhizocephalans include the genera *Sacculina* and *Peltogaster*. For those interested in the identification of *Sacculina* and other rhizocephalans, the papers of Boschma (1937) and Smith (1906) should be consulted. Most of our knowledge concerning the parasitic cirripeds has been derived from studies on the two genera mentioned.

Genus *Sacculina*

LIFE CYCLE OF *Sacculina.* Day (1935) originally reported the life history of *Sacculina* and his observations have been elaborated on by Faxon (1940). The eggs expelled from the body of the parent hatch into nauplii measuring 0.25 mm. in length. These larvae lack an alimentary tract. On molting, the nauplius metamorphoses into a cypris larva that seeks a host, usually a crab. The larva becomes attached to the host's hair by the hooked antennae of the larva. The attached cypris is commonly referred to as a kentrogen larva (Plate 17-11, Fig. 1). The cypris larva is undifferentiated sexually.

If the host is a fresh-water crab, the life cycle is somewhat altered in that the nauplius stage is suppressed and the eggs give rise to cyprii. Once attached to a host, the protoplasm of the kentrogen larva dedifferentiates and becomes a ball of embryonic cells, which is injected into the host via a style in the antennae, which penetrates the host's exoskeleton. This mass of cells is carried by the host's blood to the region of the alimentary canal in the thoracic zone. Once in this location, the mass of cells forms a tumor with rootlike processes wrapped around the alimentary canal (Plate 17-11, Fig. 2).

Further growth is directed posteriorly with the body increasing in size and the dendritic outgrowths increasing. Growth is halted when the junction between the thorax and abdomen is reached (Plate 17-11, Fig. 3). The parasite then exerts pressure against the host's exoskeleton in that region, resulting in prevention of the deposition of new exoskeletal materials. When the host molts, a hole is left in the area. In approximately 8 weeks, the parasite emerges as a saclike protrusion enclosing a brood chamber and with rootlike extensions that invade every region of the host's body. The presence of the mature parasite prevents further molting on the part of the crab.

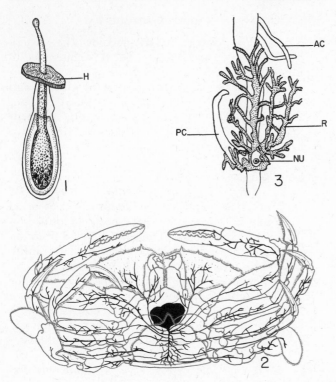

Plate 17-11   Later stages of Sacculina.
1. Kentrogon larva. (Redrawn after Delage, 1884.) **2.** Rootlike extensions of *Sacculina*, infiltrating various areas of the body of the crab host. (After Ferris.) **3.** Rootlike body of a developing specimen, situated along the gut of the crab host between the levels of the anterior and posterior caeca. (Redrawn after Smith, 1910–11.)

(AC, anterior caeca; PC, posterior caeca; NU, nucleus; R, rootlike processes of the parasite; H, host tissue.)

Although rhizocephalans have been considered hermaphroditic, Ichikawa and Yanagimachi (1958), while studying *Peltogasterella socialis,* cast some doubt on this interpretation. At times a cypris larva does not become attached to a crab host. Rather, it settles on an immature rhizocephalan adult. This "parasitized" individual then develops into a "male." The cypris injects a mass of cells into the brood chamber of the adult, and this mass then migrates to the "testes" of the young adult rhizocephalan. The individual cells of the mass differentiate into sperm when the individual reaches sexual maturity in approximately 6 weeks. Ichikawa and Yanagimachi demonstrated that the "testes" are actually seminal receptacles, and the sperm within are produced by male cells of the cypris. This discovery suggests that adult rhizocephalans are true females carrying hyperparasitic larval males. Further investigations along this line may well prove that true hermaphroditism does not exist among these animals.

Genus *Peltogaster*

Members of *Peltogaster* resemble *Sacculina* morphologically and in their pattern of metamorphosis. They parasitize the hermit crab.

Genus *Thompsonia*

Members of *Thompsonia,* which also parasitize crabs, differ from *Sacculina* in that numerous tumors are formed on the alimentary tract of the host rather than a single large one. Furthermore, *Thompsonia* does not interfere with the host's molting, and usually several saccular bodies protrude from the body of the host, each enclosing eggs that give rise to cyprii instead of nauplii. When the host molts, these saclike protrusions are caste off, but terminal swellings on the root system within the host give rise to new sacs.

Rhizocephalan Host-Parasite Relationships

PARASITIC CASTRATION AND SEX REVERSALS. Rhizocephalan parasites such as *Sacculina* and *Peltogaster* effect some severe changes in their hosts. Among these, parasitic castration is by far the most remarkable. The gonads of the host are affected in two ways—they are retarded in their development, that is, the multiplication and differentiation of the gametocytes are hindered; and actual destruction of the sex cells takes place, resulting in complete atrophy of the gonads.

Smith (1906) attributed true disintegration to cell autodigestion, while Perez (1933) attributed it to phagocytosis by the follicular cells. The recovery of partially castrated crabs is extremely interesting. Several investigators have reported that when the *Sacculina* parasite is removed, the female host generally regenerates new ovarian tissue, but the male commonly develops complete or partial ovaries instead of testes. Hence, sex reversal has taken place. Reinhard (1956) pointed out, however, that such instances of sex reversal may not be directly attributed to the parasite, because similar occurrences are known among nonparasitized crabs. Studies of this nature to determine whether the parasite induces more sex reversal than normally found should be most rewarding.

Sacculina and related genera often induce modification of secondary external sex characteristics in crab hosts. Such modifications include the broadening of the abdomen and feminization of certain appendages in males, narrowing of the abdomen and degeneration of pleopods in females. These alterations undoubtedly result from damage to gonads and manifestations of sex reversal in males.

Similarly, parasitism by *Peltogaster, Thompsonia,* and related genera effects changes in secondary sex characteristics. Reinhard (1956) has given an excellent account of sex alterations resulting from rhizocephalan infections. Various theories have been advanced to explain the alteration of sex in parasitized hosts. The more reasonable ones are based on physiological deviations from the normal, resulting from the presence of the parasite—for example, nutritional deprivation in gonadal tissue and lowering of fat content in the host.

In considering alteration of sex, one might examine the hypothesis offered by Goldschmidt (1923). He assumed that in sex determination opposing genes are present in each individual; hence, the sex of the host depends on the quantitative balance of male as opposed to female sex genes. In sex alterations due to rhizocephalans, according to Goldschmidt's postulation, the normal balance is physiologically disrupted by the presence of the parasite, and the male, or more commonly the female, genes become dominant.

PHYSIOLOGICAL ALTERATIONS. In addition to inducing morphologically appreciable alterations, rhizocephalans also cause physiological changes. For example, Robson (1911) reported an increase of lipochromes in the blood of parasitized *Inachus;* Drilhon (1936) reported that

calcium and magnesium levels in the haemolymph of *Carcinus* are almost doubled when parasitized by *Sacculina;* and Smith (1913) reported that in sacculinized *Carcinus,* the fat content in the hepatopancreas is either increased or decreased and that glycogen reserves in the liver and skin become depleted. Various other similar studies all indicate that the host's metabolism is altered by these parasitic cirripeds.

TOXICITY. It is suspected that *Sacculina* is toxic to its hosts. Lévy (1923) prepared extracts from various parts of the parasite—mantle, visceral mass, and developing embryos—and injected these extracts into healthy *Carcinus.* He reported that crabs thus treated became paralyzed and died soon after, with the mantle extracts being the most toxic.

SUBCLASS MALACOSTRACA

The Malacostraca includes an array of free-living arthropods, such as lobsters, crayfishes, crabs, and shrimps. However, a small number of malacostracans, belonging to the orders Isopoda, Amphipoda, and Decapoda, particularly the former, are parasitic.

ORDER ISOPODA

The parasitic isopods belong to one of three suborders—Epicaridea, Gnathiidea, and Cymothoidea. The gnathiid isopods are parasites as larvae, the cymothoids as adults, and the epicarids are parasites both as larvae and as adults. All the species are marine.

Suborder Gnathiidea

The gnathiids include the genera *Anceus* and *Gnathia* (Plate 17–12, Fig. 1). These animals as larvae are blood-feeding parasites of fish and are attached to the fins of their hosts. These larvae engorge themselves with blood and their bodies become so distended that the last three thoracic segments become completely obscured and remain indistinguishable until the engorged blood is digested. A molt occurs after each of two feeding periods; hence, there are three larval stages. The third larval instar undergoes a final molt and transforms into the adult.

The mouthparts of both male and female adults are completely atrophied except for a pair of powerful mandibles retained by the

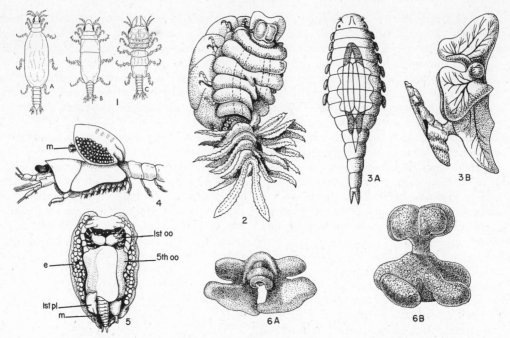

Plate 17-12   Parasitic Crustacea. 1. *Gnathia maxillaris*. **A.** Larva. **B.** Adult female. **C.** Adult male. (After Sars.) **2.** *Cepon elegans,* gravid female with dwarf male. (After Giard and Bonnier.) **3.** *Portunion maenadis*. **A.** Greatly enlarged male. **B.** Gravid female. (Redrawn after Giard and Bonnier.) **4.** *Aspidophryxus sarsi* on *Erythrops microphthalma*. **5.** *Dajus mysidis* (ventral view). (Redrawn after Giard and Bonnier.) **6.** *Ancyroniscus bonnieri*. **A.** Subadult female (before egg deposition). The two pairs of lower lobes belonging to the abdomen are lodged in the visceral cavity of the host. **B.** Adult female after laying, reduced to a lobed and closed sac filled with embryos. (After Caullery and Mesnil.)

(1st oo, first oostegite; 5th oo, fifth oostegite; e, eggs; 1st pl, first pleopod; m, male.)

males. The adults not only do not possess mouthparts, they also have no mouth or gut. The blood taken in by the larvae maintains the adults, which are buried in mud among plankton at the bottom of bodies of water. The females lay eggs that hatch into active larvae after incubation. Adult females die soon after incubating their eggs.

Suborder Cymothoidea

Adult cymothoid isopods are ectoparasitic on fishes and occasionally on cephalopods. They are found either attached to the gills or to the inside of the mouth. Members of *Ichthyoxenos*, however, are found in pairs, a male and a female, embedded in minute cavities in the host's skin. These parasitic isopods are not permanently attached, even as adults, for individuals are frequently found in plankton. Host specificity is not demonstrated by cymothoids. Sexual dimorphism occurs. The males are more similar to the larvae while the females are often asymmetrical. Protandrous hermaph-

rodites are known in *Nerocila, Anilocra, Cymothoa,* and *Ichthyoxenos*. The functional males of these protandrous hermaphrodites possess a rudimentary ovary that becomes functional only after the testis ceases to function. In this way, the males become females.

Suborder Epicaridea

The epicarid isopods require two hosts to complete their life cycles (Plate 17-13). The larva, which hatches from the egg, is known as an epicaridium. It resembles a very small isopod but is armed with piercing-sucking mouthparts. Furthermore, epicaridia possess clawlike appendages by which they attach themselves to free-swimming copepods. The larvae undergo six successive molts while attached and feed from the copepod host. There are two distinct larval stages on the copepod. The epicaridium metamorphoses into the microniscus, which in turn becomes the cryptoniscus (Plate 17-14). The cryptoniscus leaves the host and becomes attached to the second host, a

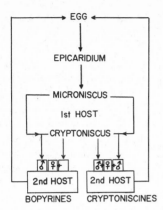

Plate 17-13   Two types of life cycles, as found among epicard isopods.

decapod crustacean living at the bottom of the sea.

The cryptoniscus of bopyrids (a family of the Epicaridea) enters either the branchial chamber or the brood pouch of the crustacean host, undergoes ecdysis, and transforms into a bopyridium, which lacks pleopods but retains pereiopods. Sex differentiation occurs when the cryptoniscus larva becomes attached to the second host. Giard and Bonnier (1887, 1893) and Reinhard (1949) demonstrated that the first larva to become attached to the crab host differentiates into a female and all subsequent larvae become males. If more than one larva

enters the crab simultaneously, these all develop into females, but only one eventually reaches sexual maturity while the others disappear. Several males, can be present with a single female. If such occurs, the female undergoes further development—the pleopods become flattened and function as breathing organs, a huge brood pouch is formed, and the size increases. The males remain as bopyridia and are considered to be neotenic larvae.

The ambipotent characteristic of the larvae was demonstrated by Reverberi and Pitotti (1942), who reported that if a young male larva is transferred into the branchial chamber of an uninfected crab, it develops into a female.

Among the cryptoniscines (a family within the suborder), the developmental pattern within the second host is different. The cryptonisci entering the crab develop into protandrous hermaphrodites. After attaining the female stage, the isopods degenerate, not as the result of parasitism, but from an excessive production of eggs.

The suborder Epicaridea includes five families. The following is a brief synopsis of these families, modified after Caullery (1952).

Family Bopyridae.   Are parasites in the branchial cavity of decapod Crustacea.
   Subfamily Bopyrinae.   Are parasites of prawns and their allies. Representative genera: *Bopyrus* and *Cepon* (Plate 17–12, Fig. 2).
   Subfamily Ioninae.   Are parasites of Brachyura and Anomura. Representative genus: *Ione*.
Family Phryxidae.   Are ectoparasitic on the abdomen of decapods (Macrura, Paguridae) and usually are very asymmetrical. Representative genera: *Phryxus* and *Athelges.*
Family Entoniscidae.   Are endoparasites of decapods, usually are found among host's viscera, greatly modified. Representative genera: *Entoniscus, Portunion* (Plate 17–4, Fig. 3), and *Priapon.*
Family Dajidae.   Are ectoparasites of schizopods. They attach to thorax, abdomen, or gills of host. They are more or less modified. Representative genera: *Aspidophryxus* (Plate 17–14, Fig. 4), *Dajus* (Plate 17–14, Fig. 5), *Notophryxus,* and *Branchiophryxus.*
Family Cryptoniscidae.   Are parasites of different types of Crustacea. Are greatly modified. Sex reversal is possible. Brood chamber is internal. Representative genera: *Hemioniscus* and *Ancyroniscus* (Plate 17–14, Fig. 6).

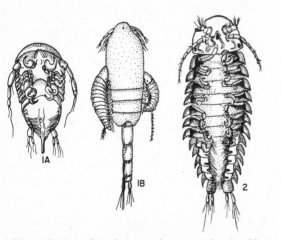

Plate 17-14   **Developmental stages of epicarids.**
1. **A.** Microniscus larva of *Cepon elegans.* (Redrawn after Giard and Bonnier, 1893.) **B.** Microniscus larvae attached to *Calanus elongatus.* (Redrawn after Sars, 1889.) **2.** Cryptoniscus larva of *Portunion kossmanni.* (Redrawn after Giard and Bonnier, 1893.)

ORDER AMPHIPODA

Certain amphipods are frequently associated with various marine invertebrates. For example, *Phronima sedentaria* is often found in colonies

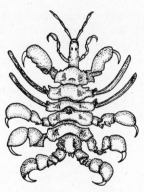

Plate 17-15 *Cyamus ceti,* **the whale louse.** (Redrawn after Bate and Westwood.)

burrowed in tunicates; and the whale louse, *Cyamus,* is found in the epidermis of whales (Plate 17–15). In *P. sedentaria,* predation, rather than parasitism, is suspected. In *Cyamus,* although nothing except its morphology is known (Lutken, 1873), the animal could well be an ectoparasite, for it appears to be specific for whales.

ORDER DECAPODA

In addition to the parasitic isopods and amphipods, certain pea crabs belonging to the genus *Pinnotheres* are parasitic in mantle cavities of oysters and related molluscs (Stauber, 1945; Christensen and McDermott, 1958; Haven, 1959). Several stages are evident during the life history of this crab. The body structure of the "first crab stage" (also known as the invasive stage) is modified and adapted for reaching the host. The mating forms possess rigid exoskeletons (and therefore are known as the hard stage). It is during the hard stage that males leave the host and seek a mate in another host. While the parasite is attached to the host, there are indications of degeneration for the body becoming soft and less motile. The presence of *Pinnotheres* in the mantle cavity of molluscs results in erosion of the host's gills, palps, and other structures.

MALACOSTRACAN HOST-PARASITE RELATIONSHIPS

Practically nothing is known about the relationship between the parasitic Malacostraca and their hosts.

CLASS TARDIGRADA

The tardigrades, or "water bears," are almost all free-living, and the majority are found in moist terrestrial and fresh-water niches. Some, however, are marine.

The cuticle of these animals lacks true chitin, and their bodies are unsegmented. Hence, they are doubtfully placed among the arthropods. In fact, the Tardigrada is often considered a distinct phylum. The bodies are generally more or less cylindrical, with rounded ends, and they measure up to 1 mm. in length. There are four pairs of stumpy, unjointed legs, with two or more claws located at the terminal of each leg. The last pair of legs is located at the posterior end of the body.

At the anterior end of the body is found a retractile snout. The mouth is situated at the anterior terminal of the snout and is usually armed with a pair of retractable stylets. Circulatory and breathing organs are absent. Materials diffuse and circulate about easily in the body fluid, and the exchange of gases occurs through the body surface. Excretion is the function of the rectal glands, which are outpockets of the rectum.

Marcus' monograph (1929) of the Tardigrada and the section in Pennak's treatise (1953) on fresh-water invertebrates that deals with the tardigrades are recommended to those desiring details on the morphology and taxonomy of this group.

The tardigrades are dioecious, and a single large saclike gonad is found in both sexes. All known tardigrade species are oviparous. Most species undergo from four to six molts during their development, and sexual maturity is usually attained sometime after the second or third ecdysis.

Tardigrades are most frequently found in lichen, damp moss, and liverwort beds, and less commonly among mosses and algae in fresh water. None of the known terrestrial and fresh-water species are symbiotic. These species are chiefly preditors, feeding upon amoeboid protozoans, nematodes, and perhaps to a certain extent on each other.

Less than 10 per cent of the known species are marine. Again, the majority of these are free-living, being found among seaweed. However, a few marine species are believed to be symbiotic. For example, Green (1950) found adults of *Echiniscoides sigismundi* in the mantle cavity of the common mussel collected at

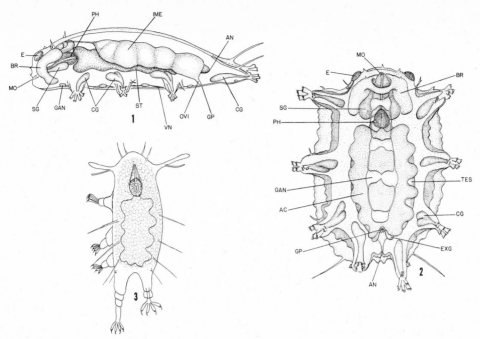

Plate 17-16   Symbiotic tardigrades. 1. *Tetrakentron synaptae* adult female, sagittal view. **2.** *T. synaptae* adult male, ventral view. **3.** *Halechiniscus guiteli* adult, dorsal view. (All figures redrawn after Marcus, 1929.)

(AC, alimentary canal; AN, anus; BR, brain; CG, ilaw glands; E, eyespot; EXG, excretory gland; GAN, ganglion of ventral nerve; GP, gonopore; IME, immature egg in saclike ovary; MO, mouth; OVI, oviduct; PH, sucking pharynx; SG, salivary gland; ST, stomach; TES, testis; VN, ventral nerve cord.)

Whitstable, England. Since Green did not find this tardigrade in the area where the mussels were obtained, despite a careful search of seaweed and other material sieved in a plankton net, he suggested that "some relationship other than a casual one exists between the tardigrades and the mussels." However, if a definite relationship exists between this tardigrade and the mussel, it is a facultative one, for *E. sigismundi* is also known to be free-living in seaweed, particularly among the green alga *Enteromorpha,* in the Mediterranean, the North Sea, the Caribbean, and even off the coast of China.

Green's discovery of a marine tardigrade associated with a host was not the first. Marcus (1936) has listed several species of marine tardigrades known to be associated with particular animals. For example, *Halechiniscus guiteli* is found in and on oyster shells (Plate 17–16, Fig. 3); *Actinarctus doryphorus* is a facultative symbiont on the echinoid *Echinocyamus pusillus;* and *Tetrakentron synaptae* appears to be a true parasite on the tentacles of the holothurian *Leptosynapta galliennei* (Plate 17–16, Figs. 1, 2).

Tetrakentron synaptae possesses a dorsoventrally flattened body that may or may not be the result of its adaptation to parasitism.

Since the symbiotic tardigrades, be they obligatory or facultative, have only been found on a few occasions, nothing beyond what has been stated is known about their relationships with their hosts.

CLASS PYCNOGONIDA

The Pycnogonida, or Pantopoda, is often considered a subphylum of the Arthropoda. The members, commonly known as "sea spiders," are all marine. Their bodies are generally small and superficially spider-like; hence, the common name, although some abyssal species may reach a length of 30 cm. Their thin and short bodies are typically divided into two conspicuous regions—the head and the thorax. The abdomen is vestigial (Plate 17–17, Fig. 1). A long, slender, tripartite feeding apparatus known as the proboscis is situated at the

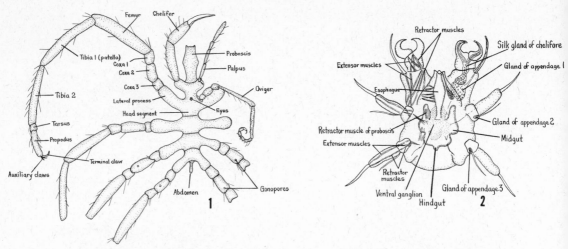

Plate 17-17   Morphology of adult and larval Pycnogonida. 1. Adult *Nymphon* (Nymphonidae), showing principal external features. **2.** Protonymphon of *Ammothea echinata* (Ammotheidae), showing muscles (left), digestive and nervous system (center), and glands (right). (Modified after Helfer and Schlottke, 1935.)

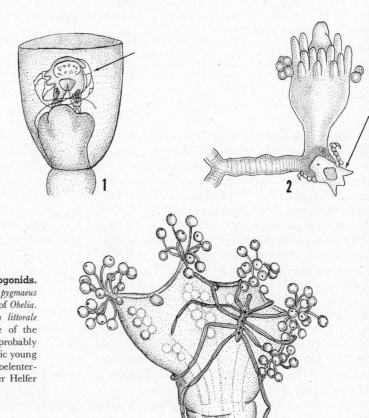

Plate 17-18   Some parasitic pycnogonids.
1. Protonymphon larva of *Anoplodactylus pygmaeus* (Phoxichilidiidae) attached to hydranth of *Obelia.*
2. Protonymphon larva of *Pycnogonum littorale* (Pycnogonidae) attached to the base of the hydrozoan coelenterate *Clava multicornis,* probably in process of penetrating. **3.** Ectoparasitic young adult of *Phoxichilidium femoratum* on the coelenterate *Lucernaria.* (All figures redrawn after Helfer and Schlottke, 1935.)

anterior end of the head segment. The suctorial mouth is located at the anterior tip of the proboscis.

There are usually three or four pairs of jointed appendages on the head segment—the pincer-like chelifers, palpi, ovigers, and the first pair of walking legs. In addition, a dorsal tubercle containing four simple eyes is located on the head segment. In certain species, either the chelifers and/or palpi are lacking.

The thorax is composed of three or four segments, which may or may not be fused, depending on the species. Generally, there are three pairs of long, jointed, walking legs attached to the thorax. In some species, an additional one or two pairs of thoracic walking legs are present. The walking legs are either eight- or nine-jointed.

The pycnogonids are dioecious and oviparous. The eggs are released in a ball-like mass, and the adult males, using their ten-jointed ovigers, carry the eggs. Ovigers are absent on the females of certain genera. Development is either direct or indirect. In indirect development, a four-legged larval stage, known as a protonymphon, occurs (Plate 17–17, Fig. 2).

All of the some 500 species of pycnogonids are marine, inhabiting areas from the littoral zone to those of more than 12,000 feet altitude. Pycnogonids are found in all seas except the inner Baltic and Caspian, and they are especially common in the polar seas. The majority of the adults are free-living, preying upon various coelenterates and other soft-bodied animals. Some pycnogonids are ectoparasitic on sea anemones.

For a detailed account of these animals, the monograph of Helfer and Schlottke (1935) is recommended to those who can read German. In addition, Hedgpeth's account (1954) of the phylogeny of the Pycnogonida is recommended.

Interest in pycnogonids is exhibited by marine parasitologists because the protonymphon larvae and juveniles of almost all the species are parasitic in or on hydroids, anemones, nudibranch and bivalve molluscs, ectoprocts, annelids, poriferans, brachiopods, echinoderms, octocorals, and ascidians (Plate 17–18, Figs. 1–3). A few species are even known to parasitize algae. In Table 17–1 some of the parasitic pycnogonids and their hosts are listed.

The physiological aspects of the relationships between larval and juvenile pycnogonids and their hosts are not known. The protonymphons, however, do possess a number of specialized glands that produce materials for attaching to, or for invading, their hosts (Plate 17–17, Fig. 2). There is no doubt that the relationships are obligatory and parasitic. Since most of the intertidal species spend their lives in association with some coelenterate as encysted, parasitic larvae or juveniles, studies on these are practical and should be forthcoming.

CLASSIFICATION

The living pycnogonids are divided into eight families. The fossil of a Devonian genus, *Palaeopantopus,* is known. Since the morphology of the parasitic larvae of the various species is still insufficiently known, the familial designations are based almost entirely on adult characteristics. A diagnosis of the eight pycnogonid families follows.

Family Nymphonidae.   Chelifers are present. Palpi are five-jointed. Ten-jointed ovigers are present on both males and females. Family includes one polymerous (that is, with many thoracic segments) genus–*Pentanymphon.*

Family Callipallenidae.   Chelifers are present. Palpi are lacking or reduced. Ten-jointed ovigers are present on both males and females.

Family Phoxichilidiidae.   Chelifers are present. Palpi are lacking. Five- to nine-jointed ovigers are present on males only.

Family Endeidae.   Chelifers and palpi are absent. Seven-jointed ovigers are present on males only. Family includes only one genus—*Endeis.*

Family Ammotheidae.   Chelifers are usually small and achelate. Palpi are well developed and comprised of four to ten joints. Nine- to ten-jointed ovigers are present on both males and females.

Family Austrodecidae.   Chelifers are absent. Palpi are composed of five to six joints. Ovigers of four to seven joints are present on both males and females. Family includes only one genus—*Austrodeus.*

Family Colossendeidae.   Chelifers are absent except on a few polymerous species. Palpi are long and composed of nine to ten joints. Ovigers are ten-jointed and present on both males and females. Family includes mostly deep-water forms with large proboscides, and includes four genera—*Pentacolossendeis, Colossendeis, Decolopoda,* and *Dodecolopoda.*

Table 17-1. Some Parasitic Pycnogonids and Their Hosts

Pycnogonid Species	Host	Phylum to Which Host Belongs	Authority
Phoxichilidiidae			
Phoxichilidium femoratum	*Clava* sp.	Coelenterata	Prell (1910)
	Bougainvillia ramosa	Coelenterata	Hallez (1905)
	Eudendrium ramosum	Coelenterata	Cole (1906)
	Coryne eximia	Coelenterata	Dogiel (1913)
	Synconyne eximia	Coelenterata	Allmann (1859)
	Tubularia larynx	Coelenterata	Loman (1907)
	Campanularia sp.	Coelenterata	Prell (1910)
	Lucernaria sp.	Coelenterata	Prell (1910)
	Crisia sp.	Ectoprocta	Prell (1910)
P. coccineum	*Bougainvillia ramosa*	Coelenterata	Allmann (1872)
	Synconyne eximia	Coelenterata	Allmann (1859)
Anoplodactylus lentus	*Eudendrium* sp.	Coelenterata	Cole (1901)
A. petiolatus	*Hydractinia echinata*	Coelenterata	Semper (1874)
	Coryne eximia	Coelenterata	Dogiel (1913)
	Stomoca dinema	Coelenterata	Lebour (1916)
	Phialidium hemisphaericum	Coelenterata	Lebour (1916)
	Obelia sp.	Coelenterata	Lebour (1916)
	Cosmetira pilosella	Coelenterata	Lebour (1916)
	"bryozoan"	Ectoprocta	Helfer (1909)
	"ascidian"	Chordata	Helfer (1909)
A. erectus	*Tubularia crocea*	Coelenterata	Dogiel (1913)
	Sertularia pumila	Coelenterata	Schlottke (1932)
A. insignis bermudiensis	*Obelia marginata*	Coelenterata	Cole (1904)
Phoxichilus spinosus	*Obelia* sp.	Coelenterata	Dogiel (1913)
	Dendrophyllia sp.	Coelenterata	Loman (1928)
	"bryozoan"	Ectoprocta	Loman (1928)
	Antedon sp.	Echinodermata	Loman (1928)
	*Laminaria**	Thallophyta (Phaeophyceae)	Dogiel (1913)
Halosoma exigua	*Podocoryne carnea*	Coelenterata	Dohrn (1881)
	Turris pileata	Coelenterata	Lebour (1916)
H. haswelli	*Brachyodontes hirsutus*	Mollusca	Flynn (1918)
Pycnosoma strongylocentroti	*Strongylocentrotus* sp.	Echinodermata	Losina O'Losinsky
Ammotheidae			
Ammothea laevis	*Obelia* sp.	Coelenterata	Dogiel (1913)
A. echinata	*Dentrophyllia* sp.	Coelenterata	Loman (1925)
A. alaskensis	*Thuiaria* sp.	Coelenterata	Cole (1910)
Ammothea sp.	*Armina variolosa*	Mollusca	Oshima (1933)
Ammothella biunguiculata	*Cucumaria frondosa*	Echinodermata	Prell (1910)
	Stichopus japonicus	Echinodermata	Oshima (1927)
Ascorhynchus arenicola	*Serialaria* sp.	Ectoprocta	Dohrn (1881)

(Data from Helfer and Schlottke, 1935. References to authorities cited can be found in Helfer and Schlottke's monograph.)

Table 17–1 continued

Pycnogonid Species	Host	Phylum to Which Host Belongs	Authority
Nymphoriidae			
Nymphon rubrum	*Clava* sp.	Coelenterata	Schlottke (1933)
	Coryne pusilla	Coelenterata	Schlottke (1932)
	Obelia geniculata	Coelenterata	Schlottke (1932)
	Demospongiae	Porifera	Hoek (1877)
N. leptocheles	*Campanularia* sp.	Coelenterata	Prell (1910)
N. strömi	*Campanulina* sp.	Coelenterata	Dogiel (1913)
N. parasiticum (=N. gracile?)	*Tethys leporina*	Mollusca	Oshima (1933)
N. tapetis	*Venus jedoënsis*	Mollusca	Oshima (1933)
N. brevirostre	*Laminaria**	Thyllophyta (Phaeophyceae)	Appellöf (1916)
N. brevicaudatum	"seaweed"		Helfer and Schlottke (1935)
N. longitarse	*Lithothamnion†*	Thallophyta (Rhodophyceae)	Appellöf (1916)
Nymphon sp.	*Lafoea*	Coelenterata	Prell (1910)
Nymphonella tapetis	*Tapes philippinarum*	Mollusca	Oshima (1927)
Pentanymphon antarcticum	Demospongiae	Porifera	Hodge (1904)
Boreonymphon robustum	*Umbellula encrinus*	Coelenterata	Stephensen (1933)
	Actiniaria sp.	Coelenterata	Stephensen (1933)
	Eunephthya sp.	Coelenterata	Stephensen (1933)
	Virgularia sp.	Coelenterata	Stephensen (1933)
Colossendeidae			
Decolopoda australis	*Tubularia* sp.	Coelenterata	Hodgson (1927)
	"brachiopod"	Brachiopoda	Gordon (1932)
D. antarctica	"brachiopod"	Brachiopoda	Gordon (1932)
Endeidae			
Endeis sp.	*Obelia dichotoma*	Coelenterata	Cole (1910)
Pycnogonidae			
Pycnogonum littorale	*Clava multicornis*	Coelenterata	Dogiel (1913)
	Urticina crassicornis	Coelenterata	Prell (1910)
	Metridium sp.	Coelenterata	Prell (1910)
	Tealia sp.	Coelenterata	Sars (1881)
	"sea anemone"	Coelenterata	Hilton (1915)
	Sabellaria sp.	Annelida	Schlottke (1932)
P. stearsi	"sea anemone"	Coelenterata	Ives (1893)

*Brown alga
†Red alga

LITERATURE CITED

Baffoni, G. M. 1948. La castrazione parassitaria da *Ione thoracica* (Montagu) e da *Parthenopea subterranea* Kossmann in *Callianassa laticauda* Otto. Arch. Oceanogr. Limnol., *5:* 1–14.

Beaumont, A. 1949. Contribution à l'étude du métabolisme de l'hemoglobine de *Gasterophilus intestinalis*. Compt. Rend. Soc. Biol., *142:* 1369–1371.

Boschma, H. 1937. The species of the genus *Sacculina* (Crustacea Rhizocephala). Zool. Mededel. Rijksmus. Nat. Hist. Leiden, *19:* 187–328.

Caullery, M. 1952. *Parasitism* and *Symbiosis*. Sidgwick & Jackson, London.

Causey, D. 1957. Parasitic copepoda from Louisiana freshwater fish. Am. Midl. Nat., *58:* 378–382.

Christensen, A. M., and J. J. McDermott. 1958. Life-history and biology of the oyster crab, *Pinnotheres astreum* Say. Biol. Bull., *114:* 146–179.

Day, J. H. 1935. The life-history of *Sacculina*. Quart. J. Micro. Sci., *77:* 549–583.

Dinulescu, G. 1932. Recherches sur la biologie des gastrophiles. Anatomie, physiologie, cycle évolutif. Ann. Sci. Nat. Zool., *15:* 1–43.

Drilhon, A. 1936. Quelques constantes chimiques et physico-chimiques du milieu intérieur de crabe Sacculine (*Carcinus moenas*). Compt. Rend Acad. Sci., Paris, *202:* 981–992.

Fasten, N. 1919. Morphology and attached stages of first copepodid larva of *Salmincola edwardsii* (Olsson) Wilson. Publ. Puget Sound Biol. Sta. Univ. Wash., *2:* 153–181.

Fox, H. M. 1945. Haemoglobin in blood sucking parasites. Nature, *156:* 475.

Fox, H. M. 1953. Haemoglobin and biliverdin in parasitic cirripede Crustacea. Nature, *171:* 162. (Also see Animal Biochromes and Structural Colours. Cambridge University Press, London.

Fox, H. M. 1957. Haemoglobin in Crustacea. Nature, *179:* 148.

Foxon, G. E. H. 1940. Notes on the life history of *Sacculina carcini* Thompson. J. Marine Biol. Assoc. U. K., *24:* 253–264.

Giard, A., and J. Bonnier. 1887. Contributions à l'étude des Bopyriens. Trav. Inst. Zool. Lille, *5:* 1–151.

Giard, A., and J. Bonnier. 1893. Contributions à l'étude des Epicarides. Bull. Sci. France Belgique, *25:* 415–493.

Goldschmidt, R. B. 1923. The Mechanism and Physiology of Sex Determination. (Transl. by W. J. Dakin). Methuen, London.

Green, J. 1950. Habits of the marine tardigrade, *Echiniscoides sigismundi*. Nature, *166:* 153–154.

Haley, A. J., and H. E. Winn. 1959. Observations on a lernaean parasite of freshwater fishes. Trans. Am. Fish. Soc., *88:* 128–129.

Harding, J. P. 1950. On some species of *Lernaea* (Crustacea, Copepoda: parasites of freshwater fish). Bull. Brit. Mus. (Nat. Hist.) Zool., *1:* 1–27.

Haven, D. 1959. Effects of pea crabs *Pinnotheres astreäm* on oysters *Crassostrea virginica*. Proc. Nat. Shellfish Assoc., *49:* 77–86.

Hedgpeth, J. W. 1954. On the phylogeny of the Pycnogonida. Acta Zool., *35:* 193–213.

Helfer, H., and E. Schlottke. 1935. Pantopoda. *In* Bronns' Klassen und Ordnungen des Tierreichs. Vol. 5, Part 4, Book 2. Akademische Verlagsgesellschaft, Leipzig.

Ichikawa, A., and R. Yanagimachi. 1958. Studies on the sexual organization of the Rhizocephala. I. The nature of the "testes" of *Peltogasterella socialis* Kruger. Annot. Zool. Japan., *31:* 82–96.

Levenbrook, L. 1950. The composition of horse bot fly (*Gasterophilus intestinalis*) larva blood. Biochem. J., *47:* 336–346.

Lévy, R. 1923. Sur la toxicité des tissus de la Sacculine (*Sacculina carcini*) vis-à-vis du crabe (*Carcinus moenas*) et sur la recherche de réactions d'immunité chez ce dernier. Bull. Soc. Zool. France, *48:* 291–294.

Lutken, C. F. 1873. Bidrag til Kundskab om Asterne af Slaegten *Cyamus* Latr. elle Hvallusene. K. Dansk Vidensk. Selsk., *10:* 231–284.

Marcus, E. 1929. Tardigrada. *In* Bronns' Klassen und Ordnungen des Tierreichs. Vol. 5, Part 4, Book 3. Akademische Verlagsgesellschaft, Leipzig.

Marshall, S. M., and A. P. Orr. 1955. The Biology of A Marine Copepod. Oliver & Boyd, Edinburgh.

Panikkar, N. K., and N. G. Sproston. 1941. Osmotic relations of some metazoan parasites. Parasitology, *33:* 214–223.

Pennak, R. W. 1953. Fresh-water Invertebrates of the United States. Ronald Press, New York.

Perez, C. 1933. Processus de résorption phagocytaire des oocytes dans l'ovaire chez les Macropodia sacculinées. Compt. Rend. Soc. Biol., *112:* 1049–1051.

Reinhard, E. G. 1949. Experiments on the determination and differentiation of sex in the bopyrid *Stegophryxus hyptius* Thompson. Biol. Bull., *96:* 17–31.

Reinhard, E. G. 1956. Parasitic castration of Crustacea. Exptl. Parasit., *5:* 79–107.

Reinhard, E. G., and T. von Brand. 1944. The fat content of *Pagurus* parasitized by *Peltogaster* and its relation to theories of sacculinization. Physiol. Zool., *17:* 31–41.

Reverberi, G. 1947. Ancora sulle trasformazione sperimentale del sesso nei Bopiridi. La trasformazione delle femmine giovanili in maschi. Publ. Staz. Zool. Napoli, *21:* 81–91.

Reverberi, G., and M. Pitotti. 1942. II ciclo biologica e la determinazione fenotipica del sesso di *Ione thoracica* Montagu, Bopiride parassito de *Callianassa laticauda* Otto. Publ. Staz. Zool. Napoli, *19:* 111–184.

Richards, A. G. 1951. The Integument of Arthropods. University of Minnesota Press, Minneapolis.

Robson, G. C. 1911. The effect of *Sacculina* upon the fat metabolism of its host. Quart. J. Micro. Sci., *57:* 267–278.

Smith, G. W. 1906. Rhizocephala. *In* Fauna und Flora des Golfes von Neapel. Monographie, *21:* 1–123.

Smith, G. W. 1913. Studies in the experimental analysis of sex. Part 10. The effect of *Sacculina* upon the storage of fat and glycogen, and on the formation of pigment by its host. Quart. J. Micro. Sci., *59:* 267–295.

Smith R. F. 1949. Notes on *Ergasilus* parasites from the New Brunswick, New Jersey, area, with a check list of all species and hosts east of the Mississippi River. Zoologica, *34:* 127–182.

Stauber, L. A. 1945. *Pinnotheres ostreum,* parasitic on the American oyster, *Ostrea (Gryphaea) virginica*. Biol. Bull., *88:* 269–291.

Van den Berghe, L. 1933. Observations sur le sang et le péristaltisme alternatif de l'intestin chez les Lernées. Bull. Acad. Roy. Med. Belg., *19:* 821–836.

von Kemnitz, G. A. H. 1916. Untersuchungen über den Stoff bestand und Stoffwechsel der Larven von *Gasterophilus equi* (Clark), nebst Bemerkungen über den Stoffbestand der Larven von *Chironomus* (spec. ?) L. (Physiologischer Teil). Ztschr. Biol., *49:* 129–244.

Waterman, T. H. (ed.). 1960. The Physiology of Crustacea. Vol. I. Metabolism and Growth. Academic Press, New York.

Waterman, T. H. (ed.). 1961. The Physiology of Crustacea. Vol. II. Academic Press, New York.

Wigglesworth, V. B. 1939. The Principles of Insect Physiology. E. P. Dutton, New York.

Wigglesworth, V. B. 1954. The Physiology of Insect Metamorphosis. Cambridge University Press, London.

Wilson, C. B. 1915. North American parasitic copepods belonging to the Lernaeopodidae, with a revision of the entire family. Proc. U. S. Nat. Mus., *47:* 565–729.

Yamaguti, S. 1963. Parasitic Copepoda and Brachiura of Fishes. John Wiley, New York.

SUGGESTED READINGS

Crustacea in General

Snodgrass, R. E. 1956. Crustacean Metamorphoses. Smithsonian Misc. Collect., *131:* 1–78. (This excellent review of the development and metamorphosis of crustaceans includes many parasitic representatives. The author has discussed in detail the morphology, factors influencing metamorphosis, and evolutionary significances of these crustaceans as only a man of his experience can do.)

Copepoda

Baer, J. B. 1952. Copepoda. *In* Ecology of Animal Parasites. University of Illinois Press, Urbana, pp. 46–59. (This section in Baer's book deals with the parasitic copepods. The information on life cycles, metamorphosis, and ecology are of particular interest.)

Pennak, R. W. 1953. Copepoda. *In* Fresh-water Invertebrates of the United States. Ronald Press, New York, pp. 383–409. (This is a general discussion of the copepods, free-living as well as parasitic. The information on the anatomy of copepods and the taxonomic keys provided are particularly useful.)

Wilson, R. W. 1953. Branchiura and parasitic copepoda. *In* Freshwater Biology (W. T. Edmondson, ed.). 2nd Ed., John Wiley, New York, pp. 862–868. (This relatively short article is concerned primarily with the parasitic copepods of North America. The references cited are particularly useful.)

Cirripedia

Baer, J. B. 1952. Cirripedia. *In* Ecology of Animal Parasites. University of Illinois Press, Urbana, pp. 59–65. (This section in Baer's book deals with the cirripeds. The information on morphology and ecology is of particular interest.)

Caullery, M. 1952. Parasitism and Symbiosis. Sidgwick & Jackson, London, pp. 33–34. (This section in Caullery's monograph deals with the Cirripedia. The information on morphology and the references listed are of particular interest.)

Reinhard, E. G. 1956. Parasitic castration of Crustacea. Exptl. Parasit., *5:* 79–107. (This is a review article in which the author has summarized and analyzed knowledge up to that time concerning crustacean-caused parasitic castration. Not only is the text informative, but the literature cited is of great value.)

Malacostraca

Baer, J. B. 1952. Isopoda and Amphipoda. *In* Ecology of Animal Parasites. University of Illinois Press, Urbana, pp. 65–72. (This section in Baer's book deals with the symbiotic Malacostraca.)

Caullery, M. 1952. Parasitism and Symbiosis. Sidgwick & Jackson, London, pp. 65–85. (The symbiotic Malacotraca are discussed in this section of Caullery's monograph.)

Tardigrada

Since only a few marine tardigrades have been reported as symbionts, no general account of these is yet available. However, the following accounts of the tardigrades in general should be of interest.

Marcus, E. 1959. Tardigrada. *In* Fresh-water Biology (W. T. Edmundson, ed.). 2nd Ed., Wiley, New York, pp. 508–521. (This short account is primarily concerned with the identification of the fresh-water species. However, the short sections devoted to morphology, especially the characteristics important in taxonomy, are useful.)

Pennak, R. W. 1953. Tardigrada (water bears). *In* Fresh-water Invertebrates of the United States. Ronald Press, New York, pp. 240–255. (This is also a general account of fresh-water tardigrades. The sections devoted to morphology, aspects of physiology, reproduction and growth, and collecting and preserving methods are useful.)

Pratt, H. S. 1935. Tardigrada. *In* Manual of the Common Invertebrate Animals. Blakiston, Philadelphia, pp. 534–536. (In this short account, the author describes the more commonly encountered fresh-water and marine tardigrades of North America.)

Shipley, A. E. 1904. Tardigrada. *In* The Cambridge Natural History. Vol. 4. Macmillan, London (reprinted in 1958 by Hafner, New York), pp. 477–487. (Although the taxonomy included in this article is outdated, the general discussion of morphology, development, and aspects of the biology of tardigrades is useful.)

Pycnogonida

Pratt, H. S. 1935. Pycnogonida. *In* Manual of the Common Invertebrate Animals. Blakiston, Philadelphia, pp. 536–538. (This is a short account of the more commonly encountered pycnogonids in North American marine waters.)

Thompson, D. W. 1909. Pycnogonida. *In* The Cambridge Natural History. Vol. 4. Macmillan, London (reprinted in 1958 by Hafner, New York), pp. 501–542. (In this general account of the Pycnogonida, the celebrated zoologist D'Arcy Thompson has reviewed the morphology, development, habits, and systematics of the group. Since relatively little has been done with this group, except for the descriptions of additional species, Thompson's account is surprisingly up-to-date.)

18

INTRODUCTION TO THE ACARINA THE IXODIDES—
The Ticks

The arthropod class Arachnoidea includes twelve orders composed of such familiar forms as scorpions, spiders, king crabs, pseudoscorpions, ticks, and mites. The ticks and mites comprise the order Acarina. All these animals are characterized by mouthparts consisting of pedipalps and chelicerae, and the absence of antennae and mandibles. Many of these animals are predaceous and are found in terrestrial and aquatic (both fresh and salt water) ecological niches. However, all ticks and a number of the mites are parasitic, mostly living on animals, both vertebrates and invertebrates. Occasionally they are found within their hosts. A number of species of mites are parasitic on plants.

The interest of parasitologists in ticks and mites stems from three avenues of investigation —that concerned with the parasitic habits of acarinas, that concerned with the role of acarinas in the transmission of microorganisms (that is, their roles as vectors), and that concerned with their role as intermediate hosts of

certain helminths (for example, anoplocephalid cestodes). To illustrate the first point, many dog owners are familiar with the skin mites that cause mange, and certain unfortunate individuals may have had first hand experience with the human-infesting itch mites. The role of ticks as vectors of rickettsial, spirochaete, and other pathogenic microorganisms is well known. One of the most feared tick-borne rickettsial diseases in the United States is Rocky Mountain spotted fever, which is transmitted from rabbits to man by *Dermacentor venustus* (=*D. andersoni*) and related species. A list of tick-borne diseases and their causative agents is given in Table 18–1.

Ticks and mites are both members of the order Acarina. Ticks are placed in the suborder Ixodides. They are characterized by a leathery integument; their larger size (when compared with mites); a more prominent gnathosoma, or capitulum—a structure formed from the fusion of the mouthparts and the basis

Table 18-1. Major Tick-borne Diseases, Their Etiological Agents, and Distribution

Disease	Etiological Agent	Tick Vector	Endemic Area
Texas cattle fever (bovine piroplasmosis, babesiosis, red water fever)	*Babesia bigemina*	*Boophilus annulatus* B. microplus	United States Southern Florida, Mexico, Central America, South America, Orient, Australia, parts of Africa
		B. decoloratus	Africa
		Rhipicephalus spp.	Africa
		Haemaphysalis punctata	Europe
Equine piroplasmosis	*Babesia caballi*	*Dermacentor* (3 spp.) *Hyalomma* (4 spp.) *Rhipicephalus* (2 spp.)	Africa, USSR, Siberia
	Babesia equi	*Dermacentor* (2 spp.) *Hyalomma* (4 spp.) *Rhipicephalus* (3 spp.)	Eastern USSR, Italy, Africa, India, Brazil
Canine babesiosis	*Babesia canis*	*Rhipicephalus sanguineus*	Many parts of the world
		Hyalomma marginatum	Russia
		Haemaphysalis leachii	South Africa
		Dermacentor reticulatus	Southern Europe
		Ixodes ricinus	Southern Europe
		Dermacentor venustus	(experimental)
East Coast fever	*Theileria parva*	*Rhipicephalus appendiculatus* R. capensis R. evertsi	Eastern, central, and southern Africa
Bovine anaplasmosis	*Anaplasma marginale*	*Boophilus annulatus* B. decoloratus B. microplus Rhipicephalus simus R. bursa R. sanguineus Ixodes ricinus Hyalomma lusitanicum Dermacentor variabilis D. andersoni D. occidentalis	Worldwide
Rocky Mountain spotted fever	*Rickettsia rickettsi*	*Dermacentor venustus* D. variabilis D. parumapertus D. albipictus D. occidentalis* Amblyomma americanum A. cajennense* Rhipicephalus sanguineus* Ornithodoros* Otobius*	United States, parts of Canada, Mexico, parts of South America

*Possible vectors.

†The various types of spirochaetes which cause relapsing fever are considered by some to be strains of *Borrelia recurrentis*.

Table 18-1 continued

Disease	Etiological Agent	Tick Vector	Endemic Area
Tick-borne typhus	*Rickettsia conorii*	*Rhipicephalus sanguineus* other spp. of *Rhipicephalus* *Amblyomma* spp. *Haemaphysalis* spp. *Hyalomma*	Area bounding the Mediterranean, other parts of Africa
Queensland tick typhus	*Rickettsia australis*	*Ixodes holocyclus*	Australia
Q fever (nine-mile fever)	*Coxiella burnetii*	*Dermacentor venustus* *Amblyomma americanum* *Haemaphysalis humerosa** *Ixodes holocyclus**	Worldwide Australia
Colorado tick fever	virus	*Dermacentor venustus* *D. parumapertus**	Western United States
Tick-borne hemorrhagic fever	viruses	*Hyalomma plumbeum* *H. anatolicum* *Dermacentor pictus* *D. marginatus*	USSR, Asia Minor, southeastern Europe
Tick-borne encephalitides	viruses	*Ixodes ricinus* (western Europe) *I. persulcatus* (eastern Europe) *Dermacentor* spp.* *Haemaphysalis* spp.*	Europe, Asia, Great Britain
Tularemia	*Pasteurella tularensis*	*Dermacentor venustus* *D. occidentalis* *D. variabilis* *Rhipicephalus sanguineus* *Amblyomma americanum* *Haemaphysalis leporispalustris* *Ixodes pacificus**	Western United States
Tick-borne relapsing fever	*Borrelia duttoni*† *B. venezuelense* *B. hispanica* *B. persica* *B. neotropicales* *B. turicatae* *B. hermsi* *B. parkeri* *Borrelia* sp.	*Ornithodoros moubata* *O. rudis* *O. erraticus* *O. talaje* *O. turicata* *O. hermsi* *O. parkeri* *O. tholozani*	Africa (central) Panama, Colombia, Venezuela, Ecuador Spain, Portugal, North Africa Panama Texas Rocky Mountain and Pacific Coast Rocky Mountain and Pacific Coast Central Asia
Avian spirochetosis	*Borrelia anserina*	*Argas persicus*	India, Australia, Brazil, Egypt, eastern Asia Minor

capitulum—in many species; a piercing hypostome with recurved teeth; lateral teeth on the movable digits of the chelicerae; a pitlike sensory organ, Haller's organ, on tarsus I; lateral stigmata without sinuous peritremes; and other minor diagnostic features.

The mites, according to the systematic interpretation of Baker and Wharton (1952), are divided among four suborders—Onychopalpida, Mesostigmata, Trombidiformes, and Sarcoptiformes. The mites are characterized by a minute size (barely visible to the naked eye); possession of one or more pairs of simple eyes, although many lack eyes; transparent or semitransparent bodies, although the Oribatei are quite opaque; a less conspicuous gnathosoma in most cases; more conspicuous, long, sensory setae and related structures on the exoskeleton; and other minor dignostic features.

MORPHOLOGY OF THE ACARINA

The body of ticks is segmented, but the segments are not readily visible. The body is more conspicuously divided into two regions: (1) the gnathosoma, sometimes referred to as the capitulum, which is the small portion that projects anteriad or anteroventrad and that bears the mouthparts (Plate 18–1, Fig. 1); and (2) the body proper. The gnathosoma is not a true head, although it is commonly referred to as such. It consists of the mouthparts and a basal chitinous segment known as the basis capitulum. This ringlike segment connects the anterior portions of the gnathosoma to the body proper. The mouthparts, which are located on the gnathosoma, include three types of structures.

(1) The elongate hypostome is usually toothed and is medially located, ventrad to the mouth. Its free end projects anteriorly.

(2) A pair of chelicerae are located on the dorsolateral surfaces of the hypostome, on each side of the mouth. Each chelicera is encased within a sheath that is directly connected with the basis capitulum. Each chelicera is typically divided into three segments, although the divisions are obscure. The free terminal of each chelicera is forked (chelate), giving rise to a fixed dorsal toothed digit—the digitus externus—and a lateral movable digitus internus. The teeth are located on the outer surfaces of each chelicera (Plate 18–1, Fig. 2). This pair of appendages function as piercing and tearing structures, by means of which the host's integument is opened and the entire gnathosoma,

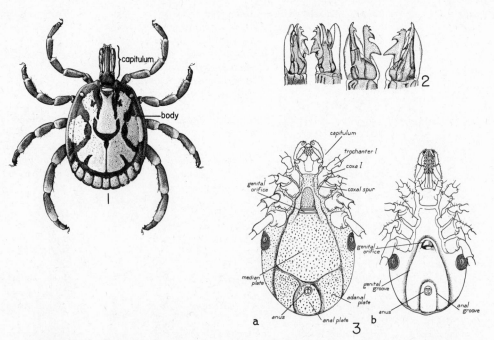

Plate 18-1   **Tick morphology.** **1.** Dorsal view of male *Amblyomma hebraeum,* showing two main regions of body. (After Whittick, 1943.) **2.** The chelicerae of *Ixodes reduvius.* Left, dorsal and ventral views of male. Right, dorsal and ventral views of female. (After Vitzthum, 1940.) **3.** *Ixodes ricinus.* **a.** Ventral view of male. **b.** Ventral view of female. (After Whittick in Smart, 1943.)

or at least the toothed hypostome, is inserted into the host. These appendages also act as anchors when the parasite is attached.

(3) A pair of palpi or pedipalps arise from the anteroventral margins of the basis capitulum. In modern ticks, each pedipalp is divided into four segments.* Among the argasid ticks, the pedipalps are flexible and not intimately associated with the hypostome. However, among the ixodid species, these palps are rigid and are intimately associated with the hypostome. Furthermore, the fourth segment is reduced and located in a pit on the ventral surface of the third segment in ixodid ticks. The function of the pedipalps is to act as counteranchors while the tick is attached to the host.

When seen from the dorsal aspect, the body proper of argasid ticks is covered with a leathery integument. This cuticle is ornamented with granulations, tubercles, and in some even circular discs. These secondary structures are quite consistent within a species and are therefore of taxonomic importance.

There is no shield (or scutum) on the dorsum of the argasid species, but among the ixodid ticks, a shieldlike scutum covers the entire dorsal surface of the body in the males and only an anteromedial portion in the females. The scutum serves primarily as a protective structure but is also a limiting one. The male ixodid ticks cannot become bloated with blood while feeding, because the nonelastic scutum holds its shape. On the other hand, females, which only possess a small scutum, can and do become greatly distended while engorging blood.

In some ticks, such as *Dermacentor* and *Amblyomma,* the scutum is decorated with silvery streaks. Such ticks are said to be ornate. The sculptures, furrows, and color patterns found on the dorsal body surface of some ticks are of taxonomic importance. The posterior and posterolateral margins of the dorsum of certain male ticks bear undulations known as festoons. Festoons are rarely found on females.

All ticks, like most mites, possess three pairs of legs as larvae, and a fourth pair appears after the larva molts. The nymphs and adults characteristically bear four pairs of legs. Each leg is subdivided into six segments—the coxa, trochanter, femur, genu, tibia, and tarsus. The coxa is the most proximal segment. In some species, some of these units are fused; thus, their number is reduced. The legs characteristically terminate in a pair of claws on the tarsi. In some, such as members of the Ixodides, a semitransparent sucker-like caruncle, or pulvillus, is found on each tarsus.

When the ventral aspect of the tick is examined, the genital pore can be seen located at the angle formed by the two genital grooves, if these are present (Plate 18–1, Fig. 3). If the grooves are absent, the genital pore is still in the same location—that is, on the midventral line between the first and second pairs of legs. The anus is also ventrally located on the midventral line, approximately equidistant from the level of the fourth pair of legs and the posterior margin of the body. In some species, such as *Dermacentor variabilis,* a post-anal groove is situated posterior to the anal orifice.

The respiratory (breathing) mechanism of adult ticks consist of tracheae that branch into tracheoles. This array of tubes infiltrate, oxygenate, and remove carbon dioxide from the various areas of the body. The main tracheae open to the exterior through two spiracles (also known as stigmata) located laterally near the coxae of the fourth pair of legs in adults. Larval forms may have more than two spiracles.

Body Wall

The cuticle of ticks and mites, like that of insects, is subdivided into layers. Most acarologists prefer the terminology of Vitzthum (1943) in referring to the four strata (Plate 18–2, Fig. 1). (1) The tectostracum is the outermost, waxy and unstainable, nonpigmented thin layer. (2) The epiostracum is the second layer and is also rather thin. It is composed of polyphenol and cuticulin. (3) The ectostracum is the middle layer, is usually pigmented, and is stainable with acid dyes. (4) The hypostracum is the innermost layer. It is usually pigmented and stainable with alkaline dyes. These four layers of the cuticle are not always distinctly recognizable in all Acarina. It is again emphasized here that the body wall is not an inert body covering. It is a dynamic structure, intimately correlated with several of the primary physiological functions of the organism—respiration, sensation, and probably the absorption of certain chemical nutrients and excretion of wastes.

Underneath the cuticle is a layer of epithelial cells—the hypodermis—which is responsible for secretion of the cuticular layers. Various glands,

---

*According to Baker and Wharton (1952), the pedipalps of modern Acarina are divided into six or less segments. For a discussion of the evolution of these appendages, the reader is referred to that monograph.

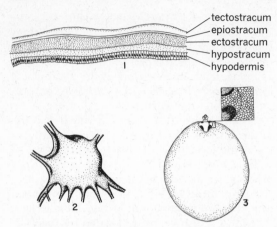

tectostracum
epiostracum
ectostracum
hypostracum
hypodermis

Plate 18-2   Tick anatomy. 1. Cross section of cuticle of a tick, showing the stratification. (Original.) **2.** Brain of a tick. (Modified after Blauvelt, 1945.) **3.** Dorsal view of *Nuttalliella namaqua* female, showing scutum and integument. (After Bedford, 1931.)

setae, pigment granules, and sense organs are derived from and associated with the hypodermis. Enlarged hypodermal cells in the form of unicellular glands that secrete onto the body surface are quite common among the ticks.

The various systems not previously mentioned in this chapter—that is, digestive, excretory, circulatory, nervous, and reproductive systems—are essentially the same in ticks and mites and are considered here as representative of both groups.

Digestive System

The alimentary canal of the Acarina can be subdivided into three portions: (1) The foregut, of stomadeal origin (ectodermal), consists of a muscular pharynx leading from the mouth into the tubular esophagus. (2) The midgut, or ventriculus, is entodermal in origin, is lined with digestive epithelium and has lateral diverticula or caeca (usually a pair) branching from it toward its posterior end. (3) The hindgut, of proctodeal origin (ectodermal), consists of the anterior thin-walled intestine and the posterior muscular rectum, which leads to the exterior through the anus. Baker and Wharton (1952) have classified the digestive system of the Acarina into three types* and consider these types to be of taxonomic importance.

*These three types are the mesostigmatid, having a small ventriculus and large diverticula, and characteristic of the Ixodides, Onychopalpida and Mesostigmata; the trombidiform, having a large ventriculus, bulbous diverticula, and hindgut modified to form an excretory organ, characteristic of the Trombidiformes; and the sarcoptiform, having a ventriculus larger than the diverticula, characteristic of the Sarcoptiformes.

Circulatory System

Although hearts are lacking in most acarinas, they are found in mites of the Holothyroidea and Mesostigmata. Circulation is accomplished by colorless blood that infiltrates the various tissues of the body. Blood cells in the form of amoeboid haemocytes are present, although they are not readily demonstrated except during quiescent stages before each molt.

Excretory System

The Acarina all possess at least two mechanisms for excretion. All members possess digestive epithelia, lining their ventriculi, that can perform the excretory function. The epithelial cells swell during digestion as the result of collecting excretory products that are later thrown back into the lumen and passed out posteriorly. The Acarina also possess one or more of three types of excretory apparati: (1) coxal glands, which are located adjacent to the coxae of certain legs and which empty to the exterior through pores located near the coxae; (2) entodermal excretory tubules, which collect the body wastes and empty into the hindgut; and (3) a modified hindgut that serves as an excretory vesicle. The suborders of Acarina and the types of excretory systems found in each are listed in Table 18-2.

Nervous System

The so-called brain of the Acarina is a large ganglionic mass formed from the fusion of large numbers of ganglia (Plate 18-2, Fig. 2). In larvae, the union of these ganglia is often not completed and individual ganglia can be recognized. The ganglionic mass is located around the esophagus. Various nerve cords arise from this mass. Those innervating the eyes (if present), pedipalps, and chelicerae originate from the portion of the brain dorsal to the esophagus. Those innervating the pharynx, legs, and internal organs originate from the ventral portion of the mass.

Certain sensory structures are found on the body surfaces of ticks and mites. The most common of these are the setae, which are hairlike projections from the sclerotized integument. The setae are located on the body proper, as well as on the various appendages. Certain specialized setae, known as sensillae, are located on certain mites in the area of the propodosoma in a segmental notch, approximately at the posterior limit of the upper third of the body proper. The notch may or may not be clearly visible. Each sensilla is rooted in a cuticular depression, the pseudostigma. The function of

Table 18-2.   The Excretory Systems Found in the Suborders of Acarina

Digestive-excretory Epithelium	Coxal Glands	Excretory Tubules	Modified Hindgut
Onychopalpida	Mesostigmata	Mesostigmata	Trombidiformes
Mesostigmata	Some Trombidiformes	Sarcoptiformes	
Trombidiformes	Some Sarcoptiformes (Oribatei)	Ixodides	
Sarcoptiformes		Onychopalpida	
Ixodides	Ixodides *(Ornithodoros)*		

such setae is presumably sensory since they are innervated.

Eyes are possessed by certain mites and a few ticks. Some acarina eyes are rather complex, although they are definitely ocelli rather than compound eyes. The simpler eyes consists of no more than a differentiated portion of the integument—the lens—and a few brown-black pigment granules that are connected to nerve fibers. In many eyeless mites, thin transparent photosensitive areas are dorsally situated.

Reproductive System

The Acarina are all dioecious. Fertilization is always internal—that is, the spermatozoa are introduced into the female. The mites, as a rule, produce a few eggs at a time, while the ticks produce numerous eggs.

The male reproductive system consists of a single testis or a pair of testes. Vasa defferentia conduct the spermatozoa from the testes into the ejaculatory duct, through which the spermatozoa are introduced into the female through the penis. Usually an accessory gland or glands feed into the vasa defferentia.

The female reproductive system includes a single or a pair of ovaries. Leading from each ovary is an oviduct, which in turn opens into the uterus. In most instances, the uterus opens to the exterior through the genital pore. During copulation, the spermatozoa are introduced into the uterus; however, in some mites, a vagina is present. A seminal receptacle and accessory glands usually are connected to the uterus. The seminal receptacle not only serves as a storage site for spermatozoa, but in most instances, is also the site where male gametes mature (sperm are not mature when they are first introduced into the female). The Acarina are either oviparous or ovoviviparous. The eggs are normally covered by a shell.

Secondary sex characteristics are found in some species. Modified chelicerae on male members of the suborder Mesostigmata help transfer sperm into the female, since peni are wanting. Many males possess modified legs (one or more pairs) that are used to grasp the female during copulation.

The genital pore of the male and the female is located between the first and second pairs of legs. The orifice is commonly covered by a genital plate.

SUBORDER IXODIDES

Members of the Ixodides, or ticks, are all parasitic and are found on all vertebrates above the fishes. As ectoparasites, they feed on the blood and lymph of their hosts.

SYSTEMATICS AND BIOLOGY

CLASSIFICATION

The taxonomy of the Ixodides has been reviewed by Nuttall et al. (1908), Nuttall and Warburton (1911), Cooley and Kohls (1944), and Baker and Wharton (1952). The volume by Baker and Wharton is especially recommended as an introduction to the subfield of Acarology. The Ixodides is subdivided into three families. A brief diagnosis of each family follows.

Family 1. Argasidae (soft-bodied ticks). Integument is leathery in nymphal and adult stages, and wrinkled, granulated, mammillated or with tubercles. Scutum is absent in all stages. Gnathosoma is either subterminal or protruding from anterior margin of body in nymphs and adults, and is subterminal or terminal in larvae. Gnathosoma lies in a distinctly or indistinctly marked depression—the camerostome— in all stages. Pedipalps freely articulate in all stages. Porose areas are absent in both sexes. Eyes are absent, or if present, are found on supracoxal folds. Stigmata near coxa III lack stigmal plates. Both sexes are distended when engorged with blood. Sexual dimorphism is slight.

Family 2.   Ixodidae (hard-bodied ticks).   Body is ovoid. Scutum is present in all stages. Scutum of adult male extends to posterior margin of body; that of adult female, like that of larvae and nymphs, is restricted to propodosomal zone. Gnathosoma is anterior and visible from dorsal view. Festoons are usually present. Eyes, if present, are located dorsally on sides of scutum. Segments of pedipalps are fused, not movable. Porose areas present on base of gnathosoma in females. Stigmatal plates are large, posterior to coxa IV. Only females distend when engorged with blood. Marked sexual dimorphism is exhibited.

Family 3. Nuttalliellidae.   Only one species, free-living under stones (parasitic habits not known). Scutum is leathery, similar to leathery integument that covers rest of body (Plate 18–2, Fig. 3). Integument has papillae. Pedipalps articulate, with groove on medial surface of second segment. Gnathosoma is anterior and visible from dorsal view. Position of stigmata is not known.

FAMILY ARGASIDAE

The Argasidae includes some sixty species of ticks. They are distributed throughout the world and are found as ectoparasites on snakes, lizards, turtles, many birds, and some mammals. The family includes four genera—*Argas, Ornithodoros, Antricola,* and *Otobius* (Plate 18–3, Figs. 1 to 4). Several species of these genera are of economical and medical importance.

Genus *Ornithodoros*

Ornithodoros, which includes some fifty species, can be distinguished by its more or less dorsoventrally flattened body, which is definitely convex dorsally, and by patterns on the integument formed by the arrangement of mammillae, which extend from the dorsal to the ventral surfaces. This genus includes the muchdreaded *O. moubata* (Plate 18–3, Fig. 2), which is the vector for *Spirochaeta duttoni,* the pathogen that causes African relapsing fever. In the Americas, *O. talajae, O. venezuelensis. O. turicata, O. hermsi, O. parkeri,* and *O. savigngi* serve as vectors for various spirochaetes that cause relapsing fevers in animals. Others, such as *O. parkeri,* have been reported by Davis et al. (1941) as possibly being able to transmit the spirochaetes to humans.

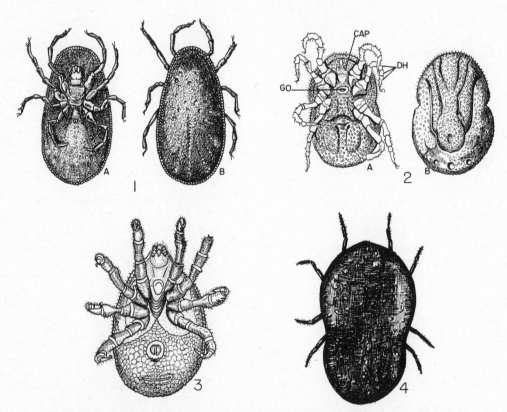

Plate 18–3   Ticks. 1. *Argas persicus* female. **A.** Ventral view. **B.** Dorsal view. (Redrawn after Bishopp, 1935.) **2.** *Ornithodoros moubata* female. **A.** Ventral view. **B.** Dorsal view. (CAP, capitulum; DH, dorsal humps; GO, genital opening.) (Redrawn after Nuttall and Warburton, 1908.) **3.** *Antricola coprophilus* female, ventral view. (Redrawn after Cooley and Kohls, 1944.) **4.** *Otobius megnini,* dorsal view. (Redrawn from photograph after Herms.)

The geographical distribution of the various species and strains of relapsing fever spirochaetes and their suitable vectors is discussed in the volume entitled *A Symposium on Relapsing Fevers in the Americas* (AAAS Publ., 18, 1942). Some of the better known of these spirochaetes are *Spirochaeta duttoni* in Africa, *S. venezuelense* in South and Central America, *S. turicatae* in Texas, and *Borrelia recurrentis,* a rather cosmopolitan species. Davis (1942) and others have demonstrated that species or strains of spirochaetes are host specific to ticks, and the recognition of different species is often based on this specificity. For example, Davis was able to separate *Borrelia hermsi* from *B. parkeri* because *B. hermsi* is carried by *Ornithodoros hermsi* and *B. parkeri* by *O. parkeri.* Rodents serve as the natural reservoirs for human-infecting spirochaetes.

LIFE CYCLE OF *Ornithodoros moubata.* Adults of *O. moubata* hide in the dust and crevices of huts in Africa. This eyeless tick is primarily nocturnal in its feeding habits and takes a relatively short time to engorge itself with the host's blood. The host may be a pig, dog, goat, sheep, rabbit, rodent, or man. Both males and females are bloated and larger than the normal size of 8 to 11 mm. long by 7 mm. wide when filled with blood. When alive, *O. moubata* varies from a brown to a greenish-brown color. Impregnated females deposit their eggs away from the host between blood meals. The eggs are deposited in batches, each batch containing 35 to 340 eggs. The maximum number of eggs a single female can produce in a lifetime is 1217.

Approximately 7 to 11 days after the eggs are oviposited, a larva is completely formed within each egg. The larva is nonmotile within the eggshell, which is split by this time. Within a few hours, the larva undergoes the first molt and transforms into the first nymphal form. The nymph escapes from the shell and attaches itself to a passing host and remains for approximately 5 to 7 days (or less), feeding on host's lymph. At the end of the feeding period, the nymph drops from the host and undergoes the second ecdysis, after which it is said to be in the second nymphal stage. Six to nine attached feeding periods ensue—each one followed by a molt—before the nymph reaches the adult stage. Although *O. moubata* does feed on the various animals mentioned, in transmission of the relapsing fever spirochaete, the cycle involves man-to-man feeding rather than animal-to-man feeding.

Variations of the feeding habit exhibited by *Ornithodoros moubata* are found in other members of the genus. For example, the larvae of some species are active and do feed.

Genus *Antricola*

Members of *Antricola* can be recognized by their flattened dorsal body wall and by their deeply convex ventral wall. The integument is shiny and smooth except for the presence of tubercles. The body covering is sometimes translucent. Furthermore, the mouthparts of *Antricola* spp. are modified for quick feeding rather than for grasping the host. The species are primarily ectoparasites of birds.

Genus *Argas*

Members of *Argas* are characterized by their flattened bodies and thin lateral margins. The body integument is leathery with minute wrinkles interrupted by rounded areas that are pitted at the top and are armed with setae set in the pits. The two species found in North America are *A. persicus* and *A. reflexus,* but these are not restricted to North America. In fact, *A. persicus* is a rather common household pest in Iran (Plate 18–4).

Argas persicus, commonly known as the fowl tick, is not only irritating to chickens and other birds because of its bite, but also is the vector for *Borrelia gallinarum,* the causative agent of avian spirochaetosis in Brazil, India, Australia, Egypt, and Iran (Plate 18–3, Fig. 1). The symptoms of the disease are diarrhea, loss of appetite, ruffled feathers, convulsions, and eventually death.

LIFE CYCLE OF *Argas persicus.* Like *Ornithodoros, Argas persicus* hides in the nests or

Plate 18-4   *Argas persicus.* Larva of the poultry tick. (Redrawn from photograph in Herms, W. B., 1961. *Medical Entomology,* Macmillan, New York.)

near the roosts of their hosts during the day. The nymphs and adults are extremely active at night, climbing onto the birds and engorging themselves with blood. The females lay their reddish-brown eggs in clumps of 25 to 100. There are usually several layings between blood meals. It has been estimated that a single female may lay as many as 700 eggs. Such eggs are deposited in the daytime hideouts and hatch in 10 to 28 days, giving rise to active larvae that bear three pairs of legs (Plate 18–4). These larvae attack birds both by day and night. Once attached to a host, the larvae may remain as many as 5 days, engorging blood until they resemble reddish balls. During this feeding process, the sites of the bites are severely irritated. After such an extended period of feeding, the larva drops off, hides, and undergoes the first molt in approximately 7 days, giving rise to the first nymphal stage, which possesses an additional pair of legs, totaling eight legs). The nymphs resemble miniature adults and are nocturnal feeders. In 10 to 12 days, the second ecdysis occurs, and the second nymphal stage is attained. There are three to four such molts, each one sandwiched between feedings. Finally, the adult form is attained. The adult males are approximately 5 mm. long by 4.5 mm. wide, and the females are 8.5 mm. long by 5.5 mm. wide. *Argas persicus* causes severe damage to birds because of drainage of blood, and the host is often killed. This tick is known to bite man, in which case dermal rashes result.

Argas reflexus, the pigeon tick, possesses a narrower anterior end than *A. persicus.* This species is ectoparasitic on pigeons and other roosting birds, and frequently attacks man. Other species of *Argas* include *A. brumpti,* the largest species, measuring from 15 to 20 mm. in length, and *A. vespertilionis.* Both species are found in Africa, and both bite man.

Genus *Otobius*

Otobius, characterized by a granulated integument and by nymphs that possess integumentary spines, includes the widely distributed *O. megnini,* the spinose ear tick, which is parasitic on the ears of cattle, horses, sheep, mules, dogs, cats, rabbits, deer, and other mammals. It is also known to bite man.

Life Cycle of *Otobius megnini.* The larvae of *O. megnini* hatch from comparatively large, dark eggs that are laid on the ground. The hatched larvae climb the host's legs and body onto the inner folds of the ear, where they assume a saccular appearance. After feeding on the host's blood, the larvae molt and transform into the nymphal stage, which is spinose. The nymphs may remain attached to the host's ear for as long as 121 days, after which they drop to the ground and undergo three molts, finally attaining the adult form.

The adults possess a vestigial hypostome and do not feed. Egg laying begins 12 to 40 days after copulation. Copulation takes place 1 to 3 days after the final molt. The laying period may last as long as 155 days, and there may be as many as 562 eggs. Herms (1917) reported that if these larvae are left unfed at room temperature, they can survive for as long as 63 days, although the average is 44 days. The bites of *O. megnini* and *O. lagophilus,* the latter found attached to the face of rabbits in western United States and Canada, are vulnerable to secondary infection. Furthermore, *O. megnini* can cause deafness, illness, and even death.

FAMILY IXODIDAE

The Ixodidae is the largest of the tick families. It includes sixteen genera, some of which are further divided into subgenera. The most important genera are *Dermacentor, Ixodes, Rhipicephalus, Haemaphysalis, Hyalomma, Boöphilus,* and *Amblyomma.* Members of these genera can readily be distinguished by the structure of the gnathosoma (Plate 18–5).

Genus *Dermacentor*

Dermacentor venustus (= D. andersoni). The Rocky Mountain wood tick, *D. venustus,* is of great importance because it serves as one of the vectors of *Rickettsia rickettsi,* the causative agent of Rocky Mountain spotted fever (Plate 18–6, Fig. 1). This tick is the principal vector of *R. rickettsi* in the Rocky Mountain states. Copulation in *D. venustus* occurs on the host—in nature is usually a horse, cow, sheep, deer, bear, or coyote. It is not host specific, however, and can be found on any mammal.

Life Cycle of *Dermacentor venustus.* Cooley (1932) has studied the complete three-host life history of *D. venustus.* After copulation, the individuals again engorge themselves. The females become greatly distended and fall off the host. In approximately 7 days, they begin to oviposit. The egg-laying period may last 3 weeks, during which approximately 6400 eggs are laid.

After 35 days of embryonic development, the

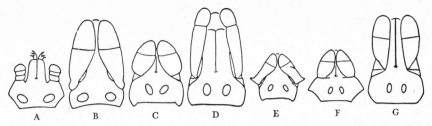

Plate 18-5   Gnathosoma of several common genera of ticks. A. *Boöphilus.* **B.** *Ixodes.* **C.** *Dermacentor.* **D.** *Amblyomma.* **E.** *Haemaphysalis.* **F.** *Rhipicephalus.* **G.** *Hyalomma.* (After Herms, W. B. 1950. *Medical Entomology,* Macmillan, New York.)

hexapod larva, commonly referred to as the seed tick, hatches. This larva actively becomes attached to a small mammal, usually a rodent, and feeds on its blood for 3 to 5 days, after which it drops off and, after a period of rest, metamorphoses into an octopod nymph. The nymph hibernates in the soil. It comes to the surface in the spring and attaches itself to a larger host, on which it engorges for 4 to 9 days. After feeding, the tick nymph drops off and undergoes the second molt in approximately 14 days. The postecdysal form is the adult. These mature individuals, which become attached to a third host (a large animal), are found in endemic areas commonly during the spring months until the end of June.

Dermacentor venustus, like many other ticks, is capable of surviving for long periods without a blood meal and hence without food. Hunter and Bishopp (1911) reported that larvae can survive for a month without feeding. In some extreme instances, larvae have survived for over 300 days. Nymphs can survive for 316 days without food, and starved adults can survive up to 413 days.

In addition to serving as a vector for the spotted fever organism, *D. venustus* serves as transport host for various other pathogenic microorganisms (Table 18–1).

Dermacentor albipictus. This species, called the winter or horse tick, differs in habit from other species of *Dermacentor* in that cold weather stimulates the larvae to seek out a host, on which they become attached throughout the winter. The larvae, nymph, and adult of this species are all found on the same host. Thus this tick has a one-host life cycle. No dropping off occurs except during the engorged adult stage. Females at this stage lay their eggs on the ground. This species is commonly and widely distributed throughout North America. It causes a general weakening of the host

and even death. Death is usually caused by the bacterium, *Klebsiella paralytica,* which is carried by the tick.

OTHER *Dermacentor* SPECIES. Other species of *Dermacentor* include *D. variabilis,* the American dog tick, which is the principal vector of the spotted fever organism in central and eastern United States. It can also serve as the vector for other organisms (Table 18–1). The seed ticks and nymphs of *D. variabilis* are usually found on the same host, a meadow mouse, *Microtus pennsylvanicus.* The adult is a parasite of many large animals, primarily dogs, and hence has a two-host cycle. *Dermacentor occidentalis,* the west coast tick, is found in California and Oregon. It has been reported on cattle, horses, mules, donkeys, deer, sheep, rabbits, dogs, and man. The immature forms attack rabbits, squirrels, field mice, and skunks.

Genus *Ixodes*

Ixodes includes some sixty species belonging to various subgenera. For those interested in the identification of the North American genera, the paper by Cooley and Kohls (1945) should be consulted. The most frequently encountered species are *I. pacificus,* which is found on deer, cattle, and dogs in California and other western states and which can bite man (Plate 18–6, Fig. 2); *I. ricinus,* the European castor-bean tick, which is distributed widely and is found on a variety of mammals; and *I. howelli,* a fairly common bird tick.

Life Cycle of *Ixodes ricinus.* This tick may take as little as 170 days or as long as 3 years to complete its life cycle, depending on environmental conditions. The three-year cycle prevails. The stages in the life cycle of this species do not feed continuously; rather, they feed for a few days once a year, usually during the spring. During the rest of the three-year life cycle, the tick is more or less quiet. Nutrients

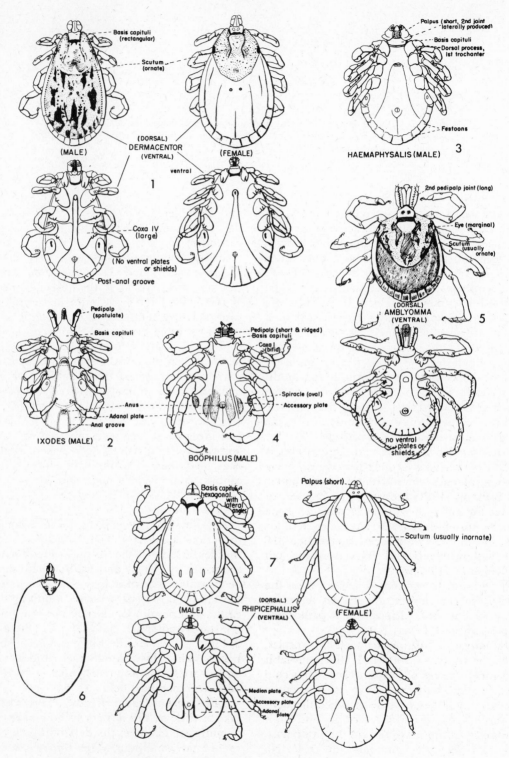

Plate 18-6 Anatomy of some common genera of ticks. 1. *Dermacentor*. 2. *Ixodes*. 3. *Haemaphysalis*. 4. *Boöphilus*. 5. *Amblyomma*. 6. *Nuttalliella*. 7. *Rhipicephalus*. (From *Labroratory Guide to Medical Entomology with Special Reference to Malaria Control*, Naval Medical School, 1945.)

taken in during the feeding periods are partially utilized by the tick and partially converted to forms required for egg formation. Immature forms of *I. ricinus* generally feed on smaller hosts than the adults do.

Genus *Rhipicephalus*

Rhipicephalus includes some forty-six species, of which *R. sanguineus,* the brown dog tick, is cosmopolitan in distribution. McIntosh (1931) has contributed an excellent article concerning this tick, which serves as vector for the malignant canine jaundice organism, *Babesia canis;* the highly fatal *Rickettsia canis;* and other microorganisms. The life cycle of this species is similar to that of *Dermacentor venustus* in that three hosts are involved.

Except for *R. sanguineus,* most species of *Rhipicephalus* are found in Africa, although a few are found in southern Europe and Asia. Most of the species are not very host specific; they can feed on a wide range of mammals. There are a few exceptions however. For example, *R. distinctus* feeds only on hyraxes. *Rhipicephalus sanguineus* can feed on carnivores and rabbits in addition to dogs, but it ignores ruminants and rarely bites man.

Genus *Haemaphysalis*

The fifty-five or more species of *Haemaphysalis* have been treated in a monograph by Nuttall and Warburton (1915). These ticks are especially abundant in Asia and Madagascar, where they primarily parasitize small mammals and birds. The body walls of these comparatively small ticks are not as tough as those found in other members of the Ixodidae.

*Haemaphysalis leporispalustris** is a widely distributed species found in North and Central America (Plate 18–6, Fig. 3). It is primarily a parasite of wild rabbits and hence is popularly referred to as the rabbit tick. Nevertheless, it reportedly parasitizes horses, dogs, cats, and even certain birds. It does bite humans on occasion, but it is not an important vector for disease organisms, although in nature it carries the tularemia and spotted fever organisms among rabbits and hence is important from the epidemiological standpoint.

OTHER *Haemaphysalis* SPECIES. *Haemaphysalis leachii,* a dog tick found in Africa,

Asia, and Australia, is of medical and veterinary importance. In addition to dogs, this tick parasitizes various carnivores, small rodents, and infrequently cattle. It is also a suitable vector for *Bebesia canis* in South Africa and tick-borne fevers (Table 18–1).

Haemaphysalis humerosa transmits the so-called Q fever, caused by *Coxiella burnetii* (= *Rickettsia burnetii*), from bandicoot to bandicoot (*Isodon* spp.) in Australia, but it does not bite humans. Nevertheless, the bandicoot is an important natural reservoir host for the pathogen.

Haemaphysalis concinna is a vector of tick-borne encephalitis in eastern USSR.

Genus *Hyalomma*

Species of *Hyalomma* are confined to Europe, Africa, and Asia. A key to the known species has been compiled by Hoogstraal (1956) and should be consulted by those interested in identification. Most of these ticks are ectoparasitic on domestic and wild animals, including horses, sheep, goats, cattle, and occasionally on tortoises, lizards, and even birds. Although *Hyalomma* spp. serve as vectors for *Theileria* (Sporozoa) and rickettsiae in domestic animals and rarely in man, they are equally important in their own right, because their bites are extremely destructive and result in bad wounds. Such wounds can cause crippling and serve as sites for invasion by screwworms.

Several species of *Hyalomma* serve as vectors for viruses that cause infectious hemorrhagic fevers in the USSR. *Hyalomma aegyptium,* the bont-leg tick, is widely distributed in Europe, Asia, and Africa. Its life cycle generally involves two hosts. The larva and nymph share the same host, commonly rabbits, rodents, and birds. The adults, developing from nymphs that drop off to molt, are attached to larger animals.

Genus *Boöphilus*

Boöphilus includes less than six species, some think only three, of which *B. annulatus* is of primary interest (Plate 18–6, Fig. 4).

Boöphilus annulatus. This parasite is the vector for *Babesia bigemina,* the Texas cattle fever haemosporidian (p. 135). It is limited to the southern United States and parts of Mexico. Although primarily a parasite of cattle, *B. annulatus* becomes attached to horses, mules, sheep, deer, and other animals. Cattle suffering from the Texas fever demonstrate weight loss,

---

*The specific name of this tick was originally written as *leporis-palustris,* but in accordance with the International Rules of Nomenclature, the hyphen has been dropped.

reduction in milk production, sterility, and even death, depending on the severity of the infection.

Life Cycle of Boöphilus annulatus. The species of *Boöphilus* are one-host ticks. When females become gravid, they drop off the host and undergo a preoviposition period before commencing to lay eggs. A single female lays between 357 and 5105 eggs, averaging 1811 to 4089. The time required for complete development of the larva fluctuates with the temperature—19 days during hot summer months and 180 days during the early autumn months. The larvae (seed ticks) hatch from the eggs and are very active. They climb up blades of grass and other vegetation and await the passing of a cow or some other large herbivore to cling to. *Boöphilus annulatus* is parasitic on the same host during its larval, nymphal, and adult stages—a typical one-host cycle. The two molts, one occurring between the larval and nymphal stages and one between the nymphal and adult stages, take place on the host.

OTHER Boöphilus VECTORS. The life history and developmental pattern of *Babesia bigemina* in the tick and in the bovine host is given in Chapter 5 (p. 135). The fatality of cattle suffering from this protozoa-caused disease may be as high as 75 per cent in some areas. The disease is endemic in Central and South America, southern Europe, India, parts of Africa, and in the Philippine Islands. *Boöphilus australis* is the vector in India, the Philippines, and parts of South America; *B. decoloratus* is the vector in Central and South Africa, Australia, the Orient, and southern Florida; and *B. microplus* is the vector in sections of South America and the West Indies. Other species of ticks can also serve as vectors for *Babesia* spp. (Table 18–1).

Genus *Amblyomma*

Amblyomma includes approximately 100 species, which have been listed and annotated by Robinson (1926).

Amblyomma americanum. The Lone Star tick, *A. americanum*, is found in Oklahoma, Louisiana, Texas, and other southern and southwestern states (Plate 18–6, Fig. 5). It is found also in Central America and Brazil. Cooley and Kohls (1944) reported that this tick is found on an array of animal hosts, wild and domesticated, ranging from birds to man. Furthermore, *A. americanum* is of economic importance because it serves as a vector for the spotted fever, Bullis fever, Q fever, and tularemia organisms. The life cycle of *A. americanum* is of the three-host type.

OTHER Amblyomma SPECIES. *Amblyomma cajennense* is found in the southern United States, Central and South America, and in the West Indies. This species parasitizes horses, cattle, sheep, hogs, and man. It is the main vector for the spotted fever rickettsia in Brazil and Colombia.

Amblyomma also includes *A. hebraeum*, the vector for tick-bite fever in South America, and *A. maculatum*, the Gulf Coast tick, found attached to the ears of cattle. Not only are the sores resulting from the bites of *A. maculatum* irritating and painful, but these lesions serve as sites for screwworm infections and secondary bacterial and fungal infections. In addition, this species serves as a suitable vector for *Rickettsia* spp. The three-host cycle is found in both *A. hebraeum* and *A. maculatum*. Nymphs of *A. maculatum* have been reported on meadow larks.

FAMILY NUTTALLIELLIDAE

The little known Nuttalliellidae has been diagnosed on p. 510. At present, it includes a single species, *Nuttalliella namaqua*, which appears to be a form intermediate between the Ixodidae and the Argasidae (Plate 18–6, Fig. 6). This species was discovered by Bedford under a stone in Little Namaqualand, Africa. Its parasitic habits, if any, remain to be determined.

PHYSIOLOGY OF IXODIDES

Comparatively little is known about the physiology of ticks. The many research papers dealing with the Ixodides are primarily concerned with the taxonomy, morphology, and control aspects of these ectoparasites. This is not surprising because concerted efforts to understand the biology of ticks are comparatively recent. As in all phases of biology, the form and classification of a group of organisms must be established before one can intelligently evaluate the physiological processes associated with them. Furthermore, since the Ixodides are of medical and veterinary importance, it is not surprising that the control aspects have been investigated extensively.

Oxygen Requirements

That ticks are true aerobes is quite obvious, for they possess well developed tracheal systems, through which gaseous exchange occurs. It would be of great interest to compare the amount of oxygen utilized by ticks during the various stages of their life cycles. It is suspected that the host's erythrocytes ingested by these blood feeders also supply a certain amount of oxygen for metabolism.

Composition of Blood

The composition of tick blood remains unknown, although it is suspected to be quite similar to that found in other arachnoids—that is, it includes either dissolved haemoglobin or haemocyanin. If such is the case, a certain amount of oxygen and carbon dioxide conduction is performed by the blood. The function of the amoeboid haemocytes (leukocytes) is not clear, but it is suspected that these are phagocytes that represent one form of internal defense mechanism.

Transovarial Transmission

Transovarial transmission among the Acarina, specifically the Ixodides, is extremely interesting. Two types of materials are transmitted in this manner.

(1) Microorganisms for which ticks serve as vectors can be transmitted from one generation to another by infestation of eggs. *Babesia* spp., for example, is passed on in this manner. The discovery of this phenomenon has explained how protozoan parasites can be transmitted from host to host by such one-host species as *Boöphilus annulatus* and *B. decoloratus,* which almost never migrate from host to host. It is through the passage of the protozoa from mother to offspring, which parasitizes other hosts, that the pathogen is spread. Similarly, spirochaetes in *Argas,* and *Babesia* in *Rhipicephalus sanguineus* are transmitted to other vertebrates via the offspring.

(2) Hyland and Hammar (1959) have demonstrated that nonliving materials can be transmitted transovarially. These investigators fed adult female *Dermacentor variabilis* glycine tagged with carbon-14. Later, radioactivity was recorded in the eggs and resulting larvae. The amount of radioactivity, however, diminished by 55 per cent between the eggs and the larvae. This clever experiment demonstrates that transovarial transmission of nonliving materials can occur.

Starvation

The ability of ticks in all stages to survive for long periods without food has been mentioned. Pavolvosky and Skrynnik (1960) reported an amazing example of this in *Ornithodoros hermsi.* These workers reported that specimens can live for 3 years without food. Starved ticks are not usually capable of ovipositing, because engorgement is necessary for egg laying.

Balashov (1957) demonstrated that in several species of ticks—*Ixodes ricinus, Haemaphysalis punctata, Dermacentor pictus, Rhipicephalus turanicus,* and *Hyalomma plumbeum*—if females are not impregnated on the third or fourth day after the final nymphal ecdysis, their feeding is slowed down or ceases, while impregnated females feed healthily. Furthermore, the amount of blood taken in by impregnated females is directly correlated with the quantity and viability of the eggs oviposited. Maximum weight is attained by engorging females before laying their eggs. If this weight is not attained through the intake of blood, the number of eggs decreases and the percentage of nonviable eggs increases.

Davis (1951) determined that *Ornithodoros moubata* can reproduce parthenogenically, the progeny being all females.

The Cuticle During Feeding

Lees (1952) demonstrated that ticks capable of ingesting large volumes of blood possess the ability to secrete new cuticle while attached to the host. He divided the periods of engorgement into two phases. During the first phase, there is a gradual increase of body weight and active cuticle synthesis, the endocuticle (ectostracum and hypostracum) increases in thickness. The moderate increase in surface area is due to the molecular growth of the cuticle and not to distention. During the second phase, cuticle deposition ceases and a large volume of blood is ingested rapidly. The body weight increases abruptly. Concurrently, the cuticle is stretched.

During cuticle synthesis in the first phase, the underlying hypodermis is greatly hypertrophied. The nuclei are enlarged, one or more nucleoli appear, and the cytoplasm becomes heavily concentrated with RNA and alkaline phosphatase. During the stretching process associated with the second phase, cuticular structures become greatly modified, especially the pore canals.

The Ixodid ticks undergo cuticle synthesis during all feeding periods, including that of all instars, and hence are slow feeders. On the other hand, among Argasid ticks, the larvae commonly undergo cuticle synthesis and therefore feed slowly. However, the nymphs and adults accommodate the smaller blood meals by simply stretching the preformed cuticle and hence are rapid feeders.

Response to Humidity

Certain species of ticks exhibit a definite orienting response in a relative humidity gradient. Sonenshine (1963), by employing multiple-choice and linear gradient chambers in which the relative humidities (RH) ranged from 23.9–28.4 per cent to 86.8–94.6 per cent, tested the reactions of seven species of ticks.

In the case of *Ornithodoros turicata*, 73 per cent of the fasting nymphs and adults placed at the 80 per cent RH position migrated and aggregated in the highest humidity zones. On the other hand, freshly engorged nymphs and adults previously maintained at 80 per cent RH were generally indifferent to the humidity choices, but 63 per cent of the freshly engorged larvae chose the highest humidity zone.

In the case of *Ornithodoros kelleyi* and *Dermacentor venustus*, a distinct avoiding reaction to high RH zones was exhibited by most specimens. Seventy-one per cent of the fasting adults of *O. kelleyi* aggregated in the lowest humidity zones, while *D. venustus* adults preferred zones with low to intermediate RHs, with 83 per cent of the ticks aggregating at humidities lower than 56 per cent, including 45 per cent in the lowest humidity zones.

Similar tests with *Ornithodoros parkeri*, *O. savignyi*, *O. delanöei delanöei*, and *Argas cooleyi* did not reveal any response.

In order to ascertain the location of the humidity receptors, Sonenshine removed the tarsi of the first pair of legs of *O. kelleyi* females and *D. venustus* males. As a result, all of these ticks failed to exhibit the avoiding reaction and wandered freely throughout all the humidity zones. Although the exact site and nature of the humidity receptors remain to be studied, Sonenshine's experiments suggest that such receptors may be present on the tarsi.

HOST-PARASITE RELATIONSHIPS

Effects of tick bites on hosts have been discussed briefly in preceding sections. Manifestations of tick bites can be classified in five categories.

Tick-Host Anemia

Certain ticks, such as *Ixodes dentatus* on wild rabbits and *Dermacentor* spp., cause a non-infectious disease known as tick-host anemia. This anemia, which has been reported in moose, jackrabbits, and foxes, causes the death of the host, which upon autopsy exhibits pale and watery blood and a definite reduction of haemoglobin. The cause of the disease remains uncertain, although it is suspected that the anemia results from drainage of blood by the parasite, for the anemia is most conspicuous in heavily infected hosts.

Tick-Host Paralysis

The bite of certain ticks results in paralysis of the host. This condition is characterized by an ascending loss of muscular function and sensation and leads to death if the respiratory centers are affected. The paralysis sets in after the female tick begins feeding. The causative agent is believed to be a neurotoxin. Apparently the toxin, if it exists, is not secreted by all females of the same species, because the bites of some females do not cause paralysis. It has been suggested that certain ideal conditions must be met to effect paralysis, but this hypothesis has not been validated. It is known that a single female tick can paralyze a 1000 pound bull by the time she is only partially engorged. If the paralysis has not advanced too far, removal of the parasite or parasites results in recovery. Investigations have revealed that age and species resistances exist. Older animals are not as apt to be paralyzed as are young animals, and certain hosts are immune.

Various ticks are known to cause paralysis. In Australia, *Ixodes holocylus* causes paralysis in dogs and man. *Dermacentor venustus* (= *D. andersoni*) bites cause paralysis in humans, cattle, sheep, and bisons in the northwestern United States and southern British Colombia. In southeastern United States, *D. variabilis* occasionally causes paralysis in man and dogs. In South Africa and occasionally in Europe, *Ixodes pilosus* has been incriminated. *Amblyomma americanum* bites can cause tick-host paralysis in various mammals. Abbot (1942) and Hughes and Philip (1958) have reviewed this subject.

Mechanical Damage

Bites of certain ticks cause severe mechanical damage to the host's integument and underlying tissues. Several instances of this have been previously cited. Furthermore, the lesions resulting from bites serve as invasion sites for bacterial and fungal infections, and as entrance sites for screwworms.

Toxins and Venoms

Among the Ixodidae, *Dermacentor occidentalis, D. variabilis,* and *Ixodes ricinus* cause systemic disturbances suggesting the secretion of some irritant during the bite. Among the Argasidae, the bite of *Ornithodorus moubata* in Africa causes severe swelling and irritation. In parts of California and Mexico, *O. coriaceus* causes a systemic disturbance known as "tlalaja," which is accompanied by severe pain and swelling. The nature of the toxin is not known, although Sabatini has demonstrated that *Ixodes ricinus* secretes an anticoagulant during feeding that prevents clotting of blood at the site of the bite, and prevents coagulation of blood within the alimentary tract of the tick. It is suspected that most ticks secrete such a substance, and this may include the irritant.

Transmitter of Microorganisms

The role of ticks as vectors for protozoa, bacteria, rickettsiae, and spirochaetes has been discussed. Specific vectors for specific microorganisms are listed in Table 18–1.

In conclusion, the author stresses that very little is known about metabolism, respiration, food synthesis, and other aspects of tick physiology. This phase of parasitology awaits the contributions of future parasitologists. Recently Arthur (1960) has contributed a monograph on the Ixodides that should be consulted as an authoritative source for serious investigators.

LITERATURE CITED

Abbot, K. H. 1942. Tick paralysis: A review. Proc. Mayo Clin., *18:* 39–45; 59–64.

Arthur, D. R. 1960. Ticks. Cambridge University Press, London.

Baker, E. W., and G. W. Wharton. 1952. An Introduction to Acarology. Macmillan, New York.

Balashov, Y. S. 1957. [Gonotropic relationships in ixodid ticks (Acarina, Ixodidae)] Ent. Obozrenie, *36:* 285–299.

Cooley, R. A. 1932. The Rocky Mountain Wood Tick. Montana State College Agric. Exp. Sta. Bull. No. 268.

Cooley, R. A. 1938. The genera *Dermacentor* and *Otocentor* (Ixodidae) in the United States with studies in variation. U. S. Pub. Health Serv. Nat. Inst. Health Bull. No. 171.

Cooley, R. A., and G. M. Kohls. 1944. The Argasidae of North America, Central America and Cuba. Am. Midl. Nat. Monogr.

Cooley, R. A., and G. M. Kohls. 1945. The Genus *Ixodes* in North America. Nat. Inst. Health Bull. No. 184.

Davis, G. E. 1942. Species unity or plurality of the relapsing fever spirochaetes. *In* A Symposium on Relapsing Fever in the Americas. AAAS Publ. No. 18, pp. 41–47.

Davis, G. E. 1951. Parthenogenesis in the argasid tick *Ornithodoros moubata* (Murray, 1877). J. Parasit., *37:* 99–101.

Davis, G. E., H. L. Harlin, and M. D. Beck. 1941. Relapsing fever: *Ornithodoros parkeri,* a vector in California. Pub. Health Rep., *56:* 2426–2428.

Herms, W. B. 1917. Contribution to the life-history and habits of the spinose ear tick, *Ornithodoros megnini.* J. Econ. Entomal., *10:* 407–411.

Hoogstraal, H. 1956. African Ixodoidea. Vol. I. Ticks of the Sudan. Research Report NM 005 050.29.07, U.S. Navy.

Hughes, L. E., and C. B. Philip. 1958. Experimental tick paralysis in laboratory animals and native Montana rodents. Proc. Soc. Exp. Biol. Med., *99:* 316–319.

Hunter, W. D., and F. C. Bishopp. 1911. The Rocky Mountain Spotted Fever Tick. Bureau Ent. Bull. No. 105, U.S.D.A.

Hyland, K. E., Jr., and J. L. Hammar. 1959. Transovarial passage of radioactivity in ticks labeled with C^{14} glycine. J. Parasit., *45:* 24–25.

Lees, A. D. 1952. The role of cuticle growth in the feeding process of ticks. Proc. Zool. Soc. London, *121:* 259–272.

McIntosh, A. 1931. The brown dog tick. North Am. Vet., *12:* 37–41.

Neumann, L. G. 1911. Ixodidae. Das Tierreich. Acarina. 26 Lieferung, pp. 1–169.

Nuttall, G. H. F., C. Warburton, W. F. Cooper, and L. E. Robinson. 1908. Ticks. A Monograph of the Ixodoidea. Part I. The Argasidae. Cambridge University Press, London.

Nuttall, G. H. F., and C. Warburton. 1911. Ticks. A Monograph of the Ixodoidea. Part II. Cambridge University Press, London, pp. 105–348.

Nuttall, G. H. F., and C. Warburton. 1915. Ticks. A Monograph of the Ixodoidea. Part III. The Genus *Haemaphysalis*. Cambridge University Press. London, pp. 349–550.

Pavolvosky, E. N., and A. N. Skrynnik. 1960. [Laboratory observations on the tick *Ornithodoros hermsi* Wheeler, 1935] Acarologia, 2: 62–65.

Robinson, L. E. 1926. Ticks. A Monograph of the Ixodoidea. Part IV. The Genus *Amblyomma*. Cambridge University Press, London.

Sonenshine, D. E. 1963. A preliminary report on the humidity behavior of several species of ticks. *In* Advances in Acarology, Vol. 1. (J. A. Naegele, ed.). Cornell University Press, Ithaca, New York, pp. 431–434.

Vitzthum, H. G. 1943. Acarina. *In* Bronns' Klassen und Ordungen des Tierreiches. 5, Sect. 4, Book 5: 1–1011.

SUGGESTED READING

Arthur, D. R. 1961. Ticks and Disease. Row, Peterson and Co., Evanston, Ill. (This is a well written text-reference in which are considered the anatomy, functions of the various organs, life cycles, and behavior of ticks. The pathogenic microorganisms that are transmitted by ticks are also considered as are various control methods.)

Baker, E. W., and G. W. Wharton. 1952. An Introduction to Acarology. Macmillan, New York, pp. 1–35; 137–145. (These sections in a book written for beginning students of Acarology discuss the morphology and taxonomy of ticks. The references listed are of particular interest for those interested in taxonomy.)

Day, M. F. 1955. Mechanisms of transmission of viruses by arthropods. Exptl. Parasit., 4: 387–418. Read pp. 394–395. (This review article discusses the relationship between viruses and their arthropod vectors. The section on the role of ticks as vectors, and the literature cited are particularly useful.)

Dethier, V. G. 1957. The sensory physiology of blood-sucking arthropods. Exptl. Parasit., 6: 68–122. Read pp. 77–87. (This is another review article by a recognized authority on insect behavioral physiology. The information accumulated on the Acarina and the literature cited are most valuable.)

Herms, W. B., and M. T. James. 1961. Medical Entomology. 5th Ed., Macmillan, New York, pp. 434–490. (M. T. James has revised and brought up to date this textbook, which was originally written by the late Dr. Herms. It is an extremely useful book, and the section devoted to the ticks should be read by all students.)

Hoogstraal, H. 1956. African Ixodoidea. Vol. I. Ticks of the Sudan. Research Report, Naval Medical 005 050.29.07, U.S. Navy. (This voluminous work on the ticks of the Sudan written by one of the world's authorities on ticks is listed here, because it is advisable for the student to become acquainted with a definitive taxonomic, morphologic, and ecological study on ticks.)

Hyland, K. E. 1963. Current trends in the systematics of acarines endoparasitic in vertebrates. *In* Advances in Acarology (J. A. Naegele, ed.). Cornell University Press, Ithaca, N.Y., Vol. I, pp. 365–374. (In this article, Hyland reviews the taxa of mites that include species endoparasitic in vertebrates. Morphological variations in certain species and the biology of others are discussed. The more recent literature pertaining to these mites is cited.)

Philip, C. B. 1963. Ticks as purveyors of animal ailments: a review of pertinent data and of recent contributions. *In* Advances in Acarology (J. A. Naegele, ed.). Cornell University Press, Ithaca, N.Y., Vol. I, pp. 285–325. (In this review article, the author points out the importance of ticks as vectors for disease-causing microorganisms. The various means by which ticks can affect their hosts and the methods by which the control of ticks can be brought about are outlined. The literature pertaining to tick-borne organisms, including viruses, rickettsiae, rickettsia-like organisms, bacteria, protozoa, and metazoan parasites, is reviewed. In addition, tick toxicosis and paralysis are discussed briefly.)

Weitz, B. 1960. Feeding habits of bloodsucking arthropods. Exptl. Parasit., 9: 63–82. Read p. 73. (This is a review article by an outstanding parasitologist who has had considerable experience in Africa and elsewhere studying parasites, particularly haemoflagellates, that utilize arthropods as vectors. The material is presented in a well synthesized manner, and the bibliography is most useful.)

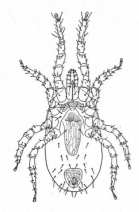

19

THE MITES

The term "mite" has no taxonomic significance. Members of the Acarina that are commonly designated as mites belong to four separate suborders. The phylogeny of these animals
is obscure. Most authorities on the group
consider them to be polyphyletic in origin.

Extensive monographs of these minute arachnids are available. That of Baker and
Wharton (1952) is most useful as is an earlier
one by Banks (1915). Ewing (1929) has listed
ectoparasitic species that are of economic importance. Radford (1950) has provided a check-
list of known genera and the type species for
each.

Mites are of interest in parasitology for two
main reasons: Some of these minute animals
are ectoparasites on animals—vertebrates and
invertebrates—and others on plants; and
certain species serve as vectors for microorganisms (Table 19–1). By far, the majority of
mites are free-living, found in every imaginable
type of ecological niche, terrestrial as well as
aquatic. Mites vary in size, ranging from 0.5 to
2.0 mm. in length.

The anatomical terminology for mites is
essentially the same as that used for the Ixodides and has been considered in the previous
chapter. Like those of the ticks, the stages
in the life history of the mites include the
larva, nymph, and adult forms. However, there
are typically a single larva, two nymphal stages

—the protonymph and the deutonymph—and
the adult. The number of nymphal generations
is increased or decreased in some species.

METHODS OF CONTACTING HOSTS

The methods by which parasitic mites make
contact with their hosts enable us to roughly
divide them into three groups (Carmin, 1963).
Members of the first group, such as the feather
mites (Analgesidae, Dermoglyphidae, Proctophyllodidae, etc., p. 542), the fur mites
(Myobiidae, p. 533), and the mange mites
(Psoroptidae, p. 541), normally spend their
entire life span on their hosts. Furthermore, they
are found on gregarious birds and mammals,
and they live through many generations on a
single host. Transmission from one host to another, when it occurs, is direct, resulting from
contact between hosts or from contact with infested materials that have been in contact with
an infested host.

Members of the second category are nest
parasites (nidicoles), which generally parasitize
nest- and burrow-dwelling vertebrates. The
members of the Dermanyssidae (p. 527) and
certain members of the Laelaptidae, which
parasitize mammals (p. 527) belong to this
group. These mites are haematophagous but

Table 19-1.   Some Representative Disease Etiological Agents Carried by Mites.

Disease	Etiological Agent	Mite Vector
Scrub typhus (tsutsugamushi fever)	*Rickettsia tsutsugamushi*	*Trombicula akamushi* (larvae) *T. deliensis* (larvae) *T. pallida** *T. scutellaris*
Rickettsialpox	*R. akari*	*Allodermanyssus sanguineus* *Liponyssus (Bdellonyssus) bacoti*†
Q fever	*Coxiella burnetii*	*L. (B.) bacoti*
Meadow mice scrub typhus	—	*Trombicula microti*

*Of minor importance.
†Potential vector.

generally are only found on their hosts during the feeding periods. They feed less frequently than do members of the first group, but the amount of blood ingested at each feeding is greater. After feeding, these mites drop off their host and are found in the host's nest or in close proximity. Thus, they can infest the same hosts when necessary. Transmission of these mites is accomplished much in the same way as in the first group, but there is greater opportunity for these mites to be transferred from one host to another, and they frequently parasitize several hosts of the same species during their life span. For this reason, the nidicolous mites are more important as vectors.

Members of the third category include the larval Trombiculidae, or chiggers (p. 533). Like most of the ixodid ticks and the nidicoles, these mites are attached to their hosts only while feeding. However, these mites feed even less frequently than the nidicoles. A great portion of their life span is therefore spent off the host. Although the chiggers also are found on gregarious vertebrates, as are members of the first category, and on nesting and burrowing vertebrates as are members of the second group, they are not as host specific and parasitize other types of hosts as well. These mites drop from their hosts practically anywhere and can survive for relatively long periods without a blood meal. When ready to feed again, they climb to some vantage point, such as on the surface of soil or the tip of a blade of grass, and await the passing of a suitable host. Thus, the members of the third category are not dependent on the gregarious or nesting habits of their hosts and have the greatest opportunity in each generation to parasitize several hosts of the same species or several species of hosts. Therefore, these acarines are the most important from the standpoint of disease transmission.

SYSTEMATICS AND BIOLOGY

All mites, free-living as well as parasitic, are subordinate to one of the four suborders listed in the following diagnosis.

Suborder 1. Onychopalpida. Pedipalps terminate as claws. Body possesses at least four lateral stigmata.

Suborder 2. Mesostigmata. Body is well chitinized, possesses dorsal and ventral plates, and is usually brown in color. Body is usually divided into anterior minute gnathosoma (or capitulum) and posterior idiosoma. Legs typically have six or seven movable joints. Tarsi usually have claws and caruncles. Body possesses two stigmata with peritremal canals leading to them, one stigma adjacent to the coxa of each of third pair of legs. Tarsus I lacks Haller's organ.

Suborder 3. Trombidiformes. Body has one pair of stigmata on or near gnathosoma; stigmata are absent in few species. Pedipalps are free and highly developed, either

as pincer-like claspers or as sensory organs. Chelicercae are usually modified for piercing. Propodosoma have two to four pseudostigmatic setae. Coxae are immovable.
Suborder 4. Sarcoptiformes. No stigmata are present (Oribatei has four pairs of stigmata sunk into the leg). Tracheal system is present in some, opening through pores on various parts of exoskeleton. Chelicerae are usually scissor-like, with strong chelae, adapted for chewing. Pedipalps are simple. Anal suckers are common on males.

SUBORDER ONYCHOPALPIDA

The Onychopalpida does not include any parasitic species. However, certain species of *Holothyrus* on the island of Mauritius, cause the death of ducks and geese (Plate 19–1, Fig. 1). Similarly, children who accidentally swallow these acarinas suffer from ill effects. The toxicity of these mites is caused by a secreted irritant.

SUBORDER MESOSTIGMATA*

The Mesostigmata includes many free-living mites. The heavily sclerotized body plates are quite characteristic (Plate 19–2). Some 200 species of mesostigmatid mites are parasitic on vertebrates and invertebrates.† Some of the species that parasitize vertebrates are of considerable economic importance and are treated in the following discussion.

The nature of this volume does not permit presentation of detailed diagnoses of the numerous families of mesostigmatid mites, nor the

*For another systematic interpretation of the Mesostigmata, the reader is referred to Camin and Gorirossi (1955).

†The true parasitic nature of some of the so-called zooparasites has not been established and undoubtedly some of these are merely epizoic species.

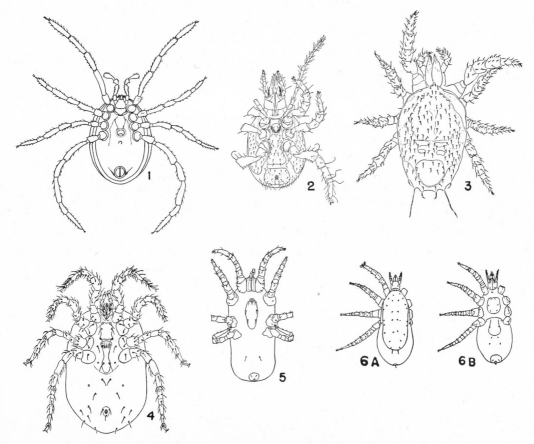

Plate 19-1   Some genera of mites. 1. *Holothyrus longipes,* ventral view of male. (After Hirst, 1922.) **2.** *Megisthanus floridanus,* ventral view of female. (After Baker and Wharton, 1952.) **3.** *Liroaspis armatus,* dorsal view of female. (After Baker and Wharton, 1952.) **4.** *Raillietia auris,* ventral view of female. (After Hirst, 1922.) **5.** *Pneumonyssus simicola,* ventral view of male. (After Vitzthum, 1931.) **6. A.** *Entonyssus glasmacheri,* dorsal view of female. **B.** Ventral view of female. (A and B after Vitzthum, 1935.)

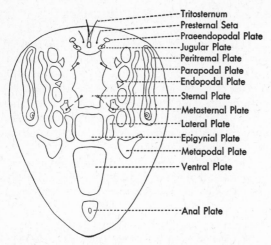

Plate 19-2   **Ventral plates that may be encountered in the Mesostigmata.** A median plate, if present, would have the same position as the epigynial plate. (After Baker, E. W., and Wharton, G. W. 1952. *An Introduction to Acarology,* Macmillan, New York.)

discussion, or even the inclusion, of the many genera. Interested readers are referred to the volume by Baker and Wharton (1952), which is most useful in introducing the beginning investigator to the available literature dealing with each taxon.

Parasitic members of this suborder are relegated to seven groups.

Gamasides Group.   Possesses forked seta at base of palpal tarsus. Epigynial plate has one pair of genital setae and is hinged to ventral plate. Male genital pore is in front of sternal plate. Chelicerae of males are modified as spermatophores.

Megisthanina Group.   Epigynial plate is primarily absent in females. Presternal setae flank the tritosternum. Sternal plate, which functions as an epigynial plate, covers genital pore. Female genital pore is crescentic fissure between sternal and ventral plates.

Liroaspina Group.   Lacks an epigynial plate. Presternal setae are lacking. Female genital pore is large, transverse slit between sternal and ventral plates.

Thinozerconina Group.   Females lack lateral plates. Epigynial plate does not articulate at base, is narrow, and has one pair of setae. Male genital pore is located in sternal plate.

Diarthrophallina Group.   Penis is biarticulated, directly posteriorly, in groove between coxae of third pair of legs. Possesses prestomal setae. Epigynial plate is enclosed in fused sternal and ventral plates, but not separated from ventral plate by suture.

Celaenopsina Group.   Possesses a pair of lateral plates developed on ventral surface as anterior elongations of ventral plate, replacing epigynial plate, which is reduced or absent. Median plate is absent. Metasternal plates are large and uncovered in some, reduced and covered in others, and they are not attached to sternal plate.

Fedrizziina Group.   Females possess median plate (scle-

rotized portion of vaginal wall) in addition to or in place of epigynial plate. Male genital pore is in center of sternal plate, closed by plate attached to anterior margin of pore.

GAMASIDES GROUP

The parasitic representatives of this extremely large group belong to fourteen families. Bregetova (1956) has contributed a monograph on the group.

Family Raillietidae

The Raillietidae includes two fairly common ectoparasites of mammals. *Raillietia hopkinsi* is found on the ears of antelopes and *R. auris* is found on the ears of cattle in North America and Europe (Plate 19–1, Fig. 4). These mites are not true parasites, for they feed on the host's ear wax and sloughed epithelia rather than on living tissues.

Family Halarachnidae

This family includes the genera *Halarachne,* *Pneumonyssus,* and *Orthohalarachne.* Species of *Halarachne* are found in the respiratory passages of seals. Species of *Pneumonyssus* are also found in the respiratory tract of mammals, particularly monkeys, apes, and dogs. *Pneumonyssus simicola* is found in the lungs of rhesus monkeys and is capable of causing inflammation (Plate 19–1, Fig. 5). Species of *Orthohalarachne* are found in the air passages of seals. In the United States, *O. zalophi* is found in the nasal passages of the California sea lion. Its presence may produce inflammation, a condition known as pulmonary or nasal acariasis. It should be apparent that the halarachnid mites are all respiratory tract parasites of mammals. They normally feed on lymph, but they may ingest blood.

Family Entonyssidae

All members of this family are parasitic in the respiratory tract, particularly in the lungs, of snakes. The family includes the genera *Entonyssus* (Plate 19–1, Fig. 6), *Hammertonia,* and *Ophiopneumicola.* The species are ovoviviparous and are widely distributed in America and Africa.

Family Rhinonyssidae

The ten genera in this family are universally distributed and are parasitic in the nasal passages of birds. Among the genera are *Rhinonyssus, Larinyssus* (Plate 19–3, Fig. 1), and

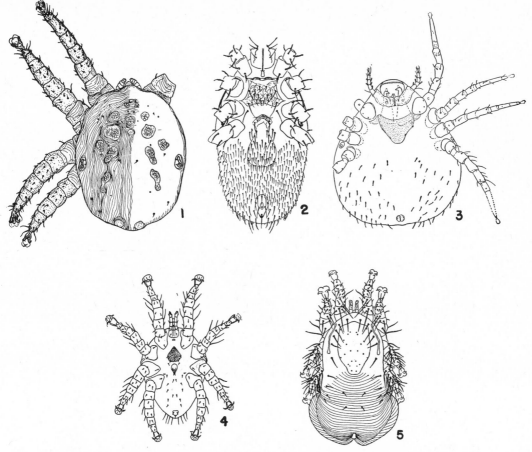

Plate 19-3   **Some genera of mites.** 1. *Larinyssus orbicularis*, dorsal view of female. (After Strandtmann, 1948.) 2. *Haemogamasus mandschuricus*, ventral view of female. (After Vitzthum, 1930.) 3. *Spelaeorhynchus* sp., ventral view. (After Baker and Wharton, 1952.) 4. *Spinturnix carloshoffmanni*, ventral view. (After Hoffmann, 1944.) 5. *Periglischrus vargasi*, dorsal view of female. (After Hoffmann, 1944.)

Sternostomum. Sternostomum includes *S. rhinoletrum,* which causes catarrhal inflammation in the respiratory passages of fowls.

Family Haemogamasidae

This family includes the genera *Haemogamasus* (Plate 19-3, Fig. 2), *Acanthochela,* and others. Almost all haemogamasids are found on various small mammals in every part of the world. Occasionally, some are found free-living and others are found on birds. Those members found on animals are true parasites, feeding on the host's blood, but their attachment to the host is intermittent, and most of the time they are found off the host and in their nests. The life cycle includes the typical larval, protonymph, deutonymph, and adult stages. Since there appears to be little, if any, host specificity among these mites, passing from one type of host to another as they do, Baker and Wharton

(1952) suggest that the haemogamasids may be of potential medical importance as vectors for the plague, typhus, and tularemia pathogens.

Families Spelaeorhynchidae and Spinturnicidae

The genus *Spelaeorhynchus* of the Spelaeorhynchidae, and the genera *Spinturnix, Periglischrus,* and *Ancystropus,* all of the family Spinturnicidae, are parasitic on bats (Plate 19-3, Figs. 3 to 5). *Spelaeorhynchus* is found in Central and South America, and the spinturnicid species are found throughout the world. Species of *Spinturnix* give birth to living young.

Family Ixodorhynchidae

This small family includes the sole genus *Ixodorhynchus.* The species are parasites of snakes. *Ixodorhynchus butantanensis* (Plate 19-4, Fig. 1) is found on snakes in Brazil, and the North

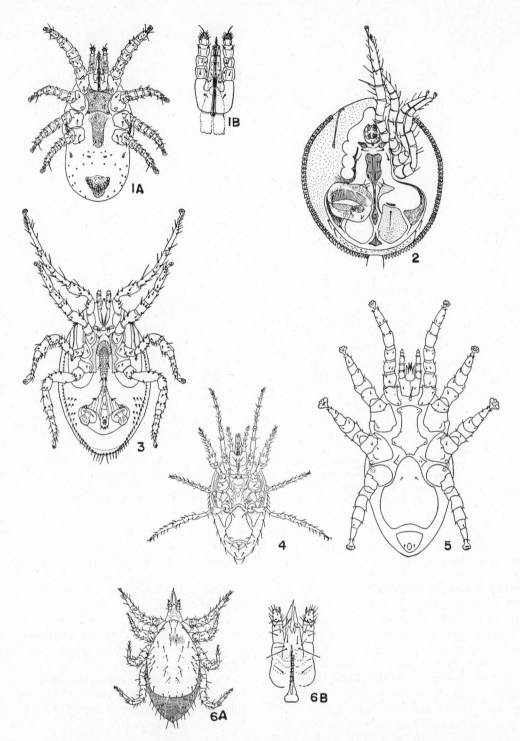

Plate 19-4   Mites. 1. A. *Ixodorhynchus butantanensis,* ventral view of female. B. Gnathostoma of *I. butantanensis.* (A and B after Fonseca, 1934.) 2. *Discozercon mirabilis,* ventral view of female. (After Berlese, 1914.) 3. *Heterozercon oudemansi,* ventral view of female. (After Finnegan, 1931.) 4. *Pachylaelaps roosevelti,* ventral view of female. (After Wharton, 1941.) 5. *Jacobsonia tertia,* ventral view of female. (After Vitzthum, 1931.) 6. A. *Myrmonyssus chapmani,* dorsal view of female. B. Ventral view of gnathosoma of *M. chapmani.* (A and B after Baker and Strandtmann, 1948.)

American *I. liponyssoides* has been reported from the eyes of a snake in Iowa. The adult males are attached to the host under the body scales, while the females and immature specimens are freely motile.

Family Laelaptidae

This family, with forty-eight or more genera, includes the largest number of parasitic genera. Many laelaptids are found on insects; others are found on mammals. *Myrmonyssus* is a representative genus found on insects (Plate 19–4, Fig. 6). Genera found on mammals include *Echinolaelaps* (Plate 19–5, Fig. 1), and *Haemolaelaps*. *Echinolaelaps* include *E. echidninus*, which is the vector for the protozoan parasite *Hepatozoon muris* of rats (p. 125). The mite transmits the protozoan from rat to rat. *Haemolaelaps* includes *H. arcuatus*, which is the vector for *Hepatozoon criceti*, a parasite of hamsters. The larvae and nymphs of parasitic laelaptid mites are mostly lymph feeders and haematophagous (blood feeders) as adults. The life cycles of these mites, including the egg, larva, protonymph, deutonymph, and adult stages, are completed between 8 and 28 days.

Family Dermanyssidae

The gamasid family Dermanyssidae is of great interest in veterinary medicine because it includes several species that inflict considerable injury to domestic animals.

Dermanyssus gallinae. The common red chicken mite, *Dermanyssus gallinae*, found on chickens throughout the world, also parasitizes turkeys, pigeons, certain wild birds, and occasionally man (Plate 19–5, Fig. 2). This pear shaped grayish mite measures between 0.6 and 0.8 mm. in length. The males are slightly smaller. Engorged specimens are larger and dark red. Chickens infested with *D. gallinae* often suffer reduced egg laying capacity; some stop laying completely. The fowls lose weight, become susceptible to other diseases, and even die. Young chicks usually die when attacked by this mite. Thus, large flocks of chickens can readily be lost when heavily infested. Furthermore, this mite serves as the vector for avian spirochaetes.

Life Cycle of *Dermanyssus gallinae*. This mite is primarily a night feeder, hiding in crevices and under debris during the day. The female begins ovipositing from 12 to 24 hours after feeding and lays up to seven eggs, which in summer temperatures, hatch in 48 to 72 hours. The hexapod larvae are sluggish and do not feed; they transform into protonymphs in approximately 24 to 48 hours. The octopod protonymphs are very active. After taking in a blood meal, the protonymphs molt and metamorphose into deutonymphs. Deutonymphs also engorge on the host's blood before molting, giving rise to adults. Third stage nymphs, although rare, have been reported. The entire life cycle may take as little as 7 days. Thus, if uncontrolled, the mite population in chicken coops multiplies rapidly.

Bdellonyssus (= Ornithonyssus) bursa. The tropical fowl mite, *B. bursa*, is widely distributed in Argentina, Brazil, China, India, parts of Africa, Colombia, the Bahamas, and in the United States. Unlike *Dermanyssus gallinae*, this species is both a day and night feeder on chickens and on the English sparrow, *Passer domesticus*. The adults, measuring approximately 1 mm. in length, remain on the host and feed intermittently. The eggs are oviposited either on the host's fluff feathers or in the nest. After 3 days of incubation, the minute six-legged larvae appear. The larva does not feed and molts in about 17 hours, giving rise to the protonymph. The protonymph is an active feeder, and after molting, gives rise to the deutonymph, which in turn feeds, molts, and gives rise to the adult. The entire life cycle takes from 8 to 12 days.

Bdellonyssus (= Liponyssus) bacoti. The tropical rat mite, *B. bacoti*, is usually found on the Norway rat, *Rattus norvegicus*, in various parts of the world including the United States (Plate 19–5, Fig. 4). Like *B. bursa*, *B. bacoti* does bite humans, resulting in pain and local inflammation. However, no severe symptoms ensue. This species serves as a vector for the Texas strain of endemic typhus, when experimentally tested on infected guinea pigs. It also serves as a vector for *Rickettsia akari* under experimental conditions with mice. It can also serve as an intermediate host for the cotton rat worm, *Litomosoides carinii* (p. 453). The life history of *B. bacoti* is quite typical—one larval, two nymphal, and an adult stage. Bertram et al. (1946) stated that the unfertilized eggs develop parthenogenically. Mites, by dropping off the host, are capable of traveling relatively long distances. Hence, they are widely dispersed.

OTHER DERMANYSSID SPECIES. *Dermanyssus americanus*, measuring 0.7 mm. in length, has been reported from English sparrows.

Allodermanyssus sanguineus, the mouse mite, measuring 0.80 mm. by 0.46 mm., is the vector for the rickettsialpox organism, *Rickettsia*

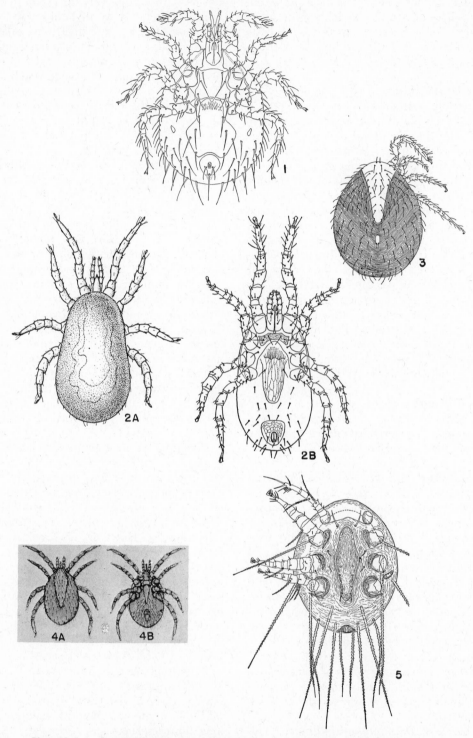

Plate 19-5   Parasitic mites. 1. *Echinolaelaps echidninus,* ventral view of female. (After Hirst, 1922.) 2. *Dermanyssus gallinae.* **A.** Dorsal view of female. **B.** Ventral view of female. (A after Herms, 1950; B after Hirst, 1922.) 3. *Allodermanyssus sanguineus,* dorsal view of female. (After Baker and Wharton, 1952.) 4. *Bdellonyssus bacoti.* **A.** Dorsal view. **B.** Ventral view. (After Dove and Shelmire, 1932.) 5. *Diarthrophallus quercus,* ventral view of nymph. (After Trägårdh, 1946.)

akari (Plate 19–5, Fig. 3). The house mouse, *Mus musculus,* serves as the reservoir host, and mites transmit the pathogen from mice to man.

GAMASID MITES OF INVERTEBRATES

Several families of the Gamasides Group include species parasitic on invertebrates. The family Discozerconidae includes the tropical and subtropical genera *Discozercon, Heterozercon,* and *Allozercon,* mostly found ectoparasitic on large millipedes, centipedes, and termites, and sometimes on snakes (Plate 19–4, Figs. 2 and 3). A few genera are free-living. The family Pachylaelaptidae includes *Pachylaelaps* and others, mostly found on insects, especially beetles (Plate 19–4, Fig. 4). Some are free-living. The family Macrochelidae includes *Macrocheles muscae,* which may or may not be a true parasite. The larvae of this species are found on the eggs of houseflies. Family Iphiopsidae includes *Iphiopsis* and *Jacobsonia,* both found on insects and myriopods, either as true parasites or as epizoic forms (Plate 19–4, Fig. 5). Since true parasites and epizoic species are found among closely related species, these mites can be of great importance as experimental animals in studying the transition between the two types of host-parasite relationships.

OTHER MESOSTIGMATE GROUPS

MEGISTHANINA GROUP. The parasitic members of this group all belong to the family Megisthanidae* and the genus *Megisthanus.* They are found as ectoparasites on large beetles in moist environments. In the United States, the common species is *M. floridanus,* found on the patent leather beetle, *Popillus disjunctus.*

LIROASPINA GROUP. All members of this group are free-living and are found primarily in the tropics. However, Fox (1947) reported finding *Liroaspis armatus* of the family Liroaspidae on rats in Puerto Rico (Plate 19–1, Fig. 3). There is considerable doubt, however, whether this species is a true parasite. It is suspected that its presence on rats is accidental and temporary.

THINOZERCONINA GROUP. Included in this small group is *Dasyponyssus neivai* of the family Dasyponyssidae. This mite was discovered in Brazil on an armadillo.

DIARTHROPHALLINA GROUP. The family Diarthrophallidae of this group includes *Diarthrophallus* and *Passelobia,* both found on various passalid bettles in North, Central, and South America, and on New Guinea. *Diarthrophallus quercus* is very common on beetles around Durham, North Carolina (Plate 19–5, Fig. 5).

CELAENOPSINA GROUP. Genus *Schizogynium* of the family Schizogyniidae of this group includes species parasitic on beetles in Africa (Plate 19–6, Fig. 1).

FEDRIZZIINA GROUP. The family Parantennulidae includes *Parantennulus* and *Diplopodophilus* (Plate 19–6, Fig. 2). Species of both

---

*Familial diagnoses are omitted herein but can be found in Baker and Wharton (1952).

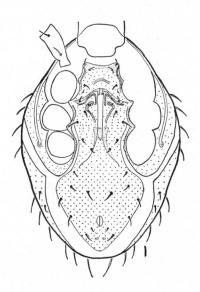
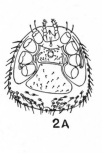
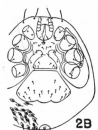

Plate 19-6   Parasitic mites. 1. *Schizogynium intermedium,* ventral view of female. (After Trägårdh, 1950.) **2.** *Diplopodophilus antennophoroides.* **A.** Ventral view of male. **B.** Ventral view of female. (After Williams, 1941.)

2A

2B

genera are found on carabid beetles and myripods.

SUBORDER TROMBIDIFORMES

Some of the species of the Trombidiformes are parasites as adults; other species are parasitic as larvae. Many other species are free-living predators. The parasitic species are found on plants as well as on both vertebrate and invertebrate animals. All trombidiform mites are assigned to one of three groups.

Group Tetrapodili. Are found on plants. Bodies are minute, wormlike, and ringed (annulated). Bodies measure up to 0.2 mm. in length. Possesses only two pairs of legs, which are without claws but possess feather claws. Body has few setae. Gnathosoma is reduced. Chelicerae are stylet-like. Pedipalps are minute, adjacent to rostrum. Possesses no respiratory system.

Group Tarsonemini. Are parasitic on plants and animals, vertebrates and invertebrates. Are minute mites, with or without usual eight legs. Chelicerae are minute and stylet-like. Pedipalps are tiny and are located behind chelicerae. Possesses a pair of clublike pseudostigmatic organs between coxae and first and second pairs of legs. Males lack tracheae and stigmata.

Group Prostigmata. Bodies are comparatively large, and shapes vary, depending on family. Gnathosoma is usually conspicuous. Usually possesses eight legs. Stigmata usually are present, at base of large chelicerae. Pedipalps are larger than those in other groups and are not closely adjacent to rostrum.

TETRAPODILI GROUP

These mites, all belonging to the family Eriophyidae, are found on various plants and include several economically important species. Whether these mites should be considered parasitic or predaceous is academic. Inasmuch as these mites do depend on the plants for nourishment and do inflict damage, they may be considered true parasites, although here the line between predation and parasitism is indeed a slim one. These mites discussed in the following section are representative of the group.

Oxypleurites aesculifoliae. The buckeye rust mite, *Oxypleurites aesculifoliae*, is of great interest biologically, because its life cycle displays an alternation of generations including two types of females—the protogyne, which resembles the males, and the deutogyne, which has no male counterpart (Plate 19–7, Fig. 1). The protogynes give rise to eggs that develop into both types of females. The deutogynes, which hibernate on the plant, only oviposit eggs that

develop into protogynes. This and other species of plant-parasitizing eriophyid mites show a strong tendency to cause gall formation on host plants.

OTHER ERIOPHYID MITES. Other economically important eriophyid mites include *Epitrimerus pirifoliae*, the pear leaf rust mite, which exhibits the same complex type of life cycle as *O. aesculifoliae; Aceria ficus,* the fig mite, which has a simple life cycle; *Eriophyes vitis,* the grape erineum mite, so called because it forms erineum patches (patches of thick hairs) on the underside of grape leaves; *Caleptrimerus vitis,* the grape rust mite, which includes deutogynes in its life cycle; *Vasates cornutus,* the peach silver mite, also with overwintering deutogynes; *V. fockeui,* the plum nursery mite, which inflicts severe damage to plum trees throughout the northern United States and Canada; and *Aceria sheldoni,* the citrus bud mite, which not only stunts the growth of citrus trees but causes leaf and fruit malformation in California, Hawaii, Java, and Australia.

Phyllocoptruta oleivorus, the citrus rust mite, is another pest of citrus trees. The damage caused by *Phytoptus avellanae* and *Cecidophyes ribis,* the big-bud filbert and currant mites, respectively, is manifested as galls, which form at the terminal buds of the plants instead of shoots, thus stunting growth. *Aceria essigi,* the redberry mite, is found on blackberries along the Pacific Coast of North America. Blackberries attacked by this mite never ripen; instead, they remain red and are worthless as food. The related *A. tulipae,* commonly known as the bulb eriophyid, parasitizes the interbulbal layers of onion, garlic, tulip, and other liliaceous plants. This mite causes shrinkage of the bulbs.

TARSONEMINI GROUP

The parasitic members of this group belong to four families.

Family Podapolipodidae

This family includes the genera *Podapolipus, Locustacarus* (Plate 19–7, Fig. 2), *Eutarsopolipus, Tarsopolipus,* and *Tetrapolipus.* All species belonging to these genera are ectoparasites of other arthropods. For example, *Podapolipus reconditus* is found under the elytra of European beetles, and *P. bacillus, P. grassi,* and *P. diander* are ectoparasites of grasshoppers.

Locustacarus trachealis is found in the tracheae

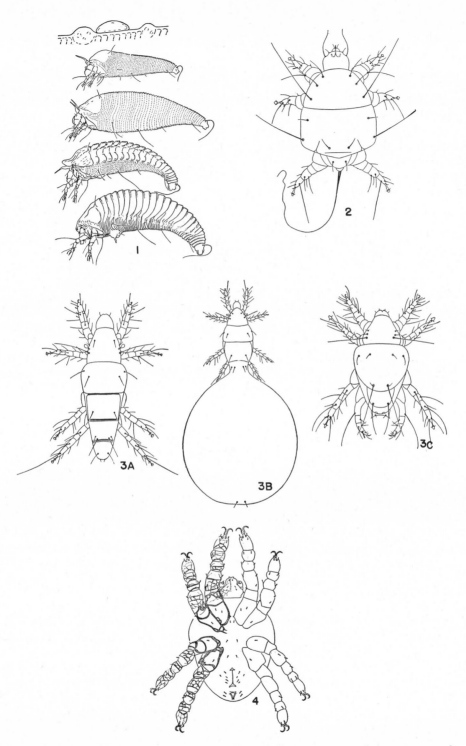

Plate 19-7   Mites.   1. *Oxypleurites aesculifoliae,* including egg, two nymphal, protogyne, and deutogyne stages. (After Keifer, 1942.) **2.** *Locustacarus trachealis,* young female. (After Baker and Wharton, 1952.) **3.** *Pyemotes ventricosus.* **A.** Dorsal view of female. **B.** Partially gravid female. **C.** Dorsal view of male. (A to C after Baker and Wharton, 1952.) **4.** *Speleognathus sturni,* ventral view of female. (After Boyd, 1948.)

and air sacs of grasshoppers in the United States and South Africa. It obtains nutrients by piercing the tracheal wall of the host and sucking blood. The genus *Tetrapolipus* includes *T. rhynchophori* found beneath the elytra of the palm weevil, *Rhynchophorus palmarum.*

Life Cycle of *Podapolipus diander.* The life cycle of *P. diander* has been studied by Volkonsky (1940). This mite is a parasite of the grasshopper *Locusta migratoria* in Algeria. The developmental pattern is unusual yet representative, of the group.

Young mites are attached to the exoskeleton of the first through the third instars of the grasshopper, under the posterior projection of the pronotum. When the host is in its fourth and fifth instar stages, the mite oviposits her eggs under the host's elytra and wings. When the host molts, attaining the adult form, the parasites' eggs have already hatched, and the young mites become attached to the new exoskeleton of the host, also under the elytra and wings. These immature female mites mature at these sites and oviposit eggs that hatch into "small" males parthenogenically. These small males copulate with parental females, which then oviposit another type of egg that hatches in 5 to 6 days to give rise to females as well as "large" males. These large males are parasitic on the females and hence are hyperparasites. The males perforate the abdomen of the females and draw their nutrients, sometimes killing the females.

The parasitized females are attached to the intersegmental membranes of the grasshopper's body, where they pierce the integument to draw out nutrient. This position, however, is not a permanent one, for the female mites gradually migrate posteriorly and congregate at the host's genitalia. The spread of infestations from host to host is accomplished during copulation. The adults are probably neotenic larvae since they possess only six legs. *Podapolipus diander* is thermosensitive, for if the temperature rises above 80.6° F., the parasite leaves the host and hides either in crevices or on blades of grass from where it can later attach to another host.

Family Scutacaridae

The Scutacaridae includes *Acarapis woodi,* the Isle of Wight disease mite of bees. This mite is of considerable economic importance in Europe, where commercial beekeeping thrives. The mite is found in the tracheae of bees, where it feeds on the hosts' body fluid, secretes a toxic substance, and clogs the air passages mechan-

ically, thus killing the host. Other genera of this family are mostly free-living, although a few species are also found on insects.

Family Pyemotidae

The genus *Pyemotes* of the Pyemotidae includes *P. ventricosus* (Plate 19-7, Fig. 3). This parasite is found on the larvae of various insect pests, such as the grain moth, *Sitotroga cerealella;* the wheat jointworm, *Harmolita grandis;* the peach twig borer, *Anarsia lineatella;* the cotton-boll weevil, *Anthonomus grandis;* and the bean and pea weevil, *Mylabris quadrimaculatus.* Because of the fatal parasitic habit of *P. ventricosus* on destructive insects, this species represents one parasite that is economically beneficial. However, this mite bites humans closely associated with the host plants, causing a type of acarodermatitis known as straw itch.

The migratory forms of the species of *Pygmephorus* are found on moles, flies, and thrips. This type of association is generally considered to be pseudoparasitic.

Family Tarsonemidae

Species belonging to the Tarsonemidae are primarily free-living predators. However, certain representatives, like the eriophyids, are found on and are destructive to plants. Some members of *Tarsonemus* are extremely destructive. For example, *T. waitei* is destructive to peach trees in the United States; *T. spirifex* is destructive to oats in Europe, in Arizona, and in Kansas; *T. laticeps,* the bulb scale mite, is destructive to narcissus bulbs in the United States and Europe; and *T. pallidis* is a hazard to strawberry plants in Europe. The genus *Hemitarsonemus* includes *H. latus,* which is parasitic on a wide assortment of plants throughout the world. It can be of great economic importance when, for example, it destroys tea plants in Ceylon.

Although none of the tarsonemid mites are true parasites of animals, Carter et al. (1944) did report finding *Tarsonemus* sp. in the lungs of a man suffering from asthma and respiratory ailments. This is undoubtedly a case of accidental parasitism.

PROSTIGMATA GROUP

Members of this extremely large group are primarily free-living, either as predators on other mites or on insects, or in damp areas such as mossy beds and in humus. However, eleven families do include species that are true parasites.

Family Ereynetidae

This family includes the interesting slug mite, *Riccardoella limacum,* in Europe and the United States. Turk and Phillips (1946), in defining the life cycle of this mite, reported that it is neotenic. The stages in its life cycle include the typical larva, protonymph, deutonymph, and adult, but it is the deutonymph that contains the fully formed eggs and is either viviparous or ovoviviparous. Eggs found in adult females are not normally developed.

Family Speleognathidae

This family includes *Speleognathus sturni* found in the nasal passages of starlings in the eastern United States (Plate 19–7, Fig. 4). The larva, unlike the other instars, is not parasitic. It is commonly lodged in the mucous secretions of the bird.

Family Pterygosomidae

This family includes some eight genera found primarily as parasites under the scales of lizards and on geckos. Representative genera include *Pterygosoma* (Plate 19–8, Fig. 1), *Geckobia,* and *Zonurobia. Pimeliaphilus podapolipophagus* is found on cockroaches and tenebrionid beetles, and *P. isometri* parasitizes scorpions in the Philippines (Plate 19–8, Fig. 2).

Families Pseudocheylidae and Cheyletidae

Members of Pseudocheylidae are all predaceous except for species of *Heterocheylus,* which are parasitic on arthropods. The same is true for members of Cheyletidae, except for some that are found on the feathers of birds and the fur of squirrels, cats, and rabbits. *Cheyletiella parasitivorax,* a species normally found in cats or on other mites parasitic on cats, can become a facultative parasite of man.

Family Myobiidae

Members of this family possess first pairs of legs that are modified as clasping appendages by which they hold onto the base of the hair of their mammalian hosts or onto the shaft of feathers of avian hosts. Representative genera include *Myobia* (Plate 19–8, Fig. 3), *Amorphacarus,* and *Syringophilus* (Plate 19–8, Fig. 4) with various species distributed throughout North America and Europe. These mites are found inside the quills of the avian host's feathers and are believed to feed on the internal cones of the quills. The genus *Harpirhynchus* includes *H. nidulans,* which is found forming colonies in the feather follicles of numerous species of birds. Its presence causes tumors and cysts. Members of *Ophioptes* are found in pits in the epidermis of South American snakes. Members of *Psorergates* are of economic significance to sheep raisers in Australia because at least one species, *P. ovis,* living at the base of the hair of sheep, causes chronic irritations.

The feeding habits of the myobiid mites are in need of clarification. Ewing (1938) reported that these parasites do not feed on the host's blood; instead, they thrive on secretions of the hair and feather follicles. However, Jameson (1948) and others have reported that specimens of *Myobia* spp., when examined, contained blood.

Family Erythraeidae

The fifteen or more genera belonging to the Erythraeidae are found as larvae on insects and arachnids and are represented here by *Leptus* (Plate 19–8, Fig. 5) and *Erythraeus.* The *Leptus atticolus* larva is attached to the legs of spiders, while that of *E. swazianus* is attached by its mouthparts to the undersurface of the wings and on the tympanic membrane of locusts. Adult erythraeids are reddish (hence the familial name) and have legs adapted for running. Adults are predaceous and are commonly found in foliage, humus, and on beach sand. The larvae of other species of *Leptus* are found attached to phelangids, pseudoscorpions, and scorpions.

Family Smaridiidae

Members of this family, represented here by *Smaris* (Plate 19–8, Fig. 6), *Fessonia,* and *Hirstiosoma,* as larvae are parasitic on insects. The adults are predaceous. The life cycles of these mites are slightly modified inasmuch as no protonymphal stage exists.

Family Trombidiidae

This extremely large family includes over 300 species (Thor and Willmann, 1947). These mites, represented here by *Allothrombium* (Plate 19–9, Fig. 1), are parasitic on arthropods as larvae. The nymphs and adults are predaceous, probably on insect eggs.

Family Trombiculidae

The Trombiculidae includes the chigger mites, which are of medical importance because their bites commonly result in dermatosis. Also,

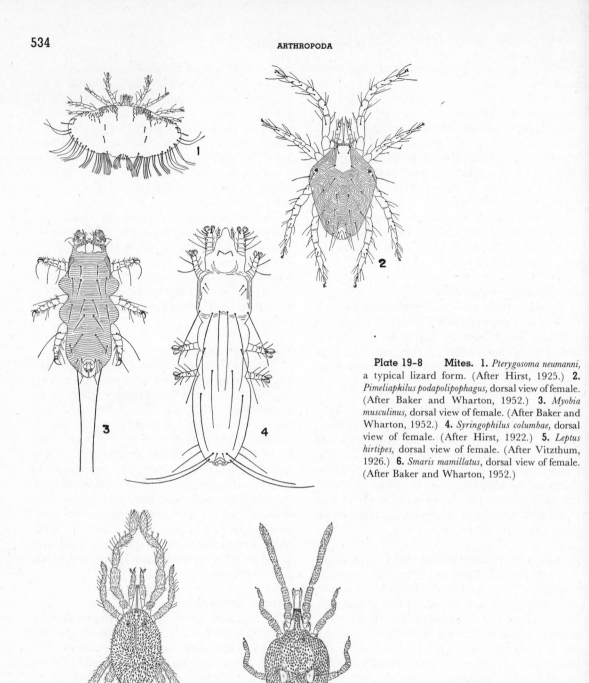

Plate 19-8   Mites. 1. *Pterygosoma neumanni,* a typical lizard form. (After Hirst, 1925.) 2. *Pimeliaphilus podapolipophagus,* dorsal view of female. (After Baker and Wharton, 1952.) 3. *Myobia musculinus,* dorsal view of female. (After Baker and Wharton, 1952.) 4. *Syringophilus columbae,* dorsal view of female. (After Hirst, 1922.) 5. *Leptus hirtipes,* dorsal view of female. (After Vitzthum, 1926.) 6. *Smaris mamillatus,* dorsal view of female. (After Baker and Wharton, 1952.)

certain species serve as vectors for pathogens. For those interested in detailed accounts of the role of trombiculid mites as vectors, the papers of Ewing (1944) and Williams (1944) should be consulted. Genera representative of the

Trombiculidae include *Euschöngastia* (Plate 19-9, Fig. 3), *Trombicula,* and *Doloisia.*

GENUS *Trombicula.* This genus includes several quite frequently encountered species. *Trombicula autumnalis,* the harvest mite, is found

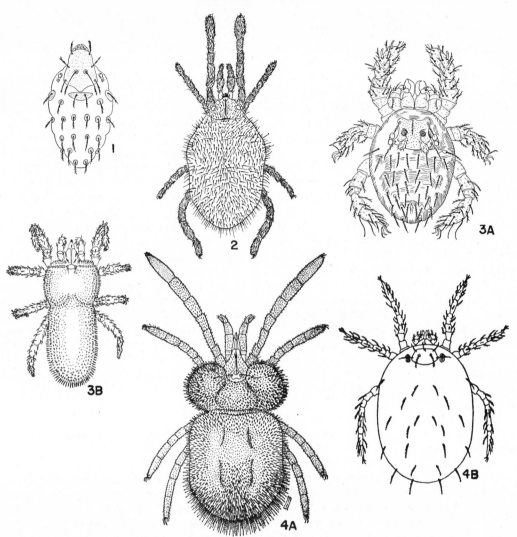

Plate 19-9   Parasitic mites. 1. *Allothrombium neapolitanum*, dorsal view of parasitic larva. (After Oudemans, 1912.) 2. *Microtrombidium hystricinum*, dorsal view of adult. (After Vitzthum, 1926.) 3. *Euschöngastia indica*. A. Dorsal view of parasitic larva. B. Dorsal view of nymph. (A and B after Wharton, 1946.) 4. *Trombicula* (= *Eutrombicula*) *alfreddugèsi*. A. Adult. B. Larva. (After Ewing.)

throughout Europe. Men working the fields, when bitten, suffer from a severe dermatosis. In the Americas, at least three species are known to attack man. *Trombicula mansoni* is found along the entire eastern coast of the United States, along the Gulf Coast to Texas, and in isolated locales in Minnesota and Michigan. *Trombicula alfreddugèsi* ranges from New England to Nebraska and south into Florida and Texas, and has also been reported in California, Mexico, and parts of Central and South America (Plate 19-9, Fig. 4). A bright

red species, *T. batatas,* is a tropical form sometimes encountered in the southern United States. These three species also cause severe dermatosis in man. The adults are free-living and predaceous, feeding primarily on insect eggs.

Dogs, horses, shrews, and various birds serve as hosts for the parasitic larva of *T. autumnalis,* and turtles, young toads, and snakes are suitable hosts for *T. alfreddugèsi.*

LIFE CYCLE OF *Trombicula batatas*. The life cycles of the species of *Trombicula* follow the same basic pattern. The dull orange-colored eggs of *T. batatas,* are oviposited singly on moist soil. In 4 to 5 days, the eggshell cracks in half, but the larva remains within the cracked shell in the deutovum (a chorionic layer secreted by the blastoderm during embryonic development) for another week before the red hexapod larva escapes and actively crawls around seeking a host. Such larvae can survive for approximately 2 weeks without food.

There appears to be little host specificity, for *T. batatas* is known to bite literally up to 100 different vertebrates, including amphibians, reptilians, birds, and mammals. The feeding mechanism is interesting in that the mite does not suck blood; rather, it secretes a lytic substance that dissolves the host's tissues. Such dissolved materials are ingested. After engorging itself on the host's digested tissues for 2 to 10 days, the larva drops off and becomes semidormant, after which it molts and transforms into the nymph.* The nymphal form is maintained for 21 to 52 days, after which the nymph molts and the free-living adult form is attained, surviving up to 45 days.

Trombicula akamushi. This species and a variety formerly known as *T. deliensis* are vectors of *Rickettsia tsutsugamushi,* the scrub typhus organism found in Japan, Formosa, Ceylon, India, the Philippines, the East Indies, and parts of Australia. Scrub typhus (tsutsugamushi fever) is a much dreaded disease as American combat troops discovered in Asia during World War II. The larval mite serves as the vector in carrying the rickettsiae from the natural reservoirs—voles, *Microtes montebelli,* and rats, *Rattus concolor browni, R. flavipectus yunanensis,* and others—to human hosts. This medically important mite is reddish as an adult and measures from 1 to 2 mm. in length. The adults are free-living and feed on insect eggs and minute arthropods. Transovarial passage of rickettsiae occurs in nature. The life history of this species parallels that of the other species of *Trombicula* in that there is only one nymphal stage.

Family Demodicidae

The Demodicidae includes the sole genus *Demodex* with many species. The demodicid mites are often referred to as "follicle mites" because they are parasites within the hair fol-

licles of their hosts. These minute (0.3 to 0.4 mm. long) mites are wormlike and have four pairs of stubby legs and a striated abdomen.

Demodex folliculorum. The follicle mite of man is found particularly around the nose and eyes (Plate 19–10, Fig. 1). It has been estimated that as high as 50 per cent of the world's population harbor this parasite. Within the hair follicle and associated sebaceous glands, these mites commonly cause inflammation resulting in an acne like condition. The entire life cycle occurs within the follicles. The typical larval, protonymphal, deutonymphal, and adult stages are present.

Other Demodex Species. *Demodex canis* parasitizes dogs around the head. Presence of this mite along with a staphylococcal bacterium causes the so-called red mange. *Demodex cati* parasitizes cats, *D. equi* parasitizes horses, and *D. bovis* is found in cattle—all in the head and neck regions. *Demodex bovis* causes depreciation in the value of the skin from these parts for leather. *Demodex phylloides* parasitizes pigs, but unlike the other species, is scattered over the entire body, causing white pustules. *Demodex muscardini* is a parasite of the dormouse.

THE HYDRACARINA

Members of the Hydracarina, or Hydrachnellae, commonly known as water mites, are a little known group of prostigmatan trombidiform mites. These mites form an ecological rather than a morphological group. All are found in water, primarily fresh water, although a few marine forms are known. Some are free-swimming, while others are nonswimming. Brightly colored species are commonly found in lakes, ponds, along shores, and in streams.

The life cycle of water mites is known in a general way. There are typically four stages—egg, larva, nymph, and adult. In many species the larvae are parasitic on aquatic insects, while the nymphs and adults are free-living, predaceous animals, feeding on crustaceans, insect larvae, and other small aquatic organisms. The adults of a few species are parasitic in the gills of fresh-water mussels and in the gill chambers of crabs. Members of Hydracarina can be found at all periods during the year, although adults are most abundant during late summer and fall.

Life Cycle Pattern. The commonly reddish-orange eggs of water mites are laid singly,

---

*Some biologists consider the quiescent stage of the larva to be the protonymphal stage.

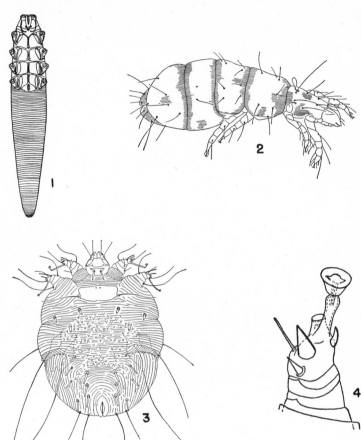

Plate 19-10   Some genera of mites. 1. *Demodex folliculorum,* ventral view. (After Herms, 1950.) **2.** *Pediuochelus raulti,* dorsal view of female. (After Baker and Wharton, 1952.) **3.** *Sarcoptes scabiei* var. *equi,* dorsal view of female. (After Hirst, 1922.) **4.** *Noto-edres cati,* tarsus I. (After Grandjean, 1938.)

in small clutches, or in masses of up to 400 or more eggs. Each egg may be encapsulated in a gelatinous matrix (Plate 19–11, Fig. 1) or two to four eggs may be arranged in a single capsule (Plate 19–11, Fig. 2). In some species, the entire egg mass, containing 100 or more eggs, may be covered with a gelatinous secretion. The encapsulated eggs may be irregularly arranged, or linearly arranged in short straight ribbons. Such egg masses are commonly attached to submerged stones, sticks, or aquatic plants. Leaves of *Sphagnum* and *Myriophyllum* are common substrates to which eggs are attached. The eggs of certain species are deposited in cavities made in plant tissues (Soar and Williamson, 1925).

The eggs of water mites hatch in less than a week to about 6 months, depending on the species and ecological factors. From each egg capsule a six-legged larva emerges. Some larvae, such as those of *Lebertia,* rupture their capsules by exerting pressure. Others, such as

Thyas, utilize spines situated on their dorsal body surface to rupture the capsule.

After a short period of free existence in most species, the larvae, which are the parasites, attach themselves to aquatic and semiaquatic insects by means of their well developed gnathosomal appendages and derive their nourishment from the host.

After the larval parasitic period, the animal undergoes metamorphosis. Each larva shrinks within its exoskeleton, and within a short period the developing nymph can be seen within. The fully developed nymph eventually escapes from the surrounding larval exoskeleton, or nymphochrysalis, either by vigorous activity of the legs or from a transverse slit that develops in the larval skin at about two-thirds of the body length from the anterior end (Crowell, 1960). The nymphs, like the adults, possess four pairs of six-segmented legs, and are generally free-swimming.

After a period of free existence, the nymphs

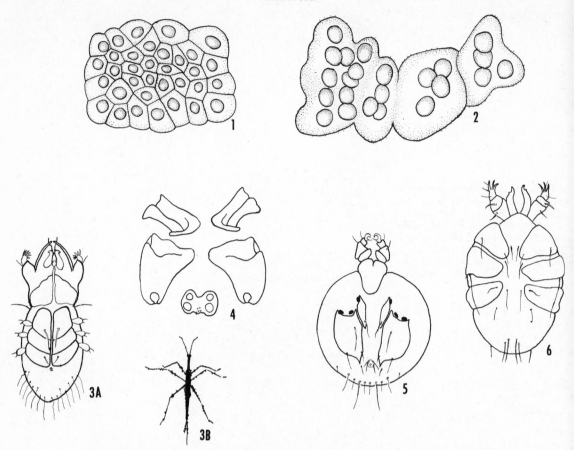

Plate 19-11 **Stages in the life cycle of Hydracarina.** **1.** Eggs of *Hydryphantes ruber*. Each egg is surrounded by a gelatinous matrix. **2.** Eggs of *Eylais extendens*. Four eggs are enveloped together within a single capsule. **3. A.** Parasitic larva of *Hydrachna magniscutata;* ventral view. **B.** Specimen of *Ranatra* sp. heavily parasitized by larvae of *Hydrachna magniscutata*. **4.** Epimera and genital area of parasitic nymph of *Limnesia undulata*. **5.** Parasitic larva of *Piona reighardi*, ventral view. **6.** Parasitic larva of *Thyas stolli*, ventral view. (All figures redrawn after Crowell, 1960.)

become quiescent (imagochrysalis stage) and are attached to plant tissues or in some other obscure niche. From this stage, the adult eventually emerges.

HOSTS OF LARVAL HYDRACARINA. Aquatic and semiaquatic insects are the favored hosts of larval water mites. Very little information is available concerning host-parasite relationships between these mites and their hosts. Marshall and Staley (1929) reported the presence of unbranched feeding tubes, or stylostomes, which connect the larvae of *Lebertia tauinsignata* to their mosquito hosts. These tubes were believed to be chitinous and of host origin. However, Wharton (1954), as a result of histochemical studies, concluded that the stylostome that connects *Trombidium* sp. to its host, the firefly

Photuris pennsylvanica, is not chitinous but is formed as the result of the precipitation of the mite's salivary secretion by the host's tissues. Solidification occurs at the interface between the insect's blood and the mite's saliva.

Among the hosts of larval water mites found by Crowell (1960) in Ohio, stoneflies (Plecoptera), various hemipterans of the families Notonectidae, Corixidae, and Nepidae, and dipterans of the families Tendipedidae and Cuclicidae were infected. In addition, dragonflies (Odonata) and caddis flies (Trichoptera) are suitable hosts.

According to Baker and Wharton (1952), the water mites are divided into 36 families. Those interested in their taxonomy are referred to that volume. Classification of water mites is based primarily on adult characteristics. Hence, the identification of parasitic larvae is not always possible.

In North America, the larvae of *Hydrachna magniscutata* (Plate 19-11, Fig. 3) is commonly found on such aquatic insects as *Arctocorixa,* the water boatman, *Ranatra,* the water scorpion, and *Notonecta undulata,* the back swimmer. The nymphs and larvae of *Limnesia* and *Piona* parasitize midges, and the larvae of *Thysas* are commonly found on mosquitoes (Plate 19–11, Figs. 4 to 6). In fact, Uchida and Miyazaki (1935) have reported that in certain areas larval mites may well serve as biological control agents. For example, anopheline mosquitoes with five or more larval mites attached to their bodies cannot be induced to bite; hence, the necessary blood meal cannot be obtained.

SUBORDER SARCOPTIFORMES

Members of the Sarcoptiformes are divided into two groups.

Acaridiae Group. Possesses thin, soft integument. Lacks stigmata and tracheae. Lacks prominent club shaped pseudostigmatic organs. Caruncles are present on tarsi, which may or may not bear one claw. Many males possess copulatory suckers on tarsi and anal region.

Oribatei Group. Possesses leathery or heavily sclerotized integument. Displays prominent pseudostigmatic organs. Lacks caruncles. Sexual dimorphism is slight. Spiracles are sunk in the leg acetabula, not readily visible.

ACARIDIAE GROUP

Many members of this group are free-living; however, representatives of some of the families are parasitic. These parasitic forms can be categorized into three types—those parasitic on invertebrates, those found in the skin and other tissues of warm-blooded vertebrates, and those found on the feathers of birds.

PARASITES ON INVERTEBRATES

There are many families that include species parasitic on invertebrates. The Ensliniellidae includes *Ensliniella parasitica* found on the larvae of *Pdynerus delphinalis* (Hymenoptera) in Germany (Plate 19–12, Fig. 1), and *Vidia undulata* on *Prosopis conformis* (Hymenoptera) in Italy. The Forcelliniidae includes *Forcellinia wasmanni* in the nests and on ants in Europe, where heavy infestations are lethal to ants (Plate 19–12, Fig. 2).

The Ewingidae includes *Ewingia cenobitae,* found on the gills of the terrestrial hermit crab, *Cenobita diogenes,* at the Dry Tortugas, Florida (Plate 19–12, Fig. 3). The Linobiidae includes *Linobia coccinellae,* found under the elytra of *Melasoma populi* in Italy (Plate 19–12, Fig. 4). The Canestriniidae includes *Photia procrustidis,* found under the elytra of *Procrustes coriacei* (Coleoptera), and *Canestrinia dorcicola* on *Dorcus parallelepipedus* (Coleoptera) in Italy.

The Myialgesidae includes *Myialges* and *Myialgopsis,* found attached by their mouthparts to the abdomen and thorax of hippoboscid flies (Plate 19–12, Fig. 5). A species of *Myialges* also parasitizes bird lice. Ferris (1928) reported that this is more than an epizoic relationship since the sites of the mite's attachment are clearly marked by scars.

PARASITES IN SKIN AND OTHER TISSUES OF WARM-BLOODED VERTEBRATES

Family Sarcoptidae

Acarid mites found in the skin and other tissues of warm-blooded vertebrates include the important family Sarcoptidae, members of which are referred to as itch mites.

GENUS *Sarcoptes.* *Sarcoptes* includes *S. scabiei,* the itch mite of humans (Plate 19–10, Fig. 3). This widely distributed mite is one of the earliest known and described parasites (see Chapter 2). The skin disease caused by *S. scabiei* is commonly referred to as scabies or the seven-year itch. Females, measuring 0.33 mm. to 0.45 mm. in length by 0.35 mm. in width, and males, measuring little more than half that size, are both involved in scabies. However, the females are by far the most irritating. These mites prefer surfaces of the body where the skin is less thick, such as the breasts, penis, shoulder blades, or between the fingers. Nevertheless, they do infect other parts of the body. Irritation to the host is caused by the burrowing of the mites, particularly females, and by the secretion and excretion of toxic substances within the host's epidermis. The irritation is often complicated by scratching and secondary infections.

Life Cycle of *Sarcoptes scabiei.* Impregnated females of *S. scabiei* lay their rather large eggs (0.15 by 0.1 mm.) in tunnels dug during their migrations in the host's epidermis. Each female oviposits from 10 to 25 eggs at 2 to 3 day intervals for about 2 months, after which she perishes. The eggs hatch in 3 to 4 days, and

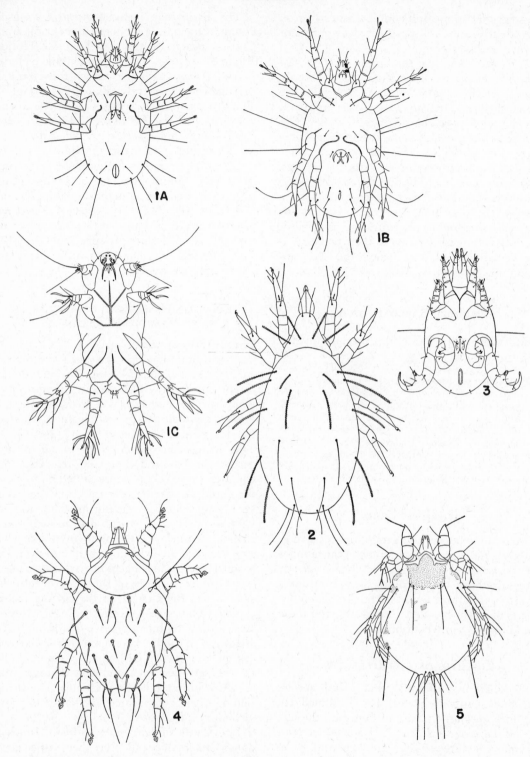

Plate 19-12   Mites. 1. *Ensliniella parasitica.* A. Ventral view of female. B. Ventral view of male.
C. Ventral view of hypopial nymph. (After Vitzthum, 1925.) 2. *Forcellinia wasmanni* female, dorsal
view. (After Michael, 1903.) 3. *Ewingia cenobitae* female, ventral view. (After Pearse, 1929.) 4. *Linobia coccinellae* female, dorsal view. (After Berlese, 1887.) 5. *Myialges caulotoon* female, dorsal view.
(After Ferris, 1928.)

the larvae actively move about, thus spreading the infection. The protonymphal and deutonymphal stages are each preceded by a molt, and the adult form is reached in 10 to 12 days. Infections are usually acquired through direct contact.

Varieties of *Sarcoptes scabiei* occur on domestic animals, each causing a skin condition known as mange. For example, *S. scabiei* var. *suis* is found on pigs, var. *equi* is found on horses, var. *bovis* on cows, and var. *canis* on dogs. *Sarcoptes scabiei* var. *equi* and var. *canis* are transmittable to man.

OTHER SARCOPTID GENERA.   Other genera of the Sarcoptidae include *Notoedres* with *N. cati,* the feline mange-causing mite (Plate 19–10, Fig. 4); and *Knemidokoptes* (= *Cnemidocoptes*) with two important species, *K. mutans,* the scaly-leg mite of chickens, and *K. laevis,* the depluming mite of chickens, pheasants, and geese.

Family Psoroptidae

Members of the Psoroptidae are scab-causing mites, primarily on mammals. *Psoroptes* includes *P. communis* with various varieties that cause scabs (Plate 19–13, Fig. 1). For example, *P. communis* var. *ovis* causes scabies in sheep. Copulation among adults of this species occurs on

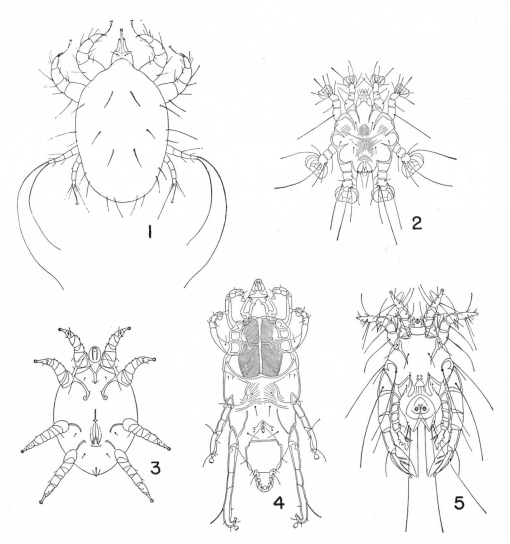

Plate 19-13   Mites. 1. *Psoroptes communis,* dorsal view. (After Herms, 1950.) **2.** *Heteropsorus pteroptopus* female, dorsal view. (After Vitzthum, 1929.) **3.** *Cytodites nudus* female, ventral view. (After Hirst, 1922.) **4.** *Campylochirus caviae* male, ventral view. (After Hirst, 1922.) **5.** *Megninia columbae* male, ventral view. (After Hirst, 1922.)

the host, but the females undergo an additional molt before ovipositing. The eggs are laid on the wool. *Psoroptes communis* var. *equi* causes the serious scab disease of horses, and *P. communis* var. *bovis* causes psoroptic mange in cattle. In rabbits, *P. communis* var. *cuniculi* causes ear canker.

Other genera of the Psoroptidae include *Caparinia; Otodectes;* and *Chorioptes* with *C. symbiotes,* which causes the foot scab disease of horses, *C. bovis,* the tail mange mite of cattle, and *C. ovis,* the foot mange mite of sheep.

Other Sarcoptiform Families

Heteropsorus pteroptopus of the family Heteropsoridae, is found in the skin of various wild birds in France and Italy (Plate 19–13, Fig. 2).

Cytodites nudus of the family Cytoditidae is found in the air sacs, respiratory system, and body cavity of chickens, canaries, and wild ruffled grouse (Plate 19–13, Fig. 3). Within the body cavity, mites of this species are attached to the visceral organs such as the liver. If large numbers are present, peritonitis and enteritis ensue. If similar large numbers are present in the respiratory system, suffocation generally results.

Laminosioptes cysticola of the family Laminosioptidae is parasitic in various tissues of domestic fowl. This mite is harmful in that it invades subcutaneous tissues in the neck, breast, and flanks. It destroys the connective tissue fibers and myofibers of birds. Whitish calcareous cysts are commonly found in the tissues of birds harboring this mite. Such cysts are not formed around living mites, but represent host tissue reaction to aggregations of dead mites accumulated within the tissues. The life cycle of *L. cysticola* is unresolved.

Members of the family Epidermoptidae are generally found on the skin of birds. Representative genera are *Epidermoptes, Dermation,* and *Dermatophagoides. Epidermoptes bilobatus* lives on the skin of chickens and causes a scaly skin condition known as pityriasis. *Dermatophagoides scheremetewskyi* attacks man and causes a mange-like inflammation (Sasa, 1950; Traver, 1951).

Psoralges liberatus, of the family Psoralgidae, is found on the fur of the mammal *Tamandua* sp. During its life cycle, the larvae and nymphs live in colonies in subcutaneous bladders. Their presence causes itching. The adults are free-living (epizoic) in the hair.

Members of the family Listrophoridae are usually found on small and medium-sized mammals. However, *Chirodiscus* is found on birds. *Labidocarpus nasicolus* is found on the nose of bats, where it feeds on the secretions of the sebaceous glands. Certain members of this family are destructive to laboratory animals. For example, *Campylochirus caviae* attaches to hair on the back of guinea pigs (Plate 19–13, Fig. 4), and *Myocoptes musculinus* causes mange (myocoptic mange) on white mice and on guinea pigs (Sengbusch, 1960).

PARASITES IN FEATHERS OF BIRDS

Most of the so-called feather mites of birds belong to three acarid families—Analgesidae, Dermoglyphidae, and Proctophyllodidae. Analgesidae includes some sixteen genera. Quite representative of this family is *Megninia columbae* found on pigeons (Plate 19–13, Fig. 5). Dermoglyphidae includes over thirty-five genera represented here by *Falculifer* and *Pterolichus,* both found on various birds (Plate 9–14, Figs. 1 and 2). Proctophyllodidae includes some nine genera, of which *Trouessartia* is a representative (Plate 19–14, Fig. 3).

Some Accidental Parasites

The family Pediculochelidae* includes *Pediculochelus raulti,* which is most commonly found on bees in Natal (Plate 19–10, Fig. 2). However, its presence has been reported on a rat in Florida and on *Gallus gallus* in the Philippines. It is not known whether this mite is a true parasite that is not very host specific, or whether it is an accidental parasite.

The family Acaridae includes species that are not actually parasites but are associated with stored grains, cereals, and milk products. *Acarus* of this family includes *A. siro,* the grain or cheese mite, so-called because it is found on these stored foods. It is known to bite man and cause a rash. Similarly *A. americanus,* the cereal mite, and *A.* (= *Tyrophagus*) *longior,* both found in grains, cereals, and dry seeds, will bite humans. Hinman and Kampmeier (1934) reported a case in which *A. longior* was found in the urinary tract. This instance of endoparasitism undoubtedly represents accidental parasitism established when contaminated food was eaten.

---

*Familial diagnoses are not given here. Interested readers are referred to Baker and Wharton (1952) or Yunker (1955).

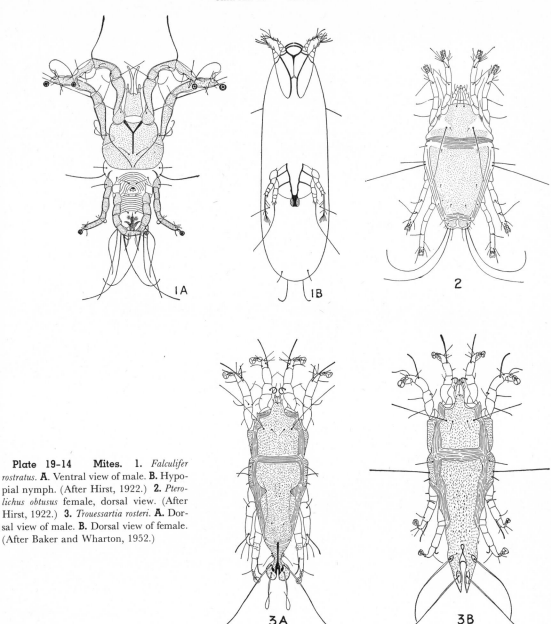

Plate 19-14   Mites. 1. *Falculifer rostratus.* **A.** Ventral view of male. **B.** Hypopial nymph. (After Hirst, 1922.) **2.** *Pterolichus obtusus* female, dorsal view. (After Hirst, 1922.) **3.** *Trouessartia rosteri.* **A.** Dorsal view of male. **B.** Dorsal view of female. (After Baker and Wharton, 1952.)

ORIBATEI GROUP

The mites of this group are all free-living, found primarily in damp places, in grass, mosses, humus, and similar habitats. Their importance in parasitology stems from the role certain members play as intermediate hosts for helminth parasites, specifically cestodes of the family Anoplocephalidae. This phase of helminthology has been discussed in Chapter 12. Kates and Runkel (1948) have reviewed the role of oribatid mites as intermediate hosts for tapeworms.

Mites of the Oribatei Group that serve as intermediate hosts belong to seven families. Some of these are listed in Table 19–2. The mites are not parasitic. Specimens infected with larval anoplocephalid tapeworms are ingested by foraging definitive hosts of the worms.

Table 19-2.   Representative Anoplocephalid Cestodes and Their Mite Intermediate Hosts

Cestode	Vertebrate Host	Mite Intermediate Host	Locality
Bertiella studeri	Primates	*Scutovertex minutus*	Germany
		Notaspis coleoptratus	Germany
		Galumna sp.	Germany
Moniezia expansa	Cattle, lambs, sheep	*Scheloribates laevigatus*	U.S., USSR
		Protoschelobates seghettii	U.S.
		Oribatula minuta	U.S.
		Galumna virginiensis	U.S.
		G. obvius	USSR
		Galumna sp.	U.S.
M. benedeni	Calves, lambs	*Scheloribates laevigatus*	USSR
		Galumna obvius	USSR
Moniezia sp.	Ruminants	*Adoristes ovatus*	USSR
Anoplocephala perfoliata	Asses, horses	*Carabodes* sp.	USSR
		Liacarus sp.	USSR
		Scheloribates laevigatus	USSR
		S. latipes	USSR
		Achipteria sp.	USSR
		Galumna nervosus	USSR
		G. obvius	USSR
A. magna	Asses, horses	*Scheloribates laevigatus*	USSR
Cittotaenia ctenoides	Common European rabbit	*Scutovertex minutus*	Germany
	(Oryctolagus cuniculus)	*Xenillus tegeocranus*	Germany
		Cepheus cepheiformis	Germany
		Liacarus coracinus	Germany
		Scheloribates laevigatus	Germany
		Liebstadia similis	Germany
		Notaspis coleoptratus	Germany
		Galumna nervosus	U.S.
		G. obvius	Germany
C. denticulata	Common European rabbit	*Scutovertex minutus*	Germany
		Xenillus tegeocranus	Germany
		Cepheus cepheiformis	Germany
		Liacarus coracinus	Germany
		Scheloribates laevigatus	Germany
Thysaniezia giardi		*Scheloribates laevigatus*	USSR
		S. latipes	USSR
Paranoplocephala mamillana	Horses, rarely tapirs	*Galumna obvius*	USSR
		Allogalumna longipluma	USSR

THE PHYSIOLOGY OF MITES

As with the ticks, the voluminous amount of material published on mites is mainly concerned with their morphology and taxonomy. Relatively little is known about the physiology and host-parasite relationships of these animals. Here lies another phase of parasitology that awaits the eager investigator.

Oxygen Requirements

The parasitic mites are undoubtedly like their free-living cousins in that they are aerobic. No studies are yet available as to the amount of oxygen the various species living in varying habitats on their hosts require. Efficient tracheal systems in some species suggest their aerobic habits. However, in species that lack such a system, it is generally accepted that gaseous exchange occurs through the thin exoskeleton.

Metabolism

Practically nothing is known about the metabolism of zooparasitic mites. In recent years, however, studies of this nature have been conducted on the two-spotted spider mite *Tetranychus urticae,* a favored experimental animal of acarine physiologists. This mite feeds on plants. In this mite, Ehrhardt and Voss (1961) have found a number of glucosidases that are capable of hydrolyzing various carbohydrates—such as maltose, sucrose, trehalose, melibiose, lactose, melezitose, and raffinose—to monosaccharides. The presence of α–glucosidase, cellulase, pectinase, and polygalacturonase, on the other hand, could not be demonstrated.

In addition, Mehrotra (1960, 1961, 1963) has shown in *T. urticae* that hexose phosphates can be utilized through the Embden-Meyerhof glycolytic pathway, as well as by the hexose monophosphate (pentose phosphate) shunt. Mehrotra has calculated that about 40 to 45 per cent of the glucose is metabolized through the hexose monophosphate pathway. Some of the enzymes of the Krebs cycle have also been shown to be present, thus suggesting that this metabolic cycle takes place in the mite.

The presence of an active hexose monophosphate pathway in *Tetranychus urticae* may have physiological significance, since Siperstein and Fagan (1958) have implicated this pathway in the synthesis of lipids. Indeed, as Mehrotra has pointed out, McEnroe's (1963) studies indicate that the respiratory quotient (RQ) of the normal summer form of *T. urticae* is suggestive of the synthesis of fats from carbohydrates.

It is not known if the glucosidases found in *Tetranychus urticae* occur in the zooparasitic species, nor is it known whether both the Embden-Meyerhof and the hexose monophosphate pathways occur in the zooparasites.

Because most zooparasitic mites feed on their host's blood, lymph, cells, and cell products, proteolytic enzymes undoubtedly occur.

Osmoregulation and Equilibrium Humidity

Wharton (1960) pointed out an important aspect of mite physiology—that of water balance. Inasmuch as these microscopic arthropods are of such minute sizes, they have great difficulty in obtaining and retaining water for use in their metabolism. The mechanism(s) employed by these animals to maintain water balance is not understood and deserves attention.

The role of equilibrium humidity in the physiology of acarinas has been reviewed by Wharton (1963). Equilibrium humidity is defined as the lowest relative humidity (RH) at which a living system can achieve equilibrium conditions and still maintain life. From the few studies now available, it appears that adult parasitic acarinas have a high equilibrium humidity. For example, Lees (1946) has shown that many adult ticks have an equilibrium humidity slightly above 90 per cent RH, and Wharton and Kanungo (1962) have shown that the females of the rodent ectoparasite *Echinolaelaps echidninus* have an equilibrium humidity of about 90 per cent RH.

The significance of equilibrium humidity in animals, especially minute animals like mites, cannot be overestimated. In most instances this is a matter of life or death. If mites are placed in desiccating humidities, they continue to lose water until they succumb to desiccation. On the other hand, if mites are temporarily exposed to an RH above its equilibrium humidity, they may replace their normal water losses by active intake of water from the atmosphere.

In addition to a matter of survival, equilibrium humidity also influences the feeding rate of mites. For example, it is known that the equilibrium humidity of *Echinolaelaps echidninus* is 90 per cent RH below temperatures of 90° F. At 90° F. and above, this mite cannot maintain its water balance at 90 per cent RH without feeding. Thus, *E. echidninus* will feed more readily at an RH below 90 per cent and at temperatures above 90° F. (Wharton and Cross, 1957). Since the damage that ectoparasitic mites inflict is almost always associated with feeding, a relative humidity above the equilibrium humidity of the parasite could possibly reduce the rate of feeding so as to render it relatively harmless.

HOST-PARASITE RELATIONSHIPS

Many ectoparasitic mites are blood ingestors; others feed on epidermal scales and lymph. It is presumed that a certain amount of oxygen is taken into the body via the ingested erythrocytes. Relative to the nocturnal or diurnal feeding habits of certain species, Harrison (1957) suggested that the feeding pattern of the mite could well be influenced by the host's activity. This investigator reported that the majority of trombiculid mite species that feed on rats—a nocturnal animal—become detached at night when the host is active. Whether departure from the host is due to a mere physical disruption or the result of physiological changes within the host remains to be determined. Harrison also reported that the feeding of trombiculid mites is influenced by the number attached to a single host. For example, the feeding time of these mites is approximately equal, but if the host is heavily parasitized, the mites show a shorter average feeding time.

Mites secrete an anticoagulant. For example, Donnadieu (1876) demonstrated that in some plant-parasitizing members of the family Tetranichidae (Trombidiformes), bunches of grapelike glands secrete a substance into the zone of the mouthparts. Aoki (1957), by using histochemical techniques, demonstrated that the mammal-biting larvae of trombiculid mites pierce the stratum corneum and stratum lucidum of their host's skin with their cheliceral blades and secrete an enzyme that acts at the point of attachment. The tissues in this area change into a hyaline substance. Interestingly enough, Aoki reported that the process is reversed when the larva detaches itself from the host. The hyaline appearance of the tissues disappears, thus suggesting that the secreted substance is no longer present. Aoki has presented some of the other theories advanced to explain the anticoagulating abilities of feed-ing mites. In *Argas persicus,* an anticoagulin is present in the salivary glands and in the gut.

The nature of this book does not warrant discussion of the histopathogenicity caused by various mites on wild and domestic animals. However, it is of interest to point out that although scalyness and similar conditions are generally present, little host tissue reaction occurs when skin-penetrating mites are present. Yunker and Ishak (1957), for example, pointed out that when *Knemidokoptes pilae* causes scaly leg or scaly face in the budgerigar *Melopsithacus undulatus* (lovebird group), an inflammatory reaction takes place in the host's stratum corneum, involving primarily polymorphonuclear leukocytes, some mononuclear leukocytes, and eosinophils, only in the very initial phase. Such tissue response soon disappears even after the mites become embedded in skin pouches and actively feed on keratin. Again, Pillers (1921) and Griffiths and O'Rouke (1950) pointed out that inflammatory lesions are absent in the initial stages of scaly-leg infections of fowls caused by *Knemidokoptes mutans.* It is postulated that the exoskeleton of mites serves as a somewhat biologically neutral shield that does not excite host tissue response.

Evolution of Parasitism Among the Acarina

Very little information is available on the evolution of parasitism among the Acarina. From what is known, parasitism among these animals appears to have developed out of their feeding habits—that is, the predators and scavengers gradually became dependent on what are now hosts. Evidence indicates that the parasitic trombidiform mites originated as parasites of reptiles. From this ancestral group, four others have arisen. The first to arise is represented by a small number of species that parasitize arthropods, particularly those species found in the same habitats as reptiles. The second group became adapted to living in the skins of amphibians. The third group, still parasitic in reptiles, became isolated in the lungs of marine snakes. The fourth group, which is by far the largest, developed as parasites of mammals and became widely distributed. It would also appear that the more primitive trombidiforms are not only found on their hosts but also in the fields where their hosts reside, while more recent forms are more intimately associated with their hosts (Audy, 1960).

LITERATURE CITED

Aoki, T. 1957. Histochemical studies on the so-called styostome or hypopharynx in the tissues of the hosts parasitized by the trombiculid mites. Acta Med. Biol. (Niigata), *5:* 103–120.

Audy, J. R. 1960. Evolutionary aspects of trombiculid mite parasitization. *In* Proceedings of the Centenary and Bicentenary Congress of Biology (R. D. Purchon, ed.). University of Malaya Press, Singapore.

Baker, E. W., and G. W. Wharton. 1952. An Introduction to Acarology. Macmillan, New York.

Banks, N. 1915. The Acarina or mites. U.S.D.A. Report, *108:* 1–153.

Bertram, D. S., K. Unsworth, and R. M. Gordon. 1946. The biology and maintenance of *Liponyssus bacoti* Hirst, 1913, and an investigation into its role as a vector of *Litosomoides carinii* to cotton rats, together with some observations on the infection in the white rats. Ann. Trop. Med. Parasitol., *40:* 228–252.

Bregetova, N. G. 1956. [Key to the families of gamasid mites, Superfamily Gamasoidea] (In Russian). Opred. Fauny SSSR, Zool. Inst. Akad. Nauk SSSR, *59:* 143–324.

Camin, J. H. 1963. Relations between host-finding behavior and life histories in ectoparasitic acarina. *In* Advances in Acarology (J. A. Naegele, ed.). Cornell University Press, Ithaca, N.Y., Vol. I, pp. 411–424.

Camin, J. H., and F. E. Gorirossi. 1955. A revision of the suborder Mesostigmata (Acarina), based on new interpretations of comparative morphological data. Spec. Publ. II. Chicago Acad. Sci.

Carter, H. F., G. Wedd, and V. St. E. D'Abrera. 1944. The occurrence of mites (Acaria) in human sputum and their possible significance. India Med. Gaz., *79:* 163–168.

Crowell, R. M., 1960. The taxonomy, distribution and developmental stages of Ohio water mites. Bull. Ohio Biol. Survey, *1:* 1–77.

Donnadieu, A. L. 1876. Recherches pour servir a l'histoire des tetranyques. Ann. Soc. Linn. Lyon, *22:* 29–163.

Ehrhardt, P., and G. Voss. 1961. Die Carbohydrasen der Spinnmilbe *Tetranychus urticae* Koch (Acari Trombidiformes, Tetranychidae). Experientia, *17:* 307.

Ewing, H. E. 1929. A Manual of External Parasites. Charles C Thomas, Springfield, Ill.

Ewing, H. E. 1938. North American mites of the subfamily Myobiinae, new subfamily (Arachnida). Proc. Ent. Soc. Wash., *40:* 180–197.

Ewing, H. E. 1944. The trombiculid mites (chigger mites) and their relation to disease. J. Parasit., *30:* 339–365.

Ferris, G. F. 1928. The genus *Myialges* (Acarina: Sarcoptidae). Ent. News, *39:* 137–140.

Fox, I. 1947. Seven new mites from rats in Puerto Rico. Ann. Ent. Soc. Amer., *40:* 598–603.

Griffiths, R. B., and F. J. O'Rouke. 1950. Observations on the lesions caused by *Cnemidocoptes mutans* and their treatment, with special reference to the use of "gammexane." Parasitology, *44:* 93–100.

Harrison, J. L. 1957. Additional feeding times of trombiculid larvae. Stud. Inst. Med. Res. Kuala Lumpur, *28:* 383–393.

Hinman, E. H., and R. H. Kampmeier. 1934. Intestinal acariasis due to *Tyroglyphus longior* Gervais. Am. J. Trop. Med., *14:* 355–362.

Jameson, E. W. 1948. Myobiid mites (Acarina: Myobiinae) from shrews (Mammalia: Soricidae) of eastern North America. J. Parasit., *34:* 336–342.

Kates, K. C., and C. E. Runkel. 1948. Observations on oribatid mite vectors of *Moniezia expansa* on pastures, with a report of several new vectors from the United States. Proc. Helminth. Soc. Wash., *15:* 8–33.

Lees, A. D. 1946. The water balance in *Ixodes ricinus* L. and certain other species of ticks. Parasitology, *37:* 1–20.

Marshall, J., and J. Staley. 1929. A newly observed reaction of certain species of mosquitoes to the bites of larval hydrachnids. Parasitology, *21:* 158–160.

McEnroe, W. D. 1963. The role of the digestive system in the water balance of the two-spotted spider mite *Tetranychus urticae* Koch. *In* Advances in Acarology (J. A. Naegele, ed.). Cornell University Press, Ithaca, N.Y., Vol. I, pp. 225–231.

Mehrotra, K. N. 1960. Carbohydrate metabolism in the two-spotted mite (*Tetranychus telarius*). Bull. Entomol. Soc. Am., *6:* 151.

Mehrotra, K. N. 1961. Carbohydrate metabolism in the two-spotted mite, *Tetranychus telarius* L. I. Hexose monophosphate cycle. Comp. Biochem. Physiol., *3:* 184–198.

Mehrotra, K. N. 1963. Carbohydrate metabolism in the two-spotted spider mite. *In* Advances in Acarology (J. A. Naegele, ed.). Cornell University Press, Ithaca, N.Y., Vol. I, pp. 232–237.

Pillers, A. W. N. 1921. Scaly leg in fowls. Vet. Rec., *33* (n.s. 1): 827–829.

Radford, C. D. 1950. Systematic check list of mite genera and type species. Union Internat. Sci. Biol. ser. C (sect. Ent.), *1:* 1–252.

Sasa, M. 1950. Mites of the genus *Dermatophagoides* Bogdanoff, 1864, found from three cases of human acariasis. Jap. J. Exp. Med., *20:* 519–525.

Sengbusch, H. G. 1960. Control of *Myocoptes musculinus* on guinea pigs. J. Econ. Entomol. *53:* 168.

Siperstein, M. D., and V. M. Fagan. 1958. Studies on the relation between glucose oxidation and intermediary metabolism. I. The influence of glycolysis on the synthesis of cholesterol, and fatty acids in normal liver. J. Clin. Invest., *37:* 1185–1195.

Soar, C. D., and W. Williamson. 1925. The British Hydracarina. Vol. I. Ray Soc. Publ. *110:* 1–216.

Thor, S., and C. Willmann. 1947. Trombidiidae. Das Tierreich Lfg. *71b:* 187–541.

Traver, J. R. 1951. Unusual scalp dermatitis in humans caused by the mite *Dermatophagoides*. Proc. Ent. Soc. Wash., *53:* 1–25.

Turk, F. A., and S. M. Phillips. 1946. A monograph of the slug mite *Riccardoella limacum* (Schrank). Proc. Zool. Soc. London, *115:* 448–472.

Uchida, T., and I. Miyazaki. 1935. Life-history of a water-mite parasitic on *Anopheles*. Proc. Imper. Acad. (Japan), *11:* 73–76.

Volkonsky, M. 1940. *Podapolipus diander,* n. sp. acarien hétérostygmate parasite du criquet migrateue (*Locusta migratoria* L). Arch. Inst. Pasteur Algérie, *18:* 321–340.

Wharton, G. W. 1954. Observations on the feeding of prostigmatid larvae (Acarina: Trombidiformes) on arthropods. Jour. Wash. Acad. Sci., *44:* 244–245.

Wharton, G. W. 1960. Water balance in mites. J. Parasit., *46:* 6.

Wharton, G. W. 1963. Equilibrium humidity. *In* Advances in Acarology. (J. A. Naegele, ed.). Cornell University Press, Ithaca, N.Y., Vol. I, pp. 201–208.

Wharton, G. W., and H. F. Cross. 1957. Studies on the feeding habits of three species of laelaptid mites. J. Parasit., *43:* 45–50.

Wharton, G. W. and K. Kanungo. 1962. Some effects of temperature and relative humidity on water balance in females of the spiny rat mite, *Enchinolaelaps echidninus* (Berlese, 1887) (Acarina Laelaptidae). Ann. Entomol. Soc. Am., *55:* 483–492.

Williams, R. W. 1944. A bibliography pertaining to the mite family Trombidiidae. Amer. Midl. Nat., *2:* 699–712.

Yunker, C. E. 1955. A proposed classification of the Acaridae (Acarina: Sarcoptiformes). Proc. Helminth. Soc. Wash., *22:* 98–105.

Yunker, C. E., and K. G. Ishak. 1957. Histopathological observations on the sequence of infection in knemidokoptic mange of budgerigars (*Melopsittacus undulatus*). J. Parasit., *43:* 664–672.

SUGGESTED READING

Baker, E.W., T. M. Evans, D. J. Gould, W. B. Hull, and H. L. Keegan. 1956. A Manual of Parasitic Mites of Medical and Economic Importance. National Pest Control Assoc., New York. (This concise volume lists and describes the various species of mites that are of economic and medical importance. In addition, the life cycles of the various species are considered along with recommended control methods.)

Baker, E. W., and G. W. Wharton. 1952. An Introduction to Acarology. Macmillan, New York, pp. 1–35. (This reference-text by two recognized acarologists is concerned primarily with the taxonomy of the Acarina. In the pages cited, the authors discuss the general morphology of mites. This section should prove to be beneficial reading for the beginning student.)

Camin, J. H. 1963. Relations between host-finding behavior and life histories in ectoparasitic Acarina. *In* Advances in Acarology. (J. A. Naegele, ed.). Cornell University Press, Ithaca, N.Y., Vol. I, pp. 411–424. (This valuable review summarizes and presents new information on the basic patterns of transmission of ectoparasitic mites. Environmental and physiological factors that affect host-parasite contact are also discussed.)

Dethier, V. G. 1957. The sensory physiology of blood-sucking arthropods. Exptl. Parasit., *6:* 68–122. Read pp. 71–77. (This review article discusses the sensory physiology of certain arthropods. Some information is included on this aspect of the physiology of the Acarina.)

Hughes, T. E. 1959. Mites or the Acari. University of London, Athlome Press. (This excellent monograph discusses the biology and classification of mites. It is an excellent reference.)

20

THE PENTASTOMIDA—
The Tongue Worms

Members of the Pentastomida, commonly referred to as the tongue worms, are of uncertain systematic position. In recent years they have been considered by some as a class of the phylum Arthropoda and by others as a distinct phylum. The pentastomids possess elongate bodies that are cylindrical in some species and flattened in others. Externally the bodies are annulated, but these rings are not true segments. Adults do not possess legs, but four or six rudimentary legs are present on larvae. Because of their vermiform bodies, these animals are often erroneously referred to as worms. There are no distinct lines of demarkation between the head, thorax, and abdomen, but the anteriormost portion is often referred to as the cephalothorax and the ringed body is referred to as the abdomen. The greatly modified form of the adults as well as of the larvae probably reflects their parasitic way of life.

Adult pentastomids are usually parasitic in the respiratory tract and lungs of vertebrates, although at least one species, *Linguatula serrata*, has been known to accidentally migrate into the brain of the definitive host. The larvae are found in the viscera (liver and mesenteric nodes) of the intermediate host, which is usually a mammal or another vertebrate. Thus, these animals are totally parasitic both as larvae and as adults. Hunter and Higgins (1960) reported the finding of an unencapsulated third stage larva of *L. serrata* floating free in the anterior chamber of a boy's eye. How the larva arrived there is unknown.

Digestive System

The mouth is located anteriorly and is subterminal. Around the lip is a chitinous ring that serves as a supporting mechanism. The mouth leads into a buccal cavity, which is linked by a narrow prepharynx with the muscular pharynx. The pharynx in turn opens posteriorly into the esophagus. The esophagus leads into a distended stomach-intestine, which extends almost the entire length of the body and opens into the anus.

Quite characteristic of the pentastomids are the two pairs of hollow fanglike hooks, one pair on each side of the mouth which can be retracted into grooves (Plate 20–1, Fig. 1). In some species, such as *Linguatula serrata,* these hooks are situated on finger-like projections, the parapodia. It has been postulated that these hooks are vestigial appendages. Frontal glands (also known as head glands) are located at the base of each hook. These secrete a lytic substance that liquefies the host's blood or dissolves tissues.

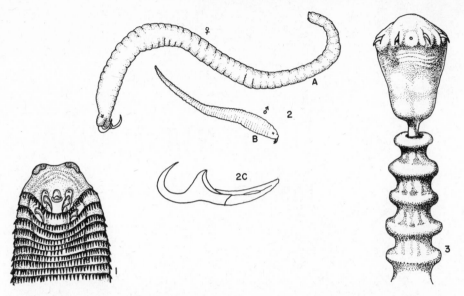

Plate 20-1   **Some parasitic pentastomids.** 1. Anterior end of third stage (mature) larva of
Linguatula serrata, showing two pairs of large hooks. 2. *Megadrepanoides varani*. **A.** Female. **B.** Male.
C. Single anterior hook. (A to C redrawn after Self and Kuntz, 1957.) 3. Anterior end of *Armillifer
annulatus*. (Redrawn after Baird.)

Nervous System

The nervous system of pentastomids is comprised of a circumesophageal ring that is connected with a ventrally located ganglion. Either
a double or a single ventral nerve extends the
entire length of the body, and branches arise
from it to innervate the various tissues. Two
ventral nerves are usually present. Lateral
commissures connect these two cords along
their lengths like rungs of a ladder. This is
obviously a rather primitive nervous system
for an arthropod. Pentastomids possess no
specialized sense organs except for the integument, which is comparatively highly innervated.

Reproductive Systems

Pentastomids are dioecious and exhibit a
certain degree of sexual dimorphism, inasmuch
as the males are usually smaller than the
females. Males possess a single tubular testis,
from which a pair of testiducts arise to conduct
the spermatozoa to a short, pear shaped vas
deferens. The vas deferens opens to the exterior
through a muscular cirrus. The testiducts serve
not only as tubes through which the spermatozoa reach the vas deferens, but also as storage
sites. Thus, they are sometimes referred to as
seminal vesicles (Plate 20–2).

In females, two oviducts arise from a single
elongate saccular ovary (Plate 20–2). The oviducts conduct the ova to the uterus, which
is short and simple in some species and long
and convoluted in others. The uterus leads
into a short muscular vagina, which opens to
the exterior through the female genital pore.
This pore is located ventrally, near the anterior end of the abdomen in some species and
near the posterior end in others. The genital
pore of the male is situated at the anterior
margin of the abdomen in all species. Fertilization is internal. That two testiducts in males lead
from a single testis and two oviducts lead from
a single ovary in females suggest that each sex
of the ancestral form possessed two gonads.
Pentastomids are oviparous.

Body Tissues

The body surface of pentastomids is covered
with a layer of chitin, which presumably consists of strata as in other arthropods. Underneath the chitinous exoskeleton is found the
hypodermis composed of discrete cells. Intermingled among the cells are unicellular glands,
which secrete a substance onto the outer surface of the exoskeleton. The body musculature
is mediad to the hypodermis. The striated
muscles are metamerically arranged.

The buccal cavity and prepharynx are lined
with chitin and are of stomodeal origin (ectodermal). The buccal cavity and the prepharynx

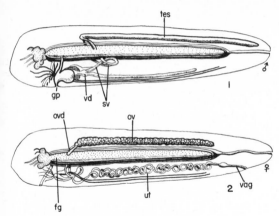

Plate 20-2   Male and female reproductive systems of pentastomids. 1. Male system of *Waddycephalus teretiusculus*. 2. Female system of *W. teretiusculus*. (Figures redrawn after Spencer in Heymons, 1935.)

(fg, frontal gland; gp, genital pore; sv, seminal vesicle; tes, testis; ut, uterus; vag, vagina; vd, vas deferens.)

are collectively known as the foregut. The stomach-intestine, or midgut, is lined with a layer of columnar cells that possess distinctly striated borders. The nuclei of these cells are basally located and are of the vesicular type. These gastrodermal cells rest on a well defined basement membrane, beneath which is found a thin muscular layer. This layer of myofibers is continuous with the mesenteries, which suspend the gut from the body wall. The pentastomids are true coelomate animals; hence, a peritoneum lines the body cavity.

Rao and Jennings (1959) reported that two types of cells make up the lining of the midgut. These cells can be distinguished by their characteristic reactions to the periodic acid–Schiff (PAS) reaction and Turnbull's blue reaction for iron. The first type of cell, designated here as PAS-positive cells, include large amounts of PAS-positive, saliva-fast, Turnbull-negative granules. Such granules collect medially within the cells (toward the lumen). Periodically these cells rupture, emptying the granules into the lumen.

The second type of cell, designated here as PAS-negative cells, contains varying amounts of colorless PAS-negative granules, which are strongly positive to Turnbull's blue reaction for iron. These iron-containing granules also concentrate at the medial pole of the cells, and eventually the entire mass of cells are extruded from the gastrodermis and passed out intact in feces.

The hindgut or rectum is also lined with chitin and is proctodeal (ectodermal) in origin.

SYSTEMATICS AND BIOLOGY

Over fifty species of pentastomids have been reported. Taxonomic reviews and monographs have been contributed by Hill (1948), Sambon (1922), and Stiles and Hassall (1927). These should be consulted by those interested in identification. According to Heymons and Vtizthum (1936), the Pentastomida is subdivided into two orders—the Cephalobaenida and the Porocephalida. A diagnosis of these two orders follows.

Order 1. Cephalobaenida.   Hooks are located on parapodia. Genital pore in both sexes is located at anteroventral margin of abdomen. Larvae possess six legs.
Order 2. Porocephalida.   Hooks are not located on parapodia, but are arranged in straight or curved line. Genital pore in female is located at posteroventral margin of abdomen. Larvae possess four legs.

ORDER CEPHALOBAENIDA

Members of the Cephalobaenida are divided into two families. Those parasitic in the lungs of snakes, toads, and lizards are assigned to the Cephalobaenidae; those found in air sacs of birds are assigned to the Reighardiidae.

Family Cephalobaenidae

This family includes the genera *Raillietiella* in Ophidia, Lacertilia, and Bufonidae in East Africa and Asia; *Sambonia* and *Kiricephalus* in water snakes (Ophidia) from the Orient and Australasian regions; and *Megadrepanoides* from the Solomon Islands (Plate 20-1, Fig. 2). No complete life history is yet available for these pentastomids. However, Gigloli (1923), in analyzing the feeding habits of the reptiles that serve as definitive hosts for *Raillietiella furcocerca*, suggested that the intermediate host could possibly be an invertebrate. Similarly, Self and Kuntz (1957) postulated that since they collected *Raillietiella* spp. from the lungs of various lizards known to be insectivorous, the intermediate host could very well be an invertebrate.

Family Reighardiidae

The family Reighardiidae includes the genus *Reighardia* with species found in the air sacs of gulls and terns (Laridae). The intermediate host, according to Sambon (1922), is probably a fish.

ORDER POROCEPHALIDA

Members of the Porocephalida are again divided into two families. Those subordinate to the Porocephalidae possess cylindrical bodies and are found in the lungs of reptiles. Those subordinate to the Linguatulidae possess flattened bodies and are generally found in the nasal passages of members of the feline and canine families.

Family Porocephalidae

The Porocephalidae includes the genus *Armillifer* (=*Nettorhynchus*) (Plate 20–1, Fig. 3). Adult members of this genus are found in the lungs, trachea, and nasal passages of snakes in eastern Africa and the Orient. The life cycle includes two vertebrate hosts. This is not surprising, for the definitive host is a carnivorous lizard or snake that feeds on small mammals in which the larvae are found.

Eggs oviposited by females in the definitive host are passed to the exterior in the nasal mucus and adhere to vegetation. When such eggs are ingested by the intermediate host, accidentally or intentionally, the larvae, which are already fully formed within the eggshells, hatch and actively burrow through the intestinal wall to become lodged in one of the visceral organs, such as lungs, liver, and kidneys. In the organ, the larvae undergo further development, molting and increasing in size. When the infective stage is reached, the larvae drop out of the organ and encyst in the abdominal or pleural cavity.

The intermediate hosts for *Armillifer* spp. include an array of mammals, such as various monkeys, antelopes, hedgehogs, rats, cats, giraffes, and even humans on some occasions. When an infected intermediate host is ingested by the definitive host, the infective larvae migrate to the lungs via the throat and trachea.

Human infections by *Armillifer* have occurred in Africa and the Far East. In Africa, *A. armillatus* larvae have been found in the liver, spleen, and lungs of humans. Such infections could have been contracted in one of three ways—by drinking water contaminated with eggs; by eating vegetables on which the eggs are found; and by handling or eating snakes that serve as the definitive host, thus become infected with the eggs. In China, the Philippines, and other Asian islands, *A. moniliformis* is the species

whose larvae are found in man. In the United States *Porocephalus crotali* is found in rattlesnakes and water moccasins, and *Kiricephalus coarctatus* occurs in colubrid snakes (Plate 20–3, Figs. 1 and 2). Penn (1942) reported that *P. crotali* utilizes muskrats (and other mammals) as the intermediate host.

Life Cycle of *Porocephalus crotali*. Esslinger (1962a, b, c) has made a detailed study of the life cycle of *P. crotali* and the response of the intermediate host to this parasite. He reported that the eggs obtained from adults in the lungs of the water moccasin *Agkistrodon piscivorus* in Louisiana possess shells composed of four distinct membranes. These eggs are highly resistant to desiccation and enclose fully formed larvae. The larvae bear four legs. From observations on the structure and function of these legs, it was concluded that their operation is based on both muscular and hydraulic mechanisms.

When pentastomid eggs are fed to albino rats, and representative infected rats are killed and examined weekly over a period of 6 months, seven immature stages can be identified within the intermediate host. The form hatching from the egg in the rat's intestine is the primary larva. It bears two pairs of legs. It actively migrates through the wall of the host's small intestine and comes to rest in the viscera and associated mesenteries. While migrating through the intestine, the larva leaves a trail of the host's neutrophils, which undoubtedly have migrated toward the parasite as a manifestation of the host's response to the parasite. Within 7 days after the infection, primary larvae are found in the liver, where their migratory path is marked by mononuclear cells and neutrophils.

Once situated in the liver or some other visceral organ, the parasite undergoes six molts, each one followed by a period of growth and differentiation. The sixth stage nymph shows marked sexual differentiation. While the parasite is undergoing ecdysis, growth, and differentiation, a granulomatous lesion is formed around it in the host's liver. During the first 3 weeks, there is macrophage proliferation, production of epithelioid and giant cells in the area of the lesion, accompanied by an accumulation of eosinophils. During the second and third months, the lesion becomes chronic. There are increasing numbers of fibroblasts, fibrous tissue, plasma cells, and lymphocytes. Finally by the fourth month, the active inflammation subsides. By the sixth month the sixth

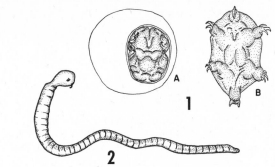

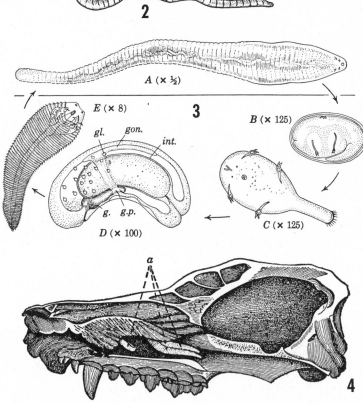

Plate 20-3   Some parasitic pentastomids. 1. *Porocephalus crotali.* **A.** Egg enclosing larva. **B.** Larva. (Redrawn after Penn, 1942.) **2.** *Kiricephalus coarctatus.* (Redrawn after Sambon.) **3.** Stages in the life cycle of *Linguatula serrata.* **A.** Adult female from nasal passage of a dog. **B.** Egg containing embryo. **C.** First-stage larva from viscera of sheep, man, etc. **D.** Third-stage larva, ninth week. **E.** Nymph from liver of sheep. **4.** Sagittal view of head of dog, showing three specimens of *L. serrata.* (Figs. 3 and 4 after Brumpt, 1949; Leuckart, 1860; and Alfort, 1884. *In* Chandler, A. C. 1955. *Introduction to Parasitology,* Wiley, New York.)

stage nymph is surrounded by a dense, hyaline fibrous capsule.

The sixth stage nymph is well developed by the third month and is infective to the reptilian definitive host from that time on. Infection is affected by ingestion of the infected rodent host.

Family Linguatulidae

The Linguatulidae includes the genera *Linguatula* and *Subtriquetra.*

GENUS *Linguatula.* The most common species is *L. serrata* (Plate 20-1, Fig. 1), found in nasal passages and frontal sinuses of canines and felines. The adult pentastomid is colorless. The females are 100 to 130 mm. long by 10 mm. wide. Within the nasal passages, these parasites dig into the lining and suck blood, causing bleeding, catarrh, and mechanical ob-

struction to normal breathing. The distribution of *Linguatula serrata* appears to be worldwide. It has been reported from Europe, Africa, South and North America, and Asia.

Linguatula rhinaria is a common parasite of livestock. It can become a facultative parasite in man in both the adult and nymphal stages.

Life Cycle of *Linguatula serrata.* Hobmaier and Hobmaier (1940) resolved the complete life history of this species. These investigators reported that the eggs, measuring 90 by 70 μ, include fully formed larvae with four rudimentary legs. The females produce enormous numbers of eggs; some report that a single female can produce several million eggs. The eggshell is resistant and wrinkled. These eggs pass out of the definitive host in nasal discharges and are deposited in water or on vegetation.

When contaminated water or vegetation is swallowed by an intermediate host, the eggs hatch, liberating acariform or primary larvae (Plate 20–3, Fig. 3C) that bore through the intestinal wall of the intermediate host (cattle, sheep, rabbits, man) and become lodged in the viscera, especially in the liver and lungs, or in the mesenteric nodes, where they are covered by host-elaborated cysts. Here the larvae undergo two molts, resulting in a pupa-like stage that is devoid of mouthparts, hooks, or body annulations. Such a larva measures from 0.35 to 0.5 mm. in length (Plate 20–3, Fig. 3D). Further growth and seven additional molts ensue.* The resultant nymph (sometimes referred to as the infective larva) (Plate 20–3, Fig. 3E) is 4 to 6 mm. long and bears two pairs of hooks and 80 to 90 annular rings. Minute spines project from the posterior margin of each ring. This is the infective form of *L. serrata*. This infective nymph migrates from the visceral organ in which it has developed and encysts in the abdominal or pleural cavity of the intermediate host.

When the intermediate host, especially if a sheep or rabbit, is eaten by the definitive host, the nymphs either escape rapidly from the cyst once they enter the definitive host and cling to the mucous membrane in the host's mouth, or more likely, migrate anteriorly when the surrounding intermediate host's tissues are digested and cling to the lining in the host's mouth. From this position they migrate to the nasal cavities of the host, where they develop rapidly into adults. After copulation, adult females begin ovipositing in about 6 months. Adults are capable of surviving for up to 2 years.

If infected intermediate hosts are ingested by an unnatural definitive host, the larvae do not migrate to the nasal passages as is normally the case. They do, however, penetrate the intestinal wall and encyst in the body cavity.

PHYSIOLOGY

Oxygen Requirements

Although pentastomids possess no respiratory system, it is quite apparent that these aberrant

arthropods are aerobic animals, because they are found in oxygen-rich location within the host—for example, nasal passages and lungs. Gaseous exchange occurs through the body wall or, as some claim in certain species, through the minute stigmata located on the thin exoskeleton.

The eggs of *Linguatula serrata* and *Porocephalus armillatus* are extremely resistant to adverse environmental conditions (Watson, 1960) and can survive a long time outside the host.

Nutrient Requirements

Rao and Jennings (1959) reported that in *Raillietiella agcoi,* a parasite in the lungs of the water snake *Natrix piscator* and other species of snakes, the food consists of host's blood drawn from the blood vessels in the lungs. The haemolytic activities of the frontal glands were confirmed by these workers. Only rarely were intact erythrocytes seen in the midgut; hence, haemolysis must have occurred soon after the cells were ingested.

Digestion is mainly intraluminar. However, the intraluminar digestion is supplemented by intracellular digestion within the PAS-negative cells of the gastrodermis. This hypothesis is verified by the presence of the iron in these cells. Intracellular digestion, however, is not complete. Further breakdown occurs after the PAS-negative cells are expelled into the lumen.

HOST-PARASITE RELATIONSHIPS

Host-parasite relationships among the Pentastomida have not been studied to any extent. No experimental evidence exists. However, clinical observations of the effects these parasites have on their hosts have been recorded in some instances. It is known that the developmental stages of *Linguatula serrata* can cause considerable trauma in intermediate hosts, resulting from their perforation of the intestine and migration into the visceral organs. If damage to the liver is severe, hepatitis ensues.

Adult pentastomids have been known to accidentally migrate into the brain of a definitive host. If this happens, meningitis ensues. Similarly, the presence of these arthropods in the lungs can cause pneumonitis. It is not uncommon for these arthropods to cause death.

Baer (1946) noted that the location of pentastomids in the air sacs of birds and in the res-

---

*Although a total of nine molts have been reported in *Linguatula serrata,* the more recent work on *Porocephalus crotali* suggests that only six molts occur. It is possible, though unlikely, that these two closely related pentastomids undergo a different number of molts.

piratory sinuses of mammals is of evolutionary significance. He postulated that these animals were originally, and most species still are, parasites of poikilothermic animals. During the transition from cold-blooded to warm-blooded hosts, they have become adapted to the coldest and most aerated localities within the warm-blooded hosts. The hypothesis that pentastomids originated as parasites in poikilothermic hosts appears to be substantiated by the large number of modern species still parasitic in such hosts. Approximately 43 per cent of the genera and 42 per cent of the species parasitize snakes; 22 per cent of the genera and 28 per cent of the species parasitize crocodiles; and 14 per cent of the genera and 18 per cent of the species parasitize lizards. Only 7 per cent of the known genera parasitize tortoises, birds, and mammals, and a significant percentage of these are parasites of tortoises that are poikilothermic.

LITERATURE CITED

Esslinger, J. H. 1962a. Morphology of the egg and larva of *Porocephalus crotali* (Pentastomida). J. Parasit., *48:* 451–462.

Esslinger, J. H. 1962b. Development of *Porocephalus crotali* (Humboldt, 1808) (Pentastomida) in experimental intermediate hosts. J. Parasit., *48:* 452–456.

Esslinger, J. H. 1962c. Hepatic lesions in rats experimentally infected with *Porocephalus crotali* (Pentastomida). J. Parasit., *48:* 631–638.

Gigloli, G. S. 1923. On the linguatulid arachnid *Raillietiella furcocerca*. Proc. Zool. Soc. London, pp. 15–18.

Heymons, R., and H. G. Vitzthum. 1936. Beiträge zur Systematik der Pentastomiden. Ztschr. Parasitenk., *8:* 1–103.

Hill, H. R. 1948. Annotated bibliography of the Linguatulids. Bull. S. Calif. Acad. Sci., *47:* 56–73.

Hobmaier, A., and M. Hobmaier. 1940. On the life cycle of *Linguatula rhinaria*. Am. J. Trop. Med., *20:* 199–210.

Hunter, W. S., and R. P. Higgins. 1960. An unusual case of human porocephaliasis. J. Parasit., *46:* 68.

Penn, G. H., Jr. 1942. The life history of *Porocephalus crotali*, a parasite of the Louisiana muskrat. J. Parasit., *28:* 277–283.

Rao, H., and J. B. Jennings. 1959. The alimentary system of a pentastomid from the Indian water-snake *Natrix piscator* Schneider. J. Parasit., *45:* 299–300.

Sambon, L. W. 1922. A synopsis of the family Linguatulidae. J. Trop. Med. Hyg., *25:* 188–206.

Self, J. T., and R. E. Kuntz. 1957. Pentastomids from African reptiles of Florida Island, British Solomon Islands (South Pacific). J. Parasit., *43:* 194–199.

Stiles, C. W., and A. Hassall. 1927. Key-catalogue of the crustacea and arachnoids of importance in public health. Bull. No. 148. Hyg. Lab., U. S. Pub. Health Serv., pp. 197–289.

Watson, J. M. 1960. Medical Helminthology. Baillière, Tindell & Cox, London.

SUGGESTED READING

Cannon, D. A. 1942. Linguatulid infestation of man. Ann. Trop. Med. Parasit., *36:* 60–167. (This article discusses the known instances in which linguatulids have parasitized man. It is of general interest.)

Hill, H. R. 1948. Annotated bibliography of the Linguatulids. Bull. S. Calif. Acad. Sci., *47:* 56–73. (This article is of value to students interested in the taxonomy of pentastomids, because it not only lists known species, but also cites literature pertaining to each species.)

Hobmaier, A., and M. Hobmaier. 1940. On the life cycle of *Linguatula rhinaria*. Am. J. Trop. Med., *20:* 199–210. (This article reports a comprehensive study of the life cycle of a pentastomid. It should be consulted by those interested in the exact morphology of the various life cycle stages.)

Penn, G. H., Jr. 1942. The life history of *Porocephalus crotali*, a parasite of the Louisiana muskrat. J. Parasit., *28:* 277–283. (This research article reports the morphology of the life cycle stages of a second pentastomid.)

21

INTRODUCTION TO THE PARASITIC INSECTS

THE SIPHONAPTERA—

The Fleas

THE MALLOPHAGA—

The Biting Lice

THE ANOPLURA—

The Sucking Lice

Insects constitute one of the largest known groups of living animals on the earth. It has been estimated that over 900,000 species of insects are in existence today. The various species are found in every imaginable type of ecological niche, be it terrestrial, fresh-water, or marine.

Man's interest in insects has formalized into that phase of biology known as entomology. Among entomologists, those interested in species that are important as pests of plants and animals have become specialized and have carved out a portion of the field known as eco-nomic entomology. Those entomologists whose interests are concentrated on species that serve either as disease-causing organisms or as vectors of pathogens have established the field of medical entomology. Along similar lines, the broad field of entomology has become subdivided into a number of subdisciplines. Within this and the following two chapters are discussions of those phases of entomology concerned with the biology of insects that lead the parasitic way of life, and the role of the haematophagous, or blood-ingesting, species as vectors.

MORPHOLOGY

The morphology of insects varies greatly from species to species. No other group of animals demonstrates so great a diversity of form as the insects. In addition to the characteristics of the phylum Arthropoda (p. 475), shared with the other classes in the phylum, members of the class Insecta are characterized by three distinct body regions—head, thorax, and abdomen.

The head bears a single pair of antennae and distinct mouthparts adapted for chewing, sucking, or lapping, depending on the feeding habits of the species. The thorax, composed of three somites, bears three pairs of jointed legs and two, one, or no pairs of wings. The abdomen, which is typically composed of eleven or less somites, bears the genitalia at its terminal.

EXTERNAL MORPHOLOGY

APPENDAGES OF THE HEAD

Other than the eyes, both compound and simple, which are discussed on page 564 with the other sense organs, the head of the "typical" insect bears a pair of antennae and mouthparts.

Antennae

The antennae are a pair of movable segmented appendages that are usually inserted between the compound eyes. The point of insertion is a socket, commonly surrounded by a sclerotized ring. The morphology of the antennae varies greatly and is of importance not only in the identification of species but also in the determination of sex in some species.

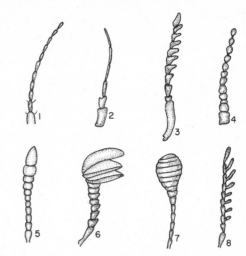

Plate 21-1   Types of insect antennae. 1. Filiform. 2. Setaceous. 3. Serrate. 4. Moniliform. 5. Clavate. 6. Lamellate. 7. Capitate. 8. Pectinate. (Redrawn after Comstock, J. H. 1949. *An Introduction to Entomology*, Comstock Publishing Co., Ithaca, N. Y.)

Antennal types include the thin and threadlike filiform antennae; the pointed setaceous antennae; the sawlike serrate antennae; the beadlike moniliform antennae; the club shaped clavate antennae; the leaflike lamellate antennae; the capitate antennae, which bear a knob or "head" at the distal ends; and the pectinate antennae, which are plumose with comblike lateral projections (Plate 21–1, Figs. 1 to 8).

Mouthparts

The mouthparts of insects vary greatly, depending on the feeding habits of the species. To properly acquaint oneself with the parts, it appears wise to use those of a familiar insect, the grasshopper, as representative of the Insecta (Plate 21–2).

Plate 21-2   Mouthparts of the grasshopper. 1. Frontal view of head, showing anatomical parts. 2. Mouthparts dissected. (After Storer, T. I., and Usinger. 1957. *General Zoology*, McGraw-Hill, New York.)

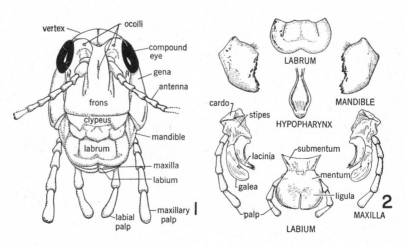

The "upper lip" of the grasshopper is the labrum, which is not an actual mouthpart. The first true mouthparts are the paired mandibles, which lie directly behind the labrum. These are heavily sclerotized and bear jagged teeth along their medial margins. Behind the mandibles are the paired maxillae. Each maxilla is jointed, being composed of the basal cardo, on which is mounted the stipes. The mesially situated lacinia and the laterally situated galea are both mounted distally on the stipes, the jointed palpus (also known as the maxilliped) is attached laterally (Plate 21–3, Fig. 1).

The hypopharynx is not a true mouthpart; it is an unsegmented outgrowth of the body wall. This tubular structure arises from the ventral membranous floor of the head. The "lower lip" of insects is the labium. This heavily sclerotized appendage is attached to the head by the submentum, which broadens out distally to form the mentum. The distal portion of the mentum is the ligula. The labial palpi arise from the lateral aspects of the mentum. The homologies and evolutionary development of the mouthparts of insects are discussed by Ross (1948, pp. 68–74).

Because the mouthparts of insects are greatly modified in many species, the principal types are listed in the following discussion.

CHEWING TYPE. Mouthparts of this type, as exemplified by those of the grasshopper, are usually found among free-living species—for example, beetles and ants. The mandibles masticate the food, and the maxillae and labium serve to push the particles into the mouth.

CUTTING-SPONGING TYPE. The tabanids, or horseflies, of the order Diptera possess mouthparts of this type (Plate 21–3, Fig. 2). The mandibles are in the form of sharp blades, and the maxillae are long and stylet-like. The mandibles and maxillae cut and tear the skin of the host. Blood is collected by a spongelike labium, conveyed to a tube formed by the hypopharynx and the epipharynx (another projection of the body wall), and sucked into the esophagus.

PIERCING-SUCKING TYPE. (Plate 21–3, Fig. 3). The mosquitoes, flies, lice (Anoplura), and bedbugs possess mouthparts of this type. The labrum, mandibles, hypopharynx, and maxillae are long and slender and fit together, forming a hollow tube. The labium is also elongate and wraps around the other parts like a rigid sheath. During feeding, the tube pierces the host's skin like a hypodermic needle, and blood is drawn through it.

CHEWING-LAPPING TYPE. Mouthparts of this type are found in bees and wasps (Plate 21–3, Fig. 4). The labrum and mandibles are similar to those found in the grasshopper; however, the maxillae and labium are modified as elongate structures, which the food is drawn up.

SPONGING TYPE. Most nonbiting dipterans possess mouthparts of this type. The parts are similar to those found in the cutting-sponging type, but the mandibles and maxillae are nonfunctional. The remaining parts form a proboscis with a spongelike apex called the labella. Liquid foods are conducted to the mouth via minute capillary channels on the labella. Solid food is ingested only after it is dissolved or suspended in deposited saliva.

The cutting-sponging and the piercing-sucking types are the most commonly found among haematophagous insects.

APPENDAGES OF THE THORAX

The thorax of insects is typically divided into three segments—the anterior prothorax, the middle mesothorax, and the posterior metathorax. The dorsal surface is covered by the notum (or tergum), the lateral aspects are covered by pleura, and the ventral surface is covered by the sternum.

Legs

The typical legs are found on the thorax, one pair per segment. Each leg consists of six joints—coxa, trochanter, femur, tibia, tarsus, and pretarsus (sometimes considered as a part of the tarsus) (Plate 21–4, Fig. 1). The coxa is the most proximal joint. The shape of the insect leg is modified in many parasitic species.

Wings

Insects are the only group of invertebrates that possess wings. Wings are actually extensions of the body wall. The "typical" insect bears two pairs—the forewings, which are attached to the mesothorax; and the hindwings, which are attached to the metathorax. Each wing exhibits a series of veins, which are actually tracheae that extend from the body proper into the wings during development but which harden and become severed at their bases when the wings complete their develop-

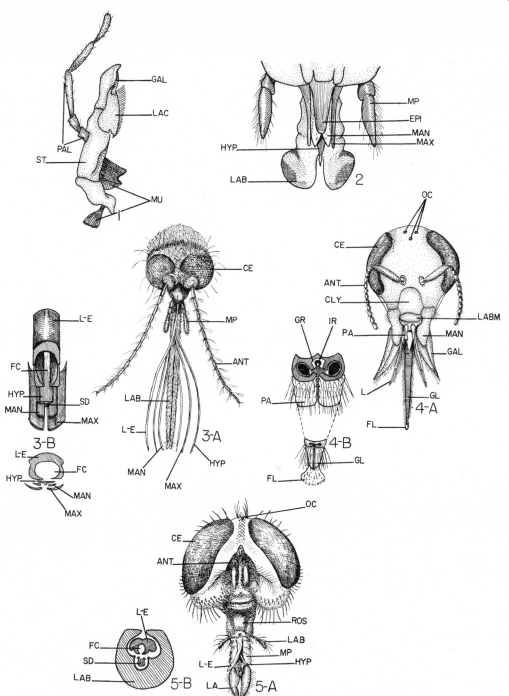

Plate 21-3   Types of insect mouthparts. 1. Maxilla of the cockroach. (Redrawn after Snodgrass.) 2. Cutting-sponging type. (Redrawn from Illinois Natural History Survey.) 3. Piercingsucking type. 4. Chewing-lapping type. 5. Sponging type. (Figs. 3 to 5 redrawn after Metcalf and Flint. 1951. *Destructive and Useful Insects,* McGraw-Hill, New York.)

(ANT, antenna; CE, compound eye; CLY, clypeus; EPI, epipharynx; FC, food channel; FL, flabellum; GAL, galeas, GL, glossa; GR, glossal rode; HYP, hypopharynx; IR, inner channel of rod; L, labial palpus; LA, labella; LAB, labium; LABM, labrum; LAC, lacinia; L-E, labrum-epipharynx; MAN, mandible; MAX, maxilla; MP, maxillary palpus; MU, muscles; OC, ocelli; PA, paraglossa; PAL, palpus; ROS, rostrum; SD, salivary duct; ST, stipes.)

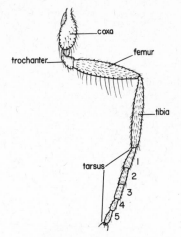

Plate 21-4   Leg of *Musca domestica*. (Original.)

ment and are expanded. The wing venation, or vein pattern, is of great taxonomic importance. The more typical veins and crossveins are depicted in Plate 21–5.

As is discussed in each order considered, the two pairs of wings are both or singly greatly modified or reduced, or even lacking, in many parasitic insects.

INTERNAL MORPHOLOGY

DIGESTIVE SYSTEM

Insects possess complete alimentary tracts. In addition to the tract, there are various associated glands—for example salivary glands, gastric caeca, and Malpighian tubules.

The alimentary canal is an asymmetrical tube, oriented lengthwise through the middle of the body (Plate 21–6, Fig. 1). It opens anteriorly through the mouth, which is located in the preoral cavity—the space enclosed by the mouthparts. The canal opens to the exterior posteriorly through the anus, which is located on the posteriormost segment of the abdomen. Between the mouth and the anus, the alimentary canal is divided into three sections.

Stomodeum

The anterior portion of the alimentary canal is the stomodeum, which in turn is divided into the anterior, tubular esophagus, followed by an enlarged crop, which opens into the narrower valvelike proventriculus. In free-living insects that ingest solid foods, the proventriculus bears a series of hooks, which aid in mastication. If such armatures exist, the proventriculus is called the gastric mill.

In most insects, two tubular glands, called the salivary or labial glands, lie in the body cavity. The ducts of these glands are directed anteriorly. They usually unite anteriorly and conduct glandular secretions into the preoral zone. In haematophagous ectoparasites, the labial glands are quite important because they secrete the anticoagulin that prevents clotting of the host's blood during feeding, and because they are storage sites for protozoan, viral, and other types of microorganisms. These microorganisms are injected into the vertebrate host while the insect vector is feeding.

Ventriculus

The middle section of the alimentary canal is the ventriculus, or stomach. This is the site of digestion. In certain hemipterans, this chamber is subdivided into three or four sections. However, in most parasitic species, the ventriculus is without secondary partitions. Associated with the ventriculus are several tubular diverticula—the gastric caeca—located at the anterior margin of the stomach. These outpocketings function primarily in digestion and to increase the surface for absorption.

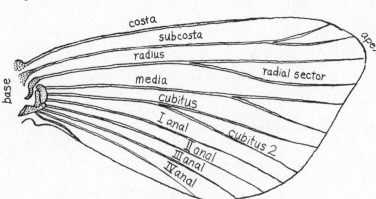

Plate 21-5   Venation of a "typical" insect wing. (Redrawn after Storer, T. I., and Usinger. 1957. *General Zoology*, McGraw-Hill, New York.)

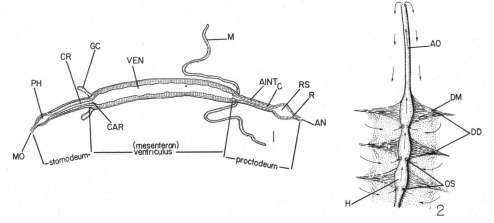

Plate 21-6   Insect morphology. 1. Alimentary tract. (Original.) **2.** Aorta and three chambers of the heart and corresponding part of the dorsal diaphragm, dorsal view. Arrows suggest the course of blood circulation. (After Snodgrass.)

(AINT, anterior portion of intestine; AN, anus; AO, aorta; C, colon; CAR, cardia; CR, crop; DD, dorsal diaphragm; DM, diaphragm muscles; GC, gastric caeca; M, Malpighian tubules; MO, mouth; OS, ostia; PH, pharynx; R, rectum; RS, rectal sac; VEN, ventriculus.)

Proctodeum

The posterior portion of the alimentary canal is the proctodeum, which leads posteriorly from the ventriculus. This tube is subdivided into the intestine, which leads from the stomach, and the rectum, which is the enlarged posterior section that communicates with the exterior through the anus. A group of long tubular structures—the Malpighian tubules—are found in most insects at the junction of the ventriculus and the proctodeum. These tubes, which vary in number depending on the species, serve an excretory function.

EXCRETORY SYSTEM

The elimination of excretory wastes in insects —that is, excess water, nitrogenous wastes, and salts—is accomplished primarily by the Malpighian tubules. Uric acid, in the form of sodium and potassium salts, is eliminated from the body tissues into the circulating blood in the haemocoel. Eventually the waste-containing blood circulates near the Malpighian tubules, which readily absorb the uric acid and discharge it into the intestinal lumen. From the intestinal lumen, the uric acid passes into the proctodeum and then to the exterior through the anus. In certain free-living species, such as lepidopterans of the family Pieridae, some body wastes are converted into pigments (uric acid derivatives) and deposited in the cuticle. This mechanism of excretion, however, has not been conclusively demonstrated in parasitic species.

CIRCULATORY SYSTEM

Insects possess an open circulatory system— that is, the blood or haemolymph is not confined within blood vessels as in vertebrates. Instead, the blood is found unrestrained within the coelom, which is referred to as the haemocoel. From the haemocoel, the blood seeps into the various tissues of the body. In most insects, however, a "heart" and "aorta" are present, and they aid in the circulation of the blood.

The heart and aorta, which represent areas on the same tube, are dorsally situated, immediately ventrad to the dorsal body wall. This circulatory tube, or blood vessel, extends from the posterior extremity to the head, and it is enlarged and muscular posteriorly, constituting the heart (Plate 21–6, Fig. 2). The heart is elongate and chambered, inasmuch as there is a slight swelling of the tube in each of the first nine body somites of the abdomen. Through the pulsatory actions of the heart muscles, blood is forced anteriorly through the aorta into the cavities in the head. From the head, the blood flows posteriorly into the haemocoelic zones of the thorax and abdomen.

Blood is returned into the elongate heart through ostia, which are paired openings on each lateral surface of the nine chambers of the heart.

Various auxiliary pulsatile organs—for example, dorsal diaphragms, ventral diaphragms, etc.—have been reported in several free-living species. However, this aspect of insect anatomy has not been critically investigated in parasitic species.

RESPIRATORY SYSTEM

Insects, like some ticks (Ixodides) and crustaceans, possess a specialized type of respiratory system in the form of a tracheal system. Although the number and arrangement of the tracheal tubes vary greatly, the basic pattern is the same in all species (Plate 21–7, Fig. 1). Opening laterally on the thoracic and abdominal segments is a series of pores known as spiracles. The aperture of these "breathing holes" is regulated either by two external movable guard plates, or internally by clamps.

The spiracles lead into individual tracheae, which connect at right angles with two longitudinally oriented lateral tracheal tubes. Secondary, tertiary, and further branches known as tracheids and trachioles arise from these lateral tracheal tubes, conducting oxygen to and removing carbon dioxide from the various tissues of the body. In diperan larvae, a pair of large dorsal tracheal trunks is present on each

side of the heart and aorta (Plate 21–7, Fig. 2). These trunks are secondary to the lateral trunks.

In some species, specialized tracheal air sacs are formed from distended areas of the tracheal trunks (Plate 21–7, Fig. 3). These sacs serve as sites for air storage. Histologically, tracheal tubes consist of a thin outer epithelial covering and an intima of cuticular spirals (Plate 21–7, Fig. 4).

The position and number of spiracles vary greatly among species. For example, on mosquito larvae, only one set of spiracles is present, located on the eighth abdominal segment. On maggots (fly larvae), two pairs of spiracles are present—one pair on the anterior portion of the thorax (known as prothoracic spiracles), and one pair on the eighth abdominal segment. When open and functional spiracles are present, the insect is said to possess an open tracheal system. In some species, however, the spiracular openings are vestigial and/or nonfunctional. In these species, gaseous exchange takes place through a thick capillary bed of tracheae located under the integument. In such instances, the insect is said to possess a closed tracheal system.

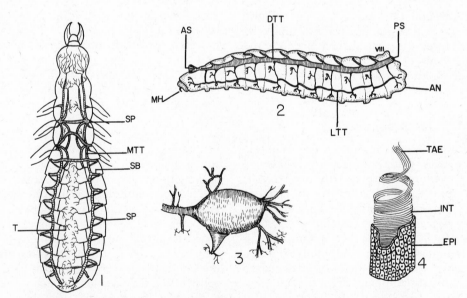

Plate 21-7   Tracheal system in insects. 1. Tracheal system of an insect. (Modified after Kolbe.) **2.** Tracheal system, as found in a fly larva. (Redrawn after Snodgrass.) **3.** A tracheal air sac. (Redrawn after Snodgrass.) **4.** Structure of a tracheal tube. (Redrawn after Snodgrass.)

(AN, anus; AS, anterior spiracle; DTT, dorsal tracheal trunk; EPI, epithelium; INT, intima; LTT, lateral tracheal trunk; MH, mouth hook; MTT, main tracheal trunk; PS, posterior spiracle; SB, spiracular branch; SP, spiracle; T, tracheoles; TAE, taenidium in spiral band of cuticular intima, artificially separated.)

NERVOUS SYSTEM

Main Nervous System

The "brain" is in the form of a supraesophageal ganglion. This nerve center is composed of three pairs of intimately fused ganglia. The first pair comprises the protocerebrum, from which nerves supply the compound eyes and ocelli; the second pair comprises the deutocerebrum, from which nerves supply the paired antennae; the third pair comprises the tritocerebrum, which controls the major sympathetic nervous system (Plate 21–8, Fig. 1).

The supraesophageal ganglion is connected to a large subesophageal ganglion by two lateral commissures that unite dorsally with the tritocerebrum. Nerve cords arising anteriorly from the subesophageal ganglion innervate the various mouthparts. The main nerves arising from the subesophageal ganglion, however, are the two intimately associated trunks that are directed caudally. Together these two trunks are known as the ventral nerve cord.

In each body somite is a fused pair of ganglia, which is joined to the ventral nerve cord by a pair of connectives. Branches arising from the segmental ganglia innervate the various tissues of the body in each segment.

Although primitively a pair of ganglia is present in each body somite, this number is

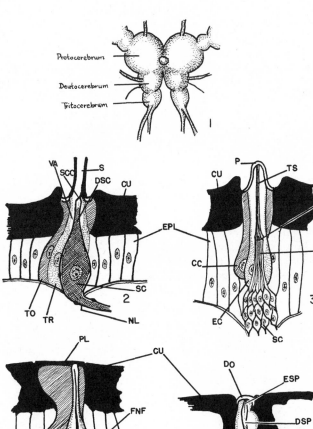

Plate 21–8   Insect morphology. 1. Insect brain. (Modified after Snodgrass, 1935. *Principles of Insect Morphology,* McGraw-Hill, New York.) 2. Histology of a seta and associated structures. 3. Histology of a peg and associated structures. 4. Histology of a plate and associated structures. 5. Histology of a dome and associated structures. (Figs. 2 to 5 redrawn and modified after Snodgrass.)

(CC, cap cell; CU, cuticle; DO, dome; DSP or DSC, distal process of sense cell; EC, enveloping cell; EPI, epithelium; ESP, end of sense cell process; FNF, fascicle of nerve fibers; MB, minute bodies; N, nerve; NL, neurilemma; P, peg; PL, plate; S, seta; SC, sense cell; SCC, connection of sense cell with cuticle; TO, tormogen cell; TR, trichogen cell; TS, terminal strands of fiber connected with cuticle; VA, vacuole.)

reduced in the Diptera and other forms in which the number of body segments is reduced. In such instances, the ganglia in fused somites also fuse; hence, the number of discrete ganglia is reduced.

Stomodeal Nervous System

The preceding discussion pertains to the main nervous system pattern found in insects. However, an auxiliary nervous system—the stomodeal nervous system—is present in most species. The stomodeal nervous system is so designated because the major bulk of the fibers are located dorsad and laterad to the stomodeum. The center of this system is a frontal ganglion located anterior to the supraesophageal ganglion. It is connected with the tritocerebrum by a pair of commissures.

Nerve fibers arising from the frontal ganglion control the involuntary motions of the stomodeum and aorta. In addition to the connectives that join the frontal ganglion to the supraesophageal ganglion, two lateral nerves infiltrate the region of the esophagus, where they are connected with small ganglionic masses. Nerve fibers from these lateral nerves also innervate portions of the stomodeum, the ducts of the salivary glands, the aorta, and certain muscles of the mouthparts.

Sensory Receptors

Sensory receptors of insects are categorically divided into sensory areas and eyes.

SENSORY AREAS. These areas are located on various parts of the body. Each area is composed of a hairlike seta that projects outward from a minute pore in the cuticle (Plate 21–8, Fig. 2). The base of the seta is connected with a sensory cell, which in turn is innervated by a nerve fiber. Such an arrangement represents a tactile sensory area. Response to pressure on the seta is via the associated nerve.

Similarly, olfactory and taste areas exist. In these, the sensory mechanism remains almost identical, except that the setae are replaced with a peg, plate, or dome (Plate 21–8, Figs. 3 to 5). The seta, peg, dome, or plate is secreted by specialized epidermal cells known as trichogen cells. Another type of cell, known as the tormogen cell, lays down the socket in which the individual seta is set.

EYES. Insects commonly possess two types of eyes—the simple eye, or ocellus, and the compound eye.

Ocellus. The simple eye (Plate 21–9, Fig. 1) differs from the compound eye in that only a single cornea (or lens)—a specialized transparent portion of the cuticle secreted by transparent corneagenous cells—is present. Nerve cells form a retina beneath the layer of corneagenous cells. The striated sensitive elements of these cells migrate to form a straight line down one side of each cell, and the lines formed in adjacent cells unite to form the rhabdom. A crystalline body lies between the cornea and the nerve cells.

Compound Eye. The compound eye is no more than an accumulation of many ocelli. Each unit of a compound eye, known as an ommatidium, can be thought of as a single ocellus, because the nerve endings innervating each unit are isolated from the retinae of surrounding ommatidia (Plate 21–9, Fig. 2). Each ommatidium has its own cornea, called a facet. Underneath each facet is a rosette of eight sense cells with a central rhabdom.

Pigment cells surround each lens and each rosette of sense cells. The pigment granules within each pigment cell migrate up and down in synchrony with those in adjacent pigment cells, resulting in unified control of the amount of light that affects the sense cells. The sense cells rest on a basement membrane, which the nerve fibers penetrate.

Insect larvae do not have compound eyes. Development of compound eyes does not commence until the insect reaches the pupal stage.

REPRODUCTIVE SYSTEM

Insects are typically dioecious. Secondary sexual dimorphism is apparent in the external genitalia along with other less prominent differences.

Male System

In males, the reproductive system consists of two testes, which are composed of tubules (or follicles). The two testes are situated dorsad to the intestine (Plate 21–10, Fig. 1). Arising from each testis is a vas deferens, which unites with its mate to form the ejaculatory duct. Prior to the union of the vasa deferentia, each vas enlarges slightly, forming a seminal vesicle.

Typically, accessory glands are present and empty into the vasa deferentia prior to their union. The ejaculatory duct opens into the penis, which communicates with the exterior through the genital pore. Inasmuch as the true penis of insects is membranous, rigidity is effected by the sclerotized aedeagus, which is part of the external genitalia forming a rigid sheath around the penis.

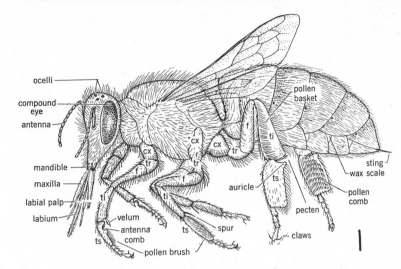

Plate 21-9 Eyes of insects. 1. The honeybee worker. **2.** The arthropod compound eye, diagrammatic drawing. (Figs. 1 and 2 after Casteel and Imms in Storer, T. I., and Usinger. 1957. *General* Zoology, McGraw-Hill, New York.)

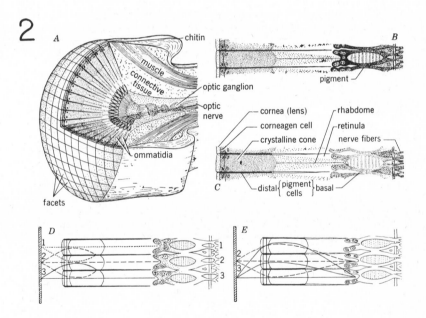

Plate 21-10 Reproductive systems of insects. 1. Male reproductive system. **2.** Female reproductive system. (Figs. 1 and 2 redrawn after Snodgrass, 1935.)

(AG, accessory glands; CAL, calyx; CO, common oviduct; ED, ejaculatory duct; GP, gonopore; LO, lateral oviduct; OV, ovary; OVL, ovarial ligament; OVR, ovariole; P, penis; SG, spermathecal gland; SP, spermathecal gland; SP, spermatheca; SV, seminal vesicle; TES, testis; VAG, vagina; VD, vas deferens.)

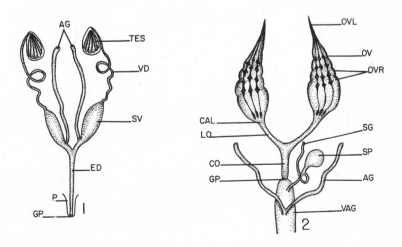

Female System

In females, a series of longitudinally oriented tubular ovaries are arranged in two bunches (Plate 21-10, Fig. 2). The posterior terminals of the ovarial units unite to form the calyx, which opens into the oviduct. The lateral oviduct from each side unites with the opposite oviduct to form the common oviduct, which opens into the vagina (or genital chamber).

Two types of diverticula empty into the vagina—an elongate spermatheca (or seminal receptacle), and a pair of colleterial glands (or accessory glands). The vagina opens into the groove of the ovipositor, which is a portion of the external genitalia.

Fertilization

Fertilization among insects is internal. During copulation, spermatozoa are introduced into the vagina and stored in the spermatheca. Ova pass down the oviducts, as the result of the peristalitic action of the muscular oviductal walls, and pass over the opening of the spermatheca. The sperm penetrate the ova at this time. As eggs are oviposited, the colleterial glands secrete an adhesive material that binds the eggs into masses, or glues the eggs to vegetation or to the hair of hosts.

LIFE CYCLE STUDIES

Embryonic development of insects is extremely interesting, but space and the nature of this volume do not permit a detailed account here. Interested students are referred to the condensed but effective account by Ross (1948, pp. 172-184). Furthermore, those interested in the physiology of insect metamorphosis are referred to the monograph by Wigglesworth (1954). Because insect parasitism is not confined to the adults—in fact, in many instances it is the larva that is parasitic—it appears advisable to discuss briefly the postembryonic, or larval, development of insects.

The exoskeleton of insects, like that of all arthropods, is a limiting factor. Increase in size or alterations in form cannot be accomplished unless these animals molt. When ecdysis occurs, the sloughed exoskeleton is known as the exuvia. The period of time in between molts is termed the stadium, and the insect during a stadium is referred to as an instar.

Insects vary in the degree of metamorphosis they undergo between the first instar and the sexually mature adult, or imago. The degree of metamorphosis can be categorized into three types—the ametabolous type, in which metamorphosis is slight and difficult to appreciate; the hemimetabolous type, in which metamorphosis is gradual or incomplete; and the holometabolous type, in which metamorphosis is complex or complete.

Ametabolous Metamorphosis

Among members of two orders of free-living insects, the Thysanura (bristletails) and Collembola (springtails), newly hatched larvae resemble miniature adults in that they are wingless. During growth practically no alteration of form, or metamorphosis, occurs. This type of development is known as ametabolous metamorphosis.

Hemimetabolous Metamorphosis

In some insects, newly hatched larvae are quite similar to, and have the same feeding habits as, the imago. There are differences, however. The young are not sexually mature and possess rudimentary reproductive structures. In winged species, the young are wingless. Acquisition of these adult structures occurs during growth. In this type of metamorphosis, the developing instars are referred to as nymphs. Hemimetabolous metamorphosis among parasitic insects is exemplified by the biting lice (Mallophaga) and the sucking lice (Anoplura).*

Holometabolous Metamorphosis

This type of metamorphosis is found in the majority of insects. The alteration of form between the postembryonic larva and the imago is quite striking. All the developing instars are wingless except for the pre-adult instar. The insect undergoes three stages during its development—the feeding grub or larva, the nonfeeding pupa, and the imago.

The larva, which is commonly elongate and wormlike, does not bear visible wings, although imaginal buds (beginning of wing development) occur internally. The antennae and eyes are often rudimentary. The thoracic legs may or may not be present, and strangely enough, larvapods may be present on the abdomen of certain species. This is primarily a feeding and growing stage, represented by a few to many instars, depending on the species.

---

*Although the Mallophaga and Anoplura are considered to undergo hemimetabolous metamorphosis, these lice do not develop wings as do other hemimetabolous insects. However, the absence of wings on lice is a secondary evolutionary adaptation.

The pupa is a nonfeeding and quiescent stage that possesses many adult characters, including appendages and wings, but these are usually held limply against the body. The pupa is the reorganizational stage, during which the body tissues are reorganized for eventual transformation into the adult form. In many insect orders, such as the Lepidoptera (butterflies and moths), the pupa is found within a cocoon spun by the last larval instar. In others, the pupa is found burrowed in soil. In still others, like some of the Diptera (flies and mosquitoes), the pupa is ensheathed within the sloughed exoskeleton of the last larval instar, which hardens and is known as the puparium.

The adult, or imago, is the definitive form of an insect. The primary function of adults is to perpetuate the species through reproduction. Among holometabolous insects, the adults generally possess mouthparts that are different from those of the larval instars. Among parasitic species, this is exemplified by the flea, which possesses chewing-type mouthparts as a scavenging larva, but possesses piercing-sucking mouthparts as an adult.

Hypermetamorphosis.   In addition to the previously mentioned three types of postembryonic metamorphosis, an additional type is found—hypermetamorphosis. This category is best considered as a specialized form of holometabolous metamorphosis. In hypermetamorphosis, two or more morphologically distinct types of larvae appear in the life cycle.

Types of Insect Parasitism

Parasitism among insects is not always an adult practice, nor is it always practiced on vertebrate animals. Insect parasites can be divided into three classes—ectoparasites on vertebrates, for example, lice, fleas, and mosquitoes; endoparasites of vertebrates, for example, botflies and warble flies; and parasites of invertebrates. In the first instance, it is the adult that is parasitic, while in the last two categories, it is commonly the larvae that are parasitic, although adult parasites of invertebrates also occur.

INSECT SYSTEMATICS AND BIOLOGY

Classification

According to Comstock (1949), there are twenty-six orders of insects. Of these, eight are known to include parasitic species, which are found attached to, and feeding on, or within vertebrates and invertebrates. Other orders may include incidental and accidental parasites. Diagnosis of eight major orders follows.

Order 1. Siphonaptera (the fleas).   Adults are small, wingless. Are ectoparasitic on birds and mammals. Bodies are laterally compressed. Legs are long, stout, and spinose. Antennae are short, clubbed, and fit in depressions along the side of the head when not extended. Mouthparts are of piercing-sucking type. Displays holometabolous metamorphosis.

Order 2. Mallophaga (the biting lice).   Are ectoparasitic on birds and mammals. Bodies are small to medium size, usually dorsoventrally flattened and wingless. Possesses chewing mouthparts. Antennae are short, and three- to five-segmented. Possesses reduced compound eyes and no ocelli. Thorax is small. Legs are stout and short. No cerci appear on abdomen. Exhibits hemimetabolous metamorphosis.

Order 3. Anoplura (the sucking lice).   Are ectoparasites of mammals. Bodies are small to medium size, dorsoventrally flattened, and wingless. Mouthparts are modified to form a piercing-sucking organ that is retractile. Antennae are short, three- to five-segmented. Some possess legs terminating as hooked claws. Thorax is fused. Abdomen of five to eight distinct segments. Exhibits hemimetabolous metamorphosis.

Order 4. Diptera (the flies, gnats, and mosquitoes).   Has ectoparasitic and endoparasitic species. Bodies are medium size. Forewing in winged species is well developed, attached to mesothorax. Hindwings are vestigial, form knobbed balancing structures known as halteres. Mouthparts are modified for piercing and sucking or for rasping and lapping. Possesses compound eyes, large antennae of three to forty segments. Exhibits holometabolous metamorphosis.

Order 5. Hemiptera (the true bugs).   Are primarily ectoparasitic. Bodies are medium size, with piercing-sucking mouthparts forming a beak. Antennae are four- to ten-segmented. Eyes are compound and large. Two pairs of wings are present. Corium (thickened portion) is present at base of outer wing. Thinner extremities of outer wing overlap on dorsum when at rest. Wing venation is reduced. Abdomen lacks cerci. Exhibits holometabolous metamorphosis.

Order 6. Hymenoptera (the bees, wasps, and ants).   Parasitic species are small, measuring approximately 0.1 mm. in length. Integument is comparatively heavily sclerotized. Mouthparts are chewing type. Possesses two pairs of well developed wings, if present. Wings are reduced or absent in some. In winged forms, hindwings are smaller than forewings. Antennae have three to sixty segments. Larvae are caterpillar-like, with chewing mouthparts. Exhibit holometabolous metamorphosis or hypermetamorphosis.

Order 7. Coleoptera (the beetles).   A few species are endoparasitic in other insects. Possesses two pairs of wings. Forewings (elytra) are veinless, hard, covering dorsal aspect of abdomen while in resting position, meeting along mid-dorsal line. Mouthparts are chewing type. Antennae have ten to fourteen segments. Compound eyes are conspicuous. Legs are heavily sclerotized. Exhibits holometabolous metamorphosis.

Order 8. Strepsiptera (the twisted-wing insects).   Species are endoparasitic in other insects. Bodies are small. Only males have wings. Forewings are reduced to club shaped appendages. Hindwings are large, fan shaped, with radiating venation. Females are legless and larviform. Mouthparts are vestigial or absent on both sexes. Exhibits hypermetamorphosis.

ORDER SIPHONAPTERA

The Siphonaptera includes the fleas. Over 1300 species of these blood-sucking ectoparasites are known. These parasitize birds and mammals. The North American species have been monographed by Ewing and Fox (1943), Fox (1940a, b), and Hubbard (1947).

The origin and evolution of fleas remain highly speculative. There is no doubt, however, that the fleas of mammals evolved from the fleas of birds. Members of *Ceratophyllus,* for example, are clearly derived from forms that parasitize squirrels and other arboreal rodents whose nests provide conditions similar to those of bird nests. It is quite possible that bird fleas, found in nests, have become adapted to tree-climbing mammals, which in turn have passed them on to terrestrial mammals.

The more common fleas measure 1.4 and 4 mm. in length, the males being slightly smaller than the females. Plate 21–11 depicts the female of *Ctenocephalides felis,* the cat flea. This illustration should provide the reader with a working knowledge of the external anatomy of a flea.

Interest in fleas among parasitologists stems from three avenues of investigation—that concerned with the blood-sucking habits of these pests, that concerned with fleas as vectors for pathogenic microorganisms, and that concerned with the fleas as intermediate hosts of helminth parasites.

LIFE CYCLE PATTERN

The life cycles of fleas all follow an essentially similar pattern. The comparatively small, whitish eggs measure approximately 5 mm. in length and are oviposited either on or off the host. If the eggs are oviposited on the host, they are not adhesive and soon are shaken off. They are commonly found in the host's abode. Flea eggs are oviposited a few at a time, usually three to twenty. However, during the life span, a female flea can lay many eggs. For example, a single female *Pulex irritans,* the human flea, can oviposit a total of 448 eggs during a period of 196 days. Because metamorphosis in the Siphonaptera is holometabolic, the hatching form is a larva.

The embryonic development and hatching process of fleas is influenced by the environmental temperature and humidity. High temperatures, (35° to 37° C.) inhibit embryonic development. Temperatures ranging from 17° to 23° C. bring about hatching in 7 to 9 days, but lower temperatures (11° to 15° C.) lengthen the process to 14 days. Bruce (1948) reported

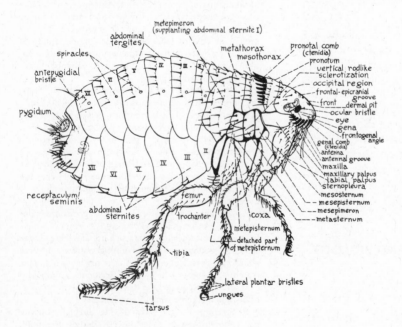

Plate 21-11   Flea anatomy. Adult female of the cat flea *Ctenocephalides felis.* (Courtesy of the Communicable Disease Center, U.S. Public Health Service, Atlanta, Ga.)

that growth in *Ctenocephalides felis* is at its optimum when they are maintained at 65 to 90 per cent relative humidity.

The larva possesses a cephalically situated spine that ruptures the eggshell. The whitish larvae of fleas are elongate and vermiform, displaying a distinct head but no legs. The body is sparsely covered with bristly hairs, and a pair of tiny hooks, known as anal struts, are situated on the last body segment.

The mouthparts of the larva are of the biting type and include mandibles (mandibles are absent in adult fleas). Such larvae are free-living, feeding on decaying animal and vegetable matter (Plate 21–12, Fig. 2). *Nosopsyllus fasciatus* larvae subsist totally on the feces of adult fleas. Bird flea larvae utilize the sheaths of feathers and epidermal scales of young birds for food. The larval growth period varies between 9 and 200 days, depending on environmental conditions—humidity, temperature, oxygen tension, etc.

Flea larvae usually undergo two molts, increasing in size after each molt. On reaching their maximum size, the third stage larvae become quiescent, spin a whitish cocoon around themselves, and pupate (Plate 21–12, Fig. 3). The pupae remain within the cocoons from 7 days to as long as a year, depending on conditions (Plate 21–12, Fig. 4). The form rupturing out of the cocoon is the adult, which is parasitic.

Emergence of the adult may not be immediate, for fully developed fleas may lie quiescent for many months within the cocoon. When disturbed, even by the slightest vibration, dormant adults are activated and leave the cocoon. Animals and birds returning to old haunts often become infested with fleas that have remained quiescent for long periods. Similarly, humans entering abandoned abodes can become infested with fleas that become activated because of the disturbance.

Because development of fleas generally occurs off of the host and the parasitic adults must have access to suitable hosts, it is not surprising that fleas are generally associated with hosts that roost, live in dens, or utilize nests, and are not associated with free-roaming animals.

SIPHONAPTERAN SYSTEMATICS AND BIOLOGY

Species of Siphonaptera parasitize birds as well as mammals. The order is divided into six families, a key to which follows.*

1. The three thoracic tergites together are shorter than the first abdominal tergite. . . . .**Hectopsyllidae**
2. The three thoracic tergites together are longer than the first abdominal tergite.
   A. Head is evenly rounded along margin. No vertical suture from dorsal margin of head to bases of antennae is evident. Abdominal tergites possess one row of setae. . . . .**Pulicidae**
   B. Head is like that in Pulicidae. Abdominal tergites possess at least two rows of setae. . . . . . .**Ceratophyllidae**
   C. Head possesses vertical suture passing from dorsal margin of head to bases of antennae. Head is strongly curved at vertex. Head has a pair of dark anteroventral flaps on each side. . . . .**Ischnopsyllidae**
   D. Head is like that in Ischnopsyllidae but lacks a pair of dark anteroventral flaps on each side. Occipital region lacks dorsal incrassation (thickening). . . . .**Hystrichopsyllidae**
   E. Head is like that in Ischnopsyllidae but lacks a pair of dark anteroventral flaps on each side. Occipital region possesses dorsal incrassation. . . .**Macropsyllidae**

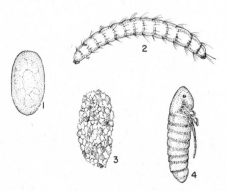

Plate 21-12   Stages in the life cycle of the flea. 1. Flea egg. **2.** Larva. **3.** Whitish cocoon. **4.** Pupa. (All figures original.)

*The key modified after Ewing and Fox (1943). In addition, Jordan (1956) presents a new system for the classification of fleas that should be consulted by those interested in Siphonopteran taxonomy.

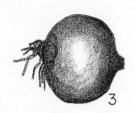

Plate 21-13   Fleas. 1. Male *Tunga penetrans*. **2.** Female *Echidnophaga gallinacea*. (Redrawn after Bishopp.) **3.** Gravid female of the jigger flea *Tunga penetrans*. (Redrawn after Ewing.) **4.** Male *Pulex irritans,* the human flea. (Redrawn after Bishopp.)

FAMILY HECTOPSYLLIDAE*

This family includes the chigoe flea, *Tunga penetrans,* and the sticktight flea of poultry, *Echidnophaga gallinacea* (Plate 21–13, Figs. 1 and 2). These unique fleas are more or less permanent parasites as adults. They are often referred to as burrowing fleas, because the impregnated females become firmly attached to the host's skin and in so doing cause such a severe irritation that the surrounding tissues become swollen, thus embedding the fleas and giving the appearance that they have burrowed into the skin.

Tunga penetrans

This flea parasite is a native of the tropical and subtropical parts of South America and has been introduced into Africa and elsewhere. There appears to be little host specificity in *T. penetrans,* for in addition to poultry, it attacks man, dogs, pigs, and other animals. However, it is strictly a parasite of warm-blooded animals. The embedded females commonly are distended because of the enclosed eggs, which when oviposited, fall to the ground and develop (Plate 21–13, Fig. 3). After laying her eggs, the female is usually expelled from the host by the pressure of the surrounding tissues and dies. The host's skin irritation often opens the way for secondary infection and may become gangrenous. Human infestations by *T. penetrans* are commonly on the foot or between the toes.

Echidnophaga gallinacea

This flea is usually parasitic on chickens and other birds, but it has been known to attack dogs, rats, man, and other animals. The adults tend to congregate in masses, usually on the host's head. It is referred to as the sticktight flea, because once attached to a host, it seldom migrates. Geographic distribution of this flea is limited to the tropical and subtropical regions of the world.

FAMILY PULICIDAE

This family includes several species that bite man. Furthermore, several species are vectors for the plague bacillus, *Pasteurella pestis. Pulex irritans,* commonly referred to as the human flea, is widely distributed and parasitizes domestic animals, as well as humans (Plate 21–13, Fig. 4). This species is capable of transmitting the plague pathogen under laboratory conditions but is not an important vector in nature. The infrequency of the blockage of its esophagus, which results in the regurgitation of alimentary tract contents including plague bacilli, renders it less effective as a vector than other fleas. The role of *P. irritans* as a vector for the filarial worm *Dirofilaria immitis* is discussed on page 451.

---

*Sometimes referred to as the Tungidae.

Genus *Ctenocephalides*

Ctenocephalides includes ten species commonly found on carnivores. The most familiar species are *C. canis,* the dog flea, and *C. felis,* the cat flea (Plate 21–14, Fig. 1). These fleas also are not host specific, for both species bite cats and dogs, as well as humans. In addition to causing dermal irritations while feeding, *C. canis* is a suitable intermediate host for the dog tapeworm, *Dipylidium caninum.*

Genus *Xenopsylla*

Over thirty species of *Xenopsylla* are known.

Xenopsylla cheopis.   This parasite, known as the Asiatic rat flea, is the most commonly encountered species in this genus (Plate 21–14, Fig. 2). *Xenopsylla cheopis* presumably originated in the Nile Valley in Africa but has spread over the entire world on their rat hosts. A major vector for *Pasteurella pestis,* both male and female fleas take in the bacillus from infected rats during feeding.

The stomach of *X. cheopis* has a capacity of 0.5 cu. mm. and is capable of receiving as many as 5000 bacilli, which continue to multiply once taken into the flea. The bacteria are limited to the stomach, intestine, and rectum; they are never found in the flea's coelom or salivary glands. Thus, it is postulated that infection is brought about in man by the rubbing of contaminated feces into fresh bite sites. This hypothesis has since been demonstrated experimentally, although it is not the only method of infection. The other, and probably more common, method of infection from *Xenopsylla cheopis* involves transmission during the bite. This is not accomplished via the salivary glands; instead, a temporary blood clot in the flea's esophagus causes regurgitation of bacteria-including materials up to the level of the clot, which then serves as a culture medium for the bacilli. Such bacteria from time to time pass into the mouthparts and from there into the victim (Plate 21–14, Fig. 3).

An average of 21 days (at least 5 days) occurs between imbibition of bacilli-containing blood and the infective bite. In *Diamanus montanus,* the ground-squirrel flea, the average time lapse is 53 days.

Other Xenopsylla Species.   *Xenopsylla braziliensis,* the African rat flea, is another important species and is found in Uganda, Kenya, and Nigeria. Its specific name arises from the fact that the flea was first described in Brazil, where it had been transported. This

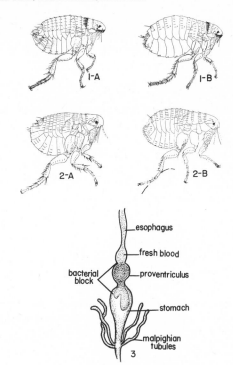

Plate 21-14   Adult fleas. 1. *Ctenocephalides felis,* the cat flea. **A.** Male. **B.** Female. **2.** *Xenopsylla cheopis,* the Oriental rat flea. **A.** Male. **B.** Female. (Figs. 1 and 2 after Herms, W. B., and James, M. T. 1961. *Medical Entomology,* Macmillan, New York.) **3.** Alimentary tract of flea, showing blocked proventriculus with bacteria. Note distention of the esophagus with fresh blood. (Redrawn and modified after Bacot and Martin.)

flea is a major vector for the plague organism in Africa and has also been reported in India.

Xenopsylla hawaiiensis is encountered in Hawaii, where it is found on the field rat, *Rattus hawaiiensis,* and not on building-inhabiting rats.

Xenopsylla astia is found in parts of Ceylon and India. Wu et al. (1936) reported that epidemiological evidence indicates that this flea serves as a vector for *Pasteurella pestis.*

Genus *Hoplopsyllus*

Hoplopsyllus anomalus is the plague vector of California ground squirrels, *Cittellus beechyi.* This flea also attacks rats.

FAMILY CERATOPHYLLIDAE*

The family Ceratophyllidae includes, among others, the genera *Diamanus, Ceratophyllus,* and *Nosopsyllus.*

---

*Sometimes referred to as the Dolichopsyllidae.

Diamanus montanus

Diamanus montanus (=*Ceratophyllus acustus, Oropsylla montana*) is a commonly encountered ectoparasite of squirrels in western United States (Plate 21–15, Fig. 1). It is indirectly of medical importance, for it aids in the maintenance of plague infections among squirrels. The egg incubation period in this species is 8 days. The first larval instar lasts for 6 days, the second for 10 days, the third for 12 days, and the pupal stage lasts for 31 days. Under experimental conditions, *D. montanus* can serve as a carrier of *Pasteurella pestis.*

Genus *Ceratophyllus*

Ceratophyllus includes *C. gallinae,* the European hen flea. This and *C. niger* are both primarily parasites of hens, but both also attack dogs, cats, and man. Unlike the sticktight fowl flea *Echidnophaga gallinacea,* the species of *Ceratophyllus* are not attached to the host's skin, except during feeding. These fleas cause serious injury to hens.

Adults of *C. styx,* a parasite of the sand martin, congregate in swarms around the entrance of burrows and await the arrival of a host.

Nosopsyllus fasciatus

The European rat flea, *N. fasciatus,* is widely distributed throughout northern Europe and North America. Its chief hosts are rodents. However, it does bite man and other mammals. Development (37 days) of this species is optimal at cool temperatures, and the larvae apparently require blood for development. Blood is acquired from the fecal droppings of adult fleas. This species is known to carry the plague pathogen, *Pasteurella pestis,* from rodent to rodent, thus maintaining natural reservoirs of the bacilli.

FAMILY ISCHNOPSYLLIDAE

Ischnopsyllid fleas include members of *Ischnopsyllus* and other host specific genera, for all these fleas are parasites of bats and only occasionally are reported from wild mice, *Peromyscus* spp. (Plate 21–15, Fig. 2). Little is known about these fleas except that they are not important as vectors for *Pasteurella pestis.*

FAMILY HYSTRICHOPSYLLIDAE

The Hystrichopsyllidae includes the common mouse flea, *Leptopsylla* (=*Ctenopsyllus*) *segnis,*

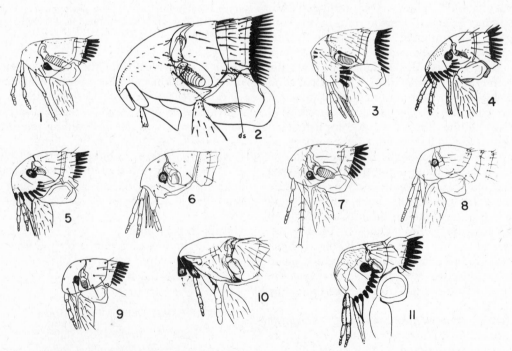

Plate 21-15   **Heads of adult fleas. 1.** *Diamanus* (=*Oropsylla*) *montanus.* **2.** *Ischnopsyllus elongatus.* (ds, dorsal sinus of prosternite.) **3.** *Leptopsylla segnis.* **4.** *Ctenocephalides felis.* **5.** *Ctenocephalides canis.* **6.** *Pulex irritans.* **7.** *Nosopsyllus fasciatus.* **8.** *Xenopsylla cheopis.* **9.** *Hoplopsyllus anomalus.* **10.** *Myodopsylla insignis.* **11.** *Cediopsylla simplex.* [After Fernow in Smart, 1943. *Insects of Medical Importance,* British Museum (Natural History).]

which is also found on rats (Plate 21–15, Fig. 3). Like all other rodent-infesting siphonapterans, *L. segnis* is distributed all over the world, especially on rodents in seaports and on ships. This species, for example, has been found on rats taken from ships in New York and New Orleans.

FAMILY MACROPSYLLIDAE*

Members of this family are not common. None is known to bite man or domestic animals, or even serve as vectors. The only member found in North America is *Rhopalopsyllus*, with two species found on dogs, rats, and opossums in the southern United States, ranging from Florida to Texas.

FLEA-BORNE DISEASES

The Plague

The disease commonly referred to as the plague (the black death of Europe during the fourteenth and seventeenth centuries) is caused by the bacillus *Pasteurella pestis*. When this bacterium is introduced into the skin, the lymph glands become inflamed. This is known as bubonic plague. Frequently the bacilli become established in the victim's blood. The condition is then referred to as septicemic plague. If the victim's lungs become involved, it is referred to as pneumonic plague. Man usually acquires his infection from rodents via a flea vector because rodents are utilized by *P. pestis* as reservoir hosts. Plague among rodents is known as sylvatic plague.

The literature concerning plague is extensive. Interested individuals are referred to the writings of Hampton (1940), Meyer (1942), and the extensive bibliography given by Jellison and Good (1942).

Murine Typhus

In addition to plague, certain fleas serve as vectors for the murine (endemic) typhus organism, *Rickettsia typhi* (=*Rickettsia mooseri*). This rickettsia is transmitted via contaminated flea feces, which are rubbed into the bite wound. Fleas contract the rickettsiae either while feeding on an infected human or on the infected rats and mice, *Rattus norvegicus, R. rattus, R. alexandrinus,* and *Mus musculus.* Furthermore, this rickettsia has been found in the opossum,

---

*Also known as Malacopsyllidae.

cottontail rabbit, fox squirrel, Florida skunk, southern weasel, dog, and even in the blue jay. Fleas found to be suitable transmitters include *Xenopsylla cheopis, X. astia,* and *Nosopsyllus fasciatus. Echidnophaga gallinacea* has been experimentally determined to be a suitable vector.

Distribution of murine typhus covers Mexico, Peru, Colombia, Venezuela, Chile, and northern Argentina. In North America, all the southeastern and southern states in the U. S., including Texas and Oklahoma and parts of southern California, are endemic, as is Hawaii. In the Old World, *Rickettsia typhi* is found in southern and western Europe, the USSR, in north, west, and south Africa, in Israel, the South Sea Islands, and central and north China.

Other Diseases

Other microorganisms associated with fleas include *Pasteurella tularensis,* the tularemia-causing organism in man, rabbit, and rodents; and *Salmonella enteritidis,* the salmonellosis-causing bacterium in man, and the virus that causes myxomatosis in wild and domestic rabbits.

Helminth Parasites

In addition to serving as vectors for bacteria, viruses, and rickettsiae, certain fleas act as intermediate hosts for helminth parasites, especially tapeworms. Some of these species and their helminth parasites are listed in Table 21–1. In addition, *Ceratophyllus fasciatus* and *Xenopsylla cheopis* are principal vectors for the haemoflagellate *Trypanosoma lewisi* in rats.

ORDER MALLOPHAGA

The Mallophaga includes the so-called biting, or bird, lice. The common name bird lice is not preferred because certain members are primarily ectoparasites of mammals. It is estimated there are over 3000 known species of biting lice. They are all ectoparasitic on birds and mammals, and are primarily, if not completely, injurious only through their bites. *Dennyus* on swifts, however, serves as intermediate host for the filarial worm *Filaria cypseli,* and *Trichodectes latus* (Trichodectidae) serves as intermediate host for the dog tapeworm *Dipylidium caninum.* The role of the Mallophaga as transmitters of helminth parasites is certainly a minor one. Lice, both Mallophaga and Anoplura, may transmit leishmanias (p. 63).

Table 21-1. Helminths That May Utilize Fleas As Intermediate Hosts

Helminth Parasite	Definitive Host	Flea Intermediate Host
Dipetalonema reconditum (nematode)	Dogs	*Ctenocephalides felis* *C. canis*
Dipylidium caninum (cestode)	Dogs, cats, certain wild carnivores	*Ctenocephalides felis* *C. canis* *Trichodectes canis* *Pulex irritans*
Hymenolepis diminuta (cestode)	Rodents, occasionally man	*Nosopsyllus fasciatus* *Xenopsylla cheopis*
H. nana (cestode)	Rodents, occasionally man	*Xenopsylla cheopis* *Ctenocephalides canis* *Pulex irritans*

The size of the biting lice ranges from approximately 1 mm. in length (males of *Goniocotes* found on pigeons) to about 10 mm. (*Laemobotkrion* found on hawks). Mouthparts of the biting lice are of the chewing type (p. 558), but they are greatly reduced and are difficult to interpret without critical study.

Mallophagan lice, as well as the anopluran lice (p. 578), are presumed to have been derived from primitive forms that lived beneath tree bark and in other similar niches. These pregenitors probably first became parasitic on birds, the nests of which the lice could have readily migrated to. Birds in turn could have passed their lice to arboreal mammals, which later passed the lice on to terrestrial mammals. On the other hand, the presence of a very primitive species of lice on a tree shrew, which is a primitive mammal, suggests that the lice infested the shrew without utilizing birds as an intermediate step. Hopkins' (1957) essay on the relationship between lice and mammals should be consulted by every student of the Mallophaga and Anoplura.

can be found attached to the host's feathers. These eggs undergo an incubation period of 3 to 5 days if they are maintained in an environmental temperature of 37° C. If the temperature is 33° C., the incubation period is 9 to 14 days; even then, the nymphs that hatch perish in 1 to 6 days. Thus, temperature is of critical importance during the embryonic period.

The young that hatches from the egg is the nymph. There are three nymphal instars, each lasting slightly less than 7 days. The third nymphal instar metamorphoses into the adult. Again, temperature is critical to survival of the adult. *C. columbae* adults live for 30 to 40 days if maintained at 37° C. Lower or higher temperatures shorten the life span.

Matthysse (1946) studied the life history of *Bovicola bovis*, the red cattle louse, and found that the stages in this species parallel those of *C. columbae*, differing only in the lengths of time required to complete each stage. Again, temperature is a critical factor. Transmission of lice from host to host occurs when the hosts' bodies are in contact.

LIFE CYCLE PATTERN

The life cycle patterns in the Mallophaga are essentially the same. The development of *Columbicola columbae*, the common pigeon louse, exemplifies the pattern. The entire life cycle of the parasite occurs on the host. As many as sixty whitish opaque eggs of the louse

MALLOPHAGAN SYSTEMATICS AND BIOLOGY

The biting lice are divided into three suborders—Amblycera, Ischnocera, and Rhynchophthirina. The last includes only one species, *Haematomyzus elephantis*, parasitic on African and Indian elephants. The Amblycera is further divided into six families, and the

Ischnocera is divided into four. The key that follows includes the more prominent families of the Amblycera and Ischnocera.

Suborder Amblycera: Are parasitic on birds and mammals. Antennae are six-jointed, short, clavate or capitate, and concealed in shallow grooves on the underside of head. Maxillary palpi are four-jointed. Mandibles are horizontally arranged.

A. Are parasitic on mammals. Possesses one claw on tarsi. . . . . **Gyropidae**

B. Are parasitic on birds. Have two claws on tarsi. . . . . **Menoponidae**

C. Are parasitic on kangaroos, wallabies, and wombats in Australia. Have two claws on tarsi. . . . . **Boöpiidae**

D. Are parasitic on birds. Have two claws on tarsi. Head is flattened. Few species exist. . . . . **Ricinidae**

Suborder Ischnocera. Are parasitic on birds and mammals. Antennae are three or five-segmented, filiform, and not concealed. Maxillary palpi are absent. Mandibles are vertically oriented.

A. Are parasitic on mammals. Antennae are three-jointed. One claw is on tarsi. . . . . **Trichodectidae**

B. Are parasitic on birds. Antennae are five-jointed. Two claws are on tarsi. . . . . **Philopteridae**

SUBORDER AMBLYCERA

FAMILY GYROPIDAE

The Gyropidae includes two species, *Gyropus ovalis* and *Gliricola percelli,* which are familiar to those who handle laboratory animals, since both are found on guinea pigs. Other members of this family are confined mainly to Central and South America.

FAMILY MENOPONIDAE*

The family Menoponidae includes the genera *Menopon, Myrsidea, Colpocephalum, Pseudomenopon, Trinoton,* and *Menacanthus.*

Genus *Menopon*

Menopon includes numerous species found on wild and domestic birds.

Menopon gallinae. The most commonly encountered species in the genus is *M. gallinae,* a chicken louse found attached to the shaft of the host's feathers (Plate 21–16, Fig. 1). Since this species is not a blood ingestor and feeds instead on the barbs and scales of feathers, it does little damage to the host by way of irritation. The females, which are about 2 mm. long, lay their eggs in clusters on the feathers. The eggs hatch in 2 to 3 weeks.

Menopon gallinae generally does not infest young chicks, presumably because chicks lack well developed feathers. It does infest ducks, turkeys, and guinea hens, at least when these birds are housed with chickens. The adult lice are extremely hardy and have been kept alive for as long as 9 months.

OTHER *Menopon* SPECIES. Other species of *Menopon* are parasitic on various birds, for example, *M. aegialitidis* on the killdeer, and *Oxyechus voriferus,* and *M. leucoxanthum* on the black duck, *Anas rubripes.*

Genus *Menacanthus*
Menacanthus stramineus. The common

* Also known as Liotheidae.

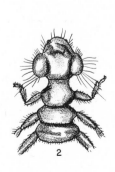
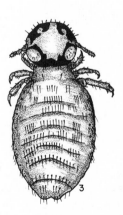

Plate 21-16   Lice. 1. *Menopon gallinae,* the common shaft louse of poultry. **2.** Anterior end of *Trinoton querquedulae* of ducks. **3.** *Trichodectes canis* of dogs.

body louse of chickens, *M. stramineus,* is also found on turkeys. It appears to prefer the host's skin to feathers. It is light yellow and is approximately 3 mm. long. It is destructive in that its bite causes droopiness, loss of weight, diarrhea, and reduced egg production. When observed on the host, this louse is extremely active and quick, and migrates over the entire body.

Other Menoponid Genera

Myrsidea includes *M. subaequalis,* commonly found on crows and hawks. *Colpocephalum* includes *C. laticeps* on the great blue heron *Corvus brachyehynchos,* and *C. pustulosum* on the pectoral sandpiper *Pisobia maculata. Pseudomenopon pacificum* is found on coots and grebes.

Trinoton querquedulae is a dark grayish species that measures approximately 4 mm. in length (Plate 21–16, Fig. 2). It is a blood ingestor found on ducks.

FAMILY BOÖPIIDAE

The Boöpiidae is a small and little known family with species found on marsupials (kangaroos and wallabies). One species, *Heterodoxus longitarsus,* has been occasionally found on dogs in Australia.

FAMILY RICINIDAE

The Ricinidae is another obscure family. The genus *Ricinius* is represented by *R. leptosomus* on the kingbird *Tyrannus tyrannus,* and *R. lineatus* on the humming bird *Archilochus colubris* in New York State. Another member of this small family is *Trochiloecetes,* represented in New York State by *T. prominens* on the hummingbird.

AMBLYCERAN HOST SPECIFICITY

Although present data still are scanty, it is becoming more evident that members of the suborder Amblycera demonstrate a certain degree of host specificity. If two avian hosts share a common species of louse, the two hosts are usually closely related. Furthermore, the mammal-parasitizing members of the family Boöpiidae are host specific and are restricted to mammals, primarily marsupials.

SUBORDER ISCHNOCERA

The suborder Ischnocera comprises two major families—the Trichodectidae with species parasitic on mammals, and the Philopteridae with species parasitic on birds.

FAMILY TRICHODECTIDAE

Genus *Trichodectes*

Several species of *Trichodectes* are commonly encountered on various domestic animals. Others are found on martins, weasels, badgers, skunks, and other small mammals. *Trichodectes canis* is an irritative louse of dogs throughout the world (Plate 21–16, Fig. 3). This species is broad, short, and approximately 1 to 2 mm. long. Other species encountered in the Americas include *T. breviceps* on llamas in South America, and *T. tibialis* on deer in the western United States (Plate 21–17, Fig. 1).

Genus *Damalinia*

Several species of *Damalinia* that infest domestic animals were at one time assigned to *Trichodectes.* However, these species have been transferred to *Damalinia* because their antennae do not demonstrate sexual dimorphism as do those of *Trichodectes,* in which the first segment of the antennae of males is enlarged. *Damalinia bovis* is the most common cattle louse in Britain and is also found in the United States (Plate 21–17, Fig. 2). During winter, this louse is found at the base of the tail, on the shoulders, and along the back of the host. In heavy infestations, the lice are uniformly distributed over the host.

Other species of *Damalinia* include *D. equi* and *D. pilosus* on horses, *D. caprae* on goats, and *D. ovis* and *D. hermsi* on sheep. Although these lice do not produce any serious injury, they do cause skin irritations that can become uncomfortable to the hosts.

Few *Damalinia equi* males have ever been found, and the females reproduce parthenogenically throughout the year. Thus, the

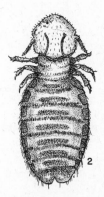

Plate 21-17   Trichodectid lice. 1. *Trichodectes tibialis* of deer. **2.** *Damalinia bovis* of cattle.

critical phases in the parthenogenic reproduction of *D. equi* are the development of eggs within the female, oviposition, morphogenesis within the shell, and hatching. Murray (1963a) found that temperature and relative humidity are of critical importance during these phases. If female lice are maintained at 16° C., no egg development within the female takes place, and exposure to 44.5° C. for only 1 hour can prevent subsequent oviposition. Fewer eggs are laid at 31° C. than at 39° C., and the majority of eggs are oviposited at between 32° C. and 37° C. with 75 per cent relative humidity or less.

Morphogenesis is also influenced by temperature and relative humidity, for only at between 31° C. and 39° C. does morphogenesis proceed to completion and hatching occur, provided the relative humidity is less than 90 per cent. A relative humidity of 90 per cent prevents hatching. If eggs are maintained between 27° C. and 31° C., less eggs develop. None reach an advanced stage of development at 42° C. Exposure of eggs at an advanced state of development for 2 hours at 49° C. is lethal, but at least 6 hours of exposure are required to kill eggs at 45° C.

Only during the winter months are temperatures near the horse's skin continuously favorable for egg development in the female louse, for oviposition, and for egg development on the horse. This probably explains the presence of *D. equi* in large numbers on the bodies of horses at the end of winter in contrast to their scarcity on the limbs.

On the other hand, the temperature within the hair coat on the horse's body during the summer is sufficient to kill the lice, or to reduce the number of eggs laid. Therefore, it's not surprising that the reproduction rate of *D. equi* is greatly reduced during the summer months.

Genus *Felicola*

Felicola includes *F. subrostratus*, which parasitizes cats. This species exhibits the generic characteristics of absence of pleural plates, and similarity of antennae in both sexes.

FAMILY PHILOPTERIDAE

Members of Philopteridae are either long and slender or are broad with rounded abdomens. Philopterid members belonging to the first category include the genera *Lipeurus*, *Ornithobius*, *Columbicola*, and *Esthiopterum*. Those possessing broad bodies and rounded abdomens include the genera *Goniodes*, *Goniocotes*, *Cuclotogaster*, and *Philopterus*.

Again, as among the amblycerid lice, the ischnocerids demonstrate a considerable degree of host specificity.

Genus *Lipeurus*

Lipeurus includes several species encountered on domestic birds. *Lipeurus caponis*, the "variable louse," measuring 2 mm. in length, is long and slender and is a parasite of chickens. *Lipeurus polytrapezius*, also slender and measuring 3 to 3.5 mm. in length, is found on turkeys. *Lipeurus humidianus* is found on guinea fowl. *Lipeurus bidentatus*, a whitish species measuring 1 mm. in length, is found on pigeons. *Lipeurus squalidus* is a large species that measures 4 mm. in length and is found on ducks and geese. *Lipeurus damicornis*, measuring 2 mm. in length, is a broad and brownish species found on pigeons.

The species of *Lipeurus* live among the feathers of both old and young birds. In heavy infestations, areas of the host's skin are made bare by the lice. The greatest amount of injury sustained by the hosts, however, does not result from the feeding habits of these insects, but from irritation of the skin. Infested birds commonly scratch themselves with their claws, thus irritating the skin further.

Kellogg, who has studied the biting lice of birds extensively, pointed out that when an infested bird is shot, the lice on it die from 2 hours to 2 or 3 days afterwards. In extremely rare instances, lice may survive on a dead bird for over a week. Kellogg also pointed out that passage of lice from one bird to another most probably occurs while the bodies of the hosts are in contact.

Genus *Ornithobius*

Ornithobius includes *O. cygni*, which measures 1 mm. in length. It possesses a reddish brown head, thorax, and legs, and a white abdomen. This louse is found on swans, while the related species, *O. icterodes*, is found on ducks and geese.

Genus *Goniodes*

Goniodes includes *G. dissimilis*, the reddish brown louse found on the feathers of chickens in southern United States. *Goniodes stylifer*, measuring 3 mm. in length, is found on turkeys. Other species include *G. minor* on pigeons, *G. breviceps* (2 mm. long) and *G. pavonis* (3 mm. long) on peacocks, and *G. meleagridis* on turkeys.

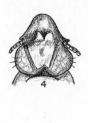

Plate 21-18   Philopterid lice. 1. Female *Columbicola columbae* of pigeons. **2.** *Esthiopterum crassicorne* of chickens. **3.** *Gonicotes gigas* of chickens. **4.** Anterior end of *Philopterus dentatus* of ducks.

Genus *Gonicotes*

Members of *Gonicotes* can be distinguished from those of *Goniodes* by the absence of prongs on the antennal segments of males. *Gonicotes* includes *G. gigas,* which is the largest of the chicken lice (Plate 21-18, Fig. 3). This species is grayish and 3 to 4 mm. long. *Gonicotes hologaster,* the fluff louse, is closely related but smaller, measuring 0.7 to 1.3 mm. in length. It is also a parasite on chickens. *Gonicotes bidentatus* is found on pigeons.

Other Philopterid Lice

Columbicola columbae, a common ectoparasite of pigeons, has been mentioned in connection with the life cycle patterns of biting lice (p. 574) (Plate 21-18, Fig. 1). This very slender species is approximately 2 mm. long.

Esthiopterum crassicorne is found on chicks (Plate 21-18, Fig. 2). The head of this species is elongate in front of the antennae and the clypeus is without dorsal spines.

Cuclotogaster heterographus, the chicken head louse, is dark grayish and approximately 2 mm. long. It is found on the head and neck of its host, and like *Menopon gallinae,* it lays eggs singly.

Philopterus dentatus, like the other members of the genus, possesses a hornlike projection situated anterior to the antennal insertions (Plate 12-18, Fig. 4). This species parasitizes ducks.

ORDER ANOPLURA

The Anoplura, or sucking lice, are quite similar to the Mallophaga. In fact, these two groups in the past were considered members of the same order. More recent systematists, however, are of the opinion that the drastically different feeding habit of the Anoplura—mouthparts modified for sucking rather than biting —is of sufficient evolutionary difference to consider these lice as members of a distinct order of the Insecta.* Members range in length from 2 to 5 mm. All are ectoparasites of mammals. Their diet consists of the host's blood and is sucked through the mouthparts, which are formed as an eversible set of five stylets (p. 558).

Approximately 250 species of sucking lice are known, of which 62 are found in the United States. The species are relegated to four or six families, depending on the systematic interpretation of the particular worker. In following the more conservative classification of Herms, four families are diagnosed below.

Family 1. Echinophthiriidae. Are parasitic on marine mammals. Bodies are robust, covered with short spines and scales. Abdomen lacks sclerotized plates except at terminal end and on external genitalia and associated segments. Antennae are four- or five-jointed. Spiracles are small. Possesses three or at least posterior two pairs of legs.

Family 2. Pediculidae. Are parasites of primates, including man. Bodies are fairly robust, not covered with dense spines. Abdomen is armed with pleural plates (paratergites) and possesses tergal and sternal plates in most species. Possesses well developed eyes, comprising lens and pigment granules. Legs are approximately equal in length or with first pair slightly smaller.

Family 3. Haematopinidae. Are parasites of mammals in-

*Another school of thought contends that separation of the Mallophaga from the Anoplura is artificial, and groups all lice under one order, Phthiraptera (see Horsfall, W. R. 1962. *Medical Entomology.* Ronald Press, N.Y., pp. 82–83).

cluding pigs, Artiodactyla, and equines. Bodies possess spines or hairs arranged in rows. Scales are absent. Abdomen has paratergites. Tergal and sternal plates are present in most species. Eyes are absent or reduced. Antennae are five-jointed. All three pairs of legs are of approximate size. Tibiae are usually with thumblike process opposing claw.

Family 4. Haematopinoididae. Are parasites on small mammals (shrews, gophers, rats, etc.). Bodies are relatively small. Abdomen has sclerotized plates. Eyes are present. All three pairs of legs are of approximate size.

FAMILY ECHINOPHTHIRIIDAE

The Echinophthiriidae includes a few species found attached to marine mammals such as seals, sea lions, and walrus. For example, *Echinophthirus phocae* is found on seals and *Antartophthirus trichechi* is found on the Pacific walrus. Not much is known about the biology of these unusual lice. Investigations on osmoregulation and salt maintenance in these animals should be of considerable interest, for unlike the other lice, these live in a marine aquatic environment.

FAMILY PEDICULIDAE

The Pediculidae includes two medically important species that feed on human blood—*Pediculus humanus,* the body louse, and *Phthirus pubis,* the crab louse.

Pediculus humanus

The males of this grayish species are 2 to 3 mm. long, and the females are 3 to 4 mm. long (Plate 21–19, Fig. 1). In the past, most parasitologists recognized two subspecies—*capitis,* found in hair on the head, and *corporis,* found on the body. However, increasing numbers of workers have come to consider the two subspecies as merely races or forms of the same

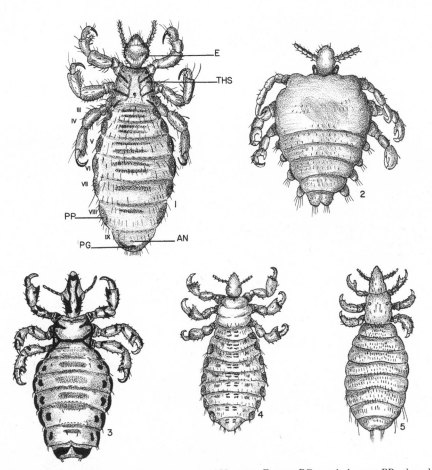

Plate 21-19   Lice. 1. *Pediculus humanus.* (AN, anus; E, eye; PG, genital pore; PP, pleural plates; THS, thoracic spiracle.) (Modified after Keilin and Nuttall, 1930.) **2.** Female *Phthirus pubis.* **3.** *Haematopinus suis.* **4.** *Haematopinus eurysternus.* **5.** *Linognathus vituli.* (Figs. 4 and 5 redrawn after Mönnig, 1949. *Veterinary Helminthology and Entomology,* Baillière, Tindall & Cox, London.)

species. Members of the two races will inter-breed. Murray reported that the color of this louse alters, depending on the coloration of the hair of the host, but this strange method of camouflage has not been confirmed.

LIFE CYCLE OF *Pediculus humanus.* Development of *P. humanus,* like that of all anopluran and mallophagan lice, is hemimetabolous, or incomplete (p. 566). The whitish eggs are less than 1 mm. long in the *capitis* race, and slightly larger in the *corporis* race. The eggs are attached by a cement-like excretion to hair or clothing. A single female oviposits between 80 and 100 eggs in the *capitis* race and between 200 and 300 in the *corporis* race. Such eggs hatch in 5 to 20 days, and the emerging nymphs are miniature replicas of adults except that their antennae are composed of three segments (five segments in adults).

There are two nymphal instars before the adult form is attained. Development, however, is rapid. The egg-to-egg cycle generally takes three weeks. Temperature is critically important during the developmental process. Leeson (1941) reported that embryonic development (within the eggshell) ceases if the environmental temperature is below 23° C. or above 38° C. Even slight changes in temperature result in marked alterations in developmental time. This phenomenon is demonstrated in Table 21–2.

Upon hatching, the nymphs require almost immediate feeding. If no host is available, they perish within 24 hours. Once reaching maturity, females live for 33 to 40 days, while the life span of adult males is slightly shorter.

Male and female *P. humanus* copulate on their host. The male crawls underneath the female from behind. When the tips of their abdomens unite, the female rises to a vertical

position, lifting the male. The two lice then return to the horizontal position and remain united for 30 minutes or more.

SKIN REACTIONS TO *Pediculus humanus.* Not only do the bites of *P. humanus* irritate, the victim can become highly sensitive, resulting in tissue reactions that are extremely irritating. Peck et al. (1943) demonstrated that the irritibility of louse bites increases with continued recurrence of bites; thus, the dermal reaction is essentially an allergic one. Human skin subjected to louse bites over long periods often becomes deeply pigmented—a condition known as vagabond's disease. When such a condition exists, irritibility does not occur; instead, the victim becomes immune.

DISEASES TRANSMITTED BY *Pediculus.* *Pediculus humanus* is a major vector for three important human diseases—relapsing fever, typhus, and trench fever.

Relapsing Fever. A cosmopolitan disease, relapsing fever can develop when the spirochaete *Borrelia recurrentis* is inoculated while the victim crushes an infected louse and scratches himself with his contaminated fingernails. This mechanism of infection is quite apparent when one considers the host-parasite relationship between spirochaete and louse. When the louse takes in spirochaetes during feeding, its gastric juices are detrimental to *B. recurrentis.* In fact, all ingested spirochaetes are killed except for the 1 to 5 per cent that penetrate the alimentary wall. Once these become established in the coelom, they begin to multiply. Spirochaetes disappear from the louse's gut 5 to 24 hours after entering but reappear in the coelom in 8 to 12 days. These pieces of evidence indicate that only through the crushing of the vector's body and the inoculation of contaminated body fluid can infection be initiated. Furthermore, attempts at infection with feces or through bites have proven unsuccessful.

Typhus. A much dreaded ancient disease, typhus is now limited to Asia, North Africa, and Central and South America. The causative agent is *Rickettsia prowazeki.* Infection of man is contracted when contaminated louse feces are rubbed into abraded skin. However, since the rickettsiae remain infective in louse feces if kept dry and at room temperature, it is also possible to contract infections when such fecal particles are inhaled.

Commonly, lice become infected with *R. prowazeki* while feeding on typhus victims during the initial stages of the disease. Once the rickettsiae enter the insect's gut, they pene-

Table 21-2. Effect of Temperature on the Incubation of Eggs of *Pediculus humanus**

Temperature	Incubation Period
22°C.	Will not hatch
24°C.	17-21 days
29°C.	9-11 days
35°C.	5-7 days
38°C.	Will not hatch

*Data from Leeson (1941).

trate into the epithelial cells and multiply so rapidly that infected cells become greatly distended and usually rupture, thus releasing the rickettsiae into the lumen. From here, the rickettsiae pass to the exterior in feces. Infected lice usually die within 10 days, but if they do not die, their infections are retained for the remainder of their life span.

Trench Fever. This disease is caused by *Rickettsia quintana.* Except for a few outbreaks in recent years, trench fever is not very common today. However, it was one of the most frequently encountered diseases during World War I. As with *R. prowazeki, R. quintana* is introduced into victims via contaminated feces. Unlike *R. prowazeki,* however, it survives and multiplies in the lumen of the louse's gut and not in epithelial cells.

Bactericidal Substances in Lice. In addition to the three human pathogens mentioned, human lice can also harbor and transmit *Pasteurella tularensis,* the causative agent of tularemia. Transmission is again via lice feces. Other than these, other bacteria are rapidly destroyed when taken into the digestive tract of lice because of bactericidal substances in the alimentary tract. Such substances are present in most insects.

The antibacterial properties of the intestinal contents, however, do not interfere with *P. tularensis.* Furthermore, these properties have no effect on various salmonellas, including the typhoid organism. Salmonellas mutiply rapidly in lice and generally kill them in 24 to 48 hours. Even after the lice die, bacteria can survive in the decaying bodies and feces for over a year.

The apparent "immunity" of *Pasteurella tularensis* and salmonellas to the gastric juices of *Pediculus humanus* exemplifies how the compatibility, or for that matter incompatibility, of the vector's chemical composition with the microorganism can influence transmission of microbes by arthropods.

Phthirus pubis

The crab louse *P. pubis* is so named because of its crablike ovoid body, which is rather wide (Plate 21–19, Fig. 2). Specimens measure 1.5 to 2 mm. in length, with the males being slightly smaller and grayish. This louse is most frequently found attached to pubic hair, but it also attaches in other hairy regions of the body. The bite of *P. pubis* is extremely irritating, and if infestations occur over long periods, the skin becomes discolored. Transmission of pubic lice occurs through direct contact or from contaminated clothing and toilet seats. A closely related species, *P. gorillae,* is found on gorillas.

LIFE CYCLE OF *Phthirus pubis.* The life history of *Phthirus pubis* parallels that of other lice. Development is of the hemimetabolous type (p. 566). A single female usually oviposits 15 to 25 eggs, which are attached to hair. The number of eggs may be greater in some instances. The eggs hatch in 6 or 7 days, and the young undergo three molts and become sexually mature in about 2 to 3 weeks. Adults usually live for about a month when on their host. If removed, they die within a day.

FAMILY HAEMATOPINIDAE

The Haematopinidae includes several important genera—*Haematopinus, Solenopotes,** *Linognathus,** and *Microthoracius.**

Genus Haematopinus

Haematopinus includes several species that parasitize domestic animals. *Haematopinus suis,* a cosmopolitan species, measuring 5 to 6 mm. in length, is the largest (Plate 21–19, Fig. 3). It is found attached in the skin folds on the neck, ears, abdomen, and legs of pigs, and it will also feed on humans.

Haematopinus tuberculatus, measuring 3.5 to 5.5 mm. in length, is found on cattle in parts of Australia and India. The short-nosed cattle louse, *H. eurysternus* measures 3.5 to 4.75 mm. in length (Plate 21–19, Fig. 4). *Haematopinus quadripertusus* is the tail louse of cattle.

Haematopinus asini, from 2.5 to 3.5 mm. long, attaches at the bases of the mane and tails of horses, mules, and donkeys. *Haematopinus ventricosus* is found on rabbits.

All these species, excepting *H. tuberculatus,* are found in North America. In fact, *H. asini* is a rather common parasite of equines in the United States.

Other Haematopinid Genera

GENUS *Solenopotes.* *Solenopotes* also includes several species that infest animals in North America. *Solenopotes capillatus,* the little blue cattle louse, 1.2 to 1.5 mm. long, is widely distributed throughout the world.

---

*The genera *Solenoptes, Linognathus,* and *Microthoracius* are considered by some as representing a separate family—Linognathidae—because members of these genera lack sclerotized abdominal plates.

Genus Linognathus. *Linognathus* includes *L. vituli,* the long-nosed cattle louse (Plate 21–19, Fig. 5); *L. stenopsis,* the goat louse; and *L. piliferus,* the common dog louse. One species, *L. pedalis,* the leg louse of sheep, has been reported to cause the host's death if they are present in large numbers.

Murray (1963b, c), while studying the ecology of sheep lice, found that specific differences exist between the behavioral patterns and survival of *Linognathus pedalis* and the closely related *L. ovillus* at different temperatures. *Linognathus pedalis,* normally found on the legs of sheep, where the temperature near the skin fluctuates greatly, is able to survive prolonged exposure to low temperatures of 2° C. to 22° C., while *L. ovillus,* normally found on the host's face and to a lesser extent on the body, cannot survive exposure to these cold temperatures.

Because the skin temperature of the legs of sheep can drop to nearly that of the environment for considerable periods in cold weather, the ability of *L. pedalis* to survive for several days without feeding at low temperatures appears to be an adaptation to survival in its habitat. Although *L. pedalis* can withstand lower temperatures and *L. ovillus* cannot, the temperatures that are favorable for reproduction of the two species are similar, being 35° C. at 54 per cent relative humidity. Furthermore, engorged females oviposit approximately twenty times more eggs than unengorged females.

Relative to behavioral patterns, Murray found that *L. pedalis* is more sedentary and tends to congregate in clusters on the part of the leg covered with hair, while *L. ovillus* never forms clusters and its populations are dispersed, being generally more dense in the region where the hair and wool on the sheep's face merge. In both species of lice, only adults are transferred from sheep to sheep.

Genus Microthoracius. *Microthoracius* includes *M. cameli,* a parasite of camels.

All of the mammal-infesting haematopinid lice lay their eggs on their hosts, and the eggs are glued to the hairs by means of a mucous secretion.

FAMILY HAEMATOPINOIDIDAE

The Haematopinoididae includes *Haplopleura aenomydis,* a species commonly found on rats in North America. Various other members of the family are found on gophers in the United States and Canada.

NUTRITION OF LICE

The nutritional physiology and the digestive processes of lice, particularly the mallophagan lice, have been reviewed by Waterhouse (1953). This investigator noted that bird lice can feed on the protective sheaths of growing feathers, feather-fiber, down, skin-scurf, scabs, blood, their own eggs, and cast skins. They can probably also feed on mucus and sebaceous matter. Some of these materials undoubtedly contain keratin, which the lice can digest with the aid of intracellular mutualistic bacteria in their bodies. Such bacteria pass from louse to louse by way of their eggs.

Some species of mammalian lice can ingest hair, although most species appear to prefer epidermal scales, skin, and wax. Some species feed on blood.

It has been postulated that the reason ant-eating mammals are nearly always free of lice is that the formic acid resulting from the digestion of the ants' bodies discourages lice. This hypothesis is in need of verification.

Other aspects of insect physiology are discussed in the last section of Chapter 23, page 646.

LITERATURE CITED

Bruce, W. N. 1948. Studies on the biological requirements of the cat flea. Ann. Ent. Soc. Amer., *41:* 346–352.

Comstock, J. H. 1949. An Introduction to Entomology. Comstock Publ. Co., Ithaca, New York.

Ewing, H. E., and I. Fox. 1943. The Fleas of North America: Classification, Identification, and Geographic Distribution of these Injurious and Disease-spreading Insects. Misc. Publ. No. 500., USDA, Washington.

Fox, I. 1940a. Fleas of Eastern United States. Iowa State College Press, Ames, Ia.

Fox, I. 1940b. Siphonaptera from western United States. J. Wash. Acad. Sci., *30:* 272–276.

Hampton, B. C. 1940. Plague in the United States. Pub. Health Rep., *55:* 1143–1158.

Hopkins, G. H. E. 1957. Host-associations of Siphonaptera. *In* First Symposium On Host Specificity Among Parasites of Vertebrates. pp. 64–87. Inst. Zool., Univ. Neuchâtel.

Hubbard, C. A. 1947. Fleas of western North America. Iowa State College Press, Ames, Ia.

Jellison, W. L., and N. E. Godd. 1942. Index to the literature of Siphonaptera of North America. Nat. Inst. Health Bull. No. 178. U. S. Publ. Health Serv., Washington.

Jordon, K. 1956. Chapters on fleas *in* J. Smart's A Handbook for the Identification of Insects of Medical Importance. 3rd Ed. British Museum (Natural History), London.

Leeson, H. S. 1941. The effect of temperature upon the hatching of the eggs of *Pediculus humanus corporis* DeGeer. Parasitology, *33:* 243–249.

Matthysse, J. G. 1946. Cattle lice, their biology and control. Agric. Exp. Sta. Bull. No. 832. Cornell University, Ithaca, N. Y.

Meyer, K. F. 1942. The ecology of plague. Medicine, *21:* 143–174.

Murray, M. D. 1963a. Influence of temperature on the reproduction of *Damalinia equi* (Denny). Austral. J. Zool., *11:* 183–189.

Murray, M. D. 1963b. The ecology of lice on sheep. III. Differences between the biology of *Linognathus pedalis* (Osborne) and *L. ovillus* (Neumann). Austral. J. Zool., *11:* 153–156.

Murray, M. D. 1963c. The ecology of lice on sheep. IV. The establishment and maintenance of populations of *Linognathus ovillus* (Neumann). Austral. J. Zool., *11:* 157–172.

Peck, S. S., W. H. Wright, and J. Q. Gant. 1943. Cutaneous reactions due to the body louse (*Pediculus humanus*). JAMA, *123:* 821–825.

Ross, H. H. 1948. A Textbook of Entomology. John Wiley, New York.

Waterhouse, D. F. 1953. Studies on the digestion of wool by insects. IX. Some features of digestion in chewing lice (Mallophaga) from birds and mammalian hosts. Austral. J. Biol. Sci., *6:* 257–275.

Wigglesworth, V. B. 1954. The Physiology of Insect Metamorphosis. Cambridge University Press, London.

Wu, L-T., J. W. H. Chun, R. Pollitzer, and C. Y. Wu. 1936. Plague, a Manual for Medical and Public Health Workers. Weishengshu National Quar. Serv., Shanghai.

SUGGESTED READING

Siphonaptera

Herms, W. B., and M. T. James. 1961. Medical Entomology. 5th Ed., Macmillan, New York. Read pp. 396–433. (This section in Herms and James' textbook discusses the fleas. All species discussed are directly or indirectly of medical importance. This information is most useful, as is the literature cited.)

Matheson, R. 1950. Medical Entomology. 2nd Ed., Comstock Publ. Co., Ithaca, New York. Read pp. 538–561. (This section in Matheson's textbook discusses the fleas. The information presented to assist in the identification of siphonapterans is particularly useful.)

Mallophaga

Comstock, J. H. 1949. An Introduction to Entomology. Comstock Publ. Co., Ithaca, New York. Read pp. 335–337. (The author discusses the Mallophaga in this section of his textbook. Although the information is of a general nature, it should aid in familiarizing the reader with the biting lice.)

Herms, W. B., and M. T. James. 1961. Medical Entomology. 5th Ed. Macmillan, New York. Read pp. 117–120. (In this section of Herms and James' textbook are discussed the biting lice that are of medical importance.)

Anoplura

Comstock, J. H. 1949. An Introduction to Entomology. Comstock Publ. Co., Ithaca, New York. Read pp. 347–349. (The author discusses the Anoplura in this section of his textbook. The information is of a general nature that will help introduce the student to the sucking lice.)

Dethier, V. G. 1957. Sensory physiology of blood-sucking arthropods. Exptl. Parasit., *6:* 68–122. Read pp. 87–92. (This is a comprehensive review article by a recognized authority. In this specific section the author discusses the sensory physiology of the lice.)

Herms, W. B., and M. T. James. 1961. Medical Entomology. 5th Ed., Macmillan, New York. Read pp. 105–117. (This section in Herms and James' textbook is devoted to the Anoplura. Medically important species are discussed in considerable detail, and there are some interesting illustrations.)

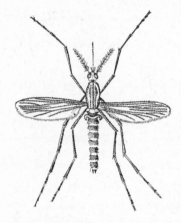

22

THE DIPTERA—
The Flies, Gnats, and Mosquitoes*

The order Diptera includes the flies, gnats, and mosquitoes. There are approximately 85,000 known species of diperans in the world, of which 16,700 are found in North America. These insects are of great interest to medical and veterinary entomologists because they serve as carriers of many important diseases. Not only are dipterans of importance as vectors, but many are ectoparasitic bloodsuckers, and still others are endoparasites.

Dipterans can be distinguished from all other insects by the possession of only one pair of membranous wings—the forewings. The hindwings are greatly reduced and appear as a pair of slender knoblike balancing organs known as halteres. The mouthparts of dipterans are of various types. In some groups, they are modified for piercing and sucking, while in others they are modified for rasping and lapping.

Hardy's (1960) monograph of the Nematocera and Brachycera should be consulted by those interested in taxonomy. For the sake of convenience, the following classification is used in this volume.

Suborder 1. Orthorrhapha.   Pupa is not enclosed in epidermis of larva. Adults emerge from the pupal case through a T shaped anterodorsal split.
  A. Nematocera Group. Possesses long antennae of at least six similar segments. Larvae have well developed heads.
  B. Brachycera Group. Possesses short antennae consisting of three segments. Third antennal segment may be annulated.
Suborder 2. Cyclorrhapha.   Pupa is enclosed in epidermis of larva (puparium). Adults escape through circular split at one terminal of puparium. Larvae are maggot-like.
  A. Aschiza Group. Lacks permanent crescent shaped mark (the lunule†) on head. Lacks frontal suture on puparium.
  B. Schizophora Group. Possesses permanent crescent shaped mark (the lunule) on head. Possesses frontal puparial suture.

SUBORDER ORTHORRHAPHA

According to Comstock (1949), the Orthorrhapha includes thirty-two families of which

---

*The physiology of parasitic insects and the relationships with their hosts are discussed at the end of Chapter 23.

†The lunule is the scar resulting from the shrinkage of the ptilinium, which is an outgrowth of the head on the pupa used in pushing out the circular opening the puparial wall during the escaping process of the adult.

fifteen are subordinate to the Nematocera and seventeen to the Brachycera. Of the thirty-two orthorrhaphan families, several include parasitic members. Six of these families are examined in the following discussion—Simuliidae, Psychodidae, Heleidae, Culicidae, Tabanidae, and Rhagionidae. The first four are subordinate to the Nematocera, and the last two are subordinate to the Brachycera. A short diagnosis precedes discussion of these families.

FAMILY SIMULIIDAE
(Blackflies)

Bodies are short and stout. Thorax is much arched, giving humpbacked appearance. Legs are comparatively short. Antennae are ten- or eleven-jointed, slightly longer than the head. Ocelli are absent. Compound eyes on males are large and contiguous; compound eyes on females are widely separated. Proboscis is not elongate. Palpi are four-jointed. Wing venation is shown in Plate 22–1, Fig. 1.

Over 600 species of simuliid flies are known (Smart, 1945; Vargas, et al., 1946). The bodies of these haematophagous, or bloodsucking, flies range from 1 to 5 mm. in length. As with most haematophagous dipterans, it is the female that possesses piercing-sucking mouthparts (p. 558) and feeds on the host. The males possess rudimentary mouthparts.

Simuliid Life Cycle Pattern

As with all dipterans, the simuliids undergo complete (holometabolous) metamorphosis (p. 566). Adult simuliid flies are generally found in the vicinity of rivers and streams. The eggs are laid either on aquatic plants or on stones beneath the surface of the water. Females of *Simulium maculatum* have been observed to submerge to a depth of 1 foot during oviposition. The eggs are glued to the substratum by a gelatinous coat.

The larvae, hatching from the eggs, are somewhat club shaped and are swollen posteriorly. They attach to stones and other objects by means of a disclike sucker at the posterior end of the body. These larvae are invariably aquatic and require swift-flowing water for their habitat. They are commonly found congregated in the vicinity of rapids and waterfalls. The larvae pupate in cone shaped cocoons that are attached in the water. The pupal respiratory organs, composed of long tubelike filaments, protrude from the cocoon and obtain oxygen

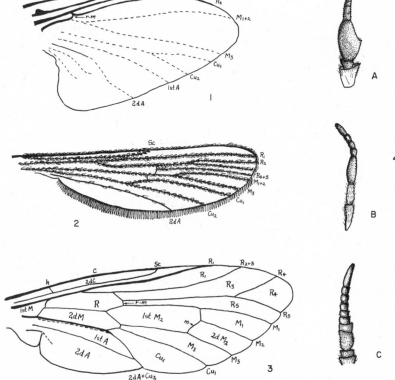

Plate 22-1   Simuliidae, Culicidae and Tabanidae. 1. Wing of *Simulium,* showing venation pattern. **2.** Wing of a mosquito, showing venation pattern. **3.** Wing of *Tabanus,* showing venation pattern. **4. A.** Antenna of *Tabanus.* **B.** Antenna of *Chrysops.* **C.** Antenna of *Pangonia.* (All figures, except Fig. 4C redrawn after Comstock, J. H. 1949. *An Introduction to Entomology,* Comstock Publishing Co., Ithaca, N.Y.)

from the moving water. The form that emerges from the cocoon is the adult. The simuliid adults are haematophagous.

There are six genera of simuliids, *Parasimulium, Prosimulium, Cnephia, Austrosimulium, Gigantodax,* and *Simulium.*

Genus *Cnephia*

Cnephia includes several species that feed on the blood of domestic animals and occasionally man. *Cnephia pecuarum,* the southern buffalo gnat, is an important pest of livestock and man in the Mississippi Valley during the spring (Plate 22–2, Fig. 1). This species is primarily a diurnal feeder. Its bite causes severe swelling resulting from the material injected during feeding. In heavy attacks, horses, mules, and even cattle have been killed in a matter of hours resulting from the general weakened condition due to blood loss and the effects of the injected substance. In the western and Pacific states, *C. minus* in the common species. This is a smaller and darker form than *C. pecuarum.*

Genus *Simulium*

Simulium includes *S. venustum,* which is a pest of man in New England, Canada, and the region surrounding the Great Lakes. During June and July, the bites of this blackfly can become quite a hazard to sportsmen.

Simulium vittatum is found in North America and quite frequently in Europe. This species attacks livestock and man. Similarly *S. colombaschense,* the goloubatz gnat, attacks livestock in middle and southern Europe. Its bite, in instances of heavy infestations, has been reported to kill pigs, sheep, cattle, and horses.

The bird-infesting species, *S. occidentale* and *S. meridionale,* commonly called turkey gnats, are found in the southern United States in the late spring. These flies attack the comb and wattles of poultry and by so doing initiate a disease similar to avian cholera.

Genus *Prosimulium*

Prosimulium hirtipes is a springtime pest of man and domestic animals in the northwestern United States.

SIMULIIDS AS VECTORS

In addition to causing irritation through their bites, the simuliid flies serve as vectors for nematode and haemosporidian parasites.

Vectors for *Onchocerca volvulus*

Onchocerca volvulus, a human-infecting nematode (p. 450), is transmitted by *Simulium damnosum* and *S. neavei* in Africa. *Simulium damnosum* is the major vector in the regions immediately south of the Sahara Desert (Plate 22–2, Fig. 2). This species breeds in large rivers and in small tributaries. *Simulium neavei* is the principal vector in the Congo. It breeds in medium-sized rivers, where the eggs are deposited in clusters on vegetation. The larvae and pupae are found attached (epizoic) on the exoskeleton of crabs of the genus *Potamonantes.*

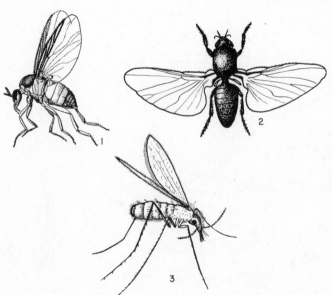

Plate 22–2　　Biting Diptera. 1. *Cnephia pecuarum,* the buffalo gnat. (After Garman. *In* Herms, W. B., and James, M. T. 1961. *Medical Entomology,* Macmillan, New York.) 2. *Simulium damnosum.* 3. *Phlebotomus papatasii,* the sand fly. (Redrawn after Byam and Archibald.)

Human onchocerciasis also occurs in Mexico, Central America, and parts of South America. In the Americas, *S. ochraceum* is the major vector. This small species measures 1.5 to 2 mm. in length. The thorax is yellowish-red, its abdomen is yellow and black, and the legs are black. Dalmat (1955) studied the development of this fly. He reported that it will breed only in small trickling streams that are relatively free of vegetation. Two other species of *Simulium*, *S. callidum* and *S. metallicum,* are capable of transmitting *O. volvulus* in the New World.

Vectors for *Onchocerca gutterosa*

Onchocerca gutterosa, the bovine onchocerciasis nematode, is transmitted by *Simulium ornatum* in Europe. Once taken into the ventriculus of the fly, the microfilariae attain the "sausage" form in approximately 10 days. By the nineteenth or twentieth day, the nematodes are found in the fly's thoracic muscles. From here they migrate anteriorly to the mouthparts and are then ready to be introduced into the vertebrate host. This passage of the microfilariae from the fly to the vertebrate host is not a passive one. The worms appear to be attracted by the warmth of the cow's blood and actively migrate from the fly. Not all the nematodes taken into the *Simulium* vector survive; only a small percentage do.

Although the vectors for other species of *Onchocerca* are not known, it is strongly suspected that in time these vectors will be shown to be simuliid flies.

Vectors for *Leucocytozoon* spp.

Species of *Simulium* also serve as vectors for the haemosporidian *Leucocytozoon* spp. For example, *L. simondi,* a parasite of ducks and geese (p. 135) is transmitted by *Simulium rugglesi* in northern United States and Canada. Similarly *L. smithi,* a species injurious to turkeys in the United States, is transmitted by *Simulium jenningsi, S. occidentale,* and *S. slossonae.*

FAMILY PSYCHODIDAE
(Moth Flies and Sand Flies)

Bodies are moth-like. Antennae are long and slender, clothed with whorls of hair, and are long in males. Wings have nine to eleven long, parallel veins, with no crossveins except at base.

This family is divided into four subfamilies, of which only the Phlebotominae includes haematophagous species.

Genus *Phlebotomus*

The largest and most important genus of subfamily Phlebotominae is *Phlebotomus.** These flies, often called sand flies, are seldom more than 4 mm. long. As with the simuliid flies, only the females possess piercing-sucking mouthparts and are haemotaphagous. The males are nonparasitic, feeding on moisture. Various species feed on mammals, lizards, and snakes.

The species of *Phlebotomus* are small slender specimens with hairy bodies. Their coloration is dull, usually yellowish. The legs are long and lanky. Of the numerous known species, 145 or more have been recorded from the Western Hemisphere, primarily from Mexico, Central, and South America. Many more species of sand flies exist in the Orient and other parts of the Old World. In general, however, these flies are limited to the warmer regions of the world.

Phlebotomus papatasii is the common sand fly in the Old World (Plate 22–2, Fig. 3). It is anthropophilic and feeds on blood. This species measures approximately 2.5 mm. in length and is yellowish gray with a dull red-brown stripe extending longitudinally down the middorsal line of the thorax and with a reddish brown spot on each lateral surface of the same region. *Phlebotomus argentipes* is widely distributed in areas of India and Burma, where it feeds primarily on cattle blood, although it attacks humans. *Phlebotomus sergenti* is widely distributed in the Near and Middle East and in North Africa.

The more common New World species include *P. intermedius,* which is widely distributed in Venezuela, Brazil, Paraguay, and Argentina; *P. diabolicus,* the only species found in North America that bites man†; and *P. verrucarum,* which is found in the high mountain canyons in Peru.

LIFE CYCLE OF *Phlebotomus* SPP.   Life cycle patterns among the various species appear to be rather similar, differing only in habitats and preferred hosts. The breeding spots of these flies are usually hidden and difficult to find. The elongate eggs are oviposited in small batches under stones, in masonry cracks, in between

---

*The generic name *Phlebotomus* should be *Flebotomus,* which is the correct spelling. However, the former is more commonly used.

†According to Addis (1945), six species of *Phlebotomus* are found in the U. S.—*P. limae,* which is widely distributed in the southern states; *P. vexator* with the same distribution; *P. diabolicus* in Texas; *P. texanus* in Texas; *P. stewarti* in California; and *P. anthrophorus* in Texas. None of these sucks human blood except *P. diabolicus.*

the walls of cesspools, and in other similar out-of-the-way places where the temperature is moderate, the environment is dark, and the humidity is high (Plate 22-3, Fig. 1). Laying habits of the females vary but can be categorized in one of three patterns. The flies feed and refeed several times before ovipositing a batch of eggs; the flies oviposit in between a single blood meal; or the flies feed, oviposit, and die. *Phlebotomus argentipes* demonstrates the third pattern.

The eggs of *P. papatasii* incubate for 9 to 12 days, after which minute whitish larvae with long anal spines and chewing mouthparts emerge (Plate 22-3, Fig. 2). Available information indicates that the incubation period in other species approximates that of *P. papatasii*.

The larvae are free-living, feeding on organic debris such as animal excreta. There are four larval instars, the stadia totaling 4 to 6 weeks. The fourth larval instar metamorphoses into the pupa which is not enclosed in a cocoon, and hence are often termed naked (Plate 22-3, Fig. 3). The pupal stadium lasts for 10 days. The egg-to-egg cycle requires 7 to 10 weeks. If cold weather sets in prior to completion of the fourth larval instar, this form undergoes diapause, which may last from several weeks to a year.

Phlebotomus SPP. AS VECTORS. Various species of *Phlebotomus* are suitable vectors for the human-infecting species of *Leishmania* (p. 63). *Phlebotomus argentipes* is the vector for *L. donovani* in India; *P. chinensis* and *P. sergenti* are the major vectors in China and Africa, respectively; and *P. major, P. perniciosus,* and *P. longicuspis* are the transmitters in the Mediterranean areas, where dogs serve as natural reservoirs

for the flagellate. As to the mechanism of transmission, Southwell and Kirshner (1938) championed the idea that human infections are acquired when flies are crushed and rubbed into the bites. However, Gupta (1948) reported that infections can be acquired through bites.

Phlebotomus papatasii and *P. sergenti* are principal vectors for *Leishmania tropica*. Again, evidence suggests that infections can be acquired both mechanically and through bites. The flies that serve as vectors for *Leishmania brasiliensis* are not as clearly defined. It is suspected that *P. intermedius, P. pessoai,* and *P. longipalpus* can serve effectively. However, in each case, there is evidence to the contrary (see Deane, 1956). *Phlebotomus cruciatus* is the most probable vector in Yucatan.

In addition to the various types of leishmaniasis, *Phlebotomus* spp. transmit the virus-caused disease commonly referred to as sand-fly fever, or pappataci fever, and for *Bartonella bacilliformis,* the causative agent of bartonellosis, which is commonly referred to as Carrion's disease, or Oroya fever.

Sand-fly fever is a nonlethal disease endemic to the Mediterranean countries, south China, parts of India and Ceylon, and sections of South America. The etiological agent is a virus that is injected into humans during the feeding of the fly, and the clinical symptoms appear after a 3 to 6 day incubation period. The virus can be demonstrated in the victim's blood 24 hours before onset of fever and for 24 hours after the onset. Flies become infective 6 to 8 days after feeding on an infected individual. Transovarial infections in the fly have been suspected; however, further investigations are necessary to verify this phenomenon. Species of *Phlebotomus* suitable as vectors include *P. papatasii, P. perniciosus,* and *P. minutus.*

Bartonellosis produces anemia that in man is commonly fatal. It is endemic to the areas along the Pacific slope of the Peruvian Andes, including parts of Columbia, Peru, Bolivia, Chile, and Ecuador. Victims of the disease exhibit cutaneous nodular eruptions. The causative agent, *Bartonella bacilliformis,** is found in, or occasionally on, erythrocytes in the circulating blood and as intracellular forms in various visceral organs, especially in the endothelial cells of lymph glands. *Bartonella bacilliformis* is transmitted by *Phlebotomus verrucarum,* generally

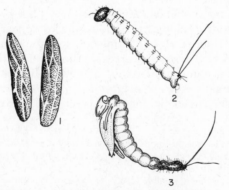

Plate 22-3   Stages in the life cycle of *Phlebotomus.* 1. Eggs of *Phlebotomus.* 2. Larva of *P. papatasii.* 3. Pupa of *P. papatasii.* (Figs. 2 and 3 redrawn after Byam and Archibald.)

---

*This is a minute rickettsia-like organism that is gram-negative, but stains well with Giemsa stain.

at night, for *P. verrucarum* is primarily a nocturnal species. *Phlebotomus noguchii* is also a suitable vector. The bionomics of the disease-causing organism needs clarification, for Herms (1950) stated that Hertig had found *Bartonella* on the proboscal tips of male and female flies. Since males are not bloodsuckers, it must still be determined where the pathogen is acquired.

FAMILY HELEIDAE*
(Biting Midges, or No-see-ums)

Bodies are very small and short, 0.6 to 5.0 mm. long, and not very hairy. Wings are broad, folded over abdomen, often mottled, and have few veins that are not all parallel.

This family includes twenty or more genera. Johannsen (1943) has contributed a synopsis of the genera found in the Americas and has listed species in North America known up till that time. Wirth (1952) has published a monograph on members of this family found in California. Not all the heleid flies are bloodsuckers. Such genera as *Helea, Leptoconops, Lasiohelea, Ceratopogon,* and *Forcipomyia* include species that are annoying pests and that attack man. These midges have been dubbed with such familiar names as punkies, no-see-ums, and black gnats.

Genus *Culicoides*

By far the most important genus of the Heleidae is *Culicoides* (Plate 22–4, Fig. 1). Vargas (1949) has listed the known species, Root and Hoffman (1937) have provided a key to species found in North America, Barbosa (1947) and Costa Lima (1937) have contributed taxonomic studies of species found in neotropical regions, Fox (1946) has provided a review of species from the Caribbean area, Foote and Pratt (1954) have catalogued species found in the eastern United States, and Campbell and Pellam-Clinton (1959) have monographed the British species of *Culicoides*.

Familiar species of *Culicoides* include *C. canithorax, C. furens,* and *C. melleus.* These species cause a serious economic problem in summer-resort areas along the Atlantic Coast. *Culicoides diabolicus* is a fiercely biting species found in Mexico. *Culicoides peliliouensis* is another fierce biter found along the Carolina coast.

LIFE CYCLE OF *Culicoides*. The larvae of *Culicoides,* hatching from elongate eggs (Plate 22–4, Fig. 2), are found in mud, sand, and debris at the edges of ponds and other bodies

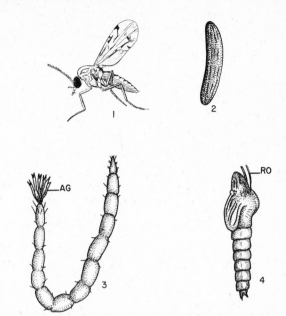

Plate 22-4   Stages in the life cycle of *Culicoides.*
1. Adult *Culicoides.* 2. Egg of *Culicoides.* 3. Larva. (AG, anal gills.) 4. Pupa. (RO, respiratory organ (breathing trumpet). (Fig. 1 after Dampf; Figs. 2 to 4 redrawn after Dove, Hall, and Hull, 1932.)

of water. The eggs of certain species are found in rotting organic material far from water. For example, one species breeds in the desert, in rotting saguaro cacti. The segmented vermiform larvae are capable of swimming with an eel-like motion, stopping to rest on floating vegetation (Plate 22–4, Fig. 3).

The larvae are free-living, being carnivorous or even cannibalistic. As pupation begins, the larvae migrate to the surface of the water, become quiescent, and metamorphose. The pupa possesses a pair of trumpet-like siphons projecting from the thorax (Plate 22–4, Fig. 4). These siphons are specialized spiracles that adhere to the water surface and through which the animal breathes. The postpupal form is the imago.

Temperature is an important factor during development of *Culicoides* spp. Dove et al. (1932) reported that larvae of the salt-marsh species they studied survived best at 50° F. In over 200 attempts to maintain larvae between 70° and 90° F., not a single specimen developed to maturity. Temperature also affects adult *Culicoides.* Travis (1949) reported that among Alaskan species, activity is greatly diminished if the temperature drops to below 55° F., an unusual condition for Alaskan insects, which usually can endure much lower temperatures. Further-

---

*Also known as Ceratopogonidae.

more, Travis reported that the midges are handicapped in their flight if the wind velocity is greater than 3.5 miles per hour. The correlation between air currents and temperature was studied by Dove et al. (1932), who noted that thermotropic responses are marked when there is little air movement. It has been fairly well established that the affinity of *Culicoides* spp. for hosts is one of body heat attraction. This is probably the reason that midges more commonly and abundantly attack men performing strenuous physical labor.

Several instances have been reported in which species differed in degree of activity, depending on the time of day. For example, Foote reported that *C. canithorax* in Mississippi is more vicious and abundant from 10 A. M. until after dark, while Hinman (1936) found that *C. mississippiensis* is most active in the early evening.

Ceratopogon stellifer is a biter of man in Arizona and New Mexico; *Leptoconops kerteszi,* the Bodega black gnat, and *Leptoconops torrens,* the valley black gnat, are both vicious attackers of man, domestic animals, and birds in many parts of the United States, particularly along the Pacific Coast, especially in California and in the southern states. Their bites often result in swellings followed by open exuding lesions.

Culicoides and Related Genera as Vectors

Forcipomyia utae and *F. townsendi* are two Peruvian species that may act as vectors for *Leishmania.*

Several species of *Culicoides* are effective vectors of filarial worms that infect humans and domestic animals. *Dipetalonema perstans,* a human nematode parasite (p. 450), is transmitted by *Culicoides austeni* (*C. milnei* pro part), a nocturnal species 2 mm. long that breeds in banana stumps. This nematode is also transmitted by *C. inornatipennis* and by *C. grahami,* an early morning and evening feeder 1 mm. long that also breeds in banana stumps. The human nematode parasite *Dipetalonema streptocerca* (p. 451) is carried by *C. grahami. Mansonella ozzardi* (p. 451), a human-infecting filarial worm, is transmitted by *C. furens,* a species that bears speckles on its mesosternum (Plate 22–5). The equine filarial worm *Onchocerca reticulata* is transmitted by *C. nebeculosus* in England. This species breeds in manure and stagnant water. The bovine filaria *O. gibsoni* is transmitted by various species of *Culicoides.*

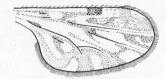

Plate 22–5   Wing of *Culicoides furens.*

In addition to serving as intermediate hosts for nematodes, some heleid midges serve as transmitters of viruses to birds and other wild animals.

FAMILY CULICIDAE
(Mosquitoes and Gnats)

Bodies are slight. Abdomen is long and slender. Wings are narrow (Plate 22–1, Fig. 2). Antennae have fifteen segments, are plumose in males. Proboscis is long and slender. Wings have fringe of scalelike setae on margins. Compound eyes are large, occupying a large portion of surface of head. Ocelli are lacking.

The mosquitoes represent the largest group of dipteran pests. There are at least 2000 known species, which are found in every part of the world. These demonstrate little discrimination while sucking blood from man and animals. Although in the past some have claimed that certain strains of mosquitoes feed only on the blood of one type of host, it is now known that almost all mosquitoes (females) feed on a variety of hosts, if such are available.

Many species not only cause great torment through their bites, but also serve as efficient vectors for such dreaded diseases as malaria, yellow fever, dengue, and encephalitis. Indeed, the scourge cast on mankind by these dipterans is beyond description.

With a few exceptions, most mosquitoes are 2.5 to 6 mm. long. The venation of the single pair of wings is quite characteristic. The veins and posterior margin of each wing are covered with a large number of scales (Plate 22–1, Fig. 2). In the author's opinion, no better monograph on mosquitoes exists than the extremely complete volume by Professor William R. Horsfall (1955) of the University of Illinois. For those interested in the physiology of mosquitoes, the monograph by Clements (1963) is especially recommended.

Life Cycle of Mosquitoes

EGGS.   Most mosquitoes oviposit in water, but

certain species such as *Aëdes* spp. and *Psorophora* spp., lay their eggs singly in moist soil. Eggs of these species are quite resistant to desiccation and remain viable in the unhatched state until they are covered with water. In *Psorophora* spp., the spinose protective coat surrounding the egg renders it viable for months or even years.

In species that deposit their eggs in water, some, such as *Anopheles* spp., release their eggs singly in loosely arranged clusters, each one armed with a float of air cells that provides buoyancy (Plate 22–6). In others, such as *Culex* spp., the eggs are deposited in masses that are vertically arranged as "egg-boats." The arrangements of mosquito eggs, at least among the better known species, are quite characteristic and are easily recognized. Some of these typical arrangements are depicted in Plate 22–6.

The number of eggs oviposited by a single female varies from species to species, ranging from forty to several hundred. Such eggs are generally oval and some bear surface markings.

LARVAE. The incubation period varies, ranging from 12 hours to several days. The escaping form is the larva. Although basically all mosquito larvae resemble one another— possessing a breathing siphon (elongate spiracle) on the posterior segment; mandibulate mouthparts; and an elongate, distinctly segmented body, bearing setae—species differences do exist, even to the extent that their positions under the water surface differ. For example, larvae of *Culex* spp. and *Aëdes* spp. are attached to the water surface by their siphons, but the bodies are directed downwards (Plate 22–7, Figs. 1 and 2); but among *Anopheles* spp., the larval bodies rest horizontally (Plate 22–7, Fig. 3).

Mosquito larvae are free-living, feeding on phyto- and zoomicroorganisms. During the warm months, they undergo three larval stadia of development. The third larval instar, after molting, transforms into the pupa. During the three larval stadia, there is a consistent increase in size. The almost microscopic first instar develops into a third instar, which measures 8 to 15 mm. in length.

PUPAE. The pupa is a nonfeeding, but an active tissue-reorganizational stage (Plate 22–8, Fig. 1). A pair of breathing tubes, located dorsally on the cephalothorax, replaces the caudal siphon of the larva. Pupae are extremely active and are very sensitive to disturbances. They will flutter up and down in the water when disturbed, hence the common designation as tumblers. Although most mosquito pupae acquire their oxygen via breathing tubes that break through the water surface, the pupae of *Mansonia* spp., like their larvae, do not adhere to the water surface. Instead, they obtain the required oxygen by piercing the air channels of the roots of certain aquatic plants with their breathing tubes.

IMAGOS. Mosquito imagos, or adults, are quite similar yet are different in minute details, thus accounting for the more than 2000 species that have been described. Plate 22–8, Fig. 2 depicts a typical adult and can familiarize the reader with the external anatomical parts. Not only do adults differ morphologically, but they also differ ecologically and in their behavior patterns and habits. Space limitation does not permit detailed descriptions of such differences here. However, the biology of the various species is authoritatively described and documented by Horsfall (1955).

All adult male mosquitoes are vegetarians, feeding on plant juices, but the females are either nectar feeders or bloodsuckers. In parasitology, our interests naturally are concentrated on the blood-ingesting species.

Natural Symbionts of Mosquitoes

In nature, mosquitoes serve as hosts for a variety of symbionts. Most of these are harmless, while a few are rather destructive and undoubtedly reduce the mosquito population. Symbionts of mosquitoes include certain microsporidian, myxosporidian, and coccidian sporozoans, as well as gregarines (Chapter 5). Flagellated protozoa, such as *Herpetomonas* (p. 67) and *Crithidia* (p. 68), are also commonly

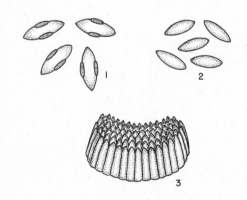

Plate 22-6   Mosquito eggs. 1. Eggs of *Anopheles*. **2.** Eggs of *Aëdes aegypti*. **3.** Eggs of *Culex*.

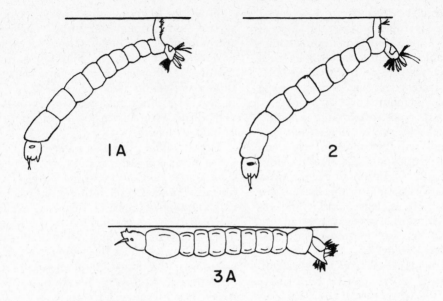

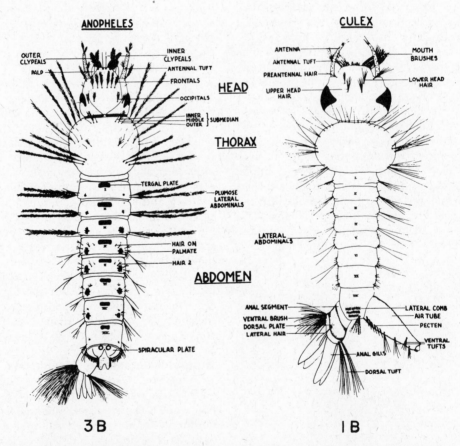

Plate 22-7   Mosquito larvae. 1. A. Larva of *Culex* adhering to water surface by its breathing siphon. **B.** *Culex* larva, showing external anatomical features. **2.** Larva of *Aëdes* attached to water
surface. **3. A.** Larva of *Anopheles* adhering to water surface. **B.** *Anopheles* larva, showing external
anatomical features. (Figs. 1B and 3B illustrations from Communicable Disease Center, U.S. Public
Health Service, Atlanta, Ga.)

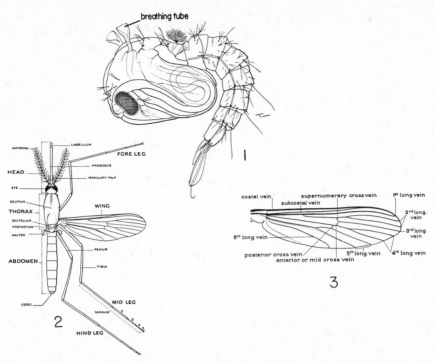

Plate 22-8   Mosquito pupa and adult. 1. Pupa of *Anopheles gambiae*. **2.** Generalized female mosquito. **3.** Mosquito wing. [All figures after Marshall in Smart, 1943. *Insects of Medical Importance*, British Museum (Natural History).]

found in mosquitoes. Ciliates, such as *Glaucoma* and *Lambornella,* are occasionally found in mosquitoes. Among metazoan parasites, nematodes, particularly filarioids, are the most common.

SYSTEMATICS AND BIOLOGY

The family Culicidae is composed of two subfamilies—the Chaoborinae and the Culicinae. The Chaoborinae includes a relatively small group of gnats that are not haematophagous and hence are not considered in this volume. The Culicinae includes the mosquitoes. These can be distinguished readily from the gnats by their mouthparts, which are several times longer than the head. Furthermore, the larvae of mosquitoes have laterally inserted antennae on the head.

Numerous taxonomic monographs are available for the identification of mosquitoes from various parts of the world. Horsfall (1955) lists most of these in his bibliography. Furthermore, he has listed almost all species known in 1955. According to this authority, the Culicinae in-

cludes 29 genera.* Of these, at least ten genera include species found in North America. The largest (number of species) and most important of these genera from the disease vector standpoint are *Culex, Aëdes, Anopheles,* and *Mansonia*.

Genus *Culex*

Culex includes over 400 species from various parts of the world. Members of the genus can be recognized by the following diagnosis.

Postnotum lacks setae. Scutellum is trilobed, one lobe bearing bristles. Palpi are short in females, less than one-fifth as long as proboscis. Body is humpbacked when at rest. Tip of abdomen is blunt in females, covered with broad scales.

---

*Chagasia Cruz, *Bironella* Theobald, *Anopheles* Meigen, *Toxorhynchites* Theobald, *Trichoprosopon* Theobald, *Goeldia* Theobald, *Tripteroides* Giles, *Sabethes* Robineau-Desvoidy, *Wyeomyia* Theobald, *Limatus* Theobald, *Topomyia* Leicester, *Harpagomyia* Meijere, *Hodgesia* Theobald, *Zengnomyia* Leicester, *Uranotaenia* Lynch Arribalzaga, *Culiseta* Felt, *Orthopodomyia* Theobald, *Ficalbia* Theobald, *Mansonia* Blanchard, *Aedolyia* Theobald, *Psorophora* Robineau-Desvoidy, *Opifex* Hutton, *Aëdes* Meigen, *Haemagogus* Williston, *Heizmannia* Ludlow, *Eretmapodites* Theobald, *Armigeres* Theobald, *Culex* Linnaeus, and *Deinocerites* Theobald.

Postspiracular bristles are absent. Wing scales are narrow. Larvae possess prominent siphon (Plate 22–7, Fig. 1), are armed with numerous tufts of hair. Eggs are usually deposited in tight, floating masses like rafts on water surface.

Culex pipiens.

The common brown house mosquito, *C. pipiens*, is found in many temperate climes. This domestic species breeds in any body of stagnant water, no matter how small, around the house and in back yards. Although the developmental period is influenced by the prevailing temperature, on the average, eggs require 18 to 24 hours to hatch. The larval instars last 7 days, and the pupal instar lasts approximately 2 days. There appears to be little host specificity on the part of this mosquito, since it feeds on domestic animals, man, and even birds. However, the type of blood ingested does influence the degree of realization of its biotic potential. For example, Woke (1937) fed 38 specimens of *C. pipiens* on human blood and found that these specimens oviposited 29 egg masses, totaling 2118 eggs, with an average of 73 eggs per mass. When 39 similar mosquitoes were fed on canary blood, these oviposited 22 egg masses, totaling 4473 eggs, with an average of 203.3 eggs per mass. This investigator computed that *C. pipiens* fed on canary blood produces twice as many eggs per gram of blood ingested.

OTHER *Culex* SPECIES. *Culex quinquefasciatus* (= *C. fatigans*) is a closely related species that is quite widespread in warmer climates, including most of the southern United States. *Culex tarsalis,* a common species in the western United States, but also found in Florida, is large and robust. It is distinguished by its dark brown to black body and its abdomen, which is ringed by basal segmental bands of yellowish-white scales.

Culex molestus is a common species found in urban areas. This species, unlike the others, can oviposit without first partaking of a blood meal. Numerous species, including some of those mentioned, are suitable vectors for microfilariae, malaria-causing sporozoa of birds, and various viruses (Table 22–1).

Genus *Aëdes*

Aëdes includes approximately 600 species, which are well represented all over the world. *Aëdes* spp. are the most numerous (number of species) in North America. Members can be identified by the following diagnosis.

Postnotum lacks setae. Scutellum is trilobed. Palpi are short in females. Body is humpbacked when in resting position. Spiracular bristles are present. Abdomen of females is pointed and nonmetallic in color, with exserted cerci. Claws are toothed in females. Larvae have short breathing siphons bearing single pair of posteroventral tuft of hair. Eggs are deposited singly on water surface or on mud.

Aëdes vexans.

This is a universally distributed species. Its coloration varies from brown to gray with uniformly brown wings and tarsi, the latter being banded basally. The females, which are the bloodsuckers, lay their eggs along the edges of rivers. Hatching occurs when water overflows the eggs, thus permitting the larvae to be totally aquatic. If the eggs are oviposited on the edges of ponds, the same mechanism holds true—water must flood over the eggs as a prerequisite for hatching. This species is a diurnal feeder.

Aëdes dorsalis.

This species is widely distributed in theUnited States, Canada, Europe, and North Africa. It can breed in floodwater pools, such as irrigation canals, and in salt marshes. The larvae of *A. dorsalis* have been found in salt pools in Oklahoma and also in pools in Norway where the salt content was 0.07 per cent NaCl. This species bites man, horses, cows, sheep, and even birds. Although usually considered a bloodfeeder, *A. dorsalis*, both males and females, will also feed on plant fluids. The females are fierce day biters.

Aëdes aegypti.

The most notorious of the *Aëdes* mosquitoes is *A. aegypti*, the yellow fever mosquito (Plate 22–9, Fig. 2). This species is distributed throughout the warm and humid parts of the world, including Louisiana, Texas, and other neighboring states. The adults are characteristically marked with transverse bands of silvery-white or yellowish-white on the abdomen and with vertical thin stripes on the dorsal surface of the thorax. The legs are banded, and the tarsi of the last pair of legs are white.

The eggs of *A. aegypti* are deposited singly on the surface of the water. They are dark in color and are surrounded by air cells. It has been estimated that a single female will oviposit approximately 140 eggs if fed on human blood. However, more eggs are produced if they feed on amphibians and reptiles (for example, frogs and turtles). The eggs are quite sensitive to low temperatures and are usually nonviable if maintained below 10° C. However, they are quite resistant to desiccation. Reed et al. (1900) reported that eggs remain viable for 30 days above the water line. Reed and co-workers were able to transport eggs from Havana to Washington, D. C., on filter paper, and 67 per cent of these eggs hatched after 3 months of

Table 22-1

Endemic Area and Species of *Anopheles*	Locality	Breeding Sites
UNITED STATES AND CANADA		
quadrimaculatus	Eastern, central, and southern U.S. (Gulf to Ontario)	Sunlit, impounded water, marshes, swamps, rice fields
freeborni	Rocky Mountains, New Mexico, Pacific Coast	Sunlit seepage water, irrigation ditches
MEXICO, CENTRAL AMERICA, WEST INDIES		
albimanus	Mexico to Colombia and Venezuela, West Indies	Sunlit brackish and fresh lagoons, swamps, ponds
pseudopunctipennis pseudopunctipennis	Southern U.S. to Argentina	Sunlit streams with green algae, pools
darlingi	Central America to Argentina	Sunlit fresh waters, marshes
aquasalis	Central America to Brazil, West Indies	Brackish marshes, irrigation ditches
punctimacula	Mexico to Brazil, West Indies	Shaded pools, swamps, streams
bellator	West Indies to Brazil	Water at bases of bromeliad leaves
aztecus	Mexico	Sunlit pools with green algae
SOUTH AMERICA		
cruzii	Brazil	Water at bases of bromeliad leaves
albitarsus	Argentina	Rice fields, marshes, ditches
EUROPE		
labranchiae labranchiae	Mediterranean Europe and North Africa	Upland streams, rice fields, brackish coastal marshes
labranchiae atroparvus	England, Sweden to Spain and northeastern Italy	Sunlit pools, ponds, marshes
maculipennis messeae	Norway, Russia, Siberia, Manchuria	Freshwater pools, ponds, marshes
superpictus	Spain, southern Europe, Greece, Asia Minor	Pools in stream beds, irrigation canals, seepages
sacharovi	Russia, Balkans	Sunlit coastal marshes, fresh and brackish water
NORTH AFRICA, MIDDLE EAST		
claviger	Ukraine, Asia Minor, North Africa	Rock pools, wells, cisterns, marshes
pharoensis	North Africa, Israel	Rice fields, swamps
sergentii	North Africa, Israel, Turkey, Syria	Rice fields, irrigation canals, borrow pits, seepage
superpictus	Asia Minor	Stream-bed pools, irrigation canals, seepage, hill district

*Data from Herms and James, 1961, *Medical Entomology;* with permission of The Macmillan Co.

Table 22–1 continued

Endemic Area and Species of *Anopheles*	Locality	Breeding Sites
CENTRAL AND SOUTH AFRICA		
funestus	Tropical Africa	Ditches, stream margins, swamps, seepage
gambiae	Tropical Africa, Eygpt, Arabia	Puddles, pools, sluggish streams
moucheti	Uganda, Congo, Cameroons	Swamps, stream margins
pharoensis	Widely distributed in Africa, Isreal	Rice fields, swamps
nili	Widely distributed in central Africa	Shady stream margins
pretoriensis	Widely distributed in central and southern Africa	Sunlit rock pools, stream beds, ditches, hoofprints
PHILIPPINE ISLANDS		
minimus flavirostris	Many islands, Java, Celebes	Foothill streams, ditches, wells
mangyanus	Many islands	Stream beds, irrigation ditches
JAPAN, NORTH CHINA, KOREA		
sinensis	Widely distributed	Open clear water, rice fields, swamps, ponds, slow streams
pattoni	North China	Beds of hill streams, rock pools
SOUTH AND CENTRAL CHINA, BURMA, FORMOSA		
minimus	Hilly regions in southern China, Formosa, Burma	Sunlit, slow streams, rice fields, irrigation ditches
sinensis	Plains in central China, Burma	Open clear water, rice fields, swamps, ponds, slow streams
jeyporiensis var. *candidiensis*	Hong Kong area	Rice fields in hill country
culicifacies	Burma	Streams, irrigation ditches
maculatus maculatus	Burma, Vietnam	Stream and river beds, rice fields, pools, lake margins
philippinensis	Burma, Vietnam	Rice fields, pits, swamps, ditches, tanks
INDIA, CEYLON		
culicifacies	India, Ceylon, Thailand	Streams, irrigation ditches
stephensi	India	Wells, cisterns, roof gutters, water receptacles
maculatus maculatus	India, Ceylon	Stream and river beds, rice fields, pools, lake margins
flaviatilis	India, Thailand	Edges of foothill streams, springs, irrigation canals
minimus	Eastern and northern Ceylon	Sunlit, slow streams, rice fields, irrigation ditches

Table 22-1 continued

Endemic Area and Species of *Anopheles*	Locality	Breeding Sites
INDIA, CEYLON—Cont'd		
philippinensis	India	Rice fields, pits, swamps, ditches, tanks
THAILAND, EAST INDIES, MALAYA		
aconitus	East Indies, Malaya, Vietnam	Rice fields, irrigation ditches, pools in creek beds, reservoirs
nigerrimus	Malaya, East Indies	Rice fields, impounded water, pits, sluggish streams
maculatus maculatus	Thailand, Malaya, East Indies	Stream and river beds, seepage, lake margins
subpictus subpictus	Malaya, East Indies	Pits, all sorts of temporary or permanent collections of water
sundaicus	Thailand, Malaya, East Indies	Sea-water lagoons, swamps
umbrosus	Malaya, Vietnam, East Indies	Shaded jungle pools, mangrove swamps
AUSTRALIA, MELANESIA, POLYNESIA		
farauti	New Guinea, Solomon Islands, New Hebrides	Fresh or brackish water, all sorts of natural or artificial collections of water, fresh or polluted
punctulatus punctulatus	New Guinea, Solomon Islands	Rain pools, stream margins, hoofprints
bancroftii	New Guinea, northern Australia	Shallow, slow streams

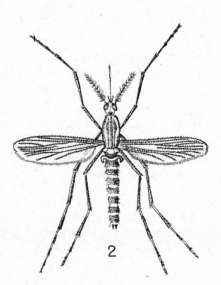

Plate 22-9   Adult mosquitoes. 1. Female of *Culex tarsalis*. (Redrawn from photograph by R. Craig in Herms, 1950.) **2.** *Aëdes aegypti*, the yellow fever mosquito. (Redrawn after Matheson, R. 1950. *Medical Entomology*, Comstock Publishing Co., Ithaca, N.Y.)

storage. Similarly, many other investigators have demonstrated the resistance of these eggs to desiccation.

The larval stadia usually last 9 to 12 days; the pupal stadium lasts for only 36 hours.

Aëdes aegypti is the principal vector for the yellow fever virus, but other species are also capable of performing this task (Table 22–1).

OTHER Aëdes SPECIES. Other common species of *Aëdes* found in North America include *A. sollicitans* distributed along the Atlantic Coast from Maine to Florida and along the Gulf of Mexico. The breeding sites of this mosquito are salt marshes. The bloodsucking females bite at any time but make no attempt to feed if the temperature drops to 10 ° C. or lower. Temperatures ranging from 20° C. are the most favorable for feeding.

Aëdes taeniorhynchus is distributed frow New England south to the Guianas along the east coast, and from Southern California to Peru in the west. This too is a salt-marsh breeding species and can be recognized by its brown body and white-banded proboscis.

Aëdes vexans, A. dorsalis, and *A. aegypti* have been cited as fresh-water breeders (*A. dorsalis* also breeds in salt marshes); *A. sollicitans* and *A. taeniorhynchus* are cited as salt-marsh breeders. A third category of *Aëdes* spp. exists—those that breed in water contained in tree holes. This type includes *A. varipalpis,* a Pacific species; *A. triseriatus,* in the eastern United States; *A. simpsoni* and *A. luteocephalus,* both found in Ethiopia; and *A. seoulensis* in the Far East.

Genus *Anopheles*

Anopheles includes over 300 species, which are widely distributed. These can be recognized by utilizing the following diagnosis.

Postnotum lacks setae. Scutellum is not lobed. Palpi of both sexes are usually as long as proboscis. Mandibles and maxillae of females are well developed and toothed. Wings are usually spotted or mottled. Body is not humpbacked when at rest. Larvae rest parallel to water surface. Eggs are laid singly with associated floats.

Anopheles quadrimaculatus. This species is the common species in eastern North America, being particularly abundant in the southeastern states (Plate 22–10, Fig. 1). The mosquito can be recognized by its dark wings, commonly possessing four black spots formed by aggregations of scales; by its palpi and hind tarsi, which are black; and by the small white "knee spots" at the tips of the femora.

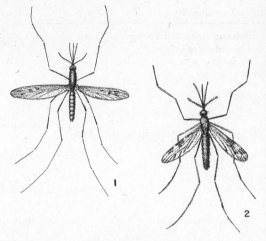

Plate 22–10   Adult mosquitoes. 1. *Anopheles quadrimaculatus.* **2.** *Anopheles punctipennis.* (Figs. 1 and 2 redrawn from photograph in Matheson, R. 1950. *Medical Entomology,* Comstock Publishing Co., Ithaca, N.Y.)

Anopheles punctipennis. This mosquito is the most abundant species in North America (Plate 22–10, Fig. 2). It ranges from southern Canada across the United States to Mexico. Environmental conditions are important in its development. For example, Horsfall and Morris (1952) reported that larvae are four times more plentiful in marshy areas where the summer mean maximum water surface temperature is 18° C., than in another area where the temperature is 25° C. Since running water aids in regulating the desirable temperature of the water surface, it is not surprising that several investigators have found numerous larvae of *A. punctipennis* in running water in Minnesota and Michigan.

Anopheles pseudopunctipennis. This mosquito is a prominent species, widely spread in South and Central America and Mexico. Its breeding sites are in clear, moving water containing large quantities of filamentous green algae. It is a vicious feeder and attacks man, cows, sheep, dogs, horses, cats, and even birds. It is an important vector for *Plasmodium* spp.

OTHER Anopheles SPECIES. *Anopheles freeborni* is a uniformly brown species found along the Pacific Coast; *A. albimanus* is an important malaria-transmitting species in the Panama Canal Zone; *A. maculipennis* is the common mosquito in Europe; and *A. sergenti* is a species common in North America and in Israel. The breeding sites of the last mentioned species are often under stones and are not easily found.

Genus *Mansonia*

Mansonia includes some 55 species, which are primarily distributed throughout tropical regions, although a few are found in temperate climes. A diagnosis for these follows.

Postnotum lacks setae. Scutellum is trilobed. Palpi in females are usually one-fourth as long or longer than proboscis. Bodies are humpbacked when in resting position. Abdomen of females is truncate and nonmetalic. Spiracular bristles are absent. Wing scales are large and broad. Eggs are deposited as masses that adhere to leaves and other objects, less commonly as rafts. Siphons of larvae penetrate air cells of plant roots.

Although species of *Mansonia* are not commonly encountered in North America, they are among the most important vectors for microfilariae (*Wuchereria bancrofti, Brugia malayi,* and *Dirofilaria immitis*) (p. 447) and the yellow fever virus in the tropics. At least two species are known in North America.

Mansonia titillans.   A tropical species, *M. titillans,* has invaded southern Florida and Texas. It is found primarily in Central and South America and the Caribbean islands.

The eggs of *M. titillans* are glued to the underside of leaves in water, because the females oviposit while sitting on a leaf with the tip of the abdomen curved beneath the leaf. Larval breathing is accomplished when the siphons puncture the roots of *Pistia.* Although larvae may breathe at the surface of water for several days, without *Pistia* they perish in 5 or 6 days.

Mansonia perturbans.   This mosquito is widely distributed in North America, ranging from southern Canada to the Gulf of Mexico. It is usually found in timbered areas. It is also found in Great Britain, continental Europe, and in Israel. The eggs are deposited on rafts, each raft containing 150 to 308 eggs. Unlike those of *M. titillans,* the larvae of *M. perturbans* can utilize a number of aquatic plants as breathing tubes. Various investigators have reported that *Typha, Limnobium, Pistia, Sagittaria, Nymphea, Pontedaria,* and *Piaropus* serve as the plants for attachment, and discovery of these plants in otherwise suitable sites for development often indicates the presence of the mosquito. In England, *Typha, Glyceria, Acorus,* and *Ranunculus* are the associated plants, but in Norway *M. perturbans* is specifically associated with *Sparganium,* thus suggesting that this Norwegian form represents a distinct strain.

Several tropical species of *Mansonia* are of medical importance as transmitters of microfilariae and viruses. Some of these are listed in Tables 22–1 and 22–2.

ORGANISMS TRANSMITTED BY MOSQUITOES

As with ticks, mites, and numerous parasitic insects, mosquitoes are not only vicious pests but also serve as vectors for various pathogenic organisms.

Malarias

The role of mosquitoes in the transmission of *Plasmodium* spp. has been discussed on p. 128. Relative to the human-infecting malarial organisms, various species of *Anopheles* serve as the only suitable vectors (Table 22–3). However, *Anopheles* spp., *Culex* spp., and *Aëdes* spp., primarily the latter two, are the major vectors for avian malarias. In North America, *Anopheles quadrimaculatus* and *A. freeborni* are the principal vectors for human malaria, when and where it occurs.

Although specific species of mosquitoes are categorically said to be compatible vectors for specific species of *Plasmodium,* strain differences do exist as far as their susceptibility to the sporozoans is concerned. Such variations in the susceptibility of mosquitoes to *Plasmodium* spp. appear to be genetically controlled. For example, Ward (1963) was able to derive a strain of *Aëdes aegypti* that was highly resistant to *Plasmodium gallinaceum,* the bird malaria organism, from a susceptible strain by genetic selection. The susceptibility of the resistant strain decreased 98 per cent over a period of 26 generations.

This study suggests that differences in the compatibility of mosquito populations for *Plasmodium* spp. may be attributed to variations in gene frequency in different areas. In areas where the mosquito populations are fairly stable, in terms of population size and absence of migration and selection, the level of susceptibility should remain constant. On the other hand, considerable variation in susceptibility might be expected in areas where extensive mosquito migration and marked shifts in the size of the population exist.

Yellow Fever

Yellow fever is a viral disease that has plagued mankind for centuries. During the building of the Panama Canal, yellow fever caused so much illness among workers that the project almost came to a standstill. It was then that Dr. Walter Reed and his associates, Drs. James Carroll, Jesse W. Lazear, and A. Agramonte, won eternal fame by proving Dr. Carlos Fin-

Table 22-2.   **Distribution and Major Mosquito Vectors of Viral Infections**

Viral Disease	Endemic Area	Mosquito Vector
Yellow fever	Primarily in the hinterland of South America and Africa although epidemics have occurred in areas of North and Central America	*Aëdes aegypti* *Haemagogus spegazzinii falco* *Aëdes leucocelaenus clarki* *Haemagogus equinus* * *H. mesodentatus* *H. splendens* * *Sabethes chloropterus* † *Aëdes africanus* *A. simpsoni* *A. triseriatus* * *A. scapularis* * *A. fluviatilis* * *A. luteocephalus* * *A. stokesi* * *A. albopictus* * *Culex thalassius* * *Eretmapodites chrysogaster* * *Mansonia africana* *
Dengue fever (breakbone fever, dandy fever)	Western Hemisphere Pacific Oceania	*Aëdes aegypti* *A. albopictus* *A. scutellaris* *A. polynesiensis*
VIRAL ENCEPHALITIS		
St. Louis encephalitis (SLE)	Western U.S., Illinois, Indiana, Ohio, Kentucky, Tennessee, Trinidad	*Culex tarsalis* *C. pipiens* *C. p. quinquefasciatus*
Western equine encephalitis (WEE)	U.S. and Canada west of the Mississippi, Illinois, Wisconsin	*Culex tarsalis* *Aëdes* spp. (including *A. aegypti*)† *Anopheles* spp.† *Culiseta* spp.†
Eastern equine encephalitis (EEE)	Atlantic Coast to Gulf Coast in U.S., Mexico, Panama, Brazil, Dominican Republic, Cuba, occasionally Kansas and Wisconsin	*Mansonia perturbans* *Culex salinarius* *Culiseta melanura* *Aëdes sollicitans*
Venezuelan equine encephalitis (VEE)	Ecuador, Colombia, Venezuela, Panama, Trinidad	*Mansonia titillans*
Japanese B encephalitis (JAP)	Far East	*Culex tritaeniorhynchus*
Murray Valley encephalitis (MVE)	Northern Australia, New Guinea	*Culex annulirostris* *C. tarsalis* *
OTHER MOSQUITO-BORNE VIRUSES		
West Nile Infection	Egypt, Sudan, Congo, Uganda, Israel, India	*Culex univittatus* † *C. antennatus* † *C. pipiens* * *C. tritaeniorhynchus* * *Aëdes albopictus* *

*Compatible vectors in the laboratory.
†Virus isolated in nature.

Table 22-2 continued

Viral Disease	Endemic Area	Mosquito Vector
OTHER MOSQUITO-BORNE VIRUSES—Cont'd		
Rift Valley Fever	South Africa, Kenya, Japan	*Aëdes caballus* *A. demeilloni*† *A. tarsalis*† *Eretmapodites* spp.†
Rabbit myxomatosis (only European rabbit, *Oryctilagus,* susceptible)		*Aëdes scapularis* *A. aegypti* *Culex annulirostris* *Anopheles annulipes*
Fowl pox (birds susceptible)		*Aëdes stimulans* *A. aegypti*

Table 22-3. Representative Nematode Parasites and Their Major Mosquito Vectors

Nematode	Mosquito Vector
Wuchereria bancrofti	*Culex* spp. including *C. quiquefasciatus* *Aëdes* spp. *Mansonia* spp. *Anopheles* spp.
Brugia malayi	*Culex pipiens quinquefasciatus* *C. pipiens pallens* *Aëdes polynesiensis* *A. togoi* *Anopheles gambiae* *A. funestus* *A. farauti* *A. pyrcanus sinensis*
Dirofilaria immitis (in dogs, cats, wild carnivores)	*Culex pipiens* *Aëdes aegypti*

lay's hypothesis that *Aëdes aegypti* serves as transmitter of the pathogen.

Mosquitoes become infected with the virus while feeding on yellow fever victims. A single female may ingest thousands of viruses at one feeding and usually remains infective for the rest of her normal life—200 to 240 days. Under field conditions, the normal incubation period within the vector is 12 hours. However, fluctuations in temperature affect the extrinsic incubation period. If the mosquitoes are exposed to temperatures of 98° F., the incubation period is reduced to 4 days, but if they are exposed at 70° F., the period is increased to 18 days.

Jungle animals, especially monkeys of the genus *Cebus,* serve as natural reservoirs for the yellow fever virus.

In addition to *Aëdes aegypti,* various other species serve as natural and experimental vectors. For example, *Aëdes vittatus* is the vector for yellow fever in Egypt. *Haemagogus spegazzinii,* a South American species found in Brazil and Colombia, is a suitable vector, especially in transmitting the virus among monkeys. *Aëdes simpsoni* and *A. africanus* have been incriminated as vectors in East Africa. Over thirty species of mosquitoes have been shown experimentally to be possible vectors. Some of these are: *Aëdes fluviatilis, A. scapularis, A. luteocephalus, A. albopictus, Mansonia africana, Haemagogus equinus,* and *H. splendens.*

Dengue Fever

Dengue fever is commonly referred to as breakbone fever. This is another viral disease transmitted by mosquitoes. Various investigators have demonstrated that a number of species are suitable vectors. Among these are *Aëdes aegypti, A. albopictus,* and *A. scutellaris. Aëdes albopictus* is prevalent in Japan, New Guinea, northern Australia, Malagasy Republic, the Philippine Islands, and Hawaii. It is distinguishable by a silvery stripe on its mesonotum and whitish irregular patches on the lateral aspects of its thorax. *Aëdes scutellaris* is a closely related species characterized by whitish wavy lines composed of scales down each side of the thoracic pleura. This is an important vector of dengue fever in Polynesia.

Equine Encephalitis

Another viral disease, equine encephalitis, is mosquito-borne. Although primarily a disease of horses, occasional outbreaks of equine encephalitis among human populations occur. Various strains of the virus exist, most of which are

Table 22–4. Common Mosquito Species That Carry Equine Encephalitis

Fresh-water Breeders	Salt Marsh Breeders
Aëdes aegypti	*Aëdes sollicitans*
A. dorsalis	*A. taeniorhynchus*
A. nigromaculis (rarely found in alkaline waters)	
A. cantator (sometimes found in brackish water)	
A. tarsalis	

experimentally infective to guinea pigs. Various mosquitoes are suitable transmitters of this virus; both fresh- and salt-water breeders are represented. Some of the more common species are listed in Table 22–4.

In addition to these mosquitoes, the conenose bug *Triatoma sanguisuga,* the tick *Dermacentor venustus,* and the bird louse *Ornithonyssus sylviarum* are also suitable vectors for this virus. The louse serves as an important transmitter of the pathogen from bird to bird in the yellow-headed blackbird *Xanthocephalus xanthocephalus,* which is a natural reservoir.

Various other viruses of man and domestic animals are transmitted by mosquitoes. Some of these are listed in Table 22–1.

The role of mosquitoes in the transmission of microfilariae has been discussed on page 447. Some of these nematodes and their vectors are listed in Table 22–2.

FAMILY TABANIDAE
(Horseflies and Deerflies)

Bodies are comparatively large, 7 to 30 mm. long. Wings are well developed with veins evenly distributed (Plate 22–1, Fig. 3). Eyes are large and widely separated (dichoptic) in females, contiguous in males (holoptic). Antennae are usually short and trijointed (Plate 22–1, Fig. 4).

The Tabanidae is one of two families of the Brachycera that includes bloodsuckers. The tabanid flies are large and stoutly built and are often beautifully colored. The more common colors are brown, black, orange, or metallic green. They are strong fliers and viciously attack cattle, horses, deer, and other warm-blooded animals, including man. Only adult females are bloodsuckers; the males feed on plant juices and nectar. The mouthparts of the female are developed for cutting skin and sucking blood that oozes from the wound.

Tabanid Life Cycle Pattern

All tabanid flies follow a basic life cycle pattern. The cylindrical eggs, 1 to 2.5 mm. long, are deposited in neatly arranged piles on stems and leaves of aquatic plants or on the leaves of trees, such as willows, that hang over bodies of water (Plate 22–11, Fig. 1). The number of eggs per pile varies from 100 to 1000, and these are cemented together with a glue-like secretion. Some species deposit their eggs in terrestrial habitats such as on logs, and mud. These eggs are oviposited during the summer and early fall.

Embryonic development is influenced greatly by environmental conditions, but during the heat of summer the average time ranges from 5 to 7 days. The escaping larvae are vermiform, composed of the head and eleven body somites (Plate 22–11, Fig. 2). Each segment bears a row of warts, on which are inserted hairs and setae. Such larvae, upon hatching, either drop into water and migrate to the substratum or burrow into the mud if the eggs are deposited thereon. These larvae are free-living animals, feeding on organic debris while undergoing rapid growth during the summer and fall. They become quiescent with the onset of winter. By the following spring, the larvae will have passed through four to nine instars and will be fully grown. The final larval stage migrates to dry ground in preparation for pupation.

Pupation ensues, and the pupae become embedded under the surface of the dryer ground (Plate 22–11, Fig. 3). The enclosed pupal stage lasts 2 to 3 weeks in most species. However, Stone (1930) reported that the pupae of *Chrysops* metamorphose into adults in less than 2 weeks. The adults rupturing from the cocoon usually hide in foliage, and the females migrate from there as bloodsuckers.

Philip (1947), Stone (1938), and Mackerras (1954-55) have contributed taxonomic studies on the Tabanidae. The family includes over 2500 species and are divided into two sub-families—the Pangoniinae, which includes genera that possess apical spurs on their hind tibiae and ocelli in addition to compound eyes; and the Tabaninae, members of which do not possess apical tibial spurs or ocelli.

SUBFAMILY PANGONIINAE

Genus *Chrysops*

Flies of the genus *Chrysops,* commonly known as deerflies, are worldwide in distribution. At least 200 species are known in North America. These are comparatively small flies with clear wings except for a dark band located vertically down the middle of the wing and a darkly-pigmented anterior border (Plate 22–12, Fig. 1). *Chrysops callida,* measuring 7 to 9 mm. in length, is a widely distributed species that is black with lateral pale yellow spots near the base of the abdomen.

Chrysops discalis, is 8 to 10.5 mm. long and is a grayish species with black spots on its abdomen. It is fairly common in the western states, including Nevada, Nebraska, and North Dakota. It has also been reported in Manitoba and Saskatchewan provinces. *Chrysops dimidiata* is a southwestern African species that measures 8.5 mm. in length and that is brownish yellow.

Genus *Silvius*

Members of *Silvius* are found primarily in Australia, although a few species are known in North America. In *Silvius* spp., the second segment of the antennae is approximately half as long as the first segment.

SUBFAMILY TABANINAE

Genus *Tabanus*

Tabanus, commonly known as the "horseflies," includes over 1200 species that are worldwide in distribution. Among the most commonly

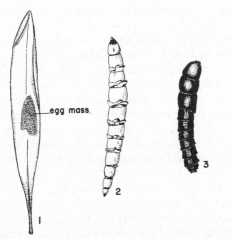

Plate 22–11   Stages in the life cycle of *Tabanus punctifer.* 1. Eggs arranged in a mass on a leaf. **2.** Larva. **3.** Pupa.

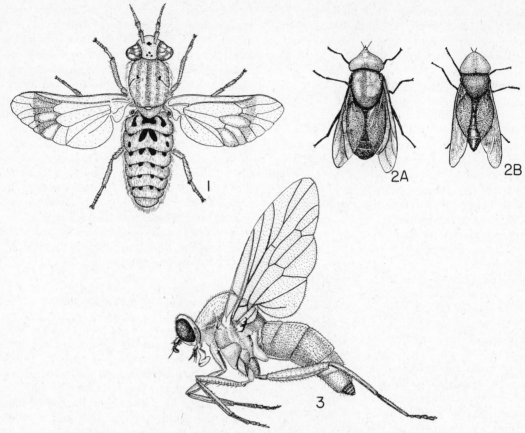

Plate 22-12   Some biting flies. 1. *Chrysops discalis.* (Redrawn after Francis.) 2. *Tabanus atratus,* the black horsefly. A. Female. B. Male. 3. *Symphoromyia atripes.* (Redrawn after Ross.)

encountered species in North America is *T. atratus,* the black horsefly, which is 16 to 30 mm. long (Plate 22–12, Fig. 2). This species is found in states east of the Rocky Mountains and in Mexico. Other species include *T. punctifer,* a black and white species found in western United States, particularly along the Pacific Coast; *T. quinquevittatus,* characterized by its green head; and *T. lineola,* characterized by its brown or black abdomen adorned with three gray stripes. The last two species are common pests of cattle in the southwestern United States. *T. striatus* is a common species in the Philippines.

TABANIDS AS VECTORS

The loss of blood (100 to 200 cc. per day) by cattle resulting from tabanid flies is a serious problem. Loss of weight and decline in milk production commonly result from the bites. In addition to the inflicted injuries, discomforts, and loss of blood, tabanids serve as vectors for bacterial, protozoan, and helminth parasites. Various tabanid flies serve as vectors for *Trypanosoma* spp. (p. 68). *Trypanosoma evansi,* the causative agent for surra of horses, cattle and dogs, is transmitted by *Tabanus striatus.* Similarly, *T. equiperdum,* the causative agent for "mal-de-caderas" in horses and other animals in South America, and *T. theileri* of cattle can be transmitted by tabanids. Furthermore, *T. vivax,* one of the haemoflagellates that cause sleeping sickness (p. 72), can be transmitted by tabanids when the normal tsetse fly vector is not present.

Tularemia and anthrax, two bacterial diseases of man and animals, are transmitted by tabanid flies, among other arthropod vectors. Tularemia is caused by *Pasteurella tularensis* and anthrax by *Bacillus anthracis.* Tularemia, or deerfly fever, is a disease of man in the western United States, Canada, northern Europe, Russia, and Japan. One of the tuleremia vectors is *Chrysops discalis.* Rabbits serve as natural reservoirs for the bacterium. Anthrax is a much dreaded disease of cattle, although various other animals and man are susceptible. *Tabanus striatus* and other tabanids are suitable hosts.

The African eye worm, *Loa loa* (p. 453), is transmitted to humans by *Chrysops dimidiata.* A second species, *C. silacea,* is also an effective vector.

FAMILY RHAGIONIDAE
(Snipe Flies)

Bodies are trim, of moderate to large size, and naked or hairy. Males usually are holoptic. Legs are comparatively long. Abdomen is cone shaped, tapering toward posterior end. Three ocelli are present. Antennae are three-jointed. Proboscis is usually short. Wings are broad, half open when at rest.

Members of the Rhagionidae, commonly called snipe flies, include both haematophagous and nonhaematophagous species. The two important ectoparasitic genera are *Symphoromyia* and *Suragina.* These flies are readily recognized by their third antennal segment, which is kidney shaped. Of the approximately 25 species of *Symphoromyia* found in North America, mostly in the mountainous western regions, *S. hirta, S. atripes, S. kincaidi,* and *S. pachyceras* are the most common. *Symphoromyia hirta,* measuring 7.5 mm. in length, is a severe biter of man and animals; *S. atripes,* a black species with reddish legs and measuring 5.3 to 8 mm. in length, is also a vicious biter (Plate 22–12, Fig. 3); and *S. kincaidi* possesses a black head and thorax but a yellow abdomen.
Suragina longipes is a Mexican species that bites viciously. In Australia, the species of *Spaniopsis* represent the bloodsucking rhagionids. The species of *Spaniopsis* possess an elongated third antennal segment that terminates in a style.

SUBORDER CYCLORRHAPHA

The Cyclorrhapha is divided into two groups —the Aschiza and the Schizophora. Comstock (1949) lists 43 families subordinate to this suborder, four belonging to the Aschiza and 39 to the Schizophora. Of these, only the family Syrphidae of the Aschiza includes parasitic species. Sixteen families* of the Schizophora include parasites, five of which are represented by larvae parasitic in invertebrates, primarily

---

*Not all the sixteen parasite-including families of the Schizophora are listed by Comstock (1949); these have been compiled from various sources.

other insects. Although the families are briefly diagnosed here, no attempt is made to give a comprehensive resumé of each one. Interested readers are referred to texts and reference volumes dealing with medical entomology for detailed discussions. The treatise by Clausen (1940) should be consulted for detailed information on species that parasitize other insects.

ASCHIZA GROUP

The Aschiza Group is represented by one family—the Syrphidae—which includes parasitic species. Suster (1960) has contributed a complete review of this family with discussions on species found in Rumania. He lists 64 genera and 260 species of syrphid flies.

FAMILY SYRPHIDAE
(Flowerflies, or Syrphid flies)

Species vary in form, are often called "mimic hymenopterous flies," because some resemble bumblebees, honeybees, and wasps. Pseudovein (or spurious vein) present between R and M veins (Plate 22–13, Fig. 1).* Antennae are three-jointed, third segment with dorsal arista or thickened style. Frontal suture on head is lacking.

The colorful adult syrphid flies are free-living, usually with dark bodies ornamented with bright-colored spots and bands. They are usually found hovering over flowers, primarily feeding on nectar. Because of their characteristic habit of continuously remaining on the wing in the proximity of flowers, the common designations "hover flies" and "flowerflies" are often used. A few genera of these flies include parasitic larvae, primarily *Syrphus* and *Tubifera.*

Genus *Syrphus*
Larvae of *Syrphus* spp. are normally predaceous, feeding on plant lice and other plant-infesting insects. A few instances of human gastrointestinal myiasis (infestation by dipteran larvae) have been reported, although these reports are in need of confirmation. Human infestations, if such reports are accurate, probably are contracted by ingesting vegetables that contain larvae.

Genus *Tubifera*
Tubifera (= *Eristalis*) includes *T. tenax, T. dimidiata,* and *T. arbustorum* (Plate 22–14, Fig. 1).

---

*The spurious vein is absent in some syrphid flies.

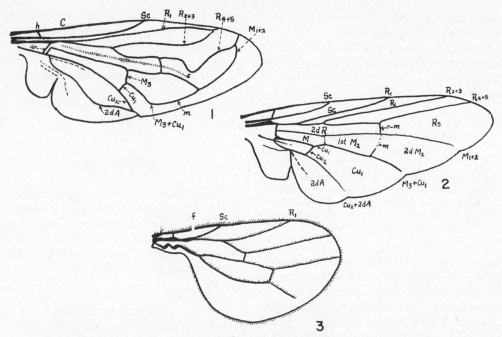

Plate 22-13   **Syrphidae, Gasterophilidae and Chloropidae. 1.** Wing of *Tubifera* (Syrphidae), showing venation. **2.** Wing of *Gasterophilus* (Gasterophilidae), showing venation. (Figs. 1 and 2 redrawn after Comstock, J. H. 1949. *An Introduction to Entomology,* Comstock Publishing Co., Ithaca, N.Y.) **3.** Wing of *Hippelates* (Chloropidae).

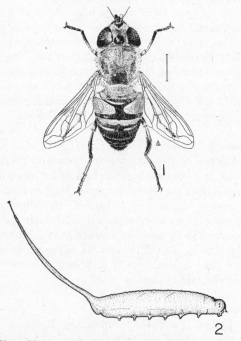

Plate 22-14   **Stages in the life cycle of *Tubifera.*** **1.** Adult drone fly *Tubifera tenax.* (After James, 1947.) **2.** Rat-tail larva of *T. dimidiata.*

The larvae of these cause gastrointestinal myiasis. *Tubifera tenax,* the drone fly, is by far the most common myiasis-causing species. It is worldwide in distribution. The adults are free-living, commonly seen hovering over cesspools, liquid manure, open privies, and bodies of water contaminated with rotting animal matter. The eggs are oviposited in these putrid sites and give rise to larvae that, like those of *Syrphus* spp., bear a long anal breathing siphon resembling a tail (Plate 22–14, Fig. 2). Thus, they are commonly called rat-tailed maggots. Animal gastrointestinal myiasis undoubtedly originates through drinking water contaminated with these maggots.

Genus *Helophilus*

Helophilus is another genus of the Syrphidae with larvae that cause myiasis. Chevrel cited a case of human urinary myiasis that he attributed to penetration up the urinary passages by the maggot. The larvae of *H. pendulus* are similar to those of *Tubifera,* but the tracheal tube (or breathing tube) of the former is undulating rather than straight (Plate 22–15, Fig. 1). *Helophilus pendulus* is distributed throughout northern and eastern Europe.

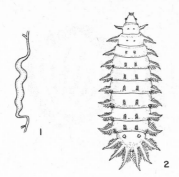

Plate 22-15   Immature flies. 1. Tracheal tube of larval *Helophilus pendulus*. (Redrawn after Johannsen, 1934.) **2.** Mature larva of *Fannia scalaris*. (After Hewitt, 1912.)

SCHIZOPHORA GROUP

Parasitism by schizophorans can be either external or internal. Ectoparasitism is manifested by the bloodsucking habits of many adult members of the group, and by the subcutaneous invasion by larvae of certain members of the Muscidae, Calliphoridae, Sarcophagidae, Gasterophilidae, Oestridae, and Cuterebridae. Endoparasitism is manifested by the larvae of species that cause internal myiasis.

MYIASIS

Not only do adults of haematophagous flies bite man and beast, the larvae of various flies invade vertebrates. Such infestations are referred to as myiasis. If the larvae, or maggots, invade the subdermal regions of their host, the condition is known as cutaneous myiasis. If the site of invasion is the host's alimentary tract, the condition is known as gastrointestinal myiasis. Similarly, ocular myiasis, urinary myiasis, and nasopharyngeal myiasis are known to occur. With only a few exceptions, the myiasis-causing flies belong to the suborder Cyclorrapha, primarily the Schizophora Group.

Among the myiasis-causing flies, those which usually invade living tissues are known as primary invaders. Eggs of these flies are commonly deposited on fresh wounds—even rather insignificant sores such as those caused by tick bites. The hatching larvae actively feed on living tissues while they burrow into the skin. Adults of these flies are undoubtedly attracted to wounds by the smell of blood. Species that invade decomposing tissues of dead animals are referred to

as secondary invaders. These maggots, however, attack healthy living tissues when dead tissues are not available.

Among the Muscidae, Calliphoridae, and Sarcophagidae, collectively known as the Muscoid Group, myiasis is manifested in four ways—by the sucking of blood; by invasion of wounds and natural cavities, such as the ears, nose, and eyes; by invasion of skin, causing boils in which the larvae dwell; and by living in, or passing through, the intestinal or urinary tracts.

Among the Gasterophilidae, Oestridae, and Cuterebridae, collectively known as the Bot Group, myiasis is manifested by invasion of the skin, resulting in boil-like lesions, known as warbles, in which the maggots survive; by penetration of the nasal passages, sinuses, or other parts of the host's head; and by living in the stomach or rectum of the host.

Myiasis of small laboratory animals is generally lethal. During primary invasions, highly toxic substances are produced by the growing larvae. These toxic substances, coupled with tissue destruction, are extremely damaging. Furthermore, the maggots of screwworms are invariably accompanied by a nonpathogenic, although proteolytic, species of bacterium, *Proteus chandleri,* which is practically in pure culture in the wounds a day or so after invasion. Hosts develop an immunity against the toxic secretions of screwworms, but not against the larvae themselves. Although *P. chandleri* is usually present, the toxins of maggots kill most other bacteria. Thus, the wounds are usually not purulent until the larvae exit, after which purulence ensues accompanied by production of a copious serosanguineous exudate.

In cases of human myiasis, particularly those caused by the invasion of screwworms up the nose, the nasopharynx, and associated sinuses, death is not uncommon. The development of nervous conditions such as delirium, convulsions, visual disturbances, and loss of speech, accompanied by great pain, generally occurs prior to death if the parasites are not removed.

Myiasis-causing maggots (larvae) are readily recognized by the shape of their posterior spiracles (Plate 22–16). James (1947) has compiled a book on various dipterans that habitually or accidentally cause myiasis in man.

The following discussion is a survey of the more commonly encountered genera of the schizophoran families that are of interest to parasitologists.

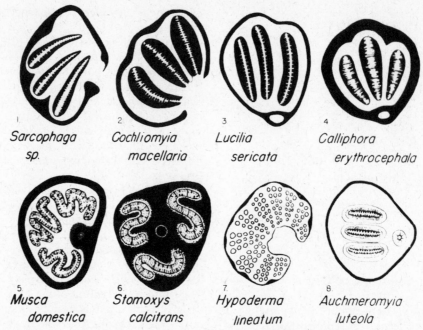

| 1. Sarcophaga sp. | 2. Cochliomyia macellaria | 3. Lucilia sericata | 4. Calliphora erythrocephala |

| 5. Musca domestica | 6. Stomoxys calcitrans | 7. Hypoderma lineatum | 8. Auchmeromyia luteola |

Plate 22-16 **Posterior spiracles of myiasis-causing maggots.** (Courtesy of U.S. Naval Medical School, Bethesda, Md.)

FAMILY MUSCIDAE
(Typical Flies)

Are typical flies. Hypopleural or pteropleural bristles are present. Basal abdominal bristles are reduced. Antennae are plumose.

Musca domestica

Family Muscidae includes the well known common housefly *Musca domestica*, which is worldwide in distribution. Adults are nonparasitic but are household pests. However, they are mechanical transmitters, by their contaminated feet, of such diseases as typhoid (etiological agent, *Salmonella typhosa**), cholera (etiological agent, *Vibrio comma†*), and yaws (etiological agent, *Treponema pertenue†*).

This fly breeds in decaying organic materials, including animal excreta. The females are oviparous, producing 120 to 150 eggs in a batch, with 5 to 20 batches oviposited during the life span. The larvae have reportedly been recovered from human vomitus and feces and passed out in urine (Plate 22–17, Fig. 1). Thus, *M. domestica* is capable of causing gastrointestinal and urinary myiasis. Furthermore,

*Bacterium
†Spirochaete

dermal myiasis, especially associated with ulcerated wounds, resulting from *M. domestica* invasions, are known.

Because the parasitic way of life is not a necessary one for this larva, these instances of myiasis are referred to as accidental myiasis. In gastrointestinal myiasis due to *M. domestica*, the infections are usually traceable to the ingestion of eggs or young larvae.‡

Genus *Glossina*

Glossina§ includes the tsetse flies, which are important not only as the vectors for certain trypanosomes (p. 71), but also because both the males and females are bloodsuckers. Although it has been determined that *Glossina* was at one time widely distributed, it is now limited to continental Africa south of the Tropic of Cancer.

LIFE CYCLE OF *Glossina*. The life cycles of *Glossina* spp. follow the basic pattern of the cyclorrhaphan flies, but a few striking differences exist. The females give birth to fully devel-

‡Similarly, several species of *Fannia*, for example *F. scalaris*, have been reported to cause accidental intestinal and urinary myiasis (Plate 22–15, Fig. 2).

§*Glossina* is considered by some to be the type genus for a separate family, the Glossinidae.

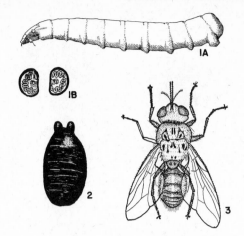

Plate 22-17   **Stages in the life cycle of some flies.**
1. *Musca domestica.* **A.** Larva. **B.** Posterior spiracles of larva.
(After James, 1947.) **2.** Pupa of *Glossina,* showing two posterior lobes. (Original.) **3.** Adult of *Glossina palpalis* in resting position. (Redrawn after Matheson, R. 1950. *Medical
Entomology,* Comstock Publishing Co., Ithaca, N.Y.)

oped living larvae. Actually the larviposited
form is the fourth larval instar, for the in utero
development involves not only embryonic development but also three larval stages. The in
utero larvae feed on the secretions of specialized glands, commonly referred to as "milk
glands." The fourth stage larvae are deposited
singly at intervals of from 10 to 12 days, with
a total of eight to ten larvae deposited by a
single female during her life span. It should be
emphasized that larvipositing females require
a blood meal between extrusions of the larvae,
and development of the larvae in utero is not
completed until blood is ingested by the mother.
The extruded larvae are off-white to pale
yellow. They are not capable of the usual
wormlike movements. Instead, they move and
burrow as the result of peristaltic movement
and longitudinal contractions. They are generally larviposited at the base of shrubs and
other vegetation, where the soil is damp and
loose.

The larvae burrow into the soil and undergo
pupation. This usually occurs within 1 hour
after birth. The pupa within the puparium is
ovoid, brownish black, and bears two characteristic posterior lobes (Plate 22-17, Fig. 2). The
usual pupal period lasts from 3 to 4 weeks.
Soil moisture and temperature are important
influencing factors. The form escaping from
the puparium is the adult, brownish in color
and bears the distinguishing characteristics
depicted in Plate 22-17, Fig 3.

Glossina Species.   Newstead (1924) has
listed and diagnosed the twenty species of
Glossina. The most prominent ones are *G. palpalis,* the major vector of Gambian trypanosomiasis (Plate 22–17, Fig. 3); *G. morsitans,* the
major vector of Rhodesian trypanosomiasis
(Plate 22–18, Fig. 1); and *G. swynnertoni,* another
vector for Rhodesian trypanosomiasis. Although
these flies feed on an array of vertebrate hosts,
they definitely demonstrate preference for
some. For example, *G. palpalis* favors crocodiles,
monitor lizards, and other reptiles, and *G.
morsitans* prefers pigs and warthogs.

Genus *Stomoxys*

Stomoxys has been monographed by Séguy
(1935). Members are grayish flies of medium
size, resembling *Musca domestica,* but possessing
long, slender horny proboscides that are spear
shaped and antennae that are pectinate. The
most common species is *S. calcitrans,* the stable
fly (Plate 22–18, Fig. 2). This is a vicious blood-
sucker that is commonly found in barns and
that feeds on domestic animals, especially
horses. It also invades houses and feeds on
human blood. Both sexes are bloodfeeders.

The life history is typically dipteran. The
females oviposit from 23 to 100 eggs (average,
25 to 50) at each of 4 to 5 layings. The bites of
large numbers of flies result in a significant loss
of blood and body weight. Instances of cutaneous and intestinal myiasis caused by the larvae
are known.

Genus *Haematobia*

The so-called horn flies belong to the genus

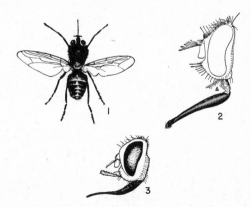

Plate 22-18   **Diptera. 1.** *Glossina morsitans.* (Drawn
from photograph after Newstead, Evans, and Potts, 1924.)
2. *Stomoxys calcitrans,* lateral view of head. (After James,
1947.) **3.** *Haematobia stimulans,* lateral view of head, showing long palpi. (Redrawn after Eldridge in Herms, W. B.,
and James, M. T. 1961. *Medical Entomology,* Macmillan,
New York.)

Haematobia. The most prevalent species in North America is *H. stimulans,* which is also found in Europe. This fly, a vicious attacker of cattle and other stable animals, is about 4 mm. long and resembles *Stomoxys* except that its labium is heavier, its palpi are long, approximating the length of the proboscis, and the antennal aristae are plumose dorsally (Plate 22–18, Fig. 3). It is called the horn fly because it commonly rests on the horns of cattle, particularly at night. It does leave the host when not feeding. The reddish brown eggs are 1.3 to 1.5 mm. long, and like those of *Stomoxys calcitrans,* are deposited in cow manure, where the larvae are found.

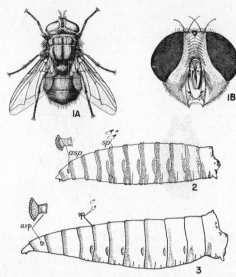

Plate 22–19   Stages in the life cycle of *Callitroga.* **1.** *Callitroga hominivorax.* **A.** Adult female. **B.** Frontal view of head of female. (After Cushman.) **2.** Lateral view of mature third stage larva of *C. hominivorax.* (After Laake, Cushing, and Parish, 1936.) **3.** Lateral view of mature third stage larva of *C. macellaria.* (Redrawn after Laake et al, 1936.) (asp, anterior spiracles; sp, spines.)

FAMILY CALLIPHORIDAE*
(Blowflies)

Bodies, especially abdomens, are metallic green or blue, less frequently violet or copper color. Are large flies. Antennae are plumose. Hypo- and pteropleural bristles are present. Posteriormost posthumeral bristle is present, and is more ventral than presutural bristle. Second ventral abdominal sclerite lies with edges overlying or in contact with ventral edges of corresponding dorsal sclerites.

The Calliphoridae includes the so-called blowflies and bluebottle and greenbottle flies. The maggots of many of these flies cause myiasis in domestic animals and man, while still others, such as the cluster fly *Pollenia rudis,* is parasitic on oligochaetes. The adult flies are not haematophagus. Members of the Calliphoridae are important not only because they cause myiasis, but also as transmitters of microorganisms carried on the hairs of their legs. Hall (1947) has contributed a taxonomic monograph of the blowflies of North America.

Genus *Callitroga*

Callitroga includes the screwworms.

Callitrogra hominivorax.   The primary screwworm, *C. hominivorax* is the most prominent American species (Plate 22–19, Fig. 1). This metallic green fly, with three dark stripes down its thorax and a yellow head and reddish eyes, is distributed from the southern United States to northern Chile. The larva is an obligatory parasite. The females oviposit on fresh wounds in man and animal. The eggs, ranging from ten to several hundred in number, are glued in

*The families Calliphoridae and Sarcophagidae are considered by some authors to be a single family, the Metapiidae.

mats along the edge of the open wound. When the larvae hatch, in 1 to 20 hours, they actively burrow into the wound and ingest the host's tissues.

Continued penetration via engorgement results in deep pockets. The posterior spiracles of the larvae are directed toward the opening of the pocket so that breathing is made possible (Plate 22–19, Fig. 2). On reaching maturity in 4 to 8 days, these flesh-eating maggots drop off, and pupation takes place in soil. It appears needless to discuss the damage screwworms inflict on their hosts, but it should be mentioned that heavy infestations can lead to the death of the hosts, especially if the larvae invade regions of the nose, eyes, and ears. Human infections by the larvae of *C. hominivorax* are known.

Callitroga macellaria.   The secondary screwworm fly, *C. macellaria,* is characterized by its predominantly orange head and by its mid-dorsal longitudinal stripe on the thorax, which does not extend over the scutellum. This species is usually not a myiasis-causing one, being primarily a scavenger in soil or on carrion, but it can become a secondary wound invader. If secondary invasion does take place, the larvae, measuring up to 17 mm. in length, do not form pockets as does *C. hominivorax* (Plate

22–19, Fig. 3). Instead, they migrate around the wound in the hair.

Genus *Chrysomya*

The larvae of *Chrysomya* spp. may be secondary invaders of sores (for example, *C. marginalis,* *C. albiceps,* and *C. putoria*), or they may cause internal myiasis (for example, *C. chloropyga* and *C. megalocephala*) (Plate 22–20, Fig. 2). These are parasites of mammals, including man. Cuthbertson (1933) has given an account of the life history of *C. marginalis* and Smit (1941) for *C. albiceps* and *C. chloropyga*. These papers should be consulted by those interested in *Chrysomya*-caused myiasis.

Genus *Phormia*

Phormia includes the black blowfly *Phormia regina,* which is characterized by its blackish-green or olive-green body, black head, orange hair on the mesothorax, and by a body length of 7 to 9 mm. Primarily a saprophagous species, *P. regina* breeds in animal carcasses. However, the larvae do invade healthy tissues and produce myiasis, especially in southwestern United States.

Other Calliphorid Genera

The larvae of certain species of *Protophormia; Cordylobia,* the Tumbu fly; and *Lucilia* can produce cutaneous myiasis (Plate 22–20, Fig. 1).

Calliphora includes two fairly common species, *C. vomitoria* and *C. vicina*. The larvae of both the calliphorans are flesh-ingestors (Plate 22–20, Fig. 3). *C. vomitoria* has black genae clothed with golden-red hairs, while *C. vicina* has fulvous genae clothed with black hairs. The eggs of both species are deposited on carrion and rarely on wounds. These hatch in 6 to 48 hours, and the growing larvae feed on flesh for 3 to 9 days. At the end of that period, the larvae are fully grown and drop off. They bury themselves

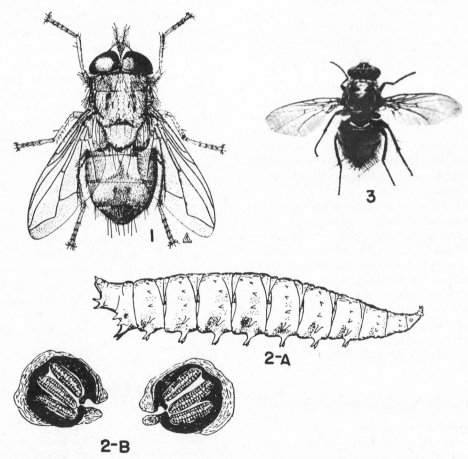

Plate 22–20   Diptera. 1. *Cordylobia anthropophaga,* adult male. (After James, 1947.) **2.** *Chrysomya albiceps.* **A.** Larva. **B.** Posterior spiracles of larva. (After Smit, 1931.) **3.** *Calliphora vomitoria.* (After Herms, 1950.)

in loose soil or debris and undergo a 2 to 7 day prepupal period. The duration of pupation varies with the environmental temperature, lasting from 10 to 17 days, after which adults emerge. Adults generally live approximately 35 days.

CALLIPHORID HOST SPECIFICITY

The calliphorid flies as a rule are not attracted to any specific host, nor do the maggots show any preference for any specific sites on their hosts, although the more readily accessible sites actually are more frequently invaded. The striking exception to the rule appears to be *Lucilia bufonivora*, larvae of which feed only on living amphibian tissue, especially on toads. In *L. bufonivora*, the female fly deposits her eggs on the surface of the host's skin, usually on the back, and here the eggs hatch within 24 hours. It is believed that hatching is induced by the chemical action of the host's skin glands.

The first stage larvae migrate along the toad's back until they reach the eyes. When the toad blinks its eyelids, the larvae are carried to the openings of the lacrimal ducts. From these ducts the larvae migrate to the lacrimal glands and from there to the nasal cavity. At this site, the second larval stage is reached. The second stage larvae feed on the host's living tissues and completely destroy the cartilaginous septum of the nasal cavity. The large cavity produced in this way is filled with crawling maggots, which eventually drop out to undergo pupation in soil.

When *L. bufonivora* females are placed among frogs, toads, salamanders, and aquatic newts, they oviposit almost exclusively on toads. This indicates that the fly is attracted by the specific odor of toads and has become adapted both ecologically and physiologically, since the larvae feed on living tissues. The other species of *Lucilia* feed on purulent tissues.

Among members of the genus *Chrysomya,* only the larvae of *C. bezziana* appear to have become obligatory parasites of mammals.

CALLIPHORID PARASITES OF INVERTEBRATES

A number of larval calliphorid flies parasitize invertebrates. In these species, an interesting form of larval migration occurs. This is strikingly demonstrated by the larva of the cluster fly *Pollenia rudis*. Adult female flies deposit their eggs in the soil, and the hatching first stage larvae penetrate the male genital pore of the earthworm *Allolobophora chlorotica*. These maggots enter either the seminal vesicles or the coelomic cavity in somites IX to XII. In this location, the maggots remain motionless for at least 8 months and are gradually encapsulated by a cyst wall comprised of the host's connective tissue and blood cells including numerous phagocytes.

In time, all encapsulated larvae are destroyed except for one. If only one larva enters the earthworm, it is not destroyed. The reason for this selective destruction remains undetermined. The single remaining larva becomes active when the end of its first larval instar period is reached. It breaks through the surrounding tissues and migrates toward the anterior end of the host. This is an unusual sort of migration, for the larva migrates backwards—with its posterior end directed forward.

Upon reaching the host's prostomial region, the parasite breaks through the body wall, extrudes its spiracular openings to obtain oxygen from the air, and begins feeding on the surrounding host tissues. As the larva increases in size, the tissues of the host that enclose it gradually disintegrate, exposing the maggot. In time, most of the host's tissues are either ingested or disintegrated, and the larva escapes into the soil and pupates. It is of interest that the third stage larva of *P. rudis* is entirely saprophagous, feeding on partly destroyed and decomposed host tissue. Larvae at this stage of development can be maintained on decomposed fragments of earthworms.

Melinda cognata, a calliphorid parasite of the snail *Helicella virgata,* possesses a similar life cycle to *Pollenia rudis* in that the fly larva feeds first on the living tissues of its host and finally devours the dead and decomposed snail. It differs from *P. rudis* in that the adult females deposit their eggs in the snail. It is apparent that both *Pollenia rudis* and *Melinda cognata* are parasites that border on being predators.

FAMILY SARCOPHAGIDAE
(Flesh Flies)

Bodies are gray or silvery. Sides of the head are hairy. Antennae are plumose above and below. Compound eyes are hairy. Proboscis is long. Palpi are rudimentary. Vein M_{1+2} has angular bend and ends considerably before the apex of the wing.

Members of Sarcophagidae, the flesh flies, like the Calliphoridae, are parasitic during larval stages. Maggots of sarcophagid flies, however, can be distinguished by a girdle of minute spines on each abdominal segment, well developed curved mouthparts, and posterior stigmal plates located in a deep cavity. There are three slits on each stigmal plate that are vertically parallel (Plate 22–21, Fig. 2).

The three major genera of the Sarcophagidae are discussed here—*Sarcophaga*, *Wohlfahrtia*, and *Titanogrypha*. Members of these genera can be distinguished by the shape of their antennae. In *Sarcophaga*, aristae are long and plumose; in *Wohlfahrtia*, aristae are short and pubescent; and in *Titanogrypha*, they are short and plumose (Plate 22–22).

Genus *Sarcophaga*

Sarcophaga haemorrhoidalis.   This species is common throughout North, Central, and South America, Great Britain, continental Europe, northern China and India, Africa, and Australia (Plate 22–23, Fig. 1). As with all the sarcophagid flies, this species is larviparous (viviparous). Larvae are deposited on carrion, feces, rotting meat, and similar breeding spots. These flies are usually scavengers, although they are capable of becoming myiasis-causing organisms by invading wounds or because of their ingestion in contaminated food by the host. The hosts are various mammals, including man.

OTHER *Sarcophaga* SPECIES.   Other myiasis-causing species of *Sarcophaga* include *S. lambens* in southern United States, Central and South America; *S. chrysostoma* in Mexico, Central and South America; *S. carnaria* in Europe; and *S. plinthopyga* in the New World (Plate 22–23, Fig. 2). The larva of *S. plinthopyga*, unlike the

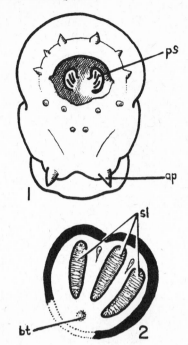

Plate 22-21   Posterior spiracles of calliphoridae. 1. Posterior view of calliphorid larva. 2. Single posterior spiracle. (Redrawn after James, 1947.)
    (ap, anal protuberances; bt, button; ps, posterior spiracles; sl, slits.)

others, is primarily parasitic in the bodies of insects. However, cases of human cutaneous myiasis have been caused by this maggot. The life cycles of these species are typically dipteran.

Genus *Wohlfahrtia*

Wohlfahrtia includes several species whose larvae produce myiasis.

Wohlfahrtia magnifica.   This species is found in northern Europe, Russia, the European and African Mediterranean countries, and eastern

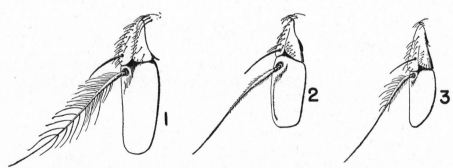

Plate 22-22   Antennae of sarcophagid flies. 1. *Sarcophaga bullata*. 2. *Wohlfahrtia magnifica*. 3. *Titanogrypha alata*. (All figures after James, 1947.)

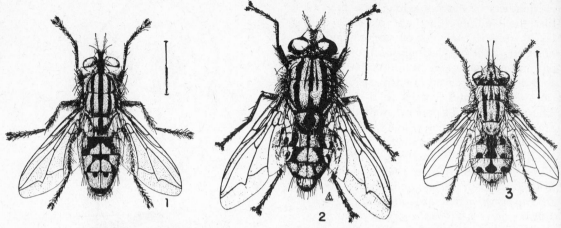

Plate 22-23   Sarcophagid flies. 1. *Sarcophaga haemorrhoidalis,* adult male. 2. *Sarcophaga plinthopyga,* adult male. 3. *Wohlfahrtia magnifica,* adult female. (All figures after James, 1947.)

Africa (Plate 22–23, Fig. 3). As in all sarcophagid species that cause wound myiasis, the adult females larviposit in wounds on man and other mammals, thus initiating the parasitic condition.

Wohlfahrtia vigil.   This species is the most important North American representative (Plate 22–24, Fig. 1). This fly displays a variation of the penetration mechanism employed in initiating cutaneous myiasis in that, unlike *W. magnifica* and the other species, the females are attached to young mammals, including man. Furthermore, larvae of *W. vigil* are deposited on healthy skin rather than in wounds, and these maggots thus penetrate unruptured skin. Once established in subdermal locations, these larvae cause small abscess-like lesions that measure 6 to 20 mm. in diameter. Even if a larva is unsuccessful at penetrating the skin, it does cause a marked dermal irritation.

Genus *Titanogrypha*

Members of *Titanogrypha* resemble small *Sarcophaga*. *Titanogrypha alata,* a species found in Florida, southern Texas, and Cuba, is capable of infesting wounds of various mammals, including man.

FAMILY CUTEREBRIDAE
(Robust Botflies)

Bodies are large and beelike. Mouth opening is small. Mouthparts usually are vestigial. Postscutellum is not developed. Squamae are large. Apical cell of wing is narrowed at margin. (For identification of parts of head refer to Plate 22–25.)

The cuterebrids, commonly called robust botflies or warble flies, are another cyclorrhaphan family, members of which are parasitic only during larval stages and thus are myiasis-causing. All cuterebrids are obligatory parasites as larvae. The major genera of this family are *Cuterebra,*[*] *Dermatobia,* and *Cephenemyia.*

Genus *Cuterebra*

Species of *Cuterebra* are limited to North America. Larvae of most of these species are parasitic on rodents and lagomorphs. Adults are among the largest muscoid flies known, measuring 20 mm. or more in length. The bodies are bumblebee-like, and the abdomen is completely, or mostly, black or blue. The thorax is usually covered with dense hair. The larva of *C. buccata* is a common dermal parasite of rabbits.

Cuterebra spp. oviposit near the entrance of the burrows of their hosts, and the hatching larvae attach themselves and proceed to burrow into the host's skin. In all known instances the eggs are oviposited in the abodes of the hosts rather than directly on the hosts. These larvae form cystlike pockets in the subdermal zone that communicate with the exterior via a pore. Human cases of nasal and dermal myiasis caused by these larvae are known.

The infective larvae possess integuments beset with spines (Plate 22–24, Fig. 2). The

---

*The genus *Cuterebra* has been subdivided into a number of genera by Bau (1931) and Townsend (1934–42), although not all these subdivisions have been widely accepted. Students interested in the taxonomy of *Cuterebra* should consult these papers.

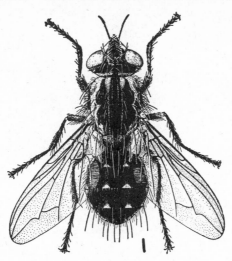

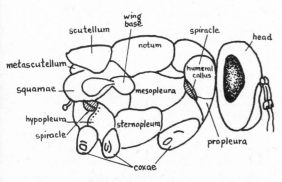

Plate 22-24   Diptera. **1.** *Wohlfahrtia vigil,* adult female. (After James, 1947.) **2.** First stage larva of *Cuterebra* sp., from a case of human myiasis. (After Beachley and Bishopp, 1942.)

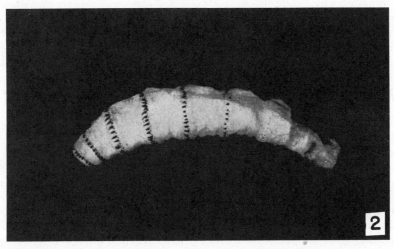

Plate 22-25   Dipteran morphology. Lateral view showing external structures in the thoracic area of a dipteran. (Redrawn and modified after Jaques, H. E. 1947. *How to Know the Insects,* Wm. C. Brown Co., Dubuque, Ia.)

older specimens are blackish in color. In addition to causing dermal, nasal, and pharyngeal myiasis, these larvae can also invade the cranial cavity. Stunkard and Landers (1956) reported such a case in a cat.

Other common species of *Cuterebra* include *C. americana* and *C. lepivora* on the western rabbit *Syvilagus audubonii sanctidiegi,* and *C. emasculator* on the eastern striped chipmonk *Tamias striatus. Cuterebra emasculator* can destroy its host's testes, causing parasitic castration. Bennett (1955) reported that *Cuterebra* species are almost specific for particular hosts.

Genus *Dermatobia*
Dermatobia hominis. *Dermatobia* includes

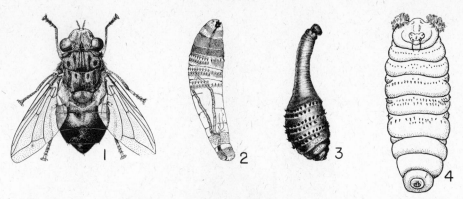

Plate 22-26   Stages in the life cycle of *Dermatobia hominis*. 1. *D. hominis,* adult female. (After James, 1947.) 2. First stage larva. (After Newstead and Potts, 1925.) 3. Second stage larva. (After James, 1947.) 4. Third stage larva, ventral view. (Redrawn after James, 1947.)

D. hominis the human botfly (Plate 22–26, Fig. 1). This large species measures 12 mm. in length and possesses a yellow head, dull blue thorax, and metallic blue abdomen. The antennal aristae are pectinate. The three parasitic larval stages are somewhat different, with the mature, elongate-oval larva being spinose (Plate 22–26, Fig. 2–4). This larva possesses posterior spiracles, each consisting of three slits located in two cavities, and anterior spiracles that are prominent and flower-like in appearance.

Life Cycle of *Dermatobia hominis*. The life cycle of this fly is unique in that the gravid females employ a fascinating method of engaging other insects, mainly dipterans, to transport their eggs to the host. This mechanism involves the capturing of other dipterans, usually *Psorophora* spp. (Plate 22–27, Fig. 1) and *Stomoxys* spp., and ovipositing and glueing the *Dermatobia* eggs onto the abdomen of the carrier. When the carrier feeds on the mammalian host—be it man, cattle, dogs, or even rarely birds (*D. hominis* seldom parasitizes members of the Equidae)—the first stage larvae, which develop within the eggshells (chorion) in 5 to 15 days, escape and enter the host through the bite of the carrier, or penetrate the host's skin via a pore or a fold.

Each larva penetrates independently and forms a boil-like pouch that communicates with the exterior through a small opening. Larval development within the pocket ensues, and as with other myiasis-causing dipterans, there are three larval instars over a period of 5 to 10 weeks. The mature larva ruptures out of the pocket by enlarging the aperture and falls to the ground to pupate.

In instances where gravid females cannot find a carrier, the eggs are oviposited on vegetation. The larvae hatching from these eggs will survive if they enter a host. However, in most instances they perish. Infestation by *D. hominis* larvae presents a serious problem in tropical and subtropical areas where cattle and dogs suffering from heavy infestations usually die.

Genus *Cephenemyia*

Cephenemyia larvae produce myiasis in deer and reindeer. The maggots most commonly form pockets in the skin of the head and neck (Plate 22–28, Fig. 2). Although previously *Cephenemyia* was suspected of infesting humans, more recent evidence suggests that *Cephenemyia* spp. do not attack man. Members of this genus are readily identified in that their head bears a narrow epistoma (Plate 22–27, Fig. 3).

FAMILY GASTEROPHILIDAE
(Horse Botflies)

Bodies are beelike. Oral opening is small. Proboscis is vestigial. Vein M_{1+2} extends in a nearly straight line toward margin of wing (Plate 22–13, Fig. 2). Wings are transparent, with dark spots and bands.

Genus *Gasterophilus*

Gasterophilidae includes the horse botflies, all of which belong to the genus *Gasterophilus*. The most common species are *G. intestinalis, G. haemorrhoidalis, G. inermis,* and *G. pecorum* (Plate 22–28, Figs. 1 and 2). The first three of these species are cosmopolitan, being found in North America in addition to other parts of

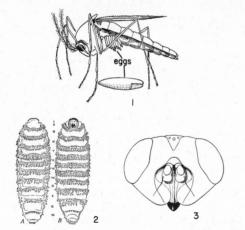

Plate 22-27   **Cuterebrid flies.** 1. The mosquito, *Psorophora* sp., with eggs of *Dermatobia hominis* attached. (Modified after James, 1947.) 2. Larva of *Cephenemyia auribarbis*. **A.** Dorsal view. **B.** Ventral view. (After Cameron.) 3. Front view of head of adult female *Cephenemyia trompe*. (After James, 1947.)

the world, while *G. pecorum* is primarily a European and African species.

LIFE CYCLE OF *Gasterophilus*. Members of the family Equidae are the preferred hosts for the parasitic *Gasterophilus* larvae. Unlike other myiasis-causing larvae, these larvae complete their development in the stomach and intestine of the horse host (thus causing gastrointestinal myiasis) as part of the normal pattern, rather than as the result of accidental ingestion. Specific differences occur in the life cycle patterns of the species but the basic pattern is the same.

The life span of the nonfeeding adults is short. Gravid females deposit their eggs on the hair of the host. These eggs become attached to the hair individually (Plate 22–28, Fig. 3). The sites of egg deposition differ among the species. The light yellow eggs of *G. intestinalis* are deposited all over the host's body but

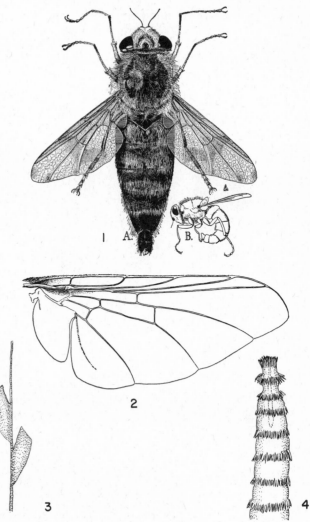

Plate 22-28   *Gasterophilus.* 1. *Gasterophilus intestinalis*. **A.** Dorsal view. **B.** Side view. (After James, 1947.) 2. Wing of *G. haemorrhoidalis*. (After James, 1947.) 3. Eggs of *Gasterophilus* attached to hair. 4. Armature at anterior end of larva of *G. intestinalis*.

especially on the inner surfaces of the knees; those of *G. haemorrhoidalis* are attached to the fine hairs around the lips; those of *G. nasalis* are attached to hairs under the jaws; those of *G. inermis* to the hairs of the cheeks; and those of *G. pecorum* are not deposited on the host, rather they are oviposited on the host's food.

The number of eggs produced by a single female is large. A single female of *G. intestinalis* may deposit 905 eggs in nearly 3 hours. The closer the eggs are laid to the horse's mouth, the smaller their number. For example, *G. haemorrhoidalis* females oviposit a mean number of 160 to 200 eggs, while females of *G. pecorum* oviposit a mean of 2300 to 2500 eggs.

The incubation period and physical stimuli required for hatching vary among the species. In *Gasterophilus intestinalis,* the eggs hatch in 7 to 14 days in warm summer temperatures, if friction and moisture are provided by the horse's tongue. Similarly, eggs of *G. haemorrhoidalis* require moisture provided by saliva. Hatching under these conditions occurs in only 2 to 4 days. The eggs of *G. nasalis* do not require moisture and hatch in 4 to 5 days.

The modes of entrance of the first stage larvae of some species differ. When the equine host licks the eggs of *G. intestinalis,* some of the hatched larvae become attached to the lips. These larvae penetrate the mucous membranes of the lips and tongue by utilizing an armature to burrow tunnel-like canals in the subepithelia (Plate 22–28, Fig. 4). From the mouth, the larvae soon migrate into the alimentary canal —stomach or small intestine—and continue their larval development until the third larval instar is attained. The larvae remain quiescent until the following spring or early summer, when they pass from the host in feces and undergo pupation in soil. The emerging pupae measure 1.5 to 2 cm. in length (Plate 22–29, Fig. 1).

In *G. haemorrhoidalis,* the path of migration to the stomach parallels that of *G. intestinalis*— that is, burrowing in the subepithelial zone. However, larvae of *G. nasalis* crawl into the mouth and form typical pockets between the molar teeth. Within such pockets the first stadium is completed, after which the larvae migrate to the stomach or duodenum, where they are commonly found in clusters. Pupation occurs in the early summer when the third larval instars pass from the host in feces.

The path of migration of *G. inermis* is unique. The hatching first larval instars penetrate the host's skin near the cheeks and migrate into

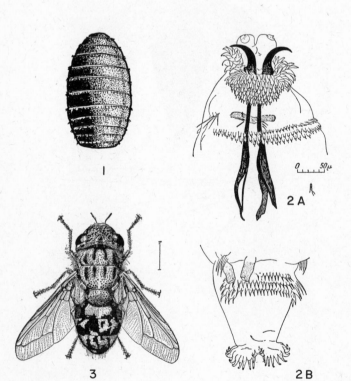

Plate 22-29   **Gasterophilid and oestrid flies. 1.** Pupa of *Gasterophilus intestinalis* (Original.) **2.** First stage larva of *Oestrus ovis.* **A.** Anterior end. **B.** Posterior end. (After Gailliard, 1934.) **3.** Adult female *Oestrus ovis.* (After James, 1947.)

the mouth by crawling through the dermis. Once within the buccal cavity, they molt underneath the mucous membrane and then proceed, not to the stomach, but to the rectum, where they mature and drop out with the onset of warm weather to pupate in soil.

The larvae of *G. pecorum* hatch from eggs that are deposited in the host's food. When the larvae come in contact with the horse's lips, they burrow into the mucous membrane and from there to the stomach and rectum.

When humans come in close contact with horses, three species of *Gasterophilus*—*G. intestinalis, G. haemorrhoidalis,* and *G. nasalis*—can infect man. In such cases, the first larval instars penetrate the skin and migrate in a serpentine, random fashion between the layers of the epidermis, causing raised red lines along paths of migration. The larvae eventually die rather than reach the alimentary tract. This migratory condition is referred to as creeping eruption, larval migrans, or preferably "myiasis linearis" to differentiate it from the subcutaneous migrations of nematodes (p. 465).

Gastric and intestinal myiasis due to *Gasterophilus* spp. are injurious to the host resulting from (1) blockage of the normal passage of chyme through the alimentary tract, (2) irritation and mechanical injury to the mucous lining of the stomach by the oral hooklets of the maggots, (3) irritation to the intestine, rectum, and anus as the maggots pass posteriorly, and (4) deprivation of some nutrients from the host. In cases of heavy infestation, death commonly occurs.

FAMILY OESTRIDAE*
(Head Maggots)

Bodies are large or medium-sized and beelike. Head is large. Mouth opening is small. Mouth parts are usually vestigial. Vein M_{1+2} is bent rather than straight as in the Gasterophilidae. Apical cell of wing is closed at margin. Postscutellum is well developed. Squamae are large.

Members of this family are commonly referred to as head maggots, because the larvae invade and parasitize the nasal cavities and frontal and maxillary sinuses of ruminants,

particularly sheep and goats, horses, antelopes, and other hoofed animals (Plate 22–29, Fig. 2). Occasionally, first larval instars parasitize humans. The larvae are robust and only slightly tapered anteriorly. The third larval instar, which is the most commonly encountered parasitic form, possesses a single pair of oral hooks, inconspicuous or nonexistant anterior spiracles, and posterior spiracles modified as two sclerotized plates with numerous perforations.

The two prominent genera of the Oestridae are *Oestrus* and *Rhinoestrus.*

Oestrus ovis

Oestrus ovis is a globally distributed species (Plate 22–29, Fig. 3). The natural host for the parasitic larvae is sheep; however, human infections are known. The adults are nonfeeders. The females are larviparous. They deposit larvae on the nostrils of sheep and goats during the summer and autumn months. A single female may give birth to as many as sixty larvae per hour. These first stage larvae actively migrate up the host's nostrils and become attached to the mucous membranes lining the nasal and frontal sinuses. In these locations, development continues, passing through two additional larval stadia. During the following spring, the mature larvae, measuring from 20 to 30 mm. in length, drop out of the host, usually aided by a sneeze, onto the ground, where they burrow into the soil and pupate. The pupal period lasts for 16 days, after which adults develop.

Rhinoestrus purpureus

The Russian bot, *R. purpureus,* is endemic to France, Spain, Italy, eastern Europe, northern Africa, USSR, northern China, India, and Central and South Africa (Plate 22–30, Fig. 1). Normal hosts are members of the horse family. The adults, like those of *Oestrus ovis,* are nonfeeders. The females larviposit first larval instars onto the eyes and nostrils of hosts. A single female can larviposit 700 to 800 larvae, placed in groups of eight to forty at a time. Larviposition usually occurs in the fall, and the two additional larval instars occur in the nasal and frontal sinuses of the host. With the onset of spring, these larvae escape, also aided by sneezes, and pupate in soil. If the larvae are deposited in the eye, severe conjunctivitis ensues, often leading to blindness. Human infections, although rare, are known.

*The familial designation Oestridae is used here in the restricted sense and does not include the Gasterophilidae, Cuterebridae, or Hypodermatidae.

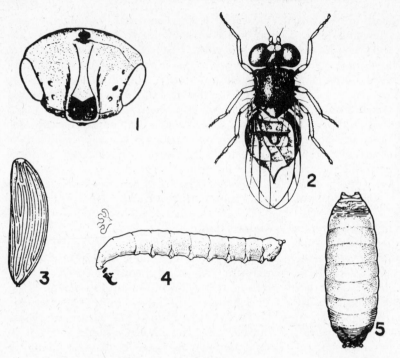

Plate 22-30   Oestrid and chloropid flies. 1. Head of female *Rhinoestrus purpureus*, showing rudimentary proboscis and palpi. (After James, 1947.) **2.** Adult *Hippelates pusio*. (After Herms, W. B., and James, M. T. 1961. *Medical Entomology*, 5th Ed, Macmillan, New York.) **3.** Egg of *H. pusio*. (After Herms and Burgess, 1930.) **4.** Larva of *H. pusio*, showing cephalopharyngeal skeleton and anterior spiracular process. (After Herms and Burgess, 1930.) **5.** Pupa of *H. pusio*. (After Herms and Burgess, 1930.)

FAMILY CHLOROPIDAE
(Frit Flies, or Eye Flies)

Bodies are small, rarely exceeding 3 mm. in length. Possess short aristate antennae. Squamae are greatly reduced or absent. Sixth longitudinal and anal veins are absent (Plate 22–13, Fig. 3).

Members of the Chloropidae, commonly known as frit flies or eye flies, are not capable of piercing the integument of their mammalian hosts. They are attracted to open wounds, sebaceous materials, and secretions about the eyes. Once attracted to such sites, these minute flies hold onto the edge of the sores or to the conjunctival epithelium and make minute lesions around the wound or eye with their spinose labella. The two important genera are *Hippelates* and *Siphunculina*.

Hippelates pusio

The eye gnat, *H. pusio*, is small (about 2 mm. long) and bears yellowish legs, eyes, and antennae (Plate 22–30, Fig. 2). This species is found in parts of California, Florida, and other southern states. It is most commonly encountered in areas of sandy or mucky soil undergoing cultivation. The curved and fluted eggs of *H. pusio* are deposited on freshly cultivated soil or decaying organic debris (Plate 22–30, Fig. 3). Such eggs measure about 0.5 mm. in length.

After an incubation period of approximately 3 days, the larvae hatch and are free-living, ingesting well aerated organic materials (Plate 22–30, Fig. 4). The conditions for normal embryonic development remain uncertain, but it is apparent that the incubation medium must be well aerated—for example, loose earth and animal feces mixed with loose earth. The larval period usually lasts for 11 days, after which the larvae migrate close to the surface of the incubation medium and pupate (Plate 22–30, Fig. 5). The pupal stadium lasts for approximately 6 days.

The direct injury caused by this and related flies is not serious. However, these dipterans are strongly suspected of being able to spread the sore-eye, or pinkeye, disease, a form of contagious conjunctivitis of man and animals. Furthermore, evidence suggests that these flies can be transmitters of *Treponema pertenue*, the yaws-causing spirochaete.

Another prominent species of *Hippelates* is *H. pallipes*, the predominent species in the West Indies.

Siphunculina funicola

Siphunculina funicola is endemic to India, Ceylon, and the East Indies. This fly is attracted to eyes and is strongly suspected of transmitting conjunctivitis. Graham-Smith

(1930) has critically reviewed the literature up to that time dealing with Chloropidae and conjunctivitis. This paper should be consulted by interested individuals.

FAMILY NYCTERIBIIDAE
(Spider-like Bat Flies)

Are parasitic on bats. Bodies are small, spider-like, wingless. Halteres are present. Head is narrow, folded back in groove on dorsum of thorax when at rest. Compound eyes and ocelli are vestigial. Antennae are short, two-jointed. Legs are long. Tarsal claws are ordinary.

The nycteribiid flies, or bat flies,* are parasites of bats in the tropics and subtropics, primarily in the Old World. The development of these flies is unique among insects. Larval development is of the pupiparous type†—that is, the larvae hatch within the body of the mother and there grow to maturity, feeding on the secretions of special milk glands. Mature larvae are either deposited on the chiropteran host's body or in the host's perch, and later they come in contact with the host.

Scott (1917) has contributed a review of the family. There appears to be a certain degree of host specificity among these wingless flies. A single species may infest bats of several genera, but these genera are usually in the same family. Furthermore, the same species of fly is usually not found on both fruit-eating and insect-eating bats. For example, Speiser (1907) pointed out that members of *Cyclopodia* are confined to frugivorous bats of the family Pteropidae. The host-parasite relationship between the bat and the fly has become so intimate that individuals removed from their hosts could not be induced to feed and rarely lived beyond 12 hours.

The family includes such representative genera as *Eremoctenia, Penicillidia, Cyclopodia,* all found in lands bordering the Indian Ocean. A few North American species are known. One of the most common North American genera is *Basilia,* a taxonomic key to the species of which is given by Peterson (1959).

The progressive atrophy of the wings of nycteribiids and streblids most probably represents a morphological adaptation to parasitism, because these flies are almost continuously attached to their host, although they are capable of a certain amount of migration on their host. The pupae are not found on bats; rather, they are deposited on the walls of the caves inhabited by the bat hosts. Their adaptation to bats is most probably of secondary origin, for their closest and more primitive relatives are found on other cave-dwelling animals, especially those that share the same caves as bats. Thus, it appears that these flies, or their immediate ancestors, have become adapted to bats only after having been initiated to parasitism on other hosts.

FAMILY STREBLIDAE
(Bat Flies)

Are parasitic on bats. Bodies are small. Head is of moderate size, with freely movable neck, but not bent back on dorsum. Compound eyes are vestigial or lacking. Ocelli are lacking. Palpi are broad, leaf-like. Wings are vestigial or lacking.

The Streblidae, also known as bat flies, are much better represented in the New World than the Nycteribiidae, although they are also found elsewhere, especially in lands bordering the Indian Ocean. The species, like those of the Nycteribiidae and the Hippoboscidae, are pupiparous. The mature adults, which are attached to bats, are wingless. Young adults are winged but lose their wings later in life.

Genus *Ascodipteron*

The members *Ascodipteron,* found in Asia and Australia, are of considerable interest, for the females are embedded in the host rather than attached to the skin. After copulation, the adult female cuts a hole in the host's skin, sheds its wings and legs, and embeds itself in the skin. Once in this position, the body increases in dimension and becomes flask shaped as the result of absorbing nutrients from the host. The head and thorax become invaginated within the bulbous body. No reaction on the part of the host has been reported. As the larvae are formed and complete their development within the embedded female, they are expelled through the gonopore at the posterior end of the body which is directed toward the opening of the cavity. These larvae fall to the ground and pupation takes place. This odd behavioral pattern of the females might be considered a type of myiasis, except that the adult, rather than the larva, is the causative agent.

---

*The nycteribiids are known as bat-ticks in the older literature.

†Although the term pupiparous is still in common use, it is actually a misnomer dating back to the early investigators who erroneously interpreted the fully grown larva that leaves the parent as the pupa. Actually, pupation does not occur until after birth of the larva.

FAMILY HIPPOBOSCIDAE
(Louse Flies)

Are continuously parasitic on birds and mammals (except pupae of *Lipoptena*). Body is winged or wingless and compressed. Head is closely attached to and fitted in notch on thorax. Antennae are single-jointed, with terminal arista or style, located in depression near mouth. Legs are stout and short, broadly separated by sternum. Tarsal claws are strongly armed.

The hippoboscid flies, or louse flies, are believed to be closely related to the nycteribiid and streblid flies. These flies are also pupiparous, but they are not limited as ectoparasites of chiropterans. Instead, they are permanent bloodsucking parasites of birds and mammals. Some hippoboscids are winged; others are not; and still others possess wings for a time before discarding them. The genera of louse flies that infest mammals include *Melophagus* and *Lipoptena*.

Genus *Melophagus*

Melophagus ovinus. The sheep tick, or ked, *M. ovinus,* is a common ectoparasite of sheep and goats the world over (Plate 22-31, Fig. 1). This wingless fly is reddish brown and measures 5 to 7 mm. in length.

Life Cycle of *Melophagus ovinus*. The entire life span of *M. ovinus* is spent on the host. It takes approximately 7 days for the fully mature larva to develop within the female. Gravid females larviposit one larva every 7 to 8 days over a period of 4 months, which is the average life span of the adult female. The larva pupates almost immediately on birth.

The pupa, which is contained within the hardened puparial envelope, is glued to the host's wool, commonly on the abdomen, thighs, and shoulders (Plate 22-31, Fig. 2). The environmental temperature influences the pupal period. For example, during the summer months, the pupa metamorphoses into an adult in 19 to 23 days. During the winter, however, if the host is kept outdoors, the pupal period lasts from 40 to 45 days. It takes 15 to 30 days for the young females to reach sexual maturity. Although a few flies do little damage to sheep, heavy infestations cause severe irritation.

Genus *Hippobosca*

There are nine species of *Hippobosca*. Of these, *H. struthionis,* the ostrich louse fly in South Africa, is a parasite of birds; the others are parasites of mammals. *Hippobosca equina* is a common species on equines in Europe; *H. rufipes* parasitizes equines in South Africa; *H. variegata* parasitizes cattle and equines in Europe, Africa, and Asia; *H. camelina* parasitizes camels and dromedaries in Africa; and *H. longipennis* parasitizes dogs in India and certain Mediterranean countries. Functional wings are present on the members of *Hippobosca*.

Genus *Lipoptena*

For detailed information on the American species of *Lipoptena,* the paper of Bequaert (1937) should be consulted. These flies possess wings when they emerge from the puparium and are known as volants. However, they lose the wings during the maturing process (Plate 22-32, Fig. 1).

Lipoptena depressa. This fly is a fairly common parasite of deer in the western United States. Its life cycle, like that of other *Lipoptena* species, is somewhat modified from that of

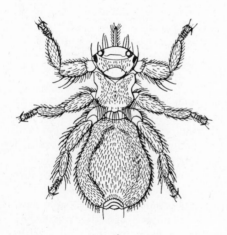

1

2

Plate 22-31   *Melophagus ovinus.* **1.** Adult of the sheep ked. [After Smart, 1943. *Insects of Medical Importance,* British Museum (Natural History)]. **2.** Pupa of *M. ovinus.*

Plate 22-32   Parasitic insects.
1. *Lipoptena.* **A.** Volant. **B.** Adult. (Redrawn from photographs in Herms, W. B., and James, M. T. 1961. *Medical Entomology,* Macmillan, New York.) **2.** *Conops.* (Redrawn after Comstock, J. H. 1949. *An Introduction to Entomology,* Comstock Publishing Co., Ithaca, N.Y.)

I A   **I B**   **2**

Hippobosca spp. in that the pupal stage is not found on the host. Instead, the puparia drop from the host to the ground. The volants, escaping from the puparia, fly about among trees. On sensing a deer, they attack it and crawl between the hairs to suck blood. They must find a host within 8 days or they will perish.

Sexual maturity is attained 12 days after feeding, and copulation occurs on the host. A single female larviposits mature larvae singly at 3-day intervals, producing a total of 30 to 35 larvae. Various authors have reported finding feeding adults in "chains,"—that is, one fly actually feeds off the host, while the mouthparts of the second fly penetrate the dorsal surface of the abdomen of the first, and the third is attached to the second, and so on.

OTHER *Lipoptena* **SPECIES.**   Other species of *Lipoptena* include *L. sabulata* on deer in North America; *L. cervi,* the deer ked, on deer in Europe and sections of eastern North America; and *L. mazamae* on deer in Central and South America and southeastern United States.

Other Hippoboscid Flies

Several species of hippoboscid flies infest birds. Among these are members of the genera *Lynchia, Pseudolynchia, Microlynchia,* and *Stilbometopa.* Representative of *Lynchia* are *L. fusca* and *L. americana,* both parasitic on owls; and *L. hirsuta,* a common parasite of the quail *Lophortyx c. californica. Lynchia hirsuta* has been shown by O'Roke (1930) to be the vector for the blood protozoan *Haemoproteus lophortyx* in quails. Similarly Herms and Kadner (1937) showed that *L. fusca* can serve as an experimental vector for this sporozoan.

Members of *Pseudolynchia* are typified here by the pigeon fly, *P. canariensis;* and *P. brunnea,* which is parasitic on nighthawks. Not only does *P. canariensis* cause much irritation in pigeons, it also serves as a vector for *Haemoproteus columbae* (p. 132).

Microlynchia pusilla is a widely distributed species found on pigeons in the New World, and *Stilbometopa impressa* is found on the California quail.

FAMILY CONOPIDAE
(Thickheaded Flies)

Head is large, broader than thorax. Body is more or less elongate and naked or sparsely covered with fine hairs. Ocelli are either present or absent. Antennae are three-jointed, prominent, and project forward. Third segment of antennae has either arista or terminal style.

The conopid flies, commonly referred to as thickheaded flies, are free-living as adults, being found on flowers. However, the larvae are parasitic in bumblebees and wasps, and a few species are parasitic in grasshoppers. Adult females deposit eggs on the host's body while in flight. When the eggs hatch, the larvae burrow into the host's abdominal cavity. An example of this family is *Conops* (Plate 22–32, Fig. 2).

FAMILY PHASIIDAE
(Phasiids)

A few species are parasitic in adult beetles; others on nymphs and adults of Hemiptera. Clypeus more or less protrudes at a low angle like a bridge. Vein M_{1+2} bent so that R_5 is narrowed or closed at margin of wing.

The Phasiidae includes a few species that are ectoparasitic on adult beetles (Coleoptera) and a few other species that are ectoparasitic on both nymphs and adults of Hemiptera. Little is known about the parasitic habits of these flies, although it is suspected that adults seek out and attach themselves to the hosts, from which they draw nutrition. Other phases of their life cycles are spent off the hosts.

FAMILY CORDYLURIDAE
(Dung Flies)

Larvae of some species are parasitic in caterpillars. Bodies are fairly small. Subcostal vein is separated from vein R_1, is nearly half as long as wing, and ends in costa.

Adult cordylurid flies are commonly referred to as dung flies, not a very exact name, since these are but one of the many families of flies observed around dung and refuse. A few cordylurid species possess larvae that are parasitic in caterpillars. These enter their hosts after hatching from eggs oviposited on the host.

FAMILY ORTALIDAE
(Ortalid Flies)

Larvae of some species are parasitic on lepidopteran larvae; a few are parasitic on plants. Wings are marked with dark spots or bands. Fronto-orbital bristles are lacking.

The Ortalidae is a large family with numerous species, most of which are free-living. The larvae of a few species have been reported on caterpillars and those of a few other species are parasites of plants. Among the plant parasites are *Tritoxa flexa* and *Chaetopsis aenea*, both occasionally found between the leaves of onions.

FAMILY TACHINIDAE
(Tachina Flies)

Larvae are chiefly parasitic in caterpillars. Bodies are usually short, stout, and bristly. Both hypopleural and pteropleural bristles are present. Ventral abdominal sclerite is more or less covered by edges of dorsal sclerites.

The tachina flies constitute a large family whose members are commonly found among flowers and rotting vegetation (Plate 22–33, Fig. 1). Some 1400 species are listed among the dipteran fauna of North America alone. Parasitologists are interested in these flies because the larvae of all the species are parasitic, primarily in caterpillars. Furthermore, they also parasitize other insects. Coquillett (1897) has provided a listing of these parasites and their hosts. The treatise by Clausen (1940) should be consulted for greater detail.

The mechanisms employed by the larvae of various species for entering their hosts fall into four categories. (1) Some oviparous species, such as *Tachina larvarum,* deposit their eggs on the integument of the host. When these eggs hatch, the larvae burrow into the caterpillar and grow to maturity. (2) Females of viviparous (larviparous) species, such as *Compsilura concinnata,* deposit their larvae inside the host by puncturing the host's integument, using the sheath of their ovipositors. (3) Some oviparous species, such as *Frontina laeta,* deposit their eggs on foliage that serves as food for the host. When such eggs are ingested, the larvae hatch within the host. (4) In a few rare but remarkable instances, as in the viviparous *Eupeleteria magnicornis,* the females deposit larvae singly in cup shaped membranous cases. The posterior end of the larva is attached to the inner surface of the cup, and the bottom of the cup (outer surface) is attached to a leaf or twig. In such a position, the larva can move around by stretch-

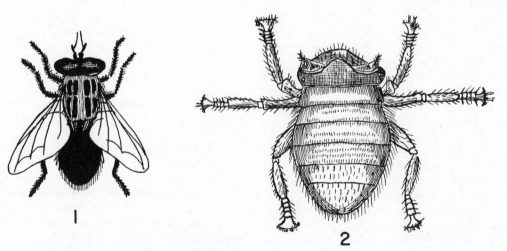

1

2

Plate 22-33   Tachinidae and Braulidae. 1. Adult tachina fly. (After Comstock, 1949.) **2.** *Braula caeca.* (After Starp and Meinert.)

ing its body. When a larva comes in contact with the silk thread on which the caterpillar host moves, it is in position to attack and penetrate the host when the host migrates past that portion of the silk tract.

FAMILY BRAULIDAE
(Braulid Flies)

Are parasitic on honeybees. Bodies are minute, approximately 1.5 mm. long. Bodies are wingless. Halteres are lacking. Head is large. Ocelli are lacking. Compound eyes are vestigial. Last segment of tarsi have a pair of comblike appendages.

Genus *Braula*

This small family includes *Braula,* commonly known as the bee louse. *Braula caeca* is the common species and is found attached like a louse to honeybees (Plate 22–33, Fig. 2). The females lay eggs that drop into the comb chambers in beehives, where they hatch and progress through the developmental stadia. Adults attach themselves to bees and remain attached throughout their life span.

Braula kohli is an African species found in the Congo attached to the African honeybee, *Apis mellifica* var. *adamsoni.* Little is known concerning the effects of this parasitic fly on its host.

LITERATURE CITED

Addis, C. J. 1945. Collection and preservation of sandflies (*Phlebotomus*) with keys to United States species. Trans. Amer. Micro. Soc., *64:* 328–332.

Aldrich, J. M. 1916. *Sarcophaga* and allies of North America. Ent. Soc. Amer., Thomas Say Foundation, Lafayette, Indiana.

Barbosa, F. A. S. 1947. *Culicoides* (Diptera: Heleidae) da Regiao Neotropica. An. Soc. Biol. Pernambuco, *7:* 3–30.

Bau, A. 1931. Über das Genus *Cuterebra,* Clark (Diptera, Oestridae); Einteilung desselben in sechs Untergattungen; Beschreibung neuer Species und Aufstellung einer Bestimmungstabelle der Mittel- und Südamerikanischen Arten. Konowia, *10:* 197–240.

Bennett, G. F. 1955. Studies on *Cuterebra emasculator* Fitch, 1856 (Diptera: Cuterebridae) and a discussion of the status of the genus *Cephenemyia* Ltr. 1818. Can. J. Zool., *33:* 75–98.

Bequaert, J. 1937. Notes on Hippoboscidae, 5. The American species of *Lipoptena.* Bull. Brooklyn Entomol. Soc., *32:* 91–101.

Campbell, J. A., and E. C. Pelham-Clinton. 1959. A taxonomic review of the British species of *Culicoides* Latreille (Diptera, Ceratopogonidae). Proc. Roy. Soc. Edinburgh, *67:* 181–299.

Clements, A. N. 1963. The Physiology of Mosquitoes. Macmillan, New York.

Comstock, J. H. 1949. An Introduction to Entomology. 9th Ed., Comstock, Ithaca, N. Y.

Coquillett, D. W. 1897. Revision of the Tachinidae of America north of Mexico. Tech. Ser. No. 7. U.S.D.A., Div. Ent.

Costa Lima, da A. 1937. Chave das especies de *Culicoides* da regiao neotropica (Diptera, Ceratopogonidae). Mem. Inst. Osw. Cruz, *32:* 411–422.

Craig, C. F., and E. C. Faust. 1951. Clinical Parasitology. Lea and Febiger, Philadelphia, Pa.

Cuthbertson, A. 1933. The habits and life histories of some Diptera in Southern Rhodesia. Rhod. Sci. Assoc. Proc., *32:* 81–111.

Dalmat, H. T. 1955. The black flies (Diptera, Simuliidae) of Guatemala and their role as vectors of onchocerciasis. Smithsonian Misc. Collect., *125:* 1–425.

Deane, L. M. 1956. Leishmaniosevisceral no Brasil. Estudos sobre reservatorios e transmissores realizados no estado do Ceara. Serv. Nac. Educ. Sanitaria, Rio de Janeiro.

Dove, W. E., D. G. Hall, and J. B. Hull. 1932. The salt marsh sandfly problem. (*Culicoides*). Ann. Ent. Soc. Amer., *25:* 505–527.

Foote, R. H., and H. D. Pratt. 1954. The Culicoides of the Eastern United States (Diptera, Heleidae). Pub. Health Monog. No. 18, U. S. Pub. Health Serv. Publ. No. 296.

Fox, I. 1946. A review of the species of biting midges of *Culicoides* from the Caribbean region. (Diptera, Ceratopogonidae). Ann. Ent. Soc. Amer., *39:* 248–258.

Graham-Smith, G. S. 1930. The Oscinidae (Diptera) as vectors of conjunctivitis, and the anatomy of their mouth parts. Parasitology, *22:* 457–467.

Gupta, P. C. S. 1948. Researches on kala-azar in India, 1938–48. Proc. 4th Internat. Cong. Trop. Med. and Malaria (Abstracts), Washington, D. C.

Hall, D. G. 1938. The blowflies of North America. Ent. Soc. Amer., Thomas Say Foundation Publ. No. 4.

Hardy, D. E. 1960. Insects of Hawaii. Diptera: Nematocera-Brachycera. University of Hawaii Press, Honolulu, Vol. 10.

Herms, W. B. 1950. Medical Entomology. 5th Ed., Macmillan, New York.

Herms, W. B., and C. G. Kadner. 1937. The louse fly, *Lynchia fusca,* parasite of California valley quail. J. Parasit., *23:* 296–297.

Hinman, E. H. 1936. Notes on Louisiana *Culicoides* (Diptera, Ceratopogonidae). Am. J. Hyg., *15:* 773–776.

Horsfall, W. R. 1955. Mosquitoes. Their Bionomics and Relation to Disease. Ronald Press, New York.

Horsfall, W. R., and A. P. Morris. 1952. Surface conditions limiting larval sites of certain marsh mosquitoes. Ann. Ent. Soc. Amer., *45:* 492–498.

James, M. T. 1947. The Flies that Cause Myiasis in Man. U.S.D.A. Misc. Publ. No. 631, Govt. Printing Office, Washington, D. C.

Johannsen, O. A. 1943. A generic synopsis of the Ceratopogonidae (Heleidae) of the Americas, a bibliography, and a list of the North American species. Ann. Ent. Soc. Amer., *36:* 763–791.

Mackerras, I. M. 1954–55. The classification and distribution of Tabanidae. I–III. Austral. J. Zool., *2:* 431–554; *3:* 439–511; *3:* 583–633.

Newstead, R. 1924. Guide to the Study of Tsetse Flies. School of Tropical Medicine, Memoir No. 1, University of Liverpool.

O'Roke, E. C. 1930. The morphology, transmission, and life history of *Haemoproteus lophortyx* O'Roke, a blood parasite of the California valley quail. Univ. Cal. Publ. Zool., *36:* 1–50.

Peterson, B. V. 1959. New distribution and host records for bat flies, and a key to the North American species of *Basilia* Ribeiro (Diptera: Nycteribiidae). Proc. Ent. Soc. Ontario, *90:* 30–37.

Philip, C. B. 1947. A catalog of the blood-sucking fly family Tabanidae of the nearctic region north of Mexico. Amer. Midl. Nat., *37:* 257–324.

Reed, W., J. Carroll, A. Agramonte, and J. W. Lazear. 1900. The etiology of yellow fever— a preliminary note. Proc. 28th Ann. Meet., Amer. Publ. Hlth Assn., Indianapolis.

Root, F. M., and W. A. Hoffman. 1937. The North American species of *Culicoides.* Am. J. Hyg., *25:* 150–176.

Scott, H. 1917. Notes on Nycteribiidae, with descriptions of two new genera. Parasitology, *9:* 593–610.

Séguy, F. 1935. Etude sur les stomoxydines et particulièrement des mouches charbonneuses du genre *Stomoxys.* Encyclopédie Entomoligique, Ser. B, 2, Diptera, *8:* 15–58.

Smart, J. 1945. The classification of the Simuliidae (Diptera). Trans. Roy. Entomol. Soc., *95:* 463–532.

Smit, B. 1931. A study of the sheep blows flies of South Africa. Onderstepoort J. Vet. Sci. Animal Indus., *17:* 299–421.

Southwell, T., and A. Kirshner. 1938. On the transmission of leishmaniasis. Ann. Trop. Med. Parasitol., *32:* 95–102.

Speiser, P. 1907. Die Fledermäuse und ihre Schmarotzer. Ber. Westpreuss. Bot. Zool. Ver., *29:* 15–24.

Stone, A. 1930. The bionomics of some Tabanidae (Diptera). Ann. Ent. Soc. Amer., *23:* 261–304.

Stone, A. 1938. The Horseflies of the Subfamily Tabaninae of the Nearctic Region. Misc. Publ. No. 305., U.S.D.A., Washington, D. C.

Stunkard, H. W., and E. J. Landers. 1956. A *Cuterebra* larva (Diptera) from the epidural space of a cat. J. Parasit., *42:* 432–434.

Suster, P. 1960. Diptera Syrphidae. Fauna Republicii Populare Romine, Insecta, *11:* 1–286.

Townsend, C. H. T. 1934–42. Manual of Myiology. São Paulo, Brazil.

Travis, B. V. 1949. Studies of mosquito and other biting insect problems in 1949. J. Econ. Ent., *42:* 451–457.

Vargas, L. 1949. Lista de los *Culicoides* del mundo (Diptera, Heleidae). Rev. Soc. Mex. Hist. Nat., *10:* 191–217.

Vargas, L., A. M. Palacios, and A. D. Najera. 1946. Simulidos de Mexico. Rev. Inst. Salub. Enferm. Trop., *7:* 101–192.

Ward, R. A. 1963. Genetic aspects of the susceptibility of mosquitoes to malarial infection. Exptl. Parasit., *13:* 328–341.

Wirth, W. W. 1952. The Heleidae of California. Univ. Calif. Publ. Ent., *9:* 95–266.

SUGGESTED READING

Clausen, C. P. 1940. Entomophagous Insects. McGraw-Hill, New York. (This treatise on insects that prey on or parasitize other insects includes extensive information on classification and biology. It is the standard reference for those interested in such insects.)

Herms, W. B., and M. T. James. 1961. Medical Entomology. 5th Ed., Macmillan, New York. pp. 362–395. (In this section of Herms and James' textbook; the authors discuss the more common dipterans that cause myiasis in man and domestic animals.)

James, M. T. 1947. The Flies that Cause Myiasis in Man. U.S.D.A. Misc. Publ. No. 631, U. S. Govt. Printing Office, Washington, D. C. (This monograph by one of the leading authorities on myiasis includes a complete listing and discussion of the various dipterans that cause myiasis in man. Not only are the discussions and taxonomic keys of great value, the references listed are also useful.)

23

THE HEMIPTERA—
The True Bugs
THE HYMENOPTERA—
The Wasps
THE COLEOPTERA—
The Beetles
THE STREPSIPTERA—
The Twisted-Wing Insects

ORDER HEMIPTERA*

There are some 30,000 hemipteran species in the world, and approximately 10,000 species are represented in the Americas. These insects are characterized by four wings. The front pair is thickened at the base, and the thinner extremities overlap at the back. Since the hindwings are completely membranous and are folded beneath the forewings, the forewings are often referred to as wing covers or hemelytra. The hindwings are completely lacking among the bedbugs, which are members of the family Cimicidae. Furthermore, the forewings are reduced to two short scalelike pads. The mouthparts of these true bugs are modified for piercing and sucking, and are col-

*The designation of Hemiptera is used here in the new restricted sense—that is, it is limited to members of the older suborder Heteroptera of the older order Hemiptera. The term does not include the Homoptera, which is considered an independent order, rather than a suborder of the older Hemiptera.

lectively known as the proboscis or beak. The proboscis is attached to the front of the head.

Comstock (1949) lists 34 families of hemipterans. Of these, the Cimicidae, Ruduviidae, and Polyctenidae include parasitic species.

FAMILY CIMICIDAE

The Cimicidae includes the bedbugs and allied forms. These bloodsucking insects are characterized by dorsoventrally flattened oval bodies; short, wide heads that are attached to the prothorax; conspicuous four-jointed antennae; proboscides that are three-jointed and lie in grooves beneath the head and thorax; compound eyes present, but without ocelli; and reduced hemelytra.

The cimicids, especially the bedbugs, are still major household pests in many parts of Europe, Asia, Africa, and South America. Occasionally, there are reports of these bugs as bedfellows in North America. Bedbugs are nocturnal—that is, they feed during the night, although occasionally they have been reported to suck blood during the day. The reactions of hosts to the bites vary. Generally the substances secreted by the salivary glands during feeding effect swelling and itching.

Bedbugs are not continuous feeders; instead, they engorge themselves in about 5 minutes and then drop off. The gregarious habit of bedbugs, which are usually found in large numbers, results in severe attacks on their hosts. The author recalls seeing "trains" of these bugs in China, climbing onto bedding like a colony of ants. Having suffered from their bites, he is well aware of the great discomfort they cause.

The resultant irritation from the piercing of the host's skin is the primary injury inflicted by bedbugs. Although various investigators have reported experimental success in getting bedbugs to serve as vectors for various pathogens, there is little evidence to support the hypothesis that they are important vectors.

Life Cycle Pattern

Cimicid life cycle patterns are similar. Metamorphosis is gradual—that is, of the hemimetabolous type (p. 566). In the common bedbug *Cimex lectularius*, the females oviposit large, operculated, yellowish-white eggs, each measuring 1.02 mm. by 0.44 mm., in batches in the crevices of bed frames, floors, walls, and similar household sites. Each batch of eggs contains ten to fifty eggs. A single female deposits 200 to 500 eggs over a period of 2 to 3 months, usually during the spring and summer.

The nymphs, which hatch from the eggs after 8 to 10 days of incubation (range 7 to 30 days), resemble adults in possessing greatly reduced hemelytra and lacking hindwings but the nymphs are white. Several nymphal instars ensue, accompanied by gradual growth, provided the environmental temperature is favorable and the nymphs are fed during each stadium. The nymphal period lasts approximately 6 weeks. This period is prolonged, however, if the environment is not favorable. Bedbug nymphs can undergo extended starvation, sometimes lasting as long as 2 months. Adults of *C. lectularius* are quite sensitive to heat. At about 60° F., activity ceases, and most specimens are killed if the temperature reaches 100° F. Adults can also live for long periods without a blood meal, surviving from 17 to 42 days.

Horvath (1912) has contributed a taxonomic account of the American Cimicidae. The most prominent genera of this family are *Cimex, Oeciacus, Haematosiphon,* and *Primicimex.*

Genus *Cimex*

Cimex lectularius is the most common bedbug, being cosmopolitan in its distribution (Plate 23–1, Fig. 2). *Cimex hemipterus,* the Indian bedbug, is limited to tropical and subtropical areas. *Cimex boueti* is the tropical species, being found in South America and Africa. All of these species attack man, but they can also feed on various mammals (rats, mice, and rabbits and birds (domestic fowls). Other species primarily infest birds and mammals. For example, *C. pipistrelli* and *C. pilosellus* are parasitic on bats in Europe and North America respectively. *Cimex columbarius* is found on pigeons in Europe and does attack man on occasion.

Genus *Oeciacus*

Members of *Oeciacus,* which are distinguished by their hairy bodies covered with long silklike coats, include several species found on birds and in their nests. *Oeciacus vicarius* is the common bedbug of swallows in North America, and *O. hirundinis* parasitizes the barn swallow in Europe and also attacks man, causing severe irritations.

Genus *Haematosiphon*

Haematosiphon inodorus is the only, but plenti-

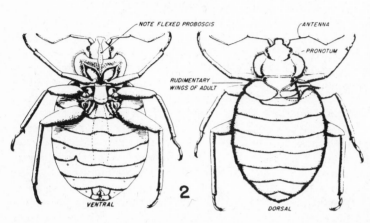

NOTE FLEXED PROBOSCIS

ANTENNA

PRONOTUM

RUDIMENTARY
WINGS OF ADULT

2

VENTRAL

DORSAL

Plate 23-1   *Cimex lectularius.* 1. Eggs of the bedbug. (After Herms, W. B., 1950. *Medical Entomology,* Macmillan, New York.) **2.** Ventral and dorsal views of an adult bedbug, showing external anatomical parts. (Courtesy of Naval Medical School, Bethesda, Md.)

ful, representative of the genus. The natural hosts for this bug in America are the California condor and the great horned owl, but it can also become a serious pest of chickens and other domestic fowl in southwestern United States and Mexico. *Haematosiphon inodorus* can invade homes and become a serious pest of man.

Other Cimicid Genera

Another widely distributed species of the Cimicidae is *Leptocimex boueti.* This species is characterized by very long legs and an elongate, ovoid body. It is widely distributed in western Africa. Other species of cimicids include *Cimexopsis nyctalis,* a parasite of the chimney swift; and *Chaetura* sp., which is widely distributed and attacks humans.

FAMILY REDUVIIDAE

There are over 4000 known species of reduviid bugs. These insects feed on the blood of other insects, and some attack man and other animals. Members of the Reduviidae are commonly large, measuring 1.5 and 2 cm. in length, and some are brightly colored. The proboscis is three-jointed, short, and is attached to the tip of the head. When not in use, the proboscis rests within a groove on the pro-

sternum. The antennae are four-jointed. Both compound eyes and ocelli are present, and both pairs of wings are well formed. These bugs are often referred to as assassin bugs, kissing bugs, or cone-nose bugs because of their attacking habits and the shape of their heads.

Life Cycle Pattern

All reduviids demonstrate a similar basic life cycle pattern. The rather large, smooth, barrel shaped eggs are deposited on the ground, on trees, or in the dirty corners of houses, depending on the habits of the adults. The eggs are deposited singly or in clusters. A single female may oviposit a few dozen to over 500 eggs, depending on the species. The incubation period varies from species to species and is influenced by the temperature. However, almost all reduviid eggs hatch in 8 to 30 days. The escaping nymph is wingless and there are generally five nymphal instars.

Both the vicious biting habits of these hemipterans and their roles as transmitters of pathogenic microorganisms have been of great interest to parasitologists.

Fracker (1914) and Usinger (1944) have contributed annotated taxonomic studies on the Reduviidae. Of the many genera, *Triatoma, Rhodnius, Panstrongylus, Melanolestes,* and *Rasahus* are the most prominent.

REDUVIIDS AS VECTORS

Genus *Triatoma*

Numerous species of *Triatoma* are naturally infected with the haemoflagellate *Trypanosoma cruzi* (p. 72) (Plate 23–2, Fig. 1). Among these, *T. sanguisuga,* found in the United States and Central America, is one of the most common vectors. This bug measures 18 to 20 mm. in length and is characterized by a flattened body that is dark brown and is splattered with reddish-orange or pinkish areas on the abdomen, the tips and bases of the hemelytra, and along the lateral and anterior margins of the pronotum. Similarly, *T. protracta,* which is widely distributed along the Pacific Coast of North America, is naturally infected with *Trypanosoma cruzi* (Plate 23–2, Fig. 2). *T. protracta* is also known to be naturally infected in Arizona and

Texas. Both of these species are vicious biters of various animals, including man. Their bites result in very painful and itchy swellings. It is known that a toxin is injected into the host during feeding.

Other species of *Triatoma* known to be naturally infected with *T. cruzi* are: *T. infestans* in southern Brazil, Uruguay, Chile, Paraguay, Argentina, and southern Bolivia; *T. dimidiata* in Mexico, Panama, Guatemala, and San Salvador; *T. hegneri, T. rubida, T. barberi,* and *T. gerstaeckeri* in Texas; and *T. rubida* and *T. recurva* in Arizona.

Since the *Trypanosoma cruzi* population in the blood of infected humans is small and difficult to detect, the diagnostic technique originated by Brumpt, known as xenodiagnosis, is widely used. This technique involves allowing uninfected *Triatoma* to bite the individual and

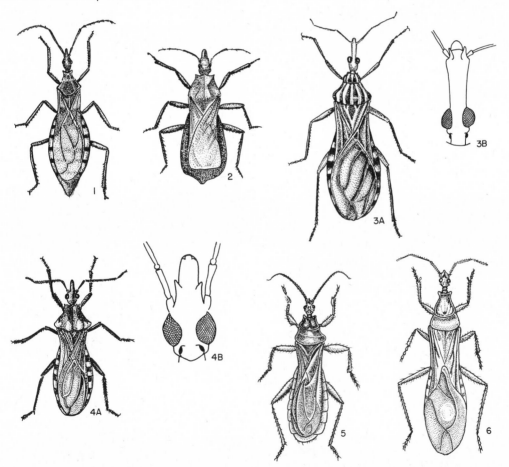

Plate 23–2   Some bloodsucking reduviids. 1. *Triatoma sanguisuga,* adult. (Redrawn after Marlatt.) **2.** *Triatoma protracta,* adult. (Redrawn after Herms.) **3.** *Rhodnius prolixus.* **A.** Adult. **B.** Head, showing origin of antennae. (Redrawn after Brumpt.) **4.** *Panstrongylus megistus.* **A.** Adult. **B.** Head, showing origin of antennae. (A redrawn after Brumpt; B redrawn after Root in Hegner, Root and Augustine, 1929. *Animal Parasitology,* Appleton-Century-Crofts, New York.) **5.** *Melanolestes picipes.* **6.** *Rasahus biguttatus.* (Figs. 5 and 6 redrawn after Matheson, 1950. *Medical Entomology,* Comstock Publishing Co., Ithaca, N.Y.)

examining the digestive tract of the bug for flagellates after a period of incubation.

Genus *Rhodnius*

Rhodnius prolixus and *R. pallescens* are two representatives of the genus that reportedly are naturally infected with *Trypanosoma cruzi* (Plate 23–2, Fig. 3). *Rhodnius prolixus* ranges from Brazil north to Colombia and is found in San Salvador and Mexico; *R. pallescens* is found in Panama. While working with *R. prolixus* in 1912, Brumpt demonstrated that *T. cruzi* is not transmitted through the bite of the bug. Rather, the infective form of the flagellate passes out in the vector's feces and is mechanically deposited via contaminated hands on the extremely susceptible mucous membranes of the nose, eyes, mouth, or is rubbed into skin perforations (p. 72).

Rhodnius brumpti and *R. domesticus* also are found in Brazil.

Genus *Panstrongylus*

This genus contains several species, including *P. megistus* and *P. rufotuberculatus*, which are suitable vectors for *Trypanosoma cruzi*. *Panstrongylus megistus*, which is widely distributed in Brazil, the Guianas, and Paraguay, is a nocturnal haematophagous species, hiding by day in cracks and crevices in houses (Plate 23–2, Fig. 4). The adults, measuring 30 to 32 mm. in length, are black with red markings on the prothorax, wings, and abdomen.

Panstrongylus rubrofasciata, another blood-feeder, is also widely distributed, being found in the Orient, Ethiopia, Central America, the West Indies, and in Florida. The bites of neither of these species result in such a severe reaction as those of *Triatoma* spp.

Genus *Melanolestes*

Melanolestes includes *M. picipes* and *M. abdominalis* (Plate 23–2, Fig. 5). *Melanolestes picipes* is a common species throughout all North America. It is black and found under stones, logs, and mosses. It bites man, and the host's reaction to its toxins is severe.

Melanolestes abdominalis has habits similar to those of *M. picipes* and is also widely distributed throughout North America. Members of this genus are not known to serve as vectors for microorganisms.

Genus *Rasahus*

Rasahus biguttatus and *R. thoracicus*, commonly referred to as the corsair bugs, are severe biters and inflict damaging inflammations (Plate 23–2, Fig. 6). Neither of them serve as vectors. *Rasahus biguttatus* is found in southern United States and in the West Indies, while *R. thoracicus* is found in western United States and Mexico.

FAMILY POLYCTENIDAE

The Polyctenidae includes the so-called bat bugs. These little-understood insects are blood-sucking ectoparasites of bats. The familial characteristics include a four-jointed rostrum, shortened three-jointed tarsi, four-jointed antennae, short or vestigial hemelytra, no eyes, and often comblike bands known as ctenidia are present on the body.

Only a very few polyctenid species are known in North America. Ferris (1919) described *Hesperoctenes longiceps* from the bat *Eumops perotis californicus* in California (Plate 23–3). Two other representatives of the genus, *H. hermsi* and *H. eumops*, are known in North America. *Hesperoctenes hermsi* is found on the bat *Tadarida macrotis* in Texas, and *H. eumops* is found on *E. perotis californicus* in southern California.

Waterhouse had placed the members of this family in the dipteran family Hippoboscidae, because the bat bugs show an affinity to the hippoboscid flies in being ectoparasites of mammals (bats), and in being viviparous, giving birth to rather advanced larvae. However, the polyctenids are definitely hemipterans rather than dipterans, although their relation-

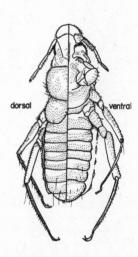

dorsal   ventral

Plate 23-3   *Hesperoctenes.* *Hesperoctenes longiceps*, female. (Redrawn after Ferris, 1916.)

ship to the other true bugs remains unclear. Their seemingly primitive form, including short legs and reduced wings, and the absence of eyes, undoubtedly reflects their parasitic habit.

ORDER HYMENOPTERA

The Hymenoptera includes the sawflies, bees, wasps, and ants. These insects are easily recognized by the extremely narrow isthmus that joins the thorax with the abdomen. Other characteristics of this order have been given on p. 567. Approximately 100,000 species of hymenopterans have been described, and some 50 per cent of these, primarily wasps, are parasitic. It is the larvae of hymenopterans that are parasitic, being found in a very great number of insects, spiders, millipedes, and other invertebrates. Many of the parasitic larvae are of economic importance in that they serve as natural controls in curbing realization of the biotic potentials of various destructive insects.

Although parasitic hymenopteran larvae begin as parasites, they very often become predators during the end of their larval period and actively eat their hosts.

Only rarely is an adult hymenopteran found to be parasitic. In one such rare instance, a female of *Riela manticida* was reported by Chopard (1929) to be ectoparasitic at the base of a wing of a praying mantis. At this site, the hymenopteran was observed to gnaw through the chitinous veins of the host's wing and feed on blood.

A rather unusual series of parasitic adaptations occurs during this relationship. On attaching themselves to the praying mantis, *R. manticida* females cast off their own wings at the bases. When the host oviposits, the eggs are deposited within a foamy mass that later hardens to form the egg capsule. As soon as the host begins ovipositing, the parasitic wasp allows itself to become engulfed within the egg mass and lays her own eggs among those of the host.

If a *R. manticida* female becomes attached to a male rather than a female praying mantis, the female wasp will not oviposit, nor will it pass from the female host to a male when the host copulates.

Life Cycle Studies

As a rule, eggs of parasitic wasps are deposited within the host after the integument of the host has been pierced by the ovipositor of the female wasp. Upon hatching, certain of the larvae emerge from and remain on their host as ectoparasites. Most of the larvae, however, remain within their host to pursue their development.

That a given larva may be either an ecto- or an endoparasite, depending on the species of host on which it is found, suggests that the nature of the host is responsible for the type of parasitism practiced by the larva. For example, when eggs of the wasp *Dentroster protuberans* are oviposited in the body of the beetle *Myelophilus,* the larvae hatching from the eggs escape to the exterior and become ectoparasitic. If eggs of the same wasp are oviposited in another beetle, *Scotylus,* the larvae remain within the host as endoparasites. Similarly, the larvae of the wasp *Oncophanes lanceolator* are ectoparasitic on the caterpillars of *Cacoecia sorbiana,* but are endoparasitic in those of *Tortrix viridana* and *Sesamia aspidiana.*

If the wasp larva is endoparasitic, it does not attempt to make contact with the respiratory organs of its host as endoparasitic dipteran larvae do, although tracheae are present in its body. The exchange of oxygen and carbon dioxide occurs through the entire surface of the hymenopteran's cuticle. This cuticle is so thin that oxygen in the host's haemolymph (blood) can be utilized.

The treatise by Clausen (1940), which includes a great deal of information on the parasitic hymenopterans, serves as a standard reference on these parasites.

SYSTEMATICS AND BIOLOGY

The order Hymenoptera, according to Muesebeck et al. (1951), is divided into two suborders—Symphyta and Apocrita. Members of the Symphyta feed on plants except for those belonging to the small, obscure family Orussidae. Members of this family are commonly known as the parasitic wood wasps. These wasps, measuring 8 to 14 mm. in length, are free-living as adults. The larvae are parasitic on the larvae of metallic wood-boring beetles of the family Buprestidae.

Suborder Apocrita includes 59 families,[*]

---

[*]The reader is referred to An Introduction to the Study of Insects by D. J. Borror and D. M. DeLong, Holt, Rinehart, & Winston Publ. Co., New York, for a key to and descriptions of these families.

the majority of which are exclusively parasitic or include parasitic species. These families are divided among eleven superfamilies, which are briefly treated in the following discussion.

SUPERFAMILY ICHNEUMONOIDEA

Members of Ichneumonoidea are wasplike in appearance, but with a few exceptions, they do not sting. All members are parasitic on or in other insects or other invertebrates. Ichneumonidea includes the large family Ichneumonidae. Adult ichneumons vary considerably in size, form, and coloration, but the majority are slender wasps (Plate 23–4, Figs. 1–5). They differ from the stinging wasps in having longer antennae, which are composed of sixteen or more segments (other wasps generally have twelve or thirteen segments); in having trochanters comprised of two instead of one joint; and in lacking a costal cell in the front wings. In most ichneumons, the ovipostor of females is very long, often longer than the body.

Life Cycle of Ichneumons

Ichneumons are parasitic as larvae. The adult female deposits her eggs on or inside the

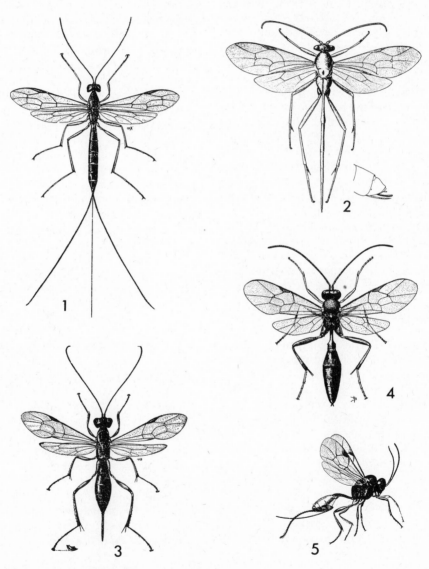

Plate 23-4 *Ichneumonidae.* **1.** *Rhyssella nitida,* female. **2.** *Casinaria texana,* female. **3.** *Phytodietus vulgaris,* female. **4.** *Phobocampe disparis,* female. **5.** *Tersilochus conotracheli,* female. (Figs. 1 and 3 courtesy of Rohwer and U.S. National Museum; Fig. 2 courtesy of Walley and *Scientific Agriculture;* Figs. 4 and 5 courtesy of USDA.)

body of the host, which is commonly a lepidopteran larva, although a great variety of immature insects and even spiders can serve as hosts. A certain degree of host specificity is displayed, for most ichneumon species attack only a few types of hosts. If the eggs are laid on the host's epidermis, the newly hatched larvae generally bore into the body. The larvae develop into legless grubs that either become ectoparasitic or remain endoparasitic, depending on the host (p. 633). When pupation begins, the larvae may either remain within the host or emerge and spin their cocoons near the host. The adult is the postpupal form.

FAMILY ICHNEUMONIDAE

Representative of the Ichneumonidae are *Rhyssella nitida,* the larvae of which parasitize xiphydriid wood wasps; *Phytodietus vulgaris,* the larvae of which parasitize tortricid moths; *Phobocampe disparis,* the larvae of which parasitize gypsy moths; and *Tersilochus conotracheli,* the larvae of which parasitize plum curculios (Plate 23–4, Figs. 1 and 3 to 5).

FAMILY BRACONIDAE

Another large and beneficial ichneumonoidean family is the Braconidae. Adult braconids are relatively small, rarely measuring over 15 mm. in length. Many braconid species have reduced wing venation. The life cycles of braconids are similar to those of ichneumons except that many of them pupate in silken cocoons on the outside of their host's body, while still others spin their cocoons entirely apart from the host.

Braconid Genera

Representative genera of the Braconidae include *Apanteles,* with *A. melanoscelus,* imported into the United States to control gypsy moth larvae; *Macrocentrus,* including *M. gifuensis,* larvae of which parasitize larvae of the European corn borer; *Chelonus,* including *C. texanus,* larvae of which parasitize larvae of various phalaenid moths; and *Phanomeris,* including *P. phyllotomae,* larvae of which parasitize bird leaf-mining sawfly larvae (Plate 23–5, Figs. 1 to 4).

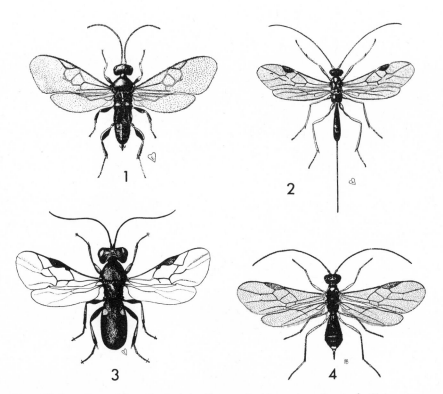

Plate 23-5   Braconidae. 1. *Apanteles diatraeae.* 2. *Macrocentrus gifuensis.* 3. *Chelonus texanus.* 4. *Phanomeris phyllotomae.* (All figures courtesy of USDA.)

SUPERFAMILY CHALCIDOIDEA

Members of the Chalcidoidea, known as chalcid flies, are actually small wasps that measure less than 1 mm. to 3 mm. in length. Their wing venation is reduced, and they usually have elbowed antennae. Chalcidoidean wasps are mainly endoparasites in eggs and larvae of lepidopterans, dipterans, coleopterans, homopterans, and other parasitic hymenopterans. Chalcidoidean wasps attack the larvae of other parasitic hymenopterans within the body of the primary host. A few chalcids develop in plant seeds or plant stems. For example, the larvae of *Bruchophagus gibbus* develops in the seeds of clover.

FAMILY PTEROMALIDAE

Mormoniella vitripennis

One of the best known chalcid wasps is *Mormoniella vitripennis,* a member of the family Pteromalidae, because it is commonly used in genetics (Whiting, 1956, 1960). This minute black wasp possesses an abdomen that appears more or less triangular in profile.

LIFE CYCLE OF *Mormoniella.* Pupae of *Sarcophaga* and other sarcophagid flies serve as hosts for *M. vitripennis,* which is parasitic during its larval and adult stages. The adult female seeks a fly puparium and punctures the puparial wall with her ovipositor. A feeding tube (or coagulation tube) is formed from secretions of the ovipositor, connecting the pupa to the tear in the puparial wall. Through this canal, the female ingests the body juices of the fly maggot. This represents the type of parasitism practiced by the adult. The adult female not only feeds on the fly pupa, but she oviposits into the puparium by making other holes in the puparial wall and inserting her ovipositor.

The eggs hatch into legless larvae that possess a small head and spiracles arranged in a row on each side of the body (Plate 23-6, Fig. 1). These larvae feed on the fly maggot, and after several molts, transform into pupae that are naked (without puparium or cocoon) (Plate 23-6, Fig. 2). The pupae are at first whitish in color but become almost completely black with age. The pupal exuviae are then shed (a process known as eclosion), and these immature forms metamorphose into imagoes, which gnaw a hole in the puparial wall to emerge (Plate 23-6, Fig. 3).

Not all larvae enclosed within a single fly puparium develop at the same rate. Many undergo larval diapause* (a quiescent period). This unique habit of *M. vitripennis* proved at first to be a drawback to geneticists employing the wasp as an experimental animal, because it reduces the number of offspring that can be scored. It is now known that larval diapause can be regulated. If puparia enclosing larvae in diapause are maintained at low temperatures (household refrigerator temperature) for 3 or more months and then placed in an incubator or at room temperature, all the larvae pupate. This discovery has greatly enhanced *M. vitripennis* as a genetic tool. In addition, if dark female pupae and freshly eclosed females are maintained under 25° C., optimally at 7° C., for 3 or more days, the subsequent offspring will undergo larval diapause. This information has also become an asset to geneticists because these parasitic wasps can now be maintained in the diapause state and made to pupate when desired.

Dibrachys boucheanus

A widely distributed pteromalid wasp, *D. boucheanus* attacks the pupae of many insects. The wasps lap the exuded juices of the para-

---

*For an excellent account of diapause in arthropods the reader is referred to A. D. Lees' The Physiology of Diapause in Arthropods, Cambridge University Press, 1955.

Plate 23-6   Stages in the life cycle of *Mormoniella.* **1.** Larva. **2.** Pupa. **3.** Adult.

sitized pupa if the pupa is resting close to the wall of the cocoon. If the pupa is not resting close enough to the wall, the wasp forms a feeding tube, as does *Mormoniella,* by secreting a mucilaginous substance through the ovipositor, which forms the tube connecting the pupa to the parasite. The ovipositor is then withdrawn, and the pupal juices flow through the tube to the exterior of the cocoon where the wasp can lap them up.

Pteromalus puparum

Pteromalus puparum is another parasitic pteromalid wasp. Only the larvae of this species is parasitic. The female wasp oviposits her eggs into the pupa of the cabbage butterfly by inserting her ovipositor through the cocoon wall. The larvae developing from the eggs parasitize the pupa. In a few weeks the larvae become adults and escape from the cocoon by chewing a hole through the wall.

FAMILY EULOPHIDAE

The Eulophidae of the superfamily Chalcidoidea includes a large group of small wasps that measure 1 to 3 mm. in length. The larvae are parasitic on a wide variety of insect hosts, including a number of major crop pests. The eulophids can be recognized by their four-segmented tarsi.

Included in this family are *Aphelinus jucundus* a parasite of aphids; and *Hemiptarsenus anementus,* a parasite of leaf-mining sawflies (Plate 23–7, Figs. 1 to 3). Some eulophids are hyperparasites. For example, the larva of *Tetrastichus bruchophagi* is a parasite of *Bruchophagus gibbus,* which is a chalcid parasite of clover seeds (Plate 23–7, Fig. 4). In the genus *Coccophagus,* the females develop as parasites of scale insects, while the males develop as hyperparasites of parasites of scale insects, often including females of their own species.

OTHER CHALCIDS

Larvae of other chalcids are either parasites or hyperparasites of other immature insects. For example, *Ooencyrtus kuwanai* of the family Encyrtidae is a parasite of the gypsy moth; *Eupelmus atropurpureus* of the family Eupelmidae is a parasite of the Hessian fly; and *Perilampus platygaster* of the family Perilampidae is a hyperparasite of *Meteorus dimidiatus,* a braconid parasite of the grape leaf folder, *Desmia funeralis* (Plate 23–8, Figs. 1 to 3).

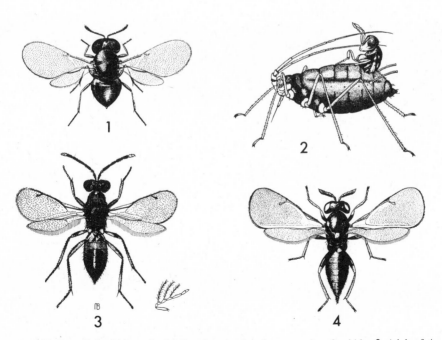

Plate 23-7   Eulophidae. 1. *Aphelinus jucundus,* female, a parasite of aphids. **2.** Adult of *A. jucundus,* emerging from an aphid. **3.** *Hemiptarsenus anementus,* female, a parasite of leaf-mining sawflies. **4.** *Tetrastichus bruchophagi,* a parasite of the clover seed chalcid. (Figs. 1, 3, and 4 courtesy of USDA; Fig. 2 courtesy of Griswald and the Entomological Society of America.)

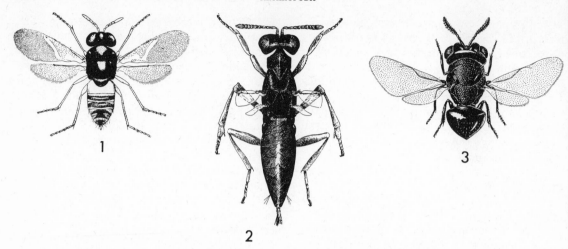

Plate 23-8   Other chalcid parasites. 1. *Ooencyrtus kuwanai,* female, a parasite of the gypsy moth. (Courtesy of Griswald and the Entomological Society of America.) **2.** *Eupelmus atropurpureus,* female, a parasite of the hessian fly. (Courtesy of USDA.) **3.** *Perilampus platygaster,* a hyperparasite of a braconid. (Courtesy of USDA.)

SUPERFAMILY PROCTOTRUPOIDEA

All larvae of members of the Proctotrupoidea are parasitic in or on the immature stages of other insects. Adult proctotrupoids are minute black wasps that measure 3 to 8 mm. in length.

Larvae of these wasps parasitize (1) egg capsules of other insects, (2) larvae of other insects, and (3) larvae of parasites of other insects. As an example of the first type of parasitism, larvae of members of the family Evaniidae, or ensign wasps, are parasitic in the egg capsules of roaches (Plate 23–9, Figs. 1 and 2). In the second category, larvae of *Pelecinus polyturator,* a member of the family Pelecinidae,

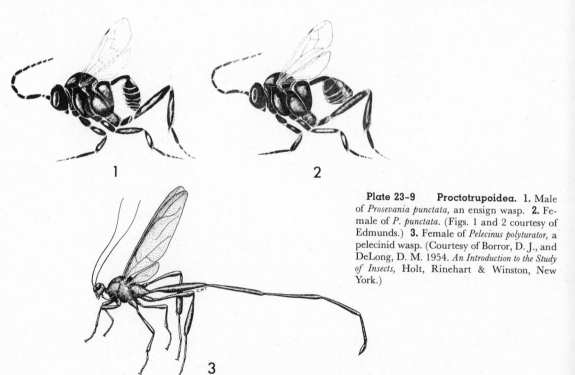

Plate 23-9   Proctotrupoidea. 1. Male of *Prosevania punctata,* an ensign wasp. **2.** Female of *P. punctata.* (Figs. 1 and 2 courtesy of Edmunds.) **3.** Female of *Pelecinus polyturator,* a pelecinid wasp. (Courtesy of Borror, D. J., and DeLong, D. M. 1954. *An Introduction to the Study of Insects,* Holt, Rinehart & Winston, New York.)

parasitizes larvae of the June beetle (Plate 23-9, Fig. 3). In the third category, some larvae of members of the family Ceraphronidae are hyperparasitic in larvae of braconid and chalcid parasites of aphids and scale insects.

SUPERFAMILY CYNIPOIDEA

Most members of the Cynipoidea are gall-forming wasps of plants. However, the larvae of a few species are parasitic in or on the immature stages of other insects. For example, larvae of members of the family Figitidae are parasitic in the cocoons of chrysopids, or lacewings; and larvae of certain members of the family Cynipidae are parasitic in the puparia of syrphid dipterans.

SUPERFAMILIES CHRYSIDOIDEA AND BETHYLOIDEA

The Chrysidoidea and the Bethyloidea include the cuckoo wasps and their relatives. Most members are parasitic on immature or mature forms of other insects. The only com-

mon members belong to the family Chrysididae. Members of this family are small, rarely over 12 mm. long, and possess metallic green or blue bodies that are coarsely sculptured. Chrysidids are ectoparasites of adult wasps or bee larvae.

SUPERFAMILY SCOLIOIDEA

All wasps belonging to the Scolioidea are parasitic. During the life cycle of scolioids, the female lays its eggs on its host, usually without particularly injuring the host, and then flies elsewhere to oviposit more eggs on other hosts. Larvae hatching from the eggs are ectoparasitic. They feed on the host and gradually destroy it. Thus, these wasps border between parasitism and predation.

FAMILY TIPHIIDAE

The major family subordinate to the Scolioidea is the Tiphiidae, which includes fair-sized wasps that measure an inch or more in length and that are somewhat hairy with short legs (Plate 23-10, Figs. 1 to 3). These wasps

1

Plate 23-10   **Tiphiid wasps. 1.** *Tiphia popilliavora* adult. (From Sweetman, after USDA.) **2.** *Tiphia* larva. (From Illinois State Natural History Society.) **3.** *Tiphia* larva, parasitizing a Japanese beetle grub. (From Sweetman, after USDA.)

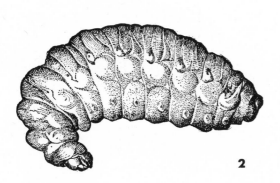

2

3

may be black, or they may be brightly colored with black and yellow. Larvae of the various species are commonly found on the larvae of scarabaeid beetles. One species, *Tiphia popilliavora,* was introduced into the United States to aid in the control of the destructive Japanese beetle (Plate 23–10, Fig. 1). The larvae of *T. popilliavora* feed on the body tissues of the grub of the beetle and thus kill it.

OTHER HYMENOPTERAN SUPERFAMILIES

Superfamilies Formicoidea (the ants), Vespoidea (the vespoid wasps), Sphecoidea (the sphecoid wasps), and Apoidea (the bees) primarily include free-living hymenopterans. Some of these, such as ants and bees, live in highly organized communities.

FAMILY DRYINIDAE

The Vespoidea does include one family— the Dryinidae—members of which are parasitic. Dryinids are unusual wasps in that the males and females are quite different morphologically. The females possess front tarsi that are modified as pincers used in holding their host during oviposition.

During the dryinid life cycle, the larvae are endoparasites of nymphs and adults of certain homopterans. Although these larvae are considered endoparasites, during most of their development, a portion of the larval body protrudes from the host in a saclike structure. The fully grown larva leaves the host and spins a silken cocoon nearby.

POLYEMBRYONY IN PARASITIC HYMENOPTERA

The consistent occurrence of polyembryony —the production of two or more embryos from the same ovum—appears to be more frequently, but not exclusively, encountered in parasites. Among parasites, this type of embryogenesis is known to occur among the Mesozoa (p. 178), the Trematoda (pp. 231 and 240), and certain Eucestoda (p. 311).* In many ways, it is surprising that polyembryony is the normal pattern in such advanced animals as certain wasps. It should not be inferred that animals that undergo polyembryony are of common ancestry.

Polyembryony in parasitic hymenopterans, although not a common phenomenon, was first discovered by Marchal (1904) among certain chalcidoid wasps. His study of this process in *Encyrtus fuscicollis,* a parasite of the caterpillars of *Hyponomeuta* spp., still remains as the classic one.

In *E. fuscicollis,* the eggs are laid within the caterpillar during July and August, and development commences before the onset of winter. Development comes to a complete stop with cold weather and is resumed the following April. Within the host, the hymenopteran egg is surrounded by a host-elaborated epithelial cyst wall.

From the very beginning, a large nucleus, rich in chromatin, known as the paranucleus, is differentiated within the ovum. In addition, a number of smaller nuclei, known as embryonic nuclei, are present (Plate 23–11, Fig. 1). The embryonic nuclei are difficult to stain.

The paranucleus undergoes extensive development, becomes lobed, and eventually divides into a number of smaller amorphous bodies. On the other hand, the embryonic nuclei give rise at an early stage to approximately 100 small aggregates of cells, each one including a germ cell. These aggregates resemble morulae (Plate 23–11, Fig. 2). Each one of these aggregates eventually becomes an embryo. If a germ cell fails to become incorporated in an embryonic cell aggregate, the resulting larva lacks rudimentary gonads and degenerates without ever metamorphosing (Patterson, 1918). Embryogenesis occurs within the egg in the middle of a cytoplasmic mass intermingled with fat-containing paranuclear bodies. The paranucleus thus serves as an amnion and as a trophic layer.

The entire egg is gradually transformed into a long tube in which the larvae are linearly arranged. The host's epithelial cyst persists. It should thus be apparent that the processes involved in the type of polyembryony found in *Encyrtus fuscicollis* are similar to those found in mesozoans, especially the orthonectids, and similar to the processes found in the formation of the larval stages of digenetic trematodes in molluscs.

Sex determination among the polyembryonic offspring of parasitic hymenopterans still remains puzzling. According to Bugnion, who

---

*The formation of many scolices on a single larval cestode (coenuri and hydatids), each of which later develops into an adult worm, may be considered a form of delayed polyembryony, because the larva, which had developed from a single ovum, gives rise to many individuals.

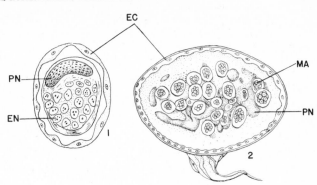

Plate 23-11   Polyembryony in *Encyrtus fuscicollis.* 1. Young egg enclosing paranucleus and embryonic nuclei. **2.** Older egg enclosing amorphous paranuclear bodies and embryonic cell aggregates. (Figs. 1 and 2 redrawn after Marchal, 1904.)

(EC, host-elaborated epithelial cyst; EN, embryonic nucleus; MA, morula-like aggregate of embryonic cells; PN, paranucleus.)

also studied *Encyrtus fuscicollis,* all offspring of the same egg are of the same sex, thus indicating that sex determination occurs at the beginning of development.

Silvestri, who studied another species, *Litomastix truncatellus,* is in agreement, but in addition reported that the offspring from fertilized eggs develop into females, while those from parthenogenetic eggs develop into males. The eggs of *L. truncatellus,* a parasite of the caterpillar of *Plusia gamma,* includes approximately 100 larvae. Patterson (1917), on the other hand, reported that among the 177 batches of eggs of the chalcidoid *Paracopidosomopsis floridanus* studied, 154 included offspring of both sexes. Analysis of his data revealed that the mixture of sexes could not be explained by the simultaneous development of several eggs of different sexes in the same host. *Paracopidosomopis floridanus* is a parasite of the caterpillar of *Pieris brassicae,* the white cabbage butterfly.

In addition to the species already mentioned, several others undergo polyembryony (Parker, 1931; Paillot, 1937; Clausen, 1940). For example, among chalcidoids, *Litomastix gelechiae,* a parasite of *Gnorimoschema salinaris; Ageniaspis testaceipes,* a parasite of *Lithocolletis* caterpillars; and *Platygaster rubi,* a parasite of dipterans living on conifers, are known to produce their young by polyembryony. The same holds true for two braconid wasps, *Macrocentrus gifuensis* and *Amicroplus collaris,* the first being parasitic in the caterpillar of *Pyralis,* and the second in the caterpillar of *Euxoa segetum.* Among the proctotrypoid wasps, *Polygnotes minutus* develops in the gastric sac of the dipterans *Cecidomyia destructor* and *C. avenae.* In *P. minutus,* each egg includes approximately fifty larvae.

The occurrence of polyembryony in certain species of parasitic hymenopterans is undoubtedly the result of evolutionary changes directed by natural selection. Polyembryony could represent a pre-adapted characteristic, carried over from an ancestral form, which benefits

the modern species in the propagation of the species, or it could be a relatively recent development. In either case, the modern parasitic hymenopterans in which polyembryony occurs are benefited in that a larger number of progeny can thus be produced. In most parasitic animals this is advantageous to species preservation, for many individuals of each generation are destroyed before another suitable host can be found.

The mechanisms responsible for the initiation of polyembryony remain undetermined. Some parasitologists favor the theory that polyembryony is a characteristic developed in parasitic wasps as the result of the conditions in which the egg of the parasite happens to develop. This theory is primarily based on the findings of Marchal, who believed that polyembryony in *Encyrtus* is associated with the arrestment of embryonic development during the winter and the resumption of development in the spring, when the caterpillar host begins to feed. When the host resumes feeding, abrupt osmotic changes occur in the medium in which the eggs are found, and such changes are thought to contribute to the initiation of polyembryony. This theory also appears to hold true in the case of *Polygnotes,* the eggs of which are in the stomach of cecidomyiid larvae, where they undergo very abrupt osmotic changes and at the same time are subjected to considerable agitation. The hypothesis that osmotic pressure changes may contribute to the initiation of polyembryony is tentative.

ORDER COLEOPTERA

The Coleoptera includes some 277,000 species of beetles and weevils, of which about 26,676 are found in the United States. These insects are readily distinguished by their leathery integument, mandibulate mouthparts (biting-chewing), and two pairs of wings. The front pair of wings, called the elytra, are horny, heavy, and nonfunctional as organs of flight. The hind pair are membranous, functional, and folded under the elytra when at rest. Although some coleopterans are wingless, most definitely possess wings. Also characteristic of these insects is the meeting of the elytra along a straight middorsal line when at rest.

Coleopteran metamorphosis is of the holometabolous type, involving an egg-larva-pupa-imago sequence (p. 566). Beetle larvae, commonly referred to as grubs, are characterized by three pairs of well developed legs. The larvae of weevils, however, are legless.

Coleopterans as Intermediate Hosts

Parasitism is rarely encountered among coleopterans. Most beetles are free-living; some, such as various weevils, are extremely destructive to economic plants. Interest in beetles stems from their role as intermediate hosts for helminth parasites and from the few parasitic species. Table 23–1 lists some of the helminth parasites and their coleopteran intermediate hosts.

Coleopterans as Parasites

A few members of the families Leptinidae and Platypsyllidae are obligatory parasites. Parasitic members of the Leptinidae include

Table 23-1.   Representative Helminth Parasites of Vertebrates That Utilize Coleopterans as Intermediate Hosts

Helminth	Vertebrate Host	Coleopteran Host
NEMATODES		
Gongylonema pulchrum	Goats, sheep, swine, cattle, occasionally man	Scarabaeidae: *Aphodius, Scarabaeus, Passalurus, Onthophagus*; Tenebrionidae: *Tenebrio molitor*
Ascarops strongylina	Swine	*Copris, Aphodius, Passalurus*
Physocephalus sexalatus	Swine	*Onthophagus, Scarabaeus, Gymnopleurus, Ataenius, Canthon, Phanaeus, Geotrupes*
Spirocerca lupi	Dogs	*Scarabaeus sacer*
Cheilospirura hamulosa	Poultry	*Alphitobius, Gonocephalum, Ammophorus, Anthrenus*, other dermestid beetles, *Alphitophagus*, other fungous beetles
Subulura brumpti	Poultry	*Alphitobius, Gonocephalum, Ammiophorus, Dermestes vulpinus*
ACANTHOCEPHALA		
Macracanthorhynchus hirudinaceus	Swine, rarely man	Scarabaeidae: *Melolontha melolontha, Cetonia aurata, Phyllophaga* spp.
Moniliformis dubius	Rats, occasionally man	*Blaps*
CESTODES		
Raillietina cesticillus	Fowl	Scarabaeidae 2 spp., Tenebrionidae 1 sp., Carabidae 38 spp. including *Amara* and *Pterostichus*
Hymenolepis diminuta	Rats, mice, occasionally man	*Tenebrio molitor* (larva), *Tribolium confusum*
H. carioca	Domestic fowl	*Aphodius, Choeridium, Hister, Anisotarsus* (?)
H. cantaniana	Turkeys	*Ataenius, Choeridium*
Choanotaenia infundibulum	Poultry	Many species of Tenebrionidae

Leptinillus validis, an ectoparasite on American beavers; *L. aplodontiae* on *Aplodontia,* a Pacific Coast rodent commonly called the mountain beaver; and *L. testaceus* on mice and shrews in North America and Europe.

The only representative of the Platypsyllidae is *Platypsyllus castoris,* which is a permanent obligatory parasite of beavers during all stages of its life cycle. This parasite inhabits both Europe and North America.

Occasionally beetles, both larvae and adults, are accidentally ingested by a mammalian host. They do not remain for long in the host, being rapidly passed out in feces. This type of accidental parasitism is termed canthariasis. Larvae of the beetle *Tenebrio molitor,* commonly known as the mealworm, are the most frequently reported accidental "parasites." Undoubtedly this grub gains entrance to the host's alimentary tract by ingestion of contaminated foods. Similarly *Onthophagus bifasciatus, O. unifasciatus,* and *Ptinus tectus* have been reported as accidental intestinal "parasites."

ORDER STREPSIPTERA

Members of the Strepsiptera, often called twisted-wing insects, are small endoparasites of other insects that include various species of Orthoptera, Hemiptera, Homoptera, and Hymenoptera. Marked sexual dimorphism exists among these insects. Only the adult males are winged. The forewings are reduced to club shaped appendages, and the fan shaped hindwings are large and folded longitudinally when in the resting position (Plate 23–12, Fig. 1). Adult females are legless and larviform. Mouthparts are greatly reduced in these insects (Plate 23–11, Fig. 2). Hypermetamorphosis is the rule (p. 567).

STREPSIPTERAN LIFE CYCLE PATTERN

The strepsipteran life cycle is extremely complex. Adult males are free-living, while adult females are endoparasites in the bodies of various insects. The male seeks out and mates with a female.

Strepsipterids are ovoviviparous and extremely prolific. A single female may contain over 2000 minute larvae in her saccular body. The eggs hatch within the female's body, giving rise to first larval instars that are campodeiform and active. These instars are referred to as triungulins and possess well developed eyes and legs. The triungulins leave the body of the female through unpaired median genital pores located on abdominal segments two through five.

Because the adult female is enveloped within the epidermis of the pupa, the triungulins do not at first escape to the exterior. Instead, they fall into the brood chamber—the space between the female and the puparial envelope. They leave the brood chamber through a slit on the cephalothorax of the puparium between the head and prothorax, and crawl over the body of the host. This escaping first larval instar represents a temporarily free-living form. It falls to the soil or to vegetation.

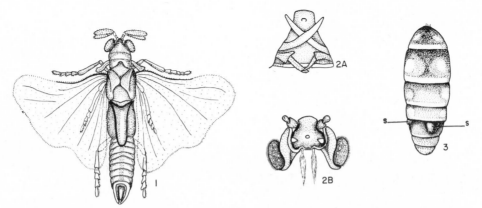

Plate 23-12   Strepsiptera.   1. *Ophthalmochlus duryi.* (Redrawn after Pierce, 1909.) **2. A.** Mouthparts of male *Acroschismus bruesi.* (Redrawn after Pierce.) **B.** Mouthparts of male *Pentozocera australensis.* (Redrawn after Perkins, 1905.) **3.** Strepsiptera projecting from between abdominal segments of insect host. (Redrawn after Comstock, J. H. 1949. *An Introduction to Entomology,* Comstock Publishing Co., Ithaca, N. Y.)

If the larva is to survive, it must seek out the larva or nymph of a suitable host and burrow into it. If the hosts are gregarious social insects as are bees or wasps, this is not too great a problem, for it only involves finding a hive. However, if the larva is to parasitize a homopteran, it must crawl over leaves and twigs until such a host is found.

Once established within a compatible host, the larva grows rapidly. After completing the first ecdysis, the second larval instar is legless and becomes increasingly cylindrical. From this stage on, development is different in males and females. There are seven larval instars in all. In males, the cephalothorax is formed during the fifth larval stadium by fusion of the distinct head and thorax, and the seventh instar is enveloped within the epidermis of the sixth. This last larval instar is distinct, for it bears strongly developed appendages. For this reason, it is sometimes referred to as the pre-pupa. At the prepupa stage, the organism first protrudes its anterior end through the intersegmental space on the host's abdomen. The pupa develops within the skin of the seventh larval instar. When the adult metamorphoses from the pupa, it pushes off the operculum present on the puparium and escapes as a winged individual. The free-living males live for only a short while, during which they seek out and copulate with parasitic females.

In females, fusion of the head and thorax also takes place during the fifth larval stadium. The seventh larval instar does not bear appendages, nor is it enveloped in the skin of the sixth. It is also at this stage that the parasite protrudes from the host, but there is no pupal stage. Instead, the larviform adult female develops directly from the seventh larval instar and remains as a permanent parasite.

The mode of fertilization of these females is not completely understood. It is strongly suspected, however, that the seminal fluid enters via the route of the triungulin's escape.

Parasitized insects are readily spotted by the trained investigator, for the parasites protrude their anterior ends from between two of the host's abdominal segments (Plate 23–12, Fig. 3). If the protrusion is flat and disc shaped, it is the head of a female; but if it is rounded and tuberculate, it is the anterior end of the cylindrical body of a male puparium. The most complete account of the life history of a strepsipterid is that given by Nassonow (1892) for *Xenos vesparum.*

EFFECTS OF STREPSIPTERANS ON HOSTS

Larvae of *Xenos vesparum,* lying between the host's organs, absorb the host's blood through their body surfaces. As they increase in size, they can push the surrounding organs out of position, although the mechanical pressure does little damage to the host. The insect host, however, may suffer from malnutrition resulting from the loss of blood.

As many as 31 strepsipteran larvae have been found within the same host. Female hymenopterans appear to be preferred over males as hosts. The heads of parasitized hymenopterans often become smaller, more globular, and more hairy. The pollen-collecting apparatus of female hosts is much reduced, their hind legs are modified to resemble those of males, and even the yellow color of the male may be acquired. Furthermore, the sting is reduced in size. Parasitic castration is suspected, because the ovaries become smaller, the oocytes in them degenerate, and there is evidence that parasitized females are infertile. In males, the copulatory apparatus is reduced, and the testes are reduced in size, although unlike the ovaries, they remain functional.

SYSTEMATICS AND BIOLOGY

Numerous species of the Strepsiptera are found in North America. The taxonomic studies of Pierce (1909, 1911) and Bohart (1941) should be consulted by those interested in classification. The volume by Clausen (1940) should also be consulted since it includes much information on the biology of strepsipterans.

The order includes four families a key to which follows.*

1. Tarsi are five-segmented, with two claws . . . .**Mengeidae**
2. Tarsi possess four or fewer segments, lack claws.
   A. Tarsi are four-segmented. Antennae are four- or six-segmented . . . . **Stylopidae**
   B. Tarsi are two-segmented. Antennae are four-segmented . . . . **Elenchidae**
   C. Tarsi are three-segmented. Antennae are seven-segmented. Third, fourth and fifth segments are prolonged laterally. Seventh segment is elongate . . . .**Halictophagidae**

---

*Essentially after Borror and DeLong (1954).

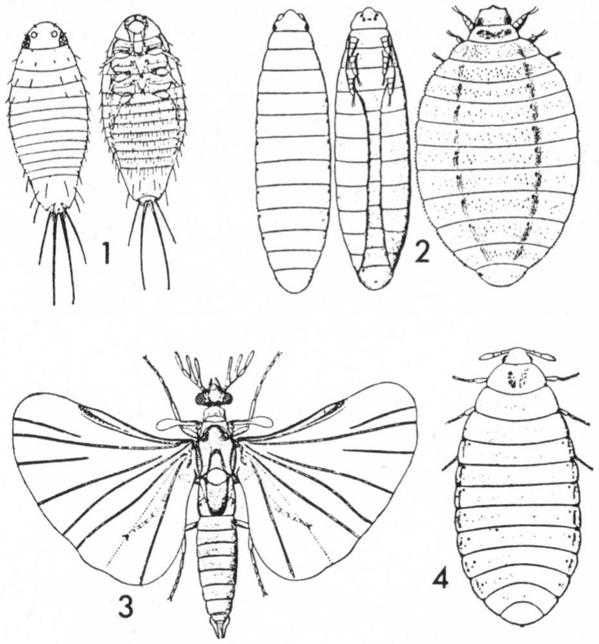

Plate 23-13   Stages in the life cycle of *Eoxenos laboulbenei.* **1.** First stage larva. **2.** Larvae from body of a thysanuran, showing the sides rolled in and expanded after the larva escapes from the host. **3.** Adult male. **4.** Wingless adult female. (All figures after Silvestri, from Baer's *Ecology of Animal Parasites,* University of Illinois Press, Urbana, Ill.)

FAMILY MENGEIDAE

Members of the Mengeidae are generally considered the least specialized of the strepsipterans. They are mostly free-living and usually found under stones.

Eoxenos laboulbenei

The larvae of one species, *Eoxenos laboulbenei,* are endoparasitic in the body cavity of thysanurans (Plate 23–13).

LIFE CYCLE OF *Eoxenos laboulbenei.* The minute larvae of *E. laboulbenei,* measuring only 200 μ in length, penetrate between the abdominal segments of the body of thysanurans, *Lepisma aurea, L. wasmanni,* and *L. crassipes.* Here the larvae metamorphose into second stage larvae that molt, after ingesting nourishment, and become third stage larvae.

Third stage larvae are readily recognizable, for their bodies are folded toward the ventral surface and appear to be cigar shaped. Each host generally includes no more than two or three larvae. The host dies when the third stage larvae emerges from it. The emerged larvae unfolds and become flattened. Pupation occurs on the ground.

Adult males are winged while adult females are wingless. Although the female possesses a genital pore, the sperm do not enter this orifice during fertilization. Instead, the male pierces the female's body cuticle with its copulatory apparatus and introduces sperm through the opening. The female's genital pore is apparently only used as a birth pore. *Eoxenos laboulbenei,* like all strepsipterans, is ovoviviparous. The larvae emerging from the female seek a new host immediately. Thus, in this mengeid strepsipteran apparently only the larvae are parasitic.

Variations of this life history pattern do occur. Parthenogenic females occur, they do not emerge from the pupal exuviae but their vaginal pores do open on the surface. It is through this pore that young larvae emerge. In addition, although thysanurans are generally infected in the autumn and the strepsipteran larvae pass the winter within their hosts, parthenogenic females, protected by the pupal exuviae are capable of overwintering in soil, and their larvae attack new hosts in the spring.

In addition to *Eoxenos,* the Mengeidae includes *Triozocera* (Plate 23–14, Fig. 1).

FAMILY STYLOPIDAE

The Stylopidae is the largest family of the Strepsiptera. Most members are parasites of bees, but a few are parasites of wasps. The stylopids are generally considered to be more specialized than the mengeids. Conversely, the

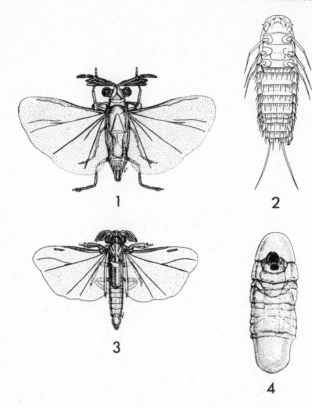

Plate 23-14   **Strepsiptera. 1.** *Triozocera mexicana*, male. **2.** *Stylops californica*, triungulin, ventral view. **3.** *Halictophagus oncometopiae*, male. **4.** *Halictophagus oncometopiae*, wingless female, ventral view. (All figures courtesy of Pierce and the U.S. National Museum.)

life cycles of stylopids are less complicated, because the number of larval stages are generally reduced. The developmental pattern is essentially that given under "Strepsipteran Life Cycle Pattern" (p. 643).

When *Stylops* (Plate 23-14, Fig. 2) and *Hylecthrus* parasitize solitary bees and *Xenos* parasitizes *Polistes metricus* and other social wasps, there is a synchronization between the life cycle of the parasite and that of the host. Usually, the parasite is in the second larval instar stage when the host larva is about to undergo its nymphal molt. Although never demonstrated, it is possible that an endocrinic synchronization takes place during these relationships.

OTHER STREPSIPTERAN FAMILIES

FAMILY ELENCHIDAE. Members of this relatively small family are parasites of plant hoppers (Fulgoridae).

FAMILY HALICTOPHAGIDAE. Members of the Halictophagidae parasitize Hemiptera, Homoptera, and crickets. This large family includes the common genus *Halictophagus* (Plate 23-12, Figs. 3 and 4).

INSECT PHYSIOLOGY AND HOST-PARASITE RELATIONSHIPS

The physiology of insects, whether of free-living or parasitic species, has become a distinct, specialized field of study. Except for some of the endoparasitic insects, such as myiasis-causing dipteran larvae, the parasitic larvae of certain hymenopterans, and the strepsipterans, the basic physiological processes within the body of various insects follow essentially comparable pathways. An attempt to survey the entire field of insect physiology has not been made here. Rather, an attempt has been made to emphasize some aspects of insect physiology that are directly correlated with host-parasite relationships. Readers interested in the general field of insect physiology should consult the volume edited by Roeder (1953) or the textbook by Wigglesworth (1939), both of which include noteworthy discussions concerning symbiotic insects. Furthermore, the textbook by Patton (1963), the comprehensive reviews by House (1958) of the nutritional requirements and by Dethier (1957) of sensory physiology should be consulted.

Oxygen Requirements

Parasitic insects, particularly the haematophagous species, are true aerobic animals well equipped with complex tracheal systems for the distribution and absorption of oxygen throughout the body tissues and for the elimination of carbon dioxide. However, the amount of oxygen required at each stage during development generally varies. The sensitivity of *Aëdes* spp. eggs to oxygen tension is well known. In eggs that are normally oviposited on moist soil or debris, the reduction of dissolved oxygen from 7 ppm (parts per million) to 3 ppm induces hatching, if the embryonic development is completed. However, a similar reduction of oxygen tension is not necessary to cause hatching of eggs in species *Aëdes* that normally oviposit in water.

The larvae of all mosquitoes require oxygen. For example, if *Culex pipiens* larvae are submerged in water of low oxygen tension, death occurs in approximately 1 hour. The survival rate of mosquito larvae when thus submerged depends to a great degree on the amount of body surface respiration and hence is directly correlated with size and permeability of the exoskeleton to oxygen molecules.

In the tracheal system, some insects possess specialized secondary mechanisms that permit more efficient transportation of gases and certain other metabolic end products. Such mechanisms are particularly pronounced among the Siphonaptera. Hefford (1938) reported that tracheal pulsations occur in certain fleas. When the oxygen is absorbed from within the closed tracheal system in these insects, in time the intratracheal pressure falls below the hydrostatic pressure of the surrounding haemocoel, resulting in collapse of the less rigid portions of the tracheal system. When the spiracles are reopened, air rushes in to fill the collapsed portions, inflating these, as well as the air sacs. Thus, the flea possesses a mechanical ventilation that supplements the normal diffusion process. Wigglesworth (1939) reported that in certain fleas and mosquito larvae, liquid is normally found within the tracheoles. This intratracheal fluid is withdrawn into the tissues during muscular activity but is released into the tracheoles again during periods of muscular relaxation. Movement of this fluid is involved in regulation of the passage of oxygen to the tissues and in removal of carbon dioxide and other metabolic end products.

Temperature is a critical factor in insect respiratory activities. In fact, it has been suggested that temperature is the only governing factor in the respiration of *Glossina*. Increases in respiratory rate generally accompany rises in temperature; however, on reaching a critical thermal point, which varies among species, heat inactivation of the animal becomes apparent. Although heat inactivation is markedly noticeable, oxygen consumption does not cease with the "death" of the animal. Instead, in some insects, such as *Calliphora* and *Sarcophaga* larvae, the rates increase concomitant with the browning of the animals' tissues for 24 hours after heat inactivation is initiated.

In insects that are parasitic in the alimentary tract of their host, respiration is microaerobic (or oligopneustic) and possibly nonaerobic (or apneustic) (Edwards, 1953).* All or most of the required oxygen is obtained by diffusion from the host's semifluid intestinal environment. The morphology and physiology of endoparasitic dipterans are greatly influenced by the fact that there are only trace quantities of oxygen within their hosts. These dipterans neither grow rapidly nor feed actively until contact is made with atmospheric air. However, respiration is definitely carried on, often by means of specialized mechanisms.

The oxygen tension in the environment governs the degree of respiratory activity pursued by the larvae. For example, in larvae of *Gasterophilus* spp., first larval instars live in the host's epithelial tissue and are metapneustic, while second larval instars are located in the host's pharynx, where there is an abundance of oxygen, and hence are amphipneustic.

In addition to diffusion of gases through the body surface of dipteran larvae, other mechanisms are employed in some instances. For example, in the larva of *Ginglymyia*, an endoparasite of the larva of *Eiophila* (Lepidoptera), the postabdominal spiracles protrude from the body surface and are in direct contact with air bubbles trapped in the web surrounding the host.

In the first larval instar of *Melinda*, which invades the kidney of snails, the posterior

---

*The respiratory activities of arthropods are commonly placed in the following categories: the apneustic type, in which no O_2 is utilized from the environment; the oligopneustic type, in which only a little O_2 is utilized; the metapneustic type, in which considerable O_2 is consumed, although not as much as among free-living forms; and the amphipneustic type in which a large quantity of O_2 is utilized.

spiracles protrude into the pulmonary cavity of the host, thus contacting an oxygen source. In dermal myiasis-causing dipteran larvae, the pore connecting the exterior with the sac in which the parasite is found serves as an entrance for atmospheric oxygen. Furthermore, the posterior end of the maggot, bearing the spiracles, is as a rule directed toward the aperture.

Since the later larval instars of *Gasterophilus* spp. are spent in the host's stomach or intestine, where there is little or no oxygen, these maggots are fortified with oxygen stored within the tracheal haemoglobin-containing cells for consumption during this period of oligopneustic or possible apneustic activity. Keilin and Wang (1946) reported that the haemoglobin of *Gasterophilus* is composed of 2 haeme globin units instead of the 4 units found in nearly all vertebrate haemoglobins.

Bloodsucking insects undoubtedly acquire a certain amount of oxygen from the oxyhaemoglobin in the ingested erythrocytes. The haemoglobin ingested by *Rhodnius* is nearly completely digested, for only a very small amount of protohaematin can be found in the feces.

Although parasitic hymenopteran larvae possess tracheae, these larvae do not attempt to reach the respiratory organs of their host, where they could obtain oxygen. All gaseous exchanges take place through the extremely thin body cuticle. Oxygen is derived from the host's haemolymph.

Metabolism

Relatively little is known about cellular metabolism in parasitic insects, although there is no reason to believe that it is very different from that of free-living species. Aerobic metabolism appears to predominate in most species. Anaerobic metabolism has been demonstrated in the larva of *Tenebrio molitor* and undoubtedly occurs in other species. Gaarder has shown that if this larva is maintained at a low oxygen tension (3 per cent) for several hours and then returned to atmospheric oxygen tension, an oxygen debt can be demonstrated, because oxygen uptake is raised above normal for some time. This phenomenon, as in certain other parasites (p. 343), is attributed to the accumulation of intermediary products of anaerobic metabolism that can and do become oxidized only after oxygen is restored. Similarly, insects maintained in complete absence of oxygen demonstrate an oxygen debt when they are returned to an oxygen-containing environment.

During aerobic metabolism, undoubtedly both carbohydrate catabolism, involving utilization of stored glycogen, and lipid catabolism provide most of the required energy. At a given temperature, the metabolic rate of a given species shows a fairly definite relation to size. In general, metabolism per gram of body weight decreases as the insect grows. The metabolic rate declines in such a manner that the respiratory rate is proportional to the mass of the insect multiplied by an exponential factor of $\frac{2}{3}$.

Although certain endoparasitic fly larvae, such as those of *Gasterophilus* (p. 616), can be maintained for surprisingly long periods in the absence of oxygen, they show almost no accumulation of lactic acid, thus suggesting an extremely low level or perhaps the absence of anaerobic fermentative metabolism. In these animals, evidence indicates that the glycogen stored in their bodies is converted to lipids, and the oxygen set free during the process is utilized.

Concerning carbohydrate uptake and metabolism in insects, it is known that the amount of blood sugars varies greatly between species. Analyses of insect blood sugars have revealed that glucose is the predominent sugar in most species, but other sugars may be present as well. Fructose, for example, often occurs in relatively high concentrations, as does the disaccharide trehalose. The presence of trehalose is of particular interest, for Treherne at Cambridge has indicated that its presence is correlated with the passage of sugar through the intestinal wall in insects. He found that glucose is absorbed from the intestine in such a manner that active transport is suggested in addition to diffusion. Glucose does not appear entirely as glucose in the blood, for when the glucose concentration in the intestine is low, nearly all sugar in the blood is in the form trehalose. Treherne considered the synthesis of trehalose from glucose a part of the active transport mechanism that permits the transfer of glucose from the intestine to the blood. It is now known that trehalose synthesis and breakdown can also occur in the insect's fat body and that trehalose can be converted to glycogen via its initial breakdown to glucose-6-phosphate (Plate 23–15).

Amino acid requirements and utilization by insects are listed in Table 23–2.

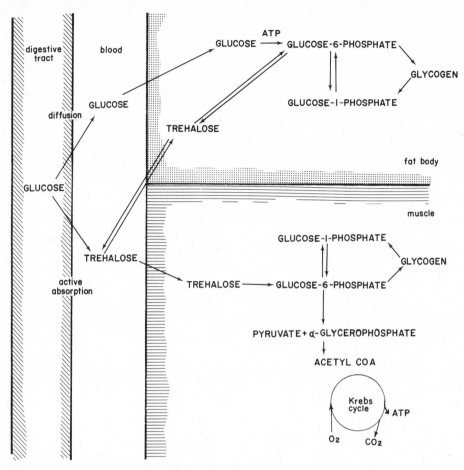

Plate 23-15   Transport and metabolism of glucose in an insect.

Water Absorption

In almost all parasitic insects, especially the ectoparasitic species, an aquatic medium is not required for the absorption of water. In *Cimex lectularius,* for example, water can be absorbed from vapor in the air, if the air is highly saturated. Flea larvae can also absorb water from vapor in the air, although the relative humidity need be only 50 per cent or slightly higher. It is presumed that absorption of water occurs through the general body cuticle—the mechanism in acarines—but specific experiments demonstrating this phenomenon remain to be contributed.

Growth Requirements

The growth requirements of parasitic insects constitute an extremely complex phase of the physiology of these animals and are by no means completely understood. An excellent review is provided by House (1958). In several instances the fecundity of the adult insect has been shown to be directly correlated with nutrition. In *Stomoxys calcitrans,* for example, Glaser (1923) reported that if flies are fed on host's serum or washed blood cells separately, no eggs are produced, but the feeding of a recombination of these two blood fractions results in normal longevity and egg production. This experiment demonstrates that it is not entirely the quantity of blood protein that influences fecundity but specific proteins or accessory substances that only the combination of serum and blood cells provide, that are the important factors. Similarly, in *Lucilia sericata,* which normally requires the ingestion of meat juices before oviposition, if the normal diet is replaced by milk, serum, or other protein-rich materials, oviposition does not occur. However, a combination of serum with auto-lyzed yeast produces oviposition, thus indicat-ing that this artificial diet includes the sub-stances normally present in meat juices that induce egg production or include sufficiently similar substances to induce egg production (Hobson, 1938).

Numerous authors have reported that various mosquitoes oviposit prior to the intake of a blood meal. This is true in *Aëdes scutellaris, A. atropalpus, A. concolor,* and *Culex pipiens.* How-ever, Weyer (1934) showed that the number of these autogenous eggs is dependent to a con-siderable extent on the adequacy of the larval diet. Even in these instances, blood meals necessarily precede further periods of oviposition and a minimal quantity of blood is necessary. In *Aëdes aegypti,* for example, the females require at least 0.82 mg. of blood to induce egg pro-duction, although a normal full meal consists of 2 mg. of blood. It is now clear that the nutritional requirements for oviposition consist of specific proteins as well as quantity.

The nature or quantity of the required pro-teins inducing egg production varies between types of blood. It has been mentioned earlier (p. 594) that *Culex pipiens* will lay twice as many eggs per milligram of blood ingested if fed on canary blood instead of on human blood. Sim-ilarly *Aëdes aegypti* will oviposit more eggs if fed on guinea pig, rabbit, canary, or frog blood instead of on human blood. These results strongly suggest degrees of host specificity as measured by egg productivity. Investigations along these lines may well lead to a better understanding of host specificity and host-parasite relationships.

Experiments designed to isolate the specific substances required for egg production have revealed that a combination of substances is required. For example, Yoeli and Mer (1938) showed that if *Anopheles sacharovi* females were fed on raisins, sugar solutions, and haemoglobin solutions, only partially developed ovaries resulted. If these females were fed serum alone, even less ovarial development took place. But if they were fed on serum and washed erythro-cytes without haemoglobin, sexual maturity and egg production followed. This suggests that haemoglobin contributes nothing. Green-berg (1951), however, showed that a diet including haemoglobin is more beneficial to *Aëdes aegypti* than blood including erythrocytes

with the pigment removed, although the latter diet will bring about egg production of lesser quality. These results indicate that haemo-globin by itself does not elicit egg production and that blood without haemoglobin is neces-sary but not ideal. The combination of the two is prerequisite for the production of large numbers of eggs. Actually it is suspected that serum, erythrocyte protoplasm, and haemo-globin, or parts of all three, contribute to normal fecundity (Woke, 1937).

Among the nutrients required for growth, the amino acids cystine and glycine play important roles in the growth of mosquitoes and probably of most insects (Table 23–2). If cystine is deprived, even if DL–methionine is present in large quantities, adult mosquitoes found within the puparia will all die with only their anterior ends projecting from the puparia. If glutathione is introduced in place of cystine, normal emergence takes place, but the growth rate and survival period of the larvae are reduced.

In addition to cystine and glycine, other substances, especially those of the vitamin B complex, play important contributary roles in growth and metabolism. For example, dietary phenylalanine and tyrosine are important for growth and pigment formation in *Aëdes,* but diets deficient in one, but not both, of these affect normal rather than aborted growth.

Trager (1948) and Lichtenstein (1948) have demonstrated in *Aëdes aegypti* and *Culex molestus* that thiamine, riboflavin, pyridoxine, niacin, pantothenic acid, biotin, pteroylglutamic acid, and choline are all required accessory growth factors. The role of biotin is of special interest, for if biotin is partially replaced by oleic acid, lecithin, and related lipids in proper concen-trations, larval growth is fairly normal but metamorphosis does not occur. A comparison of the amount of growth factors of the vitamin B complex in various animals is presented in Table 23–3.

In addition to the previously mentioned growth factors, Subbarow and Trager (1940) reported that yeast nucleic acid enhances the growth of *Aëdes aegypti.* This phenomenon has since been demonstrated in other insects as well.

What are the sources of these growth factors? Some of them undoubtedly are supplied by ingested nutrients, but in some insects, espe-cially the haematophagous species, ingested foods are deficient in some of these requirements. Numerous insects, including many parasitic

Table 23-2.   A Comparison of Amino Acid Requirements and Utilization by Bacteria, Certain Protozoa, Insects, and Vertebrates

Amino acid	Bacteria	Protozoa other than green flagellates	Insects	Vertebrates
Leucine	ru	ru	R*	R
Lysine	ru	ru	R	R
Methionine	ru	ru	R	R
Phenylalanine	ru	ru	R*	R
Threonine	ru	ru	R*	R
Histidine	ru	ru	R	R
Isoleucine	ru	ru	R	R
Tryptophan	ru	ru	R*	R
Valine	ru	ru	R*	R
Arginine	ru	ru	R	r
Cystine-cysteine	ru	u	R*	N
Glutamic acid	ru	u	r	r
Glycine	ru	ru	r	r
Proline	ru	ru	r	r
Serine	ru	ru	r	N
Alanine	ru	u	r*	N
Aspartic acid	ru	u	r*	N
Tyrosine	ru	ru	N	N

(Data from Scheer, B.T. 1963. *Animal Physiology*, Wiley, New York.)

*Some substitutions are possible; r, required by some; R, required by all tested; u, used by some; N, not required by any. Phenylalanine will substitute for threonine, tryptophan for valine, valine for leucine, tyrosine for phenylalanine, methionine for cystine (except among certain mosquitoes), aspartic acid or glutamic acid for alanine, and glutamic acid for aspartic acid in some species.

species, possess mutualists within their gut (extracellular) or in their tissues (intracellular) that supply accessory growth factors, thus enabling the insects to survive on diets that would otherwise be inadequate (Richards and Brooks, 1958). Yeast and bacteria are the most common mutualists of nonbloodsucking insects that spend their larval stages feeding on diets rich in microorganisms—for example, organic debris.

Bloodfeeders, such as *Pediculus humanus,* possess minute bacteria-like bodies, known as bacteroids, found in specialized structures known as stomach discs, or mycetomes (mycetocytes) (Plate 23–16). Aschner (1934) and Aschner and Ries (1933) have demonstrated the dependency of the louse on these mutualists. These investigators reported that if the hosts are deprived of their intracellular bacteroids while in the egg stage, they die by the fifth or

Table 23-3. Minimal Amounts of Growth Factors of the Vitamin B Complex Required for Normal Growth by Certain Insects and Selected Vertebrates*†

Species	Thiamin	Riboflavin	Pyridoxine	Niacin	Pantothenic Acid	Biotin	Pteroylglutamic Acid	Choline
Aëdes aegypti	0.1[27]	0.5[27,22]	1.0[23]	1.0[22]	1.0[23]	0.015[20]	+	+
Tribolium confusum	1.0[4]	2.0[4]	1.0[4]	8.0[4]	4.0[4]	0.05[4]	0.25[4]	+
Tenebrio molitor	+	+	+	+	+	−	0.3[5]	−
Blatella germanica	+	+	−	−	−	−	−	2000[15]
Drosophila melanogaster	0.1[27]	0.5[27,22]	1.0[23]	1.0[22]	1.0[23]	0.015[20]	+	+
Chick	0.8[12]	6.0[10]	3.0[11]	18.0[2]	9.0[9]	0.1[8]	0.5[17]	2000[14]
Rat	1.0[12]	3.0[13]	1.5[3]	0[1]	10.0[7]	+	+	200[16]
Dog	+	4.0[6]	+	10.0[31]	+	−	−	+
Monkey	+	0.25[28]	−	−	+	0.1[29]	+	−
Man	1.5[30]	3.0[21]	1.5[30]	20.0[30]	10.0[30]	+	−	−

*Quantities given as micrograms/gram of diet or per milliliter of nutrient medium.
†Data from various authors compiled by Trager in *Insect Physiology*; with permission of John Wiley.

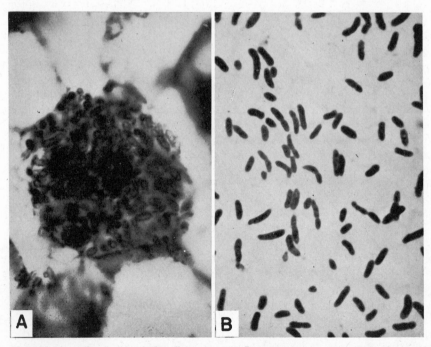

Plate 23-16   Bacteroids of *Blattella germanica*. A. A single mycetocyte enclosing bacteroids, which appear hallow as the result of fixation. **B.** Smear of fat body, showing bacteroids in various stages. (After Brooks in Roth and Willis, 1960.)

sixth day of larval life. If the bacteroids are removed from the hosts during the third larval stadium, the larvae will develop into adults. In such adults, the males are normal, but the females lay very few eggs and none of these is viable. Brooks (1956, 1960) has summarized most of the information concerning the bacteroid mutualists of cockroaches. She has demonstrated that these bacteroids are passed from one generation to the next transovarially. It is generally assumed that in *P. humanus* and other bacteroid-including insects this is also the case.

Various endoparasitic insects, such as certain strepsipteran larvae, the early stages of many tachinid larvae, and the first stage larvae of some hymenopterans, possess no buccal opening. Furthermore, in some of these, the gut is not continuous from mouth to anus. In these endoparasites, nutrient must necessarily be absorbed through the body wall. The exact requirements remain to be determined.

Digestion

Parasitic insects that are capable of feeding, unlike the helminths, are able to digest large molecules of nutrient. This is possible because of enzyme-secreting cells that line the alimentary tract. *Aëdes* is a good example in this respect. If starch or other polysaccharides are fed to this mosquito, glycogen is accumulated in the posterior half of the ventriculus before it appears in the fat bodies. This convincingly suggests that the starch and sugar molecules are split (hydrolyzed) in portions of the gut anterior to the posterior half of the ventriculus. Simple sugars are then synthesized as glycogen for storage, thus suggesting that starch-splitting enzymes at least must be present. In *Anopheles* and *Aëdes,* digestion of the complex haemoglobin molecule takes place. Similar processes are found in other bloodsucking insects. Thus, the optimal pH of the gut is of critical importance, for this complements enzymatic action. Table 23-4 compares the gut pH in several insects.

Attraction of Insects to Hosts

The attraction of bloodsucking insects to their hosts is best thought of as manifestations of the sensory physiology of these animals.

TEMPERATURE OF HOST. Temperature plays an important role in attraction. For example, Herter (1934) reported that the bedbug *Cimex* prefers and is attracted to temperatures of approximately 35° C., which is about the tem-

Table 23-4.   Hydrogen Ion Concentration of Midgut Juices of Some Insects*

Species	pH
Thysanura	
Ctenolepisma	4.8-7.0
Orthoptera	
Blattella	6.2
Carausius	6.3
Various grasshoppers	5.8-7.5
Gryllus	7.6
Tettigonia	5.9
Anoplura	
Pediculus	7.2
Odonata	
Anax	6.8-7.2
Hemiptera	
Cimex	6.2
Nezara	7.2
Hymenoptera	
Apis	6.3
Polistes	7.3

*Data from Day and Waterhouse in *Insect Physiology*; K.D. Roeder, editor; with permission of John Wiley.

perature of the host's skin. Herter also reported that fleas are optimally attracted to a temperature of ±30° C. Again, this approximates the average mammalian skin temperature.

If *Pediculus* or *Schistocerca* is placed in an experimental gradient or on a host, it undergoes restless movements until it reaches an area of optimal temperature—one ranging from 26.4 to 29.7° C. It then settles down and begins feeding. Dethier (1957) summarized experiments performed on two lice, *Pediculus humanus* and *Haematopinus suis,* stating that these blood suckers are responsive to light, temperature, humidity, odor, and contact. Normally lice are negatively phototropic, but Hase (1915) demonstrated that starved *Pediculus* are positively phototropic.

HUMIDITY.   Lice are indifferent when placed in an environment where the relative humidity ranges from 10 to 60 per cent. They choose an area of high humidity (95 per cent) if the other choices are low (10, 32, and 47 per cent). On the other hand, if the choices include 95, 85, 76, and 60 per cent relative humidity, the lice pick one of the lower zones rather than the 95 per cent zone. Wigglesworth (1941) postulated that these insects prefer a medium humidity and avoid any change once they become established to a given humidity.

ENVIRONMENTAL TEMPERATURE. Activity of biting flies is correlated with environmental temperature. In *Stomoxys calcitrans,* the preferred temperatures range from 22 to 32° C., and the peak of activity occurs at 29° C. In *Fannia canicularis,* imagoes of which appear earlier in the year, the preferred temperatures range between 10 and 28° C.

OTHER FACTORS. Rahm (1957) reported that mosquitoes are attracted to dark clothing (optical attraction), humidity and heat (physical attraction). A combination of these two factors is more attractive than each one singly. Mosquitoes are also attracted to odors (chemical attraction) given off by the hands, although they are not attracted to perspiration.

Effects of Parasite on Host

The obvious effects of parasitic insects on their hosts are (1) loss of blood to bloodsucking species; (2) introduction of toxins into the host during feeding; (3) infections and general weakening brought about by myiasis-causing species; (4) infection by pathogenic microorganisms carried by these insects; (5) inflicting of wounds that are subject to secondary infections; and (6) destruction of body tissues, even resulting in death when endoparasites are present.

INSECT TOXINS AND SECRETIONS. In *Anopheles,* each salivary gland is made up of three lobes (Plate 23–17). The lateral lobes include no haemagglutinin and little anticoagulin but do include large amounts of toxic substance. On the other hand, the median lobe contains a strong haemagglutinin and a strong anti-coagulin. The toxic secretions of the lateral lobes are responsible for the local inflammation and itchy sensation of mosquito bites.

The toxin of *Aëdes* is thermostable. Metcalf (1945) reported that the anticoagulin is also stable and is active even in a dilution of 1:10,000. He also reported that the haemagglutinin is thermolabile but is active in a dilution of 1:1,000,000. The haemagglutinin, the anticoagulin, and the toxin are not found in male mosquitoes, which are not haematophagous.

The toxic effect of bloodsucking insects is not necessarily only local. In some instances the effect is systematic, the toxin being circulated by the blood stream. Dem'yanchenko (1957) reported that if bull calves are subjected to mass attacks by the blackfly *Eusimulium pusilla,* there is a rise in blood temperature and leukocyte count; a decrease in haemoglobin, erythrocyte, and lymphocyte counts; and a disappearance of monocytes. Furthermore, he found that if an emulsion of the fly's thoracic sections including the salivary glands is injected subcutaneously, there is a distinct localized inflammation accompanied by general organic reactions. These reactions are much more severe if the emulsion is injected intravenously.

The toxicity of myiasis-causing maggots has interested parasitologists for decades. Seyderhelm and Seyderhelm (1914) and Seyderhelm (1918) reported extraction from *Gasterophilus* larvae of a toxic substance that they termed oestrin. They claimed that oestrin is responsible for pernicious anemia of horses, but du Troit (1919) and Marxer (1920) stated that the Seyderhelms were in error. Zibordi (1920) and du Troit reported that extracts of *Gasterophilus* larvae may kill horses, or at least effect transitory toxicity. Cameron (1922) stated that the symptoms of toxicity are mainly due to sensitization from a previous infection. However, Roubaud and Perard (1924) reported that they were able to effect symptoms of toxicity in small laboratory animals that positively had not previously been exposed to the fly. This question appears to have been at least partially settled by the more modern investigations of Grab (1957), who reported that in his experiments with thirty horses, symptoms typical of anaphylactic shock, accompanied by changes in the blood chemistry and pathologies of certain internal organs, are effected by single intravenous injections of extract prepared from the larvae of *Gasterophilus.* However, when sixty-two 2 to 5 month old rabbits, guinea pigs, and mice are similarly injected, no reactions occur. Only after the

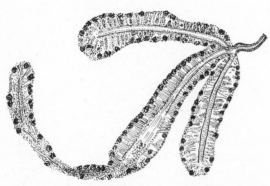

Plate 23-17   Trilobed salivary gland of anopheline mosquito. Notice inclusion of malarial sporozoites. (Redrawn after Wenyon, 1926.)

serum from one of the experimentally injected horses is first introduced into the laboratory animal, or upon second challenge with the extract, do the reactions become apparent. Grab's results appear to uphold Cameron's hypothesis that symptoms of toxicity, at least in laboratory animals, result only after a previous challenge. Why the horses reacted to the first injection is not clear, but it is possible that the horses had been previously infected with *Gasterophilus*—in other words, they were

hypersensitive—and the reactions actually represented anaphylactic shock as the symptoms suggested.

Relative to cutaneous myiasis-causing maggots, it is known that if the larvae of *Hypoderma* is crushed while in the skin of cattle, fever ensues, suggesting secretion of toxic substances. However, Roubaud and Perard (1924) reported that because small laboratory animals are only slightly sensitive to injections of the substance, the reaction in cattle may be anaphylactic.

LITERATURE CITED

Aschner, M. 1934. Studies on the symbiosis of the body louse. Elimination of the symbionts by centrifugation of the eggs. Parasitology, *26:* 309–314.

Aschner, M., and E. Ries. 1933. Das Verhalten der Kleiderlaus bei Ausschaltung ihrer Symbionten. Eine experimentelle Symbiosestudie. Ztschr. Morphol. Oekol. Tiere, *26:* 529–590.

Bohart, R. M. 1941. A revision of the Strepsiptera with special reference to the species of North America. Univ. Cal. Publ. Ent., *7:* 91–160.

Brooks, M. A. 1956. Nature and significance of intracellular bacteroids in cockroaches. Proc. 10th Intern. Congr. Ent. (Montreal), *2:* 311–314.

Brooks, M. A. 1960. Some dietary factors that affect ovarial transmission of symbiotes. Proc. Helminth. Soc. Wash., *27:* 212–220.

Cameron, A. G. 1922. Bot anaphylaxis. J. Am. Vet. Med. A. *62:* 332–342.

Chopard, L. 1923. Les parasites de la Mante religieuse. *Riela manticida* Kieff. Ann. Soc. Entomol. France, *91:* 249–264.

Clausen, C. P. 1940. Entomophagous Insects. McGraw-Hill, New York.

Comstock, J. H. 1949. An Introduction to Entomology. 9th Ed. Comstock Publ. Co., Ithaca, N. Y.

Dem'yanchenko, G. F. 1957. The toxicity of black-fly (Simuliidae) saliva on the organism of farm animals. Tr. Vses. N–I. Inst. Vet. Sanitarii Ektoparazitol., *1957:* 91–104.

Dethier, V. G. 1957. The sensory physiology of blood-sucking arthropods. Exptl. Parasit., *6:* 68–122.

Du Troit, P. J. 1919. Gastruslarven und infektiöse Anämie der Pferde. Monatsch. Prakt. Tierh., *30:* 97–118.

Edwards, G. A. 1953. Respiratory mechanisms. *In* Roeder, K. D., 1953, pp. 55–95 (see Roeder, 1953).

Ferris, G. F. 1919. Some records of Polyctenidae (Hemiptera). N. Y. Ent. Soc., *27:* 261–263.

Fracker, S. B. 1914. A systematic outline of the Reduviidae of North America. Iowa Acad. Sci., *19:* 217–252.

Glaser, R. W. 1923. The effect of food on longevity and reproduction in flies. Exptl. Zool., *38:* 383–412.

Grab, B. G. 1957. The nature of reactive charges in the organism of horses exposed to the parasitism of horse botfly (*Gasterophilus equi*) larvae. Tr. Kievsk. Vet. Inst., *1957:* 157–172.

Greenberg, J. 1951. Some nutritional requirements of adult mosquitoes (*Aëdes aegypti*) for oviposition. J. Nutrition, *43:* 27–35.

Hase, A. 1915. Beiträge zu einer Biologie der Kleiderlaus (*Pediculus corporis* de Geer *vestimenti* Nitzsch.). Z. angew. Entomol., *2:* 265–359.

Hefford, G. M. 1938. Tracheal pulsation in the flea. Exptl. Biol., *15:* 327–338.

Herter, K. 1934. Eine verbesserte Temperaturorgel und ihre Anwendung auf Insekten und Saugetiere. Biol. Zentr., *54:* 487–507.

Hobson, R. P. 1938. Sheep blow-fly investigations. Observations on the development of eggs and oviposition in the sheep blow-fly, *Lucilia sericata* Mg. Ann. Appl. Biol., *38:* 383–412.

Horvath, G. 1912. Revision of the American Cimicidae. Ann. Musei Nat. Hungarici, *10:* 257–262.

House, H. L. 1958. Nutritional requirements of insects associated with animal parasitism. Exptl. Parasit., *7:* 555–609.

Lichtenstein, E. P. 1948. Growth of *Culex molestus* under sterile conditions. Nature, *162:* 227.

Marchal, P. 1904. Recherches sur la biologie et le développement des Hymenoptères parasites. 1. La polyembryonie spécifique ou germinogonie. Arch. Zool. Exp. Gén. (Ser. 4), *2:* 257–335.

Marxer, A. 1920. Die Beziehungen der *Gasterophilus*-Larven zur infektiösen Anämie. Ztschr. Immunitatsforsch. Exper. Therap., 1. Teil: Orig., *29:* 1–10.

Metcalf, R. L. 1945. The physiology of the salivary glands of *Anopheles quadrimaculatus.* Nat. Malaria Soc., *4:* 271–278.

Muesebeck, C. F. W., K. V. Krombein, H. K. Townes, et al. 1951. Hymenoptera of America North of Mexico. Synoptic catalogue. U.S.D.A. Agric. Monogr. No. 2.

Paillot, A. 1937. Le développement embryonnaire d'*Amicroplus collaris* Spin., parasites des chenilles d'*Euxoa segetum* Schiff. Compt. Rend. Acad. Sci. Paris, *204:* 810–812.

Parker, H. L. 1931. *Macrocentrus gifuensis* Ashmead, a polyembryonic braconid parasite of the European corn borer. USDA Tech. Bull. 230, Washington.

Patterson, J. 1917. Studies on the biology of *Paracopidosomopsis.* I. Data on the sexes. Biol. Bull., *32:* 291–305.

Patterson, J. 1918. Studies on the biology of *Copidosomopsis.* IV. The asexual larvae. Biol. Bull., *35:* 362–371.

Patton, R. L. 1963. Insect Physiology. W. B. Saunders, Philadelphia, Pa.

Pierce, W. D. 1909. A Monographic Revision of the Twisted Winged Insects Comprising the Order Strepsiptera Kirby. U. S. Nat. Mus. Bull. No. 66.

Pierce, W. D. 1911. Strepsiptera. Genera Insect., Pasc. 121.

Rahm, V. 1957. Wichtige Faktoren bei Attraktion von Stechmücken durch den Menschen. Rev. Suizze Zool., *64:* 236–246.

Richards, A. G., and M. A. Brooks. 1958. Internal symbiosis in insects. Ann. Rev. Ent., *3:* 37–56.

Roeder, K. D. 1953 (ed.). Insect Physiology. John Wiley, New York.

Seyderhelm, K. R., and R. Seyderhelm. 1914. Die Ursache der perniziösen Anämie der Pferde ein Beitrag zum Problem des ultravisiblen Virus. Arch. Exp. Path. Pharmakol., *76:* 149: 201.

Seyderhelm, R. 1918. Über die Eigenschaften und Wirkungen des Oestrins und seine Beziehung zur perniziösen Anämie der Pferde. Arch. Exp. Path. Pharmakol., *82:* 253–326.

Subbarow, Y., and W. Trager. 1940. The chemical nature of growth factors required by mosquito larvae. II. Pantothenic acid and vitamin B_6. Gen. Physiol., *23:* 461–468.

Trager, W. 1948. Biotin and fat-soluble materials with biotin activity in the nutrition of mosquito larvae. J. Biol. Chem., *176:* 1211–1223.

Usinger, R. L. 1944. The Triatominae of North and Central America and the West Indies and Their Public Health Significance. Pub. Hlth. Bull. No. 288. Gov't Printing Office, Washington, D. C.

Weyer, F. 1934. Der Einfluss der Larvalernährung auf die Fortpflanzungsphysiologie verschiedener Stechmücken. Arch. Schiffs. Tropen-Hyg., *38:* 394–398.

Whiting, P. W. 1956. *Mormoniella* and the nature of the gene: *Mormoniella vitripennis* (Walker) (Hymenoptera: Pteromalidae). Proc. 10th Intern. Congr. Ent., *2:* 857–865.

Whiting, P. W. 1960. Polypoidy in *Mormoniella.* Genetics, *45:* 949–970.

Wigglesworth, V. B. 1939. The Principles of Insect Physiology. E. P. Dutton, New York.

Wigglesworth, V. B. 1941. The sensory physiology of the human louse, *Pediculus humanus corporis* de Geer (Anoplura). Parasitology, *33:* 67–109.

Woke, P. A. 1937. Effects of various blood fractions on egg production of *Aëdes aegypti.* Am. J. Hyg., *25:* 372–380.

Yoeli, M., and G. G. Mer. 1938. The relation of blood feeds to the maturation of ova in *Anopheles elutus.* Trans. Roy. Soc. Trop. Med. Hyg., *31:* 437–444.

Zibordi, D. 1920. Intorno al potere tossico degli estratti di *Gasterophilus equi.* Clin. Vet., Milano, *43:* 470–476.

SUGGESTED READING

Baer, J. G. 1952. Ecology of Animal Parasites. University of Illinois Press, Urbana, Ill., pp. 78–94. (In this section of Baer's monograph, the parasitic insects are discussed. The information is limited to representative endoparasites—primarily the strepsipterans and hymenopterans.)

Borror, D. J., and DeLong, D. M. 1960. An Introduction to the Study of Insects. Holt, Rinehart & Winston, New York. (This is a general introductory textbook on insects. The various sections devoted to the orders of insects, which include parasitic species, should prove to be valuable background material for those interested in haematophagous and endoparasitic insects. The section devoted to the parasitic hymenopterans is of particular interest since it includes effective taxonomic keys.)

Clausen, C. P. 1940. Entomophagous Insects. McGraw-Hill, New York. (This volume by a recognized authority still remains as the standard reference on the biology of insects that prey on or parasitize other insects. The sections devoted to the parasitic hymenopterans and strepsipterans should be consulted.)

Wigglesworth, V. B. 1939. The Principles of Insect Physiology. E. P. Dutton, New York. (Although somewhat outdated, this textbook is extremely well organized and should provide the beginning student with the basic principles and essentials of insect physiology.)

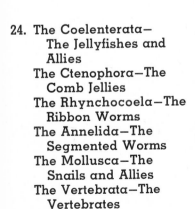

PART EIGHT

OTHER ANIMAL PARASITES

24

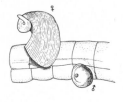

THE COELENTERATA—
The Jellyfishes and Allies
THE CTENOPHORA—
The Comb Jellies
THE RHYNCHOCOELA—
The Ribbon Worms
THE ANNELIDA—
The Segmented Worms
THE MOLLUSCA—
The Snails and Allies
THE VERTEBRATA
The Vertebrates

As stated in Chapter 1, parasitism is a way of life for which examples can be found in practically every major animal phylum. Although many of the parasitic animals have been considered separately in the foregoing chapters, the organisms discussed in this chapter are not by any means less important despite the fact that space limitations prevent their being considered in separate chapters. Some of the animals considered in this chapter demonstrate some of the most profound adaptations to parasitism known in the Animal Kingdom. This is particularly true among the molluscs.

Students of parasitology should become familiar with the animals presented in the following discussion. Undoubtedly future explorations of these relatively little studied parasites will reveal many exciting adaptations not readily appreciated among some of the better known categories of animal parasites.

Parasitism is rarely practiced by members of the phyla Porifera, Coelenterata, Ctenophora, and Rhynchocoela. However, in each of these invertebrate groups, a few species have been reported to be symbiotic, some being true parasites.

PHYLUM PORIFERA

In the Porifera, the marine *Cliona celata* bores into the shells of molluscs. Practically nothing is known about the biology of this sponge. Injured molluscs are able to repair their shells if the surrounding water temperature is above 7° C.

PHYLUM COELENTERATA

Members of the Coelenterata are all aquatic, primarily marine, and are found attached or free-floating. Their diploblastic bodies are either radial or biradial, without a head or other organ systems, and as a rule the alimentary tract is incomplete—that is, there is a mouth and enteron but no anus. The nervous system is diffuse and tactile tentacles may be present surrounding the mouth. All coelenterates possess stinging structures known as nematocysts.

The life cycles of coelenterates are interesting for they undergo metagenesis, or alternation of generations, alternating between the asexual polyp stage and the sexual medusa, or jellyfish, stage. However, as a result of evolutionary changes, the prominence of the medusa and polyp stages may not be equal. For example, in the fresh-water jellyfish *Craspedocusta sowerbyi,* the medusa is conspicuous, while the minute polyps, resting at the bottom of lakes and ponds, are seldom seen. In some species, such as the familiar fresh-water hydras, the medusa stage is completely absent. For a description of coelenterate morphology, the reader is referred to the authoritative volume by Hyman (1940).

Almost all members of the three classes of coelenterates—Hydrozoa, Scyphozoa, and Anthozoa—numbering approximately 10,000 species, are free-living. A few species have been reported to be symbiotic, but little is known about the biology of these.

CLASS HYDROZOA

Several species of the class Hydrozoa are known to be symbiotic during some phase of their life cycles. For example, the planula larva of *Cunina proboscidea* is parasitic, attached to another coelenterate, *Geryonia;* and the larva of *C. peregrina* is parasitic on *Rhopalonema velatum.*

Life Cycle of *Cunina*

There is usually no polyp stage in the life cycle of the Narcomedusae, the group to which *Cunina proboscidea* and *C. peregrina* belong. The egg produced by the maternal medusa hatches, and the escaping form is a ciliated planula larva, which differentiates into an actinula larva, which in turn, differentiates into a medusa.

In the case of *Cunina proboscidea,* Bigelow (1909) reported that the egg develops in the mesoglea (a jelly-like layer between the epidermis and gastrodermis) of the maternal medusa and is enveloped by a nurse cell, or phorocyte. The planula larva developing from the egg metamorphoses into a reduced medusa that produces gametes and then degenerates. The planulae resulting from this generation become attached to the host (to *Geryonia* in the case of *C. proboscidea,* and to *Rhopalonema* in the case of *C. peregrina*) and develop parasitically. Both *Geryonia* and *Rhopalonema* are also medusae. Each *Cunina* planula becomes flattened out as a stolon that embraces the host (Plate 24–1, Fig. 1) and buds off the definitive medusae (Plate 24–1, Fig. 2).

Nothing is known about the relationship between *Cunina* and *Geryonia* or *Rhopalonema,* although the metamorphosis of the *Cunina* planulae into flattened stolons is undoubtedly a modification adaptive to parasitism. Furthermore, this dramatic alteration of body form suggests that the relationships may be of long standing.

Life Cycle of *Polypodium*

The unusual method of medusa production by *Cunina*—that is, by budding from a stolon—also occurs in the parasitic hydrozoan coelenterate *Polypodium.* The polyp stage of this animal is free-living. It is found in the Volga River basin and in the Black and Caspian Seas.

Lipin (1911) has studied the life cycle of *Polypodium,* although its complete cycle is still unknown. The free-living polyp is solitary and migrates by employing its eight long and four short aboral tentacles (Plate 24–1, Fig. 3). Such polyps arise as buds from a stolon that is parasitic within eggs inside the ovary of the sturgeon (Plate 24–1, Fig. 4).

When the fish host lays eggs, the stolon escapes and the buds increase in size and mature by an evagination process. After the polyp buds mature and become separated, the stolon disintegrates. Gonads develop in the polyp of *Polypodium,* thus suggesting that a medusa stage

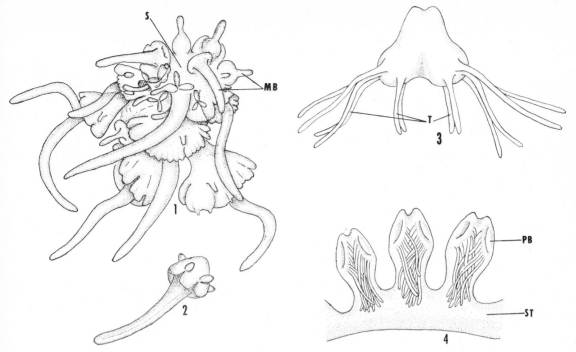

Plate 24-1   Stages in the life cycles of some parasitic coelenterates. 1. Flattened stolon of *Cunina peregrina*, removed from the medusa *Rhopalonema velatum*. **2.** Definitive medusa of *C. peregrina*, produced by budding of parasitic stolon. (Redrawn after Bigelow, 1909.) **3.** Free-living polyp of *Polypodium* in walking position. **4.** Portion of parasitic stolon of *Polypodium* with three polyp buds. (Redrawn after Lipin, 1911.)

(MB, medusal buds; PB, polyp bud; S, parasitic stolon; ST, stolon; T, tentacles.)

does not exist. Nothing is known about the fate of the free-living polyps or how sturgeons become infected. Again, the occurrence of a morphologically modified parasitic stolon in the ovarian eggs of the sturgeon suggests a relationship of long duration.

Mnestra and Hydrichthys

In addition to *Cunina* and *Polypodium,* several other hydrozoans are known to be parasitic. Very little is known about the biology of these, although in each case some anatomical modifications exist that can be interpreted as being adaptations to parasitism. For example, the parasitic stages during the life cycles of *Mnestra* and *Hydrichthys* show certain modifications of this type.

The medusae of *Mnestra* are parasitic, being attached to the pharynx of the marine snail *Phyllirhoe.* Modification of the parasitic medusa's body is apparent, for no tentacles are present.

During the relationship between *Mnestra* and *Phyllirhoe,* the latter's tissues are gradually destroyed.

Hydrichthys is a colonial hydroid coelenterate that attaches to the body of fishes. The hydroids have lost their tentacles and feed on the host's blood and tissues that have been injured by rootlike outgrowths of the parasites.

CLASS ANTHOZOA

Peachia and *Edwardsia* are two sea anemones whose larval stages parasitize other anemones or ctenophores. The coelenterate larvae are found either attached to the body surface of their host or in the gastrovascular cavity. These relationships are more than accidental, for the parasitic anemones each possess a sucker-like ring around the mouth by which they hold on to their hosts.

PHYLUM CTENOPHORA

The ctenophorans, or comb jellies, are almost all free-swimming marine animals. Their unsegmented triploblastic bodies are transparent and biradial, being oriented along an oral-aboral axis. The gastrovascular system consists of a mouth, pharynx, stomach, branched digestive canals, and two anal pores on the aboral surface. The nervous system is diffuse. An aboral sense organ, known as the statocyst, is present.

Although superficially similar to certain coelenterates, the ctenophorans lack nematocysts and characteristically bear comblike plates on their bodies at some stage during their development. These animals are hermaphroditic and reproductive cells usually are formed from endodermal cells in the digestive canals. Alternation of generation (metagenesis) does not occur. Most of the species are bioluminescent. The volume by Hyman (1940), should be consulted for morphological details.

There are approximately 80 species of ctenophorans, among which a few have been reported to be symbiotic. The larvae of *Gastrodes* is a true parasite in the tunicate *Salpa* during its larval stages. The adults are free-living.

Life Cycle of *Gastrodes parasiticum*

The life cycle of *Gastrodes parasiticum* has been studied by Komai (1922). The youngest stage found in the tunicate host, *Salpa fusiformis,* is a bowl shaped organism that is embedded in the mantle (Plate 24–2, Fig. 1). The bowl shaped form grows into a later larval form possessing four lobed, armlike canal systems (Plate 24–2, Fig. 2). This larval form metamorphoses into a cydippid type larva, possessing statocyst, tentacles, and eight rows of typically ctenophoran combs. It also possesses a gastrovascular system (Plate 24–2, Fig. 3).

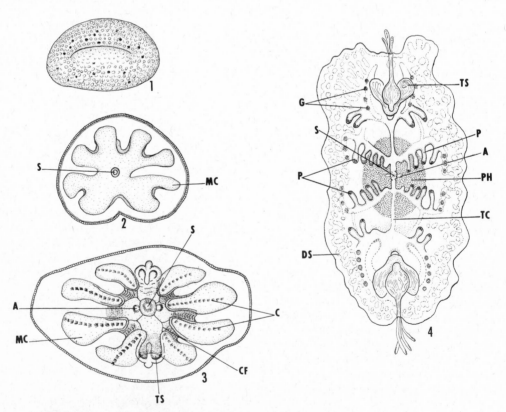

Plate 24–2   Some symbiotic ctenophorans. 1. Bowl shaped stage of *Gastrodes* parasitic in *Salpa.* **2.** Later stage showing lobed canal system. **3.** Comb-bearing stage. (Redrawn after Komai, 1922.) **4.** *Coeloplana mesnili,* ectosymbiotic on soft corals. (Redrawn after Dawydoff, 1933.)

(A, anal pore; C, comb rows; CF, ciliated furrow; DS, peripheral network of digestive system; G, gonads; MC, meridional canals; P, papillae connected with meridional canals; PH, pharynx; S, statocyst; TC, tentacular canal; TS, tentacle sheath.)

It is at this stage of development that *Gastrodes* leaves its host, settles to the bottom in sea water, casts off its rows of combs, and flattens out by everting its pharynx. This is the adult form. Eggs are produced in the pharyngeal epithelium of the adult and are believed to be of ectodermal origin, thus differing from the other ctenophorans. A typical planula larva with solid entoderm develops from each egg. Such a larva bores its way into a new host and again initiates the parasitic phase of its life cycle.

Nothing is known about the relationship between *Gastrodes* and *Salpa*. Adult *Gastrodes* species, living at the bottom of the ocean, are presumably exclusively carnivorous, as are all ctenophorans, feeding on microplankton. It is not known if the larval stages in *Salpa* derive their nutrition from their host or utilize stored nutrients.

Genus *Coeloplana*

In addition to the rare endoparasitic ctenophorans, another genus, *Coeloplana,* has been reported as an ectosymbiont, creeping about on specific species of alcyonarians, (soft corals) of the coelenterate class Anthozoa. Several species of *Coeloplana* are commonly found off the coast of Japan and are found in the Red Sea and off the coast of Vietnam.

The various species are flat and oval, measuring up to 60 mm. in length (Plate 24-2, Fig. 4). Their bodies are transparent or colored on the aboral surface. The colored *Coeloplana* may be of various shades such as red or olive. *Coeloplana* lacks rows of combs, but tentacles, tentacle sheaths, and a statocyst are present. Characteristic of the *Coeloplana* species are the erectile papillae, numbering 12 to approximately 60, depending on the species, and more or less arranged in four rows on the aboral surface. These papillae overlie the meridional canals and are connected with them. In most species, there are ciliated papillae at both poles as well.

A single testis and ovary is embedded in the wall of each of the eight meridional canals. The developing eggs are attached to the oral surface of the parent by a sticky substance. The eggs develop into typical cydippid larvae with eight rows of combs. After a free-living period, during which the larvae swim about, they attach to the body of a soft coral, lose their combs, and develop into adults.

Although *Coeloplana* is generally considered an ectocommensal of alcyonarians, the relationship is not well understood. The host specificity displayed by this ctenophoran certainly suggests that it is more than a mere epizoite.

PHYLUM RHYNCHOCOELA

The Rhynchocoela, or Nemertina, includes the so-called ribbon worms. These slender worms have soft, flat, and unsegmented bodies that are capable of extending and contracting extensively. They are triploblastic and bilaterally symmetrical. An eversible proboscis is present at the anterior end. The digestive tract is straight and complete.

The rhynchocoelans are believed to be closely related to the platyhelminths because, like the latter, they are acoelomate, possess an epidermis of ciliated epithelium like the turbellarians, and possess flame cells and a nervous system comprised of an anterior pair of ganglia from which arise a pair of lateral longitudinal nerve cords. Some species possess mid-dorsal and midventral nerve cords in addition to the lateral cords. Secondary nerve fibers arise from the primary longitudinal nerve cords.

The Rhynchocoela differs from the Platyhelminthes in that the digestive tract is complete, the reproductive system is simpler, and the sexes are separate. Furthermore, an open circulatory system is consistently present. The treatise by Hyman (1951) should be consulted for detailed morphology.

Approximately 500 species of rhynchocoelans are known. Almost all are free-living and marine, living closely coiled beneath rocks, among algae, or in burrows. Although most species live in the littoral zone, some are found in deep water.

Symbiotic rhynchocoelans are rare but a few are known. *Malacobdella* is found inhabiting the mantle cavity of clams and snails, and *Gononemertes* is found in the atrium of tunicates with its head protruding into the host's pharyngeal cavity. *Nemertopsis actinophila* lives regularly beneath the pedal disc of sea anemones, and *Carcinonemertes* is found in the gills and egg masses of crabs. Most of these rhynchocoelans do not appear to be true parasites. Rather, they could be considered commensals, although they may be approaching parasitism for they show adaptive changes characteristic of parasites, such as the loss of eyes and other sense organs, development of adhesive discs for attachment, reduction of the proboscal apparatus, and increased reproductive capacity. It is known that *Carcinonemertes* does feed on its host's eggs.

Genus *Malacobdella*

The body of *Malacobdella* is only a few millimeters long and is dorsoventrally flattened (Plate 24-3, Fig. 1). There is a conspicuous adhesive disc at the posterior terminal by which it holds onto its host. Since such a disc is absent in free-living species, its presence could be considered as a morphological adaptation to symbiosis. The adhesive disc is highly innervated, for the lateral nerve cords each display a ganglionic enlargement as they enter the disc. Within the disc, these nerve cords curve around and send secondary nerve fibers to the interior (Plate 24-3, Fig. 2). The multiplicity of gonads reflects the greater biotic potential characteristic of animal parasites (p. 21).

The circulatory system of *Malacobdella*, like that of other rhynchocoelans, consists of blood vessels (lymphatic canals) with definite walls and with lacunae in the parenchyma that are lined with a delicate membrane (Plate 24-3, Fig. 3). The system is of the open type—that is, the blood is not confined within the vessels but

is also found circulating in the parenchymal lacunae. The blood consists of a colorless fluid in which are found amoeboid lymphocytes (Plate 24-3, Fig. 4). This type of circulatory system further suggests the affinity of rhynchocoelans to certain platyhelminths, specifically certain amphistomate digenetic trematodes in which lymphatic canals enclosing lymphocytes are present in the parenchyma (p. 249).

In the United States, *Malacobdella grossa* is the common species and is widely distributed along the Atlantic Coast. It occurs in the bivalves *Mercenaria mercenaria*, *M. campechiensis*, and *Mya arenaria*, which are found from shoal water to deeper waters.

Since adults of *Malacobdella grossa* lack eyespots, do not become oriented when placed in a stream of water, and are neither attracted nor repelled by potential bivalve hosts, Ropes (1963) has suggested that dispersion of this species most likely occurs during the free-swimming lecithotropic larval phase. This larval phase is apparently of short duration, and the

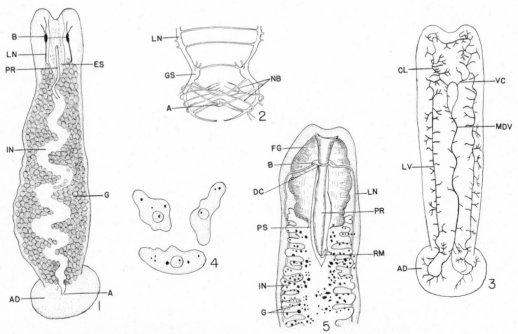

Plate 24-3   Symbiotic Rhynchocoela. 1. Adult *Malacobdella*. (Redrawn after Guberlet, 1925.) **2.** Posterior end of *Malacobdella*, showing nerve supply of adhesive disc. (Redrawn after Riepen, 1933.) **3.** Circulatory system in adult *Malacobdella*. (Redrawn after Riepen, 1933.) **4.** Blood cells (lymphocytes) of *Malacobdella*. (Redrawn after Reipen, 1933.) **5.** Anterior end of adult *Gononemertes* showing proboscal apparatus and numerous glands. (Redrawn after Brinkmann, 1927.)

(A, anus; AD, adhesive disc; B, brain; CL, cephalic lacuna; DC, dorsal commissure; ES; esophagus; FG, foregut; G, gonads; GS, ganglionic dwelling; IN, intestine; LN, lateral nerve cord; LV, lateral blood vessel; MDV, mid-dorsal blood vessel; NB, nerve branches into disc; PR, proboscis; PS, proboscal sheath; RM, retractor muscle; VC, ventral connective.

larvae appear for only a short time in the surface water. From his studies on the distribution of *M. grossa* and the water currents in Nantucket Sound, Ropes concluded that surface water current carries the larvae to sites where the molluscan hosts are found, and is thus an important factor in the distribution of *M. grossa*.

Genus *Carcinonemertes*

To those interested in marine parasitology, *Carcinonemertes carcinophila* and related species are of particular interest because they are fairly commonly found as commensals on the gills and egg masses of various species of crabs (Coe, 1902a,b; Humes, 1941, 1942). These commensals are small slender worms, varying from less than 1 mm. to 70 mm. in length (Plate 24-4, Fig. 1). A pair of ocelli, or eyespots, is present near the anterior end. The very short proboscis apparatus appears to be functionless. It is scarcely longer than the esophagus and lacks a proboscis sheath and accessory stylets (Plate 24-4, Fig. 2).

Characteristic of *Carcinonemertes* is a common sperm duct, known as Takakura's duct, into which all the testes discharge via individual vasa efferentia. The duct enlarges posteriorly

to form the seminal vesicle, posterior to which it resumes its former size and empties through the dorsal wall of the posterior end of the intestine. The sperm are discharged through the anus (Plate 24-4, Fig. 3).

Young *Carcinonemertes* live among the host's gills coiled up in mucous sheaths that they secrete. Infestation of mature crabs is most abundant throughout the summer, during the host's spawning season. When female crabs lay their eggs and their egg masses have become attached to the abdominal appendages, the young carcinonemerteans migrate onto the egg masses, on which they feed, grow to sexual maturity, and become ensheathed in mucus.

Carcinonemertean eggs, which include partially developed embryos, are oviposited within the sheaths. After ovipositing, the females move back to the gills of the crab. Pilidium-like larvae hatch from the eggs and emerge from the sheaths. These larvae are not free-swimming but develop into young worms among the egg masses of the host. The young worms either migrate to the gills of the same crab host and secrete individual sheaths or seek other crabs.

If a worm becomes attached to a young crab, its life cycle is cut short when the crab molts,

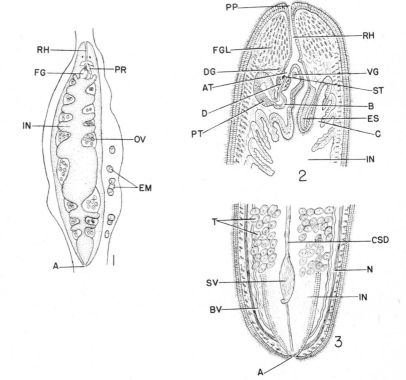

Plate 24-4   Morphology of *Carcinonemertes*. 1. Adult female *Carcinonemertes* inside mucous sheath. (Redrawn after Humes, 1942.) **2.** Sagittal section of anterior end of *Carcinonemertes*, showing frontal glands and reduced proboscis. (Redrawn after Coe, 1902.) **3.** Frontal section of posterior end of male *Carcinonemertes*, showing numerous testes and common sperm duct. (Modified after Humes, 1942.)

(A, anus; AT, anterior tube of proboscis; B, bulb; BV, lateral blood vessel; C, caecum; CSD, common sperm duct; D, diaphragm; DG, dorsal brain ganglion; EM, embryo; ES, esophagus; FG, foregut; FGL, frontal glands; IN, intestine; N, lateral nerve cord; OV, ovaries; PP, proboscis sheath; PR, proboscis; PT, posterior tube of proboscis; RH, rhynchodeum; ST, stylet; SV, seminal vesicle; T, testes; VG, ventral brain ganglion.)

because almost all the rhynchocoelans on the gills are discarded with the cast exoskeleton. If the worm becomes attached to an adult host, it develops normally. Although young encapsulated individuals increase in size, it is not clear on what they feed or if they derive their required energy from stored nutrients.

Since a phase of the development of *Carcinonemertes* is dependent on the eggs of the crab host, it is not surprising to find that young individuals that become attached to male crabs are unable to attain sexual maturity. This phenomenon suggests the influence of the host's hormones on the maturation of *Carcinonemertes*. However, this aspect has not yet been studied.

Hopkins (1947), during a survey of *Carcinonemertes* infestation of blue crabs, *Callinectes sapidus,* in the Virginia waters of the Chesapeake Bay, found that the appearance of the rhynchocoelan could be used with 97 per cent accuracy to determine whether the crab host had spawned or not. Only immature, whitish *Carcinonemertes* were found in the gills of mature crabs that had never spawned. *Carcinonemertes* found in gills of mature crabs that had spawned at least once, or in the gills and egg masses of spawning females, were large and red. Thus, in this instance, the symbiont could be utilized as an indicator of the spawning cycle of the host. The practical importance of this discovery to marine biologists and to the crab industry is obvious.

PHYSIOLOGY OF SYMBIOTIC RHYNCHOCOELANS

The physiology of symbiotic rhynchocoels has not been investigated to any extent. Most of these commensals occupy positions on their hosts where they can enjoy the ciliary currents that provide both oxygen and food for their hosts, and they thus can obtain these without exerting themselves. Except for *Carcinonemertes*, which feeds on the host's eggs, the other species feed on microplanktonic fauna carried by their host's ciliary currents.

Eggers (1936) has studied the behavior pattern of *Malacobdella grossa*. This rhynchocoelan is a sluggish animal and moves about its host in a leechlike manner by alternately attaching its anterior end and the posterior adhesive disc. When removed from the molluscan host, it only migrates for a short period, after which it becomes attached by its disc and waves its anterior end about in a seeking manner. The dorsal body cilia beat forward while the ventral

cilia beat backward. Eggers has shown that unlike other rhynchocoelans, the direction of ciliary beat of *M. grossa* cannot be altered nervously. Furthermore, severance of the lateral nerve cords or even the complete removal of the trunk does not cause the adhesive disc to become detached. This suggests that the attachment is controlled primarily by the ganglia present in the disc rather than by the anterior ganglia. When the anterior portion of *Malacobdella* is touched, the animal contracts; when the posterior end is touched, it extends. These reflexes are significant in explaining the normal leechlike movements of the animal.

PHYLUM ANNELIDA

The Annelida is comprised of segmented worms. Most annelids are free-living in aquatic and terrestrial habitats. Phylum Annelida is divided into four classes—Archiannelida, Polychaeta, Oligochaeta, and Hirudinea. None of the Archiannelida is parasitic. These small, internally-segmented worms are free-living in marine waters.

CLASS POLYCHAETA

The class Polychaeta, which should be familiar to any student who has had experience with the common laboratory animal *Nearthes* (= *Nereis*), includes the sandworms and tube worms. These annelids are predominantly marine; a few members, such as *Manayunkia speciosa* and *Nereis limnicola,* are fresh-water dwellers. In a very few instances parasitism has been reported. For an interesting account of endo- and ectoparasitism among the Polychaeta, the reader is referred to the article by Clark (1956). This author has also included an extensive bibliography on the topic.

Genus *Myzostomum*

Myzostomum includes species that are parasites on echinoderms (Plate 24–5). As the result of their adaptation to the parasitic way of life, these annelids have become so altered that they bear little resemblance to other annelids. Most *Myzostomum* species are irregularly discoid and dorsoventrally flattened. Cilia, in the form of cirri, project as tufts around the circumference. Five pairs of papillae-like projections are located on the ventral body surface, each bearing one or more setae. Although the body is circular, anterior-posterior orientation does exist. The mouth is located anteroventrally. This mouth opens into the muscular pharynx, which is protrusible. The pharynx leads into the saccular stomach, which bears three pairs of lateral, branched caeca (or diverticula). Posteriorly, the stomach opens into the short intestine, which in turn leads into the cloaca. The cloaca opens to the exterior through the anus, which is posteroventrad in position (Plate 24–5). A pair of suckers is found on each lateral margin.

The excretory system of *Myzostomum* spp. is simplified compared with that found in other annelids. A pair of nephridial tubes open into the coelom at one end and are connected with the cloaca at the other.

These aberrant annelids are hermaphroditic. Protandrism is normally the condition—that is, the male gonads develop well before the ovaries and discontinue functioning before the ovaries mature. In some species, however, the functional periods of the male and female gonads overlap.

The male system consists of two branched testes, one on each side of the alimentary tract in the coelom. A vas efferens arises from each testis, and the two unite to form the common vas deferens, which opens to the exterior through a pore located adjacent to the third parapodium.

The female system consists of two small ovaries, one on each side of the alimentary tract. These gonads discharge ova into the coelom, which functions as the uterus. A medially located tube, open at one end, collects the fertilized eggs and conducts these to the exterior either through the cloaca or through a gonopore located adjacent to the anus. During copulation, spermatozoa are introduced into the coelom of the female through the same tube.

Some species of *Myzostomum* are found encysted under the integument of echinoderms. In such forms, two individuals, one functioning as a male and the other as a female, are found within the same cyst wall. Other species have been reported endoparasitic in the intestine of echinoderms, but these cases are extremely rare.

Ichthyotomus sanguinarius

Another parasitic polychaete is *Ichthyotomus sanguinarius* found on eels. Little is known

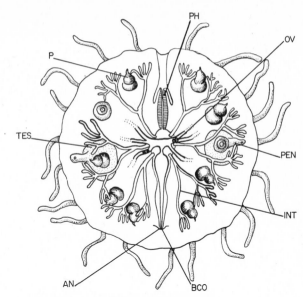

Plate 24–5   *Myzostomum glabrum.*
(AN, anus; BCO, opening of body cavity through which the ova are expelled; INT, intestine; OV, ovarian follicles; P, parapod; PEN, penis; PH, pharynx.)

concerning the biology of this worm except for its morphology. The dorsoventrally flattened and elongate body, measuring 7 to 10 mm. in length, is quite similar to that of free-living polychaetes except that the modified head lacks the usual appendages. Instead, the worm possesses a pair of crossed stylets that function like a pair of scissors. These structures undoubtedly represent specialized adaptations to parasitism.

This worm attaches to eels near the fins. The worm attaches to the eel by burrowing a hole in its body, using the stylets in the closed position. Once the puncture is made, the stylets are opened and serve as anchors for holding on. The modified perioral zone of the worm consists of a pseudosucker that becomes attached to the wound, and thus, the host's blood is sucked in. An anticoagulant is secreted by the salivary glands during the feeding process. The salivary glands, also known as haemolytic glands, are modifications of the so-called poison glands of predaceous polychaetes, and thus, must be considered another type of parasitic adaptation.

Since *Ichthyotomus* attains sexual maturity when it is only 2 mm. long and is by then composed of only some 30 of the 70 to 100 somites comprising the body of the fully grown adult, it may be considered a neotenic larva that has become precociously mature, probably as a result of feeding on the blood of its host. Neoteny is always favorable to parasites, because it enables them to produce eggs or larvae within a shorter period.

Although normally a parasite of various species of eels in the mud bottom of the Gulf of Naples in Italy, *I. sanguinarius* will become attached and feed on fish that remain motionless, and it has been shown to successfully parasitize the electric ray, *Torpedo ocellata*, thus indicating that it is not as host specific as it would first appear. Apparently the lack of rapid motility on the part of the host is an important criterion for successful parasitization.

Genus *Parasitosyllis*

Parasitosyllis is another parasitic annelid and is found on other polychaetes and nemerteans from Zanzibar. This polychaete is a tissue ingestor.

CLASS OLIGOCHAETA

Very few true parasites are known among the Oligochaeta. The biology of this class of annelids has been monographed by Stephenson (1930).

Members of the genus *Acanthobdella* are true parasites of salmon in western Siberia and northeastern Europe. The body form of *Acanthobdella* has become so modified as a result of parasitism that it was considered a leech until Michaelsen correctly identified it as an oligochaete.*

Aspidodrilus kelsalli is a minute aberrant oligochaete parasitic on earthworms in Sierra Leone. This parasite is conspicuously adapted to parasitism. The entire ventral surface of the posterior half of the body is flattened and slightly concave, thus forming an elongate adhesive disc by which it holds on. In addition, a true sucker in front of the disc also serves as an adhesive organ. *Aspidodrilus kelsalli* utilizes body surface mucus and lymphocytes exuded through the host's dorsal pores as food, in addition to ingesting mud, vegetation, and

animal debris. Similarly, *Fridericia parasitica*, found on the body surface of the earthworm *Allolobophora robustra*, feeds on mucus and lymphocytes.

A few additional examples of parasitism among oligochaetes exist. For example, Holt (1963) reported a branchiobdellid (of the family Branchiobdellidae) oligochaete, known as *Cambarinicola aliena*, parasitic in the brood pouches of females of the isopod *Asellus bicrenatus* found in Tennessee (Plate 24-6). Although almost all of the branchiobdellid oligochaetes are epizoic, the majority on the crayfish *C. aliena* appear to be true parasites, because Holt found material of granular and globular appearance in the oligochaete's gut that he suspected to be yolk from the host's eggs.

In addition to *Cambarinicola aliena*, *C. branchiophila*, and perhaps other branchiobdellids, are true parasites. These, most probably starting as epizoites, have entered their hosts and have adopted parasitism. *Cambarinicola branchiophila* is confined to the gill chambers of its crayfish host, where it feeds by clipping gill filaments off its host and sucking blood. In both *C. aliena* and *C. branchiophila*, Holt found the presence of weakened body walls and delicate jaws, which he interpreted as adaptations to parasitism.

Another greatly modified parasitic oligochaete, *Pelmatodrilus planariformis*, is known from an earthworm in Jamaica. The body of this parasite is dorsoventrally flattened and transparent. There are practically no dorsal setae present, but ventral ones are present and the animal can move about on its host by use of these.

Stiles and Hassall (1926) have listed some of the rare "parasitic" annelids reported in man. These include:

> *Fridericia bisetosa*, a pseudoparasite supposedly found in vomitus.
> *Henlea nasuta*, a pseudoparasite found in vomitus and also in a fistula.
> *Enchytraeus bucholzi*, a pseudoparasite found in saliva, presumably from the stomach.
> *Enchytraeus albidus*, found in urine.
> *Enchytraeus* sp., found in urine.
> *Eisenia foetida*, found in urine.
> *Microscolex modestus*, found in a fistula.
> *Lumbricus terrestris*, found in vomitus, and also in an ulcerated ankle.
> *Lumbricus communis cyaneus*, found in the vagina.

---

*Some biologists still consider *Acanthobdella* to be a primitive leech.

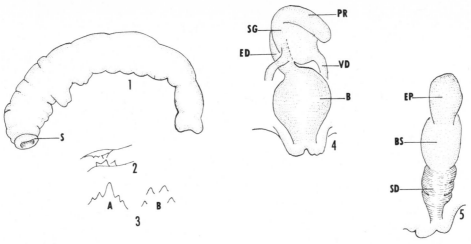

Plate 24-6   *Cambarincola aliena.* 1. Adult removed from the brood pouch of female *Asellus bicrenatus.* 2. Lateral view of jaws. 3. **A.** Dorsal jaw. **B.** Ventral jaw. 4. Lateral view of male reproductive system. 5. Spermatheca. (All figures redrawn after Holt, 1963.)

(B, bursa; BS, bulb of spermatheca; ED, ejaculatory duct; EP, ental process; PR, prostate; S, sucker; SD, ectal duct of spermatheca; SG, spermiducal gland; VD, vas deferens.)

There is serious doubt as to whether any of these species is a true or natural parasite. Several investigators have cast grave doubt on the reliability of some of the reports. At any rate, human parasites among the Oligochaeta are at best accidental.

FAMILY NAIDIDAE

A number of the Oligochaeta are epizoic or perhaps commensals, especially among members of the families Branchiobdellidae and Naididae. The family Naididae has been monographed by Sperber (1948). Several species of *Nais, Pristina,* and *Slavina* have been reported on or in sponges, the ectoproct *Plumatella,* and on other metazoan invertebrates (Plate 24–7, Figs. 1 and 2). Monticelli (1917) reported a commensal relationship between *Haplotaxis intermedia* in an ammocoetes larva of *Petromyzon planeri.* The oligochaete was found projecting outward from the host's branchial chamber, but its head was embedded in the pharyngeal canal and apparently nourished by food taken in by *Petromyzon.*

Genus *Chaetogaster*

Among other members of the Naididae known to be epicommensals or epizoic on fresh-water molluscs are species of *Chaetogaster.*

Members of this genus commonly are found in abundance on the shell, on the foot, and in the mantle cavity of fresh-water snails in North America. These microscopic annelids are primarily epizoic, feeding on protozoa, rotifers, small nematodes, crustaceans, water mites, and chironomid larvae. However, Lankester (1869) reported that *C. limnaei* can become a true parasite, feeding on the kidney cells of its host, *Limnaea* sp., during winter.

Your author has come across thousands of these microscopic annelids, crawling in and out of the mantle cavity of snails in eastern Pennsylvania. The affinity of *Chaetogaster* for the snails is most fascinating and strongly suggests that this is not a casual relationship but that some attraction exists.

The species of *Chaetogaster* are also of interest to parasitologists because they feed on trematode eggs and miracidia. Ruiz (1951) reported that specimens found on various snails ingest miracidia that attempt to penetrate the snail, including schistosomes. Hence these *Chaetogaster* species are responsible, at least to some degree, for the elimination of trematode infections.

On the other hand, Wallace (1941) reported that *Chaetogaster limnaei* can serve as the second intermediate host for the trematode *Triganodistomum mutabile,* and hence enhances the development of the fluke.

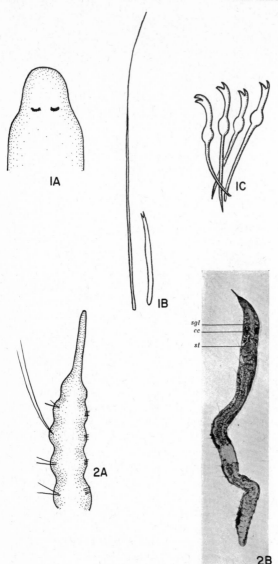

Plate 24-7   **Morphology of some epizoic Oligo-chaeta. 1.** *Nais communis.* **A.** Dorsal view of anterior end. **B.** Dorsal bundle of setae. **C.** Ventral bundle of setae. (Redrawn after Pennak, R. W. 1953. *Fresh-water Invertebrates of the United States,* Ronald Press, New York.) **2.** *Pristina.* **A.** Anterior end of *P. longiseta.* **B.** *P. aequiseta,* living specimen, slightly pressed under a cover glass. (sgl, septal gland; cc, coelomocytes; st, stomach.) (A modified after Marcus, 1943; B after Sperber, 1948.)

ENDOSYMBIOTIC NAIDIDS

At least three endosymbionts, probably parasites, exist among the Naididae. *Schmardaella lutzi* is found in the ureters of several species of the frog *Hyla,* which inhabits an area from southern Brazil to Cuba. *Nais bauchiensis* is found in the eyes of frogs, *Phrynomerus* spp., in

Africa. In the United States, Goodchild (1951) found *Schmardaella hylae* in the Wolffian ducts of the tree toad, *Hyla squirrela,* in Florida. Nothing is known about the life cycles of these parasitic naidids, although Goodchild speculated that in the case of *S. hylae,* infection of the host is achieved during the aquatic phase of the toad. It should be pointed out that these three naidids may well be immature forms of *Dero.*

OLIGOCHAETES AS HOSTS

The role of oligochaetes as hosts is also of considerable interest. For example, Codreanu and Codreanu (1928) reported a euglenoid flagellate *Astasia chaetogastris* to be parasitic in the coelom of *Chaetogaster diastrophus.*

In addition, certain marine species can serve as first intermediate hosts of digenetic trematodes, and fresh-water and semiaquatic species can serve as the intermediate host of *Dioctophyma renale* (p. 409). The role of earthworms as hosts for gregarine protozoans is well known (p. 112).

CLASS HIRUDINEA

The Hirudinea includes the leeches. These annelids are commonly found in fresh water, although marine and even a few terrestrial species exist. The leeches differ from the other annelids in that their bodies, which are commonly slender and leaf shaped, lack setae. Furthermore, a large sucker is located at the posterior end, and a smaller sucker, or pseudosucker, is found at the anterior terminal surrounding the mouth. Another characteristic of the leech is that the external body divisions, the annuli, do not correspond with the 34 internal true body segments.

Many leeches are predaceous or are scavengers. Some, however, are ectoparasitic on cold-blooded and warm-blooded vertebrates, feeding on their blood. When observed immediately after capture, leeches generally exhibit bright coloration. The pigments, however, do not persist and soon fade. Some leeches can swim, while others cannot. However, all leeches do utilize a wormlike inching crawl when placed on solid substratum. This characteristic creeping movement is facilitated by the holding ability of the anterior and posterior suckers.

Alimentary Tract

The digestive tract of the Hirudinea is complete, leading from mouth to anus. The mouth is located anteriorly in the middle of the oral sucker. It opens internally into the buccal chamber, which in turn leads into the pharynx. The pharynx may be highly muscular and acts as a suction bulb as is the case in most bloodsucking species, or it may be in the form of a slender tube. Posteriorly, it leads into the esophagus. In species possessing a large pharynx, the esophagus may not be readily visible.

The stomach of leeches generally occupies somites XIII to XIX or XX. It may be pyriform and simple, or it may bear one to fourteen pairs of lateral diverticula (or caeca). These side pouches may be simple or branched. Secondary branches are particularly common, extending from the postcaeca, which are the posteriormost diverticula, in species that engorge blood. The stomach leads into the intestine, which empties into the rectum. The rectum communicates with the exterior through the posteriorly located anus.

Coelom

Unlike the neatly septate coelom found in earthworms, the coelom of leeches is largely obliterated or reduced by the body musculature and by the parenchymatous tissues. The little space remaining is in the form of longitudinal canals interconnected by small branches. Within these canals are located the nervous, circulatory, excretory, and reproductive systems.

Circulatory System

The circulatory system of leeches varies, but the basic pattern consists of a large dorsal and a large ventral blood vessel. These two main vessels are connected anteriorly and posteriorly by a number of convoluted smaller vessels. The wall of the anterior segment of the dorsal blood vessel is thickened to function as a heart, and in some species of the Rhynchobdellida the posterior portion of the dorsal vessel is greatly expanded to form a blood sinus enveloping the intestine.

The contractions and expansions of the intestine aid in forcing the blood anteriorly in the dorsal vessel. Blood flow is directed anteriorly in the dorsal vessel and posteriorly in the ventral vessel. In members of the family Piscicolidae, there are lateral pulsating vesicles that also aid in forcing the blood to circulate in the body. Numerous minute blood vessels arise from the two main ones, and these infiltrate the body tissues to form rich beds of capillaries in the areas below the epidermis. Gaseous exchange takes place through the body wall except in a few marine species that possess lateral gill-like slits.

Excretory System

The excretory system in leeches is comparable to that found in earthworms, and should be familiar to students who have been exposed to introductory zoology. There are never more than seventeen pairs of nephridia in the Hirudinea. These are segmentally arranged along the middle somites. The collecting terminal consists of a simple ciliated funnel or of a more complex organ. In some leeches, such as *Hirudo* and *Haemopis sanguisuga,* the inner ends of the nephridial tubules have lost their connection with the ciliated organs, and these organs have no excretory function. Instead, they are the production sites for coelomic corpuscles (Mann, 1954). The nephridial tubules empty into the exterior through paired nephridiopores located in the ventral grooves between annuli.

Nervous System

The nervous system consists of an anteriorly situated "brain," located in somites V and VI. This nerve center is made up of a suprapharyngeal ganglionic mass connected to a large subpharyngeal ganglionic mass by two lateral connectives. The main nerve cord of the body is situated ventrally. It joins the brain at a posterior ganglionic mass located in somites XXV and XXVI. There is a single ganglion in each of somites VII to XXIV along the ventral nerve cord. Nerves arise from these ganglia to innervate the various tissues of the body in their immediate areas.

SENSORY ORGANS. Special sensory organs and structures found on the body surface of leeches include (1) papillae (Bayer's organs), which are minute sensory projections plentifully scattered over the body surface; (2) tubercles, which are larger retractible protruberances that involve the deeper dermal tissues and muscles and that are often beset with papillae; (3) eyes, which vary from extremely simple ocelli, consisting of a single visual cell embedded in pigment granules, to rather complex compound eyes found on the anterior end of some members of the family Hirudidae; and (4) sensillae, which are comparable to papillae except that a minute hairlike projection is present and that they are confined to certain sensory annuli.

Reproductive System

The reproductive system consists of a male and a female complex. Cross fertilization between two individuals is the rule.

FEMALE SYSTEM. This consists of two ovaries of varying sizes. A short, narrow oviduct leads from each ovary, and these ducts join to form the vagina. The vagina opens to the exterior through the female gonopore, which is located on the midventral line in somite XI. In some species, such as members of the Hirudidae, a diverticulum known as the vaginal caecum arises from the vagina and an albumin gland is connected with the muscular vagina.

MALE SYSTEM. This consists of four to eighty pairs of testes located in various somites. Arising from each testis on each side is a vas efferens. The vasa efferentia on each side connect with a single vas deferens. Each vas deferens gives rise to a seminal vesicle at its terminal end. The seminal vesicle is short or long, and straight or convoluted, depending on the species.

Spermatozoa passing into the seminal vesicles are cemented together and pass into the ejaculatory duct. The two ejaculatory ducts, one on each side, unite to form the glandular atrium. In all leeches, except in the Hirudidae, the spermatozoa are formed into spermatophores while passing down the ejaculatory duct (Plate 24–8, Fig. 1). In most species, the atrium includes an eversible bursa through which the spermatozoa are transferred to the

copulatory mate. Members of the Hirudidae possess a penis, which is the copulatory organ.

FERTILIZATION. The mechanisms of sperm penetration and ova fertilization among the leeches vary. In the Rhynchobdellida and Erpobdellidae, the spermatozoa released from the spermatophores onto the body surface of the mate actually penetrate the integument by means of local histolytic activity and reach the ovaries via the coelomic sinuses.

In the Hirudidae, the penis is extruded and the spermatozoa are introduced into the female gonopore. During the breeding season, the inconspicuous clitellum secretes rings, much in the same fashion as do earthworms. These rings collect fertilized ova while passing anteriorly over the female gonopore and eventually slip off the anterior end of the body. Such ova-bearing cocoons are deposited in water between May and August. After completing their embryonic development, young leeches escape from the cocoon and become independent. The period required for maturation varies; however, in most cases it takes years.

SYSTEMATICS AND BIOLOGY

CLASSIFICATION

According to Moore (1959), the class Hirudinea is divided into three orders.

Order 1. Rhynchobdellida. Mouth is small pore on anterior sucker through which a pharyngeal proboscis can be protruded. Possesses no jaws or denticles. Blood is colorless.

Order 2. Pharyngobdellida. Mouth is large, opening from behind into entire sucker cavity. Pharynx is not protrusible, acts as suction bulb, extending to somite XIII. Possesses three or four pairs of eyes and three muscular pharyngeal ridges. Has no true jaws or denticles. Testes are in grapelike bunches. Blood is red.

Order 3. Gnathobdellida. Mouth is large, opening from behind into entire sucker cavity. Pharynx is not protrusible, acts as suction bulb but does not extend to clitellum. Five pairs of eyes are arranged on arch in somites II to VI. Body somites are five-ringed. Muscular jaws are present (except *Haemopis*). Large testes are arranged in metameric pairs.

ORDER RHYNCHOBDELLIDA

The feeding habits of members of the Rhynchobdellida are unusual in that a muscular proboscis is present that is actually the anterior end of the pharynx. This structure is protruded and inserted in the host's tissues during feeding.

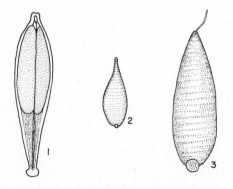

Plate 24–8   Some leeches. 1. Spermatophore of *Glossiphonia,* showing two oval bundles of spermatozoa. (Modified after Brumpt.) 2. Exterior view of *Helobdella.* 3. External view of *Glossiphonia* with extruded proboscis. (Figs. 1 and 2 modified after Pennak, R. W. 1953. *Fresh-water Invertebrates of the United States,* Ronald Press, New York.)

Rhynchobdellid Genera

Genus *Haementeria* includes *H. officinalis,* the so-called medicinal leech of South and Central America. *H. (= Placobdella) parasitica* is a species found on the snapping turtles.

The genus *Helobdella,* including *H. stagnalis, H. elongata,* and *H. fusca,* has been reported to be a suitable vector for *Trypanosoma inopinatum,* a haemoflagellate of frogs (Plate 24–8, Fig. 2).

The genus *Glossiphonia* includes *G. complanata, G. heteroclita,* and others found attached to various fresh-water snails, such as *Limaea* and *Planorbis,* and on the larvae of *Chironomus* (Plate 24–8, Fig. 3).

Genus *Pontobdella* includes species parasitic on elasmobranch fishes and some species that serve as vectors for *Trypanosoma rajae* of rays. In addition, species of *Pontobdella* may serve as vectors of trypanosomes of marine fishes including rays.

Other members of this order are vectors for trypanosomes and *Cryptobia* of fresh-water fishes. Meyer (1940, 1946) has reviewed the genera of fresh-water rhynchobdellid leeches found on fishes in North America, which include *Piscicola, Piscicolaria,* and *Illinobdella* (Plate 24–9, Fig. 1). These papers should be consulted by those interested in parasitic leeches. The presence of *Piscicola* in fish hatcheries is known to cause serious damage.

In addition to the previously mentioned ryhnchobdellid leeches, several others "parasitize" arthropods, especially decapod crustaceans. Little is known concerning the "parasitic" habits of these. It is suspected that in many instances they are merely epizoic forms. Meyer and Barden (1955) have catalogued some of the leeches found attached to decapods and have discussed the uncertainty of their parasitic nature.

ORDER PHARYNGOBDELLIDA

The Pharyngobdellida includes *Mooreobdella, Nephelopsis, Erpobdella,* and *Dina.* The last two

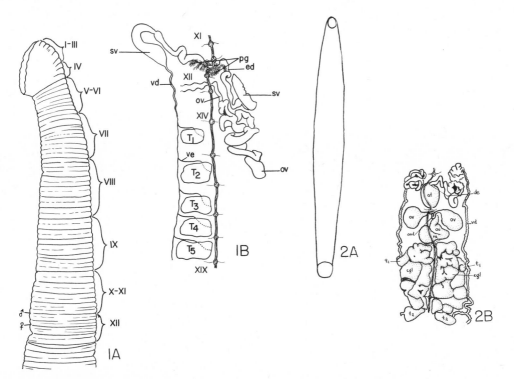

Plate 24-9   Anatomy of some leeches. 1. A. *Illinobdella moorei,* external view of body somites I to XIII, showing complete annulation. Notice male and female pores. **B.** Dissected reproductive organs showing relationship to nerve cord. (Redrawn after Moore.) (ed, ejaculatory duct; ov, ovisac; pg, prostate glands; sv, seminal vesicle; vd, vas deferens.) **2. A.** Outline drawing of body shape of *Macrobdella.* **B.** Part of reproductive organs of *M. decora.* (Redrawn after Moore.) (at, atrium; cgl, copulatory glands; ed, ejaculatory duct; t_1, 1st testisacs; t_2, 2nd testisacs; os, ovisac; ov, ovary; ovd, oviduct; va, vagina; vd, vas deferens.)

mentioned genera have been revised and mono-graphed by Pawlowski (1955).

ORDER GNATHOBDELLIDA

The Gnathobdellida includes *Hirudo medi-cinalis,* the medicinal leech. The feeding habits of this parasite vary with age. The primary food of young leeches consists of insect blood but the blood of frogs and fishes serves this function during the growing period. Adults feed primarily from warm-blooded animals, including man. In addition to robbing man of blood, this leech serves as a vector for bacteria and other micro-organisms. For example, it is strongly suspected of transmitting *Trypanosoma brucei* and *T. equiperdum* to man, as well as transmitting the anthrax bacterium.

Other prominent genera of the Pharyngob-dellida include *Macrobdella* (Plate 24–9, Fig. 2) and *Limnatis. Limnatis* includes *L. nilotica,* the large horse leech (8 to 12 cm. long), which parasitizes mammals in North Africa, middle Europe, and the Near East. It is commonly used for bloodletting in these areas. Mammals become infested with this leech while drinking contaminated water. Once within the host, it becomes attached to the nasal passages, phar-ynx, and larynx. If present in large numbers, it can cause asphyxia. Furthermore, heavily parasitized hosts can suffer from anemia be-cause of the loss of blood. In addition, bleed-ing, nausea, and vomiting, often followed by death due to anemia and suffocation are common.

Another member of *Limnatis, L. africana,* parasitizes man, monkeys and dogs in Senegal, Congo, India, and Singapore. Human infesta-tion is most commonly acquired while bathing. The leech can enter the body via the vagina and urethra and cause rather severe bleeding. Again, anemia and even death can result.

Various species of *Dinobdella* are found in India, where these leeches, when swallowed in drinking water, attack the pharynx of cattle.

The genus *Hirudinaria* includes *H. granulosa,* the Indian medicinal leech.

Haemadipsa includes the dreaded land leeches of the Far East. One species of this genus, *H. chiliani,* attacks horses and cattle in South America, and heavily parasitized hosts usually perish. Probably the best known species of *Haemadipsa* is *H. zeylandica,* which attacks all mammals in the tropical jungles of Asia, including humans. Adult leeches, measuring 2 to 3 cm. in length, are found on the surfaces of trees and grass and under stones in damp places. They readily attach themselves to the skin of man and other animals and ingest their blood. This leech is found in India, the Philip-pines, Australia, and in the Chilian Andes. Other species are found in Japan, China, Chili, and Trinidad.

The genus *Theromyzon* includes species that enter the throats and nostrils of water birds, killing geese and ducks.

The ability of bloodsucking leeches to feed is facilitated by the secretion of anticoagulants into the puncture site.

ECOLOGICAL FACTORS

Mann (1955) contributed a study of some ecological factors that influence the distribution of leeches. He reported that the amount of $CaCO_3$ in the environment influences the abundance of certain species. For example, *Erpobdella octoculata* is most abundant in "soft" waters—with 0 to 17 ml. of $CaCO_3$ per liter of water—while an abundance of *Helobdella stagnalis* is characteristic of "hard" waters—with 60 to 242 ml. of $CaCO_3$ per liter of water. These observations suggest that as is the case among most ectoparasites, the external environ-mental factors are just as important to the physiology of leeches as the internal environ-ment of the host is to endoparasites. The work of Bennike (1943) should be consulted because it contains many additional interesting obser-vations on the influence of environmental factors on the distribution of leeches. In addi-tion, the excellent monograph by Mann (1962), which includes much information on the phys-iology and ecology of leeches, should be con-sulted.

HOST-PARASITE RELATIONSHIPS

Although commonly referred to as parasites, most leeches are predators, either carnivorous or saprophagous. Only the bloodsucking species can be considered parasites. Most of these species are only temporarily attached to their hosts, abandoning them when they become engorged with blood. In a few instances, these parasites have become sedentary and never leave their hosts. This relationship is most prevalent among leeches that are attached to fishes, primarily among the rhynchobdellids. From the little information available, these leeches appear to exhibit little or no host selec-tivity. For example, *Piscicola geometra* is found on many species of fresh-water teleost fishes, on trout, and even on tadpoles. On the other hand, host specificity may be exhibited by *Theromyzon*, which has only been found on aquatic birds, and by *Ostreobdella*, which has been reported on oysters only.

Ozobranchus jantseanus is a leech commonly found attached to the aquatic turtle *Clemmys japonica*. Although the relationship is not an obligatory one, since *O. jantseanus* is also found free-living, this leech is particularly adapted to clinging to *C. japonica* because the turtle is in the habit of climbing out of water to sun itself several times a day. During these periods, the leech rapidly dries and shrivels up into a small black disc. However, when the turtle returns to water, the disc swells up and the leech resumes its normal activities. The leech loses four-fifths of its body weight when dried and can remain in a state of anabiosis up to 8 days. The ability of *O. jantseanus* to adapt to anabiosis undoubtedly explains why it can stay attached to its turtle host.

Very seldom does one find external anatomical features among leeches that suggest adaptation to parasitism. In one such instance, *Hemibdella soleae* holds on to the spines on the free edge of the scales of its host—the sole—because its mouth is very narrow and deep. Since only sole scales possess spines of the correct size to fit into the mouth of this parasite, the morphological adaptation has a selective influence in creating a host-parasite relationship. One reason given for the apparent lack of widespread adaptation by parasitic leeches is that these annelids are specialized to begin with and by coincidence their specialization permits the type of temporary parasitism that they practice.

PHYLUM MOLLUSCA

Parasitism is a rare phenomenon in adult molluscs, but in the few reported instances, the degrees of modification in the several parasitic species represent a beautiful series demonstrating progressive stages of adaptation to parasitism. Caullery (1952) has given an excellent account of parasitic molluscs.

Parasitism among larval molluscs, known as protelian parasitism, is common in fresh-water bivalves of the family Unionidae. This form of parasitism is discussed on page 682.

Adult molluscan parasites are limited primarily to members of the class Gastropoda, which includes the snails, slugs, limpets, and related forms. Parasitic gastropods are almost all limited to four families—Capulidae, Eulimidae, Entoconchida, and Paedophoropodidae.

FAMILY CAPULIDAE

The Capulidae includes prosobranchiate snails, which possess shells that are slightly coiled or in the form of a simple incurved cone. The only modern genus known is *Thyca,* containing five species found as ectoparasites of the starfish *Linckia* in the Indian Ocean and in marine waters of the Malay Archipelago. These snails still retain the form of rather typical gastropods (Plate 24–10, Fig. 1). However, the foot and the peribuccal region are modified (Plate 24–10, Fig. 2). The foot is greatly reduced and the peribuccal region is enlarged to form a large sucker by which the parasite is attached to its host. A proboscis projects from the center of this sucker to pierce the integument of the host and withdraw fluid nutrients. A radula is completely lacking. In species that possess a long proboscis, the hepatopancreas and intestine are reduced. Well developed salivary glands are present, however, suggesting the comparatively simple nature of its food, which does not require complex digestion. These animals are dioecious and the males are smaller than the females. The shells of the males and females are somewhat different.

Capulid parasites apparently are rather ancient forms. Fossils of a now extinct genus, *Platyceras,* are known on crinoids and starfishes dating back to the Silurian-Triassic era. The appearance of *Platyceras* is quite similar to that of *Thyca,* suggesting that these gastropods have undergone very little evolutionary change.

FAMILY EULIMIDAE

Members of Eulimidae possess turreted shells that are thin and translucent. The Eulimidae includes both free-living and parasitic species, the latter being either ecto- or endoparasites of echinoderms. Anatomical adaptations in eulimid snails make up a beautiful series that shows the different degrees of change caused by parasitic adaptation. The free-living species generally possess radulae,

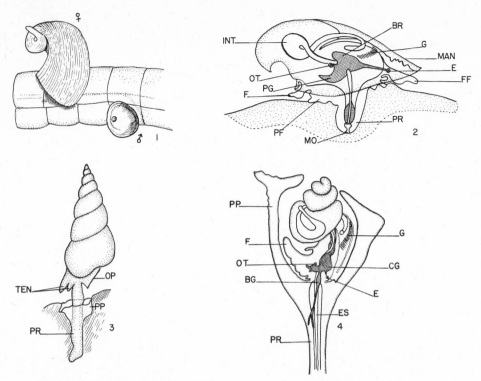

Plate 24-10   Some parasitic molluscs. 1. Male and female specimens of *Thyca stellasteris,* showing conspicuous sexual dimorphism. (Redrawn after Koehler and Vaney, 1912.) **2.** Anatomy of *Thyca ectoconcha.* (Redrawn after Sarasin and Sarasin, 1887.) **3.** *Mucronalia palmipedis.* (Redrawn after Koehler and Vaney, 1912.) **4.** *Stylifer linckiae.* (Redrawn after Sarasin and Sarasin, 1887.)

(BR, brain; E, eye; ES, esophagus; F, foot; FF, frontal fold; G, gill; INT, intestine; MAN, mantle; MO, mouth; OP, operculum; OT, otocyst; PF, pseudofoot; PG, pedal ganglion; PP, pseudopallium; PR, proboscis; TEN, tentacles.)

but these scraping structures are not found in the parasitic species.

Genus *Pelseneeria*

Members of the hermaphroditic genus *Pelseneeria* are ectoparasitic on holothurians (sea cucumbers). These parasites move over the body surface of the host but never leave it, even to oviposit. *Pelseneeria* possesses a muscular proboscis that penetrates the host's integument and through which nutrients, in the form of body fluids, are drawn out.

In one species, *P. profunda,* there is a fringed collar-like projection—the pseudopallium—in the peribuccal zone that partly covers the shell. This structure is definitely an adaption to parasitism and is encountered in other parasitic gastropods. Although the foot of *Pelseneeria* is more developed than that of *Thyca,* an operculum is also lacking in *Pelseneeria.* This

again could be considered an adaptation to parasitism, because the operculum is not found on any other parasitic snails except *Mucronalia* spp.

Genus *Megadenus*

Members of *Megadenus* are parasites of echinoderms in the Bahamas, the Indian Ocean, and in the Yellow Sea. *Megadenus voeltzkowi* and *M. holothuricola* live in the respiratory trees of holothurians, while *M. cysticola* and *M. arrhynchus* are found within tumor-like swellings on the spines of the echinoid *Dorocidaris tiara* and the asteroid *Anthenoides rugulosus,* respectively. These snails are dioecious. In *M. cysticola,* a small male and a large female are found together within the same cystic tumor. *Megadenus holothuricola* and *M. voeltzkowi* possess a proboscis that is thrust through the tracheal wall of the host into the coelom. A proboscis is also present on *M. cysticola*, but not in *M. arrhynchus*. In addition to these modifications, the foot of *Megadenus* has ceased to be a locomotory structure and an operculum is lacking. However, the pedal glands persist. A large pseudopallium is present, the intestine is shortened, and the stomach and hepatopancreas tend to fuse so as to form a single organ.

Genus *Mucronalia*

Several species of *Mucronalia* attach to ophiuroids, holothurians, sea urchins, and starfishes (Plate 24–10, Fig. 3). The shells of these gastropods are well developed with several apical whorls. An operculum is present and a pseudopallium, although present, is not very well developed. These snails remain attached to the exterior of their hosts, usually at a permanent site. A well developed, long proboscis penetrates the host's integument and draws body fluids out. *Mucronalia* spp. possess no salivary glands, hepatopancreas, or complete alimentary canals. One species, *M. variabilis,* is capable of endoparasitism and is sometimes found in the blind-sac alimentary canal of its host, *Synapta soplax,* in the Indian Ocean. These snails are dioecious.

Genus *Stylifer*

Members of the genus *Stylifer* possess thin shells and resemble *Mucronalia,* but they have no operculum, and the foot is reduced (Plate 24–10, Fig. 4). In some species, the pseudopallium is large and well developed and actually covers the shell. The various species are parasitic on starfishes and ophiuroids in Asian waters. They possess a long proboscis, which penetrates the host's integument and reaches the coelom to withdraw body fluids. Again, the hepatopancreas is vestigial or absent. The only species that has been extensively investigated is *S. sibogae.* It is a hermaphrodite and possesses a well developed male copulatory organ. In two other species, *S. linkiae* and *S. celebensis,* only the parasitic females are known. Presumably the males are free-living. The sex products of the parasitic females are flushed out by water drawn into the pseudopallial cavity by the piston action of the proboscis and/or by the contraction and expansion of the pseudopallial wall.

Genus *Diacolax*

Diacolax includes only one species—*D. cucumariae*—found as an ectoparasite of the holo-

thurian *Cucumaria mendax* in the Falkland Islands. In this greatly modified snail, the pseudopallium covers the entire body, giving the animal the appearance of an oval mass. Attached to the body is a small pointed siphon that leads to the exterior. The anterior end of the animal is embedded in the host. A shell is lacking. Within the ovoid body is the intestine, surrounded by the ovary. The remaining space is filled with developing eggs. Mandahl-Barth (1946) reported that cleavage is total and of the spiral type. The larva, known as a veliger larva, is also characteristic of several genera of the Entoconchidae (Plate 24–11).

Genus *Gasterosiphon*

Probably the most specialized of the eulimid parasites are members of the genus *Gasterosiphon* (Plate 24–12, Fig. 1). These animals are endoparasitic in holothurians found in the Indian Ocean. Koehler and Vaney (1903) described *G. deimatis* in *Deima blakei.* This gastropod has become so modified in its appearance that it can be recognized as a snail only by the trained eye. This endoparasite communicates with the exterior by means of a siphon connected to a minute pore on the body surface of the holothurian. The proximal end of the siphon is connected with the ovoid body which, if cut open, reveals a vestigial foot; an incomplete alimentary tract composed of an esophagus, stomach, and ramifying hepatopancreatic ducts; and a condensed nervous system. Another long slender tube—the proboscis—is attached to the ovoid body at the pole opposite that from which the siphon arises. The proboscis is attached distally to the marginal vessel on the intestine of the host, and blood from this vessel is thus sapped into the parasite.

Gasterosiphon deimatis is a hermaphrodite. The eggs are deposited in the pseudopallial cavity, where they undergo a period of incubation. When sufficiently developed, the eggs are discharged into the sea through the ciliated siphon.

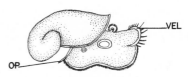

Plate 24–11   Veliger larva of *Entoconcha.* (Redrawn after Baur, 1864.) (OP, operculum; VEL, velum.)

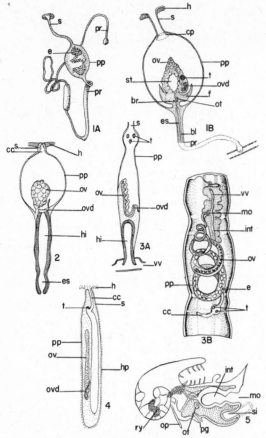

Plate 24–12   **Some parasitic molluscs. 1.** *Gasterosiphon deimatis.* **A.** Entire parasite. **B.** Cut-away section, showing internal anatomy. (Redrawn after Koehler and Vaney, 1912.) **2.** *Entocolax.* **3. A.** *Entoconcha.* **B.** *Entoconcha mirabilis* within host, attached to host's ventral blood vessel. **4.** *Enteroxenos.* **5.** Longitudinal section of veliger larva of *Entoconcha.* (Figs. 2, 3A, and 4 redrawn after Vaney; Figs. 3B and 5 after Baur.)

(bl, blood lacuna; br, brain; cc, ciliated canal; cp, calcified pseudopallial shell; e, egg mass; es, esophagus; f, foot; h, host tissue; hi, hepatic intestine; hp, sheath of host's peritoneum; int, intestine; ot, otocyst; ov, ovary; ovd, oviduct; pg, pedal gland; pp, pseudopallium; pr, proboscis; ry, residual yolk; s, siphon; si, saclike invagination; st, stomach; t, testis; vv, ventral blood vessel of host.)

FAMILY ENTOCONCHIDAE

The Entoconchidae includes several genera of molluscs that are extremely modified. None of these possesses a shell, and in many ways they resemble *Gasterosiphon.* The members of Entoconchidae include the genera *Entocolax, Entoconcha, Enteroxenos,* and *Thyonicola.*

Genus *Entocolax*

Members of the genus *Entocolax* are endo-

parasitic in the coelom of holothurians (Plate 24–12, Fig. 2). In *E. ludwigii,* a parasite of *Myriotrochus rinkii,* one end of the ovoid body is attached to the host's integument by a short siphon. The main bulk of the parasite is a hollow sac, and the pseudopallium forms the wall. Within this sac are found the ovary and the oviduct. The free end of the animal projects freely in the host's coelom as a tubular proboscis composed of a terminal esophagus and an elongate hepatic intestine.

In *E. schwanzwitschi,* a parasite of *Myriotrochus eurycyclus,* the anatomy is essentially the same as that of *E. ludwigi.* It is also located in the host's coelom, but the siphon is attached to the outer or peritoneal surface of the holothurian's gut, rather than to the integument.

Heding (1934) and Schwanzwitsch (1917) reported the presence of dwarf males attached to the inner wall of the pseudopallium. Thus, males are hyperparasitic in females. Fertilized eggs in cocoons develop into veliger larvae in the pseudopallial cavity. The larvae are typically gastropodan, with a shell, velum, and foot. These measure no more than 0.5 mm. in length.

Infection of the holothurian host occurs when a young *Entocolax* penetrates the host's surface. *Entocolax ludwigi* penetrates the body wall of the host near the dorsal tentacles, since *M. rinkii* is normally buried in mud except for its dorsal tentacles and adjacent areas. *Entocolax schwanzwitschi* enters the mouth and penetrates the gut wall of *M. eurycyclus.* The hypothesized method of entrance of this parasite into the host is depicted in Plate 24–13.

Genus *Entoconcha*

The body of *Entoconcha,* a parasite within the body cavity of holothurians in the Adriatic Sea and in the Philippines, is even more modified than that of *Entocolax.* The mouth, which opens into a hepatic intestine, is attached to the ventral vessel of the host (Plate 24–12, Fig. 3). *Entoconcha mirabilis,* the first parasitic mollusc known, is approximately 8 cm. long.

Genus *Enteroxenos*

Adults of *Enteroxenos* are tubular, measuring 100 to 150 mm. in length. They are endoparasites in the body cavity of the holothurian *Stichopus tremulus.* The younger specimens are usually found attached to the outer surface of the anterior portion of the host's gut. *Enteroxenos* is the most simplified of the parasitic gastropods as the result of adaptation. An internal elongate

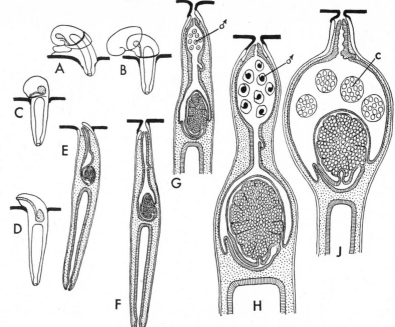

Plate   24-13   *Entocolax.*
A-F. Entrance of *Entocolax.* **G** and
H. Hyperparasitic dwarf males in
female. **J.** Cocoon filled with ova (c)
in female. (After Baer, J. G. 1952.
Ecology of Animal Parasites, University
of Illinois Press, Urbana, Ill.)

cavity extends the entire length of the body
(Plate 24–12, Fig. 4). This tubular chamber
opens to the exterior through a minute pore at
the anterior end. The gonads are embedded in
the body wall with the single elongate ovary
lying alongside the tubular cavity and the
testis located toward the proximal end. Caullery
(1952) advanced the concept that the entire
body of *Enteroxenos* corresponds to a large
pseudopallium. Although adults of this parasite are not recognizable as molluscs, the larvae
bear molluscan characteristics in the form
of coiled shells, velum, visceral hump, foot,
operculum, nervous system, and otocysts (Plate
24–12, Fig. 5).

Genus *Thyonicola*

Thyonicola   mortenseni was described by
Mandahl-Barth (1941) within the holothurian
Thyone secreta, collected at the Cape of Good
Hope, South Africa. The adults are long and
tubular, measuring a few millimeters to 8
centimeters in length, and are tangled in knots.
The anterior end of the tubular body is attached
to the host's intestine. No alimentary tract or
other intestinal organs are present except for
the gonads. The testis is situated toward the
anterior end of the body, and the ovary is at
the posterior end. Mandahl-Barth reported
that in gravid individuals the tubular body is
filled with thousands of eggs. The larva, unlike

the adult, is readily recognized as a gastropod,
for it possesses a tiny coiled shell and an
operculum.

**LIFE CYCLE AND METAMORPHOSIS OF *Thyoni-
cola mortenseni.*** Iwanow (1948) studied the
life cycle and metamorphosis of a parasitic
entoconchid, *Parenteroxenos dogieli,* which has
since been shown to be *Thyonicola mortenseni.*
The eggs are located in cocoons within the
parent's tubular body, where they undergo extensive development. Cocoons enclosing well
developed larvae are expelled in the feces of
the holothurian host. Once the cocoons come
in contact with sea water, they burst, releasing
larvae that are only about 0.1 mm. long. These
larvae are unable to survive for any length of
time. In order to survive, they must be ingested
by a holothurian along with its food.

Once in the host's gut, the larval snail
undergoes metamorphic changes. It sheds its
thin shell, mantle, and a mass of cells (probably vitelline cells). Furthermore, the primitive
stomodeum closes.

The larva now penetrates the host's gut wall
with the aid of pedal gland secretions. Once
established within the gut wall, the cilia of its
epidermis are lost, and a mass of cells—the
genital primordium—appears in the mesoderm.
As development continues, a cavity in the body
of the snail—which has been interpreted to be
the stomodeal cavity—increases in size and
progresses at one end, eventually reaching and

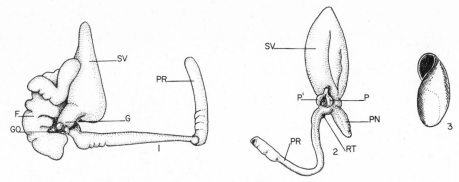

Plate 24-14 *Paedophoropus dicoelobius.* **1.** Adult female, right lateral view. **2.** Adult male, ventral surface. **3.** Larval shell. (All figures redrawn after Iwanow, 1937.)
(F, foot; G, genital regions; GO, region of genital opening; P and P′, left and right lobes of foot; PN, penis; PR, proboscis; RT, rudimentary tentacle; SV, visceral sac.)

breaking through the epidermis. This cavity communicates with the lumen of the host's gut via a ciliated canal. The large body cavity, known as the brood pouch, is thus believed to have originated from the stomodeal cavity and hence is not a pseudopallial cavity.

Concurrent with the development of the elongate brood pouch, the gonads develop from the genital primordium. The ovary, located at the posterior end, increases in size and an oviduct from it opens into the brood pouch. The testicular anlage somehow migrates to the anterior end, becoming located in the mesoderm adjacent to the base of the ciliated canal, and differentiates into the mature testis.

The larval snail, as it increases in size, expands into the host's coelom, pushing the host's peritoneum with it. Thus, the adult parasite is found projecting into the host's coelomic cavity, but with its ciliated canal connected to the host's gut.

The development of *Enteroxenos* is believed to be the same as that of *Thyonicola.* However, the eggs of *Enteroxenos* are probably not enclosed in cocoons, and the veliger larva, unlike that of *Thyonicola,* possesses a heart, statocysts, nephridium, and a better developed nervous system.

FAMILY PAEDOPHOROPODIDAE

The Paedophoropodidae includes *Paedophoropus dicoelobius,* a parasite in the respiratory tract of the holothurian *Eupyrgus pacificus* in the Sea of Japan (Plate 24-14). This gastropod is dioecious, with male and female intimately associated. There is marked sexual dimorphism, the males being less than half the size of the females. The largest known female measured 5.5 mm. in length. Both sexes possess a long

proboscis that penetrates into the host's body cavity and is attached to the host's alimentary tract. Although a shell is absent in adults, this parasitic gastropod, unlike those mentioned above, does possess a visceral mass including a nervous system, a kidney, ovary or testis, and a digestive tube and related structures. There are, however, no gills or heart. Furthermore, a pseudopallium is lacking.

There are glands located around the distal portion of the proboscis near the mouth. These glands are believed to secrete a proteolytic enzyme that aids in the digestion of nutrients. The proboscis leads into a hepatic gut. There are no stomach, terminal gut, or anus.

The larva of *P. dicoelobius* possesses a dextrally coiled shell that is thin and transparent, an operculum, and a large foot. Larvae develop in cocoons.

FAMILY UNIONIDAE

Parasitism is found among the larvae of fresh-water bivalves of the Unionidae. This way of life represents a normal stage in the life cycle of these molluscs. The female unionids incubate their eggs in brood pouches located between the gill lamellae in the water tubes. When the eggs hatch, the larvae, known as glochidia, pass out of the parent through the excurrent siphon. Most glochidia are drawn in by the breathing movements of fishes in the vicinity and become attached to the gill or to the body surface of the piscine host, where they undergo a period of development, metamorphosing into young clams. If the glochidium is of a species that possesses a pair of hooks, one on each valve (smaller auxiliary spines

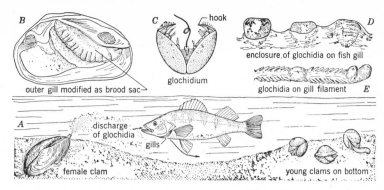

Plate 24-15   Stages in the life cycle of a unionid mollusc. A. Diagram of the life cycle. **B.** Female's outer gill modified as a brood sac. **C.** Single glochidium. **D.** Glochidia enclosed by epithelium on gill of fish host. **E.** Glochidia on a gill filament. (From Storer, T. I., and Usinger. 1957. *General Zoology*, McGraw-Hill, New York.)

may also be present), it generally becomes attached to soft exterior parts of a fresh-water fish resting at the bottom. If the glochidium does not possess hooks, it clamps onto its host's gill filaments.

Within a few hours after the glochidia become attached to a fish, they become encapsulated by host cells that respond to the presence of the parasites by undergoing mitosis and migrating to surround the molluscs. Within the capsules, the glochidia absorb nutrients from the host's epithelium and grow. After developing into young clams, the molluscs open and close their valves until the encapsulating cysts, weakened by then, rupture, and the clams fall to the bottom of the water and gradually mature. In addition to fishes, certain glochidia utilize amphibians as hosts (Plate 24–15).

Baer (1952) has given an excellent review of the host-parasite relationship between unionid glochidia and their hosts. It has been shown experimentally that glochidia become attached to many species of fish and even to tadpoles and axolotls. However, development and metamorphosis of these larvae are not completed unless they become attached to a specific species of fish, thus demonstrating host specificity. If the glochidia become attached to an incompatible host, they are sloughed off before metamorphosis is completed. Arey (1924, 1932) reported that even compatible fish hosts develop an immunity toward glochidia after the third consecutive infestation. In such instances, the molluscan larvae are sloughed off in the same way as those of an incompatible host.

Protelian parasitism occurs among such unionid pelecypods as *Unio, Anodonta, Strophitus, Proptera, Margaritana,* and *Lampsilis.* In Europe, the glochidia of *Anodonta cygnaea, Unio batavus,* and *Margaritana margaritana* are almost always found on cyprinid fishes, with *A. cygnaea* attached to the gills, and *U. batavus* and *M. margaritifera* attached to the fins. In the United

States, complete larval development of *A. cygnaea* has been known to occur on axolotls. The host specificity of parasitic glochidia is further demonstrated in the United States by *Lampsilis anodontoides,* attached to *Lepisisteus osseous,* the garpike; *Lampsilis luteola,* attached to *Micropterus salmoides,* the largemouth bass; and *Hemistema ambigua,* attached to the gills of *Necturus maculatus,* the mud puppy.

MOLLUSCAN HOST-PARASITE RELATIONSHIPS

Although our present knowledge concerning parasitic molluscs is too scanty to permit detailed elaborations on host-parasite relationships, it is apparent that these must be relationships of long duration. Among the parasitic gastropods, echinoderms appear to be the preferred hosts, which may be attributed to the fact that echinoderms are about the only potential hosts sluggish enough to permit snails to climb over them and to establish any type of association. Thus, it may be surmised that what we observe today is only the result of natural selection, concerning failure of molluscs to attach themselves to other hosts.

The somewhat similar morphological modifications exhibited by the parasitic members of the various gastropod families undoubtedly have resulted from convergent evolution.

ADAPTATIONS OF INVERTEBRATES TO PARASITISM

Although the Porifera, Coelenterata, Ctenophera, and Rhynchocoela are almost exclusively free-living invertebrates, certain species, such as those mentioned previously, have become adapted to parasitism. These adaptations presumably are not of recent occurrence, for in

most cases, dramatic anatomical modifications
have developed and these must have evolved
over a considerable period. Thus, it is apparent
that adaptation to parasitism is a possibility in
any group of animals, especially when the
situation is conducive.

SUBPHYLUM VERTEBRATA

Although vertebrates are not plentiful or
important in active roles as parasites, the
biology of these animals is intimately allied
with that of invertebrate parasites in their
roles as intermediate and definitive hosts, as
natural reservoirs, as transport hosts, and as
experimental hosts in laboratory investigations.

True parasites, in the biological sense, are
rare among the vertebrates. A few animals,
such as the lampreys and vampire bats, have
been considered by some to be parasites. However, they can just as easily be considered

predators. The lampreys, vampire bats, can-
dirus, and a few pseudoparasitic vertebrates
are briefly mentioned here.

Lampreys

The lampreys belong to the class Cyclosto-
mata, which also includes the hagfishes and
slime eels. Lampreys, however, are members of
the order Petromyzontia, and hagfishes and
slime eels belong to the order Myxinoidia. The
habitats of lampreys vary, depending upon the
species. In North American waters, *Petromyzon
marinus,* the sea lamprey, is found in the Atlantic Ocean. It migrates up streams during the
spring or early summer to spawn (Plate 24–16).
Entosphenus tridentatus is the species found along
the Pacific Coast, ranging from California to
Alaska. *Entosphenus tridentatus* also migrates to
fresh water to spawn.

In the inland lakes, such as the Great Lakes,
Petromyzon marinus unicolor is common, and its
presence represents a hazard to the fresh-
water fishing industry. This species is believed

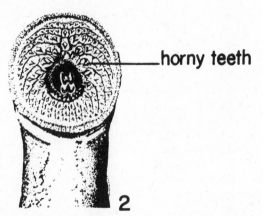

horny teeth

Plate 24–16   The lamprey. 1. *Petromyzon marinus,* the sea lamprey, attached to a whitefish.
(Courtesy of U.S.D.I. Fish and Wildlife Service.) 2. Frontal view of mouth of a lamprey, showing
circular rows of chitinous teeth. (After Gage, 1893.)

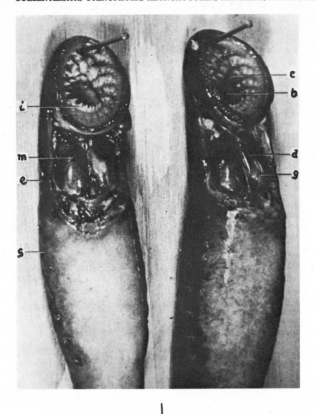

1

2

Plate 24-17   The sea lamprey. 1. Ventral view of sucking discs and buccal glands of two sexually mature sea lampreys. (b, buccal funnel; c, circumoral cusps; d, duct of buccal gland; e, eye; g, buccal gland; i, infraoral lamina; m, musculus basilaris; s, gill sac.) **2.** Lytic reactions produced in longnose suckers by subcutaneous injections of lampredin. (Figures after Lennon, 1944.)

to have arisen from marine ancestors that became landlocked during the glacial period and have adjusted to fresh-water living. It, too, migrates up streams to spawn. An anatomy and natural history of the lake lampreys have been contributed by Gage (1893). Other observations on growth and life cycles have been given by Hubbs (1924).

The mouth of the lamprey is situated anter-oventrally and is suctorial in function. Fleshy papillae or tentacles are located along the circumference of the circular mouth. When these poikilothermic parasites attack fish, they become attached by the suction of their funnel shaped mouth and by digging into the host's flesh with their buccal teeth (Plates 24–16, 24–17). A hole is ripped in the integument and flesh of the fish host by sharp lingual teeth and an anticoagulent known as lamphredin, secreted by buccal glands, is injected into the lesion to prevent the host's blood from clotting during feeding. Lamphredin not only prevents coagulation of the fish's blood but also exerts a haemolytic influence on the erythrocytes and induces a lytic action in the torn flesh (Plate 24–17, Fig. 2) (Lennon, 1954). Fish continuously parasitized by lampreys usually die. Hence, if these cyclostomes are considered parasites, they cannot be regarded as very well adapted or efficient ones, for they kill the host on which they depend.

Not all lampreys are bloodsuckers. The so-called brook lampreys, *Lampetra wilderi* and *Entosphenus latottenii,* are not.

Hagfishes and Eels

Myxine limosa, the Atlantic hagfish, is found in North America, ranging from Cape Cod northward. *Myxine glutinosa* is the European species and measures up to 3 feet in length. *Bdellostoma* spp. are found off the coast of Chile in South America. The Pacific boring hagfish, *Polistotrema stouti* is found from the coast of Lower California to Alaska (Plate 24–18). Unlike lampreys, slime eels and hagfishes actually burrow into the bodies of their piscine hosts and consume flesh, leaving only bones wrapped in integument. Without doubt, the Myxinoidia must be considered predators rather than true parasites.

The parasitic lampreys, slime eels, and hagfishes are all of considerable economic importance because they are extremely destructive to fish. Much of the work done concerning these animals has been for the purpose of eradication.

PSEUDOPARASITISM IN EELS. Pseudoparasitism is encountered among certain eels. Goude and Bean (1895) reported *Pisododonophis cruentifer* in fish; Deraniyagala (1932) identified *Ophichthus apicalis* from the body cavities of various percoid fishes; Breder and Nigrelli (1934) reported a large *Myricthys acuminatus* from the coelom of the jewfish, *Promicrops itaiara;* and Breder (1953) reported *Pisododonophis cruentifer* in a sea bass.

Walters (1955) has cited most of the known instances in which eels of the family Ophichthidae have been found in the coelom of fishes. Breder and Nigrelli postulated that such instances of "parasitism" actually represent pseudoparasitism. The engulfed eel tries to escape from the fish and in the process plunges its sharp tail through the gut wall of the host and backs into the coelom. This hypothesis is borne in that ophichthid eels found in the coelom of fish are usually dead and encapsulated within connective tissue cysts, and the anatomy of these eels does not support the idea that they are burrowers that have arrived within their hosts by penetrating from the exterior.

Candirus

Probably the only true endoparasites among vertebrates are the so-called candiru fishes found in the upper Amazon in South America. There is some doubt if these are obligatory parasites. One of these, *Vandellia cirrhosa,* a small, slender, naked catfish of the family Trichonycteridae, has been found in the gill chambers, attached to the gills of larger catfishes, where they supposedly feed on the gill epithelium and blood of the host fish. *Vandellia cirrhosa* measures no more than 2½ inches in length and has been reported to migrate up the urethra, anus, or vagina of bathers, causing severe pain when they expand their spine-bearing gill covers (opercula). It is a much feared animal among Amazon Indians, among whom much folklore about this fish has developed. Undoubtedly, some of the tales relative

Plate 24-18   *Polistotrema stouti,* **the California hagfish.** Notice the 12 pairs of gill slits.
(From Wolcott, *Animal Biology.*)

to attacks on humans by *V. cirrhosa* are merely folklore.

In a footnote, Myers (1944) reported that another small catfish, *Cetopsis candiru* of the family Cetopsidae will rasp the skin of man with its teeth when caught and suck blood. This catfish measures 8 inches or less in length.

Vampire Bats

Another group of vertebrates that could be considered parasitic is the vampire bats. These flying mammals belong to the suborder Microchiroptera of the order Chiroptera. Not all bats belonging to this suborder are bloodsuckers. For example, the brown bats *Myotis* and *Eptesicus* are insectivorous. However, the true vampire bats, *Desmodus* spp., are blood ingestors. They are found in the American tropics, where they attack (or parasitize) wild and domestic warm-blooded animals. When attacking, they dig their large canine teeth into the flesh of their victim, usually at the back of the neck or on the body proper, rupture a large blood vessel, and lap up blood, in much the same fashion as a kitten laps up milk. *Desmodus* has been known to bite fowls, particularly chickens, and also dogs, cats, cows, horses, and even man. Contrary to popular belief, the bite of the vampire bat is not fatal, nor is the loss of the relatively small quantity of blood of serious consequence. The wounds, however, are subject to secondary infection. Furthermore, a form of rabies is carried by these bats, and equine trypanosomes utilize *Desmodus* as a vector. These microorganisms are pathogenic and often lethal.

LITERATURE CITED

Coelenterata

Bigelow, H. B. 1909. The medusae. Museum Comp. Zool., Harvard Univ. Mem. 37.

Hyman, L. H. 1940. The Invertebrates: Protozoa through Ctenophora. McGraw-Hill, New York.

Lipin, A. 1911. Die Morphologie und Biologie von *Polypodium hydriforme* Uss. Zool. Jahrb., Abt. Anat. Ontog. Tiere, *31:* 317–426.

Ctenophora

Hyman, L. H. 1940. The Invertebrates: Protozoa through Ctenophora. McGraw-Hill, New York.

Komai, T. 1922. Studies on two aberrant ctenophores—*Coeloplana* and *Gastrodes.* (Published by author.) Kyoto, Japan.

Rhynchocoela

Coe, W. R. 1902a. The genus *Carcinonemertes.* Zool. Anz., *25:* 409–414.

Coe, W. R. 1902b. The nemertean parasites of crabs. Am. Nat., *36:* 431–450.

Eggers, F. 1936. Zur Bewegungsphysiologie von *Malacobdella grossa.* Ztschr. Wiss. Zool., *147:* 101–131.

Hopkins, S. H. 1947. The nemertean *Carcinonemertes* as an indicator of the spawning history of the host, *Callinectes sapidus.* J. Parasit., *33:* 146–150.

Humes, A. G. 1941. The male reproductive system in the nemertean genus *Carcinonemertes.* J. Morph., *69:* 443–454.

Humes, A. G. 1942. The morphology, taxonomy, and bionomics of the nemertean genus *Carcinonemertes.* Ill. Biol. Monogr., *18:* 1–105.

Hyman, L. H. 1951. The Invertebrates: Platyhelminthes and Rhynchocoela. McGraw-Hill, New York.

Ropes, J. W. 1963. The incidence of *Malacobdella grossa* in hard clams from Nantucket Sound, Massachusetts. Limn. Oceanogr., *8:* 353–355.

Annelida

Beunike, S. A. B. 1943. Contributions to the ecology and biology of the Danish fresh-water leeches (Hirudinea). Folia Limnobogica Scandinarica, No. 2.

Clark, R. B. 1956. *Capitella capitata* as a commensal, with a bibliography of parasitism and commensalism in the polychaetes. Ann. Mag. Nat. Hist., *9:* 433–448.

Codreanu, M., and R. Codreanu. 1928. Un nouvel euglénien (*Astasia chaetogastris* n. sp.), parasite coelomique d'un Oligochète (*Chaetogaster diastrophus* Gruith). Compt. Rend. Soc. Biol., *99:* 1368–1370.

Goodchild, C. G. 1951. A new endoparasitic oligochaete (Naididae) from a North American tree-toad, *Hyla squirrella* Latreille, 1802. J. Parasit., *37:* 205–211.

Holt, P. C. 1963. A new branchiobdellid (Branchiobdellidae: Cambarincola). Jour. Tenn. Acad. Sci., *38:* 97–100.

Lankester, E. R. 1869. The sexual form of *Chaetogaster limnaei*. Quart. J. Micro. Sci., *9:* 272–285.

Mann, K. H. 1954. The anatomy of the horse leech, *Haemopis sanguisuga* (L.) with particular reference to the excretory system. Proc. Zool. Soc. London, *124:* 69–88.

Mann, K. H. 1955. Some factors influencing the distribution of fresh-water leeches in Britain. Proc. Intern. Assoc. Theor. Appl. Limn., *12:* 582–587.

Mann, K. H. 1962. Leeches (Hirudinea). Their Structure, Physiology, Ecology, and Embryology. Pergamon Press, New York.

Meyer, M. C. 1940. A revision of the leeches (Piscicolidae) living on fresh-water fishes of North America. Trans. Am. Micro. Soc., *59:* 354–376.

Meyer, M. C. 1946. A new leech *Piscicola salmositica*. J. Parasit., *32:* 467–476.

Meyer, M. C., and A. A. Barden, Jr. 1955. Leeches symbiotic on Arthropoda, especially decapod Crustacea. Wasmann Jour. Biol., *13:* 297–311.

Monticelli, F. S. 1917. Di un curioso caso di inquilinismo di un Oligochete nell' Ammocoetes di *Petromyzon planeri*. Bull. Soc. Nat. Napoli, No. 29.

Moore, J. P. 1959. Hirudinea. *In* Freshwater Biology (W. T. Edmondson, ed.). John Wiley, New York, pp. 542–557.

Pawlowski, L. K. 1955. Revision des genres *Erpobdella* et *Dina*. Bull. Soc. Sci. Let. Lodz Cl. III, *6:* 1–15.

Ruiz, J. M. 1951. Nota sobre a cercariofagia de um Oligochaeta do genero *Chaetogaster* v. Baer, 1827. An. Fac. Farm. Odontol. Univ. San Paulo, *9:* 51–56.

Sperber, C. 1948. A taxonomical study of the Naididae. Zool. Bidrag. Fran Uppsala, *28:* 296.

Stephenson, J. 1930. The Oligochaeta. Oxford University Press, London.

Stiles, C. W., and A. Hassall. 1926. Key Catalogue of the Worms, reported from Man. Hygienic Lab. Bull., No. 142. U. S. Pub. Health Serv.

Wallace, H. E. 1941. Life history and embryology of *Triganodistomum mutabile* (Cort) (Lissorchiidae, Trematoda). Trans. Amer. Micro. Soc., *60:* 309–326.

Mollusca

Arey, L. B. 1924. Observations on an acquired immunity to a metazoan parasite. J. Exp. Zool., *38:* 377–381.

Arey, L. B. 1932. A microscopical study of glochidial immunity. J. Morph., *53:* 367–379.

Baer, J. G. 1952. Ecology of Animal Parasites. University of Illinois Press, Urbana, Ill.

Caullery, M. 1952. Parasitism and Symbiosis. Sidgwick & Jackson, London.

Heding, S. G. 1934. *Entocolax trochodotae,* n. sp., a new parasitic gastropod. Vidensk. Medd. Dansk. Naturh. For. Kbh., *98:* 207–214.

Iwanow, A. W. 1948. [Metamorphosis of the parasitic snail *Parenteroxenos dogieli* Iwanow.] Rep. Acad. Sci. USSR, *61:* 765–768.

Koehler, R., and C. Vaney. 1903. *Entosiphon deimatis,* nouveau mollusque parasite d'une holothurie abyssale. Rev. Suisse Zool., *11:* 23–41.

Mandahl-Barth, G. 1941. *Thyonicola mortensi* n. gen. n. sp., eine neue parasitische Schnecke. Vidensk. Medd. Dansk. Naturh. For. Kbh., *104:* 341–351.

Mandahl-Barth, G. 1946. *Diacolax cucumariae,* n. g., n. sp., a new parasitic snail. Vidensk. Medd. Dansk. Naturh. For. Kbh., *109:* 55–68.

Schwanwitsch, B. N. 1917. Observations sur la femelle et le mâle rudimentaire d'*Entocolax ludwigi* Voigt. J. Russe Zool., *2:* 1–147.

Vertebrata

Breder, C. M., Jr. 1953. An ophichthid eel in the coelom of a sea bass. Zoologica, *38:* 201–202.

Breder, C. M., Jr., and R. F. Nigrelli. 1934. The penetration of a grouper's digestive tract by a sharp-tailed eel. Copeia, *(4):* 162–164.

Deraniyagala, P. E. P. 1932. A curious association between *Ophichthus apicalis* and percoid fishes. Spolia Zeylanica, Sec. B, *16:* 355–356.

Gage, S. H. 1893. The Lake and Brook Lampreys of New York. Wilder Quarter-Century Book, Ithaca, N. Y., pp. 421–493.

Goude, G. B., and T. H. Bean. 1895. Oceanic ichthyology, a treatise on the deep-sea and pelagic fishes of the world. U. S. Nat. Mus. Spec. Bull. 2.

Hubbs, C. L. 1924. The life-cycle and growth of lampreys. Mich. Acad. Sci., Arts, Let., Pap., *4:* 587–603.

Lennon, R. E. 1954. Feeding mechanism of the sea lamprey and its effect on fish hosts. Fishery Bull. 98, *56:* 247–293. U. S. Printing Office, Washington, D. C.

Myers, G. S. 1944. Two extraordinary new blind nematognath fishes from the Rio Negro, representing a new subfamily of Pygidiidae, with a rearrangement of the genera of the family, and illustrations of some previously described genera and species from Venezuela and Brazil. Proc. Cal. Acad. Sci., *23:* 591–602.

Walters, v. 1955. Snake-eels as pseudoparasites of fishes. Copeia, *2:* 146–147.

SUGGESTED READING

Annelida

Baer, J. B. 1952. Annelida. *In* Ecology of Animal Parasites. University of Illinois Press, Urbana, pp. 36–42. (Baer discusses the parasitic annelids in this section of his book. The material on the morphology of these animals is particularly interesting.)

Caullery, M. 1952. Parasitism and Symbiosis. Sidgwick & Jackson, London, pp. 40–46. (This is an excellent account of the parasitic annelids.)

Mann, K. H. 1962. Leeches (Hirudinea). Their Structure, Physiology, Ecology, and Embryology. Pergamon Press, New York. (This is an excellent but advanced monograph on the leeches. Their physiology and ecology are stressed.)

Mollusca

Baer, J. B. 1952. Mollusca. *In* Ecology of Animal Parasites. University of Illinois Press, Urbana, Ill., pp. 20–33. (The discussion on the morphology and progression of adaptive changes among parasitic molluscs given in this section of Baer's book is excellent. Furthermore, the references listed should prove to be of great value to the reader.)

Caullery, M. 1952. Parasitism and Symbiosis. Sidgwick & Jackson, London, pp. 46–64. (Caullery has presented a detailed and comprehensive account of the morphology and development of parasitic molluscs in this section of his book. The adaptive evolution of these animals is also discussed authoritatively.)

AFTERWORD

One cannot overemphasize the interdisciplinary role of parasitology in biology. As is the case in increasingly more of the branches of the biological sciences, parasitologists are examining the nature of their interests, that is, parasites and parasitism, at all levels of organization, ranging from populational and macroecological to microecological and biochemical levels. Herein lies the excitement of parasitology. The pursuit of knowledge regarding natural phenomena defies curbing by man-made disciplinary boundaries, and in keeping with the philosophy of scientific research, students of parasitology must recognize that manifestations of symbiosis, including parasitism, occur at the biochemical as well as at the organismal and populational levels. However, it must be continuously borne in mind that parasitism is a way of life of whole organisms and not of molecules. It is only when one considers the entire spectrum of parasitism that one can begin fully to appreciate the nature of parasites and parasitism. Thus, host specificity and details of life cycles and development, as well as the time required for development, can only be fully appreciated and critically evaluated when the evolutionary, environmental, physiological, and biochemical factors that cause or influence these features of parasitic life are taken into consideration. Many of these factors remain unknown. The "parasitological world" awaits the biologists of tomorrow to probe its depths, for therein rest some of the greatest challenges and some of the most important processes of life and time.

INDEX

Page numbers in **bold face** indicate illustrations. Page numbers followed by the letter "t" indicate tabular information.

691